Urban Scaling

Urban allometry empirically describes how "things", for example crime, GDP, emissions, energy use, area, street length, housing prices, etc. change in cities when their size, in terms of population, increases. Urban scaling is a relatively recent area of urban science, investigating how measurable characteristics of cities vary with their sizes.

This book addresses this relatively novel but highly debated topic within urban studies and geography. It presents many results, techniques, methods, and reflections on urban scaling and allometry. The sections are organized into different sub-areas such as socio-economic, infrastructural or environmental outputs, so that there is a broad organization of the findings into recognizable sub-domains. The book is particularly timely as it is becoming increasingly urgent and necessary to understand the pro and cons of different city sizes and therefore to plan policies accordingly. The book is especially interesting from a theoretical perspective because it presents the latest developments and achievements in the field, which will help to highlight potential universal rules across cities and regions.

This book will benefit researchers in urban science, and scholars entering the field from various disciplines, such as geography, sociology, economics, mathematics, physics, or urban and regional planning. It will also find an audience among practitioners and policymakers.

Luca S. D'Acci is Associate Professor at the Department of Planning, Regional and Urban Studies, Polytechnic University of Turin, Italy; honorary research fellow at the College of Engineering and Physical Sciences, University of Birmingham; and affiliated to EHERO, Erasmus Universiteit Rotterdam.

Routledge Advances in Regional Economics, Science and Policy

Governance and Leadership in Shrinking Cities
Strategies for Managing Urban Decline
Edited by Stanisław Mazur

Regional Policy in the Southern African Development Community
Edited by J. Ernst Drewes and Mariske van Aswegen

Regional Cooperation and Resilience in East Asia
Edited by Sebastian Bobowski

The Business of Affordable Housing
Case Studies of the Commercial Supply of Affordable Homes
Alexander Styhre

Spatial Planning and the European Union
Europeanisation from Within
Eva Purkarthofer

Economic Resilience and Pandemic Response
Edited by Agnieszka Rzepka and Artur Paździor

Lagging Regions in the European Union
Structural, Productivity and Efficiency Aspects
Paweł Dobrzański

Urban Scaling
Allometry in Urban Studies and Spatial Science
Edited by Luca S. D'Acci

For more information about this series, please visit: www.routledge.com/series/RAIRESP

Urban Scaling

Allometry in Urban Studies and Spatial Science

Edited by Luca S. D'Acci

Routledge
Taylor & Francis Group
LONDON AND NEW YORK

First published 2025
by Routledge
4 Park Square, Milton Park, Abingdon, Oxon OX14 4RN

and by Routledge
605 Third Avenue, New York, NY 10158

Routledge is an imprint of the Taylor & Francis Group, an informa business

British Library Cataloguing-in-Publication Data
A catalogue record for this book is available from the British Library

Library of Congress Cataloging-in-Publication Data
Names: D'Acci, Luca S., editor.
Title: Urban scaling : allometry in urban studies and spatial science / edited by Luca S. D'Acci.
Description: New York : Routledge, 2025. |
Series: Routledge advances in regional economics, science and policy |
Includes bibliographical references and index.
Identifiers: LCCN 2024018231 (print) | LCCN 2024018232 (ebook) |
ISBN 9781032264400 (hardback) | ISBN 9781032264417 (paperback) |
ISBN 9781003288312 (ebook)
Subjects: LCSH: Cities and towns–Growth. | City planning. | System theory. | Allometry.
Classification: LCC HT371 .U7294 2024 (print) | LCC HT371 (ebook) |
DDC 307.76–dc23/eng/20240611
LC record available at https://lccn.loc.gov/2024018231
LC ebook record available at https://lccn.loc.gov/2024018232

ISBN: 978-1-032-26440-0 (hbk)
ISBN: 978-1-032-26441-7 (pbk)
ISBN: 978-1-003-28831-2 (ebk)

DOI: 10.4324/9781003288312

Typeset in Times New Roman
by Newgen Publishing UK

Contents

Figures

Tables

Contributors

Luiz G.A. Alves, Northwestern University

Kay W. Axhausen, ETH Zurich

Michael Batty, University College London

Luís M.A. Bettencourt, University of Chicago, and Santa Fe Institute

Anna F. Carbone, Politecnico di Torino

Geoffrey Caruso, University of Luxembourg

Yanguang Chen, Peking University

Sergio Luiz da Silva, Universidade Federal Fluminense

Luca S. D'Acci, Politecnico di Torino

Justin Delloye, University of Louvain, and Luxembourg Institute of Socio-Economic Research (LISER)

Amy E. Frazier, University of California

Andres Gomez-Lievano, Harvard University

Adrienne Grêt-Regamey, ETH Zurich

Agust Gudmundsson, Royal Holloway University of London

Quentin S. Hanley, Nottingham Trent University

Ricardo Hausmann, Santa Fe Institute

Limin Jiao, Wuhan University

Ruixue Jing, Universiteit Gent

Giorgio Kaniadakis, Politecnico di Torino

Peter Kedron, University of California

Christopher P. Kempes, Santa Fe Institute

Amin Khiali-Miab, ETH Zurich

Paul Kilgarriff, Luxembourg Institute of Socio-Economic Research (LISER)

Tian Lan, Southwest Jiaotong University

Weiqian Lei, Hohai University

Rémi Lemoy, Université de Rouen

Ervin K. Lenzi, Universidade Estadual de Ponta Grossa

Ruiqi Li, Beijing University of Chemical Technology

Zhilin Li, Southwest Jiaotong University

José Lobo, Arizona State University

Renio S. Mendes, Universidade Estadual de Maringá

Nahid Mohajeri, University College London

Elisa Heinrich Mora, Stanford University

Scott G. Ortman, University of Colorado Boulder

Gustavo A. Ovando-Montejo, Utah State University

Oscar Patterson-Lomba, Analysis Group, Inc., Boston

Fabien Paulus, Strasbourg University

Denise Pumain, University Paris 1 Panthéon-Sorbonne

Fabiano L. Ribeiro, Universidade Federal de Lavras

Haroldo V. Ribeiro, Universidade Estadual de Maringá

Luis E.C. Rocha, Universiteit Gent

Diego Rybski, Potsdam Institute for Climate Impact Research

Anand Sahasranaman, Sai University

Somwrita Sarkar, University of Sydney

Frank Schiller, West Coast University of Applied Science

Michael E. Smith, Arizona State University

Jack Sutton, Nottingham Trent University

Céline Vacchiani-Marcuzzo, University of Reims Champagne-Ardenne

Frank G. van Oort, Erasmus Universiteit Rotterdam

Anthony F.J. van Raan, Universiteit Leiden

Maarten J. van Strien, ETH Zurich

Gang Xu, Wuhan University

Vicky Chuqiao Yang, Massachusetts Institute of Technology

Fatemeh Zarei, Universiteit Gent

Hong Zhang, East China Normal University

Jiang Zhang, Beijing Normal University

Siyuan Zhang, Wuhan University

Tao Zhou, University of Electronic Science and Technology of China

Part I

Introduction and state of the art

1 Urban scaling

A primer on size, scale, and shape

Michael Batty

1.1 The context

One hundred years ago in thinking about how biological systems evolved, the gestalt psychologists who believed that our understanding of the world was composed of a unique ability to synthesise diverse elements in our environment, adopted the mantra that "… the whole is greater than the sum of its parts". It was Kurt Koffka [1] who is accredited with this phrase although the idea goes back to classical times, to the words of Aristotle who implied that synergy is a key property in explanation. This notion that 'more can come from less' encapsulates the idea that as a system evolves, it can change qualitatively, which is often revealed in its changing shape or morphology. The most obvious and immediate example is the human form where a newborn baby's head is proportionately much bigger than its body mass, whereas a growing child quickly stabilises in terms of the shape of its body parts as adolescence is passed. As we grow, indeed as any object grows, one critical property is its scale. Indeed as an object gets bigger or smaller, it is said to scale and in this sense, if an object scales and changes qualitatively with respect to the ways it elements form and interact, then we say that the phenomenon is '*scaling*'. This is essentially the meaning of scaling as developed in the many contributions that comprise this book.

The simplest, and in some respects the special case of scaling, is when an object increases or decreases its size linearly, that is proportionately to its mass or volume or some other measure of its geometry. If this increase is more than proportionate, the relationship is *superlinear*, while if the increase is less than proportionate, the relationship is *sublinear*. In biology, superlinear is often called positive allometry while sublinear is called negative allometry, and there is a direct correspondence between this scaling and economies and diseconomies of agglomeration in economics. In turn, these scale economies are sometimes mapped onto the positive benefits that might accrue from growth or negative benefits, and these have different interpretations and formulations [2]. Although the focus is usually on growth, scaling in spatial systems is usually defined not with respect to the processes of growth but to the emergent patterns that at any particular time display positive or negative allometry. Although systems can be seen as being organised from the top down with successive subsystems scaling in some fashion as a hierarchy of

DOI: 10.4324/9781003288312-2

parts, this can also be seen as a series of ever larger subsystems that emerge from the bottom up. In fact, scaling in this fashion is entirely coincident with the complexity sciences whose elements often display a particular motif that is replicated at ever larger scales, as fractal patterns that scale non-linearly. Although we do not have the luxury of developing these ideas here, the notion that we can define geometric scaling in mathematical terms serves to focus our initial review on the key relationships that recur again and again in the various chapters that follow. Readers can find more detailed explanations of the relationships to different morphologies, particularly cities, in the books by Batty and Longley [3] and Batty [4].

1.2 The basic scaling relations

The core relation relates the size of some set of objects, phenomena, or systems to their order, and by order we mean the relationships between the objects. The simplest order is based on arranging the objects with respect to some property such as their size (or scale) and examining the way this size distribution behaves. We first define the set of n objects where each object is defined as $P_r, r = 1,2,3,\ldots,n$, where the obvious order is simply to associate the size of the object to its rank measured with respect to its reverse order. This relates P_r to $n-r-1$, where $P_r \propto n-r-1$ and it is clear that this is a simple linear relation where size is proportional to the reverse of rank. There is no scaling in this relationship for the size of the object is the same as its reverse rank. This is almost nihilistic in its form but if we arrange the objects by size in their basic rank order, we derive the nonlinear relation

$$P_r = Kr^{-1} \tag{1.1}$$

K is a constant that determines the dimension or metric of the relation. This is the classic rank size relation associated with the frequency distribution of the set of $\{P_r\}$ objects and now known as the 'rank size' rule or *Zipf's Law* [5]. To demonstrate that the relationship is scaling, if we scale the rank r in equation (1.1) by the parameter λ as $(\lambda r)^{-1}$, this can be manipulated to show that

$$\lambda^{-1}P_r = K(\lambda r)^{-1} = K\lambda^{-1}r^{-1} \propto P_r \tag{1.2}$$

This says if we double the rank, by say $\lambda = 2$, we halve the size of the object in question and this indicates the more than proportionate decrease which is associated with the scaling.

This relation has been very widely used to examine the relative frequencies and attributes of objects that form systems where the objects compete against one another to grow; for example, the size of cities, income distribution, the frequencies of words, and the distribution of many natural and physical phenomena from animal populations, flora, and fauna, to geophysical distributions such as earthquakes and volcanoes. In terms of cities, Zipf [5] was one of the first to demonstrate that city size distributions followed the pure rank size scaling as in equation (1.1) although many others who followed him have noted that the inverse scaling is more likely to use a power law where the exponent α differs from 1. This is written as $P_r = Kr^{-\alpha}$ although it is likely that the 'true' relation is more like a lognormal with the inverse power only associated with the upper or heavy tail of the distributions where the largest objects exist.

The second form of scaling that we introduce is in some senses the opposite or even complement to the rank size rule. Imagine that the ranks no longer relate to the order of objects from large to small but to the distance from some origin or source. In other words, the objects are no longer ranked in terms of their size, but the distance of each object from some source now reflects the order. Whereas the rank size rule represents the order in which the objects are ranked from large to small, the new rule is based on an order associated with the objects that arranges them according to their position. This is exactly the way we would examine an attribute of an object at a series of successive distances from some source. It might be the density of say population at increasing distances from the central core of the city, as reflected in what is called *Clark's Law*. Clark [6], like some before and many after, argued that the density (and/or rent) of population falls off according to some inverse exponential of distance from some point, usually the central business district (CBD) of large metropolitan areas. If we now define the density of the object as P_j and the distance of the object from the CBD as $d_j, j = 1,2,3,\ldots,n$, then Clark hypothesised that the relation should be a negative exponential, that is

$$P_j = Kexp\left(-\beta d_j\right), \tag{1.3}$$

where K is the dimensional constant as before and β is the scaling parameter. In fact, in many applications of these kinds of model, an inverse power is used instead of a negative exponential and thus the complement to the rank size rule that we might call the rank distance rule is

$$P_j = Kd_j^{-\beta} \tag{1.4}$$

Note that the key difference between equations (1.1) and (1.4) is the size of the populations in (1.1) are ordered by size from $P_1 \ldots P_k \ldots P_n$ while the sizes in (1.4) are arranged in the order given by distance from the CBD $d_1 \ldots d_j \ldots d_n$.

Our third scaling function also relates to position and distance but in terms of interaction between any two locations and the flow of activity between them. In the same way that Clark's Law defines how density decays from a given locational focus, the CBD, interaction defined as T_{ij} between any two locations i and j is a function of the distance between them, d_{ij}. We can define this kind of relation from one of many gravitational equations typical of which is

$$T_{ij} = KP_iP_jd_{ij}^{-\gamma}, \tag{1.5}$$

where K and γ are appropriate parameters and the basic scaling is applied to distance d_{ij} in the same manner as we demonstrated above for both Zipf and Clark's Laws. This equation reflects the fact that interaction T_{ij} falls off with distance from i or j and this has been called *Tobler's Law* after Tobler [7] who articulated his Law as follows: He said: "… everything is related to everything else, but near things are more related than distant things …". The gravitational model in equation (1.5) can be generalised in many ways but variants have been derived in which all the independent variables of size and distance can be parameterized, which makes them subject to differential scaling. If we now define the locational variables P_i and P_j with respect to their scale as P_i^{α} and $P_i^{\beta}$and then use these in an augmented gravity model, equation (1.5) becomes

$$\tilde{T}_{ij} = KP_i^{\alpha}P_i^{\beta}d_{ij}^{-\gamma} \tag{1.6}$$

By raising the locational variables to a power, this enables the locations to reflect economies or diseconomies of scale. If we scale the locational variables by a and b and distance by λ, then it is easy to show that the interactions $\tilde{T}_{ij}$ in the new model in equation (1.6) are composed of a more complex set of functions that scale the whole equation by $a^{\alpha}b^{\beta}\lambda^{-\gamma}$, again a constant scalar.

This brings us to our fourth type of scaling and, in this context, the physical growth of the system becomes more explicit. There are many phenomena where changes to the size of the objects in question lead to variants of linear growth as we defined them earlier. Superlinear growth manifests itself if an object gets larger and some attribute of the object gets more than proportionately bigger due to its internal dynamics. Sublinear growth operates in an opposite manner for, as the object grows, some attribute in question grows less than proportionately. This kind of growth was articulated by the economist Alfred Marshall [8] in the late 19th century where he defined it implicitly as agglomeration: economics of scale if growth is superlinear or diseconomies of scale if sublinear. In various economic models, such scaling also features, but in the context of spatial systems such as cities, it is of a particularly simple form with the best examples being those demonstrated by West [2] and his colleagues for different city sizes with respect to changes in overall income. We will call this *Marshall's Law* [8] after his early discussion of economies of scale in his book *Principles of Economics.*

If we define income for a city or location i as Y_i, and assume that the size of the driver of income is population P_i, then the scaling relation that has been widely fitted to income and related population data for cities over the last 10 years or more and is reflected in several chapters in this book, is of the simplest form [9]. We can state this as

$$Y_i = KP_i^{\varphi}, \tag{1.7}$$

where the parameters K and φ act in the same way as in the other scaling relationships discussed above. This is the form of the so-called allometric equation that has been adopted in recent work on scaling in cities although there is some uncertainty about whether or not a better estimate would be of the income per capita against population, that is

$$Y_i / P_i = KP_i^{\varphi-1} \tag{1.8}$$

The parameter does not vary if the form in equation (1.8) rather than (1.7) is used, but the goodness of fit is perceived differently. In this last relationship, we introduce much stronger substantive issues than in the previous cases where the focus before has been very much on geometry, position, and location. By introducing allometry, we open this discussion of scaling to more important issues pertaining to how city and social systems function. In this introduction, we will not pursue this further for others writing in this book will take up and elaborate these themes. To round out our discussion here, we will now demonstrate empirically how we might begin to estimate the various relationships we have presented.

1.3 Demonstrating scaling for city systems and systems of cities

The four relationships that we have just introduced are applicable generically to many types of system and although our focus has been on cities and regions, the ideas do not need to be developed for spatial systems per se. For example, rank size relationships are widely applicable to firm sizes, income distributions, and large language models, while urban density functions pertain to many systems where diffusion of a rapidly decaying emission around some source needs to be modelled. Gravitational models clearly apply to how people interact within cities but they are applicable to information, demographic migration, and energy flows as well as to trips and traffic. Last but not least, allometric relations pertain directly to animal morphologies as well as to a variety of economic and infrastructural elements that make up the wider environment.

In the rest of this chapter, we will apply each of these relations to the UK urban system which is defined at the level of census tracts known as Middle-layer Super Output Areas (MSOAs) of which there are 8436 in England, Scotland, and Wales which have an average population of 7791 and average employment of 2378. These are much smaller than the 63 cities in the UK greater than 110,000 population in 2023 but they represent an elemental unit against which we can test for the existence of distributions which scale with their size. The fact that Britain is an island economy and that it is almost entirely urbanised, introduces a degree of uniformity into its spatial morphology that mirrors classic industrial cities and city regions. In the examples that follow, we define 'population' as total workplace employment from the 2011 Population Census which we consider mirrors classical urban structure much better than the distribution of residential population defined from a total head count.

The first relationship we present is based on the 8436 MSOAs which we rank in terms of employment from the largest zone (in the City of London, the square mile) which has 325,874 employees to the smallest which has 14. In fact, in these examples, we will use employment density which assumes that employment exists at a point location and in this way we can assume that the unit of analysis – the employment zone (or the 'city') – is dimensionless, that is, it is normalised to account for area. Most rank size analyses of locational distributions such as population are usually done on entire countries – systems of cities – where cities are defined according to geometric considerations and density thresholds, so the analysis we indicate here is unusual in that our zones are not cities. Nevertheless we consider them to be competitors of one another for resources, notwithstanding the well-known problems of defining their physical and socio-economic boundaries [10].

Our first application is to fit the rank size equation $P_r = Kr^{-\alpha}$ to the ranked MSOA data $(r = 1,2,3,\ldots,8436)$ which are ordered from the largest to the smallest employment density zone. In fact what we plot in Figures 1.1(a) and (b) are the inverse power equation $P_r = Kr^{-\alpha}$ and its logarithmically transformed equivalent, $\log P_r = \log K - \alpha \log r$. Noting that the fit of the equation to the observed employment density is fairly good but modest with an $R^2 = 0.844$, it is worth making the point that not much analysis of rank size at a disaggregate scale has ever been accomplished. In fact, Figure 1.1(b) illustrates that the long tail (to the right side of the graph) distorts the rank size linearity considerably and the heavy tail (to the left side of the graph) reduces the slope even further. Were we to chop off most of the long tail upwards from rank $r = 1000$, the slope looks much more like Zipf's Law with an $R^2 = 0.935$ but these results suggest that there are many, many different distributions which are defined at different spatial scales that resemble rank size. Moreover, as we begin to trim the tails to increase linearity, then the nature of the system that such scaling is applicable to begins to change. To an extent, this probably implies that estimates of this kind are not necessarily good measures of the dynamics of rank size but simply evidence of the fact that systems with limited resources inevitably always form an equilibrium which can be described by Zipf's Law.

In Figure 1.1(b) we also show the pure rank size rule normalised to ensure that the intercept of the function is the maximum employment density. The straight line thus models the equation $\log P_r = \log P_1 - \log r$ and this shows quite clearly the problem with the tails. Although our first scaling law is based on the classic inverse power, there are several ways of defining this scaling associated with the spatial distribution of activities such as employment and their densities. Instead of ranking the size of activities from largest to smallest where the rank is equally spaced as $r = 1, r = 2, r = 3,\ldots$, we order these sizes according to their location. In this application, we define location as the distance from central London where we define the first distance $d_1 = 0.5$ as the average distance within the MSOA which is Charing Cross. With all 8436 locations measured with respect to this zone, and with these distances ordered from the smallest to largest $d_1 \le d_2 \le d_3 \ldots$, we can examine the distribution of activities $E_1 \le E_2 \le E_3 \ldots$, and infer whether or not this distribution scales. Remember that in the rank size rule, activities are ranked from largest to smallest but in this second application, it is the distances that are ranked. In short this second application changes the order from size to distance where we plot rank and distance on the same horizontal axes. The most important issue here is that this transfer focuses the analysis on the morphology of the system in that its geometry – ranking the distance associated with the relevant activity at that location – provides an alternate way of looking at the same data, the distribution of employment densities in this case.

In Figure 1.1(c), we plot the employment density E_j against what we call the rank distance d_j. Whereas in the rank size of employment densities in Figures 1.1(a) and (b), there is nothing in this distribution to link it to the morphology of employment densities but when we use rank distances, it is extremely clear that the distribution of cities in Britain measured as their distance from London, mirrors the hierarchy of the city system that is well known. In Figure 1.1(c), London stands out as the origin of the UK urban system as a massive density. A total of 240 kilometres distant from London, Birmingham is located, while at 300 km Manchester can be clearly identified. Within these distances, West Yorkshire and then Newcastle can be located before the last big urban agglomeration Glasgow-Edinburgh, which is some 550 km from London. In Figure 1.1(d), we plot the logarithmic transformation, $\log P_j = \log K - \alpha \log d_j$ but this transformation masks the morphology. The further away from London, the wider the variation in densities and at greater distances from the capital, the employment density falls dramatically. In fact there is a hidden 'rank size' here if we regress $\log P_j$ against $\log d_j$ with the slope estimated as $\alpha = -0.439$ but with the R^2 falling to 0.088.

The second relationship that we have defined relates density and distance to activity distributions such as employment and population in the manner formulated by Clark [6] that we introduced previously. We have already defined these activities with respect to their distance from the UK's capital London but to demonstrate urban density scaling, we have defined rings of equal distance from the core Charing Cross in bands of 1 km distance. In each annulus, we add the total employment in the relevant MSOAs that fall predominantly in each band and then divide by the area of the annulus to extract the density. As we begin at the core point and then move successively out from London, we eventually reach the outer annulus some 1018 km from London, which includes the last zone number 8436. This method smooths the variations in density and produces a much cleaner picture of density variation in the UK. To an extent it is an alternative picture of the densities that we plot in Figures 1.1(c) and (d). However, as we move past 400 km from London, we encounter annuli which have no employment associated with them and it is therefore not possible to plot these effectively in an automated way. We therefore restrict our visual analysis to this limit which does not quite include urban Scotland although this is far enough away to make little difference to the overall scaling implied in these plots.

We show the employment density profile in Figure 1.2(a), which reveals a very clear inverse power law scaling based on $P_j = Kd_j^{-\alpha}$. The density falls dramatically within the first 50 rings up to 50 km as we show in the inset. To examine the

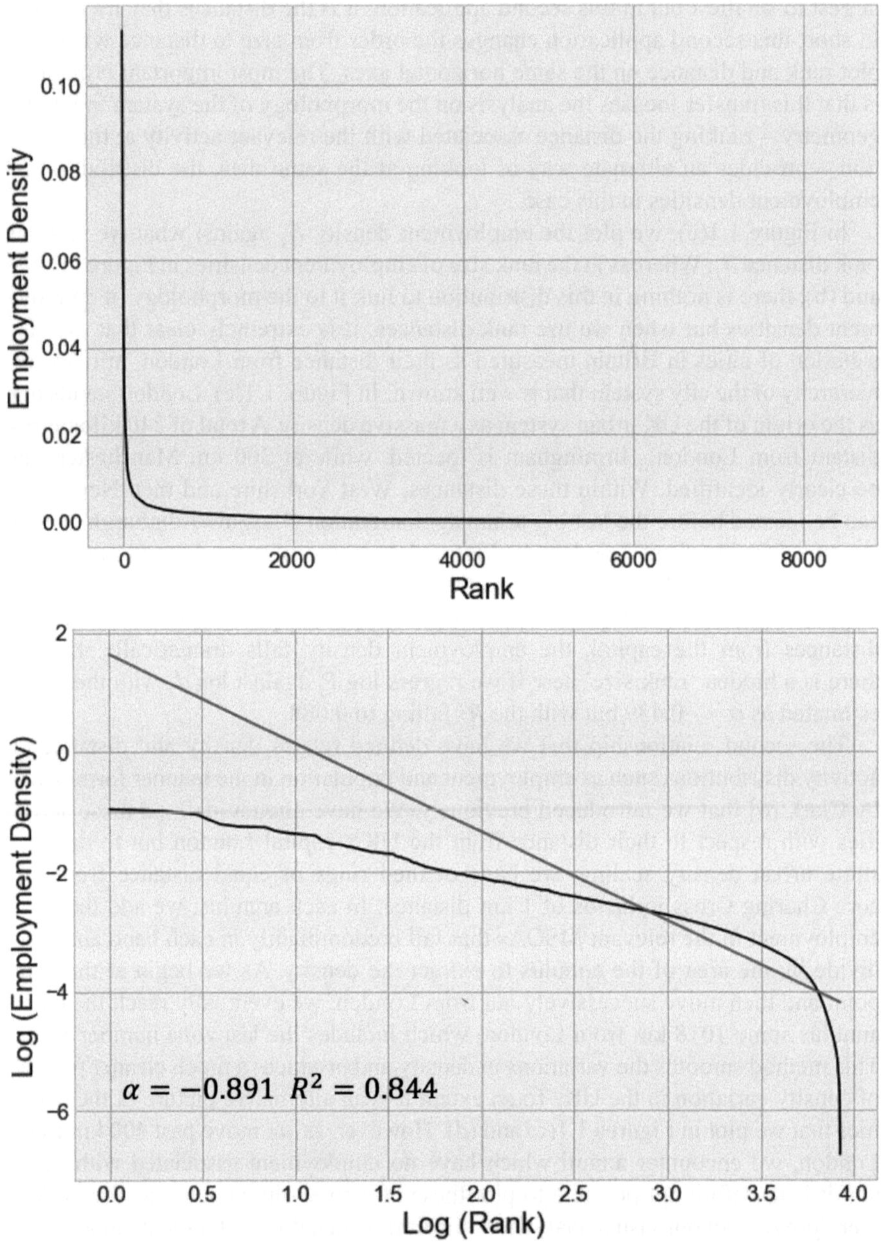

Figure 1.1 Classic scaling relationships: (a) and (b) rank size, and (c) and (d) rank distance.

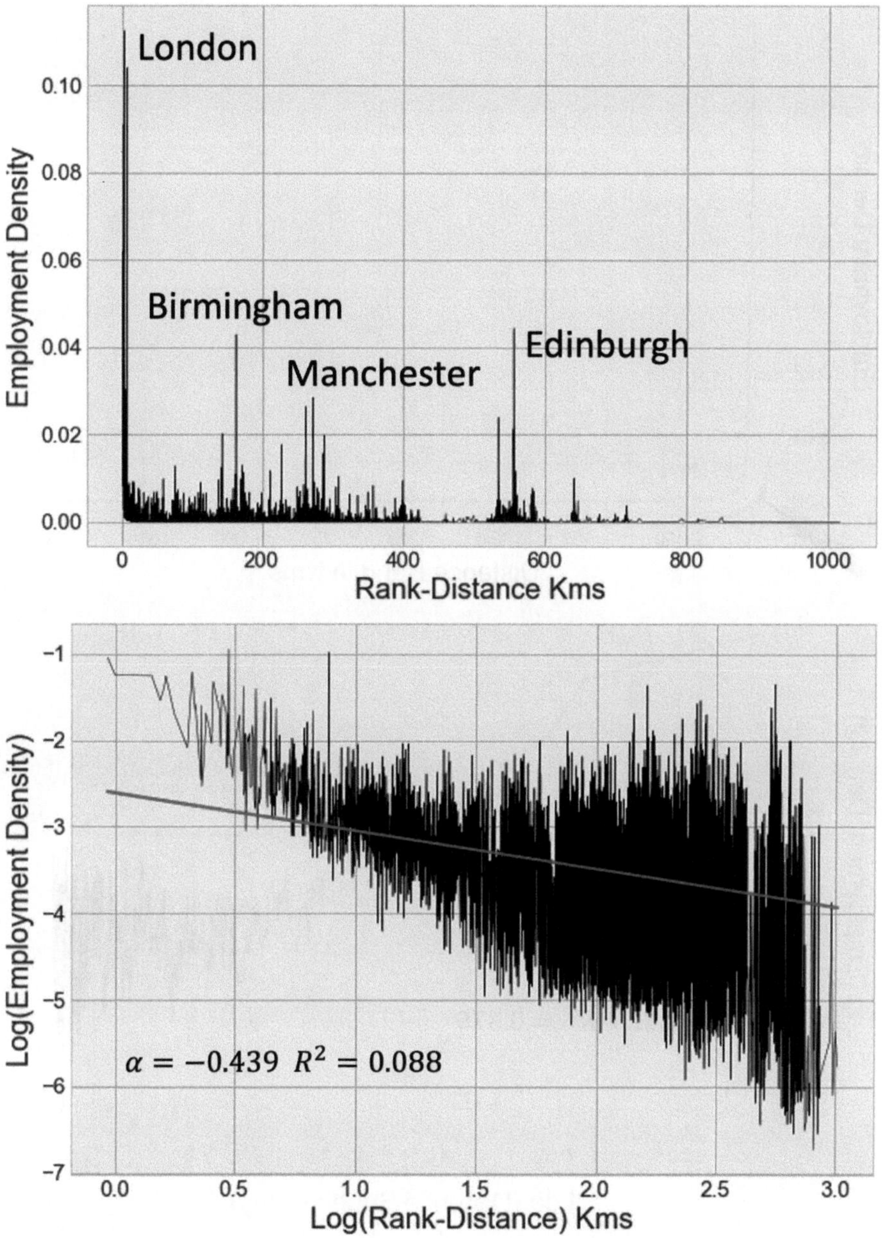

Figure 1.1 Continued

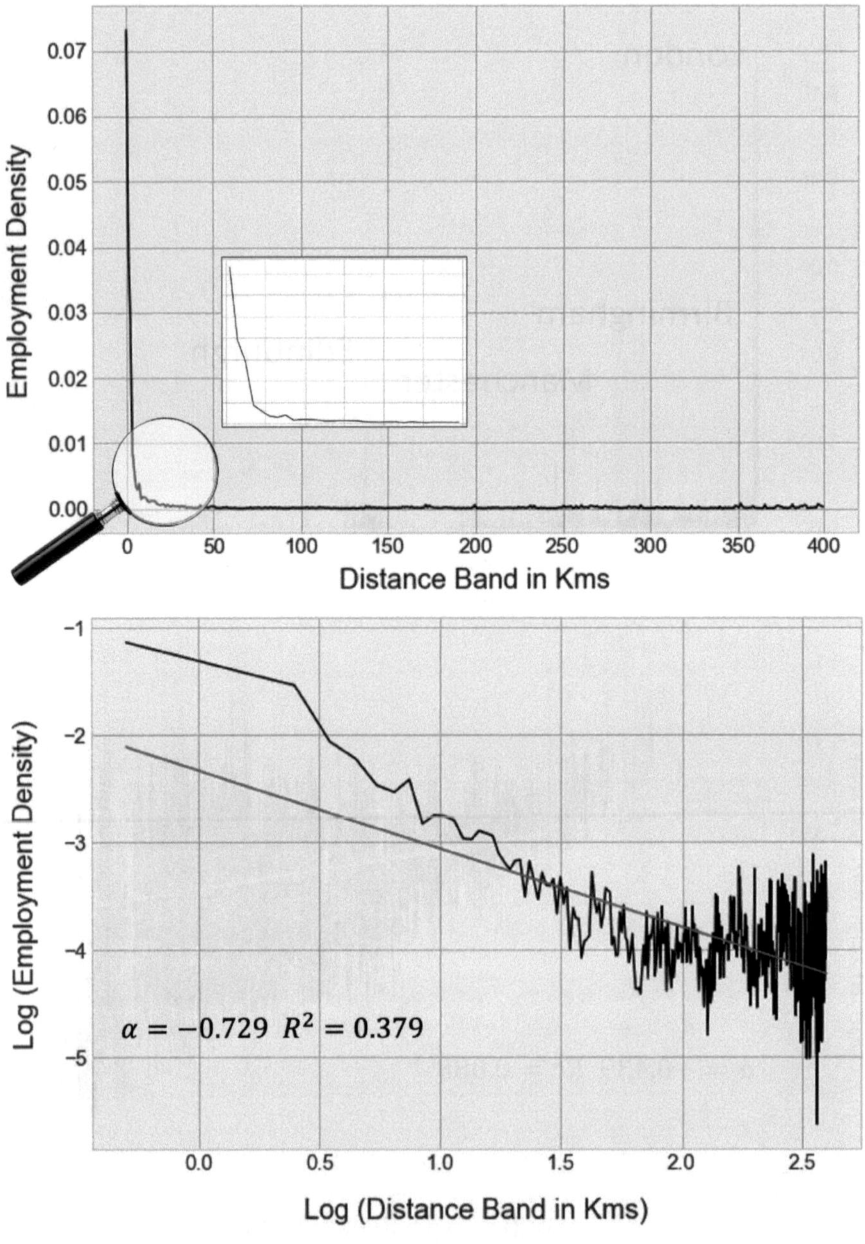

Figure 1.2 Urban density profiles for London: (a) inverse power; (b) logarithmic transformation.

stability of the relationship up to 400 km from London, we plot the logarithmic transformation $\log P_j = \log K - \alpha \log d_j$ in Figure 1.2(b) which reveals that the density accords to Clark's Law up to about 30 km from the centre (Charing Cross) with an $R^2 = 0.958$. From then on, the variations get greater although, over the entire system, the fit is good. From Figure 1.2(b), the slope of the function is $\beta = -0.729$ while the variance explained falls to about 0.379. Figure 1.2(b) can be interpreted as a continuous equivalent of the rank distance relationship that links Clark's to Zipf's Law.

Our third scaling involves the way patterns of interaction between zones that we refer to as origins and destinations scale with respect to the measure of impedance or deterrence between locations. We are not able to demonstrate this here in any quick and simple manner but it is intrinsic to the kind of scaling that is reflected in the model shown in equation (1.5). This model is the workhorse that we have developed for the urban system based on the island of Britain where the trips between origins and destinations are simulated using a model where the inverse power law has been replaced with the negative exponential that is scaling in a somewhat different manner. Then the generic model is

$$T_{ij} = E_i P_j \exp(-\gamma d_{ij}) / \sum_j P_j \exp(-\gamma d_{ij}), \tag{1.9}$$

where γ is the scaling parameter, E_i is the employment at the origin zone i and P_j is the employment at the destination zone j. The model we have built is in fact further disaggregated by different travel modes and an appropriate way of thinking about this to assume that the model in equation (1.9) is fitted separately to each of three modes of travel where the parameter values for car, bus, and rail are estimated as 0.131, 0.072, and 0.064, respectively. When we aggregate all these trips over all modes, we can work out an average flow from any zone to all others and plot these vectors for each zone, giving the picture below in Figure 1.3 which clearly shows that the cities in Britain scale according to size [11]. The picture is still impressionistic but it provides a glimpse of the fractal structure of flows that make up the urban system.

1.4 Urban allometry and scale

Our fourth and last scaling relation that we introduce here turns the relationship from a negative (inverse) one to a positive one in that it concerns the attributes of a variable as it changes in size. As cities get bigger, for example, they change qualitatively as we noted earlier when we introduced the idea of allometry. The notion that one variable changes at a different rate from another but that they are intrinsically linked lies at the core of this relation. In the examples we have identified so far, we have not discussed the need for the units that we are explaining in terms of employment and population locations to be internally consistent. In fact,

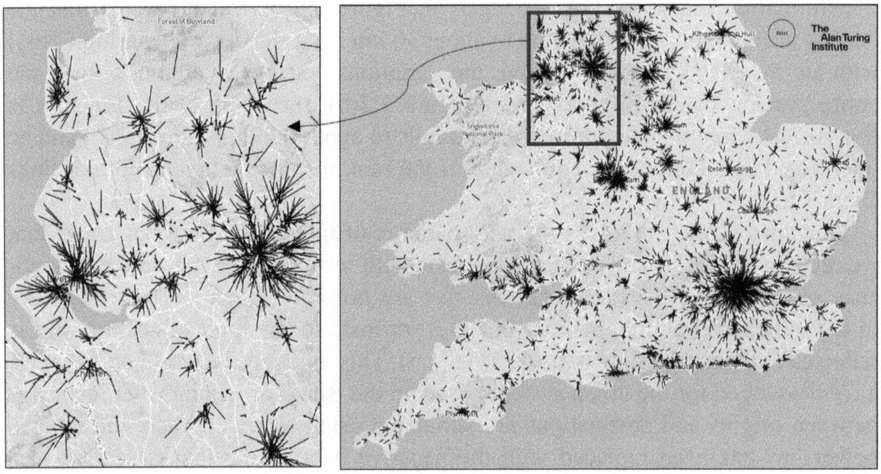

Figure 1.3 Spatial interactions patterns that scale over city size.

the rank size relation is largely applied to cities that are defined to be quite separate from one another and when it comes to positive scaling, it is essential that the units are integral objects which exist in their own right. In the examples so far, we have used partitions of cities into smaller output area units but when it comes to comparing attributes such as different features of their size, we need to ensure that the units themselves are relatively independent from one another. In this sense, here we need to ensure that we are dealing with well-defined cities. Rather than 8436 MSOAs, we will now use the 63 cities defined for the UK by the Centre for Cities (CFC) [12], which are cities greater than 110,000 in population in 2023 which can be easily compared with one another.

The idea of allometry is captured in equation (1.7), which implies that the attribute Y_i of the object i in question – a city, say – scales in a positive fashion with city size P_i^{φ}. The parameter φ is assumed to be positive; if it is between 0 and 1, the attribute increases sublinearly with city size but at a decreasing rate, whereas if φ is greater than 1, the increase is superlinear with city size, the attribute growing more than proportionately. As we noted above, this implies that growth realises economies or diseconomies of scale. This is the relation first articulated by Marshall [8] and explored extensively by Bettencourt et al. [9], which has motivated many of the chapters in this book. In Figure 1.4(a), we show the scaling relationship between the total weekly wages and population in the CfC database and what is striking is that there is hardly any evidence of scaling; in short, Figure 1.4(a) implies that wages per capita barely change as city size increases. It is also clear that London is a clear outlier with a substantial premium in terms of being associated with increasing wages compared to all the other cities in the data set.

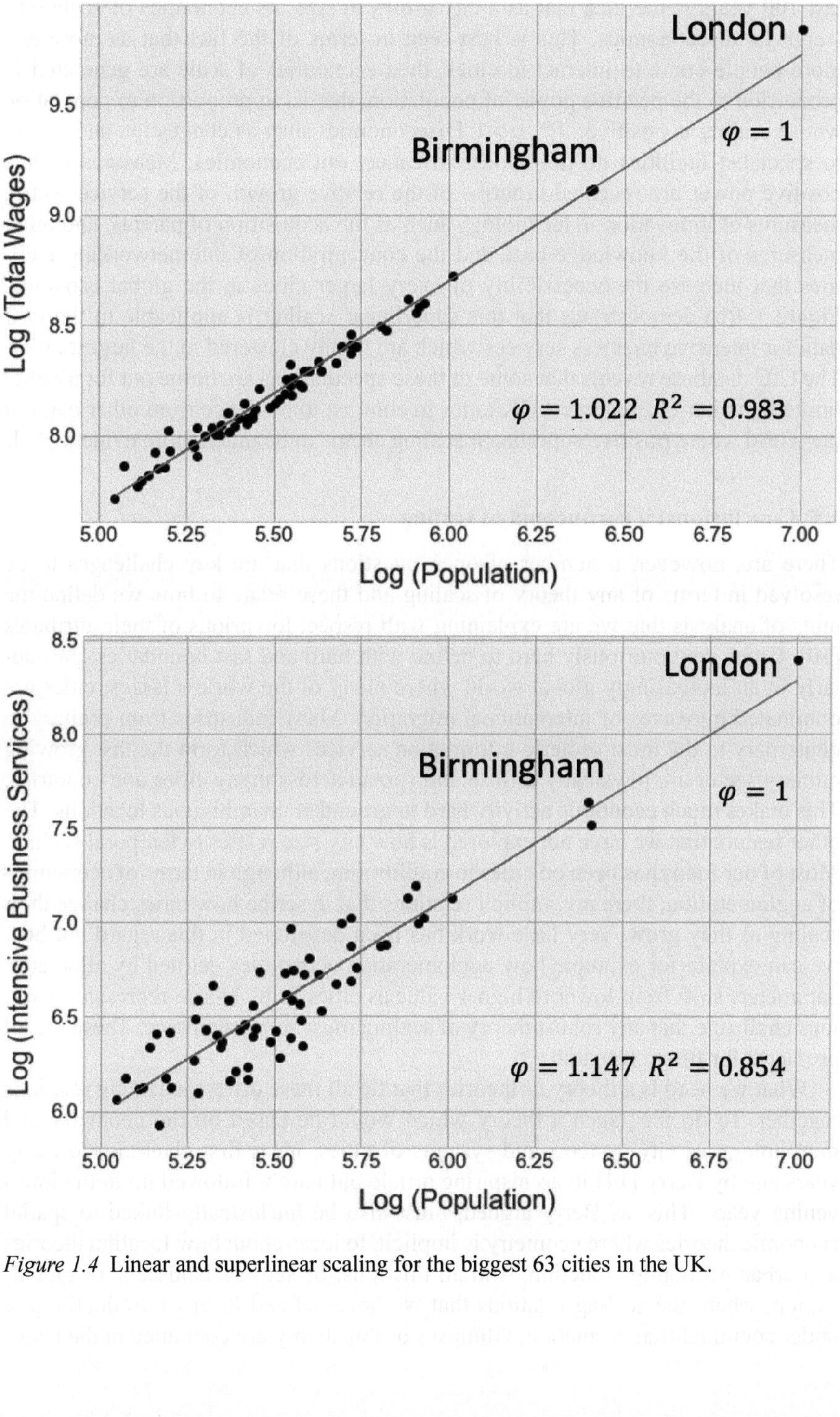

Figure 1.4 Linear and superlinear scaling for the biggest 63 cities in the UK.

In terms of city size, an old argument that has gradually gained pace during the last 100 years is the idea that as a city grows in size, its economies of scale outweigh its diseconomies. This is best seen in terms of the fact that as more and more people come to interact in cities, then economies of scale are generated in proportion to the positive power of population, that is, in proportion to population whose scaling is positive, $P_i^{\alpha}, \alpha > 1$. Diseconomies such as congestion and access to specialist facilities do not appear to cancel out economies. Measures of this positive power are revealed in terms of the relative growth of the service sector, measures of innovation in technology such as the acquisition of patents, and other measures of the knowledge base and the concentration of internetworking facilities that increase the accessibility of every larger cities in the global economy. Figure 1.4(b) demonstrates that this superlinear scaling is applicable to the CfC data for intensive business services which are highly clustered in the largest cities. The CfC database reveals that some of these speculations are borne out for a rather limited number of the largest UK cities in contrast to evidence from other parts of the world where positive superlinear scaling seems to be much more evident [13].

1.5 Conclusions: a cornucopia of scaling

There are, however, a number of open questions that are key challenges to be resolved in terms of any theory of scaling and these relate to how we define the units of analysis that we are explaining with respect to various of their attributes [10]. Cities are notoriously hard to define with hard and fast boundaries, particularly in an increasingly global world where many of the world's largest cities are dominated by waves of international migration. Many industries from primary to quaternary to the most esoteric information services which form the fast-growing quinary sector are physically diffuse and spread across many cities and countries. This makes much economic activity hard to ground at unambiguous locations. The other feature that we have not explored is how city size relates to temporal scaling. Most of our focus has been on cities in equilibrium, although in terms of economies of agglomeration, there are implicit relations that describe how cities change their scaling as they grow. Very little work has been developed in this regard but how we can explain for example how agglomeration economies defined by allometric parameters shift from lower to higher value as cities grow in size represents a serious challenge that any robust theory of scaling must surely embrace. These are all problems for future research.

What we need is a theory or theories that tie all these different scaling relations together. To do this, such a theory which would be based on the geometry and morphology of city systems and systems of cities, ideas first championed many years ago by Berry [14] in an inspiring article but barely followed up in the intervening years. This, as Berry argued, must also be intrinsically linked to spatial economic theories where geometry is implicit, to ideas about how location theories and urban economies function. And all this must be set in a landscape of globalisation, where the scaling relations that we have defined in this introduction are under continual transformation. Glimpses of this theory are contained in the pages of this book and collectively they point to a greater understanding of how scaling can be used to define ways in which we can develop more sustainable and robust approaches to the design of better cities.

Acknowledgements

This project was part-funded by the Alan Turing Institute under the *RUBICON* and *QUANT* Projects 2020–2023, ELAT2/100002 and EP/W006022/1.

References

[1] Koffka, K. *The Principles of Gestalt Psychology*. London: Routledge and Kegan Paul, 1935.
[2] West, G. *Scale: The Universal Laws of Life and Death in Organisms, Cities and Companies*. London: Weidenfeld and Nicolson, 2017.
[3] Batty, M. and Longley, P. A. *Fractal Cities: A Geometry of Form and Function*. London and San Diego: Academic Press, 1994.
[4] Batty, M. *Cities and Complexity: Understanding Cities with Cellular Automata, Agent-Based Models, and Fractals*. Cambridge: The MIT Press, 2005.
[5] Zipf, G. K. *Human Behavior and the Principle of Least Effort*. Cambridge: Addison-Wesley, 1949.
[6] Clark, C. Urban Population Densities. *Journal of the Royal Statistical Society, Series A* (General), 114, 490–496, 1951.
[7] Tobler, W. A Computer Movie Simulating Urban Growth in the Detroit Region. *Economic Geography*, 46 (Supplement), 234–240, 1970.
[8] Marshall, A. *Principles of Economics*. London: MacMillan Company, 1890.
[9] Bettencourt, L. M. A., Lobo, J., Helbing, D., and West, G. Growth, Innovation, Scaling, and the Pace of Life in Cities. *Proceedings of the National Academy of Sciences*, 104 (17), 7301–7306, 2007.
[10] Arcaute, E., Molinero, C., Hatna, E., Murcio, R., Vargas-Ruiz, C., Masucci, A. P., and Batty, M. Cities and Regions in Britain through Hierarchical Percolation. *Royal Society Open Science*, 3, 150691, 2016. DOI: 10.1098/rsos.150691
[11] Batty, M. and Milton, R. A New Framework for Very Large-Scale Urban Modelling. *Urban Studies, 58* (15), 3071–3094, 2021.
[12] CfC Cities Data Tool, London: Centre for Cities, 2023. available at www.centreforcities.org/data-tool/#graph=map&city=show-all
[13] Bettencourt, L. M. A. *Introduction to Urban Science*. Cambridge:The MIT Press, 2005.
[14] Berry, B. J. L. Cities as Systems Within Systems of Cities. *Papers of the Regional Science Association*, 13, 146–163, 1964.

2 Empirical overview of urban scaling

Urban allometry origins, critics and city performance evaluations

Luca S. D'Acci

2.1 Scaling laws

Scaling laws empirically test the functional relationship between two quantifiable variables (y, x) which scale with each other. Typically, one of these two variables is the organism, or system, as a whole (x), and the other (y) is a trait of the latter, which could be a physical quantity or a phenomenon. When x and y change at the same rate as each other, the relationship is called *isometric*, or linearly proportional, otherwise, when they do not scale linearly, namely disproportionally, it is called *allometric* [1].

A scaling relationship is a quantitative description of the change of measurable characteristics of a system when the whole system size changes. It is a measure of the *covariation* of a quantifiable trait of a system and the size of the latter. It does not designate their *causal* link, but only the nature of their *association.*

Such allometric relationships are usually following a power law function (eq. 2.1) which can also be written by using the logarithms (eq. 2.2), which allows for an easier interpretation: in a double logarithmic y–x plot if the observations align on a straight line we can describe the y–x link by a power law whose exponent is the slope of such a straight line which can be quantified via regression analysis.

$$y = ax^{\beta} \tag{2.1}$$

$$logy = loga + \beta logx \tag{2.2}$$

The interpretation of a log-log regression coefficient is in terms of percentage (a 1% change in the x, corresponds to a β% change in the y[1]) also called elasticity in economics.

In biology, allometry – called biological scaling – represents the change (e.g. metabolism, surface area, life span, heart beating, etc.) in organisms in relation to proportional changes in their body sizes (i.e., mass).

To my knowledge, the first use of allometric scale was in biology and dates back to 1891 [2]; it got general recognition in the 1920s [3], for later attracting the

DOI: 10.4324/9781003288312-3

attention of urban scholars who, during the last few decades, started to consistently investigate eventual allometries in urban settlements.

2.2 Urban scaling laws

What are the quantifiable, objective differences among typical small settlements, villages, towns, cities, and megacities within countries? Within a same region, does a typical 2 million inhabitant city, related to a typical 1 million, expect to have double the amount of crime, CO_2 emissions, GDP, built surface, street areas, patents, infections...? If so (isometric relation), or if not (allometric), why? What also happens to density, housing price, and to aspects such as life satisfaction, subjective wellbeing, and physical and mental health?

We will briefly show the state-of-the-art of urban scaling: a relatively recent area of urban science, investigating how measurable characteristics of cities vary (scale) with their sizes. When they scale linearly the relation is isometric (e.g., double population involves double built area); when not (e.g., double population involves more or less than double built area), the relation is allometric involving phenomena such as increasing returns, economies of scale, economies and diseconomies of agglomerations.

Empirical evidence indicates that a type of *universal* behaviour often appears even across countries despite historical unique individual patterns. This universality, the *systematic* scaling of y, makes urban scaling behaviour a main pillar of urban sciences.

Results are statistically robust and often consistent across countries, although attention is needed in keeping a common definition of cities, and methods to measures variables and to estimate the scaling exponent.

2.3 Empirical evidences

Within the best of my knowledge, the earliest allometric laws quantified in the social sciences was in Zipf's work [4] in cities (1949) who found a roughly scaling law between population size and economics variety (service-business, manufactures, retail stores) as well as population density, and it was known [5] since Adam Smith (1776) that occupational specialisation is linked to city sizes.

Since then more empirical findings have been accumulated and we are now reaching a status of knowledge mature enough to establish a new discipline of urban scaling on its own.

I report in Figures 2.1 and 2.2 a summary of empirical knowledge acquired in the last few decades from 46 studies indexed on Scopus.

2.4 Origins?

Reasons explaining why scaling laws empirically appear in cities are still under debate [6–23] and include the following possibilities, sometimes overlapping or mutually linked:

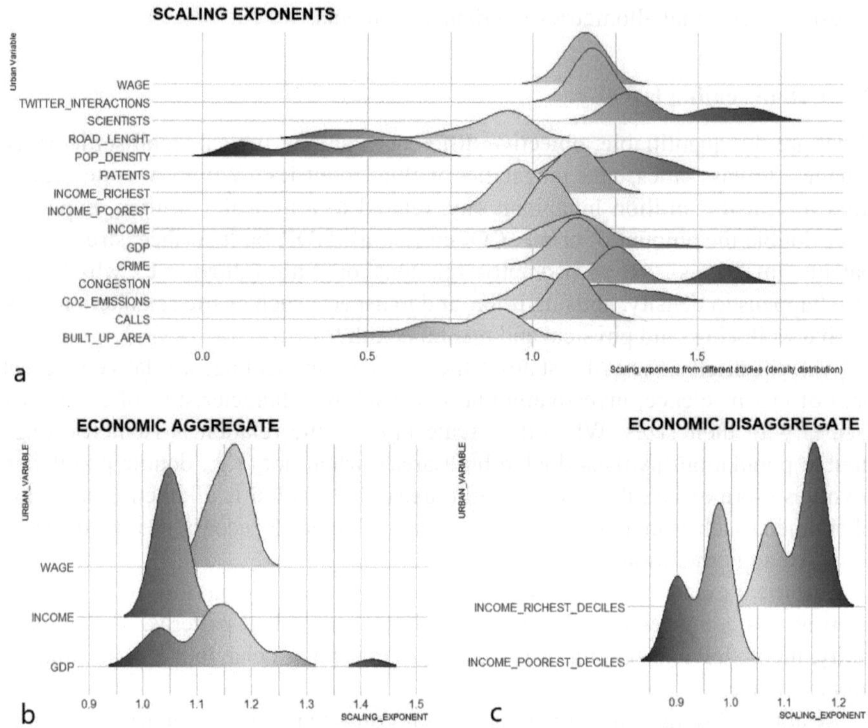

Figure 2.1 Density distribution from empirical results from 46 papers indexed on Scopus, with at least two different studies quantifing the same urban variable scaling exponent. Details about scaling exponents and sources are available at: www.urem.eu/scaling.

1. *Interactions/collaborations*: non-linear scaling of socio-economic variables might be a consequence of the amount of people interactions which typically increase superlinearly with city population size. If the range of (distance-dependent) interactions between citizens and amenities gets bigger, the socio-economic indicators improve, and the infrastructure costs decrease. Studies embracing interaction as a causal link with some urban scaling laws focus on the social network structure of cities and the probability of interactions among people. The more interactions, the more productivity. The probability of finding necessary collaborations is greater in larger populations and could explain some superlinear scaling. When, under constraints (e.g. energy, budget), the links in a network grow with the number of its nodes, scaling laws might emerge [7,15,18,20,24], specifically because *per capita* social connectivity scale-invariantly increases with city size [9].
2. *Densification*: factors such as urbanised area and some services (such as petrol stations) and infrastructures (e.g., streets, gas/electrical/water distribution)

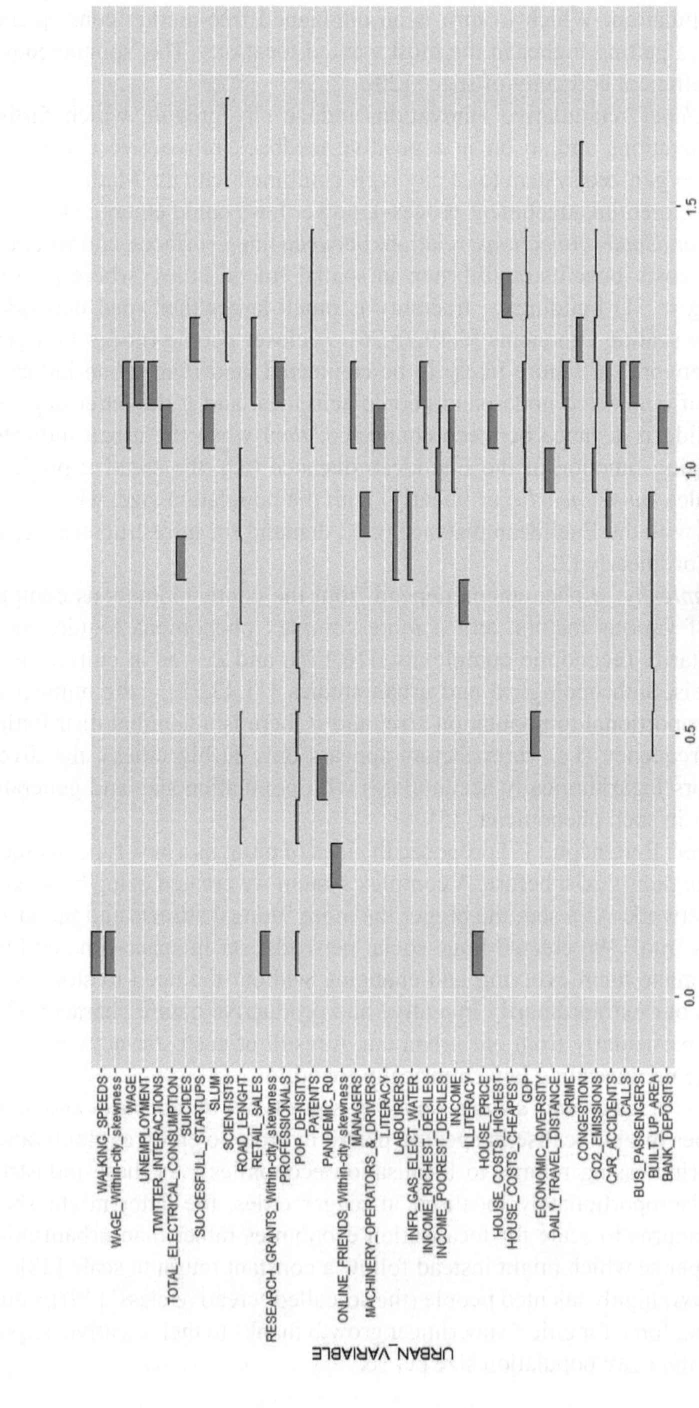

Figure 2.2 All scaling coefficients from 46 papers indexed on Scopus. Details and sources are available at: www.urem.eu/scaling.

might sublinearly scale because density typically increases when a city gets a bigger population. Which in turn is an unplanned free-market consequence of land prices getting higher in the most wanted locations. This spontaneously induces an efficient economy of space [20].

3. *Path-dependency*: cumulative innovations induce city growth, which further induces innovations and so on in a positive-feedback retroactive cycle [21]. When a self-organized system (as a city is) is combined with the Matthew effect (a type of preferential attachment process), power laws could emerge [12].
4. *Geometries and interconnections*: relations between lines, surfaces, and volumes, in a sort of costs–benefits equilibrium in spatial fractal cities (where population – living in 3D buildings – fractality is much larger than road networks) would cause scaling exponents [9,19,25,26]. *If* closer people (nodes in a geographical network) are more likely to be connected, and *if* an urban indicator is the sum of connected node-pairs people activities, and *if* the latter depends on the Euclidean distance between connected, *then* when the urban indicator is an increasing function of the Euclidean distance (e.g. the creative productivity), it scales *superlinearly* (or linearly) with the population size, while when it decreases with the Euclidean distance (e.g., demand for infrastructure) scales *sublinearly* or linearly [22].
5. *Higher complexity*: *if* phenomena depend from the contemporaneous complementarity of various factors; and *if* more complex phenomena require more complementarity (economic complexity, [16,17]); and *if* – as in cultural evolution models, anthropological and urban studies [11,13,27] – the number of factors is proportional to population size; and *if* there is a Gumbel distribution of factors frequency (i.e., rarer factors appears only in big cities); the diversity of factors logarithmically accumulates with population size and generates scaling laws in such phenomena [15].
6. *Social reactor*: Bettencourt [9] proposed the idea of cities as a new type of object in nature that didn't exist before. A complex system we created being between a star and a network. As a star, the bigger the more 'things' attracts and the faster these things 'run'. We created huge social networks set in space-time and we are able to make them evolving and changing without the need to stop them. This allows our extraordinarily inventive and productive nature characterising our species particularly from our urban era. A result of such star-network alike system is the urban scaling law empirically found.
7. *Localisation* versus *urbanisation economies*: some types of industries and occupational types might localise in specific places in order to enjoy agglomeration economies (increasing returns to localisation economies). As these industries are often disproportionately localised in bigger cities, the latter might show increasing returns to scale for localisation economies rather than urbanisation economies per se which might instead follow a constant return to scale [28].
8. *Creative class*: highly talented people (the so-called 'creative class' [29]), could be the driving force for cities' superlinear growth thanks to their creative outputs [30], rather than city population size per se.

Increasing and decreasing returns to scale have been studied by several evolutionary theories such as evolutionary economics, new economic geography, ecological economics, evolutionary transition theory, and evolutionary economic geography.

Rather than a causal variable, the size of the population might be a proxy aggregate variable [31] including all or some of the above potential sub-variables/reasons.

2.5 Planning, city performance, and urban cost–benefit evaluation

Urban scaling allows a new fundamental understanding of cities and, more importantly, in a quantitative way. It gives us tools for a new paradigm in city and regional planning. Knowing such systematic scaling between population size and certain urban factors would lead to more efficient urban management.

Planners and governments can use scaling laws to anticipate consequences of different city sizes, e.g., if a city is expected – or planned – to rapidly grow, or shrink, or be interconnected with other cities reciprocally enjoying spill over (borrow size) effects. Lot of indicators can be inferred and therefore proactively used in planning decisions.

This knowledge adds an important theoretical, empirical, and policies-oriented tool kit which any urban scholar nowadays should, if not dominate, at least be aware of. The impelling need to best accommodate a few billions of new incoming urban dwellers poses us the requirement to well understand what would likely happen to certain factors at different settlement sizes and then, by planning, how to prevent or encourage these factors in an intriguing game between self organization and planning [47]. It also provides scientific inputs to decision-making and policies for the renovation of small settlements (of which the world is full and almost ghost), and offer an intriguing new way to evaluate adjusted performance, costs, and benefits associated with urbanicity levels.

The existence of considerable variations from the regression line were evident since the above-mentioned Zipf work and the successive decades of empirical evidence till nowadays. They suggest the influence of other factors (e.g., history, planning, politics, contingencies, etc.) not taken into account from a simple covariation analysis against population size alone. These variations – which are the residuals from the expected values of equations (2.1) or (2.2) – have been proposed as a fairer evaluation of the performance of cities to measure how well a city is doing *in respect to* a typical city of her size in her region at her time (scale-independent urban indicators, SAMIs [32,33]).

2.6 Points needing attention

1. *Particular* versus *general*: there are two perspectives of viewing cities, an historical one treating each one city as a unique product of historical events which cannot be summarised with a number, being numerically translated and even identical to *n* other cities just because of having similar population size

[33–35]; and one treating cities as sharing *some* universal features regardless of individualities.

2. *Urban boundaries*: defining cities and therefore their boundaries in different ways is an obvious source of errors which sometimes results in very different scaling coefficients across researches [36]. It is therefore decisive to keep the same definition of city if we wish to *compare* results from different researches.
3. *Aggregative*: most urban scaling research uses only aggregative quantities such us *total* GDP, *total* income, etc. per city, despite the fact that different categories of such quantities (measured, for example, in terms of quantiles, such as the lowest incomes, or the highest) have specific behaviour in relations to city size. In fact, recent researches using disaggregated data, found different scaling coefficients from different categories, often even changing from sub- to superlinear (Figure 2.1b, c) across categories indicating distributional inequalities not possibly emerging from aggregative data [28,37–41].
4. *Categories*: different occupational categories as well as different industry types can show different scaling coefficients [28,41–43]. A city-wide scaling behaviour would be a consequence of specific combinations of these occupational and industry types, partially explaining distances from the expected scaling coefficients (e.g., Cambridge, Oxford, etc.).
5. *Cross-sectional (or transversal, or hierarchical) versus longitudinal (or temporal) scaling*: cross-sectional refers to the classical analysis in urban scaling, namely the functional association between an indicator (e.g. GDP, road areas, crime, CO_2 emissions, etc.) and its change across different city sizes within a region or nation at a given time. It extrapolates elasticities of urban quantifiable factors relative to urban population size at certain times. Longitudinal analysis refers to an indicator change over time for a given city as the latter grows increasing population size. They represent two different things [44].
6. *Phases of economic growth*: some urban properties might have specific scaling coefficients because being in cities during a particular *phase* of their economic growth rather than because they are stuck in universal scaling plots [45]. It will be interesting to investigate if, within regions, an association between population size (or *reciprocal* population size pattern) and economic growth phase is present.
7. *Isolated geographical entities*: studying cities as isolated entities [46] implies underestimation of socio-economic interactions across them and related spillover effects.

Note

1 The % increase of the y can be calculated by the direct substitution of the desired x values in the regression equation, or by: $100[(((100 + p)/100)^\wedge b) - 1]$, where p = %increase of the x; or by: $100[(q^\wedge b) - 1]$, where q is the multiplicative factor of x (e.g. if x doubles, $q = 2$).

References

1. Thompson, D. W., & Bonner, J. T. (2014). On growth and form. *On growth and form* (1-346).
2. Snell, O. (1891). Die Abhängigkeit des Hirnge-wichts von dem Körpergewicht und den geistigen Fahigkeiten. *Arch Psychiatr Ner-venkr, 23*, 436–446.
3. Huxley, J. S. (1925). Constant differential growth-ratios and their significance. *Nature, 114*(2877), 895–896.
4. Zipf, J. K. (1949). *Human behaviour and the principle of least effort*. Cambridge, MA.
5. Smith, A. (1776). *Inquiries into the nature and causes of wealth of nations*. London.
6. Fujita, M., Krugman P., & Venables A. J. (2001). *The spatial economy: Cities, regions, and international trade*. Cambridge, MA: The MIT Press.
7. Arbesman, S., Kleinberg, J. M., & Strogatz, S. H. (2009). Superlinear scaling for innovation in cities. *Physical Review E – Statistical, Nonlinear, and Soft Matter Physics, 79*(1), 016115. https://journals.aps.org/pre/abstract/10.1103/PhysRevE.79.016115
8. Bettencourt, L., & West, G. (2010). A unified theory of urban living. *Nature, 467*(7318), 912–913.
9. Bettencourt, L. M. A. (2013). The origins of scaling in cities. *Science, 340*(6139), 1438–1441.
10. Bettencourt, L. M. A., & Lobo, J. (2016). Urban scaling in europe. *Journal of the Royal Society Interface, 13*(116), 2016005. https://royalsocietypublishing.org/doi/10.1098/rsif.2016.0005
11. Bettencourt, L. M., Samaniego, H. & Youn, H. (2014). Professional diversity and the productivity of cities. *Scientific Reports, 4*(5393).
12. Chen, Y., Wang, Y., & Li, X. (2019). Fractal dimensions derived from spatial allometric scaling of urban form. *Chaos, Solitons and Fractals, 126*, 122–134.
13. Derex, M., Beugin, M.-P., Godelle, B. & Raymond, M. (2913). Experimental evidence for the influence of group size on cultural complexity. *Nature, 503*, 389–391.
14. Duranton, G., & Puga, D. (2004). *Chapter 48 micro-foundations of urban agglomeration economies*. NBER Working Paper 9931. www.nber.org/papers/w9931
15. Gomez-Lievano, A., Patterson-Lomba, O., & Hausmann, R. (2017). Explaining the prevalence, scaling and variance of urban phenomena. *Nature Human Behaviour, 1*(1), 0012.
16. Hausmann, R. & Hidalgo, C. A. (2011). The network structure of economic ouput. *Journal of Economic Growth, 16*, 309–342.
17. Hidalgo, C. A., Klinger, B., Barabasi, A.-L. & Hausmann, R. (2007). The product space conditions the development of nations. *Science*, 317, 482–487.
18. Mesoudi, A. (2011). Variable cultural acquisition costs constrain cumulative cultural evolution. *PLoS ONE, 6*(3), e18239.
19. Molinero, C., & Thurner, S. (2021). How the geometry of cities determines urban scaling laws. *Journal of the Royal Society Interface, 18*(176), 20200705.
20. Pan, W., Ghoshal, G., Krumme, C., Cebrian, M., & Pentland, A. (2013). Urban characteristics attributable to density-driven tie formation. *Nature Communications, 4*, 1961.
21. Pumain, D., Paulus, F., Vacchiani-Marcuzzo, C., & Lobo, J. (2006). An evolutionary theory for interpreting urban scaling laws. *CyberGeo, 2006*, 1–20.
22. Yakubo, K., Saijo, Y., & Korošak, D. (2014). Superlinear and sublinear urban scaling in geographical networks modeling cities. *Physical Review E – Statistical, Nonlinear, and Soft Matter Physics, 90*(2), 022803.

23. Yang, V. C., Papachristos, A. V., & Abrams, D. M. (2019). Modeling the origin of urban-output scaling laws. *Physical Review E, 100*(3). 032306.
24. Strumsky, D., & Lobo, J. (2015). Identifying the sources of technological novelty in the process of invention. *Research Policy, 44*(8), 1445–1461.
25. Ribeiro, F. L., Meirelles, J., Ferreira, F. F., & Neto C. R.. (2017). A model of urban scaling laws based on distance dependent interactions. *Royal Society Open Science*, 4160926160926.
26. Samaniego, H., & Moses, M. E. (2008). Cities as organisms: Allometric scaling of urban road networks. *Journal of Transport and Land Use, 1*(1), 21–39.
27. Youn, H. et al. (2016). Scaling and universality in urban economic diversification. *Journal of the Royal Society Interface, 13*, 20150937.
28. Sarkar, S., Arcaute, E., Hatna, E., Alizadeh, T., Searle, G., & Batty, M. (2020). Evidence for localization and urbanization economies in urban scaling. *Royal Society Open Science*, 7, 191638.
29. Florida, R. (2005). *Cities and the creative class*. Routledge.
30. Keuschnigg, M., Mutgan, S., & Hedström, P. (2019). Urban scaling and the regional divide. *Science Advances*, 5, eaav0042.
31. Bettencourt, L. M. A., Lobo, J., Strumsky, D., & West, G. B. (2010). Urban scaling and its deviations: revealing the structure of wealth, innovation and crime across cities. *PLoS ONE*, 5(11), e13541.
32. Alves, L. G. A., Mendes, R. S., Lenzi, E. K., & Ribeiro, H. V. (2015). Scale-adjusted metrics for predicting the evolution of urban indicators and quantifying the performance of cities. *PLoS ONE, 10*(9).
33. Hall, P. (1998). *Cities in civilization.* New York, NY: Pantheon Books.
34. Mumford, L. (1989). *The city in history: Its origins, its transformations, and its prospects*. San Diego, CA: Harcourt.
35. Benevolo, L. (1980). *The History of the City*. MIT Press.
36. Arcaute, E., Hatna, E., Ferguson, P., Youn, H., Johansson, A., Batty, M. (2015). Constructing cities, deconstructing scaling laws. *Journal of the Royal Society Interface, 12*, 20140745.
37. Arvidsson, M., Lovsjö, N., & Keuschnigg, M. (2023). Urban scaling laws arise from within-city inequalities. *Nature Human Behaviour, 7*, 365–374.
38. Heinrich Mora E., Heine C., Jackson J. J., West G. B., Yang V. C., & Kempes C. P. (2021). Scaling of urban income inequality inthe USA. *Journal of the Royal Society Interface, 18*, 20210223.
39. Sarkar, S., Phibbs, P., Simpson, R., & Wasnik, S. (2018). The scaling of income distribution in Australia: Possible relationships between urban allometry, city size, and economic inequality. *Environment and Planning B: Urban Analytics and City Science, 45*(4), 603–622.
40. Shutters, S. T., Applegate, J. M., Wentz, E. *et al.* (2022). Urbanization favors high wage earners. *npj Urban Sustain, 2*(6).
41. Rosenthal S. S., & Strange W. C. (2001). The determinants of agglomeration. *Journal of Urban Economics, 50*, 191–229.
42. Rosenthal S. S., & Strange W. C. (2003). Geography, industrial organisation, and agglomeration. *Center for Policy Research Working Papers, 107*, 1–42.
43. Mori T., Nishikimi K., & Smith T. E. (2008) The number-average size rule: a new empirical relationship between industrial location and city size. *Journal of Regulation Science, 48*, 165–211).

44. Bettencourt L. M. A., Yang V. C., Lobo J., Kempes C. P., Rybski D., & Hamilton M. J. (2020). The interpretation of urban scaling analysis in time. *Journal of the Royal Society Interface*, *17*, 20190846.
45. Strano E. & Sood V. (2016). Rich and poor cities in Europe. An urban scaling approach to mapping the European economic transition. *PLoS ONE*, *11*(8), e0159465.
46. Bonaventura, M., Aiello, L. M., Quercia, D. *et al.* (2021). Predicting urban innovation from the US Workforce Mobility Network. *Humanities and Social Sciences Communications*, *8*, 10.
47. D'Acci, L.S., Banister, D., White, R. W. (2024). Liveable urban forms: planning, self-organisation, and a third way (isobenefit urbanism). *Humanities and Social Sciences Communications*, 11, Article number: 578.

3 Scaling laws and urban systems[1]

Denise Pumain

3.1 Scale and size as fundamental features in systems of cities

Cities emerged more than 5000 years BP at a time when societies started to institutionalise and increase the complexity of their hierarchical organisation while they enlarged the territories that they controlled through developing diversified ecological, political and trading interactions [1,2]. At any historical period and in all regions of the world, cities are concentrations of diversified population, activities and artefacts that vary greatly in size and are organised in systems of cities. What is remarkable is that the statistical distribution of city sizes in any large territory is a continuum, today from a few thousand inhabitants in smaller towns to possibly tens of millions in the largest metropolises. The distribution of city size has maintained since archaeological times [3] a strongly asymmetric shape, including a large number of small towns, less cities of intermediary sizes and a small number of very large urban concentrations. As any city originated in a small settlement that went larger and larger, how can such an allometric growth can be explained? The statistical regularity of city size distributions and the relatively high persistence of urban hierarchies in all regions of the world have given rise to numerous theories [4].

Many qualitative features are associated with the quantity of inhabitants living in a city to such an extent that: "the size of a town or city is a rather synthetic indicator, which can be correlated with many aspects of city functions and urban life" [5]. Urban systems share with many other complex systems [6,7] the strong hierarchical differentiation and organisation that led the French engineer Jean Reynaud as early as 1871 to associate for the first time the term of "system" to a national set of cities[2] [8]; discovered by Robic [9]. The specific shape of the city size distribution was later coined by G.K. Zipf [10] as "the rank-size rule" and can be fitted with many other types of asymmetric distributions [11]. It has recently been the gateway to the field of urban research for many practitioners of statistical physics investigating scaling laws [12]. "Scaling refers to a set of properties associated to a type of complex systems, which exhibit nonlinear relations (often formalized as power laws) among attributes of their subsystems, either in their spatial organization or during their temporal development" [5]. Urban scaling laws are not only fits of urban attribute distributions to power functions of city size.

DOI: 10.4324/9781003288312-4

Following the inspiration given by Geoffrey West [6], they also reveal the effect of specific constraints on the evolution of complex systems. Whereas in the case of living organisms these constraints are primarily physical-chemical processes, rather stable in time and operating over the very long duration of biological evolution, in the case of cities the major constraints are those of the social organisation of interactions in interpersonal and interurban networks [13]. These constraints also are changing, on much shorter time scales than those of biological evolution.

This raises the interesting problem of transferring models from natural sciences, "whose basic requirements are not necessarily fulfilled in the case of social systems" [5]. Arguing that the question of scale deserves similar treatment to natural and societal objects, G. West elevates the theoretical framework of scaling to the status of a "grand unifying theory of sustainability" [6]. Scaling laws have become for some researchers the "cornerstone of a science of cities" [14] and are even proposed as the starting point for an "integrated theory of cities" [15]. After re-contextualising this line of research in a broader methodological approach of urban systems, I will examine the major results that were gained from the scaling laws paradigm and discuss its relevance for urban theories.

3.2 Methods: building an evolutionary theory of urban systems through multiscale simulation models

Understanding how cities can remain small towns or evolve toward very large metropolises relies on a careful observation of the urban growth process. The evolutionary theory of urban systems [12] has been constructed by taking into account a large number of empirical observations made on many cities, for long historical periods and in different regions of the world, paying the greatest attention to the coherence of the definitions and delimitations of urban entities and to the meaning of urban indicators. It explains at first the inequalities in size, close to a lognormal distribution, by a quasi-stochastic growth model, modified to take into account the effects of the process of hierarchical diffusion of innovations [16,17].

Gibrat's model [18] enables to connect the distribution of city sizes with an urban growth process that can be tested. It explains the genesis of highly unequal distributions of city size, adjustable by a lognormal distribution, by a multiplicative growth process, "the law of proportional effect". Urban growth rates are randomly distributed in a system of cities independently of their size and fluctuating over time. Tests of this model on large samples of cities observed at many time intervals for long durations ([18] for French cities late 19th–early 20th century, [19] for England and Wales 19th century, [20] for France 1831–1975, [21] for seven major regions of the world on as large as possible periods of time) have shown that this very simple model provides a rather good statistical representation of the process. This first approximation is rightly completed by including growth impulses from innovation waves and their hierarchical diffusion within the system of cities [16]. That new model helps to better understand the recurrent deviations that were observed between empirical data on urban growth and Gibrat's stochastic model, i.e., a slight positive correlation between growth rates and city size (at the beginning of each innovation wave) and a persistency of high or low growth rates in the same cities over some periods of time. This also provides an understanding of the bifurcations in the trajectories of individual cities that are created by the major functional specialisations, successively amplifying urban growth then urban decline according to the stage in the corresponding product cycles [22].

The principles of the evolutionary theory were translated into a series of dynamics models because we think that reconstructing past urban trajectories within a parsimonious description of their historical and geographical context is a first necessary step for testing the relevance of theoretical explanations. It is also a condition for ensuring the quality of projections estimating future relative positions of cities within inter-urban competition, thus for adjusting intelligent urban policies. Our experiments included at first mathematical models of systems of non-linear equations and then computational models of multi-agents systems (see [23] for a review). Through a close collaboration with computer scientists, we designed the SIMPOP series of models that was conceived to explain the hierarchical differentiation of city sizes and their functional geo-diversity. The implemented mechanisms between "agents" (i.e., collective agents that represent individual cities) are mainly: a proactive and selective propagation of innovation waves generated by interurban competition and emulation; a market exchange between urban functions; a hierarchical selection (top down and bottom up); the appearance of new urban functions (exogenous in the first models); an expanding range of interurban interaction (as a result of space-time contraction); and path dependence according to the territorial boundaries that constrain urban interaction. The development of the OpenMOLE simulation platform enabled the integration of sophisticated model validation processes, including genetic algorithms and access to parallel grid computing [24].

3.3 Results: efficiency of comparing and simulating urban growth processes

We use that knowledge for developing an interpretation, which is better anchored in geographical urban theory, of the new frame of analysis proposed under the label of "scaling laws" by physicists [25]. Instead of imagining an urbanisation process where the largest cities would simply be a replication of smaller ones constrained by universal power laws, we explain the level and observed variations in values of the exponents of urban scaling laws according to the stage of development of the considered urban attributes in the urban system [22]. Exponents of non-linear relationships between an urban attribute and city size are above 1 during the first stage of adoption of innovation in the urban system, when they are captured by and concentrate in the largest cities, and below 1 when they withdraw in smaller towns of cheaper land rents and wages after their stage of wide diffusion all over the system. Over time the exponent values evolve according to this theory of the co-evolution of cities within an integrated system of cities [26,27].

A simulation model of the SIMPOP series designed by Benoît Glisse enabled to inform some of the processes that generate diversity among systems of cities, based on a comparison of their development, respectively, over eight and three centuries in Europe and the United States [28]. Significant qualitative changes compared to the European set of parameters were necessary for simulating the evolution of American cities, identifying a system of "New World" cities, introducing the notion of a "pioneer front" for simulating the colonisation of a territory by cities and their dependence on an external demand to ensure the development of the system, in accordance with the dynamics revealed by calibrating the model on empirical data. The experiments with this model also provided further advances in explaining the evolution of systems of cities, proving the importance of urban networks in generating more urban growth (or "agglomeration economies" whose processes are described at micro-level in Ref. [29]). These results demonstrate that the inequalities in city sizes are becoming larger than those that would be predicted with a simple stochastic model and contradict other theories that predicted counter-urbanisation.

Moreover, the over-concentration in certain larger cities at given time periods was confirmed by our simulations. We comfort the intuitions of the geographer Jefferson [30] or the historians Braudel [31] and de Vries [32] on the existence of these centres of the world economy or "world cities", created by interactions whose spatial scale exceeds that of other cities. The urban primacy characterises cities that at any time have brought together different worlds that were not yet very well connected. This discovery that "global cities may exist since the Middle Age" states that some cities at the head of urban hierarchies expand a significant part of their interactions beyond the boundaries of their own system [28]. We have verified in further studies including as well the BRICS countries that "metropolisation" and "simplification from below of urban hierarchies" (leading to "shrinking cities") are common dynamics trends observed in several systems of cities in the world [33].

Another important result obtained through our simulations is in advancing modelling in the social sciences and humanities towards scientific accuracy and reproducibility [34]. Even if the ambition of these models is never to produce an exact numerical result or one that would totally optimise only one aspect of the problem, we now have powerful exploration methods that describe all the dynamic behaviours of a model, that produce satisfactory process trade-offs leading to plausible solutions, and that detect whether the contributions of certain processes and parameters to these dynamics are truly effective or not [35–37].

3.4 Discussion

Scaling laws applied to cities have been successful, when considering the multiplication of publications (more than 500 for "urban scaling laws" at spring 2023 on Google Scholar), but have they really advanced the scientific knowledge of cities? The early expectations of the framework of scaling laws for finding universal values for the parameters were not verified [38]. From a theoretical point of view, these works have above all re-formulated pre-existing knowledge in a different way. For example, the effects of centrality, i.e., the higher level of certain attributes as one considers larger cities (measured by exponents greater than

1 in the scaling laws), were already part of urban theories, such as central place theory. The allometric effects of centrality that are constructed by interaction asymmetries (unequal exchange) were long identified by regional science economists such as Roberto Camagni or Philippe Aydalot. Conversely, the scale economies revealed by exponents below 1 that are observed in the design of many urban utilities also were already well known by urban engineers, urbanists and planners. Despite the similarities of the observed regularities in terms of size inequalities, social processes are only partly self-organising, with some discernible optimisation effects under space-time constraints, but they are also partly intentional and reflexive, which creates much greater unpredictability.

When theories and models are transferred from one discipline to another, great care must be taken to avoid the temptation to make use of analogies, especially about processes. The case of the gravity model (interaction flows being proportional to the product of mass of the geographical unit at origin and destination and inversely proportional to their distance) is exemplary. This model helps to understand the spatial organisation of societies such as geographical centre–periphery configurations, it describes rather well commuting processes and regional migration flows and it helps in predicting the required size of transport infrastructures. But this does not mean that human mobility can be explained by the law of universal gravitation!

In the case of scaling laws, the research, so far, has provided neither a complete urban theory nor a practical model. There is no evidence so far that the processes having made the application of scaling laws successful in the biological domain could be transposed to cities [39]. The attempts to find fractal structures for all interaction networks and to derive urban growth trajectories from the values of scaling exponents [25] are not convincing: the suggested equations are not testable because most of their parameters refer to quantities that can hardly be measured. Perhaps in the future better estimates of social exchanges based on direct observation of interpersonal communications will be available, even if the new "social networks" provide only partial and often biased information on the behaviour of urban actors. There are deeper theoretical reasons for questioning the possibility of inferring in social sciences a longitudinal interpretation (what happens during the growth of a city) from cross-sectional data (measurements taken at a given time between cities of different sizes), claimed by the early work of physicists [40]. Whether testing theoretical hypotheses or providing decision support for cities, the combination of sound empirical data and effective modelling methods is still needed to better predict the dynamics of systems of cities.

A major interest of the research on urban scaling laws is undoubtedly that it has revived interest in the science of cities, opened the way for orienting a series of very valuable contributions along similar questions and widened its audience among a variety of disciplines that had previously been little concerned with this subject. The dynamics of urban systems is an essential component of the relationship between societies and the planet earth, in the materiality of their geographical inscription including natural resources exploitation and transformation, in the social and spatial logics of their organisation and millenary evolution and in the sustainability of this particular form of human habitat. The great urban success story can continue if we wisely use all the networks they have built, on one hand by cascading down technological and organisational innovations through national and international regulations and, on the other, irrigating every city from the bottom up with the countless local inventions that improve living conditions, environmental restraint and quality of community living. Involving everyone in this hitherto uncoordinated enterprise of self-organising territorial intelligence goes beyond what scaling laws can offer our imagination, adding ethics to our lives as we plan for our cities' future.

Notes

1 www.santafe.edu/research/results/working-papers/scaling-laws-and-urban-systems
2 In French "le système général des villes".

References

[1] Bairoch, P. (1985). *De Jéricho à Mexico: villes et économie dans l'histoire*. Paris, Éditions Gallimard.

[2] Marcus, J. & Sabloff, J. A. (eds.) (2008). *The Ancient City. New perspectives on Urbanism in the Old and New World.* SAR Press, 405 p.

[3] Fletcher, R. (1986). Settlement archaeology: World-wide comparisons. *World Archaeology*, *18*(1), 59–83.

[4] Raimbault, J., Pumain, D. (2020). Conclusion: Perspectives on Urban Theories, in Pumain D. (ed.), (2020) *Theories and Models of Urbanisation* (pp. 303–330). Springer, Lecture Notes in Morphogenesis, Cham.

[5] Pumain, D. (2004). *Scaling laws and urban systems*. Working Paper no04-02-002, Santa Fe Institute, 26 p.

[6] West, G. B. (2017). *Scale. The universal laws of growth, innovation, sustainability, and the pace of life in organisms, cities, economies, and companies*, New York, Penguin Press, 479 p.

[7] Winiwarter, P. (2009). *Neural Network Nature: Fractal hierarchies of 'Perceptrons' from Clusters of Galaxies to the World Wide Web*. www.bordalierinstitute.com/

[8] Reynaud, J. (1841). Villes, dans *Encyclopédie nouvelle, Paris, éd. par C. Gosselin, t. VIII,* 670–687.

[9] Robic, M. C. (1982–1993). A hundred years before Christaller... a central place theory. *L'Espace géographique*, *21*(1), 53–61.

[10] Zipf, G. K. (1941). *National unity and disunity*. Indiana, Bloomington Principia Press.

[11] Quandt, R. E. (1964). Statistical discrimination among alternate hypothesis and some regularities. *Journal of Regional Science*, *5*(2), 1–23.

[12] Bettencourt, L. M., Lobo, J., Helbing, D., Kühnert, C., & West, G. B. (2007). Growth, innovation, scaling, and the pace of life in cities. *PNAS – Proceedings of the National Academy of Sciences*, *104*(17), 7301–7306.

[13] Pumain, D. (1997). Vers une théorie évolutive des villes. *L'Espace Géographique*, *25*(2), 119–134.

[14] Rybski, D., Arcaute, E., & Batty, M. (2019). Urban scaling laws. *Environment and Planning B: Urban Analytics and City Science*, *46*(9), 1605–1610.

[15] Lobo, J., Alberti, M., Allen-Dumas, M., Arcaute, E., Barthelemy, M., Bojorquez Tapia, L. A., ... & Youn, H. (2020). *Urban science: Integrated theory from the first cities to sustainable metropolises*. Report submitted to the NSF on the Present State and Future of Urban Science.

[16] Favaro, J.-M., & Pumain, D. (2011). Gibrat revisited: An urban growth model including spatial interaction and innovation cycles. *Geographical Analysis*, *43*(3), 261–286.

[17] Hägerstrand, T. (1952). The Propagation of Innovation Waves. *Lund Studies in Geography, Serie B, No. 4*, 20.

[18] Gibrat, R. (1931). *Les inégalités économiques*. Paris, Sirey.

[19] Robson, B. T. (1973). *Urban growth, an approach.* Methuen, London.

[20] Pumain, D. (1982). *La dynamique des villes*. Paris, Economica, 231 p.

[21] Cura, R., Cottineau, C., Swerts, E., Ignazzi, C. A., Bretagnolle, A., Vacchiani-Marcuzzo, C., & Pumain, D. (2017). The old and the new: qualifying city systems in the world with old models and new data. *Geographical Analysis*, *49*(4) 363–386.

[22] Pumain, D., Paulus, F., Vacchiani-Marcuzzo, C., & Lobo, J. (2006). An evolutionary theory for interpreting urban scaling laws. *Cybergeo: European Journal of Geography, 343.*

[23] Pumain, D. & Sanders, L. (2013). Theoretical principles in inter-urban simulation models: a comparison. *Environment and Planning A*, *45*, 2243–2260.

[24] Reuillon, R., Schmitt, C., De Aldama, R., & Mouret, J. B. (2015). A new method to evaluate simulation models: the calibration profile (CP) algorithm. *Journal of Artificial Societies and Social Simulation, 18*(1), 12.

[25] Bettencourt, L., Lobo, J., & West, G. B. (2009). The self-similarity of human social organization and dynamics in cities, in D. Lane, D. Pumain, S. Van der Leeuw, G. West (eds.), *Complexity perspectives in innovation and social change* (pp. 221–236). Springer, Dordrecht.

[26] Finance, O. & Swerts, E. (2020). Scaling laws in urban geography. Linkages with urban theories, challenges and limitations, in Pumain D. (ed.), *Theories and Models of Urbanisation* (pp. 67–96). Springer, Lecture Notes in Morphogenesis.

[27] Paulus, F. (2004). Coévolution dans les systèmes de villes: croissance et spécialisation des aires urbaines françaises de 1950 à 2000. Thèse de Doctorat, Université Paris 1 Panthéon-Sorbonne, Paris.

[28] Bretagnolle, A., & Pumain, D. (2010). Simulating urban networks through multiscalar space-time dynamics (Europe and United States, 17th-20th centuries), *Urban Studies*, *47*(13), 2819–2839.

[29] Puga, D. (2010). The magnitude and causes of agglomeration economies, *Journal of Regional Science*, *50*(1), 203–219.

[30] Jefferson, M. (1939). The law of the primate city. *Geographical Review*, *29*, 226–232.

[31] Braudel, F. (1979). *Civilisation matérielle, économie et capitalisme (XVe – XVIIIe siècle)*, 3 vol, Paris, Armand Colin.

[32] de Vries, J. (1984). *European Urbanization 1500-1800.* London, Methuen.

[33] Pumain D., Swerts E., Cottineau C. Vacchiani-Marcuzzo C., Ignazzi A., Bretagnolle A., Delisle F., Cura R., Lizzi L, & Baffi, S. (2015). Multi-level comparison of large urban systems. *Cybergeo, European Journal of Geography*, 706.

[34] Pumain, D. & Reuillon, R. (2017). *Urban dynamics and simulation models*. Springer, International. Lecture Notes in Morphogenesis, Cham, 123 p.

[35] Cottineau, C., Chapron, P., & Reuillon, R. (2015). Growing models from the bottom up. An evaluation-based incremental modelling method (EBIMM) applied to the

simulation of systems of cities. *Journal of Artificial Societies and Social Simulation, 18*(4), 9.

[36] Raimbault, J. (2020). Indirect evidence of network effects in a system of cities. *Environment and Planning B: Urban Analytics and City Science, 47*(1), 138–155.

[37] Schmitt, C., Rey-Coyrehourcq, S., Reuillon, R., & Pumain, D. (2015). Half a billion simulations, evolutionary algorithms and distributed computing for calibrating the SimpopLocal geographical model. *Environment and Planning B, 42*(2), 300–315.

[38] Cottineau, C., Hatna, E., Arcaute, E., & Batty, M. (2017). Diverse cities or the systematic paradox of urban scaling laws. *Computers, Environment and Urban Systems, 63*, 80–94.

[39] Cottineau C. (2017). Review of "West G., 2017, Scale. The universal laws of growth, innovation, sustainability, and the pace of life in organisms, cities, economies, and companies, New York, Penguin Press, 479 p". *Cybergeo: European Journal of Geography.* doi: https://doi.org/10.4000/cybergeo.28543

[40] Pumain, D. (2012). Urban systems dynamics, urban growth and scaling laws: The question of ergodicity, in J. Portugali, H. Meyer, E. Stolk, & E. Tan, (eds). *Complexity Theories of Cities Have Come of Age: An overview with implications to urban planning and design.* (pp. 93–106). Springer, Heidelberg, Berlin.

4 Urban transitions

Scaling complex cities down to human size[1]

Frank Schiller

4.1 Introduction

Cities manifest remarkably universal features that render them quantitatively comparable. The spatial sciences have come a long way to arrive at such methodologies for spatial analysis. This chapter outlines the analysis of scaling phenomena to progress transition theory with respect to cities and urbanisation. Scaling refers to regularities across different hierarchical levels of the same entity. Typically, indicators of city development are treated independently: indicator X measures x and indicator Y measures y. The implicit assumption is an average linear increase of a given aggregated characteristic to the increase in population size, whereas scaling stands for non-linear relationships: the measurement systematically increases or decreases faster or slower than population size [1].

So far, these relationships have only been shown for some phenomena while ignoring others. For example, a key research gap relates to diseconomies of cities and the quest for sustainability. In order to move on, the chapter will address end-use technologies that closely relate to final energy consumption to present a more complete picture of cities' future. Although scaling is being studied in increasing detail, the social processes bringing these patterns about are still not well understood. This is particularly true for those phenomena that are reproduced by conglomerations of interdependent social institutions.

Complexity science has rarely provided theory explaining social self-organisation (for an exception see [2]) but it has influenced evolutionary theorising in several disciplines working towards explanatory theories, e.g., in economics, geography, and transition management. This chapter argues for socially robust theorising involving explanations of social mechanisms to manage the transition of cities [3].

4.2 Cities on a scale

Progress in network analysis has not been restricted to the domain of nature but has been applied to society and its artefacts too. In both domains some networks, so-called scale-free networks, have a logarithmic degree distribution, that is an

DOI: 10.4324/9781003288312-5

invariant relationship between one factor and a second variable signified by a power law: the same structure prevails across all hierarchical levels [4]. The relationships are remarkably stable over time but they are not necessarily static since they may change. In conjunction with increasing or decreasing returns explanations the group of analytical relationships scaling super- and sublinearly provide explanations for a variety of phenomena in cities. In both cases nodes above the median influence the system disproportionally and their median reveals little about their behaviour. By contrast, most network research in the social sciences has focused on institutionalised networks.

In natural systems scaling relationships enable the prediction of how changes of one variable will impact on a second in the network's evolution. In the social sciences such correlation-derived prediction may be considered a natural fallacy. Still, scaling has been observed in social artefacts and social structures too. It has been shown that characteristics such as economic growth and mobility vary systematically with the population size of cities [5,6]. Indeed, these relationships follow power-laws: physical infrastructure studied so far grows less than proportionally with city size, e.g., road networks [7–9], subways, or train networks [10,11]. This might also apply to other systems of provision [12]. These are typical instances of sublinear scaling and thus represent negative allometry.

Other factors scale more than proportionally with population size such as innovations, GDP, and income [13,14]. They scale superlinearly, indicating positive allometry. The superlinear scaling of GDP and innovations relate to the diversification of the socio-economic processes with cumulative effects over time [15], i.e., economics of scale and scope and agglomeration effects emerge [16]. However, we also find decreasing returns for other phenomena such as diseconomies from high land prices, congestion of infrastructure, increasing emissions, or higher infection rates.

The study of increasing and decreasing returns to scale has been pursued by several schools of evolutionary theorising in different disciplines, including, amongst others, evolutionary economics, new economic geography, evolutionary economic geography, ecological economics, and evolutionary transition theory. Within their disciplinary contexts these theories show how increasing and decreasing returns explain economic and urban growth and explain it.

Bettencourt [1] has consolidated research in urban complexity science and sharpened some of the aforementioned evolutionary theories by proposing an endogenous theory of urban growth and shrinking: cities emerge as diseconomies from transport and social interaction are overcome by social and physical networks transporting goods, people, and information creating increasing returns in socio-economic activity (superlinear scaling) and exploitation of the economies of scale in urban infrastructure (sublinear scaling but faster than city area). Accordingly, urban form and social networks feed-back on each other and we find geographic and social characteristics of cities aligned in the theory. The added-value of scaling analysis is seen in establishing baselines and null models with population size viewed "not so much a causal force, but rather a proxy aggregate variable" [17, p. 6], which is immediately supported by the greatly varying deviations from the normal scale observed for some functions, e.g., murder rates. Hence, the theory proposes a threshold where cities are most productive. Beyond this threshold social costs overcome benefits and cities decline, e.g., their GDP shrinks and the maintenance of infrastructure becomes increasingly difficult. Yet despite this theoretical openness to diseconomies of urbanisation, complexity science has scarcely engaged in the study of such diseconomies or thresholds.

4.3 Scaling phenomena and the empirical complexity of cities

Different authors have tested different parameters with respect to population size only to find that the observed scaling pattern is sensitive to the delineation of cities and hence population size itself. In particular, superlinear scaling of income and patents has been found to be highly sensitive [18]. The indicator may also fail to facilitate eco-innovations, such as low-exergy energy systems, since these depend on exogenous national policies [19]. Likewise, energy-related ex-post observations might be unsuitable for forecasting since they omit important energy-related economic mechanisms [20]. The need for a more differentiated analysis also concerns the relationship of cities to the surrounding territory [21]. Indeed, urban scaling phenomena may only be true for cities within countries due to administrative traditions, political priorities, and other factors [22]. This seems to speak for context-specific rather than generic mechanisms.

There is increasing evidence that the urban form has direct and indirect influence on the economic and the metabolic flipside of development. Following the known biologic scaling relationship between metabolic rate and the body mass of organisms ('Kleiber's law') one might expect a sublinear relationship between population size and urban metabolism. However, if the methodological challenge of defining population size functionally is considered only one study may be considered reliable so far: Oliveira et al. [23] find superlinear scaling in US cities indicating increasing urban inefficiencies: doubling the population of US cities results in an average increase of 146% in CO_2 emissions, rather than the expected efficiency gains from economies of scale in infrastructure. This suggests strong rebound effects for US cities. This is important since increasing energy-efficiency in one sector is regularly offset by growing energy use in another representing so-called rebound effects (of consumption). These are known to be particularly relevant for mobility [24,25].

4.4 Against the simplicity of allometry

Louf and Barthélémy [26] have pointed out that Bettencourt's theory implies cities with a single centre. This may, for instance, lead to an underestimation of the decreasing returns associated with increasing mobility. They suggest that delays due to congestions scale superlinearly with population (even in polycentric cities) and because CO_2 emissions correspond to commuting time rather than distance, and also the per capita emissions from commuting scale with the city size. They validate this hypothesis against limited data and call for further research on this crucial aspect of urbanisation. Other studies reveal national, regional, and global mitigation wedges [25,27] that would be more effective with policies controlling rebound effects [24].

The metabolism of urban systems has been studied too [28]. Pauliuk et al. [29] employ a fractal model to analyse water and wastewater networks and found that both total network length and mass of the network scale sublinearly and maintenance costs are dominated by small pipes at the backend of the system. Extending these methods to urban morphology Batty et al. [30] have studied allometry in buildings for correlation functions to compute the variation of particular properties of buildings, e.g., allometry has been shown to exist in respect to the ratio of wall surface-to-volume of building blocks in London. These various scaling phenomena translate into distinct hierarchical levels of urban form and morphology that allow for separating factors. For instance, density can be discriminated from behaviours of inhabitants or the building shape factor from passive volume for natural ventilation and natural lighting [31,32].

According to Brockway et al. [33] the US has experienced an "efficiency dilution" in the past 50 years with stagnating energy efficiency. Efficiency dilution signifies structural shifts to less efficient consumption that outweigh device-level efficiency gains, thus representing a specific form of rebound effect. This concerns not least urban systems of provision with supply and disposal functions. Efforts to mitigate carbon emissions from infrastructure concentrate on delivering existing services more efficiently, combining different services, terminating superseded services and recycling obsolete infrastructure or constructing new energy- and resource-efficient infrastructure [34]. These efforts are combined with the search for new business models for (energy) infrastructure in the form of energy service companies (ESCO) or multi-utility service companies (MUSC) [35,36].

Despite the appeal to explain social systems by simple rules, i.e., with low input complexity, we may have to account for the greater heterogeneity of social systems, i.e., by providing explanatory mechanisms and greater input complexity, to govern sustainable urban transitions.

4.5 Discussion

Social systems are also structured by formal institutions providing information, incentives, constraints, etc. to change behaviours, technologies, and infrastructures. We should, therefore, look for explanatory mechanisms enabling urban transitions and expect a range of such mechanisms to exist even within a unified allometric framework.

While the IPCC identified the building sector as a key contributor to energy efficiency, existing energy-efficient technologies are only diffusing slowly [37]. Diffusion is slow due to disadvantages of eco-innovations compared to ordinary innovations, a general neglect of energy-efficient end-use technologies by regulators and investors, existing path-dependencies in planning, as well as the challenges of integrating energy-efficiency technologies in mature cities and, perhaps finally, to coordinate decision-makers. Faster diffusion will require broad coordination across markets, policies, and society. To this end we need to identify mechanisms enabling sustainable urban transitions, i.e., facilitate agency viz-a-viz scale-invariant phenomena. We do not simply observe complex social systems but are and will be re-designing them in situ.

For the governance of sustainable transitions, explaining complicated institutions is equally important for success as providing complex models of social phenomena. The social realm involves multi-causalities, non-ergodic processes, and complicated mechanisms [38], and is thus best understood as a case of high input complexity. This will be crucial to move from descriptive to scenario modelling and from policy advice to implementation. Models should draw on scaling analysis in ways that enable rather than pre-empt participation, to arrive at scenario models that empower agents to practice sustainable behaviours. While scaling is scale-invariant, agency is not [3].

4.6 Conclusions

Urban allometry suggests efficiency potentials for the urban transition but it also embodies socio-economic drivers of unsustainable growth processes. This chapter has highlighted several fields where network analysis is successfully being used to reveal energy- and resource-efficiency potentials of buildings and infrastructure. It argued that these complex networks do not exist in the void but are coordinated through various formal and informal social institutions. We will therefore need explanatory social mechanisms relating human behaviours and social institutions to existing scaling phenomena in order to drive and govern cities towards sustainable pathways.

Note

1 Previously published in: www.sciencedirect.com/science/article/abs/pii/S0959652615011191

References

[1] L. M. A. Bettencourt, 'The origins of scaling in cities', *Science (80-.)*, vol. 340, no. 6139, pp. 1438–1441, Jun. 2013, doi: 10.1126/science.1235823.

[2] D. Pumain, 'Alternative explanations of hierarchical differentiation in urban systems', in *Hierarchy in Natural and Social Sciences*, vol. 3, D. Pumain, Ed. Dordrecht: Springer Netherlands, 2006, pp. 169–222.

[3] H. Nowotny, 'The increase of complexity and its reduction: Emergent interfaces between the natural sciences, humanities and social sciences', *Theory, Cult. Soc.*, vol. 22, no. 5, pp. 15–31, 2005, doi: 10.1177/0263276405057189.

[4] G. Caldarelli, *Scale-free networks complex webs in nature and technology*. Oxford University Press, Oxford, 2007, p. 336.

[5] L. M. A. Bettencourt, J. Lobo, D. Helbing, C. Kühnert, and G. B. West, 'Growth, innovation, scaling, and the pace of life in cities', *Proc. Natl. Acad. Sci. U. S. A.*, vol. 104, no. 17, pp. 7301–7306, Apr. 2007, doi: 10.1073/pnas.0610172104.

[6] M. Batty, 'The size, scale, and shape of cities', *Science (80-.)*, vol. 319, no. 5864, pp. 769–771, Feb. 2008, doi: 10.1126/science.1151419.

[7] S. Lämmer, B. Gehlsen, and D. Helbing, 'Scaling laws in the spatial structure of urban road networks', *Phys. A Stat. Mech. its Appl.*, vol. 363, no. 1, pp. 89–95, Apr. 2006, https://doi.org/10.1016/j.physa.2006.01.051.

[8] B. Jiang and C. Claramunt, 'Topological analysis of urban street networks', *Environ. Plan. B Plan. Des.*, vol. 31, no. 1, pp. 151–162, Feb. 2004, doi: 10.1068/b306.

[9] H. Samaniego and M. E. Moses, 'Cities as organisms: Allometric scaling of urban road networks', *J. Transp. Land Use*, vol. 1, no. 1, pp. 29–39, 2008, doi: https://doi.org/10.5198/jtlu.v1i1.29.

[10] C. Roth, S. M. Kang, M. Batty, and M. Barthélémy, 'A long-time limit for world subway networks', *J. R. Soc. Interface*, vol. 9, no. 75, pp. 2540–2550, 2012, doi: 10.1098/rsif.2012.0259.

[11] R. Louf, C. Roth, and M. Barthélémy, 'Scaling in transportation networks', PLoS One, vol. 9, no. 7, p. e102007, Jan. 2014, doi: https://journals.plos.org/plosone/article?id=10.1371/journal.pone.0102007.

[12] C. Kühnert, D. Helbing, and G. B. West, 'Scaling laws in urban supply networks', *Phys. A Stat. Mech. Its Appl.*, vol. 363, no. 1, pp. 96–103, Apr. 2006, doi: https://doi.org/10.1016/j.physa.2006.01.058.

[13] L. M. A. Bettencourt and G. B. West, 'A unified theory of urban living', *Nature*, vol. 467, no. 7318, pp. 912–913, 2010, doi: 10.1038/467912a.

[14] J. Lobo, L. M. A. Bettencourt, D. Strumsky, and G. B. West, 'Urban scaling and the production function for cities', *PLoS One*, vol. 8, no. 3, p. e58407, 2013.

[15] L. M. A. Bettencourt, H. Samaniego, and H. Youn, 'Professional diversity and the productivity of cities', *Sci. Rep.*, vol. 4, p. 5393, Jan. 2014, www.nature.com/articles/srep05393.pdf.

[16] D. Pumain, F. Paulus, C. Vacchiani-Marcuzzo, and J. Lobo, 'An evolutionary theory for interpreting urban scaling laws', *Cybergeo*, Jul. 2006, https://journals.openedition.org/cybergeo/251919.

[17] L. M. A. Bettencourt, J. Lobo, D. Strumsky, and G. B. West, 'Urban scaling and its deviations: Revealing the structure of wealth, innovation and crime across cities', *PLoS One*, vol. 5, no. 11, p. e13541, Nov. 2010, https://journals.plos.org/plosone/article/file?id=10.1371/journal.pone.0013541&type=printable.

[18] E. Arcaute, E. Hatna, P. Ferguson, H. Youn, A. Johansson, and M. Batty, 'Constructing cities, deconstructing scaling laws', *Interface*, vol. 12, no. iii, p. 20140745, 2015, doi: 10.1098/rsif.2014.0745.

[19] J. Noailly, 'Improving the energy efficiency of buildings: The impact of environmental policy on technological innovation', *Energy Econ.*, vol. 34, no. 3, pp. 795–806, May 2012, doi: 10.1016/j.eneco.2011.07.015.

[20] R. U. Ayres, 'The minimum complexity of endogenous growth models: The role of physical resource flows', *Energy*, vol. 26, no. 9, pp. 817–838, Sep. 2001, doi: 10.1016/S0360-5442(01)00031-7.

[21] M. Finka and T. Kluvánková, 'Managing complexity of urban systems: A polycentric approach', *Land Use Policy*, vol. 42, pp. 602–608, 2015, doi: 10.1016/j.landusepol.2014.09.016.

[22] M. Cristelli, M. Batty, and L. Pietronero, 'There is more than a power law in Zipf', *Sci. Rep.*, vol. 2, p. 812, Jan. 2012, doi: 10.1038/srep00812.

[23] E. a Oliveira, J. S. Andrade, and H. a Makse, 'Large cities are less green', *Sci. Rep.*, vol. 4, p. 4235, 2014, www.nature.com/articles/srep04235.pdf.

[24] M. Antal and J. C. J. M. van den Bergh, 'Re-spending rebound: A macro-level assessment for OECD countries and emerging economies', *Energy Policy*, vol. 68, pp. 585–590, 2014, doi: http://dx.doi.org/10.1016/j.enpol.2013.11.016.

[25] F. Creutzig, G. Baiocchi, R. Bierkandt, P. Pichler, and K. C. Seto, 'Global typology of urban energy use and potentials for an urbanization mitigation wedge', *Proc. Natl. Acad. Sci.*, vol. 112, no. 20, pp. 6283–6288, May 2015, doi: 10.1073/pnas.1315545112.

[26] R. Louf and M. Barthélémy, 'How congestion shapes cities: From mobility patterns to scaling', *Sci. Rep.*, vol. 4, p. 5561, Jan. 2014, www.nature.com/articles/srep05561.pdf.

[27] A. H. Baur, M. Thess, B. Kleinschmit, and F. Creutzig, 'Urban climate change mitigation in Europe: Looking at and beyond the role of population density', *J. Urban Plan. Develop.*, vol. 140, no. 1, p. 4013003, 2014, doi: 10.1061/(ASCE)UP.1943-5444.0000165.

[28] C. A. Kennedy, S. Pincetl, and P. Bunje, 'The study of urban metabolism and its applications to urban planning and design', *Environ. Pollut.*, vol. 159, no. 8–9, pp. 1965–1973, 2011, https://doi.org/10.1016/j.envpol.2010.10.022.

[29] S. Pauliuk, G. Venkatesh, H. Brattebø, and D. B. Müller, 'Exploring urban mines: Pipe length and material stocks in urban water and wastewater networks', *Urban Water J.*, vol. 11, no. 4, pp. 274–283, 2014, doi: 10.1080/1573062X.2013.795234.

[30] M. Batty, R. Carvalho, A. Hudson-Smith, R. Milton, D. Smith, and P. Steadman, 'Scaling and allometry in the building geometries of greater London', *Eur. Phys. J. B*, vol. 63, no. 3, pp. 303–314, 2008, doi: 10.1140/epjb/e2008-00251-5.

[31] S. Salat, 'Energy loads, CO2-emissions and building stocks: Morphologies, typologies, energy systems and behaviour', *Build. Res. Inf.*, vol. 37, no. 5–6. pp. 598–609, 2009, doi: 10.1080/09613210903162126.

[32] L. Bourdic and S. Salat, 'Building energy models and assessment systems at the district and city scales: A review', *Build. Res. Inf.*, vol. 40, no. 4, pp. 518–526, Aug. 2012, doi: 10.1080/09613218.2012.690951.

[33] P. E. Brockway, J. R. Barrett, T. J. Foxon, and J. K. Steinberger, 'Divergence of trends in US and UK aggregate exergy efficiencies 1960-2010', *Environ. Sci. Technol.*, vol. 48, pp. 9874–9881, 2014, doi: 10.1021/es501217t.

[34] D. B. Müller *et al.*, 'Carbon emissions of infrastructure development', *Environ. Sci. Technol.*, vol. 47, no. 20, pp. 11739–11746, 2013, doi: 10.1021/es402618m.

[35] J. K. Steinberger, J. van Niel, and D. Bourg, 'Profiting from negawatts: Reducing absolute consumption and emissions through a performance-based energy economy', *Energy Policy*, vol. 37, no. 1, pp. 361–370, Jan. 2009, https://doi.org/10.1016/j.enpol.2008.08.030.

[36] K. Roelich *et al.*, 'Towards resource-efficient and service-oriented integrated infrastructure operation', *Technol. Forecast. Soc. Change*, vol. 92, pp. 40–52, 2014, doi: 10.1016/j.techfore.2014.11.008.

[37] International Energy Agency, Strategies and Opportunities to 2050, *Transition to Sustainable Buildings*, Paris, 2013. https://iea.blob.core.windows.net/assets/1e300ab6-44de-41dc-8714-ee12a4800943/Building2013_free.pdf

[38] C. Andersson, A. Törnberg, and P. Törnberg, 'Societal systems – Complex or worse?', *Futures*, vol. 63, pp. 145–157, 2014, doi: 10.1016/j.futures.2014.07.003.

Part II

Socio-economic

5 Economic trajectories of cities and scaling laws[1]

Fabien Paulus, Denise Pumain, and Céline Vacchiani-Marcuzzo

5.1 Adaptive socio-economic processes in urban systems and scaling laws

We propose to bring together in a global interpretative framework the empirical facts that are available, about scaling laws on the one hand, and urban growth processes on the other. The evolutionary theory of urban systems [1] states that in a system of cities, which are connected by a large variety of physical and social networks enabling since long the exchanges of goods, persons, and information, towns and cities are engaged in a general competition for growing, or attempting to reduce the uncertainties that limit their development. This occurs mainly through the circulation of innovations, which reaches cities in two differentiated ways: the hierarchical diffusion of innovation (the largest cities capture first the benefits of innovation, and later on let them filtering down the urban hierarchy) [2], and the formation of new urban functional specializations (a few cities either create a new type of activities, or become selected for developing these, because specific amenities they have meet the location factors of the new activity). Each innovation cycle conveys impulses for urban growth when hitting cities (gains from adaptation), with variable intensity according to the stage in the cycle [3]. The size of cities and the diversity of their functional specialization are the result of this cumulative process, which is self-maintained because the interurban competition is also an incentive to innovate, as a feedback effect from the system on individual towns and cities.

In any system of cities, the largest cities became larger because they were successful in adopting many successive innovations. At the level of every city, the changes in economic activity proceed as a continuous adaptation to novelty or through sharper bifurcations in periods of more intense creativity and renewal: these major innovation cycles are often called "revolutions" in economic and historical literature. We recognize, at least for the last three centuries in the most developed countries, five of these major cycles that are narrowly connected to urbanization and diversification of urban activities: the development of planetary maritime trade and the banking sector in 17th and 18th century, the first industrial revolution of steam machines and railways at the beginning of 19th century, the electricity and automobile at the turn of 20th century, the electronic revolution in the middle of

DOI: 10.4324/9781003288312-7

20th, and the now engaged revolution in converging technologies (NBIC, nano, bio, information, and cognition) for the 21st century.

The time span of each cycle has been reduced over historical times (from hundreds of years before the industrial revolution to a few tenths of years nowadays) but in each of them three main stages are always recognizable: Emergence stage (leading technologies, highly skilled jobs); Diffusion stage (mature technologies, skilled jobs); Stage of decay (banalization and/or substitution by new products, old techniques, unskilled jobs)

Traces of this evolutionary process in systems of cities can be represented as scaling laws. Scaling laws are power-law relationships of the form $Y = cX^{\beta}$, where Y represents a variable which varies in a systematic way with the size X of subsystems and c and β are parameters. They summarize structural features of systems in a very efficient way, and they reveal the effect of universal constraints acting on the structure and development over several orders of magnitude in these systems [4]. When applied to cities, other limiting factors to their development than energy and material resources have to be considered, including a very broad variety of resources of different kinds, such as human labor and creativity, as well as institutional organization (social and cultural) and technological resources.

5.2 Methods

Assessing the validity of urban theories implies testing them over a variety of systems of cities existing in the world. A systematic comparative research was undertaken for measuring scaling laws in urban activities and professions among 331 metropolitan areas of the United States, 354 functional urban areas in France, and 87 South African urban agglomerations [5]. These countries were chosen because they are very different in size, level of development, and settlement style. They are representative of three major ideal types of systems of cities which were generated by the history of urbanization: long-standing urbanization without major external shock (France), late urbanization developed wave-like, at first in connection with an external metropolis, in a developed (USA) and less developed country (South Africa) [6]. One can thus expect that the results if converging provide insights about general properties of systems of cities.

The research data are not always readily available and have to be constructed by referring to coherent and comparable definitions and delineations of urban units. Many experiments have revealed that scaling exponents not only vary with the considered urban attributes but also are highly dependent on the chosen urban perimeter within which they were computed [7,8]. We choose here to approximate the definition of a system of cities inside the borders of each national state (thus ignoring the longer distance interactions that connect some of their cities to the rest of the world and may influence their development) and the definition of a "city" as "urban agglomeration" (i.e., continuously built-up area) or "functional urban area" (i.e., commuting zone). We shall see that this is essential information that has to be provided in any measurement of urban scaling laws for making the results usable and comparable.

We plot cities according to their size (logarithm of the number of inhabitants) on the X-axis and the logarithm of the number of employees in a given economic sector on the Y-axis. To calculate the scaling exponent (β), we estimate, using least-squares technique, the slope of the line that fits the set of points.

5.3 Results: scaling and diversification of urban functions

Table 5.1 summarizes the results of investigations comparing the scaling exponents of activity profiles of cities in three countries. The detailed economic sectors are classified in the table according to their approximate stage in the current innovation cycle. Our principal hypothesis is confirmed: at a given moment, more advanced technologies concentrate in largest cities, current ones are ubiquitous, whereas old ones remain in small towns as the exponents of adjusted power laws varies accordingly. The β values are above 1 for leading technologies (top of current innovation cycle), close to 1 for common place (or banal) technologies (diffusion stage), and below 1 for mature technologies (decay or substitution stage). Moreover, the content of each subset of activities varies according to the stage of development in national economies: manufacturing still appears as a recent economic sector and concentrates in largest cities in South Africa (that is also true for China [9] and Brazil [10, 11]) whereas it became mainly a specialization for small towns in more developed countries.

Our results also include a high negative correlation between an Isard's index measuring the specialization of economic profiles and city size. This confirms that the activity profiles of the largest cities are more diversified than those of the

Table 5.1 Scaling parameters and stage of economic sectors in the innovation cycle in three countries around 2000 (331 metropolitan areas in US, 354 "aires urbaines" in France, and 87 South African urban agglomerations; FIRE = Financial activities, Insurance, Real Estate).

Stages in innovation cycle	*France*	*USA*	*South Africa*
Innovative sectors **β > 1**	FIRE Research and development Business services Consultancy	FIRE Research and development Business services Consultancy	FIRE Manufacturing
Common sectors **β ≈ 1**	Hotels and restaurants Community, social, personal services	Hotels and restaurants Community, social, personal services	Retail trade Community, social, and personal services Utilities
Mature sectors **β <1**	Manufacturing	Retail trade Utilities	Private households

Sources: United States Census 2000; France INSEE, Recensement de la population, 1999; South Africa Data base CIS-CVM, 2003.

smallest ones. Our interpretation is even more clearly confirmed when computing the scaling exponents of the occupational groups in urban population: in all countries highly skilled jobs (such as executives) are scaling superlinearly with city size, whereas unskilled jobs (mainly workers) scale sublinearly, and average level in skills (such as teachers) is simply proportional to city size. This is illustrated for the French case in Figure 5.1.

A further test of the theory has observed the time evolution of scaling parameters. As expected, the now leading technologies can still increase their parameter value, while activities of older cycles have decreasing parameters (Figure 5.2).

5.4 Discussion

We have shown how scaling laws can be used in geography through connecting the concepts of urban function, innovation cycles, urban size, and urban growth according to an evolutionary theory of urban systems [12]. The crucial role that cities have played in the generation of innovations – intellectual and material, cultural and political, institutional and organizational – is well documented [13,14]. As Glaeser [15] points out, the creation and reposition of knowledge in cities increases their attractive pull for educated, highly skilled, entrepreneurial, and creative individuals who, by locating in urban centers, contribute in turn to the generation of further knowledge spillovers. This seemingly spontaneous process, whereby knowledge produces growth and growth attracts knowledge, is the engine by which urban centers sustain their development through unfolding innovation. The essential role of knowledge generation, recombination, and circulation within and across urban areas is at the core of our explanation for urban scaling. Figure 5.3 schematizes this interpretation of urban scaling laws. The diversity of scaling exponents according to the urban activities and their variations over time are explained by the hierarchical diffusion process of innovations in systems of cities.

Since 2006, many authors have undertaken research on urban scaling laws that introduces a concern for the evolution of scaling parameters over time. They may have been inspired by our interpretation or at least their results do not contradict it [16 –18]. Scaling laws were used to analyze the metropolization generated by the opening up of cities to global networks in Europe, demonstrating that globalization has reached a banalization stage among Western European cities while these processes still contribute to reinforce urban hierarchies in the Eastern part [19]. The search for equity in the distribution of urban services is currently inspiring many articles about cities in poor countries [20]. In China, where planning services must rapidly equip fast-growing cities, Lei et al. [21] measured the scaling exponents of a dozen attributes that cover the main urban functions (economy, finance, education, health, infrastructure, land use) in 151–297 prefectural cities between 1984 and 2019 and found results similar to ours. Further, such empirical studies that would be made comparable and reproducible are still needed to really assess the usefulness of scaling laws and their relevance for urban planning.

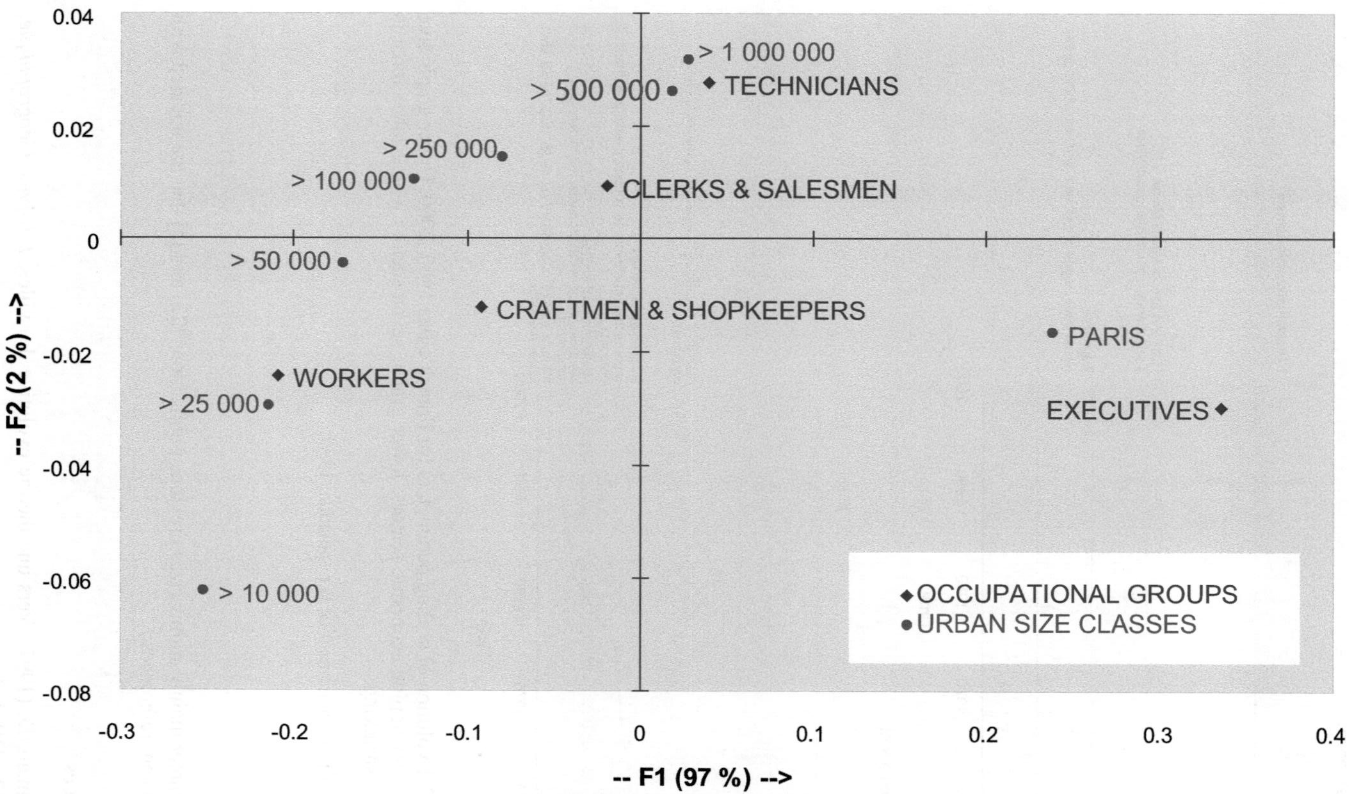

Figure 5.1 France: City size classes and occupational groups (principal component analysis on 354 functional urban areas).

Source: INSEE, Recensement de la population, 1999.

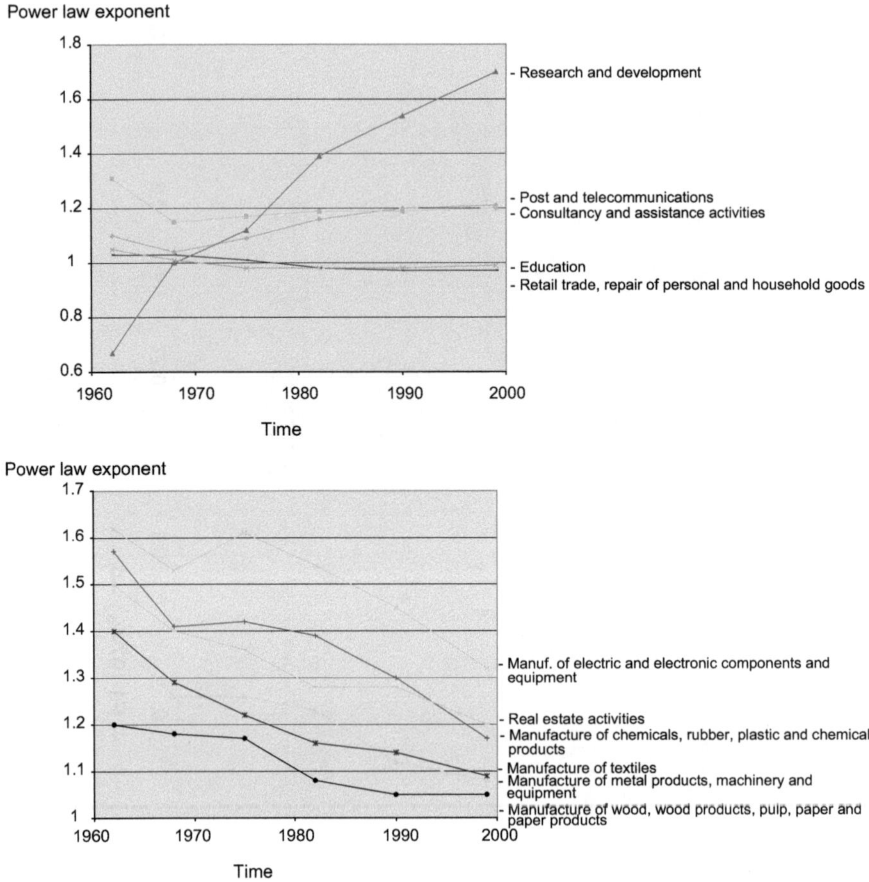

Figure 5.2 Evolution of scaling parameters for French cities 1960–2000. Upper graph: five developing economic sectors; lower graph: seven sectors whose labor force is shrinking.

Source: INSEE, Recensement de la population, 1999.

Note

1 This chapter mainly summarizes previous publications [22] and [5] that are updated with a few recent references.

References

[1] Pumain, D. (1997). Vers une théorie évolutive des villes. *L'Espace Géographique*, 26(2), 119–134.

[2] Hägerstrand, T. (1952). The propagation of innovation waves. *Lund Studies in Geography*, Serie B, No. 4, 20 p.

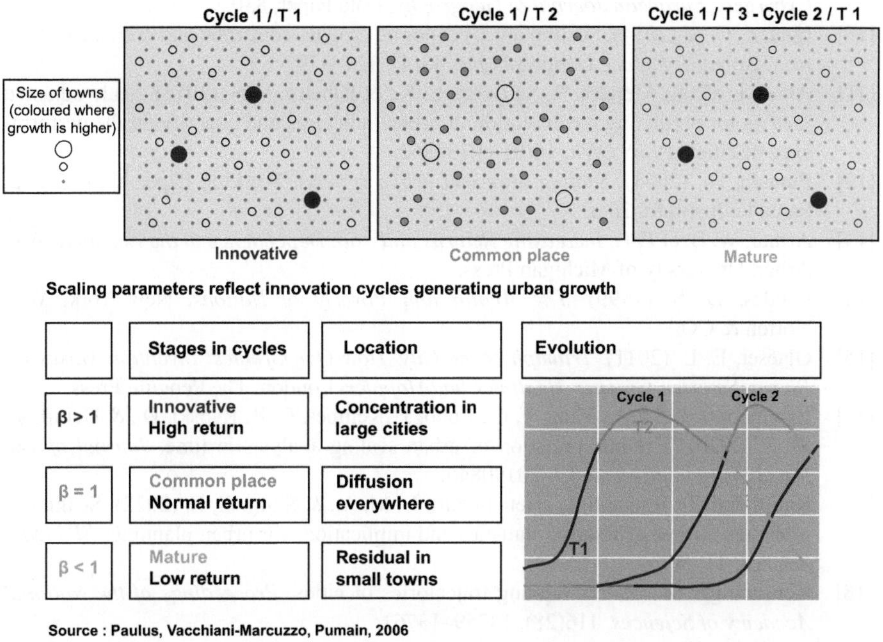

Figure 5.3 Schematic view of the theory connecting scaling laws exponents and stages in the hierarchical diffusion of innovation cycles in a system of cities. At time T1 the attributes of the innovation cycle 1 are mainly concentrated in the largest cities of the system, at time T2 they become common place after diffusing in second-tier cities, before falling back in a few small specialized towns at time 3 where another innovation cycle, C2, starts boosting further the development of large cities. The changing values of scaling laws exponents represent this hierarchical diffusion process in the system of cities.

Source: Ref. [22].

[3] Pred, A., (1977). *City Systems in Advanced Economies*. London, Hutchinson.

[4] West G. B., Brown J. H., & Enquist B. J. (1997). A general model for the origin of allometric scaling laws in biology, *Science*, 276, 122–126.

[5] Paulus, F. & Vacchiani-Marcuzzo, C. (2016). Knowledge economy and competitiveness: economic trajectories of French cities since the 1960s. In *Knowledge-creating milieus in Europe* (pp. 157–170). Springer, Berlin, Heidelberg.

[6] Bretagnolle, A., Pumain, D., & Vacchiani-Marcuzzo, C. (2009). The organization of urban systems, in: D. Lane, D. Pumain, S. Van der Leeuw, G. West (eds.), *Complexity Perspectives on Innovation and Social Change*, ISCOM, Springer, Methodos Series, Berlin, 197–220.

[7] Burghardt, K., Uhl, J. H., Lerman, K., & Leyk, S. (2022). City definition affects long-term urban scaling analyses in the United States (1900-2015). *arXiv preprint arXiv:2209.10852*.

[8] Cottineau, C., Hatna, E., Arcaute, E., & Batty, M. (2017). Diverse cities or the systematic paradox of urban scaling laws. *Computers, Environment and Urban Systems*, 63, 80–94.

[9] Swerts, E. (2017). A data base on Chinese urbanization: China Cities. *Cybergeo: European Journal of Geography,* Data Paper, 830.
[10] Ignazzi, C. A. (2014). Scaling laws, economic growth, education and crime: evidence from Brazil. *L'Espace Géographique*, 43(4), 324–337.
[11] Alves, L. G. A., Mendes, R. S., Lenzi, E. K., & Ribeiro, V. H. (2015). Scale-adjusted metrics for predicting the evolution of urban indicators and quantifying the performance of cities. *PLoS ONE*, 10(9), e0134862.
[12] Pumain, D., (2004). *Scaling laws and urban systems*, Working Paper n°04-02-002, Santa Fe Institute, 26 p.
[13] Arthur, W. B. (1994). *Increasing Returns and Path Dependence in the Economy.* Ann Arbor, University of Michigan Press.
[14] Landes, D. S. (1999). *The Wealth and Poverty of Nations.* New York, WW Norton & CO.
[15] Glaeser, E. L. (2011). *Triumph of the City, How Our Greatest Invention Makes Us Richer, Smarter, Greener, Healthier and Happier*. London, The Penguin Press.
[16] Bettencourt, L. M. A., Yang, V. C., Lobo, J., Kempes, C. P., Rybski, D., & Hamilton, M. J. (2020). The interpretation of urban scaling analysis in time. *Journal of The Royal Society Interface*, 17, 20190846.
[17] Kaufmann, T., Radaelli, L., Bettencourt, L. M. A., & Shmueli, E. (2022). Scaling of urban amenities: generative statistics and implications for urban planning. *EPJ Data Science*, 11, 50.
[18] Keuschnigg, M. (2019). Scaling trajectories of cities. *Proceedings of the National Academy of Sciences*, 116(28), 13759–13761.
[19] Pumain, D., & Rozenblat, C. (2019). Two metropolisation gradients in the European system of cities revealed by scaling laws. *Environment and Planning B: Urban Analytics and City Science*, *46*(9), 1645–1662.
[20] Ashik, F. R., Mim, S. A., & Neema, M. N. (2020). Towards vertical spatial equity of urban facilities: an integration of spatial and aspatial accessibility. *Journal of Urban Management*, *9*(1), 77–92.
[21] Lei, W., Jiao, L., Xu, G., & Zhou, Z. (2022) Urban scaling in rapidly urbanising China. *Urban Studies*, 59(9), 1889–1908.
[22] Pumain, D., Paulus, F., Vacchiani-Marcuzzo, C., & Lobo, J. (2006). An evolutionary theory for interpreting urban scaling laws. *Cybergeo: European Journal of Geography*, 343. https://doi.org/10.4000/cybergeo.2519

6 How urban allometry emerges from economic complexity and cultural evolution[1]

Andres Gomez-Lievano, Oscar Patterson-Lomba, and Ricardo Hausmann

6.1 Background

The importance of population size as a driver of output per capita (what economists call *productivity*) dates back to the work of Adam Smith. Smith hypothesized that increases in productivity would arise from greater individual specialization, itself arising from larger populations of workers. Indeed, 40 years of research in urban economics seems to suggest that such a positive relationship between urban size and productivity does exist (see, e.g., [1–5]). These gains from larger population sizes, dubbed "agglomeration economies", have been among the most intensely studied topics in urban economics [6]. Economists claim that the gains in per capita output from larger cities go beyond Smith's specialization argument, and arise from *sharing* public goods, facilities, space, and risks; from people and firms *learning* from one another; and from finding better *matches* between employers and employees, or between buyers and suppliers (see [7]).

One of the contributions of urban scaling research to this literature has been to go beyond *qualitative* assessments of whether socio-economic quantities per capita, $y = Y / N$, correlate to city size N positively or negatively. To be more precise, research in urban scaling has been interested not only in understanding why the function $y = f(N)$ increases or decreases with N, but in understanding why the function describing this relationship is a power-law $y = Y / N = Y_0 N^{\delta}$ (where Y_0 is a proportionality constant), and why the exponent δ takes values around 0.15 (see [8]). While several models reproduce the power-law relationship (for a review, see [9]), only the model proposed by Bettencourt in 2013 [10] predicts an exponent $\delta = \frac{1}{6} \approx 0.17$.

Numerical predictions like these, which go beyond qualitative assessments, are a necessary condition to developing a science of cities. Predictions based on the general concept of "output" or "output per capita", however, have been hard to verify because output can sometimes be an abstract notion, difficult to quantify. For example, the predicted value of $\delta \approx 0.17$mentioned above matches approximately the empirically observed exponent $\delta \approx 0.13$ that relates Gross Metropolitan Product (GMP) per capita in the United States with urban population size (see

DOI: 10.4324/9781003288312-8

Table S3 in [10]), but clashes with the observed exponent $\delta \approx 0.27$ relating patents per capita in the US and total population size (Table S3 in [10]).

The case of patents as the output measure is illustrative because we can test some of the basic assumptions of the model, given that it is easier to quantify the contribution of each inventor to total patenting than it is to quantify the contribution of each citizen to total GMP. When looking at data of patents per inventor, one finds that the productivity of inventors, on average, stays constant across cities. In other words, patents per inventor do not scale with population size, as the model would predict [11]. From the observation that total patents scale superlinearly with population size $Y = Y_0 N^{1+\delta}$, and that patenting per inventor is a constant, expressed as $Y / I = a$ where I is the total number of inventors and a is the average productivity per inventor, it is clear that patenting tends to be higher in larger cities not because inventors are more productive in larger cities, but because there are simply more inventors in larger cities. That is, $I = I_0 N^{1+\delta}$, where $I_0 = Y_0 / a$ is a measure of general prevalence of inventors in the system of cities. The fact that it is the number of inventors which scales with population size raises the question of whether scaling analyses should separate the study of productivity from the study of the number of people engaged in productive activities (for a study of the limitations of conducting scaling analysis on measures of productivity per capita see [12]).

Indeed, when researchers have looked at the number of individuals counted in different socio-economic activities, including cases of crime or infectious diseases (e.g., [13–15]), they have found that they also follow scaling laws. Such observations cast doubts on the mechanisms proposed by urban economists, which tend to rely on notions of optimizing behaviors, markets, and equilibria, and into Bettencourt's 2013 model, which emphasize increases of productivity at the level of individuals.

Thus, to understand the higher concentrations of socio-economic activity in larger cities, additional insights could be derived by looking at a diverse range of phenomena and calculating how many people are involved across different activities. Gomez-Lievano et al. [16] did this and analyzed more than 40 different urban activities in US metropolitan areas. We found that scaling exponents $\beta = 1 + \delta$ differed widely across activities. For example, counts of individuals with a high-school education or higher scaled with total population size with an exponent of $\beta \approx 1.00$, while those with a graduate degree or higher scaled with $\beta \approx 1.11$. The most superlinear activity in Gomez-Lievano et al.'s data is the number of individuals that produced at least a patent in the year 2011, with an exponent of $\beta \approx 1.47$. The question is: *why* do scaling exponents differ widely across activities?

6.2 Model

Bettencourt's 2013 model helps us understand which phenomena in cities scale sublinearly and, more importantly for this chapter, which scale superlinearly. According to Bettencourt's model, superlinear phenomena arise due to interaction effects. Thus, the model would suggest that the differences in scaling between the number of high-school and graduate degrees, for example, are a reflection of differences in how the number of interactions in these different populations scale with size. Our theory unpacks this phenomenon, putting an emphasis not on the number of interactions in the city, but on the diversity of interactions.

To explain why socio-economic activities scale as a power-law of population size and *do not* necessarily scale following a single universal exponent, our theory of cities is based on principles from two fields: economic complexity [17,18], and cultural evolution (see [19] and [20] for popular reviews). The theory we propose improves on previous explanations of urban allometry in that it predicts effects beyond scaling exponents. It generates specific predictions about all the characteristics of the power-law scaling. In doing so, this theory provides an integrated understanding of how socio-economic activities relate to each other.

The mathematical model emerges from three assumptions. First, any given socio-economic activity is described as the conjunction of complementary factors. For example, the activity of inventing consists of (i) having a technological problem, (ii) having a novel solution, (iii) presenting the idea clearly, (iv) applying for a patent, (v) including subsequent corrections from examiners, and (vi) satisfying all the legal requirements to earn the patent right (see, e.g., [21]). Failing on any of these factors will mean failure to invent. This idea of complementarity is key in the model, implying that a person engages in the activity only when all factors are simultaneously present. The number of different factors that an activity requires is referred to as the "complexity" of the activity. Second, everyone in the city has an individual capacity to possess some of those factors, which they can combine with factors that are readily available in the city. Third, as cities get bigger, a broader diversity of these factors accumulate in them. We will sometimes refer to factors as ingredients, skills, inputs, tasks, or capabilities, interchangeably depending on the context.

The assumptions above imply that the three essential quantities that affect scaling are how complex an activity is, how capable individuals are, and how suitable the city is for executing the activity. In our model, capabilities needed by a citizen to engage, participate, or be counted in an activity, can be provided by the citizen herself or, if available, taken from her environment, the city. Thus, our model posits that urban phenomena emerge in cities when the characteristics of individuals are complementary to the characteristics of the cities in which they live. How complementary are citizens to their cities is then modulated by the complexity of the activity they are engaging in. In the next section, we review the mathematics of the model, which will make these observations clearer.

6.3 Results

The model was first outlined by Gomez-Lievano et al. in [16] and was then further detailed by Gomez-Lievano and Patterson-Lomba in [22]. Here, we summarize the main results.

Let M be the complexity of an activity, s be the probability that an individual possesses any of the required capabilities, and r the probability that any of the capabilities are available in the city. Given these parameters, the probability, p, that a random individual participates in the activity is approximately $p = e^{-M(1-s)(1-r)}$. The number of tasks that define an activity (M), and the inherent capacity of individuals to implement any of the tasks without external help (s) are, on average, independent from the city. Thus, parameters M and s will be held constant across cities. On the other hand, the parameter r represents the idea that exposure to other people, services, tools, and institutions within the urban milieu provides citizens with a diversity of know-how, capabilities, and factors they can rely upon to participate in urban activities. It stands to reason that bigger cities, presumably, have higher r because they are more diversified.

Indeed, ideas about cultural evolution in anthropology provide a way of modeling the accumulation of know-how in a population (see, e.g., [23]). In such models, r represents the size of the cultural repertoire that a society can sustain. It is composed of so-called "cultural traits", like behaviors, rules, beliefs, tools, skills, and know-how that people can learn, use, or borrow, and is predicted to be driven by the logarithm of population size, $r = a + b\ln(N)$. We incorporate these ideas directly into our theory of cities.

Being a probabilistic model, we can use the expressions for p and r to derive the expectation (and variance) of the total number of individuals participating in an activity in a city, Y. The model, as others did previously, predicts a superlinear scaling law $E[Y \mid N] = Y_0 N^{1+\delta}$. The key result, however, is the set of predictions about how the properties of the scaling law vary with the complexity M of a given activity. The model tells us that the exponent δ, the logarithm of the general prevalence $\ln(Y_0)$, and the variance of the residuals around the scaling law σ^2 (in the log-log regression), are all three proportional to M (the complexity of activities), with the scaling exponent and the variance being larger for more complex activities with the general prevalence being smaller. Thus, differences in values for these parameters are due to changes in a single underlying variable: the complexity of the activities.

These predictions make sense. Complex activities that require many ingredients will be hard to accomplish, so one would expect to see fewer individuals engaged in them than in less complex activities. At the same time, because an individual trying to participate in a complex activity is more dependent on the availability of inputs in the urban environment, one would also expect to see the number of people in that activity to be more sensitive to changes in population size (that is, to the number of inputs available in the social environment) in contrast to low-complexity activities, for which the inherent ability of individuals can be more sufficient to perform the tasks required, and changes in the urban environment have little effect. For the same reason, one would expect differences in the cultural repertoire of cities to have big effects in the number of people engaged in high-complexity activities, even when comparing cities of the same population size.

To clarify the basic ideas, Figure 6.1 presents a couple of examples of the scaling laws for various activity groups (employment, innovation, crime, educational attainment, and sexually transmitted diseases). Each panel helps illustrate

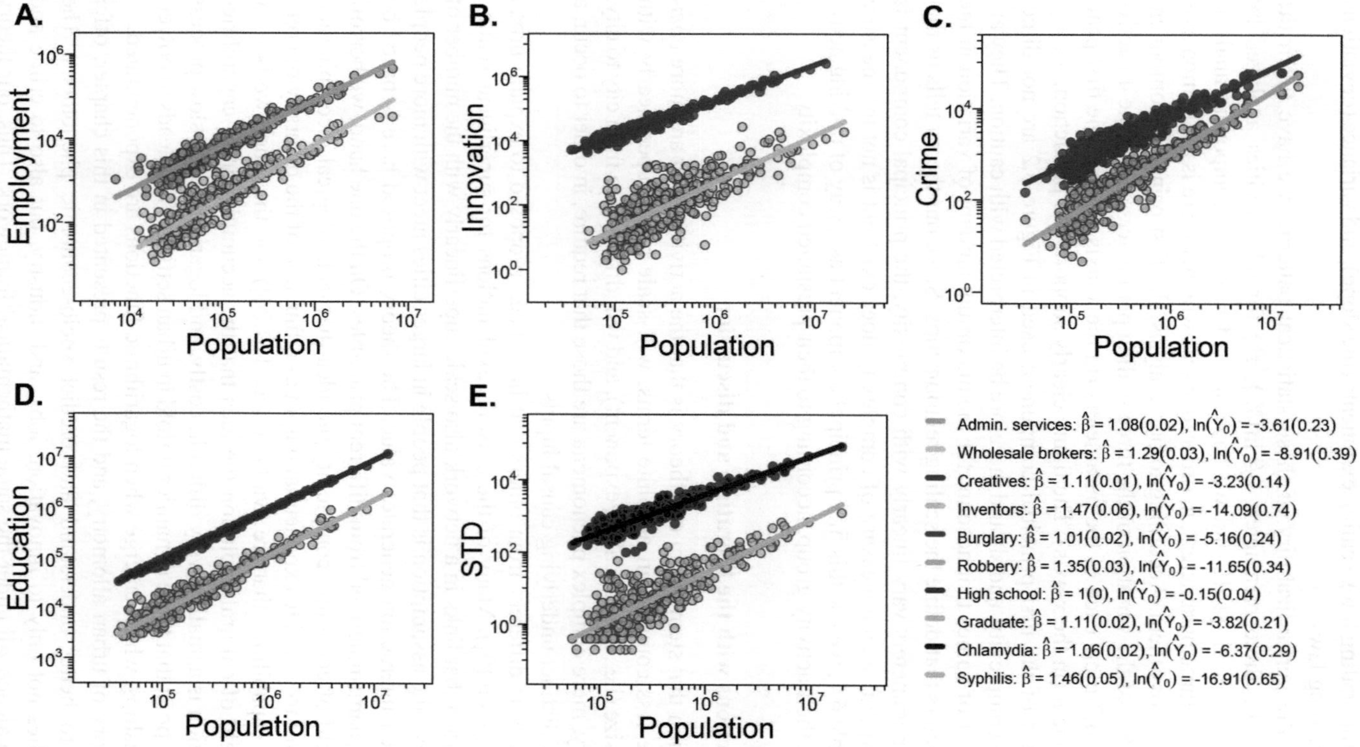

Figure 6.1 Scaling laws across socio-economic activities illustrating differences in general prevalence, scaling exponents, and variance around scaling line, predicted by theory.

Source: Gomez-Lievano et al. [16].

the dissimilarities between activities in regard to their overall prevalence (e.g., the intercept of the scaling law), scaling exponents (the slope), and variance (deviations around the scaling law).

To show the generalizability of these statistical patterns, we have taken the estimates of the three parameters $(\beta, \ln(Y_0), \sigma^2)$ for 43 activities analyzed by Gomez-Lievano et al. [16][2], and we have applied principal component analysis (PCA) to those three parameters, in order to assess whether there is a common axis of variation across them. According to our analysis, the first principal component explains 94.5% of the variation of the three scaling parameters across the 43 activities. Figure 6.2 plots each of the parameters (in the y-axis) against the first principal component (in the x-axis). The figure clearly supports the prediction.

The values of the first principal component used in Figure 6.2 are not direct measures of complexity, and should therefore be interpreted with caution. They are simply the set of values that account for the maximum amount of variation in the three parameters that define the scaling relationships. Since our theory tells us that these three parameters vary linearly with complexity, the principal component is an indication that such a measure of complexity does exist but is not the measure itself. In Table 6.1, we use this first principal component as a way of ranking activities, within their activity group, according to their presumed complexity.

6.4 Connections with the literature and discussion

The prediction that stems from our theory is that the activities that are more *complex* will be less common in absolute terms, will scale more superlinearly with population size (i.e., larger scaling exponent), and will differ more from city to city. In our theory, more complex phenomena are those that require, in order to occur, a larger set of distinct underlying causal inputs.

This theory is different from others that have been proposed to explain urban scaling laws (see [9]). Many of the existing explanations for superlinear scaling rely on the idea that links in a network also scale superlinearly with the number of nodes. Hence, the assumption is that people in larger cities meet with more people *and* that each interaction generates value. The theory proposed here is based on another mechanism derived from different principles. On the one hand, we borrow from the field of economic complexity the idea that technological recombination has the power to generate exponential output as a function of the diversity of complementary capabilities that are available (see [17,24]). On the other, we borrow from the field of cultural evolution the idea that the accumulation of capabilities in a population is actually a very difficult, costly, and logarithmically slow process [23,25]. We posit that these dynamics unfold in urban settings. This leads to power-law relationships, which emerge when logarithmic functions are exponentiated.

This theory of urban allometry, and the results presented in this chapter, offer new tools to better understand and predict socio-economic phenomena. The theory applies not only to innovation, jobs, and industry, but also to crime and disease prevalence, all under the same mathematical framework. Thus, our theory contributes to the idea that seemingly unrelated phenomena like innovation,

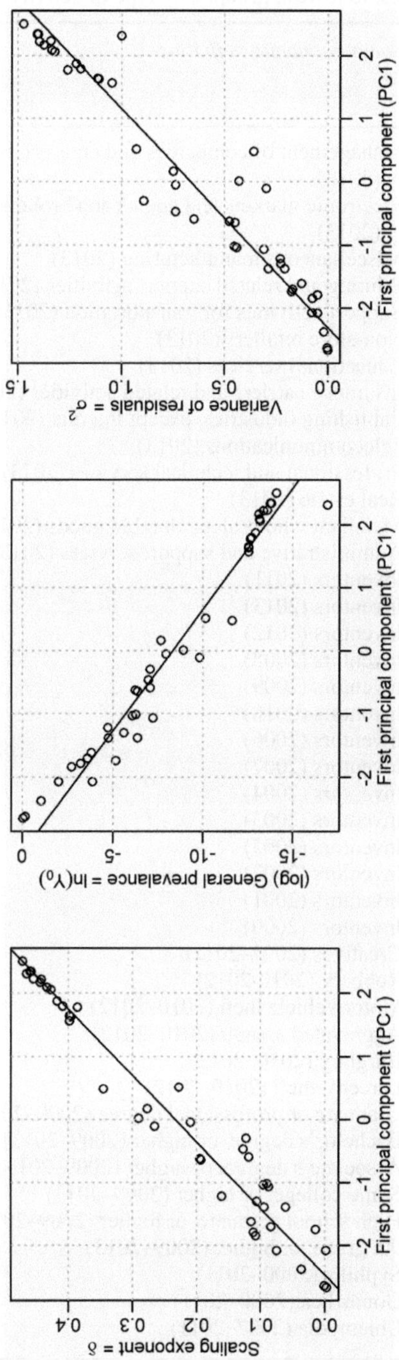

Figure 6.2 Economic complexity and cultural evolution predict scaling laws with varying parameters across socio-economic activities.

Source: Gomez-Lievano et al. [16].

Table 6.1 Socio-economic activities ranked by their presumed complexity, from highest to lowest, from highest to lowest, grouped by type of activity.

Complexity rank	*First principal component*	*Socio-economic activity*	*Activity type*
1	0.17	Management of companies and enterprises (2013)	Employment
2	0.01	Electronic markets and agents and brokers (2013)	Employment
3	–0.05	Miscellaneous manufacturing (2013)	Employment
4	–0.30	Printing and related support activities (2013)	Employment
5	–0.47	Support activities for transportation (2013)	Employment
6	–0.59	Non-store retailers (2013)	Employment
7	–0.62	Educational services (2013)	Employment
8	–0.64	Insurance carriers and related activities (2013)	Employment
9	–1.02	Publishing industries, except internet (2013)	Employment
10	–1.04	Telecommunications (2013)	Employment
11	–1.22	Professional and technical services (2013)	Employment
12	–1.30	Real estate (2013)	Employment
13	–1.38	Merchant wholesalers, durable goods (2013)	Employment
14	–1.70	Administrative and support services (2013)	Employment
1	2.50	Inventors (2011)	Innovation
2	2.34	Inventors (2013)	Innovation
3	2.34	Inventors (2012)	Innovation
4	2.23	Inventors (2008)	Innovation
5	2.22	Inventors (2009)	Innovation
6	2.17	Inventors (2010)	Innovation
7	2.09	Inventors (2006)	Innovation
8	2.06	Inventors (2007)	Innovation
9	1.87	Inventors (2004)	Innovation
10	1.79	Inventors (2003)	Innovation
11	1.77	Inventors (2005)	Innovation
12	1.64	Inventors (2002)	Innovation
13	1.63	Inventors (2001)	Innovation
14	1.56	Inventors (2000)	Innovation
15	–1.79	Creatives (2007–2011)	Innovation
1	0.48	Robbery (2010-2012)	Crime
2	–0.11	Motor vehicle theft (2010–2012)	Crime
3	–1.06	Aggravated assault (2010–2012)	Crime
4	–1.74	Burglary (2010–2012)	Crime
5	–2.07	Larceny-theft (2010–2012)	Crime
1	–1.62	Graduate or professional degree (2009–2013)	Education
2	–1.84	Bachelor's degree, or higher (2009–2013)	Education
3	–2.08	Associate's degree, or higher (2009–2013)	Education
4	–2.38	Some college, or higher (2009–2013)	Education
5	–2.63	High school graduate, or higher (2009–2013)	Education
6	–2.66	9th grade, or higher (2009–2013)	Education
1	2.31	Syphilis (2000–2011)	STD
2	0.51	Gonorrhea (2000–2011)	STD
3	–1.38	Chlamydia (2007–2011)	STD

Source: Supplementary data in Ref [16].

employment, education, crime, and disease, should not only be studied in isolation from one another, but should also be understood within an integrated framework.

Notes

1 Previously published as: Andres Gomez-Lievano, Oscar Patterson-Lomba & Ricardo Hausmann. Explaining the prevalence, scaling and variance of urban phenomena. Nature Human Behaviour volume 1, Article number: 0012 (2017).

2 The 43 activities include counts of individuals across different levels of educational attainment, levels of employment across different industries, individuals in innovative occupations, cases of sexually transmitted diseases, and reported cases across different types of violent crime. Data can be downloaded from Supplementary Data in Gomez-Lievano, A., Patterson-Lomba, O. & Hausmann, R. Explaining the prevalence, scaling and variance of urban phenomena. *Nat Hum Behav* 1, 0012 (2017). https://doi.org/10.1038/s41562-016-0012.

References

[1] Combes, P. P., & Gobillon, L. (2015). The empirics of agglomeration economies. In *Handbook of regional and urban economics* (Vol. 5, pp. 247–348). Elsevier.

[2] Davis, D. R., & Dingel, J. I. (2020). The comparative advantage of cities. *Journal of International Economics*, *123*, 103291.

[3] Rosenthal, S. S., & Strange, W. C. (2004). Evidence on the nature and sources of agglomeration economies. In *Handbook of regional and urban economics* (Vol. 4, pp. 2119–2171). Elsevier.

[4] Segal, D. (1976). Are there returns to scale in city size?. *The Review of Economics and Statistics*, *58*(3), 339–350. https://doi.org/10.2307/1924956

[5] Sveikauskas, L. (1975). The productivity of cities. *Quarterly Journal of Economics*, *89*(3), 393–413.

[6] Glaeser, E. L. (2008). *Cities, agglomeration, and spatial equilibrium*. OUP Oxford.

[7] Duranton, G., & Puga, D. (2004). Micro-foundations of urban agglomeration economies. In *Handbook of regional and urban economics* (Vol. 4, pp. 2063–2117). Elsevier.

[8] Bettencourt, L. M. A., Lobo, J., Helbing, D., Kühnert, C., & West, G. B. (2007) “Growth, innovation, scaling, and the pace of life in cities.” *Proceedings of the National Academy of Sciences*, *104*(17), 7301–7306.

[9] Ribeiro, F. L., & Rybski, D. (2023). Mathematical models to explain the origin of urban scaling laws. *Physics Reports*, *1012*, 1–39.

[10] Bettencourt, L. M. (2013). The origins of scaling in cities. *Science*, *340*(6139), 1438–1441.

[11] Bettencourt, L. M., Lobo, J., & Strumsky, D. (2007). Invention in the city: Increasing returns to patenting as a scaling function of metropolitan size. *Research Policy*, *36*(1), 107–120.

[12] Gomez-Lievano, A., Vysotsky, V., & Lobo, J. (2021). Artificial increasing returns to scale and the problem of sampling from lognormals. *Environment and Planning B: Urban Analytics and City Science*, *48*(6), 1574–1590.

[13] Gomez-Lievano, A., Youn, H., & Bettencourt, L. M. (2012). The statistics of urban scaling and their connection to Zipf’s law. *PloS One*, *7*(7), e40393.

[14] Patterson-Lomba, O., Goldstein, E., Gomez-Lievano, A., Castillo-Chavez, C., & Towers, S. (2015). Per capita incidence of sexually transmitted infections increases systematically with urban population size: A cross-sectional study. *Sexually Transmitted Infections*, *91*(8), 610–614.
[15] Rocha, L. E., Thorson, A. E., & Lambiotte, R. (2015). The non-linear health consequences of living in larger cities. *Journal of Urban Health*, *92*(5), 785–799.
[16] Gomez-Lievano, A., Patterson-Lomba, O., & Hausmann, R. (2017). Explaining the prevalence, scaling and variance of urban phenomena. *Nature Human Behaviour*, *1*(0012), 1–6.
[17] Hausmann, R., & Hidalgo, C. A. (2011). The network structure of economic output. *Journal of Economic Growth*, *16*(4), 309–342.
[18] Hidalgo, C. A., & Hausmann, R. (2009). The building blocks of economic complexity. *Proceedings of the National Academy of Sciences*, *106*(26), 10570–10575.
[19] Henrich, J. (2015). The secret of our success: How culture is driving human evolution, domesticating our species, and making us smarter. Princeton University Press. (ISBN: 9780691166858; Pages: 445).
[20] Laland, K. (2017). Darwin's unfinished symphony*: How culture made the human mind.* Princeton University Press.
[21] Shockley, W. (1957). On the statistics of individual variations of productivity in research laboratories. *Proceedings of the IRE*, *45*(3), 279–290.
[22] Gomez-Lievano, A., & Patterson-Lomba, O. (2021). Estimating the drivers of urban economic complexity and their connection to economic performance. *Royal Society Open Science*, *8*(9), 210670.
[23] Henrich, J. (2004). "Demography and cultural evolution: How adaptive cultural processes can produce maladaptive losses: The Tasmanian case". *American Antiquity*, *69*(2), 197–214. https://doi.org/10.2307/4128416
[24] Weitzman, M. L. (1998). Recombinant growth. *Quarterly Journal of Economics*, *113*(2), 331–360.
[25] Vaesen, K. (2012). Cumulative cultural evolution and demography. *PloS One*, *7*(7), e40989.

7 Explaining the socio-economic output of urban regions with a model combining urban scaling and polycentricity[1]

Amin Khiali-Miab, Adrienne Grêt-Regamey, Kay W. Axhausen, and Maarten J. Van Strien

7.1 Research question and introductory literature

Urbanisation can have a myriad of both positive and negative consequences for the social and economic status of urban regions [1–3]. It is known that the configuration of an urban region can influence a range of socio-economic factors [4], such as mobility costs [5], economic vitality [6], residential satisfaction, safety [7] and human well-being [8], and environmental sustainability [9]. However, the complex nature of urban systems makes the formulation of general principles for desirable urban configurations a difficult task. Yet, such principles are essential for urban planners to take informed decisions that maximise the chances of positive socio-economic and environmental outcomes [10].

Urban scaling law and polycentric urban development are two well-known concepts that can aid in the formulation of urban planning principles. On the one hand, the urban scaling concept finds its history in complex systems theory and describes the relationship between city size and a variety of socio-economic indicators [11,12]. For example, the population size of a city has been found to correlate positively with per capita wages, GDP, and the number of new patents [3]. On the other hand, the concept of polycentric development of urban regions originates from urban planning theory and has been advocated for its positive impact on a number of socio-economic factors [4,13,14]. For example, it has be suggested that polycentric development has positive effects on labour productivity compared to monocentric development [4].

Nevertheless, both the urban scaling and polycentricity concepts have some theoretical and practical limitations. Although it is known that functional relationships between urban centres have an effect on urban dynamics and socio-economic conditions, the urban scaling concept considers cities as isolated entities and ignores such functional relationships [15]. Certain types of polycentricity indicators explicitly take into account functional relationships between centres [4], but the polycentricity concept suffers from the ambiguity of the definition of polycentricity [16] and the lack of consensus on how best to measure polycentricity in urban regions [14]. Furthermore, when applied to real urban regions, both concepts often fail to explain socio-economic conditions accurately [e.g. 17,18]. Given that there are apparently some synergies between both concepts, combining aspects of

DOI: 10.4324/9781003288312-9

both concepts into one model may be able to overcome some of the limitations described above and improve our ability to explain socio-economic conditions in urban regions.

Here we present an overview of our study in which we combined the urban scaling and polycentricity concepts to improve the ability to explain the socio-economic status of urban regions in Switzerland [19]. Our first challenge was to delineate such regions in Switzerland, as the identified relationships between urban configuration and socio-economic conditions in both concepts seem to be sensitive to the definition of the boundaries of an urban region [14,20]. By identifying clusters in a commuter network, we were able to delineate functional urban regions to overcome sensitivities. For each region, we then calculated a new indicator of polycentricity based on the hierarchy of the commuter network. Finally, we investigated whether hierarchical linkages between urban centres (according to the polycentricity concept) and population size (according to the urban scaling concept) are complementary explanatory variables for the observed socio-economic status of urban regions.

7.2 Methods

Commuter flows are often used as an indicator of functional links between settlements or urban centres [14]. Therefore, we built a commuter network of Switzerland in which urban centres were connected by commuter flows. The nodes in this network were the 2944 zones in the Swiss national passenger transport model [NPVM; 21]. These zones generally represent Swiss municipalities, except in the more populous municipalities, which usually consist of multiple zones. Commuter flows were also determined from the NPVM [21]. We also obtained mean and median income data for each of the zones from the Federal Tax Administration. These data were used to show the socio-economic status of the urban regions. Both the income and commuting data were from 2010.

The first step in the analysis was to delineate urban regions in Switzerland. There are several ways in which urban regions can be delineated [22] and their choice can have an influence on the outcome of urban scaling or polycentricity studies [14,20]. In this study, we identified urban regions by applying a modularity maximisation algorithm to the commuter network. In an iterative process, the algorithm detects modules within the commuter network that maximise a modularity score [23]. For this analysis, the edges in the commuter network were weighted with the commuter flows. For further details on this approach we refer to Ref. [19]. Similar approaches have been used in other studies to delineate urban regions from commuter networks (e.g., [24]). As the commuter flows represent functional links between urban centres, the identified urban regions can be considered "functional urban regions" [24–26].

The second step in our analysis was to quantify the polycentricity in each of the defined urban areas. Several existing assessments of polycentricity explicitly consider functional links between urban centres, which has been coined "functional polycentricity" [4,27]. In this study, we quantified the functional polycentricity by calculating the Global Reaching Centrality (GRC) of the commuter network in each of the identified urban regions. GRC is a measure of a network's hierarchy and we argue that polycentric urban regions are less hierarchical (i.e. have a lower GRC) than monocentric regions. In Ref. [19], we give a schematic example in support of this reasoning. The GRC is calculated from the unweighted commuter network containing only links that had commuters.

In the last part of our analysis, we assessed the relationships between the population size, GRC, and mean and median income in the identified urban regions. With multivariate regression analysis, we determined how well the income was explained by the population size, the GRC, and a combination of these two variables. We also checked for collinearity between GRC and population size. For further details on the methods, we refer to Ref. [19].

7.3 Results

In the following, we give an overview of the main result found in Ref. [19]. With the modularity maximisation algorithm, we identified 16 urban regions in Switzerland (Figure 7.1), which shows considerable overlap with the 16 official Swiss labour market regions [28]. We calculated the population size for each of these regions, which ranged from 16,186 inhabitants in the region of Saanen to 3,322,387 in the region of Zurich. The GRC ranged from 0 in Schaffhausen (i.e., least hierarchical and most polycentric region) to 0.16494 around Neuchatel (i.e., most hierarchical

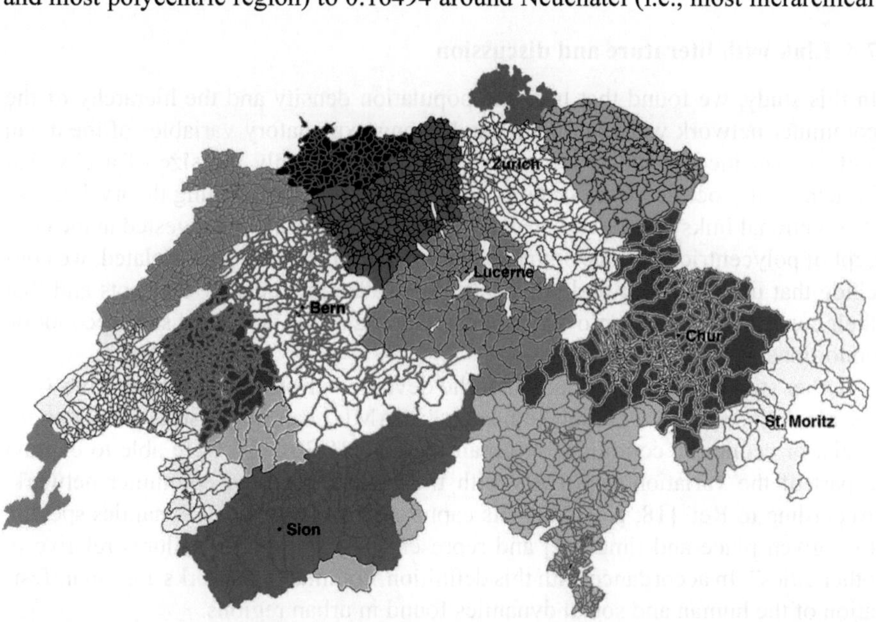

Figure 7.1 Map of the 16 urban regions identified in Switzerland by applying modularity maximisation to the commuter network.

Source: Adapted from Ref. [19].

and least polycentric region). The annual median and mean incomes ranged from 32,857 CHF (Saanen) to 45,866 CHF (Zurich) and from 39,212 CHF (Sion) to 55,118 CHF (Zurich), respectively. The rather large difference between the median and mean incomes illustrates the typically right-skewed income distribution in Switzerland.

Linear regression between log(mean income) and log(population size) revealed a significant ($p<0.05$) linear relationship (adjusted $R^2 = 0.301$; Figure 7.2A). We found that the income scaled superlinearly with the population size ($\beta = 1.04 \pm 0.01$), which is in line with scaling coefficients found in other Western European regions [29]. According to our findings, a doubling of the population in an urban region in Switzerland is associated with a 2.8% increase in mean income. We also found a significant ($p<0.05$) linear relationship between the logarithm of mean income and the GRC (adjusted $R^2 = 0.275$; Figure 7.2B). These results imply that a decrease of GRC with 0.1 is related to an approximately 5000 CHF increase in annual mean income [19].

We did not find a significant relationship between log(population size) and GRC ($p>0.05$, adjusted $R^2 = -0.06$), indicating that these two measures thus apparently explain different aspects of the income. Combining GRC and log(population size) in one linear regression model explaining log(mean income) yielded a model with a good fit (adjusted $R^2 = 0.537$; Figure 7.2C). Replacing the mean by the median income in this model produced an even higher model fit (adjusted $R^2 = 0.653$).

7.4 Link with literature and discussion

In this study, we found that both the population density and the hierarchy of the commuter network were significant and strong explanatory variables of the mean and median income in urban regions. It is thus not only the size of a city that influences its socio-economic status as suggested by urban scaling theory, but also its functional links to other urban centres within the region as suggested in the concept of polycentricity. Since both explanatory variables were uncorrelated, we conclude that urban scaling and polycentricity are complementary concepts and that their combination can improve our understanding of the drivers of socio-economic conditions in urban regions.

Other studies have also found that the deviations from urban scaling laws (i.e., "Scale-Adjusted Metropolitan Indicators"; SAMIs) can be a useful indicator for social or economic conditions in urban regions [18,30]. We were able to explain a part of the variation in SAMIs with the hierarchy of the commuter network. According to Ref. [18; p. 2] "SAMIs capture human and social dynamics specific to a given place and time [...] and represent its successes or failures relative to other cities". In accordance with this definition, commuter networks are a manifestation of the human and social dynamics found in urban regions.

We found that urban scaling relationships can be augmented with metrics calculated from commuter flows, which is in line with the findings of a recent study described in Ref. [15]. These authors demonstrate that, in addition to population size, the number of incoming commuters has a positive influence on a city's gross

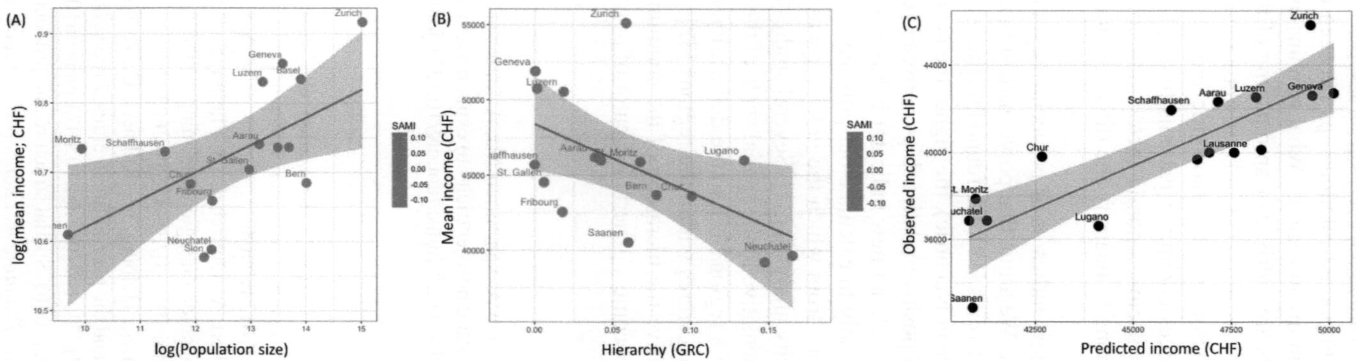

Figure 7.2 Correlation plots between (A) log(mean income) and log(population size), (B) mean income and hierarchy measured with Global Reaching Centrality (GRC), and (C) observed income and predicted income. The colours of the points in (A) and (B) indicate the Scale Adjusted Metropolitan Indicator (SAMI) [18]. The red trend-lines are identified with linear regression between the variables and the grey area represents the confidence interval.

Source: Adapted from Ref. [19].

domestic product. In our study, we do not only consider incoming commuters, but the complete commuter network within an urban region. Despite these differences, we can conclude that there are important relationships between commuter flows and socio-economic conditions in urban regions. What remains unclear, however, is whether these commuter flows are a driver or an outcome of the differences in socio-economic conditions. Whereas Ref. [15] and our study regard the commuter patterns to be an explanatory factor of socio-economic indicators, other studies demonstrate how income influences commuter patterns (e.g., [31]). There is thus most likely a feedback between socio-economic factors and commuter patterns, but more research needs to be done to quantify the direction and strength of this feedback.

In this study, we propose a new indicator of polycentricity, i.e., the hierarchy (GRC) of the commuter network. We argue that polycentric urban regions are less hierarchical than monocentric networks [19]. We found that the less hierarchical the commuter network (i.e., the more polycentric), the higher the personal income. As multiple studies have also found positive relationships between polycentricity and socio-economic indicators [4,13,14], our new indicator behaves as expectated. We used the commuter network not only to calculate our polycentricity indicator, but also to delineate the urban regions from which the indicator was calculated; both are essential steps in polycentricity analyses [32]. Several studies have shown that indicators of polycentricity are sensitive to the spatial scale of the analysis [25], to the overall population density in a region [33], to the delineation of urban regions as well as to the definition of subcentres within the regions [32]. Further research should thus point out how sensitive the hierarchy of the commuter network is to these analysis choices, for it to become a generic indicator of polycentricity.

Note

1 Previously published as: Khiali-Miab A, van Strien MJ, Axhausen KW, Grêt-Regamey A (2019) Combining urban scaling and polycentricity to explain socio-economic status of urban regions. *PLoS ONE* 14(6): e0218022. https://doi.org/10.1371/journal.pone.0218022

References

[1] Turok, I., & McGranahan, G. (2013). Urbanization and economic growth: the arguments and evidence for Africa and Asia. *Environment and Urbanization, 25*(2), 465–482. doi:10.1177/0956247813490908

[2] Thapa, P., Torralba, M., Buerkert, A., Dittrich, C., & Plieninger, T. (2021). Ecological and social outcomes of urbanization on regional farming systems: a global synthesis. *Ecology and Society, 26*(3). doi:10.5751/ES-12579-260324

[3] Bettencourt, L. M. A., Lobo, J., Helbing, D., Kühnert, C., & West, G. B. (2007). Growth, innovation, scaling, and the pace of life in cities. *Proceedings of the National Academy of Sciences, 104*(17), 7301–7306. doi:10.1073/pnas.0610172104

[4] Meijers, E. J., & Burger, M. J. (2010). Spatial structure and productivity in US metropolitan areas. *Environment and Planning A: Economy and Space, 42*(6), 1383–1402. doi:10.1068/a42151

[5] Camagni, R., Gibelli, M. C., & Rigamonti, P. (2002). Urban mobility and urban form: the social and environmental costs of different patterns of urban expansion. *Ecological Economics*, *40*(2), 199–216. doi: 10.1016/S0921-8009(01)00254-3

[6] Martino, N., Girling, C., & Lu, Y. (2021). Urban form and livability: socioeconomic and built environment indicators. *Buildings and Cities*, *2*(1), 220–243.

[7] Bramley, G., Dempsey, N., Power, S., Brown, C., & Watkins, D. (2009). Social sustainability and urban form: evidence from five British cities. *Environment and Planning A: Economy and Space*, *41*(9), 2125–2142. doi:10.1068/a4184

[8] Samuelsson, K. (2021). The topodiverse city: urban form for subjective well-being. *Frontiers in Built Environment*, *7*, 735221. doi:10.3389/fbuil.2021.735221

[9] Newton, P. (2000). Urban form and environmental performance. *Achieving Sustainable Urban Form*, *2*, 46–53.

[10] Masnavi, M. R., Gharai, F., & Hajibandeh, M. (2019). Exploring urban resilience thinking for its application in urban planning: a review of literature. *International Journal of Environmental Science and Technology*, *16*(1), 567–582. doi:10.1007/s13762-018-1860-2

[11] Han, X.-P., Hao, Q., Wang, B.-H., & Zhou, T. (2011). Origin of the scaling law in human mobility: hierarchy of traffic systems. *Physical Review E*, *83*(3), 036117. doi:10.1103/PhysRevE.83.036117

[12] Bettencourt, L. M. A. (2013). The origins of scaling in cities. *Science*, *340*(6139), 1438–1441. doi:10.1126/science.1235823

[13] González-González, E., & Nogués, S. (2016). Regional polycentricity: an indicator framework for assessing cohesion impacts of railway infrastructures. *European Planning Studies*, *24*(5), 950–973. doi:10.1080/09654313.2016.1142506

[14] Schmitt, P., Volgmann, K., Münter, A., & Reardon, M. (2015). Unpacking polycentricity at the city-regional scale: insights from Dusseldorf and Stockholm. *European Journal of Spatial Development*, *59*, 1–26.

[15] Alves, L. G. A., Rybski, D., & Ribeiro, H. V. (2021). Commuting network effect on urban wealth scaling. *Scientific Reports*, *11*(1), 22918. doi:10.1038/s41598-021-02327-7

[16] Van Meeteren, M., Poorthuis, A., Derudder, B., & Witlox, F. (2015). Pacifying Babel's tower: a scientometric analysis of polycentricity in urban research. *Urban Studies*, *53*(6), 1278–1298. doi: 10.1177/0042098015573455

[17] Veneri, P., & Burgalassi, D. (2012). Questioning polycentric development and its effects. Issues of definition and measurement for the Italian NUTS-2 regions. *European Planning Studies*, *20*(6), 1017–1037. doi:10.1080/09654313.2012.673566

[18] Bettencourt, L. M. A., Lobo, J., Strumsky, D., & West, G. B. (2010). Urban scaling and Its deviations: revealing the structure of wealth, innovation and crime across cities. *Plos One*, *5*(11), e13541. doi:10.1371/journal.pone.0013541

[19] Khiali-Miab, A., van Strien, M. J., Axhausen, K. W., & Grêt-Regamey, A. (2019). Combining urban scaling and polycentricity to explain socio-economic status of urban regions. *PLOS ONE*, *14*(6), e0218022. https://doi.org/10.1371/journal.pone.0218022

[20] Arcaute, E., Hatna, E., Ferguson, P., Youn, H., Johansson, A., & Batty, M. (2015). Constructing cities, deconstructing scaling laws. *Journal of The Royal Society Interface*, *12*(102), 20140745. doi:10.1098/rsif.2014.0745

[21] ARE. (2014). *Nationales Personenverkehrsmodell des UVEK, Aktualisierung auf den Basiszustand 2010*. Bern, Switzerland.

[22] Uchiyama, Y., & Mori, K. (2017). Methods for specifying spatial boundaries of cities in the world: the impacts of delineation methods on city sustainability indices. *Science of The Total Environment*, *592*, 345–356. doi:10.1016/j.scitotenv.2017.03.014

[23] Blondel, V. D., Guillaume, J.-L., Lambiotte, R., & Lefebvre, E. (2008). Fast unfolding of communities in large networks. *Journal of Statistical Mechanics: Theory and Experiment, 2008*(10), P10008. doi:10.1088/1742-5468/2008/10/p10008

[24] Shen, Y., & Batty, M. (2018). Delineating the perceived functional regions of London from commuting flows. *Environment and Planning A: Economy and Space, 51*(3), 547–550. doi:10.1177/0308518X18786253

[25] Brezzi, M., & Veneri, P. (2015). Assessing polycentric urban systems in the OECD: country, regional and metropolitan perspectives. *European Planning Studies, 23*(6), 1128–1145. doi:10.1080/09654313.2014.905005

[26] Ribeiro, H. V., Oehlers, M., Moreno-Monroy, A. I., Kropp, J. P., & Rybski, D. (2021). Association between population distribution and urban GDP scaling. *PLOS ONE, 16*(1), e0245771. doi:10.1371/journal.pone.0245771

[27] Vasanen, A. (2012). Functional polycentricity: examining metropolitan spatial structure through the connectivity of urban sub-centres. *Urban Studies, 49*(16), 3627–3644. doi:10.1177/0042098012447000

[28] FSO. (2019). *Arbeitsmarktregionen 2018, Erläuterungsbericht.* Retrieved from Neuchâtel, Switzerland: https://dam-api.bfs.admin.ch/hub/api/dam/assets/8948840/master

[29] Strano, E., & Sood, V. (2016). Rich and poor cities in Europe. An urban scaling approach to mapping the European economic transition. *PLOS ONE, 11*(8), e0159465. doi:10.1371/journal.pone.0159465

[30] Lobo, J., Bettencourt, L. M. A., Strumsky, D., & West, G. B. (2013). Urban scaling and the production function for cities. *PLOS ONE, 8*(3), e58407. doi:10.1371/journal.pone.0058407

[31] Bogomolov, Y., He, M., Khulbe, D., & Sobolevsky, S. (2021). Impact of income on urban commute across major cities in US. *Procedia Computer Science, 193*, 325–332. doi:10.1016/j.procs.2021.10.033

[32] Thomas, R., Schmidt, S., & Siedentop, S. (2021). Toward comparative polycentricity scores: assessing variations in regional delineation and subcenter identification. *Environment and Planning B: Urban Analytics and City Science*, 23998083211065765. doi:10.1177/23998083211065765

[33] Krasnoselskaya, D., & Timiryanova, V. (2022). Do polycentric patterns influence the economic performance of municipalities? Empirical evidence from Russia. *Regional Science Policy & Practice, 2022*, 1–22. doi:https://doi.org/10.1111/rsp3.12515

8 Comparing cities of different sizes with scale-adjusted metrics[1]

Haroldo V. Ribeiro, Luiz G. A. Alves, Ervin K. Lenzi, Fabiano L. Ribeiro, and Renio S. Mendes

8.1 Introduction

The idea of trying to understand how things change with size is definitively not new in science. Limiting ourselves to "Modern Science," we find the discourse book of Galileo [1] where Salviati talks about the impossibility of arbitrarily increasing the size of artificial and living things:

> *From what has already been demonstrated, you can plainly see the impossibility of increasing the size of structures to vast dimensions either in art or in nature; likewise the impossibility of building ships, palaces, or temples of enormous size in such a way that their oars, yards, beams, iron-bolts, and, in short, all their other parts will hold together; nor can nature produce trees of extraordinary size because the branches would break down under their own weight; so also it would be impossible to build up the bony structures of men, horses, or other animals so as to hold together and perform their normal functions if these animals were to be increased enormously in height; ... To illustrate briefly, I have sketched a bone whose natural length has been increased three times and whose thickness has been multiplied until, for a correspondingly large animal, it would perform the same function which the small bone performs for its small animal. From the figures here shown you can see how out of proportion the enlarged bone appears. Clearly then if one wishes to maintain in a great giant the same proportion of limb as that found in an ordinary man he must either find a harder and stronger material for making the bones, or he must admit a diminution of strength in comparison with men of medium stature; for if his height be increased inordinately he will fall and be crushed under his own weight.*

That is basically the same underlying idea of the work of Kleiber [2] about the relationship between animals' metabolism M and body weight W, proposed almost 300 years after Galileo. In that article, Kleiber plotted on a log-log scale the values of M versus W for 13 animals and discovered that $M \sim W^{3/4}$, a result that is now known as the 3/4 Kleiber's law. This expression indicates that by doubling the size of an animal, its energy needs will not double, but will increase only about 70 percent more, showing that large animals are more energy-efficient than small

DOI: 10.4324/9781003288312-10

ones. However, while Galileo's explanation of the impossibility of increasing the size of animals is simply based on geometry, a more complete comprehension of Kleiber's law involves the concepts of networks and self-similar fractals, and was only achieved after the works of West [3,4].

It was, however, even more recent that such "scaling ideas" have been applied to urban systems. In this case, the posed question is: *How do various characteristics of cities scale with their size?* In spite of the world's population being increasingly urban with more than half living in cities since 2007 [5], this simple question has been only recently addressed due to the availability of an unprecedented amount of data at the city level. Curiously, answers are mainly being developed by physicists, and before these works, most urban theories were largely qualitative and focused on specific cities.

This physics-inspired theory of cities can be traced back to the seminal works of West and Bettencourt [6–8] at the Santa Fe Institute 15 years ago. By using data at the city level from various countries, they demonstrated that several city indicators Y are power-law functions of the city's population N, that is, $Y \sim N^{\beta}$, where the scaling exponent β classifies city indicators in three universality classes. Indicators associated with individual needs (e.g., household energy and water consumption) have isometric relationships ($\beta = 1$) with population, infrastructure measures (e.g., road surface and petrol stations) show sublinear allometric relationships ($\beta < 1$), while social, economic, and health indicators (e.g., crime, unemployment, and AIDS cases) display superlinear allometric relationships ($\beta > 1$) with population. This result is known as the "urban scaling hypothesis," and similarly to Kleiber's law, it is attributed to the underlying structure of urban networks (e.g., transport, supply, and social networks) that mediate the interactions among city's parts [8].

Despite the intrinsic nonlinearities emerging from urban scaling theory, it is still common to find works using linear regressions between raw population and urban indicator values, and even more surprising is the ubiquity of rates (for instance, crime per 100,000 people) or per capita indicators in reports of government agencies that guide public policies and quantify the performance of cities. Ignoring urban scaling laws may lead to misguided conclusions [9–12] as rates and per capita indicators are oblivious to the urban scaling and their underlying consequences. Indeed, urban scaling implies that rates or per capita indicators are inherently biased towards large (for superlinear scaling) or small (for sublinear) cities. Furthermore, assuming urban scaling as a natural expression of how cities are organized, accounting for this phenomenon is a crucial step for obtaining a fair comparison between cities with different populations.

This chapter revisits a simple alternative metric that explicitly accounts for urban scaling and allows a fair, unbiased, and more natural comparison among cities of different sizes: the so-called scale-adjusted metropolitan indicators (SAMIs) or scale-adjusted metrics (SAMs) [10–12].

8.2 Methods

One of the main problems of defining rates for urban indicators or calculating their per capita values is that these types of normalization completely ignore the fact that urban indicators display allometric relationships (or scaling laws) with population [7]. Mathematically, we can write

$$Y_i(t) = 10^{\mathcal{A}_i} N(t)^{\beta_i}, \tag{8.1}$$

where $Y_i(t)$ is an urban indicator (e.g., urban GDP) and $N(t)$ is the urban population in a given time t, while $\mathcal{A}_i$ is a constant and β_i is the scaling exponent. This power-law relation summarizes the average effect of increasing the population on the urban indicator – it imposes cities a self-similar nature such that their properties are, to some extent, determined by their populations. Thus, we expect urban indicators to present a deterministic component with population, which in turn emerges from networks related to social and infrastructure aspects of cities [8]. Per capita values or indicator rates implicitly assume urban indicators are proportional to population ($\beta_i = 1$), which is in stark contrast to empirical behavior. Whenever the urban scaling exponent β_i is different from one, there will be a remaining component related to population in per capita values or indicator rates; for instance, the per capita indicator

$$y_i = Y_i/N \sim N^{(\beta_i - 1)}, \tag{8.2}$$

is biased towards large cities for $\beta_i > 1$ or towards small cities for $\beta_i < 1$ – this type of normalization correctly removes the effect of the population only when $\beta_i = 1$.

Urban scaling is the origin of but also the solution to this problem. Indeed, we can account for the deterministic behavior of urban allometries by following a simple and efficient recipe proposed by Bettencourt et al. [10] to define the so-called *scale-adjusted metropolitan indicators* (SAMIs) or *scale-adjusted metrics* (SAMs). This normalization approach consists in evaluating the logarithmic difference between the actual value of an urban indicator and the value expected by the urban scaling with population (Eq. 8.1), that is,

$$D_{Y_i}(t) = \log Y_i(t) - \left[\mathcal{A}_i + \beta_i \log N(t)\right]. \tag{8.3}$$

The values of $D_{Y_i}(t)$ are thus the residuals surrounding the adjustment of the urban scaling law on the log-transformed data. This simple approach explicitly takes into account the allometry between an urban indicator and the population, yielding a size-independent relative metric that is not biased by population for any value of β_i. The SAMs capture the exceptionality, either good or bad, of a place and establish a "natural" scale for comparing cities by identifying whether an urban indicator of a given city is above ($D_{Y_i} > 0$) or below ($D_{Y_i} < 0$) the expected value for cities of similar population.

This approach has proved useful in several empirical contexts [10–13] and an interesting property of these scale-adjusted metrics is that they tend to be correlated at different times, that is, the values of $D_{Y_i}(t + \Delta t)$ and $D_{Y_i}(t)$, where

Δt is a time interval, are somehow correlated such that linear functions are often good approximations for the average tendency of $D_{Y_i}(t+\Delta t)$ versus $D_{Y_i}(t)$ [12], that is,

$$D_{Y_i}(t+\Delta t) = A_i + \alpha_i D_{Y_i}(t), \tag{8.4}$$

where A_i and α_i are parameters to be estimated from the empirical data. In particular, to better understand the role of α_i, let us consider the limit where Δt is small and rewrite Eq. (8.4) as

$$\frac{d}{dt} D_{Y_i}(t) = A_i + (\alpha_i - 1) D_{Y_i}(t). \tag{8.5}$$

The solution for this differential equation is

$$f(x) = \begin{cases} A_i/(1-\alpha_i) + [k - A_i/(1-\alpha_i)]exp[-(1-\alpha_i)t], \alpha \neq 1 \\ A_i t + k, \alpha = 1 \end{cases} \tag{8.6}$$

where k is an integration constant. For $\alpha_i < 1$, Eq. (8.6) predicts that $D_{Y_i}(t)$ will exponentially approach $A_i/(1-\alpha_i)$ over time, while we expect $D_{Y_i}(t)$ to exponentially increase over time for $\alpha_i > 1$. Conversely, we find a linear behavior for the evolution of $D_{Y_i}(t)$ when $\alpha_i = 1$. Estimated values of A_i tend to be very small, such that $D_{Y_i}(t)$ is approaching zero for $\alpha_i < 1$, and thus the urban indicators are converging to the values expected by the scaling law with population (Eq. 8.1). Moreover, for $\alpha_i < 1$, the quantity $1/(1-\alpha_i)$ plays the role of a characteristic time, such that the smaller the value of α_i, the faster the changes in the urban indicator.

Besides being correlated with their own past values, scale-adjusted metrics also tend to exhibit significant cross-correlations among different urban indicators. These memory effects combined with the fact that the residuals surrounding Eq. (8.4) are well-approximated by normal distributions and make scale-adjusted metrics very useful for making forecasts via linear regressions. Indeed, an interesting possibility is to write

$$D_{Y_i}(t+\Delta t) = C_0 + \sum_{k=1} C_k D_{Y_k}(t) + \eta_i(t), \tag{8.7}$$

where C_k is the linear coefficient quantifying the predictive power of $D_{Y_k}(t)$ on $D_{Y_i}(t+\Delta t)$ (C_0 is the intercept coefficient), $\eta_i(t)$ is a noise term accounting for the effects of unmeasurable factors, and the sum goes over all urban indicators under investigation.

8.3 Results

In order to verify the usefulness of the SAMs framework, we revisit some analyses with several urban indicators (child labor, elderly population, female population, homicides, illiteracy, family income, male population, and unemployment) of Brazilian cities in three different years (1991, 2000, and 2010) [11,12]. We start by illustrating the urban scaling laws using the number of illiterate people as the urban indicator. Figure 8.1(a) shows the relation between the number of illiterate people and the population of Brazilian cities using log-transformed quantities for the three available years. We observe that Eq. (8.1) is a good fit for these data and that the adjusted urban scaling exponents are smaller than one in the three years. Thus, population size confers a "protective effect" against illiteracy as large cities have proportionally fewer illiterate people; for instance, every 1% increase in population is associated with only a 0.85% rise in the number of illiterate people in 2010.

This indicator further allows us to compare the results of an analysis based on per capita values and scale-adjusted metrics. In Figure 8.2(b), we depict the evolution of the average per capita number of illiterate people in Brazil. While there is a clear decreasing trend, these per capita values hide an interesting pattern that scale-adjusted metrics capture. To reveal these patterns, we study the evolution of the average SAM by creating two groups of cities: those whose urban indicator $Y_i(t)$ was above ($D_{Y_i}(t) > 0$) and those whose $Y_i(t)$ was below ($D_{Y_i}(t) < 0$) the urban scaling law in the year 1991. Figure 8.2(c) shows these average values for each group. We observe that the average SAM for cities above and below the scaling law is increasing over time. Thus, cities with illiteracy levels above the scaling law could not decrease this urban indicator – the number of illiterate people relative to cities of similar size has instead increased. Conversely, cities initially below the scaling law have not only managed to keep this indicator low but further decreased the number of illiterate people relative to cities of similar size.

When investigating other urban indicators, we find that almost all of them show a clear evolution in terms of their average per capita values. The elderly population, female population, homicides, and family income have increased over the years, while child labor, illiteracy, and male population have decreased over time. Unemployment is an exception and does not exhibit a clear trend. In its turn, most SAMs also present clear trends. Indeed, cities initially above the scaling laws tend to exhibit statistically significant decreasing trends, while cities initially below the scaling laws often display an increasing tendency (illiteracy is thus an exception to this pattern). For instance, cities with the number of child laborers, homicides, and unemployment above the scaling laws have successfully reduced these indicators, while cities below the scaling laws have proved unable to improve or maintain the same level of their SAMs. Remarkably, these and other patterns remain hidden or distorted when investigating only the evolution of per capita values of these urban indicators.

The trends in the average SAM values motivate an investigation of the relationship between their values at different times. As we have already expressed in Eq.

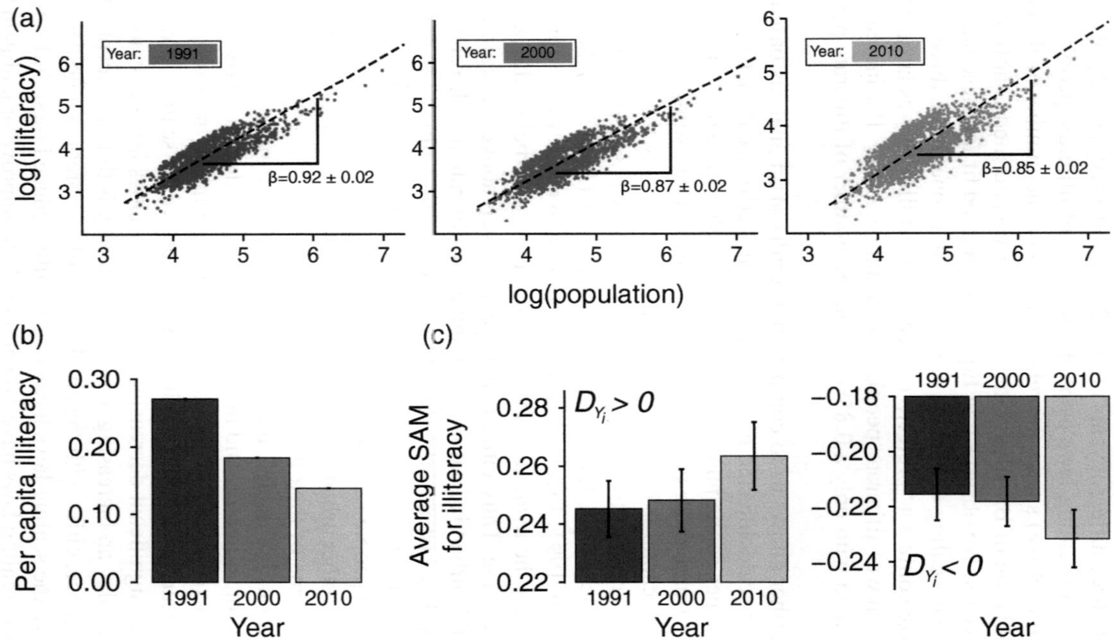

Figure 8.1 (a) Illustration of the scaling law between the number of illiterate people and the population of Brazilian cities. The markers represent the values for each city, and the dashed lines are the scaling laws (Eq. 8.1) adjusted to data with urban scaling exponents β shown within the panels. (b) Evolution of the average value of the per capita number of illiteracy people. (c) Evolution of the average SAM for illiteracy after grouping cities with positive ($D_{Y_i}(t) > 0$, on the left) and negative ($D_{Y_i}(t) > 0$, on the right) SAMs in 1991.

Source: Adapted from Ref. [12].

(8.4), the values of $D_{Y_i}(t+\Delta t)$ and $D_{Y_i}(t)$ are often correlated in a linear fashion. To confirm this pattern, we have analyzed scatter plots between SAMs in a given year versus their past values for all available urban indicators. Figure 8.2(a) shows these scatter plots considering the values of $D_{Y_i}(2010)$ versus $D_{Y_i}(2000)$. Despite the different degrees of correlation, we observe that the linear model of Eq. (8.4) is a good description of the average trends in these relationships. Moreover, very similar patterns are obtained when investigating the association between $D_{Y_i}(2000)$ and $D_{Y_i}(1991)$. We have also adjusted Eq. (8.4) to these data and the best-fitting values of α_i are shown within the panels of Figure 8.2(a). Except for illiteracy, the values of α_i are all smaller than 1. This fact agrees with the evolution of the average SAMs, that is, indicators characterized by $\alpha_i < 1$ are approaching the scaling laws, while indicators with $\alpha_i \geq 1$ exhibit a departing trend from the scaling laws.

Because the majority of the indicators have $\alpha_i < 1$, we can interpret the quantity $1/(1-\alpha_i)$ as a characteristic time for their dynamics. Indeed, as we have discussed when analyzing Eqs. (8.5) and (8.6), the smaller the value of α_i is, the faster we expect to be the changes in the urban indicators. The values of α_i for population-related indicators are among the largest ones; thus, their evolutions occur at the slowest pace, which in turn agrees with the reduction in the rate of growth of the Brazilian population. Apart from illiteracy, all other socio-economic indicators show values of α_i smaller than their population-related counterparts. This result thus indicates that socio-economic indicators are more susceptible to natural or public policies-driven changes.

The SAM values are not only autocorrelated with their past values but also display statistically significant cross-correlations with other indicators. For instance, the Pearson correlation coefficient between SAMs for illiteracy and family income is ≈ -0.8, while a correlation of ≈ -0.4 is observed between the SAMs for child labor and unemployment, both when considering the values of $D_{Y_i}(2010)$ versus $D_{Y_i}(2000)$. When combined, these memory effects show great potential for making forecasts of SAM values via simple linear regressions. Indeed, we can use the model of Eq. (8.7) by considering the relationships $(t+\Delta t) = 2000$ versus $t = 1991$ and $(t+\Delta t) = 2010$ versus $t = 2000$. We have found that these simple models account for 31–97% of the observed variance in $D_{Y_i}(t+\Delta t)$. Furthermore, as shown in Figure 8.2(b), these linear models correctly reproduce the average SAM values above and below the scaling laws for the years 2000 and 2010 only using data from the years 1991 and 2000, respectively. In addition, the model of Eq. (8.7) also replicates the distributions of the empirical values. These good agreements thus indicate that SAM values are very effective for making predictions about the evolution of urban indicators.

8.4 Summary and discussion

The global urban population surpassed the rural population in 2007, and estimates suggest that the world urbanization rate may increase by up to 90% by 2100 [14]. This urbanization process brought us several benefits as cities are usually

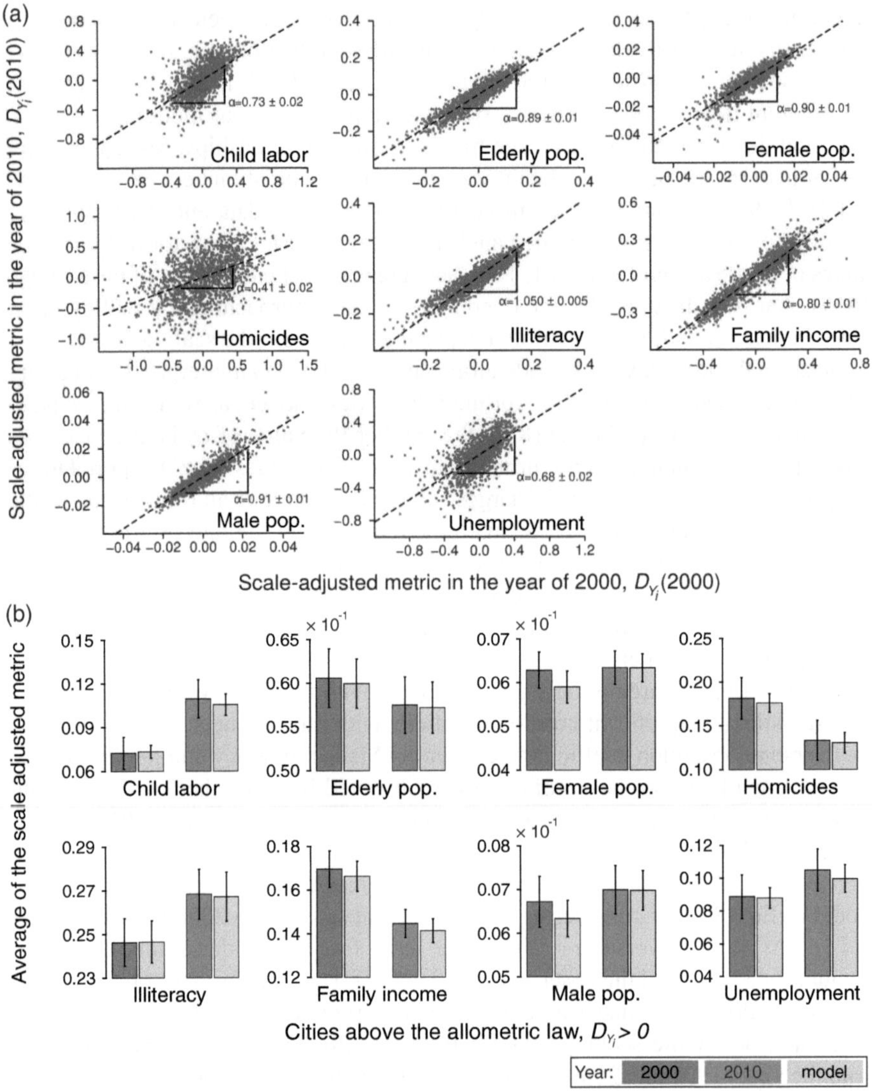

Figure 8.2 (a) Memory effects in the evolution of scale-adjusted metrics as quantified by the relationship between the values of $D_{Y_i}(2010)$ versus $D_{Y_i}(2000)$ for each Brazilian city (markers). The dashed lines are fits of the linear model of Eq. (8.4) obtained via the ordinary least-squares method. The values of α_i and their standard errors are shown within the panels. (b) Comparison between the average SAMs obtained from the linear model of Eq. (8.7) and empirical values for each urban indicator. The model of Eq. (8.7) is used for predicting the values of $D_{Y_i}(t)$ in the year 2000 only using data from the year 1991 as well as for predicting $D_{Y_i}(t)$ in the year 2010 only using data from the year of 2000. The results refer to cities above the scaling laws, but similar agreements are obtained for cities below the scaling laws.

Source: Adapted from Ref. [12].

associated with higher levels of literacy and health care, and better opportunities in general. However, cities also have a central role in humanity's most crucial problems such as climate change, pollution, environmental degradation, violence, and the rise of people living in substandard conditions. There is thus an urgent need for investigations that quantify, compare, and predict the evolution of urban indicators as these results may help in better political decisions and resource allocation. The works that have been developed by the science of cities community represent an important reply to that urgent need, and the discovery of robust scaling laws between urban indicators and population stands out among the most striking and universal findings. While these urban scaling laws categorically imply the existence of nonlinear relationships between several city indicators and population size, government agencies still very often use indicator rates or per capita values in reports and as a guide for public policies, resource allocation, and performance evaluation of cities with different sizes.

In this chapter, we have shown that urban scaling laws make indicator rates or per capita values inherently biased towards large or small cities depending on whether the scaling law is superlinear or sublinear. We have thus presented a simple alternative metric that explicitly accounts for urban scaling and allows a fair, unbiased, and more natural comparison among cities of different sizes. These relative measures, known as scale-adjusted metropolitan indicators (SAMIs) or scale-adjusted metrics (SAMs) [10–12], are simply defined by the residuals of urban allometric relationships or the "distance" to the scaling law. Despite their simplicity, we have shown that scale-adjusted metrics provide more appropriate and informative summaries about the evolution of urban regions, uncovering patterns that would go unnoticed when analyzing the evolution of the per capita values alone. By using data on eight city indicators from the three latest Brazilian censuses, we demonstrate that scale-adjusted metrics are strongly correlated with their past values in a linear fashion, which in turn allows the use of simple linear regression models for predicting their values. We show that linear models based on scale-adjusted metrics account for 31–97% of the observed variance in data and provide precise predictions for the time evolution of average values. Finally, we advocate for the extensive use of scale-adjusted metrics for government policies and resource allocation in the context of urban planning.

Note

1 Previously published as:
Alves, Mendes, Lenzi, Ribeiro (2015). Scale-Adjusted Metrics for Predicting the Evolution of Urban Indicators and Quantifying the Performance of Cities. *PLoS ONE* 10(9).
Alves LGA, Ribeiro HV, Lenzi EK, Mendes RS. (2013). Distance to the scaling law: a useful approach for unveiling relationships between crime and urban metrics. *PLoS ONE* 8, e69580.

References

[1] Galilei, G. *Discourses and Mathematical Demonstrations Relating to Two New Sciences*, Dover. (1914 – originals from Leiden, 1638).

[2] Kleiber, M. Body size and metabolism. *Hilgardia: A Journal of Agricultural Science* 6, 315–353 (1932).
[3] West, G. B., Brown, J. H. & Enquist, B. J. A general model for the origin of allometric scaling laws in biology. *Science* 276, 122–126 (1997).
[4] West, G. B. & Brown, J. H. Life's universal scaling laws. *Physics Today* 57, 36–43 (2004).
[5] Nations, U. *World Urbanization Prospects: The 2014 Revision, Highlights*. Department of Economic and Social Affairs. Population Division, United Nations (2014).
[6] Kühnert, C., Helbing, D. & West, G. B. Scaling laws in urban supply networks. *Physica A* 363, 96–103 (2006).
[7] Bettencourt, L. M., Lobo, J., Helbing, D., Kühnert, C. & West, G. B. Growth, innovation, scaling, and the pace of life in cities. *Proceedings of The National Academy of Sciences* 104, 7301–7306 (2007).
[8] Bettencourt, L. M. The origins of scaling in cities. *Science* 340, 1438–1441 (2013).
[9] Gordon, M. B. A random walk in the literature on criminality: A partial and critical view on some statistical analyses and modelling approaches. *European Journal of Applied Mathematics* 21, 283–306 (2010).
[10] Bettencourt, L. M., Lobo, J., Strumsky, D. & West, G. B. Urban scaling and its deviations: Revealing the structure of wealth, innovation and crime across cities. *PLOS ONE* 5, e13541 (2010).
[11] Alves, L. G., Ribeiro, H. V., Lenzi, E. K. & Mendes, R. S. Distance to the scaling law: A useful approach for unveiling relationships between crime and urban metrics. *PLOS ONE* 8, e69580 (2013).
[12] Alves, L. G., Mendes, R. S., Lenzi, E. K. & Ribeiro, H. V. Scale-adjusted metrics for predicting the evolution of urban indicators and quantifying the performance of cities. *PLOS ONE* 10, e0134862 (2015).
[13] Lobo, J., Bettencourt, L. M., Strumsky, D. & West, G. B. Urban scaling and the production function for cities. *PLOS ONE* 8, e58407 (2013).
[14] Jiang, L. & O'Neill, B. C. Global urbanization projections for the shared socioeconomic pathways. *Global Environmental Change* 42, 193–199 (2017).

9 Connection between Zipf's law and urban scaling[1]

Haroldo V. Ribeiro, Luiz G. A. Alves, Ervin K. Lenzi, Fabiano L. Ribeiro, and Renio S. Mendes

9.1 Introduction

Cities can occur in sizes that range from thousands of people to millions of inhabitants. Similar to other natural and socio-economic phenomena extending across multiple orders of magnitude, urban systems follow different regularities that often emerge in the form of asymptotic power-law distributions or relations [1,2]. Among the best-known examples of such regularities, we have the Zipf's law for cities [3,4] and the urban scaling relations [5]. Initially observed by Auerbach [4] and later made famous by Zipf [3], Zipf's law for cities establishes that the population of cities is distributed according to an inverse power-law function of population, reflecting the familiar fact that there are a large number of small towns and a few metropolises in a given region or country. Urban scaling, in turn, has its origins in ideas about allometry from biology [6,7] and refers to a power-law association between urban indicators and city population that is also known as urban allometry or the Bettencourt-West law [5]. According to the urban scaling hypothesis [2,5], city indicators are grouped depending on whether they present increasing returns to scale (e.g., socio-economic indicators), economy of scale (e.g., infrastructure indicators), or isometric scale (e.g., individual needs indicators).

These two scaling laws are perhaps the most fundamental paradigms of the science of cities, and a large part of literature produced by this scientific community has a direct relation either with Zipf's law [8–18] or urban scaling [19–27]. Despite the significant interest in these two scaling laws, little attention has been paid to investigating possible associations between both laws. In fact, Zipf's law and urban scaling are commonly believed to be independent matters. The very few investigations on possible connections between Zipf's law and urban scaling have, however, two distinct explanations: one probabilistic [28,29] and another one relying on country scaling constraints [30].

The first explanation is due to the seminal work of Gomez-Lievano et al. [28] showing that urban scaling is related to Zipf's law when urban indicators are power-law distributed. Gomez-Lievano et al. demonstrated the existence of an upper limit to the urban scaling exponent determined by the power-law exponents related to population distribution (Zipf exponent) and the urban indicator distribution. This result is obtained from density transformations of random variables representing

DOI: 10.4324/9781003288312-11

the city population and the urban indicator, which in turn does not imply a direct association between the Zipf and the urban scaling exponents. Instead, we may say this association has a probabilistic nature, that is, random permutations in the values of population and urban indicators have no impact on their distributions but modify the allometric association between both quantities. Still, this theoretical upper limit between both exponents holds well in the empirical data related to several urban indicators [29], indicating indeed that Zipf's law and urban scaling cannot be considered independent descriptions.

The second explanation builds upon these previous works but from a system-wide perspective. Indeed, Ribeiro et al. [30] demonstrated that the combination of Zipf's and the urban scaling laws leads to a power-law relation between total urban population and total urban indicator within an urban system. This country scaling law has an exponent determined by both the Zipf and urban scaling exponents, and because there is only one country scaling exponent, one can derive a mathematical expression relating the Zipf and urban scaling exponents.

This chapter revisits these two facets of the connection between Zipf's law and urban scaling, as well as how this connection behaves with empirical data, and some implications.

9.2 Methods

Let us start by considering an urban system (e.g., a country) composed of m cities with populations $\{s_1, s_2, \ldots, s_m\}$. Suppose now that we sort these population values s in descending order $\{s_{max}, \ldots, s, \ldots, s_{min}\}$ (where s_{max} and s_{min} are, respectively, the largest and smallest populations in the system) and associate a rank variable r defined by $\{1, 2, \ldots, r, \ldots, m\}$ to each city population. Zipf's law for cities states that the rank r and the city population s are related via [3]

$$r \sim s^{-\alpha}, \tag{9.1}$$

where $\alpha > 0$ is the Zipf exponent. Zipf's law implies that the complementary cumulative distribution of city population $F(s)$ can be written as $F(s) \sim s^{-\zeta}$, with $\zeta \approx \alpha$, and, consequently, the probability density distribution $P(S)$ of city population is a power law given by

$$P(s) \sim s^{-(\alpha+1)}. \tag{9.2}$$

In its turn, the urban scaling hypothesis [5] establishes a power-law relationship between an urban indicator y (e.g., the urban GDP) and the population s of a city, that is,

$$y = cs^{\beta}, \tag{9.3}$$

where c is a positive constant, and $\beta > 0$ is the urban scaling exponent.

Within the probabilistic connection proposed by Gomez-Lievano et al. [28], we further need to assume the urban indicator y to be power-law distributed, that is,

$$P(y) \sim y^{-(\tau+1)}, \tag{9.4}$$

where $\tau > 0$ is a power-law exponent analogous to the Zipf exponent α. Following the developments of Gomez-Lievano et al. [28], we can write

$$P(y) = \sum_{s=s_{min}}^{s_{max}} P(y|s)P(s), \tag{9.5}$$

where $P(y/s)$ is the conditional probability representing the fluctuations surrounding the urban scaling (Eq. 9.3). These fluctuations are further assumed to be log-normally distributed

$$P(y|s) = \frac{1}{y\sqrt{2\pi\sigma^2(s)}} \exp\left\{-\frac{\left[\ln y - \mu(s)\right]^2}{2\sigma^2(s)}\right\}, \tag{9.6}$$

where $\mu(s)$ and $\sigma^2(s)$ represent a possible dependence of log-normal parameters on the population s. Moreover, because of the scaling law in Eq. (9.3), we must have

$$\mu(s) = \ln(cs^\beta), \tag{9.7}$$

when $\sigma^2(s)$ is a constant. All these additional hypotheses are empirically verified in different datasets [28,29] and the log-normal fluctuations further imply the residuals of the linear regression between $\log y$ and $\log s$ are normally distributed. By plugging Eqs. (9.6) and (9.7) into Eq. (9.5), considering $s_{min} \to 0$ and $s_{max} \to \infty$, and replacing the sum by an integral, we find

$$P(y) \sim y^{-(\alpha/\beta+1)} \tag{9.8}$$

Finally, by comparing the above result with Eq. (9.4), we have

$$\beta = \alpha/\tau, \tag{9.9}$$

connecting the urban scaling exponent (β) with the Zipf exponent (α) and the exponent related to the distribution of the urban indicator (τ). The same result can be obtained using the standard change-of-variable technique for random variables, that is, $P(y)dy = P(s)ds$; however, this approach implicitly assumes the urban scaling law as an exact expression without any surrounding randomness. It is also worth remarking that the relation expressed by Eq. (9.9) is obtained by comparing probability distributions (Eqs. 9.5 or 9.8 and 9.4), which in turn implies that this connection represents an upper limit for the urban scaling exponent β, that is, random permutations in the values of population and urban indicator have no impact on their distributions but modify the allometric association between both quantities. Estimates of α vary across countries and epochs, but $\alpha \approx 1$ is typically found in empirical studies [11,16]. If $\alpha = 1$, one must have $\tau < 1$ in order to have a superlinear scaling ($\beta > 1$), and thus the mean and the variance of the urban indicator y are not finite under this condition [28]. However, this is not the only condition for superlinear scaling, as one may also have $\beta > 1$ whenever $\alpha > \beta > 1$.

We can further generalize the connection expressed by Eq. (9.9) to account for scaling relationships between pairs of urban indicators [29], that is,

$$y_i = c y_j^{\beta_{ij}}, \tag{9.10}$$

where β_{ij} represents the scaling exponent of the relation between the urban indicators y_i and y_j. Indeed, assuming that these indicators are power-law distributed, $P(y_i) \sim y_i^{-(\tau_i+1)}$ and $P(y_j) \sim y_j^{-(\tau_j+1)}$, and that the fluctuations surrounding Eq. (9.10) are log-normal (Eqs. 9.6 and 9.7), we find

$$\beta_{ij} = \tau_i / \tau_j \tag{9.11}$$

Similarly to Eq. (9.9), the above connection also has a probabilistic nature and the value of β_{ij} represents an upper limit for the scaling exponent between the indicators y_i and y_j.

Focusing now on the connection proposed by Ribeiro et al. [29], we first note that we can obtain the frequency function or the absolute number of cities with population s from Eq. (9.2) as

$$p(s) = ks^{-(a+1)} \text{ for } s_{min} < s < s_{max}, \tag{9.12}$$

where k is a normalization constant determined by

$$Y = \sum_{s_{min}}^{s_{max}} sp(s) \approx k \int_{s_{min}}^{s_{max}} s^{-\alpha} ds. \tag{9.13}$$

and S is the total population of the urban system. By combining this frequency function (Eq. 9.12) with urban scaling (Eq. 9.3), we can also write the total quantity of the city indicator y for the whole urban system (e.g., total urban GDP of a country) as

$$Y = \sum_{s_{min}}^{s_{max}} cs^{\beta} p(s) \approx kc \int_{s_{min}}^{s_{max}} s^{\beta-\alpha-1} ds. \tag{9.14}$$

To solve these equations, we assume that s_{min} and s_{max} are power-law functions of S:

$$s_{min} = aS^{\delta}, \tag{9.15}$$

$$s_{max} = bS^{\theta}, \tag{9.16}$$

where $\alpha > 0$ and $b > 0$ are constants, and $\delta > 0$ and $\theta > 0$ are country scaling exponents. Thus, by plugging Eqs. (9.15) and (9.16) into Eq. (9.14), we find

$$Y = \frac{c(\alpha-1)S}{\alpha-\beta}\left(\frac{a^{\beta}b^{\alpha}S^{\delta\beta+\theta\alpha} - a^{\alpha}b^{\beta}S^{\theta\beta+\delta\alpha}}{ab^{\alpha}S^{\delta+\theta\alpha} - a^{\alpha}bS^{\theta+\delta\alpha}}\right), \tag{9.17}$$

that in the limit of $S \gg 1$ yields

$$Y = Y_0 S^{\gamma}, \tag{9.18}$$

where Y_0 is a constant and $\gamma = \gamma(\alpha, \beta, \delta, \theta)$ is the country scaling exponent for the total total quantity of the city indicator y. Therefore, the combination of Zipf's (Eq. 9.1) and the urban scaling (Eq. 9.3) laws with country scaling relations for s_{min} and s_{max} (Eqs. 9.15 and 9.16) implies a power-law relation between total urban population S and total urban indicator Y. This country scaling law is characterized by an exponent γ that is a function of α, β, δ, and θ, which in turn yields a mathematical expression for the relation between β and α. This occurs because while α and β are intra-country exponents having different values for each country, γ, δ, and θ are inter-country exponents and there is only one value for each across all countries.

Thus, by determining the constant k from Eq. (9.13) and solving the integral in Eq. (9.14), we should obtain the country scaling of Eq. (9.18) in terms of the exponents α and β. Furthermore, if we assume γ, δ, and θ are fixed, the changes in α and β must be constrained in order to yield the particular value of γ imposed by country scaling in Eq. (9.18). However, the exact form of $\gamma(\alpha, \beta, \delta, \theta)$ depends on conditions imposed on the exponents α, β, δ, and θ.

To illustrate these calculations, we consider the general case where $\alpha \neq \beta \neq 1$. Under this assumption, Eq. (9.13) yields

$$k = \frac{(\alpha-1)Ss_{max}^{\alpha}s_{min}^{\alpha}}{s_{max}^{\alpha}s_{min} - s_{max}s_{min}^{\alpha}}, \tag{9.19}$$

and then by replacing s_{min} with Eq. (9.15) and s_{max} with Eq. (9.16), we find

$$k = \frac{(\alpha-1)(ab)^{\alpha} SS^{(\delta+\theta)\alpha}}{ab^{\alpha}S^{\delta+\theta\alpha} - a^{\alpha}bS^{\theta+\delta\alpha}}. \tag{9.20}$$

By solving the integral in Eq. (9.14), we find

$$Y = \frac{kc}{\beta-\alpha}\left(s_{max}^{\beta-\alpha} - s_{min}^{\beta-\alpha}\right), \tag{9.21}$$

and after replacing k by Eq. (9.20), s_{min} by Eq. (9.15), and s_{max} by Eq. (9.16), we have

$$\begin{aligned} Y &= \frac{c(\alpha-1)S}{\alpha-\beta}\left(\frac{a^{\beta}b^{\alpha}S^{\delta\beta+\theta\alpha} - a^{\alpha}b^{\beta}S^{\theta\beta+\delta\alpha}}{ab^{\alpha}S^{\delta+\theta\alpha} - a^{\alpha}bS^{\theta+\delta\alpha}}\right) \\ &= \frac{c(\alpha-1)S}{\alpha-\beta}\left(\frac{a^{\beta}b^{\alpha}S^{\lambda_1} - a^{\alpha}b^{\beta}S^{\lambda_2}}{ab^{\alpha}S^{\lambda_3} - a^{\alpha}bS^{\lambda_4}}\right) \\ &= \frac{c(\alpha-1)S}{\alpha-\beta}\left(\frac{\Lambda_1-\Lambda_2}{\Lambda_3-\Lambda_4}\right), \end{aligned} \tag{9.22}$$

where

$$\begin{aligned} \lambda_1 &= \delta\beta+\theta\alpha & \Lambda_1 &= a^{\beta}b^{\alpha}S^{\lambda_1} \\ \lambda_2 &= \theta\beta+\delta\alpha & \Lambda_2 &= a^{\alpha}b^{\beta}S^{\lambda_2} \\ \lambda_3 &= \delta+\theta\alpha \quad \text{and} & \Lambda_3 &= ab^{\alpha}S^{\lambda_3} \\ \lambda_4 &= \theta+\delta\alpha & \Lambda_4 &= a^{\alpha}bS^{\lambda_4}. \end{aligned} \tag{9.23}$$

Because S represents the total population of an urban system or a country, we take the limit of large S in Eq. (9.22). To do so, we need to know the conditions under which Λ_1 dominates over Λ_2 in the numerator of Eq. (9.22), that is, when

$$\begin{gathered} \lambda_1 > \lambda_2 \\ \delta\beta+\theta\alpha > \theta\beta+\delta\alpha \\ (\delta-\theta)(\beta-\alpha) > 0. \end{gathered} \tag{9.24}$$

and also the conditions under which Λ_3 dominates over Λ_4 in the denominator of Eq. (9.22), that is, when

$$\begin{aligned} &\lambda_3 > \lambda_4 \\ &\delta + \theta\alpha > \theta + \delta\alpha \\ &(\delta - \theta)(1-\alpha) > 0. \end{aligned} \tag{9.25}$$

By investigating the inequalities in Eqs. (9.24) and (9.25), we end up with the decision trees of Figures 9.1(a) and 9.1(b).

We can now follow the eight possibilities expressed by the decision trees. For instance, for $\alpha > \beta$, $\alpha > 1$, and $\delta < \theta$, we find that Λ_1 and Λ_3 dominate in Eq. (9.22), yielding

$$\begin{aligned} Y &\approx \frac{c(\alpha-1)a^{\beta-1}}{\alpha-\beta} S^{1+\lambda_1-\lambda_3} \\ &\approx \frac{c(\alpha-1)a^{\beta-1}}{\alpha-\beta} S^{1-\delta+\beta\delta}. \end{aligned} \tag{9.26}$$

By comparing the result of Eq. (9.26) with the country scaling in Eq. (9.18), we find

$$\beta = 1 + \frac{\gamma-1}{\delta} \text{ for } \{\alpha > \beta \,\&\, \alpha > 1 \,\&\, \delta < \theta\}. \tag{9.27}$$

It is worth noting that the previous conditions depend on β, but by combining $\alpha > \beta \,\&\, \alpha > 1$ and eliminating β, we can rewrite Eq. (9.27) as

$$\beta = 1 + \frac{\gamma-1}{\delta} \text{ for } \left\{\alpha > max\left(1, 1+\frac{\gamma-1}{\delta}\right) \& \, \delta < \theta\right\}. \tag{9.28}$$

Equation (9.28) thus predicts that β is a constant, that is, not dependent on α when $\{\alpha > max\left(1, 1+\frac{\gamma-1}{\delta}\right) \& \, \delta < \theta\}$.

By doing similar calculations, we find:

- For $\alpha > \beta$, $\alpha < 1$, and $\delta < \theta$:

$$\beta = \frac{\gamma+\theta-1}{\delta} + \left(1 - \frac{\theta}{\delta}\right)\alpha \text{ for } \left\{\gamma < 1 \,\&\, 1 + \frac{\gamma-1}{\theta} < \alpha < 1 \,\&\, \delta < \theta\right\}, \tag{9.29}$$

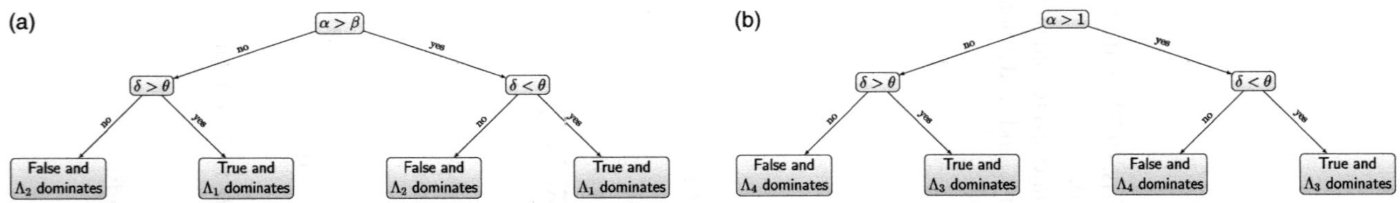

Figure 9.1 (a) Decision tree associated with the inequality $\lambda_1 > \lambda_2$ (Eq. 9.24) that defines whether Λ_1 dominates over Λ_2 (or vice-versa) in Eq. (9.22). (b) Decision tree associated with the inequality $\lambda_3 > \lambda_4$ (Eq. 9.25) that defines whether Λ_3 dominates over Λ_4 (or vice-versa) in Eq. (9.22).

predicting a linearly decreasing correspondence between β and α when $\{\gamma<1 \& 1+\frac{\gamma-1}{\theta}<\alpha<1 \& \delta<\theta\}$.

- For $\alpha<\beta$, $\alpha>1$, and $\delta<\theta$:

$$\beta=\frac{\gamma+\delta-1}{\theta}+\left(1-\frac{\delta}{\theta}\right)\alpha \text{ for}\left\{\gamma>1 \& 1<\alpha<1+\frac{\gamma-1}{\delta} \& \delta<\theta\right\}. \tag{9.30}$$

Similarly to Eq. (9.29), the result of Eq. (9.30) predicts a linearly increasing correspondence between β and α when $\{\gamma>1 \& 1<\alpha<1+\frac{\gamma-1}{\delta} \& \delta<\theta\}$. It is worth noting that the conditions underlying Eqs. (9.29) and (9.30) are mutually exclusive, that is, only one of the linear correspondences exists, depending on whether $\gamma>1$ (superlinear country scaling, Eq. 9.30) or $\gamma<1$ (sublinear country scaling, Eq. 9.29).

- for $\alpha<\beta$, $\alpha<1$, and $\delta<\theta$:

$$\beta=1+\frac{\gamma-1}{\theta} \text{ for}\left\{\alpha<min\left(1,1+\frac{\gamma-1}{\theta}\right) \& \delta<\theta\right\}, \tag{9.31}$$

indicating that β is a constant when $\{\alpha<min\left(1,1+\frac{\gamma-1}{\theta}\right) \& \delta<\theta\}$.

- for $\alpha>\beta$, $\alpha>1$, and $\delta>\theta$:

$$\beta=1+\frac{\gamma-1}{\theta} \text{ for}\left\{\alpha<max\left(1,1+\frac{\gamma-1}{\theta}\right) \& \delta>\theta\right\}, \tag{9.32}$$

predicting that β is a constant when $\{\alpha>max\left(1,1+\frac{\gamma-1}{\theta}\right) \& \delta>\theta\}$.

- $\alpha>\beta$, $\alpha<1$, and $\delta>\theta$:

$$\beta=\frac{\gamma+\delta-1}{\theta}+\left(1-\frac{\delta}{\theta}\right)\alpha \text{ for}\left\{\gamma<1 \& 1+\frac{\gamma-1}{\delta}<\alpha<1 \& \delta>\theta\right\}. \tag{9.33}$$

predicting a linearly decreasing correspondence between β and α when $\{\gamma<1 \& 1+\frac{\gamma-1}{\delta}<\alpha<1 \& \delta>\theta\}$.

- for $\alpha<\beta$, $\alpha>1$, and $\delta>\theta$:

$$\beta=\frac{\gamma+\theta-1}{\delta}+\left(1-\frac{\theta}{\delta}\right)\alpha \text{ for}\left\{\gamma>1 \& 1<\alpha<1+\frac{\gamma-1}{\theta} \& \delta>\theta\right\}, \tag{9.34}$$

Equation (9.34) predicts a linearly increasing correspondence between β and α when $\{\gamma > 1 \& 1 < \alpha < 1 + \frac{\gamma - 1}{\theta} \& \delta > \theta\}$. Similarly to cases of Eqs. (9.29) and (9.30), the conditions underlying Eqs. (9.33) and (9.34) are mutually exclusive, that is, only one of the linear correspondences exists depending on whether $\gamma > 1$ (superlinear country scaling, Eq. 9.34) or $\gamma < 1$ (sublinear country scaling, Eq. 9.33).

- for $\alpha < \beta$, $\alpha < 1$, and $\delta > \theta$:

$$\beta = 1 + \frac{\gamma - 1}{\delta} \text{ for } \left\{\alpha < min\left(1, 1 + \frac{\gamma - 1}{\delta}\right) \& \delta > \theta\right\}, \tag{9.35}$$

predicting that β is a constant when $\left\{\alpha < min\left(1, 1 + \frac{\gamma - 1}{\delta}\right) \& \delta > \theta\right\}$.

If we assume that γ, δ, and θ (with $\delta < \theta$) are fixed, the combined behavior of Eqs. (9.28), (9.29), (9.30), and (9.31) produces a functional dependence of β on α composed by three continuous line segments: an initial horizontal plateau (Eq. 9.31) followed by an increasing (Eq. 9.30, when $\gamma > 1$) or decreasing (Eq. 9.29, when $\gamma < 1$) linear function followed by another horizontal plateau (Eq. 9.28). These two behaviors are, respectively, represented by

$$\beta = \begin{cases} 1 + \frac{\gamma - 1}{\theta}, 0 < \alpha \leq 1 \\ \frac{\gamma + \delta - 1}{\theta} + \left(1 - \frac{\delta}{\theta}\right)\alpha, 1 < \alpha < 1 + \frac{\gamma - 1}{\delta} \\ 1 + \frac{\gamma - 1}{\delta}, \alpha \geq 1 + \frac{\gamma - 1}{\delta} \end{cases} \tag{9.36}$$

and

$$\beta = \begin{cases} 1 + \frac{\gamma - 1}{\theta}, 0 < \alpha \leq 1 + \frac{\gamma - 1}{\theta} \\ \frac{\gamma + \theta - 1}{\delta} + \left(1 - \frac{\theta}{\delta}\right)\alpha, 1 + \frac{\gamma - 1}{\theta} < \alpha < 1. \\ 1 + \frac{\gamma - 1}{\delta}, \alpha \geq 1 \end{cases} \tag{9.37}$$

Similarly the combined behavior of Eqs. (9.32), (9.33), (9.34), and (9.35) produces a functional dependence of β on α composed by three continuous line segments: an initial horizontal plateau (Eq. 9.35) followed by an increasing (Eq. 9.34, when $\gamma > 1$) or decreasing (Eq. 9.33, when $\gamma < 1$) linear function followed by another horizontal plateau (Eq. 9.32). In their turn, these two behaviors are, respectively, represented by

$$\beta=\begin{cases} 1+\dfrac{\gamma-1}{\delta}, 0<\alpha\leq 1 \\ \dfrac{\gamma+\theta-1}{\delta}+\left(1-\dfrac{\theta}{\delta}\right)\alpha, 1<\alpha<1+\dfrac{\gamma-1}{\theta} \\ 1+\dfrac{\gamma-1}{\theta}, \alpha\geq 1+\dfrac{\gamma-1}{\delta} \end{cases} \tag{9.38}$$

and

$$\beta=\begin{cases} 1+\dfrac{\gamma-1}{\delta}, 0<\alpha\leq 1+\dfrac{\gamma-1}{\delta} \\ \dfrac{\gamma+\delta-1}{\theta}+\left(1-\dfrac{\delta}{\theta}\right)\alpha, 1+\dfrac{\gamma-1}{\delta}<\alpha<1. \\ 1+\dfrac{\gamma-1}{\theta}, \alpha\geq 1 \end{cases} \tag{9.39}$$

Figure 9.2 illustrates these four possible relations between β and α. Furthermore, by analyzing the case in which $\alpha=1$ and $\beta\neq 1$, we find the same behaviors of Eqs. (9.27), (9.31), (9.32), and (9.35), ensuring the continuity of the behavior of β as a function of α at the point $\alpha=1$. In addition, for $\delta=\theta=\varphi$ and $\alpha>0$, we find $\beta=1+(\gamma-1)/\varphi$ regardless of $\gamma>1$ or $\gamma<1$. Thus, we have that β is constant for all values of α when $\delta=\theta$. For $\gamma=1$, we have $\beta=1$ regardless of $\gamma>1$ or $\gamma<1$. Thus, constant returns to scale at the country level imply constant returns to scale at the city level for all values of α.

9.3 Results

To empirically test the connections between the urban scaling and Zipf exponents expressed by Eqs. (9.9) and (9.11), we revisit some results related to 12 urban indicators (population, child labor, elderly population, female population, GDP, GDP per capita, homicides, illiteracy, income, male population, sanitation, and unemployment) of Brazilian municipalities [29]. Using this dataset, we first calculate the distributions of all indicators, verifying that they are all well approximated by power-law distributions (Eqs. 9.2 and 9.4). Next, we estimate the Zipf exponents α (for population) and τ (for all other indicators) using the maximum likelihood approach of Clauset-Shalizi-Newman [31]. We then investigate all possible pairs of allometric relations among our 12 indicators, from which we obtain the urban scaling exponents β (Eq. 9.3, for relations with population) and β_{ij} (Eq. 9.10, for

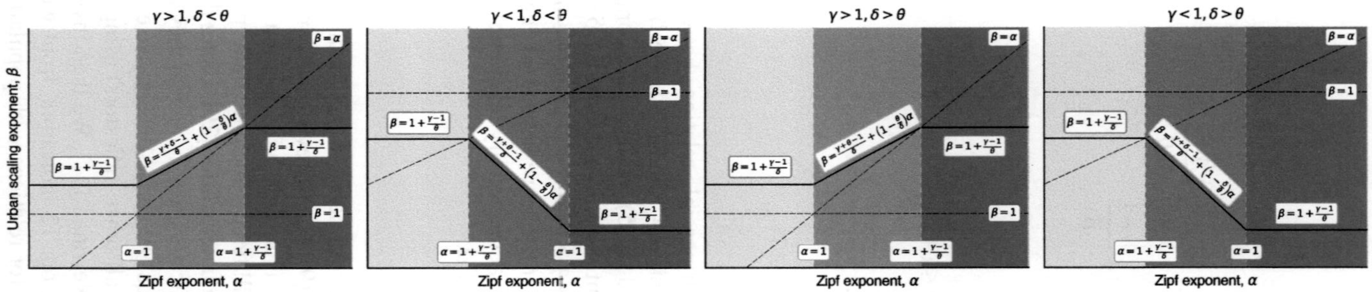

Figure 9.2 Illustration of the possible relations between β and α predicted by Eqs. (9.36) ($\gamma > 1$ and $\delta < \theta$), (9.37) ($\gamma < 1$ and $\delta < \theta$), (9.38) ($\gamma > 1$ and $\delta > \theta$), and (9.39) (and $\delta > \theta$).

all other relations) using ordinary least-square fits to the log-transformed data. Figure 9.3(a) shows a comparison between the scaling exponents estimated from the empirical data and the values obtained from the predictions of Eqs. (9.9) and (9.11) with the corresponding estimates for the Zipf exponents. In this figure, we have included all allometries with Pearson correlation coefficients larger than 0.5. We observe that the data points closely follow the 1:1 relation (dashed line), corroborating the connection proposed by Gomez-Lievano et al. [28] (Eqs. 9.9 and 9.11). However, we have also verified that the predicted exponents start to significantly underestimate the empirical values when including allometries with Pearson correlation coefficients smaller than 0.5, reinforcing the idea that Eqs. (9.9) and (9.11) are an upper limit for the allometric exponents.

Moving to the connection based on the country scaling relations, it is important to observe that we need a unified city definition across the globe for testing the models expressed by Eqs. (9.36), (9.37), (9.38), and (9.39). Following Ref. [30], we consider a generalized definition of functional urban areas (FUA) recently proposed by Moreno-Monroy et al. [32,33] and a global gridded data set for GDP [34]. After being combined, these two data sources yield the population (s) and the GDP (y) of 4571 cities from 96 countries. By aggregating the population and GDP values for each country, we can first investigate the country-scaling relations for total GDP Y, smallest city population s_{min}, and largest city population s_{max}. These scaling relations are shown in Figures 9.3(b)–(d), confirming the power-law assumptions expressed by Eqs. (9.15), (9.16), and (9.18).

Next, we investigate Zipf's law for population and scaling of urban GDP for each country in the dataset. The insets of Figure 9.3(e) illustrate these two laws when considering data from Russia and Turkey. Similarly to what was done for the first connection, we have estimated the Zipf exponents using the Clauset-Shalizi-Newman method [31], while ordinary least-square fits to the log-transformed data are used for obtaining the urban scaling exponents. Moreover, the main panel of Figure 9.3(e) depicts the values of β versus α for all countries. Considering that $\gamma > 1$ and $\delta < \theta$, the model of Eq. (9.36) is the natural candidate for describing the association between β and α. Thus, we have adjusted this model to data via the L-BFGS-B nonlinear optimization algorithm [35] and the best fitting parameters are $\gamma = 1.06 \pm 0.01$, $\delta = 0.26 \pm 0.05$, and $\theta = 0.79 \pm 0.03$. The solid line in Figure 9.3(e) represents the best fit of Eq. (9.36) and the colored background indicates the different regimes for each range of α. Despite the large variations in the data, Eq. (9.36) describes the average tendency of the empirical relation between β and α. In addition, correlations between the values of β and α are only statistically significant in the mid-range of α values, and the Akaike and Bayesian information criteria are strongly favorable to Eq. (9.36) when compared with the null-model assuming no relationship between both exponents (β = constant). More importantly, the country scaling relationships shown in Figures 9.3(b)–(d) were adjusted considering only the prefactors (a,b, and Y_0 in Eqs. 9.15, 9.16, and 9.18, respectively) as fitting parameters, all country scaling exponents (δ, θ, and γ) have been fixed to values estimated from Eq. (9.36). Taken together, these results provide robust support for

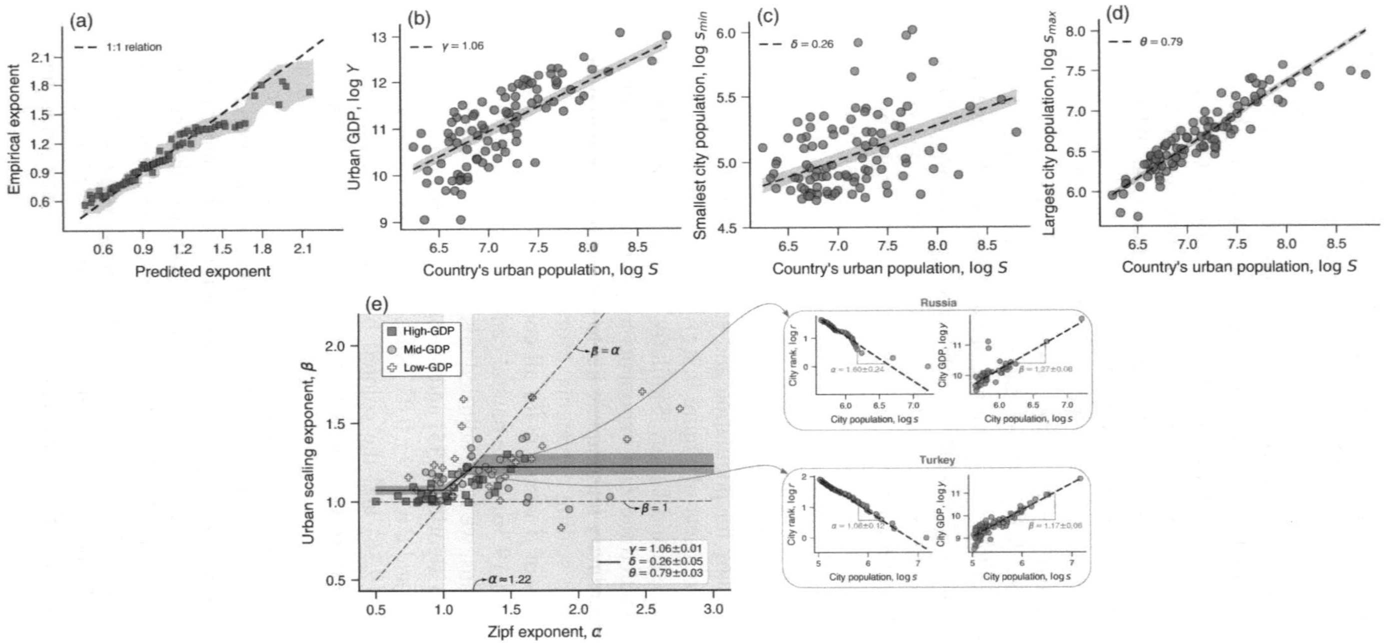

Figure 9.3 (a) Comparison between the empirical values of the allometric exponents and those predicted using the Zipf exponents in Eqs. (9.9) or (9.11). The square markers show the values obtained from pairs of relationships among 12 urban indicators from Brazilian cities and the shaded areas indicate the standard errors. (b)–(c) Country scaling relations between: total urban GDP (Y) and total urban population (S); smallest city population of a country (s_{min}) and the country's urban population (S); and largest city population of a country (s_{max}) and the country's urban population (S). The dashed lines in these three panels represent the country scaling relationships of Eqs. (9.18), (9.15), and (9.16), where the exponents γ,δ, and θ are obtained from fitting the model of Eq. (9.36) to the empirical relation between β and α. (e) Values of β versus α for each country in our dataset. The markers distinguish countries according to the tercile values of the total urban GDP distribution. The continuous line shows the model of Eq. (9.36) adjusted to data and the gray shaded region stands for the 95% confidence band. The colored background represents the different intervals of α defined in Eq. (9.36). The insets (indicated by blue arrows) illustrate Zipf's law for city population (left) and the urban scaling relationship of city GDP (right) for Russia and Turkey.

Source: Adapted from Refs. [29] and [30].

the association between the Zipf (α) and urban scaling (β) exponents as well as for the exact description of Eq. (9.36).

9.4 Summary and discussion

Zipf's law for cities and the urban scaling relations are among the best-known and most widely studied regularities emerging in urban systems. These two scaling laws are, however, commonly believed to be independent matters. This chapter has reviewed the few approaches that have tried to investigate a possible connection between Zipf's and urban scaling laws. On the one hand, we have presented the Gomez-Lievano et al. [29] connection, showing that when urban indicators are asymptotically distributed as power-laws, the urban scaling exponents can be predicted from the Zipf exponent obtained from city population and the indicator distribution. In particular, this connection shows that the urban scaling exponent has an upper limit defined by a simple function of the Zipf exponent and the power-law exponent associated with the indicator distribution. On the other hand, we have also revisited the Ribeiro et al. [30] connection, which shows that the combination of Zipf's law and urban scaling implies country scaling relationships for total urban indicator, smallest city population, and largest city population, where the exponents depend on the Zipf and the urban scaling exponents. While the Zipf and the urban scaling exponents vary from country to country, there is only one value for each country scaling exponent, which in turn implies a direct association between the urban scaling and the Zipf exponents. We have also tested both connections, finding that they hold well in empirical data.

The connection between the exponents β and α would thus imply that instead of being unrelated, Zipf's law and urban scaling are – to some extent – the two sides of the same coin. Still, the non-negligible fluctuations observed in the empirical relationships do not corroborate this simple conclusion. Instead, they suggest that other factors (such as level of socio-economic development and the particular history of an urban system) beyond population distribution may also significantly affect the urban scaling. Qualitatively, the connection between these two laws suggests that urban scaling does not solely emerge from processes occurring within the city boundaries; instead, cities do not represent a closed and non-interacting system and what happens in the entire system (such as flow of people and goods) may affect urban scaling. It remains, however, an open problem to determine the causal direction of the association between the Zipf and the urban scaling exponents.

Note

1 H. V. Ribeiro, M. Oehlers, A. I. Moreno-Monroy, J. P. Kropp, D. Rybski, Association between population distribution and urban GDP scaling, PLOS ONE, Volume 16, 2021, Article number e0245771, ISSN 1932-6203, https://doi.org/10.1371/journal.pone.0245771

References

[1] Batty, M. *The New Science of Cities* (MIT Press, Cambridge, MA, 2013).
[2] West, G. B. *Scale: The Universal Laws of Growth, Innovation, Sustainability, and the Pace of Life in Organisms, Cities, Economies, and Companies* (Penguin, New York, 2017).
[3] Zipf, G. K. *Human Behavior and the Principle of Least Effort: An Introduction to Human Ecology* (Martino Publishing, Manfield Centre, CT, 2012). (Reprint of 1949 Edition).
[4] Auerbach, F. Das Gesetz der Bevölkerungskonzentration. *Petermanns Geographische Mitteilungen* 59, 73–76 (1913).
[5] Bettencourt, L. M. A., Lobo, J., Helbing, D., Kühnert, C. & West, G. B. Growth, innovation, scaling, and the pace of life in cities. *Proceedings of the National Academy of Sciences* 104, 7301–7306 (2007).
[6] Beckmann, M. J. City hierarchies and the distribution of city size. *Economic Development and Cultural Change* 6, 243–248 (1958).
[7] West, G. B., Brown, J. H. & Enquist, B. J. A general model for the origin of allometric scaling laws in biology. *Science* 276, 122–126 (1997).
[8] Gabaix, X. Zipf's law and the growth of cities. *American Economic Review* 89 (1999).
[9] Gabaix, X. & Ioannides, Y. M. The evolution of city size distributions. In *Handbook of Regional and Urban Economics*, vol. 4 (Elsevier, Amsterdam, 2004), 2341–2378.
[10] Nitsch, V. Zipf zipped. *Journal of Urban Economics* 57, 86–100 (2005).
[11] Soo, K. T. Zipf's law for cities: A cross-country investigation. *Regional Science and Urban Economics* 35, 239–263 (2005).
[12] Batty, M. Rank clocks. *Nature* 444, 592–596 (2006).
[13] Berry, B. J. L. & Okulicz-Kozaryn, A. The city size distribution debate: Resolution for US urban regions and megalopolitan areas. *Cities* 29, S17–S23 (2012).
[14] Schmidheiny, K. & Suedekum, J. The pan-European population distribution across consistently defined functional urban areas. *Economics Letters* 133, 10–13 (2015).
[15] Li, X., Wang, X., Zhang, J. & Wu, L. Allometric scaling, size distribution and pattern formation of natural cities. *Palgrave Communications* 1, 15017 (2015).
[16] Cottineau, C. MetaZipf. A dynamic meta-analysis of city size distributions. *PLOS ONE* 12, e0183919 (2017).
[17] Zhang, L. et al. Scale-free resilience of real traffic jams. *Proceedings of the National Academy of Sciences* 116, 8673–8678 (2019).
[18] Mori, T., Smith, T. E. & Hsu, W.-T. Common power laws for cities and spatial fractal structures. *Proceedings of the National Academy of Sciences* 117, 6469–6475 (2020).
[19] Bettencourt, L. M. The origins of scaling in cities. *Science* 340, 1438–1441 (2013).
[20] Strano, E. & Sood, V. Rich and poor cities in Europe. An urban scaling approach to mapping the European economic transition. *PLOS ONE* 11, e0159465 (2016).
[21] Gomez-Lievano, A., Patterson-Lomba, O. & Hausmann, R. Explaining the prevalence, scaling and variance of urban phenomena. *Nature Human Behaviour* 1, 0012 (2017).
[22] Depersin, J. & Barthelemy, M. From global scaling to the dynamics of individual cities. *Proceedings of the National Academy of Sciences* 115, 2317–2322 (2018).
[23] Ribeiro, F. L., Meirelles, J., Ferreira, F. F. & Neto, C. R. A model of urban scaling laws based on distance dependent interactions. *Royal Society Open Science* 4, 160926 (2017).

[24] Keuschnigg, M. Scaling trajectories of cities. *Proceedings of the National Academy of Sciences* 116, 13759–13761 (2019).

[25] Pumain, D. & Rozenblat, C. Two metropolisation gradients in the European system of cities revealed by scaling laws. *Environment and Planning B* 46, 1645–1662 (2019).

[26] Balland, P.-A. et al. Complex economic activities concentrate in large cities. *Nature Human Behaviour* 4, 248–254 (2020).

[27] Bettencourt, L. M. A. et al. The interpretation of urban scaling analysis in time. *Journal of the Royal Society Interface* 17, 20190846 (2020).

[28] Gomez-Lievano, A., Youn, H. & Bettencourt, L. M. A. The statistics of urban scaling and their connection to Zipf's law. *PLOS ONE* 7, e40393 (2012).

[29] Alves, L. G. A., Ribeiro, H. V., Lenzi, E. K. & Mendes, R. S. Empirical analysis on the connection between power-law distributions and allometries for urban indicators. *Physica A* 409, 175–182 (2014).

[30] Ribeiro, H. V., Oehlers, M., Moreno-Monroy, A. I., Kropp, J. P. & Rybski, D. Association between population distribution and urban GDP scaling. *PLOS ONE* 16, e0245771 (2021).

[31] Clauset, A., Shalizi, C. R. & Newman, M. E. J. Power-law distributions in empirical data. *SIAM Review* 51, 661–703 (2009).

[32] Schiavina, M., Moreno-Monroy, A., Maffenini, L. & Veneri, P. *GHSL-OECD functional urban areas*. JRC Technical Report (2019). https://data.jrc.ec.europa.eu/dataset/347f0337-f2da-4592-87b3-e25975ec2c95

[33] Moreno-Monroy, A. I., Schiavina, M. & Veneri, P. Metropolitan areas in the world. Delineation and population trends. *Journal of Urban Economics* 125, 103242 (2021).

[34] Kummu, M., Taka, M. & Guillaume, J. H. Gridded global datasets for gross domestic product and Human Development Index over 1990–2015. *Scientific Data* 5, 180004 (2018).

[35] Byrd, R. H., Lu, P., Nocedal, J. & Zhu, C. A limited memory algorithm for bound constrained optimization. *SIAM Journal on Scientific Computing* 16, 1190–1208 (1995).

10 Density scaling laws and rural-to-urban transitions[1]

Haroldo V. Ribeiro, Jack Sutton, and Quentin S. Hanley

10.1 Introduction

The general notion that mathematics and physics can help to understand city size and behavior dates back to the work of Auerbach in the early 1900s [1]. Inspired by Auerbach's seminal work [2], Lotka (1925) [3] and Zipf (1941) [4] used 1920 and 1930 US census data to understand how city sizes are distributed [4] by rank order and noted the second-largest city in the US was half the largest (New York City) and the third-largest was one-third the largest. Zipf included economic indicators and advocated the principle of greatest gain through least effort leading to this behavior. In subsequent decades, these early studies of cities merged with ideas about allometry from biology to form the foundations of urban scaling [5]. These ideas were developed further to explain urban growth [6], and it was during this time that power laws became a ubiquitous feature of modern urban studies. Indeed, already in the 1970s, Woldenberg [7] and Nordbeck [6] used different assumptions and methods to derive the geometric and allometric growth laws for cities as well as the familiar logarithmic presentation of urban scaling laws.

More recently, methods based on allometry have become part of the urban scaling hypothesis [8,9]. In this formulation, the population of an urban area is used as a predictor for a host of economic, social, infrastructure, and health indicators. The simplicity of these relationships has made power-law scaling of urban indicators widely studied. This has led to a set of conclusions about cities, such that cities tend to exhibit superlinear relationships for economic, creativity, and transmissible disease indicators, whereas sublinear relationships emerge for certain types of infrastructure indicators.

There are, however, some known challenges current in the literature relating to the extent to which scaling truly follows simple power laws, how to deal with real-world data, particularly when a zero is reported or when there are missing data [10]. There are also issues related to what determines the boundaries of a city [11] as well as ongoing attempts to understand how the productivity of cities might relate to networks and related mathematics [12,13]. Furthermore, against this background there remain some fundamental issues and questions that need to be considered. Specifically, is there anything special about cities? Urban scaling studies have been

DOI: 10.4324/9781003288312-12

inherently biased by studying cities rather than human environments generally. Is population the key to understanding human scaling? As cities exist on a continuum of population density, if it is interactions and contact networks that drive accelerated scaling, then two cities of equal populations but different areas might not be expected to have equal behavior.

These issues lead us to explore human environments more generally as a challenge to the urban scaling hypothesis and to better understand our human environments and behavior. This chapter reviews our attempt to incorporate rural and urban regions into a coherent and unified scaling approach – what we have been calling density scaling laws [14–16] – as well as some of the opportunities it presents.

10.2 Methods

The usual approach for studying the urban scaling hypothesis relies on investigating the relationship between a given urban indicator Y and population N in an urban system with several urban units (for instance, metropolitan areas, counties, or municipalities). Within the urban scaling hypothesis [8,9], the relationship between these two quantities is assumed to be described by a power-law function, that is,

$$Y = Y_0 N^{\beta} \text{ or its linearized version } \log Y = \log Y_0 + \beta \log N, \tag{10.1}$$

where Y_0 is a constant ($\log Y_0$ would be the intercept of the linearized relationship) and β is the power-law exponent or the urban scaling exponent. Analogously to the origins of allometric scaling in biology [17], urban scaling theory attributes the emergence of urban scaling laws to intra-city networks (such as electric cable and road networks) and the superlinear scaling of human interactions within cities [18]. Furthermore, urban scaling relationships are often categorized into three classes [8]: (1) isometry ($\beta \approx 1$ for indicators related to individual needs such as household energy and water consumption); (2) superlinear allometry ($\beta > 1$ for socioeconomic and health metrics such as crime, gross domestic product, and AIDS cases); and (3) sublinear allometry ($\beta < 1$ for infrastructure indicators such as road surface and number of petrol stations).

Density scaling laws, in turn, can be thought of as an area normalizing approach. They are a simple adaptation of the standard urban scaling expression (Eq. 10.1) that considers the area A of the places by replacing N by population density, $d = N / A$, and indicator Y by indicator density, $y = Y/A$, that is,

$$y = y_0 d^{\beta} \text{ or its iinearized version } \log y = \log y_o + \beta \log d, \tag{10.2}$$

where y_0 is a constant and β is now the allometric exponent of the density scaling law. It is also worth noting that the scaling law expressed by Eq. (10.2) can be directly related to the Cobb-Douglas production function [19] when considering the urban indicator Y as a bivariate function of population N and area A expressed by

$$Y = Y_0 N^{\beta_N} A^{\beta_A}, \tag{10.3}$$

where β_N and β_A are two scaling exponents. Indeed, dividing both sides of Eq. (10.3) by A and collecting the population density term N/A on the right side, we find

$$Y/A = Y_0 (N/A)^{\beta_N} A^{\beta_A+\beta_N-1}, \tag{10.4}$$

Which, in turn, is equivalent to Eq. (10.2) when $\beta_A + \beta_N = 1$. This latter condition represents the case of a Cobb-Douglas model with constant returns to scale, that is, simultaneously doubling population N and area A of a place implies exactly doubling the value of the urban indicator Y. This and other analogies with production functions have proved quite useful to describe carbon dioxide emissions [20] and to reveal the interconnected role of population and incoming commuters on urban wealth creation [12]. Here, this connection between density scaling laws and the Cobb-Douglas production with constant returns to scale provides extra motivation for applying this alternative formulation.

Beyond a simple mathematical extension, the main point of using density scaling laws relates to the possibility of applying scaling ideas to the entire extent of human settlements, ranging from the most rural lands to the heavily urban centers. Thus, instead of implicitly ignoring rural environments, density scaling laws allow us to examine the continuum range of settings in which people live. This is a critical issue because while the proportion of the world's population living in urban areas is consistently increasing over the years [21,22], this urbanization process is not uniform across the globe such that the range of urban population varies drastically among countries; for instance, as of 2014, only 8.6% of the population of Trinidad and Tobago was urban, while Singapore was already entirely urban [21].

Furthermore, density scaling laws allow us to test whether there are fundamental differences between rural and urban areas regarding the scaling of different indicators density. To do so, we generalize Eq. (10.2) to include a possible regime change in the scaling of the indicator density y in the form of a segmented power law:

$$y = \begin{cases} y_0 d^{\beta_L}, d < d^* \\ y_1 d^{\beta_H}, d \geq d^* \end{cases} \text{ or its linearized version} \log y = \begin{cases} \log y_0 + \beta_L \log d, d < d^* \\ \log y_1 + \beta_H \log d, d < d^* \end{cases}, \tag{10.5}$$

where y_0 and y_1 are constants and d^* is the population density threshold at which the density scaling exponent changes from β_L to β_H. Here, we further assume the continuity of the two power-law regimes such that the constant y_1 can be written as a function of the other model parameters [$\log y_1 = \log y_0 + (\beta_L - \beta_H) \log d^*$]. Thus, we can verify whether the double power-law model of Eq. (10.5) represents a statistically significant improvement over the single power-law model of Eq. (10.2) for a given indicator using goodness-of-fit measures such as the adjusted R^2, the Akaike Information Criterion (AIC), or the Bayesian Information Criterion (BIC) [23]. When the double power-law model does not improve the description of a given indicator density, we say this indicator presents a *non-urban density scaling.* In this case, the behavior ascribed to urban environments is simply a continuation of the behavior already present in rural environments, and there is thus no distinction to be made between urban and rural areas for these indicators. Conversely, indicators better described by the segmented power-law model display density scaling regimes specifically rural and specifically urban that are separated by rural-to-urban transitions occurring at well-defined population density thresholds. These cases can be further classified into three categories depending on the nature of the rural-to-urban transitions:

- *accelerated urban scaling* occurs when moving to urban areas is associated with an increase in the density scaling exponent, that is, $\beta_H > \beta_L$;
- *inhibited urban scaling* occurs when moving to urban environments implies a diminished but still positive density scaling exponent, that is, $\beta_L > \beta_H > 0$;
- *collapsed urban scaling* occurs when moving to urban environments results not only in a diminished density scaling exponent but also a negative value, that is, $\beta_L > \beta_H$ with $\beta_H < 0$.

One of the most striking consequences of these nonlinearities, be they expressed by the standard urban scaling or density scaling laws, is the fact that indicators normalized by population (per capita measures, $Z = Y / P$) or normalized by area ($z = Y / A$) are efficient in correctly removing the effects of population and population density only if the indicators display isometric relations with population and population density (that is, $\beta = 1$ in Eqs. (10.1) and (10.2)). Otherwise these normalized metrics will be biased toward large population sizes and densities (for superlinear allometries) or small population sizes and densities (for sublinear allometries). Within the urban scaling framework, we can overcome this issue by defining the so-called scale-adjusted metric (SAM, also known as a scale-adjusted metropolitan indicator or SAMI) [24–27], which consists of calculating the logarithmic difference between the indicator value and the value expected from the urban scaling law (Eq. 10.1), that is,

$$Z = \log Y - [\log Y_0 + \beta \log N]. \qquad (10.6)$$

The value of Z is simply the residual following the adjustment of an observation for the urban scaling law, and therefore, it captures the "exceptionality" of the place. A city with positive SAM is above the expectation for its population, while a negative SAM shows a city below the expectation for its population.

By following the same ideas, we can define the *density scale-adjusted metrics* (DSAMs) [15] as a direct generalization of Eq. (10.6) within the context of density scaling laws, that is,

$$z = \log y - f(d), \tag{10.7}$$

where

$$f(d) = \begin{cases} \log y_0 + \beta_L \log d, d < d^* \\ \log y_1 + \beta_H \log d, d \geq d^* \end{cases} \text{or } f(d) = \log y_0 + \beta \log d, \tag{10.8}$$

depending on whether the indicator displays rural-to-urban transitions or not, respectively. Analogously to SAMs, DSAMs are simply the residuals surrounding the allometric relationship between indicator density and population density. Moreover, DSAMs are not absolute metrics but indicate how a particular area compares to the predicted behavior based on population density.

10.3 Results

In order to verify the usefulness of the density scaling approach and its implications, we revise some applications related to data from England and Wales covering indicators of crime, mortality, property values, and age [14–16]. These data refer to two different divisions of the United Kingdom: *parliamentary constituencies* and *administrative areas* (unitary authorities, non-metropolitan districts, metropolitan boroughs, and London boroughs). Parliamentary constituencies are regions with similar populations and vast variability in population density that elect the members of the lower house of the United Kingdom Parliament (House of Commons). England and Wales have 573 constituencies ranging in area from 331,440 hectares (Penrith and The Border, England) down to 738 hectares (Islington North, Greater London), while population density ranges from 0.22 people per hectare (Brecon and Radnorshire, Wales) up to 150 people per hectare (Westminster North, England). In turn, the 348 administrative regions of England and Wales range in area from 289 hectares (City of London, England) up to 518,037 hectares (Powys, Wales), while population density ranges from 0.25 people per hectare (Eden, Cumbria, England) up to 139 people per hectare (Islington, England). For both divisions, the range of population densities includes regions from very rural to highly urban environments.

Figure 10.1 shows three examples of density scaling laws for burglary, value of terraced housing transactions, and mortality from dementia and Alzheimer's disease. A single power law (Eq. 10.2) provides a more parsimonious model for burglary (as verified by AIC and BIC) with a superlinear density scaling exponent $\beta = 1.18$, such that every 1% increase in population density is associated with a 1.18% rise in the incidence of this crime type. In contrast, the double power-law

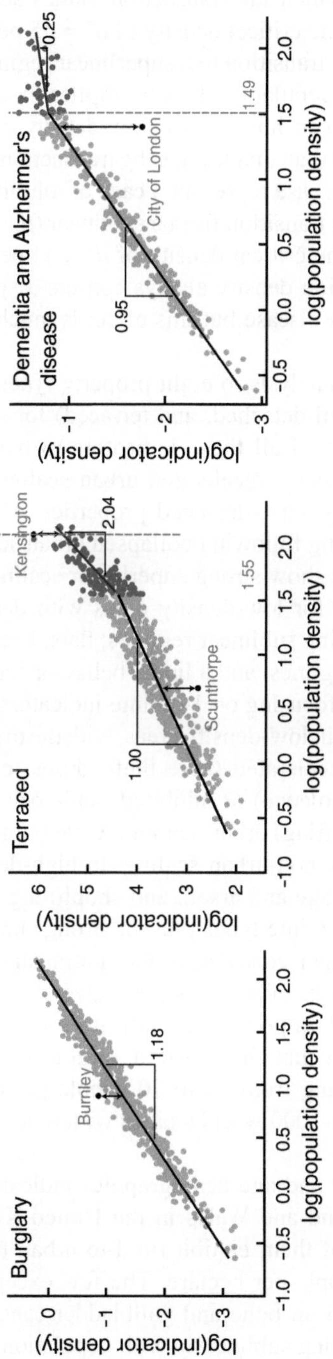

Figure 10.1 Examples of density scaling laws for indicators of crime (burglary, left), property value (terraced, middle), and mortality (dementia and Alzheimer's disease, right). The data refer to parliamentary constituencies for burglary and terraced property value, while administrative areas are used for dementia and Alzheimer's mortality. Burglary illustrates the case of non-urban density scaling where a simple power law (Eq. 10.2) with exponent $\beta = 1.18$ better describe the data. Terraced housing transaction values undergo accelerated urban scaling where the double power-law model (Eq. 10.5) with exponents $\beta_L = 1.00$ and $\beta_H = 2.04$, and critical density $d^* \approx 35$ people per hectare ($\log d^* = 1.55$) better describes the data. In turn, mortality by dementia and Alzheimer's disease illustrates the case of inhibited urban scaling where the double power-law model (Eq. 10.5) with exponents $\beta_L = 0.95$ and $\beta_H = 0.25$, and critical density $d^* \approx 31$ people per hectare ($\log d^* = 1.49$) better describes the data. Arrows in these plots illustrate the DSAMs for a few regions of England.

Source: Adapted from Refs. [15,16].

model (Eq. 10.5) better describes the indicators of terraced housing and mortality from dementia and Alzheimer's disease. Terraced housing is an example of accelerated urban scaling in which the transaction values scale linearly with population density ($\beta_L = 1$) up to the critical density of $d^* \approx 35$ people per hectare, where we observe a rural-to-urban transition to a superlinear regime with exponent $\beta_H = 2.04$. Thus, while doubling population density implies exactly doubling the transaction value density of terraced housing for low-density regions, the same change in high-density areas more than quadruples the transaction value density. In turn, dementia and Alzheimer's disease represent a case of inhibited urban scaling where we observe a rural-to-urban transition from a sublinear ($\beta_L = 0.95$) to a more sublinear ($\beta_H = 0.25$) regime at the critical density of $d^* \approx 31$ people per hectare. Therefore, an increase in population density always confers a "protective effect" against dementia and Alzheimer's disease but this effect is much more intense in highly urban environments.

Extending the density scaling analysis to eight property types (detached, flats, freehold, leasehold, new, old, semi-detached, and terraced) for all constituencies in England and Wales [14], we find all these indicators to have rural-to-urban transitions, with the majority showing accelerated urban scaling (flats, freehold, leasehold, new, old, and terraced), semi-detached properties exhibiting inhibited urban scaling, and detached housing following collapsed urban scaling. Except for the former two, all property types show strong superlinear scaling at high-density regions. Results are more mixed for low-density areas with detached, freehold, new, and old property types showing sublinear regimes; flats, leasehold, and semi-detached exhibiting superlinear regimes; and a linear behavior for terraced properties. Still with constituencies but focusing on 14 crime indicators [14], we find all exhibit superlinear scaling at least in low-density areas, with the majority presenting rural-to-urban transitions with accelerated (bike theft, drugs, order, other theft, robbery, theft from the person, violence) or inhibited (anti-social behavior, criminal damage and arson, and shoplifting) urban scaling, while burglary, other crime, vehicle crime, and weapons show non-urban scaling. In high-density areas, only antisocial behavior, criminal damage and arson, and shoplifting scale sublinearly with population density, all other crime types present strong superlinear regimes. Similar findings are observed when considering the administrative areas of the United Kingdom to define the unity of analysis [16]. Overall, these results indicate that the majority of crime and property types indicators are not scale-invariant regarding population density and that they exhibit rural-to-urban transitions at critical population densities ranging from 10 to 70 people per hectare – density values in the mid-range of the top-1000 world's cities with more than half-million inhabitants.

Focusing now on 44 mortality and age demographics indicators broken down by administrative areas of England and Wales in the United Kingdom [16], we also find that the vast majority of them exhibit rural-to-urban transitions with a median critical density of 27 people per hectare. The few exceptions presenting non-urban scaling are mortality from bone and gallbladder cancer, diabetes, cardiomyopathy, and suicide (all scaling sublinearly with population density), and the age groups 0–4 years and 20–24 years (both scaling superlinearly with population density). Furthermore, most mortality indicators exhibit inhibited urban scaling with exponents changing from weakly sublinear or approximately linear behaviors to strongly sublinear regimes.

Taken at face value, high-population density is enormously protective against a wide range of mortality indicators with dementia and Alzheimer's disease being the most striking (Figure 10.1, right panel). The evidence supporting this conclusion is sublinear scaling across all population densities. Excluding homicide, inhibited scaling is observed in all segmented mortality indicators. Defining the difference between the two scaling exponents ($\Delta\beta = \beta_L - \beta_H$) as an inhibition measure, we find $\Delta\beta = 0.70$ for dementia and Alzheimer's disease – the greatest inhibition of any mortality indicator in our study. Particularly high inhibition is observed for kidney cancer ($\Delta\beta = 0.63$), esophageal cancer ($\Delta\beta = 0.62$), cardiac arrhythmias ($\Delta\beta = 0.60$), skin cancer ($\Delta\beta = 0.54$), ovarian cancer ($\Delta\beta = 0.46$), and prostate cancer ($\Delta\beta = 0.44$). This pattern thus points to a dramatic improvement in mortality indicators in high-population density areas – a behavior partially ascribed to changes in age demographics with population density, as we next discuss.

Indeed, all age categories below 50 years scale superlinearly with population density at least in low-density areas, while sublinear regimes emerge for age categories from 50 years or older. For high-density regions, the density of young adults (aged 25–29, 30–34, and 35–39) scales strongly superlinearly with population density, while older age groups present sublinear regimes, and, the older the group, the smaller the power-law exponent. These results show that high-density regions attract young adults – who are at least in part responsible for the urban dynamism – and repel older people. Therefore, this dichotomy in the scaling of young and old age groups per se partially explains the superlinear behaviors of different socio-economic indicators (such as the crime types we investigated previously) and the protective effect against different mortality types observed in high-density areas. Still, the changes in the exponents of some mortality indicators are so extreme that we cannot rule out the effects of other factors, such as a more than proportional increase in number and quality of health infrastructure in high-density regions [28].

When evaluating any protective effect of high-population density, dementia is a useful example. Dementia is overwhelmingly a disease affecting the elderly. Standard approaches to understanding scaling assume the population is homogeneous and hence total population or total population density is a sufficient predictor of indicators as diverse as income, petrol stations, homicide, and AIDS. Since dementia does not affect all age groups equivalently, the assumption of homogeneous population must be challenged. Our results make clear that the population of England and Wales is not homogeneous: the higher the population density, the lower the proportion of elderly people. Putting this together, age heterogeneity leading to inhibition of scaling in ages 50 and over ($\Delta\beta = 0.10 - 0.45$) explains much of the protective effect of population density on this set of conditions ($\Delta\beta = 0.44 - 0.70$). However, the inhibition of scaling values of even the 85+ age group ($\Delta\beta = 0.45$) and dementia ($\Delta\beta = 0.70$) are incommensurate, leaving a potentially strong protective effect of high-population density. Conversely, conditions where there is no segmented scaling and no inhibition and (diabetes, gallbladder cancer, and cardiomyopathy) need a more critical look. What initially appears unremarkable may be masking a substantial increase in risk. These cases make clear the profound impact of age heterogeneity on scaling exponents.

As we have already mentioned, a critical consequence of the nonlinearities manifested by these scaling laws is the emergence of systematic bias in per capita indicators. Still, this type of normalization remains widely used in different contexts. For instance, in the United Kingdom, the distribution of healthcare resources uses a per capita allocation model adjusted for mortality and other factors [29]. This per capita model thus likely underestimates the economies of scale and the demographic changes discussed above, delivering fewer resources than needed to rural and low-density regions. Density scale-adjusted metrics (DSAMs) are a simple and effective approach to considering the scaling laws and correctly removing the deterministic effect of population density on different indicators. More than that, the normalization provided by DSAMs allows us to compare regions with different population densities and reveal the complex inter-relationships among various indicators. To illustrate this possibility, we revisit an approach used to create a complex network representation based on a cross-correlation analysis of DSAMs calculated from 67 indicators of crime, property values, age, and mortality related to the administrative areas of England and Wales [16]. Each indicator is mapped into a network node in this representation, and the connections among them indicate pairs of significantly positively correlated indicators (as estimated by bootstrapping the Pearson correlation coefficient at the 99% confidence level).

Figure 10.2 shows a visualization of this network comprising a giant connected component with 66 nodes and one isolated node associated with the mortality indicator by bone cancer (that is, this particular indicator does not significantly correlate to any other). Out of the 2211 possible connections among the 67 indicators, this network presents 784 connections which in turn indicate pairs of metrics that are significantly and positively correlated to each other. By applying the Girvan-Newman algorithm [30] to detect community structure, we find that this network can be partitioned into three modules (with a modularity score equal to 0.472) represented by the different colors in Figure 10.2. These groups contain: (1) mortality and age groups associated with elderly (purple nodes); (2) property types and age groups associated with children and middle-aged people (green nodes); (3) crime indicators and age groups related to young adults. Exceptions to these patterns include only homicide (clustered in group 1) and suicide and cancer of the larynx (clustered in group 3). The examination of these complex inter-relationships reveals a number of intriguing patterns. The more obvious are already highlighted by the modular structure, such as the associations among elderly and mortality as well as among age indicators of young adults and crime. Other more intriguing patterns include the association between suicide and behavioral crimes [anti-social behavior (ASB), criminal damage and arson (CD&A)]. But overall, these patterns suggest that mortality indicators may be susceptible to prevention strategies focused on long-term responses to violence, stress, and mental illness.

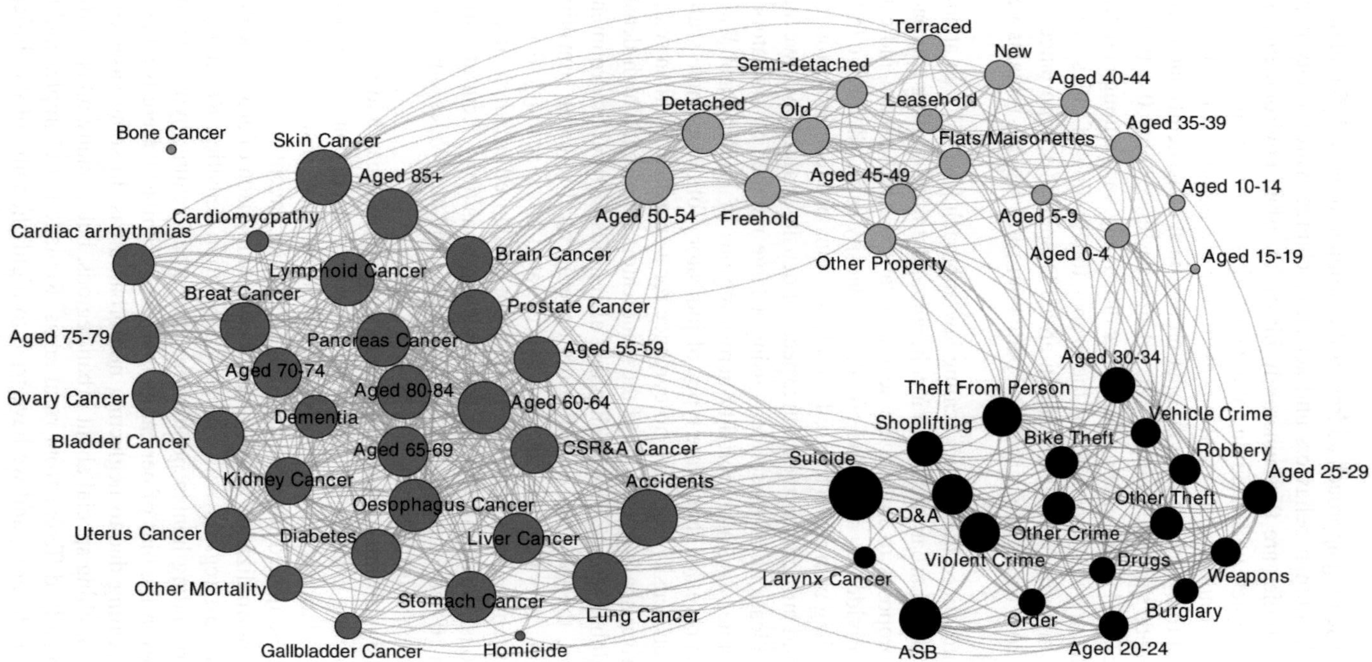

Figure 10.2 Complex network representation of the positive correlations among 67 indicators of crime, property values, age, and mortality. The data refer to the 348 administrative regions of England and Wales. In this visualization, node sizes are proportional to their degrees, while the colors indicate the community structure of this network.

Source: Adapted from Ref. [16].

10.4 Summary and discussion

The standard urban scaling approach addresses the problem of how different urban indicators related to human behaviors and activities change with the city population size. These studies are thus inherently biased to urban environments and cannot provide a complete understanding about the full range of human settlements which exist in a continuum from rural places to densely populated urban cores. While it is true that the world's urban population has been consistently increasing and currently exceeds the rural one [21,22], urban areas cover only 0.4–0.9% of global land surfaces [31], and urbanization rates drastically vary among countries [21]. Rural regions are also essential for the proper functioning of cities as they provide food and material security for urban areas. Despite this importance, our understanding of how (non-urban) scaling operates in rural regions remains very limited.

This chapter introduced the density scaling law approach [14–16] – an attempt to incorporate rural and urban areas into a coherent and unified scaling approach. This framework proposes to investigate scaling relationships between indicator density (indicator divided by area) and population density as an alternative to the standard urban scaling approach (focused on relationships between indicators and population). Beyond introducing the main aspects of density scaling laws, we have also reviewed applications of these ideas using a large number of indicators of crime, property value, age, and mortality across regions of England and Wales. These applications revealed that some types of indicators follow a single scaling law with population density, showing no evidence for a specifically urban scaling law, that is, the urban scaling relations of these indicators represent a high-density subsection of a global scaling relationship that also holds in rural environments. On the other hand, the majority of indicators undergo rural-to-urban transitions in which the scaling exponent may increase (accelerated urban scaling), decrease (inhibited urban scaling), or even become negative (collapsed urban scaling) in high-density regions. Intriguingly, these urban scaling transitions occur at critical densities between 10 and 70 people per hectare in England and Wales, suggesting an underlying universal mechanism.

In addition to significantly refining our understanding of urban and non-urban scaling, density scaling laws further contribute to the problem of comparing places with different population sizes or densities. Indeed, we have discussed how to define density scale-adjusted metrics – an extension of the concept of scale-adjusted metrics – and this normalization allows an unbiased comparison of urban and non-urban indicators across regions with different population densities. Reflecting on progress in understanding human populations, the urban scaling hypothesis has unequivocally proven the bias of per capita measures. Similarly, there is a bias in studies of urban scaling due to neglecting non-urban areas. In some cases (e.g., burglary), there is nothing special about urban regions, but in many others, urban regions are profoundly different from rural areas. Remarkable examples include age demographic indicators, and we have tried to highlight some of the difficulties introduced by population age heterogeneity when seeking to interpret scaling exponents. Finally, we hope this chapter has contributed to shedding some light on the problems of ignoring low-density areas in scaling studies and that it motivates further investigations of different indicators with different country data within the density scaling law framework or any other approach capable of handling the entire range of human settlements.

Note

1 J. Sutton, G. Shahtahmassebi, H.V. Ribeiro, Q. S. Hanley, Rural -urban scaling of age, mortality, crime and property reveals a loss of expected self-similar behaviour. Scientific Reports 10, 16863 (2020).

References

[1] Auerbach, F. Das Gesetz der Bevölkerungskonzentration. *Petermanns Geographische Mitteilungen* 59, 73–76 (1913).

[2] Rybski, D. Auerbach's legacy. *Environment and Planning A* 45, 1266–1268 (2013).

[3] Lotka, A. J. *Elements of Physical Biology* (Waverly Press, Baltimore, 1925).

[4] Zipf, G. K. *National Unity and Disunity: The Nation as a Bio-Social Organism* (Principia Press, Bloomington, 1941).

[5] Beckmann, M. J. City hierarchies and the distribution of city size. *Economic Development and Cultural Change* 6, 243–248 (1958).

[6] Nordbeck, S. Urban allometric growth. *Geografiska Annaler: Series B, Human Geography* 53, 54–67 (1971).

[7] Woldenberg, M. *Part II in Concepts and Applications - Spatial Order* (Harvard University Press, Cambridge, 1967).

[8] Bettencourt, L. M. A., Lobo, J., Helbing, D., Kühnert, C. & West, G. B. Growth, innovation, scaling, and the pace of life in cities. *Proceedings of the National Academy of Sciences* 104, 7301–7306 (2007).

[9] West, G. B. *Scale: The Universal Laws of Growth, Innovation, Sustainability, and the Pace of Life in Organisms, Cities, Economies, and Companies* (Penguin, New York, 2017).

[10] Finance, O. & Cottineau, C. Are the absent always wrong? Dealing with zero values in urban scaling. *Environment and Planning B: Urban Analytics and City Science* 46, 1663–1677 (2019).

[11] Arcaute, E., et al. Constructing cities, deconstructing scaling laws. *Journal of the Royal Society Interface* 12, 20140745 (2015).

[12] Alves, L. G., Rybski, D. & Ribeiro, H. V. Commuting network effect on urban wealth scaling. *Scientific Reports* 11, 22918 (2021).

[13] Prieto Curiel, R., Cabrera-Arnau, C. & Bishop, S. R. Scaling beyond cities. *Frontiers in Physics* 10, 858307 (2022).

[14] Hanley, Q. S., Lewis, D. & Ribeiro, H. V. Rural to urban population density scaling of crime and property transactions in English and Welsh parliamentary constituencies. *PLOS ONE* 11, e0149546 (2016).

[15] Ribeiro, H. V., Hanley, Q. S. & Lewis, D. Unveiling relationships between crime and property in England and Wales via density scale-adjusted metrics and network tools. *PLOS ONE* 13, e0192931 (2018).

[16] Sutton, J., Shahtahmassebi, G., Ribeiro, H. V. & Hanley, Q. S. Rural–urban scaling of age, mortality, crime and property reveals a loss of expected self-similar behaviour. *Scientific Reports* 10, 16863 (2020).

[17] West, G. B., Brown, J. H. & Enquist, B. J. A general model for the origin of allometric scaling laws in biology. *Science* 276, 122–126 (1997).

[18] Bettencourt, L. M. The origins of scaling in cities. *Science* 340, 1438–1441 (2013).

[19] Cobb, C. W. & Douglas, P. H. A theory of production. *American Economic Review* 18, 139–165 (1928).

[20] Ribeiro, H. V., Rybski, D. & Kropp, J. P. Effects of changing population or density on urban carbon dioxide emissions. *Nature Communications* 10, 1–9 (2019).

[21] United Nations. World Urbanization Prospects: Urban population (% of total). Available: http://data.worldbank.org/indicator/SP.URB.TOTL.IN.ZS. Accessed: May 2022.

[22] Jiang, L. & O'Neill, B. C. Global urbanization projections for the Shared Socioeconomic Pathways. *Global Environmental Change* 42, 193–199 (2017).

[23] Burnham, K. P. & Anderson, D. R. *Model Selection and Multimodel Inference: A Practical Information-Theoretic Approach* (Springer, New York, 2002).

[24] Bettencourt, L. M., Lobo, J., Strumsky, D. & West, G. B. Urban scaling and its deviations: Revealing the structure of wealth, innovation and crime across cities. *PLOS ONE* 5, e13541 (2010).

[25] Lobo, J., Bettencourt, L. M., Strumsky, D. & West, G. B. Urban scaling and the production function for cities. *PLOS ONE* 8, e58407 (2013).

[26] Alves, L. G., Ribeiro, H. V., Lenzi, E. K. & Mendes, R. S. Distance to the scaling law: A useful approach for unveiling relationships between crime and urban metrics. *PLOS ONE* 8, e69580 (2013).

[27] Alves, L. G., Mendes, R. S., Lenzi, E. K. & Ribeiro, H. V. Scale-adjusted metrics for predicting the evolution of urban indicators and quantifying the performance of cities. *PLOS ONE* 10, e0134862 (2015).

[28] Ribeiro, H. V., Sunahara, A. S., Sutton, J., Perc, M. & Hanley, Q. S. City size and the spreading of COVID-19 in Brazil. *PLOE ONE* 15, e0239699 (2020).

[29] Advisory Committee Allocation Resource. Public health grant: Exposition book for proposed formula for 2016–17 target allocations – Technical Guide (2016). Available: https://assets.publishing.service.gov.uk/media/5a80bdca40f0b623026953e4/3_Public_health_proposed_formula_2016-17_Technical_Guide_-_amended.pdf. Accessed: May 2022.

[30] Girvan, M. & Newman, M. E. Community structure in social and biological networks. *Proceedings of the National Academy of Sciences* 99, 7821–7826 (2002).

[31] Esch, T. et al. Breaking new ground in mapping human settlements from space – The global urban footprint. *ISPRS Journal of Photogrammetry and Remote Sensing* 134, 30–42 (2017).

11 Exploring socio-economic inequalities in cities through the lens of urban scaling[1]

Somwrita Sarkar

11.1 The measurement of socio-economic inequalities

The discipline of economics has a rich and long history focused on the measurement of socio-economic inequalities [1]. A diversity of measures has been proposed, starting from the simplest to the very complex. The problem is posed as follows: Given an income distribution, in which people are arranged in ascending order by their income, poorest to richest, assign a single number to such a distribution that summarises how unequal this distribution is. This is a one-dimensional problem, where the inequality measure I is an output, given the incomes $x_i, i = 1, 2, \ldots, n$ as input:

$$I = f(x_1, x_2, \ldots, x_n) \tag{11.1}$$

This function f can take several forms. The simplest are the measures of central tendency and dispersion, e.g., the mean, median, range, or variance of a distribution. The more complex measures incorporate more information about the complexity of a distribution. For example, the entropy measure shows whether the distribution is very concentrated (unequal), or very spread out (equal). Similarly, the Gini coefficient shows by how much a given distribution sits away from a completely equal distribution in which every person earns the same.

11.2 Measuring inequalities for cities

Socio-economic inequalities can be measured at different geographical and political scales. Primarily, economics has concentrated upon inequalities between countries, inequalities within a country, inequalities between cities (metropolitan areas), and inequalities within cities. The actual measure used usually defaults to any of the established measures [1], with the Gini coefficient being one of the most used.

A fundamental paradoxical result is that local spatial inequality, say at the city scale, is the inverse of larger area level inequality, say at the national scale [2]. For example, if all the cities within a country were integrated with very rich to very poor living in the same city, then this would push up the inequality at the

DOI: 10.4324/9781003288312-13

national level. On the other hand, holding the national inequality constant, if all the rich clustered in one city and all the poor in another, then the local inequalities measured would be low for at the city scale.

This paradox points to an important missing dimension: *the effect of city size on inequalities*. Do inequalities grow as cities grow in population size? Or do they decrease? Is a larger city more unequal than a smaller city? Because our existing inequality measures give us one number that summarises inequality for one distribution, how do we compare across multiple distributions that are all differently sized (i.e., the n in Equation (11.1) is different for a small city and a big city). The answer is not as simple as simply computing an inequality number for a small city and big city and comparing them, because of the above-mentioned paradox. If, when cities grow bigger, they begin to accumulate the highest-income earners, pushing out moderate- and low-income earners, and the spatial sorting by income occurs between cities rather than within a city, then we might end up observing that inequalities fall as city sizes grow!

The above effect can take place in many ways. Inequalities in cities are fundamentally of a different nature from national inequalities for many other reasons. First, mobility between cities is more probable than mobility across countries [2]. This means that spatial sorting by income classes can occur more easily between cities. Secondly, spatial sorting between cities is related to the industrial and occupational bases of individual cities, which may attract or repel populations with specific skills, with populations exercising locational choice. Since occupational and industrial categories are themselves sorted by income, this leads to an indirect spatial sorting by income, as many high-income occupations and industries (especially those with knowledge economy jobs) tend to cluster in bigger cities. Third, housing and land prices in bigger cities are generally higher, which again indirectly leads to spatial sorting by affordability. If the premium on land and housing rises sharply by city size, even workers in skilled and key occupations may still be unable to afford living close to their work in a big city and may be forced to live in satellite cities. In effect, this again will have an indirect outcome of spatial sorting by affordability, via income.

These complex effects are hidden when a standard inequality measure like Gini coefficient is used, since the inequality measures only capture the range, spread, or variance (of income distribution, housing costs, etc.) within a single city. How does scaling theory provide a view on city-level income inequalities?

11.3 The scaling of income distributions

Scaling theories on cities posit that a dependent socio-economic indicator will scale either superlinearly, linearly, or sublinearly with population size, following the equation:

$$y = \alpha X^{\beta},$$

where y is the socio-economic indicator, X is the population of a city, α is a proportionality constant, and β is the critical exponent value which decides whether the indicator y will scale superlinearly ($\beta > 1$), linearly ($\beta = 1$), or sublinearly ($\beta < 1$) with X. In general, it was found that socio-economic outputs like total income or GDP, or total number of patents filed, scaled superlinearly, along with negative externalities such as congestion and pollution, and any socio-economic inputs that go in to make a city like the length of infrastructure networks, road networks, numbers of petrol stations, etc. all scaled sublinearly.

A principal observation arising from scaling studies was that larger cities are in general wealthier – income, wages, and wealth increase superlinearly with city size. If a city of a 100 people generates a total income of $100, then, a city of 200 people would generate not $200, but around $215, showing that a doubling of the number of people leads to more than a doubling of the total income.

But the question of inequalities arises almost hand-in-hand with this observation – how is the extra $15 generated being distributed between the income classes. Do all income classes fare equally when city size grows?

Figure 11.1 shows that when instead of total income, the scaling of income earned in different income categories is studied, there is clear evidence that while there is superlinear scaling of income in the highest income categories, income only scales linearly or sublinearly in the lower or moderate-income categories. Thus, there is clear evidence to show that that $15, the extra wealth generated by a larger city, is accumulating in the highest income categories – the others do not fare as well [3,4].

This finding was tested across multiple time points and countries. The findings were very similar for Australia (2016) and for the metropolitan areas of the USA [4]. In addition, the scaling of housing costs, mortgages, and rents were studied in a similar way. Figure 11.2 shows that the higher housing cost categories scale highly superlinearly with city size. Since the quality of housing and shelter directly varies with the cost, the scaling of housing costs in the higher categories implies that this section of housing is only available to the section of the high-income population that can afford these costs. There is, thus, not only an inequality here, but also an issue of affordability connected to this inequality: more and more people in moderate- and low-income work would be either forced into or locked into low-cost, often poor(er)-quality housing, or face extremely long mortgage terms, high costs, and high rents under significant affordability stress, or move out of a large city into satellite cities where higher quality housing is more affordable at lower costs, but face long commutes to work.

In addition, there is also evidence that larger cities agglomerate more skilled workers in the higher income occupations and industries [2,5]. On the other hand, a host of lower and moderate-income key services host large numbers of workers, which support the higher-skilled higher-income occupations – this set of workers on low or moderate incomes would then face the above trade-offs and forced locational choice.

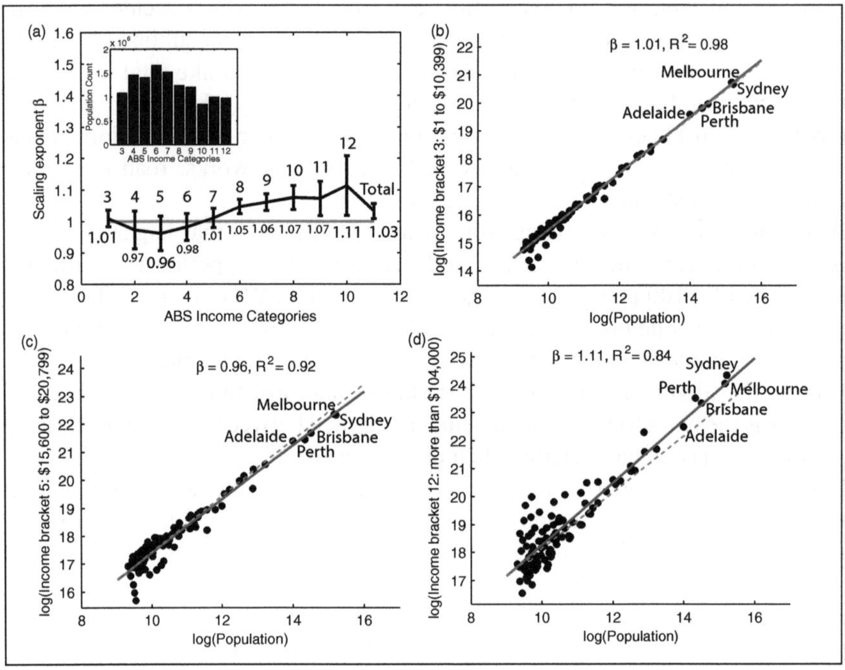

Figure 11.1 The scaling of income in different income categories for significant urban areas (SUAs) in Australia. (a) The exponent β values for 12 income categories in the Australian 2011 census, the scaling of (b) income in a low-income category, (c) income in a moderate–low-income category, and (d) income in the highest income category.

Source: Ref. [4].

These findings were followed up with several studies around the world. All these studies corroborated the principle finding that larger cities tend to be more unequal by favouring higher income or wage earners [6,7].

Thus, overall, the findings point to a tight link between income scaling, housing cost scaling, and the spatial concentration of the economic base in terms of occupations and industries. Combining these findings throws light on socio-economic inequalities in ways that the traditional single measures of inequality miss, namely that people's locational choice and capability sets may be highly constrained by the incomes they earn and the occupations they choose. Spatial concentrations of high-, low-, and moderate-income earners in different cities may show that within city inequalities are low (since there is spatial sorting and segregation between cities, rather than within cities). Nonetheless, this hides the effect of why there is spatial sorting occurring between cities rather than within cities in the same degree. A scaling theory lens sheds light on this between cities inequality, showing that socio-economic quantities scale differently by city size depending upon the specific socio-economic class a person may belong to.

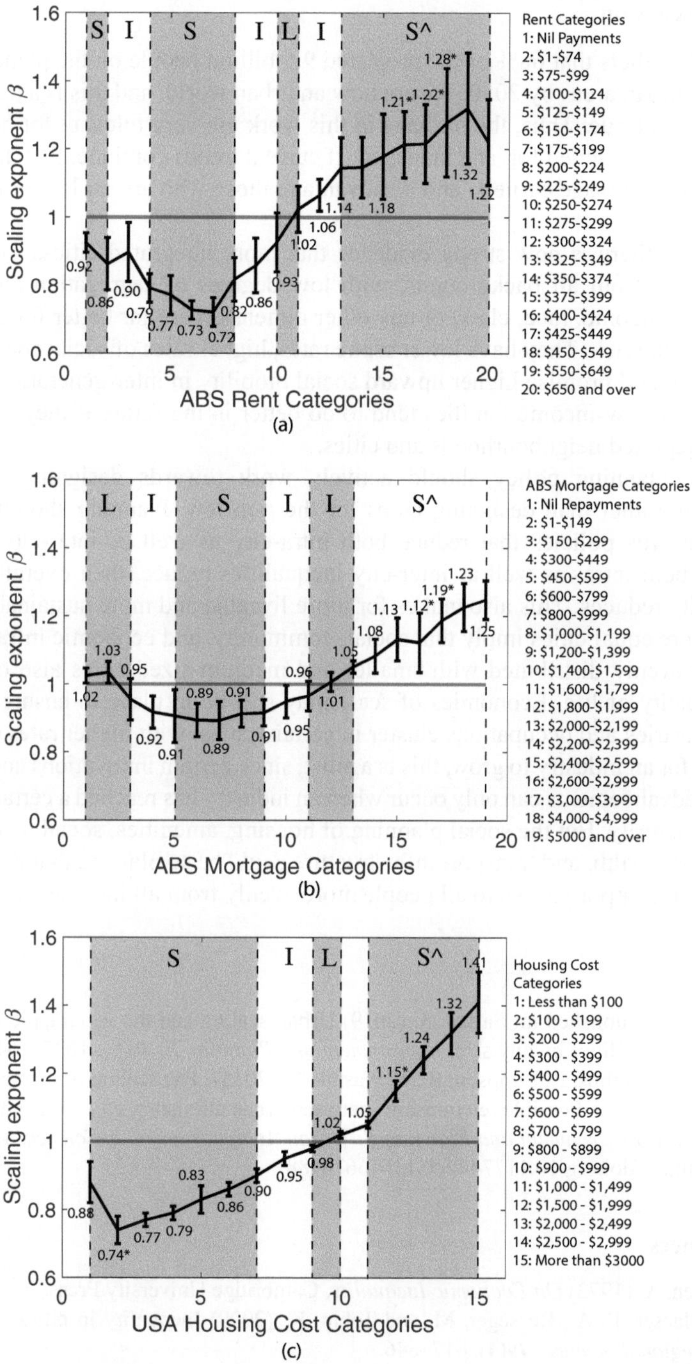

Figure 11.2 The scaling of housing costs in different (a) rent and (b) mortgage categories for the significant urban areas (SUAs) of Australia, and across (c) different housing cost categories for the metropolitan statistical areas (MSAs) of the USA.

Source: Ref. [5].

11.4 Discussion

The UN predicts that 68% of the projected 9.5 billion people on the planet will be living in urban areas by 2050. We are now an urban world, and this is a trend that's likely to continue. Thus, the findings in this work are very relevant for how cities are designed, planned for, and managed. If current trends continue, they favour the higher income/wage earners, and disadvantage those who are on low or moderate incomes.

Further, there is now strong evidence that more integrated cities, with mixed populations from all backgrounds, with low degrees of segregation and spatial sorting by income, race, class, or any other dimension are far better for everyone, including the rich. They have lower crime rates, higher rates of social cohesion and wellbeing, and promise higher upward social mobility in inter-generational terms. Children of low-income families tend to do better in the future if they are part of more integrated neighbourhoods and cities.

Thus, planning policy should actively work towards designing cities for everyone, rather than designing cities for the rich few. Planning should actively work towards policies that reduce both intra-city as well as inter-city inequalities. If both intra- as well as inter-city inequalities reduce, then overall national inequality reduces. This also makes for more liveable and more sustainable cities, since more equal cities imply that social, community, and economic infrastructure is more evenly distributed with smaller and medium-sized cities also offering a good quality of life. Economies of scale may still be in place to ensure that certain industries and occupations cluster in certain cities, with higher rates of return. Indeed, for an industry to grow, this is a must, since certain innovations and technological advancements can only occur when an industry has reached a certain critical size or maturity. But the social planning of housing, amenities, social, community, education, health, and transport infrastructure could be so planned that they benefit and provide opportunities to all people more evenly from all income classes.

Note

1 Previously published in: Sarkar, S. (2019) Urban scaling and the geographic concentration of inequalities by city size. *Environment and Planning B*, *46*(9), 1627–1644.
Sarkar, S., Phibbs, P., Simpson, R., & Wasnik, S. (2018). The scaling of income distribution in Australia: Possible relationships between urban allometry, city size, and economic inequality. *Environment and Planning B: Urban Analytics and City Science, 45*(4), 603–622. https://doi.org/10.1177/0265813516676488

References

[1] Sen, A. (1973) *On Economic Inequality*, Cambridge University Press.

[2] Glaeser, E. A., Resseger, M. and Tobio, K. (2009) Inequality in cities. *Journal of Regional Science*, *49*(4), 617–646.

[3] Sarkar, S., Phibbs, P., Simpson, R. and Wasnik, S. (2018) The scaling of income distribution in Australia: Possible relationships between urban allometry, city size, and economic inequality. *Environment and Planning B*, *45*(4), 603–622.

[4] Sarkar, S. (2019) Urban scaling and the geographic concentration of inequalities by city size. *Environment and Planning B*, *46*(9), 1627–1644.

[5] Sarkar S., Arcaute E., Hatna E., Alizadeh T., Searle G. and Batty M. (2020) Evidence for localization and urbanization economies in urban scaling. *Royal Society Open Science*, 7, 191638.

[6] Shutters, S. T., Applegate, J. M., Wentz, E. and Batty, M. (2022) Urbanization favors high wage earners, *NPJ Urban Sustainability*, *2*(6), Article 6.

[7] Heinrich Mora E., Heine C., Jackson J. J., West G. B., Yang V. C., and Kempes C. P. (2021) Scaling of urban income inequality in the USA. *Journal of the Royal Society Interface*, *18*, 20210223.

12 Scaling in Indian cities[1]

Anand Sahasranaman and
Luís M. A. Bettencourt

12.1 Introduction

The Indian subcontinent has seen multiple waves of urbanisation. We know now that the major sites of the Indus Valley civilisation (3300–1300 BCE) like Harappa, Dholavira, Mohenjodaro, and Rakhigarhi were sophisticated urban cultures, with evidence of well-developed public infrastructures such as drainage systems, baths, and warehouses, as well as private houses with wells and bathrooms [1]. The Vedic period heralded the "second" urbanisation, this time in the Indo-Gangetic plain, with cities like Pataliputra and Varanasi, which yielded the emergence of philosophical and religious movements such as Buddhism and Jainism [2]. Since then, through the ancient and medieval periods, cities grew across the length and breadth of the subcontinent. The colonial era saw the emergence of yet newer urban centres such as Mumbai, Chennai, and Kolkata, which are today some of the largest cities in the world. Indeed, going forward, the UN projects that the urban population in India could reach 800 million by 2050 [3].

This leads us to an intriguing question: Despite the interplay of complex social, political, and economic forces over time that have resulted in the urban Indian landscape of today, is it possible to study the network of Indian cities as a system? In this chapter, we explore the possibility of using the framework of urban scaling to quantitatively characterise the system of Indian cities and lay a baseline for future studies.

Urban scaling analysis uses population size as the basis of isolating agglomeration effects operating in cities, essentially characterising economies of scale in infrastructure and urban services, and increasing returns to scale arising from network effects in socioeconomic interactions [4,5].

An urban indicator $Y_i(t, N_i)$, such as GDP or crime count or road length, for any city i, with population size $N_i(t)$, can be described as:

$$Y_i(t, N_i) = Y_0(t) N_i^{\beta} e^{\xi_i(t)}, \tag{12.1}$$

where $Y_0(t)$ is independent of population size (but time varying) and can be interpreted as an underlying or systemic effect that applies to all cities under consideration, such as the general economic environment or social relations [6].

DOI: 10.4324/9781003288312-14

The scaling exponent β is the elasticity of $Y_i(t)$ to the population $N_i(t)$. Scaling theory yields the following expectations for the exponent β:

i. $\beta \simeq 7/6 > 1$,for socioeconomic properties such as income, innovation, and crime.
ii. $\beta \simeq 5/6 < 1$, for infrastructure quantities such as road length, as well as for spatial density.
iii. $\beta \simeq 1$, for individual or household properties such as number of houses or water consumption

Finally, the quantities $\xi_i(t)$ in Eq. (12.1) are the scale-independent (but also time-dependent) deviations from the scaling law (residuals), which can be interpreted as the idiosyncratic effects particular to individual cities in the analysis, as opposed to the systemic common effects captured by Y_0. We denote these city-specific residuals as Scale Invariant Metropolitan Indicators (SAMIs) [6]:

$$\xi_i(t) = \ln \frac{Y_i}{Y_0 N_i^{\beta}} \tag{12.2}$$

We will use the scaling exponent β to measure the nature of agglomeration effects in operation in the Indian city system, and the notion of SAMIs to explore the regional patterns of variation across various indicators under study.

12.2 Scaling results for Indian cities: expectation and exception

Table 12.1 presents the estimated values of the scaling exponent β across a range of urban quantities, including social and economic rates, as well as quantities of infrastructures, public and private [7,8]. Overall, we find empirical agreement with the expectations from urban scaling theory.

As is apparent, public infrastructures such as roads, educational institutions, and bank branches are found to scale sublinearly, in line with theory and empirical observations across other nations [5,6]. We find that household infrastructures (related to urban services) like toilets and electricity connections exhibit slightly superlinear scaling, where we would have expected linearity. These discrepancies between expectation and outcome are likely attributable to the fact that while larger cities are better served with basic household services, smaller cities see a deficit of these services (toilets and electricity connections). We expect that the exponent will tend towards unity over time, as development spreads across the urban hierarchy, from larger to smaller cities [9].

It is the scaling exponents for crime (both all crimes and serious crimes) that stand out most in the analysis, because they run counter to expectation. Crime is a social phenomenon, and urban scaling theory would have us expect superlinear scaling of crime, something which is empirically confirmed in other contexts [4,10]. In India,

Table 12.1 Summary of scaling exponents.

Quantity (Y)	*β*	*95% CI*	R^2	*Number of observations*	*Data source*
Road length	0.96	0.92–1.01	0.64	903	Census 2011
Total area	0.88	0.84–0.93	0.61	909	Census 2011
Number of educational institutions	0.87	0.83–0.90	0.78	909	Census 2011
Number of bank branches	0.88	0.85–0.92	0.72	908	Census 2011
Number of private toilets	1.02	0.96–1.07	0.58	909	Census 2011
Number of private electricity connections	1.04	1.01–1.07	0.84	909	Census 2011
Number of patents	1.53	1.22–1.83	0.95	320	IPI 2004, 2006, 2008, 2011
Number of crimes	0.87	0.81–0.93	0.70	317	NCRB 1991, 1996, 2001, 2006, 2011
Number of serious crimes (murder and culpable homicide)	0.78	0.69–0.87	0.46	317	NCRB 1991, 1996, 2001, 2006, 2011
Gross domestic product (GDP)	1.14	0.98–1.30	0.92	22	Created by authors

however, we observe that the scaling exponent for crime is sublinear (Table 12.1). What explains this discrepancy?

One possible explanation is that the nature of socialisation in Indian cities is markedly different from their Western counterparts. More specifically, the study of caste and gender relationships in the context of crime offers us two lenses to examine the sociology of urban crime in India. Governments in post-independence India have attempted to counter the caste system – one of the major fault lines of Indian society – through affirmative action and specific legislation on crimes against the most vulnerable populations in society. Specifically, this refers to Scheduled Caste (SC) and Scheduled Tribe (ST) communities, which have been traditionally placed at the bottom of the caste hierarchy and consequently suffer from extreme marginalisation due to long-term lack of access to basic health, education, and infrastructure. Extensive government intervention to improve the situation of these communities has, on average, resulted in improved redistribution and provision of public goods [11,12], but the very fact of social organisation amongst SC and ST citizens has also led to violent feudal backlashes. Gender and crime are found to be linked through the negative relationship between female–male ratios and murder rates [13,14]. Violent crime is also found to manifest at the conjunction of caste and gender, in the form of "honour" killings, which are generally a response to inter-caste marriages [15]. While crime and gender help understand the nature of scaling of crime in India, it is also likely that these differences in socialisation are particularly relevant to rural areas and smaller cities, and less so in the larger cities [16].

This sociological narrative possibly contextualises the difference in scaling results for crime in India, but leaves open the question of whether the trends suggested by the narrative are reflected in the scaling analysis?

12.3 An urban geography of crime, income, and innovation

In order to answer this question, we go back to the residuals (SAMI for crime), and construct the urban geography of their variation for Indian cities. The SAMIs reflect the performance of individual urban areas, distinct from any systemic effects operating across all cities.

A visual inspection of crime SAMIs (Figure 12.1, left) reveals that there is a geographical pattern for crime in India. Essentially, cities in north and central India, have high crime SAMIs (grey) indicating an excess relative to the scaling law, while those in western and southern India have much lower crime SAMIs (red) indicating a deficit. This geographical pattern of crime SAMIs is concordant with empirical evidence from the ground: (i) reports from the National Council for

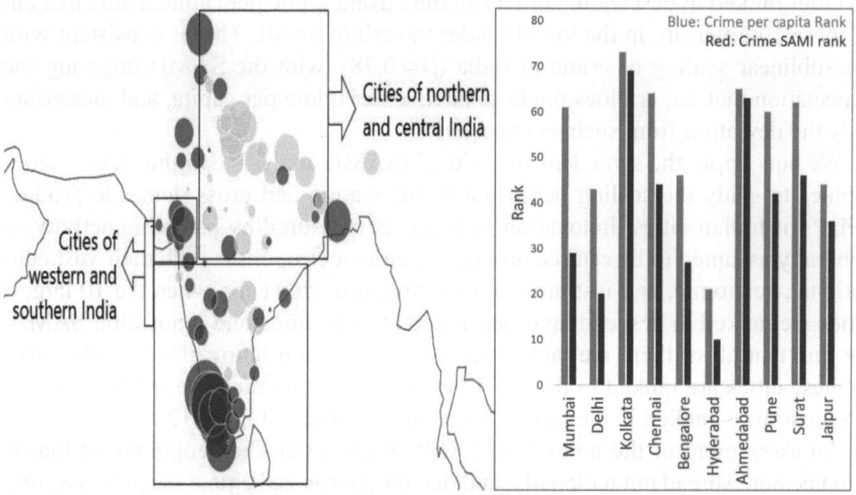

Figure 12.1 Scaling residual analysis of crime across Indian cities. Left: Urban geography of crime SAMIs: Red dots correspond to lower-than-expected crimes and grey dots correspond to higher-than-expected crimes. Expected crime for a given city size is based on the scaling exponent $\beta = 0.78$, meaning that crimes per capita decrease on average with city size. The size of the dot denotes the magnitude of Crime SAMI. Right: Rank ordering of 10 large Indian cities based on crime per capita (blue columns) and crime SAMI (red columns).

Scheduled Castes [16], show that ~ 60% of the crimes against SCs occur in four states of northern and central India – Uttar Pradesh, Rajasthan, Bihar, and Madhya Pradesh, and (ii) studies on "honour" killings report that while it is a pan-Indian phenomenon, such killings are especially prevalent in the northern states of Uttar Pradesh, Delhi, Rajasthan, and Haryana.

Even as smaller cities of northern and central India have higher SAMIs, indicating higher than expected crime, they also have a higher proportion of vulnerable SC and ST populations – the Scheduled Caste population scales sublinearly with city size, with an $\beta = 0.96$. This again ties in with the evidence on the ground, which finds that most atrocities including hate crimes, rape, and murder occur predominantly in small urban settlements [16].

This concordance between ground-level evidence on the nature and geographical spread of serious crimes in India and the SAMIs derived from the scaling analysis suggests that the urban scaling framework is potentially revelatory of specific underlying dynamics of societies, even (or maybe especially) when the scaling exponent deviates from theory.

Finally, we also see how the residual (SAMI) analysis reveals a different comparative reality, when contrasted to the standard per capita measure of crime for the 10 largest Indian cities. We find that each one of these cities performs worse when ranked by SAMIs than by the per capita measure (Figure 12.1, right). Using the SAMI reveals that larger cities in India are, on average, more violent than revealed by the per capita crime measure – only one of these 10 cities is in the top 40 cities ranked in descending order of crime using crime per capita, while five out of these 10 cities are in the top 40 under the crime SAMI. This is consistent with the sublinear scaling of crime in India ($\beta = 0.78$), with the SAMIs implying the expectation that larger cities ought to have lesser crime per capita, and measuring only the deviation from such an expectation.

We now apply the same lens of residual (SAMI) analysis defining urban geographies to study the scaling behaviour of innovation and gross domestic product (GDP) of Indian cities. Innovation in India, as measured by patenting activity, is generally assumed to be centred around the large metropolises with their vast educational, economic, and institutional infrastructure. However, when the 10 largest cities are ranked in descending order of patents per capita and innovation SAMIs, we find that all of them are ranked as less inventive on innovation SAMIs – five of these cities are ranked in the top 10 by the per capita measure, while only one (Bengaluru) is ranked in the top 10, when using SAMIs (Figure 12.2, left)

An assessment of the innovation SAMIs reveals that the geography of innovation is more spread out nationally, and that medium-sized cities – such as Mysuru, Salem, Trichy, and Jamshedpur – are in fact amongst the most inventive in India. Once again, this is related to the superlinear scaling expectation for innovation ($\beta = 1.53$), meaning that the largest cities are expected to have more than proportional levels of inventiveness, and that it is the smaller cities, with SAMIs having accounted for their population size, where we find evidence of over-performance of patenting activity.

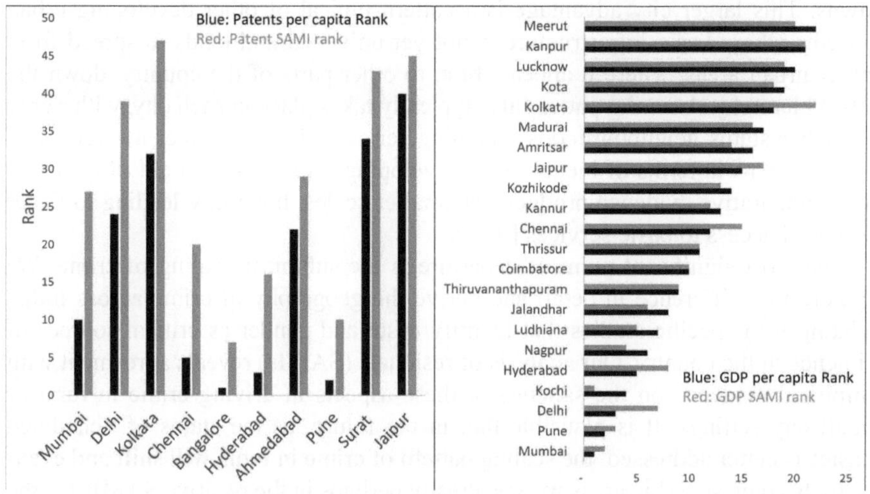

Figure 12.2 Residual analysis of innovation and income. Left: Rank ordering of 10 large Indian cities based on patents per capita (blue columns) and patent SAMI (red columns). Right: Rank ordering of 22 Indian cities based on GCP per capita (blue columns) and GDP SAMI (red columns).

A similar trend is observable when we consider the GDP of cities (Figure 12.2, right). Comparing the rank of cities based on per capita GDP and GDP SAMI, we find that the largest cities – Mumbai, Delhi, Kolkata, Chennai, Hyderabad, Pune, and Jaipur – rank slightly worse under SAMI than per capita GDP, which is explained by the expectations of superlinear scaling of GDP ($\beta = 1.14$).

We also find that, just as in the case of crime, there is a distinct urban geography of innovation in India. An analysis of residuals for innovation and GDP reveals that the cities of southern and western India, on average, tend to over-perform scaling expectations, while those in northern and central Indian under-perform.

12.4 Conclusion

We studied the system of Indian cities using the urban scaling framework to explore underlying statistical patterns and uncover resultant signals of urbanisation in terms of agglomeration economies and geographic varying patterns. Broadly, we find that scaling relationships for various urban quantities for the Indian system of cities are in line with theoretical expectation and empirical evidence from other contexts [6].

However, there are important points of difference, which point to features specific to India and to its present state of development and set expectations for future dynamics. Access to basic services such as toilets and electricity, which are expected to scale linearly, but show a slightly superlinear scaling exponent for

India, essentially mean that large Indian cities have an advantage relative to smaller towns. This larger city advantage is a pattern typical of other developing urban systems where basic infrastructure is not yet universal and tends to spread from larger urban areas, where it appears first, to other parts of the country, down the urban hierarchy. A similar pattern also typically takes place in each city, with richer or higher status neighbourhoods obtaining services first. A greater awareness of these patterns in terms of inequities is developing, especially in light of quantitative comparative evidence produced at smaller scales, hopefully leading to faster universal access to basic services [9,17].

The most significant point of departure is the sublinear scaling of crime. We explore this difference in detail and derive the geography of crime across India, relating it to specific studies that identify caste and gender as critical sources of violence in the country. Our analysis of residuals (SAMIs) reveals agreement with empirical evidence on the salience of these aspects in driving crime in rural or small city settings. It is plausible that in the future, as the status of Scheduled Castes is better addressed, the scaling pattern of crime in India will shift and eventually become superlinear, as we see already perhaps in the positive SAMIs for the nation's largest cities.

The scaling of patenting activity is significantly superlinear, meaning that larger cities are more than proportionally inventive. The large exponent indicates that on average technological innovation in India is strongly concentrated in its largest cities. However, the analysis of residuals also provides new evidence of many medium-sized cities being highly inventive relative to their size.

We find that crime also shows a strong regional signature with distinct urban behaviour in northern and central India vis-à-vis southern and western India. A similar regional pattern emerges for the scaling of innovation and GDP. These patterns reflect a larger and well-known differential reality of development patterns, cultural variation, and state government across the vast continental country that is India. Scaling analysis allows us to see how these general features are expressed in greater detail.

One crucial gap in India is the creation and availability of quality data at the appropriate scale, especially the lack of reliable urban economic data. The studies reported here were based to a large extent on the Census of India 2011, which did produce systematic datasets for Urban Agglomerations, but currently the 2021 census has been delayed because of the COVID pandemic. Collection of data at the level of urban agglomerations and neighbourhoods, modernisation of data records, and the use of technologies such as digital mapping and remote sensing, will be essential to creating consistent and reliable evidence on a rapidly urbanising and developing India, a country soon to be the most populous in the world.

Note

1 Based on the following publications: Sahasranaman, Anand, and Luís MA Bettencourt. "Urban geography and scaling of contemporary Indian cities." *Journal of the Royal Society Interface* 16.152 (2019): 20180758.

Sahasranaman, Anand, and Luís MA Bettencourt. "Economic geography and the scaling of urban and regional income in India." *Environment and Planning B: Urban Analytics and City Science* 48.3 (2021): 540–554.

References

[1] G. Possehl, *The Indus Civilization: A Contemporary Perspective*, Rowman Altamira, 2002.
[2] G. Samuel, *The Origins of Yoga and Tantra*, Cambridge University Press, 2010.
[3] UN DESA, *World Urbanization Prospects: The 2017 Revision*, UN, 2017.
[4] L. Bettencourt, J. Lobo, D. Helbing, C. Kühnert and G. West, "Growth, innovation, scaling, and the pace of life in cities," *PNAS*, p. 7301–7306, 2007.
[5] L. Bettencourt, "The origins of scaling in cities," *Science*, p. 1438–1441, 2013.
[6] L. Bettencourt, *Introduction to Urban Science: Evidence and Theory of Cities as Complex Systems*, MIT Press, 2021.
[7] A. Sahasranaman and L. Bettencourt, "Economic geography and the scaling of urban and regional income in India," *Environment and Planning B*, p. 540–554, 2021.
[8] A. Sahasranaman and L. Bettencourt, "Urban geography and scaling of contemporary Indian cities," *Journal of the Royal Society Interface*, p. 20180758, 2019.
[9] C. Brelsford, J. Lobo, J. Hand and L. Bettencourt, "Heterogeneity and scale of sustainable development in cities," *PNAS,* 2017.
[10] A. Gomez-Lievano, H. Youn and L. Bettencourt, "The Statistics of Urban Scaling and Their Connection to Zipf's Law," *PLoS ONE*, p. e40393, 2012.
[11] S. Sharma, "Caste-based crimes and economic status: Evidence from India," *Journal of Comparative Economics*, p. 204–226, 2015.
[12] T. Besley, R. Pande, L. Rahman and V. Rao, "The politics of public good provision: Evidence from Indian local governments," *Journal of the European Economic Association*, p. 416–426, 2004.
[13] J. Drèze and R. Khera, "Crime, gender, and society in India: Insights from homicide data," *Population and Development Review*, p. 335–352, 2000.
[14] P. Oldenburg, "Sex ratio, son preference and violence in India: A research note," *EPW*, p. 2657–2662, 1992.
[15] Jamia Millia Islamia, "Discriminatory and derogatory practices against women by khap panchayats, shalishi adalts, and kangaroo courts in India: An empirical study in the states of Haryana, UP (West), West Bengal, and Rajasthan," 2022. [Online]. Available: www.ncw.nic.in/sites/default/files/ReportbyJamiaMilia.pdf.
[16] NCSC, "Investigation of atrocities," 2022. [Online]. Available: https://ncst.nic.in/content/investigation-atrocities.
[17] A. Sahasranaman and L. Bettencourt, "Life between the city and the village: Scaling analysis of service access in Indian urban slums," *World Development,* p. 105435, 2021.

13 Urban allometries in archaeology

The Social Reactors Project[1]

Scott G. Ortman, José Lobo, and Michael E. Smith

13.1 Introduction

Economists have long been aware that concentrated populations tend to be more productive than dispersed populations. Several classic treatments of this phenomenon argue that the principal agglomeration benefit of cities arises from human capital spillovers [1–3]. Figure 13.1 presents a summary of current thinking. Much work has been done in the ensuing decades to identify and measure these effects at the level of the firm and the individual, using very sophisticated econometric techniques and micro-level data. The data and modeling frameworks used in these studies (e.g., production and wage functions) are tailored to specific characteristics of contemporary capitalist economies; but urban economists acknowledge that agglomeration effects must have also occurred in past cities for which many contemporary economic institutions were absent [4]. Despite this recognition, evidence from cities of the past has not been considered by urban economists in the development of general theory.

The benefits of agglomeration are widely assumed to stem from the variety, intensity, and quality of interactions, social and economic, which are facilitated by spatial proximity. This suggests the manner in which aggregated individuals produce greater value, innovate more rapidly, and utilize infrastructure more efficiently is transposable between modern and pre-modern contexts [4]. Population size and density are considered major facilitators of these effects. Indeed, there is nothing in the basic concept of agglomeration that necessarily restricts its effects on wages or firm-level productivity – rather, it has simply been the case that economists have focused on measuring these specific effects using available, high-quality micro-level data from contemporary urban settings. The research program in urban economics and economic geography has been to identify and measure the strength of the determinants of agglomeration effects. As a result, the modeling framework of urban economics does not easily accommodate the type of data available for ancient settlement systems. The presence of agglomeration effects, resulting from generalized social interactions and not necessarily from interactions occurring in firms or labor markets, are reflected in the scaling coefficients and are detected at the aggregate (i.e., city- or settlement-wide) level rather than the level of firms or individual workers.

DOI: 10.4324/9781003288312-15

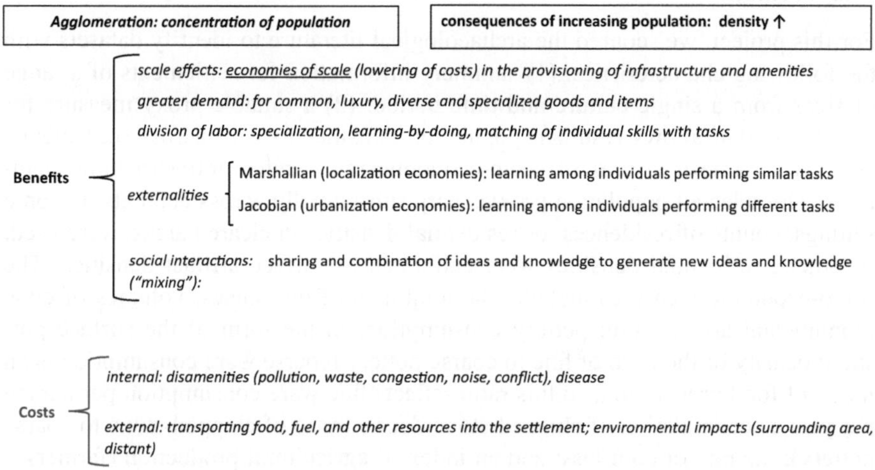

Figure 13.1 Summary of the current view of agglomeration effects in urban economics.

Since 2014, the Social Reactors Project has been investigating the consequences of agglomeration effects in a wide range of non-industrial and non-capitalist societies of the past. No presupposition is made, as it is not necessary to make it, that the costs and benefits engendered by agglomeration are monetized, nor that costs and benefits are experienced and compared within a market system. As shown in Figure 13.1, the concepts and phenomena underpinning the study of agglomeration effects in urban economics are also relevant for non-market economies.

We have focused on measuring agglomeration effects using simple aggregate properties of settlements as they have been documented through archaeology and history. The theoretical framework of settlement scaling theory – founded on first principles common to most of urban economics, economic geography, and regional science [5] – generates hypotheses and specific predictions as to what the relationship should be between the measurable aggregate properties and population scale given the putative presence of agglomeration effects. One notable aspect of the research program of settlement scaling is that it derives a value for the scaling coefficient of the relationship between aggregate properties of settlements and population size (turning the aggregate property into a dependent variable in a power function equation with population size as the independent variable). Thus far, project collaborators have published more than two dozen studies using data from across the world, including pre-Columbian Latin America, Native North America, Classical Antiquity, Medieval Europe, Bronze Age China, and Medieval Angkor. All Project publications and data are available through the project website (www.colorado.edu/socialreactors/). Here, we summarize these results and their implications for a general model of agglomeration effects.

13.2 Methods

For this project, we scoured the archaeological literature to identify datasets with the following characteristics: (1) summary information for settlements of a range of sizes from a single culture and time period; (2) a suitable proxy measure for population that allows resultant population densities to vary across settlements; and (3) suitable measures of socio-economic rates and/or infrastructural quantities. The selected population proxies vary substantially across contexts. In some settings, counts of residences, or residential densities in cleared areas, were used. In others, residential densities were calibrated to surface artifact densities. The socio-economic measures include: the total area of residences; volumes of civic monumental architecture; pottery consumption, in the form of the surface potsherd density or the ratio of fine to coarse pottery (coarse ware consumption is an index of food preparation, so this ratio reflects fine ware consumption per person per year); accumulation of chipped-stone debris (ratio of chipped-stone to coarse pottery); the rate of coin loss; and an index of agricultural production (farmers × land × irrigation inputs). Finally, the infrastructural measures include: the areas of interaction spaces, including plaza area, epicenter area, forum/agora area, and street network area; and total circumscribing or built areas, as defined by the total extent of artifacts and features. Details of the linking arguments for these measures are summarized in Table 13.1.

To estimate the elasticities of aggregate properties relative to population we generally apply ordinary least-squares regression to the log-transformed data, using the white correction for heteroskedasticity when necessary to estimate standard errors of the regression parameters. The slope of the fit line to the log-transformed data is an estimate of the elasticity of the dependent variable relative to settlement population. We also assessed the degree of fit of the observed elasticities to those expected for various aggregate properties of settlements based on formal models of urban scaling developed by Bettencourt [6,7] and adapted to an archaeological context by Ortman, Lobo, and others [5,8]. These models are much more general than those typically used in urban economics; and yet, we find that they account for data across a wide range of past societies and contemporary industrialized nations.

13.3 Results

Table 13.1 presents a summary of published results to date. Each row of the Table summarizes a specific relationship between a population proxy and an aggregate property of past settlements; arguments that link the archaeological observations to economic phenomena of interest; the expected elasticity of the relationship under settlement scaling theory; the number of cases where the observed empirical elasticity was found to be within the range of statistical tolerance of the expected value; and references to the source studies. To the extent that the relationships between aggregate output and population and areal extent and population conform the predicted scaling coefficient, the results suggest that agglomeration effects were present in societies very different in scale, institutional arrangements, and levels of technological development than modern ones. We note that there are empirical cases in which the expected relationship has not been found, indicating either a situation where the foundational assumptions are not met or the use of spatial units which do not in effect constitute social networks embedded in physical space.

Figure 13.2 provides further detail on the first row of Table 13.1. The top panel displays the relationship between population, as proxied by the total house count, and total socio-economic output, as proxied by the total area of these houses, across settlements from a range of New World societies. House count is a suitable population proxy because households are fundamental socio-economic units; and total house area is a reasonable proxy measure of aggregate incomes because in these societies almost all economic output was physical (food, manufactured goods), such that more productive households needed more space in which to store their product. These data encompass six millennia of time, sixty degrees of latitude, and six orders of magnitude in settlement population. As the top panel shows, the intercepts of these relationships vary a fair bit (due to differences in the baseline productivity of individual households in various technological and ecological settings), but their slopes are remarkably consistent. In fact, if one centers the data to equilibrate the intercepts and then re-calculates the slope across the entire dataset, the point estimate of the agglomeration elasticity turns out to be 1.162. This is within five one-thousandths of the value of 1.167 predicted by settlement scaling theory. This is a remarkably precise match between a theoretical expectation and archaeological data, especially given the many issues that affect their quality, from time averaging to sparse sampling intervals [9]. This result does not necessarily mean that the settlement scaling model is the right one, but it does mean that a plausible alternative would need to account for these results, and a better model would need to account for additional patterns that this approach does not account for.

13.4 Discussion

It is important to emphasize that the empirical patterns we observe in the archaeological record, with elasticities as expected from settlement scaling theory, also occur in some contemporary urban systems. For example, the income elasticity of $\beta \cong 7/6$ illustrated in Figure 13.2 is also apparent in relationships between population and productivity (GDP) across contemporary European metropolitan areas, US metropolitan statistical areas, Japanese metropolitan areas, and Chinese prefectural cities [7,10]. There has been some debate regarding the extent to which scaling effects in contemporary cities are an artifact of spatial unit construction [11,12], but we note that this issue is minor with respect to the smaller and simpler societies of the past, where it is straightforward to determine settlement boundaries [5,13]. We also acknowledge that there are contemporary systems (such as Micropolitan Areas in the USA) and salient urban indicators (such as metropolitan patenting output) where the observed scaling coefficients do not conform to this theory. Overall, our results suggest that, at least with respect to agglomeration effects, contemporary capitalist economies represent a special case of a much

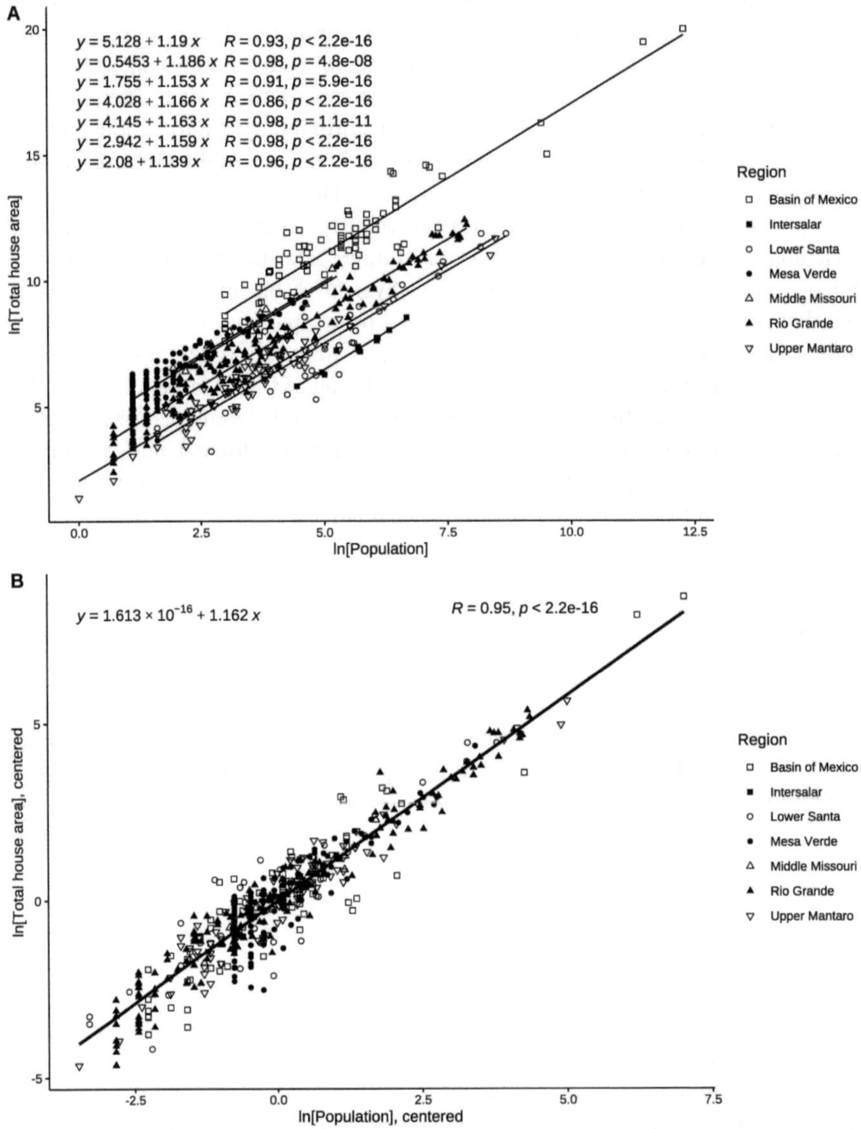

Figure 13.2 Relationship between settlement population (house count) and aggregate socio-economic outputs (total house area) in seven non-industrial New World societies. In A, above, fits are listed in the same order as the legend items.

Table 13.1 Summary of Social Reactors Project results.

Socio-economic measure	*Linking arguments*	*Expected elasticity*	*Number of cases*	*Locations*	*Sources*
Total house area (m^2)	More productivity leads to more stuff, which needs more space	7/6	7	Mesa Verde, N. Rio Grande, Middle Missouri, Central Mexico, Central Andes, Coastal Peru	[14–18]
Civic monument construction rate (architectural m^3/year)	Most construction effort is reflected in the accumulated mass	7/6	3	Central Mexico, Maya, Coastal Peru	[13,16,19]
Pottery consumption (amount/year)	More socializing with food leads to faster accumulation of broken pottery	7/6	3	N. China, N. Rio Grande, Roman Britain	[15,20,21]
Coin loss (coins/year)	Lost small change is proportional to the total money in circulation	7/6	1	Roman Britain	[21]
Chipped-stone debris accumulation (amount/year)	Debris is proportional to tools produced; tool sharing increases with network size	5/6	1	N. Rio Grande	[15]
Agricultural production (product of land, labor, and irrigation inputs)	Coordinated labor increases aggregate output per laborer	7/6	1	Angkor	[22]
Plaza/epicenter/ forum/street area	Space for social mixing	2/3	2	Roman Empire, Classic Maya	[19,23]
Circumscribing/ built area	Spatial equilibrium of costs and benefits of social interchange	2/3–5/6	10	Mesa Verde, Middle Missouri, Central Mexico, Mixteca Alta, Central Andes, coastal Peru, Roman Empire, Medieval Europe, N. China, NW coast	[24,25]

more general phenomenon: human sociality embedded in physical and infrastructural space. What the consequences of this generality are for the design of policies related to urban development and planning remain to be seen.

Note

1 A summary of results available at www.colorado.edu/socialreactors/publications.

References

[1] R. E. Lucas (1988). On the mechanics of economic development. *Journal of Monetary Economics* **22**(1), 3–42. doi:https://doi.org/10.1016/0304-3932(88)90168-7

[2] J. V. Henderson (1988). *Urban Development: Theory, Fact and Illusion.* (Oxford University Press, New York).

[3] E. L. Glaeser, H. D. Kallal, J. A. Scheinkman, A. Shleifer (1992). Growth in cities. *Journal of Political Economy* **100**, 1126–1152.

[4] E. L. Glaeser (2011). *Triumph of the City: How Our Greatest Invention Makes Us Richer, Smarter, Greener, Healthier, and Happier.* (Penguin Press, New York).

[5] J. Lobo, L. M. A. Bettencourt, S. G. Ortman, M. E. Smith (2020). Settlement scaling theory: Bridging the study of ancient and contemporary urban systems. *Urban Studies* **57**, 731–747.

[6] L. M. A. Bettencourt (2021). *Introduction to Urban Science: Evidence and Theory for Cities as Complex Systems.* (The MIT Press, Cambridge).

[7] L. M. A. Bettencourt (2013). The origins of scaling in cities. *Science* **340**, 1438–1441.

[8] S. G. Ortman, A. H. F. Cabaniss, J. O. Sturm, L. M. A. Bettencourt (2014). The prehistory of urban scaling. *PLOS-One* **9**, e87902.

[9] C. Perreault (2019). *The Quality of the Archaeological Record.* (University of Chicago Press, Chicago).

[10] L. M. A. Bettencourt, J. Lobo (2016). Urban scaling in Europe. *Journal of the Royal Society Interface* **13**, 20160005.

[11] E. Arcaute *et al.* (2015). Constructing cities, deconstructing scaling laws. *Journal of the Royal Society Interface* **12**, 2014745.

[12] C. Cottineau, E. Hatna, E. Arcuate, M. Batty (2016). Diverse cities or the systematic paradox of urban scaling laws. *Computers, Environment and Urban Systems* **63**, 80–94.

[13] S. G. Ortman, M. E. Smith, J. Lobo, L. M. A. Bettencourt (2020). Why archaeology is necessary for a theory of urbanization. *Journal of Urban Archaeology* **1**, 151–167.

[14] S. G. Ortman, G. D. Coffey (2017). Settlement scaling in middle-range societies. *American Antiquity* **82**, 662–682.

[15] S. G. Ortman, J. Lobo (2020). Smithian growth in a nonindustrial society. *Science Advances* **6**, eaba5694.

[16] S. G. Ortman, A. H. F. Cabaniss, J. O. Sturm, L. M. A. Bettencourt (2015). Settlement scaling and increasing returns in an ancient society. *Science Advances* **1**, e1400066.

[17] S. G. Ortman *et al.* (2016). Settlement scaling and economic change in the Central Andes. *Journal of Archaeological Science* **73**, 94–106.

[18] S. G. Ortman (2019). A new kind of relevance for archaeology. *Frontiers in Digital Humanities* **6**, https://doi.org/10.3389/fdigh.2019.00016.

[19] M. E. Smith *et al.* (2021). The low-density urban systems of the classic period Maya and Izapa: Insights from settlement scaling theory. *Latin American Antiquity* **32**, 120–137.

[20] S. G. Ortman, Z. Cooper (2021). Artifact density and population density in settlement pattern research. *Journal of Archaeological Science: Reports* **39**, 103189.

[21] S. G. Ortman *et al.* (2024). Identification and measurement of intensive economic growth in a Roman Imperial Province. *Science Advances* 10(27):eadk5517.

[22] S. Klassen, S. G. Ortman, J. Lobo, D. Evans (2021). Provisioning an early city: Spatial equilibrium in the agricultural economy at Angkor, Cambodia. *Journal of Archaeological Method and Theory*. doi:10.1007/s10816-021-09535-5.

[23] J. W. Hanson, S. G. Ortman, L. M. B. Bettencourt, L. C. Mazur (2019). Urban form, infrastructure and spatial organization in the Roman Empire. *Antiquity* **93** (369), 702–718. doi:10.15184/aqy.2018.192.

[24] S. G. Ortman, J. Lobo, M. E. Smith (2020). Cities: Complexity, theory and history. *PLOS ONE* **15**, e0243621.

[25] J. Lobo *et al.* (2022). Scaling of hunter-gatherer camp size and human sociality. *Current Anthropology* **63**(1), 68–94.

14 Socio-economic strength and governance

Influence of the number of municipalities in an urban agglomeration[1]

Anthony F.J. van Raan

14.1 Introduction and research question

This study focuses on the urban scaling of cities in the Netherlands by analyzing the scaling behavior of major cities in two governance modalities: (1) the municipality of the central city and (2) its urban agglomeration with a number of autonomous municipalities. In other words, a compact, seamlessly connected urban area can be a *one-governance structure*, i.e., the central city and its (former) suburbs are one municipality, or a *multi-governance structure*, i.e., the central city and its suburbs are separate municipalities.

Our research question is whether we can find a significant relation between socio-economic strength and governance. We take two approaches. First, by comparing urban scaling measurements applied to cities (one-governance) and their agglomerations (multi-governance). The second approach is about governance fragmentation of the agglomeration and this approach is central in our study. In an OECD study [1,2] it was found that cities defined as urban agglomerations with fragmented governance structures tend to have lower levels of productivity. For instance, for a given population size, a metropolitan area with twice the number of municipalities is associated with around six percent lower productivity. Here we investigate on the basis of the urban scaling methodology the relation between urban agglomeration performance and the number of municipalities in the agglomeration.

The structure of this chapter is as follows. Section 14.2 addresses the method and data. In Section 14.3 the results are presented and discussed, and we conclude this chapter with our main findings in Section 14.4.

14.2 Method and data

For a discussion of the urban scaling methodology, the calculation of scaling residuals and relevant references we refer to earlier work[2] [3,4] and to our chapter *Regional and sectorial diversity of employment urban scaling* in this handbook. This chapter is a further elaboration of our work on the socio-economic urban scaling behavior of municipalities in the Netherlands discussed in Ref. [4]. In the textbox here below we present a short overview of the methodology.

DOI: 10.4324/9781003288312-16

The socioeconomic performance of cities tends to increase superlinearly (power law relation) with population size. More specifically, for a set of cities the scaling relation between, for instance, the gross urban product (G) and population (N) can be written as:

$$G(N) = aN^{\beta} \tag{14.1}$$

The values for the coefficient a and the power-law exponent β follow from the empirically determined scaling equation. Eq. (14.1) means that for a specific city i with population N_i the *expected* value for the gross urban product is $G(N_i) = aN_i^{\beta}$, whereas the *real* value of the gross urban product of this city is G_i. The residual ξ_i of the scaling relation is given by the logarithm of the ratio between the real and the expected value:

$$\xi_i = ln\left[G_i / G(N_i)\right] = ln\left[G_i / aN_i^{\beta}\right] \tag{14.2}$$

The Netherlands, with around 17,500,000 inhabitants, is administratively divided into 12 provinces and 342 municipalities (January 2023). The Central Bureau of Statistics (CBS) defines for 21 major cities (population above 100,000) their urban agglomerations. In total, the urban agglomerations of these 21 major cities comprise 40 municipalities. We collected [5,6] for the period 2014–2016 for all municipalities (the central cities and the suburban cities) the number of inhabitants (population size) as well as the gross urban product (GUP). In addition, we collected for all municipalities the land surface areas (in km^2, total surface area corrected for water surface area) and for each of the 40 suburban cities the distances (in km) to the center of the central city.

14.3 Results and discussion

14.3.1 Scaling of major cities and their agglomerations

In Figure 14.1 we present the scaling of GUP[3] for the 21 major cities and for their urban agglomerations. We see that the major cities scale with the following exponents [4]: 1.20 (95%CI [1.17–1.23], R^2=0.94) for cities as a municipality (*C*), and 1.16 (95%CI [1.10–1.22], R^2=0.92) for the urban agglomerations of these cities (*A*). But it is not (a difference in) the scaling exponents that is most important in this measurement. What matters is the difference in GUP values. We see in Figure 14.1 that the average value of the gross urban product for the urban agglomeration is lower than for the central cities as municipalities. Thus, although the multi-governance urban agglomerations do scale with population, they, on average, underperform as compared to the one-governance central cities. In other words, an urban agglomeration consisting of one municipality (one-governance, the definition of the central city) performs substantially better as compared with an urban

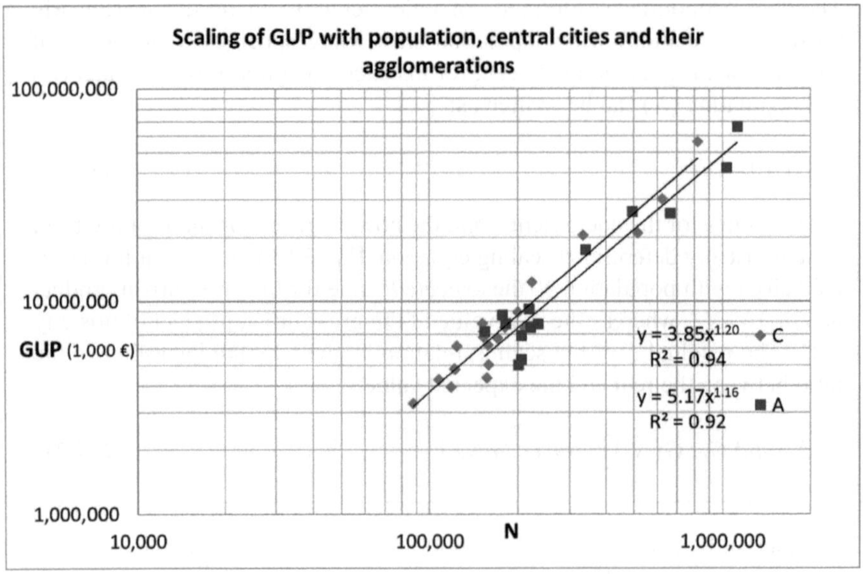

Figure 14.1 Scaling of GUP with population size N for the major cities. The central cities are indicated with blue diamonds (C), their urban agglomerations with red squares (A).

agglomeration with the same number of inhabitants but consisting of several municipalities. And this difference is large in terms of GUP. For instance, the expected value for *C* (one-governance) is in the case of 200,000 inhabitants around 20% higher than the expected value for *A* (multi-governance). This gives a first indication of the profit that can be made by the municipal merging of a central city with its directly connected suburban municipalities in the agglomeration. Even if only a small part (say 10%) of these expectations is fulfilled, we are still talking about an amount of 100 million Euros per medium-sized city.

An important further indication of the benefits of municipal merging can be found by analyzing the relation between the urban agglomeration residuals and the number of municipalities in the agglomeration. In this sense, we look at the relation between the socioeconomic strength of an urban agglomeration and its size in terms of the number of municipalities within the agglomeration. In other words, does the performance of an urban agglomeration depend on the number of municipalities in the agglomeration? This is the central theme of this chapter, and we discuss this in the next section. Our approach is in line with the previously mentioned work by Ahrend et al. [1,2].

Are multi-governance urban agglomerations less densely populated than one-governance cities? If so, it could be an explanation why most of the urban agglomerations in the Netherlands are characterized by underperformance. But this is not the case. A detailed analysis in our earlier study showed that population density does not relate significantly to the measured residuals. In other words, over- and underperformance of cities as compared to the expected GUP values cannot be attributed to population density [4]. A few examples. The Rotterdam agglomeration has eight municipalities, and the overall density is 2680 inhabitants/km^2. Compare this with two German harbor cities, Hamburg and Bremen, both are *kreisfrei*, i.e., central city plus agglomeration is one municipality. The densities of these *one-governance* urban areas are for Hamburg 2304 inhabitants/km^2 and for Bremen 1682 inhabitants/km^2, well below the *multi-governance* Rotterdam agglomeration. The densities of the multi-governance The Hague agglomeration (four municipalities) and the multi-governance Leiden agglomeration (five municipalities) are 3656 and 2775 inhabitants/km^2, considerably higher than the population densities of Hamburg and Bremen or of Cologne and Düsseldorf with 2542 and 2744 inhabitants/km^2, respectively. Again, we conclude that population densities are most probably not a main factor in the difference of GUP between one-governance and multi-governance urban areas.

With the empiric determination of the scaling equations (given in Figure 14.1) we calculate the residuals for the individual cities and agglomerations. For this calculation we refer to the textbox in the previous section. We distinguish the following residuals.

(1) ξ_{iC}, the residual of city *i* related to the scaling of the whole set of cities, i.e., the residual calculated with the scaling equation of the *C*-regression line in Figure 14.1. It is a measure of *over- or underperformance* of a city (as municipality) in a national context. Using Eq. (14.2) we write:

$$\xi_{iC} = ln\left[G_{iC} / a(C) N_{iC}^{\beta(C)}\right] \tag{14.3}$$

where $a(C)$ and $\beta(C)$ indicate the coefficient and the power-law exponent of the *C*-regression line, G_{iC} is the gross urban product of city *i* and N_{iC} its population size.

(2) ξ_{iA}, the residual of the *urban agglomeration of city i* related to the scaling of the whole set of agglomerations, i.e., the residuals calculated with the scaling equation of the *A*-regression line in Figure 14.1. It is a measure of over- or underperformance of the urban agglomeration (central city with the immediately connected suburban cities that are separate municipalities), again in a national context. We write:

$$\xi_{iA} = ln\left[G_{iA} / a(A) N_{iA}^{\beta(A)}\right] \tag{14.4}$$

where $a(A)$ and $\beta(A)$ indicate the coefficient and the power-law exponent of the *A*-regression line, G_{iA} is the gross urban product of the agglomeration of city *i* and N_{iA} its population size.

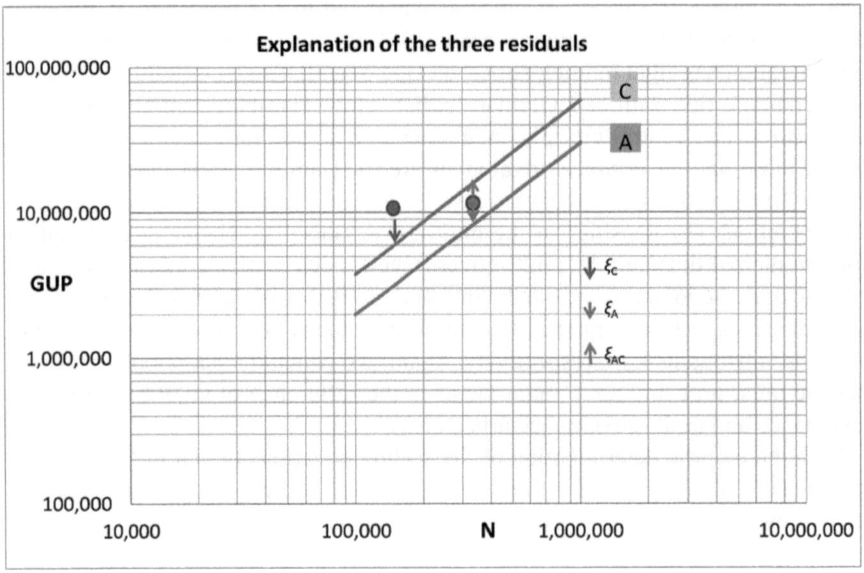

Figure 14.2 Explanation of the three residuals in relation to the regression lines of the major cities and their agglomerations.

(3) ξ_{iAC}, the residual of the *urban agglomerations of city i* but now related to the scaling of the cities, i.e., related to the *C*-regression line. If an urban agglomeration would be a one-governance (i.e., one municipality) urban area, the *expected position* should be on the *C* regression line. Thus this residual is a measure of the difference in gross urban product between what the agglomeration could "earn" if it was a one-governance city, and what it actually earns now, in a fragmented, multi-governance urban agglomeration. Thus we can write:

$$\xi_{iAC} = ln\left[G_{iA} / a(C) N_{iA}^{\beta(C)}\right] \tag{14.5}$$

We illustrate these residuals with Figure 14.2.

14.3.2 Urban agglomeration performance and number of municipalities

In the previous section we formulated our research question: Does the performance of an urban agglomeration depend on the number of municipalities in the agglomeration? In order to investigate this, we need to take the socio-economic strength of the central city into account. The performance of the urban agglomeration largely depends on the performance of its central city. Thus we define

$$\Delta\xi_i = (\xi_{iAC} - \xi_{iC}) \tag{14.6}$$

as a measure of under- or over-performance of an urban agglomeration relative to the performance of the central city *i* of the agglomeration. From Eqs. (14.3), (14.5), (14.6) follows:

$$\Delta\xi_i = ln\left[G_{iA} / a(C) N_{iA}{}^{\beta(C)}\right] - ln\left[G_{iC} / a(C) N_{iC}{}^{\beta(C)}\right]$$
$$= ln\left\{\left[\frac{G_{iA}}{a(C) N_{iA}{}^{\beta(C)}}\right] / \left[\frac{G_{iC}}{a(C) N_{iC}{}^{\beta(C)}}\right]\right\} \tag{14.7}$$

which shows that $\Delta\xi_i$ is the performance of the *urban agglomeration of city i* (related to the city scaling, *C*-regression line) normalized to the performance of the city (also related to the city scaling, *C*-regression line).

Next, we look at the relationship between $\Delta\xi_i$ and the number of municipalities (*n*) in the urban agglomeration for the 21 major cities in the Netherlands. Seven cities do not have an agglomeration mainly because the former agglomeration municipalities have been merged with the central city in the past. In these cases we have

$$\xi_{iAC} = \xi_{iC} \text{ so that } \Delta\xi_i = 0 \tag{14.8}$$

and we set the number of municipalities in the urban agglomeration at n=1. One of the 21 urban agglomerations is in fact a double-city structure which makes it an exception compared to all other urban agglomerations. The result without the exceptional case is shown in Figure 14.3.

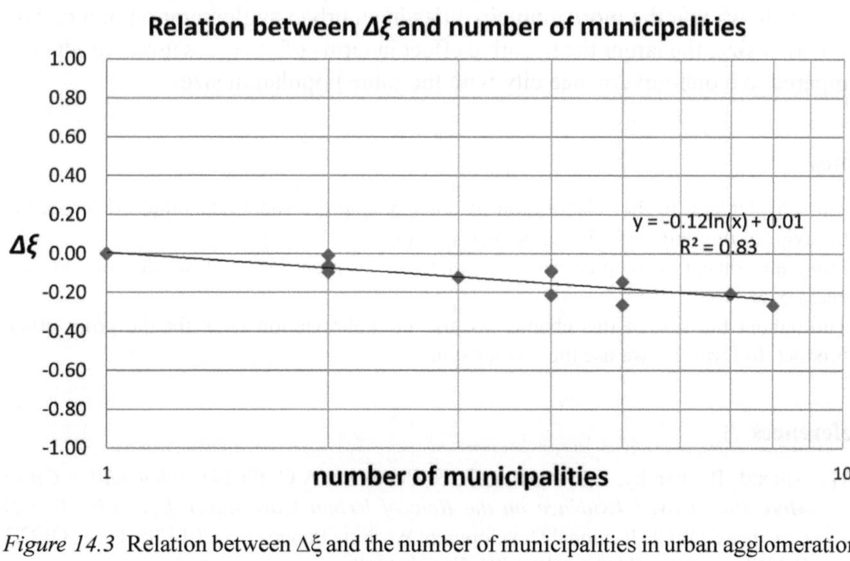

Figure 14.3 Relation between Δξ and the number of municipalities in urban agglomerations.

We find with a reasonable significance (R^2=0.83) that $\Delta\xi$ has a negative, logarithmic relation with the number of municipalities *n*:

$$\Delta\xi = -0.12 ln(n) + 0.01 \tag{14.9}$$

We emphasize that the number of municipalities *does not play any role* in the urban scaling equations used in this study, and thus the relation between $\Delta\xi$ and *n* is an independent empirical finding. This measurement shows that the more municipalities in an urban agglomeration of a certain population size, the larger the negative effect in terms of GUP as compared to a one-governance city with the same population size. This finding is in line with the results of the previously mentioned OECD study [1,2].

14.4 Concluding remarks

This study focuses on the urban scaling of cities in the Netherlands by analyzing the scaling behavior of major cities in two governance modalities: (1) the municipality of the central city and (2) its urban agglomerations with a number of autonomous municipalities. In other words, a compact, seamlessly connected urban area can be a *one-governance structure*, i.e., the central city and its (former) suburbs are one municipality, or a *multi-governance structure*, i.e., the central city and its suburbs are separate municipalities.

In both cases significant superlinear scaling is measured but there is a substantial difference in GUP values between the two modalities at the same population size. While confirming our previous measurements that one-governance urban areas perform better than multi-governance urban areas, we focused in this study on the relation between socio-economic strength and governance by investigating the influence of the number of municipalities in an urban agglomeration. Our measurement shows that the more municipalities in an urban agglomeration of a certain population size, the larger the negative effect in terms of the gross urban product as compared to a one-governance city with the same population size.

Notes

1 This chapter is a further elaboration of our work on the socio-economic urban scaling behavior of municipalities in the Netherlands discussed in [4].

2 From this recent work pieces of text that can be regarded as basic descriptions are taken over.

3 Throughout the text of this chapter we use the abbreviation GUP for the gross urban product. In formulas we use the shorter symbol *G*.

References

[1] Ahrend, R., Farchy, E., Kaplanis, I., & Lembcke, A.C. (2014). *What Makes Cities More Productive? Evidence on the Role of Urban Governance from Five OECD Countries*. OECD Regional Development Working Papers, No. 2014/05. Paris: OECD Publishing. https://doi.org/10.1787/5jz432cf2d8p-en.

[2] Ahrend, R., Farchy, E., Kaplanis, I. & Lembcke, A.C. (2017), What Makes Cities More Productive? Evidence From Five OECD Countries on the Role of Urban Governance. *J Regional Sci* 57: 385–410. https://doi.org/10.1111/jors.12334.

[3] van Raan, A.F.J., van der Meulen, G., & Goedhart, W. (2016). Urban Scaling of Cities in the Netherlands. *PLoS ONE* 11(1): e0146775. https://doi.org/10.1371/journal.pone.0146775.

[4] van Raan, A.F.J. (2020). Urban Scaling, Geography, Centrality: Relation with Local Government Structures. *PLoS ONE* 15(9): e0238418. https://doi.org/10.1371/journal.pone.0238418.

[5] LISA. (2018). Database of Business Locations in the Netherlands. www.lisa.nl/home.

[6] CBS. (2020). Central Bureau of Statistics Netherlands. https://opendata.cbs.nl/statline.

15 Regional and sectorial diversity of employment urban scaling

Anthony F.J. van Raan

15.1 Introduction and research question

Recent studies show a *more than proportional* (superlinear) increase in the socioeconomic performance of cities in relation to population size [1–3]. This *urban scaling* relation of a set of cities is described by a power-law dependence of, for instance, the gross urban product on population size given by the relation

$$G(N) = aN^{\beta} \tag{15.1}$$

where G is the gross urban product[1] and N the population size of a city. The coefficient a and the exponent β follow from the measurement; in most cases, values of the exponent are between 1.10 and 1.20. This means that the socioeconomic strength of cities increases more than proportionally with increasing population size. Urban scaling behavior is also found for employment (number of jobs) and human interactions in general, for knowledge production activities in cities [1,4,5] and also universities show a size-dependent performance scaling behavior similar to cities [6]. In this chapter we focus on urban scaling of the gross urban product (GUP) and of employment.

In this chapter we build on our recent empirical work[2] on urban scaling of German cities [7,8] which implies that we use the term city *only* for cities defined as municipalities [9,10]. Thus we focus on typical *one-governance cities* and not on *multi-governance* cities defined as urban agglomerations such as the US metropolitan statistical areas [2] or the European functional urban agglomerations [11–13], or urban areas defined by population density statistics. Different "city" definitions, whether or not with population-size cut-offs, may considerably influence the measured scaling [14–19] and recently it also led to heated debates [20–22]. Multi-governance "cities" consist of many independent, autonomous municipalities that may or may not cooperate optimally. Inter-municipality collaboration within urban agglomerations may differ substantially per municipality in form, duration, and effectiveness for the many different social, economic, and infrastructural urban sectors, resulting in a weakening of the decision-making cohesion between all these sectors. This

DOI: 10.4324/9781003288312-17

problem of *governance fragmentation of urban areas* is largely underestimated in the urban scaling literature [23–25].

Our research question is what an empirical study can tell us about the influence of regions on the measured socioeconomic urban scaling exponent, and in particular the influence of regions in relation to business sectors on the measured scaling exponent of employment. The structure of this chapter is as follows. Section 15.2 addresses the method and data. In Section 15.3 the results are presented and discussed, first on scaling of the gross urban product and next on the scaling of several types of employment in relation to regions. We conclude this chapter with our main findings in Section 15.4.

15.2 Method and data

This chapter presents follow-up work of our recent investigation of urban scaling in Germany [7,8]. Germany, with 83 million inhabitants, consists of sixteen federal states. These federal states have a specific administrative structure in which cities and districts (Kreise) play a central role. Most larger cities (particularly those above 100,000 inhabitants) are *kreisfrei* ("district-free"), i.e., cities of which the surrounding urban area belongs to the municipality of the city. Therefore we have in these cases a *one-governance urban area* (which is in fact the definition of the concept "kreisfrei"). The country currently has 107 *kreisfreie* cities. Together these cities have a population of about 27 million, which is about 32 percent of the total German population. The kreisfreie cities cover a large range of inhabitants: the smallest have a population of around 40,000, the largest over a million. For our urban scaling analysis of the western, southern, middle, northern, and eastern regions[3] of Germany and of the country as a whole we apply the same approach as described in our recent papers on urban scaling [7,8] and we refer to those papers for details of the method. The German Federal Bureau of Statistics [26] provided data for all (kreisfreie) cities on the gross urban product (GUP), number of inhabitants, and number of employees in different business sectors. This study relates to the period 2017–2019.

In this chapter we also focus briefly on socioeconomic strength. In urban scaling *observed* (i.e., real) positions of cities will always deviate from the *expected* positions given by the regression line through all measuring points of a specific set of cities. These deviations can be measured by the residuals: using Eq. (15.1) (which is the scaling relation for a *set* of cities) we find that $G(N_i)$ is the *expected* gross urban product of an *individual* city (*i*) with population N_i. By denoting the *observed* (real) value of the gross urban product of a city with G_i, we calculate the residuals ξ_i of the scaling distribution for each of the cities as follows:

$$\xi_i = ln\left[G_i / G(N_i)\right] = ln\left[G_i / aN_i^{\beta}\right] \tag{15.2}$$

Positive residuals indicate that a city performs better than expected, a negative residual means underperformance. Thus, *these residuals can be considered as an indicator of socioeconomic strength.* Indeed, we find a strong relation of residuals with other measures of socioeconomic strength [7]. The full list of residuals of German cities calculated on the basis of Eq. (15.2) can be found in Table S1 in [8].

15.3 Results and discussion

15.3.1 Gross urban product scaling diversity by region

In many studies urban scaling is measured for a set of cities in a whole country, and countries are compared with each other on the basis of whole-country scaling exponents [11]. In our previous studies we already demonstrated the large differences in urban scaling exponents but also in absolute GUP values between major regions in Germany. We here present a short overview and an update of these measurements. Other work on regional urban scaling differences has been done, for example, for India [27].

Figure 15.1 shows the scaling of cities in the five German regions (Figure 15.1, upper-left part), and for the whole country (Figure 15.1, upper-right part). In all cases the gross urban product (GUP) scales superlinearly with population, the scaling exponent ranges between and 1.03 and 1.34 (90% CI interval +/– 0.03). As we can clearly see, in urban scaling not only the power law exponent is a crucial parameter, but also *the absolute difference* in GUP between two sets of cities, i.e., the distance between the regression lines of the two sets. For instance, the difference in both the scaling exponent as well as the absolute GUP value between the old industrial western region and the economically booming southern region of Germany is striking.

Is the scaling exponent of a group of regions, for instance all regions in a country, a simple combination (e.g., approximately an average) of the constituent exponents? This certainly is not the case. We see that although the scaling exponents of all German regions are ≥1.06, the combined set of cities in all five regions (i.e., the whole country) have a low scaling exponent of 1.03. In Figure 15.1 (lower part), we show how this is possible. Here we combine the western, southern, and middle regions, all with high scaling exponents (1.33, 1.08, and 1.28, respectively), but the combination (which is the largest part of Germany) again gives the low value 1.03. It is clear that the *substantial difference in absolute GUP values* forces, as it were, the slope of the regression line of the combined regions to a less steep slope and thus to a lower scaling exponent. Thus, superlinear scaling as an effect of aggregating many cities from different locations in the same analysis, as suggested by Strano and Sood [28], is unlikely. It is rather the opposite, as we see in our above-discussed measurements, aggregating cities tend to remove superlinearity. We also see that the urban scaling exponent is larger for the more prosperous southern (1.08) and middle (1.28) regions of Germany than for the least prosperous eastern region (1.06). This contradicts the findings by Strano and Sood [28] on European cities. They found that for “rich” cities (i.e., West EU cities) the urban scaling exponent is about 1.03, while for the “poorer” post-communist cities (i.e.,

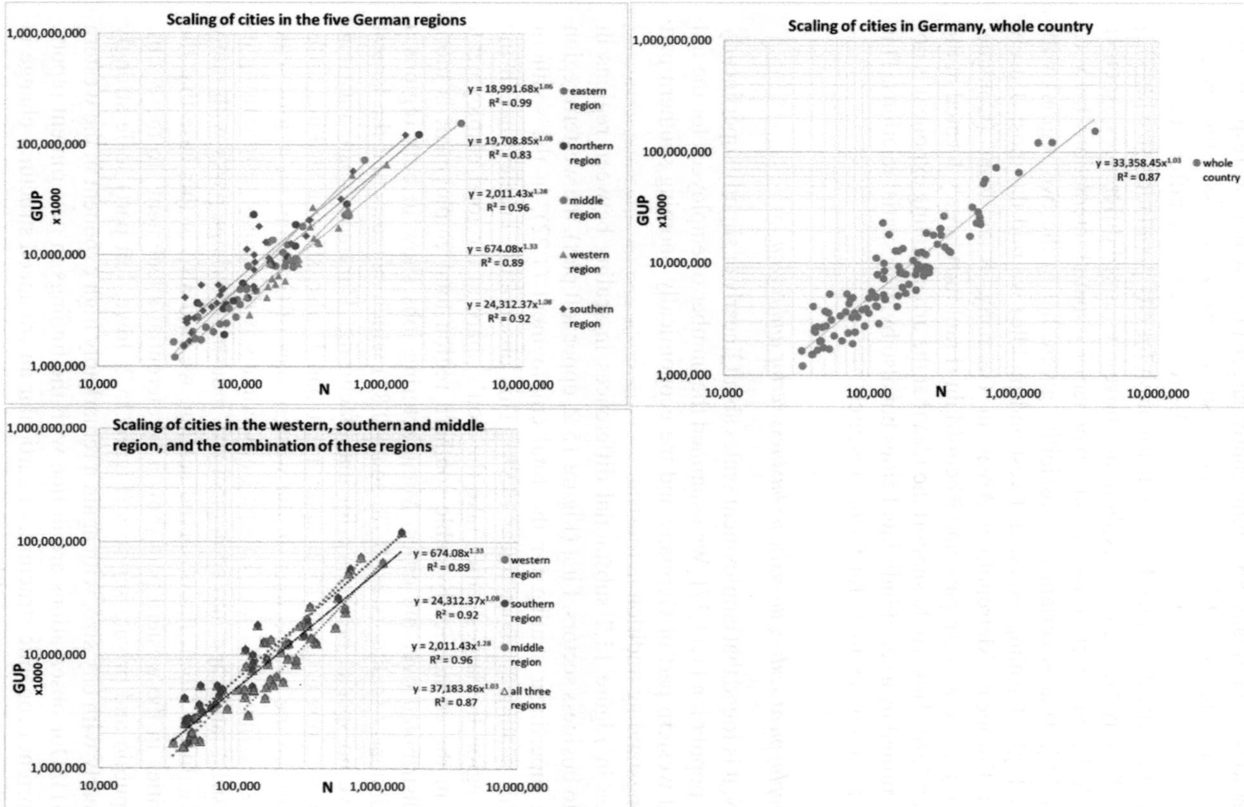

Figure 15.1 Urban scaling of the gross urban product. Upper-left part: scaling of the five regions; upper-right part: scaling of the whole country (the five regions combined); lower part: illustration how the scaling of a combination of regions is influenced by the substantial differences in absolute GUP values between the regions.

East EU cities) the exponent is considerably higher and increases in the measured period (2005–2010) from 1.25 to 1.42.

Nevertheless, differences in prosperity cannot explain differences in urban scaling exponents given our finding that the exponents for cities in the western and middle regions of Germany are significantly larger (1.33 and 1.28, respectively) than for the other regions of Germany (north, south, east: 1.08, 1.08, 1.06, respectively). Currently, we are investigating what the reason for these differences could be. The first results show that the Zipf distribution for city population size [29–32] as well as for city GUP cannot explain the above-mentioned differences. Another cause could be an effect on the scaling exponent by spatial interactions between cities [33–35]. That is certainly a possibility given that in the two regions with by far the highest scaling exponent (west and middle) we find the most densely populated European Metropolitan Areas in Germany, Rhein-Ruhr (Cologne, Düsseldorf) in the western part, and Rhein-Main (Frankfurt) largely located in the middle part [36]. This would support the idea that the urban scaling exponent is not only determined by a set of individual cities but also by their spatial relations. This is clearly an important topic for further research.

15.3.2 Employment scaling diversity by business sector and region

Generally, it is found that employment scales about linearly or slightly superlinearly with city population [1,11,37]. We examined the number of employees for the old industrial western part of Germany and the economically booming southern part with a longstanding tradition in tourism.

We see in Figure 15.2 substantial differences in scaling between regions in relation to business sectors. First (Figure 15.2, upper-left part), the western region shows a superlinear scaling for the total employment (1.22), in the southern region this scaling is about linear (0.98). This observation implies that in the western region the largest cities take the lion's share in the total employment, whereas in the economically stable southern region total employment is more evenly distributed over the cities. Manufacturing jobs show in both regions a clear sublinearly scaling (west 0.78, south 0.83) which suggests that the largest cities have no special preference for manufacturing. The trade, hospitality, and traffic sector jobs (Figure 15.2, upper-right panel) also show a striking difference between the two regions: in the western part of Germany these jobs scale strongly superlinearly (1.26). This part of Germany is rigorously restructuring its old industrial landscape into ecological and industrial heritage parks with many leisure facilities. Given the observed scaling, we find also in this case that the largest cities in the western part show a "preferential attachment" to these jobs. Jobs in public and private services (Figure 15.2, lower-left part) scale strongly superlinearly with city size, with again a remarkably high exponent in the western part (1.61). Our observations are in line with the findings in government reports on the current economic structure, in particular an advanced structural change in favor of the service sector [38].

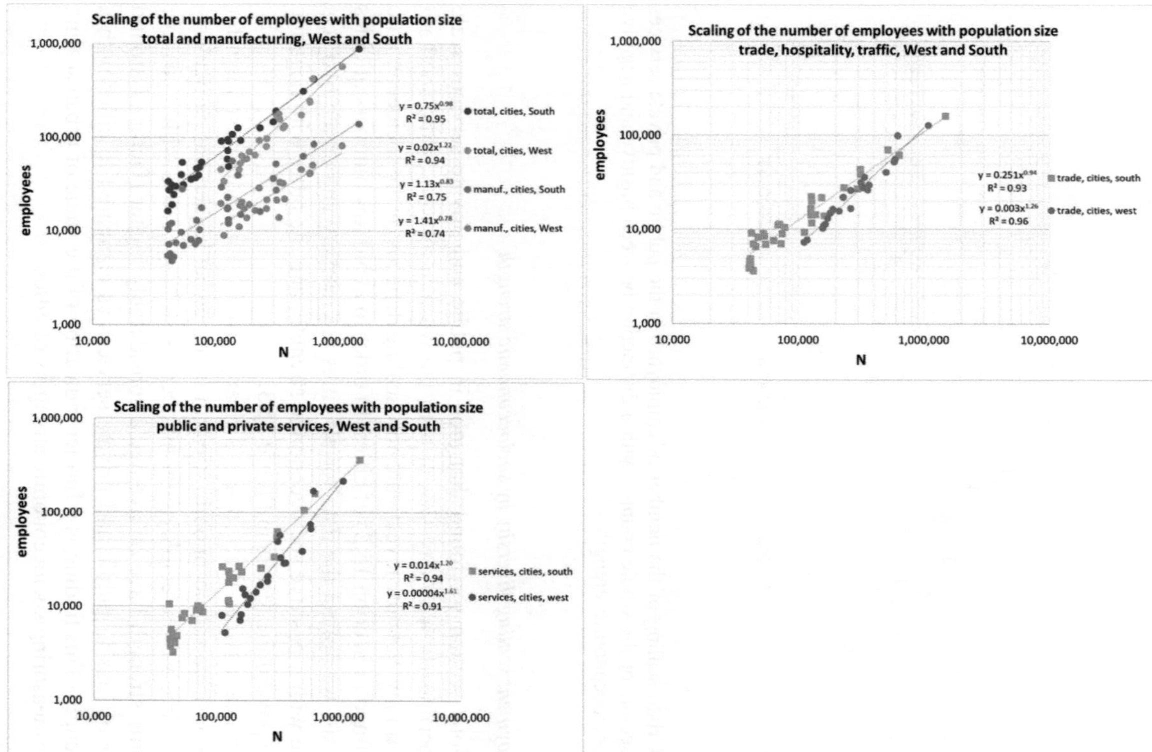

Figure 15.2 Urban scaling of the number of employees.[4] Upper-left part: scaling of the total number of employees and of the number of employees in the manufacturing sector for the western and southern regions; upper-right part: scaling of the number of employees in the trade, hospitality, and traffic sectors for the western and southern regions; lower part: scaling of the number of employees in the public and private services sector for the western and southern regions.

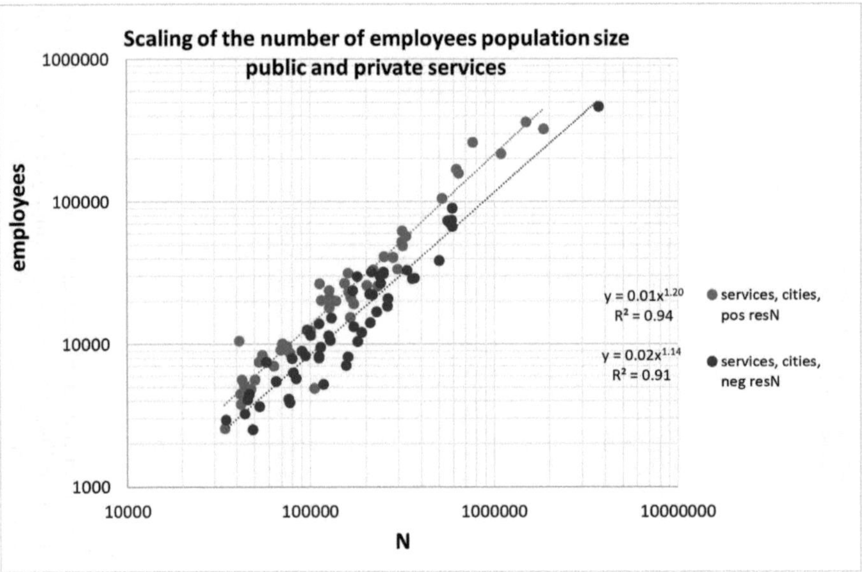

Figure 15.3 Urban scaling of the number of employees in the public and private services sector for the whole country with a distinction between positive and negative socioeconomic strength.

15.3.3 Employment scaling diversity by socioeconomic strength

In the previous section we found that jobs in public and private services scale strongly superlinearly with city size in both the western as well as the southern region of Germany. We now investigate how scaling depends on the socioeconomic strength (defined in Section 15.2) of cities. In order to avoid low numbers of cities in our analysis, we collect the data for all cities in Germany and create two sets of cities, one with a positive socioeconomic strength, and the other with negative strength. We present the results in Figure 15.3.

The difference between the two sets is clearly visible. The scaling exponent for cities with a positive socioeconomic strength is somewhat higher, but particularly the difference in absolute employment numbers is striking. Cities with a positive socioeconomic strength have on average a considerably higher (factor of around 1.6) number of jobs in public and private services as compared to cities with a negative strength. This finding is a further indication of the value of urban scaling residuals for measuring socioeconomic strengths of cities.

15.4 Concluding remarks

In our analysis of urban scaling characteristics of around 100 German cities we find a substantial influence of regions on both the measured socioeconomic urban scaling exponent as well as on the absolute value of the dependent variables, gross urban product, and employment. Next to the influence of regions, the business sector also influences the measured scaling exponent for employment. We compare the old industrial western region with the economically booming southern region of Germany for total employment, employment in the manufacturing industry, employment in trade, hospitality, and traffic, and employment in public and private services. In the next step we use the scaling residuals as a measure of socioeconomic strength. We find that the scaling exponent for cities with a positive socioeconomic strength is somewhat higher, but particularly the difference in absolute employment numbers is striking. This finding demonstrates the use of urban scaling residuals as a measure of the socioeconomic strength of cities. Our study shows that in one and the same country large regional and sectorial differences in scaling exist.

Notes

1 Throughout the text of this chapter we use the abbreviation GUP for the gross urban product. In the case of mathematical equations we use the shorter symbol G.
2 From this recent work pieces of text that can be regarded as basic descriptions are taken over.
3 North Rhine-Westphalia, western region of Germany; Baden-Württemberg and Bavaria, southern region; Hesse, Rhineland-Palatinate, and Saarland, middle region; Bremen, Hamburg, Lower Saxony, and Schleswig-Holstein, northern region; Berlin, Brandenburg, Mecklenburg-Vorpommern, Saxony, Saxony-Anhalt and Thuringia, eastern region.
4 Employees who are subject to social security contributions (social security employees), i.e., all employees who are subject to health, pension, or nursing care insurance contributions under the labor law.

References

[1] Bettencourt, L.M.A., Lobo, J., Helbing, D., Kühnert, C., & West, G.B. (2007). Growth, innovation, scaling, and the pace of life in cities. *Proc Natl Acad Sci USA* 104(17): 7301–7306. https://doi.org/10.1073/pnas.0610172104.
[2] Bettencourt, L.M.A., Lobo, J., Strumsky, D., & West, G.B. (2010). Urban scaling and its deviations: Revealing the structure of wealth, innovation and crime across cities. *PLoS ONE* 5(11): e13541. https://doi.org/10.1371/journal.pone.0013541.
[3] Lobo, J., Bettencourt, L.M.A., Strumsky, D., & West, G.B. (2013). Urban scaling and the production function for cities. *PLoS ONE* 8(3): e58407. https://doi.org/10.1371/journal.pone.0058407.
[4] Arbesman, S., Kleinberg, J.M., & Strogatz, S.H. (2009). Superlinear scaling for innovation in cities. *Phys Rev E* 68: 066102. https://doi.org/10.1103/PhysRevE.79.016115.
[5] Nomaler, Ö., Frenken, K., & Heimeriks, G. (2014). On scaling of scientific knowledge production in U.S. metropolitan areas. *PLoS ONE* 9(10): e11080. https://doi.org/10.1371/journal.pone.0110805.
[6] van Raan, A.F.J. (2013). Universities scale like cities. *PLoS ONE* 8(3): e59384. https://doi.org/10.1371/journal.pone.0059384.
[7] van Raan, A.F.J. (2020). Urban scaling, geography, centrality: Relation with local government structures. *PLoS ONE* 15(9): e0238418. https://doi.org/10.1371/journal.pone.0238418.

[8] van Raan, A.F.J. (2022). German cities with universities: Socioeconomic position and university performance. *Quantitative Science Studies* 3(1): 265–288. https://doi.org/10.1162/qss_a_00182.

[9] Cebrat, C., & Sobczyński, M. (2016). Scaling laws in city growth: Setting limitations with self-organizing maps. *PLoS ONE* 11(12): e0168753. https://doi.org/10.1371/journal.pone.0168753.

[10] Meirelles, J., Neto, C.R., Ferreira, F.F., Ribeiro, F.L., & Binder, C.R. (2018). Evolution of urban scaling: Evidence from Brazil. *PLoS ONE* 13(10): e0204574. https://doi.org/10.1371/journal.pone.0204574.

[11] Bettencourt, L.M.A., & Lobo, J. (2016). Urban scaling in Europe. *J R Soc Interface* 13: 2016.0005. https://doi.org/10.1098/rsif.2016.0005.

[12] OECD (2019). Functional urban areas by country, available from www.oecd.org/cfe/areaal-policy/functionalurbanareasbycountry.htm.

[13] Eurostat (2019). City Statistics, available from: https://ec.europa.eu/eurostat/web/cities/data/database

[14] Batty, M., & Ferguson, P. (2011). Defining city size. *Environ Plann B* 38(5):753–756. https://journals.sagepub.com/doi/pdf/10.1068/b3805ed.

[15] Louf, R., & Barthelemy, M. (2014). Scaling: Lost in the smog. *Environ Plann B* 41(5): 767–769. https://journals.sagepub.com/doi/pdf/10.1068/b4105c.

[16] Arcaute, E., Hatna, E., Ferguson, P., Youn, H., Johansson, A., & Batty, M. (2015). Constructing cities, deconstructing scaling laws. *J R Soc Interface* 12: 20140745. http://dx.doi.org/10.1098/rsif.2014.0745.

[17] Cottineau, C., Hatna, E., Arcaute, E., & Batty, M. (2017). Diverse cities or the systematic paradox of Urban Scaling Laws. *Comput Environ Urban Syst* 63: 80–94. http://dx.doi.org/10.1016/j.compenvurbsys.2016.04.006.

[18] Cottineau, C., Finance, O., Hatna, E., Arcaute, E., & Batty, M. (2019). Defining urban clusters to detect agglomeration economies. *Environ Plann B Urban Anal City Sci* 46(9): 1611–1626. https://doi.org/10.1177/2399808318755146.

[19] Cottineau, C., & Vanhoof, M. (2019). Mobile phone indicators and their relation to the socioeconomic organisation of cities. *ISPRS Int J Geo-Inf.* 8(1): 19. https://doi.org/10.3390/ijgi8010019.

[20] Stier, A.J., Schertz, K.E., Rim, N.W., Cardenas-Iniguez, C., Lahey, B.B., Bettencourt, L.M.A., & Berman, M.G. (2021). Evidence and theory for lower rates of depression in larger US urban areas. *Proc Natl Acad Sci USA* 118(31): e2022472118. https://doi.org/10.1073/pnas.2022472118.

[21] Stier, A.J., Schertz, K.E., Rim, N.W., Cardenas-Iniguez, C., Lahey, B.B., Bettencourt, L.M.A., & Berman, M.G. (2022). Reply to Huth et al.: Cities are defined by their spatially aggregated socioeconomic networks. *Proc Natl Acad Sci USA* 119(2): e2119313118. https://doi.org/10.1073/pnas.2119313118.

[22] Huth, K.B.S., Finnemann, A., van den Ende, M.W.J., & Sloot, P.M.A. (2022). No robust relation between larger cities and depression. *Proc Natl Acad Sci USA* 119(2): e2118943118. https://doi.org/10.1073/pnas.2118943118.

[23] Cheshire, P.C., & Magrini, S. (2009). Urban growth drivers in a Europe of sticky people and implicit boundaries. *Journal of Economic Geography* 9: 85–115. https://doi.org/10.1093/jeg/lbn044.

[24] Ahrend, R., Farchy, E., Kaplanis, I., & Lembcke, A.C. (2014). *What Makes Cities More Productive? Evidence on the Role of Urban Governance from Five OECD Countries*. OECD Regional Development Working Papers, No. 2014/05. Paris: OECD Publishing. https://doi.org/10.1787/5jz432cf2d8p-en.

[25] Ahrend, R., Farchy, E., Kaplanis, I. & Lembcke, A.C. (2017). What makes cities more productive? Evidence from Five OECD countries on the role of Urban Governance. *J Regional Sci* 57: 385–410. https://doi.org/10.1111/jors.12334.

[26] German Federal Bureau of Statistics (2021). Data on the gross domestic product and number of inhabitants of cities and Kreise, available from: www.statistikportal.de/en/node/109978#alle-ergebnisse.

[27] Sahasranaman, A., & Bettencourt, L.M.A. (2021). Economic geography and the scaling of urban and regional income in India. *Environ Plann B Urban Anal City Sci* 48(3): 540–554. https://doi.org/10.1177/2399808319879463.

[28] Strano, E., & Sood, V. (2016). Rich and poor cities in Europe. An urban scaling approach to mapping the European economic transition. *PLoS ONE* 11(8): e0159465. https://doi.org/10.1371/journal.pone.0159465.

[29] Shutters, S.T., Lobo, J., Muneepeerakul, R., Strumsky, D., Mellander, C., Brachert, M., Farinha, T., & Bettencourt, L.M.A. (2018). Urban occupational structures as information networks: The effect on network density of increasing number of occupations. *PLoS ONE* 13(5): e0196915. https://doi.org/10.1371/journal.pone.0196915.

[30] Gomez-Lievano, A., Youn, H., & Bettencourt, L.M.A. (2012). The statistics of urban scaling and their connection to Zipf's Law. *PLoS ONE* 7(7): e40393. https://doi.org/10.1371/journal.pone.0040393.

[31] Cottineau, C. (2017). MetaZipf. A dynamic meta-analysis of city size distributions. *PLoS ONE* 12(8): e0183919. https://doi.org/10.1371/journal.pone.0183919

[32] Cura, R., Cottineau, C., Swerts, E., Ignazzi, C.A., Bretagnolle, A., Vacchiani-Marcuzzo, C., Pumain, D. (2017). The old and the new: Qualifying city systems in the world with classical models and new data. *Geograph Anal* 49: 363–386. https://doi.org/10.1111/gean.12129.

[33] Ribeiro, F.L., Meirelles, J., Ferreira, F.F., & Neto, C.R. (2017). A model of urban scaling laws based on distance-dependent interactions. *R Soc Open Sci* 4: 160926. http://dx.doi.org/10.1098/rsos.160926.

[34] Altmann, E.G. (2020). Spatial interactions in urban scaling laws. *PLoS ONE* 15(12): e0243390. https://doi.org/10.1371/journal.pone.0243390.

[35] Khiali-Miab, A., van Strien, M.J., Axhausen, K.W., & Grêt-Regamey, A. (2019). Combining urban scaling and polycentricity to explain socioeconomic status of urban regions. *PLoS ONE* 14(6): e0218022. https://doi.org/10.1371/journal.pone.0218022

[36] Vergleich der Metropolregionen in Deutschland (2019). Amt für Stadtforschung und Statistik für Nürnberg und Fürth, Nürnberg. www.nuernberg.de/imperia/md/statistik/dokumente/veroeffentlichungen/berichte/sonderberichte/sonderbericht_2019_s263_vergleich_der_metropolregionen_nbg.pdf.

[37] Keuschnigg, M., Mutgan, S., Hedström, P. (2019). Urban scaling and the regional divide. *Sci Adv* 5, eaav0042. https://www.science.org/doi/10.1126/sciadv.aav0042.

[38] Wirtschaft in Nordrhein-Westfalen im Regionalvergleich (2017). Information und Technik Nordrhein-Westfalen, Düsseldorf. www.it.nrw.

16 The non-causal scaling of health indicators and city size[1]

Luis E. C. Rocha, Fatemeh Zarei, and Ruixue Jing

16.1 Introduction

The search for healthier and wealthier lives, the so-called urban advantage, drives the influx of migrants from rural areas to urban centres in developed and developing economies [1]. Urban centres provide more job opportunities, quality education and health, and better access to essential and non-essential services. Research suggests that cities with larger populations can optimise resources like schools and hospitals, transportation and sanitation infrastructure [2], and promote social interactions [2,3], collectively leading to economic development, innovation [2,4], and population well-being [5,6]. Rapid urban growth is also known to generate uneven development [7], with increased carbon emissions [8,9], criminal activity [10], and homicides [11] in larger cities, reducing the mental health of citizens [12].

The contrasting effects of cities on health, society, and economics call for novel methodologies to study how population size affects macroscopic indicators, considering the complexity of human behaviour. An implicit assumption in health sciences and policymaking is that a linear relationship exists between the dependent (health indicator) and independent (population size) variables [2], leading to the analysis of per-capita rates. This linear assumption is acceptable if the quantity under observation is size-independent, meaning that the per-capita rates explain population differences. The allometric theory relaxes the linearity assumption to study the relationship between city size and urban indicators [2,13], with the underlying assumption that a health quantity scales non-linearly with the city size [14–16]. The urban advantage may thus be quantified by estimating the relative per-capita increase or decrease of the health indicator H with the city size P, where β is a proportionality constant (Eq. 16.1).

$$\mathrm{H} = \beta \mathrm{P}^{\alpha} \tag{16.1}$$

Urban scaling provides additional explanatory information but only for some indicators [17]. To analyse the scaling properties, the relationship between

DOI: 10.4324/9781003288312-18

socioeconomic inequalities and the city size can be examined using distributions of those aggregate quantities (e.g., income distributions). The city size can be the main reason for differences in income distributions, housing costs, and the concentration level of people [18]. The number of social contacts also scales superlinearly with group size for social interactions with different social functions [3]. Based on the proposed economic convergence model under stable political conditions, a linear scaling can be expected for the gross metropolitan product and population [19]. However, research shows that it is not only the size that matters but also the changes. Variations in CO_2 emissions associated with proportional changes in population may depend on the magnitude of these changes and the initial values of these quantities. The larger the city, the higher the impact of changing its population on emissions. However, population changes always have a higher effect on emissions than population density [20]. Positive correlations between pairs of indicators can be leveraged to attain the UN sustainable development goals, and the trade-offs need to be overcome by more profound changes in the current development strategies [21].

In this chapter, we focus on the scaling properties of relevant health indicators in Brazil from the traditional cross-sectional perspective (multiple cities each year) and the longitudinal analysis (the same city for subsequent years). We use the scaling exponents to question the idea of urban advantage. We also hypothesise that although non-linear scaling exponents can be determined at the country level, individual cities follow their evolutionary trajectories with population growth that cannot be explained by the same exponents, thus lacking universal patterns. Such mismatches indicate non-causal relationships between the increase in health indicators and population growth, highlighting that scaling relations should be carefully interpreted.

16.2 Methods

16.2.1 Data

Our analysis uses the population size and health indicators of Brazilian cities based on the absolute number of events, e.g., deaths or infections, at the place of residence or on the available infrastructure, e.g., the number of clinics or services. We follow the governmental definition of the city for census purposes, that in Brazil means the lowest political-administrative territorial level and corresponds to 5550 locations. Due to the large variability of the indicators for small cities and the under-representation of very large cities, our sample contains only the cities with population sizes in the interval [50,000–5,000,000]. If no events are observed in a specific city for a given health indicator, the city is also removed from the respective analysis [2]. The data set, available at the aggregated city level (no personal data were processed), is public and has been made available by the Brazilian public healthcare system (www2.datasus.gov.br).

16.2.2 Scaling analysis

To perform the cross-sectional scaling analysis, we first define one vector for the population size (*P*) and another for each health indicator (*H*) whose entries p_i and h_i contain the respective data of each city *i* for a given year T. For the longitudinal scaling analysis, we define one vector for the population size (*P*) and one for the health indicator (*H*) for each city, where the entry *i* now corresponds to a given year. We then linearise Eq. (16.1) by taking the logarithm on both sides (Eq. 16.2) because the population sizes are spread over several orders of magnitude. This operation reduces the importance of these values and allows the estimation of the parameters using linear regression analysis with higher statistical power.

$$\log(\mathrm{H}) = \log(\beta) + \alpha \log(\mathrm{P}) \qquad (16.2)$$

We define three levels of deviation from linearity: $0.95 \leq \alpha \leq 1.05$ (weak), $0.85 \leq \alpha < 0.95$ and $1.05 < \alpha \leq 1.15$ (medium), and $\alpha < 0.85$ and $\alpha > 1.15$ (strong). The relative increase of an indicator *H* for an increase in the population size ($P_2 = \delta P_1$, where δ is a proportionality constant) is given by:

$$\frac{H_2 - H_1}{H_1} = \frac{P_2^{\alpha} - P_1^{\alpha}}{P_1^{\alpha}} = \delta^{\alpha} - 1 \qquad (16.3)$$

This relation shows the asymmetric effect of super- and sublinearity on the indicators. If the population doubles ($\delta = 2$), the output indicator also doubles if $\alpha = 1.0$, but it increases by 114.35% (for $\alpha = 1.1$) and by 86.61% (for $\alpha = 0.9$). The statistical software R (www.r-project.org) estimates the equation parameters (Eq. 16.1) using the linear least squares method.

16.3 Results

16.3.1 Scaling exponents for health indicators

Table 16.1 shows the estimated exponents (Eq. 16.2) for various health indicators. The number of cases of infectious diseases generally scales superlinearly, being strongly superlinear for HIV and meningitis [22] while not as strong for Hep-C, but this possibly reflects the well-known under-reporting of Hep-C. Although leprosy is also under-reported, it is linked to poverty and is more prevalent in rural areas with poor diagnostics [23]. Dengue spreads via mosquitos (vectors) and is more common in areas lacking proper sanitation. Although some locations within urbanised areas (e.g., slums) may be associated with a higher risk of infection [24], there is a weak superlinear relation with the population size. Recent studies with COVID-19 also indicate superlinear scaling [25]. Infectious diseases spread mainly

Table 16.1 Scaling exponents of health indicators.

Indicator	*α*	*95% C.I.*	*β*	*95% C.I.*	*Adj. R^2*
Infectious diseases					
HIV	1.38	[1.31, 1.45]	1.77e-6	[–3.00, 3.00]	0.71
Pandemic influenza	1.00	[0.89, 1.11]	3.77e-5	[–3.88, 3.88]	0.41
Meningitis	1.39	[1.26, 1.52]	5.63e-7	[–4.28, 4.28]	0.51
Hepatitis C	1.06	[0.93, 1.19]	2.99e-5	[–4.41, 4.41]	0.37
Dengue	1.03	[0.82, 1.24]	3.73e-4	[–6.95, 6.95]	0.14
Leprosy	0.77	[0.64, 0.90]	1.74e-3	[–4.35, 4.35]	0.18
Causes of Death					
Infant mortality (0–1 year)	0.98	[0.94, 1.03]	2.33e-4	[–2.53, 2 53]	0.77
Child mortality (1–9 years)	0.94	[0.88, 1.00]	9.47e-5	[–2.84, 2.84]	0.60
Car accidents	0.89	[0.84, 0.94]	8.03e-4	[–2.59, 2.59]	0.70
Suicides	0.92	[0.84, 1.01]	9.78e-5	[–3.32, 3.33]	0.50
Diabetes	0.97	[0.92, 1.02]	3.87e-4	[–2.65, 2.65]	0.70
Heart attack	1.04	[0.98, 1.09]	2.34e-4	[–2.71, 2.71]	0.70
Cerebrovascular accident	1.00	[0.97, 1.04]	4.62e-4	[–2.44, 2.44]	0.83
Lung cancer	1.16	[1.09, 1.22]	1.58e-5	[–2.95, 2.96]	0.65
Chronic respiratory insufficiency	1.07	[1.00, 1.14]	7.40e-5	[–2.99, 2.99]	0.59
Violence					
Rapes	1.29	[1.19, 1.38]	2.04e-6	[–3.56, 3.56]	0.55
Domestic physical violence	1.28	[1.13, 1.43]	1.02e-5	[–4.82, 4.82]	0.32
Domestic moral violence	1.18	[1.04, 1.32]	1.32e-5	[–4.53, 4.53]	0.34
Health Providers					
Physicians	1.45	[1.38, 1.53]	5.13e-6	[–3.03, 3.03]	0.72
Primary care physicians	1.28	[1.20, 1.35]	1.54e-5	[–3.06, 3.06]	0.65
Dentists	1.19	[1.12, 1.26]	4.84e-5	[–2.96, 2.96]	0.65
Mental health providers	1.29	[1.20, 1.37]	6.64e-6	[–3.20, 3.20]	0.61
Nutritionists	1.21	[1.14, 1.29]	5.37e-6	[–3.01, 3.01]	0.65
Primary care clinic	1.10	[1.03, 1.17]	1.59e-4	[–2.95, 2 95]	0.62
Private insurance	1.69	[1.59, 1.79]	4.42e-5	[–3.63, 3.63]	0.63

through proximity or physical contact between an infected and a susceptible host [26]. Social contacts scale superlinearly with group size [3] with relatively high scaling exponents (α = 1.5) for proximity contacts, contributing significantly to positive deviations from linearity.

The number of deaths by non-infectious diseases or external causes also deviates from the linear trend. Still, the exponents depend not only on the grounds of death or underlying disease (Table 16.1) but also on the country [16]. Diabetes and heart attacks are, respectively, weakly sublinear and weakly superlinear. Both indicators have decreased in recent years [16]. Lung cancer and chronic respiratory insufficiency are consistently superlinear. This likely reflects not only the local behaviour (e.g., healthier lifestyle in larger cities) but also the disproportionally higher access to health care in larger cities [16]. Larger cities have relatively fewer deaths by external causes such as car accidents, injury, or suicides [27] and relatively higher levels of violence, linked not only to the higher density of people and social interactions but also to more reporting of cases.

16.3.2 Scaling patterns on individual cities

The scaling analysis is typically done across cities by aggregating reported data during the same period, e.g., during a year. Such methodology implicitly assumes that the microscopic dynamics generate macroscopic universal patterns across the system. This cross-sectional methodology based on correlations between variables cannot explain potential causal links of city size on health, for example, the impact that increasing a city's population would have on health indicators. To analyse the evolution of the scaling of health with population size, we analyse the evolution of individual cities over $n = 32$ years.

Table 16.2 shows that the scaling exponents of selected cities vary significantly for the same indicator. Cities follow individual evolutionary dynamics (e.g., migration, investment, development) that affect health and other social and economic indicators differently. We divided HIV into two periods because it increased substantially in the early 1980s and followed a slowdown after the peak of epidemics in the early 1990s. Infant mortality was the only studied indicator that experienced a decrease in the scaling exponents, indicating a favourable pattern with decreasing number of deaths over the years. Superlinear exponents for diabetes were observed in all cities but Belo Horizonte, whereas the number of heart attacks varied in all cities. Colon and lung cancer were generally strongly superlinear for all cities except colon cancer in Campinas and Belo Horizonte.

16.4 Discussion

Larger cities are known to generate knowledge and capital, optimise resources [2], and boost productivity [28,29] and innovation [30]. This is due to a disproportionate increase in the number of social interactions, which is the cornerstone of a functioning society [3]. The densification of social interactions directly affects the spread of infectious diseases that uses social interactions as the primary channels for transmitting infections. To optimise resources and economics, cities concentrate on high-quality, specialised healthcare centres and health professionals. Healthcare providers like primary care physicians, dentists, mental health practitioners, and nutritionists are more abundant (per capita) in larger cities. Larger cities also concentrate a relatively higher number of specialists per capita. Although health care is public and completely free in Brazil, the wealthier population tend to register for private health care that is less overloaded and typically more responsive. The number of privately insured individuals is also highly superlinear, a factor linked to the higher income observed in larger cities. In general, relatively greater access to health care services is observed in large cities, which may result in more offers and support of health care and contribute to a relatively lower burden of non-communicable diseases, suicides, and child and infant mortality.

Table 16.2 Scaling exponents for individual cities. The HIV analysis was split into two time periods. The symbols ♮, ◊, ♭, and ♯ correspond, respectively, to more than 50 cases, less than 50 cases, more than 200 cases, and less than 200 cases.

	Small cities		*Medium-sized cities*		*Large cities*	
	Londrina	*Cuiaba*	*Campinas*	*Sao Luis*	*Fortaleza*	*Belo Horizonte*
	α 95%C.I.	*α 95%C.I.*	*α 95%C.I.*	*α 95%C.I.*	*α 95%C.I.*	*α 95%C.I.*
HIV	27.3 [14.9, 39.7] ♮	5.50 [4.78, 6.27]	30.7 [24.5, 36.8] ♭	7.60 [6.85, 8.35]	20.1 [17.7, 22.4] ♭	3.25 [1.82, 4.69] ♮
	1.49 [0.68, 2.29] ◊		0.94 [0.18, 1.70] ♯		4.18 [3.48, 4.88] ♯	7.89 [5.72, 10.0] ◊
Infant mortality	–2.96 [–3.29, –2.62]	–0.52 [–1.08, 0.03]	–3.10 [–3.39, –2.81]	–1.68 [–1.90, –1.46]	–3.06 [–3.42, –2.69]	–7.84 [–8.41, –7.27]
Diabetes	3.63 [2.75, 4.52]	4.17 [3.70, 4.64]	1.48 [1.11, 1.85]	2.88 [2.62, 3.15]	2.73 [2.42, 3.05]	0.89 [0.21, 1.57]
Heart attack	0.17 [–0.34, 0.68]	1.62 [1.26, 1.99]	1.80 [1.46, 2.15]	0.45 [–0.02, 0.92]	0.42 [0.18, 0.65]	0.55 [0.17, 0.93]
Colon cancer	2.19 [1.28, 3.11]	2.19 [1.28, 3.11]	–1.77 [–2.69, –0.86]	3.68 [2.54, 4.83]	2.83 [2.33, 3.33]	0.32 [–0.40, 1.05]
Lung cancer	3.12 [2.68, 3.57]	2.25 [1.87, 2.63]	1.99 [1.62, 2.36]	1.91 [1.67, 2.16]	2.73 [2.49, 2.97]	2.65 [2.29, 3.00]

Our results highlight that one must be careful when linking the observed scaling relationships with causal dynamics, particularly the impact of city growth on health and likely other indicators. Although a cross-sectional analysis shows the disproportionate macroscopic effect of larger cities, likely due to macroscopic stimulus, the longitudinal analysis shows that cities have their own development path. The impact of the increasing population of cities is generally not universal and far from the linear scaling. Complex social and economic interactions at the microscopic level, combined with other microeconomic variables (e.g., local investment, climate, migration), affect the evolution of cities in different ways, not leading to universality. People tend to have a healthier lifestyle in large cities, including proportionally less smoking, more physical activity, and facilitated access to healthy food. Such activities have a vital social component and benefit from robust social networks. Some studies suggest that social networks influence obesity [31] and smoking habits [32] through complex contagion processes and reinforcement of healthy behaviour. However, people in larger cities are more exposed to infectious diseases and violent crime and report disproportionately higher numbers of rape and household problems, including domestic violence. Urban living may also make people stressed and follow a faster pace of life, which reduces mental health and increases the consumption of alcohol and other drugs. Social networks might be denser in larger groups, but their structures are not identical in urban and rural cities [3]. Differences in the cohesiveness of social networks, such as connectivity and clustering, may explain why health behaviour and infectious diseases spread differently in those contexts.

Note

1 Updated from: Rocha LEC, Thorson AE, Lambiotte R. The Non-linear Health Consequences of Living in Larger Cities. *J Urban Health*. 2015; 92: 785. pmid:26245466

References

[1] D. Vlahov, S. Galea, E. Gibble, and N. Freudenberg, "Perspectives on Urban Conditions and Population Health," *Cadernos de Saúde Pública*, vol. 21, no. 3, pp. 949–957, 2005.

[2] L. M. A. Bettencourt, J. Lobo, D. Helbing, C. Kühnert, and G. West, "Growth, Innovation, Scaling, and the Pace of Life in Cities," *Proceedings of the National Academy of Sciences*, vol. 104, no. 17, pp. 7301–7306, 2007.

[3] L. E. C. Rocha, J. Ryckebusch, K. Schoors, and M. Smith, "The Scaling of Social Interactions Across Animal Species," *Scientific Reports*, vol. 11, no. 1, pp. 1–10, 2021.

[4] J. Jacobs, *The Economy of Cities*. Vintage Publisher, 1970.

[5] S. Cyril, J. C. Oldroyd, and A. Renzaho, "Urbanisation, Urbanicity, and Health: A Systematic Review of the Reliability and Validity of Urbanicity Scales," *BMC Public Health*, vol. 13, no. 513, 2013.

[6] Y. Rydin, A. Bleahu, M. Davies, J. D. Dávila, S. Friel, et al., "Shaping Cities for Health: Complexity and the Planning of Urban Environments in the 21st Century," *The Lancet*, vol. 379, no. 9831, pp. 2079–2108, 2012.

[7] L. Sun, J. Chen, Q. Li, et al. "Dramatic Uneven Urbanization of Large Cities Throughout the World in Recent Decades," *Nature Communications*, vol. 11, no. 5366, 2020. https://doi.org/10.1038/s41467-020-19158-1
[8] A. Sarzynski, "Bigger is Not Always Better: A Comparative Analysis of Cities and Their Air Pollution Impact," *Urban Studies*, vol. 49, pp. 3121–3138, 2012.
[9] M. Fragkias, J. Lobo, D. Strumsky, and K. C. Seto, "Does Size Matter? Scaling of CO2 Emissions and U.S. Urban Areas," *PLoS ONE*, vol. 8, no. 6, p. e64727, 2013.
[10] L. M. A. Bettencourt, J. Lobo, D. Strumsky, and G. West, "Urban Scaling and Its Deviations: Revealing the Structure of Wealth, Innovation and Crime Across Cities," *PLoS ONE*, vol. 5, no. 11, p. e13541, 2010.
[11] A. Gomez-Lievano, H. Youn, and L. M. A. Bettencourt, "The Statistics of Urban Scaling and Their Connection to Zipf's Law," *PLoS ONE*, vol. 7, no. 7, p. e40393, 2012.
[12] J. Peen, R. A. Schoevers, A. T. Beekman, and J. Dekker, "The Current Status of Urban-Rural Differences in Psychiatric Disorders," *Acta Psychiatrica Scandinavia*, vol. 121, no. 84-93, 2009.
[13] A. W. Shingleton, "A Shingleton Allometry: The Study of Biological Scaling," *Nature Education Knowledge*, vol. 3, no. 10, p. 2, 2010.
[14] J. Martinez, R. Pampalon, D. Hamel, and G. Raymond. *Does Living in Rural Communities Rather than Cities Really Make a Difference in People's Health and Wellness*? Institut National de Santé Publique du Québec, 2004.
[15] S. Galea, N. Freudenberg, and D. Vlahov, "Cities and Population Health," *Social Science & Medicine*, vol. 60, no. 5, pp. 1017–1033, 2005.
[16] L. E. C. Rocha, A. E. Thorson, and R. Lambiotte, "The Non-Linear Health Consequences of Living in Larger Cities," *Journal of Urban Health*, vol. 92, pp. 785–799, 2015.
[17] V. Akuraju, P. Pradhan, D. Haase, J. P. Kropp, and D. Rybski, "Relating SDG11 Indicators and Urban Scaling–An Exploratory Study," *Sustainable Cities and Society*, vol. 52, p. 101853, 2020.
[18] S. Sarkar, "Urban Scaling and the Geographic Concentration of Inequalities by City Size," *Environment and Planning B: Urban Analytics and City Science*, vol. 46, no. 9, pp. 1627–1644, 2019.
[19] E. Strano and V. Sood, "Rich and Poor Cities in Europe: An Urban Scaling Approach to Mapping the European Economic Transition," *PLoS ONE*, vol. 11, no. 8, p. e0159465, 2016.
[20] H. V. Ribeiro, D. Rybski, and J. P. Kropp, "Effects of Changing Population or Density on Urban Carbon Dioxide Emissions," *Nature Communications*, vol. 10, no. 1, pp. 1–9, 2019.
[21] P. Pradhan, L. Costa, D. Rybski, W. Lucht, and J. P. Kropp, "A Systematic Study of Sustainable Development Goal (SDG) Interactions," *Earth's Future*, vol. 5, no. 11, pp. 1169–1179, 2017.
[22] F. J. Antonio, S. D. P. Jr., J. J. V. Teixeira, and R. S. Mendes, "Growth Patterns and Scaling Laws Governing AIDS Epidemic in Brazilian Cities," *PLoS ONE*, vol. 9, p. e111015, 2014.
[23] W. J. Britton and D. N. Lockwood, "Leprosy," *The Lancet*, vol. 363, no. 9416, pp. 1209–1219, 2004.
[24] D. J. Gubler, "The Economic Burden of Dengue," *American Journal Tropical Medicine Hygiene*, vol. 86, no. 5, pp. 743–744, 2012.
[25] H. V. Ribeiro, A. S. Sunahara, J. Sutton, M. Perc, and Q. S. Hanley, "City Size and the Spreading of COVID-19 in Brazil," *PLoS ONE*, vol. 15, no. 9, p. e0239699, 2020.

[26] L. E. C. Rocha and N. Masuda, "Individual-Based Approach to Epidemic Processes on Arbitrary Dynamic Contact Networks," *Scientific Reports*, vol. 6, no. 31456, pp. 1–10, 2016.
[27] H. P. M. Melo, A. A. Moreira, E. Batista, H. A. Makse, and J. S. Andrade Jr, "Statistical Signs of Social Influence on Suicides," *Scientific Reports*, vol. 4, no. 6239, pp. 1–5, 2014.
[28] J. Lobo, L. M. A. Bettencourt, D. Strumsky, and G. B. West, "Urban scaling and the production function for cities," *PLoS ONE*, vol. 8, no. 3, p. e58407, 2013.
[29] D. Sornette, T. Maillart, and G. Ghezzi, "How Much is the Whole Really More Than the Sum of Its Parts 1 + 1 = 2.5: Superlinear Productivity in Collective Group Actions," *PLoS ONE*, vol. 9, no. 8, p. e103023, 2014.
[30] F. Zarei, J. Ryckebusch, K. Schoors, and L. E. C. Rocha, "Social Network Heterogeneity Benefits Individuals at the Expense of Groups in the Creation of Innovation," *Journal of Physics: Complexity*, vol. 3, p. 045002, 2022.
[31] N. A. Christakis and J. H. Fowler, "The Spread of Obesity in a Large Social Network over 32 Years," *New England Journal of Medicine*, vol. 357, pp. 370–379, 2007.
[32] N. A. Christakis and J. H. Fowler, "The Collective Dynamics of Smoking in a Large Social Network," *New England Journal of Medicine*, vol. 358, pp. 2249–2258, 2008.
DOI: 10.1056/NEJMsa0706154

17 A framework of multi-scaling allometric analysis for city development

Yanguang Chen

17.1 Introduction

Allometric growth law is an important scaling law for understanding urban development. Allometric scaling relations can be found everywhere in urban studies. With the aid of fractal theory [1] and general system theory [2], I proposed a multi-scaling allometric analysis (MSA) method for evaluating city development [3–5]. As far as mathematical process is concerned, this method bears an analogy with the analytical hierarchy process (AHP) developed by Saaty [6, 7]. The essential difference between MSA and AHP is as follows: the former is based on the scaling exponent matrix coming from objective allometric analysis, while the latter is based on a pairwise comparison matrix resulting from subjective consideration and thinking of decision-makers.

Urban systems are complex networks with a hierarchical structure. An urban system can be divided into two levels. One is a system of cities (urban network) belonging to interurban geography, and the other is a city as a system (city system) belonging to intraurban geography [8,9]. Two postulates should be stated as follows. First, the allometric growth law dominates any pair of cities (city pair) in a system of cities or any pair of elements in a city by a given measure, Q. Although the urban allometric scaling relations in the real world may partly degenerate, it can be approximately treated as allometric relation. Second, any element of the system undergoes nonnegative growth in the mass, i.e., $\mathrm{d}Q/\mathrm{d}t \geq 0$, where t denotes time. Thus the scaling exponents are positive forever. Although real urban growth may partly retrogress, the allometric relations will be acceptable if the time series can be fitted to an increasing function, namely, take on monotonic increasing curves. Based on these postulates, the model and method are constructed as follows.

17.2 Model and method

Suppose there is a city as systems, or a system of cities, with n elements. For a city, the elements may be population, land use, roads, etc.; for a system of cities, the elements are cities and towns. For simplicity of expression, let's examine a system of cities consisting of n cities. We can quantify the system by making a measurement. For example, we can describe the size of each city by population in different years. If the system of cities follows the allometric scaling law, we have

DOI: 10.4324/9781003288312-19

$$Q_i = \beta_j Q_j^{\alpha_{ij}} = \beta_j Q_j^{D_{(i)}/D_{(j)}} \tag{17.1}$$

where Q_i, Q_j refer to two time series of some measurements of cities i and j, β_j to the proportionality coefficient, α_{ij} to an allometric scaling exponent, and $D_{(i)}$ and $D_{(j)}$ to the generalized fractal dimension of Q_i and Q_j, respectively. According to the principle of dimension consistency [1,10,11], we have

$$\alpha_{ij} = \frac{D_{(i)}}{D_{(j)}} \tag{17.2}$$

This is the dimension equation based on the allometric growth of an urban system [3]. If the relation between each pair of cities follows the allometric scaling law, Equation (17.1), we can make an allometric scaling exponent (ASE) matrix such as

$$\mathbf{M} = \left[\alpha_{ij}\right]_{n\times n} = \begin{bmatrix} \alpha_{11} & \alpha_{12} & \cdots & \alpha_{1n} \\ \alpha_{21} & \alpha_{22} & \cdots & \alpha_{2n} \\ \vdots & \vdots & \cdots & \vdots \\ \alpha_{n1} & \alpha_{n2} & \cdots & \alpha_{nn} \end{bmatrix} = \left[D_{(i)} / D_{(j)}\right]_{n\times n} \tag{17.3}$$

where $\mathbf{M}$ denotes the scaling exponent matrix (SEM), and n, the number of elements in the system. Allometric scaling exponent is actually a share coefficient [2]. In this sense, the ASE values reflect the sizes of the share space of an element in a geographical system [3]. In theory, the relationships of ASEs are as below

$$\alpha_{ii} = \alpha_{jj} = 1, \alpha_{ij} = 1/\alpha_{ji}, \alpha_{ij} = \alpha_{is} / \alpha_{js} \tag{17.4}$$

where $i, j, s = 1, 2, \cdots, n$. This suggests that $\mathbf{M}$ is a positive reciprocal matrix. Suppose that the fractal dimensions of cities form a vector in the form

$$\mathbf{D} = \left[D_{(1)} \quad D_{(2)} \quad \cdots \quad D_{(n)}\right]^{\mathrm{T}} \tag{17.5}$$

Apparently, multiplying $\mathbf{M}$ on the right by $\mathbf{D}$ yields $n\mathbf{D}$, namely

$$\mathbf{MD} = \begin{bmatrix} D_1/D_1 & D_1/D_2 & \cdots & D_1/D_n \\ D_2/D_1 & D_2/D_2 & \cdots & D_2/D_n \\ \vdots & \vdots & \cdots & \vdots \\ D_n/D_1 & D_n/D_2 & \cdots & D_n/D_n \end{bmatrix} \begin{bmatrix} D_1 \\ D_2 \\ \vdots \\ D_n \end{bmatrix} = n \begin{bmatrix} D_1 \\ D_2 \\ \vdots \\ D_n \end{bmatrix} = n\mathbf{D} \tag{17.6}$$

which is a scaling relation of fractal dimension matrix. This implies that **D** is just one of the eigenvectors of $\mathbf{M}=\mathbf{D}\mathbf{D}^{*\mathrm{T}}$, and $n=\mathbf{D}^{\mathrm{T}}\mathbf{D}^{*}$, the maximum eigenvalue corresponding to **D**. Here $\mathbf{D}^{*}$ represents the reciprocal vector of fractal dimension values, that is $\mathbf{D}^{*}=[1/D_{(1)}, 1/D_{(2)},\ldots, 1/D_{(n)}]^{\mathrm{T}}$.

In theory, we can evaluate **D** and thus evaluate city development. However, in many cases, it is hard to estimate values of $D_{(i)}$ or $D_{(j)}$. On the other hand, the ratio of $D_{(i)}$ to $D_{(j)}$ is easier to work out and more important in the practice of urban analysis [12,13]. After all, the value of a measurement, including fractal dimension, rests with comparison and relation. The allometric scaling exponent is just the ratio of fractal dimension. Therefore, we can calculate the α_{ij} values rather than $D_{(i)}$ and $D_{(j)}$ values for application.

In order to evaluate the scaling exponent, we must solve the equation (M – n**I**)**A**=0. The equation has a nontrivial solution if and only if n is an eigenvalue of **A**, in that case the determinant of (**M** – n**I**) vanishes. It is clear that all the eigenvalues except one are zero. Here **M** has unit rank because every row is a constant multiple of the first row. As we known, the sum of the eigenvalues equals the trace of **M**. This implies that n is the maximum and unique eigenvalue of **M** and we have a nontrivial solution consisting of positive entries. In short, based on the second postulate given above, all the elements of matrix **M** are nonnegative numbers. According to the positive matrix theory, the matrix **M** has a nonnegative largest eigenvalue $\lambda_{\max}=n$ since it conforms to the rule defined by Equation (17.4). If the urban system follows the laws of allometric growth completely, the goodness of fit of the double logarithmic linear regression, R^2, is close to 1 in theory. For a perfect fit, we have

$$\lambda_{\max}=\sum_{i=1}^{n}\lambda_i=\sum_{i=1}^{n}\alpha_{ii}=\sum_{i=1}^{n}D_{(i)}/D_{(i)}=n \tag{17.7}$$

where λ_i denotes the ith eigenvalue.

17.3 Application to four cities of China

17.3.1 Algorithm and results

The MSA method can be used to evaluate city development and generate a rank of the relative growth potential for cities or elements of a city. As a teaching example, the four municipalities directly under the Central Government of China, Beijing (BJ), Tianjin (TJ), Shanghai (SH), and Chongqing (CQ), are employed to make a case study (Figure 17.1). The basic measurement is gross regional product (GRP) (Table 17.1). It is not difficult to estimate the allometric scaling exponent value of any pair of cities by using Equation (17.1). Thus, step by step, the values of entries in the upper triangular matrix (UTM) of the scaling exponent matrix (SEM) and goodness of fit (GOF) can be given. The GOFs form a symmetric matrix and the

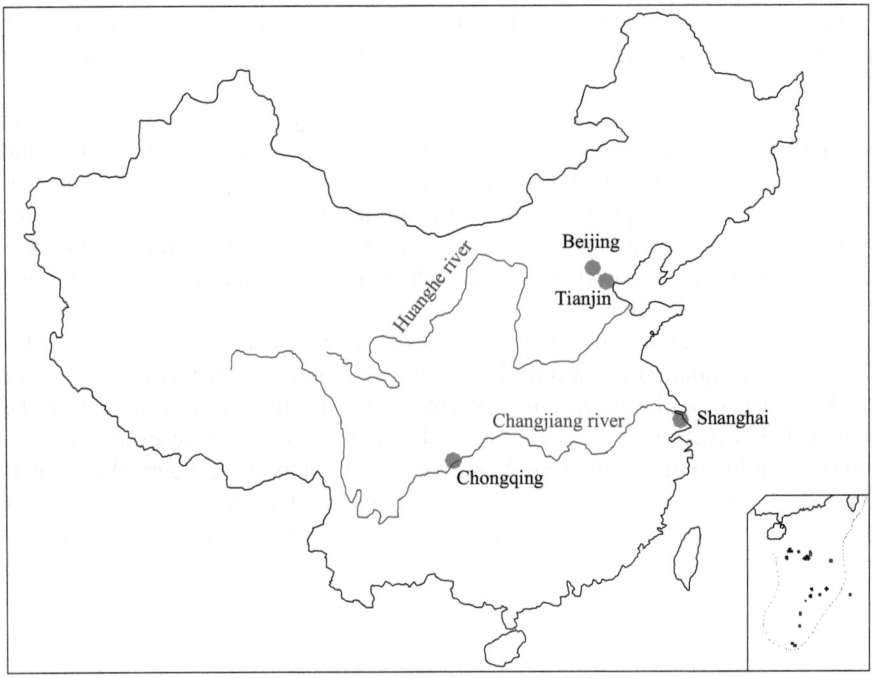

Figure 17.1 A sketch map for the geographical locations of the four municipalities directly under the Central Government of China.

lower triangular matrix (LTM) can be created by transposing it. As for the LTM of SEM, the entries can be evaluated by Equation (17.4) in theory. However, in empirical analysis, it should be given by [4]

$$\widehat{\alpha}_{ji} = R_{ij}^2 / \widehat{\alpha}_{ij} \tag{17.8}$$

where R_{ij}^2 denotes GOFs, i.e., the correlation coefficient square for the allometric scaling relation between cities i and j, and the hat "^" suggests the values come from estimation. The scaling relations of city pairs are displayed in Figure 17.2, and the ASE and GOF matrices are shown in Table 17.2. Using Matlab or Mathcad, we can find the maximum eigenvalue, λ_{max}, and the corresponding normalized eigenvector, **W**, which is given by

$$\widehat{W}_i = \widehat{D}_{(i)} / \sqrt{\sum_{i=1}^{n} \widehat{D}_{(i)}^2} \tag{17.9}$$

For convenience, we can write a Matlab program to calculate the eigenvalue and eigenvector. The Matlab function is **[W, n]** = eig(**M**).

Table 17.1 The gross regional product (GRP) of four Chinese municipalities (1998–2018).

Unit: 100 millions yuan

Year	*Beijing*	*Tianjin*	*Shanghai*	*Chongqing*
1998	2816.818	1463.445	3994.190	1630.671
1999	3045.308	1587.933	4369.718	1688.230
2000	3471.477	1795.232	4928.734	1813.309
2001	3985.302	2015.059	5361.584	1996.347
2002	4499.366	2246.187	5857.495	2249.095
2003	5219.790	2692.410	6830.032	2568.725
2004	6296.744	3248.995	8236.599	3043.394
2005	6969.520	3905.640	9247.660	3467.720
2006	8117.780	4462.740	10,572.240	3907.230
2007	9846.810	5252.760	12,494.010	4676.130
2008	11,115.000	6719.010	14,069.860	5793.660
2009	12,153.030	7521.850	15,046.450	6530.010
2010	14,113.580	9224.460	17,165.980	7925.580
2011	16,251.930	11,307.280	19,195.690	10,011.370
2012	17,879.400	12,893.880	20,181.720	11,409.600
2013	19,800.810	14,442.010	21,818.150	12,783.260
2014	21,330.830	15,726.930	23,567.700	14,262.600
2015	23,014.590	16,538.190	25,123.450	15,717.270
2016	25,669.130	17,885.390	28,178.650	17,740.590
2017	28,014.940	18,549.190	30,632.990	19,424.730
2018	30,319.980	18,809.640	32,679.870	20,363.190
Mean	13,044.3874	8489.9158	15,216.7986	8047.7481
Stdev	8844.3701	6371.8483	9180.3043	6374.8384

Source: National Bureau of Statistics of China, available from: www.stats.gov.cn/tjsj/ndsj/.

The simple approach to estimating the eigenvector and the maximum eigenvalue of SEM is the geometric averaging method. The calculating process can be outlined as below. The first step is to calculate the geometric mean by row. The formula and results are

$$\widehat{\mathbf{W}} = \left(\prod_{j=1}^{n} \alpha_{ij}\right)^{1/n} = \begin{bmatrix} 0.9600 & 1.1181 & 0.8445 & 1.0898 \end{bmatrix}^{\mathrm{T}} \tag{17.11}$$

which represents the eigenvector. The second step is to normalize the entries in the eigenvector. That is

$$\widehat{\mathbf{w}} = \widehat{\mathbf{W}} / \sum_{i=1}^{n} W_i = \begin{bmatrix} 0.2393 & 0.2787 & 0.2105 & 0.2716 \end{bmatrix}^{\mathrm{T}} \tag{17.12}$$

which gives the numerical values of evaluating the cities. The third step is to compute the maximum eigenvalue. The formula and result are

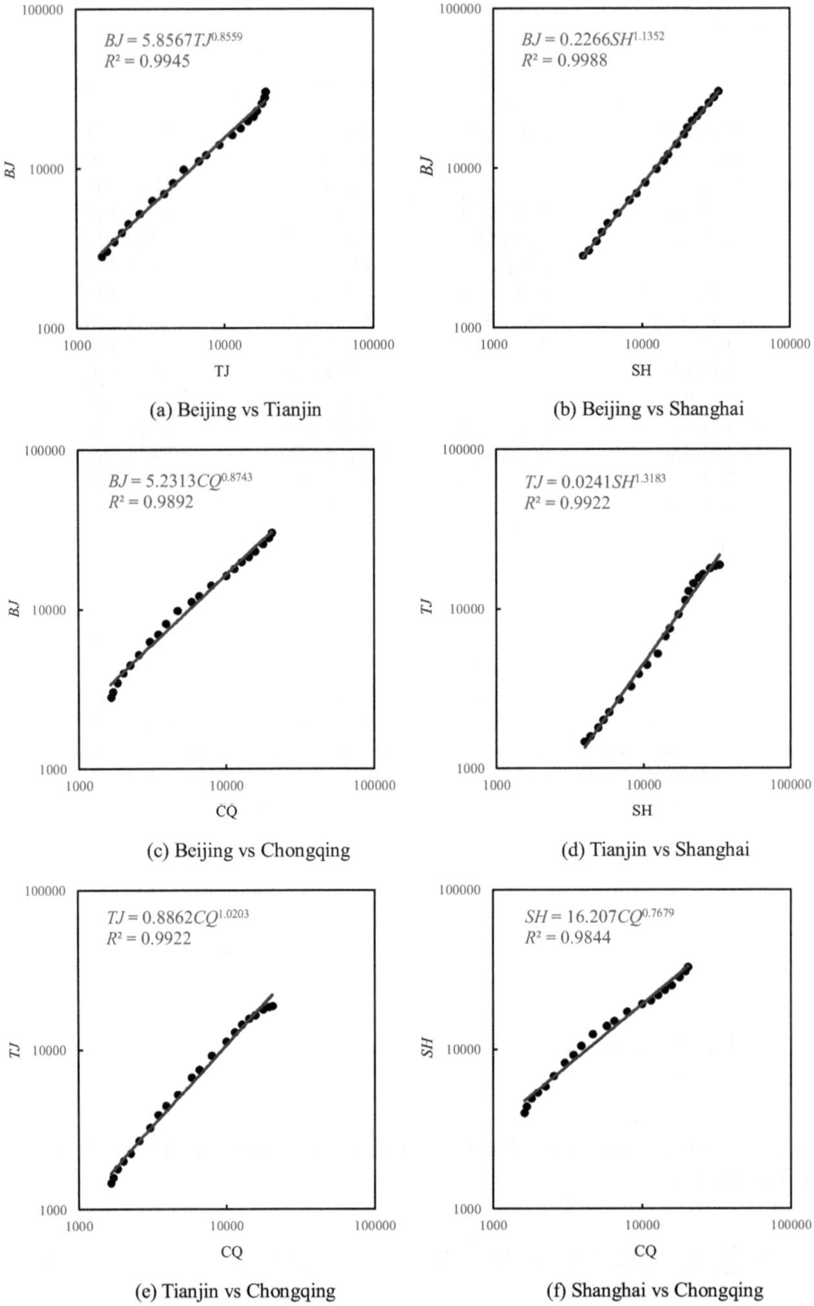

Figure 17.2 The allometric scaling relations between cities of China in terms of GRP (1998–2018).

Note: The numerical unit of the coordinate axes is "100 millions *yuan* (RMB)".

Table 17.2 The matrices of allometric scaling exponents and corresponding values of goodness of fit.

City	*Allometric scaling exponent (ASE)*				*Goodness of fit (GOF)*			
	BJ	*TJ*	*SH*	*CQ*	*BJ*	*TJ*	*SH*	*CQ*
BJ	1	0.8559	1.1352	0.8743	1	0.9945	0.9988	0.9892
TJ	1.1620	1	1.3183	1.0203	0.9945	1	0.9922	0.9922
SH	0.8799	0.7527	1	0.7679	0.9988	0.9922	1	0.9844
CQ	1.1314	0.9724	1.2820	1	0.9892	0.9922	0.9844	1

Table 17.3 The matrices of allometric scaling exponents, geometric mean, and normalized eigenvector.

City	*BJ*	*TJ*	*SH*	*CQ*	*Geometric average*	*Eigenvector*	*ASI*
BJ	1	0.8559	1.1352	0.8743	0.9600	0.4757	0.2393
TJ	1.1620	1	1.3183	1.0203	1.1181	0.5541	0.2787
SH	0.8799	0.7527	1	0.7679	0.8445	0.4185	0.2105
CQ	1.1314	0.9724	1.2820	1	1.0898	0.5400	0.2716

$$\lambda_{\max} = \sum_{i=1}^{n} (\mathbf{M}^* \widehat{\mathbf{w}})_i = 3.9878 \tag{17.13}$$

where $\mathbf{M}^*$ refers to the matrix of allometric scaling exponents, as indicated above, and $\mathbf{w}$, to the normalized eigenvector (Table 17.3).

17.3.2 Tests

The process of allometric scaling analysis is based on the following postulate: each pair of elements in an urban system follows the allometric scaling law. Due to spatial heterogeneity, which results in space-time translational asymmetry of geographical mathematical laws, we cannot guarantee that any pair of elements in a city or cities in a network always absolutely follows the allometric growth law (Figure 17.2). Therefore, it is necessary to make tests before implementing the evaluation of city development. The allometric scaling exponent matrix bears an analogy with the pairwise comparison matrix of the analytical hierarchical process (AHP) of Saaty [6,7]. So the test of AHP for positive reciprocal matrix consistency can be employed to carry out basic evaluation for the model. Defining a scaling consistency index (SCI) [3,4], we have

$$SCI = \frac{|\lambda_{\max} - n|}{n-1} = 0.0041 \tag{17.14}$$

According to Saaty [7], for $n = 4$, the random consistency index (RCI) is RCI = 0.9040. Thus, the scaling consistency ratio (SCR) is SCR = SCI/RCI = 0.0045 < <0.1. The result is satisfying and the allometric scaling exponent matrix passed the consistency test.

The second test is to make use of the matrix of goodness of fit (GOF). The average correlation coefficient is

$$R^* = \left[\frac{1}{n(n-1)}\left(\sum_{i=1}^{n} R_{ij}^2 - n\right)\right]^{1/2} = 0.9959 \quad (17.15)$$

Then, input the formula "=((FINV(α, 1, $T-2$)/($T-2$))/(1 + FINV(α, 1, $T-2$)/($T-2$)))^0.5" into any cell in a sheet of Microsoft Excel, we can gain the critical value of R^*. For example, for significance level $a = 0.05$ and degree of freedom (DOF) df = $T - 2 = 19$, we should input the following formula "= ((FINV(0.05,1,19)/19)/(1+FINV(0.05,1,19)/19))^0.5" in a cell. Pressing the enter key gives $R_c^* = 0.4329$. Since $R^* = 0.9959 >> 0.4329$, the GOF matrix passes the test.

17.3.3 Evaluation

The average value of GRP within the 21 years can be employed to describe the absolute level of economic development, while the allometric scaling indexes, i.e., ASE, can be used to characterize the relative level and future potential of city development. Where absolute level is concerned, Shanghai is higher than Beijing, which is in turn higher than Tianjin, and Chongqing is at the bottom of the ranking. Where relative level is concerned, Tianjin is the best one, the next is Chongqing. Beijing is higher than Shanghai, and Shanghai is the most lagging (Figure 17.3). Comparatively speaking, on the whole, Tianjin has a larger share space to develop in future.

17.4 Conclusion remarks

By analogy, MSA can be applied to intraurban development. The same method can be used to evaluate the relative potential of different industrial sections in a city. For example, we can rank the development of the primary industry, secondary industry, and tertiary industry of a city such as Beijing. If we adopt different variables (say population, transport, greenbelt) to carry out MSA on cities as systems and systems of cities, we can develop a multilevel comprehensive evolution framework with cascade structure based on allometric scaling law for city development.

Acknowledgments

This research was sponsored by the National Natural Science Foundation of China (Grant No. 42171192). The support is gratefully acknowledged.

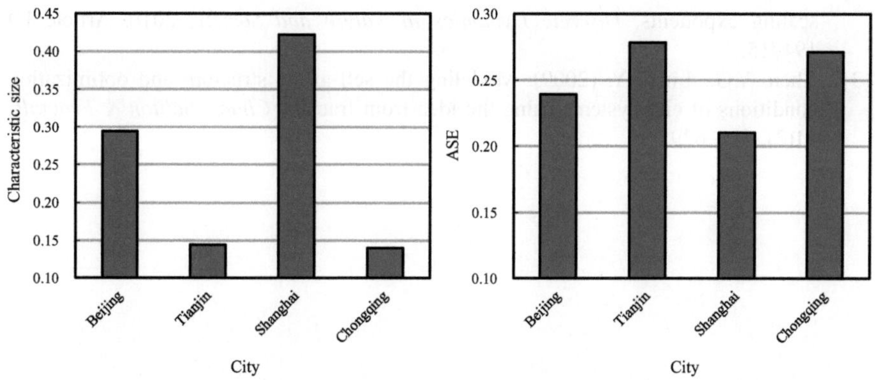

(a) Absolute development level (b) Relative development level

Figure 17.3 The absolute and relative development levels of the four China's cities measured by average GDP and dimension scale (1998–2018).

References

[1] Mandelbrot, B.B. (1982). *The Fractal Geometry of Nature*. New York: W. H. Freeman and Company.

[2] Bertalanffy, L. von. (1968). *General System Theory: Foundations, Development, and Applications*. New York: George Braziller.

[3] Chen, Y.G. (2008). *Fractal Urban Systems: Scaling, Symmetry, and Spatial Complexity*. Beijing: Science Press [In Chinese].

[4] Chen, Y.G. (2017). Multi-scaling allometric analysis for urban and regional development. *Physica A*, 465, 673–689.

[5] Chen, Y.G., Jiang, S.G. (2009). An analytical process of the spatio-temporal evolution of urban systems based on allometric and fractal ideas. *Chaos, Soliton & Fractals*, 39(1), 49–64.

[6] Saaty, T.L. (1999). *Decision Making for Leaders: The Analytic Hierarchy Process for Decisions in a Complex World*. Pittsburgh: RWS Publications.

[7] Saaty, T.L. (2008). Relative measurement and its generalization in decision making: Why pairwise comparisons are central in mathematics for the measurement of intangible factors. *RACSAM*, 102(2), 251–318.

[8] Batty, M., Longley, P.A. (1994). *Fractal Cities: A Geometry of Form and Function*. London: Academic Press.

[9] Berry, B.L.J. (1964). Cities as systems within systems of cities. *Papers of the Regional Science Association*, 13, 147–163.

[10] Lee, Y. (1989). An allmetric analysis of the US urban system: 1960–80. *Environment and Planning A*, 21(4), 463–476.

[11] Takayasu, H. (1990). *Fractals in the Physical Sciences*. Manchester: Manchester University Press.

[12] Chen, Y.G. (2010). Characterizing growth and form of fractal cities with allometric scaling exponents. *Discrete Dynamics in Nature and Society*, 2010, Article ID 194715.

[13] Chen, Y.G., Lin, J.Y. (2009). Modeling the self-affine structure and optimization conditions of city systems using the idea from fractals. *Chaos, Soliton & Fractals*, 41(2), 615–629.

18 Urban scaling law of the COVID-19 epidemic in the United Kingdom

Gang Xu, Siyuan Zhang, and Limin Jiao

18.1 Introduction

Human activity is increasingly concentrated in urban areas, with projections indicating that the world's urban population could reach more than 90% by the end of the century [1]. In addition to increasing urbanization, we are living in an unprecedentedly interconnected and highly mobile world [2]. Cities are typically complex systems, and urban systems consisting of multiple cities are also complex systems [3–5]. Cities are based on extensive and intense face-to-face socioeconomic interactions [6]. Many measurable attributes of cities are mediated by socioeconomic interactions and are influenced by the well-known population size effect.

The idea that population size affects different urban indicators has been extensively studied and can be summarized by the city size theory [4,5,7,8]. This theory suggests that urban indicators and urban population can be measured by a scaling law [7,9,10]. The mathematical form of the scaling law of the urban system is a power function ($Y = Y_0N^\beta$), where Y is the urban indicator, N is the population size, and β is known as the scaling exponent [8]. According to the relationship between β and 1, urban indicators can be divided into three categories: (1) social interaction type indicators have a superlinear scaling relationship with population sizes ($\beta > 1$), e.g., economic output, infectious diseases [11]; the scaling exponent of these urban indicators is around 1.15. (2) Infrastructure type indicators have a sublinear scaling relationship ($\beta < 1$) with population size, e.g., roads, length of pipe networks, etc. [12]; the scaling exponent of such urban indicators is around 0.85 [8]. (3) Individual demand type indicators have a linear scaling relationship with population size, such as residential electricity consumption.

The spread of infectious diseases cannot be separated from human interactions, which increases superlinearly with the size of the urban population [13]. Although some exceptions exist [14], non-infectious diseases (e.g., diabetes) are typically less prevalent in large cities, whereas infectious diseases (e.g., AIDS) are relatively more common in large urban areas. This differential behavior may reflect the fact that infectious diseases are more prevalent in large cities [14,15]. This has been demonstrated in the early epidemic case growth of AIDS [16]. It has also been found that the number of infectious diseases such as HIV, influenza, and dengue

DOI: 10.4324/9781003288312-20

fever in the United States, Brazil, and Sweden has a superlinear scaling relationship with urban population size [14].

The COVID-19 epidemic has been spreading globally for more than 2 years. The United Nations report (2020) states that more than 90% of global COVID-19 cases are from cities, while the global urban population share in 2020 is only 56% [17]. Cities are breeding grounds for the growth and spread of COVID-19 [18]. The COVID-19 pandemic poses an unprecedented health and economic threat to our society, and understanding its transmission patterns may find important factors to mitigate or control the epidemic [19]. In this context, studies have confirmed a scaling relationship between COVID-19 cases and urban population size [20,21]. Analyses based on data from the United States, Brazil, and Germany have pointed out that large cities have a higher per capita exposure rate, which in turn exacerbates the COVID-19 epidemic in large cities [22]. Also, studies have shown that large cities in the United States experienced more pronounced growth rates during the first weeks of the introduction of COVID-19 cases [23]. Therefore, large cities need to respond faster to new infectious diseases, which would help to curb the spread of the epidemic and spillover spread in large cities [6,23].

Although there is a consensus that there is a scaling relationship between the number of infectious disease cases and population size, it can be expected that there should be a superlinear scaling relationship between confirmed COVID-19 cases and urban population size. However, government interventions have led to multiple and reciprocal fluctuations in urban social interaction [24], in this context of the dynamic development of COVID-19, the quantitative relationship between the number of COVID-19 cases and urban population size remains unclear, and the evolutionary characteristics and spatial variation of the scaling exponent over time are unclear.

18.2 Methods

Here, we obtained daily COVID-19 confirmed cases and deaths from March 1, 2020, to August 31, 2020, for 380 lower tier local authorities in the UK and 2020 population data for each region (https://coronavirus.data.gov.uk/) to explore the scaling law of COVID-19 cases and city size and their evolution over time.

Scaling laws are power law relationships of the form:

$$Y = Y_0 N^{\beta} \tag{18.1}$$

Y in equation (18.1) is the cumulative cases/deaths of COVID-19 at the county unit up to a certain date, N is the urban population size, Y_0 and β are parameters, where β is the scaling exponent [25].

Taking the base logarithm of 10 for both sides of equation (18.1) simultaneously, we obtain:

$$lgY = \beta \cdot lgN + lgY_0 \tag{18.2}$$

Equation (18.2) is a linear function. After taking the logarithm of cases/deaths and population size, a linear function is fitted and the slope of the fitted straight line is the scaling exponent (β), which is denoted as β_{case} and β_{death}, respectively. Although other nonlinear fitting methods are also available [26,27], linear fitting is widely used in scaling law fitting because of its simplicity and ease of operation [28,29]. In this study, we set at least 10 lower tier local authorities where COVID-19 cases/deaths existed and the scaling exponent obtained from the fit was recorded as a valid value only when the adjusted R^2 of the double log linear fitting equation was greater than 0.3. This study focused on the magnitude of β versus 1 and its temporal variation.

18.3 Results

18.3.1 Spatio-temporal variations of the COVID-19 epidemic

The daily and 7-day averagely added COVID-19 cases/deaths in the UK are shown in Figure 18.1. The period we have chosen is the complete first wave of the COVID-19 epidemic in the UK from March 1, 2020, to August 31, 2020. Daily added COVID-19 cases remained high for about 1 month before they started to

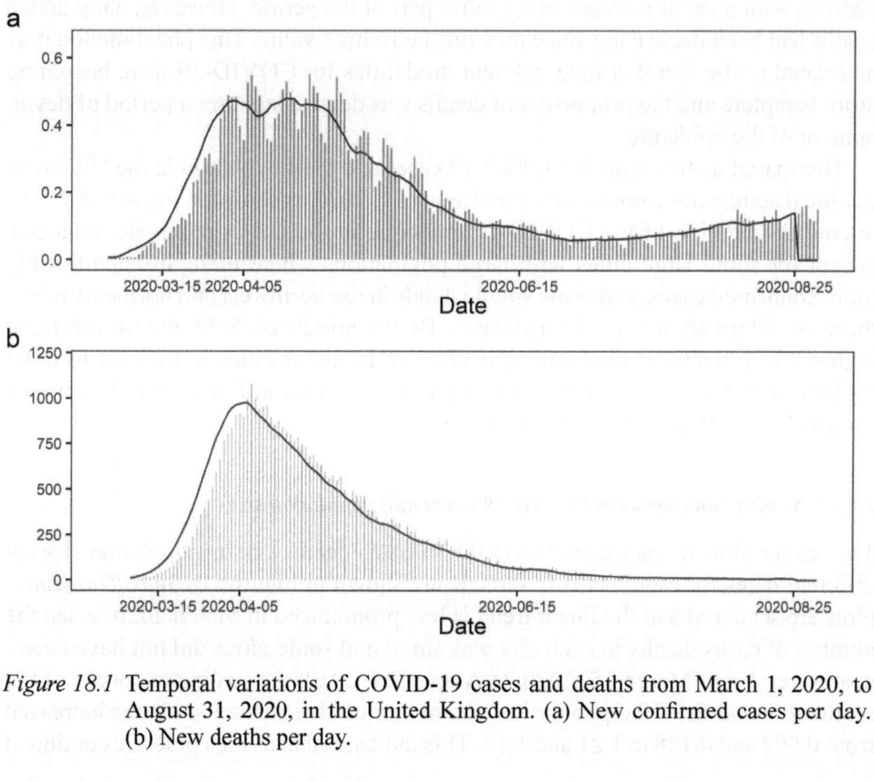

Figure 18.1 Temporal variations of COVID-19 cases and deaths from March 1, 2020, to August 31, 2020, in the United Kingdom. (a) New confirmed cases per day. (b) New deaths per day.

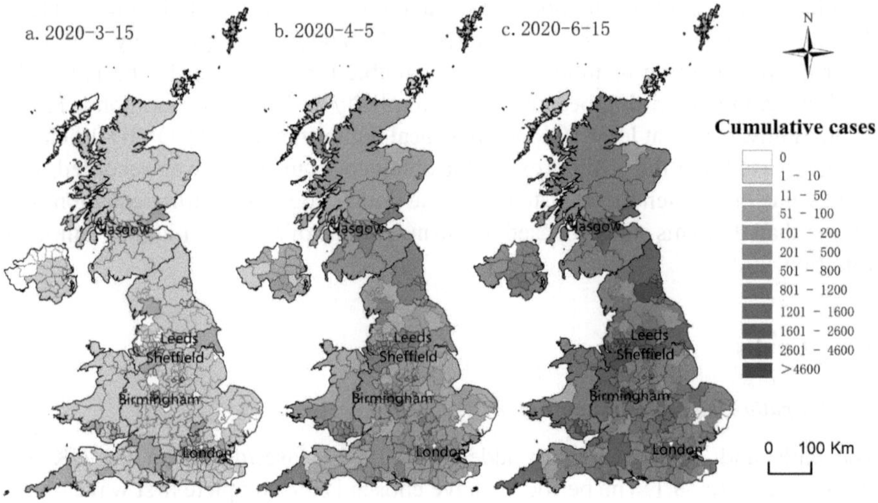

Figure 18.2 Spatial distributions of COVID-19 cases at three representative dates in the United Kingdom.

decline, with a small increase in the latter part of the period. However, daily added deaths had been decreasing since they reached a high value. This phenomenon may be related to the fact that the treatment modalities for COVID-19 were becoming more complete and the proportion of deaths was decreasing after a period of development of the epidemic.

The spatial distribution of COVID-19 cases and their evolution in the UK lower tier local authorities from March 1 to August 31, 2020, is shown in Figure 18.2. The overall distribution of the COVID-19 epidemic in the UK is relatively balanced, except for some large cities with large populations where there are significantly more confirmed cases, and some small islands in the northwest and northeast where there are relatively few confirmed cases. By the middle of 2020, the overall trend is that the epidemic is gradually spreading from major cities in the east to other regions, with the most serious outbreaks in major cities in England and Scotland, such as Leeds, Birmingham, and Glasgow.

18.3.2 Scaling laws between COVID-19 cases and population sizes

The scatter plots of cumulative COVID-19 cases/deaths versus population sizes at different dates for each LTLA in the UK are shown in Figures 18.3a,b. The scatter plots are scattered and the linear trend is less pronounced in March 2020, when the number of cases/deaths in each city was small and some cities did not have cases/deaths yet. From March 15, 2020, to August 25, 2020, the scaling exponent of the scattered linear fit of the population size of cumulative cases and deaths increased from 0.997 and 0.148 to 1.21 and 1.15. This indicates that as the epidemic continued

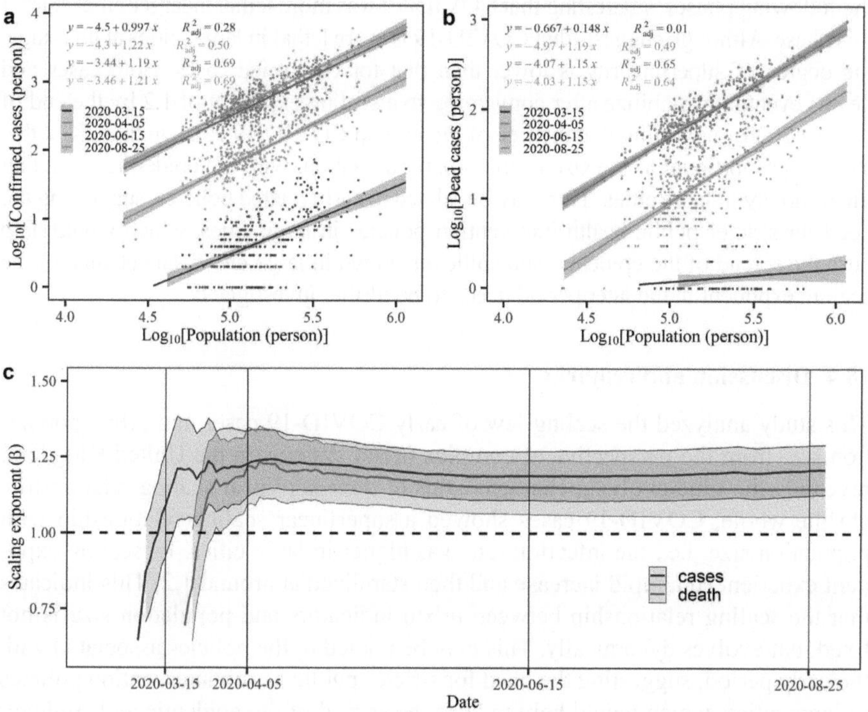

Figure 18.3 Scaling laws of the COVID-19 epidemic in the United Kingdom. (a) Scaling laws of COVID-19 cases and population. (b) Scaling laws of COVID-19 deaths and population. (c) Temporal variations of scaling exponents of COVID-19 cases and deaths from March 1, 2020, to August 31, 2020.

to develop, the number of cases/deaths in each city increased, and the scattered linear trend increased and eventually became superlinear.

Figure 18.3c shows the temporal trend of the scaling exponent of COVID-19 cases/deaths in the UK, with the 95% confidence interval of the estimated scaling exponent shaded in gray. Early in the epidemic β_{case} is less than 1, when the scaling relationship between the spread of the COVID-19 epidemic and population size is not evident and the scaling effect of higher incidence of infectious diseases in large cities is not yet apparent. Subsequently, the β_{case} rose rapidly and exceeded 1. From April to August 2020, the β_{case} stabilized at around 1.2, showing a superlinear relationship, and the scaling effect of higher incidence of COVID-19 epidemic in large cities was very obvious at this time.

The time series changes in the UK COVID-19 mortality scaling exponent followed roughly the same trend as the confirmed case scaling exponent, but the information flowing from the values at certain stages was not the same. β_{case} also underwent a rapid rise and continued to stabilize at around 1.15 (Figure 18.3c). The rise in β_{death} lagged behind that of β_{case}, which rose rapidly in the second phase of the epidemic, whereas

β_{case} rose rapidly to about 1.15 in the third phase of the epidemic and remained stable in the following phases, suggesting that COVID-19 was more lethal in larger cities during this phase. Although suggests that COVID-19 is more lethal in larger cities at this stage, the degree of superlinearity is lower than that for confirmed cases. Both cases and deaths eventually stabilize after converging to a scaling exponent of 1.2 by the end of August 2020, suggesting that the rate of increase in COVID-19 cases in the UK at this stage is proportional to the size of the urban population, with the epidemic spreading more rapidly in large cities. This may be related to early related policies, suggesting the need for stricter public health intervention policies in large cities, which would help curb the spread of the epidemic and spillover spread in large cities. The change of the scaling exponent in the later period needs to be further investigated.

18.4 Discussion and remarks

This study analyzed the scaling law of early COVID-19 cases and urban population size from the perspective of complex urban systems in the United Kingdom, revealing the time-evolving characteristics of their nonlinear scaling relationship. On the whole, COVID-19 cases showed a superlinear scaling relationship with population size, i.e., the infection rate was higher in large cities. Its scaling exponent experienced a rapid increase and then stabilized at around 1.2. This indicates that the scaling relationship between urban indicators and population size is not fixed, but evolves dynamically. This may be related to the policies associated with the early period, suggesting the need for stricter public health intervention policies in large cities, which would help to curb the spread of the epidemic and spillover spread in large cities. The change of scaling exponent in the later period needs to be further investigated. This study uses the scaling law theory to reveal the scale effect of COVID-19 epidemic spread, and the discovery of the scaling exponent time evolution pattern also enriches the theory of urban scaling law, which is an interactive combination of practice and theory.

This superlinear relationship is not expected to persist in the later stages of the pandemic, as non-pharmacological interventions such as travel restrictions were commonly implemented in cities across countries after the COVID-19 epidemic [30,31]. When mitigation measures are implemented, social distance and blockades can disrupt social networks in cities, especially by reducing contact, which can affect transmission rates [6]. In conclusion, the COVID-19 epidemic is still evolving and these observations can inform national, regional, and local responses to the evolving COVID-19 epidemic and contribute to the development of future response plans for novel infectious diseases. First, large cities need to be able to act more quickly to contain the surge in cases, and large cities need to respond faster, which may include some policies that work [32,33]. Second, social distancing policies and other actions in response to a pandemic should take into account the nonlinear effects of city size on COVID-19 transmission [19,22,23,34]. In the future, we need to integrate epidemic prevention and control measures, vaccination levels, and virus transmission attributes to uncover the driving mechanisms of the temporal evolution of the epidemic scaling exponent and reveal the synergistic evolution of the scaling exponent of cases and deaths.

References

[1] Jiang, L. W., & O'Neill, B. C. (2017). Global urbanization projections for the Shared Socioeconomic Pathways. *Global Environmental Change-Human and Policy Dimensions*, 42, 193–199. doi: 10.1016/j.gloenvcha.2015.03.008

[2] International Civil Aviation Organization. (Civil Aviation Statistics of the World and ICAO staff estimates.

[3] Berry, B. J. (1964). Cities as systems within systems of cities. *Papers of the Regional Science Association*, 1(13), 146–163.

[4] Michael, B. (2013). *The New Science of Cities*: Cambridge: MIT Press.

[5] West, G. (2017). *Scale: The Universal Laws of Growth, Innovation, Sustainability, and the Pace of Life in Organisms, Cities, Economies, and Companies*: New York: Penguin.

[6] Angel, S., & Blei, A. (2021). Why pandemics, such as COVID-19, require a metropolitan response. *Sustainability*, 13(1). doi: 10.3390/su13010079

[7] Bettencourt, L. (2013). The origins of scaling in cities. *Science*, 340(6139), 1438–1441. doi: 10.1126/science.1235823

[8] Bettencourt, L., Lobo, J., Helbing, D., Kuhnert, C., & West, G. B. (2007). Growth, innovation, scaling, and the pace of life in cities. *Proceedings of the National Academy of Sciences of the United States of America*, 104(17), 7301–7306. doi: 10.1073/pnas.0610172104

[9] Bettencourt, L., & West, G. (2010). A unified theory of urban living. *Nature*, 467(7318), 912–913. doi: DOI 10.1038/467912a

[10] Li, R. Q., Dong, L., Zhang, J., Wang, X. R., Wang, W. X., Di, Z. R.,... Stanley, H. E. (2017). Simple spatial scaling rules behind complex cities. *Nature Communications*, 8. doi: 10.1038/s41467-017-01882-w

[11] Lei, W. Q., Jiao, L. M., Xu, G., & Zhou, Z. Z. (2022). Urban scaling in rapidly urbanising China. *Urban Studies*, 59(9), 1889–1908. doi: 10.1177/00420980211017817

[12] Xu, G., Xu, Z. B., Gu, Y. Y., Lei, W. Q., Pan, Y. P., Liu, J.,... Jiao, L. M. (2020). Scaling laws in intra-urban systems and over time at the district level in Shanghai, China. *Physica A-Statistical Mechanics and its Applications*, 560. doi: 10.1016/j.physa.2020.125162

[13] Schlapfer, M., Bettencourt, L., Grauwin, S., Raschke, M., Claxton, R., Smoreda, Z.,... Ratti, C. (2014). The scaling of human interactions with city size. *Journal of the Royal Society Interface*, 11(98). doi: 10.1098/rsif.2013.0789

[14] Rocha, L., Thorson, A. E., & Lambiotte, R. (2015). The non-linear health consequences of living in larger cities. *Journal of Urban Health-Bulletin of the New York Academy of Medicine*, 92(5), 785–799. doi: 10.1007/s11524-015-9976-x

[15] Tizzoni, M., Sun, K. Y., Benusiglio, D., Karsai, M., & Perra, N. (2015). The scaling of human contacts and epidemic processes in metapopulation networks. *Scientific Reports*, 5. doi: 10.1038/srep15111

[16] Antonio, F. J., de Picoli, S., Teixeira, J., & Mendes, R. D. (2014). Growth patterns and scaling laws governing AIDS epidemic in Brazilian cities. *PLOS ONE*, 9(10). doi: 10.1371/journal.pone.0111015

[17] United Nations. (2020). *Policy Brief: COVID-19 in an Urban World.*

[18] Acuto, M., Larcom, S., Keil, R., Ghojeh, M., Lindsay, T., Camponeschi, C.,... Parnell, S. (2020). Seeing COVID-19 through an urban lens. *Nature Sustainability*, 3(12), 977–978. doi: 10.1038/s41893-020-00620-3

[19] Ribeiro, H. V., Sunahara, A. S., Sutton, J., Perc, M., & Hanley, Q. S. (2020). City size and the spreading of COVID-19 in Brazil. *PLOS ONE*, 15(9). doi: 10.1371/journal.pone.0239699

[20] Lai, S. K., & Huang, J. Y. (2022). Why large cities are more vulnerable to the COVID-19 pandemic. *Journal of Urban Management*, 11(1), 1–5. doi: 10.1016/j.jum.2022.02.001

[21] Angel, S., & Blei, A. (2020). COVID-19 Thrives in larger cities, not denser ones. *Journal of Extreme Events*, 7(4).

[22] Cardoso, B. H., & Gonçalves, S. (2020). Urban scaling of COVID-19 epidemics. *arXiv:200507791.*

[23] Stier, A. J., Berman, M. G., & Bettencourt, L. M. A. (2021). Early pandemic COVID-19 case growth rates increase with city size. *npj Urban Sustainability*, 1(1), 1–6. doi: 10.1038/s42949-021-00030-0

[24] Sutton, J., Shahtahmassebi, G., Ribeiro, H. V., & Hanley, Q. S. (2022). Population density and spreading of COVID-19 in England and Wales. *PLOS ONE*, 17(3). doi: 10.1371/journal.pone.0261725

[25] Louf, R., & Barthelemy, M. (2014). Scaling: lost in the smog Commentary. *Environment and Planning B-Planning & Design*, 41(5), 767–769. doi: 10.1068/b4105c

[26] Leitao, J. C., Miotto, J. M., Gerlach, M., & Altmann, E. G. (2016). Is this scaling nonlinear? *Royal Society Open Science*, 3(7). doi: 10.1098/rsos.150649

[27] Xiao, Y. X., & Gong, P. (2022). Removing spatial autocorrelation in urban scaling analysis. *Cities*, 124. doi: 10.1016/j.cities.2022.103600

[28] Keuschnigg, M. (2019). Scaling trajectories of cities. *Proceedings of the National Academy of Sciences of the United States of America*, 116(28), 13759–13761. doi: 10.1073/pnas.1906258116

[29] Meirelles, J., Neto, C. R., Ferreira, F. F., Ribeiro, F. L., & Binder, C. R. (2018). Evolution of urban scaling: Evidence from Brazil. *PLOS ONE*, 13(10). doi: 10.1371/journal.pone.0204574

[30] Jia, J., Lu, X., Yuan, Y., Xu, G., Jia, J. M.,... Christakis, N. A. (2020). Population flow drives spatio-temporal distribution of COVID-19 in China. *Nature*, 582(7812), 389. doi: 10.1038/s41586-020-2284-y

[31] Tian, H. Y., Liu, Y. H., Li, Y. D., Wu, C. H., Chen, B., Kraemer, M.,... Dye, C. (2020). An investigation of transmission control measures during the first 50 days of the COVID-19 epidemic in China. *Science*, 368(6491), 638. doi: 10.1126/science.abb6105

[32] Gatto, M., Bertuzzo, E., Mari, L., Miccoli, S., Carraro, L., Casagrandi, R.,... Rinaldo, A. (2020). Spread and dynamics of the COVID-19 epidemic in Italy: Effects of emergency containment measures. *Proceedings of the National Academy of Sciences of the United States of America*, 117(19), 10484–10491. doi: 10.1073/pnas.2004978117

[33] Glaeser, E. L., Jin, G. Z., Leyden, B. T., & Luca, M. (2021). Learning from deregulation: The asymmetric impact of lockdown and reopening on risky behavior during COVID-19. *Journal of Regional Science*, 61(4), 696–709. doi: 10.1111/jors.12539

[34] Heroy, S. (2020). Metropolitan-scale COVID-19 outbreaks: How similar are they? *arXiv:200401248*

19 Scaling of urban income inequality in the USA[1]

Elisa Heinrich Mora, Vicky Chuqiao Yang, and Christopher P. Kempes

19.1 Research question and introductory focused literature

For many urban outputs, the scaling exponent suggests greater economic productivity in more populated cities which has generally been seen as a benefit to larger cities [1, 2–7]. However, an additional and important question is how the return to scale benefits different sectors of the population. Analyses of aggregated city totals gives us insight into average scaling effects but loses important information about heterogeneity that might elucidate the different mechanisms that drive scaling patterns. One such example is economic inequality [8–10].

In this chapter, we address a few key questions related to urban income inequality: (1) how does income inequality (adjusted for shifting average income) systematically change with city size? (2) How different is the income of rich and poor people (measured by population percentiles) in small and large cities, and how does this difference scale with city size? (3) Are poor/rich sectors in larger cities better off than poor/rich sectors in small cities, after adjusting for the cost of living?

We study the scaling of inequality by analysing income scaling in population percentiles. Also, we introduce systematic considerations of the entire distribution of income to show which income distribution features change with city size. Our results indicate that city growth has no positive effect on income growth for the poorest income deciles. For the lower income deciles, income growth only follows the null expectation of a linear increase. These results illustrate that the benefits of larger cities are increasingly unequally distributed. We find that these conclusions hold, or are exacerbated, after adjusting for the cost of living.

19.2 Methods

19.2.1 Data

We use empirical data from the 2015 American Community Survey conducted by the US Census Bureau. We use income data reported on the level of census tracts. To aggregate census tracts into cities, we gather the geographical definitions of

DOI: 10.4324/9781003288312-21

urban areas from the United States Office of Management and Budget. We assign all census tracts that intersect within the territory of each urban area, including cases where multiple urban areas intersect simultaneously. We define the population of an urban area as the sum of their census tracts' populations. We infer the individual-level income distribution in cities by applying the Gaussian kernel density estimator with a widened Silverman bandwidth function on census-tract-level data.

19.2.2 Analysis

We use these data to tackle different avenues to understand scaling effects on income inequality outcomes. We include the following analyses.

19.2.3 Analysis of income scaling in deciles

We propose a new method to investigate the scaling of income aggregated by deciles in each city [1]. We group the data on the income distributions of each city into deciles. We then estimate the scaling exponent of total income for all deciles. We estimate the scaling exponents and corresponding confidence intervals. The number of individuals in decile n of city i is, $N_i^{(n)} = \frac{N_i}{10}$, where N_i is the population of city i. The total income in decile n of city i, $Y_i^{(n)}$ is,

$$Y_i^{(n)} = \sum_{j \in D^{(n)}} y_{i,j}, \tag{19.1}$$

where $D^{(n)}$ are the individuals in income decile n, and $y_{i,j}$ is the income of individual j in city i.

19.2.4 Adjusting income by housing cost

To adjust income for the cost of living, we use housing cost data from the 2015 American Community Survey. The total housing cost in a census tract is calculated as 12 times the sum of the average monthly rent or owner costs for each residence. We then multiply this value by the number of residences in the census tract to infer the total housing cost in the census tract. This adjusted income is the part of income not spent on housing.

19.2.5 Analysis of income distributions

To further analyse the shapes of the income distribution, we compared them with population size. This analysis is done by computing the first four statistical moments of each city's income distributions – mean, variance, skewness, and kurtosis. We compute, furthermore, the Kullback–Leibler (KL) divergence between the largest city and the rest of the cities, which systematically measures a general statistical distance between two distributions. Mathematically, the KL divergence between two distributions of random variables x, $P(x)$ and $Q(x)$ is,

$$KL(P \parallel Q) = \sum_x P(x)\log\left(\frac{P(x)}{Q(x)}\right) \tag{19.2}$$

19.3 Results

19.3.1 Scaling of income in deciles

Figure 19.1 summarizes income scaling results by deciles. The scaling exponent β is linear or weakly sublinear (0.97) for the lowest two deciles and consistently superlinear (up to 1.16) for the upper deciles. Meanwhile the total income scales superlinearly (β = 1.07), consistent with prior findings [2]. This shows varying scaling effects across population segments. The poorest two deciles' per-capita income does not increase as cities get larger, while the wealthiest deciles earn more in larger cities, and the wealthier groups benefit more from larger cities.

19.3.2 Scaling of decile income adjusted by housing cost

While the income scaling differences we observed are significant, they may not solely capture an urban residents' lived experiences. Variations in the cost of living

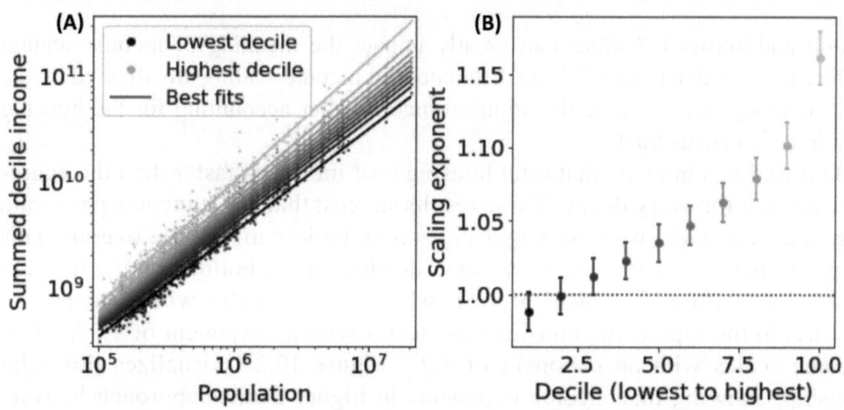

Figure 19.1 Scaling of aggregated income (in US dollars) by population for deciles of US cities. (A) Scaling of total income in deciles. (B) Scaling exponents (β) of each decile and corresponding 95% confidence intervals. The dashed line represents linear scaling for reference. Higher-income deciles exhibit greater scaling exponents than lower-income deciles, and the lowest deciles exhibit near-linear scaling. The scaling exponents for aggregated income in city, combining all deciles, is 1.07.

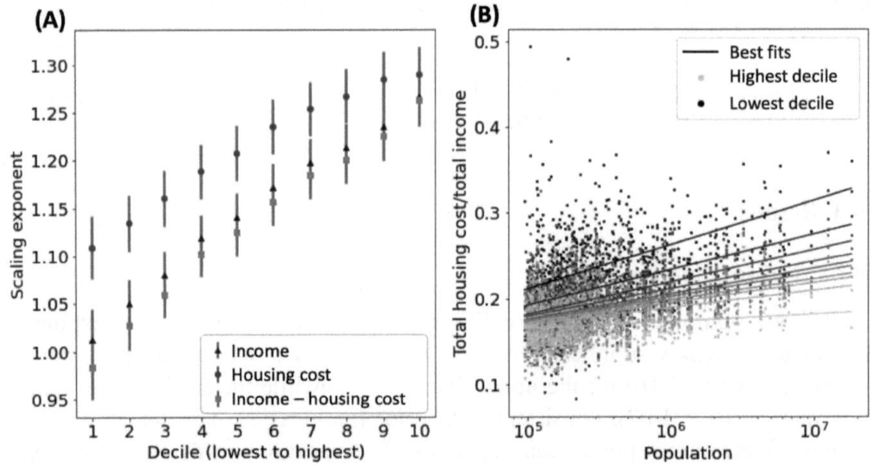

Figure 19.2 Comparing the scaling of housing cost and income. (A) The scaling of aggregated income, aggregated housing cost, and the difference between aggregated income and housing cost, for each decile. Housing cost scales with greater exponents than income for all deciles. The housing-adjusted income exhibits similar variation across deciles as total income. (B) Ratio between housing cost and household income as a function of city population. In the poorest deciles (dark brown), the proportion of income spent on housing increases sharply with city size; in the wealthiest deciles (orange), this proportion remains stagnant.

within and across US cities can greatly impact the meaning of income scaling differences. To determine if these differences in income scaling are affected by the cost of living, we examine the adjusted income after accounting for the housing cost in each census tract.

Our findings indicate that total housing cost increases faster than the aggregate income for every decile. These results suggest that while income per capita may increase with city size, larger cities may be less affordable overall. This disparity is more pronounced for lower deciles. In the bottom decile, housing cost scales with an exponent of 1.11, while income scales with an exponent of 1.01; in the top decile, housing cost scales with an exponent of 1.29, while income scales with an exponent of 1.27. Figure 19.2A visualizes this relationship, showing that income exponents in higher deciles approach housing cost exponents, but do not catch up. Figure 19.2B shows that the ratio of total housing cost to total income increases with city size for every decile. However, the increase is more pronounced for lower deciles. These results collectively suggest a widening affordability gap between richer and poorer residents in larger cities.

19.3.3 Analysis of income distribution characteristics

We analyse how cities' income distributions vary with population by examining the first four statistical moments of income distributions – mean, variance, skewness, and kurtosis. The results, shown in Figure 19.3, indicate that per capita income generally increases with city size, as expected. In larger cities, income inequality tends to increase, with greater variability, asymmetry, and tail heaviness in the income distributions. These results indicate a widening income gap and more pronounced differences in income levels among people living in larger cities. This trend is particularly evident in the third and fourth moments, indicating pronounced growth in the high-income tail of the income distributions.

We also compare the income distributions of each city with that of the largest city using the Kullback–Leibler (KL) divergence, a measure that accounts for the shape of the entire distribution. Figure 19.4 shows that the KL divergence generally decreases with increasing city population, indicating that smaller cities have increasingly dissimilar income distributions compared to that of the largest cities. The Pearson correlation between the log-transformed city population and the KL divergence is –0.259, and the Spearman correlation is –0.718. The Pearson correlation measures the linear correlation between two variables, while the Spearman correlation measures the rank correlation, and assesses how well the relationship between two variables can be described by a monotonic function, regardless of linearity. This finding suggests that population and the KL divergence tend to change together, but not necessarily at a constant rate. While we can identify a general scaling trend, our data also exhibit frequent outliers and deviations.

19.4 Link with literature and discussion

In this study, we propose a new method to analyse income distributions and income inequality in urban areas. We find that the aggregated income in income deciles scales systematically with city size, and the return to scale of cities is not evenly distributed. The bottom decile scales with an exponent slightly below 1 and the top decile with an exponent of 1.15, indicating that the benefits of larger cities are increasingly unequally distributed. These results suggest that cities have no positive effect on the incomes of the poorest deciles beyond the null expectation of a linear increase. Income distributions show systematic variations in distribution characteristics, with larger cities exhibiting greater spread, asymmetry, and heavier tails in income distributions. Additionally, we provide additional information on how urban agglomeration effects vary for different income groups. Our method disentangles the systematic shift in mean income from the study of income inequality and allows us to understand how income scaling effects differ between relatively rich and poor people. We achieve this after accounting for the systematically increasing mean with population size.

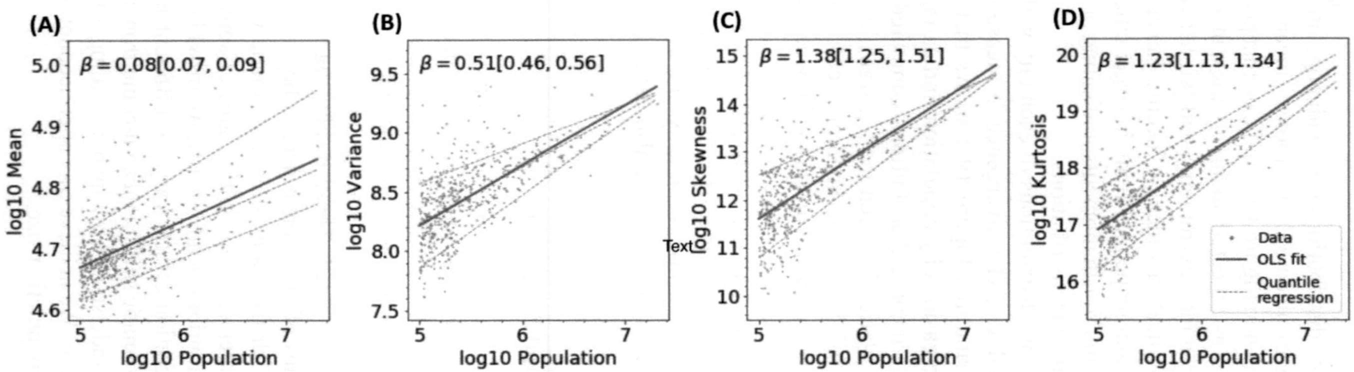

Figure 19.3 First four statistical moments of the estimated income distributions as a function of city size. The texts in each panel display the scaling exponent, β, and in the bracket, corresponding 95% confidence intervals. The dashed lines represent quantile regression results from 10%, 50%, and 90% percentiles.

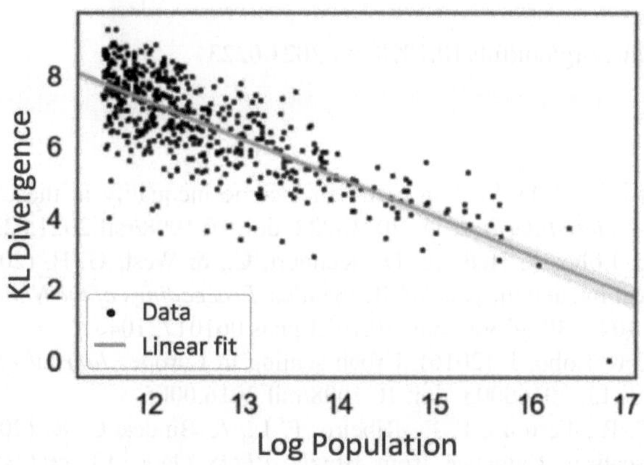

Figure 19.4 Kullback–Leibler divergence between the estimated income distributions and that of the largest city, as a function of log population. The Spearman correlation is –0.718, and the Pearson correlation –0.259.

Our analysis shows that larger cities are less affordable for people of all income levels. This phenomenon particularly affects lower-income individuals, as they allocate a larger proportion of their income toward housing. These results hold despite the income agglomeration effects, indicating that affordability challenges persist in bigger cities regardless of income deciles. We also analyse more complex properties of income distributions, such as statistical moments and KL divergence, and show systematic variations with city size. Our findings highlight the necessity of expanding the current understanding of urban agglomeration effects, moving beyond theories that exclusively focus on homogeneous densifying interactions. Incorporating the role of heterogeneity in urban dynamics is crucial for a more comprehensive understanding of this phenomenon.

Understanding why income inequality systematically scales with city size has important implications for the future. Most urban scaling theory proposes densifying social interactions within cities as the fundamental process leading to the superlinear increase of many features [7,11–14]. Our analysis reveals that income's superlinear scaling is inconsistent across income deciles. The top income deciles primarily drive the increase in total wealth, while the lowest deciles do not exhibit proportional growth. Our findings shed light on an additional dimension of urban scaling theory, highlighting questions about the processes driving the unequal distribution of wealth in larger cities. We propose that city heterogeneity, as an indirect proxy for heterogeneous interaction rates, may play a role in this phenomenon. We hypothesize that cities with high levels of economic segregation, inhibiting mixing between diverse populations, may under-perform with respect to income scaling. Our conclusions encourage future research to consider heterogeneous models of interactions to gain a more comprehensive understanding of urban scaling.

Note

1 https://royalsocietypublishing.org/doi/full/10.1098/rsif.2021.0223

References

1. Heinrich Mora, E., et al. (2021). Scaling of urban income inequality in the USA. *Journal of The Royal Society Interface*, 18, 20210223. doi: 10.1098/rsif.2021.0223
2. Bettencourt, L. M. A., Lobo, J., Helbing, D., Kuhnert, C., & West, G. B. (2007). Growth, innovation, scaling, and the pace of life in cities. *Proceedings of the National Academy of Sciences*, 104, 7301–7306. doi: 10.1073/pnas.0610172104
3. Bettencourt, L. M. A., & Lobo, J. (2016). Urban scaling in Europe. *Journal of the Royal Society Interface*, 13, 20160005. doi: 10.1098/rsif.2016.0005
4. Meirelles, J., Neto, C. R., Ferreira, F. F., Ribeiro, F. L., & Binder, C. R. (2018). Evolution of urban scaling: Evidence from Brazil. *PLOS ONE*, 13, e0204574. doi: 10.1371/journal.pone.0204574
5. Zund, D., & Bettencourt, L. M. A. (2019). Growth and development in prefecture-level cities in China. *PLOS ONE*, 14, e0221017. doi: 10.1371/journal.pone.0221017
6. Sahasranaman, A., & Bettencourt, L. M. A. (2019). Urban geography and scaling of contemporary Indian cities. *Journal of the Royal Society Interface*, 16, 20180758. doi: 10.1098/rsif.2018.0758
7. Yang, V. C., Papachristos, A. V., & Abrams, D. M. (2019). Modeling the origin of urban-output scaling laws. *Physical Review E*, 100, 032306. doi: 10.1103/PhysRevE.100.032306
8. Behrens, K., & Robert-Nicoud, F. (2014). Survival of the fittest in cities: Urbanization and inequality. *The Economic Journal*, 124, 1371–1400. doi: 10.1111/ecoj.12096
9. Cottineau, C., Finance, O., Hatna, E., Arcaute, E., & Batty, M. (2019). Defining urban clusters to detect agglomeration economies. *Environment and Planning B: Urban Analytics and City Science*, 46, 1611–1626. doi: 10.1177/2399808319836065
10. Baum-Snow, N., & Pavan, R. (2013). Inequality and city size. *Review of Economics and Statistics*, 95, 1535–1548. doi: 10.1162/REST_a_00326
11. Pumain, D., Paulus, F., Vacchiani-Marcuzzo, C., & Lobo, J. (2006). An evolutionary theory for interpreting urban scaling laws. *Cybergeo: European Journal of Geography*, Document 343. doi: 10.4000/cybergeo.4896
12. Bettencourt, L. M. A. (2013). The origins of scaling in cities. *Science*, 340(6139), 1438–1441. doi: 10.1126/science.1235823
13. Gomez-Lievano, A., Patterson-Lomba, O., & Hausmann, R. (2016). Explaining the prevalence, scaling, and variance of urban phenomena. *Nature Human Behavior*, 1(9), 1–6. doi: 10.1038/s41562-016-0001
14. Pan, W., Ghoshal, G., Krumme, C., Cebrian, M., & Pentland, A. (2013). Urban characteristics attributable to density-driven tie formation. *Nature Communications*, 4, 1961. doi: 10.1038/ncomms2961

20 Mathematical model explaining variations in urban scaling exponents

Vicky Chuqiao Yang

20.1 Research question and introductory focused literature

It has long been known that superlinear scaling behavior occurs in a wide range of urban outputs [1,2]. Figure 20.1A shows several examples – the number of murder cases, new patents, and new AIDS cases all scale superlinearly with city size in the United States.[1] Increases in these outputs can be primarily beneficial, as with GDP and patents, or primarily harmful, as with crime or contagious disease [2–6].

The scaling of serious crime was previously reported to be superlinear [2,7] with a power law exponent of approximately 1.16. When we break down the data and compare across the seven FBI crime report categories,[2] however, the scaling behavior varies significantly: some categories show approximately linear scaling, while others are strongly superlinear. These differences persist for all years since 1999, the earliest year for which data are available. See Figure 20.2 for the scaling exponents and their 95% confidence intervals in each year for all seven types of crime. One illustrative example is the comparison between robbery and rape, as shown in Figure 20.1B. Robbery scales superlinearly with city size, while rape scales close to linearly.

It has remained unclear why some quantities are affected by city population more than others: previous efforts at understanding superlinear scaling in urban outputs have focused mainly on the similarities rather than differences [7–11]. In addition, many models [7,9–12] rely on a power law assumption for the scaling behaviors, which was later challenged [13].

Explaining the variations in the scaling behavior and formulating a non-power-law framework are now two significant challenges in developing a scientific understanding of urban scaling. Here, we propose a novel model that explains and predicts the variation in scaling among different urban outputs, without relying on a power law hypothesis and test the model's predictions with novel empirical observations on crime.

DOI: 10.4324/9781003288312-22

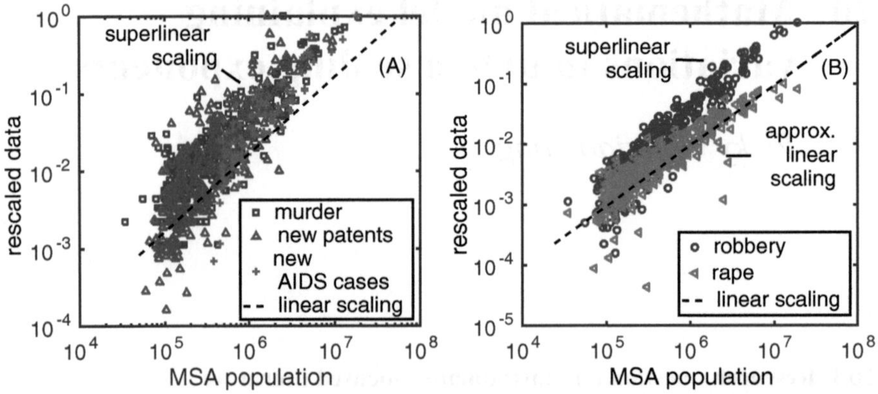

Figure 20.1 Urban outputs versus city size. (A) Number of new patents, murder cases, and AIDS cases in US Metropolitan Statistical Areas (MSA's) vs. population. These three urban outputs exhibit superlinear scaling – as MSA population doubles, the amount of output more than doubles. (B) Number of robbery cases and rape cases vs. MSA population. Robbery scales superlinearly, while rape scales close to linearly. All data are scaled to have maximum value 1.

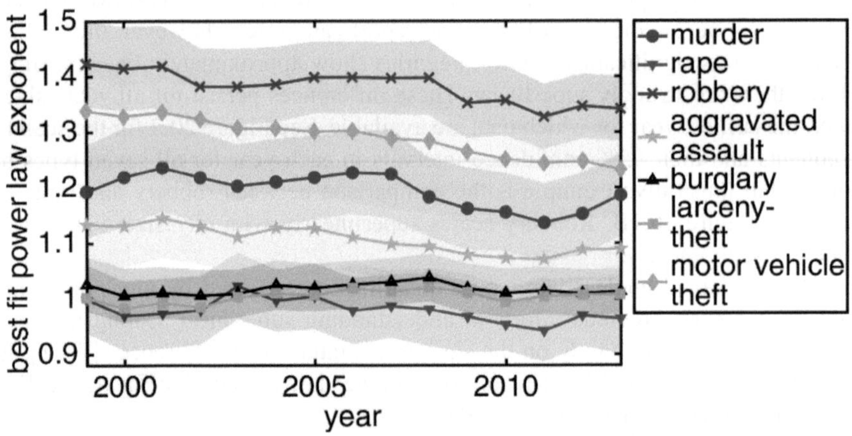

Figure 20.2 Scaling exponents of all seven FBI crime categories over time. The shaded regions show 95% confidence intervals. Exponents differ considerably among crime categories, and are consistent over time.

20.2 Methods

20.2.1 Summary of the mathematical model

Since most urban outputs, such as AIDS infection, patenting, and many types of crime have social components [14–19], we are motivated to incorporate existing knowledge about these social processes into our model. Granovetter's landmark work *The Strength of Weak Ties* [20] argues that weak ties play an important role in providing information novel to one's social network that fosters outputs such as finding a job or starting a business. Motivated by this and direct empirical evidence for the importance of weak ties in innovation and crime [21,22], we base our model on the assumption that finding the right collaboration is key to human productivity: one must meet all the necessary collaborators for an output in order to produce. Mathematically, this key concept is expressed as

$$y(N) \sim NP_n[u(N)] \tag{20.1}$$

where $y(N)$ denotes the volume of an urban output (such as the total number of robbery cases or the number of patents) for a city with population N. The parameter n is the number of partners needed for the output, $u(N)$ is the average number of unique contacts for a person living in the city, and $P_n[u(N)]$ is the probability of finding all required n collaborators among $u(N)$ contacts.

Here, we give an overview of the model's general conclusions, without functional form assumptions. From treating social interactions as a sampling process, we can show, that P_n depends on u in the form of

$$P_n \sim u^n(N) \tag{20.2}$$

Please see Ref. [1] for detailed derivations. Combining Eqs. (20.1) and (20.2), we have,

$$y(N) \sim Nu^n(N)$$

Taking the logarithm of both sides and differentiating with respect to $\ln(N)$, we have

$$\beta \equiv \frac{d\ln(y)}{d\ln(N)} \sim 1 + n\frac{d\ln(u)}{d\ln(N)} \tag{20.3}$$

We shall discuss the implication of this equation in the Results section.

20.2.2 Data

We use empirical data to test the agreement of the model and its predictions, which requires the knowledge of the number of individuals needed for each activity. We focus on crime as an example because of the high quality and quantity of the data available. In addition to using the 14 years of crime instances data (Figure 20.2), we compile an additional dataset of the average co-offending group sizes of the seven FBI crime types.

We compile the new dataset from crime reports of two independent sources: the National Incident Based Reporting System (NIBRS) in 2014 and the Chicago Police Department arrest records from 1999 to 2012. Both sources report incident-level records for a variety of crime types. Note that since the Chicago Police Department does not participate in NIBRS, the two datasets are mutually exclusive. The co-offending group size of each incident is defined as the number of unique offenders reported in that incident. We average over all incidents of each type to reach the average group size. The parameter n, the number of partners, is calculated by average group size minus one. Note that average group sizes vary only over a small range in our crime data. This is primarily due to inherent limitations in offender reporting: for many crimes committed by groups, only a subset of the co-offenders are arrested or listed in crime reports (a single arrestee is the most common case). Despite this limitation, the data do show significant and consistent variation in group sizes, but the average values we use should be interpreted as correlates of, rather than direct estimates of, true co-offending group sizes. To ensure the robustness of our results, we use both sources for model validation.

20.3 Results

20.3.1 Predictions of the mathematical model

Equation (20.3) derived from our model leads to the following three predictions.

Superlinear scaling. $\beta \equiv d\ln(y)/d\ln(N)$ is the scaling exponent of y. Eq. (20.3) predicts that if $d\ln(u)/d\ln(N) > 0$, meaning residents of more populated cities have more contacts (supported by empirical findings in Ref. [23]), and $n > 0$, meaning the activity typically requires more than one participant, then $\beta > 1$, giving rise to superlinear scaling.

Variation in scaling exponents. Eq. (20.3) suggests that β should increase with n. For fixed N, β grows linearly with n. Thus Eq. (20.3) predicts that urban outputs requiring more participants should exhibit more pronounced superlinear scaling. This explains the variation across scaling exponents of different outputs.

Possibility of non-power-law superlinear scaling. Individuals in bigger cities have the chance to meet more people, but cognitive limits restrict them to only interacting with a small subset [24]. It is thus likely for $d\ln(u)/d\ln(N)$ to decrease as N increases. As a result, β is expected to be larger when measured among small cities, and smaller when measured among large cities. This resulting behavior is diminishing return in the scaling exponents, predicting the scaling exponents approximate 1 for infinitely large cities.

Considering typical patterns of collaboration can resolve the puzzle of why scaling behaviors vary across different urban outputs. The three predictions above hold for any general increasing function of $u(N)$. For the sections below, where we compare the model with empirical data, we adopt a numerical estimation for $u(N)$ derived from treating social interactions as a biased sampling process. The general behavior of this function is that $u(N)$ is an increasing function with N (which is consistent with empirical data from phone contact networks in a number of cities [23]), and shows diminishing return with N.

20.3.2 Comparing model prediction with data

Our model agrees well with US FBI data on all seven crime categories across 14 years; typical comparisons are shown in Figure 20.3. The model explains not only the observed superlinear scaling for some urban outputs (e.g., robbery in Figure 20.3A), but also close-to-linear scaling in others (e.g., rape in Figure 20.3B). Note that the model makes these distinct predictions while using the same set of parameters except one, which is the number of co-offenders involved in the crime type, which is given by the data.

As predicted by the model, the scaling exponent of a crime type should increase linearly with the number of co-offenders. It is the case in the empirical data. Figure 20.4 shows the relationship predicted by the model and observed in the data between the average co-offending group sizes with the degree of superlinearity of the scaling relationship for all seven crime types. Superlinearity is quantified for ease of comparison by the best-fitting power-law exponent (in the range where the data are available) minus one – though note that our model *does not* predict power law scaling. The two panels in Figure 20.4 use two independent sources of data for the co-offending group size – NIBRS in Figure 20.4A and Chicago Police Department in Figure 20.4B. The Pearson correlation between average co-offending group size and superlinearity in the data is 0.764 (p-value 0.046) in Figure 20.4A, and 0.761 (p-value 0.047) in Figure 20.4B. The Spearman's rank

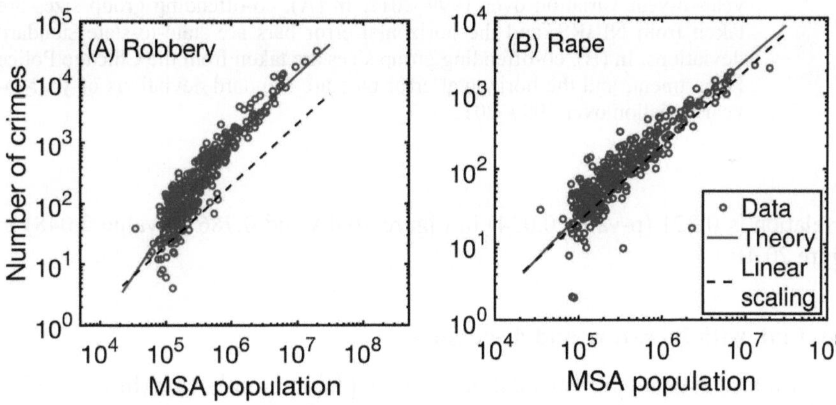

Figure 20.3 Model predictions compared with data. (A) Number of robbery cases versus MSA population. (B) Number of rape cases versus MSA population. Both for the USA in 2012. Red solid curves show model predictions (not power law), blue dots show data points, and the black dashed curves are reference lines of unit slope. Our model predicts superlinear scaling for robbery, and approximately linear scaling for rape. The difference between the model predictions in (A) and (B) is a result of the differing average co-offending group sizes. This figure uses co-offending group size calculated from the NIBRS dataset.

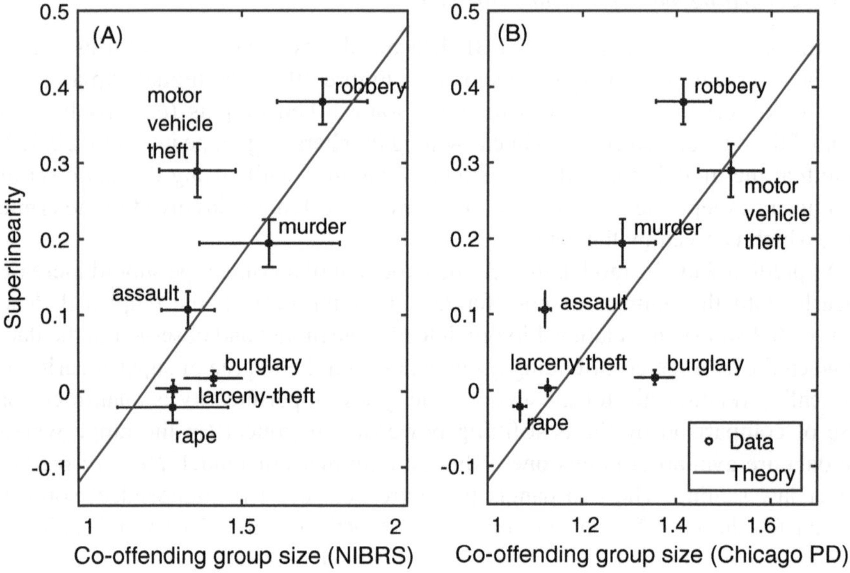

Figure 20.4 Superlinearity as a function of average group size for crimes. Superlinearity is quantified as the exponent of the best-fit power law minus 1; this is for convenience – our model does not predict power law scaling. Red solid line shows model prediction. Vertical error bars in both panels are standard deviations of year-to-year variation over 1999–2012. In (A), co-offending group sizes are taken from NIBRS, and the horizontal error bars are state-to-state standard deviations. In (B), co-offending group sizes are taken from the Chicago Police Department, and the horizontal error bars are standard deviations of year-to-year variation over 1999–2012.

correlation is 0.821 (p-value 0.034) in Figure 20.4A and 0.786 (p-value 0.048) in Figure 20.4B.

20.4 Link with literature and discussion

Here, we proposed a mathematical model to explain not only superlinear scaling in urban outputs, but also how the exponents should increase with the number of participants needed for the output. Our model offers a non-power-law framework to study urban scaling relations. We validated the model's predictions using novel datasets on the co-offending group size of several types of crimes.

Some prior work has attributed superlinear scaling to the hypothesis of hierarchy in infrastructure and social networks [7,9], or differences in population density [8]. Our model suggests that superlinear scaling arises due to the increased social connectivity of larger cities facilitating the complementarity required in socioeconomic activities.

Our model predicts diminished return in scaling exponents as city population gets larger. Data such as those shown in Figure 20.1 display a reduced slope for the largest cities. This result suggests that, with limited resources, populating smaller cities would have a bigger impact on overall urban productivity than populating already big ones.

This chapter relies heavily on crime as an example because of the abundance and quality of data we were able to compile. However, the principle of the model can be generalized to other urban outputs driven by forming collaborations, such as inventions and starting new businesses. We applied our model to patent scaling laws, while extracting empirical average group sizes from patent co-authorship. We find good agreement between our model and patent scaling behavior (see Ref. [1]).

Our model, in agreement with previous models [7,8], implies that the dual aspects of cities are not separable: both positive and negative urban outputs (e.g., inventions and crimes) share common driving mechanisms rooted in social interaction. Future research – especially in the study of crime, law, deviance, and other sources of urban inequality – would do well to consider how scaling models such as ours might be further calibrated to capture differences within cities, especially across neighborhoods or communities.

Notes

1 Note that, for convenience, we frequently use the simpler but more ambiguous term "city" to refer to a Metropolitan Statistical Area (MSA) throughout this chapter.

2 FBI crime categories are murder, rape, robbery, aggravated assault, burglary, larceny-theft, and motor vehicle theft.

References

1. Yang, V. C., Papachristos, A. V. & Abrams, D. M. Modeling the origin of urban-output scaling laws. *Physical Review E* **100**, 032306 (2019).
2. Bettencourt, L. M. A., Lobo, J., Helbing, D., Ku¨hnert, C. & West, G. B. Growth, innovation, scaling, and the pace of life in cities. *Proceedings of the National Academy of Sciences* **104**, 7301–7306 (2007).
3. Jacobs, J. *The Death and Life of Great American Cities* (Random House, New York, 1961).
4. Bettencourt, L. M. A. & Lobo, J. Urban scaling in Europe. *Journal of The Royal Society Interface* **13**, 20160005 (2016).
5. Rocha, L. E. C., Thorson, A. E. & Lambiotte, R. The non-linear health consequences of living in larger cities. *Journal of Urban Health* **92**, 785–799 (2015).
6. Hanley, Q. S., Lewis, D. & Ribeiro, H. V. Rural to urban population density scaling of crime and property transactions in English and Welsh Parliamentary Constituencies. *PloS ONE* **11**, e0149546 (2016).
7. Bettencourt, L. M. A. The origins of scaling in cities. *Science* **340**, 1438–1441 (2013).
8. Pan, W., Ghoshal, G., Krumme, C., Cebrian, M. & Pentland, A. Urban characteristics attributable to density-driven tie formatione. *Nature Communications* **5**, 1961 (2013).
9. Arbesman, S., Kleinberg, J. M. & Strogatz, S. H. Superlinear scaling for innovation in cities. *Physical Review E* **79**, 016115 (2009).

10. Duranton, G. & Puga, D. Micro-foundations of urban agglomeration economies. *Handbook of Regional and Urban Economics* **4**, 2063–2117 (2004).
11. Arbesman, S. & Christakis, N. A. Scaling of prosocial behavior in cities. *Physica A: Statistical Mechanics and its Applications* **390**, 2155–2159 (2011).
12. Gomez-Lievano, A., Patterson-Lomba, O. & Hausmann, R. Explaining the prevalence, scaling and variance of urban phenomena. *Nature Human Behavior* **390**, 2155–2159 (2017).
13. Arcaute, E. *et al.* Constructing cities, deconstructing scaling laws. *Journal of The Royal Society Interface* **12**, 20140745 (2015).
14. US Centers for Disease Control and Prevention. *HIV Surveillance Reports* (2013).
15. LeFevre, K. B. *Invention as a Social Act* (SIU Press, Carbondale, Illinois, 1987).
16. Glaeser, E. *Triumph of the City: How Our Greatest Invention Makes US Richer, Smarter, Greener, Healthier and Happier* (Pan Macmillan, London, UK, 2011).
17. Warr, M. *Companions in Crime: The Social Aspects of Criminal Conduct* (Cambridge University Press, New York, 2002).
18. Reiss, A. J. Co-offending and criminal careers. *Crime and Justice* **10**, 117–170 (1988).
19. Stolzenberg, L. & D'Alessio, S. J. Co-offending and the age-crime curve. *Journal of Research in Crime and Delinquency* **45**, 65–86 (2008).
20. Granovetter, M. S. The strength of weak ties. *American Journal of Sociology* **78**, 1360–1380 (1973).
21. Hauser, C., Tappeiner, G. & Walde, J. The learning region: The impact of social capital and weak ties on innovation. *Regional Studies* **41**, 75–88 (2007).
22. Patacchini, E. & Zenou, Y. The strength of weak ties in crime. *European Economic Review* **52**, 209–236 (2008).
23. Schl¨apfer, M. & et al. The scaling of human interactions with city size. *Journal of The Royal Society Interface* **11**, 20130789 (2014).
24. Milgram, S. The experience of living in cities. *Science* **167**, 1461–1468 (1970).

21 Characteristics and mechanisms of urban scaling in rapidly urbanizing China

Limin Jiao, Weiqian Lei, and Gang Xu

21.1 Urban scaling in China

The empirics and the theory of urban scaling are sufficiently mature to be formulated and measured in many urban systems around the world [1,2]. As a typical developing country, China has been experiencing rapid urbanization since the 1980s with a complex urbanization pattern that has attracted the world's attention. It is necessary and interesting to focus on the comprehensive characteristics of urban growth in a rapidly urbanizing country and to analyze the dynamic evolution of cities by verifying Chinese cities as social entities whether conform to the predictions of the scaling framework. This chapter intends to capture how the unique scaling characteristics in China vary from those in developed countries to reveal the distinct development pattern of rapidly urbanizing countries which can be explained by evolutionary theory.

It is noted that scaling relationships are highly dependent on urban ontology and measurement contexts and methods [3,4]. Properly defining urban boundary and choosing appropriate statistical data are important prerequisites for a systematic quantitative analysis of urban scaling. Our statistical unit is Chinese prefecture-level cities with frequent social interactions, consistent with the definition of functional cities fundamentally (Figure 21.1) [5–8].

More than 90 urban indicators in ten categories, including infrastructure, land use, education, medical and healthcare, energy, employment, economy, company, innovation and environmental press, from 275 Chinese cities were used to systematically explore the integrated characteristics of the Chinese urban system using scaling analysis. Power-law distributions describe well a multitude of the indicators in China (Figure 21.2). The general proposition of increasing returns to size for social-economic attributes and economies of scale for infrastructure holds true for our urban attributes in the Chinese urban system. In general, the scaling exponent values of attributes related to education, medical and healthcare, land use and public services indicators are less than one, following the sublinear regimes and indicating that there is a higher infrastructure sharing rate in Chinese large cities. Urban attributes related to economy and company present superlinear regimes as expected. These results enrich the choice of a new set of attributes compared with previous studies, such as the number of employees in different

DOI: 10.4324/9781003288312-23

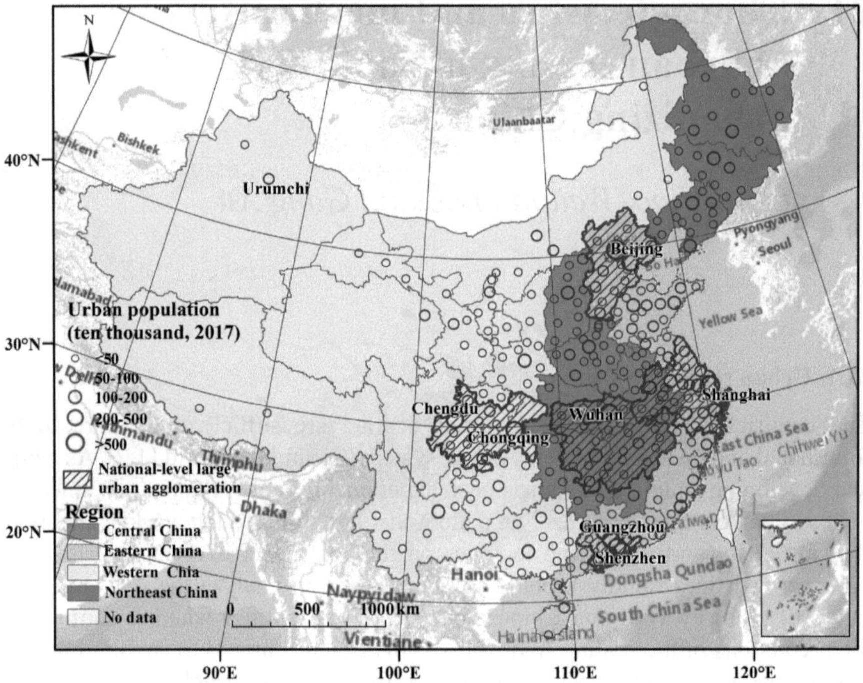

Figure 21.1 The spatial distribution of the urban population of 275 Chinese cities in 2017. Figure created by the author.

sectors (manufacturing, services), different types of urban construction land area, finance and economy development (revenue, tax, expenditure).

Figure 21.3 shows the scaling exponents of the 12 main chosen representative sets of indicators. These scaling exponents derived from OLS regression on logarithmic indicators broadly agree quantitatively with the simplest predictions from scaling regimes. All indicators related to social interactions (i.e., patents, GDP) and numerous indicators for infrastructure follow the empirical superlinear and sublinear scaling regimes, respectively. With the increase of urban size, both positive (i.e., GDP, patents and the number of industrial enterprises) and negative (i.e., annual quantity of wastewater discharged) social output attributes have increased significantly.

Indicators related to individual need, which are expected to exhibit a linear scaling regime, slightly deviate from the expectation. Employment (the number of employees) scales superlinearly against population. Household water consumption also scales superlinearly against population. Urban residents living in large cities have superior living conditions, which also makes them have a greater per capita household water consumption.

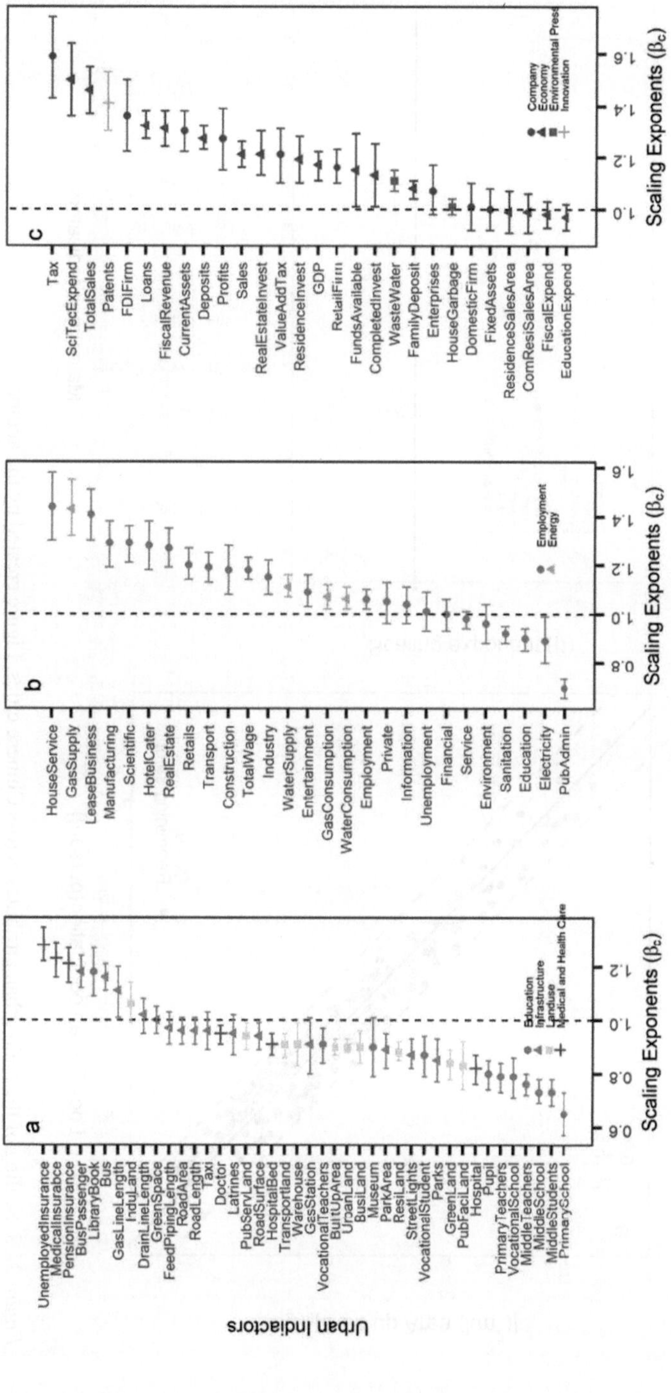

Figure 21.2 Urban scaling exponents for 97 indicators across the Chinese urban system. Figure created by the author.

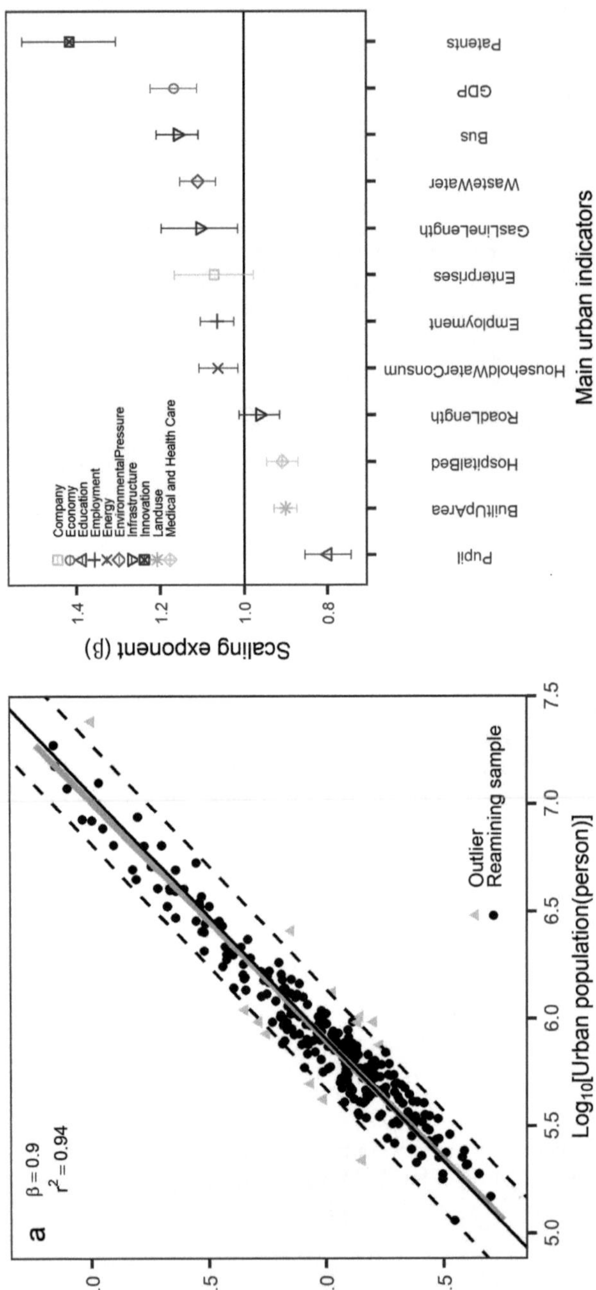

Figure 21.3 Scaling of the main urban attributes across Chinese cities. Figure created by the author.

Built-up area, pupils, hospital beds and road length follow the sublinear regimes as expected. But other indicators, such as the number of buses and the length of gas supply pipeline, surprisingly scale superlinearly against population. These public resources in China tend to be gathered towards large cities and fail to reflect economies of scale. It is surprising but common in rapidly urbanizing country that large cities have comparative advantages in public service construction, resulting in an uneven development of infrastructure configuration among districts.

21.2 Spatial disparities and temporal evolution of scaling

We selected three main representative urban indicators (built-up area, employment and GDP), and obtained the scaling exponents by regions (Western, Central, Eastern, and Northeast China), so as to explore spatial disparities of scaling exponents in China (Figure 21.4). Built-up area in four regions scaled sublinearly with population size (β<1) as expected. As for individual need indicators, the expected scaling exponent value of employment is supposed to be equal to 1. However, there are some exceptions in different regions in China. Employment in the NE appears to have superlinear scaling behavior with β=1.12, contrary to the prediction. Meanwhile, employment in Central China shows a significant sublinear relationship with the urban population (β=0.95), showing a slower growth with the increase in urban population. Scaling exponent values of GDP in all regions are greater than 1, which is consistent with the expected superlinear scaling behavior. Among all regions, the NE shows the most significant agglomeration effects for economic outputs with β=1.44.

Five major national-level urban agglomerations, including the Beijing-Tianjin-Hebei (BTH), Chengdu-Chongqing (CY), Pearl River Delta (PRD), Yangtze River Delta (YRD) and Yangtze River Middle-Reach (MYR) Urban Agglomerations, were selected as the typical urban agglomeration analysis units. Figure 21.5 shows that built-up area in MYR presents a significant sublinear scaling relationship with urban population (β=0.77). From small cities to large cities, there is a greater average population density within MYR. When it comes to individual need indicators, employment in BTH unexpectedly shows a superlinear scaling behavior with β=1.22. Large cities in BTH are more attractive to labor resources. Relatively, employment in the MYR and PRD scales sublinearly against population size with the scaling exponent values less than 1. As for social outputs, there is a clear sublinear and linear scaling behavior of GDP, respectively, in the PRD and CY. These results stand in stark contrast to the expected superlinear scaling regime. In contrast, GDP of BTH strongly scales superlinearly against population size with β=1.21, indicating a significant agglomeration effect of economic productivity.

In order to make a horizontal comparison of urban agglomeration development, we collected 19 urban agglomerations following *The 13th Five-Year Plan for Economic and Social Development* besides samples of five national urban agglomerations, and normalized the data for each urban agglomeration by the average logarithmic city size and attribute magnitude within the sample. These comparisons take urban agglomerations as units for fitting, giving us a sense of their

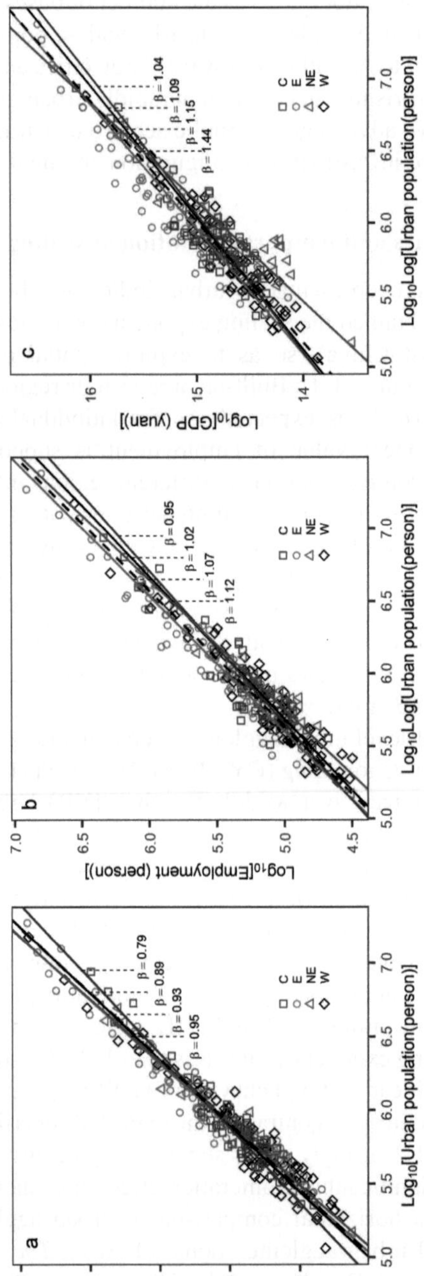

Figure 21.4 Spatial disparities of scaling of main urban attributes by regions. Figure created by the author.

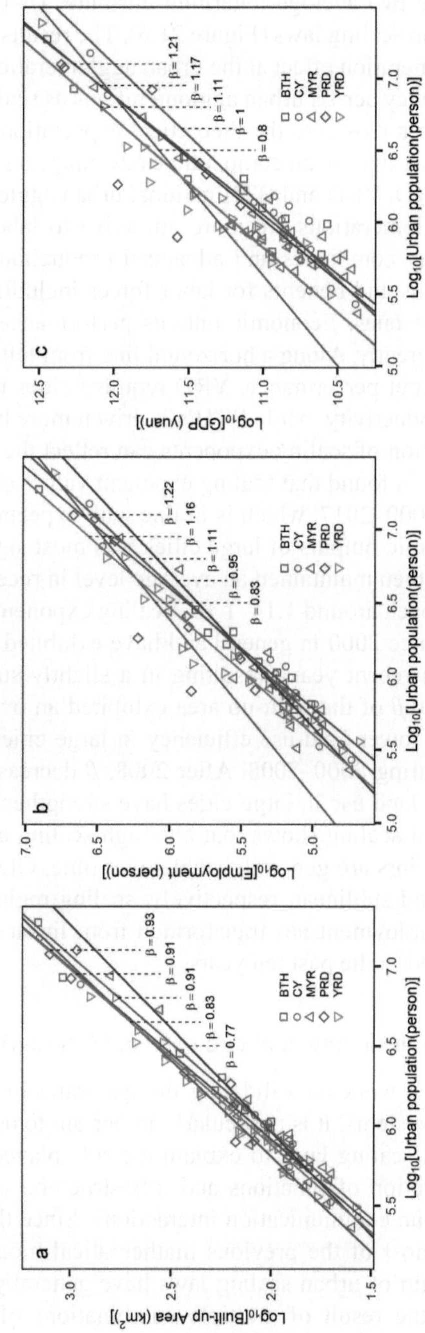

Figure 21.5 Spatial disparities of scaling of main urban attributes by urban agglomerations. Figure created by the author.

convergence or divergence across the urban system. Scatter points show a strong correlation between the two average logarithm attributes ($p<0.001$), and are still consistent with the urban scaling laws (Figure 21.6). The results show that there is a more significant agglomeration effect at the urban agglomeration level. There is an average land use efficiency across urban agglomerations as scaling exponent value for *centered* built-up area closed to the theoretical expectation ($\beta=0.85$). In terms of employment, there is a significant comparative advantage on working conditions and bonus in mature PRD, YRD and BTH national urban agglomerations, with $\beta=1.35$. These urban agglomerations are more attractive to labor force, especially to senior talents, quality companies and advanced production, because they can provide better conditions and benefits for labor forces including work provisions not available in smaller ones. Economic outputs performance of different urban agglomerations varies greatly. Along a horizontal line from left to right, to achieve a similar economic output performance, YRD requires cities to improve the efficiency of economic productivity, while BTH's is driven more by size.

The temporal evolution of scaling exponents can reflect the variations in urban system (Figure 21.7). It is found that scaling exponent values of GDP were always greater than 1 during 2000–2017, which is in line with expectations. The agglomeration effect of economic outputs of large cities was most significant in 2009; it weakened slightly and then maintained an average level in recent years, as scaling exponent values have been around 1.14–1.16. Scaling exponent values of employment have increased since 2000 in general and have exhibited robustness without obvious fluctuations in recent years, resulting in a slightly superlinear behavior. From 2000 to 2008, the β of the built-up area exhibited an overall upward trend. There was a relatively lower land-use efficiency in large cities with a higher per capita land-use area during 2000–2008. After 2008, β decreased slightly and the economies of scale for land use in large cities have strengthened. The above analysis of the evolution of scaling shows that although scaling exponent values are dynamic, scaling behaviors are generally stable over time. GDP and built-up area maintain superlinear and sublinear, respectively, scaling regimes over time. The scaling behavior of employment has transformed from linearity to superlinearity and has been maintained in the past ten years.

21.3 Scaling arises from the internal and external interactions

In addition to extensive work on validating the generalizability of scaling laws across different urban systems, it is particularly important to develop a model that can simulate empirical scaling laws to explain the role played by urban population size in the distribution of functions and infrastructure, and to model urban heterogeneity and human communication interactions. Since the essence of a city is interaction [9,10], most of the previous mathematical models concerning the explanation of the origin of urban scaling laws have generally considered socio-economic activity as the result of multiple combinations of population, urban geometry, and the possibility of human interaction [11,12].

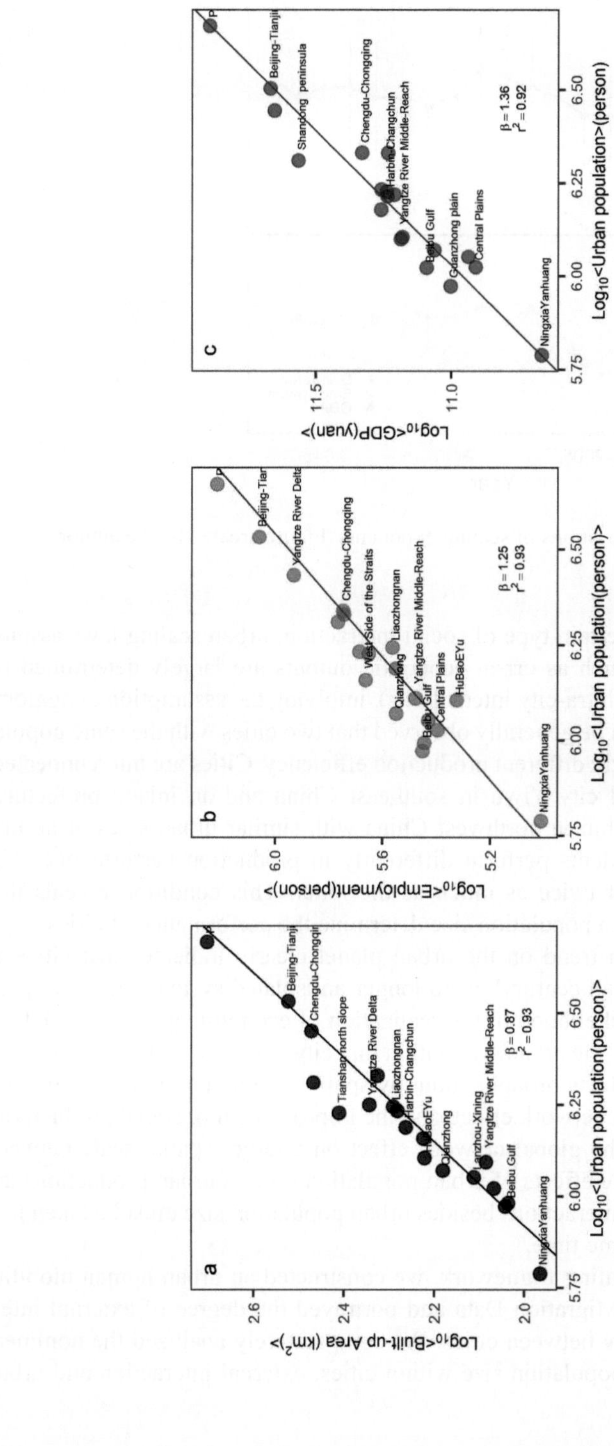

Figure 21.6 The average logarithm indicators and population size of cities in 19 different urban agglomerations across the Chinese urban system. Figure created by the author.

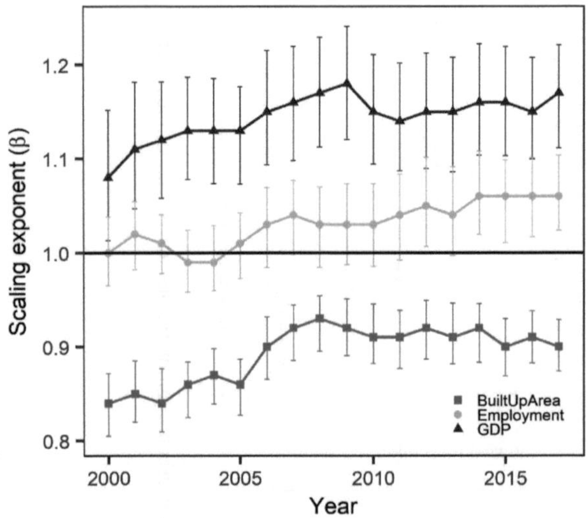

Figure 21.7 Temporal variations of scaling exponents. Figure created by the author.

As a product of a certain type of social interaction, urban scaling laws assume that urban attributes such as urban economic outputs are largely determined by urban population size (intra-city interactions), implying the assumption of agglomeration economy. It can be generally observed that two cities with the same population size may have vastly different production efficiency. Cities are interconnected. A coastal county-level city Yiwu in southeast China and an inland prefecture-level inland city Tianshui in northwest China with similar urban sizes of around 1.3 million urban residents perform differently in production performance. The former produces about twice as much as the latter. This condition reveals that factors apart from urban population size determine the performance of cities.

A new urbanization trend on the urban planet clearly indicates that cities in contemporaneous "urban century" is no longer an isolated system, but "the space of the flow" [9]. The likelihood of the realization of economic growth of a city is determined not only by the urban size within that city, but also by the benefits from the spatial spillover effects brought about by spatial interaction. Urban agglomeration represents a local network effect, and the improvement of social productivity should also consider the global network effect on a larger spatial scale between cities. That is, when the effects of urban population size on urban productions are measured, interurban interactions besides urban population size must be taken into consideration at the same time.

Under the urban scaling framework, we constructed an urban human mobility network using Baidu Migration Data and portrayed the degree of external interaction by total mobility between cities. We comparatively analyzed the nonlinear relationship between population size within cities, external interaction and urban economic outputs. Urban population size $N_i(t)$ is replaced by the urban external interaction strength $S_i(t)$ to measure the nonlinear effect of urban external interaction on urban economic output $Y_i(t)$. Further, inspired by the Cobb–Douglas production function equation, $Y_i(t)$ is defined as the function of the interaction between urban population size and external interaction, i.e., $Y \sim F(N, S)$, to measure the synergistic effect of urban population size and external interaction on urban elements, and the following formulas are obtained:

$$Y_i(t) \sim Y_0 N_i(t)^{\beta_N} S_i(t)^{\beta_S} \tag{21.1}$$

$$LogY_i(t) \sim \beta_N LogN_i(t) + \beta_S LogS_i(t) + LogY_0 \tag{21.2}$$

The results show that there is a significant scaling relationship between interurban interaction and urban economic outputs including GDP, exports, secondary and tertiary industrial production, retail sales and total wages (Figure 21.8), and all the scaling exponents are larger than one ($\beta>1$), presenting a significant superlinear scaling regime. All the scaling exponent values obtained by interaction intensity and urban growth are larger than by urban size. The scaling relationship between urban economic production and urban population size is more robust, but the external interaction strength of cities has a higher multiplier effect and agglomeration advantage on urban economic output. This finding verifies the hypothesis that the urban scaling law is derived from the interaction within and outside the city and makes up for the deficiency of the traditional scaling law in mechanism interpretation [13].

We considered both population mobility and urban population size in the regression, and compared the coefficients to obtain the respective contribution to urban economic outputs (Table 21.1). We compare the coefficients of the independent variables after normalizing the coefficients and measure the relative contributions of urban population size and interurban interactions on urban production by the Lindeman–Merenda–Gold (LMG) method of "relaimpo" package in R. There is little collinearity among independent variables (VIF<3). For the socio-economic attributes such as GDP, secondary and tertiary industry products and total wage, urban population size has a greater influence on them and the relative contribution of urban size is concentrated in 60–65%. Meanwhile, interurban interaction has a lower impact with a contribution rate of between 35–40%. This proves that urban economic output is definitely dominated by the urban population size. More importantly, interurban interaction also affects and contributes to urban growth.

However, there is an exception for the export volume of goods, population mobility intensity is of greater importance to exports with a larger normalized coefficient and relative contribution of 52%. In other words, intercity interactions have a greater impact on the export volume of goods than urban size. Regional trade and the exports of goods are closely linked to population mobility and connections; thus, population mobility is conducive to the export of enterprises. The opposite example is the social total retail sales of consumer goods. Urban population size

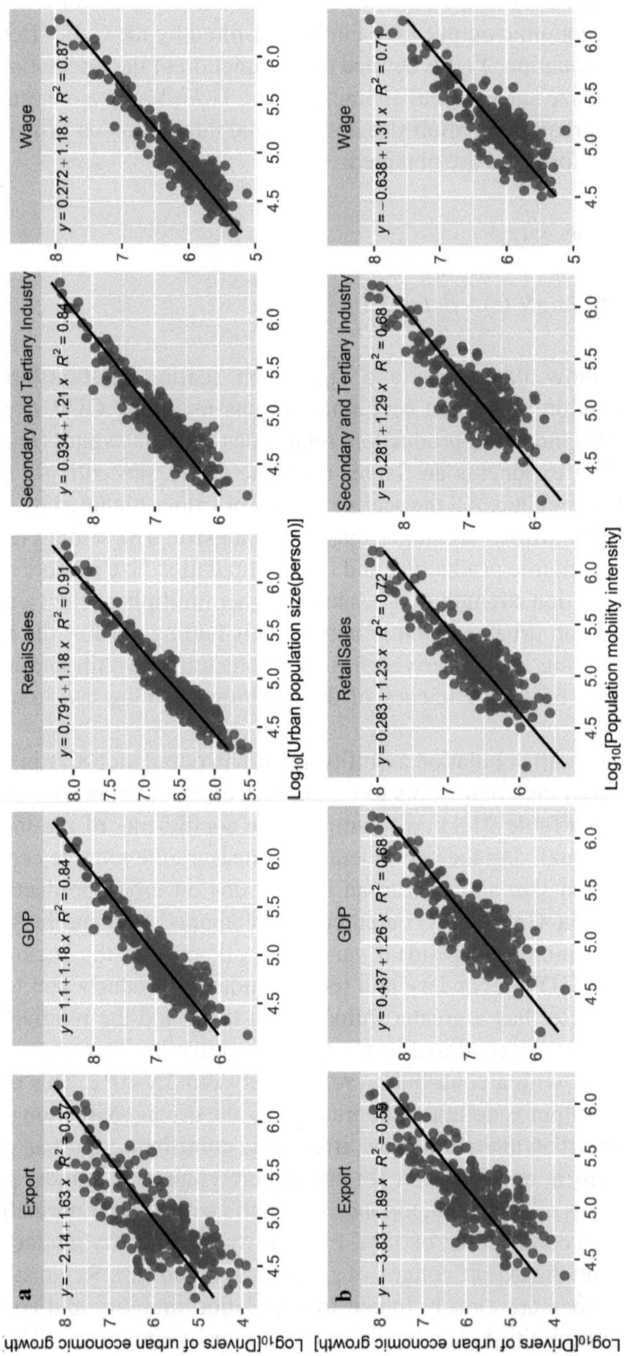

Figure 21.8 The scaling relationships between urban productions and (a) urban population size and (b) interurban interaction. Figure created by the author.

Table 21.1 Regression coefficients and relative contributions deriving from multiple regression of productions.

Explained variable	*Explaining variables*						
	Urban population size			*Population mobility*			*VIF*
	Coefficient	*Normalized coefficient*	*Relative contribution*	*Coefficient*	*Normalized coefficient*	*Relative contribution*	
Export	0.800***	0.352***	0.481	1.094***	0.425***	0.518	2.816
GDP	0.992***	0.770***	0.614	0.263***	0.182***	0.385	2.869
Secondary and tertiary industry product	1.026***	0.778***	0.618	0.254***	0.171***	0.382	2.869
Retail sales	1.081***	0.852***	0.647	0.119*	0.084*	0.353	2.880
Wage	0.994***	0.783***	0.615	0.268***	0.184***	0.385	2.873

plays a more significant role in the process of urban growth than population mobility. The purchasing power of goods is affected by the wage level and consumption concept of dwellers. Urban residents living in larger cities have greater purchasing power, resulting in the greater consumption of goods.

References

[1] Bettencourt, L. M., Lobo, J., Helbing, D., Kuhnert, C., & West, G. B. (2007). Growth, innovation, scaling, and the pace of life in cities. *Proceedings of the National Academy of Sciences*, *104*(17), 7301–7306. doi: 10.1073/pnas.0610172104

[2] Bettencourt, L. M. A., & Lobo, J. (2016). Urban scaling in Europe. *Journal of The Royal Society Interface*, *13*(116), 20160005. doi: 10.1098/rsif.2016.0005

[3] Arcaute, E., Hatna, E., Ferguson, P., Youn, H., Johansson, A., & Batty, M. (2015). Constructing cities, deconstructing scaling laws. *Journal of The Royal Society Interface*, *12*(102), 20140745. doi: 10.1098/rsif.2014.0745

[4] Batty, M., & Ferguson, P. (2011). Defining city size. *Environment and Planning B: Planning and Design*, *38*(5), 753–756. doi: 10.1068/b3805ed

[5] Lei, W., Jiao, L., Xu, G., & Zhou, Z. (2022). Urban scaling in rapidly urbanising China. *Urban Studies*, *59*(9), 1989–1908.

[6] Jiao, L., Xu, Z., Xu, G., Zhao, R., Liu, J., & Wang, W. (2020). Assessment of urban land use efficiency in China: A perspective of scaling law. *Habitat International*, *99*, 102172. doi: 10.1016/j.habitatint.2020.102172

[7] Zund, D., & Bettencourt, L. M. A. (2019). Growth and development in prefecture-level cities in China. *PLOS ONE*, *14*(9), e0221017. doi: 10.1371/journal.pone.0221017

[8] Zhao, S., Liu, S., Xu, C., Yuan, W., Sun, Y., Yan, W., ... Fang, J. (2018). Contemporary evolution and scaling of 32 major cities in China. *Ecological Applications*, *28*(6), 1655–1668. doi: 10.1002/eap.1760

[9] Batty, M. (2013). *The new science of cities*: MIT Press.
[10] Lobo, J., Bettencourt, L. M. A., Smith, M. E., & Ortman, S. (2019). Settlement scaling theory: Bridging the study of ancient and contemporary urban systems. *Urban Studies*, *57*(4), 731–747. doi: 10.1177/0042098019873796
[11] Bettencourt, L. M. A. (2013). The origins of scaling in cities. *Science*, *6139*(319), 399–407. doi: 10.1126/science.1235823
[12] Ribeiro, F. L., & Rybski, D. (2023). Mathematical models to explain the origin of urban scaling laws. *Physics Reports*, *1012*, 1–39.
[13] Lei, W., Jiao, L., Xu, Z., Zhou, Z., & Xu, G. (2021). Scaling of urban economic outputs: insights both from urban population size and population mobility. *Computers, Environment and Urban Systems*, *88*, 101657.

Part III

Environment

22 Urban carbon dioxide emissions and the roles of population, area, and density[1]

Haroldo V. Ribeiro and Diego Rybski

22.1 Introduction

World population is becoming increasingly concentrated in urban areas. Indeed, since 2007, there have been more people living in cities than in rural areas [1], and with the current pace, the world urban population could surpass 90% by the end of this century [2]. This worldwide urbanization process brought us many benefits but also complex problems related to pollution and environmental degradation. Earth's climate change is among the most urgent ones, and carbon dioxide (CO_2) emissions are considered the primary driver of this problem [3]. Furthermore, the rise of cities is strongly linked to this issue as urban areas account for more than 70% of CO_2 emissions [4,5] even covering less than 1% of global land surfaces [6]. Cities and the urbanization process have thus a critical role in the global climate change problem, making the question of whether urbanization promotes or mitigates climate change ubiquitous among researchers from several disciplines.

The literature about the effects of urbanization on CO_2 emissions can be roughly organized into two main groups of works whose approaches are perceived as different issues although they are closely related by scaling ideas. As in the *urban scaling* hypothesis [7,8], one of these approaches assumes that city emissions (C) are a power-law function of population size (P) [9–16], that is, $C \sim P^{\beta}$, where β is the power-law exponent. The other approach (known as *per capita density scaling*) investigates the association between emissions per capita (C/P) and population density (P/A, where A is the urban area) by also assuming a power-law function between C/P and P/A [17–19], that is, $C/P \sim (P/A)^{\alpha}$, where α is the scaling exponent. Underlying this methodological difference is the fact that urban scaling assumes population size as the most important feature for modeling urban emissions, while the per capita density scaling considers population density as the most significant variable. The urban scaling approach has produced dissonant results about the effects of population on urban emission as manifested by isometric ($\beta \approx 1$), superlinear ($\beta > 1$) or sublinear ($\beta < 1$) relationships between population and CO_2 emissions (see Table 22.1). In its turn, per capita density scaling more harmoniously asserts that an increase in population density is associated with a decrease in emissions per capita ($\alpha < 0$), although the intensity of this association varies significantly from study to study (see Table 22.1).

DOI: 10.4324/9781003288312-25

Table 22.1 Exponents associated with the urban scaling (β) and per capita density scaling (α). Abbreviations: Reduced Major Axis Regression (RMA), Ordinary Least-Squares Regression (OLS), Prais-Winsten Regression (PW), City Clustering Algorithm (CCA), Global Rural-Urban Mapping Project (GRUMP), and Global Land Cover Dataset (GLC).

Method, reference	*Country*	*Year*	*Urban Units*	*Sample Size*	*Sector*	*Value (Lower, Upper)*
Urban scaling						β
RMA [16]	Annex 1	2005	Large cities	22	N/A	0.87 (0.59, 0.95)
RMA [16]	Non-Annex 1	2005	Large cities	39	N/A	1.18 (0.90, 1.49)
OLS [14]	US	1999–2011	Metropolitan areas	1875	Local CO_2 and five air pollutants	0.75 (0.71, 0.79)
OLS [13]	US	1982–2011	Urban centers	101	Excess CO_2 from congestion	1.27 (1.21, 1.33)
PW [13]	US	1982–2011	Urban centers	101	Excess CO_2 from congestion	1.14 (1.38, 1.44)
OLS [15]	US	N/A	N/A	122	N/A	0.92 (0.90, 0.95)
OLS [15]	India	N/A	N/A	42	N/A	1.13 (1.02, 1.23)
OLS [15]	UK	N/A	N/A	35	N/A	0.76 (0.68, 0.83)
OLS [12]	GB	2010	City and administrative boundaries	28	Transport CO_2 emissions	1.02 (0.96, 1.08)
OLS [11]	US	2010	Metropolitan areas	101	Excess CO_2 from congestion	1.26 (1.17, 1.35)
OLS [11]	OECD countries	2014	Metropolitan areas	268	Transport CO_2 emissions	1.21 (1.11, 1.31)
OLS [10]	US	2002	CCA clusters ($l = 5$km, $D = 1000$)	2281	All Vulcan sectors	1.38 (1:35, 1.41)
OLS [10]	US	2002	CCA clusters ($l > 10$ km, $D = 1000$)	N/A	All Vulcan sectors	1.46 (1.44, 1.48)
OLS [9]	US	1999–2008	Metropolitan Areas	933	All Vulcan sectors	0.93 (0.92, 0.95)
Per capita density scaling						α
OLS [19]	US	2000	CCA/GRUMP/GLC ($l = 1$ km)	4585	Buildings and on-road emissions	–0.78 (N/A, N/A)
OLS [19]	US	2000	CCA/GRUMP/GLC ($l = 5$ km)	3285	Buildings and on-road emissions	–0.79 (N/A, N/A)

Table 22.1 (Continued)

Method, reference	*Country*	*Year*	*Urban Units*	*Sample Size*	*Sector*	*Value (Lower, Upper)*
OLS [19]	US	2000	CCA/GRUMP/ GLC ($l = 10$ km)	2786	Buildings and on-road emissions	–0.82 (N/A, N/A)
OLS [19]	US	2000	CCA/GRUMP ($l = 1$km)	5182	Buildings and on-road emissions	–0.90 (N/A, N/A)
OLS [19]	US	2000	CCA/GRUMP ($l = 5$km)	2156	Buildings and on-road emissions	–1.10 (N/A, N/A)
OLS [19]	US	2000	CCA/GRUMP ($l = 10$ km)	1538	Buildings and on-road emissions	–1.13 (N/A, N/A)
OLS [17]	Global	1980	World cities	32	Gasoline consumption	–0.92 (–0.85, –0.99)
OLS [18]	EU	2007–2009	European cities	134	Transport CO_2 emissions	–0.19 (N/A, N/A)
OLS [18]	EU	2007–2009	France	24	Transport CO_2 emissions	–0.39 (N/A, N/A)
OLS [18]	EU	2007–2009	Spain	22	Transport CO_2 emissions	–0.40 (N/A, N/A)

A large part of the discrepancies in the literature can be ascribed to different methodologies related to adjusting scaling laws, diverse definitions of urban units, small sample sizes, and different emission sectors under investigation (see Table 22.1). In addition, both urban scaling and per capita density scaling approaches ignore the fact that population and area are correlated [20,21], which in turn yields confounding effects and biased estimates for the scaling exponents β and α. Furthermore, by assuming either population or population density as the most relevant urban feature for describing CO_2 emissions, both approaches completely neglect the holistic possibility of an interconnected effect of population and area on urban emissions.

In this chapter, we revisit a recently proposed model for investigating urban emissions that simultaneously accounts for the effects of population and area along with possible interactions between these urban quantities [22]. This approach is inspired by the economic theory of production functions, a mathematical relationship between inputs (capital, labor, land, etc.) and output of goods (iron, cars, wheat, etc.) in some production process [23]. Thus, as in a standard economic model where the output good is a combination of capital and labor, this generalized model assumes that urban emissions are described by a two-factor production function ($C = F(P, A)$) of urban population and area. We discuss this analogy by considering the main forms of production functions (Cobb–Douglas, transcendental logarithm, and constant elasticity of substitution models) and how this generalized approach recovers urban scaling and per capita density scaling of CO_2 emissions as particular cases. By analyzing emissions in the United States, we argue that models based on production functions provide significantly better descriptions of empirical data, revealing the crucial role of interactions between population and area in the scaling of CO_2 emissions. Among other findings, this theory shows that emissions may scale sublinearly or superlinearly with population (P) and area (A) depending on whether the product $\Omega = PA$ exceeds a particular threshold Ω^*. Moreover, this approach further indicates that proportionate changes in emissions associated with proportionate changes in population and area depend on the initial values of P and A, meaning that the most important covariate for describing urban emissions also depends on the values of population and area (or population density).

22.2 Methods

The approach proposed by Ribeiro, Rybski, and Kropp [22] relies on a simple analogy with the economic theory of production functions [23]. In general terms, a production function establishes a mathematical relationship between inputs (capital, labor, land, etc.) and output of goods (iron, cars, wheat, etc.) in some production process. By putting forward this analogy, we consider urban emissions (C) as the output and population (P) and area (A) as the inputs of a two-factor production process, that is

$$C = F(P, A), \tag{22.1}$$

where $F(P, A)$ represents the form of the production function that we borrow from the theory of production functions [23]. Within this context, we can define the elasticity of scale ε as the ratio between a proportionate change in the output (emissions) and a proportionate change in the inputs (population and area), that is, $\varepsilon = (dF/F)/(dP/P)$, where $dP/P = dA/A$ represents the proportionate change in the inputs. The values of ε quantify the impact of changing population and area on emissions such that $\varepsilon < 1$ indicates decreasing returns to scale (doubling P and A implies less than doubling C), $\varepsilon > 1$ indicates increasing returns to scale (doubling P and A implies more than doubling C), and only for $\varepsilon = 1$ we have constant returns to scale (doubling P and A implies exactly doubling C). Another interesting quantity we can borrow from the theory of production functions is the marginal product. The marginal product of an input is defined as the infinitesimal change in the output resulting from an infinitesimal change in one of the inputs. Because we have two inputs, we can define the marginal product of population as $\Delta_P = dF/dP$ while the marginal product of area is $\Delta_A = dF/dA$. These quantities can also be defined in terms of logarithmic quantities, that is, $\Delta_P = d\log F/d\log P$ and $\Delta_A = d\log F/d\log A$. We can borrow other interesting quantities from the theory of production functions (such as the technical rate of substitution or the elasticity of substitution); however, the elasticity of scale and the marginal products are the most suitable for our results. Furthermore, it is worth mentioning that we can replace the variable area by population density (P/A) in our general form of production function (Eq. 22.1) as well as in the particular forms we shall consider in this chapter.

As a first example, we consider the Cobb–Douglas production function [24], that is,

$$C \sim P^{\beta_P} A^{\beta_A} \text{ or } \log C \sim \beta_P \log P + \beta_A \log A, \tag{22.2}$$

where β_P and β_A are two independent exponents. This production function recovers the usual urban scaling ($C \sim P^{\beta}$) by setting $\beta_P = \beta$ and $\beta_A = 0$ (ignoring the effect of area) and the per capita density scaling [$C/P \sim (P/A)^{\alpha}$] if $\beta_P = \alpha + 1$ and $\beta_A = -\alpha$. Similarly to these more standard scaling models, the Cobb–Douglas production function yields a scale-invariant elasticity $\varepsilon = \beta_P + \beta_A$, such that proportionate changes in emissions associated with proportionate changes in population and area are independent of P and A. Moreover, we have decreasing returns to scale for $\beta_P + \beta_A < 1$, increasing returns to scale for $\beta_P + \beta_A > 1$, and constant returns to scale if $\beta_P + \beta_A = 1$. This latter result thus reveals that per capita density scaling is a particular case of the Cobb–Douglas model with constant returns to scale, a crucial constraint that would pass unnoticed within usual scaling frameworks. From a more technical standpoint, we can further interpret the Cobb–Douglas model as the result of including urban area as a confounding variable in the usual urban scaling via a multiple linear regression in the log-transformed variables.

The interconnected role of population and area on CO_2 emissions becomes evident by noticing that isolines of the Cobb–Douglas model are straight lines on logarithmic scale, that is, $\log A \sim -(\beta_P/\beta_A)\log P$. Thus, if the population of a city increases, its population density must also increase to keep emissions unaltered. To better understand this implication, we first remark that Eq. (22.2) can be rewritten as

$$C \sim P^{\beta_P+\beta_A} (P/A)^{-\beta_A} \quad \text{or} \quad \log C \sim (\beta_P + \beta_A)\log P - \beta_A \log(P/A) \tag{22.3}$$

and thus, by assuming $\beta_P > 0$ and $\beta_A > 0$, it becomes clear that an increase in population must be followed by an increase in population in order to keep the same level of urban emissions. Equation (22.3) also allows us to conclude that, within the Cobb–Douglas hypothesis, proportionate changes in population will always impact more on CO_2 emissions than a proportionate change in density, since $|\beta_P + \beta_A| > |\beta_A|$. This latter condition simply states that the absolute value of the marginal product of population ($\beta_P + \beta_A$) is always larger than the absolute value of the marginal product of population density ($-\beta_A$).

While the Cobb–Douglas production function allows a more flexible description of urban emissions in terms of population and area (or population density), it also imposes some constraints on these emissions that may not necessarily hold in empirical data. The slope of the isolines – a quantity known as the technical rate of substitution in economics [23] – represents one of these limitations. For Eq. (22.2), this quantity is $\frac{dA}{dP} = -\frac{\beta_P}{\beta_A(P/A)}$, and thus, it is completely determined by the city density. Therefore, how much a population should change in response to alterations in area to keep the same level of emissions in a city will only depend on its population density in the Cobb–Douglas approach. Another limitation of the Cobb–Douglas model refers to the so-called elasticity of substitution [23]. This dimensionless quantity reflects the shape of the isolines, and mapped to our context, measures the efficiency at which population and area substitute each other. L-shaped isolines indicate low elasticity of substitution (that is, there is no room for replacing A by P while keeping emissions constant), whereas more linear/smooth isoquants tend to have high elasticity of substitution (it is easy to replace A by P while keeping emissions constant). It turns out that the Cobb–Douglas production function always has a unitary elasticity of substitution [23].

One possibility of overcoming these limitations is by considering the transcendental logarithmic (translog) production function [23,25]

$$\log C \sim \beta_P \log P + \beta_A \log A + \beta_C \log(P)\log(A) \tag{22.4}$$

where β_C is an additional parameter. The translog production function generalizes the Cobb–Douglas model (recovered by setting $\beta_C = 0$) by including an interaction term between population and area. This interaction term allows population effects on emissions to depend on the urban area as well as the effects of area on emissions to depend on population. Indeed, a small proportionate increment in population [$P \to (1+x)P$, with $x \ll 1$] implies a proportionate increment in emissions that depends on urban area [$C \to (1 + x(\beta_P + \beta_C \log A))C$]. Similarly, a small proportionate increment in urban area [$A \to (1+x)A$] also results in a proportionate increment in emissions that depends on population [$C \to (1 + x(\beta_A + \beta_C \log P))C$]. In other words, the marginal products of population ($\Delta_P = \beta_P + \beta_C \log A$) and area ($\Delta_A = \beta_A + \beta_C \log P$) related to the translog production function are not constants as in the Cobb–Douglas model.

Also in contrast to Eq. (22.2), the translog model presents elasticity of scale dependent on population and area, that is, $\varepsilon = \beta_P + \beta_A + \beta_C \log(PA)$. Thus, variations in urban emissions associated with proportionate changes in population and area are dependent not only on the magnitude of these changes but also on the initial values of P and A. According to this model, the more populous and the more widespread a city is, the larger the impact of a proportionate change in its population and area on its emissions. Even more intriguing is the fact that this non-constant elasticity of scale allows cities to display decreasing ($\varepsilon < 1$), increasing ($\varepsilon > 1$), or constant ($\varepsilon = 1$) returns to scale depending on whether the product $\Omega = PA$ is respectively smaller, larger, or equal to the critical value

$$\Omega^* = 10^{\frac{1-\beta_P-\beta_A}{\beta_C}}. \tag{22.5}$$

In terms of density, we can rewrite Eq. (22.4) as

$$C \sim P^{\beta_P+\beta_A+\beta_C \log P}\left(P/A\right)^{-\beta_A-\beta_C \log P}, \tag{22.6}$$

and from this expression, we find that the elasticity of scale in terms of population and density is $\varepsilon = \beta_P + \beta_C \log A$. Thus, the more widespread a city is, the larger the impact of a proportionate change of population and density on its emissions. Furthermore, in terms of population and density, decreasing ($\varepsilon < 1$), increasing ($\varepsilon > 1$), or constant ($\varepsilon = 1$) returns to scale are possible when urban area is, respectively, smaller, larger, or equal to the critical value

$$A^* = 10^{(1-\beta_P)/\beta_C}. \tag{22.7}$$

The translog model expressed in terms of population and population density further allows us to verify whether changes in population have more impact on the emissions than changes in density. To do so, we just need to compare the marginal products of population $\left[\frac{d\log C}{d\log P} = \beta_P + \beta_A + \beta_C \log(PA)\right]$ and density $\left[\frac{d\log C}{d\log(P/A)} = -\beta_A - \beta_C \log P\right]$. Assuming $\beta_P, \beta_A, \beta_C > 0$ and $A, P > 1$ and solving the inequality $\left|\frac{d\log C}{d\log P}\right| > \left|\frac{d\log C}{d\log(P/A)}\right|$, we find that population size has more impact on emissions than population density whenever urban area exceeds the threshold value

$$\widetilde{A^*} = 10^{-\beta_P/\beta_C}, \tag{22.8}$$

Table 22.2 compares and summarizes the main properties of the Cobb–Douglas and translog models, both in terms of population and area as well as in terms of population and population density.

22.3 Results

Having presented our analogy with production functions, Eqs. (22.2) and (22.4), and their main properties, we now focus on applying these models to empirical data. To do so, we use a dataset related to CO_2 emissions in US urban areas in the year 2000 [19,22]. This dataset was built using gridded population obtained from the Global Rural-Urban Mapping Project (GRUMP) [26] and the Global Land Cover Dataset (GLC) [27], and gridded sectoral emissions data (building and transportation) from the Vulcan Project [28]. From these gridded sources, the city

Table 22.2 Summary of the main properties of the Cobb–Douglas (Eq. 22.2) and translog (Eq. 22.4) models. All marginal products are expressed in logarithmic scale.

Property	*Cobb–Douglas model (Eq. 23.2)*	*Translog model (Eq. 23.4)*
Elasticity of scale in terms of P and A	$\beta_P + \beta_A$	$\beta_P + \beta_A + \beta_C \log(PA)$
Elasticity of scale in terms of P and P/A	β_P	$\beta_P + \beta_C \log A$
Technical rate of substitution between P and A	$-\dfrac{\beta_P}{\beta_A(P/A)}$	$\dfrac{-1}{(P/A)}\left(\dfrac{\beta_P + \beta_C \log A}{\beta_A + \beta_C \log P}\right)$
Elasticity of substitution	1	$-\dfrac{\beta_P + \beta_A + \beta_C \log(PA)}{C(\beta_P + \beta_A + \beta_C \log(PA) - 2\beta_C)}$
Marginal product of population (in terms of P and A)	β_P	$\beta_P + \beta_C \log A$
Marginal product of area (in terms of P and A)	β_A	$\beta_A + \beta_C \log P$
Marginal product of population (in terms of P and P/A)	$\beta_P + \beta_A$	$\beta_P + \beta_A + \beta_C \log(PA)$
Marginal product of density (in terms of P and P/A)	$-\beta_A$	$-\beta_A - \beta_C \log P$
Condition for population dominates over density	$\lvert\beta_P + \beta_A\rvert > \lvert\beta_A\rvert$	$A > 10^{-\beta_P/\beta_A}$ (if $\beta_P, \beta_A, \beta_C > 0$ and $P, A > 1$)
Condition for decreasing returns to scale (in terms of P and A)	$\beta_P + \beta_A < 0$	$PA < 10^{\frac{1-\beta_P-\beta_A}{\beta_C}}$
Condition for decreasing returns to scale (in terms of P and P/A)	$\beta_P < 0$	$A < 10^{\frac{1-\beta_P}{\beta_P}}$

clustering algorithm (CCA) [29] was used to define the urban units. This clustering algorithm assigns any two cells to the same cluster if their distance is smaller than or equal to a predefined threshold distance l, which in turn is a parameter of the method. After that, we end up with the population size (P in raw counts), area (A in square kilometers), and CO_2 emissions (C in tonnes of CO_2) for each urban unit for a given value of l. The results we describe here refer to $l = 5$ km (yielding 3285 urban units), a threshold distance that does not overestimate nor underestimate the urban extents [19]; however, similar results are obtained for l ranging from 1 km to $l = 10$ km.

We start by investigating the usual scaling relation between population and emissions on logarithmic scale, as shown in Figure 22.1A. This figure also shows the adjusted scaling law ($\log C \sim \beta \log P$) with parameter $\beta = 0.48 \pm 0.01$ (red dashed line) obtained from the usual least-squares method. From an initial analysis, this value of β is much smaller than other estimates from different datasets (Table 22.1) and indicates a strong sublinear trend between emissions and population. However, by closely inspecting the empirical data, we find that the scaling law deviates systemically from the data points and underestimates the emissions in largely populated

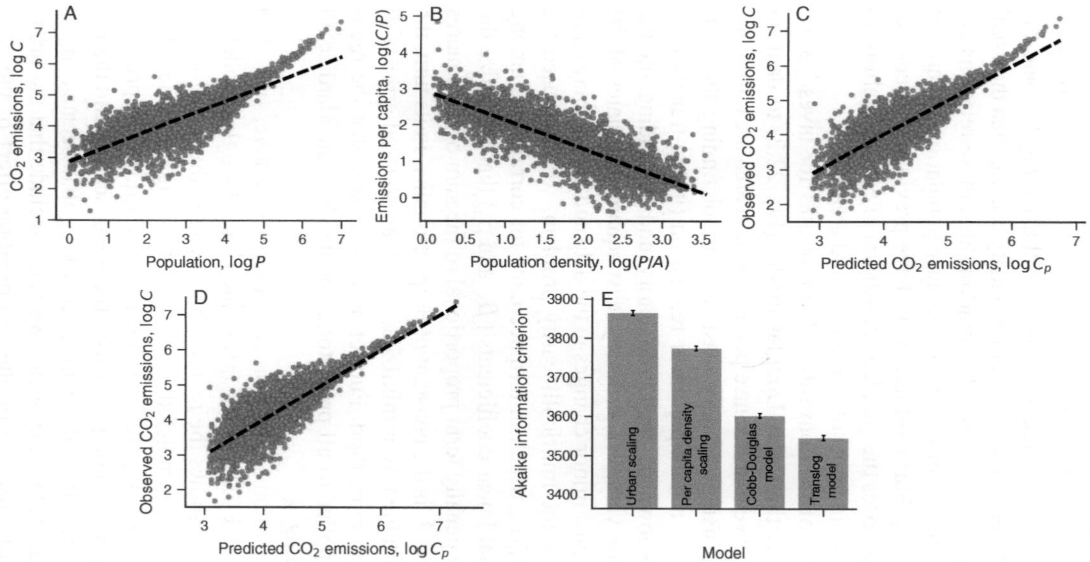

Figure 22.1 (A) Urban scaling relation between CO_2 emissions (C) and population size (P). The dashed line represents a power-law fit ($C \sim P^{\beta}$) with an exponent $\beta = 0.48 \pm 0.01$. (B) Per capita density scaling relation between CO_2 emissions per capita (C/P) and population density (P/A). The dashed line is a power-law fit [$C/P \sim (P/A)^{\alpha}$] with an exponent $\alpha = -0.79 \pm 0.01$. (C) Scatter plot of the observed values of CO_2 emissions (C) and those predicted (C_P) by the Cobb–Douglas model (Eq. 22.2 with $\beta_P = 0.31 \pm 0.01$ and $\beta_A = 0.45 \pm 0.03$). (D) Scatter plot between the observed and predicted CO_2 emissions obtained from the translog model (Eq. 22.4 with $\beta_P = 0.28 \pm 0.02$, $\beta_A = 0.14 \pm 0.05$, and $\beta_C = 0.07 \pm 0.01$). All quantities in panels (A)–(D) are expressed in base-10 logarithmic scale, and dashed lines in panels (C) and (D) represent the 1:1 relationship. (E) Comparing the goodness-of-fit among the models of urban scaling, per capita density scaling, Cobb–Douglas (Eq. 22.2), and translog (Eq. 22.4). The bars show the average Akaike information criterion (AIC) estimated from 1000 different random samplings (with replacement) of our data, while the error bars are 95% bootstrap confidence intervals. The smaller the values of the AIC, the better is the quality of fit.

Source: Adapted from Ref. [22].

areas. Moving to the per capita density scaling framework, Figure 22.1B shows the relationship between emissions per capita and population density on a logarithmic scale. In this figure, the blue dashed line shows the adjusted scaling relation ($\log C/P \sim \alpha \log P/A$), where the scaling exponent $\alpha = -0.79 \pm 0.01$ is obtained by fitting the data with the ordinary-least-squares method. This negative value of α agrees with other estimates from the literature (Table 22.1) and indicates that every increase in the population density of a city associates with a reduction in its CO_2 emissions per capita. While the agreement between the scaling law and the empirical data is significantly better for the per capita density scaling than the usual scaling approach (see Figure 22.1E), it is worth remarking that these relations are likely to be biased by the confounding effect of area because population and area of urban units are correlated [20,21]. Furthermore, as we have previously discussed, the per capita density scaling imposes the "hidden" constraint of constant returns to scale when expressing emissions in terms of population and area.

To overcome the limitations of the conventional approaches for investigating urban emissions, we first adjust the Cobb–Douglas model (Eq. 22.2) to data. In this case, it is important to observe that because population and area are correlated to each other, one must avoid using ordinary least-squares for finding the best-fitting parameters β_P and β_A via a multiple linear regression (in log-transformed variables). This problem is known as multicollinearity and depending on the degree of correlation among the variables, ordinary least-squares estimates of the parameters can be unstable against minor changes in the data and also display large standard errors. To account for the multicollinearity problem, we have used the ridge regression approach [30,31], which in turn accounts for correlations among the variables by finding optimal linear coefficients (β_P and β_A) that minimize the residual sum of squares plus a penalty term proportional to the sum of the squares of the linear coefficients, where λ is the constant of proportionality. In its turn, the optimal value of $\lambda = \lambda^*$ is obtained by minimizing the mean squared error with the leave-one-out cross-validation method. Furthermore, to ensure that the regularization term is uniformly applied to all predictors, one needs to standardize all predictor variables before finding λ^*.

By using the ridge regression approach as described above, we find $\beta_P = 0.31 \pm 0.01$ and $\beta_A = 0.45 \pm 0.03$ when fitting the Cobb–Douglas model to the empirical data. Figure 22.1C shows the relationship between the actual values of the urban emissions and those predicted by the Cobb–Douglas model. The Akaike information criterion (AIC, Figure 22.1E) shows that Eq. (22.2) provides a significantly better fit to data when compared with the urban scaling and the per capita density scaling approaches. It is also worth remarking that because β_P is much smaller than β (the usual scaling exponent) we can conclude that the urban scaling approach is significantly affected by the confounding effect of the area. Moreover, because $\beta_P + \beta_A = 0.76$, the association between emissions and population and area displays diminishing returns, such that every 1% increase in both the population and area of a city associates with a 0.76% increase in its emissions. In terms of population and population density (Eq. 22.3), our estimates indicate that if the population of a given city decreases by 1% while its density remains constant (that is, a 1.01% increase in its area), its emissions would decrease 0.76%; whereas a 1% rise in its density while population is unaltered (that is, a 1% reduction in its area), implies only a 0.45% decrease in its CO_2 emissions. This result thus confirms that, according to the Cobb–Douglas model, a proportionate change in population always has more impact on emissions than a proportionate change in density.

Although the Cobb–Douglas model improves the description of our empirical data, it also imposes constraints on the behavior of emissions in terms of population and area that may not necessarily hold. As discussed, these limitations include a constant elasticity of scale (ε) and unitary elasticity of substitution. Furthermore, the Cobb–Douglas description of data shows a systematic bias for large emission values that is similar to what we have found for the usual urban scaling but with a smaller degree. In the context of this chapter, the next logical step toward a more flexible function for modeling emissions in terms of population and area is the translog production function (Eq. 22.4). The translog model has an additional parameter β_C compared with the Cobb–Douglas model (recovered for $\beta_C = 0$) that introduces an interaction term [$\beta_C \log(P)\log(A)$, in Eq. 22.4] between population and area, allowing the effects of population and area on emissions to vary with population and area.

To avoid the multicollinearity problem, we have also fitted the translog model to our data with the ridge regression approach, finding $\beta_P = 0.28 \pm 0.02$, $\beta_A = 0.14 \pm 0.05$, and $\beta_C = 0.07 \pm 0.01$ as the best-fitting parameters. Figure 22.1A shows the relationship between the actual values of emissions and those predicted by the translog model. We observe that Eq. (22.4) refines the quality of the predictions and reduces the bias observed for the Cobb–Douglas model in urban areas with high emissions. A more rigorous comparison of goodness-of-fit using the Akaike information criterion (AIC) confirms that the translog model is a significantly better description compared to urban scaling, per capita density scaling, and Cobb–Douglas, as shown in Figure 22.1E. Moreover, because the interaction term is significantly different from zero and positive, we can conclude that the effect of population and area on emissions intensifies with the increase of urban population and area. This fact becomes clear by using the adjusted parameters to estimate the elasticity of scale ε, which in turn yields $\varepsilon = 0.42 + 0.07\log(PA)$. Thus, the more populous and the more widespread a city is, the larger is the impact of a proportionate change in its population and area (a growth with constant density) on its emissions.

As we have already discussed, this change in behavior with population and area allows the translog model to display decreasing, increasing, or constant returns to scale depending on whether the product $\Omega = PA$ is respectively smaller, larger, or equal to the critical value Ω^* defined in Eq. (22.5). By plugging the adjusted values of β_P, β_A, and β_C into Eq. (22.5), we find $\Omega^* \approx 1.93 \times 10^8$, thus making it possible to find cities that display decreasing ($\Omega < \Omega^*$) and increasing ($\Omega > \Omega^*$) returns to scale. For instance, a large metropolitan area about the dimensions of Chicago ($P = 8 \times 10^6$ and $A = 6000$ km^2) has $\Omega = 4.8 \times 10^{10} > \Omega^*$ and thus presents increasing returns to scale – every 1% increase in its population and area is associated with a 1.17% rise in its emissions. Conversely, a relatively small city about the dimensions of Santa Fe ($P = 90,000$ and $A = 140\,\text{km}^2$) has $\Omega = 12.6\times10^6 < \Omega^*$ and thus presents decreasing returns to scale – the same 1% increase in population and area associates now only with a 0.92% rise in its emissions. This behavior is in stark contrast with the scale-invariant elasticity of the Cobb–Douglas model and emphasizes that proportionate changes in emissions caused by changes in both population and area depend not only on the intensity of the changes but also on the initial values of population and area.

In terms of population and population density (Eq. 22.6), the translog model yields an elasticity of scale $\varepsilon = 0.28 + 0.07\log A$, and thus, the more widespread a city is, the larger is the impact of a proportionate change of population and density (that is, area remains constant) on its emissions. For instance, a 1% increase in population and density of a large city with 6,000 km^2 associates with a 0.54% increase in its emissions, while the same change in a city with 140 km^2 correlates with a 0.42% rise in its emissions. Furthermore, we analyze the conditions for increasing and decreasing returns to scale in terms of population and density by calculating the critical area A^* defined in Eq. (22.7). By using the adjusted parameters, we find $A^* \approx 1.93\times10^{10}$ km^2 for our data – an area roughly corresponding to 38 times the area of Earth – such that only decreasing returns to scale are possible when emissions are described in terms of population and density. Thus, for the US data, any increase in the population of a city that keeps area constant leads to decreasing returns to scale.

In addition, the translog written in Eq. (22.6) allows us to compare the impacts of individual changes in population or population density via the marginal products of these input variables. As we have discussed in the previous sections, for $\beta_P, \beta_A, \beta_C > 0$ and $A, P > 1$ – assumptions that agree with our estimates – the marginal product of population is larger than the marginal product of density whenever the urban area exceeds the critical area $\widetilde{A^*}$ defined in Eq. (22.8). From the estimated values of β_P and β_C, we find $\widetilde{A^*} \sim 10^{-4}$ km^2, and therefore proportionate changes in population always have more impact on emissions than proportionate changes in density. Note that the same conclusion was obtained from the Cobb–Douglas model. However, differently from the Cobb–Douglas model, the translog model predicts that the impact of population and density on emissions increases with population and density. Thus, the densification of large urban areas impacts proportionally more on emissions than the increase of density of small towns. For instance, the translog model predicts that a 1% densification of a small city with 10,000 inhabitants associates with a 0.42% reduction in its emissions, while the same densification in a large city with 1 million inhabitants associates with a 0.56% reduction in its emissions. The impact of the densification of large populated urban areas on the reduction of urban emissions becomes even more critical in absolute terms and when considering that large metropolitan areas are expected to grow more than their small counterparts.

22.4 Summary and discussion

Carbon dioxide emissions are one of the leading causes of Earth's climate change, and over 70% of such emissions are associated with activities occurring in urban areas [4,5]. This fact assigns cities a central role in the global climate change problem, which in turn motivates a growing scientific literature about the effects of urbanization on emissions. As discussed, part of this literature is divided into two main groups whose approaches are perceived as different issues although closely related by scaling ideas. One of these approaches – *urban scaling* [9–16] – assumes city emissions as a power-law function of population size. The other approach – *per capita density scaling* [17–19] – investigates the association between emissions per capita and population density by also assuming a power-law relation between these quantities. Thus, the first group assumes population size as the most important feature for modeling urban emissions, while the second considers population density as the most significant variable. Both approaches have led to controversial results about the effects of population or population density on urban emissions (Table 22.1), and part of these discrepancies is caused by correlations between urban population and urban area as well as their interconnected role on urban emissions.

This chapter has described an approach that combines ideas from these two bodies of the urban emissions literature into a coherent approach that simultaneously considers the effects of population and area or population and density as well as interactions between these pairs of quantities [22]. The core of this novel approach is an analogy with the economic theory of production functions [23]. In the same way that different combinations of capital and labor may lead to a similar output of goods in a factory, our approach considers that urban emission is mediated by a process involving population and area or population and density. By borrowing classical forms of production functions from economic theory, we have shown that this analogy not only accounts for confounding factors ignored by the standard scaling approaches but significantly refines the description of the emissions in terms of urban quantities. These models further reveal intriguing aspects about the interplay between population and area or population and density on urban emissions that are entirely neglected under the standard scaling approaches. Among these findings is the possibility of having an elasticity of scale dependent on population and area, such that changes in emissions caused by proportionate changes in population or density may not only depend on the magnitude of these changes but also on the initial values of these quantities. This behavior in turn allows urban emissions to display increasing or decreasing returns. Using US data, we have verified that emissions scale superlinearly or sublinearly with population and area depending on whether the product between these quantities exceeds $\Omega^* \approx 1.93 \times 10^8$. However, when describing emissions in terms of population and population density, results indicate that urban emissions can only display decreasing returns to scale – simultaneous doubling population and density of a city is always associated with less than doubling its emissions. Moreover, for US urban areas, we find that population changes always have a greater impact on emissions than population density.

We believe that the framework described here has great potential for investigating urban emissions in other regions and opens a wide range of possibilities for exploring the interplay between population and area (or population and density) in urban scaling in other indicators. Indeed, some recent studies have shown that this analogy with production functions is also useful for investigating the interconnected role of population and incoming commuters on urban wealth creation [32]. Similarly to our findings for urban emissions, Ref. [32] has shown that increasing returns to scale of urban GDP is only possible when the product between population and number of incoming commuters exceeds a well-defined threshold – a condition that is verified for approximately 63% of all urban areas in the US and Brazil. Thus, beyond improving the description of urban emissions, these models inspired by production functions can further help us achieve a better understanding of cities as complex interconnected systems.

Note

1 Ribeiro, H.V., Rybski, D. & Kropp, J.P. Effects of changing population or density on urban carbon dioxide emissions. *Nat Commun* 10, 3204 (2019).

References

[1] United Nations. World urbanization prospects: Urban population (% of total). Available: http://data.worldbank.org/indicator/SP.URB.TOTL.IN.ZS. Accessed: May 2022.

[2] Jiang, L. & O'Neill, B. C. Global urbanization projections for the Shared Socioeconomic Pathways. *Global Environmental Change* 42, 193–199 (2017).

[3] Schellnhuber, H. J., Cramer, W., Nakicenovic, N., Wigley, T. & Yohe, G. *Avoiding Dangerous Climate Change* (Cambridge University Press, New York, 2006).

[4] Johansson, T. B., Patwardhan, A. P., Nakicenovic, N. & Gomez-Echeverri, L. *Global Energy Assessment: Toward a Sustainable Future* (Cambridge University Press, Cambridge, 2012).

[5] Seto, K. *et al.* Chapter 12 – Human Settlements, Infrastructure and Spatial Planning. In *Climate Change 2014: Mitigation of Climate Change. IPCC Working Group III Contribution to AR5* (Cambridge University Press, New York, 2014).

[6] Esch, T. *et al.* Breaking new ground in mapping human settlements from space – The Global Urban Footprint. *ISPRS Journal of Photogrammetry and Remote Sensing* 134, 30–42 (2017).

[7] Bettencourt, L. M. A., Lobo, J., Helbing, D., Kühnert, C. & West, G. B. Growth, innovation, scaling, and the pace of life in cities. *Proceedings of the National Academy of Sciences* 104, 7301–7306 (2007).

[8] West, G. B. *Scale: The Universal Laws of Growth, Innovation, Sustainability, and the Pace of Life in Organisms, Cities, Economies, and Companies* (Penguin, New York, 2017).

[9] Fragkias, M., Lobo, J., Strumsky, D. & Seto, K. C. Does size matter? Scaling of CO_2 emissions and U.S. urban areas. *PLOS ONE* 8, e64727 (2013).

[10] Oliveira, E. A., Andrade, J. S. & Makse, H. A. Large cities are less green. *Scientific Reports* 4, 4235 (2014).

[11] Louf, R. & Barthelemy, M. How congestion shapes cities: From mobility patterns to scaling. *Scientific Reports* 4, 5561 (2014).

[12] Mohajeri, N., Gudmundsson, A. & French, J. R. CO_2 emissions in relation to street-network configuration and city size. *Transportation Research Part D: Transport and Environment* 35, 116–129 (2015).

[13] Chang, Y. S., Lee, Y. J. & Choi, S. S. B. Is there more traffic congestion in larger cities? – Scaling analysis of the 101 largest US urban centers. *Transport Policy* 59, 54–63 (2017).
[14] Muller, N. Z. & Jha, A. Does environmental policy affect scaling laws between population and pollution? Evidence from American metropolitan areas. *PLOS ONE* 12, e0181407 (2017).
[15] Rybski, D. *et al.* Cities as nuclei of sustainability? *Environment and Planning B* 44, 425–440 (2017).
[16] Gudipudi, R. *et al.* The efficient, the intensive, and the productive: Insights from urban Kaya scaling. *Applied Energy* 236, 155–162 (2019).
[17] Newman, P. W. C. & Kenworthy, J. R. Gasoline consumption and cities. *Journal of the American Planning Association* 55, 24–37 (1989).
[18] Baur, A. H., Thess, M., Kleinschmit, B. & Creutzig, F. Urban climate change mitigation in Europe: Looking at and beyond the role of population density. *Journal of Urban Planning and Development* 140, 04013003 (2013).
[19] Gudipudi, R., Fluschnik, T., Ros, A. G. C., Walther, C. & Kropp, J. P. City density and CO_2 efficiency. *Energy Policy* 91, 352–361 (2016).
[20] Stewart, J. Q. Suggested principles of 'social physics'. *Science* 106, 179–180 (1947).
[21] Batty, M. & Ferguson, P. Defining city size. *Environment and Planning B* 38, 753–756 (2011).
[22] Ribeiro, H. V., Rybski, D. & Kropp, J. P. Effects of changing population or density on urban carbon dioxide emissions. *Nature Communications* 10, 1–9 (2019).
[23] David F. Heathfield, S. W. *An Introduction to Cost and Production Functions* (Macmillan, London, 1987).
[24] Cobb, C. W. & Douglas, P. H. A theory of production. *American Economic Review* 18, 139–165 (1928).
[25] Christensen, L. R., Jorgenson, D. W. & Lau, L. J. Transcendental logarithmic production frontiers. *Review of Economics and Statistics* 55, 28–45 (1973).
[26] Center for International Earth Science Information Network – CIESIN – Columbia University, International Food Policy Research Institute – IFPRI, The World Bank, and Centro Internacional de Agricultura Tropical – CIAT. 2011. *Global Rural-Urban Mapping Project, Version 1 (GRUMPv1): Population Density Grid.* Palisades: NASA Socioeconomic Data and Applications Center (SEDAC). Available: http://sedac.ciesin.columbia.edu/data/set/grump-v1-population-density. Accessed: May 2022.
[27] Global Land Cover 2000 Project (GLC 2000). Available: http://forobs.jrc.ec.europa.eu/products/glc2000/glc2000.php. Accessed: May 2022.
[28] Gurney, K. R. *et al.* Vulcan Science Methods Documentation, Version 2.0. Available: http://vulcan.project.asu.edu. Accessed: May 2022.
[29] Rozenfeld, H. D. *et al.* Laws of population growth. Proceedings of the National *Academy of Sciences* 105, 18702–18707 (2008).
[30] Hastie, T., Tibshirani, R. & Friedman, J. *The Elements of Statistical Learning: Data Mining, Inference, and Prediction*, 2nd edn (Springer, New York, 2016).
[31] Hoerl, A. E. & Kennard, R. W. Ridge regression: Biased estimation for nonorthogonal problems. *Technometrics* 12, 55–67 (1970).
[32] Alves, L. G., Rybski, D. & Ribeiro, H. V. Commuting network effect on urban wealth scaling. *Scientific Reports* 11, 1–10 (2021).

23 The impacts of urbanisation and travel behaviour on transport CO_2 emissions

From scaling relations to urban sustainability[1]

Nahid Mohajeri and Agust Gudmundsson

23.1 Introduction and background

The total population of the United Kingdom is expected to increase from 63 million in 2011 to 73 million people in 2037 – the (2023) population being estimated at about 69 million. A population growth from 63 to 73 million is a 16% increase in only 26 years. An increase by 16% in 26 years puts the urban infrastructure, particularly the transportation infrastructure, under significant pressure. The infrastructure of urban areas, particularly the transport infrastructure, basically determines the overall shapes, productivity, and sustainability of cities. Additionally, transport is a major source of greenhouse gas emissions. More specifically, transport-related CO_2 emissions are about 30% of the total for developed countries and 23% of the total worldwide anthropogenic CO_2 emissions. Transport on roads constitutes about 20% of the EU's total emissions of CO_2. Transport is the largest emitting sector of GHG emissions, producing 24% of the UK's total emissions in 2020 from UK territorial greenhouse gas emissions national statistics in 2022.

Some 91% of emissions from domestic transport are from vehicles on roads. More specifically, the biggest contributors to GHG emissions from domestic transport were cars and taxis (responsible for 52%), heavy goods vehicles (HGVs) responsible for 19%, and vans responsible for 16% of the emissions. In view of this, it is clearly of great importance to understand the relation between different transport modes and carbon dioxide (CO_2) emissions [1].

There has been considerable work on the relations between urban growth, city size, and transport-related CO_2 emissions [2,3]. Few studies, however, have analysed the scaling relations between urban travel behaviour and transport CO_2 emissions. In this study, we report the results of estimated transport-related CO_2 emissions (at local authority district level, LAD) from 347 LADs in England (see Figure 23.1). The focus is on the relationship between urbanisation (ratio between urban and rural areas) and travel behaviour. The main aims of this study are two-fold. First, to explore how urbanisation affects transport-related energy use and associated CO_2 emissions. Second, to analyse the scaling relations between travel behaviour, CO_2 emissions, and fuel consumption.

DOI: 10.4324/9781003288312-26

23.2 Data and method

There is no clear-cut agreed-on definition as to what should count as a city boundary. The definitions used vary depending on the applications. In this chapter we use the administrative boundaries for all the 347 (LADs) as determined by the United Kingdom Office for National Statistics. The CO_2 emissions and fuel consumption datasets used here were provided by the UK government and are based on the administrative boundaries that cover both urban and (occasionally large) rural areas. The focus of the present study is only on the CORINE urban fabric (continuous and discontinuous), rather than areas defined by administrative boundaries, as obtained from the Environmental Information Data Centre. The continuous urban fabric class is assigned when urban structures and transport networks dominate the surface area (>80% of the land surface). By contrast, the discontinuous urban fabric class is assigned when urban structures and transport networks associated with vegetated areas and bare surfaces are present and occupy significant parts of the surface in a discontinuous spatial pattern (30–80% land surface) [4,5].

We use the CORINE urban areas so as to avoid overestimation of urban area when using administrative boundaries. Also, using CORINE, the CO_2 emissions and fuel consumptions are then related solely to the cities themselves and not contaminated by the inclusion of part of their surrounding rural areas. Transport fuel consumption from Sub-national Consumption Statistics in 2018 and associated CO_2 emissions datasets from Local Authority CO_2 emissions estimates in 2018 were provided by the UK Department of Energy and Climate Change (Open Government License) for 2010 at a spatial resolution of 1×1 km. Transport fuel consumption for 2010 is estimated for two fuel types, namely petrol and diesel, type of vehicle – namely motorcycle, car, bus, HGVs, and LGVs (light goods vehicles) – and the type of road (motorways, A roads, and minor roads). We classify buses, diesel cars, HGVs, and diesel LGVs as diesel-consuming vehicles. By contrast, motorcycles, petrol cars, and petrol LGVs are classified as petrol-consuming vehicles. The estimations refer to where the fuel was consumed and not to where it was purchased. It follows that, for example, road fuel purchased abroad and consumed in the UK is included in these data, whereas road fuel purchased in the UK and consumed abroad is excluded. Therefore, the methods used here for calculating fuel consumption by road vehicles combine traffic activity data (from the Department for Transport [DfT]'s national traffic census) with fleet composition data and fuel consumption/emission factors.

Allometry as originally used in biology [6–8] describes how and in what way organisms, as they grow, maintain certain ratios among the various geometric aspects of their bodies. Today allometry has a wider meaning as to the growth of some parts relative to a standard (or, in biology, an entire organism). Allometric scaling shows how the quantity of interest, Y, depends on the size of a system X [2,9,10] through the following relation:

$$Y = AX^{\alpha} \tag{23.1}$$

or, by taking logarithms on both sides,

$$\log(Y) = A + \alpha \log(X) \tag{23.2}$$

where α is the allometric or scaling exponent and A is a normalisation constant. A bi-logarithmic (log–log) plot of two variables X and Y that yields a straight line indicates an allometric power-law relationship between the two variables. In Eqs. (23.1, 23.2) the parameter α is the slope of the regression line in the log–log plot and is particularly important for quantifying the allometric relationship between the two variables. Many human activities fit into three categories based on the value of α in Eqs. (23.1) and (23.2), namely: (i) A linear relation, in which case the scaling exponent α is roughly equal to 1. This is applicable to many human needs (water, houses, and jobs) that scale with city or population size. (ii) A sublinear relation, in which case α is less than 1. This relation implies that the quantity of interest grows at a slower rate than the population. For example, sublinear relations exist between city size and the number of gasoline stations, the cumulative length of electrical cables, and cumulative road surface (material and infrastructure). (iii) A superlinear relation, in which case α is greater than 1, occurs when the social activity pattern influences the urban indicator. For example, superlinear relations exist between city size [11] and income and wages, gross domestic product, bank deposits, and rates of invention measured by the number of patents [12,13]. Superlinear relations imply that larger cities generate proportionally more economic activity and human productivity.

23.3 Results

The results are presented in the three following sections.

23.3.1 Scaling relations between travel behaviour (distance commuted to work) and urbanisation (defined by CORINE urban area)

Figure 23.1 shows that as the CORINE urban area become larger, the distance to work increases, but not at the same rate as the area increases, for the following reasons. (i) As population increases the area becomes more urbanised which means the distances for many to the working places decrease. (ii) When the CORINE urban area expands it may change to a multi-centre which, again, contributes to the distances to work being comparatively short. Also, as an area becomes more urbanised the CORINE urban area increases proportionally to the rural area. As a consequence, the use of cars/vans/taxis decreases and the use of public transport and walking and cycling increases.

23.3.2 Scaling relations between travel behaviour (modes of transport) and urbanisation

Modes of transport to work show clear relationships with the size of CORINE urban area. The share for cars/taxis/vans (private transport) increases as the area

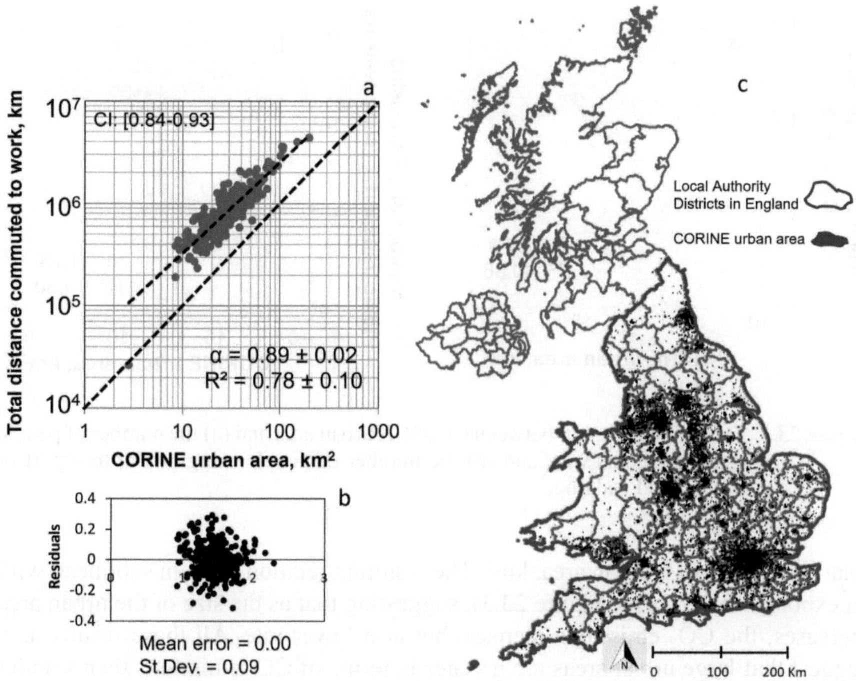

Figure 23.1 Scaling relations between the urbanised part of each LADs, that is, the CORINE urban areas, with (a) the total distance travelled to work and (b) associated error estimation (b). The CORINE urban area for each LAD is shown in (c).

becomes more urbanised, but in a sublinear fashion (see Figure 23.2). This means that the use of cars/taxis/vans increases at a lower rate than the size of the CORINE urban area. Public transport, as well as cyclic and walking, by contrast, increases in a superlinear fashion with increasing urbanisation, that is, with growth of CORINE urban area. These results indicate that as the size of the CORINE urban area increases – which generally indicates an increasing city size – there is some shift from private to public transport, the latter also including walking and cycling.

23.3.3 Scaling relations between travel behaviour, urbanisation, transport CO_2 emission, and fuel consumption

The transport CO_2 emissions (in metric tonnes) and fuel consumption (tonnes) show clear sublinear relations with total travel distance commuted to work, that is, with the scaling exponents of 0.82 and 0.84, respectively (see Figure 23.3). The results imply that as the travel distance increases, transport CO_2 emissions grow but at a much lower rate. We also analysed the transport CO_2 emissions in

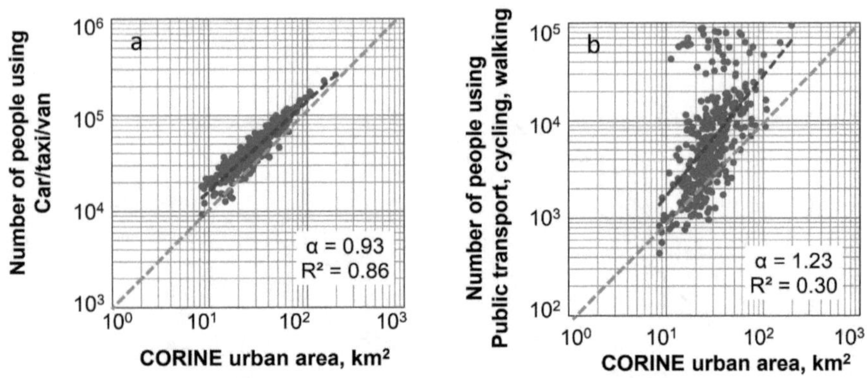

Figure 23.2 The scaling relation between CORINE urban area and (a) the number of people using cars/taxis/vans and (b) the number of people using public transport or cycling and walking.

relation to CORINE urban area, km^2. The resulting relation is again sublinear, with an exponent of 0.78 (see Figure 23.3), suggesting that as the size of the urban area increases, the CO_2 emissions increase but at a lower rate. All these results may suggest that large urban areas are greener in terms of CO_2 emissions than smaller urban areas. However, calculated population sizes depend on city-boundary definitions, and there is not at present a general agreement as to how city boundaries should be defined. Thus, populations may not necessarily be the best parameter to measure CO_2 against, and the results need to be put into a wider context before firm conclusions can be reached.

23.4 Discussion and conclusions

In this study, allometric scaling relations are used to address the question whether environmental impacts of transport in cities become proportionally less or greater with increasing urbanisation and reduced travel distance. More specifically, are large urban areas more or less sustainable than smaller urban areas as regards transport energy (fuel) use and the CO_2 emissions? Here we address the above questions in two ways using scaling relations. First, we consider the scaling relations between the CORINE urban areas and (i) travel distance and (ii) travel modes. Second, we compare the transport fuel consumption and CO_2 emissions with the travel distance and the size of the CORINE urban area.

Some studies show contrasting results as to the scaling relation between CO_2 emissions and city size. The results may partly depend on how a city is defined and whether the city boundary is regarded as the administrative boundary [2] or based on the City Clustering Algorithm (CCA) [3]. The present results, however, show clear sublinear relations between transport CO_2 emissions and fuel consumption,

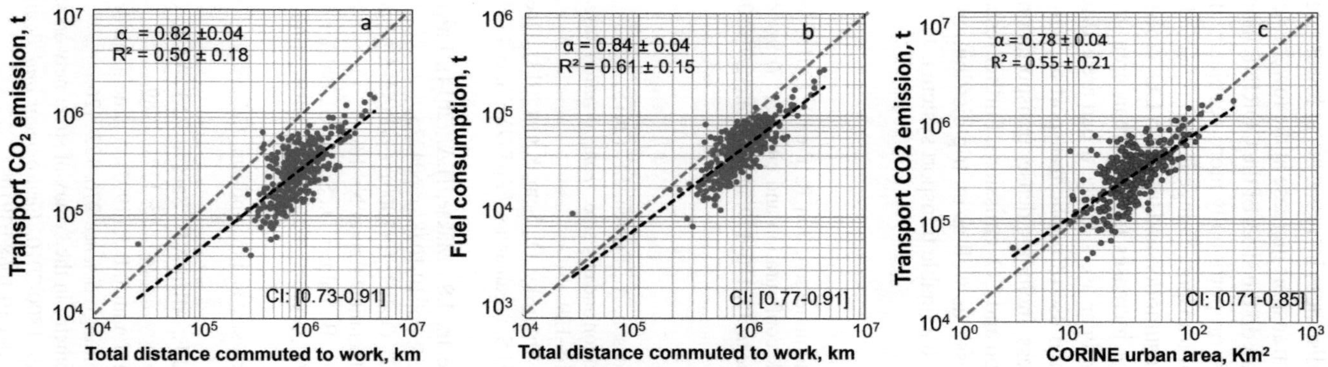

Figure 23.3 The scaling relations between total distance commuted to work (in km) and (a) transport CO_2 emission and (b) fuel consumption (both in metric tonnes [t], where 1 tonne = 1000 kg). (c) The scaling relation between CORINE size of the urban area (in km^2) and transport CO_2. CI shows the lower and upper limit of confidence intervals for α, scaling exponent.

on one hand, with the travel distances and the sizes of the CORINE urban areas, on the other. Thus, the total fuel consumption and CO_2 emissions both increase as the urbanisation and travel distances increase, but at lower rates. More specifically, travel distances and private transport increase at the lower rate (but public/cycling/walking at a higher rate) than do the sizes of the CORINE urban areas. This means that as the urban area grows, proportionally more people are using public than private transport. This mode of transport change is also reflected in fuel consumption and CO_2 emissions. Fuel consumption and transport CO_2 emissions grow at a lower rate than the travel distance increases (as the urban area grows), which implies proportionally fewer cars and car users. Large urban areas discourage transport by private car and encourage the use of public transport as well as walking/cycling. Increasing urban compactness, including denser transportation networks, may thus help reduce fuel consumption and CO_2 emissions. Further research on low and high urban densities (compactness), as well as on trip distributions, should help in the effective planning of more sustainable transport systems.

Note

1 Nahid Mohajeri, Agust Gudmundsson, Jon R. French (2015, March). CO_2 emissions in relation to street-network configuration and city size. *Transportation Research Part D: Transport and Environment*. 35, 116–129. https://doi.org/10.1016/j.trd.2014.11.02

References

[1] Mohajeri, N., Gudmundsson, A., French, J.F. (2015). CO2 emissions in relation to street-network configuration and city size. *Transportation Research Part D: Transport and Environment* 35, 116–129.

[2] Fragkias, M., Lobo, J., Strumsky, D., Seto, K.C. (2013). Does size matter? Scaling of CO2 emissions and U.S. urban areas. *PLoS ONE* 8, e64727. doi:10.1371/ journal.pone.0064727.

[3] Oliveira, E.A., Andrade Jr., J.S., Makse, H.A. (2014). Large cities are less green. *Scientific Reports* 4, 4235. doi:10.1038/srep04235.

[4] Bossard, M., Feranec, J., Otahel, J. (2000). *CORINE land cover technical guide – Addendum 2000*. EEA Technical Report No 40.

[5] Cole, B., King, S., Ogutu, B., Palmer, D., Smith, G., Balzter, H. (2015). *Corine Land Cover 2012 for the UK, Jersey and Guernsey*. NERC Environmental Information Data Centre.

[6] Kleiber, M. (1932). Body size and metabolism. *Hilgardia: A Journal of Agricultural Science* 6, 315–351.

[7] Brown, J.H., Gillooly J.F., Allen A.P., Savage V.M., West, G.B. (2004). Toward a metabolic theory of ecology. *Ecology* 85, 1771–1789.

[8] West, G.B., Brown, J.H. Enquist, B.J. (1997). A general model for the origin of allometric scaling laws in biology. *Science* 276, 122–126.

[9] Shpuza, E. (2014). Allometry in the syntax of street networks: Evolution of Adriatic and Ionian coastal cities 1800-2010. *Environment and Planning B: Planning and Design* 41(3), 450–471. doi:10.1068/b39109.

[10] Yakubo, K., Saijo, Y. (2014). Superlinear and sublinear urban scaling in geographical network model of the city. *arXive.1401.3956v1* [physics.soc.ph].
[11] Batty, M. (2008). The size, scale, and shape of cities. *Science* 319, 769–771.
[12] Bettencourt L.M.A., Lobo L., Helbing, D., Ku¨hnert, C., West, G.B. (2007). Growth, innovation, scaling, and the pace of life in cities. *Proceedings of National Academics of Science* 104, 7301–7306.
[13] Bettencourt, L.M.A., West, G.B. (2010). A unified theory of urban living. *Nature* 467, 912–913.

Part IV
Infrastructure

24 Allometric relations between structural fractal dimensions of road networks and urban quantities[1]

Tian Lan, Zhilin Li, and Hong Zhang

24.1 Introduction

Cities are evolving complex systems composed of people and activities [1]. As fundamental elements of cities, urban roads not only form the skeletons for the physical extension of cities but also distribute energy, materials, and people to locations [2]. Previous studies have shown that road networks are fractals (i.e., statistically self-similar objects), and a variety of quantitative relations between geometric fractal dimension D_g (i.e., a measure describing the space-filling capacity of an object in its geometric form) of road networks and urban quantities have been discovered [3–5]. However, the complexity of road networks is not only related to their geometric forms, but also to their topological structures, which can be described by structural fractal dimension D_s (i.e., a measure describing the complexity of an object with its topological connections) [6,7]. To the best of our knowledge, whether some potential relations (such as allometric relations) exist with D_s of road networks in a growing individual city is still unclear. It has been reported that "our understanding of how cities evolve is still woefully inadequate" [8]. In fact, exploring how the complexity of road networks evolves with urban environmental, social, and economic quantities is helpful to understand how cities evolve.

This study aims to study potential allometric relationships between D_s of urban road networks and urban quantities for a growing individual city during a long period. The reminder of this chapter is organized as follows. Section 24.2 introduces the structural representation of road networks in topological space and illustrates the box-counting approach for calculating structural fractal dimensions. Section 24.3 presents the discovered allometric relations with structural fractal dimensions of urban road networks. Finally, some discussions and conclusions are provided in Section 24.4.

24.2 Roads in topological space

24.2.1 Structural representation of roads

In the past few years, some road representation methods have been developed based on semantic (e.g., road names), geometric (e.g., road shapes), and structural (e.g.,

DOI: 10.4324/9781003288312-28

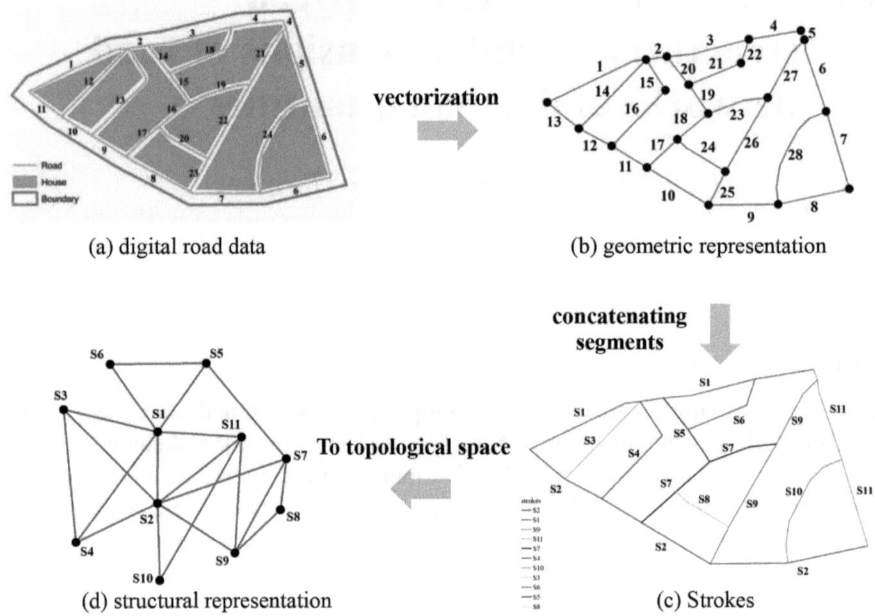

Figure 24.1 Transforming representations of road networks.

road intersections) properties of road networks [9–12]. Those representations based on semantic and geometric properties are embedded in the geographic space where accurate geometric information of road networks can be acquired (e.g., shape and direction). However, the connection relations between roads are not emphasized in such ways. The structural representations are embedded in topological space where road networks are represented by abstract graphs made up of vertices and edges. In this way, some new properties of road networks have been found, such as small-world and scale-free [13,14].

In this study, structural representation is employed. The acquired digital road data are first vectorized into the geometric representation. Then, the road segments are concatenated into strokes (i.e., long roads). Finally, these strokes are transformed into topological space where vertices and edges refer to the previous strokes and connection relations between strokes, respectively. The whole transformation process has been clearly illustrated in Figure 24.1 modified from Lan et al. [15].

24.2.2 Computing structural fractal dimensions: box-counting approach

In this study, 10 sets of Hong Kong topographic maps (hard copies) from 1971 to 2011 were obtained from the Lands Department of Hong Kong (www.landsd.gov.hk/en/). By extracting road networks from these paper maps (see Figure 24.2) and

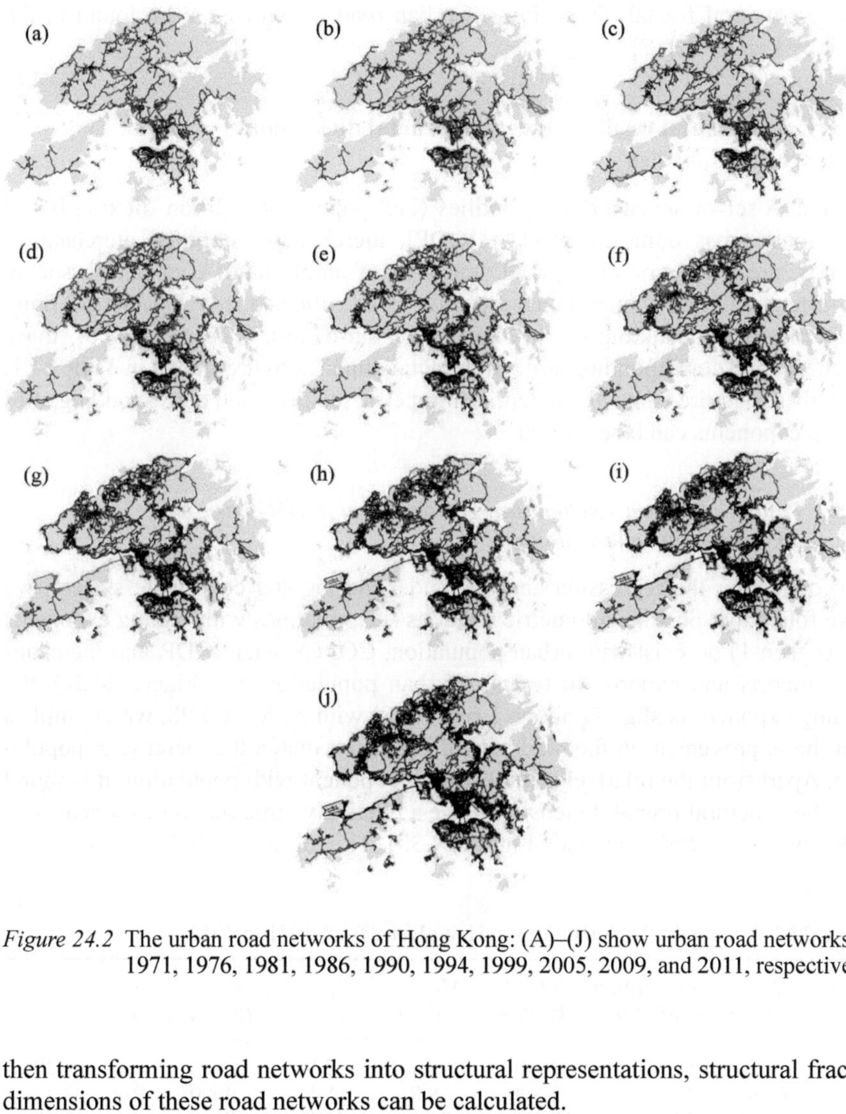

Figure 24.2 The urban road networks of Hong Kong: (A)–(J) show urban road networks in 1971, 1976, 1981, 1986, 1990, 1994, 1999, 2005, 2009, and 2011, respectively.

then transforming road networks into structural representations, structural fractal dimensions of these road networks can be calculated.

The box-counting approach developed by Song et al. [16] has been widely employed to calculate structural fractal dimensions of various complex networks. In the calculation process, the structural representations of road networks are tiled by the least number of nonoverlapping boxes N_s with size of l_s. It should be noted that L_s refers to topological distance. By progressively reducing the box size L_s, a series of N_s can be acquired. The relations between L_s and N_s are as follows:

$$N_s \propto L_s^{-D_s}, \qquad (24.1)$$

where D_s is the box-counting structural fractal dimension. More details of calculating structural fractal dimensions of urban road networks can be found in the work by Lan et al. [17].

24.3 Experimental results: structural fractal dimensions versus urban quantities

In total, a set of seven urban quantities (i.e., population, carbon dioxide [CO_2] emissions, gross domestic product [GDP], merchandise imports, merchandise exports, areas of agricultural land, and area of arable land) considering social, environmental, and economic aspects have been collected from The World Bank (http://data.worldbank.org/country/hong-kong-sar-china). The details of these quantities and corresponding structural fractal dimensions are shown in Table 24.1. With these acquired data, the potential allometric relations and corresponding allometric exponents can be explored.

24.3.1 Positive allometric relations between structural fractal dimensions and socio-economic quantities

By conducting the regression analysis under the log–log coordinate system, we have found that positive allometric relations (i.e., relations with scaling exponents larger than 1) do exist with urban population, CO_2 emission, GDP, and merchandise imports and exports. In terms of urban population (see Figure 24.3a), the scaling exponent is slightly above 1 (i.e., 1.58) with an R^2 of 0.98, which implies that the improvement in the road network does not match the increase in population. Apart from the relatively small scaling exponent with population, it is found that the structural fractal dimensions have a relatively large scaling exponent (i.e., 4.30) with CO_2 emissions (see Figure 24.3b). This discovery indicates that slow

Table 24.1 Acquired urban quantities in Hong Kong from 1971 to 2011.

Year	*GDP (billion)*	*Population (million)*	*CO_2 (kilotons)*	*M_I (billion)*	*M_E (billion)*	*A_1 (hectare)*	*A_2 (km^2)*	D_s
1971	4.5	4.0	9160	3.4	2.9	11,000	120	2.281
1976	12.9	4.5	12,508	8.8	8.5	9000	100	2.474
1981	31.1	5.2	18,691	26.1	21.8	7000	90	2.626
1986	41.1	5.5	25,698	35.9	36.1	7000	90	2.749
1990	76.9	5.7	27,660	84.7	82.4	6000	80	2.897
1994	135.8	6.0	31,430	165.9	151.5	6000	80	2.930
1999	165.8	6.6	42,754	180.7	174.4	5000	70	3.020
2005	181.6	6.8	40,546	300.2	292.1	5000	70	3.172
2009	214	7.0	36,996	352.2	329.4	4000	60	3.218
2011	248.5	7.1	40,275	510.9	455.6	3500	55	3.281

Note: M_I and M_E refer to merchandise imports and exports; A_1 and A_2 refer to areas of arable and agricultural land; D_s refers to structural fractal dimension.

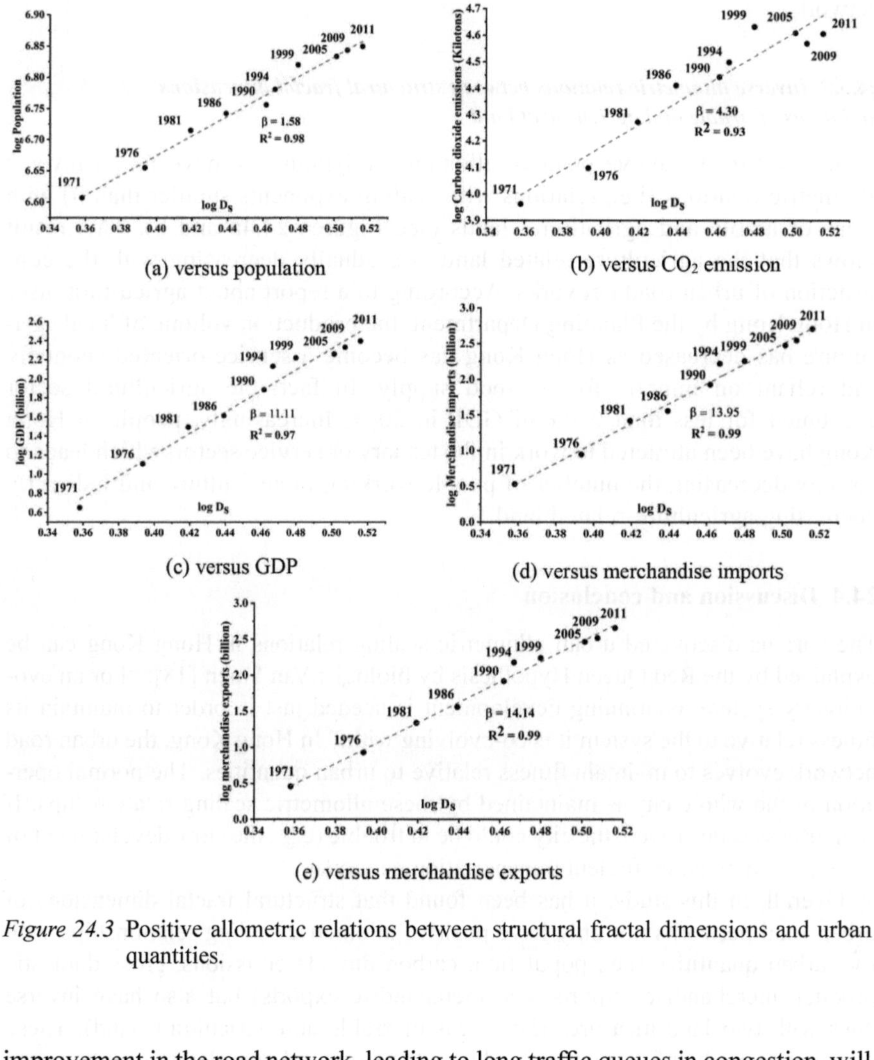

(a) versus population

(b) versus CO_2 emission

(c) versus GDP

(d) versus merchandise imports

(e) versus merchandise exports

Figure 24.3 Positive allometric relations between structural fractal dimensions and urban quantities.

improvement in the road network, leading to long traffic queues in congestion, will worsen roadside air quality (reflected in the increase of CO_2 emissions). Compared to the above two scaling exponents, the scaling exponents for the cases of structural fractal dimension versus three economic quantities (i.e., GDP, merchandise imports, and exports) are much larger (see Figures 24.3c, d, and e). These results imply that the improvement of the road transportation network has great impacts on the urban economic development. In fact, the economy of Hong Kong is externally oriented and highly dependent on international trade. With the construction of undersea tunnels and roads in Lantau island and other locations, the connectivity of the whole urban road network is increasing. Merchandise from different locations of Hong Kong can be easily transported by roads to airports or to ports for export.

Similarly, imported goods can easily be distributed to other places through the road network.

24.3.2 Inverse allometric relations between structural fractal dimensions and areas of arable and agricultural land

In addition to the above positive allometric relations, we have found inverse allometric relations (i.e., relations with scaling exponents smaller than 0) with areas of arable and agricultural lands (see Figures 24.4a and b). This result shows that the agriculture-related land is gradually decreasing with the construction of urban road networks. According to a report about agricultural uses in Hong Kong by the Planning Department, the production volume of local agriculture has decreased as Hong Kong has become a service-oriented economy and reliant on imports for its food supply. In fact, the agricultural sector accounted for less than 0.1% of GDP in 2014. Increasingly, people in Hong Kong have been attracted to work in the tertiary or service sector, which leads to directly decreasing the number of people working in agriculture and indirectly decreasing agriculture-related land.

24.4 Discussion and conclusion

The various discovered urban allometric scaling relations in Hong Kong can be explained by the Red Queen Hypothesis by biologist Van Valen [18]: "For an evolutionary system, continuing development is needed just in order to maintain its fitness relative to the system it is co-evolving with." In Hong Kong, the urban road network evolves to maintain fitness relative to urban quantities. The normal operation of the whole city is maintained by these allometric scaling relationships. If such fitness is destroyed, the city could be in trouble (e.g., the slow development of trade caused by an inefficient transportation network).

Overall, in this study, it has been found that structural fractal dimensions of urban road networks not only have positive allometric scaling relationships with five urban quantities (i.e., population, carbon dioxide emissions, gross domestic product, merchandise imports, and merchandise exports) but also have inverse ones with two land measures (i.e., areas of arable and agricultural land). These discoveries are helpful to understand how the structural complexity of urban road network interacts with urban quantities in the self-organized evolution of an individual city. They may form another basis for the study of urban evolution and provide empirical guidance for urban planning.

Acknowledgments

This work was supported by the National Natural Science Foundation of China (42101442, 41471383) and the Hong Kong Research Grant Council (PolyU 152233/15E).

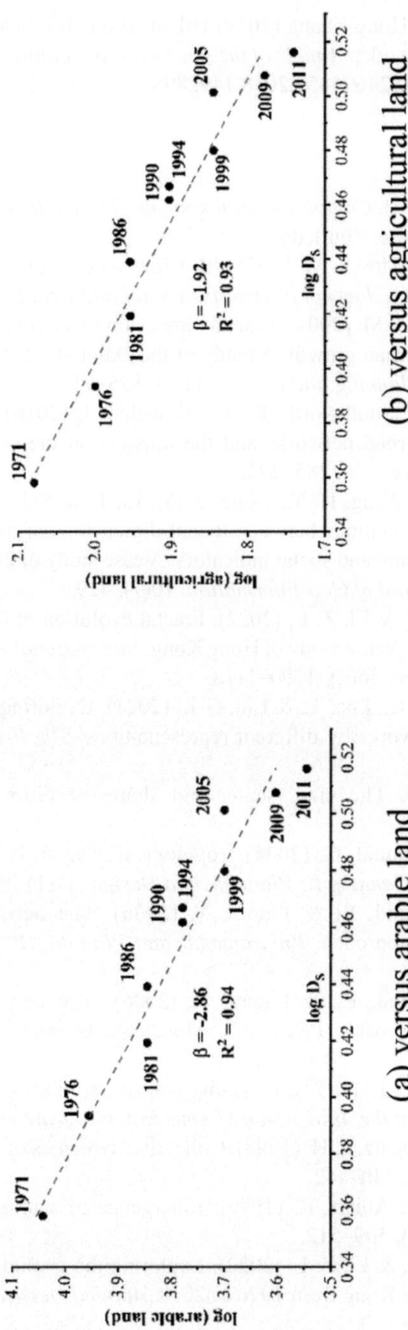

Figure 24.4 Inverse allometric relations between structural fractal dimensions and arable and agricultural land.

Note

1 Tian Lan, Zhilin Li & Hong Zhang (2019) Urban Allometric Scaling Beneath Structural Fractality of Road Networks, *Annals of the American Association of Geographers*, 109:3, 943–957, DOI: 10.1080/24694452.2018.1492898

References

[1] Wilson, A. G. (2014). *Complex spatial systems: The modelling foundations of urban and regional analysis*. Routledge.

[2] Samaniego, H., & Moses, M. E. (2008). Cities as organisms: Allometric scaling of urban road networks. *Journal of Transport and Land Use*, 1(1), 21–39.

[3] Lu, Y. M., & Tang, J. M. (2004). Fractal dimension of a transportation network and its relationship with urban growth: A study of the Dallas-Fort Worth area. *Environment and Planning B: Planning and Design*, 31(6), 895–911.

[4] Lu, Z., Zhang, H., Southworth, F., & Crittenden, J. (2016). Fractal dimensions of metropolitan area road networks and the impacts on the urban built environment. *Ecological Indicators*, 70, 285–296.

[5] Lan, T., Peng, Q., Wang, H. Y., Gong, X. Y., Li, J., & Shi, Z. C. (2021). Exploring allometric scaling relations between fractal dimensions of metro networks and economic, environmental and social indicators: A case study of 26 cities in China. *ISPRS International Journal of Geo-Information*, 10(7), 429.

[6] Zhang, H., Lan, T., & Li, Z. L. (2022). Fractal evolution of urban street networks in form and structure: A case study of Hong Kong. *International Journal of Geographical Information Science*, 36(6), 1100–1118.

[7] Zhang, H., Gao, P. C., Lan, T., & Liu, C. L. (2021). Exploring the structural fractality of urban road networks by different representations. *The Professional Geographer*, 73(2), 348–362.

[8] Batty, M. (2008). The size, scale, and shape of cities. *Science*, 319(5864), 769–771.

[9] Jiang, B., & Claramunt, C. (2004). Topological analysis of urban street networks. *Environment and Planning B: Planning and Design*, 31(1), 151–162.

[10] Porta S., Crucittiand, P., & Latora, V. (2006). The network analysis of urban streets: A primal approach. *Environment and Planning B: Planning and Design*, 33(5), 705–725.

[11] Porta S., Crucittiand, P., & Latora, V. (2006). The network analysis of urban streets: A dual approach. *Physica A: Statistical Mechanics and its Applications*, 369(2), 853–866.

[12] Zhang, H., & Li, Z. L. (2012). Fractality and self-similarity in the structure of road networks. *Annals of the Association of American Geographers*, 102(2), 350–365.

[13] Watts, D. J., & Strogatz, S. H. (1998). Collective dynamics of 'small-world'networks. *Nature*, 393(6684), 440–442.

[14] Barabási, A. L., & Albert, R. (1999). Emergence of scaling in random networks. *Science*, 286(5439), 509–512.

[15] Lan, T., Zhang, H., & Li, Z. L. (2022). Exploring the evolution of road centrality: A case study of Hong Kong from 1976 to 2018. *Applied Geography*, 146, 102767.

[16] Song, C. M., Gallos, L. K., Havlin, S., & Makse, H. A. (2007). How to calculate the fractal dimension of a complex network: The box covering algorithm. *Journal of Statistical Mechanics: Theory and Experiment*, 2007(03), 1–16.
[17] Lan, T., Li, Z. L., & Zhang, H. (2019). Urban allometric scaling beneath structural fractality of street networks. *Annals of the American Association of Geographers*, 109(3), 943–957.
[18] Van Valen, L. 1973. A new evolutionary law. *Evolutionary Theory*, 1, 1–30.

25 The scaling of urban land and density profiles

Empirical facts and theory[1]

Geoffrey Caruso, Paul Kilgarriff, Justin Delloye, and Rémi Lemoy

25.1 Introduction

Most of the urban scaling literature relates a single or composite indicator to city size. Often this indicator directly represents the social, economic, or environmental outcome of a city, such as emissions, GDP, income, or crimes. They thus provide direct evidence, in the form of statistically robust scaling laws, to the normative question of knowing whether it is best to accommodate future migration and urban growth in a few large cities or rather across a larger set of smaller cities.

Some indicators for which scaling laws are looked after also depict the structure of the city itself, with indicators that are essentially neutral a priori. The connectivity or fractal dimension of the road network or the average density of the population, for example, aren't good or bad as such. Examining how these attributes scale with city size is a positive description of the effects of urban growth or agglomeration. Most of those physical or infrastructural elements of cities are themselves embedded in their own theory of "infra" (or "intra") urban structure. Those theories build on urban planning principles or on formal behavioral processes such as spatial interaction theory or micro-economic urban theory, from which one can then draw normative policy lessons. When, later, a statistical link is drawn between those "infra"-structural indicators and city size, the normative statements one can make about the socio-economic and environmental outcome of larger or smaller cities are then enlightened with micro-foundations at the intra-urban scale. This, we believe is a very important step in the making of an urban science [1,2] that would be completely integrated across scales.

This chapter is devoted to this second trend of research that seeks to understand the within urban structure of cities. Yet it diverges in two significant and recent manners from the majority of this literature. First, it is about micro-foundations but is not agnostic to city size, so a behavioral understanding of intra-urban processes is explicitly contributed to the urban scaling or allometric literature. Second, it does not consider the scaling of a single aggregate indicator but the scaling of an entire function defined within the city: a profile along the center–periphery dimension of a city. Although limited to one spatial dimension only, this profile is already more

DOI: 10.4324/9781003288312-29

than a single point estimate. The approach smooths out some of the 2D spatial heterogeneity that does not necessarily require much explanation (such as the effects of rivers, mountains, history, etc.) but captures accessibility, which is a key trade-off within cities. Beyond the case of urban land and density profiles analyzed here, this chapter more generally portrays an example of how urban allometry research can be progressed if an entire function rather than a single indicator is considered along city size and shows how existing behavioral theories can be plugged into allometric research.

We examine the profile of urban land and population density as one moves away from the main city center of a city. The population density profile is a feature that has long been analyzed [3] and easily linked with standard urban economics, especially the Alonso–Muth–Mills framework [4]. The behavioral rationale is simple: as they move away from the center, households trade-off a larger living space against commuting costs. As a result, population density and rent per surface unit both decrease from the center to the periphery. Even if some very large cities can be considered to be polycentric [5,6], the distance effect above still holds within properly defined scales after zooming into sub-parts of the city. Polycentricity in that sense is an extra dimension that does not rule out a radial perspective [7].

Much less well explained than the density profile or rent gradient, is the reason for leaving some land undeveloped at each distance as the city grows: the share of developed land is decreasing in every farther ring around the center. While the land footprints of cities are broadly circular because transportation costs are a pull factor, they are no full discs. As we know well from urban fractal dimension < 2, vacant land is left behind in some ordered fashion. This is puzzling as a behavior because it means that more transport or servicing costs are generated for a given population and their activities. In sum, if the population distribution within urban land is well understood, the distribution of developed land itself, onto which the population is organized, is less clear, at least from a micro-economic perspective. We don't bring new behavioral insights into this question here but we document the empirical pattern for a large set of cities in Europe and explain what changes would be needed in urban economic theory for the density profile to fit this reality rather than assuming a fully urbanized disc.

This chapter quickly sketches the data and methods underpinning the empirical approach before showing its main results. We invite the reader to consult Lemoy and Caruso [8,9] for more details about the empirical methods of this work and Delloye et al. [10] for a deeper exposé of the theoretical connections. These studies were using the 2006 Urban Atlas dataset, including 300 European cities with over 100,000 inhabitants. This chapter expands and updates the analysis with the 2012 version of the dataset and cities with over 50,000 inhabitants. Kilgarriff et al. [11] have analyzed the proportion of the urban development change between those two years, confirming Gibrat's rule of proportionate growth for land, a rule usually only considered for population [12–14]. They also show differences in change locations across the hierarchy of cities.

25.2 Methods

25.2.1 Empirics

Our empirical analysis consists in (i) building radial profiles for urban land and population density for all European cities and (ii) stretching one or both axes as a function of city size to reduce variance around the mean profile.

The main input is the 5 m resolution Copernicus Urban Atlas land use data of 2012 with population assigned to each cell [15]. We consider 585 cities, each delineated as a Functional Urban Area (FUA), which assumes a commuting link (i.e., transport costs) to the city center. We compute the share of artificial land within the surface of rings placed regularly (every 500 m) at increasing distances r from the main center to obtain an urban land profile $s(r)$ for each city. The city hall is used as a proxy for the main center (see Ref. [8] for a robustness check of this definition). Similarly, we compute a population density profile $\rho(r)$ after summing the population in each ring and dividing it by the total surface of the ring.

The second stage consists in rescaling the two sets of profiles by stretching the horizontal axis (r) for urban land and both axes (ρ and r) for the density. This rescaling is made as a function of city size, thus drawing an empirical link between the intra-urban structure literature and the classical aggregate scaling literature. Lemoy and Caruso [8] found numerically and Lemoy and Caruso [9] confirmed econometrically that the best rescaling of the distance axis for land use is obtained with the square root of the city population. For density, the best result is obtained by stretching the vertical and horizontal axes of the profile with the cube root of the population.

Formally, the rescaling consists in applying homothetic transformations to the land use $s(r)$ and population density $\rho(r)$ profiles of each city of population N, which changes them to $s'(r')$ and $\rho''(r'')$:

$$s'(r') = s(r) \quad \text{with} \quad r' = r(N_{ref}/N)^{1/2}, \tag{25.1}$$

$$\rho''(r'') = (N_{ref}/N)^{1/3}\rho(r) \quad \text{with} \quad r'' = r(N_{ref}/N)^{1/3}. \tag{25.2}$$

N_{ref} is a reference population (which is used to transform all other city sizes), for instance, the population of the largest city in the dataset ($N_{ref} \approx 1.2 \times 10^7$ for Paris urban region in this case).

25.2.2 Theory

In the urban economic tradition, the radial profile of density $\rho(r)$ results from the residential decision of every household constituting the population N. All households are identical and choose a location r after maximizing a utility function subject to a budget constraint. Their utility $U(z,s)$ increases with the consumption of two goods: a surface s dedicated to housing and a composite commodity z. Note that we equate housing to land here as did Alonso [16], thus discarding for simplification the housing development feature added by Muth [17]. Each household earns a wage Y_N from their job, for which they commute to the center, thus bearing transport costs: $T_N(r)$. The price of z is unitary and the rent per unit of s is endogenous and denoted by $R(r)$. Using the common log-linear form for the utility function, the decision program of households is thus defined as follows [see 10, for the general case]:

$$\max \quad U(z,s) = (1-\beta)\ln z(r) + \beta \ln s(r) \tag{25.3}$$

$$\text{subject to} \quad z + R(r)s(r) = Y_N - T_N(r). \tag{25.4}$$

$0 < \beta < 1$ is the only utility parameter. It is the share of the budget net of transport costs (i.e. $Y_N - T_N(r)$) spent on housing (i.e. $R(r)s(r)$) and assumed constant in space and across city sizes N. β values around 25% or 30% are commonly accepted empirically.

The above is a standard form of the monocentric model and results [4] in the housing consumption $s(r)$ increasing with distance to compensate for transport costs, so that every household reaches the same utility level. Density $\rho(r)$, being the inverse of the housing consumption, thus decreases with distance.

We now modify the model to account for (i) the fact that the land used for urban activities is not a full disc, (ii) the homothetic rescaling as in the empirical radial analysis, and (iii) both income and transportation vary with city size.

First, we formalize the rescaling of the urban land consumption profile along its horizontal axis and the density profile along the two axes:

$$s_N(r) = s_1(rN^{-\gamma}), \tag{25.5}$$

$$\rho_N(r) = N^{\alpha}\rho_1(rN^{-\alpha}), \tag{25.6}$$

where $s_1(r)$ and $\rho_1(r)$ are, respectively, the land consumption and density profiles of a theoretical one-person city, a reference to which the scaling is then established using the scaling exponents γ and α (those we examined empirically). Note that since the empirical approach transforms many city sizes towards one reference size, while the theoretical approach transforms the city of size 1 into many cities of different sizes N, we have opposite signs for the scaling exponents.

Second, both wages Y_N and transport costs T_N are assumed to depend on city size N. It is well agreed in economic geography [e.g., 18] and in the scaling literature [e.g., 19] that agglomeration leads to higher wages and transport costs and to use power laws for these. Hence we define wages according to city size:

$$Y_N = N^{\phi}Y_1 \tag{25.7}$$

where Y_1 is the reference wage in a unitary city, and ϕ is its elasticity with respect to city size. Similarly, we define the transport cost function $T_N(r)$ with θ its elasticity with respect to city size while further assuming that commuting is a linearly increasing function of r using the transport cost c per unit of distance. Conversely to wages, transport is a function of distance r and thus, instead of using the unitary city as a reference, we account for the distance stretching as of the density profile (Eq. 25.6), thus a definition that comprises α:

$$T_N(r) = cN^{\theta-\alpha}r \tag{25.8}$$

From equilibrium conditions between cities (to avoid endless migrations between large and small cities), Delloye et al. [10] demonstrate that the condition $\phi = \theta = \beta/3/(1 - \beta)$ must hold. Considering β is empirically close to 1/3, the income and transport costs' elasticities ϕ and θ are then close to 1/6, which is consistent with the superlinear scaling of socio-economic attributes of cities reported by Bettencourt [20].

With the standard Alonso model, one would then solve the model to find the equilibrium density over a full disc of land. Here, we impose the developed land to decrease and scale with population size, hence a model now named "Alonso-LU". Unfortunately, Delloye et al. [10] demonstrate that it is not possible for the density (Eq. 25.6) to scale with $\alpha = 1/3$ while the land use (Eq. 25.5) would scale with $\gamma = 1/2$ as of the empirical evidence (Eqs. 25.1, 25.2). Our Alonso-LU model thus uses $\gamma = 1/3$, which squeezes the land supply into a smaller scaling than expected from European data.

25.3 Results

25.3.1 Empirics

The artificial land profile of each of the 585 European cities is depicted on the left panel of Figure 25.1. Artificial land represents around 85% of surfaces in the very first rings around the center of cities on average, but this average drops very quickly with only 50% of the land being urbanized at 2 or 3 km from the center and only 10% at around 10 km. This is in sharp contrast to the general wisdom, or modeling assumption, that cities are fully urbanized discs!

Most interesting for us is the systematic progression of the colors with a clear ordering of the curves by city size. The color scale (linear with the log of the city population), shows very well that the share of artificial land in small cities (yellow) is of a lower level at any given distance r from the center compared to large cities (blue/purple). Yet, the general form seems to remain the same. Only the two highest ranked cities, Paris and London, are detached from the others given they are twice as big as the next-tier cities (Madrid, the Ruhr region, Milan, Barcelona, Berlin), which is well known from the rank-size rule, and because they show a plateau near the center.

The land profile is then displayed on the right panel of Figure 25.1 after transforming the distance axis (Eq. 25.1), i.e. using "Paris-km" (r') for each city. First, we see the colors are fully re-shuffled, meaning there is no longer an effect of city size on the ordering of the curves. Second, the standard deviation is limited,

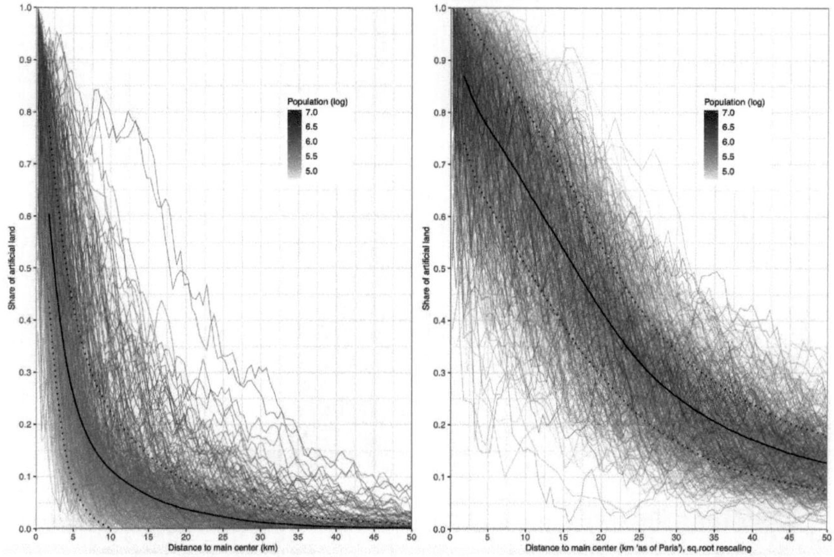

Figure 25.1 Artificial land share. Radial profile of 585 largest European cities. Left: distance profile. Right: rescaled distance profile. Black lines: Mean profile +/– 1 standard deviation (dotted). Data: Copernicus Urban Atlas 2012. Computation by the authors.

with a range of variation of only 10% around the mean, and is homoscedastic. This indicates the central value obtained after the square-root transformation represents a robust law for land use profiles.

A similar process is conducted for population density in Figure 25.2. The left panel displays every density profile in a classical manner. The general shape is close to a negative exponential as suggested long ago by Clark [3]. London and Paris again stand out after 10 km, but the two diverge very much closer to the center, with Paris respecting the general exponential form and offering among the highest density values ($\approx 30 \times 10^3$ *inh/km*^{2}) next to the center while London shows a density crater around 10×10^3 *inh/km*^{2}. A crater we can also find in other large cities such as Berlin or Roma for instance. This disruption is no surprise and led Newling [21] to modify Clark's law.

Overall, there is still also a progression of colors with city size as for land use. Conversely to land use, however, the intercept is not capped at 100%. Regardless of interactions with offices at the center (i.e., craters), the same quantity of urban land is used more intensively to house the population (higher buildings) in larger cities. Any re-scaling, in order to achieve a good overlay of the curves and reshuffling of the colors, must therefore be applied on both axes. In other words, density is a 3D cone, the envelope of which inflates with population.

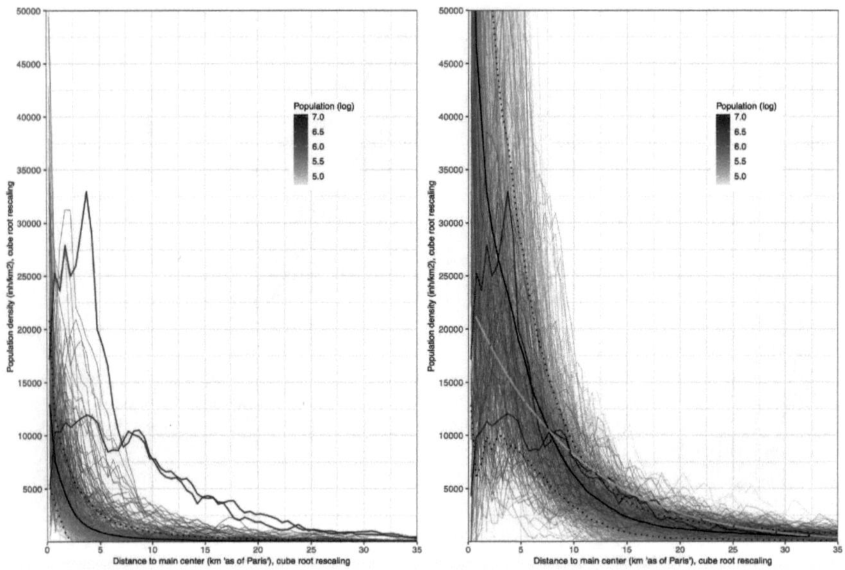

Figure 25.2 Population density. Radial profile of 585 largest European cities. Left: distance profile. Right: rescaled distance profile. Black lines: Mean profile +/– 1 standard deviation (dotted). Light gray: Calibrated Alonso-LU model. Data: Copernicus Urban Atlas 2012. Computation by the authors.

The right panel of Figure 25.2 shows the result of applying such a volume transformation with the scaling exponent 1/3 according to Eq. (25.2). With respect to mixing the colors, i.e., cities of different sizes, it is overall quite successful. The mean is also close to a negative exponential, although probably flatter in the periphery, which is also why we limited the focus up to 40 Paris-km. Beyond, densities are very low and heterogeneities appear that are due to cities' delineations.

25.3.2 Theory

Deloye et al. [22] derive the equilibrium density profile that results from assuming that artificial land is not a disc but decreases from the city center and scales horizontally with the cube root of the city population (stretching the horizontal axis less strongly than in Figure 25.1). The density is expressed for a city of unitary population and then its scaling is applied with the cube root exponent on both axes as in Figure 25.2. The density profile for a city of population N is then

$$p_N(r) = \frac{N^{1/3}}{2\pi} e^{-r_1/d} (f_1 - r_1)^{\frac{1}{\beta}-1} \left[\beta f_1^{\frac{1}{\beta}+1} - (\beta f_1 + d) e^{-f^{1/d} d^{1/\beta}} Q \right]^{-1} \tag{25.9}$$

which relates to a unitary city's distance ($r_1 = r/N^{1/3}$) and outer fringe ($f_1 = Y_f/c$). The economic parameters of the model (wages and transport costs) are introduced for all cities via this fringe f_1. The formal link with the land profile is made through *d*, the characteristic decay distance of the land profile. *Q* is a constant given by the following

$$\text{integral}: \boldsymbol{Q} = \int_0^{f1/d} e^x x^{1/\beta} dx$$

In order to see how this extended Alonso model output fits with empirical observations, some calibration is in need. After fixing the housing expenditure to a third of the available budget, i.e., $\beta = 1/3$, only *d* and f_1 are unknown. *d* is calibrated after a nonlinear regression of the equilibrium housing consumption function using the observed average urban land profile of Figure 25.1, assumed to refer to a city of around 7×10^5 inhabitants. And then f_1 is calibrated after fitting Eq. (25.9) to the observed density profile of Figure 25.2.

The resulting curve is plotted on the left panel of Figure 25.2 (light gray curve) for a city of 1.16×10^7 inhabitants, which is about the size of both Paris and London (dark blue curves). From 8 km onward, i.e., beyond the crater mentioned above, the model is very convincing for London and Ref. [10] shows there is also a good fit for many smaller-sized cities (100×10^3 and more). It is less convincing though for Paris, where densities are much higher at the center to the expense of the close periphery.

25.4 Discussion

Our empirical analysis shows how entire curves, instead of an aggregate index, can be used in scaling and allometry research to better represent the form of cities and their change when cities grow. Our scaling empirical exponents for land and density, respectively 1/2 and 1/3, are reminiscent of the urban allometry parameters suggested by pioneers in the field [23,24]. They are here calibrated on a large sample of cities, and distance (accessibility) is explicitly made an element of the form.

The land use profile curve is particularly robust and the interpretation of this law is important for resource and land use planning. Indeed, it means that the surface of land used for urban activities at different distances from the center can be considered a constant per inhabitant, hence challenging the idea of environmental benefits of agglomeration where larger cities would use land more efficiently than smaller cities. The density law, which results from an additional stretching of the vertical axis, shows that larger cities reorganize their population with higher densities, which calls for further research about how this is actually done, especially whether each plot of land is more fully used, or whether compensation is done mostly through increased building heights.

In addition to providing a set of empirical evidence about the "infra"-structure of cities, identifying those generic profiles along the distance to the center also comes with a practical advantage. One can now compare cities of different sizes on the same ground. For example, if the focus of a study is set on inner cores, one can pick a threshold of urbanized land (e.g., 50% artificial) or rescaled density (e.g., 10,000 inh/km^2) and then use the population size to find the distance at which data are to be gathered for large and small cities, thus making sure the cities, despite their size, are comparable. Comparability and coherent delineation of cities is a huge challenge in scaling and urban science research [e.g., 25,26]

Finally, we show that the scaling and allometry literature can indeed be linked with classical urban theory and thus behavior. It is difficult to assume behavior to a complex aggregate body like a city but when we envisage its structure as the outcome of the decision of multiple agents (even assuming they are in equilibrium) then the effect of decisional variables such as housing preferences, transportation costs, or income can be questioned. Similarly, the effect on land use or density of any policy or exogenous chock that would modify these variables can then be predicted across the hierarchy of cities.

To date, however, this work is still very incomplete, a more robust test of the urban economic model would typically require that housing rent profiles be estimated and contrasted with observed rent profiles. Also, our calibrated profile is not perfect, which particularly questions the linearity of transportation costs with distance. Finally, while we document how urbanized land decreases with distance and across cities, it is still puzzling why this happens. Some land is left over close to the center despite it implying lower transport costs than some land already developed farther away. The urban land supply process definitely needs further investigation as well as the preferences for keeping nature (or undeveloped land) within cities, for example, to counteract negative effects of density such as a lack of green space or induced pollution [e.g., 27].

Note

1 Lemoy, R., & Caruso, G. (2018). Evidence for the homothetic scaling of urban forms. *Environment and Planning B: Urban Analytics and City Science*. https://doi.org/10.1177/2399808318810532
Delloye, J., Lemoy, R. and Caruso, G. (2019), Alonso and the Scaling of Urban Profiles. Geogr Anal. doi:10.1111/gean.12191

References

[1] Batty, M. (2013). *The New Science of Cities*. MIT Press.
[2] Thisse, J.-F. (2014). The new science of cities by Michael Batty: The opinion of an economist. *Journal of Economic Literature*, 52(3):805–819.
[3] Clark, C. (1951). Urban population densities. *Journal of the Royal Statistical Society. Series A (General)*, 114(4):490–496.
[4] Fujita, M. (1989). *Urban Economic Theory*. Cambridge University Press.
[5] Arribas-Bel, D. and Sanz-Gracia, F. (2014). The validity of the monocentric city model in a polycentric age: Us metropolitan areas in 1990, 2000 and 2010. *Urban Geography*, 35(7):980–997.

[6] Louf, R. and Barthelemy, M. (2013). Modeling the polycentric transition of cities. *Physical Review Letters*, 111(19):198702.

[7] Caruso, G., Pumain, D., and Thomas, I. (2022). No "Prêt à Porter" but a multiscalar perspective of "smart cities". In Laurini, R., Nijkamp, P., Kourtit, K., and Bouzouina, L., editors, *Knowledge Management for Regional Policymaking*, pp. 123–147. Springer International Publishing, Cham.

[8] Lemoy, R. and Caruso, G. (2020). Evidence for the homothetic scaling of urban forms. *Environment and Planning B: Urban Analytics and City Science*, 47(5):870–888.

[9] Lemoy, R. and Caruso, G. (2021). Radial analysis and scaling of urban land use. *Scientific Reports*, 11(1):1–8.

[10] Delloye, J., Lemoy, R., and Caruso, G. (2020). Alonso and the scaling of urban profiles. *Geographical Analysis*, 52(2):127–154.

[11] Kilgarriff, P., Lemoy, R., and Caruso, G. (2021). Gibrat's law and the change in artificial land use within and between european cities. In Reggiani, A., Schintler, L.A., Czamanski, D., and Patuelli, R., editors, *Handbook on Entropy, Complexity and Spatial Dynamics*, pp. 213–233. Edward Elgar Publishing Limited. Cheltenham, UK.

[12] Eeckhout, J. (2004). Gibrat's law for (All) cities. *The American Economic Review*, 94(5):1429–1451.

[13] Rozenfeld, H. D., Rybski, D., Andrade, J. S., Batty, M., Stanley, H. E., and Makse, H. A. (2008). Laws of population growth. *Proceedings of the National Academy of Sciences*, 105(48):18702–18707.

[14] Favaro, J. M. and Pumain, D. (2009). Gibrat revisited: An urban growth model incorporating spatial interaction and innovation cycles. *Geographical Analysis*, 43:261–286.

[15] European Environment Agency (2012). Copernicus Urban Atlas. https://land.copernicus.eu/local/urban-atlas.

[16] Alonso, W. (1964). *Location and Land Use*. Harvard University Press.

[17] Muth, R. F. (1969). *Cities and Housing*. University of Chicago Press.

[18] Richardson, H. W. (1995). Economies and diseconomies of agglomeration. In Giersch, H., editor, *Urban agglomeration and Economic Growth*, pp. 123–155. Publications of the Egon-Sohmen-Foundation. Springer, Berlin, Heidelberg. https://doi.org/10.1007/978-3-642-79397-4_6.

[19] Louf, R. and Barthelemy, M. (2014). How congestion shapes cities: from mobility patterns to scaling. *Scientific Reports*, 4(1):5561.

[20] Bettencourt, L. M. (2013). The origins of scaling in cities. *Science*, 340(6139): 1438–1441.

[21] Newling, B. E. (1969). The spatial variation of urban population densities. *Geographical Review*, 59:242–252.

[22] Delloye, J., Lemoy, R., and Caruso, G. (2017). *Alonso and the scaling of urban profiles*. Technical report, Université catholique de Louvain, Center for Operations Research and Econometrics (CORE).

[23] Nordbeck, S. (1971). Urban allometric growth. *Geografiska Annaler. Series B, Human Geography*, 53(1):54–67.

[24] Tobler, W. R. (1969). Satellite confirmation of settlement size coefficients. *Area*, 1(3):30–34.

[25] Cottineau, C., Hatna, E., Arcaute, E., and Batty, M. (2016). Diverse cities or the systematic paradox of urban scaling laws. *Computers, Environment and Urban Systems*, 63(May 2017):80–94.

[26] Thomas, I., Jones, J., Caruso, G., and Gerber, P. (2018). City delineation in european applications of luti models: Review and tests. *Transport Reviews*, 38(1):6–32.

[27] Schindler, M. and Caruso, G. (2022). Urban interventions to reduce pollution exposure and improve spatial equity. *Geographical Analysis*, 54(2):309–332.

26 Active population and spatial scaling laws within cities

Ruiqi Li and Jiang Zhang

26.1 Introduction

Urban scaling laws, which state various urban quantities scale nonlinearly with population, have proved to be a powerful framework for urban science [1–11]. Generally, infrastructure-related variables scale sublinearly with population, which reflects the economy of scale [1,2,4]. Socioeconomic-related variables scale superlinearly, which is unique in urban systems and is a reflection of increasing return to scale [1,2,4]. For more complex phenomena, there is a stronger agglomeration in larger cities indicated by a higher scaling exponent [6,9]. Urban scaling laws focus on macroscopic behaviors and treat the whole city as an entity, which is regarded as integrated socioeconomic networks of interactions embedded in physical space [12]. A city is a typical dynamic system, having a better sensing on human interactions is crucial for understandings on the collective dynamics and growth of urban systems [1,13], and we were lacking good knowledge about universal laws regarding spatial distributions of various urban elements within each individual city at the mesoscopic level [1,14], e.g., population, road segments, interactions.

Some pioneering works touched upon related subjects decades ago. After scrutinizing spatial distribution of residential population in dozens of cities, Clark found that population density decreases exponentially from the city center to the urban fringe in most cities [15], but noted that, in some cities, the population density still deviates from the exponential distribution near the city center, where fewer people can afford to live. Later, Smeed argued that if taking suburbs (i.e., a larger range) into consideration, then the power-law is a better fit to the population density profile [16]. Batty and Kim also pointed out that if the population density does not decrease in a power-law form, then the total population integrated from the city center to the fringe will not be in a power-law relation with respect to the radius R of the city. If so, there will be a theoretical conflict between the population density profile and the area-population sublinear relation with the exponent roughly equal to $2/3$ [17],[1] as the built-up area of a city is proportional to R^d with $d \in (1, 2)$ [20].

DOI: 10.4324/9781003288312-30

Though the form of population density is controversial, it is crucial to urban modeling, including evolution of road networks [21] and cities [22]. However, most works only investigate the residential population, and few study focus on both residential and working population, which can be quite different [23] and engage in different economic and social interactions [12]. However, we are still lacking a unified theoretical framework for the interplay among urban elements at the mesoscopic level and the relationship between spatial scaling laws within cities, and macroscopic urban scaling laws across cities remain outstanding problems. Addressing them is important to both urban science and practical applications, including urban planning [24,25], traffic engineering [23,26–29], epidemic intervening [30–32], and emergency management [33].

26.2 Methods

26.2.1 Estimating active population

We all know that people in cities are moving almost constantly [2], thus the population of each location is dynamic and there are hotspot locations [34] that attract many people and might also change over time in a day [23]. With the development of telecommunication technology and high penetration rate of mobile phones, massive call and data detailed records (CDDR) data enable us to make accurate estimations of the mobility trajectory of individuals at the level of locations partitioned by cellphone towers [35–37].

However, the raw CDDR data are subject to noises due to tower-to-tower call traffic balancing to improve their service by telecommunication operators. When the nearest tower is busy, the signal might be routed to a less busy tower farther away. This generates signal jumps that introduce noise, appearing as fast and long movements beyond a travel speed limit. To filter such noises, various methods have been reviewed in Refs. [36,37]. One of the simplest yet most effective methods is to remove the next record if the inferred speed between two records is beyond the reasonable speed limit. However, this relies heavily on the correctness of the first record. To improve its accuracy, we check if the first record is noisy (i.e., the speed between the first and second records is beyond a predefined speed limit). If so, we then remove the first record and repeat the process until there are no artificial jumps between two records [38,39].

After obtaining mobility trajectories of individuals, we can aggregate them to locations to estimate the active population (AP) in a certain place over a certain period (e.g., an hour, a day, or even longer). When the CDR data are sparse, which is usually the case when the network is 2G or 3G, mobility modeling is usually necessary [40]; but when upgrading to 4G or 5G, the CDDR data per se are already of a quite high spatio-temporal resolution. However, CDDR data are usually not easy to obtain due to privacy and business concerns. When there are no massive cellphone data available, AP can be estimated by weighting residential and working populations in a certain place [1].

26.2.2 A simple dynamic spatial growth model

The concept of active population (AP) also provides us a more dynamic perspective for urban modeling. A city grows when more people are arriving. Attractions of a city sometimes can be specific: some places or buildings (which can be regarded as historical), some resources (e.g., gold mines in San Francisco), some people (maybe friends or relatives), some events or traditions (sorts of collective attractions emerged from previous interactions). Sometimes, attractions can be quite vague: just "It is Beijing!" might be enough. Though they may not be that specific, there is definitely something or many things that attract people to a location. Also, it is intriguing to find out that after roughly 100 years, the reasons that why people come to a city are the same as in the 1920s according to a survey from that period (e.g., for greater economic opportunity, better public schools, a secure and comfortable retirement, a more fulfilled social life) [41].

In order to explain the discovered spatial scaling laws within cities, in Ref. [1] we propose a bottom-up dynamic spatial growth model with four simple assumptions. (i) Spatial attraction: the social and environmental attractions of a place are approximated by the AP and a parameter, respectively. (ii) Matching growth: in addition to attractions, constraints also apply. A new node that attempts to join the city will not survive if it is too far away from current settlements. (iii) Road networks generation: for simplicity, we employ the Voronoi tessellation based on spatial distribution of settlements. Though simple, it can yield the sublinear relation, $l \propto p^{1/2}$, between road length l and population density ρ in locations that agrees well with empirical findings [21]. (iv) Socioeconomic output: the output g of a location is proportional to the number of interactions happening there, which can be approximated by the product of population density ρ and road length l, i.e., $g \propto \rho l \propto \rho^{3/2}$ [5]. Here, AP is more appropriate for estimating the number of interactions [1]. Based on such a simple model, we are able to explain both the observed spatial scaling laws within cities [1] and urban scaling laws across cities [4,5].

26.3 Results

26.3.1 Spatial distribution of active population

Empirical results derived from massive CDR data indicate that population density difference can be quite obvious between day and night (see Figures 26.1a–c), and hotspot locations that attract people change over time [23,42]. This signifies the dynamic nature of population [2] and when estimating the interactions happening in a certain place, simply residential or working population is not enough. With the help of cellphone data, we can obtain active population (AP) at a finer temporal resolution. We discovered a robust Zipfian distribution of hourly AP at the location level within cities (see Figure 26.1d and Ref. [42]). Given the fact that people are almost constantly moving in cities, the stability of such Zipfian distributions on population concentration is non-trivial.

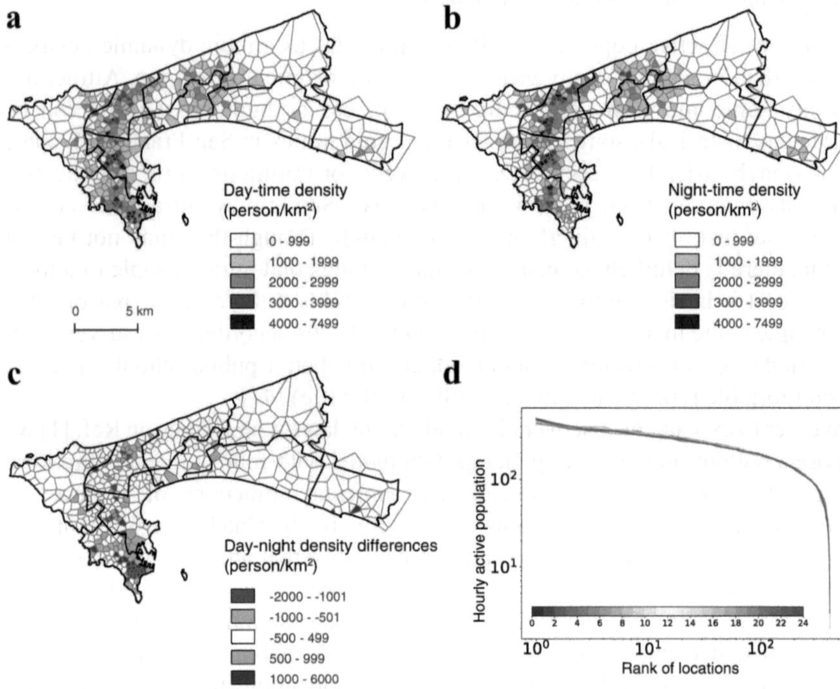

Figure 26.1 The dynamic nature of population and hourly active population (AP) distributions. (a) Day- and (b) night-time population density maps estimated from cellphone data in Dakar [23]. (c) The difference between the day and night density maps (day minus night). Red areas indicate that the day-time population density is greater than the night-time population density, and blue areas mean the opposite. Hotspot locations are changing over time. (d) Zipfian distribution of hourly AP over the whole day for each location in Dakar, which almost collapse together (same behaviors also observed in other cities [42]).

Source: Figures (a)–(c) are adapted from Ref. [23], and (d) is from Ref. [42].

When summing hourly AP over the whole day for each location, we can obtain their daily AP, which is more appropriate for estimating interactions in a certain place. For example, the residential population of Washington DC in the United States is only around 0.69 million, but the size of population entering in a day is far more than that, including commuters for work[2] and visitors for tourism. Thus the AP there is more informative for explaining various phenomena. For example, when estimating the CO_2 emissions, using only the residential population is not accurate [43,44].

Note that AP can be averaged over a much longer period than just one day, if fluctuations during longer periods need to be incorporated (e.g., over a week, month, or even a year). For example, in some tourist cities, the populations of some locations will only be high during certain periods of time [45]. Washington DC is again an interesting example, where the seasonal changes in population are also drastic. When I first went there during Christmas holidays, DC was more like a ghost town, with very few people wandering on the streets. But when I went there again in April, it was crowded with visitors from around the world for the blooming cherry flowers and various attractions.

26.3.2 Spatial scaling laws within cities

Previous works on population density profile mainly focus on residential population [15,16,46], due to the cohesive development of fast transportation systems and industry, and impacted by urban terrain and hydrological conditions, the population density profile can change dramatically. For example, the residential population in London is neither in an exponential nor power-law form (see Figure 26.2a), but when we weight residential and working population to approximate active population, we find that they follow a power-law distribution:

$$\rho(r,t) = r^{-\beta}\left(R(t)^{1+\beta} - r^{1+\beta}\right) \sim r^{-\beta}, \tag{26.1}$$

where $\rho(r,t)$ is the average density at distance r from the city center, and $R(t)$ is the radius of the entire city at time t. This reconciles the conflict between area-size allometry [17] and the exponential decay of population from the city center to the urban fringe [46].

In addition, the power exponent β is informative on the structure of cities. The β of Beijing is smaller than that of London, which suggests that Beijing is undergoing a more flat expansion than London. In London and many other typical Western cities, there is usually a dense core that channels a broad suburban area. Beijing expands in a high-density urban way, if you had a chance to wander near the urban fringe around the fifth Ring Road, you might still find many tall buildings or even some skyscrapers. We suspect that Paris might be quite similar to Beijing on AP density profile, but this would be due to a different reason – strict restrictions on the height of buildings, which eventually will limit the volume of interaction space, especially in the central area. Thus the β value is an important characteristic of a city because it can capture both the static spatial patterns of the elements and the developmental status of the city.

When accumulating urban quantities from the city center, clear spatial scaling relations are observed (see Figures 26.2c,d). For example, making integration of AP $\rho(r,t)$shown in Eq. (26.1) gives the cumulative quantity

$$P(r,t) = \int_0^r \rho(x,t)\, x\mathrm{d}x \propto r^{2-\beta}\left(\frac{R(t)^{1+\beta}}{2-\beta} - \frac{r^{1+\beta}}{3}\right) \sim r^{2-\beta} \tag{26.2}$$

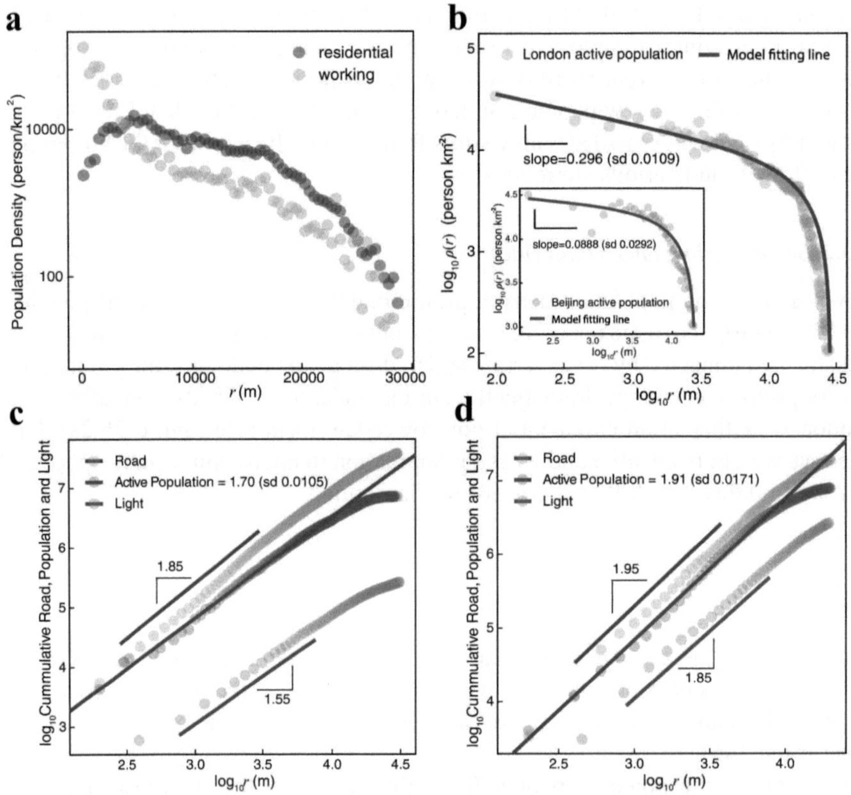

Figure 26.2 Active population (AP) density profile and spatial scaling laws in Beijing and London. (a) The working (red) and residential population (blue) density distributions in Greater London, UK. r is the distance to the city center. (b) The AP density profile for London and (inset) Beijing. The power exponents β for London and Beijing are 0.296 and 0.0888, respectively. The spatial scaling results for (c) London and (d) Beijing. According to our theory [1], the spatial scaling exponents of road length and socioeconomic interactions captured by night-time lights are $2-\beta/2=1.85(1.95)$ and $2-3\beta/2=1.55(1.86)$ for London (Beijing), which are very close to empirical results.

Source: Figure (a) is adapted from the supplementary information of Ref. [1], and (b)–(d) are from Ref. [1].

where $P(r,t)$ is the cumulative AP within the circle with a radius r. Similarly, the cumulative road length and socioeconomic interactions can be obtained as

$$L(r,t)=\int_0^r l(x,t)x\mathrm{d}x \sim r^{2-\frac{\beta}{2}} \tag{26.3}$$

and

$$P(r,t) = \int_0^r g(x,t)\,x\mathrm{d}x \sim r^{2-\frac{3\beta}{2}} \tag{26.4}$$

with power exponents equal $2-\beta/2$ and $2-3\beta/2$, respectively [1]. Based on Eqs. (26.2)–(26.4) we can obtain all the other spatial scaling exponents from any single observation. Based on the same analytical framework, we can also derive macroscopic scaling laws across cities. By simply changing the upper limit of integration in Eqs. (26.2)–(26.4) from a certain distance r to the radius of the whole city $R(t)$, we can obtain corresponding macroscopic quantities $Y(t)$ of a city:

$$Y(t) = \int_0^r \rho^{\eta}(x,t)\,x\mathrm{d}x \sim R(t)^{2+\eta} \tag{26.5}$$

where η equals $0, 1, 1/2$, and $3/2$ for calculating total area $A(t)$, population $P(t)$, road length $L(t)$, and socioeconomic interactions $G(t)$, respectively. Then subsisting $P(t)$ into other quantities, we can obtain the macroscopic scaling exponents as $2/3$, $5/6$, and $7/6$ for total area, road length, and socioeconomic interactions, respectively, which agree well with empirical findings [5].

26.4 Discussion and outlook

We might all have a feeling that many urban quantities are fundamentally related to each other, for example, the spatial distributions of population density and house price or traffic volume or night light luminosity might be quite similar. In this work, based on the concept of active population (AP), the revealed spatial scaling relations allow us to infer the distribution of other types of urban elements from any single observation. This deepens our understanding of complex urban systems and can be aggregated to more sophisticated urban models to predict the evolution of cities.

In addition, the concept of AP can be of contributions to both urban theory and practical applications. Urban scaling laws are macroscopic regularities across cities, a recent study discovered that within cities, at a mesoscopic level with a spatial scale of a few kilometers, the infrastructure volume and socioeconomic activity scale sublinearly and superlinearly with the AP of locations (e.g., a location can corresponds to a region with 2 km × 2 km), respectively [14]. AP also can be applied in various practical scenarios, for example, for better estimating the energy consumption of different types of buildings [47] or energy demands for charging electric vehicles [48].

The density of AP and intensity of human interactions are also important for epidemic interventions [31,32,49,50] in cities. Interactions are systematically stronger in larger cities [50], which scale superlinearly with urban population, and have a great influence on designing effective epidemic intervention strategies. In addition, by constructing the spatio-temporal interaction networks between residents from spatio-temporal co-occurrence, and further making community partitions [51,52], we discover that cities are switching between active and sleeping states [42]. In the active state, most people are concentrated in a fewer larger communities, while in the sleeping state, people are scattered in more smaller communities. And larger cities have a shorter sleeping time [42], which is also consistent with the observations that the pace of life is faster in larger cities [4]. In most human mobility models, the attraction of a location is approximated by the population there, using AP instead of residential population can have a better prediction on both mobility patterns and individual interactions dynamics [42].

Beyond spatial scaling laws within cities [31], at much larger spatial scales, cumulative quantities (e.g., total area of urban impervious surfaces) also manifest spatial scaling relations with staircase-like patterns (i.e., the scaling exponents would be different beyond a certain distance) [53]. Such spatial scaling laws reveal a fundamental structure behind complex cities and the system of cities. These simple scaling relations, which are also ubiquitous in other systems [54–56], significantly increase our ability to understand and intervene with complex systems. In addition, apart from the traditional geometric view, the impacts of various networks are increasingly more profound in urban studies [25]. With the rapid development of rapid transportation systems, interactions between cities that are geometrically remote from each other can be quite strong, which will "distort" the Euclidean space and have great impacts on various dynamics, including epidemic spreading [31,57] and spatial spill-over effects [58]. For example, for high-tech industries, the "spatial" spill-over effects are much stronger when we look at them from a network perspective (e.g., focus on the volume of labor flow) instead of from a geometrical view (e.g., the distance between city centers or the length of borders between cities) [58].

Notes

1 It is worth noting that based on different definitions of urban area [18], or more fundamentally, what a city is [2], the exponent varies from 0.56 to 1.04 – from sublinear to almost linear [18]. If we consider the temporal evolution of each city, such exponents vary more significantly, with some cities of even having a superlinear scaling relation [19].

2 According to the Bureau of Labor Statistics, there were 774,600 jobs in DC as of December 2015, which is more than the resident population.

References

[1] Li, R., Dong, L., Zhang, J., Wang, X., Wang, W. X., Di, Z., & Stanley, H. E. (2017). Simple spatial scaling rules behind complex cities. *Nature Communications*, *8*, 1841.

[2] West, G. (2018). *Scale: The universal laws of life, growth, and death in organisms, cities, and companies*. Penguin.

[3] Bettencourt, L. M. (2021). *Introduction to urban science: evidence and theory of cities as complex systems*. MIT Press.

[4] Bettencourt, L. M., Lobo, J., Helbing, D., Kühnert, C., & West, G. B. (2007). Growth, innovation, scaling, and the pace of life in cities. *Proceedings of the National Academy of Sciences*, *104*(17), 7301–7306.

[5] Bettencourt, L. M. (2013). The origins of scaling in cities. *Science*, *340*(6139), 1438–1441.

[6] Gomez-Lievano, A., Patterson-Lomba, O., & Hausmann, R. (2016). Explaining the prevalence, scaling and variance of urban phenomena. *Nature Human Behaviour*, *1*, 0012.

[7] Keuschnigg, M. (2019). Scaling trajectories of cities. *Proceedings of the National Academy of Sciences*, *116*(28), 13759–13761.

[8] Keuschnigg, M., Mutgan, S., & Hedström, P. (2019). Urban scaling and the regional divide. *Science Advances*, *5*, eaav0042.

[9] Balland, P. A., Jara-Figueroa, C., Petralia, S. G., Steijn, M. P., Rigby, D. L., & Hidalgo, C. A. (2020). Complex economic activities concentrate in large cities. *Nature Human Behaviour*, *4*(3), 248–254.

[10] Bettencourt, L. M. (2020). Urban growth and the emergent statistics of cities. *Science Advances*, *6*(34), eaat8812.

[11] Li, R., Lu, L., Cui, T., Gu, W., Ma, S., Xu, G., & Stanley, H. E. (2021). Assessing the attraction of cities on venture capital from a scaling law perspective. *IEEE Access*, *9*, 48052–48063.

[12] Strumsky, D., Lobo, J., & Mellander, C. (2021). As different as night and day: Scaling analysis of Swedish urban areas and regional labor markets. *Environment and Planning B: Urban Analytics and City Science*, *48*(2), 231–247.

[13] Xu, F., Li, Y., Jin, D., Lu, J., & Song, C. (2021). Emergence of urban growth patterns from human mobility behavior. *Nature Computational Science*, *1*(12), 791–800.

[14] Dong, L., Huang, Z., Zhang, J., & Liu, Y. (2020). Understanding the mesoscopic scaling patterns within cities. *Scientific Reports*, *10*, 21201.

[15] Clark, C. (1951). Urban population densities. *Journal of the Royal Statistical Society. Series A (General)*, *114*(4), 490–496.

[16] Smeed, R. J. (1961). The traffic problem in towns. *Manchester Statistical Society*, *8*, 1–59.

[17] Nordbeck, S. (1971). Urban allometric growth. *Geografiska Annaler: Series B, Human Geography*, *53*(1), 54–67.

[18] Louf, R., & Barthelemy, M. (2014). How congestion shapes cities: from mobility patterns to scaling. *Scientific Reports*, *4*, 5561.

[19] Xu, G., Zhou, Z., Jiao, L., Dong, T., & Li, R. (2019). Cross-sectional urban scaling fails in predicting temporal growth of cities. *arXiv preprint arXiv:1910.06732*.

[20] Shen, G. (2002). Fractal dimension and fractal growth of urbanized areas. *International Journal of Geographical Information Science*, *16*(5), 419–437.

[21] Barthélemy, M., & Flammini, A. (2008). Modeling urban street patterns. *Physical Review Letters*, *100*(13), 138702.

[22] Makse, H. A., Havlin, S., & Stanley, H. E. (1995). Modelling urban growth patterns. *Nature*, *377*(6550), 608–612.

[23] Dong, L., Li, R., Zhang, J., & Di, Z. (2016). Population-weighted efficiency in transportation networks. *Scientific Reports*, *6*, 26377.

[24] Batty, M. (2008). The size, scale, and shape of cities. *Science*, *319*(5864), 769–771.

[25] Batty, M. (2013). *The new science of cities*. MIT Press.

[26] de Dios Ortúzar, J., & Willumsen, L. G. (2011). *Modelling transport*. John Wiley & Sons.

[27] Qiu, X., Gao, T., Yang, Y., Luo, A., Zhang, Y., Shang, F., & Li, R. (2022). Understanding urban congestion with biking traffic and routing detour ratio. *arXiv preprint arXiv:2205.08118.*

[28] Li, R., Gao, S., Luo, A., Yao, Q., Chen, B., Shang, F., Jiang, R., & Stanley, H. E. (2021). Gravity model in dockless bike-sharing systems within cities. *Physical Review E, 103*, 012312.

[29] Gao, T., Xu, Z., Liu, C., Yang, Y., Shang, F., & Li, R. (2022). Quantifying relation between mobility patterns and socioeconomic status of dockless sharing-bike users. *arXiv preprint arXiv:2204.03894.*

[30] Eubank, S., Guclu, H., Anil Kumar, V. S., Marathe, M. V., Srinivasan, A., Toroczkai, Z., & Wang, N. (2004). Modelling disease outbreaks in realistic urban social networks. *Nature*, *429*(6988), 180–184.

[31] Li, R., Wang, W., & Di, Z. (2017). Effects of human dynamics on epidemic spreading in Côte d'Ivoire. *Physica A: Statistical Mechanics and its Applications*, *467*, 30–40.

[32] Li, R., Richmond, P., & Roehner, B. M. (2018). Effect of population density on epidemics. *Physica A: Statistical Mechanics and its Applications*, *510*, 713–724.

[33] Lu, X., Bengtsson, L., & Holme, P. (2012). Predictability of population displacement after the 2010 Haiti earthquake. *Proceedings of the National Academy of Sciences*, *109*(29), 11576–11581.

[34] Louail, T., Lenormand, M., Cantu Ros, O. G., Picornell, M., Herranz, R., Frias-Martinez, E., Ramasco, J. J., & Barthelemy, M. (2014). From mobile phone data to the spatial structure of cities. *Scientific Reports*, *4*, 5276.

[35] Gonzalez, M. C., Hidalgo, C. A., & Barabasi, A. L. (2008). Understanding individual human mobility patterns. *Nature*, *453*(7196), 779–782.

[36] Zheng, Y., & Xie, X. (2011). Learning travel recommendations from user-generated GPS traces. *ACM Transactions on Intelligent Systems and Technology (TIST)*, *2*(1), 1–29.

[37] Jiang, S., Fiore, G. A., Yang, Y., Ferreira Jr, J., Frazzoli, E., & González, M. C. (2013, August). A review of urban computing for mobile phone traces: current methods, challenges and opportunities. In *Proceedings of the 2nd ACM SIGKDD International Workshop on Urban Computing* (pp. 1–9).

[38] Xu, Y., Li, R., Jiang, S., Zhang, J., & González, M. C. (2017). Clearer skies in Beijing–revealing the impacts of traffic on the modeling of air quality. In *Proceedings of the Transportation Research Board (TRB) 96th Annual Meeting*, 17, 05211.

[39] Xu, Y., Jiang, S., Li, R., Zhang, J., Zhao, J., Abbar, S., & González, M. C. (2019). Unraveling environmental justice in ambient PM2. 5 exposure in Beijing: A big data approach. *Computers, Environment and Urban Systems*, *75*, 12–21.

[40] Jiang, S., Yang, Y., Gupta, S., Veneziano, D., Athavale, S., & González, M. C. (2016). The TimeGeo modeling framework for urban mobility without travel surveys. *Proceedings of the National Academy of Sciences*, *113*(37), E5370–E5378.

[41] Boehm, L. K., & Corey, S. H. (2014). *America's urban history*. Routledge.

[42] Liu, C., Yang, Y., Chen, B., Cui, T., Shang, F., Fan, J., & Li, R. (2022). Revealing spatiotemporal interaction patterns behind complex cities. *Chaos: An Interdisciplinary Journal of Nonlinear Science*, *32*(8), 081105.

[43] Peña, G., Puente-Ajovín, M., Ramos, A., & Sanz-Gracia, F. (2022). Log-growth rates of CO2: An empirical analysis. *Physica A: Statistical Mechanics and its Applications*, *588*, 126550.

[44] Ribeiro, H. V., Rybski, D., & Kropp, J. P. (2019). Effects of changing population or density on urban carbon dioxide emissions. *Nature Communications*, *10*, 3204.

[45] Deville, P., Linard, C., Martin, S., Gilbert, M., Stevens, F. R., Gaughan, A. E., Blondel, V. D., & Tatem, A. J. (2014). Dynamic population mapping using mobile phone data. *Proceedings of the National Academy of Sciences*, *111*(45), 15888–15893.

[46] Batty, M., & Kim, K. S. (1992). Form follows function: reformulating urban population density functions. *Urban Studies*, *29*(7), 1043–1069.

[47] Barbour, E., Davila, C. C., Gupta, S., Reinhart, C., Kaur, J., & González, M. C. (2019). Planning for sustainable cities by estimating building occupancy with mobile phones. *Nature Communications*, *10*(1), 3736.

[48] Xu, Y., Çolak, S., Kara, E. C., Moura, S. J., & González, M. C. (2018). Planning for electric vehicle needs by coupling charging profiles with urban mobility. *Nature Energy*, *3*(6), 484–493.

[49] Hazarie, S., Soriano-Paños, D., Arenas, A., Gómez-Gardeñes, J., & Ghoshal, G. (2021). Interplay between population density and mobility in determining the spread of epidemics in cities. *Communications Physics*, *4*, 191.

[50] Schläpfer, M., Bettencourt, L. M., Grauwin, S., Raschke, M., Claxton, R., Smoreda, Z., West, G. B., & Ratti, C. (2014). The scaling of human interactions with city size. *Journal of the Royal Society Interface*, *11*(98), 20130789.

[51] Blondel, V. D., Guillaume, J. L., Lambiotte, R., & Lefebvre, E. (2008). Fast unfolding of communities in large networks. *Journal of Statistical Mechanics: Theory and Experiment*, *2008*(10), P10008.

[52] Shang, F., Chen, B., Expert, P., Lü, L., Yang, A., Stanley, H. E., Lambiotte, R., Evans, T. S., & Li, R. (2022). Local dominance unveils clusters in networks. *arXiv preprint arXiv:2209.15497*.

[53] Ma, Q., Wu, J., He, C., & Hu, G. (2018). Spatial scaling of urban impervious surfaces across evolving landscapes: From cities to urban regions. *Landscape and Urban Planning*, *175*, 50–61.

[54] Barzel, B., & Barabási, A. L. (2013). Universality in network dynamics. *Nature Physics*, *9*(10), 673–681.

[55] Sornette, D. (2006). *Critical phenomena in natural sciences: chaos, fractals, selforganization and disorder: concepts and tools*. Springer Science & Business Media.

[56] Li, R., Luo, A., Shang, F., Lv, L., Fan, J., Lu, G., Pan, L., Tian, L., & Stanley, H. E. (2022). Emergence of scaling in dockless bike-sharing systems. *arXiv preprint arXiv:2202.06352*.

[57] Brockmann, D., & Helbing, D. (2013). The hidden geometry of complex, network-driven contagion phenomena. *Science*, *342*(6164), 1337–1342.

[58] Wang, C., Wang, L., Xue, Y., & Li, R. (2022). Revealing spatial spillover effect in high-tech industry agglomeration from a high-skilled labor flow network perspective. *Journal of Systems Science and Complexity*, *35*(3), 839–859.

27 Scaling laws in human mobility[1]

Tao Zhou

27.1 Introduction

Scaling laws, in particular the power-law displacement distributions, are widely observed in human mobility [1], ranging from local movements captured by GPS [2] and daily travel surveys [3], to the mixture of both intra-city trips and worldwide travels recorded by self-reported trajectories of individual bills [4], mobile phones [5] and location-based social network services [6], to distant migrations surveyed by national censuses [7]. Most known models to explain the observed scaling laws focus on either short-distance movements (mostly driven by interests or routine purposes) [8–14] or migrations due to career changes or other significant reasons (mostly affected by population-induced competition) [7,15], while intercity and worldwide travels are rarely discussed.

This chapter introduces a layered geographical network model (named the hierarchical traffic network model, HTN model for short), which is inspired by the hierarchical organization of real traffic systems [16]. For example, when I was a joint-trained student, I had to frequently travel between the University of Science and Technology of China (USTC) and the University of Fribourg (UF), the former located in a small city (Hefei) in China and the latter lying in an even smaller city (Fribourg) in Switzerland. However, there is no straight way connecting USTC and UF. If one wants to go from USTC to UF, as presented in Figure 27.1(a), a typical journey involves many intermediate locations and traffic modes. Therefore, the actual traveling distance is usually much longer than the geographical distance, in particular for long-distance travels.

More precisely, human traffic systems are hierarchically organized, with a megalopolis rounded by cities, cities rounded by counties, counties rounded by towns and villages, and so on. Some empirical studies have already revealed such hierarchical organization patterns, such as road networks [17] and air transportation networks [18]. This chapter tries to simplify the complex real traffic systems and complex human behaviors to a solvable dynamical process, which mainly consists of two parts, the HTN model and random walk dynamics. Later analyses indicate that the hierarchy of traffic systems may be one origin of the scaling laws in human travel.

DOI: 10.4324/9781003288312-31

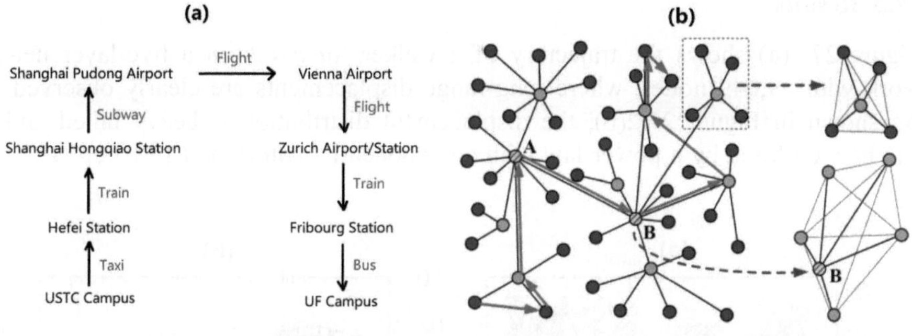

Figure 27.1 (a) An example of the real journey resulting from the hierarchy of known traffic systems. The red words indicate corresponding traffic modes. (b) Illustration of an eight-step travel in a three-layer system ($K = 2, N = 3, M = 5$), where yellow, green, and blue nodes are the first-, second- and third-layer nodes, respectively. For clarity, links are between nodes in the same layer, except for the one between the two first-layer nodes, A and B. Two subplots respectively show links in the domain of a second-layer node and a first-layer node. After Ref. [16].

27.2 Model

In the model, geographical units, including megalopolis, cities, counties, towns, villages and so on, are represented by nodes in different layers. Assuming the network has N layers, the first layer (i.e., the top layer) contains K nodes, and the ratio of the next-layer nodes to the current-layer nodes is M, then there are in total KM^{N-1} nodes, including K first-layer nodes, $K(M-1)$ second-layer nodes, ..., $KM^{n-2}(M-1)$ nth-layer nodes, ..., and $KM^{N-2}(M-1)$ Nth-layer nodes. All those nodes are randomly distributed in a continuous square. The first-layer nodes are fully connected with each other, and each nth-layer node ($1 < n \leq N$) is connected to its nearest higher-layer node. Two nth-layer nodes ($1 < n \leq N$) are connected if they are connected to the same higher-layer node. A network with 50 nodes ($K = 2, N = 3, M = 5$) is illustrated in Figure 27.1(b).

The human mobility behaviors are modeled by a weighted random walk process [19]. At each time step, a random walker jumps from the current node to a randomly selected neighboring node. Inspired by the gravity law in human mobility [20], the selecting probability of a neighbor is proportional to its attractiveness. As in the network, nodes are only different in associated layers, an nth-layer node's attractiveness is assumed to be

$$w_n = r^{N-n}, \tag{27.1}$$

where $r \geq 1$ is a free parameter. When $r > 1$, a higher-layer node (corresponding to a smaller n) is of greater attractiveness. The displacement L of the walker in one step is defined as the corresponding geometric distance, and the central target concerned in this research is the distribution of displacements, say $P(L)$.

27.3 Results

Figure 27.2(a) shows the trajectory of a walker for $r = 2.0$in a five-layer network with 59,049 nodes, where long-range displacements are clearly observed. As shown in Figure 27.2(b), the displacement distribution is heavy tailed and can be well fitted by a power law with an exponential cutoff, as $P(L) = cL^{-\beta}e^{-\lambda L}$.

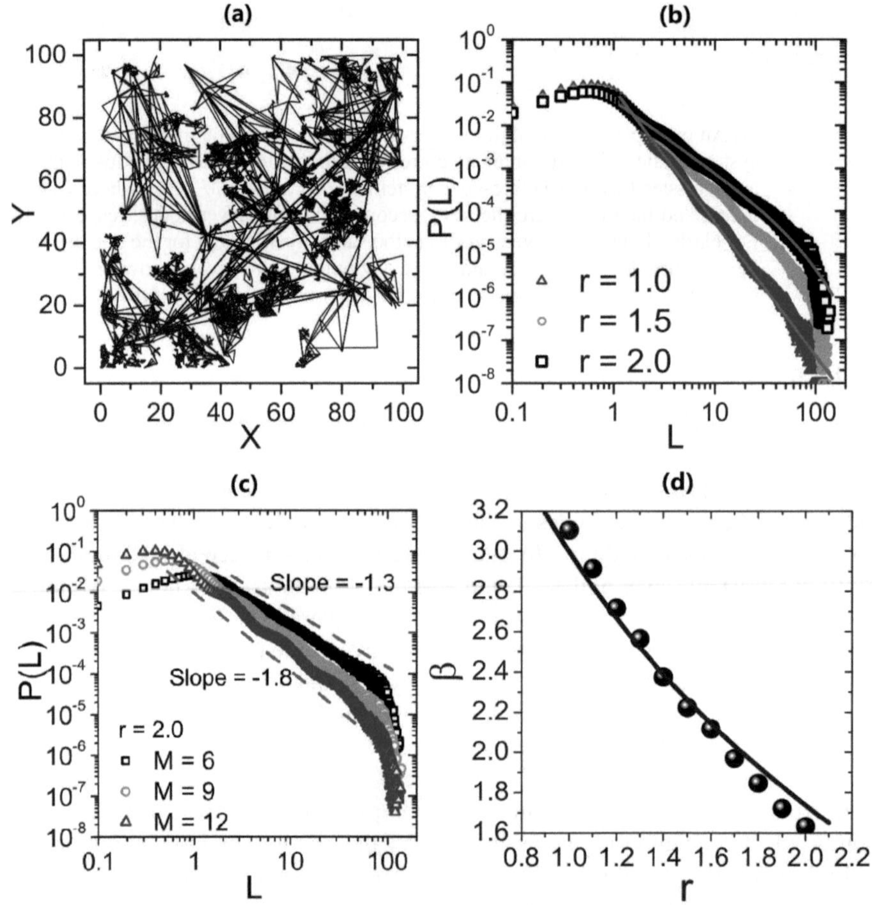

Figure 27.2 (a) The trajectory of a walker in 5000 consecutive steps with $r = 2.0$. (b) Displacement distribution $P(L)$, averaged over 1000 independent runs, each of which lasts 10^5 time steps. The red solid lines denote the fitting function: $f(L) = 0.070L–3.11e^{-0.000L}$ for $r = 1.0$, and $f(L) = 0.038L^{-1.63}e^{-0.015L}$ for $r = 2.0$. Other parameters for (a) and (b) are $K = 9, N = 5, M = 9$. (c) The displacement distribution $P(L)$ for varying M with $K = 9$ and $N = 5$ being fixed. (d) Comparison between the analytical solution of the power-law exponent β and the simulation with varying r, Other parameters are fixed as $K = 9, N = 5, M = 9$. After Ref. [16].

The parameters β and λ are obtained by using the maximum likelihood estimation [21]. When r increases from 1.0 to 2.0, the power-law exponent β monotonously decreases from 3.11 to 1.63, covering the range of empirical observations [4,5,22]. It can be inferred from the model that smaller M will make travel between lower-layer and higher-layer nodes more frequent, and thus enhances the long displacements. This effect is more remarkable when $r > 1$, because in the case of a larger r, travel to higher-layer nodes is more frequent. Figure 27.2(c) shows the effects of M for $r = 2.0$, in agreement with the inference.

As the model involves complicated details, to directly obtain the analytical solution of $P(L)$ is difficult. Note that, if $P(L)$ can be approximated by a power law in a large range, a part of data points sampled from $P(L)$ still follows the power law with the same exponent. Accordingly, instead of all possible displacements, we focus on two kinds of specific displacements: (i) the maximum likelihood displacements $d_{*,n}$ $(n > 1)$ from an nth-layer node to its nearest higher-layer node; and (ii) the maximum likelihood displacements $l_{*,n}(n \geq 1)$ between two nth-layer nodes. The theoretical analysis indicates that both distributions of d_* and l_* follow power laws with the same exponent

$$\beta = 3 - 4\log_M r. \tag{27.2}$$

The detailed mathematical deviation can be found in Ref. [16]. As shown in Figure 27.2(d), the theoretical prediction agrees well with the simulation.

27.4 Discussion

Uncovering regularities in human mobility helps understand various spatiotemporal phenomena [1,23,24], and can find valuable applications in the design of traffic systems [25], emergence management [26], the recommendation of friends and products [27], the understanding and control of infectious diseases [28], and so on. The hierarchical structure is widely observed in real and artificial networks [29–33], wherein some traffic-related networks are known to be hierarchical for years [17,18]. However, early studies missed the connection between the hierarchy of traffic systems and the scaling laws in human mobility. The present model integrates the hierarchical structure of a traffic network and the geographical movements of humans. Both theoretical predictions and simulation results indicate that the hierarchy of traffic systems can lead to the observed scaling laws in human mobility. At the same time, readers should be aware of the fact that the observed mobility patterns result from a number of complex factors, and traffic hierarchy is just one of them.

Note

1 Han XP, Hao Q, Wang BH, Zhou T. Origin of the scaling law in human mobility: hierarchy of traffic systems. *Phys Rev E*. 2011;83(3):036117

References

[1] Barbosa, H., Barthelemy, B., Ghoshal, G., James, C. R., Lenormand, M., Louail, T., Menezes, R., Ramasco, J. J., Simini, F., & Tomasini, M. (2018). Human mobility: Models and applications. *Phys. Rep.*, 734, 1–74.

[2] Rhee, I., Shin, M., Hong, S., Lee, K., Kim, S. J., & Chong, S. (2011). On the levy-walk nature of human mobility. *IEEE/ACM Trans. Netw.*, 19, 630–643.

[3] Yan, X.-Y., Han, X.-P., Wang, B.-H., & Zhou, T. (2013). Diversity of individual mobility patterns and emergence of aggregated scaling laws. *Sci. Rep.*, 3, 2678.

[4] Brockmann, D., Hufnagel, L., & Geisel, T. (2006). The scaling laws of human travel. *Nature*, 439, 462–465.

[5] Gonzalez, M. C., Hidalgo, C. A., & Barabasi, A.-L. (2008). Understanding individual human mobility patterns. *Nature*, 453, 779–782.

[6] Noulas, A., Scellato, S., Lambiotte, R., Pontil, M., & Mascolo, C. (2012). A tale of many cities: universal patterns in human urban mobility. *PLoS One*, 7, e37027.

[7] Simini, F., Gonzalez, M. C., Maritan, A., & Barabasi, A.-L. (2012). A universal model for mobility and migration patterns. *Nature*, 484, 96–100.

[8] Song, C., Koren, T., Wang, P., & Barabasi, A.-L. (2010). Modelling the scaling properties of human mobility. *Nat. Phys.*, 6, 818–823.

[9] Hu, Y., Zhang, J., Huan, D., & Di, Z. (2011). Toward a general understanding of the scaling laws in human and animal mobility. *EPL*, 96, 38006.

[10] Yan, X.-Y., Han, X.-P., Zhou, T., & Wang, B.-H. (2011). Exact solution of the gyration radius of an individual's trajectory for a simplified human regular mobility model. *Chin. Phys. Lett.*, 28, 120506.

[11] Pappalardo, L., Simini, F., Rinzivillo, S., Pedreschi, D., Giannotti, F., & Barabasi, A.-L. (2015). Returners and explorers dichotomy in human mobility. *Nat. Commun.*, 6, 8166.

[12] Gallotti, R., Bazzani, A., Rambaldi, S., & Barthelemy, M. (2016). A stochastic model of randomly accelerated walkers for human mobility. *Nat. Commun.*, 7, 12600.

[13] Yan, X.-Y., & Zhou, T. (2019). Destination choice game: A spatial interaction theory on human mobility. *Sci. Rep.*, 9, 9466.

[14] Xu, F., Li, Y., Jin, D., Lu, J., & Song, C. (2021). Emergence of urban growth patterns from human mobility behavior. *Nat. Comput. Sci.*, 1, 791–800.

[15] Yan, X.-Y., Wang, W.-X., Gao, Z.-Y., & Lai, Y.-C. (2017). Universal model of individual and population mobility on diverse spatial scales. *Nat. Commun.*, 8, 1639.

[16] Han, X.-P., Hao, Q., Wang, B.-H., & Zhou, T. (2011). Origin of the scaling law in human mobility: Hierarchy of traffic systems. *Phys. Rev. E*, 83, 036117.

[17] Kalapala, V., Sanwalani, V., Clauset, A., & Moore, C. (2006). Scale invariance in road networks. *Phys. Rev. E*, 73, 026130.

[18] Sales-Pardo, M., Guimera, R., Moreira, A. A., & Amaral, L. A. N. (2007). Extracting the hierarchical organization of complex systems. *PNAS*, 104, 15224–15229.

[19] Ou, Q., Jin, Y.-D., Zhou, T., Wang, B.-H., & Yin, B.-Q. (2007). Power-law strength-degree correlation from resource-allocation dynamics on weighted networks. *Phys. Rev. E*, 75, 021102.

[20] Zipf, G. K. (1946) The P1P2/D hypothesis: on the intercity movement of persons. *Am. Sociol. Rev.*, 11, 677–686.

[21] Clauset, A., Shalizi, C. R., & Newman, M. E. J. (2009). Power-law distributions in empirical data. *SIAM Rev.*, 51, 661–703.

[22] Jiang, B., Yin, J., & Zhao, S. (2009). Characterizing the human mobility pattern in a large street network. *Phys. Rev. E*, 80, 021136.
[23] Gao, J., Zhang, Y.-C., & Zhou, T. (2019). Computational socioeconomics. *Phys. Rep.*, 817, 1–104.
[24] Jusup, M., Holme, P., Kanazawa, K., Takayasu, M., Romic, I., Wang, Z., Gecek, S., Podobnik, B., Wang, L., Luo, W., Klaujscek, T., Fan, J., Boccaletti, S., & Perc, M. (2022), Social physics, *Phys. Rep.*, 948, 1–148.
[25] Barthelemy, M., & Flammini, A. (2006). Optimal traffic networks. *J. Stat. Mech.*, L07002.
[26] Lu, X., Bengtsson, L., & Holme, P. (2012). Predictability of population displacement after the 2010 Haiti earthquake. *PNAS*, 109, 11576–11581.
[27] Lian, D., Xie, X., Zhang, F., Yuan, N. J., Zhou, T., & Rui, Y. (2015). Mining location-based social networks: A predictive perspective. *IEEE Data Eng. Bull.*, 38(2), 35–46.
[28] Tan, S., Lai, S., Fang, F., Cao, Z., Sai, B., Song, B., Dai, B., Guo, S., Liu, C., Cai, M., Wang, T., Wang, M., Li, J., Chen, S., Qin, S., Floyd, J. R., Cao, Z., Tan, J., Sun, X., Zhou, T., Zhang, W., Tatem, A. J., Holme, P., Chen, X., & Lu, X. (2021). Mobility in China, 2020: A tale of four phases. *Natl. Sci. Rev.*, 8, nwab148.
[29] Ravasz, E., Somera, A. L., Mongru, D. A., Oltvai, Z. N., & Barabasi, A.-L. (2002). Hierarchical organization of modularity in metabolic networks. *Science*, 297, 1551–1555.
[30] Ravasz, E., & Barabasi, A.-L. (2003). Hierarchical organization in complex networks. *Phys. Rev. E*, 67, 026112.
[31] Andrade, J. S. Jr, Herrmann, H. J., Andrade, R. F., & Silva, L. R. Da. (2005). Apollonian networks: Simultaneously scale-free, small world, Euclidean, space filling, and with matching graphs. *Phys. Rev. Lett.*, 94, 018702.
[32] Zhou, T., Yan, G., & Wang, B.-H. (2005). Maximal planar networks with large clustering coefficient and power-law degree distribution. *Phys. Rev. E*, 71, 046141.
[33] Clasuet, A., Moore, C., & Newman, M. E. J. (2008). Hierarchical structure and the prediction of missing links in networks. *Nature*, 453, 98–101.

28 Geographical space based on urban allometry and fractal dimension

Yanguang Chen

28.1 Introduction

Three basic laws are important in geographical analysis, that is, distance decay law, rank-size law, and allometric growth law. The first law is a spatial law, the second law is a hierarchical law, and third law is originally a temporal law. Nowadays, the law of allometric growth has been generalized to allometric scaling law and can be used to associate space and time with hierarchy. In urban studies, allometric scaling law has been employed to describe urban growth, urban form, and urban systems. The law of allometric growth initially implies that the rate of relative growth of an organ is a constant fraction of the rate of relative growth of the total organism [1,2]. In general system theory, allometry means a constant ratio of one relative growth rate to another relative growth rate [3]. We can find two types of allometric scaling relations: First, the ratio of the relative growth rate of a part to the relative growth rate of the whole is a constant. For example, the relationships between a central city and a system of cities [1,4]. Second, the ratio of the relative growth rate of one part to the relative growth rate of another part is a constant. For example, the relationships between urban perimeter and urban area [5,6], the relationships between urban area and population [2,5], the relationships between two cities [4], and so on [7].

The question is how to interpret the allometric scaling exponent. This involves two basic principles about dimension, that is, dimension consistency principle and dimension uniqueness principle. Allometric relation always takes on power laws, and a power law is in essence a geometric measure relation, which obeys the principle of dimensional consistency. In this sense, an allometric scaling exponent is a ratio of one dimension value to another dimension value. Unfortunately, it is difficult to explain the empirical values of allometric scaling exponents using the concepts from traditional mathematics. It is fractal geometry rather than Euclidean geometry that can be adopted to effectively interpret the allometric scaling exponents in scientific research [5,8–11]. On the other hand, dimension is a kind of geometric characteristic quantity of space. A dimension value corresponds to a spatial form. A geometric object and an aspect of the object bear only one dimension value. This is the principle of dimension uniqueness. However, in geographical analysis, we can obtain several dimension values for the same geographical object.

DOI: 10.4324/9781003288312-32

To solve the problem of dimension paradox, we necessarily reconsider the concepts of geographical space. This work is devoted to deriving three types of geographical space from different allometric scaling relations. With the help of new results of space classification, some specious problems in geographical research can be clarified, including the confusion between the box dimension and the similarity dimension of an urban system.

28.2 Allometry models of cities

28.2.1 Allometric scaling classification

Allometric scaling relations can be divided into three categories, that is, longitudinal allometry, transversal allometry, and isoline allometry. The transversal allometry can be equivalently expressed by cross-sectional allometry and hierarchical allometry (Table 28.1). The urban area–population allometric growth is a simple and good example to illustrate the three types of geographical allometric relations. Using the allometric scaling relation between urban area and population size, we can derive three concepts of geographical space. The urban area–population allometric relation is well known to geographers [12,13]. The model can be formulated as

$$A = aP^b = aP^{D_\mathrm{a}/D_\mathrm{p}}, \tag{28.1}$$

in which a refers to the proportionality coefficient, and b=$D_\mathrm{a}/D_\mathrm{p}$ to the allometric scaling exponent [2]. According to the principle of dimension consistency, the allometric exponent is a ratio of two fractal dimensions [5,9], that is

$$b = \frac{D_\mathrm{a}}{D_\mathrm{p}}, \tag{28.2}$$

where D_a refers to the fractal dimension of urban area, and D_p to the fractal dimension of urban population. The allometric scaling relation between urban area and population size can be examined from three angles of view.

The first is the isoline allometry based on spatial distribution, which reflects the spatial pattern of urban form. For a given city at a certain time, Eqs. (28.1) and (28.2) should be replaced by

$$A(r) = a'P(r)^{b'} = a'P(r)^{D'_\mathrm{a}/D'_\mathrm{p}}, \tag{28.3}$$

where r denotes the radius from the city center, $A(r)$ refers to the land-use area within a radius of r unit from the center ($0 \leq r \leq R$, where R is the maximum radius of a cities), and $P(r)$ to the population within the same sphere as $A(r)$, a' is the proportionality coefficient, and $b' = D_a'/D_p'$ is the scaling exponent. Eq. (28.3) can be derived from two fractal models as follows

$$A(r) = A_1 r^{D_a'}, P(r) = P_1 r^{D_p'}, \tag{28.4}$$

where A_1 and P_1 are two proportionality constants, D_a' is the fractal dimension of urban land use form, and D_p' is the fractal dimension of population distribution of the city. This suggests that the fractal dimensions D_a' and D_p' belong to the real geographical space ($0 \leq D_a', D_p' \leq 2$), which is always confined in a two-dimensional Euclidean space by maps or digital maps [14].

The second is the longitudinal allometry based on time series, which reflects the dynamic process of urban growth. For a given city at a certain time, Eqs. (28.1) and (28.2) should be replaced by

$$A(t) = a'' P(t)^{b''} = a'' P(t)^{D_a''/D_p''}, \tag{28.5}$$

where t denotes the time (t=1, 2, …, n), $A(t)$ refers to the land-use area in the tth time within a radius of R unit from the center, and $P(t)$ to the population in the same time within the same sphere as $A(t)$, a'' is the proportionality constant, and $b''=D_a''/D_p''$ is the scaling exponent [9]. Eq. (28.5) can be derived from two models such as

$$A(t) = A_T R(t)^{D_a''}, P(t) = P_T R(t)^{D_p''}, \tag{28.6}$$

where A_T and P_T are two proportionality constants, $R(t)$ is the largest radius of a city in the tth year, D''_a is the average fractal dimension of urban land use form in the n year, and D''_p is the average dimension of population distribution of the city in the same period. If the area within an urban envelope is A, the largest radius can be defined by $R=F/2=(A/\pi)^{1/2}$, where F denotes Feret's diameter [5]. This implies that the fractal dimensions D''_a and D''_p belong to a generalized geographical space – phase space ($0 \leq D''_a, D''_p \leq 3$), which is always determined with one or more time series.

The third is the transversal allometry based on cross-sectional data, which reflects the rank-size distribution or hierarchical structure of urban systems. For N cities within a region in a given time, Eq. (28.1) should be replaced by

$$A(k) = a''' P(k)^{b'''} = a''' P(r)^{D_a'''/D_p'''}, \tag{28.7}$$

where k denotes the rank of a city (k=1, 2, …, N), $A(k)$ refers to the land-use area within an urban envelope, and $P(k)$ to the population size inside the same urban boundary, a''' is the proportionality constant, and $b'''=D_a'''/D_p'''$ is the scaling exponent. Eq. (28.7) can be derived from two power laws

$$A(k) = A_1 R(k)^{D_a'''}, P(k) = P_1 R(k)^{D_p'''}, \quad (28.8)$$

where A_1 and P_1 are two proportionality constants, D_a''' is the average fractal dimension of urban land use form of the *N* cities, and D_p''' is the average dimension of population distribution of the same urban system. This implies that the fractal dimensions D_a''' and D_p''' belong to another generalized geographical space – order space ($0 \leq D_a'''$, $D_p''' \leq 3$), which is always determined by one or more rank-size series. In fact, Eq. (28.7) can be equivalently expressed as the following hierarchical scaling relation

$$A(m) = a''' P(m)^{b'''} = a''' P(m)^{D_a'''/D_p'''}, \quad (28.9)$$

which can be derived from

$$A(m) = A_1 R(m)^{D_a'''}, P(m) = P_1 R(m)^{D_p'''}, \quad (28.10)$$

where m=1,2,3,... represents the order number of levels in a hierarchy [9,15]. This suggests that the rank-size series that is/are used to define an order space can be substituted with one or more hierarchical series. What is more, Eq. (28.7) can be derived from two Zipf laws, area-based Zipf's law and population-based Zipf's law (Table 28.1).

28.2.2 Allometric scaling exponents and fractal dimension

According to the principle of dimension consistency, the allometric scaling exponent is a ratio of one fractal dimension to another fractal dimension. In geometry, a measure (e.g., length) is proportional to another measure (e.g., area) if and only if the two measures bear the same dimension. For example, length is not proportional to area, but length is proportional to the square root of area. Generally speaking, we have a geometric measure relation as below

$$L^{1/1} \propto A^{1/2} \propto V^{1/3}, \quad (28.11)$$

where *L*, *A*, and *V* represent length, area, and volume, respectively. Eq. (28.11) can be generalized to fractal measure relation such as [16,17]

$$L^{1/1} \propto A^{1/2} \propto V^{1/3} \propto M^{1/D}, \quad (28.12)$$

where *M* refers to generalized volume, and *D* to fractal dimension. Here Euclidean dimension is regarded as the special case of fractal dimension. Suppose that the dimension of urban area is d=2, and the dimension of urban population is d=3. According to Eq. (28.11), we have a geometric measure relation between one measure *A* and another measure *V* such as $A=aV^{2/3}$, where *a* denotes a proportionality

Table 28.1 The spatial, longitudinal, and transversal allometric scaling relations of cities and the related growth or distribution functions.

Item	*Type*	*Sub-type*	*Basic models*	*Main model*	*Parameters*
Space	**Isoline allometry**	**Spatial allometry**	$S(r)=S_1r^{D_s}$ $A(r)=A_1r^{D_a}$	$A(r)=aS(r)^b$	$a=A_1S_1^{-b}$ $b=D_a/D_s$
Time	**Longitudinal allometry**	**Exponential allometry**	$S_t=S_0e^{ut}$ $A_t=A_0e^{vt}$	$A_t=aS_t^b$	$a=A_0S_0^{-b}$ $b=v/u$
		Logistic allometry	$S_t=\frac{S_{\max}}{1+(S_{\max}/S_0-1)e^{-vt}}$ $A_t=\frac{A_{\max}}{1+(A_{\max}/A_0-1)e^{-ut}}$	$\frac{A_t}{A_{\max}-A_t}=a(\frac{S_t}{S_{\max}-S_t})^b$	$a=\frac{A_0}{A_{\max}-A_0}\div(\frac{S_0}{S_{\max}-S_0})^b$ $b=v/u$
Hierarchy	**Cross-sectional allometry**	**Power allometry**	$S_k=S_1k^{-q}$ $A_k=A_1k^{-p}$	$A_k=aS_k^b$	$a=A_1S_1^{-b}$ $b=p/q$
	Hierarchical allometry	**Exponential allometry**	$S_m=S_1r_s^{1-m}$ $A_m=A_1r_a^{1-m}$	$A_m=aS_m^b$	$a=A_1S_1^{-b}$ $b=\ln r_a/\ln r_s$
		Power allometry	$S_m=S_1N_m^{-q}$ $A_m=A_1N_m^{-p}$	$A_m=aS_m^b$	$a=A_1S_1^{-b}$ $b=p/q$

Note: The symbols are as follows: t, time; r, distance; k, rank; m, level; S, (population) size; A, urban area; a, b, p, q, u, v, r_a, r_p, A_0, A_1, $A_{\max}$, D_a, D_s, S_0, S_1, $S_{\max}$ are all parameters (proportionality coefficient, fractal dimension, scaling exponent, ratio, capacity, etc.).

coefficient. According to Eq. (28.12), we have a general proportional relation between one measure *A* and another measure *M* such as $A=aM^{\beta/D}$.

In short, an allometric scaling model can be decomposed into two growth processes, or two spatial distributions, or two probability distributions. Based on spatial data, an allometric scaling process can be decomposed into a pair of power law distributions; based on time series, an allometric growth can be decomposed into a pair of exponential growths or logistical growth; based on cross-sectional data, an allometric scaling process can be decomposed into a pair of exponential distributions or power law distributions of probability. Thus we have isoline allometry indicative of spatial patterns, longitudinal allometry indicative of temporal process, and transversal allometry indicative of hierarchical structure (Table 28.1). From each allometry, we can derive a pair of fractal parameters indicating the dimension of some types of geographical space.

28.3 Geographical space based on allometric models

28.3.1 Three types of geographical space

Since there are three types of fractal dimensions for a city as a system or a system of cities, the notion of generalized space should be introduced into geography. Given different spatio-temporal conditions, the allometric scaling model suggests three types of urban geographical space: real space, phase space, and order space [18]. The first geographical space is the *real space* (R-space). This is the conventional, concrete geographical space, which can be described by field investigation, map, remote sensing image data, etc. Using the spatial data of a city or an urban system, we can model it through real space. The second geographical space is the *phase space* (P-space). This is the first abstract geographical space, which can be depicted by one or more time series. Using the observational data of a temporal process of a city or an urban system, we can model it through phase space. The third geographical space is the *order space* (O-space). This is the second abstract geographical space, which can be characterized by rank-size series or hierarchical series. Using the cross-sectional data of a city or an urban system, we will be able to model it through order space. Different types of geographical space correspond to different types of fractal dimension (Table 28.2).

In theory, the same kind of fractal dimension of different spaces should be equal to one another. For a given city at a given time (*t* is determined), if the urban radius is defined according to certain criterion (*r*=*R*), we will have

$$b=\frac{D'_{\mathrm{a}}}{D'_{\mathrm{p}}}=\frac{D''_{\mathrm{a}}}{D''_{\mathrm{p}}}=\frac{D'''_{\mathrm{a}}}{D'''_{\mathrm{p}}}, \tag{28.13}$$

However, because of random disturbance and varied human factors, the observational data do not always support this equation. In practice, Eq. (28.13) should be replaced by an approximate relation in the following form

Table 28.2 Three types of geographical space: real space, phase space, and order space.

Space	*Description*	*Physical base and data*	*Basic fractal dimension*	*Dimension value range*
Real space (R-space: the first space)	Empirical space	Spatial series or random observational data based on maps, digital maps, remotely sensed images, etc.	Box dimension, radial dimension, correlation dimension	$0 \leq D \leq 2$
Phase space (P-space: the secondspace)	Abstract space	Temporal series based on daily/monthly/yearly observations and measurements, etc.	Similarity dimension, correlation dimension	$0 \leq D \leq 3$
Order space (O-space: the third space)	Abstract space	Cross-sectional data based on regional observations and measurements, etc.	Similarity dimension, correlation dimension	$0 \leq D \leq 3$

$$b = \frac{D'_{\mathrm{a}}}{D'_{\mathrm{p}}} \approx \frac{D''_{\mathrm{a}}}{D''_{\mathrm{p}}} \approx \frac{D'''_{\mathrm{a}}}{D'''_{\mathrm{p}}}, \tag{28.14}$$

which can be validated with the statistical average of large-sized samples.

28.3.2 Fractal methods of spatial analysis

In the past, we used distance to characterize geospatial space. If a geographical phenomenon bears characteristic scales, distance will be an effect measure for the spatial description of geographical systems. On the contrary, if a geographical phenomenon possesses no characteristic scale, the distance measurement will be invalid for geographical spatial analysis. In this case, the characteristic scale should be replaced by scaling, and distance-based space should be replaced by dimension-based space. Anyway, dimension is the characteristic parameter of space. Euclidean dimension has no more geographical information, but fractal dimension give us useful geographical information for spatial analysis. In short, fractal geometry provides a powerful tool for scaling analysis in geography, especially in urban studies. We have various fractal parameters, which can be applied to geographical analysis of different types of space (Table 28.3).

28.3.3 Empirical evidence

Three typical examples can be presented to illustrate the allometric scaling defined in different types of geographical space. The first case is the spatial allometric relation between urban area and total length of streets based on spatial distribution data. This type of allometry reflects the real space (R-space) of urban geographical

Table 28.3 Methods of urban fractal dimension estimation of three types of space based on time series, spatial structure, and hierarchical structure.

Object	*Method*	*Object*	*Fractal dimension*
R-space for pattern: Spatial structure, texture, and distribution	Box counting method	Form/network	Box dimension
	Sandbox	Growth	Sandbox dimension
	Radius–area/number scaling (cluster growing)	Growth	Radial dimension
	Wave spectral analysis	Form/network	Image dimension
	Walking–divider method	Boundary	Boundary dimension
	Perimeter-area scaling	Boundary	Boundary dimension
	……	……	……
P-space for process: Time series	Power spectral analysis	Process	Self-affine dimension
	Reconstructing phase space	Dynamics	Correlation dimension
	Elasticity relation	Growth	Similarity dimension
	……	……	……
O-space for cascade: Hierarchical structure	Size distribution function	Hierarchy	Similarity dimension
	Hierarchical scaling	Hierarchy	Similarity dimension
	Allometric scaling	Relation	Dimension ratio
	Renormalization	Structure	Network dimension
	……	……	……

systems. Two Chinese cities, Changchun and Jinan, are taken into account [14]. Based on different searching radius r, a number of urban envelopes of a city can be identified. Each urban envelope gives an urban area, $A(r)$, and a total length of streets, $L(r)$, of the city. The relationships between urban area and corresponding street length follow spatial allometric scaling law (Figure 28.1). The scaling exponent is the ratio of the fractal dimension of street network and the fractal dimension of urban form in the real geographical space.

The second example is the longitudinal allometric growth relation between urban population size and built-up area based on time series data. This type of allometry reflects the phase space (P-space) of urban geographical systems. Two Chinese cities, Beijing and Shanghai, are taken as cases [15]. For a city, urban population and urban built-up area data can be extracted every year. In principle, the relationships between urban population, P_t, and urban area, A_t, follow the law of allometric growth. The scaling exponent is the ratio of the fractal dimension of urban form to the fractal dimension of urban population in geographical phase space. Unfortunately, owing to the unstable statistical caliber of Chinese cities, the allometric scaling relationships based on time series exhibit significant variability. Nevertheless, this example can be utilized to show the allometry growth defined in phase space (Figure 28.2).

The third example is the transversal allometric relation between urban population size and built-up area based on cross-sectional data. This type of allometry is associated with rank-size distribution and reflects the order space (O-space) of urban systems. Chinese cities in two years, 2011 and 2014, are

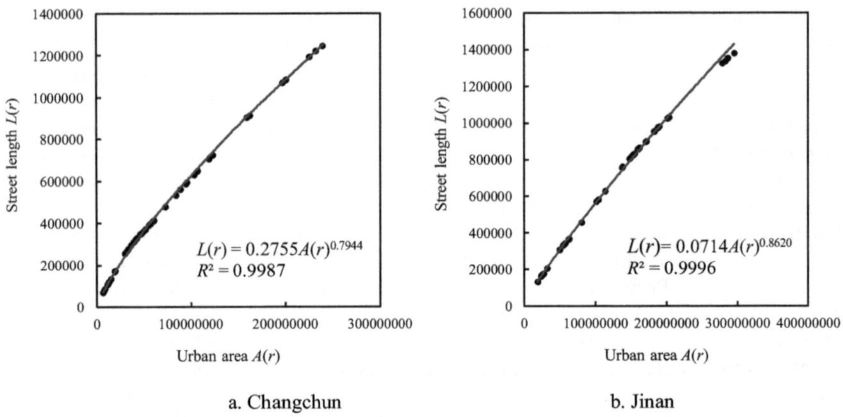

Figure 28.1 The allometric scaling relations between urban area and total street length for two Chinese cities defined in real space (2011).

Note: Different searching radius r yields different urban boundaries for a city. A set of urban areas $A(r)$ and corresponding street lengths $L(r)$ can be extracted in terms of different urban envelopes.

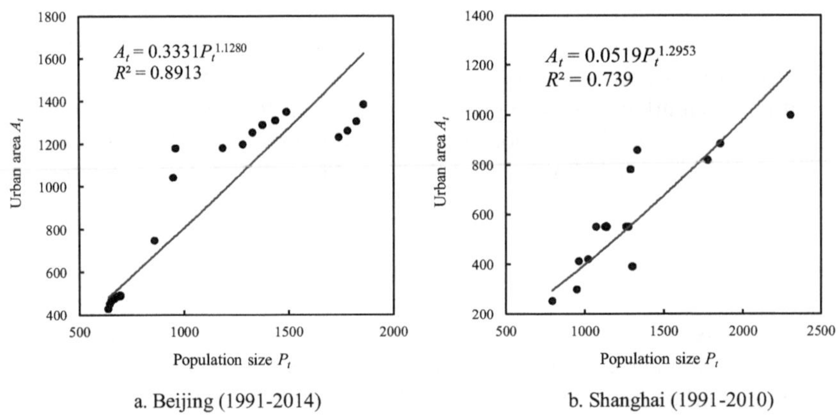

Figure 28.2 The allometric scaling relationships between population size and area of built district for Chinese cities defined in phase space.

Note: Only comparable data from 1991 to 2014 are available. Beijing lacks data on urban area for 2010. Shanghai lacks urban area data for 2008 and 2009. From 2010 to 2014, the urban area data of Shanghai did not change.

taken as cases [15]. Suppose that the rank of urban population size is k, the city size of the kth city is P_k, and the corresponding urban area is A_k. The relationships between urban population and urban area follow the rank-size allometric scaling law (Figure 28.3). The scaling exponent is the ratio of the

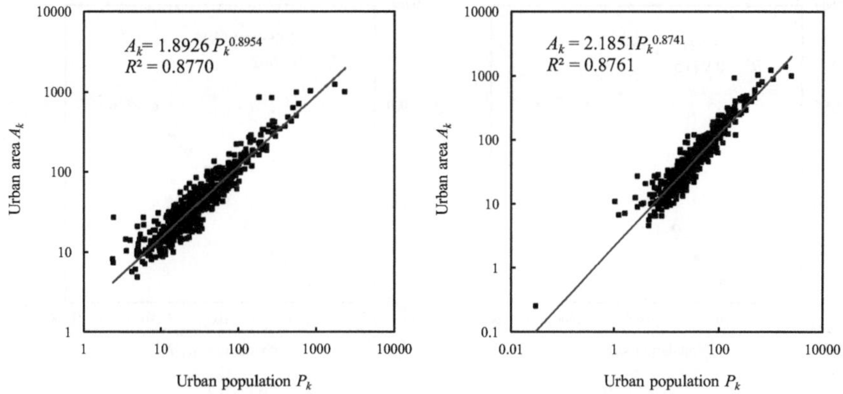

a. 2011 (657 cities) b. 2014 (658 cities)

Figure 28.3 The rank-size allometric scaling relationships between urban population and urbanized area of Chinese cities for two years defined in order space.

Note: Only comparable data of 657 to 658 Chinese cities from 1991 to 2014 are available.

fractal dimension of urban form to the fractal dimension of urban population in geographical order space.

The cross-sectional allometry can be equivalently transformed into the hierarchical allometry of cities. The hierarchical allometry also reflects the order space of urban geographical systems. Suppose that the level order of urban hierarchy is numbered as m, the average city size of the mth level is P_m, and the corresponding average urban area is A_m. The relationships between average urban population and urban area follow the hierarchical allometric scaling law (Figure 28.4). The scaling exponent is also the ratio of two fractal dimensions of geographical order space.

28.4 Questions and discussion

Dimension is a measurement in space indicative of length, width, or height. Generally speaking, dimension implies the magnitude of something in a particular direction, e.g., length, width, or height. In mathematics and science, dimension is a spatial concept, which is used to describe points, lines, and solids. In Euclidean geometry, the dimensions of points, lines, areas, and cubes are 0, 1, 2, 3, respectively. In analytic geometry, a dimension represents one of three Cartesian coordinates that determine a position in space. If we talk about the dimensions of an object or place, we always refer to its aspects, sizes, or proportions. In Euclidean geometry, dimension is apriori and cannot provide much spatial information for scientific research due to the dimension value of each Euclidean object is known. However, in fractal geometry, things are different. Fractal dimension is empirical and no longer a known quantity, but an unknown

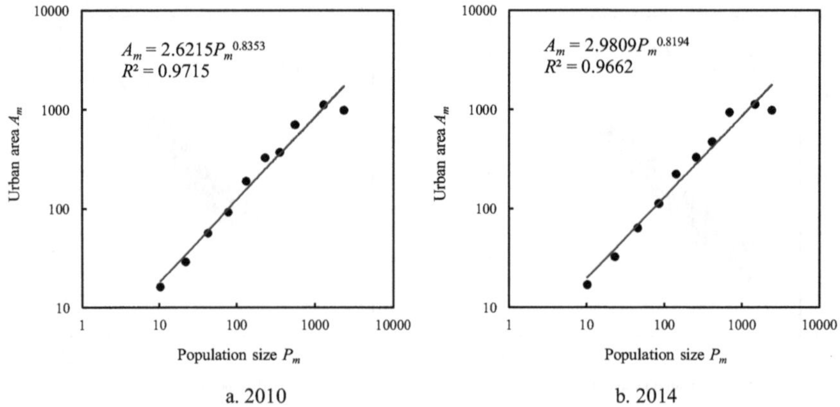

Figure 28.4 The hierarchical allometric scaling relationships between population size and area of built district of Chinese cities for two years defined in order space.

Note: The hierarchical allometric scaling relation is equivalent to the rank-size allometric scaling relation because Zipf's law reflects a self-similar hierarchy with cascade structure.

quantity to be measured. Thus, fractal dimension can provide useful information for spatial analysis. Two basic principles, which were known in Hellenic times, are important for understanding fractal dimension. One is the *principle of dimension uniqueness*. For a given object (e.g., a line), or an aspect of an object (e.g., perimeter or area of a circle), the dimension is unique. The other is the *principle of dimension consistency*. As indicated above, one measure (e.g., length, area) is in proportion to another measure (e.g., area, volume) if and only if the two measures share the same dimension.

In geospatial analysis, we have encountered and still face a series of problems to be solved. Power laws can be found in geographical world everywhere. However, the power exponent is difficult to be explained by means of traditional mathematical notions in many cases (Table 28.4). The typical difficult problems are the relationship between the allometric exponent of urban area vs. population growth and the distance exponent of gravity models. Suppose that the dimension of an urban area is d=2, and the dimension of an urban population is d=3. According to the principle of dimension consistency, we have a geometric measure relation between urban area and population such as $A=aP^{2/3}$. However, a large number of observational datasets do not lend support to this measure relation based on Euclidean dimension. Generally speaking, the allometric scaling exponent values come between 2/3 and 1, and approach 0.85 [8,9,19]. In other words, urban form and growth are fractal patterns and processes. If so, it is easy to explain the values of the allometric scaling exponent. Suppose that a fractal city is defined in a two-dimensional space. Assuming the dimension of urban form is D=1.7, and the dimension of urban population is d=2, we have $b=D/d$=0.85.

If we employ an inverse power law as an impedance function of spatial interaction, the gravity model will encounter a difficult problem of dimension. It is hard to interpret the experimental results of distance exponent value using Euclidean geometry. According to the principle of dimension consistency, the distance exponent is supposed to be an integer or an integer ratio. However, the calculation results based on the observation data are arbitrary values ranging from 0 to 4. In fact, distance exponent σ proved to the fractal dimension of city size, D_p, or the product of Zipf exponent, q, and the fractal dimension of central place network, D_f. That is, we have $\sigma=D_p=qD_f$. Today, many such problems can be solved by using the ideas from fractals. However, the phenomenon of fractal dimension values violating the principle of dimension uniqueness is impossible to be interpreted yet. For the same city at a given time, we can obtain a fractal dimension value from spatial measurement, and we can get another fractal dimension value from time series. The only solution to the problem of dimension uniqueness is to distinguish one type of geographical space from another type of geographical space. Different types of geographical space correspond to different types of fractal dimensions, which depend on different types of observational data and calculation methods (Table 28.4). On the other hand, different types of fractal dimension can be employed to make different types of spatial analysis for geographical systems.

28.5 Conclusions

So far, we have had four paradigms for scientific research, that is, mathematical theory, laboratory experiment, computer simulation, and data-intensive computing. The four paradigms represent mathematical method, controlled experimental method, simulation method, and computational method, respectively. Among these four paradigms, the mathematical method is most basic and very important paradigm. However, scientific research comprises two correlated processes: description and understanding. With no exact description, there is no correct understanding. Mathematical modeling is the precondition for effective description and deep understanding. There are three difficult problems against mathematical modeling in scientific research: spatial dimension, time lag (response delay), and interaction (coupling). The three-parts method of geographical space is helpful for the effective mathematical modeling of geographical phenomena. The introduction of fractal dimension is helpful for spatial characterization of geographical systems. Only when the concept of geospatial space is clarified can fractal dimension be effectively used. Based on three types of allometric scaling of cities, geographical space was divided into three categories: real-space (R-space), phase-space (P-space), and order space (O-space). The real space can be described with box dimensions and radial dimensions, the phase space can be depicted by correlation dimensions, and the order space can be characterized by similarity dimensions. In the future, new geo-spatial theory and analytical methodologies could be developed on the basis of three-space concepts.

Table 28.4 Several typical scientific conundrums associated with dimensions in geography.

Principle	*Meaning*	*Parameter*	*Traditional explanation*	*New explanation*
Dimension consistency	Measure X is proportional to measure Y if and only if X and Y share the same dimension value	Scaling exponent of allometry	A ratio of one Euclidean dimension to another Euclidean dimension	A ratio of one fractal dimension to another fractal dimension
		Distance exponent of gravity model	An integer or fraction based on integers	Fractal dimension or fractal dimension ratio
Dimension uniqueness	The dimension of measure X is unique	Scaling exponent based on spatial data	Integer dimension or ratio of integer dimensions	Fractional dimension or ratio of fractional dimensions
		Scaling exponent based on time series data	Integer dimension or ratio of integer dimensions	Fractional dimension or ratio of fractional dimensions
		Scaling exponent based on cross-sectional data	Integer dimension or ratio of integer dimensions	Fractional dimension or ratio of fractional dimensions

Acknowledgments

This research was sponsored by the National Natural Science Foundation of China (Grant No. 42171192). The support is gratefully acknowledged.

References

1. Beckmann, M.J. (1958). City hierarchies and distribution of city sizes. *Economic Development and Cultural Change*, 6(3), 243–248.
2. Lee, Y. (1989). An allometric analysis of the US urban system: 1960–80. *Environment and Planning A*, 21(4), 463–476.
3. Bertalanffy, L. von. (1968). *General System Theory: Foundations, Development, and Applications*. New York: George Braziller.
4. Chen, Y.G. (2017). Multi-scaling allometric analysis for urban and regional development. *Physica A: Statistical Mechanics and its Applications*, 465, 673–689.
5. Batty, M., Longley, P.A. (1994). *Fractal cities: A geometry of form and function*. London: Academic Press.

6. Benguigui, L., Blumenfeld-Lieberthal, E., Czamanski, D. (2006). The dynamics of the Tel Aviv morphology. *Environment and Planning B: Planning and Design*, 33, 269–284.
7. West, G.B. (2017). *Scale: The Universal Laws of Growth, Innovation, Sustainability, and the Pace of Life in Organisms, Cities, Economies, and Companies*. London: Penguin Press.
8. Chen, Y.G., Xu, Q.H. (1999). Studies on the fractal geometric model of allometric growth relationships between area and population of urban systems. *Journal of Xinyang Teachers College (Natural Science Edition)*, 12(2), 198–203 [in Chinese].
9. Chen Y.G. (2010). Characterizing growth and form of fractal cities with allometric scaling exponents. *Discrete Dynamics in Nature and Society*, 2010, Article ID 194715.
10. West, G.B., Brown, J.H., Enquist, B.J. (1997). A general model for the origin of allometric scaling laws in biology. *Science*, 276, 122–126.
11. West, G.B., Brown, J.H., Enquist, B.J. (1999). The fourth dimension of life: fractal geometry and allometric scaling of organisms. *Science*, 284, 1677–1679.
12. Nordbeck, S. (1971). Urban allometric growth. *Geografiska Annaler B*, 53(1), 54–67.
13. Lo, C.P., Welch, R. (1977). Chinese urban population estimates. *Annals of the Association of American Geographers*, 67(2), 246–253.
14. Chen, Y.G., Wang, Y.H., Li, X.J. (2019). Fractal dimensions derived from spatial allometric scaling of urban form. *Chaos, Solitons & Fractals*, 126, 122–134.
15. Chen Y.G., Feng, J. (2017). A hierarchical allometric scaling analysis of Chinese cities: 1991–2014. *Discrete Dynamics in Nature and Society*, 2017, Article ID 5243287.
16. Mandelbrot, B.B. (1982). *The Fractal Geometry of Nature*. New York: W. H. Freeman and Company.
17. Takayasu, H. (1990). *Fractals in the Physical Sciences*. Manchester: Manchester University Press.
18. Chen, Y.G. (2014). The spatial meaning of Pareto's scaling exponent of city-size distributions. *Fractals*, 22(1–2), 1450001.
19. Louf, R., Barthelemy, M. (2014). How congestion shapes cities: from mobility patterns to scaling. *Scientific Reports*, 4, 5561.

29 Spatial allometric scaling of cities based on variable urban boundaries

Yanguang Chen

29.1 Introduction

Scientific description used to be based on typical scales, which is termed characteristic lengths in mathematical modeling and quantitative analysis. Unfortunately, a city is a fractal system and the characteristic scales can hardly be found in many cases [1,2]. Scaling analysis is an effective way of exploring a scale-free system such as cities. Allometric growth is one of the scaling behaviors earliest revealed from cities [1,3]. Today, scaling represents an important hot and controversial topic in urban studies [4–11]. Allometry opens a special window for understanding urban scaling. However, there is a functional deficiency in the research on urban allometry. Urban systems (a city as a system and a system of cities) can be quantified by spatial data, temporal data, and hierarchical data series. Based on time series of dynamical evolution, longitudinal allometry is modeled; based on rank-size series of hierarchical structure, transversal allometry is modeled [12,13]. However, few allometric relations have been really explored through spatial series of urban morphology [14]. In theory, we should have spatial allometry that is associated with the fractal structure of a city. Years ago, a new method termed city clustering algorithm (CCA) was proposed by Rozenfeld et al. [15] to identify urban boundaries. The method was improved by Jiang and Jia [16]. The results from the improved CCA depend on the length of the searching radius [17]. This seems to be a shortcoming for sketching an urban boundary. However, the disadvantage of a method for the study based on characteristic scales becomes an advantage for scaling studies. Using improved CCA, we can delineate a series of boundary lines for a city. Based on the set of urban boundaries, several sets of urban area and size data can be extracted. With these datasets, we can examine the geometric measure relation between urban area and size from the angle of view of variable boundaries. If the relation follows power law, new allometric scaling will be brought to light.

29.2 Spatial allometry models

29.2.1 Three types of allometric scaling relations

Allometric scaling relations of cities can be divided into three major types: longitudinal allometry, transversal allometry, and spatial allometry. The first one is based

DOI: 10.4324/9781003288312-33

Table 29.1 Classifications of allometric scaling for cities as systems and systems of cities.

Type	*Series*	*City*	*Latent variable*	*Variable pair*	
				X	Y
Longitudinal allometry	Time series	City	time t=1	X_1	Y_1
			time t=2	X_2	Y_2
			…	…	…
			time t=T	X_T	Y_T
Transversal (cross-sectional) allometry	Rank-size series for cross-sectional allometry	City 1	rank k=1	X_1	Y_1
		City 2	rank k=2	X_2	Y_2
		…	…	…	…
		City n	rank k=n	X_n	Y_n
	Hierarchical series for hierarchical allometry	Class 1	level h=1	X_1	Y_1
		Class 2	level h=2	X_2	Y_2
		…	…	…	…
		Class m	level h=m	X_m	Y_m
Spatial allometry	Spatial series	City	boundary j=1	X_1	Y_1
			boundary j=2	X_2	Y_2
			…	…	…
			boundary j=B	X_B	Y_B

on time series for an individual city, the second is based on rank-size or hierarchical series for a system of cities, and the third is based on spatial series for an individual city. Among the three allometric relations, transversal allometry is also termed cross-sectional allometry and can be further divided into two subtypes: rank-size allometry and hierarchical allometry. The former is based on a pair of rank-size distributions of cities, and the latter is based on the hierarchical systems of cities derived from the rank-size distributions. Suppose that the time series are numbered t=1, 2,…, T, the rank-size series are numbered k=1,2,…, n, the hierarchical series are numbered h=1,2,…, m, and the variable urban boundaries are numbered j=1,2,…, B, where T is the length of the sample path, n is the number of cities, m is the number of city levels, and B is the number of urban boundary lines. The classification results of allometric scaling of cities can be tabulated as shown in Table 29.1.

29.2.2 Spatial allometric scaling

Spatial allometric scaling can be revealed from the pattern of a city based on variable boundaries. If a boundary is figured out, we will have at least three spatial measurements: urbanized area within the boundary (surface), total length of streets (lines), and number of street nodes (points). However, according to the improved CCA principle [15,16], an urban boundary depends on the searching radius [17]. A different searching radius (cut-off length, threshold value) yields a different urban boundary and gives different measurements of urban area, street length, and node number [14]. Thus, we will have three sets of data, including a dataset of urban area, a dataset of urban road length, and a dataset of traffic node number. The growth curve of the three spatial measurements can be modeled with exponential functions. From the three exponential models, we can derive three power-law relations as follows:

$$L(s) = \mu A(s)^b, \tag{29.1}$$

$$N(s) = \eta A(s)^v, \tag{29.2}$$

$$N(s) = \xi L(s)^\sigma, \tag{29.3}$$

where s refers to the searching radius length, $A(s)$ is urban area, $L(s)$ is street length, and $N(s)$ is node number, the powers b, v, and σ represent scaling exponents, and $\mu=L_0A_0^{-b}$, $\eta=N_0A_0^{-v}$, and $\xi=N_0L_0^{-\sigma}$ are proportionality coefficients.

An allometric scaling exponent indicates a pair of fractal parameters. The boundary identification is based on improved CCA, and improved CCA is based on a spatial searching process. The spatial search seems to be involved with spatial correlation, which results in scaling behavior under certain conditions [18,19]. The scaling in an urban system is always associated with fractal structure [12]. The dimension of urban area can be regarded as $D_a=d=2$. Suppose that the fractal dimension of a network of streets is D_s, and the fractal dimension of node distribution is D_n. According to the fractal measure relation [20], the relationships between the scaling exponents and fractal dimensions are as follows: $b=D_s/D_a= D_s/2$, $v= D_n/D_a= D_n/2$, $\sigma=D_n/D_s=v/b$. Using these parameter equations, we can evaluate the allometric scaling exponents directly and estimate the fractal dimensions indirectly for urban form.

29.3 Data and results

29.3.1 Material and methods

The materials are elaborate digital maps of urban traffic networks that include streets and roads. The objects of this study are 10 Chinese cities, which are all located on the eastern coastal areas of China (Table 29.2). The methodology is involved with two algorithms. The first, as indicated above, is CCA developed by Rozenfeld et al. [15] and improved by Jiang and Jia [16], which is employed to process images and extract spatial data. CCA is originally based on raster data, but it can be improved to process vector data [16]. The improved CCA is an excellent approach for delineating boundary lines of urban agglomerations, but it bears a deficiency, that is, the identified boundary depends on the search radius length. However, where scaling analysis is concerned, the significant disadvantage can be turned into a great advantage. Applying the variable searching radius to vector images of a city, we can outline a series of boundaries (Figure 29.1). Based on a

Table 29.2 The allometric scaling relations, scaling exponents, and goodness of fit of 10 Chinese cities.

City	*Scaling relation*	*Parameter and statistic*		*City*	*Scaling relation*	*Parameter and statistic*	
		Scaling exponent	*Goodness of fit R^2*			*Scaling exponent*	*Goodness of fit R^2*
Changchun	$A(s)$-$L(s)$	b=0.7944	0.9987	Kunshan	$A(s)$-$L(s)$	b=0.7474	0.9956
	$A(s)$-$N(s)$	b=0.6621	0.9927		$A(s)$-$N(s)$	v=0.5190	0.9880
	$L(s)$-$N(s)$	σ=0.8347	0.9972		$L(s)$-$N(s)$	σ=0.6963	0.9979
Changzhou	$A(s)$-$L(s)$	b=0.8124	0.9990	Nanjing	$A(s)$-$L(s)$	b=0.7958	0.9994
	$A(s)$-$N(s)$	v=0.6949	0.9976		$A(s)$-$N(s)$	v=0.6716	0.9984
	$L(s)$-$N(s)$	σ=0.8556	0.9991		$L(s)$-$N(s)$	σ=0.8442	0.9996
Guangzhou	$A(s)$-$L(s)$	b=0.9526	0.9995	Shanghai	$A(s)$-$L(s)$	b=0.7482	0.9997
	$A(s)$-$N(s)$	v=0.9508	0.9986		$A(s)$-$N(s)$	v=0.5550	0.9980
	$L(s)$-$N(s)$	σ=0.9984	0.9997		$L(s)$-$N(s)$	σ=0.7420	0.9992
Hangzhou	$A(s)$-$L(s)$	b=0.8740	0.9996	Weifang	$A(s)$-$L(s)$	b=0.8842	0.9990
	$A(s)$-$N(s)$	v=0.8034	0.9989		$A(s)$-$N(s)$	v=0.8373	0.9954
	$L(s)$-$N(s)$	σ=0.9194	0.9998		$L(s)$-$N(s)$	σ=0.9480	0.9984
Jinan	$A(s)$-$L(s)$	b=0.8620	0.9996	Yangzhou	$A(s)$-$L(s)$	b=0.7823	0.9991
	$A(s)$-$N(s)$	v=0.7669	0.9989		$A(s)$-$N(s)$	v=0.6460	0.9983
	$L(s)$-$N(s)$	σ=0.8898	0.9998		$L(s)$-$N(s)$	σ=0.8256	0.9988

Note: Kunshan city is in fact a special case: the data points on log–log plots display two scaling ranges.

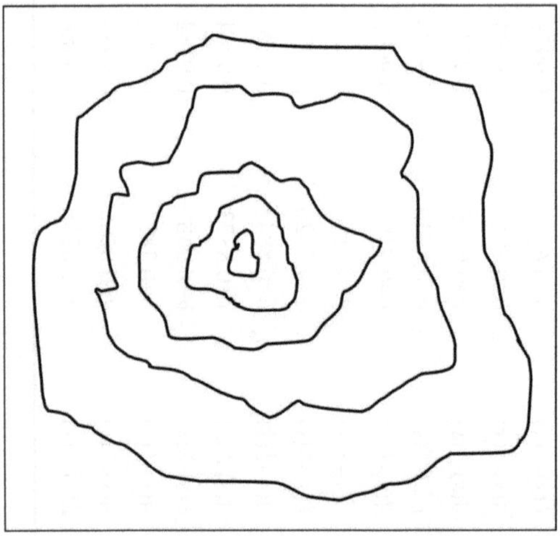

Figure 29.1 A sketch map of variable urban boundary lines based on different search radii of improved CCA.

set of boundary lines, several sets of spatial measurements, such as urban area and population size, can be extracted for allometric analysis. The second algorithm is the ordinary least squares (OLS) calculation, which is utilized to estimate allometric scaling exponents.

The results of CCA depend on searching radius, so we can create spatial data series by changing the radius length. Combining ArcGIS technology with CCA, we can delineate a set of boundary lines for a city (Figure 29.2). The isolines of a city's boundary set look likes tree rings on a digital map, from which we can extract three spatial series including urban area, street length, and node number. The steps of data processing and analysis are as follows. **Step 1**: scanning maps to generate vector graphs for urban traffic networks. **Step 2**: calibrating data by selecting a reference point on each urban digital map. **Step 3**: generating normal maps including traffic points and terminals. **Step 4**: collating a spatial dataset for each cities. **Step 5**: estimating model parameters by means of the OLS method [14]. Using Eqs. (29.1), (29.2), and (29.3), we can make log–log linear regression analyses and evaluate the allometric scaling exponents.

29.3.2 Results and analysis

The spatial allometric scaling relations can be verified by the datasets of the 10 Chinese cities. Applying Eqs. (29.1), (29.2), and (29.3) to the spatial data series of a city's urban area $A(s)$, street length $L(s)$, and road node number $N(s)$, we will build three power law models. For example, for the largest city in China, Shanghai, the spatial allometric relations are as follows

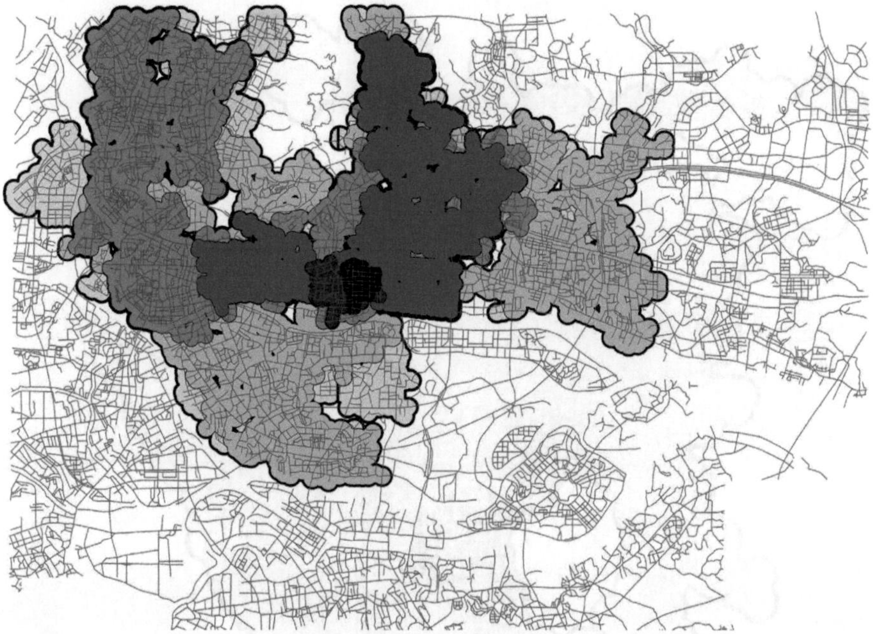

Figure 29.2 Four Chinese cities with variable boundaries: (a) Guangzhou; (b) Hangzhou; (c) Nanjing; (d) Shanghai.

Note: The digital maps were published in 2012. The area of these cities depends on the search radius. The longer the searching radius, the larger the urban area.

$$\hat{L}(s) = 0.7724A(s)^{0.7482}, \tag{29.4}$$

$$\widehat{N}(s) = 0.0736A(s)^{0.5550}, \tag{29.5}$$

$$\widehat{N}(s) = 0.0887L(s)^{0.7420}, \tag{29.6}$$

where the hat "^" indicates predicted value. The scaling exponents are b=0.7482, v=0.5550, σ=0.7420. The corresponding fractal parameters are $D_s=2b\approx1.4965$, $D_n=2v\approx1.1100$, $D_n/D_s\approx0.7417 \rightarrow \sigma=0.7420$. The ratio of fractal dimension is theoretically equal to the ratio of relative growth rates of cities [12]. According to the parameter values, the relative growth rates of total street length and node number are less than the relative growth rate of urban area, and the relative growth rate of node number is less than the relative growth rate of total street length. The other cities can be treated by analogy. The results show that all of the 10 cities follow the spatial allometric scaling laws. The power laws can be well fitted to the numerical relations between urban area, street length, and

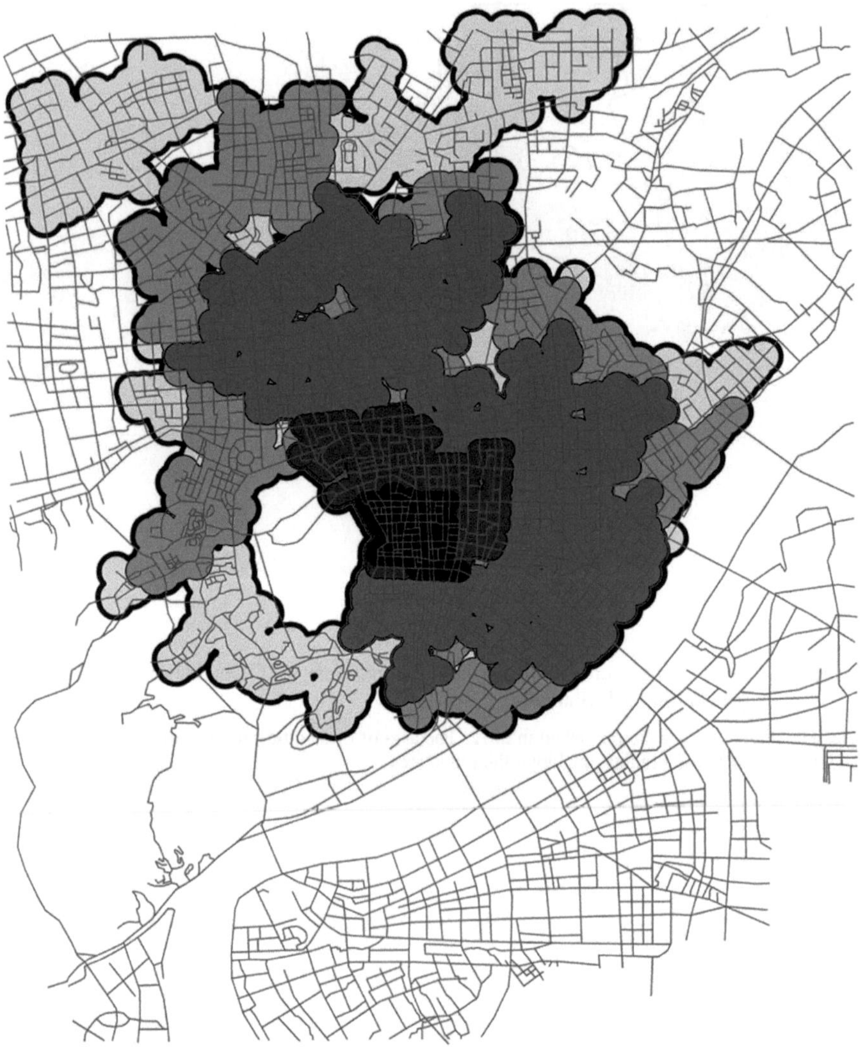

Figure 29.2 Continued

node number. Typical relations are displayed in Figures 29.3 and 29.4, and the results of scaling exponents and the coefficient of determination are tabulated in Tables 29.2 and 29.3.

29.4 Questions and discussion

The spatial allometric scaling relation has been revealed on the base of variable boundaries of urban agglomerations. The relationships between urban area,

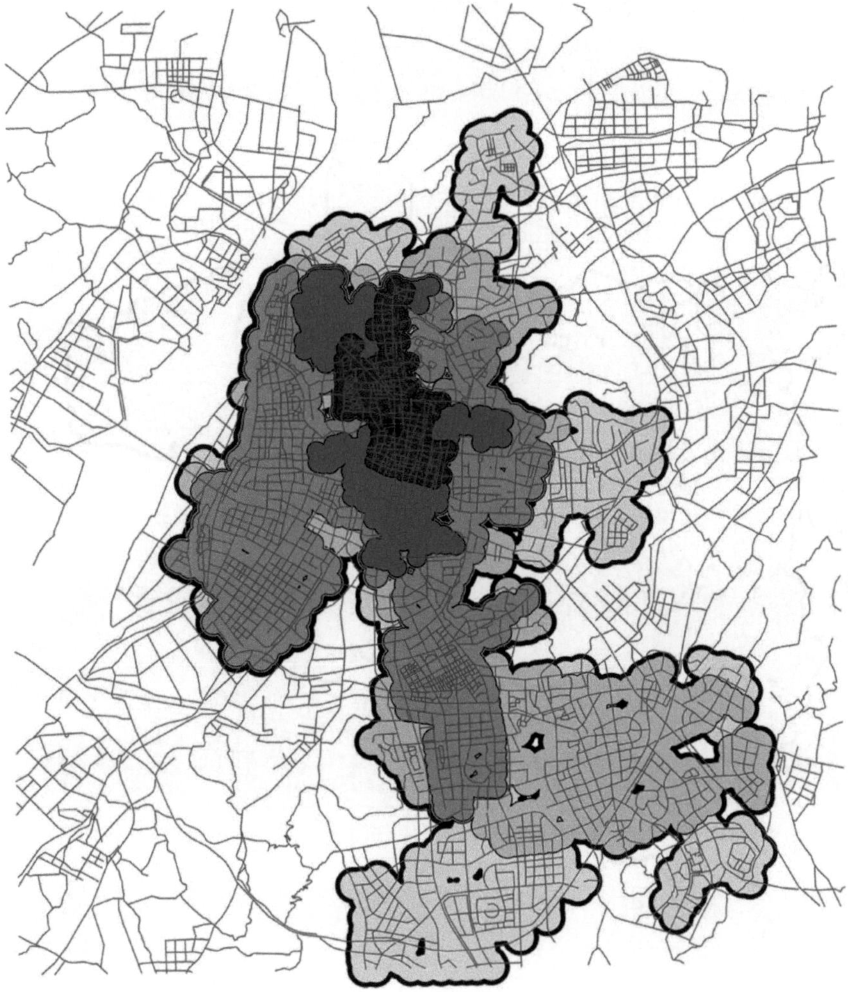

Figure 29.2 Continued

street length, and node number follow power laws. As far as the 10 Chinese cities are concerned, the power functions can be globally fitted to the datasets of nine cities. The city of Kunshan is a special case. The power function can be locally fitted to the observational data due to self-affine process. Despite this, the spatial allometry can be testified by these cities. The above results suggest a new way of looking at allometric scaling in cities. The relationships between fractals and allometry can be brought to light well from the perspective of spatial allometry [14].

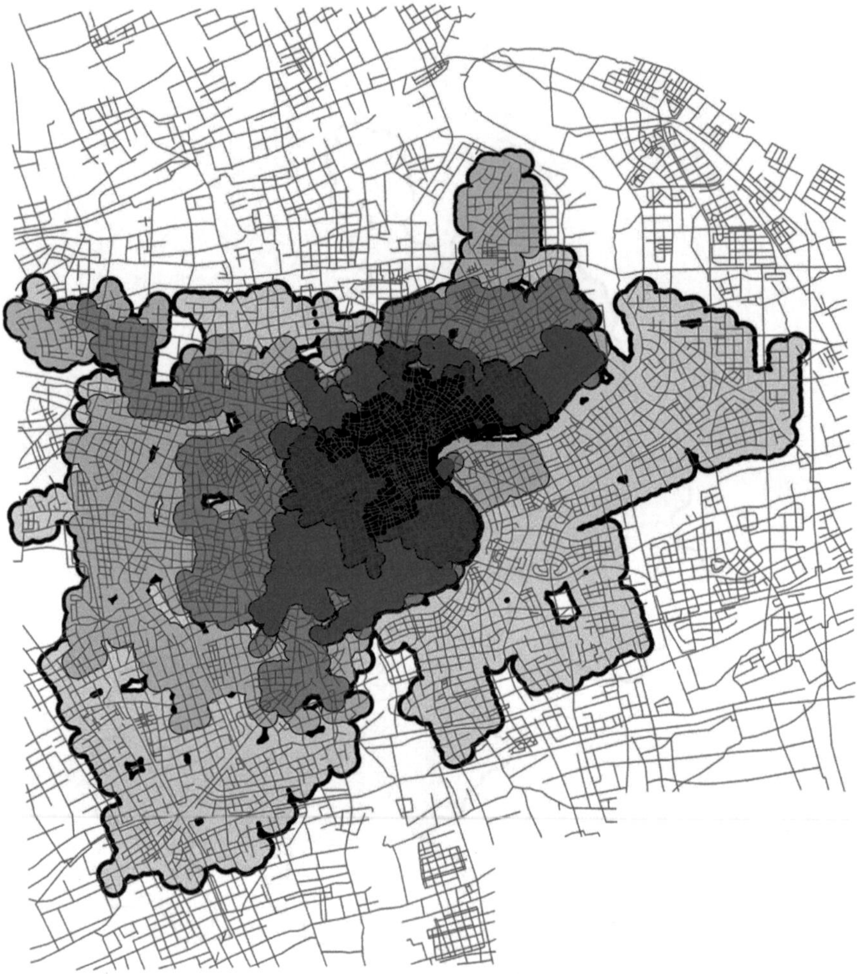

Figure 29.2 Continued

Spatial allometry is different from longitudinal allometry and transversal allometry. Longitudinal allometry indicates scaling in a temporal process of urban growth, reflecting the phase space of urban evolution, and transversal allometry indicates scaling in the hierarchical structure, reflecting the order space of rank-size distributions. Spatial allometry suggests scaling in spatial patterns of urban form, relating to fractality and reflecting the real space of cities [14]. The shortcomings of this study rest with two aspects. First, no Western city is investigated owing to an absence of data. Second, the relationships between

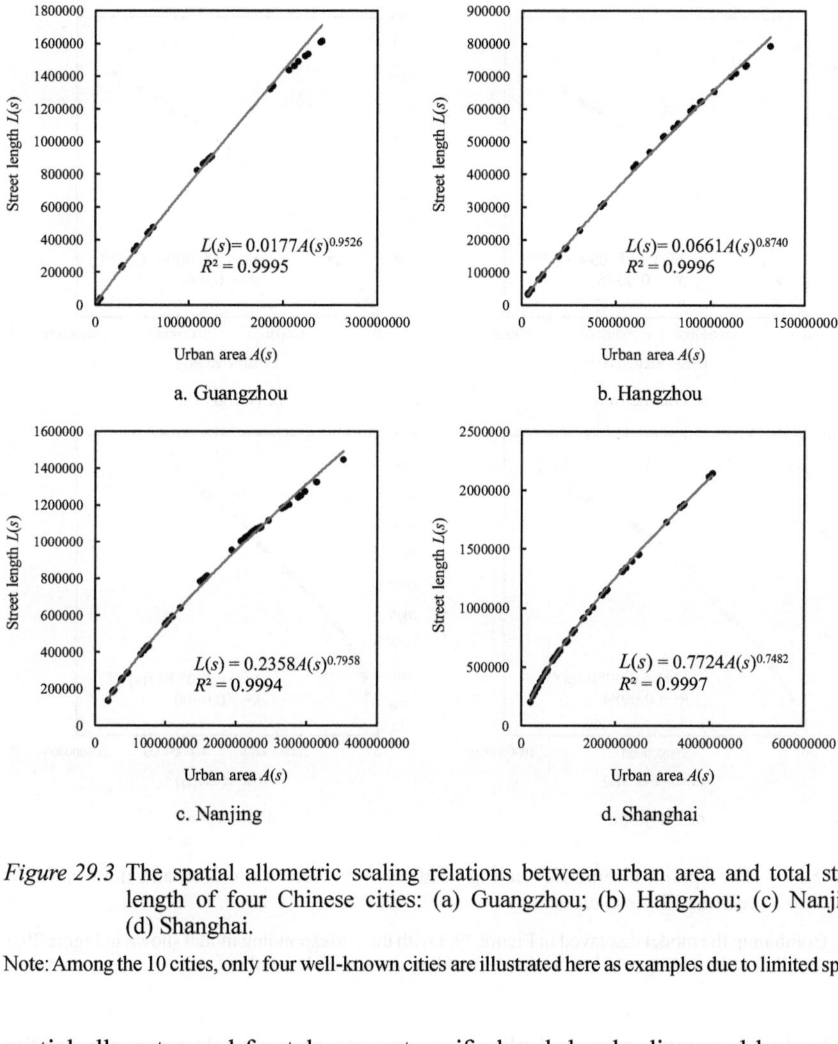

Figure 29.3 The spatial allometric scaling relations between urban area and total street length of four Chinese cities: (a) Guangzhou; (b) Hangzhou; (c) Nanjing; (d) Shanghai.

Note: Among the 10 cities, only four well-known cities are illustrated here as examples due to limited space.

spatial allometry and fractals are not verified and deeply discussed because of limited space.

29.5 Conclusions

Spatial allometry is an indispensable allometric scaling process in addition to longitudinal allometry and cross-sectional allometry of cities in geographical analysis. Based on the logic and empirical analyses, the main conclusions can be reached as follows. First, urban allometry can be modeled by three types of scaling relations. Spatial allometry and longitudinal allometry are based on individual cities, while transverse allometry is based on systems of cities. Second, spatial allometry is

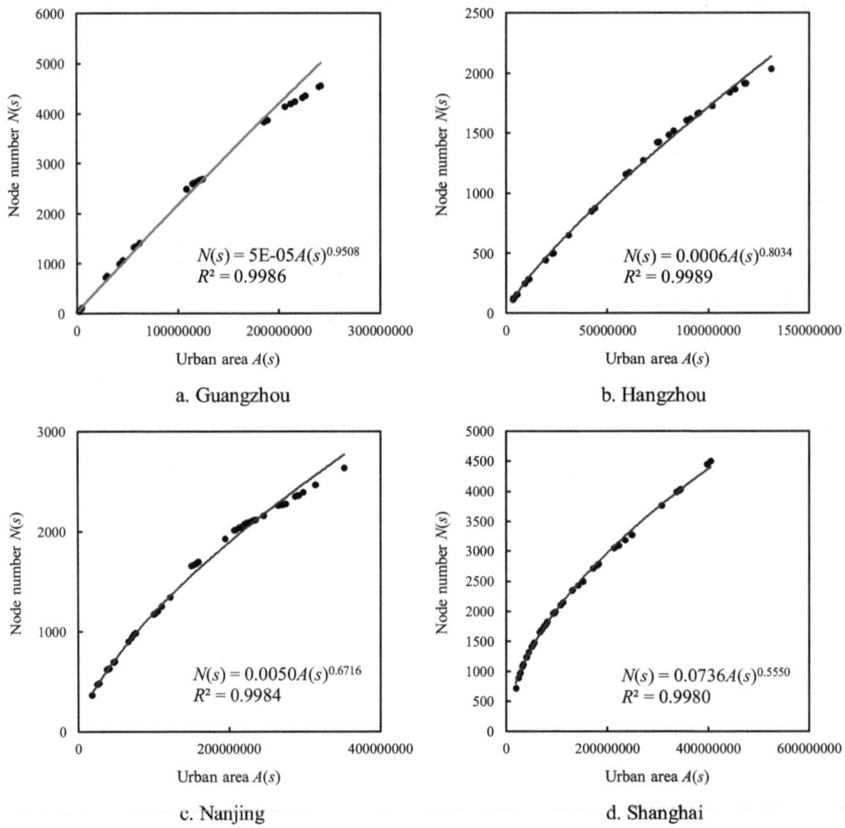

Figure 29.4 The spatial allometric scaling relations between urban area and node number of four Chinese cities.

Note: Combining the model displayed in Figure 29.3 with the corresponding model shown in Figure 29.2 gives the allometric scaling relation between street lengths and node numbers.

involved with points, lines, and planes of urban form. This allometry mirrors the scaling relations between urban area (plane), street length (line), and node number (points) of a city. The allometric scaling exponents reflect the fractal dimension ratios and relative growth rate ratios. Third, spatial allometry is a kind of evolutive law. Not all cities follow the allometric scaling law globally. The anisotropic growth may result in a self-affine process and lead to bi-scaling ranges on a log–log plot. In the long run, the self-affine patterns will gradually evolve to self-similar patterns.

Acknowledgments

This research was sponsored by the National Natural Science Foundation of China (Grant No. 42171192). The support is gratefully acknowledged.

Table 29.3 The numerical relationships between allometric scaling relations and the fractal dimension ratios of 10 Chinese cities.

City	*Parameter*		*City*	*Parameter*	
	Scaling exponent	*Fractal dimension ratio*		*Scaling exponent*	*Fractal dimension ratio*
Changchun	σ=0.8347	D_n/D_s=0.8334	Kunshan	σ=0.6963	D_n/D_s=0.6944
Changzhou	σ=0.8556	D_n/D_s=0.8554	Nanjing	σ=0.8442	D_n/D_s=0.8439
Guangzhou	σ=0.9984	D_n/D_s=0.9981	Shanghai	σ=0.7420	D_n/D_s=0.7417
Hangzhou	σ=0.9194	D_n/D_s=0.9192	Weifang	σ=0.9480	D_n/D_s=0.9470
Jinan	σ=0.8898	D_n/D_s=0.8896	Yangzhou	σ=0.8256	D_n/D_s=0.8258

References

[1] Batty, M., Longley, P.A. (1994) *Fractal Cities: A Geometry of Form and Function.* London: Academic Press.

[2] Frankhauser, P. (1994). *La Fractalité des Structures Urbaines (The Fractal Aspects of Urban Structures)*. Paris: Economica.

[3] Naroll, R.S., Bertalanffy, L. von. (1956). The principle of allometry in biology and social sciences. *General Systems Yearbook*, 1(part II), 76–89 [see also: *Ekistics*, 1973, 36: 244–252]

[4] Arcaute, E., Hatna, E., Ferguson, P., Youn, H., Johansson, A., Batty, M. (2015). Constructing cities, deconstructing scaling laws. *Journal of the Royal Society Interface*, 12(102), 20140745.

[5] Batty, M. (2008). The size, scale, and shape of cities. *Science*, 319, 769–771.

[6] Batty, M. (2013). A theory of city size. *Science*, 340, 1418–1419.

[7] Bettencourt, L.M.A. (2013). The origins of scaling in cities. *Science*, 340, 1438–1441.

[8] Bettencourt, L.M.A., Lobo, J., Helbing, D., Kühnert, C., West, G.B. (2007). Growth, innovation, scaling, and the pace of life in cities. *Proceeding of the National Academy of Sciences of the United States of America*, 104(17), 7301–7306.

[9] Chen, Y.G. (2014). An allometric scaling relation based on logistic growth of cities. *Chaos, Solitons & Fractals*, 65, 65–77.

[10] Louf, R., Barthelemy, M. (2014). How congestion shapes cities: from mobility patterns to scaling. *Scientific Reports*, 4, 5561.

[11] Louf, R., Barthelemy, M. (2014). Scaling: lost in the smog. *Environment and Planning B: Planning and Design*, 41, 767–769.

[12] Chen, Y.G. (2017). Multi-scaling allometric analysis for urban and regional development. *Physica A: Statistical Mechanics and its Applications*, 465, 673–689.

[13] Pumain, D., Moriconi-Ebrard, F. (1997). City size distributions and metropolisation. *GeoJournal*, 43(4), 307–314.

[14] Chen, Y.G., Wang, Y.H., Li, X.J. (2019). Fractal dimensions derived from spatial allometric scaling of urban form. *Chaos, Solitons & Fractals*, 126, 122–134.

[15] Rozenfeld, H.D., Rybski, D., Andrade, Jr. D.S., Batty, M., Stanley, H.E., Makse, H.A. (2008). Laws of population growth. *PNAS*, 105(48), 18702–18707.

[16] Jiang, B., Jia, T. (2011). Zipf's law for all the natural cities in the United States: a geospatial perspective. *International Journal of Geographical Information Science*, 25(8), 1269–1281.

[17] Chen, Y.G., Wang, J.J., Long, Y.Q., Zhang, X.H., Li, X.S. (2022). Defining urban boundaries by characteristic scales. *Computers, Environment and Urban Systems*, 46, 101799.

[18] Chen, Y.G., Jiang, S.G. (2010). Modeling fractal structure of systems of cities using spatial correlation function. *International Journal of Artificial Life Research*, 1(1), 12–34.

[19] Makse, H., Havlin, S., Stanley, H.E. (1995). Modelling urban growth patterns. *Nature*, 377, 608–612.

[20] Mandelbrot, B.B. (1983).*The Fractal Geometry of Nature*. New York: W. H. Freeman and Company.

30 The allometry of urban configuration

Scaling evidence from a Latin American city system[1]

Gustavo A. Ovando-Montejo, Peter Kedron, and Amy E. Frazier

30.1 Introduction

The conversion of natural lands to urban impervious surfaces is a main driver of global environmental change [1], and assessing how impervious surfaces are distributed across space is critical for understanding growth patterns and potential environmental consequences [2]. The configuration of urban impervious surfaces plays a key role in the sustainability of cities by moderating ecosystem services through surface urban heat islands, energy consumption, and CO_2 emissions [3–6]. More complex impervious surface configurations can signal less efficient use of space and greater resource use. However, little is known about how the configuration of urban impervious surfaces changes across an urban hierarchy.

Uncovering allometric relationships that relate the spatial configuration of urban areas to their relative size can help predict how city characteristics will change as a city grows, making it possible to anticipate how that growth will impact other facets of the built environment and urban life. This scalability can ultimately help researchers and policy makers understand the mechanisms driving urban growth and plan for more sustainable cities in the future. Identifying thresholds of city size beyond which cities no longer adhere to these scaling relationships can also spark insights into where critical growth inflection points occur. Evidence that demonstrates how the configuration or urban space changes with city size and assesses whether those relationships are allometric is needed to inform future planning for sustainable cities as the world adapts to global environmental change.

We present empirical evidence that UIS configuration scales predictably with city size. Using Mexico as a case study, we determine the range of city sizes over which impervious surface area (ISA) follows a univariate power law distribution and then employ standard major axis regression to determine which configuration metrics are allometrically related to ISA. We interpret our findings in the context of urban growth and discuss whether such scaling relationships might apply universally across urban systems.

30.2 Methods

Mexico is a primarily urban country, with around 80% of the population living in cities [7]. The country also contains a hierarchy of urban places, with Mexico

DOI: 10.4324/9781003288312-34

City – the primate capital – comprising a disproportionate share of the population and economic activity. We obtained impervious surface data for the 668 cities in Mexico with at least 10,000 people from the GlobeLand30 database [8] and binary reclassified the 10 classes into impervious surface and all others (Figure 30.1). Population and impervious surfaces for each city were extracted using a vector file representing urban localities obtained from the Mexican census INEGI (Instituto Nacional de Estadistica y Geografia).

We established whether a univariate power law is a viable description of ISA in Mexico following Clauset et al. [9] and estimated the threshold of the power law distribution as 294 ha. A goodness-of-fit test indicated that observed ISA data were generated by a power law, so we applied the 294 ha threshold to remove the smallest 160 cities (average population 15,060), limiting our investigation to 508 cities. We then compared the fit of alternative distributional models using Vuong's [10] normalized log-likelihood ratio test. The test statistic from our comparisons indicated that while both log-normal and power law models were viable for ISA, there was a clear preference for the power law model over an exponential model. establishing that power law was an appropriate model to compare ISA and configuration, we chose a minimally redundant set of 11 landscape metrics representing three categories of configuration: size, shape, and distribution (Table 30.1). We computed each metric for each city using FRAGSTATS v4 [11, 12] with an 8-neighbor rule for defining patches.

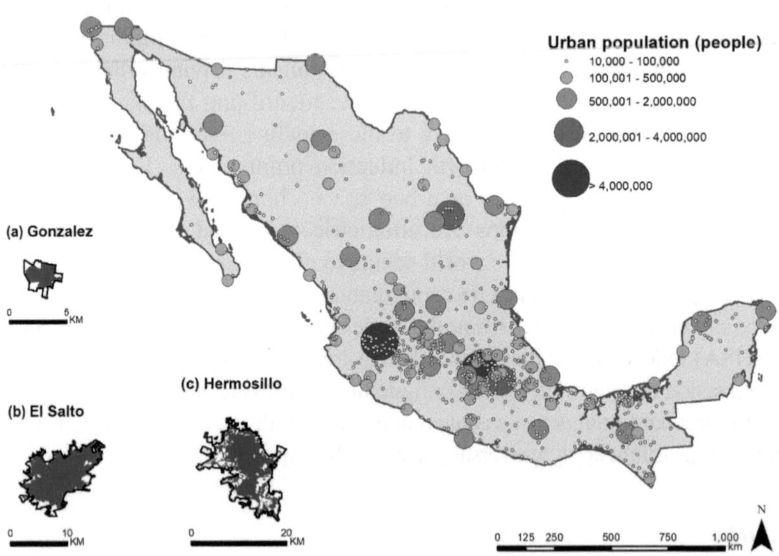

Figure 30.1 Mexico's 668 study cities with at least 10,000 inhabitants and impervious surface area for three cities: (a) Gonzalez, (b) El Salto, and (c) Hermosillo.

Table 30.1 Configuration metrics with abbreviations and descriptions. Equations are available in Ovando-Montejo et al. [20]. All metrics are computed at the urban class level except cohesion (landscape level).

Category	*Abbreviation*	*Metric name*	*Description*
Size	PLAND	Percentage of the landscape	Percent of the landscape covered by all urban patches
	LPI	Largest patch index	Percent of the landscape comprising the largest urban patch
	MNAREA	Mean patch area	Average size of urban patches
	AWAREA	Area-weighted mean patch area	Average (area-weighted) size of the urban patches
Shape	ED	Edge density	Total perimeter of urban land divided by total landscape area. Higher values indicate irregular shapes
	MNSHAPE	Mean shape index	Measure of shape complexity based on patch perimeter and area. Higher values indicate more complex shapes
	AWSHAPE	Area-weighted mean shape index	Area-weighted measure of shape complexity
Distribution	NP	Number of patches	Count of the number of urban patches. Higher values indicate fragmentation
	MNGYRATE	Mean radius of gyration	Mean distance between each patch cell and patch centroid. Lower values indicate form compaction; higher values elongation
	AWGYRATE	Area-weighted mean radius of gyration	Area-weighted mean distance between each cell in the patch and patch centroid
	MESH	Effective mesh size	Based on probability that two points, randomly chosen, are in the same patch. Lower values indicate fragmentation

We used standard major axis regression (SMA) to test for the existence of bivariate allometric relations between ISA and configuration. Biologists frequently use SMA to examine scaling relationships between body size and physical characteristics such as limb length or biting force [13,14]. Ma et al. [2] showed SMA can also be applied to urban allometry. The allometric relation between ISA and each configuration metric, y, is defined by:

$$y = \alpha ISA^{\beta} \tag{30.1}$$

where α is a normalization constant, and β is the scaling exponent representing the proportional change in y per unit change in ISA. Eq. (30.1) can be log transformed and re-expressed as Eq. (30.2), which is advantageous for interpreting size variables since growth is multiplicative. Transformation also allows the relationship between

x and y to be expressed linearly, which simplifies estimation [15]. Using Eq. (30.2), we estimate α and β for each metric.

$$\ln y = \ln \alpha + \beta \ln ISA \tag{30.2}$$

Reliable SMA estimates require a linear relationship between the variables as well as normality and homoscedasticity of the residuals [15,16]. We checked both and excluded PLAND, ED, LPI, MNGYRATE, and MNSHAPE. For NP, we also excluded cities with only a single contiguous urban area, as these cities were systematically underfit by the SMA regression. This change removed 215 additional cities for NP (average population = 19,737). The remaining six metrics met normality and homoscedasticity criteria, so the full set of 508 cities was used.

We estimated SMA regression coefficients using the *smatr* R package [17]. We then tested for allometric isometry (β=1) following Warton et al. [15] and Taskinen and Warton [18], paying particular attention to sublinear ($\beta < 1$) relationships where metric values y increased at a slower rate than *ISA*, and superlinear ($\beta > 1$) relationships where metric values y grew at a faster rate than *ISA*.

30.3 Results

Mexico generally follows a Zipf distribution for population rank versus population and area rank versus area (Figure 30.2). The relationship is particularly strong for smaller cities for population and mid-sized cities for area. Both relationships stray from the dotted line for some larger cities, particularly for area.

All metrics had moderate to strong model fits (0.4–0.9) for bivariate power law relationships with ISA (Table 30.2). Isometry tests show that the estimated relationships are allometric, with most metrics having a sublinear relationship with ISA, meaning their configuration values grow slower than the overall growth of impervious surface. Two metrics, AWAREA and MESH, are superlinear. A test

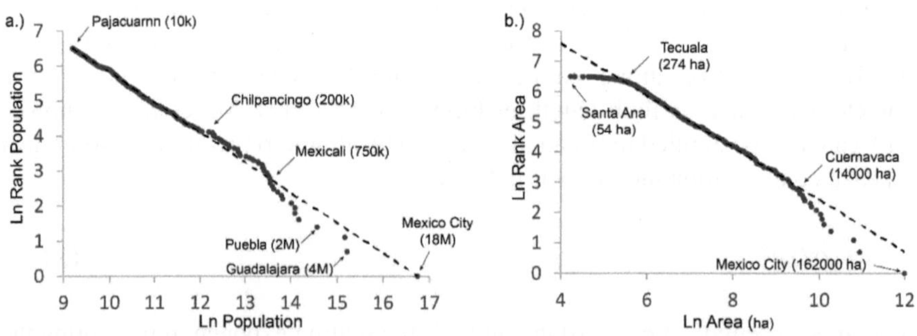

Figure 30.2 Univariate relationships for (a) population and (b) area for Mexican cities greater than 10,000 people. Zipf distributions will follow the dotted line.

Table 30.2 Standardized major axis regression estimates of the allometric relation between ISA and configuration. Only metrics with significant Spearman correlation coefficients (ρ) are included. All reported estimates significant at $p = 0.05$.

Metric category	*Configuration metric*	*Spearman's ρ*	*SMA regressions*		
			r^2	$\hat{a}$	$\hat{\beta}$
Size	MNAREA	0.398	0.204	0.226 *(0.053, 0.398)*	0.741 *(0.685, 0.801)*
	AWAREA	0.888	0.900	–0.191 *(–0.276, –0.107)*	1.036 *(1.008, 1.065)*
Shape	AWSHAPE	0.614	0.540	–0.633 *(–0.699, –0.568)*	0.369 *(0.347, 0.391)*
Distribution	NP[1]	0.607	0.532	–1.493 *(–1.645, –1.341)*	0.727 *(0.678, 0.778)*
	AWGYRATE	0.854	0.870	1.508 *(1.458, 1.558)*	0.534 *(0.518, 0.552)*
	MESH	0.807	0.800	–0.754 *(–0.887, –0.621)*	1.157 *(1.116, 1.206)*

[1] Relationship estimated with 294 cities where NP > 1 and ISA > 294 ha.

for β = 0.75 for NP shows that the relation for this metric could not be statistically distinguished from the ¾ power law commonly observed in biological allometry [19].

Bivariate plots for AWAREA and MESH, which had superlinear scaling, show a clear mathematical limit along the 45 degree line (Figure 30.3). This limit relates to the saturation of impervious surface within the urban boundary (see [20]) as both metrics are derived from the sum of all patches. As the area within the urban boundary fills with ISA and patches merge, a city will approach this natural limit. In the Mexican system, most cities lie along or near this limit. A similar upper bound exists for MNAREA, but the lack of an area-weighted size correction for this metric means there is a wider spread of values and a poorer model fit.

30.4 Link with literature and discussion

Allometry can provide insights into how system characteristics, or the processes shaping them, scale with size. Applied to urban systems, this knowledge elucidates the predictability of urban patterns, which can inform future urban development planning and resource allocation. Unlocking the laws governing spatial patterns in cities begins with observing scaling relationships. Two types of relationships are commonly discussed in the allometry literature. Quarter-power scaling relationships (i.e., exponents are multiples of ¼) are well established in biology [19,21,22] and are related to the rate at which networks deliver resources to cells in organisms. Samaniego and Moses [23] showed that biological explanations may also extend to city systems, as cities, like organisms, distribute resources over space through infrastructure networks. We also found evidence supporting "cities as organisms"

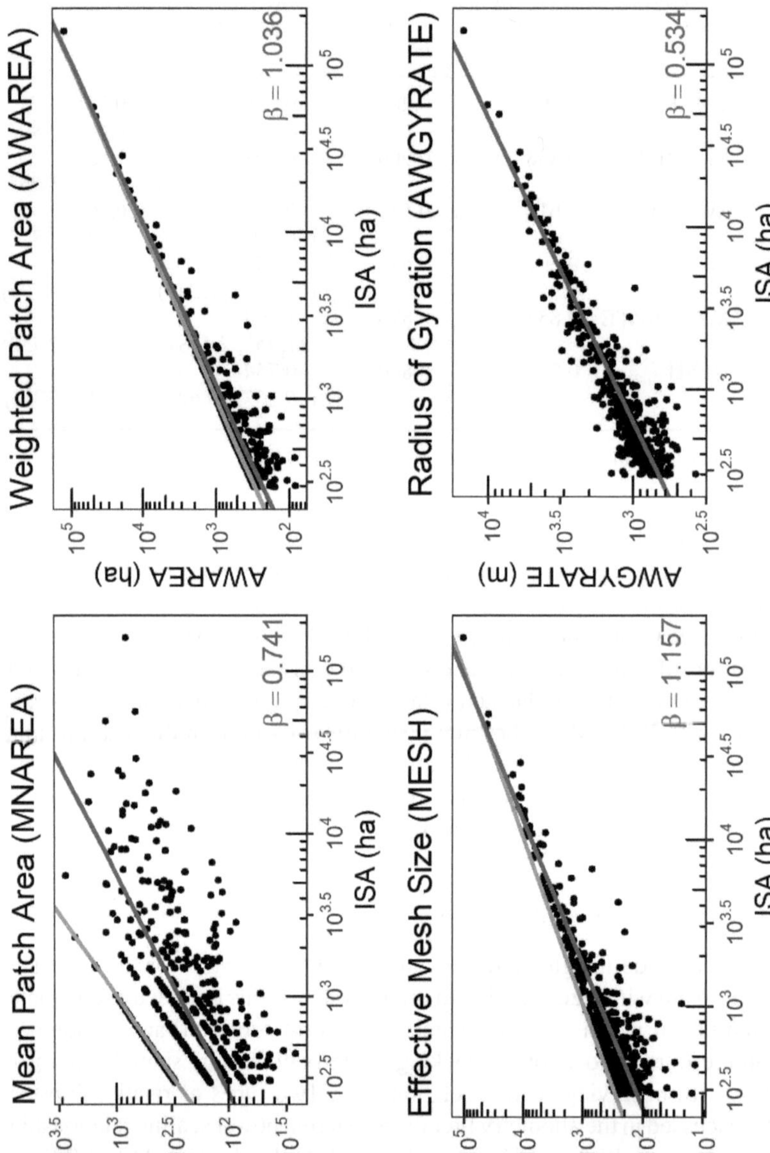

Figure 30.3 Scatter plots of configuration vs. ISA. Red lines are SMA regression models with the estimated slope of each line, β. The 45° line is shown in light blue. The NP plot was produced using 294 cities.

in the 0.75 scaling exponents of NP and MNAREA. The second type of relationship, third-power scaling, is driven by geometric similarity and is characteristic of Euclidean objects [24]. Despite the geometric basis of landscape metrics, we did not find evidence of third-power scaling (AMSHAPE was not statistically significantly similar to 1/3), which conforms to earlier studies [25,26].

Four metrics scale sublinearly with ISA in Mexico, suggesting infill development may be offsetting sprawl as cities grow. We found that configuration complexity increases at a greater rate relative to changes in city size for smaller cities where infill development opportunities are less. This relationship supports the idea that different forms of urban infrastructure are characterized by economies of scale that may be beneficial for sustainable growth (e.g., roads, utilities; [27]). The infill process may indeed be driving those economies of scale as it is often cheaper to build adjacent to existing infrastructure. Infill development may also be environmentally beneficial as it constrains the impacts of urban areas within urban areas. Our findings therefore have important implications for development planning, as they suggest that the development of new urban areas may be more costly and environmentally impactful per unit of ISA in smaller cities. Since allometric predictions have not always held across all urban contexts [28], these findings need replication in other city systems.

An outstanding question about the scaling relationships we observed in Mexico is how different types of settlements are reflected in ISA. Past research [29,30] has established that larger Latin American cities often have numerous informal settlements along their peripheries. These outlying areas develop without formal urban planning but are classified as ISA in remotely sensed imagery, and it is difficult to distinguish them from formally planned areas. Distinguishing between these types of development is important in the context of the scaling of urban configurations because these informal settlements often form irregular shapes discontiguous from the urban core [12,31]. While researchers still debate the socio-economic drivers producing this type of urban expansion, these informal settlements may be contributing complex growth patterns along city edges. The extent to which these informal settlements drive scaling patterns is not yet known and would be a fruitful avenue for future research, particularly for relating findings from Latin America to other areas around the world.

Note

1 www.sciencedirect.com/science/article/abs/pii/S0143622821000783?via%3Dihub

References

1. Seto, K. C., Güneralp, B., & Hutyra, L. R. (2012). Global forecasts of urban expansion to 2030 and direct impacts on biodiversity and carbon pools. *Proceedings of the National Academy of Sciences*, *109*(40), 16083–16088.
2. Ma, Q., Wu, J., He, C., & Hu, G. (2018). Spatial scaling of urban impervious surfaces across evolving landscapes: From cities to urban regions. *Landscape and Urban Planning*, *175*, 50–61.

3. Fang, C., Wang, S., & Li, G. (2015). Changing urban forms and carbon dioxide emissions in China: A case study of 30 provincial capital cities. *Applied Energy*, *158*, 519–531.
4. Sharifi, A. (2019). Resilient urban forms: A macro-scale analysis. *Cities*, *85*, 1–14.
5. Stuhlmacher, M., Andrade, R., Turner, B. L., Frazier, A. E., & Li, W. (2020). Environmental outcomes of urban land systems: comparing Riparian design approaches in the Phoenix Metropolitan Area. Land Use Policy, *99*, Article number 104615.
6. Wang, M., Madden, M., & Liu, X. (2017). Exploring the relationship between urban forms and CO2 emissions in 104 Chinese Cities. *Journal of Urban Planning and Development*, *143*(4), 04017014.
7. Instituto Nacional de Estadistica y Geografia [INEGI] (2018). Población. Retrieved August 30, 2018. Retrieved online from www.beta.inegi.org.mx/temas/estructura/
8. Chen, J., Chen, J., Liao, A., Cao, X., Chen, L., Chen, X., & Mills, J. (2015). Global land cover mapping at 30m resolution: A POK-based operational approach. *ISPRS Journal of Photogrammetry and Remote Sensing*, *103*, 7–27.
9. Clauset, A., Shalizi, C. R., & Newman, M. E. (2009). Power-law distributions in empirical data. *SIAM Review*, *51*(4), 661–703.
10. Vuong, Q. H. (1989, March). Likelihood ratio tests for model selection and non-nested hypotheses. *Econometrica: Journal of the Econometric Society*, *57*(2), 307–333.
11. McGarigal, K., Cushman, S., & Ene, E. (2012). *FRAGSTATS v4: Spatial pattern analysis program for categorical and continuous maps*. Amherst: Computer software program produced by the authors at the University of Massachusetts. www.umass.edu/landeco/research/fragstats/fragstats.html.
12. Ovando-Montejo, G. A., & Frazier, A. E. (2020). Geographic assessment of urban quality of life in Mexico City using socio-economic and environmental factors. *International Journal of Applied Geospatial Research (IJAGR)*, *11*(3) 68–86.
13. Chamoli, U., & Wroe, S. (2011). Allometry in the districution of material properties and geometry of the felid skull: why larger species may need to change how they may achieve it. *Journal of Theoretical Biology*, *283*(1), 217–226.
14. Price, C. A., Wing, S., & Weitz, J. A. (2012). Scaling and structure of dicotyledonous lead vention networks. *Ecology Letters*, *15*(2), 87–95.
15. Warton, D. I., Wright, I. J., Falster, D. S., & Westoby, M. (2006). Bivariate line-fitting methods for allometry. *Biological Reviews*, *81*(2), 259–291.
16. Legendre, P. & Legendre, L. (2012). *Numerical ecology. Number 24 in Developments in Environmental Modelling*. Elsevier, Amsterdam, 3rd edition.
17. Warton, D. I., Duursma, R., Falster, D., & Taskinen, S. (2018). Package 'smatr', Available at: https://cran.r-project.org/web/packages/smatr/smatr.pdf
18. Taskinen, S., & Warton, D. I. (2013). Robust tests for one or more allometric lines. *Journal of Theoretical Biology*, *333*(21), 38–46.
19. West, G. B., Brown, J. H., & Enquist, B. J. (1997). A general model for the origin of allometric scaling laws in biology. *Science*, *276*(5309), 122–126
20. Ovando-Montejo, G. A., Kedron, P., & Frazier, A. E. (2021). Relationship between urban size and configuration: Scaling evidence from a hierarchical system in Mexico. *Applied Geography*, *132*, 102462.
21. Enquist, B. J., Brown, J. H., & West, G. B. (1998). Allometric scaling of plant energetics and population density. *Nature*, *395*(6698), 163.
22. Savage, V. M., Gillooly, J. F., Woodruff, W. H., West, G. B., Allen, A. P., Enquist, B. J., & Brown, J. H. (2004). The predominance of quarter-power scaling in biology. *Functional Ecology*, *18*(2), 257–282.

23. Samaniego, H., & Moses, M. E. (2008). Cities as organisms: Allometric scaling of urban road networks. *Journal of Transport and Land Use*, *1*(1), 21–39.
24. Wu, J., & Li, H. (2006). Perspectives and methods of scaling. In J. Wu, B. Jones, H. Li, & O. L. Loucks (Eds.). *Scaling and uncertainty analysis in ecology*, 17–44. Dordrecht, The Netherlands: Springer.
25. Arcaute, E., Hatna, E., Ferguson, P., Youn, H., Johansson, A., & Batty, M. (2015). Constructing cities, deconstructing scaling laws. *Journal of the Royal Society Interface*, *12*(102), 201–207.
26. Strano, E., & Sood, V. (2016). Rich and poor cities in Europe. An urban scaling approach to mapping the European economic transition. *PloS one*, *11*(8), e0159465.
27. Bettencourt, L. M., Lobo, J., Helbing, D., Kühnert, C., & West, G. B. (2007). Growth, innovation, scaling, and the pace of life in cities. *Proceedings of the National Academy of Sciences*, *104*(17), 7301–7306.
28. Zhao, S., Liu, S., Xu, C., Yuan, W., Sun, Y., Yan, W., & Fang, J. (2018). Contemporary evolution and scaling of 32 major cities in China. *Ecological Applications*, *28*(6), 1655–1668.
29. Aguilar, A. G. (2008). Peri-urbanization, illegal settlements and environmental impact in Mexico City. *Cities*, *25*(3), 133–145.
30. Bejarano, M. S. (2016). Tipología de invasiones urbanas. Una propuesta a partir del caso de Cali, Colombia. *Entorno Geográfico, 12*(1), 70–100.
31. Ruíz-Gómez, M. (2006). El crecimiento de los asentamientos irregulares en áreas protegidas. *La delegación Tlalpan. Investigaciones Geográficas*, *60*(1), 83–109.

31 Capturing urban scaling laws via spatio-temporal correlated clusters[1]

Anna Carbone, Sérgio Luiz da Silva, and Giorgio Kaniadakis

31.1 Introduction

A variety of urban features have been reported to exhibit quite universal behaviour depending on population size N. Scaling laws $Y \sim N^{\beta}$ linking socio-economic and infrastructural features to population size, either with $\beta > 1$ or with $\beta < 1$, imply that a more concentrated population corresponds to better socio-economic performances and less costly infrastructural investments [1–4]. The probability density function (pdf) of the population size follows a power-law of N with an exponent approximately equal to 2 [5,6]. Models of monocentric cities have been proposed where individuals commute from home to a central business district (CBD) and back by private or public transportation in a homogeneous isotropic space [7–10]. In such models, population density shows an exponential dependence on the distance from the CBD. Recently, urban landscapes with distinct multicentric activity centres have been envisioned to emerge as population size increases [11] with the monocentric urban organization stable up to a threshold value N^* when a transition to a multicentric structure takes place characterized by a number of business clusters varying with population size as $C_e = N^{\sigma}$ with $\sigma = \mu / (\mu + 1) < 1$ and $0 < \mu < 1$ depending on the congestion level [12,13].

Overall, the scaling features indicate that urban organizations behave as heterogeneous complex systems. Hence, understanding urban microstructure and its evolution over multiple spatio-temporal scales has become a scientific priority with direct practical implications for the sustainable management of big cities [14–17]. The focus of the scientific community has been increasingly drawn towards urban feature description in terms of pointwise rather than cumulative functions of the population size N. In this scenario, the increasing availability of high-resolution spatio-temporal data (phone, satellites) can contribute to investigating models of urban areas and quantifying related phenomena at the local level.

Statistical physics concepts put forward within the subfield of complex systems science have proved relevant to the description of socio-economic and infrastructural urban systems featured by increasing population size and heterogeneity. The investigation of inter- and intra-urban features in heterogeneous multicentric structures has been carried out in terms of spatio-temporal clustering driven by socio-economic

DOI: 10.4324/9781003288312-35

and/or geographical/infrastructural phenomena. A growing number of studies have been addressed to the application of clustering methods in relation to percolation, fractality, self-similarity, self-organization concepts and their statistical significance in the context of urban modelling [18–37]. The Diffusion Limited Aggregation (DLA) model is among the early attempts to describe urban growth phenomena in terms of only one large fractal cluster with a tree-like dendritic structure developed around the central business district, where additional units are randomly added at the periphery. Models where long-range correlated rather than random clusters add to form the city topology could better suit the real urban organization. A percolation process with long-range correlation and an exponential dependence on the distance from the central business district is proposed in [35,36]. A two-dimensional fractional Brownian field is adopted to model the urban grid infrastructure where a set of long-range correlated clusters is generated according to the approach proposed in Ref. [37]. This method is able to reproduce the heterogeneous self-similar urban structure without requiring the assumption of an exponential distribution of the population density with respect to the city centre. Furthermore, it does not operate via a constant thresholding clustering approach, as it is based on a locally varying average function of the spatial field.

This work aims to provide a brief review focused on the adoption of statistical clustering concepts to quantify complexity features of urban landscapes. Special attention will be paid to how scaling laws emerge from long-range correlated clusters with a specific focus on the works [35–37]. This chapter is organized as follows. In Section 31.2 (*Statistical clustering*) the main concepts of clustering algorithms are briefly recalled. In Section 31.2.1 the main steps of the (*Detrending moving average*) algorithm are presented. In Section 31.3 (*Discussion*), a comparison among the methods is provided and the main outcomes, potential implications, and directions for future work are summarized.

31.2 Statistical clustering

Clustering is becoming increasingly relevant for making sense of large amounts of correlated data, where the main aim is identifying patterns intrinsically emerging in the data (natural clusters) rather than building artificial partitions. Several methods and optimization criteria have been proposed that in turn lead to different classes of clustering algorithms. In general, clustering refers to partitioning a dataset into subsets according to some criterion. Let $X = \{\mathbf{x}_1, ..., \mathbf{x}_n\}$ be a set of n data points. Centre-based clustering operates via a partition $C = \{C_1, ..., C_k\}$ of X into k clusters with corresponding centres $\mathbf{c}_1, ..., \mathbf{c}_k$ and allocating data points according to some optimization criterion. The k-centre, k-median, and k-means methods minimize, respectively, the maximum, the sum, and the sum of squares of distances between $\mathbf{c}_k$ and any data point. Despite extensive interesting applications of centre-based clustering, the method suits convex-shaped clusters and requires prior knowledge of the number of cluster k input parameters. An alternative is offered by density-based clustering, which is not affected by these drawbacks as the clusters are built as varying density areas of some relevant feature of the data surrounded by density values lower than a threshold. Density-based clusters are usually built as sets of points resulting from the intersection through a density function $\delta(r)$ relevant for the data at a certain density level $\bar{\delta}(r)$ (threshold level). Each intersection generates separate connected regions in the feature space where the probability density is higher than the threshold value (see Figure 31.1). Each region corresponds to a cluster defined over all the data points falling into this region. The threshold $\bar{\delta}(r)$ is usually defined as a constant over the whole data domain. If the threshold density level is too small, several clusters will result in being merged together. If the threshold density level is too large, large clusters will not show up. The choice of the threshold is critical to the cluster region definition. In particular, the assumption of a constant threshold is an issue when the relevant feature is not a constant but varies as a long-range correlated quantity of space and time. Such a situation occurs in many real-world systems and is particularly interesting for urban data (e.g., the population size N).

31.2.1 Detrending moving average algorithm

For the sake of completeness, before discussing the application of the detrending moving average (DMA) algorithm to urban landscapes, the main concepts underlying the algorithm together with the essential analytical relationships will be briefly recalled [39,40]. The DMA can be classified as a density-based clustering method with a position-dependent threshold.

Two-dimensional long-range correlated data, such as those featuring urban landscapes, can be modelled in terms of random fields [41,42]. Interesting classes of models for random fields are the fractional Gaussian noise (fGn) and fractional Brownian motion (fBm). A fractional Brownian field $f_H(r)$ is a scalar function with $r=(x_1,x_2,\ldots,x_d)$ the spatial coordinates, d the dimension of the Euclidean domain. The fractional Gaussian noise (*fGn*) is obtained from the fBm increments $f_H(r+1)-f_H(r)$. The fGn is a stationary process with zero mean and covariance given by:

$$\begin{aligned}\rho(\lambda) &= \frac{\sigma^2}{2}\left[(\lambda+1)^{2H}-2\lambda^{2H}+|\lambda-1|^{2H}\right]\\ &\sim H(2H-1)\lambda^{2H-2}\end{aligned} \tag{31.1}$$

where $\lambda=(\lambda_1,\lambda_2,\ldots,\lambda_d)$ is the scale factor and $|\lambda| = (\lambda_1^2+\lambda_2^2+\ldots+\lambda_d^2)^{1/2}$. The parameter $H\in[0,1]$ is called the Hurst exponent and is linked to the fractal dimension D_f by the relationship $D_f = d - H$. The above properties indicate that fractional Brownian motion and fractional Gaussian noise exhibit long-range correlation and self-similarity.

According to Refs. [39,40] the density threshold is defined by the moving average function $\widetilde{f}_H(r)$, that for a two-dimensional space with $d = 2$, $r = (x_1, x_2)$ and $\lambda = (n_1, n_2)$ writes:

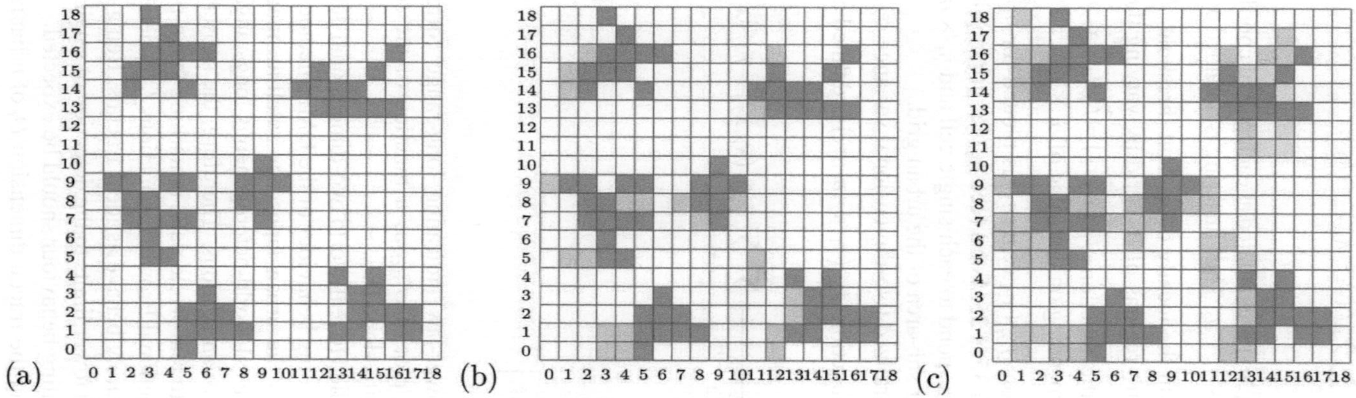

Figure 31.1 Density-based clusters are generated by the intersection between a relevant density function defined at each cell and a threshold. The standard density-based clustering operates with a constant valued threshold. Panels (a), (b), and (c) show how the characteristic size of the clusters scale up as the threshold value decreases. In Refs. [37,38] the threshold is defined as a locally dependent average. The threshold value is determined by the window size $n_1 \times n_2$, which also provides an estimate of the average area of the clusters. In Refs. [35,36] the threshold is a constant.

$$\widetilde{f}_H(x_1, x_2; n_1, n_2) = \frac{1}{n_1 n_2} \sum_{k_1=0}^{n_1-1} \sum_{k_2=0}^{n_2-1} f(x_1 - k_1, x_2 - k_2). \tag{31.2}$$

The function $\widetilde{f}_H(x_1, x_2; n_1, n_2)$ is evaluated at each pair of coordinates x_1, x_2 over sub-arrays with different sizes $n_1 \times n_2$. The clustering is obtained by the intersection of the function $f_H(x_1, x_2)$ with the locally dependent threshold $\widetilde{f}_H(x_1, x_2; n_1, n_2)$ estimated recursively over sub-regions of the grid by varying the values of $n_1 \times n_2$. The difference between the function $f_H(x_1, x_2) - \widetilde{f}_H(x_1, x_2; n_1, n_2)$ generates clusters of increasing area depending on the value of $n_1 \times n_2$.

In Figure 31.2, the function $\widetilde{f}_H(x_1, x_2; n_1, n_2)$ is plotted for $n_1 \times n_2$ equal to (a) 15×15, (b) 25×25, and (c) 35×35. For a rectangular urban grid with size $N_1 \times N_2$, the coordinates x_1, x_2 correspond to each single cell and $n_1 \times n_2$ corresponds to a cell array, i.e., a rectangular sub-area of the urban grid.

In Refs. [39,40], the generalized two-dimensional variance σ^2_{DMA} of $f_H(x_1, x_2)$ around the moving average function $\widetilde{f}_H(x_1, x_2; n_1, n_2)$ is defined as:

$$\sigma^2_{DMA}(n_1, n_2) = \frac{1}{(N_1 - n_{1_{max}})(N_2 - n_{2_{max}})} \sum_{x_1=n_1}^{N_1} \sum_{x_2=n_2}^{N_2} \left[f_H(x_1, x_2) - \widetilde{f}_H(x_1, x_2; n_1, n_2) \right]^2, \tag{31.3}$$

which can be rewritten as:

$$\sigma^2_{DMA}(n_1, n_2) \sim \left[\sqrt{n_1^2 + n_2^2} \right]^{2H}. \tag{31.4}$$

Eq. (31.4) is again a power-law indicating long-range correlation and self-similarity. Hence a log–log plot of σ^2_{DMA} as a function of the scale $s = n_1^2 + n_2^2$ would yield a straight line with slope H.

The procedure can be applied to real-world two-dimensional data as for example done in Refs. [37,38]. The scaling behaviour of the DMA method (Eq. 31.4) when implemented on real data as the urban landscape satellite images provides the Hurst exponent of the data. Real-world heterogeneous long-range correlated data are not ideal fractional Brownian motions. Therefore, the subscript H is dropped when the method is applied to real-world data, remarking that a-priori data are not ideal fBms. Contrarily to fractional Brownian functions $f_H(r)$ defined to exist at all scales, real-world datasets barely behave as ideal fractals. Being characterized by finite sizes, setting upper and lower limits to the detection of small and large scales, deviations from the ideal scaling behaviour should be expected.

The Hurst exponent H and the fractal dimension D_f of urbanized regions have been estimated by implementing the two-dimensional detrending moving average

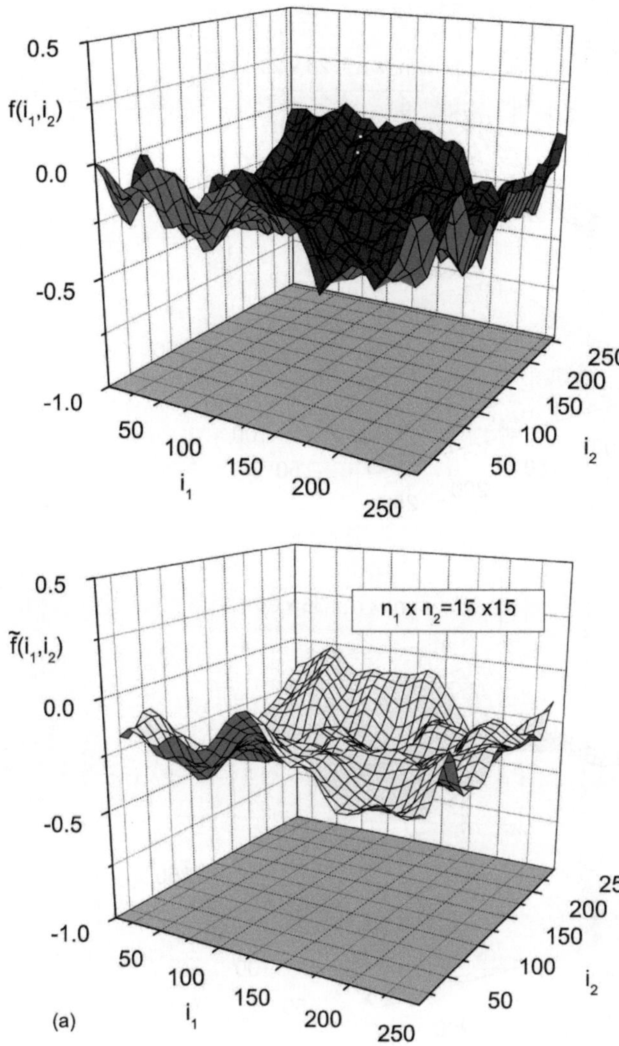

Figure 31.2 Two-dimensional ($d = 2$) Fractional Brownian motion field with $H = 0.5$ (a) and moving averages $\widetilde{f}_H(x_1, x_2; n_1, n_2)$ estimated by using Eq. (31.2). The size $n_1 \times n_2$ refers to the local areas over which the moving average is estimated. Values of $n_1 \times n_2$ are (a) 15×15, (b) 25×25, and (c) 35×35.

(DMA) algorithm on satellite images in Refs. [37,38]. The purpose of the investigation is twofold: to provide accurate estimates of H and D_f and shed light on the models of interurban and intraurban scaling laws. The analysed urbanized or rural areas are drawn from satellite images. Before implementing the DMA algorithm, raw data are converted from the *unit8* to the *double* format. The algorithm is

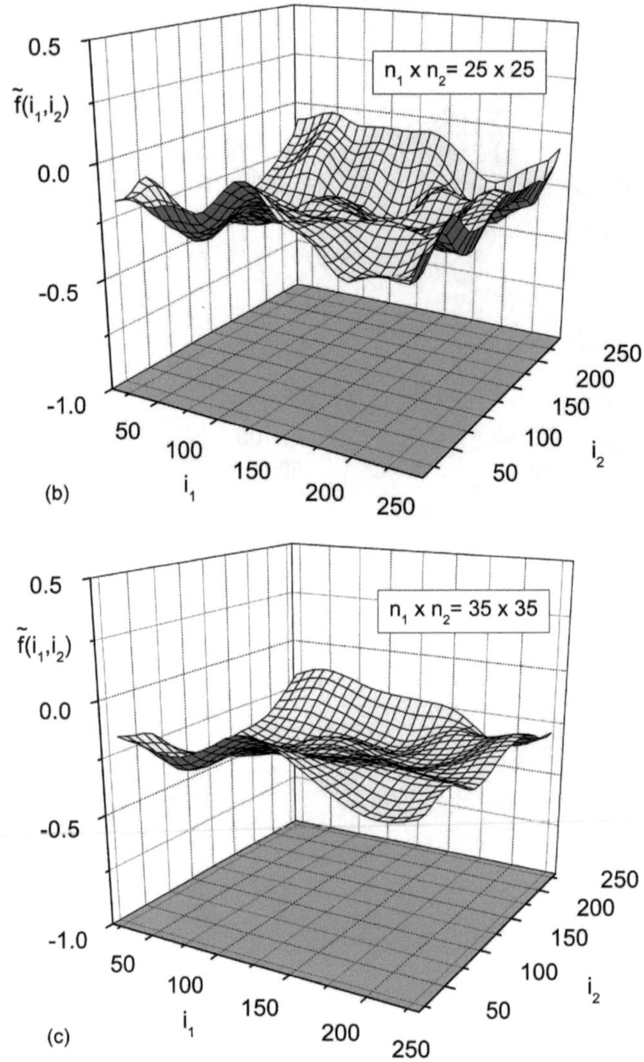

Figure 31.2 Continued

implemented separately on each sub-image, to grasp the variability of the scaling properties of different areas (partially mountainous, suburban, and centrally located areas). Further technical details and results for several intraurban regions of different cities can be found in Ref. [37] and are not repeated here.

The *moving average clustering* optimization criterion can be interpreted as a minimization of an information measure over a partition generated by the threshold $\widetilde{f}_H(x_1,x_2;n_1,n_2)$ which is a coarse-grained description of the observed system obtained by smoothing out the fine details of the real data [43]. As the system becomes coarser, randomness and entropy increase. In the *detrending moving average clustering* threshold $\widetilde{f}_H(x_1,x_2;n_1,n_2)$ is obtained by performing a local average over each cell of the partition in phase space (Figure 31.3).

The difference $f(x_1,x_2)-\widetilde{f}_H(x_1,x_2;n_1,n_2)$ generates a set of regions for each sub-array $n_1 \times n_2$ corresponding to a finite partition $C_{n,j}=\{C_{n,1}, C_{n,2}, \ldots\}$ of clusters. The difference $f(x_1,x_2)-\widetilde{f}_H(x_1,x_2;n_1,n_2)$ quantifies the error, i.e., the loss of information of the coarse-grained two-dimensional structure compared to the real data. The spatial coordinates (x_1, x_2) where the difference $f(x_1,x_2)-\widetilde{f}_H(x_1,x_2;n_1,n_2)$ becomes zero correspond to the cluster boundaries (Figure 31.4).

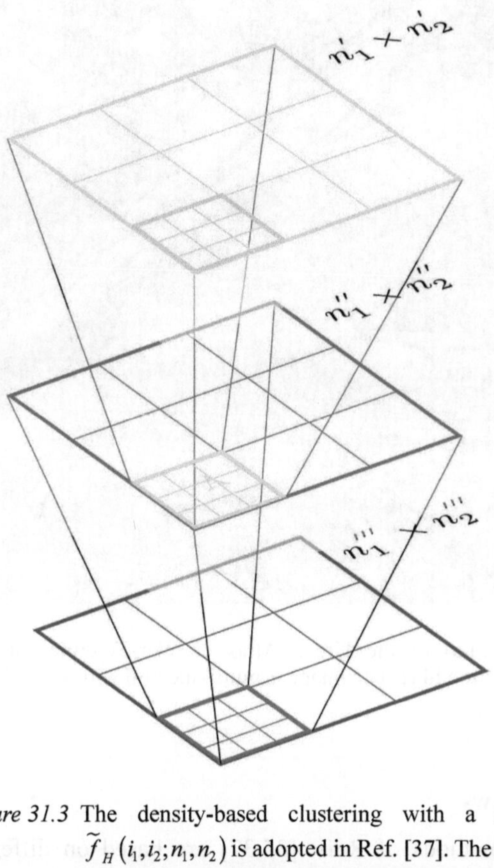

Figure 31.3 The density-based clustering with a non-constant threshold function $\widetilde{f}_H(i_1,i_2;n_1,n_2)$ is adopted in Ref. [37]. The threshold function $\widetilde{f}_H(i_1,i_2;n_1,n_2)$ is defined as a local average and is estimated over a rectangular subset of area $n_1 \times n_2$. The threshold function yields smoother replicas of the original density function as shown in Figure 31.2 where the procedure is implemented on a fractional Brownian motion random field with $H = 0.5$.

Figure 31.4 Image N48-181 (Vienna) of the Urban Atlas of WorldView-2 satellite European Cities collection [44]. The image is multi-spectral with size 1080 × 1080.

31.3 Clustering and scaling laws

The density-based clustering methods of Refs. [35,37] are based on different models: the former adopts percolation, while the latter has a fractional Brownian motion description. Despite this difference, they share the common statistical feature of introducing a two-point long-range correlation among urban cells. The outcome of the two approaches provides the correlation exponent that has been used to estimate the exponent β of the scaling laws. In particular, the correlation exponent is related to exponent of the Gibrat law in Ref. [35], while in Ref. [37] a relationship between the correlation exponent is discussed against the models [45–47]. The main features of the two approaches will be discussed and compared in this section. The cluster construction starts with the identification of a relevant feature corresponding to a discrete function $f(x_1, x_2)$ at each cell (x_1, x_2) of the urban grid. Next a suitable threshold $\bar{f}(x_1, x_2)$ is defined at each cell. A constant threshold $\bar{f}(x_1, x_2) = 0$ is used in Ref. [35], while the procedure Ref. [37] adopts is a locally dependent threshold $\bar{f}(x_1, x_2) = \tilde{f}(x_1, x_2; n_1, n_2)$ defined in Eq. (31.2). The difference between the data and the threshold quantifies the fluctuations of the relevant urban feature as, for example, the pointwise population density. The fluctuations are found to be scale-invariant, obeying a scaling law with a given correlation exponent.

The common assumption is that the clusters are long-range correlated, hence the two-point correlation is expressed by:

$$\left(f\left(x_i,x_j\right)-\bar{f}\left(x_i,x_j\right)\right)\left(f\left(x_{i'},x_{j'}\right)-\bar{f}\left(x_{i'},x_{j'}\right)\right)\sim\frac{\Delta^2}{\left|\left(x_i,x_j\right)-\left(x_{i'},x_{j'}\right)\right|^{\alpha}} \quad (31.5)$$

where $\left(x_i,x_j\right)$ and $\left(x_{i'},x_{j'}\right)$ denote a pair of cell coordinates of the urban grid and α is the correlation exponent ($0 < \alpha < 2$). For fluctuations modelled as fractional Gaussian noise, as in Ref. [37] the correlation exponent is related to the Hurst exponent H (see Eq. 31.1). The correlation of the relevant urban feature (e.g., the population density) decays as a power-law of the distance between cells, implying long-range scale-free correlations in the clustering process.

According to Ref. [35], a cluster is defined through the following main steps. A populated cell is selected. The cluster is built by adding all nearest-neighbour cells with a population density larger than a constant threshold. The cluster stops growing when there is no neighbouring cell outside the cluster with population density larger than the threshold which is usually set to zero. The population in a cluster N_i is defined as the sum of the population of all the cells within the cluster.

The *continuum* CCA [36] proceeds as in the above case but the cluster stops growing when no cell with population density larger than the threshold is found at a distance smaller than the coarse graining level. For a population growth rate lower than 1, the mean μ and the standard deviation of the populations $\sigma_1(N_i)$ vary according to a scaling law. For large clusters, one has:

$$\sigma_1^2=\sum_{j,k}^{N_i}\frac{\Delta^2}{\left|\left(x_i,x_j\right)-\left(x_{i'},x_{j'}\right)\right|^{\alpha}}\rightarrow\Delta^2\frac{N_i}{a^2}\int\frac{rdr\,d\theta}{r^{\alpha}}\approx\Delta^2\frac{N_i}{a^2}\frac{r^{-\alpha+2}}{(2-\alpha)} \quad (31.6)$$

where a^2 is the area of each cell and r_c the radius of the cluster. Since $r_c \sim N_i a^2$, one can write:

$$\sigma_1^2 \sim N_i^{2-\alpha/2} \tag{31.7}$$

with the exponent $2-\alpha/2$ larger than 1 and smaller than 2 being $0<\alpha<2$.

The standard deviation of the population density σ_1^2 can be related to the standard deviation of the growth rate $\sigma_0^2 \sim S_0^{-\beta}$. By using $S_0 = N_i n$, it results in $\beta = \alpha/4$, with $0 < \beta < 1/2$ as $0 < \alpha < 2$. If $\alpha = 0$, the standard deviation of the populations growth rates has no dependence on the population size ($\beta = 0$), as expected by Gibrat's law.

The long-range correlation exponents yield in Ref. [37] have been used to estimate the scaling exponents β of the scaling law $Y \sim N^\beta$ proposed in Refs. [45–47]. This comparison is made by expressing the exponent β of the scaling law in terms of the fractal dimension D_f of the urban landscape. The infrastructural and socio-economic features are written as power laws of the population size $Y \sim N^\beta$ respectively with exponents $\beta_i < 1$ and $\beta_s > 1$. According to Ref. [45], the scaling law exponents are defined as:

$$\beta_i = 1 - \frac{D_f}{d(d+D_f)} \quad \text{and} \quad \beta_s = 1 + \frac{D_f}{d(d+D_f)} \tag{31.8}$$

that can be rewritten in terms of the long-range correlation exponent by using the relationship $D_f = d - H$. According to Eq. (31.3), the clustering is obtained by the intersection of the density function mapped from the satellite image with the locally dependent threshold estimated recursively over sub-regions of the grid (pixel by pixel) by varying the values of $n_1 \times n_2$. The log–log plot of σ_{DMA}^2 as a function of the scale $s = n_1^2 + n_2^2$ provides the H value.

Acknowledgments

This work received financial support from the TED4LAT project (a WIDERA initiative within the Horizon Europe Programme, Grant Agreement: 101079206).

Note

1 https://iopscience.iop.org/article/10.1088/2632-072X/ac718e

References

[1] Newling, B. E. (1969). The spatial variation of urban population densities. *Geographical Review*, 59(2), 242–252.

[2] Nordbeck, S. (1971). Urban allometric growth. *Geografiska Annaler. Series B, Human Geography*, 53(1), 54–67.

[3] Bettencourt, L. M. A., Lobo, J., Helbing, D., Kühnert, C., & West, G. B. (2007). Growth, innovation, scaling, and the pace of life in cities. *Proceedings of the National Academy of Sciences*, 104(17), 7301–7306.

[4] Rybski, D., Arcaute, E., & Batty, M. (2019). Urban scaling laws. *Environment and Planning B: Urban Analytics and City Science*, 46(9), 1605–1610.

[5] Zipf, G. K. (1949). *Human behavior and the principle of least effort*. Cambridge, MA (USA): Addison Wesley Press.

[6] Gabaix, X. (1999). Zipf's law for cities: An explanation. *Quarterly Journal of Economics*, 114(3), 739–767.

[7] Alonso, W. (1964). *Location and Land Use. Toward a General Theory of Land Rent*. Cambridge (USA): Harward University Press.

[8] Mills, E. S. (1972). *Urban Economics*. Glenview. Scott: Foreman, & Company.

[9] Muth, R. F. (1969). *Cities and Housing: The Spatial Pattern of Urban Residential Land Use*. Chicago and London: The University of Chicago Press.

[10] Brueckner, J. K. (1987). The structure of urban equilibria: a unified treatment of the muth-mills model. *Handbook of Regional and Urban Economics*, 2, 821–845.

[11] Dubin, R. (1991). Commuting patterns and firm decentralization. *Land Economics*, 67(1), 15–29.

[12] Louf, R., & Barthelemy, M. (2013). Modeling the polycentric transition of cities. *Physical Review Letters*, 111(19), 198702.

[13] Louf, R., & Barthelemy, M. (2014). How congestion shapes cities: From mobility patterns to scaling. *Scientific Reports*, 4, 5561.

[14] Cumbers, A., & MacKinnon, D. (2004). Introduction: Clusters in Urban and Regional Development. *Urban Studies*, 41(5–6), 959–969.

[15] Phelps, N. A. (2021). Which city? Grounding contemporary urban theory. *Journal of Planning Literature*, 36(3), 345–357.

[16] Wu, H., Levinson, D., & Sarkar, S. (2019). How transit scaling shapes cities. *Nature Sustainability, Nature*, 2(12), 1142–1148.

[17] Keuschnigg, M., Mutgan, S., & Hedström, P. (2019). Urban scaling and the regional divide. *Science Advances*, 5(1), eaav0042.

[18] Barthelemy, M. (2019). The statistical physics of cities. *Nature Reviews Physics*, 1(6), 406–415.

[19] Reia, S. M., Rao, P. S. C., Barthelemy, M., & Ukkusuri, S. V. (2022). Spatial structure of city population growth. *Nature Communications*, 13(1), 5931.

[20] Lengyel, J., Roux, S. G., Abry, P., Sémécurbe, F., & Jaffard, S. (2022). Local multifractality in urban systems-the case study of housing prices in the greater Paris region. *Journal of Physics: Complexity*, 3(4), 045005.

[21] Portugali, J. (1997). *Self-Organization, Cities, Cognitive Maps and Information Systems*. In: Hirtle, S.C., Frank, A.U. (eds), Spatial Information Theory A Theoretical Basis for GIS. COSIT 1997. Lecture Notes in Computer Science, vol 1329. Berlin, Heidelberg: Springer. https://doi.org/10.1007/3-540-63623-4_59

[22] Rauws, W., Cozzolino, S., & Moroni, S. (2020). Framework rules for self-organizing cities: Introduction. *Environment and Planning B: Urban Analytics and City Science*, 47(2), 195–202.

[23] Delloye, J., Lemoy, R., & Caruso, G. (2020). Alonso and the scaling of urban profiles. *Geographical Analysis*, 52(2), 127–154.

[24] Portugali, J. (2012). *Self-organization and the city*. Berlin, Heidelberg: Springer Science & Business Media. https://doi.org/10.1007/978-3-662-04099-7

[25] Haken, H., & Portugali, J. (2021). Urban Scaling, Urban Regulatory Focus and Their Interrelations. In: Hermann H., Portugali J. (eds), *Synergetic Cities: Information, Steady State and Phase Transition*. Cham: Springer Series in Synergetics. Springer, 199–215. https://doi.org/10.1007/978-3-030-63457-5

[26] Batty, M., & Longley, P. A. (1987). Fractal-based description of urban form. *Environment and Planning B: Planning and Design*, 14(2), 123–134.

[27] Frankhauser, P. (1998). The fractal approach. A new tool for the spatial analysis of urban agglomerations. *Population: An English Selection*, 10(1), 205–240.

[28] Shen, G. (2002). Fractal dimension and fractal growth of urbanized areas. *International Journal of Geographical Information Science*, 16(5), 419–437.

[29] Tannier, C., & Thomas, I. (2013). Defining and characterizing urban boundaries: A fractal analysis of theoretical cities and Belgian cities. *Computers, Environment and Urban Systems*, 41, 234–248.

[30] Lemoy, R., & Caruso, G. (2021). Radial analysis and scaling of urban land use. *Scientific Reports*, 11, 22044.

[31] Liang, B., & Weng, Q. (2018). Characterizing urban landscape by using fractal-based texture information. *Photogrammetric Engineering & Remote Sensing*, 84(11), 695–710.

[32] Yakubo, K., Saijo, Y., & Korošak, D. (2014). Superlinear and sublinear urban scaling in geographical networks modeling cities. *Physical Review E*, 90(2), 022803.

[33] Dong, L., Huang, Z., Zhang, J., & Liu, Y. (2020). Understanding the mesoscopic scaling patterns within cities. *Scientific Reports*, 10, 21201.

[34] Altmann, E. G. (2020). Spatial interactions in urban scaling laws. *PLoS One*, 15(12), e0243390.

[35] Rozenfeld, H. D., Rybski, D., Andrade, J. S., Jr, Batty, M., Stanley, H. E., & Makse, H. A. (2008). Laws of population growth. *Proceedings of the National Academy of Sciences of the United States of America*, 105(48), 18702–18707.

[36] Rozenfeld, H. D., Rybski, D., Gabaix, X., & Makse, H. A. (2011). The area and population of cities: New insights from a different perspective on cities. *American Economic Review*, 101(5), 2205–25.

[37] Carbone, A., Murialdo, P., Pieroni, A., & Toxqui-Quitl, C. (2022). Atlas of urban scaling laws. *Journal of Physics: Complexity*, 3(2), 025007.

[38] Valdiviezo-Navarro, J. C., Castro, R., Cristóbal, G., & Carbone, A. (2014). Hurst exponent for fractal characterization of LANDSAT images. In Remote Sensing and Modeling of Ecosystems for Sustainability XI. *International Society for Optics and Photonics*, 9221, 922103.

[39] Carbone, A., Castelli, G., & Stanley, H. E. (2004). Analysis of clusters formed by the moving average of a long-range correlated time series. *Physical Review E*, 69(2), 026105.

[40] Carbone, A. (2007). Algorithm to estimate the Hurst exponent of high-dimensional fractals. *Physical Review E*, 76(5), 056703.

[41] Isichenko, M. B. (1992). Percolation, statistical topography, and transport in random media. *Reviews of Modern Physics*, 64(4), 961.

[42] Hristopulos, D. T. (2020). *Random Fields for Spatial Data Modeling: A Primer for Scientists and Engineers*. Netherlands: Springer.

[43] Carbone, A., & Ponta, L. (2022). Relative cluster entropy for power-law correlated sequences. *SciPost Physics*, 13(3), 076.

[44] Urban Atlas, last visit on 07/2021. The ESA third party mission collection of the largest European urban areas recorded by the WorldView-2 satellite https://tpm-ds.eo.esa.int/ oads/access/collection/WorldView-2.

[45] Bettencourt, L. M. A. (2013). The origins of scaling in cities. *Science*, 340(6139), 1438–1441.

[46] Ribeiro, F. L., Meirelles, J., Ferreira, F. F., & Neto, C. R. (2017). A model of urban scaling laws based on distance dependent interactions. *Royal Society Open Science*, 4(3), 160926.

[47] Molinero, C., & Thurner, S. (2021). How the geometry of cities determines urban scaling laws. *Journal of the Royal Society Interface*, 18(176), 20200705.

Part V

Conclusion

Regional economics, science and policy

32 Bridging scaling with agglomeration economies

Frank G. van Oort

32.1 Identifying agglomeration economies

Despite covering half a percent of the Earth's total terrestrial surface, cities are home to approximately 58% of the global population and generate nearly 80% of the world's gross domestic product (GDP). This concentration of people and economic activities in cities cannot be solely explained by variations in physical geography or the distribution of natural resources, or by the reduction in transportation costs resulting from proximity alone [1,2]. Complementary explanations point at the presence of increasing returns to scale within cities, which benefit individuals and firms by enhancing their wages, productivity, and overall economic performance. These returns are known as agglomeration economies [3,4]. They are external to the firms and individuals located within the urban space and contribute to a cumulative process that drives the gradual concentration of economic activities, accompanied by a pronounced clustering of the population, resulting in significant spatial disparities [5]. One of the main theoretical justifications for implementing place-based policies alongside or instead of people-based policies is the recognition of market failures or spatially driven market processes. In microeconomic terms, these failures or processes entail costs and benefits that arise from various activities conducted by individuals or institutions, which impact the welfare of third parties who are not directly involved [6].

A substantial body of literature provides evidence regarding the positive impact of agglomeration on economic growth, productivity, wages, and other socioeconomic dimensions. These benefits encompass a wide range of factors, including a higher propensity for innovation, a reduction in per capita pollution emissions, improved accessibility to amenities, and enhanced energy efficiency [7]. However, once cities surpass certain thresholds in terms of size and population density, the incremental gains from agglomeration benefits become marginal, while the associated costs, both monetary (such as land and housing prices) and non-monetary (such as crime, traffic congestion, or pollution), increase [8]. These costs, known as agglomeration diseconomies, counterbalance the advantages of size and density. In addition to addressing the question of defining the optimal size of cities where the economies and diseconomies of agglomeration are balanced [9], research in the field of urban economics has focused on explaining the impact of agglomeration on

DOI: 10.4324/9781003288312-37

economic performance, with particular attention to the observed increase in productivity. This emphasis is partly driven by the interconnected relationship between urban agglomeration and theories of regional economic growth [10].

The available empirical evidence generally supports the notion that agglomeration has a positive impact on productivity. However, it is important to consider that the magnitude of agglomeration size elasticities is influenced by various contextual factors. Scholars such as Melo et al. [11] emphasize the significance of country-specific effects, the specific industry being analysed, and the choice of model when determining these elasticities. As a result, it is not realistic to expect similar magnitudes across different sectors, cities, or countries. In the United States, productivity gains can be as high as 10% [12], with an average range typically falling between 3–8% [13]. In Europe, agglomeration elasticities usually range between 4–6% on average [14], with larger urban agglomeration dominating (overshadowing) scale-economies of interconnected polycentric settings [15]. A meta-analysis conducted by Donovan et al. [16], which examined the productivity advantages of cities across 54 countries, suggests that while there are variations in productivity due to methodological differences and country-specific effects, it is likely that agglomeration elasticities fall within the range of 3–6%. These findings align with other studies estimating productivity gains of approximately 4–6%, depending on whether labour productivity or total factor productivity is being measured [7,17,18]. It should be noted that the effects of agglomeration on productivity exhibit significant variations in developing or low-income countries. For instance, doubling the size of a city is estimated to lead to productivity improvements of between 6–16% in Latin American nations. In China, the increase can reach up to 19%, while in India it stands at 12%, and in African countries it amounts to 17%. These estimates indicate that the productivity gains in these regions are two to four times higher compared to those observed in developed countries [2]. These findings are not inconsistent with the existing body of literature on urban scaling.

32.2 Matching, sharing, and learning as externalities mechanisms

Agglomeration economies literature has tried to deepen our understanding of these elasticities. In the field of urban economics, three main sources of agglomeration economies that contribute to enhanced urban productivity are recognized: sharing, matching, and learning. Sharing pertains to the indivisibility of certain goods, services, infrastructures, and amenities in cities due to high fixed production costs. It encompasses the benefits derived from shared suppliers of diverse inputs, specialization, and risk mitigation. Matching involves the advantages gained by employers and job seekers, buyers and sellers, and business partners as the size of markets expands, increasing the likelihood of finding suitable matches that meet their needs and quality expectations. Lastly, the learning process refers to the generation, dissemination, and accumulation of knowledge in cities, driven by the development and widespread adoption of new technologies, practices, and processes [19]. Transitioning from the theoretical definition of these three sources of agglomeration to their empirical estimation poses a challenge due to the intertwined nature of their effects on productivity [4].

McCann and Van Oort [10] and Steijn et al. [20] differentiate various agglomeration scenarios that provide a deeper understanding of the processes involved in transferring knowledge, input–output relationships, and labour skills. These concepts partly overlap with the matching, sharing, and learning distinction. Whether attributable to a company's size or a considerable initial number of local enterprises, a notable level of local factor employment can nurture the emergence of external economies within the cluster of local firms within a specific sector. These phenomena are commonly known as localization economies. The strength of these local externalities is presumed to vary, with some sectors experiencing stronger effects while others exhibit weaker ones [21]. The associated economies of scale encompass elements that decrease the average production cost within the particular region. To enhance the understanding of localization economies, it is beneficial to explicitly consider the market structure [22]. Furthermore, externalities characterized by knowledge spillovers among firms in a geographically concentrated industry are commonly referred to as Marshall–Arrow–Romer (MAR) externalities. In a dynamic context, the MAR theory predicts that local monopoly fosters growth more effectively than local competition by constraining the dissemination of ideas to external entities, enabling innovators to internalize them. Porter [23] supports the importance of localization economies and argues that knowledge spillovers in specialized, geographically concentrated industries stimulate growth. Conversely, urbanization economies materialize as external economies experienced by enterprises, resulting from cost savings derived from the large-scale operation of the agglomeration or the city as a whole, irrespective of the industry structure. The density of institutions, encompassing not only economic aspects but also social, political, and cultural dimensions, facilitates the generation and assimilation of know-how, stimulating innovative behaviour and influencing varying rates of interregional growth. The diverse blend of industries within an urbanized area enhances opportunities for interaction, the adoption and adaptation of practices, and innovative behaviour within the same or related sectors. In her theory of urban growth, Jane Jacobs [24] identifies diversity as a fundamental source of agglomeration economies and, in contrast to the MAR theory, suggests that the most substantial knowledge transfers originate from outside one's own industry. The interplay of specialization, diversity, and competition represents one of the extensively researched themes in the field of agglomeration economies, given its significant implications for economic policies and urban planning [25].

Each of these elements pertaining to agglomeration economies also presents a potential explanation for why regions characterized by agglomeration generally experience higher levels of growth compared to regions lacking such characteristics. Moreover, cities possess additional attributes that contribute to the growth potential of a city-region [10]. One way to perceive the structure of a regional or urban economy is through an analogy to corporate diversification in product portfolios. Regional diversity can be viewed as a portfolio strategy aimed at safeguarding regional income against sudden asymmetric shocks specific to specific sectors.

This strategy is particularly effective in protecting labour markets and preventing persistent unemployment. Consequently, an increase in regional industrial diversity would reduce regional unemployment rates and foster regional economic growth, while specialization would elevate the risk of unemployment and lead to a slow-down in growth. Similarly, for firms, a fundamental question arises regarding the most rewarding approach to diversification – whether it should be related or unrelated. Scholars such as Baldwin and Brown [26] explore whether related industries, more frequently than not (although not as an absolute rule), experience correlated demand shocks. Therefore, from a portfolio strategy perspective, diversifying risk across unrelated sectors is generally preferable. However, it is crucial to consider the potential benefits derived from related diversification as well. Comparable to economies of scope at the firm level, one can anticipate that knowledge spillovers within a region primarily occur among sectors that are related, and to a limited extent among unrelated sectors. In the realm of agglomeration theory, it is expected that Jacobs' externalities would be more pronounced in regions characterized by a related variety or cognitive relatedness of sectors compared to regions with an unrelated assortment of sectors [27,28]. Additionally, technological development and the diffusion of knowledge and innovation are regarded as central to the modern concept of regional growth. A large literature argues that there is an urban product cycle notion in that new products are more easily developed in large diverse metro areas with a diversified industrial structure and skill base, whereas mature products eventually are decentralized to hinterland or peripheral areas [29,20].

32.3 Beyond scaling: bridging disciplines

The scaling literature and the economic agglomeration literature share many common features: both observe a 5–10% premium in economic outcomes for larger cities (when doubling in size or moving along a logarithmic scale). These economic outcomes include productivity, employment, and other positive factors, as well as related problematic issues like crime, congestion, and segregation (for recent urban economic applications, see Refs. [30,31]). However, despite these similarities, these two literatures do not integrate much as to date, although an interdisciplinary approach offers clear learning advantages. The agglomeration literature suggests that scaling outcomes depend on a delicate balance between agglomeration advantages and disadvantages. The advantages can be divided into two types: first-nature (natural) and second-nature (man-made) advantages. The latter are influenced by micro-based sorting of talented people and entrepreneurs, accompanied by meso-based local matching, sharing, and learning externalities related to specialization, diversity, and competition. Understanding the complexity of this build-up forms a starting point for a common research agenda. To gain a deeper understanding of the building blocks of scaling premiums, it is crucial to advance the joint discussion on urban (dis)advantages. This also has implications for policymaking. People-based policies might focus on attracting talent and entrepreneurs. However, these individuals are mobile and may move away from areas once they have improved their personal abilities and skills, which are often fuelled by policies. Therefore, it is equally important to introduce place-based policies that support the development of cities and regions that are not targeted by the most talented workforce [32,33]. Ultimately, people and entrepreneurs in cities and regions are those who drive, benefit from, and bear the consequences of scaling effects. Thus, local policies and governance structures play a critical role in shaping significant economic and social developments, as well as addressing societal challenges, as both literatures suggest [34,35]. More research is needed from both disciplines to identify the impacts of policies and guide effective governance. Understanding the mechanisms and determinants of agglomeration and sorting effects is crucial. This includes gaining insights into labour mobility as carriers of knowledge, dependencies on trade networks, and the factors that attract people to local qualities of life, sustainability, and inclusive prosperity. Finally, the concept of polycentricity, as an alternative to urban concentration, has been a subject of fierce debate. For effective planning purposes, it is also essential to pay more attention to polycentricity, especially ensuring that medium-sized and smaller urban nodes are well-connected through infrastructure and functional (complementary) relations [15].

References

[1] Henderson, J.V., Squires, T., Storeygard, A., Weil, D. (2017). The global distribution of economic activity: nature, history, and the role of trade. *Quarterly Journal of Economics*, 133(1), 357–406.

[2] Grover, A., Lall, S.V., Maloney, W.F. (2022). *Place, productivity, and prosperity: Revisiting spatially targeted policies for regional development.* Washington, D.C., World Bank.

[3] Fujita, M., Thisse, J. (2013). *Economics of agglomeration: cities, industrial location, and globalization.* Cambridge, University Press.

[4] Puga, D. (2010). The magnitude and causes of agglomeration economies. *Journal of Regional Science*, 50, 203–219.

[5] Duranton, G., Puga, D. (2020). The economics of urban density. *Journal of Economic Perspectives*, 34(3), 3–26.

[6] Goolsbee, A., Levitt, S., Syverson, C. (2015). *Microeconomics*. New York, Worth Publishers.

[7] Ahlfeldt, G.M., Pietrostefani, E. (2019). The economic effects of density: a synthesis. *Journal of Urban Economics*, 111, 93–107.

[8] Frick, S.A., Rodríguez-Pose, A. (2018). Big or small cities? on city size and economic growth. *Growth and Change*, 49(1), 4–32.

[9] Batty, M. (2008). The size, scale, and shape of cities. *Science*, 319(5864), 769–771.

[10] McCann, P., Van Oort, F.G. (2019). Theories of agglomeration and regional economic growth: a historical review. In: Capello, R., Nijkamp, P. (eds.). *Handbook of Regional Growth and Development Theories.* Revised and extended second edition. Cheltenham, Edward Elgar, pp. 6–23.

[11] Melo, P.C., Graham, D.J., Noland, R.B. (2009). A meta-analysis of estimates of urban agglomeration economies. *Regional Science and Urban Economics*, 39(3), 332–342.

[12] Meijers, E., Burger, M. (2010). Spatial structure and productivity in US metropolitan areas. *Environment and Planning A*, 42(6), 1383–1402.

[13] Rosenthal, S., Strange, W.C. (2004). Evidence on the nature and sources of agglomeration economies. In: Henderson, J.V., Thisse, J.F. (eds.). *Handbook of Regional and Urban Economics*, Amsterdam, Elsevier, pp. 2119–2171.

[14] Artis, M., Curran, D., Sensier, M. (2011). Investigating agglomeration economies in a panel of European cities and regions. SERC Discussion Papers 0078, Centre for Economic Performance, LSE.

[15] Ouwehand, W., Van Oort, F.G., Cortinovis, N. (2022). Spatial structure and productivity in European regions. *Regional Studies*, 56(1), 48–62.

[16] Donovan, S., De Graaff, T., De Groot, H., Koopmans, C. (2022). Unravelling urban advantages—A meta-analysis of agglomeration economies. *Journal of Economic Surveys*, 38(1), 12543.

[17] Ciccone, A. (2002). Agglomeration effects in Europe'. *European Economic Review*, 46(2), 213–227.

[18] Wheeler, C. (2001). Search, sorting, and urban agglomeration. *Journal of Labor Economics*, 19(4), 879–899.

[19] Duranton, G., Puga, D. (2004). Micro-foundations of urban agglomeration economies. In: Duranton, G., Henderson, J.V., Strange, W.C. (eds.). *Handbook of Regional and Urban Economics*. Amsterdam, Elsevier, pp. 2063–2117.

[20] Steijn, M., Koster, H., Van Oort, F.G. (2022). The dynamics of industry agglomeration: evidence from 44 years of co-agglomeration patterns. *Journal of Urban Economics*, 130, 103456.

[21] Combes, P.P., Gobillon, L. (2015). The empirics of agglomeration economies. In: Duranton, G., Henderson, J.V., Strange, W.C. (eds.). *Handbook of Regional and Urban Economics*. Amsterdam, Elsevier, pp. 247–348.

[22] Gordon, I.R., McCann, P. (2000). 'Industrial clusters: complexes, agglomeration and/or social networks? *Urban Studies*, 37, 513–32.

[23] Porter, M. (1990). *The competitive advantage of nations*. New York, Free Press.

[24] Jacobs, J. (1969). *The economy of cities*. New York, Vintage.

[25] Van Oort, F.G. (2004). *Urban growth and innovation. Spatially bounded externalities in the Netherlands.* London, Ashgate.

[26] Baldwin, J.T., Brown, W.M. (2004). Regional manufacturing employment volatility in Canada: the effects of specialisation and trade. *Papers in Regional Science*, 83, 519–541.

[27] Frenken, K., Van Oort, F.G., Verburg, T. (2007). Related variety, unrelated variety and regional economic growth. *Regional Studies*, 41, 685–697.

[28] Boschma, R.A. (2005). Proximity and innovation: a critical assessment. *Regional Studies*, 39, 61–74.

[29] Duranton, G., Puga, D. (2001). Nursery cities: urban diversity, process innovation, and the life cycle of products. *American Economic Review*, 91(5), 1454–1477.

[30] Kuiper, N. (2023). *Externalities, place-based policies and urban regeneration*. PhD-Thesis, University of Groningen.

[31] Donovan, S. (2023). *Ties that bind and fray: agglomeration economies and location choice*. PhD-thesis, Vrije Universiteit Amsterdam.

[32] Neumark, D., Simpson, H. (2015). Place-based policies. In: Duranton, G., Henderson, J.V., Strange, W.C. (eds.). *Handbook of Regional and Urban Economics*. Amsterdam, Elsevier, pp. 1197–1287.

[33] McCann, P. (2023). *How have place-based policies evolved to date and what are they for now*?. Paris, OECD Working Group.

[34] Van Raan, A.F.J. (2020). Urban scaling, geography, centrality: relation with local government structures. *Plos One*, 1–23.

[35] Rodriguez-Pose, A. (2018). The revenge of the places that don't matter (and what to do about it). *Cambridge Journal of Regions, Economy, and Society*, 11(1), 189–209.

Index

Note: Page numbers in **bold** refer to tables and those in *italic* refer to figures.

COMMISSIONS OF INQUIRY

This timely and pertinent collection looks at the variety of questions involved in the operation of Commissions of Inquiry (CoIs). Traditionally existing as pure fact-finding bodies, in recent times the function of CoIs has arguably shifted and broadened so as to provide a form of legal adjudication. This shift in their application merits scrutiny and this edited collection of essays addresses institutional and procedural aspects of CoIs, as well as issues in regards to the application and interpretation of the substantative law applied to them. Essay topics include the relationship of CoIs with, and impact upon, traditional forms of adjudication, the influences of international law upon the work of CoIs, through to issues of procedural fairness. Drawing upon the expertise of scholars working within in the field, it offers an insightful and critical analysis of CoIs.

Commissions of Inquiry

Problems and Prospects

Edited by
Christian Henderson

• HART •
OXFORD • LONDON • NEW YORK • NEW DELHI • SYDNEY

HART PUBLISHING
Bloomsbury Publishing Plc
Kemp House, Chawley Park, Cumnor Hill, Oxford, OX2 9PH, UK

HART PUBLISHING, the Hart/Stag logo, BLOOMSBURY and the Diana logo are trademarks of Bloomsbury Publishing Plc
First published in Great Britain 2017

First published in hardback, 2017
Paperback edition, 2019

A catalogue record for this book is available from the British Library.

ISBN: HB: 978-1-78225-876-6
PB: 978-1-50993-220-7
ePDF: 978-1-78225-879-7
ePub: 978-1-78225-877-3

Typeset by Compuscript Ltd, Shannon

Foreword

THE HON. MICHAEL KIRBY AC CMG*

In October 1904 naval ships of the Imperial Russian Fleet in the Baltic Sea left their home ports on their way to the Far East to participate in a war with the Empire of Japan. Approaching the Dogger Bank area of the North Sea, and allegedly basing their action on 'intelligence' reports, the ships opened fire on a harmless collection of British fishing vessels, causing death and destruction.[1]

When the news broke in England, the Russian excuse that they had mistaken the fishing boats for torpedo-carrying Japanese warships was dismissed contemptuously. Few believed that anyone claiming to be a mariner could make such a mistake, especially thousands of miles from the warzone and given the huge disparities between the sizes of the ships concerned. In consequence, there was a real risk of war. As a result of French intervention, the parties concerned agreed to convene a commission of inquiry under the *Hague Convention* of 1899. The commission met in Paris. Its investigations unveiled the nervousness of the Russian sailors and the rumours that unleashed the attack (which was soon followed by other disasters enroute to the warzone, when real vessels of Japan's navy trounced the Russians in combat.

The commission of inquiry met and reported promptly. Its findings were prudently written in an understated style. They even included face-saving remarks about the Russian admiral. Russia paid compensation, substantial for the times, to the families of the dead fishermen. A memorial, of which there were shortly to be many more, was erected in Kingston upon Hull. War was avoided. Honour was saved. The *Entente* between France, Russia and Britain was preserved to await the Great War which lay just around history's corner.

Ironically, the Great War itself also involved a proposed commission of inquiry. Everyone knows that the war arose following the murder of Grand Duke Franz Ferdinand and his Duchess, following shots fired

* Chair of the UN Commission of Inquiry on Human Rights in the Democratic People's Republic of Korea (2013–14).

[1] RN Lebow, 'Accidents and Crises: The Dogger Bank Affair' (1978) 31 *Naval War College Review*, 66. The incident is referred to by Frederick Pollock Sir, *The League of Nations* (Stevens, London, 1920), 51.

in Sarajevo in June 1914. The immediate *casus belli*, however, was the refusal of Serbia (that agreed to many other terms) to bow to Austrian demands about the constitution of a commission of inquiry to investigate the Sarajevo incident.[2] One commission of inquiry worked perfectly. The other never got off the ground. Unimaginable suffering, reaching right up to the current age, might have been avoided if only time had allowed wiser counsel to prevail in 1914. The mechanism was promising, given the successful recent demonstration. However, the execution was imperfect, overtaken by events and squabbling over the details.

The idea of creating commissions of inquiry to investigate dangerous incidents of international circumstances was in the air much earlier, indeed at the Congress of Vienna (1814–1815). After the prolonged and costly Napoleonic wars, the European powers, 'tired out with war',[3] sought to establish effective institutional means to resolve dangerous conflicts and to restrain wars and the causes of war. The central idea was that the law of nations would provide an effective alternative to unbridled power. In the century of substantial peace that followed Vienna, many international arbitration treaties emerged. Eventually, the *Hague Convention* of 1899 was adopted, designed to promote peaceful solutions to conflicts. The success of the Dogger Bank Inquiry was in the minds of President Woodrow Wilson and other leaders when they gathered at Versailles and Paris following the Armistice of 1918, to create the League of Nations. The *Covenant of the League of Nations* was agreed to. Yet Wilson predicted in 1918 that peace would only be assured if it was built on foundations of law and justice:[4]

> It must be a justice that plays no favourites and knows no standard but the equal rights of the several peoples concerned.

The League Council used good offices, mediation, conciliation and commissions of inquiry in various combinations. Occasionally, these mechanisms produced useful results.[5] And yet the League failed and war returned to Europe. When the *Charter* of the United Nations was agreed in 1945, it expressly envisaged the utilisation by the Security Council, in any dispute the continuance of which was likely to endanger the maintenance of international peace and security, of a search for a solution by nominated means. The second of these stated means was 'inquiry'.[6] Moreover, the Security Council was expressly authorised to 'investigate

2 C Clark, *The Sleepwalkers: How Europe Went to War in 1914* (Harper, London, 2013).

3 Pollack, above n 1.

4 President Wilson quoted by Pollock, above n 1 at 241.

5 JG Starke, *An Introduction to International Law* (Butterworths, London, 5th Edition, 1963), 384. JG Starke QC, an Australian, was reputed to be the last surviving officer of the Secretariat of the League of Nations at the time of his death in 2006.

6 United Nations *Charter*, art 33.1.

any dispute or any situation which might lead to international friction or give rise to a dispute, in order to determine whether the continuation of the dispute or situation is likely to endanger the maintenance of international peace and security'.[7] The Council was empowered to decide what measures should be taken, as deemed necessary for the performance of its functions.[8] Clearly these provisions envisaged the establishment and use by the Security Council of commissions of inquiry. So it was no surprise that they were created.

The broad powers of the Secretary-General[9] also envisaged such a facility. Whilst there is no express grant of the power of inquiry to the General Assembly, the ambit of that body's functions, together with the necessarily implied powers to discharge its responsibilities, extended to the conduct of inquiries. These included by the initiation of studies and the making of recommendations (amongst other things) for 'promoting international cooperation … and assisting in the realisation of human rights and fundamental freedoms for all'.[10]

The creation by the General Assembly of the Human Rights Commission, and later the Human Rights Council, also envisaged the establishment of commissions of inquiry when deemed necessary to discharge their respective functions. Given the preceding history in the 19th Century, in the League of Nations and in the necessities presented on the creation of the United Nations in 1945, it would have been astonishing if the new organisation had not moved quickly to create commissions of inquiry where that mechanism was deemed appropriate and necessary.

However, to the preceding history and the express and implied powers granted by the *Charter*, was added an additional dimension. This was the significant relationship envisaged by the *Charter* between the several 'common ends' recognised in the 'Purposes of the United Nations' stated in Article 1. These were, relevantly, to maintain international peace and security; to develop friendly relations among nations based on respect for the principle of equal rights and self-determination of peoples; and to:[11]

> … achieve international cooperation in solving international problems of an economic, social, cultural or humanitarian character, and in promoting and encouraging respect for human rights and for fundamental freedoms for all without distinction as to race, sex, language or religion.

Although human and peoples' rights preceded the adoption of the United Nations *Charter*, it was the devastating evidence of war crimes, crimes

[7] *Charter*, art 34.
[8] *Charter*, art 39.
[9] Under the *Charter*, art 97 (chief administrative officer of the Organization; 'performance of such other functions as are entrusted to him'. See also art 101.3 'highest standards of efficiency, competence and integrity'.
[10] *Charter* art 13.1(b) see also art 14.
[11] *Charter*, 1.1, 1.2, 1.3.

against humanity and genocide (together with the horrifying dangers of nuclear weapons) that made the potentially dangerous interconnections between such rights and international peace and security much clearer and more urgent. Initially, it was envisaged that the United Nations *Charter* itself would include human rights provisions.[12] When that proved impossible to achieve, work was continued separately on the *Universal Declaration of Human Rights* (UDHR), adopted in December 1948. Having adopted the UDHR, and the treaty law that was to follow, it became inevitable that institutions would be needed to refine the applicable rules, to provide for the receipt of complaints about derogations; to facilitate investigations; to reach and express findings, conclusions and recommendations; to determine and implement responses; to adjudicate at least some of the ensuing accusations; to punish and sanction a number of those responsible; to derive lessons from the entire process; and to record, publicise and educate others on the lessons learned.

Mandate holders were needed to discharge various steps on the pathways to these responses. At the more formal and serious end of the spectrum of mandate holders were those appointed to commissions of inquiry.

During my judicial service in Australia, I was appointed to United Nations mandates involving fact-finding and conciliation[13] and to a mandate under the Human Rights Commission.[14] However, after the conclusion of my judicial service I received, for the first time, a mandate to chair a UN commission of inquiry. I was surprised by the relative lack of materials available to the Commissioners (and for that matter to their independent secretariats) to provide academic and other insights and afford guidance on the discharge of their respective duties.[15] How helpful it would have been, in preparing for our work, to have had the collection of papers now published in this book. Woven throughout the chapters are questions which both scholars and mandate holders in future COIs may need to ask themselves and to debate and resolve, including:

— Are there steps that they should take to ensure greater diversity of participants and viewpoints?;
— How should they resolve disputed issues of fact when they arise and accord procedural fairness to relevant actors?;

[12] Mark Mazower, 'The Strange Triumph of Human Rights, 1933–1950' *This Historical Journal*, vol 47, no 2 (2004), 379.

[13] As member of the International Labour Organization Fact Finding and Conciliation Commission on Freedom of Association in South Africa 1991–92.

[14] As Special Representative of the UN Secretary General for Human Rights in Cambodia (1993–96).

[15] Subsequently the OHCHR issued *Commissions of Inquiry and Fact-Finding Missions*. See OHCHR, *Commissions of Inquiry and Fact-Finding Missions on International Human Rights and Humanitarian Law: Guidance and Practice*, 2015, available at www.ohchr.org/Documents/Publications/CoI_Guidance_and_Practice.pdf.

— Have they adequately explored the history, procedures and outcomes of at least those COIs most similar to their own?;
— Have they familiarised themselves with the UNHCR Code of Practice and ensured that it is observed, where relevant, by all players?;
— Is a recommendation of referral to the ICC or any other court or tribunal competent, appropriate and desirable in the case of their COI?;
— Can accountability for human rights violations be secured without destroying the chances for change in the state of human rights and in safeguarding peace and security?;
— What can/should they do to avoid the perils of geopolitics and to stick to a more useful if subsidiary, role in fulfilling their mandate?;
— How may they inform themselves of non-Western and minority viewpoints, so as to contribute to the legitimacy of their COI, and COIs generally, in the wider world?;
— How can their report reach out beyond the asymmetries and misalignments that sometimes accompany the politics of human rights?;
— Are there any steps that they can take to contribute in practical ways to the de-escalation of tensions—as for example adopting a strictly legal and confined analysis?;
— Do their terms of reference permit only backward looking issues of accountability? Or can they address future looking issues and problem solving?;
— How may one reconcile adherence to the rule of international law with practical contributions to human rights in the present and future?;
— Are COI members themselves the best people to conduct the inquiry? Or should more suitable persons be engaged to support and supplement their investigations?;
— Have the COI members retained an independent voice in the selection and supervision of their secretariat and other contributors?;
— Have they thought through and applied the applicable standard of proof for the resolution of factual conflicts and contested evidence?;
— Are the powers that they enjoy adequate to the discharge of their inquiries? Or should they propose new and different powers and if so what?;
— How do COI members control a natural sympathy for victims but also win respect by true adherence to the rule of law, including where that law is unclear or doubtful?;
— How do COI members constantly impose reality checks on evidence, witnesses and themselves in reaching factual conclusions?;
— Do COI members truly understand the differences between their role in a COI and the respective functions of prosecutors, tribunals and courts?;

— How do COI members protect themselves from stepping beyond fact-finding into an inappropriate and excessive prosecutorial or judgmental posture?;
— How do COIs make wise decisions on the potentially damaging publication of names, before appropriate prosecutorial and judicial decisions have been reached by persons with specific authority to do so?;
— What connection, if any, should COI members have with the ICC, prosecutors, or other courts and tribunals?;
— Does membership of a COI afford those members an appropriate command of the applicable rules of international human rights and humanitarian law? Or do the COI members need to look outwards and further afield?;
— How will COI members be faithful to the limitations, as well as the opportunities of the mandate they have received. How will they put a break on exceeding their jurisdiction, where that is a risk?;
— Whilst discharging their own functions, how will COI members make a beneficial contribution to the credibility and legitimacy of UN COIs generally and the global pursuit of human rights and justice?;
— Do COI members sometimes need, within their mandate, to consider balancing accountability and immunity? Can accountability ever be achieved without some selectivity and occasional provision of immunity?;
— Do COI members have authority, by their mandates or in international law, to push the envelope of expressing culpable wrongdoing? Or should they reject 'activism' of that kind as damaging to the credibility of fragile new human rights institutions?;
— What approach should be taken in fact-finding and adjudication to contribute to a coherent development of related areas of international law?;
— How do COIs fulfil the basic obligation first to do no harm? How should they act to balance a policy of transparency against full protection for victims?;
— In one sided inquiries, what can be done to maintain objectivity and to avoid capture by an understandable empathy and symbiosis?;
— How do the members of a COI ensure full integrity and independence, including in relation to each other? When is dissent in reasoning and outcomes justified or necessary? When will it simply undermine the findings and delay any practical action?;
— What formal procedures should be put in place to reinforce natural justice and high standards of procedural fairness?;

— When is it appropriate to give notice of adverse conclusions to permit those accused a right of response? And when might such procedural niceties simply delay or impede the conduct of efficient investigations?[16];
— How will COI members write a report at once accurate but also readable? How will clarity be assured whilst avoiding inappropriate emotion and prejudgment?;
— What are the appropriate delineations between the functions of COIs and the functions of other UN human rights mandate-holders (eg special rapporteurs)? Where does the balance lie between thoroughness, fairness and speedy responses to shocking revelations that call out for early responses?;

The book affords its readers a thread of Ariadne: to guide the future members of COIs and to provide those working with them a means through the maze as well as measures of protection to avoid the ever threatening minotaurs of error, prejudgment, partiality and unprofessionalism.

Several authors in their respective chapters disagree with what others have written. Of course, the starting point in each inquiry must be the precise language of the mandate. Even here those appointed to a COI may adopt different approaches because of their individual backgrounds, experience and culture. A former judge from a common law jurisdiction may place a greater store on transparency than an appointee from the civilian inquisitorial tradition. A person whose background has been diplomacy may lay emphasis on resolving underlying tensions. One whose experience has been in criminal law may emphasise accountability and the emphatic exposure of wrongdoing. Thus, many of the innovations in procedures adopted by the COI on DPRK were a reflection on my own professional experience. And yet, they were readily agreed to by the two other members of that COI, each from civilian countries and one with high experience as an advocate in that tradition. Unanimously, we considered that transparency was the antidote to our exclusion from, and non-cooperation by, the country subject to our inquiry.[17] Our mandate

[16] F Wilmot-Smith, 'Blame Robert Maxwell—On How Public Inquiries Go Wrong' *London Review of Books*, 17 March 2006, 33. The reference is to the litigations brought by publisher Robert Maxwell in the English Court of Appeal challenging inquiries for failing to give him due notice. See also *Air New Zealand Limited v Mahon* [19] AC.

[17] MD Kirby, 'United Nations Report on North Korea and the Security Council: Interface of Security and Human Rights' (2015) 89 *Australian Law Journal*, 714. See also M.D. Kirby, 'The UN Report on North Korea: How the United Nations Met the Common Law' (2015), 27 *Judicial Officers' Bulletin* (Australia—NSW), #8, 69. The United Nations report of the detailed findings of the Commission of Inquiry on Human Rights in the Democratic People's Republic of Korea (United Nations, Geneva, 7 February 2014) (A/HRC/25/CRP.1).

was express and emphatic in relation to accountability. We were not at liberty to ignore it or to turn a blind eye.

In international jurisdiction, as in municipal jurisdiction, inquiries are proliferating, and this book turns the spotlight of inquiry upon international inquiries themselves. If this results in the strengthening of the lawfulness, consistency and professionalism in the conduct of COIs, this will itself be an important contribution to the goal of universal human rights expressed in the UN *Charter*. That goal was spelt out in the eloquent language of Eleanor Roosevelt, René Cassin, John Humphrey and others in the text of the UDHR and in the law that has followed. For the contribution that this book makes to the evolution of global human rights we should be truly grateful.

Silent, voiceless, suffering victims do not need bleeding hearts and emotional demands from COIs. If the global protection of human rights, justice, peace and security are to be attained, the needs are different. They include lawfulness, integrity, experience, professionalism, calm analysis, and contextual appreciation and insight. To the extent that the writers in this book contribute to these goals they contribute to a better, safer and less violent world.

Acknowledgements

Commissions of inquiry have arguably come of age. They have evolved—and continue to evolve—and have now reached the point where they are not only consistently resorted to but also relatively regularly make the front pages of newspapers and other media, as well as often forming the focus of academic attention. Their prominence within the international community and the varied functions they now serve, including arguably through providing a form of legal adjudication, leads one to question various aspects of their establishment, composition, functioning, rules of procedure, authority, and overall impact, both actual and intended. It therefore became apparent that the concept of commissions of inquiry could form the basis of a collaborative research project within the International Law and Human Rights Unit at the University of Liverpool. This edited collection is the resulting product and aims to contribute to the emerging debates regarding commissions of inquiry within the legal realm, and thus contains various chapters on different aspects of the legal significance of their existence and functioning.

The idea of pooling our respective expertise into a project on international commissions of inquiry was taken up by members of the Unit with enthusiasm, so my thanks to them for being receptive and engaging. However, the workshop that took place in January 2015 at the Liverpool Law School was made possible through the support of the Economic and Social Research Council's Transformative Research fund. In particular, this support enabled the project to incorporate the expertise of many participants external to the Unit and who have made such a significant contribution to it, so my thanks to all the participants involved.

The organisation and coordination of the project was greatly facilitated by April Longstaffe, a former LL.M student within the Liverpool Law School. April not only single-handedly organised the workshop but also provided invaluable research assistance ahead of it to various participants engaged with the project. Chosen Onyekachi, a Ph.D student within Sussex Law School, also assisted in drawing the final manuscript together, so my thanks go to him for his work during the final stages of the project.

I would also like to thank Michael Kirby AC CMG, former Chair of the Commission of Inquiry on Human Rights in the Democratic People's Republic of North Korea, for his comments on the book and for so

graciously agreeing to write a Foreword to it. The pressures on his time are immense, which makes his contribution to this project a valuable one. Finally, I would like to thank Sinead Moloney and the team at Hart Publishing, who have been very supportive, not to mention patient, from the outset.

Christian Henderson
Sussex Law School
October 2016

Contents

List of Contributors

Alison Bisset is Associate Professor in International Human Rights Law at the University of Reading

Théo Boutruche is currently a legal adviser with the MENA Programme of the International Commission of Jurists

Russell Buchan is a Senior Lecturer in International Law at the University of Sheffield

Patrick Butchard is a doctoral candidate in law at the University of Liverpool

Shane Darcy is a Senior Lecturer at the Irish Centre for Human Rights at the National University of Ireland Galway

Michelle Farrell is a Senior Lecturer in Law at the University of Liverpool

Rob Grace is a Senior Associate at the Harvard Humanitarian Initiative, Harvard University

James A Green is Professor of Public International Law at the University of Reading

Corinne Heaven is a Postdoctoral Research Fellow in the Department of Politics and International Relations at the University of Reading

Christian Henderson is Professor of International Law at the University of Sussex

Dr Triestino Mariniello is a Senior Lecturer in Law at Edge Hill University

Ben Murphy is a doctoral candidate and Lecturer in Law at the University of Liverpool

Marco Odello is a Reader in Law at Aberystwyth University

Alexander Orakhelashvili is a Senior Lecturer in Law at the University of Birmingham

Stephen Samuel is a doctoral candidate in law at the University of Reading

Christine Schwöbel-Patel is a Senior Lecturer in Law at the University of Liverpool

Introduction

CHRISTIAN HENDERSON

TODAY, MORE THAN ever, there are forums and mechanisms in existence for the consideration, deliberation and adjudication of international disputes, breaches of international law, and allegations of international crimes.[1] In the context of the legal issues involved these are given attention, *inter alia*, in the International Court of Justice,[2] the ad hoc International Criminal Tribunals[3] and Claims Commissions,[4] and the International Criminal Court.[5] However, while at first glance these judicial forums appear to potentially have jurisdiction over allegations of violations of the laws of war, international human rights law, and international criminal law there are various obstacles that exist that often ultimately prevent them from exercising it. For example, the decentralised nature of the international system and the non-compulsory nature of the Court means that the legality of a State's forcible actions very rarely end up being heard by the International Court of Justice.[6] The jurisdictions of the International Criminal Tribunals and Claims Commissions are limited both temporally and geographically[7] and the mechanisms for bringing charges of the perpetration of international crimes before the International Criminal Court means that the Court's jurisdiction cannot be relied upon.[8]

1 For a discussion of the contemporary issues regarding dispute settlement in international law, see D French, M Saul and ND White, *International Law and Dispute Settlement: New Problems and Techniques* (Oxford, Hart Publishing, 2010).

2 See, for example, *DRC v Uganda* [2005] ICJ 116 (19 December).

3 These consist primarily of the International Criminal Tribunal for the Former Yugoslavia and the International Criminal Tribunal for Rwanda.

4 In particular, the Eritrea-Ethiopia Claims Commission. See C Gray, 'The Eritrea/Ethiopia Claims Commission Oversteps Its Boundaries: A Partial Award?' (2006) 17 *European Journal of International Law* 699.

5 See, for example, W Schabas, *An Introduction to the International Criminal Court* (3rd edn, Cambridge, Cambridge University Press, 2007).

6 Only three key judgments in contentious cases and two advisory opinions on the issue of self-defence have been given by the Court in over 60 years despite the numerous incidences of the use of force with this as the justification.

7 That is, they are established to deal with a particular incident over a particular time.

8 This arises if either the accused's home state or the state where the alleged crime took place is a party to the Rome Statute (1998) or the United Nations Security Council refers a case to the chief prosecutor.

Furthermore, while various organs of the United Nations, in particular the Security Council, provide a forum for the deliberation of disputes and violations of international law,[9] these are political organs, regardless of the fact that condemnation by them is arguably a potential indicator as to illegality.[10] However, the political nature of these organs means that condemnation, or even consideration, is patchy at best. Additionally, domestic courts, for example in the United Kingdom, have some role to play in this context, but have notably refrained from addressing certain issues, both for constitutional and jurisdictional reasons. Consequently, there is often seemingly an uncomfortable accountability deficit.

Nevertheless, despite the various difficulties in possible violations of international law in the context of internal disturbances, armed conflicts and human rights atrocities being formally heard in these forums, this does not mean that they necessarily go entirely unchecked. Indeed, as a result of the decentralised international system other less formal methods of deliberation are available. For example, other actors within the international community are very often drawn in, and occasionally at the forefront, in offering judgments as to the legality of the actions of those involved. While individual states are regularly the key actors in this respect, international legal scholars are also very often involved in this process of assessment.[11]

However, the commission of inquiry is another key actor involved in this process, an actor which, although increasingly utilised, and which has arguably recently attained greater prominence, has thus far been given relatively little attention by legal scholars. Today, these bodies of inquiry, which may be domestic, international, or non-governmental in nature, are increasingly the forums, often to the exclusion of others, where issues are heard and given exposure, as well as having a role in '[f]ostering increased conformity with international standards'.[12]

Although not an entirely new phenomenon—indeed, they attracted some relatively early academic attention[13]—commissions of inquiry

[9] Perhaps the most notable example in this regard was that surrounding the use of force against Iraq by the United States and United Kingdom in 2003.

[10] A point made by Christine Gray. See C Gray, 'The Use of Force and the International Legal Order' in M Evans (ed), *International Law* (3rd edn, Oxford, Oxford University Press, 2010) 617.

[11] Indeed, as is well known, Art 38(1)(d) of the Statute of the International Court of Justice includes the writings of 'highly qualified' scholars as 'subsidiary means for the determination of rules of law'.

[12] A Cassese, 'Fostering Increased Conformity with International Standards: Monitoring and Institutional Fact-Finding', in A Cassese (ed), *Realizing Utopia: The Future of International Law* (Oxford, Oxford University Press, 2012) 295.

[13] B Kaufman, 'The necessity for rules of procedure in *ad hoc* United Nations Investigations' (1969) 18 *American University Law Review* 747; R Miller, 'United Nations Fact-Finding Missions in the Field of Human Rights' (1970–73) *Australian Yearbook of International Law* 40;

appear to have become an increasingly prominent feature of the international landscape in the post-Cold War era. In particular, they have become a regularly resorted to forum or mechanism for determining not only the factual issues of a particular incident or conflict, but also—either intentionally or as a by-product—the responsibility of both states and individuals for violations of international law, most notably international human rights, international humanitarian law, and international criminal law. Indeed, today, although often termed or referred to as 'fact-finding missions', commissions of inquiry are either mandated to do more than this or ultimately go further than this in their work, for example in making determinations on the legal framework that is applicable to the factual situations they are called upon to investigate and on the scope of the relevant legal rules and norms at issue, as well as engaging in analysis as to whether particular acts amount to violations of the particular branch or rule of international law under focus.[14]

Commissions of inquiry have not replaced more formal modes of adjudication, and, for now, at least, their prospects of doing so in the future would appear slim. Nonetheless, they often enhance and contribute to the work of international organisations and existing courts and tribunals, either by providing the impetus for calls of referral to the International Criminal Court, as we have witnessed in the context of the conflict in Syria, and also with the publication of the commission of inquiry on North Korea, or through their factual findings and legal determinations being drawn upon by other bodies and adjudicative mechanisms.[15] However, and in the absence of an alternative mechanism or forum to carry out such work, commissions of inquiry do seem to be an important tool for clarifying the factual situation on the ground and obtaining an authoritative

SD Bailey, 'UN Fact-Finding and Human Rights Complaints' (1972) 48 *International Affairs* 250; TC van Boven, 'Fact-Finding in the Field of Human Rights' (1973) 3 *Israel Yearbook on Human Rights* 93; TM Franck and H Scott Fairly, 'Procedural Due Process in Human Rights Fact-Finding by International Agencies' (1980) 74 *American Journal of International Law* 308; D Weissbrodt and J McCarthy, 'Fact-Finding by International Nongovernmental Human Rights Organizations' (1981) 22 *Virginia Journal of International Law* 1; BG Ramcharan (ed), *International Law and Fact-Finding in the Field of Human Rights* (The Hague, Nijhoff, 1982); H Thoolen and B Verstappen, *Human Rights Missions: A Study of the Fact-Finding Practice of Non-Governmental Organisations* (Dordrecht, Martinus Nijhoff, 1986); DF Orentlicher, 'Bearing Witness: The Art and Science of Human Rights Fact-Finding' (1990) 3 *Harvard Human Rights Journal* 83; KJ Partsch, 'Fact-Finding and Inquiry' in R Bernhardt (ed), *Encyclopedia of Public International Law* (Amsterdam-London, North-Holland, 1992) 343; M Cherif Bassiouni, 'Appraising UN Justice-Related Fact Finding Missions' (2001) 5 *Journal of Law and Policy* 35.

[14] D Akande and H Tonkin, 'International Commissions of Inquiry: A New Form of Adjudication?' (*EJIL: Talk!* 6 April 2012), available at www.ejiltalk.org/international-commissions-of-inquiry-a-new-form-of-adjudication/.

[15] Akande and Tonkin (n 14).

determination of whether violations of international law have taken place and who is responsible.[16] Furthermore, these determinations are influential on public perceptions of the legal issues involved, and the reports of commissions of inquiry, though not formally binding, may end up being perceived by many as an authoritative determination of the legal issues as well as providing an historical record of the facts. As a consequence, and given that they are unlikely to come before a court of law, the fact that the legal issues are examined in a commission of inquiry is of some significance, as it provides what may be the only, or at least most formal, treatment of them.

Within what would seem a relatively short space of time, the idea of fact-finding and the establishment of commissions of inquiry to this end has seen a rapid rise. In the post-Cold War era they have been established not just by the UN, but also by states and regional organisations. And within the UN they have been established by the Security Council, the Secretary General and, more frequently, the Human Rights Council. In line with this there has been a rise of interest in the concept and work of commissions of inquiry from an academic perspective, with the publication of numerous books and articles,[17] manuals, guidelines and field handbooks for those working within commissions of inquiry,[18] the

[16] Akande and Tonkin (n 14).

[17] See, for example, M Bothe, 'Fact-finding as a means of ensuring respect for international humanitarian law' in W Heintschel von Heinegg and V Epping (eds), *International Humanitarian Law Facing New Challenges* (Berlin, Springer, 2007) 249; JG Stewart, 'The UN Commission of Inquiry on Lebanon: A Legal Appraisal' (2007) 5 *Journal of International Criminal Justice* 1039; C Henderson and JA Green, 'The *Jus ad Bellum* and Entities Short of Statehood in the Report on the Conflict in Georgia' (2010) 59 *International and Comparative Law Quarterly* 129; T Boutruche, 'Credible Fact-Finding and Allegations of International Humanitarian Law Violations: Challenges in Theory and Practice' (2011) 16 *Journal of Conflict and Security Law* 105; A Cassese, 'Fostering Increased Conformity with International Standards: Monitoring and Institutional Fact-Finding' in A Cassese (ed), *Realizing Utopia: The Future of International Law* (Oxford, Oxford University Press, 2012) 295; Z Yihdego, 'The Gaza Mission: Implications for International Humanitarian Law and UN Fact-Finding' (2012) 13 *Melbourne Journal of International Law* 1; M Frulli, 'Fact-Finding or Paving the Road to Criminal Justice?: Some Reflections on United Nations Commissions of Inquiry' (2012) 10 *Journal of International Criminal Justice* 1323; LJ van den Herik, 'An Inquiry into the Role of Commissions of Inquiry in International Law; Navigating the Tensions between Fact-Finding and International Law-Application' (2014) 13 *Chinese Journal of International Law* 507; P Alston and S Knuckey (eds) *The Transformation of Human Rights Fact-Finding* (Oxford, Oxford University Press, 2015).

[18] See, for example, M Cherif Bassiouni et al (eds), *Siracusa Guidelines for International, Regional and National Fact-Finding Bodies* (Cambridge, Intersentia, 2013); DJ Ravindran et al (eds), *Handbook on Fact-Finding and Documentation of Human Rights Violations* (Bankgok, Asian Forum for Human Rights and Development, 1994); International Bar Association: Raoul Wallenberg Institute of Human Rights and Humanitarian Law, *Guidelines on International Human Rights Fact-Finding Visits and Reports* (The Lund-London Guidelines) (1 June 2009), available at www.factfindingguidelines.org/; M Bergsmo (ed), *Quality Control in Fact-Finding*, (Florence, Torkel Opsahl Academic EPublisher, 2013); OHCHR, *Commissions of Inquiry and*

initiation and conclusion of various studies and projects,[19] and several conferences.[20]

This book aims to contribute to the burgeoning literature on contemporary commissions of inquiry through consciously seeking to address these bodies through the perspective of international law, both in terms of analysing their various forms and functions, where they fit within—and their contribution to—the legal landscape, their engagement with and impact upon international law, and, given their particular nature, procedural issues that may arise in the international legal context. More specifically, numerous questions arise around their selectivity, both in terms of the situations that they address and the facts and evidence chosen in each investigation, their mandates, their legal basis, the selection of commissioners, their procedures for investigations and standard of proof, the legal conclusions reached, and the utilisation and impact of the inquiries and their reports. In this sense, through its various chapters, it both seeks to highlight the problems of these bodies within international law and also their prospects for the future.

The book is divided up into four sections. The first section is on the diversity of contemporary commissions of inquiry. Diversity in this sense can be seen from two complimentary angles. Patrick Butchard and Christian Henderson begin by looking at diversity from the perspective of the functions that commissions of inquiry have had, and do have today. In their chapter, 'A Functional Typology of Commissions of Inquiry' they set out what they perceive to be the key identifiable functions of commissions of inquiry in the form of fact-finding, arbitration, informing, public accountability, monitoring, alerting, and recommending. As this chapter attempts to highlight, commissions of inquiry are far from monolithic in nature and are, in that sense, difficult to define. However, while fragmentation

Fact-Finding Missions on International Human Rights and Humanitarian Law: Guidance and Practice (2015), 43, available at www.ohchr.org/Documents/Publications/CoI_Guidance_and_Practice.pdf.

[19] See, for example, Harvard Group of Professionals on Monitoring, Reporting, and Fact-Finding, Program on Humanitarian Policy and Conflict Research (Harvard University), www.hpcrresearch.org/research/monitoring-reporting-and-fact-finding; 'From Fact-Finding to Evidence: Harmonizing Multiple Investigations of International Crimes', The Hague Institute for Global Justice, available at thehagueinstituteforglobaljustice.org/index.php?page=Projects-Projects-Current_Projects-From_Fact-Finding_to_Evidence:__Harmonizing_Multiple_Investigations_of_International_Crimes&pid=122&id=2.

[20] See, for example, American Society of International Law's 105th Annual Meeting (2010), panel on 'Commissions of Inquiry into Armed Conflict, Breaches of the Laws of War and Human Rights Abuses: Process, Standards, and Lessons Learned'; Centre for Human Rights and Global Justice 'International Human Rights Fact-Finding in the Twenty-First Century' (NYU School of Law, conference 1–2 November 2013); the UN Human Rights Council, *Commissions of Inquiry Conference Brief* (1 December 2011).

in the functions of commissions of inquiry may give rise to problems for the coherence of international law, a 'one size fits all' option is equally inappropriate.

The remaining chapters in this section look at diversity in terms of the political actors who have established the commissions of inquiry. The second chapter, by Michelle Farrell and Ben Murphy, is titled 'Hegemony and Counter-Hegemony: The Politics of Establishing United Nations Commissions of Inquiry'. In their chapter Farrell and Murphy argue that while there is discernible hegemony at play within the bodies of the UN, the UN Human Rights Council, in particular, through its establishment of various commissions of inquiry, acts as what they describe as 'an institutional counter-balance' to the effects of the 'power asymmetries' that characterise relations that exist between Western and other, notably developing, states. Following on from this, Rob Grace places a focus on commissions of inquiry established by regional bodies and organisations in his chapter titled 'Lessons from Two Regional Missions: Fact-finding in Georgia and South Sudan', while Steve Samuel and James A Green focus their attention, instead, on commissions of inquiry of a 'domestic' nature in their chapter on 'Domestic Commissions of Inquiry and International Law: The Importance of Normative Authority'. While Grace argues that through an examination of the commissions of inquiry in both Georgia and Sudan 'one can point to, on the one hand, novel innovations that improved upon typical fact-finding practice, and on the other hand, problematic practices that fly in the face of trends of professional practice that have emerged in recent years', Samuel and Green suggest, in emphasising the importance of 'normative authority', that 'it is only where the international legal claims of domestic commissions of inquiry are made with a degree of normative authority that they can be, or should be, viewed as being of value'.

Section two of the book offers some perspectives on the relationship commissions of inquiry have with other international courts and tribunals. Alexander Orakhelashvili, in chapter five, examines 'Commissions of Inquiry and Traditional Mechanisms of Dispute Settlement'. In particular, Orakhelashivili looks at the inquiry function and how the work of commissions of inquiry compares with that of more traditional mechanisms of dispute settlement and argues that while commissions of inquiry have real potential in filling gaps left open by more traditional means of dispute settlement, they must nonetheless take caution so as not to overstep their mandates while also being careful in their use of standards of proof. The next two chapters turn to examining the role of commissions of inquiry in the context of international criminal justice and the courts and tribunals that exist therein. Christine Schwöbel-Patel, in her chapter 'Commissions of Inquiry: Courting International Criminal Courts and Tribunals', takes a critical perspective in arguing that commissions of inquiry have effectively

'courted' international criminal tribunals and that, rather than being part of an intervention check list, they may—through further inquiries in connection with the more deep-rooted causes of conflict—instead be a check on intervention. On the other hand, Triestino Mariniello in chapter seven looks at 'The Impact of Commissions of Inquiry on the Proceedings before the International Criminal Court'. In this chapter, Mariniello examines the work of various commissions of inquiry whose work has been connected with that of the International Criminal Court, and argues that while commissions of inquiry and their findings have played a very real role in the work of the International Criminal Court, a certain distance, nonetheless, needs to be maintained between them and the Court so as not to provide the impression that their findings are simply rubber-stamped by the prosecutor or the Court.

Section three of the book looks more at issues in the substantive engagement of commissions of inquiry with international law. Indeed, the way in which they have engaged with relevant branches of international law has proved controversial. First, in chapter eight, Marco Odello seeks to untangle the interplay between international human rights law and international humanitarian law in the practice of commissions of inquiry. This is important to understand, as many commissions are mandated to address violations of both branches of the law, while some begin addressing violations of international human rights law when events on the ground require it to broaden its scope so as to address international humanitarian law. While Odello notes particular problems with commissions of inquiry engaging with these branches of international law, he is also optimistic about the role of commissions of inquiry in dealing with these sensitive areas of the law, providing that they are appropriately mandated and equipped to do so.

Secondly, it is an unavoidable aspect of international life that while the decisions and opinions of international courts and tribunals are often not binding, or are at least not precedent setting, they nonetheless have an impact upon the way states and the epistemic international community view and apply international legal rules and norms. In this sense, Shane Darcy seeks to address, in chapter nine, if, and if so how, commissions of inquiry have simply applied or gone further so as to develop international law in certain respects. It is one thing to apply the law, but the place of commissions of inquiry within the international legal context will be made more significant and perhaps further entrenched if they can also be witnessed developing the law.

However, and thirdly, whether they apply the law or develop it, their activities pose real questions for the coherence of international law. Indeed, it could be argued that while on the one hand having additional accountability mechanisms is a positive thing on the other hand they also simply further the fragmentisation of international law. Russell Buchan, in chapter ten, addresses precisely this question and, in characterising

commissions of inquiry as the 'third generation of international adjudication', argues that '[w]hilst undoubtedly commissions of inquiry provide an important contribution to the adjudication of international law, especially given the relative unavailability of the International Court of Justice and even specialised treaty tribunals, ... commissions of inquiry can threaten the unity and coherence of the international legal order where they provide differing interpretations of international law.'

Finally, section four of the book looks at procedural questions and working methods of commissions of inquiry. There has been much controversy regarding issues such as the standard of proof to which they work, which is potentially very significant given the conclusions that they often draw. Théo Boutruche begins this section in chapter eleven by addressing selectivity fact-finding in his chapter titled 'Selectivity and Choices in Human Rights Fact-Finding: Reconciling Subjectivity with Objectivity?', and whether it is possible and desirable to reconcile subjectivity with objectivity. In particular, Boutruche looks at what subjectivity and objectivity mean and the inherent tension between them in the context of fact-finding. He argues that 'despite the exponential professionalisation and standardisation of the field of fact-finding, further work is needed to address persistent mistakes and risks associated directly or indirectly with matters of selectivity and subjectivity'. Closely following on from this, Alison Bissett takes as the focus of her chapter, titled 'Commissions of Inquiry and Procedural Fairness', the notion of procedural fairness in the actual practice of commissions of inquiry. However, as opposed to regarding procedural fairness as a notion, Bisset on the contrary argues that this is a strict requirement for the work of commissions of inquiry, and highlights not only many weaknesses of this element in the practice of commissions to date, but also ways in which its prominence may be increased. Lastly, Corinne Heaven, in her chapter 'A Visible College: The Community of Fact-Finding Practice', addresses whether there is a discernable 'community' of fact-finding practice. Indeed, by exploring communities of practice within international law and international relations Heaven convincingly demonstrates that through an examination of the concepts of standardisation, professionalism and transparency there is a 'community of fact-finding practice'. Together, it is hoped that this volume of essays contributes both to understanding some of the problems that the existence and functioning of commissions of inquiry present for international law and the international legal systems but also their prospects for contributing to the resolution of disputes and the search for justice and accountability into the future.

Section 1

The Diversity of Contemporary Commissions of Inquiry

1

A Functional Typology of Commissions of Inquiry

PATRICK BUTCHARD AND CHRISTIAN HENDERSON

1.1. INTRODUCTION

COMMISSIONS OF INQUIRY have existed in one form or another over the course of the last two centuries. From inter-state dispute settlement to providing a means of public accountability, these bodies of investigation have transformed over the years to encompass a wide range of tasks and functions. They have been established between states,[1] by individual states,[2] regional organisations,[3] and have now found a place as a well-established tool of the United Nations (UN).[4] Today, they are established with notable frequency, and while they may be established with a mandate containing a single function, they may alternatively have several, or may have originally been established with a single function but through choice or necessity go on to incorporate others.

The aim of this short chapter is to briefly set out a typology of these commissions of inquiry, in particular to highlight the different functions that they have had over time as the practice of establishing and utilising them has developed. It intends, in this respect, to set the scene for the other chapters within this volume. While it is impossible to be entirely comprehensive, as each commission of inquiry is inherently unique and established in different contexts and by different entities in the pursuit of different aims, the chapter nonetheless intends to trace and set out *in general* the various types of functions that commissions of inquiry possess and their distinguishing features in this respect, and assesses the extent

[1] See, for example, section 1.3 below.

[2] See Ch 4: S Samuel and JA Green, 'Domestic Commissions of Inquiry and International Law: The Importance of Normative Authority'.

[3] See Ch 3: R Grace, 'Lessons From Two Regional Missions: Fact-finding in Georgia and South Sudan'.

[4] See Ch 2: M Farrell and B Murphy, 'Hegemony and Counter-Hegemony: The Politics of Establishing United Nations Commissions of Inquiry'.

to which their diversity of functions and attributes have made them a permanent fixture on the international landscape. Of course, and as will become clear, these functions cannot be entirely separated and there are some inherent overlaps between them.

The chapter first looks at the fact-finding function, which may be seen to be the elementary function of any commission of inquiry.[5] However, this function is rarely employed in isolation and forms the basis for the operation of other functions and the attainment of other ends. Indeed, as section 1.3 highlights, with added formalisation commissions of inquiry quickly took on something resembling an arbitral function. While finding facts was often at the heart of these commissions, this was not always the case. Furthermore, although perhaps more prevalent in the context of commissions of inquiry that have been established by international organisations, although, again, based upon their basic fact-finding function, commissions of inquiry have been employed as a means of informing a particular entity or section of the public, as discussed in section 1.4. Similarly, in section 1.5 their function in providing a form of public legal accountability will be highlighted, in particular addressing the question of whether particular types of inquiry have developed into a new form of (legal) adjudication.

The functions of commissions of inquiry in monitoring particular situations (section 1.6), alerting an establishing body to the occurrence of an event (section 1.7), and as is very often the case today, making recommendations (section 1.8) will also be addressed. As discussed further in later chapters within this book, there is a relationship—and, occasionally, uneasy tension—between commissions of inquiry and more traditional mechanisms of dispensing international criminal justice.[6] Indeed, while they have been established as a prelude to the establishment of a more formal tribunal,[7] they have also begun to contribute to the work of the International Criminal Court (ICC).[8] However, the extent to which they have contributed, and should contribute, in this respect is debatable, and whether through their engagement with international law they actually end up causing more fragmentation is open to question.

[5] While this chapter will generally employ the term 'commissions of inquiry' there does not appear to be any generally distinguishing features of these bodies from those officially titled as 'fact-finding' missions.

[6] See, in particular, Ch 6: C Schwöbel Patel, 'Commissions of Inquiry: Courting International Criminal Courts and Tribunals' and Ch 7: T Mariniello, 'The Impact of International Commissions of Inquiry on the Proceedings before the International Criminal Court'.

[7] See, for example, the Commission of Experts for the former Yugoslavia which was established by the Security Council in UN Security Council Resolution 780, *Establishing a Commission of Experts to Examine and Analyze Information Submitted Pursuant to Resolution 771*, UN Doc S/RES/780 (1992) (6 October 1992) para 2. The interim report of this commission of inquiry triggered the establishment of the International Criminal Tribunal for the former Yugoslavia.

[8] See, in general, Ch 7.

1.2. FACT-FINDING

The most basic function of any commission of inquiry is to find 'facts' in one form or another, and it can be witnessed in virtually every commission. Fact-finding might be seen as the sole function of formative commissions of inquiry. For example, the *Maine* inquiries of 1898, which were established by the US and Spain to investigate the sinking of the *Maine*, a US vessel, were purely fact-finding, in that they focused almost exclusively on discovering factual evidence.[9] The fact-finding function was evident not only in their mandates, but also in the appointment of their personnel, as none of their members were lawyers, as well as in their outcomes, and in that their role was to present a factual narrative of the conflict concerned and present the circumstances that led to the sinking of the *Maine* to the state parties involved.[10]

However, while the earliest function of commissions of inquiry could thus be seen as 'pure' fact-finding, this function had the more indirect function of providing a veiled or outsourced diplomacy between states, with the commissions of inquiry directing their factual findings towards the states concerned so as to settle a dispute. The focus was thus upon finding facts, but doing so in a way in which a dispute might be settled. They, in this sense, could be said to employ their fact-finding function to achieve pacifying ends. As a result, the working methods which they employed 'sufficiently impressed the delegates to the Hague Peace Conference of 1899 for them to give serious attention to the issue of fact-finding in international disputes.'[11] However, these formative commissions of inquiry of a purely fact-finding nature led to the 1899 Hague Convention for the Peaceful Settlement of Disputes envisaging such inquires to be used solely for settling disputes of fact and not questions of law.[12]

The value of fact-finding was acknowledged in the context of violations of the laws of war, in that Article 90 of the 1977 Additional Protocol I to the Geneva Conventions established an International Fact-Finding Commission which 'shall be competent to … enquire into any facts alleged to be a grave breach as defined in the Conventions and this Protocol or other serious violation of the Conventions or of this Protocol.'[13] Despite the fact that it has never been resorted to, it is still in existence and is ready to be called upon if necessary.[14] In the context of the United Nations,

[9] See *The Annual Register: A Review of Public Events at Home and Abroad for the Year 1898* (New York, Longmans, Green and Co, 1899) 362–63.

[10] JG Merrills, *International Dispute Settlement* (5th edn, Oxford, Oxford University Press, 2011) 41–42.

[11] Merrills (n 10) 42.

[12] The Hague Convention for the Pacific Settlement of International Disputes 1899, Art 14.

[13] Art 90(2)(c)(i).

[14] See, in general, F Kalshoven, 'The International Humanitarian Fact-Finding Commission: A Sleeping Beauty?' (2002) 4 *Humanitäres Völkerrecht—Informationsschriften* 213.

the General Assembly adopted in 1991 the Declaration on Fact-finding by the United Nations in the Field of the Maintenance of International Peace and Security.[15] In this resolution the delegates of the General Assembly encouraged organs to undertake fact-finding:

> In performing their functions in relation to the maintenance of international peace and security, the competent organs of the United Nations should endeavor to have full knowledge of all relevant facts. To this end they should consider undertaking fact-finding activities.[16]

This competence has been exercised particularly by the UN Security Council, Human Rights Council, and the UN General Assembly, each of whom have established fact-finding missions with increasing frequency.[17] For example, commissions of inquiry have been established by both the UN Security Council and Human Rights Council to investigate whether violations of international human rights law and international humanitarian law have occurred.[18] While determining whether violations of the law have taken place is the ultimate aim of these particular commissions of inquiry, they are premised upon an inherent fact-finding function and are also, as stipulated by the 1991 resolution, arguably situated within their respective peace and security functions. Similarly, the Bahrain Independent Commission for Investigation, established by the King of Bahrain, was 'established to investigate and report on the events occurring in Bahrain in February/March 2011, and any subsequent consequences arising out of the aforementioned events, and to make such recommendations as it may deem appropriate'.[19] In this respect '[t]he Commission's mandate [was] to engage in fact finding'.[20]

1.3. ARBITRATION

As noted above, the 1899 Hague Convention for the Peaceful Settlement of Disputes envisaged commissions of inquiry being established to settle

[15] UN General Assembly Resolution 46/59, *Declaration on Fact-Finding by the United Nations in the Field of the Maintenance of International Peace and Security*, UN Doc A/RES/46/59 (9 December 1991) ('*Declaration on Fact-finding*').

[16] ibid para 1.

[17] See, in general, Ch 2.

[18] See, for example, the International Commission of Inquiry on Darfur, established by the UN Security Council in UN Security Council Resolution 1564 (2004), UN Doc S/RES/1564 (2004) (18 September 2004) para 12, and the Independent International Commission of Inquiry on the Syrian Arab Republic, established by the Human Rights Council in Resolution S-17/1 (2011), UN Doc A/HRC/RES/S-17/1 (23 August 2011), available in UN Doc A/HRC/S-17/2 (23 November 2011).

[19] Royal Order No 28 of 2011, Art one.

[20] ibid, Art four. Although see Art nine, which sets out the purposes for which this fact-finding is ultimately intended, including whether any human rights violations had taken place during the period under examination.

disputes of fact and not questions of law and that their findings should not be obligatory. In addition, the UN Declaration on Fact-Finding made clear that:

> The decision by the competent United Nations organ to undertake fact-finding should always contain a clear mandate for the fact finding mission and precise requirements to be met by its report. *The report should be limited to a presentation of findings of a factual nature.*[21] (emphasis added)

Yet, we also saw how fact-finding is very often a means to an end as opposed to an end in itself. For example, the UN has encouraged its organs to resort to fact-finding in performing their functions specifically 'in relation to the maintenance of international peace and security', while commissions of inquiry of a more contemporary nature often employ fact-finding in determining whether violations of international law have taken place.

However, fact-finding has also formed the basis for what might be described as an 'arbitration' function. The Hague Convention, for example, provided that the commissions should be composed of two commissioners selected by each party and then by a fifth who had been jointly selected.[22] While this composition resembles that of an arbitral body, commissions of inquiry also more generally shifted on a functional level from pure fact-finding bodies further towards those of an arbitral nature, including through having at least some engagement with the law. Indeed, given their common inter-state nature they began to go beyond 'simple' fact-finding functions to increasingly looking like arbitral bodies, including through producing reports of a legally binding nature.

Following on closely from the *Maine* inquiries and the Hague Convention came the *Dogger Bank* inquiry of 1904, which involved a naval dispute between England and Russia whereby a Russian warship had fired at a UK fishing fleet under the erroneous belief that it was comprised of Japanese torpedo boats.[23] While the commission was requested to look at the incident as a whole, it was specifically mandated to determine where responsibility lay for the incident and to apportion blame. As Merrills notes, '[t]he duty to apportion "blame" appeared to assign the Commission an arbitral as well as a fact-finding function'.[24]

The shift towards commissions of inquiry developing an arbitral function was heightened by the further change in personnel. For example,

[21] *Declaration on Fact-finding* (n 15) para 17.

[22] Hague Convention for the Pacific Settlement of International Disputes 1899, Art 32.

[23] For its terms of reference see *Declaration between Great Britain and Russia, relating to the constitution of an international commission of inquiry on the subject of the North Sea incident*, signed at St Petersburg, 12/25 November 1904, Art 2. See also JB Scott, *The Hague Court Reports* (New York, Oxford University Press, 1916) 411.

[24] Merills (n 10) 44.

while for many years these commissions of inquiry were composed almost exclusively of naval officers, the *Tubantia* inquiry of 1921 between Germany and the Netherlands was the 'first case in which a commission of inquiry had included a lawyer among its members',[25] although it did not resort to determining issues of blame with regard to whether a Dutch U-Boat had been torpedoed knowingly by Germany or as a result of error.[26] However, despite the parties not accepting the commission's report as binding, it was nonetheless 'notable for the extent to which the proceedings resembled arbitration'.[27]

Furthermore, despite the stipulations of the 1907 Hague Convention it was not long before the findings of the reports of commissions of inquiry began to take on a binding nature. Indeed, in rejecting one of the stipulations of Article 35 of the Hague Convention which provided that '[t]he report of the commissions is limited to a statement of facts, and has in no way the character of an award',[28] the *Tiger* inquiry of 1917, between Germany and Norway, on the contrary, was the first commission of inquiry in which the report was accepted as binding upon the parties.[29] Things developed further in the *Red Crusader* inquiry of 1961, a dispute involving an incident at sea between a Danish warship, the *Niels Ebbesen*, and a British trawler, the *Red Crusader*.[30] In response to alleged illegal fishing by the *Red Crusader* and in it attempting to avoid arrest, the *Niels Ebbesen* had opened fire. Subsequently, a commission of inquiry was established to settle the dispute. What was notable was that 'in respect of its composition, its procedure and its findings', which went beyond its factual mandate and made several evaluations of a legal nature, 'the … Commission was a fundamentally judicial operation. A majority of the Commission were jurists and had the tribunal been a court of arbitration its blend of legal and non-legal expertise would have been in no way unusual'.[31]

However, occasionally commissions of inquiry have been established exclusively with an arbitral mandate and function, without being underpinned by a fact-finding function. The *Letelier and Moffitt* Commission of 1988, for example, between the US and Chile,[32] 'was essentially judicial and this was reflected in all stages of its work'.[33] In particular, it had no fact-finding role to speak of, being restricted in its mandate to determining

[25] Merills (n 10) 47.

[26] See JB Scott, *The Hague Court Reports* (2nd series, New York, Oxford University Press, 1932) 135.

[27] Merills (n 10) 47.

[28] Hague Convention for the Pacific Settlement of International Disputes 1907, Art 35.

[29] The report of the *Tiger* commission of inquiry was not published.

[30] For the terms of reference of the inquiry, see Exchange of Notes of 15 November 1961, para (b), UKTS No 118 (Cmnd 1575, 1961).

[31] Merills (n 10) 50.

[32] 63 ILR 378.

[33] Merills (n 10) 52.

the amount of compensation payable by Chile to the family of a former foreign minister, which the US had pursued Chile for on behalf of the deceased's family. Indeed, and as observed by Merrills:

> the Commission which was eventually set up functioned less as an inquiry commission and more like a court of arbitration, producing a binding decision, being dominated by international judges, including an International Court of Justice judge as president and a judge from the European Court of Human Rights, and deciding issues of law as well as fact.[34]

Not only did it identify and apply the relevant international legal rules and principles to the facts of the case in resolving the dispute between the parties, but it also was described by one of the commissioners as 'advancing the frontiers of international law'.[35] Consequently,

> [i]t was, in essence, a notable departure from the concept and function of the commission of inquiry as envisaged in the 1899 Hague Convention, manifesting a discernible shift in their nature from being non-legal and non-binding bodies towards operating increasingly like courts of law, albeit of a temporary nature, arbitrating disputes between two states.[36]

1.4. INFORMING

Fact-finding missions also have an important function of 'informing', in the sense that they provide an account—sometimes viewed as an *official* account, depending on the establishing body—of the facts relating to a particular situation. Similarly, according to the Office of the United Nations High Commissioner for Human Rights (OHCHR), information reported by such inquiries might also provide a historical record of serious violations of human rights and international humanitarian law.[37]

The 'informing' function of an inquiry could be seen as a sub-function of fact-finding itself, in that the inquiries relay facts to their establishing body as per their mandate.[38] However, and particularly at the institutional level, 'informing' may also serve as a function in and of itself in that most UN inquiries provide, and are seen as providing, an official account of the facts—useful to states, the general public, and indeed the media as an authoritative and impartial source of information. Within the UN, such information is intended to be presented in an impartial manner,

34 Merills (n 10) 53.
35 Merills (n 10).
36 C Henderson, 'Commissions of Inquiry: Flexible Temporariness or Permanent Predictability?' (2015) 45 *Netherlands Yearbook of International Law* 287, 291.
37 UN OHCHR, *Commissions of Inquiry and Fact-Finding Missions on International Human Rights and Humanitarian Law: Guidance and Practice* (New York, United Nations, 2015) 7.
38 It is also closely related to the accountability function, as discussed below in section 1.5.

as emphasised by the Declaration on Fact-Finding, which was clear that 'Fact-Finding missions have an obligation to act in strict conformity with their mandate and to perform their task in an impartial way …'.[39] This is, however, something that can also be witnessed in commissions of inquiry established by individual states. For example, the Chilcot Inquiry was established as an independent, and to that extent impartial, body that provided a narrative and historical record of the UK's involvement in Iraq, including the forcible intervention in March 2003, that extended to 12 volumes in length.[40]

The OHCHR identifies a number of other key principles that it suggests UN commissions of inquiry should abide by, including: independence; impartiality; transparency; objectivity; confidentiality; credibility; visibility; integrity; professionalism; and consistency.[41] These principles are said to be based upon years of UN practice and doctrine,[42] as well as specific UN declarations[43] and practice manuals such as the Minnesota Protocol[44] and the Istanbul Protocol.[45] If these are witnessed in the establishment and functioning of commissions of inquiry then it is of no surprise that such standards might underline the authority, credibility, and attractiveness of UN fact-finding and commissions of inquiry as reliable sources of information.

Whether such standards apply to non-institutional fact-finding outside of the UN, for example within a state or NGO, is dependent upon the institution itself. Guidelines have been adopted by non-governmental institutions, such as the International Bar Association,[46] which have also

[39] *Declaration on Fact-finding* (n 15) para [25].

[40] See Report of a Committee of Privy Counsellors, *The Report of the Iraq Inquiry: Executive Summary* (6 July 2016), available at www.iraqinquiry.org.uk/the-report/, accessed 1 October 2016 (hereinafter, the *Chilcot Report*).

[41] OHCHR, *Guidance and Practice* (n 37) 33–35.

[42] OHCHR, *Guidance and Practice* (n 37) 33.

[43] See, eg, UN General Assembly Resolution 55/89, *Principles on the Effective Investigation and Documentation of Torture and Other Cruel, Inhuman or Degrading Treatment or Punishment*, UN Doc A/RES/55/89 (22 February 2001) Annex.

[44] United Nations Centre for Social Development and Humanitarian Affairs, *Manual on the Effective Prevention and Investigation of Extra-Legal, Arbitrary, and Summary Executions* (New York, United Nations, 1991), available at www.ohchr.org/Documents/Issues/Executions/UNManual2015/Annex1_The_UN_Manual.pdf, accessed 1 October 2016 (The Minnesota Protocol). See also, United Nations Economic and Social Council Resolution 1989/65, *Principles on the Effective Prevention and Investigation of Extra-legal, Arbitrary and Summary Executions*, (24 May 1989) Annex, available at www.unodc.org/documents/commissions/CCPCJ/Crime_Resolutions/1980-1989/1989/ECOSOC/Resolution_1989-65.pdf, accessed 1 October 2016.

[45] OHCHR, *Istanbul Protocol: Manual on the Effective Investigation and Documentation of Torture and Other Cruel, Inhuman or Degrading Treatment or Punishment* (New York, United Nations, 2004) UN Doc HR/P/PT/8/Rev.1.

[46] International Bar Association (Raoul Wallenberg Institute), *Guidelines on International Human Rights Fact-Finding Visits and Reports by Non-Governmental Organisations (The Lund-London Guidelines)* (International Bar Association, 2015), available at www.ibanet.org/Fact_Finding_Guidelines.aspx, accessed 1 October 2016.

been acknowledged by the UN in recent drafts of the revised principles relating to the Minnesota Protocol.[47]

1.5. PUBLIC ACCOUNTABILITY

While commissions of inquiry may be seen as authoritative sources of information, they may in this sense also provide, and act as a mechanism for, public accountability, and they have done so in a number of ways. Today, commissions of inquiry are very rarely established *between* states, but by individual states, regional organisations, and perhaps most frequently by the UN, in particular the Human Rights Council.[48] As opposed to being established simply to provide an authoritative account of the truth to the parties concerned through a process of finding facts on the ground or as a mechanism of dispute settlement, their aim often appears to be to inform, and direct their findings towards, broader domestic and international audiences.

In the case of commissions of inquiry established by states, this perhaps can be seen, rather cynically, simply as an attempt at exoneration, although one should be cautious in drawing such a conclusion too hastily, as the commission of inquiry established by the authorities in Bahrain perhaps demonstrates.[49] Indeed, while a perceived lack of impartiality may scupper any chances of obtaining a credible and legitimate form of public accountability, the commission on Bahrain 'was established and funded by the King of Bahrain, but the commission conducted investigations and administered its budget independently, and ultimately delivered a report that was highly critical of the ruling regime'.[50] This is not always the case, as was perhaps witnessed in the final reports of the Turkel Commission, which was established by the Israeli government to investigate

[47] UN Human Rights Council, *Draft Report of the Special Rapporteur on extrajudicial, summary or arbitrary executions—The Minnesota Protocol on the Investigation of Potentially Unlawful Deaths: The Revised United Nations Manual on the Effective Prevention and Investigation of Extra-legal, Arbitrary and Summary Executions*, UN Doc A/HRC/32/39/Add.4 (June 2016) para [10], available at www.ohchr.org/Documents/Issues/Executions/UNManual2015/A.HRC.32.39.Add.4.docx, accessed 1 October 2016. Note: at the time of writing, the full draft of the report and the revised Protocol had not yet been published, and so the document was not included in the Special Rapporteur's annual report.

[48] See Farrell and Murphy (n 4), around n 57.

[49] See Royal Order No 28 of 2011, Art one and, in general, the Report of the Bahrain Independent Commission of Inquiry, 23 November 2011, available at www.bici.org.bh/, accessed 1 October 2016.

[50] D Akande and H Tonkin, 'International Commissions of Inquiry: A New Form of Adjudication?' (*EJIL Talk!*, 6 April 2012), available at www.ejiltalk.org/international-commissions-of-inquiry-a-new-form-of-adjudication/, accessed 1 October 2016.

and report upon its actions during the Flotilla incident of 31 May 2010.[51] Yet the public accountability aspects of the Chilcot (Iraq) Inquiry report seemed to be clear, in that the Inquiry was critical of the UK government and military in virtually every aspect of its involvement in Iraq between 2001 and 2009, and came close to suggesting the Iraq war was unlawful without expressly stating such.[52] In this latter respect, the Dutch inquiry, established to examine the role of Holland within the same conflict, was more explicit.[53] Whatever the lasting legacy of the Chilcot Report may ultimately turn out to be, its process and final report provided a form of public, if not ultimately legal, accountability and historical record of the conflict.

In the case of commissions of inquiry established by the UN, regional organisations, and NGOs, their aim appears to be to provoke a reaction from the international community, or a particular section of it. But simply exposing facts would not necessarily provoke a reaction. Instead, these facts, which are often seemingly predetermined to exist by the mandating body,[54] are qualified or interpreted by commissions of inquiry through the utilisation of relevant and *prima facie* applicable legal frameworks. In this respect, commissions of inquiry have certainly become a part of the legal accountability process. Indeed, in light of their factual findings, and as highlighted below,[55] they very often make recommendations to the parties concerned, for example domestic prosecutions, but also to the international community, including referral to the ICC. For example, in finding

[51] See *The Public Commission to Examine the Maritime Incident of 31st May 2010*, January 2011, available at www.turkel-committee.com/index.html. There was widespread criticism of the Turkel Commission as a tool to justify the raid and the blockade of Gaza. See 'The public has a right to know: The government's efforts to avoid a thorough and credible investigation of the flotilla affair seem more and more like a farce'(*Haaretz*, 13 June 2010), available at www.haaretz.com/print-edition/opinion/the-public-has-a-right-to-know-1.295797, accessed 1 October 2016.

[52] *Chilcot Report* (n 40), *Executive Summary*, para 810, see also vol 5, section 5 generally. The Inquiry did not ultimately offer such an express view on the legality of the war as this was not part of its mandate.

[53] *Report of the Dutch Committee of Inquiry on the War in Iraq* (12 January 2010), available at www.onderzoekscommissie-irak.nl, accessed 1 October 2016 (for the text of the report in Dutch as well as an executive summary and the conclusions in English).

[54] For example, while the UN Human Rights Council '*strongly condemn*[ed] the recent gross and systematic human rights violations committed in Libya' (para 1) and '[s]*trongly call*[ed] upon the Government of Libya to meet its responsibility to protect its population, to immediately put an end to all human rights violations, to stop any attacks against civilians, and to fully respect all human rights and fundamental freedoms' (para 2) it then '[d]*ecide*[d] to urgently dispatch an independent, international commission of inquiry … to investigate all *alleged* violations of international human rights law in Libya, to establish the facts and circumstances of such violations and of the crimes perpetrated, and, where possible identify those responsible' (para 11 (second emphasis added)). See UN Human Rights Council Resolution S-15/1, *Situation of Human Rights in the Libyan Arab Jamahiriya*, UN Doc A/HRC/RES/S-15/1 (25 February 2011).

[55] See section 1.8 below on the 'recommending' function.

violations of international human rights law the commission of inquiry on the DPRK subsequently recommended—indeed, urged—that the situation be referred to the ICC.[56] While this would have led to a form of legal accountability for those concerned, it cannot be denied that the report of the commission of inquiry by itself represents a form of public accountability, and stands as an authoritative and formal examination of the situation within the DPRK.

But while we may restrict our enthusiasm for commissions of inquiry to being simply a *part* of the accountability process in this context or a *precursor* to further, perhaps harder, accountability measures, we might instead perhaps perceive of them as more than this and as a mechanism of *legal* accountability *in their own right*. Some commissions have expressly identified themselves as taking an approach akin to a judicial body, as the Commission on Darfur did,[57] although others have very much sought to downplay their identity in this respect, the UNSG's Palmer commission on the Flotilla raid providing a good example.[58] Yet, regardless as to how they identify themselves, commissions of inquiry nearly always are either mandated to address issues of international law, or go on to do so regardless, the Palmer commission included. Ultimately, the four functions of international adjudication that have been identified by Alvarez (that is, dispute settlement, fact-finding, law making, and governance) can be seen to have been performed by commissions of inquiry, albeit to varying degrees, meaning that at the very least we might describe them as quasi-judicial.[59]

They also occasionally engage with international law to a rather extensive depth. A good example of this is provided in the mandate for the commission of inquiry in Darfur in which it was:

> … to investigate reports of violations of international humanitarian law and human rights law in Darfur by all parties, to determine also whether or not acts of genocide have occurred, and to identify the perpetrators of such violations with a view to ensuring that those responsible are held accountable…[60]

[56] See UN Human Rights Council, *Report of the Commission of Inquiry on Human Rights in the Democratic People's Republic of Korea*, UN Doc A/HRC/25/63 (7 February 2014) para 94.

[57] The commissions of inquiry on Darfur stated that 'in classifying the facts according to international criminal law, the Commission adopted an approach proper to a judicial body'. See *Report of the International Commission of Inquiry on Darfur to the United Nations Secretary-General*, UN Doc S/2005/60 (1 February 2005) para 14.

[58] *Report of the Secretary-General's Panel of Inquiry on the 31 May 2010 Flotilla Incident* (September 2011) para 5, available at www.un.org/News/dh/infocus/middle_east/Gaza_Flotilla_Panel_Report.pdf, accessed 1 October 2016.

[59] A Alvarez, *International Organisations as Law Makers* (Oxford University Press, 2005) 516.

[60] UN Security Council Resolution 1564 (2004); UN Doc S/RES/1564 (2004) (18 September 2004) para 12. Frulli notes that this a good example of an 'accountability driven mandate': M Frulli, 'Fact-Finding or Paving the Road to Criminal Justice? Some Reflections on United Nations Commissions of Inquiry' (2012) 10(5) *Journal of International Criminal Justice* 1323, 1329. See also the mandate for the commissions of inquiry on the Gaza Conflict above at n 30.

This is a significant shift from the arbitral nature that commissions of inquiry formerly occasionally possessed, as identified above, and is also very different to many of the other identified functions of commissions of inquiry. Within the international context, the discernible rise in contemporary commissions of inquiry offering a form of public accountability, as opposed to dispute settlement, could be attributed to the general shift from inter-state to intra-state conflicts. In addition, there has been a general recognition that many of the laws and obligations under focus are *erga omnes* in nature. These two factors have arguably given rise to the Responsibility to Protect concept, which set out the primary responsibility of states to protect those within their borders, along with a secondary responsibility upon the international community.[61] In this atmosphere, there are of course increased expectations of accountability within the international community, but at the same time with several limitations in connection with the emerging international criminal justice system, leaving space for the emergence of other mechanisms designed to ensure accountability and compliance with international obligations. While many, perhaps justifiably, perceive the secondary responsibility to protect as being the Security Council's, and in particular to react forcibly, the Human Rights Council appears to have instead stolen the show and reacted to suspected breaches of the responsibility through the establishment of commissions of inquiry.

1.6. MONITORING

As has become clear, fact-finding missions or commissions of inquiry may be mandated with a task that requires more than 'fact-finding'. On occasion, such investigative bodies have been set up to complete a task that could accurately be described as requiring a 'monitoring' function. This function includes the monitoring, inspection, and verification of a state or situation as part of a mandate that investigates a subject's compliance with a particular obligation, and is most often found within the setting of an institutional commission of inquiry.

Early in the life of the UN, a number of investigative commissions of inquiry were commissioned by the General Assembly to undertake such tasks as the monitoring of conditions for elections in Germany in the 1950s.[62] A similar Commission had previously been created to monitor and

[61] See, in general, The Report of the International Commission on Intervention and State Sovereignty, *The Responsibility to Protect* (December 2001), available at responsibilitytoprotect.org/ICISS%20Report.pdf.

[62] This was undertaken by the Impartial International Commission under United Nations Supervision to Investigate Elections in Germany, as established by UN General Assembly Resolution 510 (VI) *Appointment of an impartial international commission under United Nations*

observe elections in Korea in 1947.[63] Both these Commissions were made up of representatives of Member States, and were originally intended to oversee important transition phases in the rebuilding or establishment of each state.[64]

As well as observation and monitoring, some bodies were mandated to actively assist in the peaceful settlement of a dispute, as undertaken by the Special Committee on the Balkans in 1947.[65] This Special Committee was mandated: '(1) To observe the compliance by the four Governments concerned with the foregoing recommendations; (2) To be available to assist the four Governments concerned in the implementation of such recommendations'.[66]

Of course, such practical tasks have been largely assumed by peacekeeping missions and other special envoys in more recent years.[67] In addition, many regional organisations have their own methods of investigating a Member State's compliance with a particular legal obligation, and some international bodies, such as the International Atomic Energy Agency[68] (IAEA) or the Organisation for the Prohibition of Chemical Weapons[69] (OPCW), are set up specifically to carry out such investigations in their particular area of expertise.

Thus, today, the use of the monitoring function has been principally focused upon the observance and verification of a state's compliance with a particular obligation or duty. Similarly, there have been occasions, particularly involving the Security Council, where ad hoc investigations have been set up to monitor and verify a State's compliance with its own resolutions. For example, the Security Council established the United Nations Special Commission (UNSCOM) in 1991, and later the United Nations Monitoring, Verification and Inspection Commission (UNMOVIC) in 1999,

supervision to carry out a simultaneous investigation in the Federal Republic of Germany, in Berlin, and in the Soviet Zone of Germany in order to determine whether existing conditions there make it possible to hold genuinely free elections throughout these areas, UN Doc A/RES/510(VI) (20 December 1951).

[63] This was undertaken by the United Nations Temporary Commission in Korea, established by UN General Assembly Resolution 112 (II) *The Problem of the Independence of Korea*, UN Doc A/RES/112(II) (14 November 1947) Parts A and B.

[64] In the German Commission, the representatives were Brazil, Iceland, the Netherlands, Pakistan and Poland. In the Korean Commission, the representatives were Australia, Canada, China, El Salvador, France, India, Philippines, Syria, and the USSR.

[65] See, UN General Assembly Resolution 109 (II) *Threats to the political independence and territorial integrity of Greece*, UN Doc A/RES/109(II) (21 October 1947).

[66] ibid, para 6.

[67] See, eg, United Nations Department of Peacekeeping Operations, 'Peacekeeping Issues', www.un.org/en/peacekeeping/issues/, accessed 1 October 2016; and United Nations Department of Peacekeeping Operations, 'What is Peacekeeping', available at www.un.org/en/peacekeeping/operations/peacekeeping.shtml, accessed 1 October 2016.

[68] See www.iaea.org/ourwork, accessed 1 October 2016.

[69] See www.opcw.org/our-work/, accessed 1 October 2016.

which were mandated with the task of verifying Iraq's compliance with its obligations under Security Council Resolution 687 (1991), and establishing a system of *ongoing* monitoring and verification of Iraq's disarmament obligations following its invasion of Kuwait.[70] This particular work required these inspection commissions to work closely with the IAEA, but the establishment of the Security Council's own ad hoc body of investigation demonstrates the existence of a particular 'monitoring' function that may be undertaken by commissions of a certain nature.

After initial investigations suggested that the Syrian government had used chemical weapons in 2013,[71] it emerged that Syria did indeed have a chemical weapons program that existed in violation of its international obligation to disarm of such weapons.[72] In response to this revelation, a Joint Mission between the OPCW and the UN was established to monitor the timely elimination of this weapons program, mandated by the OPCW[73] and the Security Council.[74] This Mission[75] arguably had more of a monitoring function than the original investigation into the chemical weapons attacks, in that its primary task was to oversee the destruction of Syria's weapons program and provide monthly reports of its progress to the Security Council. Nonetheless, the reason for including such missions within this typology of the functions that commissions of inquiry may possess is based upon the following factors. Firstly, the Mission had fact-finding functions in the sense that it oversaw the development of the facts on the ground as the weapons program was dismantled. Secondly, while the Joint Mission was paired with the institutional tools of the OPCW, it was 'commissioned' in the sense that it could correctly be described as an ad hoc investigation. This inquiry was not just a simple fact-finding

[70] See UN Security Council Resolution 687 (1991), UN Doc S/RES/687 (1991) (3 April 1991), and UN Security Council Resolution 1284 (1999), UN Doc S/RES/1284 (1999) (17 December 1999) respectively.

[71] See discussion below at nn 86–87 and accompanying text.

[72] Syria had acceded to the Protocol for the Prohibition of the Use in War of Asphyxiating, Poisonous or Other Gases and of Bacteriological Methods of Warfare, signed at Geneva on 17 June 1925, on 22 November 1968, and, following its revelation that it had maintained stockpiles of chemical weapons in September 2013, acceded to the Convention on the Prohibition of the Development, Production, Stockpiling and Use of Chemical Weapons and on their Destruction, notifying the UN on 14 September 2013. See Framework for Elimination of Syrian Chemical Weapons, in *Letter dated 19 September 2013 from the Permanent Representatives of the Russian Federation and the United States of America to the United Nations addressed to the Secretary-General*, UN Doc A/68/398–S/2013/565 (24 September 2013) Annex; see also UN Security Council Resolution 2118 (2013), UN Doc S/RES/2118 (2013) (27 September 2013).

[73] OPCW Executive Council decision EC-M-33/DEC.1, *The Destruction of Chemical Weapons* (27 September 2013), available at www.opcw.org/fileadmin/OPCW/EC/M-33/ecm33dec01_e_.pdf, accessed 1 October 2016.

[74] UN Security Council Resolution 2118 (2013), UN Doc S/RES/2118 (2013) (27 September 2013).

[75] See OPCW-UN Joint Mission, available at opcw.unmissions.org/AboutOPCWUNJoint-Mission/MandateandTimelines.aspx, accessed 1 October 2016.

mission—it had a particular function unique to the type of mandate it was given. This function, as discussed, is best described as a 'monitoring' function, in that the Mission was involved with the verification of a particular act or duty.

Alternatively, this particular aspect of the monitoring function of commissions of inquiry may also help to prevent such atrocities by forming a part of the UN's 'preventive diplomacy'.[76] It has previously been acknowledged that the presence of such commissions of inquiry alone can help to diffuse tensions, by showing the parties that the UN is actively seised of the matter.[77] It might also be argued as an extension of this that the presence and existence of a commission of inquiry within a region of tension might encourage compliance with human rights law or international humanitarian law. Indeed, the UN Secretary General has noted the role of investigations in 'preventive diplomacy' as 'helping to shift the calculations of the parties, defuse tensions and build confidence.'[78]

1.7. ALERTING

The monitoring function, however, does not simply encompass missions that oversee and encourage compliance. Commissions of inquiry with a monitoring function may have an additional 'alerting function'.[79] When investigating and monitoring a particular situation, an inquiry is often best positioned to alert the international community to threats to international peace and security, and also to the risk of genocide, war crimes and crimes against humanity, for example. In this sense, the supervisory function may form part of the UN's capacity for a system of 'early warning'.[80] The Secretary General has also noted that these investigations are a method of implementing the 'prevention' aspects of the Responsibility

[76] On the role of 'preventive diplomacy' in the UN, see for example: Report of the Secretary General, *Preventive Diplomacy: Delivering Results*, UN Doc S/2011/552 (26 August 2011), generally, and at para 32.

[77] See, eg Report of the Secretary-General, *An Agenda for Peace: Preventive Diplomacy, Peacemaking and Peacekeeping*, UN Doc A/47/277-S/24111 (17 June 1992) para 25.

[78] *Preventive Diplomacy* Report (n 76).

[79] LJ van den Herik and C Harwood, 'Sharing the Law: The Appeal of International Criminal Law for International Commissions of Inquiry' in S Knuckey and P Alston (eds), *Human Rights and Fact-Finding in the 21st Century* (forthcoming); *Grotius Centre Working Paper No 2014/016-ICL* papers.ssrn.com/sol3/papers.cfm?abstract_id=2387554, accessed 1 October 2016, 8–9.

[80] In 2005, the international community unanimously agreed to 'support the United Nations in establishing an early warning capability': see *2005 World Summit Outcome Document*, UN Doc A/RES/60/1 (15 September 2005) para 138; see also Report of the Secretary General, *Early Warning, Assessment, and the Responsibility to Protect*, UN Doc A/64/864 (14 July 2010) para 10(b).

to Protect,[81] where investigations looking into the human rights situation within a state are able to highlight such violations of fundamental rights as a cause of tension, or a threat of crimes against humanity, or even uncover the early warning signs of genocide or widespread unrest.

One clear example of this function would be the outcome of the commission of inquiry for North Korea.[82] This commission found evidence of widespread violations of human rights, some of which may have amounted to crimes against humanity, conducted by the Democratic People's Republic of Korea.[83] Following the release of the report, the head of the commission, Michael Kirby, made several public statements calling on the international community to take decisive action in response to the findings, and implored states not to let the findings go unnoticed.[84] For the first time in its history, the Security Council voted to formally adopt the human rights situation in North Korea as an item on its agenda.[85]

As a further example, when allegations of the use of chemical weapons arose during the Syrian civil war in early 2013, and then again in August 2013, the 'United Nations Mission to Investigate Allegations of the Use of Chemical Weapons in the Syrian Arab Republic' was the Secretary General's answer to calls for investigation by members of the international community.[86] This particular mission worked alongside the World Health Organisation and the OPCW to investigate several instances of alleged uses of chemical weapons, in particular investigating Syria's compliance with its obligations under international law.[87] These initial investigations helped to confirm and alert the international community to the fact that

[81] Or 'R2P'. See, eg, Report of the Secretary General, *Implementing the Responsibility to Protect*, UN Doc A/63/677 (12 January 2009) paras 52–53.

[82] Human Rights Council, *Report of the Commission of Inquiry on Human Rights in the Democratic People's Republic of Korea*, UN Doc A/HRC/25/63 (7 February 2014).

[83] ibid, paras 24–73. See also *Report of the detailed findings of the commission of inquiry on human rights in the Democratic People's Republic of Korea*, UN Doc A/HRC/25/CRP.1 (7 February 2014).

[84] See, eg *Statement by Mr Michael Kirby Chair of the Commission of Inquiry on Human Rights in the Democratic People's Republic of Korea to the 25th session of the Human Rights Council*, (Geneva, 17 March 2014), available at www.ohchr.org/EN/NewsEvents/Pages/DisplayNews.aspx?NewsID=14385&LangID=E, accessed 1 October 2016.

[85] UN Security Council Verbatim Record, SC Meeting 7353, UN Doc S/PV.7353 (22 December 2014).

[86] See, *Letter dated 22 March 2013 from the Secretary General addressed to the President of the Security Council*, UN Doc S/2013/184 (25 March 2013), available at www.un.org/en/ga/search/view_doc.asp?symbol=S/2013/184, accessed 1 October 2016.

[87] For the Reports of this Mission, see: *Report of the United Nations Mission to Investigate Allegations of the Use of Chemical Weapons in the Syrian Arab Republic on the alleged use of chemical weapons in the Ghouta area of Damascus on 21 August 2013*, UN Doc A/67/997–S/2013/553 (16 September 2013); and Final Report Annexed to, *Identical letters dated 13 December 2013 from the Secretary-General addressed to the President of the General Assembly and the President of the Security Council*, UN Doc A/68/663–S/2013/735 (13 December 2013) Annex.

chemical weapons had been, and were being, used during the civil war in Syria, paving the way for further investigations and operations.[88]

It seems clear, therefore, that commissions of inquiry that undertake a monitoring function thereby may also be in a much better position to 'alert' their founding bodies or the international community in general to ongoing violations of international law, or to the possibility of future violations based upon their findings and observations during an investigation.

1.8. RECOMMENDING

The making of recommendations by a commission of inquiry is a function that is often mandated by the simple phrase asking it to 'make recommendations' relevant to its overall investigatory mandate.[89] Such commissions of inquiry often combine a fact-finding or investigative function with an evaluation of the possible solutions relevant stakeholders might adopt in response to its findings. In fact, on occasion the making of recommendations is done without even being mandated to do so.[90] According to the OHCHR's recent guidance, 'the issuing of recommendations to different entities' has been a task consistently included in the work of commissions of inquiry within the UN, despite the variations in the formulation of mandates.[91] The *scope* and *addressees* of recommendations made by inquiries is also often determined by the inquiry itself rather than the mandate that establishes it.[92] One area that has, in particular, witnessed commissions of inquiry making recommendations is the field of international criminal justice.

1.8.1. International Criminal Justice and the UN Security Council

To explore this function, our discussion will firstly highlight the use of recommendations for the purposes of international criminal justice and how they have been utilised by the UN Security Council, demonstrating the potential scope and impact that recommendations by a commission of inquiry may have.

[88] See above, nn 71–75 and accompanying text.

[89] For example, see below at n 94 and accompanying text, regarding the Commission of Experts for Yugoslavia, where the Secretary General was requested to make appropriate recommendations based upon the findings of the Commission.

[90] This was the case with the Commission of Inquiry for Darfur. See below, nn 112–115 and accompanying text.

[91] OHCHR, *Guidance and Practice* (n 37) 10–11.

[92] OHCHR, *Guidance and Practice* (n 37) 94–99.

When the Security Council established the Commission of Experts for Yugoslavia, this particular commission of inquiry was mandated to examine and analyse evidence relating to breaches of the Geneva Conventions and international humanitarian law committed during the crisis in the former Yugoslavia.[93] Notably, the Secretary General was asked to take into account the conclusions of the Commission when recommending appropriate measures to the Council.[94] Originally, the Secretary General, Member States, and international humanitarian organisations were requested to collate substantiated information relating to these grave violations, and the Secretary General in particular was requested to recommend additional measures that might have been appropriate in light of the information that could be collated.[95] In a Note on the situation of human rights in the former Yugoslavia,[96] the Secretary General highlighted the need for a Commission to investigate the breaches of international humanitarian law, but also highlighted that the multiplicity of international activities in the region was limiting the efficiency of efforts to resolve the crisis.[97] In response to this suggestion, the Security Council then decided to authorise the Secretary General to establish the aforementioned Commission of Experts. It was during the course of the Commission's work that the possibility of holding perpetrators of international criminal law to account was discussed, with the Commission's interim report explicitly suggesting that it was within the Security Council's power to establish an ad hoc international tribunal to prosecute these violations of international humanitarian law, basing its suggestion upon the universality principle.[98]

In the letter accompanying the Commission's interim report to the Council, the Secretary General noted the importance of the Commission's suggestions 'even through the interim report is not the report foreseen in [the Council's original mandate for the Commission]'.[99] The Security Council's response was to agree with the Commission's recommendation and declare that, for the first time in its existence, it would establish an international tribunal for the prosecution of persons responsible for serious violations of international humanitarian law committed in the territory of the former Yugoslavia since 1991.[100] Three months later,

[93] UN Security Council Resolution 780 (1992), UN Doc S/RES/780 (1992) (6 October 1992) para 2.

[94] ibid paras 2–4.

[95] See UN Security Council Resolution 771 (1992), UN Doc S/RES/771 (1992) (13 August 1992) paras 5–6.

[96] Note by the Secretary General, *The Situation of Human Rights in the Territory of the Former Yugoslavia*, UN Docs A/47/418-S/24516 (3 September 1992).

[97] ibid at Section VII and VIII, paras 69–73.

[98] Commission of Experts for Yugoslavia, *Interim Report of the Commission of Experts Established Pursuant to Security Council Resolution 780 (1992)*, UN Doc S/25274 (10 February 1993) Annex, paras 72–74.

[99] ibid 2.

[100] UN Security Council Resolution 808 (1993), UN Doc S/RES/808 (1993) (22 February 1993) para 1.

Resolution 827 (1993)[101] formally established the International Criminal Tribunal for the former Yugoslavia (ICTY) alongside the Statute of the Tribunal. With this development, the task of the initial Commission of Experts was adapted so as to continue collecting the information and evidence that it was originally mandated to, but with the role of the ICTY in mind.[102] This in itself represented a new function for a commission of inquiry—the preparation of evidence and information suitable for use by an international tribunal.[103]

What is perhaps important to note from this series of events is the role that the Commission of Experts played in 'unlocking' a power of the Security Council that had never before been used or perhaps even considered by the Council itself. By making such a recommendation to establish an international tribunal, the Commission changed the way in which the Security Council approached subsequent investigations like this. This is evident from the Council's approach to the subsequent Commission of Experts on Rwanda,[104] and indeed the International Commission of Inquiry for Darfur, as will be discussed below.[105] The Commission of Experts for Rwanda had a very similar mandate to the Commission of Experts for Yugoslavia,[106] but this time with the precedent of the establishment of the ICTY as an undoubtedly relevant consideration. In fact, this precedent had a clear influence on the Commission of Experts, because in its preliminary report on 1 October 1994 it made the following recommendations:

> 150. The Commission of Experts strongly recommends that the Security Council take all necessary and effective action to ensure that the individuals responsible for the serious violations of human rights in Rwanda during the armed conflict triggered on 6 April 1994 are brought to justice before an independent and impartial international criminal tribunal.
>
> …
>
> 152. The Commission of Experts recommends that the Security Council amend the Statute of the International Criminal Tribunal for the former Yugoslavia to ensure that its jurisdiction covers crimes under international law committed during the armed conflict in Rwanda that began on 6 April 1994.[107]

[101] UN Security Council Resolution 827 (1993), UN Doc S/RES/827 (1993) (25 May 1993).
[102] ibid Preamble.
[103] See, in particular, the chapters by Schwöbel Patel and Mariniello in this volume (Chs 6 and 7 respectively).
[104] See below, n 106 and accompanying text.
[105] See below, n 112 and accompanying text.
[106] UN Security Council Resolution 935 (1994), UN Doc S/RES/935 (1994) (1 July 1994).
[107] Commission of Experts for Rwanda, *Preliminary Report of the Independent Commission of Experts Established in accordance with Security Council Resolution 935 (1994)*, UN Doc S/1994/1125 (4 October 1994) Annex, paras 150 and 152.

Following this preliminary report, and prior to the final report of the Commission even reaching the Security Council,[108] Resolution 955 (1994) was adopted on 8 November 1994, establishing the International Criminal Tribunal for Rwanda (ICTR) as a separate UN organ.[109] Thus, the practice of establishing a commission of inquiry in the Security Council had evolved—from the creation of investigations of facts and violations of the law into the establishment of commissions with the added directive to recommend solutions to the situations that they were also investigating.[110]

Since 1994, the ICC has come into existence, and so there is now the possibility of a permanent court being utilised in response to investigations into violations of international humanitarian law and other international crimes. In fact, we witnessed the ICC being used by the Security Council in response to the crisis in Darfur, on the express recommendation of the International Commission of Inquiry on Darfur.[111] This Commission was established on 18 September 2004, at which point it was provided with the mandate by the Security Council to: (i) *investigate* reports of violations of international humanitarian *and* international human rights law in Darfur; (ii) to *determine* whether or not acts of genocide had occurred; and (iii) to *determine* responsibility and *identify* the perpetrators of such violations, with a view to ensuring that those responsible are held accountable.[112] The findings of this Commission[113] ultimately led to the referral of the situation in Darfur to the ICC by the Security Council in Resolution 1593 (2005), even though the Council did not expressly request such recommendations to be made.[114] In fact, the Commission on Darfur did not just recommend measures to the Security Council, but also included a comprehensive set of recommendations relating to what action should be taken by the Sudanese authorities, and indeed other bodies.[115] For example, it was recommended that Sudanese laws be brought into conformity with

[108] For the Final Report, see Commission of Experts for Rwanda, *Final Report of the Commission of Experts established pursuant to Security Council Resolution 935 (1994)*, UN Doc S/1994/1405 (9 December 1994) Annex.

[109] UN Security Council Resolution 955 (1994), UN Doc S/RES/955 (1994) (8 November 1994) and Annex: Statute of the International Tribunal for Rwanda.

[110] For the contribution of commissions of inquiry to international criminal justice and international law see, in particular, Chs 6–10.

[111] *Report of the International Commission of Inquiry on Darfur to the United Nations Secretary-General*, UN Doc S/2005/60, 1 February 2005, Section IV (Accountability Mechanisms) 5–6, and paras 647–49.

[112] See UN Security Council Resolution 1564 (2004), UN Doc S/RES/1564 (2004) (18 September 2004) para 12.

[113] *Report of the International Commission of Inquiry on Darfur to the United Nations Secretary-General*, UN Doc S/2005/60 (1 February 2005) 5.

[114] UN Security Council Resolution 1593 (2005), UN Doc S/RES/1593 (2005) (31 March 2005) para 1.

[115] *Report of the International Commission of Inquiry on Darfur* (n 113) paras 647–53.

human rights standards, and to strengthen the independence and impartiality of the judiciary and confer on courts adequate powers to address human rights violations.[116] Similar recommendations were made in the final report of the Human Rights Council's 2011 commission of inquiry on the situation in Libya, and again in the 2016 report of the investigation established following a breakdown of stability in Libya.[117]

Of course, the practice of international commissions of inquiry making recommendations for courses of action is not limited to Commissions on violations of international criminal law or humanitarian law, but this particular chronology of examples demonstrates most clearly the development of practice since the 1990s. Where the Commissions of Experts for Yugoslavia and Rwanda respectively were touching upon novel ground, we have seen that newer Commissions, such as the one for Darfur, have been employed to develop much more comprehensive recommendations that the Security Council and other international entities can follow.

Such Commissions that are granted the task of offering solutions to international problems seem to be most effective when established by the Security Council, for the simple reason that the Security Council can ensure that states and other parties cooperate fully with them through a legally binding Resolution.[118] However, as we can see by the two commissions of inquiry addressing the situation in Libya, there are of course precedents for commissions having a recommending function when established by entities other than the Security Council.

1.8.2. Other Types of Recommendations

Other types of inquiry utilise the recommending function in different ways, and the types of recommendations made by such inquires can be wide-ranging and far-reaching, addressing any range of bodies from the organ of the United Nations which may have established it, to authorities within a state concerned, or even non-state actors within that state.[119] For

[116] ibid.

[117] *Report of the International Commission of Inquiry to investigate all alleged violations of international human rights law in the Libyan Arab Jamahiriya*, UN Doc A/HRC/17/44 (12 January 2012 (late submission)) paras 258–61; see also *Investigation by the Office of the United Nations High Commissioner for Human Rights on Libya*, UN Doc A/HRC/31/47 (15 February 2016) paras 81–86.

[118] See, eg United Nations Charter, Art 25, where all members are required to accept and carry out the 'decisions' of the Security Council.

[119] See, eg, the 2016 Commission of Inquiry *Report on Libya* (n 117) para 82 which addressed 'all parties to the conflict' when it recommended that they '[d]esist immediately from all violations of international human rights law and international humanitarian law and abuses of human rights…'. The commission of inquiry for Syria has also produced over 12 reports since its inception in 2011, reiterating in its recommendations to 'all parties to the conflict',

example, the UK's Iraq Inquiry (*Chilcot Report*),[120] which was set up to investigate the UK's role in the 2003 Iraq war, was primarily focused on a very context-specific situation, and so did not make 'recommendations' in the traditional sense. Instead, the Chilcot Inquiry's mandate focused on 'lessons' that could be learned from any failings of the UK government in the run up to, and during, the Iraq war—some of which were largely 'recommendatory' in nature in the final report.[121]

The more far-reaching manifestations of the recommending function are particularly evident in commissions of inquiry of a more 'international' nature. The most extreme example may be seen from the recommendations provided by the UN Human Rights Council's Commission of Inquiry for the Democratic People's Republic of Korea (North Korea).[122] After establishing that crimes against humanity have been widespread and systematic throughout North Korea, the Commission provided detailed and extensive recommendations directed at the international community, the relevant UN organs, and the policies of North Korea itself. For example, this Commission recommended that North Korea undergo a profound political and institutional reform,[123] effectively advocating for a complete reestablishment of the state's domestic institutions. It also directed recommendations at China about its refugee policy in the region,[124] and called upon the Security Council to refer the situation to the ICC.[125] In response, China refused to recognise the jurisdiction of the Commission and the findings of the report.[126]

Other commissions of inquiry, for example the Goldstone Report (United Nations Fact-Finding Mission on the Gaza Conflict), have included recommendations of a similarly extensive nature.[127] In particular, the Goldstone Report recommended that Israel should initiate a review of the rules of engagement, standard operating procedures, open fire regulations and

but also directly addressing recommendations to 'anti-government armed groups' to 'repudiate extreme elements and apply effective leverage for compliance with international law': see eg *Report of the Independent International Commission of Inquiry on the Syrian Arab Republic*, UN Doc A/HRC/31/68 (11 February 2016) paras 153–55 and 157; see also OHCHR, *Guidance and Practice* (n 37) 94–99.

120 *Chilcot Report* (n 40) Executive Summary.

121 *Chilcot Report* (n 40) 129–41.

122 See Human Rights Council, *Report of the Commission of Inquiry on Human Rights in the Democratic People's Republic of Korea*, UN Doc A/HRC/25/63 (7 February 2014) (*Report on DPRK*).

123 *Report on DPRK* (n 122) para 89.

124 *Report on DPRK* (n 122) para 90.

125 *Report on DPRK* (n 122) para 94.

126 *Report on DPRK* (n 122) Annex II, Correspondence with China, paras 33–36.

127 Human Rights Council, *Report of the United Nations Fact-Finding Mission on the Gaza Conflict*, UN Doc A/HRC/12/48 (25 September 2009) Chapter XXXI (hereinafter, *Goldstone Report*).

other guidance for military and security personnel.[128] Furthermore, as Israel itself noted,[129] the report called for an urgent discussion on the 'future legality of the use of certain munitions'[130] and in doing so also called upon on Israel to 'undertake a moratorium in the use of such weapons.'[131] Clearly, these are far-reaching recommendations that not only address issues of international law, in particular the methods and means of warfare, but also specifically call upon a sovereign state to either alter or review their behavior in this regard.

Responses to such reports have varied. Israel, in response to the Goldstone Report, completely rejected that report's conclusions and findings.[132] However, the DPRK responded to the commission of inquiry on the human rights situation within the state with the suggestion that the report was 'a product of political confrontation and a plot against the DPRK', and part of politically motivated action by states to 'behave as "human rights judges" trampling on the sovereignty and interfering in the internal affairs of those countries they dislike.'[133] Such responses inevitably call into question the effectiveness and place of the recommending function of commissions of inquiry in certain circumstances—with some bodies producing non-binding reports, we need to ask what is the place of these recommendations and how effective are the subsequent follow-up procedures? Some commissions of inquiry, established to investigate a topic of controversy, are the result of a failure to find unity in the Security Council—thus producing reports and recommendations that would not perhaps have the same political and legal weight as those backed by the Security Council itself. Nonetheless, the making of recommendations, regardless of if and how they are taken up and implemented, feeds into the discourse surrounding a particular incident or situation. While this may seem like they are meddling in the internal affairs of a state to some, it certainly provides an interesting focal point in the accountability process for others.

[128] *Goldstone Report* (n 127) para 1972(c).

[129] See Israel's Initial Response (n 132) 23–24.

[130] *Goldstone Report* (n 127) para 1971(d).

[131] *Goldstone Report* (n 127) para 1971(d).

[132] See, eg, Israel Ministry of Foreign Affairs, *Initial Response to Report of the Fact Finding Mission on Gaza Established Pursuant to Resolution S-9/1 of the Human Rights Council* (24 September 2009), available at mfa.gov.il/MFA_Graphics/MFA%20Gallery/Documents/GoldstoneReportInitialResponse240909.pdf, accessed 1 October 2016.

[133] See, *Letter dated 3 February 2014 from the Permanent Representative of the Democratic People's Republic of Korea to the United Nations Office at Geneva addressed to the President of the Human Rights Council*, UN Doc A/HRC/25/G/6 (12 February 2014) 1 and 4; see also, eg, 'North Korea: We totally reject the UN report' (*USA Today* 18 February 2014), available at www.usatoday.com/story/opinion/2014/02/18/democratic-peoples-republic-of-korea-editorials-debates/5591393/, accessed 1 October 2016.

1.9. CONCLUDING THOUGHTS

From the above it might be said that a metamorphosis has occurred in the overriding function of commissions of inquiry, for while traditional commissions 'aimed to conciliate and pacify', contemporary commissions seek to 'condemn and provoke'.[134] Yet, while we might be able to identify a change in the contexts in which they are established, the entities that establish them, the personnel involved, the legal basis for their establishment, and their overall outcome aims, these changes have simply meant that the functional typology of commissions of inquiry has broadened as necessary over the centuries, thus increasing their versatility and utility, as opposed to representing a single type of commission of inquiry that has simply changed in nature.

This fragmentation in the functions of commissions of inquiry is not new, and will arguably continue, but may well have an impact upon the coherence of international law, with so many different bodies providing interpretations of relatively few legal frameworks. While calls for a permanent commission of inquiry may well be made in response to this, given the various functions identified it would be difficult, if not impossible, to have a 'one size fits all' commission of inquiry, and would not in any event prevent states from simply establishing them as and when they felt inclined to do so. In this respect, despite problem it is perhaps wiser to continue having various commissions of inquiry established by different bodies and then to accord them the legitimacy that they deserve, in particular through an assessment of their independence, impartiality, membership, the constructive interpretation of their mandate, the quality of the reasoning and handling of the law, and the recommendations, if any, that are made.

[134] LJ van den Herik, 'An Inquiry into the Role of Commissions of Inquiry in International Law: Navigating the Tensions between Fact-Finding and Application of International Law' (2014) 13 *Chinese Journal of International Law* 507.

2

Hegemony and Counter-Hegemony: The Politics of Establishing United Nations Commissions of Inquiry

MICHELLE FARRELL AND BEN MURPHY

2.1. INTRODUCTION

THIS CHAPTER IS concerned with the interplay between law and politics in the establishment of commissions of inquiry by United Nations (UN) institutions, particularly by the Security Council and the Human Rights Council.[1] Frulli notes that 'in recent years, there has been a gradual shift and many UN commissions of inquiry—even those that were mainly tasked with the investigation of alleged violations of international humanitarian law—have been established by the Human Rights Council and not by the Security Council'.[2] It is true to say that the Human Rights Council has become increasingly prolific in the establishment of commissions of inquiry. 2014 was its most active year to date; it established five commissions in relation to alleged human rights violations in the Central African Republic,[3] Sri Lanka,[4] Eritrea,[5] Iraq (with abuses committed by the so-called Islamic State specifically targeted)[6] and, most controversially, in relation to the ongoing situation in the Occupied Palestinian Territory.[7] It is not at all clear, however, that this proliferation of Human Rights Council-established commissions is the result of some kind of 'shift', as Frulli suggests. The Security Council has not, it seems, consciously delegated responsibility for establishing commissions to the

[1] Where relevant, we will also address commissions of inquiry established both by the General Assembly and the Secretary General.
[2] M Frulli, 'Fact-Finding or Paving the Road to Criminal Justice? Some Reflections on United Nations Commissions of Inquiry' (2012) 10 *Journal of International Criminal Justice* 1323, 1323.
[3] UN Human Rights Council Resolution S-20/1 (20 January 2014).
[4] UN Human Rights Council Resolution 25/1 (27 March 2014).
[5] UN Human Rights Council Resolution 26/24 (26 June 2014).
[6] UN Human Rights Council Resolution S-22/1 (1 September 2014).
[7] UN Human Rights Council Resolution S-21/1 (23 July 2014).

Human Rights Council, nor has the Human Rights Council wrestled this function out of the arms of the Security Council; it is also not clear or obvious that the Security Council is unwilling to establish commissions of inquiry when political context allows.[8] Van den Herik contemplates the contextual possibilities at play in the proliferation of Human Rights Council-established commissions of inquiry vis-à-vis the Security Council. She points out:

> It may in fact also be that, occasionally, these Geneva-based commissions rather function as a correction mechanism to New York dynamics and in particular to a paralysed Security Council. In such a case, they would represent public opinion and have the *de facto* aim to express condemnation, to present a compelling conflict narrative so as to counter the Security Council inaction or to elicit alternative involvement by the International Criminal Court.[9]

Following van den Herik's line of argument, this suggests that the increased activity of the Human Rights Council in this area may stem from the fact that the Security Council is *unable* to establish a commission of inquiry, as opposed to it being *unwilling*. To draw this out further, in certain cases, the Security Council may be unable to establish a commission of inquiry because of the unwillingness of *individual* members of the Council. In this light, the increased activity of the Human Rights Council could potentially even be viewed as a form of institutional burden sharing.

All this is not to say, however, that the identity of the institution or office establishing a commission of inquiry is irrelevant. Far from it; the establishing institution will potentially have a great impact on how a commission is perceived, and ultimately upon the ability of a commission to realise its mandate. This is best illustrated by the juxtaposition between the perception of the Human Rights Council in this regard and that of other UN institutions and offices. The commission-establishing activity of the Human Rights Council is greeted in the (admittedly minimal) literature with great suspicion. Commentators tend to view the proliferation of commissions established by the Human Rights Council as a highly politicised activity. These commissions are often criticised on the grounds of being 'selective' and holding a 'biased mandate'. These accusations allege that the commissions depart from the impartiality requirement central to the Hague Convention[10] and to other more recent pronouncements

[8] See eg, UN Security Council Resolution 1564 (18 September 2004) (establishing commission of inquiry for Darfur).

[9] LJ van den Herik, 'An Inquiry into the Role of Commissions of Inquiry in International Law: Navigating the Tensions between Fact-Finding and Application of International Law' (2014) 13 *Chinese Journal of International Law* 507, 528.

[10] The Preamble to Hague Convention XIII (1907) declares that 'it is, for neutral Powers, an admitted duty to apply these rules impartially to the several belligerents'. Art 9 of the same Convention reads: 'A neutral Power must apply impartially to the two belligerents the conditions, restrictions, or prohibitions made by it in regard to the admission into its ports, roadsteads, or territorial waters, of belligerent war-ships or of their prizes.'

on such commissions, such as the General Assembly Declaration on Fact-finding.[11] The 2009 UN Fact-Finding Mission on the Gaza Conflict, or Goldstone Commission, for example, came under fire in these respects,[12] as did the 2014 Gaza commission.[13] Other commissions have also been criticised along the same lines, particularly the International Commission of Inquiry on Libya[14] and the International Commission of Inquiry on the Syrian Arab Republic.[15] To a great extent, these criticisms echo those made more generally of the Human Rights Council and of its predecessor, the Commission on Human Rights. Criticisms levelled at the Human Rights Council may not be unjustified per se, but it is extremely difficult to distinguish the Human Rights Council from any other international institution as regards so-called politicisation. Yet, commissions of inquiry established by the Secretary General or the Security Council do not tend to receive comparable levels of criticism. On the one hand, the Security Council may be deemed the most authoritative UN institution to establish such inquiries, vested as it is with the power to make decisions that are binding on the international community at large.[16] On the other hand, the Security Council is itself constantly criticised for its unrepresentative permanent membership and its veto power. This begs the question: why does the Security Council—itself an overtly political institution—escape the charges directed at the Human Rights Council—also an overtly political institution—when it comes to the establishment of commissions of inquiry?

In this chapter we hypothesise that the different reactions to UN institutions in their commission-establishing activity can be understood as a challenge to the legitimacy of the Human Rights Council, whilst the legitimacy of the Security Council or of the Secretary General is not similarly challenged. This legitimacy challenge is levelled both at the lawfulness of the Human Rights Council's establishment of such commissions and at the procedures by which they are established. We argue that the charge of

[11] UN General Assembly Resolution 46/59, *Declaration on Fact-finding by the United Nations in the Field of the Maintenance of International Peace and Security 1991* (9 December 1991) (hereafter *Declaration on Fact-finding*).

[12] See eg, Frulli (n 2) 1334. See also A Jachec Neale, 'Human Rights Fact-Finding into Armed Conflict and Breaches of the Laws of War' (2011) 105 *Proceedings of the Annual Meeting (American Society of International Law)* 85, 86.

[13] See eg, J Weiler, 'Editorial: After Gaza 2014: Schabas' (2014) 25(3) *European Journal of International Law* 641, 641–43.

[14] See eg, KJ Heller, 'The International Commission of Inquiry on Libya: A Critical Analysis' in J Meierhenrich (ed) *International Commissions: The Role of Commissions of Inquiry in the Investigation of International Crimes* (Oxford, Oxford University Press, forthcoming), available at SSRN: ssrn.com/abstract=2123782, accessed 4 August 2016.

[15] See eg, T Marauhn, 'Sailing Close to the Wind: Human Rights Council Fact-Finding in Situations of Armed Conflict—The Case of Syria' (2013) 43(2) *California Western International Law Journal* 401, 455.

[16] UN Charter (1945), Art 25.

a legitimacy-deficit levelled at the Human Rights Council but not at the Security Council is itself evidence of a form of politicisation, which can best be understood as an acceptance and perpetuation of the hegemonic order that exists within the UN. In order to establish our hypothesis and to test our argument, in section 2.2, we provide the background to and the legal basis for the establishment of commissions of inquiry across the UN institutions. In section 2.3, we consider the commentary on UN commissions of inquiry, especially those established by the Human Rights Council, to establish the variations in reaction to the institutions. With this in mind, in section 2.4, we contextualise this commentary as a legitimacy challenge and undertake an examination of the meaning of legitimacy as it concerns the Commission-establishing activity of the Human Rights Council. As our examination focuses on the establishment of commissions of inquiry, we limit our discussion to so-called 'input legitimacy'. Finally, we argue that this legitimacy critique of the Human Rights Council is actually best understood as discomfort with the counter-hegemonic challenge posed by this increasingly active body.

2.2. THE LEGAL BASIS FOR ESTABLISHING COMMISSIONS OF INQUIRY

Commissions of inquiry are not a particularly new phenomenon in international law.[17] Their introduction onto the international landscape can be traced to the *Maine* inquiries, which were established by both the United States and Spain following the sinking of the US battleship, Maine, in 1898.[18] In the aftermath of that incident, commissions of inquiry were viewed as a means of pre-empting exacerbation of a conflict and clarifying facts.[19] The legal genesis of international commissions of inquiry as a construct of dispute settlement can be found in the 1899 Hague Convention. According to the Hague Convention, the function of the commission of inquiry is to 'facilitate a solution of disputes by elucidating the facts by means of an impartial and conscientious investigation'.[20] By the time of the adoption of the UN Charter in 1945, at least two functions of commissions of inquiry were apparent. First, Article 33 of the Charter lists 'enquiry' as one mechanism amongst a number of other forms of dispute settlement that the Security Council may call upon states to engage in, in the event of such a dispute. As such, commissions of inquiry have been established

[17] For a good historic overview see JG Merrills, *International Dispute Settlement* (3rd edn, Cambridge, Cambridge University Press 1998) 44.

[18] van den Herik (n 9) 511; C Henderson, 'Commissions of Inquiry: Flexible Temporariness or Permanent Predictability?' (2014) 45 *Netherlands Yearbook of International Law* 287, 288.

[19] van den Herik (n 9) 511.

[20] Convention for the Pacific Settlement of International Disputes, Art 9 (adopted 29 July 1899, entered into force 4 September 1900).

as free-standing dispute resolution processes between states. The General Assembly has also repeatedly promoted the use of fact-finding as a means of dispute settlement for states.[21] Second, commissions of inquiries have increasingly been established by international institutions, in accordance with the broadening functions of international organisations generally, most notably the UN. The introduction of UN commissions of inquiry should be understood in the context of the 'march towards international institutionalisation that marked the turn of the century'.[22] Xiaodan has contextualised the rise in the resort to commissions of inquiry in light of the end of the Cold War. According to Xiaodan, the UN 'with a renewed sense of responsibility for international legal accountability and civilian protection'[23] has acknowledged the importance of timely and accurate knowledge of all relevant facts and has progressively employed fact-finding mechanisms when exercising its functions in relation to the maintenance of international peace and security and the protection of human rights.[24]

This institutionalisation of fact-finding practice was recognised and encouraged in the 1991 General Assembly Declaration on Fact-finding by the UN. Article 1 declares:

> In performing their functions in relation to the maintenance of international peace and security, the competent organs of the United Nations should endeavour to have full knowledge of all relevant facts. To this end they should consider undertaking fact-finding activities.[25]

The Declaration asserts that formal fact-finding commissions 'may be undertaken by the Security Council, General Assembly and Secretary General, in the context of their respective responsibilities for the maintenance of peace and security in accordance with the Charter'.[26] The primary

[21] See eg, General Assembly Resolution 2329 (XXII) (18 December 1967), para 1, which 'Urges Member States to make more effective use of the existing methods of fact-finding'.

[22] van den Herik (n 9) 510. See generally, D Kennedy, 'The Move to Institutions' (1987) 8 *Cardozo Law Review* 841.

[23] W Xiaodan, 'Quality Control and the Selection of Members of International Fact-Finding Mandates' in M Bergsmo (ed), *Quality Control in Fact-Finding* (Torkel Opsahl Academic EPublisher, 2013) 194. See also M Aksenova and M Bergsmo, 'Non-Criminal Justice Fact-Work in the Age of Accountability' in M Bergsmo (ed), *Quality Control in Fact-Finding* (Torkel Opsahl Academic EPublisher, 2013) 1, who argue that: 'The mounting reliance on fact-finding in international law can be explained by several factors, including generally increased expectations of accountability and some limitations in the emerging international criminal justice system', and Henderson (n 18) at 289, who opines that the rise in the establishment of commissions of inquiry 'perhaps represent[s] an important shift in the *modus operandi* of the international community in seeking at least some accountability for violations of international law'.

[24] Xiaodan (n 23) 194.

[25] *Declaration on Fact-finding* (n 11) para 1.

[26] *Declaration on Fact-finding* (n 11) para 7. See also Report of the Secretary General, *Agenda for Peace, Preventive Diplomacy, Peace-making and Peacekeeping*, UN Doc A/47/277 (17 June 1992) para 25(c).

organs of the UN have thus interpreted their competences so as to establish commissions of inquiry on an ad hoc basis; however, their precise constitutional basis under the Charter perhaps invites greater scrutiny.

At first glance, the legal basis for the establishment of commissions of inquiry may appear to be Article 7(2) of the Charter, which provides for the establishment of subsidiary organs by the principal organs of the UN. Although the term 'subsidiary organ' is not defined in the Charter,[27] there is some support for the proposition that certain commissions of inquiry may constitute subsidiary organs for the purposes of Article 7(2).[28] Indeed, commissions of inquiry—at least those established by the General Assembly, Security Council and the Secretary General—apparently meet Sarooshi's two preconditions for the lawful establishment of a UN subsidiary organ: they are established by a principal organ of the UN, and they are under the authority and control of a principal organ.[29] However, having said that, it is not insignificant that all commissions of inquiry established by the Human Rights Council fall outside of the above definition; the Human Rights Council is, after all, not a principal organ of the UN.[30] In addition, as Lippold and Paulus note, although Article 7(2) constitutes a 'constitutional authority' for establishing subsidiary organs, 'the power to create them is not unlimited. Rather it depends on the power and competences of the Organization and of the respective organ'.[31] It is therefore necessary to explore the legal competences, both express and implied,

[27] See, *Repertory of Practice of United Nations Organs (1945–54)* vol 1, 224, which points out that the term 'subsidiary organ' has not been defined by any organ of the UN, but, in the practice of the organisation, 'such expressions as "commissions", "committees", "subsidiary organs", and "subsidiary bodies" have been used interchangeably'. See also, General Assembly Resolution 231 (III) (8 October 1948), App A, which lists as subsidiary organs 'commissions of inquiry or conciliation as instituted by the General Assembly or Security Council'.

[28] See, specifically, E Fromageau, 'Collaborating with the United Nations: Does Flexibility Imply Informality?' (2010) 7 *International Organizations Law Review* 405, 417–18, who states that recent commissions established by the Secretary General 'were presumably created on the basis of Article 7(2) of the UN Charter'. See further, M Lippold and A Paulus, 'Article 7', in B Simma et al (eds), *The Charter of the United Nations: A Commentary* (3rd edn, Oxford, Oxford University Press, 2012), who list 'UN Observer Missions in areas of international conflict or civil war, in particular those verifying the implementation of ceasefire, armistice or peace agreements or monitoring human rights situations, *or for other fact-finding purposes*', among the 'typical categories' of subsidiary organs.

[29] D Sarooshi, 'The Legal Framework Governing United Nations Subsidiary Organs' (1996) 67 *British Yearbook of International Law* 413, 416.

[30] Notwithstanding comments of the President of the Human Rights Council that 'at the next institutional review in 2021, mandated by the General Assembly, UN member States should make it a primary organ of the UN, because politically … it has somewhat "outgrown" its current role of a subsidiary organ of the General Assembly', the Council obviously does not currently enjoy this status. See, Human Rights Council, *Statement attributable to President of the Human Rights Council, Ambassador Joachim Ruecker (Germany) 21 December 2015*, (21 December 2015), available at www.ohchr.org/EN/NewsEvents/Pages/DisplayNews.aspx?NewsID=16912&LangID=E#sthash.gW5plKcT.dpuf, accessed 4 August 2016.

[31] Lippold and Paulus (n 28).

of the individual UN institutions, in order to ascertain whether they are vested with the legal competence to establish commissions of inquiry. In the following sections, we will address the legal competences of the Security Council, General Assembly, Secretary General and Human Rights Council in turn.

2.2.1. The Security Council

The Security Council is the only primary organ of the UN that has been expressly vested with an inquiry competence. Under Article 34 of the Charter, the Security Council

> may investigate any dispute, or any situation which might lead to international friction or give rise to a dispute, in order to determine whether the continuance of the dispute or situation is likely to endanger the maintenance of international peace and security.

The wording of Article 34 appears to suggest that the provision only authorises the Security Council to establish whether these preconditions exist.[32] However, the Security Council clearly regards itself as having broader powers to engage in fact-finding missions that stray beyond the parameters of Article 34, and it is accepted that the Security Council is empowered to acquire information by other means of investigation and for purposes other than those mentioned in Article 34.[33] In any event, as a result of the potentially restrictive nature of Article 34, the provision has largely fallen into disuse in the Security Council's contemporary practice of establishing commissions. In fact, the Security Council has only established a commission of inquiry explicitly through this mechanism in two cases: the Commission of Investigation on Greek Frontier Incidents[34] and the Commission of Inquiry for India and Pakistan.[35]

[32] van den Herik (n 9) 524, refers to the restrictive nature of Art 34 in order to explain the limited use of the Art 34 mechanism. According to this interpretation, the Security Council's investigative power under Chapter VI can only be used to determine competence, ie to determine whether a given situation is of such a nature that it merits Security Council engagement. According to this reasoning, any investigatory mandate that is broader than this procedural question would therefore be outside the scope of Art 34.

[33] See generally, EL Kerley, 'The Powers of Investigation of the United Nations Security Council' (1961) 55 *American Journal of International Law* 892, 905. Kerley focuses particularly on the Provisional Rules of Procedure of the Security Council, specifically citing r 28, which states that the Security Council 'may appoint a commission or committee or a rapporteur for a specified question' (and provides no other procedural limitations) and r 39, which empowers the Security Council to 'invite members of the Secretariat *or other persons, whom it considers competent for the purpose,* to supply it with information or to give it other assistance in examining matters within its competence' (emphasis added).

[34] UN Security Council Resolution 15 (19 December 1946).

[35] UN Security Council Resolution 39 (20 January 1948).

The Security Council has, instead, relied on its implied powers in order to establish commissions of inquiry. Under Article 29, for example, the Security Council may 'establish subsidiary organs as it deems necessary for the performance of its functions'. This provision, conceivably, grants the Security Council the authority to determine that the establishment of commissions is necessary for the performance of its Charter-derived functions and that this, in turn, entitles it to assign investigative functions to such subsidiary organs.[36] Arguably, the Security Council may also find the authority to establish commissions of inquiry under Article 39, in order to ascertain whether the pre-conditions for determining the existence of a 'threat to the peace, breach of the peace or act of aggression' have been fulfilled.[37] However, the Security Council generally avoids a precise indication of the Charter-basis for its decision to establish a commission of inquiry and, instead, seemingly assumes, under a broad interpretation of its implied powers, that it has a mandate to do so. The implied powers theory was accepted by the International Court of Justice in the *Reparations* case, where the Court held that UN member states have entrusted certain functions to the Security Council and 'have clothed it with the competence required to enable those functions to be effectively discharged.'[38] In addition, the Court held that:

> The rights and duties of an entity such as the Organization must depend upon its purposes and functions as specified or implied in its constituent documents and developed in practice…Under international law, the Organization must be deemed to have those powers which, though not expressly provided in the Charter, are conferred upon it by necessary implication, as being essential to the performance of its duties.[39]

It has been accepted, therefore, that the Security Council, by using its implied powers, has a general competence to establish commissions of inquiry.[40]

2.2.2. The General Assembly

Unlike the Security Council, the General Assembly is not granted an express investigatory competence, although its ability to 'establish

[36] See eg, T Schweisfurth, 'Article 34' in B Simma, *The Charter of the United Nations: A Commentary* (2nd edn, Oxford, Oxford University Press, 2002) 596.

[37] Schweisfurth (n 36) 595–96.

[38] *Reparations Suffered in the Service of the United Nations* (Advisory Opinion) [1949] ICJ Rep 174, 179.

[39] ibid 180–82.

[40] Schweisfurth (n 36) 595–96.

such subsidiary organs as it deems necessary for the performance of its functions' is reaffirmed in Article 22. The General Assembly also has a subsidiary role—to the Security Council—in the maintenance of international peace and security. Under Article 11(2) of the Charter, for example, the General Assembly may 'discuss any questions relating to the maintenance of international peace and security brought before it by any Member of the United Nations, or by the Security Council, or by a state which is not a Member of the United Nations…' As Klein and Schmahl put it,

> the importance of Article 11(2) … lies in the fact that it assigns to the [General Assembly] a share of the responsibility to counter breaches of the peace or imminent threats to the peace as quickly and effectively as possible by giving the [Security Council] a chance to act.[41]

The provision confirms the common responsibility of the two organs in maintaining peace and security and, arguably, does so in a pragmatic way which recognises the possibility of Security Council political paralysis or simple inaction, for whatever reason.[42] With the explicit limitation under Article 1—stipulating the primary responsibility of the Security Council in the maintenance of peace and security—the General Assembly is further authorised by Article 14 to 'recommend measures for the peaceful adjustment of any situation'. This provision would certainly provide the scope for the use of fact-finding machinery and, in practice, the General Assembly has established commissions of inquiry on a variety of occasions.[43] The legal basis of the General Assembly to establish commissions of inquiry is, therefore, not questioned. However, in recent times, since its establishment in 2006, the Human Rights Council, itself a subsidiary organ of the General Assembly, has formed the majority of commissions of inquiry.[44]

[41] E Klein and S Schmahl, 'The General Assembly Function and Powers, Article 11' in Simma (n 28).

[42] ibid.

[43] UN General Assembly Resolution 616 A (VII) (5 December 1952) (investigating the politics of apartheid in South Africa); UN General Assembly Resolution 1601 (VX) (15 April 1961) (investigating the circumstances surrounding the death of Patrice Lumumba, the first legally elected prime minister of the Democratic Republic of Congo); UN General Assembly Resolution 1628 (XVI) (26 October 1961) (investigating the circumstances surrounding the deaths of Secretary General Dag Hammerskjöld and 15 UN officials in 1961); UN General Assembly Resolution 1627 (XVI) (23 October 1961) (investigating and the assassination of the prime minister of Burundi in the same year). See generally, van den Herik (n 9) 525.

[44] See text at section 2.2.4 (on the legal basis of these commissions) and section 2.3 (on how these commissions have been received).

2.2.3. The Secretary General

The Declaration on Fact-finding encourages the Security Council and the General Assembly to entrust the establishment of commissions of inquiry to the Secretary General:

> The Security Council and the General Assembly should, in deciding to whom to entrust the conduct of a fact-finding mission, give preference to the Secretary-General, who may, inter alia, designate a special representative or a group of experts reporting to him. Resort to an ad hoc subsidiary body of the Security Council or the General Assembly may also be encouraged.[45]

The formal legal basis for such requests lies in Article 98 of the Charter, which states that the Secretary General 'shall perform such other functions as are entrusted to him by [primary] organs'. While the Secretary General is the 'chief administrative officer' of the UN,[46] such 'other functions' are seemingly not limited to administrative matters, but have been interpreted to include non-administrative and political duties as well.[47] The Security Council, in particular, has resorted to this approach on a number of occasions to establish commissions of inquiry.[48]

In addition, the Secretary General may, under Article 99, 'bring to the attention of the Security Council any matter which in his opinion may threaten the maintenance of international peace and security'.[49] It is accepted that Article 99 not only confers upon the Secretary General a right to bring matters to the attention of the Security Council, but that this right carries with it a broad discretion to conduct inquiries unilaterally and to engage in informal diplomatic activity in regard to matters which may threaten the maintenance of international peace and security.[50] The Declaration on Fact-finding also acknowledges the Secretary General's freestanding role: it states that the Secretary General should consider using fact-finding 'to contribute to the prevention of disputes and situations'[51] and that the Secretary General, 'on his own initiative or at the request of

[45] *Declaration on Fact-finding* (n 11) para 15.

[46] UN Charter (1945), Art 97.

[47] MC Bourloyannis, 'Fact-finding by the Secretary-General of the United Nations' (1991) 22 *New York Journal of International Law and Politics* 641, 645.

[48] See eg, UN Security Council Resolution 780 (6 October1992) (establishing commission of inquiry for the former Yugoslavia); UN Security Council Resolution 885 (16 November 1993) (establishing commission of inquiry for Somalia); UN Security Council Resolution 935 (July 1994) (establishing commission of inquiry for Rwanda); UN Security Council Resolution 1564 (18 September 2004) (establishing commission of inquiry for Darfur).

[49] UN Charter (1945), Art 99.

[50] See, EA Plunkett, 'UN Fact-Finding as a Means of Settling Disputes' (1968) 9 *Virginia Journal of International Law* 154, 172; *cf* van den Herik (n 9) 525, who suggests that the Secretary General's inquiry competence is 'implied and ad-hoc'.

[51] *Declaration on Fact-finding* (n 11) para 12.

the States concerned, should consider undertaking a fact-finding mission when a dispute or a situation exists'.[52]

Fact-finding initiatives by the Secretary General have derived, in most cases, from this expansive interpretation of Article 99.[53] The broad but practical interpretation of Article 99 given by Trygve Lie, the United Nations' first Secretary General, first provided a foundation for the extensive practice of fact-finding on the initiative of the Secretary General:

> I hope that the Council will understand that the Secretary-General must reserve his right to make such enquiries or investigations as he may think necessary, in order to determine whether or not he should consider bringing any aspect of this matter to the attention of the Council, under the provisions of the Charter.[54]

Thirty-six years after Trygve Lie's expansive interpretation of Article 99, Secretary General Javier Perez de Cuellar announced his intent to expand further the Secretary General's fact-finding capabilities:

> In order to avoid the Security Council becoming involved too late in critical situations, it may well be that the Secretary-General should play a more forthright role in bringing potentially dangerous situations to the attention of the Council within the general framework of Article 99 of the Charter … In order to carry out effectively the preventive role foreseen for the Secretary-General under Article 99, I intend to develop a wider and more systematic capacity for fact-finding in potential conflict areas.[55]

In fact, writing in 1991, Bourloyannis opined that 'the Secretary-General has been by far the most active in this field [fact-finding]—both by fulfilling various mandates entrusted to him by other UN organs' and by undertaking fact-finding activities on his own initiative'.[56]

2.2.4. The Human Rights Council

The Secretary General may, in the past, have been the most active office in the establishment of commissions of inquiry; however, that is most certainly no longer the case. Charter and treaty-based human rights bodies have frequently established commissions of inquiry to investigate alleged human rights abuses, with the Human Rights Council being most active in this regard. Under the former Commission on Human Rights, fact finding was developed under the auspices of the UN Economic and Social Council

52 *Declaration on Fact-finding* (n 11) para 13.

53 See, generally, Bourloyannis (n 47) 646–47.

54 Security Council Official Records (1st session, 70th meeting) (20 September 1948) 404.

55 *Report of the Secretary-General on the Work of the Organization* General Assembly Official Records (37th session, supp 1) (7 September 1982) UN Doc A/37/1, at 3.

56 Bourloyannis (n 47) 646.

through special procedures, including rapporteurs, working groups and expert committees.[57] The Human Rights Council, which replaced the Commission in 2006, has developed—expanded even—this practice.

On the one hand, the specific legal competence of the Human Rights Council to establish commissions of inquiry is not immediately apparent. Express provision was not included in the mandate of the former Commission on Human Rights. Likewise, explicit authorisation to establish commissions of inquiry is not included either in the constitutive instrument of the Human Rights Council[58] or in the resolution setting out its working practices.[59] However, on the other hand, the authority of the Human Rights Council to establish commissions of inquiry can perhaps be readily inferred from its functions and from its status as a subsidiary body of the General Assembly. At least three primary observations stand to support this proposition. First, in accordance with its founding resolution, the Human Rights Council is mandated 'to address situations of violations of human rights, including gross and systemic violations, and make recommendations thereon'.[60] This mandate is arguably reliant upon an investigatory function. Second, it is accepted that the Council 'assume[d] the mandates, mechanisms, functions and responsibilities of the Commission'.[61] The competence of the Commission's parent organ, the Economic and Social Council to establish commissions of inquiry is expressly supported by the Charter;[62] widespread scholarly opinion would suggest that this extended to the Commission, and there is no reason to suggest that the Human Rights Council has not inherited this competence.[63] Finally, the Human Rights Council was set up as a subsidiary body of the General Assembly—unlike the Commission, which was established under the Economic and Social Council. It is no great leap to suggest that the Human Rights Council, therefore, shares the functions of the General Assembly, including its residual responsibility for international peace and security and its authority to establish commissions of inquiry.[64]

[57] ECOSOC Res 1503 (XLVIII) (27 May 1990), subsequently revised by ECOSOC Res 2000/3 (19 June 2000). See generally, C Chinkin, 'UN Human Rights Council Fact-Finding Missions: Lessons from Gaza' in MH Arsanjani, J Cogan, RD Sloane and S Wiessner (eds) *Looking to the Future: Essays on International Law in Honor of W Michael Reisman* (Martinus Nijhoff, 2010) 479–80.

[58] UN General Assembly Resolution 60/251 (3 April 2006)

[59] UN Human Rights Council Resolution 5/1 (18 June 2007).

[60] UN General Assembly Resolution 60/251 (3 April 2006) para 6.

[61] ibid.

[62] UN Charter (1945), Art 68 states that: 'The Economic and Social Council shall set up commissions in economic and social fields and for the promotion of human rights, and such other commissions as may be required for the performance of its functions'.

[63] See eg, F Ermacora, 'The Competence and Functions of Fact-Finding Bodies' in BG Ramcharan (ed), *International Law and Fact-Finding in the Field of Human Rights* (Martinus Nijhoff, 1982, revised and reprinted 2014) 86; R Miller, 'United Nations Fact-Finding Missions in the Field of Human Rights' (1973) 1970-3 *Australian Yearbook of International Law* 40, 43–44.

[64] Chinkin (n 57) 481.

Going further, Chinkin locates the authority of the Human Rights Council to establish fact-finding inquiries in the connection between human rights and international peace and security.[65] This linkage is present in the Charter and is reiterated clearly in the Preamble to the Human Rights Council's constitutive resolution, where the General Assembly '[acknowledges] that peace and security, development and human rights are the pillars of the United Nations system and the foundations for collective security and well-being, and [recognises] that development, peace and security and human rights are interlinked and mutually reinforcing'.[66] Chinkin also relies on the theory of implied powers and endorses Emacora's (we submit authoritative) observation that:

> International organizations possess an implied power to establish fact-finding bodies if the statute [or other constitutive instrument] of the international organization allows it to conclude that the investigation of facts is a pre-condition for fulfilling accurately the main function of the organization.[67]

In summary, then, the legal basis for the establishment of fact-finding bodies or commissions of inquiry derives primarily from the assumption of such invested authority under various provisions of the Charter by three of the primary organs of the UN. The Human Rights Council has, similarly, assumed such authority even though it is not expressly provided. However, while the legal basis behind their establishment is, as we have shown, not always particularly straightforward, criticism of fact-finding is rarely, at any rate, couched in legal terms. In fact, the commission-establishing conduct of the two Councils—the two bodies which receive the most attention on this issue—is, instead, generally grounded in a legitimacy critique that targets the political competences, rather than the legal authority, of the establishing body.

2.3. THE HUMAN RIGHTS COUNCIL UNDER FIRE

In the literature, there is a discernible sense of unease about the fact-finding activity of the Human Rights Council. In relation to the function of commissions of inquiry established by the Human Rights Council, van den Herik remarks: 'Whereas the traditional commissions of inquiry were principally meant to pacify and defuse a conflict, contemporary human rights commissions rather aim to stir, to evoke action, to opine and to condemn. Their inquiry is to a certain extent predisposed'.[68] Van den

65 Chinkin (n 57) 480–81.
66 UN General Assembly Resolution 60/251 (3 April 2006).
67 Ermacora (n 63) 85.
68 van den Herik (n 9) 536.

Herik's comments are rooted in her effort to detect what the primary purpose of today's commissions might be. Her tone is not condemnatory of the Human Rights Council's approach per se, although she is fairly confident that contemporary human rights commissions are inflammatory rather than de-escalating in their objective. Frulli is more explicitly condemnatory of the Human Rights Council's fact-finding activity compared to other UN organs, particularly the Security Council. Frulli identifies a shift from Security Council initiated fact-finding to Human Rights Council initiated fact-finding, and is perceptibly suspicious of the merits of this 'shift'.[69] Like van den Herik, Frulli characterises the purpose of Human Rights Council fact-finding as provocative or pressurising, and doubts the capabilities of the Human Rights Council to adequately address situations involving violations of international humanitarian law. These concerns lead Frulli to suggest that: 'These considerations should induce reflection on whether the Human Rights Council is the appropriate body to establish a fact-finding mission to investigate situations where serious [international humanitarian law] violations are on-going'.[70] As an alternative, Frulli ponders whether 'a Security Council mandated commission would be a better tool to make a rapid preliminary assessment on the perpetration of serious crimes and provide the Security Council with all necessary information to decide on future steps to be taken'.[71]

The language that Frulli uses in describing the fact-finding activities of both Councils is revealing. She speaks of the commissions of inquiry established by the Security Council in positive terms; as, variously, 'paving the way towards prosecutions',[72] holding an 'accountability-driven mandate',[73] a 'watershed',[74] a 'model',[75] and a 'persuasive assessment … by an independent and competent body'.[76] Indeed, this resonates with a general belief that the Security Council is the most authoritative body to establish commissions of inquiry and that the binding nature of Security Council decisions means commissions of inquiry are more likely to be effective—thus increasing the credibility of the final outcome.[77] The language adopted to describe Human Rights Council commission-establishing

[69] Frulli (n 2) 1333.
[70] Frulli (n 2) 1334.
[71] Frulli (n 2) 1334.
[72] Frulli (n 2) 1328.
[73] Frulli (n 2) 1329.
[74] Frulli (n 2) 1330.
[75] Frulli (n 2) 1330.
[76] Frulli (n 2) 1331.
[77] As the Human Rights Council lacks binding powers, member states are under no obligation to comply with a commission of inquiry. See eg, UN Human Rights Council, *Report of the Independent International Commission of Inquiry on the Syrian Arab Republic*, UN Doc A/HRC/22/59 (5 February 2013), which states, at para 5, that: 'Lack of physical access to the country undermined the commission's ability to fulfil its mandate. Its access to Government

activity is far less flattering: 'one-sided missions', 'unbalanced mandates' and 'bad effects on subsequent criminal prosecution' are some of the descriptions Frulli provides in relation to specific Human Rights Council established commissions.[78]

Frulli's critique of Human Rights Council commission-establishing practice is not uncommon, and it follows a trend in that the authority, including the legal authority, of the Human Rights Council to establish commissions of inquiry is not necessarily questioned; instead scepticism is directed at its competence more generally. This scepticism is often framed in terms of the 'politicisation' of the Human Rights Council.[79] Indeed, given the historical and contextual background of its establishment, and given the grounds for the dissolution of its predecessor, the Commission on Human Rights, the fact that the Human Rights Council faces this charge is hardly surprising.

By the time of its demise, the Commission on Human Rights had become almost completely discredited. UN Secretary General, Kofi Annan, in his landmark 2005 report, *In Larger Freedom*, stated that:

> The Commission's capacity to perform its tasks has been increasingly undermined by its declining credibility and professionalism. In particular, States have sought membership of the Commission not to strengthen human rights but to protect themselves against criticism or to criticize others. As a result, a credibility deficit has developed, which casts a shadow on the reputation of the United Nations system as a whole.[80]

The Human Rights Council's mandate, founding principles and structure were seemingly designed to overcome the above-mentioned flaws. The preamble to its founding resolution, General Assembly Resolution 60/251, recognised 'the importance of ensuring universality, objectivity and non-selectivity in the consideration of human rights issues, and the elimination of double standards and politicization', and reaffirmed that 'all human rights must be treated in a fair and equal manner, on the same footing and with the same emphasis'. Whether wholly justified or not, the Human Rights Council has, however, been unable to escape the perception of politicisation associated with its predecessor. Cox, for example, notes that:

officials and to members of the armed and security forces was limited. Victims and witnesses inside the country, especially those allegedly abused by anti-Government armed groups, could not be interviewed in person'.

[78] Frulli (n 2) 1335–36.

[79] See particularly, the work of R Freedman, *The United Nations Human Rights Council: An Early Assessment* (Routledge, 2013); *Failing to Protect: The UN and the Politicisation of Human Rights* (London, Hurst, 2014); 'The United Nations Human Rights Council: More of the Same?' (2013) 31(2) *Wisconsin International Law Journal* 208.

[80] Report of the Secretary General, *In Larger Freedom: Towards Development, Security and Human Rights for All*, UN Doc A/59/2005/Add.3 (21 March 2005) para 182.

> The impetus behind the creation of the [Human Rights Council] was the shortcomings of the [Commission on Human Rights]: its failure to engage human rights abuses around the world to a sufficient degree; its inclusion of human rights abusers among its members; and its production of politicized decisions. Nevertheless, the [Human Rights Council] does not really address these issues … it would appear that the outcome of the Human Rights Council was, in many ways, predetermined.[81]

The criticisms of 'politicisation' levelled against Human Rights Council fact-finding practice raise the question as to whether the Human Rights Council is simply 'more of the same',[82] offering 'new wine in old bottles'.[83] The very charge of 'politicisation' encapsulates the idea of a failure to observe the principles of 'universality', 'non-selectivity' and 'objectivity' that the Human Rights Council's founding Resolution 60/251 so forcefully recognised. These principles offer useful tools of reference for coming to terms with the charges against the Human Rights Council in relation to the establishment of commissions of inquiry.

2.3.1. Universality

The capacity of the Human Rights Council to investigate alleged human rights violations 'universally' has been called into question. Similar to its predecessor, the Human Rights Council was created along customary UN lines of equitable geographical distribution; member states enjoy sovereign equality and geographic groups are represented proportionately. Like in other international institutions, geographically and politically aligned states tend to vote collectively; as such, the political aims of large groups or blocs gain more attention. African and Asian members enjoy a comfortable majority (at least 26 out of 48 votes) and it has been argued that these states have used this majority to set the agenda.[84] Critics point to bloc-voting as an example of the politicisation charge, as it impedes a 'sensible regrouping of the majority of voices, which should change from issue to issue'.[85] Instead, large groups of states tend to vote in favour of their policy preferences—for example, to establish a commission of inquiry

[81] E Cox, 'State Interests and the Creation and Functioning of the United Nations Human Rights Council' (2010) 6 *Journal of International Law & International Relations* 87, 117.

[82] See generally, Freedman, 'More of the Same?' (n 79).

[83] N Schrijver, 'The UN Human Rights Council: A New "Society of the Committed" or Just Old Wine in New Bottles?' 20(4) *Leiden Journal of International Law* 809.

[84] See, Y Terlingen, 'The Human Rights Council: A New Era in UN Human Rights Work?' (2007) 21 *Ethics & International Affairs* 167, 171; Freedman, 'More of the Same?' (n 79) 220. See also Schrijver (n 83) 812, who describes the current state of play as 'the Rest against the West'.

[85] T Weiss, *What's Wrong with the United Nations and How to Fix It* (Polity Press, 2009) 51–52.

against a particular state—as opposed to voting in a manner that reflects objectively the situation in that state. As a result, there is a perception that human rights standards are not applied 'universally', not least because the decision of whether or not to establish a commission of inquiry to investigate alleged human rights violations is inherently partial to the subjective political preferences of the African and Asian majority. This universality deficit manifests for many most glaringly in the manner by which 'very large blocs of Israel's adversaries, and their allies, push their own states off the agenda while keeping Israel on it'.[86]

2.3.2. Selectivity

This perceived lack of universality is, it is argued, reflected in apparent selectivity in determining which situations to investigate, and, once the decision has been made, to establish a commission of inquiry. Franck and Fairley have developed key indicators of impartiality in international fact-finding that usefully contextualise these charges.[87] Selectivity in the choice of situations to be examined, according to Franck and Fairley, 'has a negative effect on the credibility of investigations that do go forward'.[88] Indeed, 'fact-finding is likely to gain in credibility when it occurs within a broader matrix'.[89] Given the large number of situations that might merit investigation and the small number of international commissions of inquiry that are typically established, the decision to investigate a particular situation requires particular justification. Franck and Fairley emphasise that, as a consequence, 'any suspicion of "ad hoc-ery" undermines the efficacy of the fact-finding process'.[90]

Freedman argues that regional and political alliances have used their collective influence to ensure that the Human Rights Council has devoted selective and disproportionate attention to particular countries.[91] The Council's record in the establishment of commissions of inquiry does reveal disproportionate attention to the Middle East. Scannella and Splinter argue that bias and selectivity has 'been most evident in the Council's

86 E Heinze, 'The Reality and Hyper-reality of Human Rights: Public Consciousness and the Mass Media', in R Dickinson et al, *Examining Critical Perspectives on Human Rights* (Cambridge, Cambridge University Press, 2012) 193, 204.

87 See TM Franck and HS Fairley, 'Procedural Due Process in Human Rights Fact-Finding by International Agencies' (1980) 74(2) *American Journal of International Law* 308, 311–23: 'Both critics and defenders of the current state of international fact-finding tend to identify five key indicators of procedural probity: (1) choice of subject, (2) choice of fact finders, (3) terms of reference, (4) procedures for investigation, and (5) utilization of product'.

88 Franck and Fairley (n 87) 312.

89 Franck and Fairley (n 87) 312.

90 Franck and Fairley (n 87) 312.

91 Freedman, 'More of the Same?' (n 79) 210.

handling of situations involving Israel'.[92] Of the 18 commissions of inquiry established by the Human Rights Council since its inception in 2006, five commissions concern Africa (27.8 per cent), two relate to Asia (11.1 per cent), and eleven concern the Middle-East region (61.1 per cent). Israel, in particular, has been the subject of no less than eight of the eleven commissions of inquiry established in the region (72.7 per cent).[93] Terlingen, for example, is concerned that the nearly exclusive focus on Israel 'at the cost of disregarding equally if not more egregious human rights situations elsewhere in the world, [has] started to raise serious questions regarding the council's credibility'.[94] Such concern is, to a certain extent, vindicated in practice. In a continuation of the practice of its predecessor, the Human Rights Council did place Israel on its permanent agenda, the only country-specific mandate to be treated in that way.[95] In addition, the human rights situation in Palestine and other occupied Arab territories is singled out to be discussed at every regular Council session.[96] Finally, quantitatively, simply more resolutions are passed concerning Israel than any other state. Resolutions on Israeli violations have often either been the sole country-specific resolutions adopted at a specific Council session or have collectively amounted to more than all other country-specific resolutions adopted within a particular session.[97] Freedman argues that this demonstrates the grossly disproportionate scrutiny of Israel not only in terms of the discussions on that country 'but also the use of Council powers and mechanisms to deal with that state'.[98] This is, of course, potentially problematic in terms of the perception of the Human Rights Council vis-à-vis the international community. In the words of Franck and Fairley:

> There may be honest differences of opinion as to whether these do, indeed, constitute the most flagrant abuses of human rights; but reasonable persons are unlikely to believe that they are the only problems. Consequently, the paucity

[92] P Scannella and P Splinter, 'The United Nations Human Rights Council: A Promise to be Fulfilled' (2007) 7 *Human Rights Law Review* 41, 61.

[93] UN Human Rights Council Resolution S-1/1 (6 July 2006); UN Human Rights Council Resolution S-2/1 (11 August 2006); UN Human Rights Council Resolution S-3/1 (15 November 2006); UN Human Rights Council Resolution S-9/1 (12 January 2009); UN Human Rights Council Resolution 13/9 (14 April 2010); UN Human Rights Council Resolution 14/1 (2 June 2010); UN Human Rights Council Resolution 19/17 (10 April 2012); UN Human Rights Council Resolution S-21/1 (23 July 2014).

[94] Terlingen (n 84) 174.

[95] UN Human Rights Council Resolution 5/1 (18 June 2007) 'Framework for the programme of work', item 7.

[96] ibid.

[97] Freedman, 'More of the Same?' (n 79) 243.

[98] Freedman, 'More of the Same?' (n 79) 243. In May 2012, Israel ceased engagement with the Human Rights Council altogether. Although Israel reversed that position within 18 months, its disengagement demonstrates the degree to which the Council had isolated and ostracised that country.

> of human rights fact-finding activity directed elsewhere has a negative effect on the credibility of the investigations that do go forward.[99]

2.3.3. Objectivity

Weiler identifies 'the manner in which our normative sensibilities and sensitivities condition the very way we experience both facts and the law'.[100] With this in mind, he strongly suggests, however, that:

> When the firing and killing ceases and judicial inquiry takes over it is in the interest of justice and the credibility of the bodies who administer it to adopt those other idioms of the law—dispassionate, 'blind', fair—and to heed the wisdom of justice needing not only to be done but to be seen to be done.[101]

From this perspective, in order to maintain credibility, it is imperative that a commission is seen to be conducting its inquiry objectively. The scope of a commission's mandate, or its 'terms of reference' will, therefore, also clearly impact upon this perception.[102] Indeed, in this regard, Franck and Fairley explicitly warn against 'conclusory language that palpably interfere[s] with the integrity of the fact-finding process by violating the essential line between political assumptions and issues to be impartially determined'.[103] They continue:

> Although such a strict rule of *sub judice* may not invariably be appropriate to activity that is no more than quasi-judicial, a fact-finding group created by terms of reference that seek to direct its conclusions is essentially a waste of time. Its findings, at most, will reassure those whose minds are already made up.[104]

As such, it is central to the arguments of Human Rights Council critics that disproportionality is evident not only in the number of commissions of inquiry established that concern Israel, but also in the fact that commissions have, in the past, only been mandated to investigate one party to the conflict; in short, that the outcome is predetermined and the inquiry lacks objectivity. In its very first special session, the Council, expressing 'grave concern at the violations of the human rights of the Palestinian people caused by the Israeli occupation, including the current extensive Israeli military operations against Palestinians in the Occupied Palestinian Territory'[105] decided 'to dispatch an urgent fact-finding mission headed by the Special Rapporteur on the situation of human rights in the Palestinian

99 Franck and Fairley (n 87) 312.
100 Weiler (n 13) 641.
101 Weiler (n 13) 641–2.
102 Franck and Fairley (n 87) 315–17.
103 Franck and Fairley (n 87) 316.
104 Franck and Fairley (n 87) 316.
105 UN Human Rights Council Resolution S-1/1 (6 July 2006) para 1.

territories occupied since 1967'.[106] The commission was mandated to investigate alleged human rights violations *in* Palestine, but not alleged violations committed *by* Hamas. This theme has developed through Human Rights Council fact-finding practice. In its second special session, the Council established a high-level mission to investigate the targeting of civilians by Israel in Lebanon, the types of weapon used by Israel and their conformity with international law, and the extent and impact of Israeli attacks on human life, property, critical infrastructure, and the environment.[107] This resolution was deemed to be unbalanced in that it strongly condemned 'grave Israeli violations of Human Rights and breaches of International Humanitarian Law in Lebanon'[108], but did not mention potential human rights violations committed by Hezbollah. To Terlingen, this 'was a clear example of the "selectivity" and "double standards and politicization" that Resolution 60/251 seeks to eliminate'.[109]

There is a striking correlation between (largely Western) scholarly criticisms and those forwarded by (largely Western) states within the Human Rights Council. A study of the explanations of votes to resolutions which establish Human Rights Council commissions of inquiry indeed demonstrates the fact that a lack of universality, selectivity and unbalanced mandates presents a common thread in state opinion also. In reference to the establishment of the above-mentioned commission of inquiry in Lebanon, for example, the Canadian delegation stated:

> Canada firmly reiterates our desire to employ this new Council for constructive not divisive ends … Rather than fall back into non-productive habits, it must work to ensure universality, objectivity and non-selectivity in the consideration of human rights issues, and to eliminate double standards and politicization.[110]

The United States has been particularly damning in its consideration of the 'unbalanced' approach to commissions of inquiry against Israel. For example, in 2010, the Human Rights Council established a commission of inquiry to investigate the attack by the Israeli forces against the humanitarian flotilla of ships (the so-called 'flotilla incident'), which resulted in the killing and injuring of many innocent civilians from different countries.[111] The representative of the United States remarked that the establishing

[106] ibid para 6.
[107] Human Rights Council Resolution S-2/1 (11 August 2006) para 7.
[108] ibid para 1.
[109] Terlingen (n 84) 174.
[110] Government of Canada, *Statement by Ambassador Paul Meyer of Canada to Special Session of the UN Human Rights Council* (11 August 2006).
[111] The 'International Fact-Finding Mission to Investigate Violations of International Law Resulting from the Israeli Attacks on the Flotilla of Ships Carrying Humanitarian Assistance' was established by UN Human Rights Council Resolution 14/1 (23 June 2010) (32 votes in favour, 3 votes against and 9 abstentions).

resolution 'rushes to judgment on a set of facts that … are only beginning to be discovered and understood … [which] thereby risks further politicizing a sensitive and volatile situation'.[112] Most recently, in relation to the commission of inquiry established to investigate all violations of international humanitarian law and international human rights law in the Occupied Palestinian Territory in 2014,[113] the United States, the lone state among 48 who voted against the establishment of the inquiry, argued that 'once again the Council had failed to address the situation in Israel and Palestinian territories with any semblance of balance'.[114]

Other Human Rights Council-established commissions have also been criticised. For example, the ad hoc commission of inquiry established by the Human Rights Council and mandated to investigate human rights violations in Syria in 2011 illustrates how perceived selectivity and unbalanced terms of reference are recurring problems.[115] In an explanation of the vote the Cuban representative commented that 'Once again the Human Rights Council was examining a political draft resolution which was selective and confrontational' and that this reminded them of similar practices which had led to the dissolution of the previous Commission on Human Rights.[116]

Cuba argued that 'developing countries could not be silent accomplices to the hypocrisy, double standards and politicization'.[117] Russia labelled the resolution as 'one-sided and politicized'[118] and lamented the fact that the resolution ignored the willingness of the Syrian authorities to engage in dialogue.[119] Syria, speaking as a concerned country, regretted the fact that the resolution 'remained political and unbalanced'.[120] They argued that the resolution sent a mistaken message which poorly described the situation.[121] The Syrian representative argued that Syria had declared that

[112] Statement by the Delegation of the United States of America, *Explanation of Vote: The Grave Attacks by Israeli Forces against the Humanitarian Boat Convoy* (2 June 2010), available at geneva.usmission.gov/2010/06/02/hrc-resolution/, accessed 4 August 2016.

[113] The UN Independent Commission of Inquiry on the 2014 Gaza Conflict was established by UN Human Rights Council Resolution S-21/1 (23 July 2014) (29 votes in favour, 1 vote against and 17 abstentions).

[114] UN Human Rights Council, *Human Rights Council establishes Independent, International Commission of Inquiry for the Occupied Palestinian Territory* (23 July 2014), available at www.ohchr.org/en/NewsEvents/Pages/DisplayNews.aspx?NewsID=14897&LangID=E#sthash.e4yqQece.dpuf, accessed 4 August 2016.

[115] The Independent International Commission of Inquiry on the Syrian Arab Republic was established by UN Human Rights Council Resolution S-17/1 (22 August 201) (33 votes in favour, 4 votes against and 9 abstentions).

[116] UN Human Rights Council, *Human Rights Council Decides to Dispatch a Commission of Inquiry to Investigate Human Rights Violations in the Syrian Arab Republic* (23 August 2011).

[117] UN Human Rights Council (n 116).

[118] UN Human Rights Council (n 116).

[119] UN Human Rights Council (n 116).

[120] UN Human Rights Council (n 116).

[121] UN Human Rights Council (n 116).

it was prepared to receive a mission of inquiry from the Office of the High Commissioner, but that this statement had not been favourably welcomed by the states who prepared the draft resolution and this confirmed their determination to politically condemn Syria.[122] The Chinese representative stated that 'the correct way to protect human rights was not through accusations'.[123]

Undoubtedly linked to these charges of imbalance, critics also argue that the already accusatory tone of Human Rights Council-established commissions is further perpetuated by an (emerging) tendency of the Council to phrase its resolutions in legalistic language. Van den Herik points to what she sees as an increasing trend whereby the mandates of commissions of inquiry 'are inherently contradictory as they seemingly predetermine that violations have been committed and encourage the commissions to use legal language to establish facts'.[124] For van den Herik, questions thus arise as to whether commissions are primarily acting as fact-finders or rather as de facto law-applying authorities.[125] The Goldstone Commission of 2009 was particularly criticised in this regard.[126] The establishing resolution mandated the commission:

> to investigate all violations of international human rights law and international humanitarian law by the occupying Power, Israel, against the Palestinian people throughout the Occupied Palestinian Territory, particularly in the occupied Gaza Strip, due to the current aggression.[127]

In addition to the charge of an apparently one-sided mandate, which does not purport to investigate all parties to the conflict,[128] this is seen to mark a departure from the traditional understanding of a commission

[122] UN Human Rights Council (n 116).
[123] UN Human Rights Council (n 116).
[124] van den Herik (n 9) 509.
[125] van den Herik (n 9) 509.
[126] The UN Fact-Finding Mission on the Gaza conflict was established by UN Human Rights Council Resolution S-9/1 (12 January 2009) (33 votes in favour, 1 vote against and 13 abstentions).
[127] ibid para 7.
[128] The fact that the resolution addressed 'only one side of the conflict' was cited in the explanation of all European Union members, who abstained collectively: European Union, *Explanation of Vote with regard to the draft resolution A/HRC/S-9/L.1/Rev.* 2 (12 January 2009). Although see Henderson (n 18) 298; Frulli (n 2) 1334. See also Heller (n 14) 9, who notes that 'a commission can compensate for a biased mandate by expanding the scope of its investigation'. Indeed, Richard Goldstone agreed to chair the commission only after rebalancing the mandate. Subsequently, in the final report, *Report of the United Nations Fact Finding Mission on the Gaza Conflict*, UN Doc A/HRC/12/48 (25 September 2009), para 152, the mandate was stated as being to investigate:

> *all violations of international human rights law and international humanitarian law that might have been committed at any time* in the context of the military operations that were conducted in Gaza during the period from 27 December 2008 and 18 January 2009, whether before, during, or after (emphasis added).

of inquiry as an impartial 'fact-finding' body; the use of legal language such as 'aggression' in a quasi-judicial sense before a situation has in fact been investigated is to come to a conclusion before completing the investigation. Explaining their abstention, Germany, on behalf of the European Union, voiced its regret that 'some paragraphs use legal terms with very specific meanings without full evidence of whether definitions are met'.[129] According to van den Herik, 'International law is … used as the predominant language of communication and construction of facts in a quest to make the facts more objective and to create political effects'.[130]

In closing this section, Human Rights Council commissions of inquiry have, in recent years, come under heavy fire. The charge of 'politicisation' could be viewed as the overarching critique, with the more specific criticisms that Human Rights Council commissions lack universality, that member states are selective in the situations in which they opt to establish a commission of inquiry and, once a commission is established, it is often based on a one-sided mandate, with legal judgments being made even before an inquiry has taken place.

2.4. LEGITIMACY AS IDEOLOGY: A TWAIL PERSPECTIVE

As we have seen, commissions of inquiry established by the Human Rights Council have come under heavy fire in recent times. But it is not necessarily the legal basis of these commissions that is questioned. Rather the 'politicised' nature of Human Rights Council decision-making compared, apparently, to other UN institutions is at stake. In reality, the critique targets somewhere in between international law and international politics, which resonates with D'Amato's conception of 'legitimacy', 'as the space between international law and international politics'.[131] The charges of politicisation against the Human Rights Council thus represent a critique of the legitimacy of this institution in relation to its commission establishing activity. In this final section, we do not aim to defend the Human Rights Council against this legitimacy critique; rather our aim is to demonstrate that the critique, examined through the lens of a third world approach to international law and institutions, is itself deeply representative of the hegemonic, Western, powerful state order. The critique, we argue, is ideological insofar as it perpetuates a continuation of the propriety of that order.

[129] European Union, *Explanation of Vote with regard to the draft resolution A/HRC/S-9/L.1/Rev. 2* (12 January 2009).

[130] van den Herik (n 9) 536.

[131] A D'Amato, 'On the Legitimacy of International Institutions' in R Wolfrum and V Röben, *Legitimacy in International Law* (Springer, 2008) 83.

2.4.1. Understanding the Legitimacy Critique

Legitimacy is, of course, a contested concept.[132] International institutions are, nevertheless, generally assessed and criticised on a legitimacy basis. Indeed, legitimacy is often viewed as central for the effectiveness of political institutions.[133] In relation to the utilisation of the concept of legitimacy in this context, two overlapping caveats are in order. First, the sources of institutional legitimacy are conventionally divided into 'output' and 'input' legitimacy.[134] Output legitimacy refers to the achievement of the substantive purposes of the institution, be that, for example, the advancement of international human rights (Human Rights Council) or the maintenance of international peace and security (Security Council). Input legitimacy refers to the processes by which decisions are reached—whether they have certain attributes regarded as important to the international community. The criticisms of Human Rights Council commissions of inquiry generally target features of their establishment; that is to say, it is the input legitimacy—the politics behind the establishment of commissions of inquiry—as opposed to the substance of the commissions' reports (output) that is most often at issue.

Second, the concept of legitimacy has two generally agreed facets, or forms. On the one hand, there is the constitutive aspect of legitimacy; this refers to the normative basis upon which an institution is established, or its 'right to rule'.[135] We have demonstrated that all UN institutions surveyed possess the normative (legal) competence to establish commissions of inquiry.[136] The constitutive aspect of legitimacy is not, therefore, what concerns us here. Instead, we are concerned with legitimacy in the *sociological* sense.[137] At its root, the legitimacy of an organisation or institution is inextricably dependent upon its social perception and recognition. From this perspective, the social acceptance of states of the establishing institution is pivotal, for, as Franck has argued, 'Legitimacy exerts a pull

[132] A Hurrelmann, S Schneider and J Steffek, 'Conclusion: Legitimacy—Making Sense of an Essentially Contested Concept' in A Hurrelmann, S Schneider and J Steffek (eds), *Legitimacy in an Age of Global Politics* (Palgrave Macmillan, 2007). See seminally, WB Gallie, 'Essentially Contested Concepts' (1956) 56 *Proceedings of the Aristotelian Society* 167.

[133] M Weber, *Economy and Society: An Outline of Interpretive Sociology* (first published 1922, University of California Press, 1978).

[134] See originally, F Scharpf, *Governing in Europe: Effective and Democratic?* (Oxford, Oxford University Press, 1999).

[135] A Buchanan and RO Koehane, 'The Legitimacy of Global Governance Institutions' in LH Meyer (ed), *Legitimacy, Justice and Public International Law* (Cambridge, Cambridge University Press, 2010) 29, 29.

[136] See text at 2.2.

[137] ibid. See also, C Reus-Smit, 'International Crises of Legitimacy' (2007) 44 *International Politics* 157, 158–59: 'The critical thing that differentiates legitimacy is the necessity of social recognition. No action can be coherently described as legitimate if it is not socially recognised as rightful'.

towards compliance which is powered by the quality of the rule or of the rule making institution not by coercive authority'.[138] From this perspective, if a commission of inquiry is established 'legitimately', this will improve compliance with the commission's mandate. Perhaps the most important question, therefore, is *why* states opt to comply; or, in other words, what are the key markers against which states will (subjectively) decide whether an institution, or the establishment of a commission of inquiry by that institution, is 'legitimate'. This question is at the centre of Weber's conception of legitimacy, which is concerned with the subjective state of those directly affected by decisions. For Weber, in order for an authority to exert its authority, obedience to that authority is required—legitimation is, thus, 'the process by which authority comes to be seen as valid and appropriate'.[139] The establishment of a UN commission of inquiry, from this viewpoint, would be legitimate if those states subject to the inquiry considered that commission and the commission-establishing institution to be authoritative and therefore acceptable and justified. The legitimacy underpinning the establishment of commissions of inquiry is, consequently, based on the establishing institution's performance against objectivity, non-selectivity and balance.

Many argue that the Human Rights Council fares particularly poorly against these markers. This criticism is often rooted in discomfort with the voting blocs of the Human Rights Council. As Buchanan and Keohane put it:

> [w]hen someone asserts or denies that a particular global governance institution is legitimate, part of what is at stake is whether those who occupy key roles in the institution are morally justified in performing the functions attached to those roles,[140] including formulating rules and attempting to ensure that they are complied with.[141]

From this perspective, therefore, the Human Rights Council can be said to suffer a 'crisis of legitimacy', which, according to Reus-Smit, arises 'when the level of social recognition that its identity, interests, practised, norms, or procedures are rightful declines to the point where it must either adapt … or face disempowerment'.[142]

[138] T Franck, *The Power of Legitimacy Among Nations* (Oxford, Oxford University Press, 1990) 26.

[139] S Marks, *The Riddle of all Constitutions: International Law, Democracy and the Critique of Ideology* (Oxford, Oxford University Press, 2003) 19.

[140] In this regard, the membership of the Human Rights Council is regularly contested. It is argued that due to their human rights records certain states are not entitled to a seat on the Council. The 2016 election of Saudi Arabia to the council was particularly controversial in this respect in the light of its human rights record as well as its actions in Yemen. See, for example, UN Human Rights Council, 'UN: Suspend Saudi Arabia from Human Rights Council' (29 June 2016).

[141] Buchanan and Koehane (n 135) 32–33.

[142] Reus-Smit (n 137) 158–59.

2.4.2. Tipping the Scales: Legitimacy Critique as Ideology

Bassiouni, reflecting on the politics of UN fact-finding, emphasises the political backdrop: 'The [UN] was established as a political organisation, and, as such, it is largely governed by political considerations'.[143] He notes that the 'human rights component of the [UN] system reflects the values of justice, while systemically it functions as a *political process*, thus conditioning the upholding of these values to political oversight' (emphasis added).[144] The justice 'goals' of fact-finding, he suggests then, can become subservient to politics, threatening the effectiveness and impartiality of fact-finding. Fact-finding missions, he points out, must take this context into consideration. In that regard, he argues, the establishment, methods and goals of fact-finding depend on the organ or body that establishes it, the mandate given to it and the extent of political support from the permanent Security Council members, particularly the Western ones 'which determines its real authority and effectiveness'.[145] Bassiouni's observations require consideration, particularly the connection he makes between the permanent (Western) Security Council member states and the authority and effectiveness of commissions of inquiry. Indeed, we argue that the organ and, therefore, the states responsible for creating or supporting the establishment of a commission of inquiry determine, to a great extent, the perception of the legitimacy of that commission.

The criticisms of the Human Rights Council are illustrative. Overall, the calls to balance out resolutions and commission of inquiry mandates by ensuring enhanced objectivity, invoking all parties to the conflict and by neutralising the legal language are sensible ones.[146] There is, however, some disingenuousness to these calls given the underpinning claims that the Human Rights Council is characterised by, amongst other things, political selectivity and non-universality. The accusations of imbalance or lack of objectivity are made within a context in which the Human Rights Council is already viewed as uniquely politicised. In other words, the idea that a greater geographic spread of commissions of inquiry or 'more balanced mandates' would change the critics' perceptions is a fallacious one. The perceived illegitimacy of particular commissions of inquiry rests on

143 M Cherif Bassiouni, 'Appraising UN Justice-Related Fact-Finding Missions' (2001) 5 *Washington University Journal of Law and Policy* 35, 37.

144 Cherif Bassiouni (n 143) 38.

145 Cherif Bassiouni (n 143) 38.

146 However, the Independent Commission of Inquiry on the 2014 Gaza Conflict showed that charges of bias can appear no matter how carefully the resolution and mandate are worded. In this case, charges of non-objectivity were directed from the outset at the appointed Commission Chair, William Schabas, who was forced to resign as a consequence in February 2015. See, UN Human Rights Council, *Press Statement on the Resignation of the Chairperson of the Commission of Inquiry on the 2014 Gaza Conflict* (3 February 2015).

a general perception of the Human Rights Council as illegitimate. The calls to balance out the Human Rights Council's commission establishing-practices obfuscate the deeply-embedded hegemonic dynamics not just of the Human Rights Council and of the UN more generally, but also of the prevailing academic commentary. The member states of the Human Rights Council are not alone in churning out resolutions and establishing commissions of inquiry that reflect the political interests and concerns of those member states. To take just one example, the United States' role in and backing of Security Council Resolution 1564 on Darfur in 2004 and, in particular, its push for the inclusion of the 'g-word' in the resolution establishing the commission of inquiry exemplifies this 'phenomenon' elsewhere and with different consequences.[147] This commission was equally politically-motivated (stands to reason, one might say) as was the resolution's inclusion of the spectre of genocide, a legal term with potent rhetorical currency and a conclusive tenor.

The frame of analysis that is applied to the examination of the Human Rights Council is, therefore, a central aspect of the construction of the legitimacy critique. Critics rely on decontextualised discussion and an absence of comparative scrutiny. These silences in the analysis powerfully limit our perception of the Human Rights Council from the perspective of both its activities or workings and its politics. In other words, the charges of political selectivity and non-universality train our perception, providing an effective firewall inside which charges are able to mount. The analytical standpoint when it comes to scrutiny of the Human Rights Council is crucial. The charges against it serve as a challenge to its legitimacy and its consequent capability to do analogous work to the other UN organs. Critics of Human Rights Council commissions of inquiry, while indeed representing the traditional orthodoxy in Western scholarship, are therefore limited by the lack of contextualisation that they offer. Their comments are directed squarely at the Human Rights Council and not at the Human Rights Council in the context of the UN or in comparison to other UN institutions. This leaves the impression that the Human Rights Council is uniquely beset by these charges of non-universality and political selectivity—a charge that may be merited but is itself revealing of a different kind of politicisation. Linked to this, but perhaps more importantly, the voting blocs, the disproportionate attention to Israel and other practices of the Human Rights Council may be understood differently when the frame of analysis shifts from a hegemonic to a 'third world' (and arguably more international) conception of international institutions.

[147] UN Security Council Resolution 1564 (18 September 2004). On the consequences, see D Luban, 'Calling Genocide by its Rightful Name: Lemkin's Word, Darfur and the UN Report' (2006) 7 *Chicago Journal of International Law* 1.

Although it is important to emphasise the diversity within third-world perspectives, the approach is in a sense unified by:

> A shared ethical commitment to the intellectual and practical struggle to expose, reform, or even retrench those features of the international legal system that help create or maintain the generally unequal, unfair, or unjust global order … a commitment to centre the *rest* rather than merely the *west*, thereby taking the lives and experiences of those who have self-identified as Third World much more seriously than has generally been the case.[148]

The criticisms of the Human Rights Council reproduce the hierarchies built in to the UN system, where the 'Good West' is pitted against the 'Bad Rest'.[149] The discourse stands to reproduce the binary dichotomy that ruptures the international sphere into two conceptual communities, one 'heavenly' and the other 'hellish'.[150] In reality—a reality masked in the literature by attention to the issue of Human Rights Council bias vis-à-vis Israel—contemporary commissions of inquiry disproportionately target third world states. The practice, consequently, fosters the impression that serious human rights violations almost always occur in, or are committed by, developing states, dismissing those occurring in, or committed by, Western states.[151] As Orakfor explains, this 'leaves the impression in the undiscerning mind' that there is little need to focus on fact-finding in Western or powerful states.[152] This reinforces what has been referred to as the 'one-way traffic paradigm'. According to this paradigm, human rights knowledge, scrutiny and supervision tends to flow from the West to the Third World.[153] The one-way traffic paradigm, and the heaven/hell binary that it reinforces, is factually flawed. However, beyond this, a deeper problem exists insofar as this discourse:

> helps to foster a racialised hierarchy in which Third World societies are endemically and perpetually viewed as the sites of human rights violations and

[148] OC Okafor, 'Newness, Imperialism and International Legal Reform in our Time: A TWAIL Perspective' (2005) 43 *Osgoode Hall Law Journal* 171, 176 (emphasis in original). See further, M Mutua, 'What is TWAIL?' (2000) 94 *Proceedings of the American Society of International Law* 31.

[149] OC Okafor, 'International Human Rights Fact-Finding Praxis in its Living Forms: A TWAIL Perspective' (2014) 1 *The Transnational Human Rights Review* 59, 67.

[150] M Mutua, 'Savages, Victims and Saviors: The Metaphor of Human Rights' (2001) 42 *Harvard International Law Journal* 201. This binary logic constructs historical imperatives of the 'superior' and the 'inferior', the 'barbarian' and the 'civilised', the 'traditional' and the 'modern'. Within this narrative, history is a linear progression with the superior western states leading and paving the way for others to follow. See D Slater, 'Contesting Occidental Visions of the Global: The Geopolitics of Theory and North-South Relations' (1994) 4 *Beyond Law* 97, 100–101.

[151] Okafor (n 149) 69.

[152] Okafor (n 149) 68.

[153] Okafor (n 149) 72. See also Mutua (n 150).

> investigations, and Third World peoples are not adequately appreciated as agents of human rights knowledge production, fact-finding, and dissemination.[154]

Okafor challenges this hierarchy by asking:

> If Third World subalterns could speak, if they could author the dominant human rights narratives, how would we see the human rights situation in many Western states? And would not more human rights knowledge flow from the Third World toward the West?[155]

TWAIL helps to identify the myriad ways in which the 'gaze' of western states disproportionately constitutes how we conceive of the world order and its concerns. Third World contributions to the understanding and development of human rights and third world conceptions of governance, democracy and other practices fall outside of the frame of this Western perception. In the same way, the orientation of the 'western gaze' tends to determine the need for, and the legitimacy of, UN commissions of inquiry. In the words of Okafor once more:

> It is wherever the Western eye goes, on whatever it sees, that tends to motivate, frame, constitute and legitimize [international fact-finding]. Whatever the Western eye does not see, is not primed to see, or regards with studied ignorance, does not tend to motivate, frame, constitute and legitimize [international fact-finding].[156]

Aspects of the Human Rights Council—its geographic spread of membership and consequent inclusion of third world perspectives as well as the Universal Periodic Review—do challenge (and are adapting) this Western or powerful state control of the international discourse. The accusations against the Human Rights Council's practices in establishing commissions of inquiry demonstrate discomfort with this challenge to western and powerful state hegemony and reveal themselves as a general distrust of the Council's political composition and of its non-western viewpoint.

The question of legitimacy of commissions of inquiry and of the office or institution responsible for establishing such commissions takes us to the heart of the hierarchies and hegemony that constitutes the existing international order. There is ideology at work in the legitimacy critiques of the Human Rights Council when those critiques are examined in light of corresponding silences in relation to the Security Council. Marks, drawing on Thompson, uses the concept of 'ideology' to refer to the 'ways in which meaning serves to establish and sustain relations of domination'.[157] Domination manifests in asymmetrical or unequal power relations. The international system is constituted by an asymmetry of power that is crudely

[154] Okafor (n 149) 74.
[155] Okafor (n 149) 73.
[156] Okafor (n 149) 74.
[157] Marks (n 139) 10.

represented by the opposition between developed and developing states or western and third world states. Thompson purports that ideology:

> Calls our attention to the ways in which meaning is mobilized in the service of dominant individuals and groups … to establish and sustain structured social relations from which some individuals and groups benefit more than others, and which some individuals and groups have an interest in preserving while others may seek to contest.[158]

Legitimacy, Marks explains, is one of the means by which such meaning is mobilised.[159] A legitimacy critique in the context of the establishment of commissions of inquiry should, therefore, be cause for suspicion as it is ideologically mobilised to do the work of preserving the ideas, concerns and hierarchies of the existing international order or status quo.

2.5. CONCLUSION

It may be that no reform to the composition or procedures of the Human Rights Council can overcome its (perceived) political legitimacy challenge in the establishment of commissions of inquiry. Where Cox proffers that the 'politicisation' of the Council was 'pre-determined', it may be, instead, that it is in fact the legitimacy critique itself that is pre-determined by virtue of the fact that the Human Rights Council is dominated by non-western states. Criticisms of the Human Rights Council commission-establishing activity thus demonstrate a hegemonic viewpoint both of that Council and, to a certain extent, of the conceptualisation of legitimacy itself. This chapter has sought to show that the proliferation of Human Rights Council-established commissions of inquiry could, productively, be viewed through a counter-hegemonic lens; one does not have to like or agree with the all of the practices of the Human Rights Council in order to appreciate it as an institutional counter-balance to the effects of the power asymmetries that characterise the relationship between western and developing states.

[158] JB Thompson, *Ideology and Modern Culture* (Stanford University Press, 1991) 72–73, cited in Marks (n 139) 15.

[159] Marks (n 139) 19.

3

Lessons From Two Regional Missions: Fact-finding in Georgia and South Sudan

ROB GRACE

3.1. INTRODUCTION

THIS CHAPTER FOCUSES on efforts of regional organisations to mandate and implement fact-finding missions and commissions of inquiry to investigate alleged violations of human rights, international humanitarian law, and international criminal law. The analysis included in this chapter builds on a foundation of research undertaken as part of a multi-annual initiative by the Program on Humanitarian Policy and Conflict Research (HPCR), a program of the Harvard Humanitarian Initiative at the Harvard TH Chan School of Public Health. This research project—based on an assessment of 15 monitoring, reporting, and fact-finding missions, as well as extensive engagement with fact-finding practitioners—focused on several particularly challenging aspects of fact-finding practice and culminated in the publication of a field-based handbook: the *HPCR Advanced Practitioner's Handbook for Commissions of Inquiry*.[1]

Before outlining the chapter, this introduction first briefly comments on two main themes that emerged through HPCR's research. First, the departure point for the HPCR initiative was the ad hoc state of the domain of international fact-finding. In short, in the absence of a centralised mandating authority, international fact-finding missions have arisen from multiple entities, leading to a state of affairs in which fact-finding practitioners

[1] The author of this chapter served as the lead researcher on this initiative, as well as the lead drafter of the handbook. See generally program on Humanitarian Policy and Conflict Research, *HPCR Advanced Practitioner's Handbook on Commissions of Inquiry* (Harvard University, March 2015), available at hhi.harvard.edu/sites/default/files/publications/handbook-hpcr-mrf.pdf.

must devise mission-specific methodologies each time a new mandate is adopted, and limited capacity exists for building institutional memory after a mission concludes.[2] Second, numerous challenges arise from the dual nature of fact-finding missions as both political and technical exercises. To elaborate briefly on this notion, the purpose of fact-finding is to initiate a technically sound investigation, insulated from the politics of the surrounding environment, with the aim of producing an authoritative account of events that have occurred. However, for fact-finding missions created by governmental or inter-governmental bodies, political factors play a role in the consensus building process that leads to the mandate's adoption. Moreover, politics shape how members of the mandating body, the actors engaged in the conflict, and other members of the international community respond to fact-finding reports. In this sense, somewhat paradoxically, fact-finding reports aim to be political by being apolitical. The potential for political impact hinges on the perception that the report is an objective and methodologically sound undertaking.

In an effort to shed additional analytical light on these issues, this chapter offers an assessment of two of the highest profile regional missions created in recent years. The first is the Independent International Fact-Finding Mission on the Conflict in Georgia (IIFFMCG), mandated by the Council of the European Union (EU) in 2008 in response to the Russia-Georgia War. The second is the African Union Commission of Inquiry on South Sudan (AUCISS), mandated by the Peace and Security Council of the African Union in 2013 after the outbreak of the South Sudanese Civil War.

These missions, of course, constitute merely two cases in a rich history of monitoring, reporting, and fact-finding activities undertaken at the regional level. Indeed, the Organization of American States has decades of experience in gathering information about alleged violations of international law, particularly under the rubric of the Inter-American Commission on Human Rights, as does the African Commission on Human and People's Rights (ACHPR).[3] The Organization for Security and Co-operation in Europe (OSCE) has mandated a wide array of monitoring

[2] See generally R Grace and C Bruderlein, 'Building Effective Monitoring, Reporting, and Fact-Finding Mechanisms' *Program on Humanitarian Policy and Conflict Research* (Harvard University, 2012), available at papers.ssrn.com/sol3/papers.cfm?abstract_id=2038854.

[3] For the Inter-American Commission on Human Rights, see generally D Shelton, 'Improving Human Rights Protections: Recommendations for Enhancing the Effectiveness of the Inter-American Commission and Inter-American Court of Human Rights' (1988) 2 *American University International Law Review* 2. For the ACHPR, see generally R Murray and D Long, *The Implementation of the Findings of the African Commission on Human and People's Rights* (Cambridge, Cambridge University Press, 2015).

missions.[4] And entities such as the Organization of Islamic Cooperation and the League of Arab States have also created ad hoc investigative bodies during armed conflicts.[5]

This chapter focuses attention on the IIFFMCG and the AUCISS for two key reasons. First, both of these missions constituted the first time that these regional organisations—namely, the Council of the EU and the African Union Peace and Security Council—engaged in efforts of this nature. In this sense, examining these case studies allows one to examine the implications of an entity undertaking its first foray into the landscape of ad hoc international fact-finding related to international humanitarian law, human rights, and international criminal law.[6] This dimension is particularly relevant in light of the continued proliferation of fact-finding missions and commissions of inquiry as components of international responses to international and non-international armed conflicts. As state reliance on such missions persists, governmental and inter-governmental bodies undertaking maiden fact-finding efforts in the future will benefit from lessons learned in the past.

Second, both the EU and the African Union, before mandating these missions, had been significantly engaged in the relevant context—the Russia-Georgian War and the South Sudanese Civil War, respectively—at the political level. Given that, in both instances, the fact-finding mandate grew out of conflict resolution efforts, these cases illustrate the tensions between the political and technical aspects of fact-finding work. As this chapter will examine, the involvement of the mandating entity at the political level can strain the process of compartmentalising these political and technical dynamics.

[4] See generally M Huber, D Lewis, R Oberschmidt, and Y du Pont, 'The effectiveness of OSCE Missions: The Cases of Uzbekistan, Ukraine and Bosnia and Herzegovina' (February 2003) *Netherlands Institute of International Relations 'Clingendael' Conflict Research Unit*, available at www.clingendael.nl/sites/default/files/20030200_cru_paper_huber.pdf.

[5] For example, see generally *Report of the OIC Mission to Assess the Situation in the Darfur Region of the Sudan*, available at reliefweb.int/sites/reliefweb.int/files/resources/761A7E3E1B0E01134925702D00205E56-oic-sdn-27jun.pdf; *Report of the Independent Fact Finding Committee on Gaza: No Safe Place* presented to the League of Arab States (30 April 2009), available at www.tromso-gaza.no/090501ReportGaza.pdf; and *Report of the Head of the League of Arab States Observer Mission to Syria for the period from 24 December 2011 to 18 January 2012* (27 January 2012), available at www.columbia.edu/~hauben/Report_of_Arab_League_Observer_Mission.pdf.

[6] Although the Peace and Security Council had created fact-finding missions with more limited mandates before, the AUCISS was the first time that the body created a commission of inquiry tasked to gather information about violations of international law. For an example of a previous panel mandated by the Peace and Security Council, see generally African Union, *Report of the African Union High-Level Panel on Darfur (AUPD)* (29 October 2009), available at www.refworld.org/docid/4ccfde402.html.

In this sense, both of these missions speak directly to the two overarching themes mentioned above: (1) the ad hoc state of fact-finding practice; and (2) the hybrid 'political-technical' nature of fact-finding work. In its examination of these issues, this chapter proceeds in four parts. Section 3.2 presents an overview of the experiences and methodological choices of the IIFFMCG. Section 3.3 offers a similar examination of the AUCISS. Section 3.4 extrapolates lessons learned. Section 3.5 offers concluding remarks.

3.2. INDEPENDENT INTERNATIONAL FACT-FINDING MISSION ON THE CONFLICT IN GEORGIA

3.2.1. Creating the Mission

The creation of the IIFFMCG marked a significant moment in a years-long process of increased EU engagement in the South Caucasus region. After the eruption of the war in August 2008, the EU—in particular, through the efforts of Nicolas Sarkozy, who then held the rotating office of the presidency of the Council of the EU—assumed the lead role in mediating the ceasefire that ended the conflict on 12 August 2008. The following month, the Council of the EU, first, mandated a small-scale fact-finding mission to Georgia as a preliminary measure, and then mandated the EU Monitoring Mission to undertake stabilisation, normalisation, and confidence building activities in Georgia.[7]

Previously, the EU had no significant monitoring presence in Georgia. In the wake of the 1992–1993 Abkhazia War and the 1991–1992 South Ossetia War, it was not the EU but rather the United Nations (UN) Security Council and the OSCE that mandated on-the-ground monitoring missions in the form of the UN Observer Mission in Georgia and the OSCE Mission to Georgia, respectively. After the 2008 war, despite EU objections, Russia opposed renewing the mandates of both the UN Observer Mission in Georgia and the OSCE Mission to Georgia, and both missions withdrew from the country in the summer of 2009, solidifying the EU's role as a key third-party actor.

Public calls for fact-finding emerged over the course of the final months of 2008, as the EU more fully enmeshed itself in this context, and as tensions lingered in the wake of the conflict, in particular after Russia, first, exhibited reluctance to fully adhere to the troop withdrawal element of the

[7] For the mandate of the EU Monitoring Mission, see EU Monitoring Mission, *Council Joint Action 2008/736/CFSP of 15 September 2008 on the European Union Monitoring Mission in Georgia*, available at eur-lex.europa.eu/LexUriServ/LexUriServ.do?uri=OJ:L:2008:248:0026:0031:EN:PDF.

ceasefire agreement, and second, recognised the independence of South Ossetia and Abkhazia. Representatives of the Georgian government spoke about the issue with particular forcefulness, as evidenced by Georgian President Mikheil Saakashvili's comments during the 63rd Session of the UN General Assembly in September 2008:

> There should be an exhaustive, independent investigation of the origins and causes of this war. Investigators must have unimpeded access to all officials, documents, and intelligence. Georgia welcomes such an investigation. My government is ready to share every piece of evidence and provide access to every witness sought by investigators. We call on the other party to this conflict to fully cooperate and not obstruct this investigation. This is how democracies behave. The truth must come out not only to clarify how events unfolded last month, but to help us answer the fundamental questions that this invasion has raised.[8]

However, calls for international investigations initially overlooked the EU and instead were directed toward other potential fact-finding actors, such as the OSCE, the UN Secretary General, the International Criminal Court, and the International Humanitarian Fact-Finding Commission.[9] A perception emerged within the EU, though, that an authoritative account of the conflict could facilitate EU cohesiveness about the route forward and bolster the legitimacy of ongoing EU mediation efforts.[10] Hence, on 2 December 2008, the Council of the EU adopted Council Resolution 2008/901/CSSP, which established the IIFFMCG, stating:

> The aim of the fact-finding mission shall be to investigate the origins and the course of the conflict in Georgia, including with regard to international law,

[8] *Statement by HE Mr Mikheil Saakashvili President of Georgia*, The General Debate of the 63rd Session of the UN General Assembly, Georgia (23 September 2008), available at www.un.org/ga/63/generaldebate/pdf/georgia_en.pdf.

[9] For examples, see 'Russia vs Georgia: The Fallout', Europe Report No 195 (22 August 2008) p iii, available at www.crisisgroup.org/~/media/Files/europe/195_russia_vs_georgia___the_fallout.pdf; 'Georgia: International Groups Should Send Missions' (*Human Rights Watch*, 18 August 2008), available at www.hrw.org/legacy/english/docs/2008/08/17/georgi19633_txt.htm; 'Sarkozy Seeks Russian Troop Pullout From Georgia' (*Deutsche Welle*, 8 September 2008), available at www.dw.com/en/sarkozy-seeks-russian-troop-pullout-from-georgia/a-3626092; 'Georgia/Russia Conflict: Counting the Cost of War: Return, Security and Truth Still a Long Way Off' (*Amnesty International*, 18 November 2008), available at www.amnesty.org/en/press-releases/2008/11/georgiarussia-conflict-counting-cost-war-return-security-and-truth-still.

[10] Within the EU, divisions arose between Member States about the extent to which the EU should explicitly or implicitly condemn Russia for the conflict, and this lack of consensus within the EU persisted in the wake of the ceasefire. See H Dijkstra, 'EU External Representation in Conflict Resolution: When does the Presidency or the High Representative Speak for Europe?' 15(1) *European Integration Online Papers* 13, available at eiop.or.at/eiop/pdf/2011-001.pdf. See also 'Did Saakashvili Lie? The West Begins to Doubt Georgian Leader' Spiegel Online International (15 September 2008), available at www.spiegel.de/international/world/did-saakashvili-lie-the-west-begins-to-doubt-georgian-leader-a-578273-2.html.

> humanitarian law and human rights, and the accusations made in that context. The geographical scope and time span of the investigation will be sufficiently broad to determine all the possible causes of the conflict. The results of the investigation will be presented to the parties to the conflict, and to the Council, and the [UN] in the form of a report.[11]

One can discern from this language, as well as from statements included in the mission's final report, that the mandate married two core objectives. First, the mission would aim to produce an authoritative factual account of the conflict with the goal of easing political tensions. Toward this end, the mission's final report states:

> [B]y presenting the sequence of events on the basis of the information available at the time of its writing, and by discussing the responsibility for them, the Report will provide a firm basis from which to arrive at a sober assessment of the situation as it really is. This is the starting point for all serious and responsible politics, and in that sense the Report will make a contribution to the stable and peaceful environment the South Caucasus needs as a prerequisite for the development of all the countries and nations sharing the region. It is the Mission's hope that all sides in the conflict will understand and accept these principles, even if some of their actions may be reviewed in a critical manner.[12]

Second, the mission would aim to facilitate accountability efforts, as suggested by the mandate's reference to specific legal lenses—in particular, international humanitarian law, human rights, 'allegations of war crimes', and the Helsinki Final Act.[13]

One final important point about the surrounding political environment is that the EU's overall response to the 2008 war occurred in the context of UN Security Council gridlock.[14] A lack of consensus emerged between the five permanent members of the UN Security Council over how the Security Council should react, and the EU stepped into the resulting vacuum. By doing so, the EU was able to capitalise on the fact that, as one author asserts, 'In the eyes of the conflict parties the EU enjoyed a reasonable degree of impartiality at least when compared to other possible actors, such as the US, NATO [North Atlantic Treaty Organization], the UN or OSCE.'[15] Given the delicate nature of gathering information about allegations of violations of international law, and the prevalence of accusations of bias that

[11] *Independent International Fact-Finding Mission on the Conflict in Georgia Report* (*IIFMCG Report*) vol 1 (September 2009) 3, (IIFFMCG Report) available at echr.coe.int/Documents/HUDOC_38263_08_Annexes_ENG.pdf.

[12] *IIFMCG Report* (n 11) 9.

[13] *IIFMCG Report* (n 11) 3.

[14] See T Forsberg, 'The EU as a Peace-Maker in the Russo-Georgian War' (*Fifth Pan-European Conference on EU Politics*, June 2010) 3–4, available at www.jhubc.it/ecpr-porto/virtualpaperroom/136.pdf.

[15] Forsberg (n 14) 6.

fact-finding missions face,[16] the perception of the EU as relatively objective had the potential to situate the IIFFMCG well for the task at hand. The rest of this section will examine the extent to which this proved to be true.

3.2.2. Implementing the Mandate

The IIFFMCG was led by a solitary Head of Mission who relied on a core team of three members, various experts hired as contractors, and a Senior Advisory Board composed of prominent European diplomats. Personnel recruiting difficulties arose due to the lack of a sufficient pool of qualified practitioners able to make themselves available at short notice, and as the Head of Mission wrote after the mission's conclusion, 'procedural and financial matters tend[ed] to absorb the limited staff, to the detriment of the delicate and demanding fact-finding exercise'.[17] Nevertheless, the mission succeeded in fulfilling its mandate and produced a final report that was published in September 2009.[18]

The mission's approach to gathering and analysing information seems to have been fairly ad hoc. For example, although the mission was attentive to issues of witness and victim protection and staff security,[19] according to the one of the mission's investigators, 'There were no formal [staff security] guidelines', only 'a common understanding that I would apply security procedures'.[20] Similarly, there was no mission-wide discussion about how the mission would approach standards of proof.[21]

[16] See generally R Grace, 'Communication and Report Drafting in Monitoring, Reporting, and Fact-Finding Missions' *Program on Humanitarian Policy and Conflict Research* (Harvard University, 2014), available at papers.ssrn.com/sol3/papers.cfm?abstract_id=2462590.

[17] H Tagliavini, 'The August 2008 Conflict in Georgia' (2011) 105 *American Society of International Law* 92.

[18] The report's publication was launched with a public relations effort—including an editorial that that the Head of Mission wrote for *The New York Times*—geared toward raising the visibility of the mission. See H Tagliavini, 'Lessons of the Georgia Conflict', *The New York Times* (30 September 2009), www.nytimes.com/2009/10/01/opinion/01iht-edtagliavini.html?_r=0&adxnnl=1&adxnnlx=1383686542-DmN+dP5xC9k6Ay6bky8sfw. A webpage was created for the mission that hosted the report online, but the webpage is no longer active.

[19] The Head of Mission wrote, 'In order to protect the mission members and the witnesses, we negotiated a diplomatic status agreement with Switzerland, where the mission was based, granting privileges and immunities for our members. To negotiate it with the parties to the conflict, which in fact was even more important for the mission, took quite some time.' See Tagliavini (n 17) 93.

[20] Interview with Théo Boutruche, IHL/Human Rights Expert, Independent International Fact-Finding Mission on the Conflict in Georgia (13 August 2013) (on file with author).

[21] Although, as one of the mission's investigators stated, 'Even if the mission had all met together and discussed a common approach to standards of proof, we could still have wound up applying different standards, depending on the area being researched. For example, for issues such as passportization, the use of force, self-defence, and military questions, they

In terms of drawing from institutional memory, it is important to note that fact-finding was not unprecedented within the EU. Previously, the EU had engaged in information gathering on human rights practices in the context of its Generalised System of Preferences, which offers developing countries low tariffs or completely duty-free imports, conditioned on the countries' respect for human rights.[22] On six occasions under this mechanism, the EU has initiated investigations into human rights practices, three of which led to the suspension of trade privileges. However, the methodologically ad hoc nature of the IIFFMCG, as well as the aforementioned issues of garnering human resource and logistical capacities, suggest the limited institutional infrastructure within which the mission operated.

The rest of this section addresses two notable points regarding the mission's approach to addressing the politically sensitive issue of responsibility for the conflict. First, the report actually provides two different answers to the question of who was responsible for the war. On the specific question of whether the Georgian attack on Russian peacekeeping forces on 7–8 August 2008 was justified, Volume I asserts that, since the mission could not verify allegations that Russian armed forces were preparing for a major attack, Russian peacekeeping forces had not lost their legal protection from attack, meaning that Georgia's attack violated international law.[23] In contrast, Volume II declares the IIFFMCG unable to reach a conclusion on this point due to a lack of factual clarity.[24]

Why does the *IIFFMCG Report* seem to contradict itself? One curious, and often overlooked, aspect of the report's structure informs the answer to this question. The report is divided into three volumes. Volume I provides

were using specific documents or were investigating less conflicting accounts. For human rights and international humanitarian law, I would have applied a strict balance of probabilities test because the conflict in Georgia was, like many other conflicts, plagued by allegations and counter-allegations': Interview with Théo Boutruche (n 20).

[22] See generally EC Directorate-General for Trade, *The European Union's Generalised System of Preferences* (2004), available at trade.ec.europa.eu/doclib/docs/2004/march/tradoc_116448.pdf. For an overview of issues faced in these efforts, as well as examination of the EU's approach to Myanmar case study, see L Beke, 'The EU GSP: A Preference for Human Rights and Good Governance? The Case of Myanmar' (2015) Leuven Centre for Global Governance Studies Working Paper No 155/2015, available at ghum.kuleuven.be/ggs/publications/working_papers/new_series/wp151-160/wp155-beke-hachez.pdf. See also B Brandtner and A Rosas, 'Trade Preferences and Human Rights' in P Alston (ed), *The EU and Human Rights* (New York, Oxford University Press, 1999) 717; and E Fierro, *The EU's Approach to Human Rights Conditionality in Practice* (New York, Martinus Nijhoff Publishers, 2003).

[23] *IIFMCG Report* (n 11) vol I, 23.

[24] *IIFMCG Report* (n 11) vol II, 326–27. This point was made in A Lott, 'The Tagliavini Report Revisited: Jus ad Bellum and the Legality of the Russian Intervention in Georgia' (2012) 28 *Utrecht Journal of International and European Law* 63.

a description of the creation of the mission, articulates the mission's aims, and offers the mission's key findings. Volume II contains an extensive examination of various issues, such as the conflict's historical background, alleged violations of international humanitarian law and human rights, and Russia's passportisation policy. Volume III includes voluminous submissions to the mission solicited from the four parties concerned—Georgia, Russia, South Ossetia, and Abkhazia—preceded by an introduction that specifies, 'This Volume is simply a compilation of the material received from the sides, and is not intended to be comprehensive.'[25]

Although commentaries on the report have tended to place both Volumes I and II on equal footing, a caveat similar to that included in Volume III appears also at the beginning of Volume II. This caveat states:

> This volume contains a selection of contributions by experts in the military, legal, humanitarian, human rights, political and historical fields. They were critically reviewed by the Fact-Finding Mission and constitute the basis for this Report on the Conflict in Georgia.
>
> The elaboration, findings and opinions expressed in these texts do not necessarily reflect the views of the Mission. In this regard, the views and findings as laid out in Volume I shall be considered as authoritative.[26]

Essentially, this declaration makes clear that Volume II, which many readers treat as the bulk of the report itself, is actually intended to be an annex of supporting materials that one should not necessarily deem to be authoritative. Similar to the documents included in Volume III, Volume II's findings, authored by the experts who worked as contractors for the mission, do not represent the mission's conclusions. This choice leaves ambiguous the reasons why these contrasting findings were reached and has the potential to create confusion about which conclusions are valid.

Second, the IIFFMCG opted to examine the issue of ascribing responsibility for initiating the conflict through the lens of *jus ad bellum*. The mandate did not require the mission to draw legal, as opposed to only factual, conclusions about this question. Indeed, the mandate makes no mention of *jus ad bellum*, although it specifically references other relevant bodies of law, as noted earlier in this chapter.

The incorporation of *jus ad bellum* into a fact-finding report is somewhat unusual. One of the few UN reports that offers a *jus ad bellum* legal analysis is that of the Secretary General's Panel of Inquiry on the 31 May 2010 Flotilla Incident. However, in this report, the Panel opted to place the legal analysis in an appendix, based on the rationale that the legal

[25] *IIFMCG Report* (n 11) vol III, 3.
[26] *IIFMCG Report* (n 11) vol II, 1.

analysis was 'too exhaustive' and that relegating the legal analysis to the end of the report would 'place more emphasis on factual findings and what should happen next'.[27] The IIFFMCG could have made a similar choice to foreground factual findings, especially given the mission's aim 'to improve the prospects for securing a lasting, peaceful solution to the conflict in Georgia', as the *IIFFMCG Report* states.[28] Instead, by incorporating *jus ad bellum* into the report, the IIFFMCG examined one of the most politically pertinent issues of the report through the lens of a body of law that is highly contested among states. As various scholarly critiques of the IIFFMCG's legal analysis have noted, the report, at some points, takes stances on disputed questions of *jus ad bellum* without explicitly acknowledging the potential for alternate interpretations, and at other points, misstates or misinterprets the law entirely.[29]

On the one hand, such complexities are not particular to *jus ad bellum*. Indeed, fact-finding practitioners frequently operate under mandates that require the mission to make determinations about unsettled or evolving areas of international humanitarian law or human rights law. Many such reports have not been sufficiently transparent about these inherent complexities, and some have made blatant errors of legal analysis.[30] On the other hand—given the response to the report by the parties to the conflict, as the next section will examine—one could consider the experience of the IIFFMCG to constitute a cautionary tale regarding the limited utility of *jus ad bellum* for generating consensus amidst disparate perceptions of a conflict's origins.

3.2.3. Aftermath

The Head of Mission of the IIFFMCG has credited the mission with leading to a '[d]e-escalation of pressure in the highly controversial and heated debates over what had really happened'.[31] Overall, though, the rift between the contrasting narratives promoted by the parties to the conflict endured

[27] Interview with Sir Geoffrey Palmer, Chair, Secretary-General's Panel of Inquiry on the 31 May 2010 Flotilla Incident (4 April 2013) (on file with author).

[28] *IIFMCG Report* (n 11) vol I, 9.

[29] For example, see generally Lott (n 24), and C Henderson and JA Green, 'The *Jus Ad Bellum* and Entities Short of Statehood in the Report on the Conflict in Georgia' (2010) 59(1) *International Comparative Law Quarterly* 129.

[30] See generally T Boutruche, 'Selecting and Applying Legal Lenses in Monitoring, Reporting, and Fact-Finding Missions' *Program on Humanitarian Policy and Conflict Research* (Harvard University, October 2013), available at papers.ssrn.com/sol3/papers.cfm?abstract_id=2365435.

[31] Tagliavini (n 17) 94.

even after the report's publication. On the question of responsibility for starting the war, representatives from both Russia and Georgia claimed that the report cast blame on the other side.[32] Indeed, state representatives and fact-finding practitioners alike have criticised the *IIFMCG Report* for its lack of forcefulness on this issue. The Russian ambassador to NATO stated, 'This report has a pseudo-balanced approach… All the parties are criticized a little, including the Ossetians, the Russians and Georgia's Western patrons. But one no longer sees the wood for the trees.'[33] And one high-level fact-finding practitioner has similarly commented on the report's overly cautious approach:

> I think the Georgia exercise is a good example as something that went well. At the same time, one has to admit that because everything was drafted so cautiously and carefully that in terms of the political impact of the report, it has been somewhat limited. When you read between the lines, you understand that, for instance, the Georgian armed forces fell into a trap. They took an initiative that they should not have taken. But it's said in a very careful way. So you don't have an article in the press. It did not trigger the major re-evaluation. It was said so softly that nobody had an interest in dotting the I's. It systematically avoided any statements that could lead to some polemics.[34]

The mission's impact might be more readily discernible in relation to accountability. On 27 January 2016, the Pre-Trial Chamber of the International Criminal Court authorised the Prosecutor to proceed with an investigation of alleged war crimes and crimes against humanity committed before, during, and after the 2008 conflict.[35] The Prosecutor's request for authorisation of an investigation cites the *IIFFMCG Report* throughout,

[32] Georgia's viewpoint was, 'Almost all of the facts in the report do confirm the Georgian version of events … The report goes into detail in confirming the obvious-that Russia invaded Georgia; Georgia never attacked Russia or any other country.' See M Champion, 'Tblisi Started '08 War, but Moscow Also at Fault, EU Finds' *The Wall Street Journal* (1 October 2009), available at www.wsj.com/articles/SB125431087432152321. In contrast, Russia's ambassador to the EU asserted that the report 'provides an unequivocal confirmation—an unequivocal answer to the main question: who started the war … And it says squarely that it was the Georgian massive shelling and artillery attack on the city of Tskhinval [known in Georgia as Tskhinvali] on the night of the 7th to 8th August 2008'. See 'EU Report On 2008 War Tilts Against Georgia' (*Radio Free Europe* 30 September 2009), available at www.rferl.org/content/EU_Report_On_2008_War_Tilts_Against_Georgia/1840447.html.

[33] B Bidderm 'New Report on Russia-Georgia War: EU Investigators Debunk Saakashvili's Lies' *Spiegel Online International* (1 October 2009), available at www.spiegel.de/international/world/new-report-on-russia-georgia-war-eu-investigators-debunk-saakashvili-s-lies-a-652512.html.

[34] Confidential Interview with a High-Level Fact-Finding Practitioner (name of interviewee on file), (Summer 2013).

[35] For the Pre-Trial Chamber's decision, see International Criminal Court, 'Situation in Georgia: Decision on the Prosecutor's request for authorization of an investigation' Pre-Trial Chamber I (27 January 2016), available at www.icc-cpi.int/iccdocs/doc/doc2195945.pdf.

and includes all three volumes of the report in full in the document's annexes, indicating the important role that the IIFFMCG has come to play in the context of the Prosecutor's case.[36]

3.3. AFRICAN UNION COMMISSION OF INQUIRY ON SOUTH SUDAN

3.3.1. Creating the Mission

The African Union Peace and Security Council's adoption of the AUCISS mandate followed decades of involvement by the AU—and before 2002, by the African Union's predecessor, the Organization of African Unity—in South(ern) Sudan. Throughout South Sudan's years-long journey toward independent statehood, which culminated in 2011 with the country's declaration of independence, as well as through post-independence economic and institutional development efforts, African Union support and involvement in South Sudan has been driven by a policy emphasis on 'African Solutions to African problems.'[37]

After the eruption of the South Sudanese Civil War in December 2013, a plethora of Africa-based and UN entities responded to the deteriorating humanitarian situation. The Intergovernmental Authority on Development (IGAD) served as the institutional umbrella for international mediation efforts between South Sudanese governmental and opposition representatives.[38] Various UN entities, including the UN Mission in South Sudan (UNMISS), the UN Children's Fund, and the Office of the High Commissioner for Human Rights, gathered information about and reported on alleged violations of international law and civilian vulnerabilities.[39] The UN Security Council voted to bolster UNMISS's civilian protection capacities by increasing its military personnel to 12,500.[40]

36 See International Criminal Court, 'Situation in Georgia: Request for Authorization of an Investigation Pursuant to Article 15' (corrected version), ICC-01/15-4-Corr, Pre Trial Chamber I (16 October 2015), available at www.icc-cpi.int/iccdocs/doc/doc2160852.pdf.

37 GK Komey, AA Osman, and N Melakedingel, 'Operationalizing African-led Solutions in Peace and Security: Case Studies from South Sudan and Somalia' (2013) *Institute for Peace and Security Studies* 45.

38 See generally KP Apuuli, 'IGAD's Mediation in the Current South Sudan Conflict: Prospects and Challenges' (2015) 8(2) *African Security* 120.

39 See 'UN hopes to have peacekeeping reinforcements in strife-torn South Sudan within 48 hours' *UN News Centre* (26 December 2013), available at www.un.org/apps/news/story.asp?NewsID=46829#.VwKrTBGofzJ; and C Hauser, 'In South Sudan, Reports of Massacres and Mass Graves' The Lede, *International New York Times* (24 December 2013), available at thelede.blogs.nytimes.com/2013/12/24/in-south-sudan-reports-of-massacres-and-mass-graves/?ref=africa.

40 See UN Security Council Resolution 2132, UN Doc S/RES/2132 (24 December 2013).

African Union engagement included the participation of the African Union Commissioner for Peace and Security in the IGAD mediation efforts.[41] Additionally, the Chairperson of the African Union Commission and the African Union Peace and Security Council issued statements expressing concern about the violence and emphasising the importance of resolving the political dispute underlying the crisis.[42] On 31 December 2013, within weeks of the outbreak of the conflict, the Peace and Security Council adopted the AUCISS mandate, which:

> Requests the Chairperson of the Commission, in consultation with the Chairperson of the African Commission on Human and Peoples' Rights (ACHPR) and other relevant AU structures, to urgently establish a Commission to investigate the human rights violations and other abuses committed during the armed conflict in South Sudan and make recommendations on the best ways and means to ensure accountability, reconciliation and healing among all South Sudanese communities. Council requests that the above-mentioned Commission submit its report to Council within a maximum period of three months…[43]

Similar to the mandate for the IIFFMCG, this decision created a mission oriented toward multiple aims—in this instance, 'accountability,

[41] African Union, 'The African Union Welcomes the IGAD Ministerial Mission to South Sudan' (*Peaceau.org*, 19 December 2013), available at www.peaceau.org/en/article/the-african-union-welcomes-the-igad-ministerial-mission-to-south-sudan.

[42] For statements of the Chairperson of the African Union Commission, see African Union, 'The African Union Deeply Concerned About the Ongoing Developments in South Sudan' (*Peaceau.org*, 17 December 2013), available at www.peaceau.org/uploads/auc-southsudan17.12.2013.pdf; African Union, 'The African Union Welcomes the IGAD Ministerial Mission to South Sudan' *Press Release* (19 December 2013), available at www.peaceau.org/uploads/auc-com-south-sudan-19-2013.pdf; 'African Union calls for Christmas truce in South Sudan' *Reuters* (21 December 2013) available at www.reuters.com/article/southsudan-unrest-africanunion-idUSL6N0K00D920131221; African Union, 'The AU and IGAD reiterate the call for an immediate ceasefire in South Sudan and urgent dialogue between the parties' (*Peaceau.org*, 25 December 2013), available at www.peaceau.org/en/article/press-release-the-au-and-igad-reiterate-the-call-for-an-immediate-ceasefire-in-south-sudan-and-urgent-dialogue-between-the-parties; and African Union, 'Report of the Chairperson of the Commission on the situation in South Sudan: 411th meeting of the Peace and Security Council' (*Peaceau.org*, 30 December 2013), available at www.peaceau.org/en/article/report-of-the-chairperson-of-the-commission-on-the-situation-in-south-sudan-411th-meeting-of-the-peace-and-security-council. For press statements of the African Union Peace and Security Council, see African Union, 'Press Statement of the 409 Meeting of the Peace and Security Council on the situation in South Sudan' (*Peaceau.org*, 18 December 2013), available at www.peaceau.org/en/article/press-statement-of-the-409-meeting-of-the-psc-on-the-situation-in-south-sudan; and African Union, 'Press Statement of the 410th Meeting of the Peace and Security Council on the situation in South Sudan' (*Peaceau.org*, 24 December 2013), available at www.peaceau.org/en/article/press-statement-of-the-410th-meeting-of-the-peace-and-security-council.

[43] Peace and Security Council, '411th Meeting at the Level of Heads of State and Government' (*Peaceau.org*, 30 December 2013), available at www.peaceau.org/uploads/psc-com-411-south-sudan-30–12-2013.pdf.

reconciliation and healing.' The mission perceived these aims to feed into one another. As the final report states:

> It is the Commission's view that while reconciliation merits attention as an independent pursuit, when considered as a 'by-product' of other initiatives and processes related to accountability including criminal accountability and reparations as well as institutional reforms, reconciliation finds expression in various aspects of the Commission's mandate.[44]

However, as this section will explain, tensions between these aims nevertheless emerged, leading to uncertainty about the fate of the mission's final report.

3.3.2. Implementing the Mandate

The AUCISS, compared to the IIFFMCG, conformed to a more traditional organisational structure for a commission of inquiry. Five commissioners, one of whom served as the chairperson, led the mission with the support of a secretariat. The commissioners' eclectic professional backgrounds, including the former president of Nigeria, high-level African Union actors, and academics, reflected the mission's multi-pronged focus on accountability and reconciliation. The mandate also specifically authorised the involvement of the ACHPR, offering the mission the opportunity to benefit from decades of ACHPR experiences in developing and refining systematised procedures for gathering information about alleged violations of international law.[45]

The systematised investigative methodology detailed in the mission's final report suggests the benefits that the AUCISS derived from its engagement not only with the ACHPR but also with a wide array of other institutional actors, including the Office of the High Commissioner for Human Rights, the Office of the Special Advisor of the Secretary General of the UN on the Prevention of Genocide, and United Nations Women.[46] In stark contrast to the IIFFMCG, the *AUCISS Report* specifies an overarching standard of proof ('reasonable suspicion'), and in the annex, includes an

[44] *Final Report of the African Union Commission of Inquiry on South Sudan* (October 2014) 32 (*Final AUCISS Report*).

[45] For information about the ACHPR's rules and procedures, see generally African Commission on Human and People's Rights, 'Rules and Procedure of the African Commission on Human and People's Rights' (2010), available at www.achpr.org/files/instruments/rules-of-procedure-2010/rules_of_procedure_2010_en.pdf. For an overview of the role of the ACHPR, see generally S Gumedze, 'Bringing Communications before the African Commission on Human and Peoples' Rights' (2003) 3 *African Human Rights Law Journal* 118, available at www.corteidh.or.cr/tablas/R21582.pdf.

[46] *Final AUCISS Report* (n 44) 3.

eight-page protocol outlining the process by which commissioners would make decisions, the roles of the different staff members, and extensive details about the mission's investigative policies.[47]

However, similar to the IFFMCG, the AUCISS suffered from a dearth of logistical capacity that hampered its operations. The three-month timeline specified in the mandate proved to be unfeasible, and in June 2014, after undertaking visits to South Sudan as well as to neighboring countries, the AUCISS produced only an interim report that refrained from offering conclusions about alleged violations of international law. This report elaborates at length the challenges that the mission faced:

> The Commission has faced several problems, some of which are linked to the nature of the institution itself and where it is headquartered. The Commission was created in the midst of a crisis, which has meant that it had limited time to set up internal structures to enable it begin its work. Equally, the fact that the members of the Commission were not appointed on fulltime basis has posed some scheduling problems as members have had to find time within their regular engagements. While the nature of the work requires assemblage of varied expertise, this is not readily available within the AU. A fair amount of time was expended, in conditions demanding urgency, in procuring required expertise. The Commission has also been hamstrung by lack of adequate resources, which has among other things, resulted in inadequate logistical arrangements in the field.[48]

These difficulties fueled perceptions of various stakeholders in South Sudan and throughout the region that the AUCISS would prove to be an impotent entity.[49] The Peace and Security Council extended the AUCISS's mandate through September 2014,[50] and the mission continued its work and produced a final report during this timeframe.

Three particular choices that the AUCISS made departed in an interesting manner from traditional fact-finding practice. First, the mission integrated gender analysis into its work to an extent that surpasses the typical fact-finding mission.[51] The protocol included in the report's annex directly

[47] *Final AUCISS Report* (n 44) 208–315.

[48] African Union, *Interim Report of the African Union Commission of Inquiry on South Sudan*, International Criminal Court (June 2014) 5, (*Interim AUCISS Report*), available at www.icc-now.org/documents/Final_-_Interim_Report_Assembly_AU_19_(XXIII)__E.pdf.

[49] American Bar Association, 'Assessment of Justice, Accountability and Reconciliation Measures in South Sudan' *Rule of Law Initiative* (June 2014) 11–12, available at www.americanbar.org/content/dam/aba/directories/roli/sudan/aba_roli_sudan_assessment_final_report_0614.authcheckdam.pdf. See also O-O Alex, 'Interim report of the AU commission of inquiry on South Sudan below expectations' *Pambazuka News* (31 July 2014), available at www.pambazuka.org/governance/interim-report-au-commission-inquiry-south-sudan-below-expectations.

[50] 'African Union extends mandate of inquiry commission on South Sudan' *Sudan Tribune* (11 July 2014), available at www.sudantribune.com/spip.php?article51641.

[51] Indeed, see *Final AUCISS Report* (n 44) 12, which states that the mission adopted a 'gendered approach to all aspects of its work'.

specifies, 'In keeping with the Commission's gender policy investigators shall pay particular attention to allegations of sexual and gender based violence (SGBV).'[52] In addition to SGBV, the mission also addressed other issues with a gender dimension, including the importance of incorporating women into the reconciliation process and gender-based workforce discrimination.[53] This focus on gender is likely a reflection of the importance that the African Union has placed on promoting gender equality,[54] as well as the professional profiles of the practitioners selected to serve on the mission—in particular, one of the commissioners was the African Union Chairperson's Special Envoy on Women, Peace and Security,[55] and a sexual and gender-based violence expert was deployed from the roster of Justice Rapid Response.[56]

Second, the report presents direct quotes from people who offered statements to the mission. Some of these sources are identified by name, some by generic identifying information (eg, 'key SPLM official'),[57] and some are kept anonymous (indicated by footnotes that state, 'Details of witness on file with the Commission').[58] The potential benefit of this choice is to enrich the report with the voices of various people from whom the mission gathered information. One potential drawback, though, is the resulting witness protection issues. Indeed, a portion of the mission's report was leaked prematurely, and concerns arose about witness confidentiality due to the fact that the leaked document seemed to include identifiable information linked to witnesses who had given statements to the mission.[59]

Third, the report was published along with a separate opinion drafted by one of the commissioners, indicating the lack of consensus that had

52 *Final AUCISS Report* (n 44) 314.

53 *Final AUCISS Report* (n 44) 243 and 285.

54 See generally *African Union Gender Policy*, available at www.un.org/en/africa/osaa/pdf/au/gender_policy_2009.pdf; BJ Omotosho, 'African Union and Gender Equality in the Last Ten Years: Some Issues and Prospects for Consideration' (2015) 1(5) *Journal of Integrated Social Sciences* 92, available at www.jiss.org/documents/volume_5/issue_1/JISS%20 2015%205(1)%2092-104%20African%20Union.pdf; O Martin, 'The African Union's Mechanisms to Foster Gender Mainstreaming and Ensure Women's Political Participation and Representation' (2013) *International IDEA*, available at www.idea.int/resources/analysis/loader.cfm?csModule=security/getfile&pageid=58486; and African Commission on Human and People's Rights, *Declaration on Gender Equality*, available at www.achpr.org/instruments/declaration-on-gender-equality-in-africa.

55 See *Final AUCISS Report* (n 44) 4 and 10.

56 Justice Rapid Response, *Annual Report 2014* 10, available at www.justicerapidresponse.org/wp-content/uploads/2015/03/Annual_Report_Final_Email.pdf.

57 *Final AUCISS Report* (n 44) 98.

58 For example, see *Final AUCISS Report* (n 44) 135.

59 JM Jok, 'The African Union and the Botched Responsibility to Act on Behalf of South Sudan's Victims of Conflict' *The Sudd Institute* (17 March 2015) 5, available at www.suddinstitute.org/assets/Publications/ResponseAUCISSJok.pdf.

existed within the commission.[60] One key difference between these two documents relates to a central aspect of the mission's mandate: the question of how accountability should be pursued. An assertion included only in the separate opinion, and not in the *AUCISS Report*, states, 'Key to the pursuit of political justice in the transitional period is the exclusion from high office of all those held politically accountable for the mass violence that followed the crisis of December 15, 2013.'[61]

The fact that the commissioners were unable to agree on all aspects of the final report deprived the mission of the powerful seal of authoritativeness that would have derived from their full consensus. In short, in the 'commissioner' model of fact-finding mission design, much of the mission's legitimacy hinges on the perception that the commissioners are eminent and trusted figures able to lead the mission in an unbiased manner. The commissioners' role is traditionally to jointly shoulder public responsibility for the report's findings and recommendations. Numerous missions mandated by the UN Human Rights Council have followed this model, although the standard design for such missions is for three commissioners, whereas the AUCISS had five. The AUCISS experience suggests that, on missions with a greater number of commissioners, and with a higher degree of professional eclecticism among them, the difficulties in consensus building can become more severe.

3.3.3. Aftermath

The African Union Peace and Security Council initially made a controversial choice not to publish the mission's report, evidently due to a belief that the report's release could stymie ongoing IGAD-led peace efforts. As a consequence, worries that the AUCISS would fail to meet expectations further escalated, fueled by a perception that the Council was unnecessarily sacrificing justice for the possibility of peace.[62] The salience of this

[60] The report was released on 27 October 2015. See African Union, 'The African Union Releases the Report of the AU' (27 October 2015), available at www.peaceau.org/en/article/abc. For the separate opinion, see generally M Mamdani, 'Separate Opinion of The AU Commission of Inquiry on South Sudan' (20 October 2014), available at paanluelwel2011.files.wordpress.com/2015/10/separate-dissenting-opinion-of-the-auciss-by-mamdani.pdf.

[61] See 'Separate Opinion', Mamdani (n 60) 58. Also see *Final AUCISS Report* (n 44) 230 and 301, which reference the disparity in the commissioners' opinions.

[62] See LB Deng, 'The AU Commission of Inquiry on South Sudan: Justice First or Peace?' *The New Nation* (25 June 2015), available at www.newnationsouthsudan.com/opinion/the-au-commission-of-inquiry-on-south-sudan-justice-first-or-peace.html; 'South Sudan's peace process: One step forward, two steps backward?' *Solomondersso* (4 February 2015), available at solomondersso.wordpress.com/2015/02/04/south-sudans-peace-process-one-step-forward-two-steps-backward; 'Will the report of AU Commission of Inquiry on South Sudan be released?' *Sudan Tribune* (20 July 2015), available at www.sudantribune.com/spip.

'peace versus justice' outcry became amplified after August 2015, when South Sudanese government and opposition representatives signed a peace deal that included an agreement to establish a hybrid court to try alleged perpetrators of war crimes committed during the conflict.[63] The conflict continued despite the peace agreement, but the possibility arose that the AUCISS's findings could prove useful in the context of this hybrid accountability mechanism. The Peace and Security Council reversed its decision in September 2015, when the body finally adopted a decision that established the Hybrid Court of South Sudan and requested that the AUCISS report be released.[64] The report was made public the following month.

In terms of impact, at the time of the writing of this chapter, progress on both accountability and reconciliation remains elusive. The African Union has yet to move forward with establishing the hybrid court.[65] Furthermore, despite the fact that the conflict in South Sudan has intensified, the African Union has not established a follow-up mission to the AUCISS. Instead, the locus of fact-finding in relation to this context has shifted definitively to the UN.[66] Indeed, the UN Human Rights Council decision in March 2016 to establish a UN commission of inquiry on South Sudan solidified the

php?article55760; DK Deng, 'No Peace, No Justice: How the African Union is failing South Sudan' *African Arguments* (2 February 2015), available at africanarguments.org/2015/02/02/no-peace-no-justice-how-the-african-union-is-failing-south-sudan-by-david-k-deng; S Wheeler, 'Opinion: AU report should be made public now' *Radio Tamazuj* (15 December 2014), available at radiotamazuj.org/en/article/opinion-au-report-should-be-made-public-now; East and Horn of Africa Human Rights Defenders, 'State of human rights in East and the Horn of Africa: Statement by the East and Horn of Africa Human Rights Defenders Project to 56th Ordinary Session of the Africa Commission on Human and Peoples' Rights Banjul, Gambia' (21 April 2015), available at www.pambazuka.org/activism/state-human-rights-east-and-horn-africa; 'Why is AU sitting on South Sudan inquiry report?' *Pambazuka News* (5 March 2015); and 'UN official demands AU report on S. Sudan crimes' *Sudan Tribune* (15 January 2015), available at www.sudantribune.com/spip.php?article53653, which quotes the UN Assistant Secretary General for Human Rights, Ivan Simonovic, as saying that an AU decision to keep the report from the public would be a 'very disturbing development'.

[63] See 'Joint Letter to the African Union Commission Chairperson Regarding South Sudan' (*Human Rights Watch*, 24 September 2015), available at www.hrw.org/news/2015/09/24/joint-letter-african-union-commission-chairperson-regarding-south-sudan.

[64] African Union, 'Communiqué of 547th meeting of the PSC, at the level of Heads of State and Government, on the situation in South Sudan' (26 September 2015), available at www.peaceau.org/en/article/communique-of-547th-meeting-of-the-psc-at-the-level-of-heads-of-state-and-government-on-the-situation-in-south-sudan.

[65] 'UN Human Rights Council: Joint NGO Letter on South Sudan' (*Human Rights Watch*, 4 March 2016), available at www.hrw.org/news/2016/03/04/un-human-rights-council-joint-ngo-letter-south-sudan.

[66] N Cumming-Bruce, 'Mass Rape, a Weapon of War, Traumatizes South Sudan' *International New York Times* (11 March 2016), available at www.nytimes.com/2016/03/12/world/africa/un-reports-systematic-rape-in-south-sudan-conflict.html.

fact that, in the wake of the AUCISS, fact-finding efforts directed toward the South Sudanese Civil War would be not African- but rather UN-led.[67]

3.4. LESSONS LEARNED

This section revisits the two overarching themes introduced at the beginning of this chapter, in light of the experiences of the IIFFMCG and the AUCISS. First, the section addresses the ad hoc nature of the domain of international fact-finding; second, the section focuses on the tension between the political and technical aspects of fact-finding practice. Through this examination, this section seeks to discern what lessons one can extrapolate from these cases to inform our understanding of fact-finding work.

3.4.1. The Ad Hoc Nature of the Domain of International Fact-Finding

Both the IIFFMCG and the AUCISS reveal the positive and negative aspects of the ad hoc state of the domain of international fact-finding. Potential benefits include the ability to adapt and tailor missions to the needs of particular contexts and to explore innovations in how missions are designed and conducted. The overarching risk, though, is that this methodological flexibility could lead to missions that are ineffective or undertaken in a professionally irresponsible manner. Indeed, through the recent proliferation of guidance and practice documents, practitioners and policymakers have sought to clarify generally accepted limits to flexibility.[68]

In many ways, the IIFFMCG and the AUCISS both followed paths that diverged from recent trends of fact-finding practice. Some of these divergences constituted welcome developments that could inform future fact-finding practice, for example, the prominence of gender analysis included

[67] UN Office of the High Commissioner for Human Rights, 'Human Rights Council establishes Commission on Human Rights in South Sudan' (23 March 2016), available at ohchr.org/EN/NewsEvents/Pages/DisplayNews.aspx?NewsID=18528&LangID=E.

[68] For example, see generally *HPCR Handbook on Commissions of Inquiry*; M Cherif Bassiouni and C Abraham (eds), *Siracusa Guidelines for International, Regional and National Fact-Finding Bodies* (Cambridge, Intersentia, 2013); 'Guidelines on International Human Rights Fact-Finding Visits and Reports' (Lund-London Guidelines), *Raoul Wallenberg Institute of Human Rights and Humanitarian Law* Lund University and the International Bar Association, available at www.factfindingguidelines.org/guidelines.html; and Office of the High Commissioner for Human Rights, *Commissions of Inquiry and Fact-Finding Missions on International Human Rights and Humanitarian Law: Guidance and Practice* (2015), available at www.ohchr.org/Documents/Publications/CoI_Guidance_and_Practice.pdf.

throughout the AUCISS report. Other choices, such as the confusion-inducing report structure of the IIFFMCG, were less successful. In other ways, both missions confronted issues with which the broader domain of fact-finding continues to grapple. For example, the leaked partial draft of the AUCISS report raised questions about how missions should handle potentially identifiable information given by witnesses, an issue that has been subject to a great deal of professional dialogue between fact-finding practitioners.[69] Similarly, the IIFFMCG's lack of a systematic approach to standards of proof speaks to questions that the domain of international fact-finding has been confronting about how, if at all, fact-finding practitioners should consider standards of proof in their work.

The overall benefit of methodological flexibility is that each context that a fact-finding mission examines is, to a certain extent, *sui generis*. Therefore, a rigid methodological template applicable to all fact-finding missions would likely prove to be unnecessarily constraining and unrealistic. Furthermore, with flexibility comes the possibility for innovation. The organisational structure of the IIFFMCG is a great example of seizing this opportunity. In contrast to the 'commissioner' model that guides the design of most fact-finding missions, the IIFFMCG was led by one Head of Mission and included a Senior Advisory Board that, as the Head of Mission wrote, 'was involved in all major decisions, and acted as a sort of protective shield against all kinds of attacks and attempts to discredit the mission'.[70] In the 'commissioner' model, the commissioners play the 'protective shield' role, serving the dual purpose of endowing the mission with both technical expertise and legitimacy. The novelty of the IIFFMCG's organisational structure is that Board members served this legitimising function but without the full spectrum of technical responsibilities accorded to the usual commissioner. Although the Senior Advisory Board was heavily involved in the mission's decisions, the consensus of Board members was evidently not required in the same way that it would have been if the mission had accorded with the more traditional 'commissioner' model. Given the consensus building difficulties that commissioners sometimes face, as evidenced by the experience of the AUCISS, a model along the lines of the IIFFMCG could warrant consideration for future missions.

[69] See generally C Petrigh, 'Protection of Witnesses, Victims, and Staff in Monitoring, Reporting, and Fact-Finding Missions' *Program on Humanitarian Policy and Conflict Research* (Harvard University, February 2014), available at papers.ssrn.com/sol3/papers.cfm?abstract_id=2392493.

[70] Tagliavini (n 17) 93.

The question facing the domain of international fact-finding is whether those who mandate, design, and implement fact-finding missions can capitalise on the potential benefits of agility and flexibility while mitigating the negative ramifications inherent in the lack of methodological systematisation. The experience of the AUCISS holds a lesson in this regard. By engaging extensively with other entities with expertise in gathering information about alleged violations of international law, the AUCISS situated itself well (albeit still imperfectly) to devise its own methodologies in a manner conducive to avoiding the methodological mistakes of the past.

3.4.2. The Political and Technical Dimensions of Fact-finding

The experiences of the IIFFMCG and the AUCISS underscore a disparity that sometimes exists between the aims of fact-finding professionals (as technically oriented practitioners) and those of the bodies that adopt fact-finding mandates (as primarily political entities). On the one hand, as fact-finding missions have proliferated in recent years, a perspective has emerged among many fact-finding practitioners and human rights advocates about the inherent utility of fact-finding reports for serving various ends—such as establishing a publicly available historical record, putting normative pressure on parties to a conflict to address alleged violations of international law, and gathering information that can feed into formal accountability efforts. On the other hand, the structure of the domain of international fact-finding, which lacks a centralised mandating authority, relegates decisions about creating missions, and about the scope of these missions' mandates, to different governmental and inter-governmental bodies.

Similar to the ad hoc aspects of fact-finding discussed above, the involvement of political bodies brings forth both opportunities and potential drawbacks. The opportunity, as the IIFMCG example indicates, is that the domain of international fact-finding allows for something comparable to forum shopping for the mandating entity most likely to be deemed legitimate. Indeed, as mentioned earlier in this chapter, during the 2008 Russia-Georgian War, in the midst of UN Security Council gridlock, the EU seized an opportunity to respond on various fronts, including mediation and fact-finding, benefiting from the perception that it could do so in a reasonably fair manner, at least relative to other third-party actors engaged in the context.

The risk, though, is that the domain of fact-finding becomes a battleground for institutional competition between different bodies vying for influence. For example, as one analyst notes, in the context of the violence that erupted in Libya in 2011, the African Union Peace and Security

Council announced its intention to send a fact-finding mission to Libya but delayed in doing so, which:

> …set the basis upon which it came to be marginalized by the UN SC. Had the PSC [Peace and Security Council] immediately established the fact-finding mission, it would have been very difficult for the UN SC to ignore it in the conflict… Thus, the failure of the PSC to immediately establish the fact-finding mission paved the way for the UN SC to pull the rug from the feet of the AU in the Libya crisis.[71]

This example suggests the political interests that could be at play in the adoption of fact-finding mandates. Indeed, the actual institutional impetus for creating a mission might have little to do with the aims that the mission's mandate articulates.

Furthermore, the experience of the AUCISS demonstrates the reality that the mandating entity constitutes a node through which a fact-finding report must first pass before reaching the public. Fact-finding practitioners tend to be sensitive to the notion that their primary audience is the mandating entity itself. As the Head of Mission of the IIFFMCG stated in an interview at the beginning of the mission, 'It's a report to the EU… I believe it's the EU that will choose the function of this.'[72] But, as occurred during the controversy surrounding the publication of the AUCISS report, the mandating body's priorities can collide with those of advocates and practitioners who prioritise the importance of issues such as human rights protection and accountability.

This tension is less salient for an entity such as the UN Human Rights Council, which has a more narrowly-delineated substantive area of focus geared toward promoting respect for human rights protection, addressing human rights violations, and promoting human rights coordination and the mainstreaming within the UN.[73] It would be unusual for the UN Human Rights Council to keep a fact-finding report confidential due to concerns about potentially adverse political consequences. In practice, UN Human Rights Council-mandated reports have been published, even in the absence of an explicit policy toward this end.[74] In contrast, the African Union Peace and Security Council 'is a standing decision-making organ for the prevention, management and resolution of conflicts'.[75] Similarly,

[71] KP Apuuli, 'The Principle of "African Solutions to African Problems" under the spotlight: The African Union (AU) and the Libya Crisis' (2011) *Open Society Institute* 3.

[72] P Runner, 'Swiss diplomat outlines Georgia war probe' (*euobservor*, 3 December 2008), available at euobserver.com/foreign/27221.

[73] For the mandate of the UN Human Rights Council, see UN General Assembly Resolution 60/251, UN Doc A/RES/60/251 (15 March 2006).

[74] Interview with Sonia Bakar, Peace Mission Support, Rapid Response Section, Office of the High Commissioner for Human Rights (20 January 2014).

[75] Protocol Relating to the Establishment of the Peace and Security Council of the African Union, Art 2(1), available at www.peaceau.org/uploads/psc-protocol-en.pdf.

the broad scope of the Council of the EU's activities encompasses economic, fiscal, education, and security policy.[76] Such a multi-faceted mandate can lead a mandating entity to downplay the utility of fact-finding in relation to other competing, more politically oriented, priorities.

3.5. CONCLUSION

Since neither the Council of the EU nor the African Union Peace and Security Council had previously mandated missions geared toward gathering information about alleged violations of international law, the IIFFMCG and the AUCISS were extremely ad hoc. For this reason, these cases constituted a test, of sorts, of the institutionally fragmented state of international fact-finding. As this chapter has described, for both the IIFFMCG and the AUCISS, one can point to, on the one hand, novel innovations that improved upon typical fact-finding practice, and on the other hand, problematic practices that fly in the face of trends of professional practice that have emerged in recent years.

Herein lies a true challenge for future fact-finding practice. As practitioners and policymakers continue to direct attention toward improving the methodological soundness of fact-finding work, how can innovation not be strangled? Efforts to save future missions from repeating errors made in past practice have, by necessity, been backward looking—indeed, the successes and failures of past missions can and should inform our understanding of how fact-finding should be undertaken. But there is still the issue of what has not yet been tried, what has not yet been envisaged as a possibility for future practice, and how innovative thinking can be promoted. In this sense, speaking directly to the overarching theme of this book, the ad hoc nature of fact-finding missions presents both a prospect and a challenge. Each mission starts anew, and the risk is prevalent that the lack of systemisation across the domain of international fact-finding will prove to be disadvantageous. But there are also opportunities for reinvention in this state of affairs. This more forward-thinking aspect of fact-finding should be highlighted in ongoing efforts to promote more effective practices in the future. The task will be to harness the prospects for innovation while being mindful of the challenges inherent in undertaking fact-finding work in a methodologically sound and professional, yet still ad hoc, manner.

[76] See generally General Secretariat of the Council of the European Union, *The Council of the European Union – 1952–2012: Sixty years of law and decision-making* (2013), available at www.consilium.europa.eu/en/documents-publications/publications/2013/council-european-union-1952-2012-sixty-years-law-decision-making/.

4

Domestic Commissions of Inquiry and International Law: The Importance of Normative Authority

STEPHEN SAMUEL AND JAMES A GREEN

4.1. INTRODUCTION

THE MAJORITY OF commissions of inquiry that are created can be considered to be 'domestic' in nature, in that most are established within a single state and in relation to internal concerns, rather than being 'international' in form or scope.[1] This chapter examines these domestic commissions of inquiry and, in particular, offers a critique of their intersection with international law. There is relatively little literature devoted to this subject.[2] Scholars have certainly engaged with 'domestic commissions of inquiry', but this has tended to be in relation to particular commissions or groups of commissions created within a single state, rather than with regard to domestic commissions *tout court*.[3]

Moreover, appraisals of domestic commissions of inquiry have tended to focus on the suitability of a commission's procedural mechanisms for ascertaining facts, and its ability to legitimately establish accountability

[1] JE Méndez, Human Rights Council, *Report of the Special Rapporteur on Torture and Other Cruel, Inhuman or Degrading Treatment or Punishment*, UN Doc A/HRC/19/61 (18 January 2012), 7 ('[m]ost commissions of inquiry are established at the initiative of national Government authorities'). See section 4.2 for further discussion of what makes a commission of inquiry 'domestic'.

[2] Although there has been notable scholarly engagement on the question of the interaction between international law and international commissions of inquiry. See, eg, LJ van den Herik, 'An Inquiry into the Role of Commissions of Inquiry in International Law: Navigating the Tensions between Fact-Finding and Application of International Law' (2014) 13 *Chinese Journal of International Law* 507.

[3] See, eg, J Beer, *Public Inquiries* (Oxford, Oxford University Press, 2011); C Campbell and F Ní Aoláin, 'Local Meets Global: Transitional Justice in NI' (2003) 26 *Fordham International Law Journal* 871; G Gilligan, 'Royal Commissions of Inquiry' (2002) 35 *Australian and New Zealand Journal of Criminology* 289; and A Hegarty, 'The Government of Memory: Public Inquiries and the Limits of Justice in Northern Ireland' (2003) 26 *Fordham International Law Journal* 1148.

and 'wrong-doing'.[4] This focus means that there has been comparatively little attention devoted to the role of domestic commissions of inquiry as a form of social settlement or political reform.[5] A consideration of the underlying politics of commissions of inquiry stands in contrast to an analysis of 'wrong-doing'—albeit that there are obvious overlaps—and, instead, draws attention to a process that involves complex normative decisions.

The primary aim of this chapter is to emphasise that the engagement by domestic commissions of inquiry with international law is hugely dependant on the relevant social context, which generates consequent implications for the *normative authority* of those inquiries. The intersection of domestic commissions of inquiry and international law thus must be viewed through the prism of political and social choice. For reasons of space, this chapter is necessarily an exploratory sketch: our analysis is intended to act as a starting point for further research.

Section 4.2 begins by briefly outlining what 'domestic commissions of inquiry' are, at least to the extent that we refer to them herein and as distinct from 'international' commissions. In section 4.3, we explore the fact that national commissions of inquiry are influenced by their domestic context, giving them a clear political dimension. It is argued that the domestic political scene affects, on many levels, the normative authority accorded to any given commission and its findings. Sections 4.4–4.7 then explore how normative authority, particularly in relation to international law, is framed through the creation, mandates, composition and substantive findings of domestic commissions. We acknowledge that these frames are somewhat artificial, and there are certainly overlaps between them. However, they are not entirely arbitrary: our selection in sections 4.4–4.7 can be seen as something of a 'chronological survey', in that the sections chart key moments within the timeline of a domestic commission of inquiry.

Overall, our objective is not to argue that the use of (or reference to) international law in a domestic commission cannot have the potential to generate normative authority, nor to argue that there are no benefits to domestic commissions engaging with international law. Instead, we simply wish to highlight that 'benefit' in this regard should not be taken as a given.

4.2. WHAT MAKES A COMMISSION OF INQUIRY 'DOMESTIC'?

The umbrella term 'domestic commission of inquiry' is used in this chapter to denote any national-level or non-international body mandated to

[4] See, eg, *Report of the Special Rapporteur* (n 1) (providing a detailed assessment of the 'value' of commissions of inquiry, and particularly domestic commissions).

[5] A notable exception is the literature dealing with truth and reconciliation commissions. See, eg, W Schabas and S Darcy (eds), *Truth Commissions and Courts: The Tension Between Criminal Justice and the Search for Truth* (Dordrecht, Kluwer Academic Publishers, 2004).

investigate particular factual circumstances and report upon them.[6] However, it is important to note that this understanding is necessarily imprecise, and that domestic commissions can—in most instances—only be identified and described based on their individual characteristics.

Distinguishing 'domestic' commissions from their 'international' counterparts usually must be based on the factual circumstances of their creation. Any attempt to identify jurisdictional or normative differences between the two forms of inquiry is difficult, particularly in meta-theoretical or overarching terms. Many international commissions of inquiry necessarily concern 'international' issues, and thus—at the legal level—will almost inevitably relate to matters governed by international law.[7] Some domestic commissions of inquiry concern exclusively 'domestic' questions, and so only trigger questions of domestic law.[8] However, given the fact that commissions are usually set up in exceptional circumstances comprising issues of significant social or political concern,[9] many domestic commissions will commonly also trigger international legal questions.[10]

Where a domestic commission's mandate relates to international law, and especially where a commission expressly *engages with* international law, the juridical significance of a formal distinction between 'domestic' and 'international' commissions of inquiry is undermined. No difference may be drawn as to the relevant law: leaving aside potentially divergent interpretations, the provisions of international law are identical whether an international or a domestic body is applying them. The distinction between domestic and international commissions of inquiry is, thus, a factual matter based on how the body was created, and who created it.

While they can be distinguished from international commissions based on the circumstances of their creation, it is clear that domestic commissions of inquiry—as a mechanism—defy a singular definition. As Gilligan has noted, such commissions 'are too diverse in their effects to be tied

[6] See, eg, M Aksenova and M Bergsmo, 'Non-Criminal Justice Fact-Work in the Age of Accountability' in M Bergsmo (ed), *Quality Control in Fact-Finding* (Florence, Torkel Opsahl, 2013) 1, 2 ('the terms "fact-finding" and "inquiry" refer to the methods of ascertaining facts used … for differing purposes … [including] work processes to identify, locate, obtain, verify, analyse, corroborate, summarise, synthesise, structure, organise, present and disseminate these facts').

[7] See, generally, D Jacobs and C Harwood, 'International Criminal Law outside the Courtroom: The Impact of Focusing on International Crimes for the Quality of Fact-Finding' in Bergsmo (n 6) 325.

[8] See, eg, Special Commission of Inquiry into the Greyhound Racing Industry in New South Wales, 2015, available at www.greyhoundracinginquiry.justice.nsw.gov.au/.

[9] See *Phillips v Nova Scotia (Commission of Inquiry into the Westray Mine Tragedy)* [1995] 2 SCR 97, para 62, per Justice Cory (commissions of inquiry 'are often convened, in the wake of public shock, horror, disillusionment, or scepticism…').

[10] As will be seen throughout this chapter, however, international law will not necessarily be considered or applied by domestic inquiries when fulfilling their mandate simply because international legal questions are 'triggered'.

down to a uniform explanatory model…'[11] Domestic commissions take a wide range of forms and operate under a variety of mandates. As such, any attempt to define them runs the risk of being too general and open to exceptions, as well as being normatively abstract (irrespective of the extent to which procedural elements are defined with regard to any particular commission).

Of course, all of this can be said in relation to 'international' commissions of inquiry too,[12] but it is worth noting that such diversity is more pronounced for commissions of inquiry in the domestic context.[13] Given the comparatively underdeveloped and decentralised mechanisms at the international level for both fact-finding and legal determination,[14] the creation of commissions of inquiry has become commonplace and is a useful governance technique at the international level: a fact with which much of this book engages from a range of perspectives. This, in turn, has led to a number of guidelines being developed for commissions of inquiry in the international context,[15] which has begun to foster at least some degree of cross-body coherence.

Domestic commissions of inquiry, in contrast, operate in the context of the existing institutional and legal framework of the state concerned. They are created precisely to respond, on an ad hoc basis, to exceptional intervening events that would not otherwise receive adequate treatment by the extant institutional mechanisms of the state in question.[16] Inevitably, the exceptional nature of the circumstances of their creation raises incident-specific and context-specific questions, particularly with regard to the manner in which notions of procedure and justice are understood by inquiries and societies when making determinations of fact and law.

[11] Gilligan (n 3) 289 (in reference to the limited context of Australian Royal Commissions of Inquiry).

[12] For the difficulties of generalising commissions of inquiry, see D Orentlicher, 'International Norms in Human Rights Fact-Finding' in P Alston and S Knuckey (eds), *The Transformation of Human Rights Fact-Finding* (Oxford, Oxford University Press, 2016) 501, 503–506. For a discussion of the various types of commissions of inquiry, see Ch 1: C Henderson and P Butchard, 'A Functional Typology of Commissions of Inquiry'.

[13] See F Morstein Marx, 'Commissions of Inquiry in Germany' (1936) 30 *The American Political Science Review* 1134, 1134 (domestic '[i]nquiries are ventures into the unknown' and 'officially organised investigations are a relatively recent addition to the mechanism of politics').

[14] See, generally, K Oellers-Frahm, 'Multiplication of International Courts and Tribunals and Conflicting Jurisdiction—Problems and Possible Solutions' (2001) 5 *Max Planck Yearbook of United Nations Law* 67.

[15] See, eg, UN Human Rights Office of the High Commissioner, *Commissions of Inquiry and Fact-Finding Missions on International Human Rights and Humanitarian Law: Guidance and Practice* (Geneva, UN, 2015).

[16] See RA Macdonald, *An Analysis of the Forms and Functions of Independent Commissions of Inquiry (Royal Commissions) in Canada: Executive Summary and Bibliography* (Montreal, McGill Faculty of Law, 2011) 11–12, available at www.mcgill.ca/roled/files/roled/roled_commissioninquiries_en_-roderick_macdonald.pdf.

The processes that concern domestic commissions of inquiry—including their creation, their mandates and the overall scope of their authority—not only vary significantly from state to state but also, perhaps unsurprisingly, from commission to commission.[17] This inherent plurality and the widely different social and political contexts in which different domestic commissions are created underpin the analysis throughout this chapter.

4.3. NORMATIVE AUTHORITY AND THE IMPORTANCE OF SOCIAL CONTEXT

We contend in this chapter that a central feature of all commissions of inquiry should be that the inquiries themselves, and the respective societies that they address, mutually recognise and share notions of *normative authority*. The notion of 'normative authority' is an admittedly broad one,[18] but we employ it in reference to the product of a range of considerations and potential interaction between law, politics and morality: a product that provides weight and credibility to normative determinations and the subsequent real-world effects of those determinations.

For commissions of inquiry to have meaningful value,[19] the findings that they present (legal or otherwise) must be the product of some degree of legitimate, recognised authority. The need for commissions of inquiry to be normatively authoritative is commonly—albeit largely implicitly—assumed.[20] More than that, however, scholarship has tended to assess commissions of inquiry as transitional or procedural forms of justice,

[17] Given the diverse range of circumstances in relation to which commissions of inquiry can be and have been created, this plurality can be viewed as being appropriate. In 2014, the UK's Select Committee on the Inquiries Act 2005 concluded, in a line from the Report highlighted in bold, 'that there neither can nor should be fixed criteria regulating the setting up of inquiries': Select Committee on the Inquiries Act 2005, House of Lords, Report of Session 2013–14, *The Inquiries Act 2005: Post-Legislative Scrutiny* (London, The Stationery Office Limited, 2014) para 51. However, as will be examined herein, such plurality also poses significant challenges for assessing the 'value' of domestic commissions of inquiry.

[18] The term 'normative authority' is used in the literature, but its meaning is more conceptual rather being open to practical definition. See, eg, M Koskenniemi, 'Hierarchy in International Law: A Sketch' (1997) 8 *European Journal of International Law* 566, 569 ('[s]ystematization aims to make explicit the origin and relationships of norms so as to answer questions about normative authority and to solve problems of normative conflict'); and LO Gostin, D Sridhar and D Hougendobler, 'The Normative Authority of the World Health Organization' (2015) 129 *Public Health* 854, 854 ('[b]y normative authority, we mean the Organization's power to shape or influence global rules and norms and to monitor compliance').

[19] We use the term 'value' in this chapter both in relation to practical dispute settlement and social justice and the integrity of the wider 'project of international law'.

[20] See, generally, eg, I Lassée, 'Coherence in the Design and Implementation of the Mandates of International Fact-Finding Commissions: Internal and External Dimensions' in Bergsmo (n 6) 167.

inherently supported by notions of fairness and due process.[21] Where domestic commissions of inquiry have faced critique regarding their normative character, this has predominantly focused on perceived political failings that are considered 'outside' of the formal character of the inquiry.[22] It is understandable, particularly where fast-moving changes to governments alter their commitment to supporting inquiries and implementing their findings, that one would accept the suggestion that the loss of normative authority may have little to do with the character of the commissions themselves. Lawyers are predisposed to look at 'law' and 'facts' as being 'a-political' and 'objective', and scholarship has been inclined to view formal, quasi-legal inquiries as inherently embodying those characteristics.[23] This lawyerly stance often leans towards a presumption that a domestic commission is either 'supported' or 'failed' by external politics.

On this basis, domestic commissions of inquiry are at times perceived as being 'considerably tainted',[24] especially when it comes to their engagement with international legal standards. In a statement made to the United Nations (UN) Human Rights Council in 2010, for example, Professor Philip Alston asserted that where 'national-level commissions had been established', the overall 'track record of such inquiries' have been 'remarkably poor'.[25] Alston, who was addressing the UN Human Rights Council as Special Rapporteur on Extrajudicial, Summary or Arbitrary Executions, noted gravely that in many instances, such inquiries 'had in fact resulted in comprehensive impunity'.[26]

It is certainly true that domestic commissions of inquiry have—in some instances—reached highly dubious legal conclusions, seemingly because of the political motivation of the government of the state in which they were created. An example that neatly highlights this involves the violent

[21] For discussion and critique, see A Bisset, *Truth Commissions and Criminal Courts* (Cambridge, Cambridge University Press, 2012) 10–19; and M Freeman, *Truth Commissions and Procedural Fairness* (Cambridge, Cambridge University Press, 2006) 108–54.

[22] See, eg, JS Sarkar, *Commissions of Inquiry: Practice and Principle* (New Delhi, Ashish, 1990, reprint 2001) particularly at 5–10.

[23] Scholars have questioned this through various analytical frames, perhaps most notably through the notion of 'fragmentation'. See, eg, International Law Commission, ILC Study Group on the Fragmentation of International Law, *Fragmentation of International Law: Difficulties Arising from the Diversification and Expansion of International Law*, UN Doc A/CN.4/L.682 (2006); A Fischer-Lescano and G Teubner, 'Regime-Collisions: The Vain Search for Legal Unity in the Fragmentation of Global Law' (2004) 25 *Michigan Journal of International Law* 999; and M Koskenniemi, 'The Fate of Public International Law: Between Technique and Politics' (2007) 70 *Modern Law Review* 1.

[24] C Hellestveit, 'International Fact-Finding Mechanisms: Lighting Candles or Cursing Darkness?' in CM Bailliet and K Mujezinović Larsen (eds), *Promoting Peace Through International Law* (Oxford, Oxford University Press 2015) 368, 370.

[25] 'Statement by UN Special Rapporteur on Extrajudicial, Summary or Arbitrary Executions before the Human Rights Council' (3 June 2010), available at www.extrajudicial-executions.org/application/media/Statement-Alston1.pdf, 1.

[26] ibid.

events that occurred in Conakry, Guinea in 2009.[27] An independent UN Fact-finding Mission indicated that crimes against humanity had very likely occurred in Guinea,[28] and recommended referrals to the International Criminal Court.[29] However, a national fact-finding commission into the same events came to completely the opposite conclusion.[30] The domestic commission's findings were broadly dismissed by the wider international community as being biased.[31]

However, we argue that the heuristic that domestic commissions of inquiry are 'tainted' by the influence of 'politics' can be unhelpful, at least in itself. When it comes to critical discussions of domestic and international influences upon commissions of inquiry, the implied distinction between 'objective' commissions and the 'subjective' political realities in which they function ignores the fact that any given domestic commission does not merely function within a particular political and social context; it is also the product of it. For a domestic commission of inquiry to acquire normative authority, experts and societies must grasp a relational self-awareness: one that appreciates that normative authority is ultimately given form by comprehensive social deliberation of legal, political and moral concerns. Thus, the value or desirability of a domestic commission of inquiry's engagement with international law depends on the purpose for which the inquiry was created, how it was created, and the wider public consciousness surrounding international law/international legal expertise.

Indeed, rather obviously, it is the inherent subjectivity of the social context that (at least in part) *leads* to calls for commissions of inquiry to be neutral and objective. The need to stand apart from context is referenced through a variety of synonyms in commentary, as exemplified by the following statement by Heller: '[a]ll scholars—and common sense indicates—that, to be credible, [a] … commission of inquiry must be both politically independent and procedurally impartial.'[32] It is difficult to dispute the desirability of such neutrality when it comes to the engagement

[27] See Hellestveit (n 24) 370 (referencing this example in this way).

[28] *Report of the International Commission of Inquiry Mandated to Establish the Facts and Circumstances of the Events of 28 September 2009 in Guinea*, UN Doc S/2009/693 (18 December 2009) paras 180–200 (*Report of the Guinea International Commission*).

[29] ibid, paras 266 and 278.

[30] See 'National Commission's Findings', Coalition of the International Criminal Court Report (10 February 2010), available at www.iccnow.org/?mod=newsdetail&news=3764.

[31] See Hellestveit (n 24) 370; and *Report of the Guinea International Commission* (n 28) 3 (the 'Government established a National Commission of Inquiry. Its strong-arm tactics, and particularly those of its military wing, seem to intimidate witnesses rather than encouraging them to come forward').

[32] KJ Heller, 'The International Commission of Inquiry on Libya: A Critical Analysis' (2012), SSRN paper, forthcoming in J Meierhenrich (ed), *International Commissions: The Role of Commissions of Inquiry in the Investigation of International Crimes*, available at papers.ssrn.com/sol3/papers.cfm?abstract_id=2123782 (discussing international commissions).

by commissions of inquiry with international law, but it is important to recognise that characterisations of neutrality (or of other similar concepts) are necessarily a matter of degree. Engagement with international law is not 'a-political' or 'objective'. Policy choices exist (and are made) regarding the extent of that engagement. These policy choices, either to have 'more' or 'less' engagement, not only delimit the institutional powers of any given commission. They are also influenced by attitudes towards international law and inform the nature of a commission's normative voice; moreover, they inform the extent to which that normative voice achieves any degree of subsequent authority in the respective social context.

For obvious reasons, choices regarding the extent of engagement with international law are far more pronounced in relation to domestic commissions of inquiry than is the case for international inquiries. Domestic commissions are likely to have 'distinct domestic political purposes or … additional objectives',[33] which, for practical reasons, lie outside the standard purview of international legal standards. While it would be naïve to suggest that international commissions do not also operate in a politically charged milieu, one must keep in mind that the *uniqueness* of each individual domestic commission of inquiry is far more pronounced. The unique context of any given commission has a direct effect upon the manner in which its normative authority is both constructed and construed. There are four identifiable moments where domestic commissions' intersection with international law is most acute: at their creation; within their mandates; in relation to the composition of their members; and their substantive findings. Consequently, in the next four sections, we explore the manner in which engagement with international law and international legal expertise impact domestic commissions of inquiry, particularly as they seek to acquire normative authority within their situational contexts.

4.4. THE CREATION OF DOMESTIC COMMISSIONS OF INQUIRY

Normative authority is not inherent in any given commission of inquiry. The entity that creates a commission defines its purposes, and bestows formal authority (of whatever sort) upon it. While normative authority is generally 'assumed' simply on the basis that a body *is* a commission of inquiry, practice indicates that the real picture is more dynamic and contextual.[34]

[33] Hellestveit (n 24) 370.

[34] The composition of, and powers given to, any given commission stem from its social context, and, indeed, can change in relation to political changes within that context. For example, the Public Commission to Examine the Maritime Incident of 31 May 2010 (Turkel Commission), reports available at www.turkel-committee.gov.il/index-eng.html, created by Israel in 2010, originally lacked powers of subpoena, but such powers were

Domestic commissions of inquiry are created in a wide variety of ways. Most commonly, the process of creation is ad hoc and un-formalised. In South Africa, for example—a state that has been referred to as 'the Commission capital of the world',[35] because of the high number of commissions of inquiry that have been created there since 1994—the Constitution provides that the President has authority to create commissions of inquiry.[36] However, the only notable regulation of these commissions in South Africa remains the Commissions Act 1947,[37] which gives the President (or, in 1947, Governor-General as then was) almost unlimited power to set their procedures, mandates and rules. Recent high-profile commissions in South Africa, such as the 2011 Arms Procurement Commission[38] or the 2012 inquiry into the massacre of the miners at the Lonmin Marikana Shaft,[39] were therefore created by the presidential order of Jacob Zuma, with ad hoc terms of reference and rules of procedure.[40]

Other domestic commissions are created with even less structural background or guiding legislation. The Bahrain Independent Commission of Inquiry,[41] for example, was simply born of a royal order by the King of Bahrain, on 29 June 2011.[42] There was no existing framework for such commissions in Bahrain: *everything* about the Commission's mandate, procedures and terms of reference stemmed from that royal order.[43] Another similar example is the Ad Hoc Inquiry Commission in Charge of the Question of

later bestowed upon it by the Israeli government because of public criticism and resulting political pressure. See B Ravid, 'Government Expands Authority of Gaza Flotilla Probe Commission' *Haaretz* (4 July 2010), available at www.haaretz.com/israel-news/government-expands-authority-of-gaza-flotilla-probe-commission-1.299955.

[35] DT McKinley, 'Commissions of Inquiry or Omission?' South African Civil Society Information Service (14 April 2015), available at www.sacsis.org.za/site/article/2347.

[36] Constitution of the Republic of South Africa, 1996, s 84(2)(f).

[37] Commissions Act 8 of 1947, 18 April 1947 (as amended).

[38] Commission of Inquiry into Allegations of Fraud, Corruption, Impropriety or Irregularity in the Strategic Defence Procurement Packages (SDPP), 2011, www.armscomm.org.za/index.html.

[39] Marikana Commission of Inquiry, 2012, www.marikanacomm.org.za/index.html.

[40] See Government Notice, Department of Justice and Constitutional Development, No R 926 4, November 2011, President of the Republic of South Africa, Staatskoerant, 4 November 2011 No 34731 3, available at www.armscomm.org.za/docs/20111104-gg34731-r926-terms-comms.pdf (Arms Procurement Commission); and Proclamation by the President of the Republic of South Africa, No 50, Staatskoerant, 12 September 2012, No 35680 3, available at www.justice.gov.za/legislation/notices/2012/20120912-gg35680-nor50-marikana.pdf (Marikana Commission).

[41] See *Report of the Bahrain Independent Commission of Inquiry* (23 November 2011), available at www.bici.org.bh.

[42] Bahrain, Royal Order No 28 of 2011, available at www.bici.org.bh/wp-content/uploads/2011/08/RoyalOrder28of2011.pdf.

[43] On the legal framework of the Commission, see www.bici.org.bh/indexa2d7.html?page_id=313.

Disappearances,[44] created in Algeria by presidential decree, again entirely ad hoc, in 2003.[45]

In some states, however, there is a degree of standardisation and formality to the creation of commissions of inquiry, which can help to strengthen neutrality and objectivity, and, thus, impact upon the normative authority of the findings of the commission in question. In Canada, for example, Royal Commissions of Inquiry are formally created by the government under statute. The Inquiries Act 1985 retains a measure of flexibility for the creation of Canadian domestic commissions, while at the same time providing a set of framework rules governing scope, procedure and evidence.[46] The Act is buttressed by a series of federal or provisional acts—the most recent of which being the 2011 Ontario Public Inquiries Act[47]—that provide more bespoke regulation for inquiries focused on matters of regional public concern.[48]

While there is no constitutional, or even legal, guarantee of independence of Royal Commissions (or, indeed, other public commissions) in Canada, their formalised yet flexible nature has contributed to them being highly valued internally, and thus to a corresponding (deeply rooted) social norm of *expected* independence.[49] The public perception of domestic inquiries in Canada is an extremely positive one.[50] The consequent normative authority, acquired from this social context, has allowed some Canadian commissions to apply international legal rules in a notably credible, court-like manner. A good example of this is the Arar Report's evaluation of the prohibition of torture and unqualified assertion of that prohibition's *jus cogens* status.[51]

The formalisation of the creation of domestic commissions of inquiry can be a double-edged sword, however. It can mask policy choices in a way that may undermine that value of a commission's work. In the UK, for example, a clear distinction is drawn between 'statutory' and

[44] Commission d'Enquête ad hoc chargée de la question des disparus, 2003–2005. The final Report of the Commission was confidential, but public data of its work is available from the United States Institute of Peace, www.usip.org/publications/commission-of-inquiry-algeria.

[45] Presidential Decree, available at www.joradp.dz/JO2000/2003/055/F_Pag.htm.

[46] Inquiries Act, RSC, 1985, c I–11.

[47] Public Inquiries Act, 2009, SO 2009, c 33, Sch 6.

[48] For discussion, see ZF Ahmed, 'UN Fact-Finding Inquiry Commissions for Assassinations of Prominent Individuals' (unpublished thesis, University of Toronto, 2012) 6–13, available at tspace.library.utoronto.ca/bitstream/1807/33314/1/Ahmed_Zahra_F_201211_LLM_thesis.pdf.

[49] Macdonald (n 16) 13–14.

[50] ibid, 20–21. Having said this, some fears of partiality persist, see nn 102–104 and accompanying text.

[51] *The Report of the Commission of Inquiry into the Actions of Canadian Officials in Relation to Maher Arar, Report of the Events Relating to Maher Arar, Analysis and Recommendations* (2006) particularly at 52, available at publications.gc.ca/collections/Collection/CP32-88-1-2006E-AR.pdf.

'non-statutory' inquiries.[52] In recent years, the former primarily have been set up under the Inquiries Act 2005,[53] although a few have also been created under other pre-existing statutory provisions.[54] The general academic perception has been that the 2005 Act and the subsequent, extensive, Inquiry Rules 2006[55] have been 'good', because such formalisation has improved the transparency and procedural certainty of commissions in the UK.[56]

In practice, however, even under the 2005 Act, ministers retain a huge range of powers in relation to commissions of inquiry: they can limit the attendance of the public, restrict the disclosure of documents, withhold material from publication and bring inquiries to premature conclusions.[57] More than this, non-statutory inquires can still be created, and commonly still *are* created,[58] often based on dubious assertions of efficiency (of both cost and speed).[59] Public confusion as to the statutory or non-statutory nature of any given inquiry in the UK—and the lack of formalisation of non-statutory inquiries in particular—has meant a corresponding lack of confidence in relation to inquiries per se.[60]

The *partial* formalisation of domestic inquiries in the UK has in fact given, at least in some instances, the British government a strategic choice regarding the extent of public scrutiny, especially in circumstances where public inquiries intersect with matters of national security. The Iraq (Chilcot) Inquiry, for example, was a non-statutory inquiry into the events that led to the 2003 intervention and its aftermath.[61] Chilcot was repeatedly presented as an 'open', 'public' inquiry,[62] yet—at the same time—it

52 J Simson Caird, *Public Inquiries: Non-Statutory Commissions of Inquiry*, Commons Briefing Papers SN02599 (London, House of Commons Library, 2016), available at researchbriefings.parliament.uk/ResearchBriefing/Summary/SN02599, particularly at 3–6.

53 Inquiries Act 2005.

54 See Select Committee Report (n 17) App 5 for a list of the statutory inquiries between 1990 and 2014 that were created under legislation other than the Inquiries 2005.

55 Inquiry Rules 2006, SI 2006/1838.

56 See E Ireto, 'The Inquiries Act 2005—Fit for Purpose?', *Law Society Gazette* (27 March 2014), available at www.lawgazette.co.uk/law/the-inquiries-act-2005-fit-for-purpose/5040566.fullarticle.

57 Select Committee Report (n 17) 6.

58 See Ireto (n 56). A list of the non-statutory inquiries that were created in the UK between 1990 and 2014 is appended to the Select Committee Report (n 17) App 5.

59 Select Committee Report (n 17) 6.

60 See, eg, A Hamilton, 'The One Thing Chilcot Won't Reveal is the Truth' *The Independent* (26 November 2009).

61 See *The Report of the Iraq Inquiry (Report of a Committee of Privy Counsellors)* (6 July 2016) (*Chilcot Inquiry Report*), available at www.iraqinquiry.org.uk/the-report (comprising 12 volumes and executive summary).

62 See, eg, ibid, vol 1, Introduction, paras 8, 54 and 59; and Statement by Sir John Chilcot, Chairman of the Iraq Inquiry, at a news conference on 30 July 2009, available at www.iraqinquiry.org.uk/the-inquiry/news-archive/2009/2009-07-30-opening/statement-by-sir-john-chilcot-chairman-of-the-iraq-inquiry-at-a-news-conference-on-thursday-30-july-2009/.

was constituted and conducted in a way that obscured many aspects of the Inquiry's work (particularly prior to the publication of its Report in July 2016).[63]

The normative authority of the findings of domestic commissions of inquiry in general is significantly weakened by the ad hoc and comparatively unregulated way in which they are often created. Equally, it is also important to note that *more* regulation or increased 'formalisation' of the creation process is not necessarily a remedy for this issue. The creation and ultimate findings of the Bahrain Independent Commission of Inquiry, for example, have generally been considered to be credible and legitimate,[64] irrespective of the fact that the Commission was created entirely ad hoc. There are certainly instances where domestic commissions have valuably engaged with international law irrespective of how they were set up; however, it may broadly be said that the way(s) in which such bodies are created will often mean that the application and elucidation of international law may have been strategically excluded.

4.5. INTERNATIONAL LAW IN THE MANDATES OF DOMESTIC COMMISSIONS OF INQUIRY

As Aksenova and Bergsmo have stated, '[t]he diversity of fact-finding missions manifests itself … in the scope of their mandates, which can be formulated in very broad or very narrow terms'.[65] For the purposes of this chapter, our focus is with the possibilities that some of the (diverse) mandates of domestic commissions of inquiry may or may not provide for engagement with international law.

Not every domestic commission will have a mandate to engage with legal questions: for some, their terms of reference will not provide for this, or will explicitly exclude it.[66] It is generally not the case, however, that a domestic commission's terms of reference will allow for engagement with domestic law but preclude the consideration or application of international

[63] A statement by Gordon Brown at the Inquiry's launch in 2009 is telling in this regard, see HC Deb 15 Jun 2009, vol 493, col 23 ('evidence will be heard in private. I believe that that will also ensure that evidence given by serving and former ministers, military officers and officials is as full and candid as possible').

[64] It is worth noting that while the Bahraini Commission's Report itself was seen in this way, there has been significant criticism of the implementation of the Report's findings. See J Kinninmont, *Bahrain: Beyond the Impasse* (London, The Royal Institute of International Affairs, 2012), particularly at xi, 1 and 11.

[65] Aksenova and Bergsmo (n 6) 9.

[66] See, eg, Commission for Investigation of the Events in and around Srebrenica between 10th and 19th July 1995, Republic of Serbia, (June 2004) 6, available at www.justiceinperspective.org.za/images/bosnia/Srebrenica_Report2004.pdf ('[t]he Commission is not a judicial body and has no mandate to consider legal issues…').

law.[67] For the most part, once 'law' is on the table, commissions can generally consider international as well as domestic law.

Yet, even where a domestic commission's terms of reference leave the door open for the consideration of international law in this way (either implicitly or explicitly), when a commission's mandate allows for or requires legal appraisal, domestic law commonly will be the 'first port of call': indeed, international law may well not be a port of call at all.[68] A commission's *interpretation* of its own mandate in this regard is likely to be crucial. For example, one might consider the Linden Commission in Guyana, which was created in 2012 and reported in February 2013.[69] The Commission was created by presidential order[70] to investigate the events that occurred at the Mackenzie-Wismar Bridge, Linden, in July 2012, and particularly the deaths, at the hands of police, of a number of persons who were protesting energy-rate increases.[71]

While the Linden Commission's terms of reference did not expressly refer to either 'international law' or, indeed, 'law' per se, they did not exclude legal analysis.[72] As such, the Commission directly applied Guyanese domestic law at a number of points in its Report.[73] However, it ultimately decided to reference international human rights law standards only extremely obliquely.[74] In the Commission's view, it was beyond its

[67] Although this does happen on occasion. See, eg, the 2010 New Zealand Royal Commission on the Pike River Coal Mine Tragedy (which had a mandate that required its engagement with 'the law' to be limited to domestic provisions concerning 'underground coal mining and related operations … [and] health and safety in underground coal mining and related operations'). See pikeriver.royalcommission.govt.nz/Terms-of-reference.

[68] It is perhaps telling that Beer (n 3)—the leading comprehensive text on commissions of inquiry set up in the UK—does not even mention international law. Such lack of engagement with international law can be contrasted with international commissions where any legal focus will inevitably be on international law. See, eg, the Independent International Commission of Inquiry on the Syrian Arab Republic, which was created by the UN Human Rights Council with an explicit mandate to 'investigate all alleged *violations of international human rights law* since March 2011 in the Syrian Arab Republic' (emphasis added), Resolution adopted by the Human Rights Council at its seventeenth special session, *Situation of human rights in the Syrian Arab Republic*, UN Doc A/HRC/S-17/1 (22 August 2011) para 13. This was the only reference to law in the Commission's terms of reference.

[69] Linden Commission of Inquiry, Appointed to Inquire into the Death of Allan Lewis, Ron Somerset and Shemroy Bouyea and the Injuries of Several Other Persons on July 18, 2012 at the Mackenzie-Wismar Bridge, Linden, *Report of the Commission*, presented in Georgetown, Guyana (28 February 2013), available at www.guyana.org/govt/THE_LINDEN_COMMISSION_OF_INQUIRY_FINAL_REPORT.pdf (*Linden Commission Report*).

[70] *Linden Commission Report* (n 69) para 6.

[71] 'Linden Protest Turns Deadly … Four Dead, Two Dozen Injured', *Kaieteur News Online* (19 July 2012), available at www.kaieteurnewsonline.com/2012/07/19/linden-protest-turns-deadly-four-dead-two-dozen-injured/.

[72] *Linden Commission Report* (n 69) para 8.

[73] ibid, throughout, but, eg, at paras 164–65 (applying the Constitution of the Co-operative Republic of Guyana).

[74] ibid, paras 188–91. For further discussion, see nn 126–127 and accompanying text.

mandate to consider international law, even though the mandate itself could certainly have been interpreted so as to allow for this.

One might therefore argue that a commission's mandate can have as much to do with its own interpretation of its terms of reference as its terms of reference themselves. However, as was noted in the previous section,[75] the 'nature' of commissions of inquiry is heavily dependent on the entity that creates them, and this extends not just to the framing of a commission's terms of reference, but also how the commission then interprets them. This can again be seen with the Linden Commission's Report, which—while being notably critical of the police[76]—was essentially exoneratory in relation to the Guyanese government and, particularly, the Minister of Home Affairs.[77] Leaving aside the merits of its findings in that regard, one may certainly say that there was no political will on the part of the Linden Commission to interpret its mandate so as to meaningfully engage with international human rights law: the *reasons* for this lack of political will, however, undoubtedly stemmed from beyond the Commission itself.

In some instances, one can observe that domestic inquiries have been set up to rival other inquiries, to act as a more acquiescent alternative to the courts,[78] or generally to offer a false perception of impartiality or justice 'being done'. We have, for example, already seen this with regard to the domestic commission in Guinea, concerning the 2009 Conakry protests.[79] The mandate of the commission in question in such cases is designed to provide the preferred political outcome of its creator.

Of course, not all domestic commissions are, or are designed to be, at odds with their international counterparts (or other mechanisms for dispute settlement) in this way. At times, the function of a domestic commission is fully intended to be complimentary in this regard. Canada is a good example here: the Inquiries Act 1985 explicitly envisages the complimentary interaction between domestic and international commissions, by allowing for the conference 'on an international commission or tribunal all or any of the powers conferred on commissioners [in a domestic one]'.[80] In a similar vein, the Supreme Court of Canada made it clear in *Starr v Houlden* that '[t]he inquiry process cannot be used to circumvent the federally prescribed criminal procedure'.[81]

[75] See section 4.4, particularly n 34 and accompanying text.
[76] *Linden Commission Report* (n 69) throughout, but, eg, at para 261.
[77] ibid, paras 114–30.
[78] Macdonald (n 16) 16 ('investigative inquiries are sometimes accused of acting as a substitute for criminal proceedings…').
[79] See nn 27–31 and accompanying text.
[80] Inquiries Act 2005, s 14(1).
[81] *Starr v Houlden* [1990] 1 SCR 1366, 1368 (per Dickson CJ and Lamer, La Forest, Sopinka, Gonthier and Cory JJ).

An illustration of the complexity inherent in assessing the mandates of domestic commissions in relation to international law is the Turkel Commission, which was appointed by the Israeli government in June 2010 to examine the naval blockade of the Gaza Strip and the steps taken by Israel to enforce that blockade.[82] Somewhat unusually for a domestic commission, international law was at the very forefront of its terms of reference. Israel explicitly tasked the Commission with assessing *the conformity with international law* of: (1) the imposition of the naval blockade on the Gaza Strip; (2) the actions taken by Israel to enforce the naval blockade on 31 May 2010; and (3) Israel's mechanism for examining and investigating complaints and claims raised in relation to violations of the laws of armed conflict (generally and in relation to the enforcement of the blockade).[83]

The Turkel Commission's purported *raison d'etre* was thus predicated on the application of international law. Its two final Reports were certainly extremely detailed and involve significant factual and legal analysis.[84] On that basis, it has been argued that they 'might have a meaningful impact [in relation to international law] beyond the concrete Israeli context'.[85] Equally, the Commission was clearly set up as an indirect response to the 2009 UNHCR-instigated Goldstone Report.[86] The substantive findings of the Turkel Commission go beyond the scope of this section, but suffice to say here that its legal conclusions were highly contentious,[87] and—from inception—the Commission had limited international credibility.[88] To

[82] Turkel Commission (n 34).

[83] Turkel Commission, Commission's Mandate, www.turkel-committee.gov.il/content-189.html.

[84] See Turkel Commission, *Report—Part 1*, (January 2011), available at www.turkel-committee.gov.il/files/wordocs//8707200211english.pdf; and Turkel Commission, *Report—Part 2*, (February 2013), available at www.turkel-committee.gov.il/files/newDoc3/The%20Turkel%20Report%20for%20website.pdf.

[85] A Margalit, 'Some Observations on the Turkel Report and the Investigation of Wrongdoing by the Armed Forces' (*EJIL:Talk!*, 13 March 2013), available at www.ejiltalk.org/some-observations-on-the-turkel-report-and-the-investigation-of-wrongdoing-by-the-armed-forces/. See also M Lesh, 'A Critical Discussion of the Second Turkel Report and How It Engages with the Duty to Investigate Under International Law' (2013) 16 *Yearbook of International Humanitarian Law* 119.

[86] UN Human Rights Council, *Report of the United Nations Fact-Finding Mission on the Gaza Conflict* (*Goldstone Report*), UN Doc A/HRC/12/48 (25 September 2009). See Margalit (n 85); and A Dworkin, 'Goldstone and After: Judicial Intervention and the Quest for Peace in the Middle East' European Council on Foreign Relations, Background Paper (November 2013), available at www.ecfr.eu/ijp/case/israel_palestine.

[87] For just one example of the academic critique, see A Cohen and Y Shany, 'The Turkel Commission's Flotilla Report (Part One): Some Critical Remarks' (*EJIL:Talk!*, 28 January 2011), available at www.ejiltalk.org/the-turkel-commissions-flotilla-report-part-one-some-critical-remarks/. See also Ch 10: R Buchan, 'Quo Vadis? Commissions of Inquiry and their Implications for the Coherence of International Law' (particularly in relation to the Report's conclusion that customary international humanitarian law recognises the right to impose a naval blockade in non-international armed conflicts).

[88] UN Secretary General Ban Ki-Moon notably asserted that the Commission was 'not sufficient enough to have international credibility'. See N MacFarquhar, 'UN Leader

assert a lack of credibility in this way is only partially based on a technical legal conclusion; it equally reveals contrasts between cross-institutional perspectives on the appropriate manner in which international disputes ought to be investigated and determined.

However much it may seem valuable to have international law 'front and centre' in the mandate of a domestic commission (especially in relation to such fundamental issues of humanitarian and human rights law), the wider societal and political context surrounding the Turkel Commission clouds the extent to which its creation and mandate may be said to be of true benefit for the implementation of international law (both specifically in relation to the Gaza blockade, and more generally).

For the creator of a domestic commission of inquiry (usually the national executive)[89] to prescribe the commission's terms of reference so as to require or allow it to engage with legal questions is for it to give an ad hoc body quasi-judicial powers: no small matter. The creator is thus only likely to do so where there is: (1) a genuine willingness on its part for an independent finding/legal appraisal; or (2) a desire to create and control an authoritative interpretation of international law as it applies within the domestic context. This requires a high degree of 'trust' in the commission on the part of its creator, either in it 'correctly' and 'impartially' applying the law, or in it being willing to 'play ball' and reach legal conclusions that reflect the preferences of the creator (and, perhaps, the preferences of the wider domestic society). It is precisely because such 'trust' is so often absent that the mandates of domestic commissions commonly will not provide for the engagement with international law (or why commissions themselves will refrain from interpreting their mandates so as to provide for this).

4.6. INTERNATIONAL LEGAL EXPERTISE IN DOMESTIC COMMISSIONS

International commissions of inquiry are often composed, at least in part, of international law experts.[90] This is not commonly so for domestic commissions. Indeed, where domestic commissions of inquiry have members

Criticizes Israeli Plan for Inquiry' *New York Times* (18 June 2010), available at www.nytimes.com/2010/06/19/world/middleeast/19nations.html?_r=0.

[89] See *Report of the Special Rapporteur* (n 1) 7.

[90] For example, consider the 2004 International Commission of Inquiry on Darfur, where all five members of the commission—Antonio Cassese, Mohamed Fayek, Hina Jilani, Dumisa Ntsebeza and Therese Striggner-Scott—had significant legal expertise and at least some (and in some cases, a lot) of international law expertise: *Report of the International Commission of Inquiry on Darfur to the United Nations Secretary-General Pursuant to Security Council Resolution 1564 of 18 September 2004*, (Geneva, 25 January 2005), available at www.un.org/news/dh/sudan/com_inq_darfur.pdf.

with legal expertise, such expertise is often in the domestic law of the state concerned.

The independent 9/11 Commission,[91] created in the US in 2002, is illustrative of the conventional composition of domestic commissions when it comes to legal expertise. Half of its members were—or had been—'lawyers' of one sort or another.[92] However, none had a meaningful international law background. This absence of international legal expertise seems incongruous with the fact that aspects of the Commission's mandate[93] prima facie engaged a range of international legal standards. Ultimately, aside from a passing reference to Common Article 3 of the 1949 Geneva Conventions,[94] the Commission's near-600 page report was silent on international law; it had a good deal to say, however, on the application and enforcement of the law of the United States.[95]

Domestic commissions of inquiry tend to reflect any nation's (and given government's) conventional practices of administrative review. There is good reason for this in straightforward practical terms. Technical expertise and support is often a matter of availability: the type and existence of expert resources is significantly dependent on social circumstances.[96]

From a general point of view, there is no doubt that expertise is a cornerstone of normative authority.[97] A society's confidence in the findings of an inquiry only goes as far as its confidence in the expertise of the commission's commissioners, to the point that it has been argued that '[t]he success or failure of a Commission of Inquiry depends mainly on the proper selection of personnel'.[98] It is worth noting that—in spite of the fact that independence and autonomy need to be preserved—the existence of

[91] National Commission on Terrorist Attacks upon the United States, created 22 November 2002, govinfo.library.unt.edu/911/report/index.htm.

[92] For official biographies of the 9/11 Commission's members, see govinfo.library.unt.edu/911/about/bios.htm.

[93] See Public Law 107-306, Nov 27, 2002 116 Stat 2383, s 602 ('purposes'), govinfo.library.unt.edu/911/about/107-306.title6.pdf.

[94] *Final Report of the National Commission on Terrorist Attacks upon the United States* (22 July 2004), available at govinfo.library.unt.edu/911/report/911Report.pdf, 380.

[95] See, generally, ibid.

[96] Such complexity may be illustrated in reference to the UK's Independent Inquiry into Child Sexual Abuse (IICSA), see www.iicsa.org.uk/. The UK government was forced to seek foreign professional expertise after the Inquiry's first two Chairs stepped down. Furthermore, the Home Affairs Select Committee asserted that the Home Secretary's nondisclosure of the Chair's salary package was 'not in line with the open and transparent approach we would expect in the course of a pre-appointment process'; Home Affairs Committee, *Appointment of the Chair of the Independent Inquiry into Child Sexual Abuse* (11 February 2015) (2014–15, HC 710) para 15.

[97] See, generally, M Bódig, 'Doctrinal Knowledge, Legal Doctrinal Scholarship and the Problem of Interdisciplinary Engagement' in H Dedek and S Van Praagh (eds), *Stateless Law: Evolving Boundaries of a Discipline* (Farnham, Ashgate, 2015) 61, 62–65; and AS Greene, *Against Obligation: The Multiple Sources of Authority in a Liberal Democracy* (Cambridge, Harvard University Press, 2012) 31.

[98] Sarkar (n 22) 49.

governmental pathways for the scrutiny and oversight of any technical expertise is of critical importance. For example, in the UK, members of parliament regularly participate in the process of scrutiny and oversight of domestic commissions of inquiry, such as during the deliberative process of parliamentary debates.[99]

For the purposes of this section, the potentially esoteric nature of expertise raises a significant question about the extent to which there can be reasonable public scrutiny and oversight of expert knowledge. The proceedings of the Chilcot Inquiry exposed this difficulty in relation to international law and international legal expertise. This was profoundly highlighted when a member of the Inquiry asked Sir Michael Wood (giving oral evidence in 2010 as former Legal Adviser to the Foreign and Commonwealth Office): 'Would you agree with the Foreign Secretary's characterisation that international law is an uncertain field?'[100] Notwithstanding Sir Michael's reasoned reply at the time, the very fact that this question was asked in the first instance—and then considered in some detail in the Chilcot Inquiry's 2016 Report[101]—underlines that one ought not to presume that there is a shared understanding of even very basic axioms of professional expertise.

Thus, the exact manner in which expert knowledge feeds into normative authority depends on how well the 'knowledge' in question is understood by those wishing to scrutinise such use of expert tools. Clearly, for normative authority to be grasped, some minimum understanding of expertise is required by other members of society (both governmental and general public).

Beyond the general problems of translating knowledge between experts and non-experts, there is no doubt that expertise is a tool that brings value to commissions of inquiry. This importance can be seen from the 2010 Protocol issued by the Canadian Judicial Council (Canada's chief judicial governing body).[102] The Protocol provided a set of guidelines on the appointment of judges to domestic commissions following concerns

[99] An example of such deliberation is the following contribution from John Mann MP in one such debate: '[w]e can learn a lot from abroad. …Whoever is the Minister, and whoever sits on the Select Committees and all the rest, should get out there, steal their good ideas, bring them back and implement them here. … I need from the Government a clear undertaking that the resources and expertise will be there' HC Deb 17 March 2015, vol 594, col 245 (emphasis added).

[100] Iraq Inquiry, Sir Michael Wood Transcript, Oral evidence of Legal Adviser, Foreign and Commonwealth Office, 2001–2006 (26 January 2010), available at umbr2.cabinetoffice.gov.uk/media/44205/20100126am-wood-final.pdf.

[101] See *Chilcot Inquiry Report* (n 61) vol 5, section 5, paras 341–95.

[102] *Protocol on the Appointment of Judges to Commissions of Inquiry*, adopted by the Canadian Judicial Council August 2010, available at www.cjc-ccm.gc.ca/cmslib/general/JIC-CIsc-protocol-finalE-Augsut-2010.pdf.

raised in relation to a number of high-profile inquiries.[103] Although the Protocol was focused on the integrity of legal expertise per se (and not international law expertise specifically), it nonetheless demonstrates that notable fears persist as to the normative authority even of Canadian domestic commissions,[104] particularly in relation to concerns over the perception of legal expertise in the public consciousness.

The discussion so far in this section has considered more prosaic elements of expertise. However, as noted in section 4.3,[105] one ought to remember that starker political tensions might be at play. Furthermore, such tensions may have a causal link with regard to the absence of international legal expertise; or, at least, certainly there are perceivable substantive and normative effects when international legal expertise is absent. When internationalised expertise or standards contrast with national political moralities or goals, inherently political choices are made as to respective prioritisation. As noted above,[106] it should perhaps not be a surprise that the context-specific social interests that underpin the creation of domestic commissions of inquiry mean that there they are often composed without international lawyers as part of their membership. However, this fact may significantly undermine the normative authority of international legal claims made by a commission.

The Malaysian Commission on Immigrants in Sabah (2012–2014),[107] for example, was composed largely of legal experts,[108] but—as with the 9/11 Commission—none of its members had any meaningful *international law* expertise. This was in spite of the implications for international law of the Commission's terms of reference relating to immigration and citizenship. In the view of the present authors, the substantive 'international law' findings of the Commission—at least on refugee status and on the status of stateless persons[109]—were wholly unsatisfactory, both in terms of their brevity and lack of understanding of customary international law obligations in these areas beyond treaties to which Malaysia is not party.[110]

[103] See C Forcese, 'Judicial Supervision of Anti-Terrorism Laws in Comparative Democracies' in B Saul (ed), *Research Handbook on International Law and Terrorism* (Cheltenham, Edward Elgar, 2014) 521, 527–28.

[104] Which are generally positively viewed in the Canadian public consciousness, see n 50 and accompanying text.

[105] See section 4.3, particularly nn 31–33 and accompanying text.

[106] See n 96 and accompanying text.

[107] *Report of the Commission of Enquiry on Immigrants in Sabah*, presented to Seri Paduka Baginda Yang di-Pertuan Agong (3 December 2014), available at www.sapp.org.my/rci/RCI-Eng.pdf.

[108] ibid, iii.

[109] See ibid, 227–29.

[110] For example, the Commission dismissed the definition (and notion) of a stateless person on the basis that 'the Convention on the Status of Stateless Persons 1951 [sic, 1954] and the Convention on the Reduction of Statelessness 1961… [are treaties to which] Malaysia is not a signatory'. See *Report of the Commission of Enquiry on Immigrants in Sabah* (n 107) 228–29.

Interestingly, where domestic commissions *have* included members with suitable international legal expertise (when international law questions are at issue), this has at times directly fed not only into the substantive quality of the legal conclusions reached by these commissions, but also the wider perception of credibility with which those conclusions have been received. The 2011 Kyrgyzstan Inquiry Commission (KIC)[111] serves as an example of this. The *KIC Report* engaged in detail with international law, and produced a number of credible and balanced legal findings, particularly with regard to international criminal law.[112]

The international community—including the European Union, the Organisation for Security and Co-operation in Europe (OSCE), the United States and Russia—commended the quality of the KIC's report and its findings.[113] Undoubtedly, the reason for the international credibility of the Report is in no small part due to the presence of *specific* international legal expertise in the Commission. There are three notable reasons for this. First, the KIC's terms of reference explicitly stipulated that it would 'be composed of a panel of eminent personalities as well as a group of experts', and further specified the need for 'requisite expertise in human rights, conflict analysis, international humanitarian law and international criminal law'.[114] Secondly, the Commission's ultimate composition included notable legal expertise, including but not limited to international legal expertise.[115] Thirdly, the Crisis Management Initiative (CMI) 'assisted [the Commission] by [providing] the necessary administrative and technical staff' and served as the Secretariat for the KIC.[116] In spite of all this, however, in terms of normative authority, such embedded international legal expertise was not enough to alter the Kyrgyzstani government's ultimately critical view of the Report.[117]

However, as the International Law Commission has made very clear, the 1954 definition of a stateless person 'can no doubt be considered as having acquired a customary nature', obliging all states to adopt it: UN, *Draft Articles on Diplomatic Protection with Commentaries* (2006), text adopted by the International Law Commission at its fifty-eighth session, UN Doc A/61/10, 48–49.

[111] KIC, *Report of the Independent International Commission of Inquiry into the Events in Southern Kyrgyzstan in June 2010*, (3 May 2011), available at www.cmi.fi/images/stories/activities/blacksea/kic/kic_report_english_final.pdf.

[112] See nn 136–139 and accompanying text.

[113] See A Matveeva, 'Kyrgyzstan: Balancing on the Verge of Stability' (2011) 19 *EUCAM* 1, 3.

[114] *KIC Report* (n 111) para 4.

[115] For a list of the KIC's members, including their expertise, see *KIC Report* (n 111) para 5.

[116] For more information, see www.cmi.fi/en/about-us/who-we-are/history/past-projects/kyrgyzstan-inquiry-commission. The CMI is a non-profit organisation founded by Finland's Nobel Peace Prize winning President Martti Ahtisaari, who had extensive prior mediation and peace brokering experiences in Namibia, Kosovo and Aceh.

[117] See n 152 and accompanying text.

Sri Lanka's Paranagama Commission[118] serves as a contrast to the KIC example. Whereas there was a presence of international legal expertise embedded within the KIC and around it, international legal expertise—in the form of an 'Advisory Council'—was only appointed belatedly to assist the Paranagama Commission.[119] Though there were some concerns about whether this additional support, having finally been provided, was prematurely taken away, the Advisory Council brought a wealth of legal assistance to the Commission.[120]

However, because the President of Sri Lanka appointed the Advisory Council belatedly, externally (to the Commission), and conspicuously *after* the Office of the UN High Commissioner for Human Rights (OHCHR) formally established its own investigation,[121] questions were raised about the move. One Sri Lankan government official opined that the appointment of the Advisory Council was 'just to advise the commission', which would 'decide whether to accept the advice or to set it aside'.[122] The same official went further in stating that the Advisory Council's role was 'to double check … and to get some international backing … not a re-correction.'[123] Another Sri Lankan official was altogether more critical, saying that the Sri Lankan government 'was under pressure' and that this pressure was why it 'had to resort to these measures [of appointing the Advisory Council part way through the Commission's work]'.[124]

The Paranagama Commission highlights how international legal expertise may not necessarily be received neutrally, particularly where it has been brought in ad hoc. It seems likely that the external reliance on international legal expertise would have faced less criticism if the Commission itself had appointed the Advisory Council, instead of the President. This would have helped with the credibility of such an initiative and would have had a more positive influence on the Commission's normative authority (dependant, as that is—in part—on wider perceptions of credibility).

118 Presidential Commission to Investigate into Complaints Regarding Missing Persons, created in August 2013. For the terms of reference of the Paranagama Commission and biographies of its members, see web.archive.org/web/20160519045508/http://www.pcicmp.lk.

119 'Sri Lanka to investigate war crimes; appoints foreign experts', *Reuters* (17 July 2014), available at www.reuters.com/article/us-sri-lanka-warcrimes-idUSKBN0FM1M820140717.

120 See 'Sir Desmond's Mandate was Not Extended', *Colombo Gazette* (23 August 2015), available at colombogazette.com/2015/08/23/sir-desmonds-mandate-was-not-extended/.

121 The OHCHR received its mandate to establish the OHCHR Investigation on Sri Lanka (OISL) from the UN Human Rights Council: 'to undertake a comprehensive investigation into alleged serious violations and abuses of human rights and related crimes by both parties in Sri Lanka during the period covered by the Lessons Learnt and Reconciliation Commission'. UN Human Rights Council Resolution, *Promoting reconciliation, accountability and human rights in Sri Lanka*, UN Doc A/HRC/RES/25/1 (9 April 2014) para 10.

122 'Sri Lanka to Investigate War Crimes; Appoints Foreign Experts', *Reuters* (17 July 2014), available at uk.reuters.com/article/uk-sri-lanka-warcrimes-idUKKBN0FM1MM20140717.

123 ibid.

124 ibid.

By way of summary, international law expertise certainly has the potential to impart upon domestic commissions of inquiry a degree of normative authority. This potential ought not to be uncritically assumed, however. As has been discussed in this section, international legal expertise might not necessarily be available, it may not be adequately understood and it may ultimately not be received without criticism. The discussion in this section is merely an illustrative guide to the normative significance that international legal expertise might bring to domestic commissions of inquiry. In the limited space available here, it has not been possible to flesh out good lawyerly techniques in greater detail.[125]

4.7. SUBSTANTIVE ENGAGEMENT WITH INTERNATIONAL LAW IN DOMESTIC COMMISSIONS

Previous sections have explored the main technical barriers that determine the extent to which domestic commissions of inquiry have (or have not) engaged with international law. Insofar as engagement with international law has occurred, there are two standpoints from which one could assess the quality of such engagement: firstly, by considering the commission's expressed substantive findings themselves, and, secondly, by examining the manner in which those findings are received. Although some of the representative examples given in previous sections have alluded to these two ways in which appraisal can be undertaken, this section looks in greater detail at both the manner and extent of commissions' engagement with international law, and the reception and implementation of their findings and reports.

It will be recalled, for example, that the findings of the Linden Commission in Guyana demonstrated a lack in political will on the part of the Commission to meaningfully engage with international law; this was irrespective of the fact that its mandate would have allowed for such engagement, and that questions of international human rights law were undoubtedly at issue.[126] Indeed, the Commission explicitly noted that international law standards might be applicable to the facts under investigation but then refrained even from identifying what these standards were:

> It would serve no useful purposes for us to attempt to…reinvent the wheel. It [ie 'the wheel', meaning international human rights law] exists…We are of the clear

[125] Though not directly relating to commissions of inquiry per se, international law scholarship does contain numerous examples where such good practices have been discussed. See, eg, UN, *Collection of Essays by Legal Advisers of States, Legal Advisers of International Organizations and Practitioners in the Field of International Law* (New York, UN Office of Legal Affairs, 1999); and C Wickremasinghe (ed), *The International Lawyer As Practitioner* (London, British Institute of International and Comparative Law, 2000).

[126] See nn 69–77 and accompanying text.

> view that the United Nations has adequately provided guidance on how to deal with the pernicious and pervasive practice of human rights abuse.[127]

Examples of this sort are relatively commonplace: international law being referenced only to a limited extent, or sometimes even being ignored, in instances where one might perhaps expect engagement. Nonetheless, there are, of course, instances where extensive international legal findings have been reached by domestic commissions. The *value* of such findings, though, is dependent on the overall normative authority possessed by the commission in question: that level of normative authority both includes and influences the wider perception of those findings (in the media, expert opinion and the public consciousness).

In the following analysis in this section, we consider aspects of the substantive engagement with international and the reception of that engagement by referencing three examples: domestic commissions of inquiry set up in Nigeria, Kyrgyzstan and the Netherlands. These are selected as illustrations rather than as an in-depth comparative survey.

The Oputa Panel,[128] which was created by the Obasanjo government in Nigeria in 1999,[129] engaged extensively with international legal standards: in particular, it considered international human rights law in depth (both treaty law and customary international law).[130] The Panel had a clear mandate to do so,[131] and had wide-ranging investigative powers of summons/subpoena.[132] However, it was also given an extremely limited time to produce its Report,[133] and had only a negligible budget to conduct its work.[134] The international legal conclusions that were reached in the (leaked) Oputa Panel Report, while extensive, read as being rather rushed: indeed, much of the analysis involves an appraisal of *how Nigeria has perceived* its international human rights obligations, rather than a truly objective assessment of those obligations and Nigeria's compliance with

[127] *Linden Commission Report* (n 69) paras 188–89.

[128] *Report of the Human Rights Violations Investigation Commission* (May 2002) (nine volumes, plus Summary, Conclusions and Recommendations), never officially released: available as a private publication by the Nigerian Democratic Movement and Nigeria-based Civil Society Forum at www.dawodu.com/oputa1.htm (*Report of the Oputa Panel*).

[129] See United States Institute of Peace, 'Truth Commission: Nigeria' (14 July 1999), available at www.usip.org/publications/truth-commission-nigeria.

[130] *Report of the Oputa Panel* (n 128) vol 2, Chs 3–6.

[131] ibid, vol 1, 29–30 (setting out the Panel's sweeping mandate).

[132] ibid, vol 1, 31–32.

[133] Initially, this was a mere three months, although it was then extended to one year: see ibid, vol 1, 30.

[134] The Panel's budget was never formally agreed, but see 'Nigeria: Oputa Panel Wraps Up Hearings', (*WikiLeaks*, 24 November 2001) para 3, available at wikileaks.org/plusd/cables/01ABUJA2973_a.html, (leaked statement of a Panel Member, making it clear that it had a 'limited budget').

them.[135] While it would perhaps be unfair to admonish the Panel itself for this—given its obvious attempts to accurately identify and apply international human rights law—the value of its substantive international legal conclusions are ultimately rather limited.

As previously identified in section 4.6,[136] the Kyrgyzstan example—KIC—illustrates significant and meaningful engagement by a domestic commission with international law. The *KIC Report* examined and applied international human rights law, international humanitarian law and international criminal law, each in notable depth.[137] It ultimately took the view 'that the violence of June [2010] does not qualify as either war crimes or genocide' but that certain acts, if conclusively proven in law, 'would amount to crimes against humanity'.[138] The Commission also held that 'serious human rights violations have occurred and are still occurring within Kyrgyzstan'.[139] More importantly, it reached these various conclusions—in the view of the present authors—based on rigorous and detailed analysis of the law, and balanced application of that law to the facts.

The 2010 Independent Dutch Committee of Inquiry on the War in Iraq (Davids Committee)[140] serves as an example where the normative authority of a commission is even more extensive.[141] The Committee can be distinguished from the Oputa Panel and the KIC, not merely in terms of the extent of its substantive engagement with international law, but also based on the characteristics of its normative authority within the given social context.[142] Unlike the two prior examples, there were no domestic human rights abuses or instances of domestic violence for the Davids Committee to investigate.

In procedural terms, the Committee primarily 'perceived its task as one of fact-finding'.[143] It is worth noting, however, the Committee's broad

[135] See, eg, *Report of the Oputa Panel* (n 128) vol 2, 16–17 ('*Nigeria demonstrated in practice* her commitment to the implementation of IHL … *Nigerian state practice recognizes* the distinction between a combatant and a civilian', emphasis added).

[136] See nn 111–117 and accompanying text.

[137] *KIC Report* (n 111) particularly paras 236–300.

[138] ibid, Executive Summary, para 5.

[139] ibid, para 300.

[140] *Rapport Commissie-Davids, Rijksoverheid* (Dutch Government) (12 January 2010), available at www.rijksoverheid.nl/binaries/rijksoverheid/documenten/rapporten/2010/01/12/rapport-commissie-davids/rapport-commissie-irak.pdf (*Davids Committee Report*).

[141] The *Davids Committee Report* contains a summary, in English, including its 49 conclusions. See ibid, 517–33. In addition, Ch 8 of the Report was translated into English, which dealt with international law questions. See 'Report of the Dutch Committee of Inquiry on the War in Iraq' (2010) 57 *Netherlands International Law Review* 81.

[142] For this chapter's purposes, we have focused our discussion on the context of the Committee's findings. For analysis of the substantive international law content of the Davids Committee Report, see J Nijman, 'After 'Iraq': Back to the International Rule of Law? An Introduction to the NYIL 2011 Agora' (2011) 42 *Netherlands Yearbook of International Law* 71; and TE Aalberts, 'Forging International Order: Inquiring the Dutch Support of the Iraq Invasion' (2011) 42 *Netherlands Yearbook of International Law* 139.

[143] *Davids Committee Report* (n 140) 521.

remit of investigation: 'with regard to the Netherlands' political support for the invasion of Iraq in general, and with regard to matters pertinent to international law, to intelligence and information provision and to alleged military involvement in particular.'[144] The Davids Committee thus not only engaged with issues of public international law in depth—Chapter 8 of its Report dealt expressly with the legal basis for military intervention in Iraq under international law[145]—but it also was able to take a critical view of the Dutch government (with which the Committee had a candid debate),[146] as well as being able to itself present a nuanced and diverse analysis.[147] All of this is noteworthy, as it reveals demonstrable maturity of the democratic context in the Netherlands, which allowed for in-depth governmental scrutiny, as well as scrutiny of the complex topics of foreign policy and international law. In our view, the mature socio-political context of the Netherlands—allowing for democratic deliberation—was key to the manner in which the normative authority of the Davids Committee was framed.[148]

In addition to highlighting the influence of the domestic context on the extent of substantive international law engagement, the three examples also reveal that the domestic context is key to the reception and implementation of the findings of commissions of inquiry. This is evident in relation to the Report of the Oputa Panel, which was essentially disavowed and 'annulled' by the Nigerian government. Moreover, *none* of the Panel's recommendations were implemented[149] and, tellingly, its Report has never officially been made public.[150] One could at least argue that the creation of the Oputa Panel did more harm than good to the *implementation* of international human rights law in Nigeria, despite there being a clear attempt

[144] ibid, 521.

[145] ibid, 215–73.

[146] See 'PM Survives Iraq No Confidence Motion' *Dutch News* (17 February 2010), available at www.dutchnews.nl/news/archives/2010/02/pm_survives_iraq_no_confidence/; and 'Balkenende Oneens met Conclusies Davids over Irak' *NU* (12 January 2010), available at www.nu.nl/politiek/2160846/balkenende-oneens-met-conclusies-davids-irak.html.

[147] For example, the Report contained a separate comment by one of the Committee's members, much like minority dissenting opinions in judicial judgments. Peter Walsum endorsed the Committee's conclusion that there lacked legal basis for intervention, however, he refrained 'from concluding that hence the Dutch government was wrong in its political support for the invasion': see Aalberts (n 142) 170.

[148] Importantly, the Davids Committee itself took a broader view of the whole Iraq question to the Netherlands, asserting that '[t]he Government's reasoning was influence by public opinion to a significant extent, Accordingly [sic] the Committee felt it appropriate to describe public opinion on Iraq in the Netherlands (and elsewhere) and to consider the extent to which the government used public opinion research to shape its policy': *Davids Committee Report* (n 140) 522.

[149] HO Yusuf, *Transitional Justice, Judicial Accountability and the Rule of Law* (Abingdon, Routledge, 2010), 45.

[150] See 'Oputa Panel Report: Matters Arising—Guardian Editorial', *Nigerian Muse* (28 December 2006), available at www.nigerianmuse.com/nigeriawatch/oputa/?u=Guardian_editorial_Oputa_panel_December04.htm.

on the part of the Panel to apply human rights standards to the factual circumstances that it was investigating.[151]

In the case of the KIC, which reached rather more compelling international law conclusions than did the Oputa Panel, the Kyrgyzstani government rejected much of the substance of the 2011 Report produced by the KIC (a Commission that it had, of course, itself created), *especially* regarding the KIC's findings concerning international law.[152] Kyrgyzstan also has failed to implement any of the recommendations made. In contrast, the implementation of the Davids Committee's conclusions was more encouraging. Not only did the Committee's work lead to public deliberations, it also resulted in substantive reforms relating to the manner in which ministers receive legal advice in the Netherlands.[153]

Overall, it may be said that substantive engagement with international law is beneficial in terms of the credibility and functionality of a commission and its findings. The three examples highlighted in this section demonstrate this, but they also indicate that any wider benefits must be understood in terms of the interaction between public deliberation and governmental techniques. The whole process of a commission's engagement international law not only operates in narrow 'legal' terms—such as fact-finding and quasi-judicial capacities—but also has a capacity to transform the wider normative arena. This helps to explain why we have chosen to analyse commissions of inquiry from the perspective of *normative authority*. The engagement with international law and other international standards is often the first and only time that a new standard of appreciating a domestic issue occurs. This potentially leads—as was the case in the Davids Committee example—not just to the critical appraisal of particular state practice (or practices), but to reform.

Of course, holding domestic practices to an external standard is fraught with difficulty. Nonetheless, engagement with international law can be seen as a form of normative entrepreneurism. For international law to have a positive effect with regard to the normative authority of domestic commissions—both in terms of engagement and implementation—the domestic context needs to be actively deliberating on international legal

[151] Yusuf (n 149) 44–45 (alluding to this position rather than explicitly adopting it).

[152] 'Comments by the Government of Kyrgyzstan in Response to the Report of the Kyrgyzstan Inquiry Commission into the Events in Southern Kyrgyzstan in June 2010', available at www.ndi.org/files/KG-comments-final-ENG.pdf, particularly at paras 56–72 (rejecting most of the KIC's conclusions regarding international law, other than that no war crimes or acts genocide had been established).

[153] Specifically, an independent legal adviser (who could provide both solicited and unsolicited advice to the Minister) was appointed. 'André Nollkaemper benoemd tot externe volkenrechtelijk adviseur', Rijksoverheid (Dutch Government) (25 May 2011), available at www.rijksoverheid.nl/actueel/nieuws/2011/05/25/andre-nollkaemper-benoemd-tot-externe-volkenrechtelijk-adviseur/.

standards. Both the general public and government of the state in question must be willing to deliberate upon the international legal standards that domestic commissions of inquiry might refer to, so as not to merely pay lip service to them.

4.8. CONCLUSION

It is perhaps axiomatic that 'fact-finding missions are diverse, plentiful, geographically dispersed, and established by different bodies and under different circumstances.'[154] Domestic commissions of inquiry are unsurprisingly a product of the varied social and political contexts in which they are established. Their engagement with international law (or lack of) is similarly a product of that context, as is the *desirability* of that engagement (which will be dependent on the nature of the inquiry in question and, thus, the social context that bore it and in which it exists).

It is tempting for an international lawyer to view engagement with international law in commissions of inquiry as being inherently 'positive', especially with respect to potential violations of human rights or humanitarian norms, and especially given that such a commission may well be the most formal and 'authoritative' forum in which international law standards are considered in relation to the given factual circumstances. However, commissions of inquiry—whether domestic or international—ought not to be perceived as an automatic legal panacea for dealing with severe social injustices. Similarly, it is a mistake to view their engagement with international law as being inherently desirable.

It is worth noting that the establishment of any given commission of inquiry may belie a genuine attempt to revitalise commitment to social standards that had not been followed or affirmed sufficiently in past practice. In some instances, the circumstances that enabled injustices to arise continue to be present within society. The character of the prevailing sociological context, whether one wishes to emphasise its strengths or weaknesses, is not entirely separable from the historic problems that brought about the need to conduct an inquiry in the first instance.

We have argued in this chapter that it is only where the international legal claims of domestic commissions of inquiry are made with a degree of normative authority that they can be, or should be, viewed as being of value. The ultimate composition of such normative authority in domestic commissions—which, after all, are ad hoc bodies—is complex and varied,

[154] Aksenova and Bergsmo (n 6) 5.

and involves developing a consensus of political, legal and moral considerations. Not all domestic commissions will be irredeemably 'tainted' by any means; valuable contributions to international law can and have been made by them. However, the notable increase in number of these commissions over the last 20 years and the engagement by them with international law must be treated with extreme caution, and approached contextually. Members of commissions of inquiry, and of the societies that they address (including the international community), must be acutely aware of the nature of legal objectivity and political consensus in these highly diverse, and largely unregulated, investigatory bodies. Ultimately, 'international law' should not be uncritically transposed to the substantive national context, and more scholarly attention needs to be paid to the selectivity that is inherent in such transpositions.

Section 2

Commissions of Inquiry and International Courts and Tribunals

5

Commissions of Inquiry and Traditional Mechanisms of Dispute Settlement

ALEXANDER ORAKHELASHVILI

5.1. INTRODUCTION

AT VARIOUS STAGES of international legal history, a 'commission of inquiry' would not be invariably seen to refer to the same thing. The older, more traditional forms of commission of inquiry would be established through inter-state agreement and with a mandate that would be reflective of the parameters of state consent on which their existence and operation was founded. The modern commissions of inquiry set up within the United Nations (UN) system, to deal with politically contentious situations involving allegations of violations of international human rights law and international humanitarian law, are mostly not supported by the consent of states whose conduct and practices they expose both in factual and legal terms. They instead operate in conditions where the states involved are opposed to their investigative tasks being performed. This prompts, among others, the question as to the extent to which these modern commission of inquiry can be described as dispute settlement bodies, and as to their place and feasibility within the international legal system.

In the overall global legal and political landscape of international organisations and of dispute settlement mechanisms, the emergence of any new type of institution tends to alter some elements of that overall landscape. A new mechanism of accountability prompts questions not only as to its own essence, but also as to its implications for other, older accountability institutions. Therefore, when we set out to examine commissions of inquiry in relation to, or in comparison with, traditional dispute settlement mechanisms, the accuracy of the comparison requires some certainty as to the essence of each pertinent category of dispute-settlement institution.

In a way, commissions of inquiry themselves have originated as part of the traditional dispute settlement framework that was one of the products of the 1899 Hague Peace Conference. The relevance of the commission

of inquiry found its expression in the 1899 Hague Convention on the Pacific Settlement of International Disputes. Article 9 of the 1899 Hague Convention determined that:

> In differences of an international nature involving neither honor nor vital interests, and arising from a difference of opinion on points of fact, the Signatory Powers recommend that the parties, who have not been able to come to an agreement by means of diplomacy, should as far as circumstances allow, institute an International Commission of Inquiry, to facilitate a solution of these differences by elucidating the facts by means of an impartial and conscientious investigation.

Article 10 of the Hague Convention 1899 prescribed that 'International Commissions of Inquiry are constituted by special agreement between the parties in dispute'. This agreement would define the facts to be examined in the process of the inquiry, 'and the extent of the powers of the Commissioners'.

The Hague Convention 1899 provided for a number of other dispute settlement modes, each of them distinguished from others by its institutional characteristics, extent of authority and nature of its decisions. The relevance and role of the commission of inquiry had a number of assets in the political and ideological context at the end of the nineteenth and beginning of the twentieth centuries, especially manifested by the purported limitation of the commissions' legal authority to the ascertainment of the facts in dispute, and by the lack of the binding force of their findings, which factor was supposed to make them more attractive to states that would not ordinarily be expected to submit to binding judicial or arbitral settlement. A number of controversies were handled through such commissions of inquiry in the early twentieth century.[1]

At subsequent stages, especially over the past few decades, the proliferation of international courts and tribunals has somewhat coincided with the relative decline in relevance of the commission of inquiry of the traditional type, as foreseen under the 1899 Hague Convention, instead leading to the enhancement of the relevance of judicial settlement of disputes between states as well as between states and non-state actors through multiple petition and adjudication procedures within the UN, regional or other frameworks. The current commissions of inquiry, such as those dealing with violations of human rights and humanitarian law, have developed not as discrete free-standing institutions consensually set up by states-parties to the relevant dispute, but as parts of a broader framework of the UN system.

[1] See J Merrils, *International Dispute Settlement* (5th edn, Cambridge, Cambridge University Press, 2011) 41; LJ van den Herik, 'An Inquiry into the Role of Commissions of Inquiry in International Law: Navigating the Tensions between Fact-Finding and International Law Application' (2014) 13 *Chinese Journal of International Law* 507.

Therefore, the international legal system has witnessed both the relative decline of the traditional role of commission of inquiry, and the merger of the inquiry function with the broader institutional framework of international organisations, deployed at the service of their broader goals of the maintenance of international peace and security, or the protection of human rights in peace as well as armed conflict. This was manifested by the embodiment of the inquiry function as part of the UN Security Council's peace and security mandate under Chapters VI and VII of the UN Charter (especially Article 34), as well as more lately as part of the framework of the UN Human Rights Council.

The practical importance of modern commissions of inquiry is that when there is little prospect of bringing the relevant state before an international court, because that state would not submit to the relevant court's jurisdiction, the UN organs may decide to establish a commission of inquiry to examine the legality of that state's relevant conduct, especially in relation to human rights and humanitarian law violations. The dilemma that obtains in this context relates to the need to balance the response to the accountability gap against the principle that no state should be subjected to international jurisdiction without its consent.

5.2. INQUIRY: FUNCTION OR INSTITUTION?

There is no authoritatively prescribed legal definition of 'inquiry'. Literally speaking, inquiring refers to asking for information, or to an official investigation.[2] The definition of a commission of inquiry is possible either by reference to the express designation of its mandate or by reference to its tasks and functions. Thus, Merrills suggests that inquiry can refer to two different phenomena. Inquiry in the operational sense is a major element of all arbitration and adjudication proceedings. But inquiry can also refer to a specific institutional arrangement.[3]

If we approach 'inquiry' as a function, some instruments, such as the 1899 Hague Convention, provide the description of its rationale and criteria. The commissions of inquiry have to impartially examine facts and deal with evidence. It stands to reason to say that the inquiry function involves the assessment of facts on the basis of evidence, and therefore presupposes the requirement of impartiality, in that particular respect at least, from all organs that exercise the inquiry function whether as the task discretely or ad hoc entrusted to them, or whether they act as part of the broader institutional framework such as the UN Security Council.

[2] *Compact OED* (Oxford, Oxford University Press, 2005) 331, 523.
[3] Merrils (n 1) 41.

The independence element can operate in relation to states (with the older commissions of inquiry) or in relation to international organisations (with the newer commissions of inquiry) who establish them.

To what extent could the older commissions of inquiry be properly described as dispute settlement organs, given that they were merely supposed to state facts? The express reference is made in Article 9 of the Hague Convention to 'difference of opinion on points of facts', and the definition of a dispute by the Permanent Court of International Justice in the *Mavrommatis* case refers to a disagreement as to the point of fact *or* law.[4] Thus a mere disagreement as to the relevant facts, their occurrence, scale and nature could, in principle, as such constitute a dispute to be resolved through the relevant dispute settlement mode provided for under the Hague Convention or, subsequently, under the UN Charter (Chapter VI).

But the purely factual nature of the commission of inquiry findings also has implications for whether the *lis pendens* rule could apply to situations where a commission of inquiry deals with the matter and an international tribunal also tries to resolve it. The *lis pendens* rule, when relevant, could ordinarily apply only in situations when the same dispute is pending before more than one judicial (including arbitral) organ, and then when the relevant tribunal's constituent instrument so requires (in terms of declining jurisdiction accordingly). The International Court of Justice has generally rejected the claims that it should decline to hear a case because another international organ is also dealing with it. In the cases of *Tehran Hostages* and *Nicaragua*, the International Court has rejected the approach that the UN Security Council's involvement in the relevant situation could prevent it from adjudicating on it.[5] In *Cameroon-Nigeria* (Preliminary Objections), the International Court suggested that 'the Lake Chad Basin Commission cannot be seen as a tribunal. It renders neither arbitral awards nor judgments and is therefore neither an arbitral nor a judicial body'.[6]

On the other hand, whether any international tribunal would be necessarily bound by the fact-related findings of any commission of inquiry is questionable. In the exercise of its own jurisdiction, any international tribunal would need to establish facts independently and thus perform its own inquiry function. Nevertheless, and apart from the sphere of international adjudication proper, the definitive settlement of the factual issue within the commission of inquiry framework would tie hands and restrain the political freedom of states to the extent that those facts have been transparently investigated and established. Once the facts on the ground are

4 *Mavrommatis* PCIJ (1924) Series A no 2, 11.

5 *Hostages* (Merits) [1980] ICJ Rep 22 (para 40); reaffirmed in *Nicaragua* (Jurisdiction and Admissibility) [1984] ICJ Rep 433–34 (para 93).

6 *Cameron-Nigeria*, Preliminary Objections [1998] ICJ Rep 307.

established, the lack of binding force of the commission of inquiry's report to that effect matters precious little, because the lack of such binding force of the report cannot undo the facts that the report has established. This consideration could have some importance in the context of commissions of inquiry that operate as part of the UN system.

Where does the inquiry function stand in relation to the international adjudication process performed by arbitral and judicial organs? It is clear that the judicial or quasi-judicial nature of an organ refers to its function before it refers to its express designation. According to Rosenne, international adjudication refers to the judicial function of an international tribunal to do justice with the case submitted to it and resolve it with completeness, finality and binding force.[7]

It is not crucial how an organ is expressly designated or how its functions were envisaged at the stage of its establishment. An organ initially designed or intended as a fact-finding organ could end up operating as a quasi-judicial organ. To illustrate, the World Bank Inspection Panel was initially intended as a fact-finding body to assist the Bank's management in the observance of Bank's policies in relation to Bank's projects,[8] but has effectively ended up operating as a quasi-judicial organ dealing with disputes on the basis of the applicable international law.[9]

A treaty-based organ that is not expressly designated as a court could effectively exercise functions which are inherently judicial, and thus resolve disputes with finality. No direct binding force discretely accrues to decisions of the UN Human Rights Committee operating under the 1966 International Covenant on Civil and Political Rights (ICCPR), yet the correctness of the interpretation placed by the Committee on the relevant provisions of the Covenant could be as good as binding force of its decisions. This is in accordance with the position that the Committee has been tasked, under the ICCPR, by states-parties to ensure the uniform and effective interpretation of the Covenant's provisions.

A political organ such as the UN Security Council could exercise quasi-judicial functions in resolving a dispute. However, under the UN Charter the scope of quasi-judicial activities of the Security Council is rather limited and strictly functional. While the Security Council could recommend the terms of resolution of a particular dispute that may lead to a threat to international peace and security, it has no direct authority to resolve any

[7] S Rosenne, *The Law and Practice of the International Court, 1920–1996* (Kluwer Law International, 1997) 536.

[8] Merrills describes it as 'standing inquiry procedure'; (n 1) 56.

[9] A Orakhelashvili, 'The World Bank Inspection Panel in Context: Institutional Aspects of the Accountability of International Organisations' (2005) *International Organisations Law Review* 57.

inter-state dispute in a binding manner.[10] This could, however, lead to the consideration of the issue of *vires* of the Security Council.

Despite some significant structural diversities, what unites the above three various organs is the possibility of the referral of complaints to them, and the possibility of them dealing with those complaints impartially and on the basis of international law. If a political organ assumes quasi-judicial functions, it has to conform to relevant adjudication requirements such as fair hearing requirements and proof and evidence requirements.[11]

As part of the discrete institutional context dealing with international peace and security, the nature and requirements of 'inquiry' could also contribute to the ascertainment of the very essence of the UN Security Council's Chapter VII powers. The establishment of the relevant facts and state conduct through the inquiry or investigation under Article 34 of the UN Charter, within the Chapter VI framework, could pave the way for the adoption of Chapter VII measures against the relevant state. However, Chapter VII itself is not free of the requirement that facts amounting to a 'threat to the peace' under Article 39 of the Charter should be duly and properly established, so as to justify the further use of the Security Council's statutory coercive powers under Chapter VII. The lack of the proper investigation of the factual aspect of the relevant matter could draw adversely on the legality and propriety of the Security Council's use of its own Chapter VII powers. The legality of these statutory powers is dependent on the proper ascertainment of facts.

The General Assembly and Security Council, as well as the Secretary General, could use inquiry and fact-finding both for their preventive diplomacy and quasi-judicial tasks,[12] as well as for the purposes of determining whether any enforcement action is warranted. However, in the institutional sense, the nature of 'inquiry' is premised not only on the essential importance of inquiry and fact-finding commissions for the proper discharge of the principal organs' statutory powers under the Charter, but also on the degree of independence of these commissions from the will and position of the organs that establish them.

The 1991 UN Declaration on Fact-finding, adopted by the General Assembly, could be seen as an authoritative interpretation of the principal organs' powers under the Charter when dealing with situations that require the proper establishment of underlying facts. Article 1 of the Declaration proposes that,

[10] See A Orakhelashvili, *Collective Security* (Oxford, Oxford University Press, 2011) Chs 2 and 5.

[11] Orakhelashvili (n 10) Ch 2.

[12] The view is also expressed in academic writings that such use of inquiry functions is premised on the implied power of the General Assembly and Secretary General, *cf* van den Herik (n 1) 524–25.

> In performing their functions in relation to the maintenance of international peace and security, the competent organs of the United Nations should endeavour to have full knowledge of all relevant facts. To this end they should consider undertaking fact-finding activities.

Furthermore, the Declaration specifies that,

> Unless a satisfactory knowledge of all relevant facts can be obtained through the use of the information-gathering capabilities of the Secretary-General or other existing means, the competent organ of the United Nations should consider resorting to a fact-finding mission.

And then it is specified that 'Fact-finding should be comprehensive, objective, impartial and timely'.[13] Article 25 of the Declaration further suggests that

> Fact-finding missions have an obligation to act in strict conformity with their mandate and perform their task in an impartial way. Their members have an obligation not to seek or receive instructions from any Government or from any authority other than the competent United Nations organ.

These provisions are indications of what the good administration of these organs' Charter-based functions would be and how well and impartially they discharge it. The least these provisions suggest is that, even at the service of UN principal organs that are in the first place guided by the political discretion originating from political instructions that state representatives in these organs receive from their governments, the commission of inquiry should remain politically impartial, even at the cost of not delivering on whatever the prevailing political expectation in the relevant principal organ is. But more importantly, the above provisions from the Declaration also incorporate the inherent requirements under the Charter for the Security Council's use of its coercive authority under Chapter VII. Even if the Security Council possesses discretion under the relevant Charter provisions such as Article 39, the good faith requirement inherently attendant to the exercise of that discretion requires that due regard should be had to all facts on the ground. Without such, there would be little prospect of properly ascertaining what the threat to international peace and security is in the relevant situation. To illustrate, the fact that the Security Council rejected the option to establish a fact-finding or commission of inquiry in relation to the Lockerbie aerial incident, went hand in hand with the doubts that could arise as to whether the Council had correctly identified the existence of a 'threat to the peace' under Article 39 in that situation.[14] In such or similar contexts, the findings made by commissions of inquiry established within the UN Human Rights Council framework

[13] 1991 Declaration, Art 3.
[14] See for detail and analysis, Orakhelashvili (n 10) Ch 4.

on the matter of violations of human rights and humanitarian law could also be useful for the Security Council's handling of the context in which those violations were alleged or established to have occurred.

What all this shows also is that in relation to any inquiry task by the Security Council it is bound by the impartiality principle even in the course of making its political decisions under Chapters VI or VII of the UN Charter. There are inquiry organs that work on the basis of the parties' submissions and involve some elements of adversarial process, and those that do not have such an institutionalised procedure expressly built into them. Commissions of inquiry could thus be institutionally arranged as adversarial (state-to-state) or directorial (UN-directed) organs. Yet that is merely a difference of form. In terms of the tasks that they undertake, the requirement of impartiality, as derived from the above-cited provisions of the 1899 Convention, and further reinforced by the 1991 Declaration, applies to all inquiry and fact-finding organs and missions, including those utilised by the principal organs of the UN.

The relativity of the above institutional difference is further underlined by the requirement stated in Article 26 of the 1991 Declaration, that

> The States directly concerned should be given an opportunity, at all stages of the fact-finding process, to express their views in respect of the facts the fact-finding mission has been entrusted to obtain. When the results of fact-finding are to be made public, the views expressed by the States directly concerned should, if they so wish, also be made public.

And further, as emphasised in Article 27, 'Whenever fact-finding includes hearings, appropriate rules of procedure should ensure their fairness.'

Modern human rights commissions of inquiry operate mostly within the framework of the UN Human Rights Council. The General Assembly has established the Human Rights Council as an organ that 'should address situations of violations of human rights, including gross and systematic violations, and make recommendations thereon.' The Council 'should address situations of violations of human rights, including gross and systematic violations, and make recommendations thereon.'[15] It stands to reason that, as an integral part of the broader UN human rights protection system, the Human Rights Council should be able to pursue this task effectively and independently, and thus any commission of inquiry it establishes should be able to pursue its tasks undeterred from preconceptions or past precedents as to the nature and function of commissions of inquiry.

The Human Rights Council is a subsidiary organ of a principal organ of the UN—the General Assembly;[16] but not necessarily its subordinate

15 UN Doc A/RES/60/251 (3 April 2006) operative paras 3 and 5.
16 UN Doc A/RES/60/251 (n 15) operative para 1.

organ. In the advisory opinion on *Effect of Awards*, the International Court of Justice has found that it is not the subsidiary character of an organ that is decisive, but its tasks, functions and powers, as well as the intentions underlying its establishment.[17] A subsidiary organ may also have the power to make decisions binding on principal organs.[18] Therefore, the Human Rights Council is not necessarily under a strict obligation to replicate the legal findings or even political positions that would prevail within any principal organ of the UN, whether the General Assembly or Security Council, were these organs themselves to be called to pronounce on the matters under investigation by the particular commission of inquiry.

Overall, the relationship between the principal (political) and subsidiary (non-political) organs on the *Effect of Awards* equation is a mirror image of the limits on the principal organs' discretion that their decision to establish a non-political subsidiary organ inevitably generates. Once a principal organ commits itself to the handling of particular matters by a non-political subsidiary organ, it must be deemed to have agreed to the limiting of its own discretionary powers to the extent required to enable the relevant subsidiary organ to complete its task and make the required difference inherent to its mandate. The same legal equation seems to be fully applicable to the relations between the Human Rights Council and the commissions of inquiry that it establishes from time to time.

After all, the independence of the subsidiary organ is precisely the emanation of the will of the principal organ that the latter organ has established. An inquiry organ must be deemed to have been intended to effectively discharge its tasks and purposes. The main reason a principal organ establishes a subsidiary organ is that the principal organ may either lack the specialist expertise to deal with underlying matters, or not possess the independence and impartiality that is required for the resolution of the relevant disputes or controversies.

5.3. THE INQUIRY PROCESS AND THE PRINCIPLE OF CONSENT

Even though there is no set or authoritative definition of a judicial organ in international law, judicial organs are distinguished from other dispute settlement bodies by the consensual basis of their jurisdiction and by their ability to adopt decisions that legally bind the parties to the litigation.[19] It seems that, on such adjudication equation, satisfying the consensual basis for a tribunal's jurisdiction is a strict requirement because it leads to the adoption of binding decisions by that tribunal. A coherent and

[17] *Effect of Awards* [1954] ICJ Rep 56–58.
[18] *Effect of Awards* [1954] ICJ Rep 60–61.
[19] As specified, for instance, in the Statute of the International Court of Justice, Arts 36 and 59.

transparent viewing of the consensual principle could be that no binding determination of a state's rights and obligations should be performed without that state first giving its consent to that.

It is worth querying why a state's consent is required for the third-party dispute settlement. Is it because the relevant procedure involves some binding pronouncement? Or because the mere fact that its pronouncement affects the interests of the relevant state without imposing on that state any binding obligation? To illustrate this distinction, in some institutional contexts the principle of consent may, at times, be discarded altogether. The World Bank Inspection Panel's pronouncements as to the World Bank's accountability might very well involve pronouncements as to the conduct of the state in whose territory the Bank's project was implemented. Yet, the lack of the territorial state's consent is not seen as an impediment for the Panel's performance of its mandate.

The exact requirements of the principle of consent could similarly be relevant in relation to commissions of inquiry. There is, however, no authoritative definition of the principle of consent in international law, or specification of its ambit, either. This is natural, as consent itself operates as a way of creating international rules and institutions. So, these rules and institutions cannot feasibly define the scope and ambit of that which creates them, and international judicial jurisdiction can be no more consensual than any other international legal rule or instrument that is created through state consent. The true ambit of international judicial competence depends on the interpretation of rules and instruments that form part of the discrete legal framework within which the relevant international tribunal operates.[20]

The 1899 Hague Convention has determined that commissions of inquiry possess jurisdiction based on the consent of states that would establish them and be parties to their proceedings. Modern commissions of inquiry established as part of the UN system do not necessarily enjoy the same consensual backing from states. Instead, on occasions they may be bitterly opposed by the state whose conduct they attempt to evidence and publicise.

Article 33 of the UN Charter generally endorses the consensual principle in relation to all modes of dispute settlement, and also endorses the principle that states have free choice as to the use of particular modes of dispute settlement. The Manila Declaration 1982, operative paragraph 2 suggests that

> International disputes shall be settled on the basis of the sovereign equality of States and in accordance with the principle of free choice of means in conformity

[20] For a general discussion of the merit of the consensual basis of international judicial jurisdiction see A Orakhelashvili, 'The Concept of International Judicial Jurisdiction: A Reappraisal' (2003) 3 *The Law and Practice of International Courts and Tribunals* 50.

> with obligations under the Charter of the United Nations and with the principles of justice and international law. Recourse to, or acceptance of, a settlement procedure freely agreed to by States with regard to existing or future disputes to which they are parties shall not be regarded as incompatible with the sovereign equality of States.

This prompts the question whether, if modern commissions of inquiry assume some adjudicative or quasi-judicial functions,[21] to what extent should they observe the consensual principle in relation to states who do not consent to the inquiry being carried out? Is the principle of consent the same throughout and in relation to all kinds of proceedings and modes of dispute settlement? The discussion of the principle of state consent to judicial jurisdiction in relation to advisory opinions delivered by the International Court of Justice could be useful in clarifying the essence of the problem. The advisory opinion procedure is somewhat akin to the task of commissions of inquiry, in the sense that the statute of the International Court of Justice does not require the specific acceptance of the Court's jurisdiction from states the way it does in relation to the Court's contentious jurisdiction under Article 36 of the Statute. Moreover, the imperative of the impartial statement of law underlies international judicial function both in relation to contentious and advisory proceedings; whatever the procedural differences, the task of 'law-finding' is essentially the same.

The Permanent Court of International Justice (PCIJ) in the *Eastern Carelia* case placed emphasis on the issue of 'whether questions for an advisory opinion, if they relate to matters which form the subject of a pending dispute between nations, should be put to the Court without the consent of the parties.' For, 'the opinion which the Court has been requested to give bears on an actual dispute between Finland and Russia.' Relevant to the advisory proceedings was

> a principle which is a fundamental principle of international law, namely, the principle of the independence of States. It is well established in international law that no State can, without its consent, be compelled to submit its disputes with other States either to mediation or to arbitration, or to any other kind of pacific settlement. Such consent can be given once and for all in the form of an obligation freely undertaken, but it can, on the contrary, also be given in a special case apart from any existing obligation.

The Permanent Court further elaborated that,

> solution [of a dispute involving States] according to the methods provided for in the Covenant, could take place only by virtue of their consent. Such consent, however, has never been given by Russia. On the contrary, Russia has, on several occasions, clearly declared that it accepts no intervention by the League of Nations in the dispute with Finland. The refusals which Russia had already

[21] On which see below section 5.4.

> opposed to the steps suggested by the Council have been renewed upon the receipt by it of the notification of the request for an advisory opinion. The Court therefore finds it impossible to give its opinion on a dispute of this kind.[22]

One could query whether the above deals with the principle of consent pure and simple or with the host of relevant factors and considerations involved in this case specifically. The matter was already, in essence, a contentious dispute, in that Soviet Russia was not a member of the League of Nations, and it had indicated its opposition to the judicial settlement of this issue. Thus the principle of consent arguably barred judicial pronouncement, even via the Court's advisory opinion. The statement that 'no State can, without its consent, be compelled to submit its disputes with other States either to mediation or to arbitration, *or to any other kind of pacific settlement*' (emphasis added) presumably confirms the relevance of the principle of consent in relation to commissions of inquiry as well.

But in other advisory opinions such as *Western Sahara* and *Wall*,[23] the International Court of Justice did not consider that the principle of consent precluded the exercise of its advisory jurisdiction. It seems now that, in practice at least, the International Court will not invariably adhere to a broad understanding of the principle of consent in relation to its advisory proceedings the way it did in *Eastern Carelia*.

It could be objected that advisory opinions do not result in the 'settlement' of a dispute, and hence state consent should not be a precondition for them to be rendered. Advisory opinions relate to 'any legal question',[24] while contentious proceedings relate to 'all legal disputes'.[25] The former term is broader than the latter and therefore advisory opinions could effectively deal with disputes. The only distinguishing factor is their lack of binding force. The 'settlement' of a dispute requires, on this view, some binding force or conclusive effect accruing to the act that purports to settle it.

But perhaps the most pertinent distinction to be drawn is that, whatever the merit of the principle of consent in relation to commissions of inquiry that could be established under the 1899 Convention, the commissions of inquiry established under the UN framework are not premised on state consent in a similar manner. This is so not least because these commissions operate as part of the broader institutional framework of the UN, as elements of principal and subsidiary organs of international organisations to exercise their competence in a proper and effective manner. Unlike the states-parties within the 1899 Convention framework, the UN organs

[22] *Status of Eastern Carelia*, Advisory Opinion, PCIJ (1923) Series B no 5 (July 23) 7 at 27–28.

[23] Western Sahara, Advisory Opinion [1975] ICJ Rep 12; *Wall in the OPT*, Advisory Opinion [2004] ICJ Rep 136.

[24] Statute of the International Court of Justice, Art 65.

[25] Statute of the International Court of Justice, Art 36.

are not the interested parties in the outcome of the inquiry either. And, unlike the inspection missions which require the territorial state's consent to enter into and operate in their territory, commissions of inquiry do not seem to require such consent for merely pronouncing on the relevant state's conduct.

5.4. THE JURISDICTION OF COMMISSIONS OF INQUIRY: BETWEEN FACT-FINDING AND LAW-DETERMINATION

Voicing the widespread perception about the role of commissions of inquiry, Ian Brownlie suggested that

> The purpose of the Commissions of Inquiry is provisional and political. The device is linked to the idea that the resort to an inquiry provides a cooling off period and reduces the risk of counter-measures or breaches of the peace. Moreover, the Report on the facts de facto facilitates the settlement of the dispute.[26]

If this position is generalised to all inquiry exercises, then the relevance of commissions of inquiry in the international legal system should be viewed as rather minor, having little to do with the clarification of the merit of the controversies the modern commissions of inquiry deal with. On that vision, a commission of inquiry would merely state facts and leave the rest to be adjusted, if at all, through the political process. While in the context of adjudication, which relies on the separation of factual and legal aspects of litigation, that could be a sensible approach, the same outcome would be less adequate if, after the performance of fact-finding, the legal aspects of the issue were to remain uncertain and hang in the air.

It is noteworthy that, except for the requirement of limiting the inquiry findings to facts and their lack of binding force, the 1899 and 1907 Conventions did affiliate the essence of commissions of inquiry, in almost every possible aspect, to the manner in which arbitral tribunals would be formed and operate. One crucial distinction is that, as suggested in Article 11 of the 1899 Hague Convention,

> The report of the International Commission of Inquiry is limited to a statement of facts, and has in no way the character of an Arbitral Award. It leaves the conflicting Powers entire freedom as to the effect to be given to this statement.

In principle, the effect that a statement of facts produces is no more than those facts being stated. Unless they are disproved or rebutted, for instance by demonstrating that the relevant commission of inquiry did not apply the proper standard of proof, they cannot be undone. There is little parties could do in order not to give effect to a report that states those facts.

[26] I Brownlie, 'The Peaceful Settlement of International Disputes' (2009) *Chinese Journal of International Law* 267, 272.

States are politically, as well as legally, constrained by such determination of facts and blame. After the report has been published, they cannot dispute these facts anymore, and in principle the way is paved for legal claims, including those as to remedies and reparation. Quite simply, the 'entire freedom as to the effect to be given to this statement' means precious little in relation to statements that merely elaborate upon facts and do not prescribe any legally required conduct.

Moreover, it is questionable whether inquiry as a discrete process invariably has to be limited to fact-finding issues. For the relevant organ might as well be required to 'inquire' into the aspects of legal responsibility of the relevant actors and entities, effectively exercising some functions akin to adjudication. Whatever the merit of this argument in relation to the commissions of inquiry established and operating under the 1899 Convention, in relation to other commissions of inquiry (or indeed in relation to all commissions of inquiry), there is no comparable rule under any other source of international law that would require *any* commission of inquiry to adhere to the strict separation of fact and law the way that the 1899 Convention requires from the commissions that operate under that Convention. And, moreover, we have seen above that quasi-judicial functions have been exercised by organs that have not initially been designated as such.[27] Furthermore, as Merrils commented on an early inquiry enterprise, 'The duty to apportion "blame" appeared to assign to the Commission an arbitral as well as a fact-finding function.'[28]

While the establishment of facts could be seen as the principal task of commissions of inquiry, some facts are of discrete relevance and others have more far-reaching implications. Establishing a fact could, at times, be practically, even if not nominally or formally, tantamount to the finding that international law has been violated. For instance, a factual finding that a person has been tortured, a vessel has been sunk or a plane has been shot down by a particular state and its agents, would not be too far away from determining the underlying violation of international law. On its face, this 'fact-finding' exercise would be merely a determination of the attribution of conduct to the state, which is a separate issue from finding a violation of a rule of international law.[29] Then early commissions of inquiry have also engaged in the moral, ethical, or operational assessment of conduct, and did so in addition to their task of determining underlying facts. As the *Red Crusader* report suggested, 'Commander Griffiths and the other Officers of the British Royal Navy made every effort to avoid any

27 See section 5.2.
28 Merrils (n 1) 44.
29 2001 ILC Articles on States Responsibility, Art 3.

recourse to violence between "Niels Ebbesen" and "Red Crusader". Such an attitude and conduct were impeccable'.[30]

There is nothing inherent in the essence of the modern human rights inquiry process to require that its findings should be limited to facts alone. This has to be increasingly borne in mind, given the proliferation of commissions of inquiry and the diversity of their mandates, as a factor expressive of the diversity of expectations of those who establish these commissions, whether governments or organs of international organisations. If a UN organ establishes a commission of inquiry, and in the absence of a clear indication to the contrary, it makes every sense to presuppose that such organ is interested in hearing both about factual and legal aspects of the pertinent controversy.

The UN Human Rights Council does not seem to care too much about the precise delineation between fact-finding and law-finding, or adjudicatory and non-adjudicatory elements in the mandates of commissions of inquiry. The commissions of inquiry address the law applicable to pertinent violations of international law, whether human rights law or international humanitarian law. That approach was confirmed in the report of the Gaza Flotilla Commission of inquiry, where:

> The members of the Mission have decided to interpret their mandate as ascertaining the facts surrounding the Israeli interception of the Gaza-bound flotilla to determine whether any violations of international law, including international humanitarian and human rights law, took place.[31]

The report contains a detailed section of legal analysis of the facts it deals with.[32] The UN Secretary General's Flotilla inquiry report went even further than that, by outlining rapprochement recommendations with a substantial remedial dimension,[33] to some extent similar to ordinary international legal remedies.

[30] *Investigation of certain incidents affecting the British trawler Red Crusader*, Report of 23 March 1962 of the Commission of Enquiry established by the Government of the United Kingdom of Great Britain and Northern Ireland and the Government of the Kingdom of Denmark on 15 November 1961 (23 March 1962) 29 *RIAA* 521 at 539.

[31] *Report of the international fact-finding mission to investigate violations of international law, including international humanitarian and human rights law, resulting from the Israeli attacks on the flotilla of ships carrying humanitarian assistance*, UN Doc A/HRC/15/21, 57 (27 September 2010) para 4.

[32] ibid para 162ff.

[33] 'x. An appropriate statement of regret should be made by Israel in respect of the incident in light of its consequences.

xi. Israel should offer payment for the benefit of the deceased and injured victims and their families, to be administered by the two governments through a joint trust fund of a sufficient amount to be decided by them.

xii. Turkey and Israel should resume full diplomatic relations, repairing their relationship in the interests of stability in the Middle East and international peace and security. The establishment of a political roundtable as a forum for exchanging views could assist to this end.' *Report of the Secretary-General's Panel of Inquiry on the 31 May 2010 Flotilla Incident* (September 2011) para 169.

The risk of drawing the opposition of particular governments to such findings seems to constitute one of the occupational hazards in the work of the commissions of inquiry. It is probably also true that too much emphasis on legalities could induce the state in question to reject the commission of inquiry's report (especially if it is on a matter in relation to which that state would not agree to adjudication). However, it is not uncommon that the state may be averse to the adverse or critical finding by any international organ, or indeed to the adverse position under any source of international law regulating its rights and obligations if that position entails the undesirable limitation on that state's interest- or policy-driven conduct. Thus, a State may be just, or almost, as wary of having facts established by an independent third-party organ as it would be in relation to a binding determination of legal rights and obligations.

However, and depending on the terms of their mandates, commissions of inquiry are established and their tasks are determined so that they contribute to resolving relevant controversies by making the difference that cannot be made in their absence. Political relations are fluid anyway, and by adding yet another layer of fluidity by producing a legally ambiguous report, a commission of inquiry would be even less able to contribute to the resolution of the relevant controversy than it would do by plain report even at the cost of irritating some state(s).

The UN-established commissions have asserted and maintained their broadly defined power to determine their own jurisdiction. To illustrate, the Eritrea Commission first specified that its mandate was outlined in paragraph 8 of Resolution 26/24, which states that 'the Commission of inquiry will investigate all alleged violations of human rights in Eritrea, as outlined in the reports of the Special Rapporteur'. Then the Commission said that, 'As part of the definition of its methods of work, the Commission further delineated the scope of its mandate and its competences as follows', after which the description of its particular tasks stated in terms of describing the commission's competence *ratione materiae*, *ratione personae* and *ratione loci* with regard to ascertaining the commission of pertinent violations of international law.[34] Similarly, the Sri Lanka Commission saw itself as tasked to

> undertake a comprehensive investigation into alleged serious violations and abuses of human rights and related crimes by both parties in Sri Lanka during the period covered by the Lessons Learnt and Reconciliation Commission (LLRC), and to establish the facts and circumstances of such alleged violations and of the crimes perpetrated with a view to avoiding impunity and ensuring

[34] *Report of the Detailed Findings of the Commission of Inquiry on Human Rights in Eritrea*, UN Doc A/HRC/29/CRP.1 (5 June 2015) paras 9–10.

accountability, with assistance from relevant experts and special procedures mandate holders.[35]

This is yet another incidence of an commission of inquiry viewing its tasks broadly. For the commission refers to inherently legal tasks suitable to be determined or investigated or otherwise looked into by a court or magistrate. Defining the subject-matter of investigations as 'violations', rather than merely as facts, conveys the intention to enable the relevant commissions to examine both factual and legal matters.

There is definitely a degree of institutional confidence as to the jurisdictional independence of commissions of inquiry both from the will and vision of states whose conduct may be assessed in the course of inquiry, and from the position of the organ of an international organisation that has established the relevant commission of inquiry. For all dispute settlement organs, judicial, inquiry or other, are established and operate within the pre-existing normative frameworks, and all enjoy the ability to determine their own competence independently from the contemporaneous will of the state or organ that has conferred that competence to them.

Some commissions of inquiry have stated that they are different from a court of law and therefore cannot make definitive legal findings as to the characterisation of particular conduct in the light of international criminal law. Generally it has been noted that the commissions' approach to the issues of international criminal law is less detailed and less sophisticated than usually is the case with the reasoning of international criminal tribunals.[36] On their face, and structurally, the international criminal justice and commission of inquiry refer to different processes, which emphasises not only the limits on the law-identifying activities of commissions of inquiry, but also the potential for some useful patterns of the division of labour between them and international criminal tribunals. It is pointed out that the operation of commissions of inquiry could lead to the establishment of an international criminal tribunal, as was the case with ICTY, and also to the facilitation of their work and the performance of their mandate, as has been the case with the ICC's DRC-related investigations, or with the STL's investigation process.[37] In certain cases the findings by commission of inquiry could prompt international criminal tribunals to proceed with investigation or prosecution. Furthermore, the findings of the commission of inquiry could provide some indications

[35] *Comprehensive Report of the Office of the United Nations High Commissioner for Human Rights on Sri Lanka*, UN Doc A/HRC/30/61 (28 September 2005) para 1.

[36] LJ van den Herik and C Harwood, 'Commissions of Inquiry and the Charm of International Criminal Law' in P Alston (ed), *The Transformation of the UN Human Rights Fact-finding* (Oxford, Oxford University Press, 2015) 233, 244.

[37] C Stahn and D Jacobs, 'The Interaction between Human Rights Fact-Finding and International Criminal Proceedings' in Alston (n 36) 256, 259–60.

as to whether the relevant criminal proceedings should be launched at national or international level, for instance in terms of the complementarity equation under the ICC Statute.[38] That could depend on how the relevant commission of inquiry would assess the reliability of particular national criminal justice systems.

In terms of the identification of substantive points of international criminal law, an international criminal tribunal would not be bound by the finding of a commission of inquiry as to the fact of the commission of an international crime or the legal characterisation of the pertinent act under international criminal law. International criminal tribunals are independently under the duty to administer the relevant law, as opposed to having their judgment second-guessed by an inquiry organ. Overall, there seems to be no direct jurisdictional link between commissions of inquiry and international (criminal) tribunals, and their institutional interaction could only be an outcome of voluntary cooperation among them. The interaction between commissions of inquiry and international criminal tribunals does not reveal any obvious pattern of normative or institutional connection between the tasks, mandates and jurisdictions of various institutions.

5.5. THE APPLICABLE STANDARD OF PROOF

The relevance of the applicable standard of proof arises, in the first place, from the nature of the commission of inquiry's tasks and mandate. As we saw above, in *Eastern Carelia*, the PCIJ cited the difficulties in ascertaining facts properly in relation to the matter handled by it, owing to Russia's lack of consent and cooperation. The question arising in relation to commission of inquiry is the extent to which the failure to cooperate, from the relevant state whose conduct is being investigated, should produce an impediment for the discharge of the commission of inquiry's tasks and mandate in relation to the particular controversy. The failure of the state to cooperate with the relevant commission of inquiry inevitably runs into the issue of which pattern of the standard of proof the relevant commission should adopt. In the absence of the determination of such standards of proof in any written instrument that binds the relevant commission, or by the establishing body, the selection of the standard of proof becomes a matter of legal certainty, as well as that of the operational strategy, for the commissions to perceive and perform their role relatively efficiently in an environment which does not invariably support the performance of their mandate and tasks.

Therefore, the standard of proof is key to fact-finding, but also material to the nature of the commissions' other tasks, whether the establishment

[38] ICC Statute, Art 17.

of state liability or other pertinent issues. The required standard of proof may differ depending on whether the relevant commission of inquiry sees itself in a quasi-adjudicatory or law-determining role in relation to particular violations of international law, or as an organ that reviews the relevant situation and then recommends the relevant strategies, policies and options for its overall adjustment and resolution. Moreover, whatever the standard of proof and evidence the relevant commission has used could be important in whether any international court or tribunal would find its factual findings persuasive for the purposes of the performance of their own adjudicatory tasks.

The 1899 Hague Convention's above-emphasised affiliation of the essence of commissions of inquiry with arbitral tribunals has not been without importance to the nature of the work of the commissions in relation to the facts and evidentiary standards they deal with. To illustrate, the range of issues dealt with by some older commissions of inquiry, such as the *Dogger Bank* or *Tubantia* (as to who perpetrated the relevant incident and who was supposed to know what in the relevant circumstances) is strikingly similar—in terms of their substance as well as standard of proof issues—to what proper international tribunals have to deal with. For instance, the International Court of Justice used the higher standard of proof in *Oil Platforms*, and required that the state involvement in the unlawful use of force has to be proved through the establishment of that state's ownership of weapons and vehicles involved in the relevant situation.[39] The reason for this is that the involvement of a state in violent attacks perpetrated against another state will not be established unless the involvement of the state in such attacks is conclusively proved. This approach is matched by the policy statement made by the International Court in *Bosnia v Serbia*, to the effect that 'claims against a State involving charges of exceptional gravity must be proved by evidence that is fully conclusive. The Court requires that it be fully convinced of allegations made in the proceedings'.[40] But the main lesson from the Court's recent practice in *Oil Platforms* and *DRC v Uganda* is that the standard of proof is adequate if it is aimed at proving the commission of that specific act and conduct which is alleged in the proceedings, ruling out the relevance of contextual or circumstantial headings of evidence.

The *Tubantia* commission of inquiry has used such a high standard of proof, addressing the need to the prove concrete facts and occurrences, and suggesting that:

> The Commission has been unable to arrive at the conviction that calculations of this nature could be conclusive and could furnish proof for an object of concrete

[39] *Oil Platforms* (Iran v USA) [2003] ICJ Rep 161.
[40] *Application of the Genocide Convention*, Judgment of 26 February 2007 [2007] ICJ Rep 129.

> observation, and it believes that in spite of the most minute observations of currents and winds it will not be possible to find a torpedo which has been launched and has remained afloat for ten days at the point where it ought to be according to the calculations. The Commission cannot, consequently, decide that it is impossible that a floating torpedo struck the Tubantia at the point where this vessel sank.[41]

Note especially the expression 'in spite of the most minute observations of currents', which should be seen as an inclination against proving the involvement of the state in a wrongful act by relying on circumstantial evidence. Furthermore,

> there is not the least proof for admitting that a vessel of a power hostile to Germany torpedoed the Tubantia and that, subsequently, fragments of the German torpedo No. 2033, recovered by the enemy vessel, were surreptitiously placed in the boats. It is evident that such a procedure, as complicated as it is perfidious and destined to prejudice Germany in the eyes of the neutral countries and to provoke anti-German feelings there, could never be presumed. In default of all proof this hypothesis must be discarded.[42]

Consequently, the

> question of determining whether the torpedoing took place knowingly or as the result of an error of the commander of the submarine must remain in suspense. It has not been possible to determine that the loss of the Tubantia was caused by striking a torpedo that had remained afloat. Although it cannot be denied that a certain number of indications militate in favor of the latter possibility, the Commission, after examining them conscientiously and comparing them with the other proofs, cannot recognize that these indications are conclusive and have the force of proof.[43]

And then the Commission added that 'No indication permitting the assumption of any other cause for the loss of the *Tubantia* could be produced.' This approach was replicated in *Oil Platforms* on strikingly similar terms, when the International Court of Justice ruled that no involvement of Iran in the attacks on the US vessels could be proved, despite the fact that Iran's military arsenal did include the kind of weapons and mines used to attack those vessels.[44] Whether any third state was the author of these attacks could not be established in these proceedings. It seems that the use of such a high standard of proof is due to the duty of fairness any institution of whatever kind owes to the state whose conduct it examines. Whether or not the inquiry findings are binding on states, the institutional

[41] *Loss of the Dutch Steamer 'Tubantia' (Germany v The Netherlands)* (1922) 16 *American Journal of International Law* 485 (ICI Report of 27 February 1922) para 8.
[42] *Tubantia* (n 41) para 11.
[43] *Tubantia* (n 41) para 12.
[44] See n 39.

credibility of the organ that authors them requires that the standard of proof is properly used and discharged. Even if the UN-established commissions of inquiry have to prioritise human rights and humanitarian concerns, they still operate in the state-centric legal system in which the prevention of the turning of the relevant commission into a tool of parochial political agenda and the preservation of its legitimacy is possible only if it blames states for what it can prove. This compellingly evidences the need for UN-established commissions of inquiry to display a careful approach in relation to the proper use of the standard of proof.

Against the background of the lack of any statutory definition of the standard of proof, the human rights inquiry organs have displayed a degree of independence in adopting a particular evidentiary standard. The Sri Lanka Commission decided to use the 'reasonable ground to believe' standard of proof. Thus, the Commission emphasised that:

> There are reasonable grounds to believe that an incident or pattern of violations or crimes occurred if the OISL has obtained a reliable body of information, consistent with other information, indicating their occurrence. This standard of proof may be sufficiently high to call for judicial investigations into violations of international humanitarian and human rights law and international crimes.[45]

The North Korean Commission proposed to adopt the 'reasonable grounds' standard thus defined:

> The commission bases its findings on a 'reasonable grounds' standard of proof. It concluded that there are reasonable grounds establishing that an incident or pattern of conduct had occurred whenever it was satisfied that it had obtained a reliable body of information, consistent with other material, based on which a reasonable and ordinarily prudent person would have reason to believe that such an incident or pattern of conduct had occurred.[46]

The Commissions do not coherently, let alone uniformly, define the 'reasonable grounds' standard. Nor is such clear definition available under general international law. The Human Rights Council similarly has not determined the standard of proof issue in relation to commissions of inquiry it establishes and thus, the commissions' approach should be seen as yet another aspect of the broad assertion of their *competence de la competence*.

On substantive terms, the 'reasonable ground to believe' standard is not that far away from the 'balance of probabilities' standard. Both tests are similar in their lack of conclusive proof, and thus also from the 'beyond reasonable doubt' standard used in national legal proceedings. The latter tests endorse outcomes arrived at after the opposite possibilities and

[45] See n 35.

[46] *Report of the Commission of Inquiry on Human Rights in the Democratic People's Republic of Korea*, UN Doc A/HRC/25/63, para 22.

competing considerations are engaged, weighed and disproved, while the 'reasonable ground to believe' standard reveals no such reflection to be strictly required from the decision-maker.

As we saw above, the 'reasonable grounds' standard is used for findings that lead to requesting criminal investigations. The North Korean Commission has thus suggested that

> The commission is neither a judicial body nor a prosecutor. It cannot make final determinations of individual criminal responsibility. It can, however, determine whether its findings constitute reasonable grounds establishing that crimes against humanity have been committed so as to merit a criminal investigation by a competent national or international organ of justice.[47]

Curiously enough, the standards of 'reasonably believing' in, and of 'reasonable grounds establishing' are used for the same purpose of encouraging the criminal investigation of underlying facts and incidents. The Sri Lanka commission's 'reasonably believing' standard seems to be more contextual and circumstantial than the North Korean commission's 'reasonable grounds establishing' standard, which seems to focus on more on underlying facts and less on the underlying context. However, the difference between the two articulated standards is rather relative, and given that each commission of inquiry is an independent organ pursuing its own discrete mandate, it is difficult to identify any coherent uniform ground on which the selection and use of a particular standard of proof by the relevant commission of inquiry could be rationalised and explained. Moreover, believing in a fact and establishing it are two different things. Still, the commission says that crimes against humanity have been committed, pursuant to policies established at the highest level of the North Korean State,[48] as opposed to recommending that an investigation into whether they have been committed is appropriate or necessary. Against this background, any international or national criminal tribunal, which would deal with the issues formulated this way by a commission of inquiry, would still have to examine facts as part of their adversarial proceedings, in order to prove the blame of the accused.

International criminal tribunals are not bound by the evidentiary standards accepted in national legal systems. They are generally supposed to apply the higher standards of evidence, premised on the approach that 'a high evidentiary standard is important for the legitimacy of any court'. This is the position, among others, which ensures a fair trial of the accused.[49] It could, therefore, be alleged that the commission of inquiry's approach towards the standard of proof is somewhat loose, if compared

[47] UN Doc A/HRC/25/63, para 74.
[48] UN Doc A/HRC/25/63, para 75.
[49] R Cryer et al, *International Criminal Law and Procedure* (3rd edn, Cambridge, Cambridge University Press, 2014) 468.

to the standard of proof ordinarily required in criminal proceedings. This problem could be corroborated by the commissions' expansive use of their mandate to cover both factual findings and the findings of violations of international law. Therefore, depending on the ways in which commissions of inquiry deal with evidentiary standards, their activities could result either in a useful and legitimate way of dividing the labour between them and international criminal tribunals, or in a somewhat needless reduplication of the latter's tasks and functions by the former.

In principle, the proper establishment of the same set of facts, say in the human rights law or international criminal law context, could bear some probative value in terms of demonstrating the commission of wrongs under human rights law, humanitarian law, and international criminal law. The International Court of Justice in *Bosnia v Serbia* was in principle receptive to the ICTY's determination of facts and regarded them as helpful and persuasive, though against the background that 'The Court must itself make its own determination of the facts which are relevant to the law which the Applicant claims the Respondent has breached'.[50] The implication, therefore, is that these facts are established through the use of the correct standard of proof so that findings made as part of one body of law could be recognisable within another relevant body of law. Multiple killings, imprisonments or tortures, if properly established, could amount to wrongs under several bodies of international law, each of which would then attach to them their own qualification.

It may be queried whether the commissions' approach to proof is somewhat similar to the human rights tribunals' use of evidentiary standards that may not be as strict as the ones used by the International Court of Justice and criminal tribunals, as examined above. It is said that the European Court of Human Rights adheres to the 'beyond reasonable doubt' standard, defined as the standard that refers to doubts arising from or in relation to the facts presented, and not from theoretical possibilities. But this standard is not the same as the one used in criminal proceedings in national legal systems. For instance, the fact that a police officer's liability has not been established in national proceedings will not prevent the European Court from making the opposite finding.[51]

To illustrate, in *Cyprus v Turkey* the European Court of Human Rights considered that the killing of the missing Greek Cypriot persons by Turkish or Turkish Cypriot armed forces could not be proved and therefore no breach of Article 2 could be present on this account. Nevertheless, the Court examined the applicant government's allegations 'in the context of a Contracting State's procedural obligation under Article 2 to protect the

[50] *Bosnia v Serbia* [2007] ICJ Rep 130, 134.

[51] DJ Harris, M O'Boyle, EP Bates and CM Buckley, *Law of The European Convention on Human Rights* (3rd edn, Oxford, Oxford University Press, 2014) 148.

right to life'.[52] Although the Court found no proof that any of the missing persons were unlawfully killed, it concluded that the above-mentioned procedural obligation may arise merely upon proof of an arguable claim in this respect.[53] The same attitude has been reaffirmed in *Assenov* with regard to the scope of Article 3 of the European Convention on Human Rights. The Court considered that Bulgaria breached Article 3 merely by its failure to investigate claims of alleged torture, despite the fact that the actual fact of torture was never proved.[54] In both cases the Court was careful to separate the commission of particular acts (which could not be directly proved) from the failure to investigate them (which was duly established). To that extent, it could be suggested, the standard of proof used by the Strasbourg Court is not radically different from the standards used in other international tribunals.

But matters could arise in the Strasbourg jurisprudence, similar to the tasks encountered by commissions of inquiry, when the Strasbourg court has to deal not just with individual violations and state conduct, but with general characteristics of that state's legal system. The Court may use contextual inferences alongside the proof of perpetration of particular acts by particular officials or individuals. To illustrate, the finding that local remedies are not effective is hardly limited to the conditions in which the relevant single individual was treated by national authorities.[55] In relation to such systemic issues, it could be suggested that all pertinent international tribunals could find the relevant commission of inquiry findings to be useful and instructive.

5.6. CONCLUSION

The experience of the UN organs demonstrates that the function of inquiry can no longer be suitably limited to fact-finding, as narrowly understood, for an organ that establishes the commissions wants to obtain factual as well as legal answers. The commissions' proactivity in determining standards of proof on their own is understandable.

The lack of the binding force of the commissions' reports is not crucial. The state affected by the commission of inquiry's findings has no legal cause for grievance on the basis of the lack of the report's binding force alone. The binding force does not constitute the legal merit of the

[52] Case 25781/94 *Cyprus v Turkey* (2001) para 131.

[53] Case 25781/94 *Cyprus v Turkey* (2001) para 132; lack of investigation with regard to disappearances and alleged killings further resulted in violation of Art 3 with regard to the victims' relatives in that the latter have been subjected to a moral agony and pressure arising out of the lack of information about the alleged victims: paras 156–57.

[54] Case 24760/94 *Assenov v Bulgaria* (28 October 1998) paras 90–106.

[55] *Akdivar v Turkey* 99/1995/605/693 (16 September 1996) paras 71–76.

commission's report. If the commission's report transparently states the content of rules that are applicable in the relevant situation and which have been violated by the relevant state, and accurately describes facts that have constituted those violations, it only declares and re-states the binding force and legal consequences of those rules and the fact or their violation. Overall, it would be far more suitable to be less attached to semantics and preconceptions evoked in this process, and to focus with more seriousness on the legal frameworks that underlie the establishment and operation of particular commissions of inquiry.

Commissions of inquiry may end up being politically controversial, but they are by-products of the inaction by states at more fundamental levels, not letting human rights and humanitarian law considerations interfere with bilateral relations with the states whose conduct the commissions investigate, or not being willing to create more enhanced mechanisms of international accountability. This way, the revival of the inquiry function witnessed in older frameworks originating in the early twentieth century, now within the UN framework, could entail the narrowing of the accountability gaps that persist in our times, owing to the lack of the comprehensive compulsory judicial jurisdiction over states.

While it is true that commissions of inquiry are mechanisms with limited powers and lacking the enforcement powers or one to make binding decisions, it should also be right to say that, in performance of their tasks, commissions of inquiry should not be seen as impotent but as organs designed to make the required difference, at the service of the international institutions which establish them and endow them with their mandates. Once the material and evidence is amassed, and the relevant commission's legal assessment is made and publicised, provided that it both is, and is seen to be, impartial, the political climate and the will of states and institutions could be significantly altered, towards the more enhanced drive of securing the international accountability of the relevant state. Governments can put up some resistance or even ignore the findings of a commission of inquiry. Non-binding mechanisms cannot transform the essence of the international legal system, but can constitute a motivating force by providing an impartial statement of fact and the relevant legal issues, by streamlining political opinion and strengthening the drive towards securing more effective accountability of the relevant state. Commissions of inquiry may be stepping stones towards that purpose, in the absence of any more robust jurisdictional arrangement to encompass the activities of states in relation to the investigation of whose conduct the commissions of inquiry have been established. To achieve these tasks in a reliable, sustainable and legitimate manner in the state-centric environment of the international legal system also requires an increasing emphasis by commissions on the legal terms of their mandates and the accurate use of the standards of proof.

6

Commissions of Inquiry: Courting International Criminal Courts and Tribunals

CHRISTINE SCHWÖBEL-PATEL

6.1. INTRODUCTION

THIS CHAPTER TAKES a critical look at what has been referred to as the 'criminalisation' of international commissions of inquiry.[1] International commissions of inquiry, particularly United Nations (UN) Security Council-established as well as UN Human Rights Council-established commissions of inquiry, are increasingly acting as either international criminal quasi-tribunals or (more commonly) as an investigative arm of international criminal courts and tribunals (ICCTs). I argue that these commissions of inquiry are directing too much attention to a narrow set of international crimes with a view to seeing their findings used by ICCTs—a practice which I describe as 'courting'. Commissions of inquiry are not only consequently implicated in the limitations and biases of international criminal law itself, they are also increasingly part of an 'intervention formula', a formulaic interventionism by international organisations.

I examine the so-called 'judicialisation' of commissions of inquiry first and then turn to the phenomenon described as 'criminalisation'. I demonstrate that commissions of inquiry (on the basis of external pressures and internal preferences) are increasingly narrowing their focus to acts which may qualify as international crimes.[2] Much of the current critique of this

[1] See, eg LJ van den Herik and C Harwood, 'Sharing the Law: The Appeal of International Criminal Law for International Commissions of Inquiry' in S Knuckey and P Alston (eds), *The Transformation of Human Rights Fact-Finding* (New York, Oxford University Press, 2016).

[2] This trend, has been observed by several commentators in the field: M Frulli, 'Fact-Finding or Paving the Road to Criminal Justice? Some Reflections on United Nations Commissions of Inquiry' (2010) 10 *Journal of International Criminal Justice* 1323; van den Herik and Harwood (n 1).

trend, what Larissa van den Herik and Catherine Harwood refer to as a 'turn to international criminal law', has revolved around questions of procedure—concerning critiques which are ultimately about improving the quality and effectiveness of fact-finding through rigour or standardisation.

In this chapter, I take a step back from concerns about procedure and instead raise some structural questions concerning the criminalisation of fact-finding and the courting of ICCTs. The narrow scope which comes with a focus (although this is not an exclusive focus) on international crimes is exposed as being problematic, in that it implicates commissions of inquiry in international criminal law's limitations and biases. Of these, I single out what I call the 'options critique' and the 'politics critique'. International criminal law's narrow scope of individual criminal responsibility is turning attention away from other mechanisms of accountability, such as conciliation, and peace-making (options critique). Despite claiming to be engaged in law, and not politics, the politically charged nature of the field is sustaining and creating political and economic discrepancies between the powerful and the disenfranchised (politics critique).

On a more general level, in courting ICCTs, commissions of inquiry find themselves as part of an 'intervention formula' of the big military and economic powers. The intervention formula can be understood as a check list of UN interventionist measures which are engaged in order to ultimately, if need be, legitimate military intervention. This not only makes commissions of inquiry complicit in a narrowing of the understanding of accountability, it also makes them complicit in a global power struggle in favour of the great political and economic powers.

I come to the conclusion that so long as commissions of inquiry are able to resist the courting of ICCTs, they could focus more on fact-finding of structural problems around conflict, including its root causes. This would involve fact-finding on questions of key socio-economic causes of conflict such as resource and power legacies of colonialism, corporate interests, causes and consequences of climate change, resource contract rivalries, provisions of arms, and financial institutional investment. Rather than being part of an intervention check-list, commissions of inquiry could be a check on intervention.

6.2. COMMISSIONS OF INQUIRY AND THE LAW: JUDICIALISATION

In the case of disputed events, a commission of inquiry can be established to investigate and ascertain the facts. The establishment of commissions of inquiry is common as a response to crises, both domestically and internationally. The object of inquiry can be vast; it can refer to territorial disputes, to trading disputes, or to allegations of human rights violations. Undoubtedly, commissions of inquiry have become an increasingly

prominent component of international, regional, and national responses to allegations of infringements of international human rights law and international humanitarian law in the context of armed conflicts and internal disturbances.[3] The asserted benefits of fact-finding include their effectiveness when there is a political deadlock, flexibility in terminology, access to vast amounts of evidence, and a related flexibility in conducting investigations.

The relationship between fact-finding and law is a complicated one. In theory, fact-finding outfits should have no adjudicative function in that they are, historically, not supposed to test the facts against possible violations of law.[4] However, the relationship between fact and law is immediately complicated and entwined when international organisations which oversee infringements of international law set up commissions of inquiry. Not only do they inevitably view the facts through a legal lens, they also draw legal conclusions on the basis of these facts.

Several organisations and bodies have the competence to establish commissions of inquiry under international law. The two leading bodies with competence to set up fact-finding missions under international law are the UN Human Rights Council and the UN Security Council. The Human Rights Council is 'the mandating body for over 60 per cent of all UN commissions established since 2006'.[5] Some prominent examples of Human Rights Council commissions of inquiry include the Commission of Inquiry on Lebanon,[6] the High-Level Mission on the situation in Darfur,[7] the Fact Finding Mission on the Gaza Conflict,[8] the UN Independent Commission of Inquiry on Libya,[9] and the Independent International Commission of Inquiry in the Syrian Arab Republic.[10] The Human Rights Council is an inter-governmental body responsible for the promotion and protection of human rights. That fact-finding commissions set up by the Human Rights Council should be concerned with human rights violations, and therefore question of law, is, from a common-sense point of view, unsurprising.

[3] *HPCR Advanced Practitioner's Handbook on Commissions of Inquiry. Monitoring, Reporting and Fact-Finding* (Program on Humanitarian Policy and Conflict Research, Harvard College, 2015) p 1, available at www.hpcrresearch.org/sites/default/files/publications/HPCR%20 Handbook%20March%202015.pdf, accessed 11 July 2016.

[4] Larissa van den Herik states boldly: 'In theory, of course, fact-finding commissions should not engage with law at all', in LJ van den Herik, 'An Inquiry into the Role of Commissions of Inquiry in International Law: Navigating the Tensions between Fact-Finding and Application of International Law' (2014) 13 *Chinese Journal of International Law* 507, 528.

[5] van den Herik and Harwood (n 1).

[6] Constituted following UN Human Right Council Resolution S-2/1 (11 August 2006).

[7] Constituted following UN Human Rights Council Resolution S-4/10 (13 December 2006).

[8] Constituted following UN Human Rights Council Resolution S-9/1 (12 January 2009).

[9] Constituted following UN Human Rights Council Resolution S-15/1 (25 February 2011).

[10] Constituted following UN Human Rights Council Resolution S-17/1 (22 August 2011).

The UN Security Council is a further organ which establishes commissions of inquiry to investigate whether international law has been violated, although it has been doing this less and less as the Human Rights Council has become more and more active. Recent commissions of inquiry set up by the Security Council include commissions to inquire into conflicts in Darfur,[11] East Timor,[12] Lebanon[13] and the Central African Republic.[14] Given that the UN Security Council has primary responsibility for the maintenance of international peace and security in the international sphere, it is again unsurprising that fact-finding missions established by this organ should concern questions of international law.

Indeed, the particular focus on violations of international law is made explicit in some of the commissions' mandates, also referred to as the 'terms of reference'. The commission of inquiry on Lebanon, for example, explicitly states that the mandate, along with investigating the targeting of civilians and the impact on human life, property, infrastructure and the environment, is 'to examine the types of weapons used by Israel and their *conformity with international law*'.[15] The fact-finding mission established by the UN Secretary General and tasked with inquiring into the flotilla incident of 2010 even has international law in its (rather long-winded) title: 'The international fact-finding mission to investigate *violations of international law*, including international humanitarian and human rights law, resulting from the Israeli attacks on the flotilla of ships carrying humanitarian assistance' (emphasis added).[16]

The perspective from which the facts are considered not only depends on the mandate but also on the members appointed to the commission. It should, therefore, not seem surprising that the Commission on Darfur waded through the elements of international crimes (genocide and crimes against humanity) given that Antonio Cassesse, a foremost scholar of international criminal law, was chairman. It should also not be surprising that Cherif Bassiouni, a long-standing scholar and advocate of international criminal law, injected his enthusiasm for international criminal law when he served on the Commission of Experts for the former Yugoslavia, the Commission of Inquiry on Libya, and the Bahrain Commission of Inquiry. International Criminal Law professor William Schabas, who headed the UN commission of inquiry for the 2014 attack on Gaza,[17] unsurprisingly

[11] Constituted following UN Security Council Resolution 1564 (18 September 2004).

[12] Constituted following UN Security Council Resolution 1690 (20 June 2006).

[13] Constituted following UN Security Council Resolution 1595 (7 April 2005).

[14] Constituted following UN Security Council Resolution 2127 (5 December 2013).

[15] Constituted following UN Human Rights Council Resolution S-2/1 (11 August 2006).

[16] Constituted following UN Human Rights Council Resolution 14/1(2 June 2010).

[17] Shortly before the report was due, Schabas, under pressure, resigned from the commission. It had been alleged that he was biased given previous consultancy work for the PLO. See R Falk, 'Interview with William Schabas, former Chair, UN Commission of Inquiry for

noted that the difference between this commission of inquiry on the Israel-Palestine conflict and the previous ones lay in the fact that the International Criminal Court (ICC) was 'standing in the wings'.[18] Carla del Ponte, one of the commissioners of the UN commission of inquiry on Syria, recently called for an ad hoc tribunal in Syria. Del Ponte is of course former chief prosecutor of the ad hoc International Criminal Tribunal for the former Yugoslavia and the ad hoc International Criminal Tribunal for Rwanda.[19] The facts deemed relevant and the recommendations made on the basis of the fact-finding are therefore naturally determined by the expertise of the commissioners. Indeed, the commissioners are appointed on the basis of this very expertise.

In terms of the relationship between fact-finding and the drawing of legal conclusions, it is of note that the practitioner's handbook recently published by the Program on Humanitarian Policy and Conflict Research (HPCR), a Harvard-based research project on 'Monitoring, Reporting, and Fact-Finding', is entirely unapologetic about this close connection between fact-finding and legal analysis, stating boldly:

> The processes of gathering information and drawing legal conclusions are interrelated. The mission's decisions about planning the investigation, selecting legal frameworks, and adopting a standard of proof all inform one another and cannot be conducted in isolation.[20]

The interim conclusion on commissions of inquiry and the law is, rather banally, that in theory fact-finding should remain independent of judicial considerations of accountability, but, in practice fact-finding is determined by the institution which has established it, its mandate, and its commissioners. The legal lens adopted for fact-finding and the legal nature of the recommendations has been described as 'judicialisation'.[21] Given that organisations which have established commissions of inquiry are often charged with the identification and safeguarding of violations of (international) law, the judicialisation of commissions of inquiry is, although contestable, not remarkable.

2014 Israeli Attack on Gaza' *Global Justice in the 21st Century* blog (16 February 2015), available at richardfalk.wordpress.com/2015/02/16/interview-with-william-schabas-former-chair-un-commission-of-inquiry-for-2014-israeli-attack-on-gaza/, accessed 11 July 2016.

[18] ibid.

[19] J Borger, 'Call for special tribunal to investigate war crimes and mass atrocities in Syria', *The Guardian.com* (17 March 2015), available at www.theguardian.com/world/2015/mar/17/call-for-special-tribunal-to-investigate-war-crimes-and-mass-atrocities-in-syria, accessed 11 July 2016.

[20] *Practitioner's Handbook* (n 3) 20.

[21] Beginning the tradition of lengthy commission names, the Commission on the Responsibility of the Authors of the War and on Enforcement for Penalties for Violations of the Laws and Customs of War was established by a decision adopted at the Paris Peace Conference on 25 January 1919.

The main critique of judicialisation has been of a largely technical nature, concerning standards of proof, due process,[22] evidence collection,[23] sharing of witnesses.[24] It is believed that commissions of inquiry do not display adequate legal technique in their analysis and recommendations. This brings with it an assumption that commissions of inquiry would be improved if they did better law.

The standard of proof critique deserves a brief study since this has in particular come under some scrutiny. It is believed that it is paramount for the purpose of accuracy and procedural integrity, for commissions to address the standard of proof required for a commission of inquiry.[25] The standard of proof under criminal law would be that the prosecution must prove 'beyond reasonable doubt' that responsibility is to be attributed for certain behaviour, which is forbidden by criminal law, and was caused by the defendant. In addition, the prosecution must prove 'beyond reasonable doubt' that the defendant had a defined state of mind in relation to the behaviour. Largely, commissions of inquiry apply the 'balance of probabilities' test or the test which determines whether there are 'reasonable grounds to believe' that a particular incident occurred or that a given pattern of violations prevailed.[26] This test is, of course, not as strict as the 'beyond reasonable doubt' test.[27] Along with calls for the standardisation of practises amongst commissions of inquiry, there are commonly

[22] See TM Franck and HS Fairley, 'Procedural Due Process in Human Rights Fact-Finding by International Agencies' (1980) 74 *American Journal of International Law* 308.

[23] See eg DF Orentlicher, 'Bearing Witness: The Art and Science of Human Rights Fact-Finding' (1990) 3 *Harvard Human Rights Journal* 83, 109.

[24] In regard to procedural fairness and consent to jurisdiction see H Tonkin, 'International Commissions of Inquiry: A New Form of Adjudication?' (*EJIL Talk!* 6 April 2012), available at www.ejiltalk.org/international-commissions-of-inquiry-a-new-form-of-adjudication/, accessed 11 July 2016.

[25] S Wilkinson, 'Standards of Proof in International Humanitarian and Human Rights Fact-Finding and Inquiry Missions' (Geneva, Geneva Academy of International Humanitarian Law and Human Rights, 2012), available at www.geneva-academy.ch/docs/reports/Standards%20of%20proo%20report.pdf, accessed 11 July 2016; Franck and Fairley (n 22) 310.

[26] S Wilkinson, '"Finding the Facts": Standards of Proof and Information Handling in Monitoring, Reporting and Fact-Finding Missions', *Program on Humanitarian Policy and Conflict Research* (Harvard, Harvard University, 2014), available at papers.ssrn.com/sol3/papers.cfm?abstract_id=2400927, accessed 13 November 2016. The Human Rights Council recommended the use of the 'balance of probabilities' test in 'Commission of Inquiry Conference Brief' (1 December 2011) 3.

[27] 'Reasonable grounds to believe' has been defined to mean that the information gathered 'would justify a reasonable or ordinarily prudent man to believe that a suspect has committed a crime' and 'raise a clear suspicion of the suspect being guilty of a crime'. Judge R Sidhwa of the International Criminal Tribunal for the former Yugoslavia, quoted in *Report of the International Commission of Inquiry on Darfur to the United Nations Secretary-General* p 12 (Darfur Report), available at www.un.org/news/dh/sudan/com_inq_darfur.pdf.

statements as to the need for a quality control of admission of evidence for reasons of credibility.[28]

Overall, there seems to be more concern over *procedure* in the critique and only very little over *subject-matter*. It is notable that, for example, the legal analysis of the aforementioned Flotilla Report was lamented for its 'poor quality' and 'sloppiness'.[29] Similarly, the legal findings of the commission of inquiry on Libya were described as 'either incorrect or at best debatable'.[30] This kind of technical critique strengthens the assumption that if commissions of inquiry were to address their procedural faults, they could be 'one of the best ways of obtaining authoritative pronouncements' on issues of violations of human rights, international humanitarian law and other rules of international law.[31] The purpose of this chapter is to direct attention away from technicalities and toward the issue of subject-matter: ie an understanding why a focus on international criminal law might be problematic in the first place.

6.3. COURTING INTERNATIONAL CRIMINAL COURTS: CRIMINALISATION

In 1980, Thomas Franck and H Scott Fairley stated that the purpose of the fact-finders' report, 'serves to clarify misconceptions, absolve or embarrass the investigated party, influence public opinion, and, where appropriate, facilitate further expressions of community disapprobation'.[32] Arguably, since the rise of ICCTs, an additional purpose of the reports has been to call for individual accountability and to facilitate the institutions established for this purpose.[33]

[28] eg L Daqun, 'Quality Control in Truth and Reconciliation Processes' in M Bergsmo (ed), *Quality Control in Fact-Finding* (Florence, Torkel Opsahl Academic EPublisher, 2013) 146.

[29] Y Shany, 'Know Your Rights! The Flotilla Report and International Law Governing Naval Blockades', (*EJIL: Talk!* 12 October 2010), available at www.ejiltalk.org/know-your-rights-the-flotilla-report-and-international-law-governing-naval-blockades/, last accessed 18 July 2016.

[30] KJ Heller, 'The International Commission of Inquiry on Libya: A Critical Analysis' in J Meierhenrich (ed) *International Commissions: The Role of Commissions of Inquiry in the Investigation of International Crimes* (Oxford, Oxford University Press, *forthcoming*).

[31] Tonkin (n 24).

[32] Franck and Fairley (n 22) 308.

[33] Dov Jacobs and Catherine Harwood state there are three main bases for the criminalisation of human rights commissions: (1) the inclusion of international criminal law concepts in the mandates set out for commissions of inquiry; (2) the interrelated nature of international criminal law with other areas of international law; and (3) the desire to ensure accountability for violations of international law: D Jacobs and C Harwood, 'International Criminal Law outside the Courtroom: The Impact of Focusing on International Crimes for the Quality of Fact-Finding by International Commissions of Inquiry' in M Bergsmo (ed), *Quality Control in Fact-Finding* (Florence, Torkel Opsahl Academic EPublisher, 2013) 325.

It would be overstated to say that the criminal law outlook of commissions of inquiry is a recent phenomenon.[34] Indeed, one of the first international commissions of inquiry documented, established in the wake of World War I in 1919 for the purpose of determining responsibility for the outbreak of war, concerned considerations of modern international criminal law, including command responsibility and the impunity of heads of state.[35] Despite these early considerations, individual accountability has really only become central since the establishment of the ad hoc tribunals of Rwanda and the former Yugoslavia and the emergence of international criminal law as a discipline.[36]

Of note in this disciplinary context is that the majority of commissions of inquiry, according to their parent institution and their mandate, remain concerned with violations of international human rights law and international humanitarian law, and not *explicitly* violations of international criminal law.[37] This harks back to a time when international criminal law was considered the enforcement arm of these disciplines. Considering the specific crimes enumerated in the constituting statutes and resolutions of international criminal courts and tribunals, the institutions themselves, the growing jurisprudence, and the number of practitioners and academics identifying as international criminal lawyers, international criminal law certainly seems to have become a discipline in its own right.[38] One can go further and claim that international criminal law is eclipsing international human rights law and that the latter discipline is increasingly being reinterpreted as concerning individual criminal responsibility rather than state responsibility (as was traditionally the case). Karen Engle has observed this shift in regard to human rights NGO *Amnesty International*, demonstrating how the NGO has changed its mandate from promoting impunity (amnesties) to fighting impunity.[39] It appears that the Human

[34] van den Herik traces this as a historical development from fact-finding to judicialisation and criminalisation, which begins with 'the archetype' of dispute settlement in the 1899 Hague Convention to the contemporary commissions of inquiry with a strong accountability focus: van den Herik (n 4).

[35] Commission on the Responsibility of the Authors of the War and on Enforcement of Penalties, established at the Paris Peace Conference, 26 January 1919; report available at (1920) 14(1) *American Journal of International Law* 95.

[36] Jacobs and Harwood state that the increased attention to 'fighting impunity' and the rise of international criminal law has caused individual criminal accountability to be a tool of semantic legitimacy resonating in the work of commissions of inquiry (n 33).

[37] See also the *Practitioner's Handbook*, which purports to concern commissions of inquiry established in light of international human rights law and international humanitarian law violations (n 3).

[38] On the relationship between human rights law and international criminal law, see C Schwöbel, 'The Comfort of International Criminal Law' (2013) 24(2) *Law and Critique* 169.

[39] K Engle, 'Self-critique, (Anti)politics and Criminalization: Reflections on the History and Trajectory of the Human Rights Movement' in JM Beneyto and D Kennedy (eds) *New Approaches to International Law: The European and American Experiences*, (The Hague, TMC Asser, 2013) 41.

Rights Council, which has established several commissions of inquiry and tasked them with investigating crimes, is undergoing a similar transition. The General Assembly resolution which established the Human Rights Council in 2006, for example, makes no mention of international criminal law or fighting impunity.[40] Yet, the website of the Office of the UN High Commissioner for Human Rights, which oversees the Human Rights Council, sets out 'fighting impunity' as one of its thematic priorities.[41] In addition, the High Commissioner for Human Rights has in recent years called for the UN Security Council to refer the situation in Syria to the ICC, as well as the Democratic People's Republic of Korea.[42]

Despite the continued reference to human rights law and international humanitarian law, 'criminalisation' is increasingly a feature of mandates. It was mentioned above that the commission of inquiry mandates task the committees with investigating international law; moreover, there certainly seems to be a trend for them to increasingly mention the investigation of individual criminal accountability. The Libyan commission of inquiry's mandate states that it has been constituted 'to establish the facts and circumstances of [human rights] violations and of the *crimes perpetrated*, and where possible identify those responsible to make recommendations, in particular, on accountability measures, all with a view to ensuring that *those individuals responsible are held accountable*…'. The mandate for the (second) Syrian commission of inquiry set up by the Human Rights Council also explicitly refers to an investigation *of the crimes perpetrated* but goes even further in that it provides a concrete crime to investigate in the crime against humanity.[43] Recent UN Security Council mandates are similar. The commission of inquiry on the Central African Republic, for example, was set up by the UN Security Council in part 'to help identify the perpetrators of such violations and abuses, point to their possible *criminal responsibility* and to help ensure that *those responsible are held accountable*'.[44] The commissions of inquiry on the Israeli-Palestinian conflict stand out in their silence on the criminalisation of perpetrators.

To address the concerns about technicalities, politics and 'ad hocery', there have in recent years been several attempts at a harmonisation of the

40 UN General Assembly Resolution A/Res/60/251 (3 April 2006).

41 See www.ohchr.org/EN/AboutUs/Pages/WhoWeAre.aspx, accessed 18 July 2016.

42 Perhaps not surprising given that the former High Commissioner also served as judge at the ICC and as President of the International Criminal Tribunal for Rwanda. 'North Korea must be referred to ICC, UN human rights chief says', *The Telegraph.co.uk* (11 December 2015), available at www.telegraph.co.uk/news/worldnews/northkorea/12045075/North-Korea-must-be-referred-to-ICC-UN-human-rights-chief-says.html, accessed 18 July 2016.

43 UN Human Rights Council Resolution on Syria (n 10).

44 UN Security Council Resolution on CAR (n 14) para 24.

methods used by fact-finding missions.[45] Despite the good intentions of transparency and predictability, this type of harmonisation is also leading down a further path of 'criminalisation'—and a further narrowing of the scope to individual accountability.

The Hague Institute for Global Justice has a particular angle on international criminal law with its project titled 'From Fact-Finding to Evidence: Harmonizing Multiple Investigations of International Crimes'. On its website it frames the central question as:

> Can criminal investigators and prosecutors interact more effectively with each other and with other investigators (including commissions of inquiry, UN panels of experts and the OHCHR, truth commissions etc), without compromising their respective mandates? And if so, how?[46]

This type of project is further converging fact-finding with international criminal law.

In 2015, the HPCR published a practitioner's handbook on commissions of inquiry in a bid to set out best practices, including key methodological principles and modalities of application.[47] Even if this is in subtle rather than explicit terms, there appears to be a distinct bias for recommending international criminal law enforcement. For example, the HPCR handbook cautions practitioners drafting their recommendations that 'offering too many recommendations could render this section of the report less readable adversely affecting its impact'. The preference for readability and impact is also, almost by definition, a preference for recommending those measures 'with teeth', ie criminal procedure.

An emerging practice has been for commissions of inquiry to compile lists of alleged perpetrators of international crimes, commonly when there are reasonable grounds to believe that a crime or violation has occurred. The commissions of inquiry for Cote d'Ivoire, Libya and Sudan compiled

[45] There have been repeated calls for a permanent commission of inquiry, which is presented as a possibility due to the fact that there now is a permanent ICC, see eg C Henderson, 'Commissions of Inquiry: Flexible Temporariness or Permanent Predictability' in M Ambrus and R Wessel (eds), *Netherlands Yearbook of International Law* (The Hague, TMC Asser Press, 2015) 307, 308. In 2013, M Cherif Bassiouni and C Abraham published a set of guidelines, which articulate rules and principles applicable to different types of fact-finding endeavors. M Cherif Bassiouni and C Abraham (eds) *Siracusa Guidelines for International, Regional and National Fact-Finding Bodies* (Cambridge, Intersentia, 2013). In 2015, the Office of the High Commissioner for Human Rights (OHCHR), produced a manual titled *Commissions of Inquiry and Fact-Finding Missions on International Human Rights and Humanitarian Law: Guidance and Practice* (New York, Office of the High Commissioner for Human Rights, 2015). This publication provides information about standard operating procedures and guidelines relevant to each stage of UN commissions of inquiry and fact-finding missions.

[46] Available at thehagueinstituteforglobaljustice.org/index.php?page=Projects-Projects-Current_Projects-From_Fact-Finding_to_Evidence:__Harmonizing_Multiple_Investigations_of_International_Crimes&pid=122&id=2.

[47] HPCR *Practitioner's Handbook* (n 3).

lists containing the names of individuals it believed had committed international crimes. The commission of inquiry on Syria has gone back and forth on whether it will release such a perpetrator list. First the list was mysteriously locked up in a safe in Geneva; then it was announced in a report that a fifth list would be added to the existing list;[48] shortly after this, the Commission chair Paulo Sérgio Pinheiro was widely cited as stating that the release of the list would put 'alleged perpetrators on notice' and could 'serve to maximise the potential deterrent effect'.[49] The latest statement by Pinheiro was that the Commission would not be releasing the list of names publicly.[50] This compiling of lists also appears to be an emerging practice in non-UN commissions of inquiry. A commission of inquiry set up by the Kenyan government to investigate the violence of the post-presidential elections of 2007/2008, the so-called Waki Commission, handed over a sealed envelope of suspects to Kofi Annan with the request to deliver it to the ICC Prosecutor.[51]

Against this background of mandates seeking accountability, of standardisation, and of drafting ominous perpetrator lists, it appears crucial to consider which facts are sought and, more importantly perhaps, which facts are ignored. More concretely, if commissions of inquiry and their mandating bodies are narrowing their gaze to international criminal law, are they then only deeming those facts as relevant which have a bearing on the elements of accepted international crimes? Such a bias for finding the facts on genocide, crimes against humanity, and war crimes could blind fact-finders to other relevant facts which not only elucidate the root causes of the conflict but also potential paths to peace. This may be facts on economic inequalities which lead to conflict; it may be facts regarding religious and cultural sensitivities and tensions; it may be facts regarding the structural biases in a society for a particular elitist class; it may be facts concerning the colonial encounter and the consequential political and economic dependencies; it may be facts regarding the allegiances and sentiments of the population.

[48] *9th Report of the Commission of Inquiry on Syria*, UN Doc A/HRC/28/69 (5 February 2015) para 101.

[49] 'UN "prepared" to name Syria "war criminals"', *The New Arab* (21 February 2015), available at www.alaraby.co.uk/english/news/2015/2/21/un-prepared-to-name-syria-war-criminals, accessed 18 July 2016.

[50] Statement by Mr Paolo Sérgio Pinheiro, Chair of the Independent Commission of Inquiry on the Syrian Arab Republic, (17 March 2015), available at www.ohchr.org/EN/NewsEvents/Pages/DisplayNews.aspx?NewsID=15843&LangID=E, accessed 18 July 2016.

[51] *The Report of the Commission of Inquiry into Post-Election Violence*, 18, available at www.kenyalaw.org/Downloads/Reports/Commission_of_Inquiry_into_Post_Election_Violence.pdf. See, for further analysis, Ch 7: T Mariniello, 'The Impact of International Commissions of Inquiry on the Proceedings before the International Criminal Court'.

Theo Boutruche, himself involved in several fact-finding missions, has drawn attention to the biases in fact-finding, stating that they are sought in order to *confirm* the laws in question: 'Ultimately, the facts covered through the inquiry are framed by the elements of the very rule allegedly violated.'[52] The mentioned practitioner's handbook produced by a group of academics and former commissioners (including Boutruche) clearly states that 'the norms themselves determine the type of factual information needed'.[53] With an increasing focus on international crimes, it is these norms which are determining the type of factual information needed. The Executive Summary of the commission of inquiry on the Central African Republic, for example, states that:

> The Commission has, throughout its work, always kept in mind the fact that the one thing that the Security Council particularly wished to put an end to the reigning climate of impunity.[54]

If ending impunity is always 'kept in mind' in its fact-finding, what is it that is 'kept out of mind'?

In their focus on international crimes, commissions of inquiry take up one of two identities, either they act as international criminal quasi-tribunals or they act as investigative arms of international criminal tribunals. I will explain these in turn.

6.4. INTERNATIONAL CRIMINAL QUASI-TRIBUNALS

Bassiouni, who has been a frequent commissioner on commissions of inquiry, has stated that 'fact-finding and investigation are a means to an end. With respect to the values of truth and justice, the end is accountability of the perpetrators [...]'.[55] This interpretation would be more in line with the rationale of an international criminal tribunal than a fact-finding and investigative body.

Prompted by a structural bias, their mandates and a self-understanding as accountability bodies, commissions of inquiry use (international) criminal legal methods of determining whether a crime has been committed. In criminal law, the prosecution must prove that certain elements of a crime are given. Generally, the elements of a crime are split into the act or omission (*actus reus*) and the state of mind of the accused (*mens rea*).

52 T Boutruche, 'Credible Fact-Finding and Allegations of International Humanitarian Law Violations: Challenges in Theory and Practice' (2011) 16 *Journal of Conflict and Security Law* 111.

53 HPCR *Practitioner's Handbook* (n 3) 20.

54 UN Security Council Resolution S/2014/928, *The International Commission of Inquiry on the Central African Republic* (*CAR Report*) (22 December 2014) 7.

55 M Cherif Bassiouni, 'Appraising UN Justice-Related Fact-Finding Missions' (2001) 5 *Journal of Law & Policy* 35, 45.

The commission of inquiry which was most explicit in the criminal law investigation of the given facts was the commission of inquiry on Darfur. The report walks the reader through the different elements of the crimes under investigation in a systematic way, as any criminal lawyer might. In a rather illuminating self-reflective turn, the report states that: 'Although clearly it is not a judicial body, in classifying the facts according to international criminal law, the Commission adopted an approach proper to a judicial body.'[56]

One of the clues that commissions of inquiry not only have a self-understanding as quasi-tribunals but are thought of as such within the UN system, is that the UN Security Council, which has the power to establish commissions of inquiry, has done so less since the establishment of the International Criminal Court in 1998. This would seem to indicate that the UN Security Council sees a conflict of competence in the bodies. Between 1989 and 1999 nine commissions of inquiry were set up. In the following ten years, only four commissions of inquiry were set up. However, despite this adjudicative function, commissions of inquiry seem to largely be interested in *courting* international criminal courts and tribunals rather than *replacing* them.

6.5. INVESTIGATIVE ARMS OF INTERNATIONAL CRIMINAL TRIBUNALS

Commissions of inquiry, while generally not taking up the strict testing of elements of crimes themselves, are most likely to pave the way for an international prosecutor to do so. There is much historical precedent for this. The UN War Crimes Commission, established in 1943 at a diplomatic conference of Allied and Dominion countries in London, gathered large swathes of information on the Second World War, and according to its Chairman Robert Wright, prepared the groundwork for the prosecution and punishment of war criminals, which was of course to take place at the Nuremberg trials of 1945/6.[57] The commission even drafted a statute for a proposed UN War Crime Court.[58] The Commission of Experts concerning the former Yugoslavia, the so-called 'Bassiouni Commission', created in order to investigate grave breaches of international humanitarian law committed in the territory of the former Yugoslavia, was the first which

[56] *Darfur Report* (n 27) 11.

[57] *History of the United Nations War Crimes Commission* (London, HM Stationery Office, 1948), available at www.unwcc.org/wp-content/uploads/2014/11/UNWCC-history-ch1.pdf.

[58] See further Ch 9: S Darcy, 'Laying the Foundations: Commissions of Inquiry and the Development of International Law', and WA Schabas, 'The United Nations War Crimes Commission's Proposal for an International Criminal Court' (2014) 25 *Criminal Law Forum* 171.

explicitly recommended the establishment of an international criminal tribunal.[59]

Not all commissions are set up for the purpose and legitimation of establishing international tribunals; the main mechanism through which commissions of inquiry court international criminal courts and tribunals is through recommendations for referral to the ICC or recommendations for the establishment of a new tribunal. It simply is an argument of common sense to state that they therefore must believe that the fact-finding and legal reasoning would be *of use* to the relevant international criminal courts and tribunals.[60]

In many cases an explicit recommendation for referral to judicial bodies is made. The special inquiry into Al-Houla (the first Syria Commission), the Independent International Commission of Inquiry on the Syrian Arab Republic (the second Syria Commission), the Burundi Commission, the Darfur Commission, the Commission of Experts concerning the former Yugoslavia, have all expressly referred to the potential use of their findings for prosecution. The second Syria Commission has gone beyond the recommendation for prosecution and has repeatedly called upon the Security Council to refer the situation to the ICC or to an ad hoc international tribunal.[61] In their reports, the commissions do much of the work that a prosecutorial or investigator team would need to do in order to confirm the need for opening an investigation.

The commission of inquiry on the Central African Republic explicitly referred to its role as an investigative arm. It stated that it is:

> neither a prosecutor nor a court. Instead, its task in relation to alleged perpetrators is to marshal a reliable body of information […] in order to provide the foundations for a full-fledged criminal investigation to be undertaken in the future by the appropriate national and/or international authorities.[62]

It then proceeds to fulfil this purpose by considering, in much depth, the extent to which genocide, crimes against humanity and war crimes have been committed according to the standards of the Rome Statute. In determining whether genocide or ethnic cleansing took place, it even explicitly, and rather helpfully for the ICC, mentions that its findings are based on the same standard of proof utilised under the Rome Statute, Article 58(1)(a) relating to the issuance of an ICC arrest warrant or summons to appear.[63] This is interesting, given that the report acknowledges a memorandum

[59] The Commission of Experts established pursuant to UN Security Council Resolution 780 (1992) concerning former Yugoslavia.

[60] Since the establishment of the ICC, the pattern is that in the event that the state being investigated has signed up to the Rome Statute, a referral to the ICC would be recommended. If not, a recommendation for domestic prosecution or a hybrid ad hoc tribunal is made.

[61] *9th Report on Syria* (n 48) para 96.

[62] *CAR Report* (n 54) para 16.

[63] *CAR Report* (n 54) para 456.

between the Minister of Justice of the CAR and the Special Representative of the Secretary General which commits the CAR government to establishing a Special Criminal Court, to be incorporated into the existing legal system of the CAR.[64] Several reservations about this agreement are spelled out in the commission's report, including whether there will be adequate resources and the fact that the current CAR Penal Code (if that were to apply) 'does not mirror the provisions of the Rome Statute'.[65] Although the report goes on to state some of the benefits of a domestic process, such as the fact that more perpetrators can be tried, the advantage of being closer to the local population and the ability to establish precedents for future accountability measures, this section is concluded with a rather pessimistic final sentence which states that

> in any event, it is clear that if the State, on the basis of the work of the Special Criminal Court and other relevant bodies, can be deemed to be unwilling or unable [...], the ICC will be empowered [...] to step in.[66]

It is almost as though the commission of inquiry is here willing the domestic process to fail, so that the ICC may step in.

The vested interests in seeing a situation referred to the institutions of international criminal justice are all to obvious, considering the choice of commissioners—as already noted above. Of particular note is the International Commission of Inquiry on Libya. Two out of three of the commissioners were undoubtedly interested in the success of the ICC.[67] Canada's Pilippe Kirsch was the first President of the International Criminal Court and Cherif Bassiouni was the Vice-Chairman of the Drafting Committee at the Rome Conference. As Kevin Jon Heller observes, the suspicion that the commission had a vested interest in finding war crimes and crimes against humanity had been committed, would only be strengthened by the report stating that the commissioners 'consulted with the Office of the Prosecutor of the International Criminal Court',[68] although failing to note what it was they consulted about.

This admiration for international criminal courts and tribunals is, however, rather one-sided. For, like a secret lover, the courts and tribunals have been somewhat unwilling to acknowledge any connection with these bodies. Although undoubtedly linked, and undoubtedly influenced by commissions of inquiry, the judgments of the formal adjudicative bodies very rarely make any reference to this link or influence. The practice of distance

64 *CAR Report* (n 54) para 63 ff.

65 *CAR Report* (n 54) paras 65, 66.

66 *CAR Report* (n 54) para 71.

67 Heller (n 30) 8.

68 *Report of the International Commission of Inquiry to Investigate All Alleged Violations of International Human Rights Law in the Libyan Arab Jamahiriya* (*Libya Report*), UN Doc A/HRC/17/44 (31 May 2011) para 18 (the first report filed with the Human Rights Council).

and denial goes back to the UN War Crimes Commission set up during the Second World War. As Shane Darcy observes: 'it was sidelined by the main Allied powers when it came to the preparation of the Nuremberg Charter, and was not referenced in the Nuremberg judgment.'[69]

The ICC has been quite vocal in its rejection of the findings of fact-finding missions. The *Ngudjolo* judgment, for example, dismisses the evidence of human rights investigations in no uncertain terms.[70] This outright rejection is interesting given that the ICC has been described as having 'an evidence problem'.[71] Referring, inter alia, to the overwhelming scope of potential evidence, the understaffing of the investigation teams, the short-term missions from The Hague, and the high rate of charges dismissed or withdrawn due to lack of evidence, De Vos states that 'more attention must be paid to the investigative practices of the Office of the Prosecutor'.[72] Perhaps it is precisely the inadequacy of the investigative process which prevents the direct acknowledgment of cooperation. The ICC may simply not be willing to draw attention to part of the process which it knows to be vulnerable to critique.

Despite the unrequited love, one can see the appeal of international criminal law as a discipline 'with teeth'. The enforcement of the commission of inquiry's recommendations on prosecution can easily be tracked: have prosecutions occurred or not? Yet, it is of note that any reservations in regard to the narrow scope of international criminal law, disrupted peace processes through international criminal justice interventions, the failing recognition and legitimacy of the ICC with the African Union, the worry over neo-colonial exercises of power, and the inability of gathering sufficient evidence are all left unsaid in the reports of commissions of inquiry.

6.6. THE PROBLEMS OF INTERNATIONAL CRIMINAL LAW

As noted above, the predominant critique of commissions of inquiry generally concerns questions on whether they make 'good law': Have

[69] See Darcy, Ch 9, referencing D Plesch and S Sattler, 'A New Paradigm of Customary International Criminal Law' (2013) 2 *International Criminal Law Review* 203.

[70] '[T]he Chamber wishes to emphasise that conducting an investigation into human rights violations is not subject to the same rules as those for a criminal investigation. Reports are prepared in a non-adversarial manner; they are essentially based on oral testimony, sometimes derived from hearsay, and the identity of sources is always redacted.' *The Prosecutor v Mathieu Ngudjolo* ICC-01/04–02/12 (18 December 2012) para 294. Also quoted in C Stahn and D Jacobs, 'Human Rights Fact-Finding and International Criminal Proceedings: Towards a Polycentric Model of Interaction' (2014) *Grotius Centre Working Paper* 2014/017-ICL, 3.

[71] C de Vos, 'Investigating from Afar: The ICC's Evidence Problem' (2013) 26 *Leiden Journal of International Law* 1009.

[72] de Vos (n 71) 1009.

commissions of inquiry reasoned correctly in regard to their interpretations of the elements of a crime? Have commissions of inquiry used a standard of proof which is appropriate? Is the evidence presented by commissions of inquiry appropriate for an international criminal trial? Rather than critiquing the facts considered, the law applied is critiqued. This kind of critique seems both unfair and rather myopic. It is unfair in that commissions of inquiry (perhaps despite their efforts to *pose* as adjudicative bodies) *are not* adjudicative bodies. They should not be measured against something they are not set up to be. It is a myopic critique in that it does not consider the many limitations of international criminal law itself—using instead international criminal law jurisprudence as the correct benchmark with which to test commissions of inquiry. The premise is that if commissions of inquiry adopted better standards of international criminal law, they would be more transparent, more predictable, and ultimately more effective.[73] Interestingly, those voices who critique commissions of inquiry on their sloppy use of international criminal law, are often critics of international criminal law themselves.

There is a growing literature which takes issue with the attention to an effectiveness critique in international criminal law and instead draws attention to the biases and limitations of international criminal law. Although such a critique of international criminal law has been around since the very beginnings of the discipline, it was particularly through the idea of a network of scholars dedicated to critique, the Critical Approaches to International Criminal Law (CAICL) network, that the critique became more pronounced and identifiable.[74] Taking issue with the seemingly self-congratulatory, uncritical, and over-confident tone of the proponents of international criminal law, the CAICL literature seeks to shift the debate to the possible complicities of international criminal law in injustice, conflict, exclusion and bias.[75] In light of the recognition that technical disputes often strip issues of any social or political dimension and generally blind towards other ways of perception which might raise larger objections, the CAICL approach has been to move away from technical disputes.[76]

[73] Jacobs and Stahn, for example, take the effectiveness argument even further in that they write of methods of collaboration between commissions of inquiry and ICCTs which are 'mutually supportive' for the purpose, primarily, of the effectiveness of international criminal trials: Stahn and Jacobs (n 70).

[74] The first conference dedicated to the theme took place in Liverpool in 2012.

[75] See C Schwöbel, 'Introduction' in C Schwöbel (ed), *Critical Approaches to International Criminal Law. An Introduction* (Oxford, Routledge, 2014).

[76] See a reflexive engagement with critique and introductory thoughts on the above themes in C Schwöbel, *Critical Approaches to International Criminal Law. An Introduction* (Oxford, Routledge, 2014).

Many charges brought against the 'effectiveness critique' of international criminal law and its neglect of exploring an 'assumptions critique' apply to the problem of the commission of inquiry's courting ICCTs. If commissions of inquiry are increasingly narrowing their focus on international criminal law, then they also inherit some of its limitations.

I would like to single out two points brought up by the critical turn in international criminal law which seem particularly relevant for a critique of commissions courting ICCTs. First, international criminal law's narrow focus on individual criminal responsibility is turning attention away from other mechanisms of accountability, conciliation, and peace-making. And second, despite claiming to be engaged in law, and not politics, the politically-charged nature of the field is sustaining and creating political and economic discrepancies between the powerful and the disenfranchised.

Sarah Nouwen and Wouter Werner have observed the 'monopoly' which international criminal law has created in regard to questions of global justice. This narrow focus on individual accountability is, according to them, risking the marginalisation of alternative conceptions of justice.[77] Alternative conceptions of justice may, be found in the restoration of relationships (rather than a punitive approach), in putting an end to on-going violence (and the amnesties which may be necessary for this), in redistribution, and in non-criminal forms of punishment and equality.[78] As mentioned above, international criminal law is appealing because it is regarded as 'having teeth'. But it is also appealing because of its narrative: 'There are bad guys out there, who have committed grave crimes harming many people, these bad guys need to be locked up'. The narrative and the attendant roles of perpetrator, victim and legal representative are easy to understand and easy to convey. Moreover, the list of crimes recognised as the core crimes, those 'shocking the conscience of mankind', namely genocide, crimes against humanity and war crimes, are widely accepted—and easily recounted.[79] Criminalisation proceeds through the principle of legality: Did the facts match these crimes? 'This leads to a narrowing of the investigative focus,' observe Jacobs and Harwood, 'as only some incidents that may be characterised as violations of human rights law and international humanitarian law form the constitutive elements of crimes against humanity and war crimes'.[80] Through their focus on international criminal law, commissions of inquiry are therefore complicit in

[77] SMH Nouwen and WG Werner, 'Monopolizing Global Justice. International Criminal Law as Challenge to Human Diversity' (2015) 13 *Journal of International Criminal Justice* 157.
[78] Nouwen and Werner (n 77).
[79] See Schwöbel (n 38) in regard to the 'comfort' in these attributes of international criminal law and a call for more 'discomfort'.
[80] Jacobs and Harwood (n 33) 17.

the deepening of the monopoly of international criminal law in regard to matters of global justice and are further narrowing the scope of alternative justice mechanisms. Conversely, and rather bizarrely, the focus on the procedural short-comings of commissions of inquiry give (undue) credibility and legitimacy to international criminal tribunals.

This monopolising effect of international criminal law is not only due to the appeal of enforcement and simplicity but also because it sits within a widely accepted development narrative of international criminal law, and international law in general. International law is believed to have progressed from consensus and dispute resolution in the early League of Nations days, to foregrounding human rights accountability from mid-century to the end of the twentieth century, and an increasing focus on international criminal accountability at the beginning of the twenty-first century. Within international criminal law, the development narrative views the Nuremberg Tribunal after the Second World War as the beginning of a progressive path, which led from Nuremberg's victors' justice, via the ad hoc tribunals of Yugoslavia and Rwanda to the permanent International Criminal Court in The Hague. Stahn and Jacobs, for example, write of the 'maturing' of procedural standards in international justice as the standard with which commissions of inquiry should be tested. A development narrative of this kind implies that history has been overcome, that the current focus and institutions are better than those which were before.[81] There appears to be a parallel development narrative of commissions of inquiry: commissions of inquiry were, at the beginning of the twentieth century, directed towards dispute resolution; they then became largely about naming and shaming; and today, as the number of commissions of inquiry established is at its peak, are about attributing accountability. Recommendations made by commissions of inquiry in the past have ranged from mediation to administering compensation. However, the narrowing of the understanding of their purpose means that a follow-up prosecution is becoming the prime rationale for their existence. Alternative recommendations are thought of as less mature. In this context, it is important to note that proliferation does not necessarily mean 'maturing' and international criminal accountability does not necessarily mean 'progress'. The proliferation of bodies which investigate or adjudicate as a response to international crises of a violent nature, can also distract from structural crises. 'Not a single government, whether monarchy or bourgeois republic, has yet ventured to undertake a serious inquiry into the position of the French working class,' Karl Marx

[81] For a critique of the progress narrative in international criminal law, see G Simpson, 'Linear Law: The History of International Criminal Law' in Schwöbel (n 76) 159; T Skouteris, *The Notion of Progress in International Law Discourse* (The Hague, TMC Asser, 2010).

lamented. 'But what a number of investigations have been undertaken into crises—agricultural, financial, industrial, commercial, political!'[82] This draws attention to the problem that investigations and judicial proceedings are structurally incapable or unwilling to investigate root causes and are instead focused on symptoms. In particular, the key socio-economic roots of conflict are largely ignored and even obscured. Such root causes may be conditions caused through colonisation and the extraction of resources to meet the demands of the colonial state, they may be the erosion of agriculture due to 'cash crops' and other uses of land to meet corporate interests, they may be movements of people due to environmental strains brought on by climate change or pollution, or they may be other rivalries over access to land and resources. Mahmoud Mamdani, in a comment on the Darfur commission of inquiry, reflects on how Darfur is largely constructed in the public imagination as a place without a history and politics.[83] In its focus on whether genocide occurred, the international institutions glossed over some important aspects of Darfur's history. For example, that there was a struggle for power within the political class in Sudan; and that there was a community-level split inside Darfur, between nomads and settled farmers, who had abandoned their cooperation due to sustained droughts and a consequent intense struggle over diminishing resources. Far from individual accountability, Mamdani notes that anyone wanting to end the spiralling violence 'would have to bring about power sharing at the state-level and resource-sharing at the community level, land being the key resource'.[84]

A related issue concerns the fact that despite ICCTs' continued declarations of being a legal rather than a political tool, they have been highly political bodies. This may not of itself be problematic, considering that all institutions of international law are, by default, political organisations. However, the *kind of politics* engaged in matters. It has emerged in recent years that the international criminal justice system, and particularly the ICC, is neither the self-proclaimed legal-institutional David against the politically maverick Goliath,[85] nor a pawn in the global political game of delegitimising political opponents;[86] it is rather itself contributing to the

[82] K Marx, 'A Workers', Inquiry (20 April 1880) *La Revue socialiste*.

[83] M Mamdani, 'The Politics of Naming: Genocide, Civil War, Insurgency' (2007) 29 *London Review of Books* 5. See also M Mamdani, *Saviors and Survivors: Darfur, Politics and the War on Terror* (London, Verso, 2009).

[84] Mamdani (2007) (n 82).

[85] The narrative which was favoured by former Prosecutor Luis Moreno-Ocampo, for example in the film *Prosecutor: Law. No Order* (Barry Stevens, 2010).

[86] This argument on the politics of the ICC tends to be traced back to SMH Nouwen and W Werner, 'Doing Justice to the Political: The International Criminal Court in Uganda and Sudan' (2011) 21(4) *European Journal of International Law* 941.

great political and economic divide.[87] Tor Krever has examined the context of the ICC's establishment, identifying the key states involved in its political and economic backing and, crucially, in its *shaping* so that they would be shielded from prosecution.[88] The power of monetary support and cut-throat diplomacy at the Rome Conference, where its founding treaty the Rome Statute was negotiated, helped certain states (like Germany and Canada) to claim a grip on appointments to key positions. Although much has been made of the US not having signed up to the Rome Statute, US officials were closely involved in the setting up of the ICC—mainly to ensure that US military personnel could not be made accountable before it.[89] The ICC's role in 'ignoring Iraq' and 'shielding Israel', alongside shielding Americans are further clues to the significant power politics at play.[90] In this bowing to and enabling of imperial concerns, the ICC is further legitimising the interventionist agenda and the civilising mission of the great economic and military powers of the global North. Seen as a body of work, it is undeniable that the interventions of the ICC in Africa have been most controversial in the *receiving* states of international criminal justice as opposed to the *dispensing* states of international criminal justice.

With their close work with the ICC and other tribunals, commissions of inquiry could be tainted with similar criticisms. Commissions of inquiry, in their often narrow focus on individual accountability, could be understood as part of international law's post-World War II rise of liberal internationalism and institutionalism which has hinged on a discourse of development and modernisation of the Third World. Commissions of inquiry could, therefore, be implicated in international law's entwinement in a civilising mission. This is set against the background of international commissions' work largely focusing on countries in the global South and the persistent immunity of Israeli violence, despite the work of several commissions of inquiry on the Israel-Palestine conflict. Indeed, the response to commissions of inquiry in the countries in which they are investigating is painfully familiar to the neo-colonial arguments brought forward by the African Union and African states in which the ICC has intervened. Asked about the Syrian commission of inquiry's report, Syria's ambassador to

[87] See T Krever, 'Dispensing Global Justice' (2014) 85 *New Left Review* 67 and T Krever 'International Criminal Law. An Ideology Critique' (2013) 26 *Leiden Journal of International Law* 701.

[88] Krever (2014) (n 86).

[89] Hot on the heels of the entering into force of the Rome Statute in 2002 came the enactment of The American Service-Members' Protection Act, which provides for the protection of US soldiers by 'all necessary means'. The Act is more colloquially referred to as The Hague Invasion Act.

[90] Krever (2014) (n 86).

the UN, Bashar al-Jaafari, dismissed the inquiry as 'propaganda' aimed at demonising his government.[91] Regardless of whether one sees commissions of inquiry as directly implicated in a civilising mission, courting of ICCTs means that their rationale must be punishment and deterrence, and therefore also justice system reform within the country investigated.

6.7. COIS AS PART OF AN INTERVENTION FORMULA

Commissions of inquiry which court ICCTs are not only tainted by the problems of international criminal law; they have themselves become part of what I call an *intervention formula*. Recent conflicts which have experienced military and non-military intervention go through a check-list of intervention options, often with a view to using military intervention 'as the last resort'. The UN Security Council will most likely begin with resolutions expressing concern and warning; it might impose measures such as sanctions; pressures for military intervention will rise; either the UN or another UN body might then set up a commission of inquiry which may recommend prosecution of international crimes; the UN Security Council might then refer the case to the International Criminal Court; lastly, military intervention may be authorised by the UN Security Council or, in the event of a Security Council dead-lock, may be exercised by a group of aligned (big power) states.

The intervention formula is not fixed in regard to the institutions involved or in regard to the order suggested. Indeed, part of the contemporary intervention formula includes concurrent investigations of violations of international (human rights, humanitarian, or criminal) law by different bodies.[92] Rather than proposing that there is always a predetermined 'plan of attack' (although there may be), I wish, first, to draw attention to the fact that such commissions of inquiry can only adopt a retrospective view—it is already a part of a process of narrating a transition from one governing power to another. As van den Herik observes, human rights commissions of inquiry have a public nature, raising awareness and mobilising public opinion, thus imposing a certain conflict narrative and preparing a case for action.[93] This conflict narrative of commissions of inquiry corresponds with the conflict narrative of the other intervention

[91] 'UN investigators ready to release secret Syria "war criminals" list', *The Telegraph.co.uk* (20 February 2015), available at www.telegraph.co.uk/news/worldnews/middleeast/syria/11426334/UN-investigators-ready-to-release-secret-Syria-war-criminals-list.html, accessed 18 July 2016.

[92] See for example the case of Libya.

[93] van den Herik (n 4) 510.

mechanisms in its identification of perpetrators, victims and appropriate judicial institutions. It also works through an acceptable check-list of interventions, with military intervention being the last resort. A problematic part of this retrospective perspective is that rather than focusing on the situation *as it unfolds*, commissions of inquiry are already considering juridical mechanisms of accountability as they would apply *after a conflict*. Bassiouni claimed, for example, that the Commission of Experts on Rwanda was in essence window-dressing for the Security Council's intention to create another ad hoc international criminal tribunal.[94] Thomas Franck and H Fairley speak of fact-finding as an alternative to international organisations' effective *law-enforcing sanctions*.[95] This raises the above-mentioned tensions with peace-building processes and a narrowing of the transitional justice options to individual criminal accountability.[96]

But the temporalities of fact-finding are not the only problem with commissions of inquiry being part and parcel of an intervention formula: the problem also lies in the political alignment of this intervention. Intervention, whether militarily or in terms of international criminal law, is mostly exercised at the behest of 'the international community'. However, in reality the part of the international community which intervenes is always the same part: the military and economic great powers.

The intervention formula has become such accepted practice that it gives the impression of the dual mechanisms of criminalisation and military intervention being the natural way of approaching peace and security. However, focusing on individual accountability is a distinct liberal tradition, entrenched within a Western history; a Western history which is marred by colonialism and its narration and legitimation as 'the white man's burden'. Intervention of a military nature has often served colonial or neo-colonial interests and intervention through criminalisation is appearing to follow its footprints. Indeed, the chronicling of atrocities, as done in 'criminalised' fact-finding missions, often provides the moral pretext for intervention.[97] Ultimately, commissions of inquiry, when they court international courts, whether by design through their mandates or through their own volition, are therefore implicated in underlying civilising and military purposes. Commissions of inquiry dealing with human rights violations are therefore firmly entrenched in the intervention formula, serving the interests of big powers, rather than as a means to determine unfolding and evolving events and how they can be contextualised in an economic and political landscape.

94 Cherif Bassiouni (n 55) 47.

95 Franck and Fairley (n 22) 308.

96 A further problem which emerges, for which there is too little space to delve deeper into here, is the issue of victims and witnesses being interviewed by different organisations multiple times. This cannot only lead to a narration fatigue but also a problematic professionalisation of victimhood.

97 Mamdani (n 82).

6.8. OPPORTUNITIES AND PROSPECTS

However, the criminalisation trend could also be countered. Commissions of inquiry *not* being judicial bodies is precisely where the opportunity lies for their credibility: investigations into a broad set of facts, and the root causes of context, as well as proposals on a variety of mechanisms for a resolution are a distinct possibility. Rather than working *for* international prosecutors, commissions of inquiry could act as a check on keen prosecutors. Rather than being a handmaiden to the big power players, commissions of inquiry could be a means of requiring accountability of big powers. Rather than being part of an intervention formula, they could unsettle the naturalised presumption that criminalisation and militarisation are the only options for peace. Indeed, commissions of inquiry have historically demonstrated the ability to do precisely these things. The Libyan commission of inquiry, for example, boldly sent a series of letters to NATO asking it to justify bombing attacks which had resulted in civilian casualties.[98] Furthermore, the Libyan commission of inquiry put then Prosecutor of the ICC Luis Moreno-Ocampo in his place for fuelling rumours that, prior to the intervention in Libya, Colonel Gaddafi's troops were engaging in Viagra-fuelled mass rape. Moreno-Ocampo had made a statement to reporters at the UN that there were strong indications of mass rape as well as indications that the government was handing out doses of Viagra to soldiers to encourage sexual attacks.[99] Only weeks later, Cherif Bassiouni, who led the UN inquiry, suggested that the Viagra and mass rape allegations were part of a 'massive hysteria'.[100] In the report by the commission, it is stated that, although sexual violence did occur, 'The Commission was not able to authenticate' whether soldiers were encouraged to rape and that there were 'unsubstantiated allegations' of Gaddafi's troops raping victims.[101]

Although the February 2016 report of the Syrian commission of inquiry also foregrounds individual accountability, it shows welcome glimpses of context and nuance. For example, it states that the international and regional stakeholders that are 'ostensibly pushing for a peaceful solution

[98] UN Human Rights Council, *Report of the International Commission of Inquiry on Libya*, UN Doc A/HRC/19/68 (8 March 2012), Annex II, 139–147, available at www.ohchr.org/documents/hrbodies/hrcouncil/regularsession/session19/a.hrc.19.68.pdf, accessed 13 November 2016.

[99] 'Gaddafi faces new ICC charges for using rape as weapon in conflict', *The Guardian.com* (9 June 2011), available at www.theguardian.com/world/2011/jun/08/gaddafi-forces-libya-britain-nato, accessed 30 March 2015.

[100] 'Libya rape claims "hysteria"—investigator', *The Herald Sun.com* (10 June 2011), available at www.heraldsun.com.au/news/breaking-news/libya-rape-claims-hysteria-investigator/story-e6frf7jx-1226072781882?nk=b871befc4b54dff8dc4cdc366f264eb9, accessed 30 March 2015.

[101] *Report of the International Commission of Inquiry on Libya* (n 97).

to the war are the same that continue to feed the military escalation.'[102] Later, in a section on the collapse of the country's economy, accounts by residents are mentioned, according to which 'young men had joined ISIS primarily to generate income'.[103] Such facts are crucial in resisting international criminal law's blunt casting of characters in conflict as either perpetrators or victims.

With a nudge away from individual criminal responsibility and towards context and diplomacy, commissions of inquiry could make the potential of being a check on power a reality. These potentially anti-hegemonic features of commissions of inquiry should be encouraged and extended in the future if commissions of inquiry are not simply to be regarded as investigative arms of international courts and tribunals and as forming part of an intervention formula. Rather than the narrow criminal approach, and despite the fact that commissions of inquiry are still always a form of intervention, they could provide for a broader scope of recommendations. Commissions of inquiry could, for example, be involved in peace negotiations rather than accountability mechanisms; they could invoke possible diplomatic channels, and alternative models for social and transitional justice which include ideas for the redistribution of goods and power.

6.9. CONCLUSION

It has been argued that commissions of inquiry which court ICCTs are at risk of being tainted by the limitations and biases of international criminal law. Where commissions of inquiry are believed to fail, tribunals are believed to succeed. This not only blinds us to many of the shortcoming of international criminal courts and tribunals but also creates the fiction that international criminal adjudication is the end to be aspired to. Moreover, it was argued that the courting of ICCTs implicates commissions of inquiry in an intervention formula which serves the interests of the big political, economic and military powers. Commissions of inquiry are increasingly part of a check-list of intervention rather than a check on intervention. Historically, recommendations made by commissions of inquiry have ranged from mediation to administering compensation. This chapter has argued that fact-finding in a less juridical and non-criminalised form could provide a welcome means for investigating and exposing the key socio-economic root causes of conflict.

[102] *Report of the Independent International Commission of Inquiry on the Syrian Arab Republic*, UN A/HRC/31/68 (11 February 2016) para 17.

[103] *Report of the Independent International Commission of Inquiry on the Syrian Arab Republic* (n 101) para 132.

to the war are the same that continue to feed the military, as shown.[168] Later, in a section on the collapse of the country's economy, accounts by residents are mentioned, according to which young men had joined IS primarily to generate income.[169] Such facts are crucial in resisting international criminal law's blunt casting of characters in conflict as either perpetrators or victims.

With a nudge away from individual criminal responsibility and towards context and diplomacy, commissions of inquiry could make the potential of being a check on power a reality. These potentially anti-hegemonic features of commissions of inquiry should be encouraged and extended in the future. Commissions of inquiry are not simply to be regarded as investigative arms of international courts and tribunals and as forming part of an intervention formula. Rather than the narrow criminal approach, and despite the fact that commissions of inquiry are still always a form of intervention, they could provide for a broader scope of recommendations. Commissions of inquiry could, for example, be involved in peace negotiations rather than accountability mechanisms; they could invoke possibly diplomatic channels; and alternative models for social and transitional justice which include ideas for the redistribution of goods and power.

6.9 CONCLUSION

It has been argued that commissions of inquiry which court ICCTs are at risk of being tainted by the limitations and biases of international criminal law. Where commissions of inquiry are believed to fail, tribunals are believed to succeed. This not only blinds us to many of the shortcomings of international criminal courts and tribunals but also creates the fiction that international criminal adjudication is the end to be aspired to. Moreover, it was argued that the courting of ICCTs implicates commissions of inquiry in an intervention formula which serves the interests of the big political, economic and military powers. Commissions of inquiry are increasingly part of a checklist of intervention rather than a check on intervention. Historically, recommendations made by commissions of inquiry have ranged from mediation to administering compensation. This chapter has argued that fact-finding in a less juridical and non-criminalised form could provide a welcome means for investigating and exposing the key socio-economic root causes of conflict.

[168] *Report of the Independent International Commission of Inquiry on the Syrian Arab Republic*, UN Doc A/HRC/31/68 (11 February 2016) para 17.

[169] *Report of the Independent International Commission of Inquiry on the Syrian Arab Republic* (n 168) para 112.

7

The Impact of International Commissions of Inquiry on the Proceedings before the International Criminal Court

TRIESTINO MARINIELLO

7.1. INTRODUCTION

ON 18 SEPTEMBER 2004, the United Nations (UN) Security Council requested the Secretary General to appoint an international commission of inquiry in order to investigate reports of violations of international humanitarian law and human rights law in Darfur.[1] In February 2008, the Kenyan government decided to establish an international commission of inquiry to provide recommendations on the measures in bringing to justice those persons responsible for acts of violence that occurred immediately after the presidential elections results were announced.[2] In 2011, the Human Rights Council decided to dispatch two commissions of inquiry on the allegations of serious violations of human rights law that occurred in Libya and Ivory Coast.[3]

These commissions were vested with the authority to make a first legal evaluation of the facts that occurred in the situations in question. Despite the fact that they were established by different bodies and had to deal with very different contexts, their mandates presented a common denominator: they received an *accountability driven-mandate*. Indeed, rather than being

[1] UN Security Council Resolution 1564 (2004) 12.

[2] The Commission of Inquiry into the Post Election Violence began on 23 May 2008 with an announcement published in the Kenya Gazette Notice No 4473 vol cx-no 41.

[3] The International Commission of Inquiry on Libya was created by the Human Rights Council at its 15th session on 25 February 2011 by Resolution S-15/1, UN Doc A/HRC/S-15/1, 11. The International Commission of Inquiry on Côte d'Ivoire was established by UN Human Rights Council Resolution 16/25 on 13 April 2011, UN Doc A/HRC/RES/16/25, 10.

mere fact-finding missions they were instructed to identify the alleged perpetrators of international violations and ensure that they were held accountable.

This chapter critically assesses the relationship between the Sudan, Kenya, Libya, and Ivory Coast commissions of inquiry and the International Criminal Court (ICC). Such commissions were tasked to investigate allegations of international violations within the context of situations that are still open before the ICC. Therefore, this study examines the mandate and work of these commissions vis-à-vis (pre-trial) decisions of the ICC. In so doing, it aims to explore whether and to what extent the commissions' investigations impacted upon the different phases of the ICC's pre-trial proceedings, namely from the referral of a situation to the confirmation of charges. Since no case related to the situations in Sudan, Kenya, Libya and Ivory Coast has been completed, this study does not investigate the weight of the commissions' information at the trial stage.

In light of this ambition, section 7.2 provides a brief description of the evolution of the role of international commissions of inquiry from plain fact-finding to (quasi) judicial bodies, entrusted with the authority to provide legal evaluation of the relevant facts and secure prosecution-oriented criminal evidence. Section 7.3 offers a general overview on the use of international criminal law by international commissions of inquiry since 1993. It examines how international criminal law has been applied not only by those UN Commissions which were explicitly instructed to assess the perpetration of international crimes, but also by fact-finding missions whose mandate was confined to ascertaining violations of international human rights law and international humanitarian law.

Following a presentation of the main international criminal law findings by the commissions of inquiry in Sudan, Kenya, Libya and Ivory Coast (section 7.4), section 7.5 provides the first comprehensive analysis of the relevant pre-trial jurisprudence related to the situations in question, in order to assess the significance of the commissions' sources in the different phases of the ICC proceedings. In particular, it shows how the commissions' information, although not binding on the ICC, played a key role within the context of both pre-investigative and investigative phases before the Court. In light of the relevance that commissions' documents assumed in the decisions to issue arrest warrants or summons under Article 58 of the Rome Statute, Section 7.6 argues the necessity that the Prosecutor does not heavily rely on the fact-finding sources. As fact-finding missions' information appeared very persuasive to the decisions under Article 58, this section recommends that the Prosecutor submit the application for an arrest warrant or summons only if she is able to conduct an independent investigation, producing evidence which might corroborate third-party findings.

7.2. THE EMERGING SYNERGY BETWEEN FACT-FINDING MISSIONS AND INTERNATIONAL CRIMINAL JUSTICE: THE COMMISSION OF EXPERTS ON THE FORMER YUGOSLAVIA

The functions of international commissions of inquiry have significantly evolved in the last 30 years. Traditionally, the role of commissions was confined to making factual determinations, in order to encourage the peaceful resolution of international disputes.[4] As enshrined in Article 9 of the 1907 Hague Convention for the Pacific Settlement of International Disputes, when an international dispute exists because of a difference of opinion on points of fact, states should establish an international commission of inquiry to 'facilitate a solution of these differences by elucidating the facts by means of an impartial and conscientious investigation'. The role of fact-finding missions was confined to the presentation of findings of a factual nature, while the possibility of drawing legal conclusions exceeded the commissions' mandates.

The Charter of the United Nations confirms this traditional understanding of fact-finding missions as enshrined in the 1907 Hague Conventions. In particular, according to Article 33 of the UN Charter, fact-finding missions may constitute a distinct means for the resolution of a dispute. The UN organs may, therefore, rely on detailed fact-finding to gather information, which could be useful for exercising effectively their role in restoring and maintaining international peace and security.

The 1991 Declaration on Fact-finding by the United Nations in the Field of the Maintenance of International Peace and Security recognised this function of fact-finding missions:

> In performing their functions in relation to the maintenance of international peace and security, the competent organs of the [UN] should endeavour to have full knowledge of all relevant facts. To this end they should consider undertaking fact-finding activities.[5]

The establishment of a Commission of Experts for the former Yugoslavia (Yugoslavia Commission) in 1993 represented a turning point, as it introduced a new model of commission vested with authority to investigate violations of international law and recommend measures to ensure

[4] For a detailed historical-comparative analysis of commissions of inquiry, see LJ van den Herik, 'An Inquiry into the Role of Commissions of Inquiry in International Law: Navigating the Tensions between Fact-Finding and Application of International Law' (2014) 13 *Chinese Journal of International Law* 507. See also LJ van den Herik and C Harwood, 'Sharing the Law: The Appeal of International Criminal Law for International Commissions of Inquiry' in P Alston and S Knuckey (eds), *The Transformation of Human Rights Fact-Finding* (Oxford, Oxford University Press, 2016) 233.

[5] UN General Assembly Resolution 46/59, *Declaration of Fact-Finding by the United Nations in the Field of the Maintenance of International Peace and Security 1991*, UN Doc A/RES/46/59 (9 December 1991) 1.

accountability for those violations.[6] Indeed, the Yugoslavia Commission was entrusted by the UN Security Council with the power to inquire into violations of the Geneva Conventions and other violations of international humanitarian law committed in the territory of the former Yugoslavia.[7] The same Commission decided to extend its analysis into violations of international criminal law and recommended the establishment of an international criminal tribunal (ICT).[8] In so doing, it performed the investigation in order to secure prosecution-oriented criminal evidence. The Commission also clarified legal concepts related to the investigated facts, such as genocide, crimes against humanity, command responsibility, superior orders, reprisals, rape and other forms of sexual assault.[9]

The interim report of the Commission triggered the establishment of the first ICT after Nuremberg and Tokyo.[10] Although there was no formal institutional link between the Commission and the International Criminal Tribunal for the former Yugoslavia (ICTY), the Commission's work had a significant influence on the law and practice of the Court.[11] With respect to the applicable law, the ICTY Statute included legal formulations, as indicated by the Commission of Inquiry. This is true in relation to the definition of command responsibility and the concept of superior orders, which, as suggested by the commissions, do not represent a ground to exclude criminal liability of the subordinate, but may be taken into account as a mere mitigating circumstance.[12] With regard to the influence on the practice of the ICTY, the Prosecutor could start his work on the basis of the material collected by the Commission of Experts. As argued by Frulli, 'the findings of the Commission contributed greatly to a quick and efficient start of the work of the ICTY prosecutor, who took office almost fourteen months after the establishment of the ICTY'.[13]

In particular, the relevance of the information collected by the Commission to the ICTY lay in the fact that it revealed that grave breaches of the Geneva Conventions and other violations of international humanitarian law had been committed on a large scale.[14] In addition, the Commission

[6] UN Security Council Resolution 780 (1992), UN Doc S/RES/780 (1992) (6 October 1992) 2.

[7] ibid.

[8] *Interim Report of the Commission of Experts Established Pursuant to Security Council Resolutions 780 (1992)*, UN Doc S/25274 (10 February 1993) (*Yugoslavia Interim Report*).

[9] *Final Report of the Commission of Experts Established Pursuant to Security Council Resolution 780 (1992)*, UN Doc S/1994/674 (27 May 1994) (*Yugoslavia Final Report*).

[10] *Yugoslavia Final Report* (n 9).

[11] M Frulli, 'Fact-Finding or Paving the Way to Criminal Justice? Some Reflections on the UN Commissions of Inquiry' (2012) 10 *Journal of International Criminal Justice* 1323, 1327.

[12] See the *Yugoslavia Interim Report* (n 8) 51–53 and the ICTY Statute, Art 7.

[13] Frulli (n 11) 1327.

[14] *Yugoslavia Final Report* (n 9) 311.

provided a significant contribution to the investigation of international violations as it found the systematic nature of the commission of rape and sexual assault.[15]

7.3. THE USE OF INTERNATIONAL CRIMINAL LAW BY INTERNATIONAL COMMISSIONS OF INQUIRY: A GENERAL OVERVIEW

The vast majority of UN commissions of inquiry established since 1993 followed on from the Yugoslavia experience, as their mandates were no longer confined to factual determinations, but also included the possibility for providing legal evaluations, in particular to investigate whether the relevant facts constituted violations of international law. It can be argued that the Yugoslavia Commission started a process of 'juridification' or 'criminalisation' of commissions of inquiry,[16] instructed to go beyond the ascertainment of the responsibilities of legal entities as states and non-state armed groups and make a preliminary evaluation of the facts based on international legal parameters, so that individuals who were responsible for the violations are held accountable.

Some commissions were expressly requested to ascertain whether the investigated facts amounted to international crimes.[17] Other commissions were instructed to assess international humanitarian law and human rights violations.[18] Still, they decided to cover also alleged violations of international criminal law, on the basis of the possibility of framing international humanitarian law and human rights violations as international crimes.

[15] *Yugoslavia Final Report* (n 9) pt IV, section F.

[16] PG Alston, 'The Criminalization of International Human Rights Fact-Finding' (Key Note Address at the Conference on Fact-finding on Gross Violations of Human Rights During and After Conflicts, Oslo, Norwegian Centre for Human Rights, 17–18 November 2011). For a critical analysis of this process of 'criminalisation' of international commissions of inquiry, see Ch 6: C Schwöbel-Patel, 'Commissions of Inquiry: Courting International Criminal Courts and Tribunals'.

[17] See, inter alia, UN Security Council Resolution 935 (1994), Commissions of Experts for Rwanda (1 July 1994); Darfur Commission (n 1); Independent International Commission of Inquiry on the Syrian Arab Republic, UN Doc A/HRC/S-17/L.1 (22 August 2011); Commission of Inquiry on Human Rights in the Democratic People's Republic of Korea (DPRK), UN Doc A/HRC/RES/22/13 (21 March 2013).

[18] See, inter alia, Libya Commission (n 3); UN Human Rights Council Resolution S-9/1, Independent Commission of Inquiry on the 2014 Gaza Conflict (12 January 2009). For a detailed analysis of the migration of international criminal law concepts into the work of international commissions of inquiry, see also, D Jacobs and C Harwood, 'International Criminal Law outside the Courtroom: The Impact of Focusing on International Crimes for the Quality of Fact-Finding by International Commissions of Inquiry' in M Bergsmo (ed), *Quality Control in Fact-Finding* (Torkel Opsahl Academic EPublisher, 2013) 325.

With respect to fact-finding missions established to assess the perpetration of international crimes, for instance, a few months after the Yugoslavia Commission the UN Security Council requested the Rwanda Commission to gather evidence of grave violations of international humanitarian law committed in the territory of Rwanda, including the evidence of *possible acts of genocide* (emphasis added).[19] In contrast to the Yugoslavia experience, it does not appear that the Rwanda Commission played any role in prompting the establishment of the international criminal tribunal. Indeed, the International Criminal Tribunal for Rwanda was established before the submission of the Commission's final report.[20] However, the final findings of the Commission confirmed that genocide and other systematic, widespread and flagrant violations of international humanitarian law had been perpetrated in Rwanda.[21] Similarly, the Darfur Commission was instructed, inter alia, to ascertain whether acts of genocide had occurred,[22] while the Syria Commission was tasked with identifying those responsible for international violations, particularly crimes against humanity.[23] The Democratic People's Republic of Korea Commission was mandated to 'investigate systematic, widespread and grave violations of human rights, with a view to ensuring full institutional and personal accountability, in particular where violations may amount to *crimes against humanity* (emphasis added)'.[24]

Other commissions were established to determine alleged violations of international humanitarian law and/or human rights violations. However, even if their mandates did not explicitly include international criminal law, these commissions also investigated allegations of international crimes. The commissions justified their decisions to exceed their mandates by stressing that international criminal law constitutes an enforcement measure for serious violations of human rights and international humanitarian law. For instance, the International Commission of Inquiry for Libya stated that international criminal law is the 'means of enforcement at the international level of penalties for grave violations of customary law, [human rights] and serious violations of [international humanitarian law] which are recognized as attracting individual liability'.[25]

[19] Rwanda Commission (n 17).

[20] The Report of the Commission was finalised on the 9 December 1994, whilst the ICTR had already been established on 8 November 1994. See *Final Report of the Commission of Experts Submitted Pursuant to Resolution 935 (1994)*, UN Doc S/1994/1405 (9 December 1994) Annex.

[21] ibid.

[22] Darfur Commission (n 1).

[23] Syria Commission (n 17) 12.

[24] See DPRK Commission (n 17) 5.

[25] UN Human Rights Council, *Report of the International Commission of Inquiry to investigate all Alleged Violations of International human rights law in the Libyan Arab Jamahiriya*, UN Doc A/HRC/17/44 (1 June 2011) 23 (*Libya Report*).

The so-called Goldstone Commission, instructed to investigate violations of international humanitarian law and human rights during the Gaza Conflict, found that:

> International criminal law has become a necessary instrument for the enforcement of IHL and (human rights). Criminal sanctions have a deterrent function and offer a measure of justice for the victims of violations. The international community increasingly looks to criminal justice as an effective mechanism of accountability and justice in the face of abuse and impunity. The Mission regards the rules and definitions of international criminal law as crucial to the fulfilment of its mandate to look at all violations of IHL and IHRL by all parties to the conflict.[26]

The Eritrea Commission of Inquiry explicitly admitted that its mandate was confined to investigate only violations of human rights and, as such, did not establish whether such violations amounted to international crimes.[27] However, it concluded that international crimes might have been committed and recommended further investigations.[28]

The commission established by the UN Human Rights Council to investigate violations of international humanitarian law and human rights law, resulting from the interception by Israeli forces of the humanitarian aid flotilla bound for Gaza (Flotilla Commission), concluded that these violations constituted (war) crimes under Article 147 of the Fourth Geneva Convention.[29]

In the proposal to establish a fact-finding mission in East Timor, the same UN Commission on Human Rights clearly stated that 'all persons who committed or authorised violations of human rights or international humanitarian law were individually responsible and accountable for those violations'.[30] In its final report, the East Timor Commission stated that victims have a right to an effective remedy for violations of human rights, which includes also the state's responsibility to use criminal law measures against those responsible of such violations.[31]

Several fact-finding missions established after the Yugoslavia Commission received an explicit accountability driven-mandate, since they were

[26] *Report of the United Nations Fact-Finding Mission on the Gaza Conflict*, UN Doc A/HRC/12/48 (25 September 2009) 286.

[27] *Report of the Commission of Inquiry on Human Rights in Eritrea*, UN Doc A/HRC/29/42 (4 June 2015) 8.

[28] ibid.

[29] *Report of the international fact-finding mission to investigate violations of international law, including international humanitarian and human rights law, resulting from the Israeli attacks on the flotilla of ships carrying humanitarian assistance*, UN Doc A/HRC/15/21 (27 September 2010) 265.

[30] See The Commission on Human Rights, *Report of the Fourth Special Session*, E/CN.4/RES/1999/S-4/1 (27 September 1999).

[31] *Report of the International Commission of Inquiry on East Timor*, UN Doc A/54/726, S/2000/59, 148.

instructed to ensure that those responsible of such violations were held accountable. For instance, the Burundi Commission was also established to recommend measures to bring to justice persons responsible for 'the assassination of the President of Burundi on 21 October 1993, the massacres and other related serious acts of violence',[32] and the Sri Lanka Commission was requested to investigate allegations of the crimes perpetrated in order to avoid impunity and ensuring accountability.[33] The Cambodia Commission was mandated to 'determine the nature of the crimes committed by Khmer Rouge leaders' and 'to explore legal options for bringing them to justice before an international or national jurisdiction'.[34]

Occasionally, this accountability-driven mandate included also the authority to identify those responsible for the crimes committed. The Central African Republic Commission, established by the UN Security Council in 2013, was entrusted with the identification of perpetrators of violations of international humanitarian law and international human rights law, and the assessment of their possible criminal responsibility, with a view to ensuring that those responsible were held accountable.[35] The 2009 Guinea Commission was established to ascertain which crimes had been committed and identify their perpetrators.[36]

7.4. ACCOUNTABILITY-DRIVEN MANDATES IN PRACTICE: THE CASES OF SUDAN, KENYA, IVORY COAST AND LIBYA

The UN commissions of inquiry in Sudan, Libya, and Ivory Coast were also instructed to ensure accountability and identify the alleged perpetrators of international violations. Before assessing the relationship between commissions of inquiry and international criminal proceedings, the next section will briefly discuss the findings of these fact-finding missions, as they investigated the alleged commission of international crimes within the context of situations that are still open before the International Criminal Court. For the same reason, the analysis will cover also the work of the

[32] The Commission was created by UN Security Council Resolution 1012, UN Doc S/RES/1012 (28 August 1995).

[33] See UN Doc A/HRC/25/L.1/Rev.1, 10(b).

[34] The Group of Experts for Cambodia was established pursuant to UNGA Resolution 52/135 (27 February 1998), UN Doc A/RES/52/135(1).

[35] See UN Doc S/RES/2127 (2013).

[36] On 28 September 2009, a violent crackdown on a pro-democracy rally in the Guinean capital of Conakry resulted in the deaths of at least 150 people as well other violent incidents. The Commission was mandated to establish the facts and circumstances of the events of 28 September 2009 and the related events in their immediate aftermath, qualify the crime perpetrated, determine responsibilities and, where possible, identify those responsible. See *Letter from the Secretary General*, UN Doc S/2009/556 (28 October 2009).

international commission of inquiry in Kenya, the so-called Waki Commission, which significantly paved the road to international criminal justice.

In line with the evolution of the role and functions of commissions of inquiry post-1993, beyond being plain fact-finding missions, these commissions were called to ensure that those responsible for heinous conduct were brought to justice. As we will analyse in the following subsections, the mandate of the Darfur Commission provided that it had to identify the perpetrators of violations of international humanitarian law and human rights law with a view to ensuring that those responsible were held accountable. In Kenya, according to the terms of reference, the Commission had to issue recommendations on the measures with regard to bringing to justice those persons responsible for acts of violence occurring immediately after the presidential elections results were announced. The Libya Commission had to identify those responsible for violations of international human rights law and ensure that those individuals responsible were held accountable. In Ivory Coast, the Commission also had to identify those responsible for serious abuses and violations of human rights law committed in Côte d'Ivoire following the presidential election of 28 November 2010.

7.4.1. The UNSC Darfur Commission

The Darfur Commission admitted that in classifying the facts according to international criminal law, it adopted an approach proper to a judicial body.[37] It excluded the commission of genocide, as it stressed that attacking, killing and forcibly displacing members of some tribes was not perpetrated in order to annihilate, in whole or in part, a racial, ethnic, national or religious group, as required by the genocide definition.[38] However, the Commission concluded that the investigated facts amounted to war crimes and crimes against humanity.[39] With respect to these core crimes, the Commission provided a detailed analysis of their contextual elements and underlying offences. Indeed, it reported the existence of the armed conflict for war crimes,[40] and of widespread or systematic attacks against the civilian population for crimes against humanity.[41] It also defined the

[37] *Report of the International Commission of Inquiry on Darfur to the United Nations Secretary-General* (25 January 2005) 14 (*Darfur Report*).
[38] *Darfur Report* (n 37) 518.
[39] *Darfur Report* (n 37) section VI (1–6).
[40] *Darfur Report* (n 37) 74–76.
[41] *Darfur Report* (n 37) section VI (1–6).

nature of the conflict, in order to establish which set of rules of international humanitarian law were applicable in each case.[42]

The Commission also found that most attacks were deliberately and indiscriminately directed against civilians.[43] Moreover, it relied on the jurisprudence of ad hoc tribunals and the Statute of the ICC in classifying the relevant facts as underlying offences of international crimes.[44] In particular, it ascertained the perpetration of underlying offences of war crimes and crimes against humanity, such as killing of civilians, torture, enforced disappearances, destruction of villages, rape and other forms of sexual violence, pillaging and forced displacement.[45]

The Commission claimed its authority not only to find material perpetrators of alleged crimes but also those who bore the greatest responsibility. Therefore, it identified a number of possible suspects for serious violations of international human rights law and international humanitarian law. However, it decided to withhold the names of these suspects from the public domain, on the basis of:

> 1) the importance of the principles of due process and respect for the rights of the suspects; 2) the fact that the Commission has not been vested with investigative or prosecutorial powers; and 3) the vital need to ensure the protection of witnesses from possible harassment or intimidation.[46]

The list of likely suspects of international crimes was filed with the UN Security Council, with the recommendation that it should have been delivered to the ICC Prosecutor for future investigations and possible indictments.[47]

7.4.2. The International Commission of Inquiry into the Post-Election Violence in Kenya

In Kenya, the so called Waki Commission of Inquiry reached the conclusion that crimes against humanity had been committed in Kenya after the 2007 presidential elections.[48] In particular, the Commission found that murder, destruction of property, serious injuries, sexual violence, and forcible transfer of population had been perpetrated.[49] According to the

[42] *Darfur Report* (n 37) 74–76.
[43] *Darfur Report* (n 37) 238–68.
[44] *Darfur Report* (n 37) section VI (1–6).
[45] *Darfur Report* (n 37) section VI (1–6).
[46] *Darfur Report* (n 37) 645.
[47] *Darfur Report* (n 37) 525.
[48] *The Report of the Commission of Inquiry into Post-Election Violence* was handed over to president Mwai Kibaki and Prime Minister Raila Odinga on 15 October 2008 (*Kenya Report*).
[49] *Kenya Report* (n 48).

Commission, criminal cases should have been brought against persons bearing greatest responsibility for these crimes.[50] The Commission extensively described that the post-election violence was not a mere juxtaposition of citizen-to-citizen opportunistic assaults, but it found that there were systematic attacks on civilians based on their ethnicity and political leanings.[51] These findings were crucial to show that acts of violence in Kenya could amount to international crimes, as they were not sporadic or isolated. Indeed, the widespread or systematic nature of the attacks against the civilian population, which constitutes the contextual element of crimes against humanity under the Article 7 of the Rome Statute, draws a borderline between crimes against humanity falling within the jurisdiction of the ICC, and ordinary crimes, which are punishable only before domestic courts. The Commission also recommended the establishment of a special tribunal to prosecute crimes as a result of post-election violence.[52]

Similar to the Darfur Commission, the Waki Commission identified a list of alleged perpetrators and decided to not publish the list with names of alleged perpetrators in its report.[53] This list was placed in a sealed envelope, which was sent to the Panel of African Eminent Personalities, with the recommendation to forward the names of likely suspects to the Prosecutor of the ICC, if the proposed special tribunal had not been set up.[54]

7.4.3. The UNHRC Libya Commission

The Libya Commission classified the investigated facts as international crimes. In its first report, the Commission had already found that Gadhafi forces had used excessive force against demonstrators in February 2011.[55] In the final report, the Commission concluded that Gadhafi forces had committed crimes against humanity and war crimes in Libya.[56] According to the Commission, acts of murder, enforced disappearance and torture had been perpetrated within the context of a widespread or systematic attack against a civilian population.[57] The Commission also established additional violations as unlawful killing, individual acts of torture and ill-treatment, attacks on civilians, and rape.[58] The fact-finding mission

50 *Kenya Report* (n 48) pt III.
51 *Kenya Report* (n 48) pt V.
52 *Kenya Report* (n 48) pt V.
53 *Kenya Report* (n 48) pt V.
54 *Kenya Report* (n 48) pt V.
55 *Libya Report* (n 25).
56 *Report of the International Commission of Inquiry on Libya*, UN Doc A/HRC/19/68 (2 March 2012) (*Final Libya Report*).
57 *Final Libya Report* (n 56) pt III (A–D).
58 *Final Libya Report* (n 56) pt III (B, D, F).

stated also that the anti-Gadhafi forces (Thuwar) were responsible for war crimes and breaches of international human rights law.[59] These forces, according to the Commission's findings, had committed unlawful killing, arbitrary arrest, torture, enforced disappearance, indiscriminate attacks, and pillage.[60]

The Commission also assessed the Libyan legislation and judicial system. In particular, it found that the domestic legislation did not adequately provide for the prosecution of international crimes.[61] In addition, it established that Libya lacked a functioning justice system, so that international crimes would have likely been unpunished.[62] Lastly, the Libya fact-finding mission decided not to include the names of the alleged perpetrators of international crimes in the final report, apart from senior figures who are publicly known. The Commission sent the confidential list of the alleged responsible for international violations to the High Commissioner for Human Rights.[63]

7.4.4. The UNHRC Ivory Coast Commission

As mentioned above, the Ivory Coast Commission was established to investigate the facts and circumstances surrounding the allegations of serious abuses and violations of human rights committed in Côte d'Ivoire following the presidential election of 28 November 2010, in order to identify those responsible for such acts and to bring them to justice.[64] The Commission did not confine its role to assessing violations of human rights law, but also covered violations of international humanitarian law and international criminal law.[65] Even if more superficially compared to other commissions examined in this section, the Ivory Coast Commission provided a legal characterisation of these abuses, by determining that war crimes and crimes against humanity had been committed at the relevant time. With regard to crimes against humanity, the Commission established that serious crimes such as murder and rape had been perpetrated within the context of a widespread and systematic attack against the civilian population, which was targeted on the basis of their supposed ethnicity or political sympathies.[66]

[59] *Final Libya Report* (n 56) 810.
[60] *Final Libya Report* (n 56) 810.
[61] *Final Libya Report* (n 56) 771–774.
[62] *Final Libya Report* (n 56) 779–784.
[63] *Final Libya Report* (n 56) 760.
[64] See UN Doc A/HRC/16/L.33 (18 March 2011) 10.
[65] *Rapport de la Commission d'enquête Internationale Indépendante sur la Côte d'Ivoire*, UN Doc A/HRC/17/48 (1 July 2011) (*Ivory Coast Report*).
[66] *Ivory Coast Report* (n 65) 91.

The Commission did not provide detailed findings on why the post-election period amounted to a non-international armed conflict. Still, it concluded that some of the investigated abuses such as violence to life and person, cruel treatment and torture and humiliating and degrading treatment amounted to serious violations of common Article 3 to the Geneva Conventions, and as such, constituted war crimes under Article 8 of the Rome Statute.[67] The Commission stressed that other serious violations of the laws and customs applicable in armed conflicts had been committed, such as intentionally directing attacks against the civilian population not taking direct part in hostilities, intentionally directing attacks against buildings, material, units and medical transports, attacks intentionally directed against personnel, installations, material, units or vehicles involved in a peace-keeping mission, intentionally directing attacks against buildings dedicated to religion, education and hospitals, looting of towns and villages, as well as rape and other forms of sexual violence.[68]

7.5. COMMISSIONS OF INQUIRY AS NEW ACTORS ON THE STAGE OF THE ICC

Before moving to an assessment of the impact of the work of commissions of inquiry on the ICC, it is necessary to remove the work of the Libya from the scope of this research. Indeed, although the scenario addressed by the Commission is the same of the Situation open before the ICC, I believe the investigation of the Libya fact-finding mission did not assume any relevance to the proceedings before the ICC. The investigation in Libya displays a lack of cooperation between the Commission of Inquiry and the ICC, as well as among other UN bodies, namely the Security Council and the Human Rights Council. The same Commission admitted that it consulted with the Court, but at the same time it stated no information had been shared with the ICC. Indeed, the UN Security Council referred the situation in Libya to the ICC the day after the Human Rights Council had established the Commission.[69] Therefore, it appears that the work of the Libya commission of inquiry did not influence the Security Council's choice of referring the situation to the ICC. In other words, the UN Security Council's decision to trigger the ICC's jurisdiction under Article 13(b) was taken independent of the findings of the Commission.

In addition, the Prosecutor's decision to initiate the investigation was taken with unprecedented expeditiousness, only seven days after

[67] *Ivory Coast Report* (n 65) 92–93.

[68] *Ivory Coast Report* (n 65) 92–93.

[69] UN Security Council Resolution 1970 (2011), UN Doc S/RES/1970(2011) (26 February 2011).

the Security Council's referral. The same report of the Commission was published two weeks after the Prosecutor had submitted a request for three arrest warrants to the Pre-Trial Chamber.[70] Thus, the Prosecutor did not have the possibility to use the Commission's report in supporting his request for warrants of arrest against Muammar Gaddafi, Abdullah Al Sanussi, and Saif Al-Islam Gaddafi.

Therefore, this section will focus on the relationship between the ICC and the Sudan, Ivory Coast and Kenya Commissions. In order to assess the impact of the commissions' sources on international criminal proceedings, it is necessary to discuss separately the different pre-trial stages before the ICC: (i) triggering the jurisdiction of the Court; (ii) authorisation of the investigation; (iii) issuance of arrest warrant or summon to appear; (iv) confirmation of the charges; (v) admissibility of the cases.

7.5.1. Triggering the ICC Jurisdiction

The UN Security Council, a state party or the Prosecutor may trigger the ICC's jurisdiction.[71] The Sudan Situation was referred to the ICC by the Security Council,[72] while in both the Kenya and Ivory Coast contexts the Prosecutor decided to initiate an investigation using his *proprio motu* powers under Article 15.[73] In the Sudan, Kenya and Ivory Coast Situations, the Commissions' reports constituted the basis of the allegations leading to criminal prosecutions before the ICC. The detailed assessment of facts, which were made in particular by the Sudan and Kenya Commissions, raised the necessity of further investigation by the ICC Prosecutor and the need to ensure accountability for alleged international crimes committed.

Indeed, the Darfur Commission's work prompted the Security Council to approve Resolution 1593 (2005), which activated the jurisdiction of the ICC.[74] The Security Council was persuaded by the detailed report of the Cassese Commission that international crimes had allegedly been committed. Therefore, the Commission's findings on the necessity of further investigations to be conducted by an international Prosecutor convinced the Security Council to approve its first referral to the ICC under Article 13(b) of the Rome Statute.

[70] *Libya Report* (n 25).

[71] Rome Statute, Art 13.

[72] UN Security Council Resolution 1593 (2005), UN Doc S/RES/1593 (2005) (31 March 2005).

[73] See *Situation in the Republic of Kenya, Request for an Authorization of Investigation Pursuant to Article 15*, ICC-01/09-3 (26 November 2009); *Situation in the Republic of Ivory Coast, Request for an Authorization of Investigation Pursuant to Article 15*, ICC-02/11-3 (23 June 2011).

[74] UN Security Council Resolution 1593 (n 72).

The Kenya situation can be considered as an emblematic example of the strict cooperation between the ICC and the Commission of Inquiry. Indeed, the Waki Commission had handed over a sealed envelope naming the suspects to former UN Secretary General Kofi Annan, requesting him to deliver the envelope to the ICC Prosecutor should the Kenyan authorities fail to establish a special court to try the likely suspects of crimes committed during the post-election violence.[75] It was only following the failure by domestic authorities to establish this special tribunal that the ICC Prosecutor decided to use his powers under Article 15 of the Statute.[76] Prior to this decision, the Prosecutor had agreed with the Kenyan government to not intervene, if the Special Tribunal had been established in order to seek accountability against persons bearing the greatest responsibility for crimes, particularly crimes against humanity, relating to the 2007 General Elections in Kenya.[77] After receiving the sealed envelope and supporting material compiled by the Commission, on 26 November 2009 the ICC Prosecutor requested the Pre-Trial Chamber II to grant the authorisation to start an investigation on the crimes against humanity allegedly committed during the post-election violence in Kenya.[78] In his request for the authorisation under Article 15, the same Prosecutor extensively used the Commission's allegations regarding the perpetration of crimes against humanity in Kenya.

With respect to the Ivory Coast Situation, the UN Commission's report is not the main fact-finding document, as it constituted one of several materials submitted by third parties investigating the post-election violence in Ivory Coast. Together with reports presented by a number of non-governmental organisations, the Commission's materials were used by the Prosecutor as evidence for the contextual elements of an 'attack' for the purposes of establishing the commission of crimes against humanity, and of a non-international armed conflict with regard to the existence of war crimes.[79]

7.5.2. Decision of the Pre-Trial Chamber to Authorise the Investigation

Article 15(4) of the Rome Statute provides that

> If the Pre-Trial Chamber, upon examination of the request and the supporting material, considers that there is a reasonable basis to proceed with an

[75] *Kenya Report* (n 48) pt V.
[76] *Situation in the Republic of Kenya* (n 73).
[77] ICC, Agreed Minutes of the meeting between Prosecutor Moreno-Ocampo and the delegation of the Kenyan Government, 3 July 2009.
[78] *Situation in the Republic of Kenya* (n 73).
[79] *Situation in Côte d'Ivoire* (n 73) 61–173.

investigation, and that the case appears to fall within the jurisdiction of the Court, it shall authorise the commencement of the investigation…

In light of the low standard of proof required at this stage of proceedings, all the evidentiary materials presented by the Prosecutor are subject to a minimum judicial review by the competent Pre-Trial Chamber.

In its decision to authorise the investigation into the Ivory Coast situation, the Pre-Trial Chamber II accepted the Prosecutor's request.[80] In line with the OTP allegations, the Chamber made a significant use of the Commission's report to establish that there was a reasonable basis to believe that the contextual element of war crimes, consisting of the existence of an armed conflict of a non-international character, was met.[81]

The Waki Commission's report had a noteworthy influence on the same decision of the Pre-Trial Chamber authorising the Prosecutor to initiate the investigation in Kenya.[82] First, the Pre-Trial Chamber used the Commission's sources to define the temporal, material and territorial parameters of the investigation, which could have been conducted by the Prosecutor.[83] Second, the fact-finding mission's report assumed significant relevance to the Pre-Trial Chamber's ascertainment of the *chapeau* elements of crimes against humanity, as: (i) the attack directed against the civilian population;[84] (ii) the organisational policy;[85] (iii) the widespread and systematic nature of the attack;[86] and (iv) the link between the individual conduct and the attack.[87] Similarly, the Chamber relied on the Commission's information also to establish that there was a reasonable basis to believe that murder, rape, forcible transfer, and other inhumane acts causing serious injuries had been committed within the context of the widespread and systematic attack against the civilian population.[88]

7.5.3. Issuance of Arrest Warrant and Summons to Appear

As already mentioned, the Sudan, Kenya, and Ivory Coast Commissions each submitted a list of alleged perpetrators of international crimes to the

80 *Situation in Côte d'Ivoire, Decision Pursuant to Article 15 of the Rome Statute on the Authorization of an Investigation into the Situation in the Republic of Côte d'Ivoire*, ICC-02/11-14 (3 October 2011) (*Authorisation Investigation Côte d'Ivoire*).

81 *Authorisation Investigation Côte d'Ivoire* (n 80).

82 *Decision Pursuant to Article 15 of the Rome Statute on the Authorization of an Investigation into the Situation in the Republic of Kenya*, ICC-01/09-19 (31 March 2010) (*Authorisation Investigation Kenya*).

83 *Authorisation Investigation Kenya* (n 82) 201–11.

84 *Authorisation Investigation Kenya* (n 82) 100–14.

85 *Authorisation Investigation Kenya* (n 82) 115–28.

86 *Authorisation Investigation Kenya* (n 82) 129–34.

87 *Authorisation Investigation Kenya* (n 82) 135–38.

88 *Authorisation Investigation Kenya* (n 82) 139–71.

ICC Prosecutor. However, they decided to keep these lists confidential. Whether the people identified by the Prosecutor as alleged perpetrators were the same as those listed in the commissions' materials is a matter of speculation. However, we cannot fail to note that the profile of the likely suspects identified by the commissions is very similar to those people prosecuted before the ICC. This is true with regard to the Darfur Commission, which pointed to the responsibility of members of the government and Janjaweed Militias for crimes against humanity and war crimes.[89] Indeed, since 2009, most senior leaders of the State and Janjaweed have been accused by the Prosecutor of international crimes.[90] The Commission had also stressed the responsibility of members of two rebel groups: the Sudan Liberation Army (SLA) and Justice for Equality Movement (JEM). In line with the Commission's findings, in 2010, the Prosecutor started an investigation against Banda and Jerbo, considered as the military commanders respectively of JEM and SLA.[91]

In Ivory Coast, the relationship between the Commission's work and the suspects against whom the Prosecutor brought a case appears evident. Indeed, the public report frequently mentioned the role played by the former President of Ivory Coast, Laurent Gbagbo, and Charles Blè Goude', former Minister of Youth Affairs.[92] In particular, the Commission reported the involvement of the militias and mercenaries working for Gbagbo in the commission of abuses during the post-election violence.[93] Gbagbo and Goudè were committed to trial in 2014.[94]

It is worth to remembering that third party fact-finding sources constitute indirect evidence, whose probative value appears to be sufficient in order to establish the standard of proof under Article 58, namely that there are reasonable grounds to believe that the suspect has committed the crimes falling within the Rome Statute. Indirect evidence encompasses hearsay evidence, reports of international and non-governmental organisations (NGOs), as well as reports from national agencies, domestic intelligence services and the media.[95] Similar to the stage of proceedings

[89] *Darfur Report* (n 37) 630–39.

[90] See the Darfur cases: *Prosecutor v Omar Hassan Ahmad Al Bashir* ICC-02/05-01/09; *Prosecutor v Ahmad Muhammad Harun ('Ahmad Harun') and Ali Muhammad Ali Abd-Al-Rahman ('Ali Kushayb')* ICC-02/05-01/07; *Prosecutor v Abdel Raheem Muhammad Hussein* ICC-02/05-01/12.

[91] *Prosecutor v Abdallah Banda Abakaer Nourain* ICC-02/05-03/09. Proceedings against Saleh Mohammed Jerbo Jamus were terminated by Trial Chamber IV on 4 October 2013 after receiving evidence pointing towards his death.

[92] *Ivory Coast Report* (n 65) 23–28.

[93] *Ivory Coast Report* (n 65) 23–28.

[94] See *Prosecutor v Laurent Gbagbo*, Decision on the Confirmation of Charges against Laurent Gbagbo, ICC-02/11-01/11-656-Red (12 June 2014); *Prosecutor v Charles Blé Goudé*, Decision on the Confirmation of Charges against Charles Blé Goudé, ICC-02/11-02/11-186 (11 December 2014).

[95] *Prosecutor v William Samoei Ruto, Henry Kiprono Kosgey and Joshua Arap Sang*, Decision on the Confirmation of Charges Pursuant to Article 61(7)(a) and (b) of the Rome Statute, ICC-01/09-01/11-373 2 (23 January 2012) 69.

regarding the authorisation to open an investigation under Article 15, Article 58 entails a low standard of proof and low level of judicial oversight in terms of arrest warrant or summons to appear. Article 58 of the Rome Statute provides two requirements for the issuance of a warrant of arrest: there must be reasonable grounds to believe that a person has committed a crime within the jurisdiction of the Court and that an arrest is necessary. If the arrest warrant is not deemed necessary, as one of the three conditions provided under Article 58(1)(b) should fail, a summons to appear may be issued.[96] The issuance of an arrest warrant or summons to appear marks the beginning of a case before the ICC.

As stated in the *Lubanga* and *Katanga* cases, the first limb for the purposes of the issuance of an arrest warrant is a two-fold test, which requires that there are reasonable grounds to believe: (1) that one of the crimes within the ICC jurisdiction has been committed; and (2) that the alleged perpetrator is criminally liable for such a crime under one of the modes of liability enshrined in the Rome Statute.[97]

An examination of the different cases related to the situation in Sudan show how the commission of inquiry's information assumed significant probative value in establishing the perpetration of one of the crimes within the jurisdiction of the ICC. In the Darfur cases, the OTP had notably relied on the Cassese Commission's material in its applications under Article 58.[98] In the application for an arrest warrant against Hussein, the evidence provided by the OTP included open source material, witness statements, material obtained from the Darfur Commission of Inquiry, and documents provided by the government of Sudan.[99] In the application for summons to appear in the *Harun* and *Kushayb* case, the Prosecutor admitted to having 'benefited greatly from the information furnished by the UNCOI' and the National Commission of Inquiry.[100] The Prosecution

[96] According to the Rome Statute, Art 58(1)(b), the arrest is necessary when of the following condition is met: '(i) To ensure the person's appearance at trial; (ii) To ensure that the person does not obstruct or endanger the investigation or the court proceedings; or Where applicable, to prevent the person from continuing with the commission of that crime or a related crime which is within the jurisdiction of the Court and which arises out of the same circumstances.'

[97] *Situation in the Republic of Congo, Decision on the Prosecutor's Application for Warrants of Arrest, Article 58*, Lubanga, ICC-01/04-01/07 (10 February 2006) 93; *Decision on the Evidence and Information Provided by the Prosecution for the Issuance of a Warrant of Arrest for Germain Katanga*, Katanga, ICC-01/04-01/07 (5 November 2007) 24.

[98] See *Situation in Darfur, the Sudan, Public Redacted Version of the Prosecutor's Application under Article 58*, Al Bashir, ICC-02/05-157-AnxA (14 July 2008).

[99] *Situation in Darfur, the Sudan, Public Redacted Version of Prosecutor's Application under Article 58* filed on 2 December 2011 with Public Annexes 1 & 2, Hussein, ICC-02/05-237-Red (24 January 2012) 7.

[100] *Situation in Darfur, the Sudan, Public Redacted Version Prosecutor's Application under Article 58(7)*, ICC-02/05-56, Harun and Ali Kushayb (27 February 2007).

stated that he had 'evaluated the conclusions of the UNCOI and the NCOI, and the materials underlying the findings of those commissions'.[101]

In light of this, the Pre-Trial Chamber mainly followed the Prosecutor's reasoning and recognised the relevance of the Commission's sources to the issuance of the arrest warrants. Still, a significant difference between the Chamber's findings and the Prosecutor's application is related to the crime of genocide. Indeed, in the first arrest warrant decision against Al Bashir, the Pre-Trial Chamber appeared more persuaded by the Commission's findings when it rejected the Prosecutor's submissions that there were reasonable grounds to believe that genocide had been committed in Darfur.[102]

In particular, in the *Al Bashir* case, the Pre-Trial Chamber I used the Commission's materials to establish the contextual element and the underlying offences of both war crimes and crimes against humanity.[103] In the Darfur cases, the Pre-Trial Chamber I relied on the Commission's sources, not only to find that there were reasonable grounds to believe that crimes had been committed, but also in order to establish a link between the perpetration of these crimes and the alleged perpetrators.[104]

It appears more problematic to establish the weight of the commissions' findings in the Kenya and Ivory Coast cases. This is due to the fact that the prosecutorial applications for summons to appear in the Kenya cases are heavily redacted,[105] while the OTP's request for arrest warrants related to the situation in Ivory Coast are still under seal. This prevents us from knowing which types of evidence have been presented and in particular, the role that the commissions' documents may have played in supporting the Prosecutor's applications.

Nevertheless, in the case against Gbagbo, it is the Pre-Trial Chamber's decision on the arrest warrant to reveal that the Prosecutor had mainly relied on third party sources, in particular reports by several NGOs.[106]

[101] ibid 13: 'On 5 April 2005, the Prosecution received more than 2,500 items, including documentation, video footage and interview transcripts which had been gathered by the UNCOI, together with a sealed envelope containing the conclusions reached by that commission as to persons potentially bearing criminal responsibility for the crimes in Darfur'.

[102] See *Prosecutor v Omar Al Bashir*, Decision on the Prosecution's Application for a Warrant of Arrest against Omar Hassan Ahmad Al Bashir, ICC-02/05-01/09-3 (4 March 2009) 204–05.

[103] ibid 55–109.

[104] See, inter alia, *Situation in Darfur* (n 100) 209–23.

[105] *Situation in the Republic of Kenya, Prosecutor v William Samoei Ruto, Henry Kiprono Kosgey and Joshua Arap Sang*, Prosecutor's Application Pursuant to Article 58 as to William Samoei Ruto, Henry Kiprono Kosgey and Joshua Arap Sang, ICC-01/09-30-Red2 (15 December 2010); *Situation in the Republic of Kenya*, Prosecutor's Application Pursuant to Article 58 as to Francis Kirimi Muthaura, Uhuru Muigai Kenyatta and Mohammed Hussein Ali, ICC-01/09-31-Red2 (15 December 2010).

[106] *Prosecutor v Laurent Koudou Gbagbo*, Decision on the Prosecutor's Application Pursuant to Article 58 for a warrant of arrest against Laurent Koudou Gbagbo, ICC-02/11-01/11-9-Red (30 November 2011).

In line with the Prosecutor's application, the Commissions' information, together with a number of documents provided by NGOs, was persuasive to the Pre-Trial Chamber III's findings, particularly with regard to the establishment of a widespread or systematic attack against the civilian population and of individual conduct constituting crimes against humanity, as inhumane acts and murder.[107] In the case against Simone Gbagbo, in the establishment of criminal liability for the crimes alleged by the Prosecutor, the Chamber used, inter alia, the UNHRC's report to conclude that the suspect had played a key role in recruiting, arming and integrating thousands of volunteers and enlisting them into the Defense and Security Forces FDS chain of command.[108]

7.5.4. Confirmation of Charges

The confirmation of charges constitutes one of the main innovations introduced by the drafters of the Statute in the field of international criminal justice.[109] Statutes of other international or internationalised criminal tribunals do not contain such a procedure. The confirmation of charges is the stage at which a Pre-Trial Chamber makes a determination whether the case is to be sent for trial.[110] The Prosecutor and the Defence are the parties to the confirmation procedure and, as such, they may submit their evidence and call witnesses.[111] Pursuant to Article 61(6) of the Statute, the suspect may also object to the charges, challenge the evidence presented by the Prosecutor and submit evidence. In addition, victims who have suffered personal harm linked to the charges against the accused may participate in the confirmation proceedings through their legal representatives.[112]

In contrast to the arrest warrant or summons to appear procedure, the confirmation of charges is deliberately envisaged as an adversarial hearing, whereby the person charged has the right to be present and contest the evidence before a Pre-Trial Chamber composed of three judges. Thus, ICC Pre-Trial Chambers are vested with the authority to assess

[107] ibid 28–61.

[108] *Prosecutor v Simone Gbagbo*, Decision on the Prosecutor's Application Pursuant to Article 58 for a Warrant of Arrest against Simone Gbagbo ICC-02/11-01/12-2-Red (2 March 2012) 33.

[109] T Mariniello, 'Questioning the Standard of Proof: The Purpose of the ICC Confirmation of Charges Procedure' (2015) 13 *Journal of International Criminal Justice* 579.

[110] Rome Statute, Art 61.

[111] Rome Statute, Arts 61(5) and 61(6)(c).

[112] Rome Statute, Art 68(3).

evidence, including the power to determine its relevance, admissibility, and weight.[113]

These factors characterising the confirmation of charges procedure—the higher standard of proof, the judicial scrutiny of the evidence submitted by the parties and the role of the Defence, who can challenge the prosecutorial evidence—have the effects of reducing the impact of indirect evidence, including the commissions' information, on the decision to commit an individual to trial. The Darfur cases have not reached the stage of confirmation of charges before the ICC. However, the Kenya and Ivory Coast decisions on the confirmation of charges reveal how third party fact-finding sources have a lesser weight in the proceedings, if compared to the previous stage relating to the arrest warrant or summons to appear.[114]

In the Kenya cases, the Chamber clarified that the decision on the confirmation of charges cannot be based solely on a piece of indirect evidence,[115] whilst a single piece of direct evidence may be decisive for the Chamber's determination.[116] According to the Chamber, 'more than one piece of indirect evidence, which has low probative value, is preferable to prove an allegation to the standard of substantial grounds to believe'.[117]

Saying that, in both cases, it appears that the majority (Judge Trendafilova and Judge Tarfusser) used the commissions' materials as corroborating evidence of witness statements submitted by the Prosecutor. In

[113] For instance, r 63(2) of the Rules and Procedures of Evidence establishes that any Chamber, including the Pre-Trial Chamber, 'shall have the authority, in accordance with the discretion described in Article 64, paragraph 9, to assess freely all evidence submitted in order to determine its relevance or admissibility in accordance with Article 69 …'. In addition, Article 69(4) of the Statute, which applies also at the confirmation hearing, provides that '[t]he Court may rule on the relevance or admissibility of any evidence, taking into account, *inter alia*, the probative value of the evidence and any prejudice that such evidence may cause to a fair trial or to a fair evaluation of the testimony of a witness, in accordance with the Rules of Procedure and Evidence'.

[114] With regard to the situation in Kenya, see *Prosecutor v William Samoei Ruto, Henry Kiprono Kosgey and Joshua Arap Sang*, Decision on the Confirmation of Charges Pursuant to Article 61(7)(a) and (b) of the Rome Statute, ICC-01/09-01/11-373, Pre-Trial Chamber II (23 January 2012) (Ruto, Kosgey and Sang Confirmation Decision); *Prosecutor v Francis Kirimi Muthaura, Uhuru Muigai Kenyatta and Mohammed Hussein Ali*, Decision on the Confirmation of Charges Pursuant to Article 61(7)(a) and (b) of the Rome Statute, ICC-01/09-02/11-382-Red (23 January 2012) (Muthaura, Kenyatta and Ali Confirmation Decision). With respect to the situation in Ivory Coast, see *Prosecutor v Charles Blè Goudè*, Decision on the Confirmation of Charges against Charles Blè Goudè, ICC-01/09-02/11-382-Red (23 January 2012); *Prosecutor v Laurent Koudou Gbagbo*, Decision on the Confirmation of Charges against Laurent Gbagbo, *Gbagbo* (ICC-02/11-01/11-656-Red), Pre-Trial Chamber I (Gbagbo Confirmation Decision) (12 June 2014); *Prosecutor v Laurent Koudou Gbagbo*, Decision adjourning the hearing on the confirmation of charges pursuant to Art 61(7)(c)(i) of the Rome Statute, ICC-02/11-01/11-432, Pre-Trial Chamber I (3 June 2013) (Gbagbo Adjournment Decision).

[115] Ruto, Kosgey and Sang Confirmation Decision (n 114) 74.

[116] Ruto, Kosgey and Sang Confirmation Decision (n 114) 74.

[117] Ruto, Kosgey and Sang Confirmation Decision (n 114) 75.

particular, in the case against Muthaura, Kenyatta and Ali, the Pre-Trial Chamber found the Commission's documents persuasive as corroborating evidence in relation to the underlying offences of crimes against humanity, murder, deportation and other inhuman acts.[118]

In the *Gbagbo* case, the Pre-Trial Chamber adopted an even stricter approach in the assessment of the probative value of indirect evidence for the confirmation of charges.[119] The Chamber expressed its concern that the Prosecutor had relied heavily on NGO reports and press articles with regard to key elements of the case, including the contextual elements of crimes against humanity.[120] The Chamber found that these pieces of indirect evidence did not constitute the fruits of a proper investigation conducted by the Prosecutor in accordance with Article 54(l)(a) of the Statute.[121] According to the majority of judges sitting in the Pre-Trial Chamber, NGO reports and press articles may be a useful means to clarify the historical context of a conflict situation.[122] However, they do not usually constitute a valid substitute for the type of evidence that is required to meet the evidentiary threshold for the confirmation of charges.[123] This is due to the fact that NGOs reports are mainly based on anonymous hearsay, which cannot be investigated and challenged by the Defence. The Chamber also expressed its doubts that anonymous hearsay contained in NGOs' reports could be useful to corroborate other types of indirect evidence, since it is problematic to establish whether these sources are truly independent of each other.[124]

7.5.5. Admissibility

The Darfur Commission condemned the inaction of both the Sudanese authorities and the rebels to prosecute and try those allegedly responsible for the serious crimes committed.[125] It found that the government had not put in place any real and effective response to large-scale criminality linked to the armed conflict.[126] Therefore, considering the nature of international crimes, which are committed by state officials or with their complicity, as well as the shortcomings of the Sudanese criminal justice

[118] Muthaura, Kenyatta and Ali Confirmation Decision (n 114) 240, 247, 262, 276.
[119] Gbagbo Adjournment Decision (n 114).
[120] Gbagbo Adjournment Decision (n 114) 35.
[121] Gbagbo Adjournment Decision (n 114) 35.
[122] Gbagbo Adjournment Decision (n 114) 35.
[123] Gbagbo Adjournment Decision (n 114) 35.
[124] Gbagbo Adjournment Decision (n 114) 30.
[125] *Darfur Report* (n 37) 567–68.
[126] *Darfur Report* (n 37) 567–68.

system, the Commission concluded that Sudan was unwilling and unable to prosecute and try the alleged offenders.[127] The Kenya Report emphasised the weaknesses and difficulties of the domestic criminal justice system to investigate and prosecute crimes allegedly committed during the post-election violence.[128] The Ivory Coast Commission highlighted that domestic authorities had failed to adopt any measures to put an end to impunity.[129]

This type of information by fact-finding commissions on states' unwillingness to prosecute and investigate alleged perpetrators of serious crimes, or on the state of domestic justice systems, may be very useful in making a preliminary evaluation of the admissibility of a case before the ICC. The ICC could be called to deal with questions related to the admissibility from early stages of the proceedings up until trial. At the situation stage, the prosecutorial decision to start the investigation and prosecution entails also the evaluation of the admissibility of the case under Article 17.[130] Similarly, the Pre-Trial Chamber's authorisation for the Prosecution to start the investigation under Article 15 encompasses also the examination of the admissibility conditions. At this stage of the proceedings, where there is no identified suspect, the admissibility test requires an assessment as to whether the state is conducting, or has conducted, national proceedings in relation to a potential case, namely in relation to the groups of persons and the crimes allegedly committed during those incidents.[131] Therefore, the material provided by fact-finding commissions might be crucial in providing significant information on whether the relevant state is willing and/or able to investigate and prosecute certain categories of potentially accused, as those identified as alleged perpetrators by the same commissions.

Therefore, commissions of inquiry's findings might also be used by the ICC to evaluate the quality and state of a domestic judicial system, in order to establish its capability to conduct effective criminal proceedings. Indeed, as it stems from the detailed reports in Darfur and Kenya, the work of the commissions' may provide the ICC with useful insights on the shortcomings of a domestic judicial system, which would be unable to carry out impartial criminal proceedings, also in light of the general security situation.

127 *Darfur Report* (n 37) 568.
128 *Kenya Report* (n 48) Ch 12.
129 *Ivory Coast Report* (n 65) 120.
130 According to the Rome Statute, Art 53(1)(b) 'In deciding whether to initiate an investigation, the Prosecutor shall consider whether: the case is or would be admissible under Article 17'. Under Art 53(2)(b), 'If, upon investigation, the Prosecutor concludes that there is not a sufficient basis for a prosecution because: The case is inadmissible under Article 17'.
131 See, inter alia, *Authorisation Investigation Kenya* (n 82) 48–50.

7.6. A CONCLUDING APPRAISAL OF THE RELATIONSHIP BETWEEN FACT-FINDING SOURCES AND ICC PROCEEDINGS

This chapter assessed the influence of the information provided by commissions of inquiry on the pre-trial proceedings before the ICC. Even if commissions' material is not binding on international criminal tribunals, their investigations appeared to be very persuasive with regard to the Prosecutor's decisions as well as to the Chamber's findings. The analysis conducted in section 7.5 shows how the significance of the material provided by commissions of inquiry before the ICC varies in the course of proceedings on the basis of the rising standards of proof. As indirect evidence, fact-finding materials appeared to have a stronger impact on the ICC during those preliminary phases of the proceedings that require the lowest standards of proof to be satisfied. Indeed, the Rome Statute establishes four different, progressively higher, evidentiary thresholds in Articles 53(1)(a), 58(1), 61(7) and 66(3).[132] The lowest test is provided in the early stage of the proceedings, namely, in Article 53(1)(a) regarding the initiation of an investigation, where the Prosecutor has to assess whether or not there is a '*reasonable basis* to believe that a crime within the jurisdiction of the Court has been or is being committed' (emphasis added).[133] At the next, higher, standard the issuance of a warrant of arrest pursuant to Article 58(1) requires that there are 'reasonable grounds to believe that the person has committed a crime within the jurisdiction of the Court'. Situated immediately above, there is Article 61(7) providing a 'substantial grounds to believe' test for the purposes of the confirmation of charges. Finally, the highest threshold is enshrined in Article 66(3), according to which 'in order to convict the accused, the Court must be convinced of the guilt of the accused beyond reasonable doubts'.

By providing the first comprehensive analysis of the relevant pre-trial jurisprudence related to the situations in Sudan, Kenya, and Ivory Coast, this paper confirms Stahn and Jacobs' argument that the impact of fact-finding sources decreases in the progression of the proceedings.[134] They

[132] See Ruto, Kosgey and Sang Confirmation Decision (n 114) 40. However, in the Bemba Confirmation Decision, Pre-Trial Chamber II found that there are only three evidentiary threshold, by omitting any references to Art 53(1)(a). In this regard, see *Prosecutor v Jean-Pierre Bemba Gombo*, Decision Pursuant to Article 61(7)(a) and (b) of the Rome Statute on the Charges of the Prosecutor Against Jean-Pierre Bemba Gombo, ICC-01/05-01/08-424 (15 June 2009) 27.

[133] The same evidentiary threshold is enshrined in Art 15 with regard to the Pre-Trial Chamber's authorisation for the Prosecutor to commence investigations *proprio motu*.

[134] C Stahn and D Jacobs, 'Human Rights Fact-Finding and International Criminal Proceedings: Towards a Polycentric Model of Interaction', Grotius Centre Working Paper Series, 2014/017-ICL.

also bring into the picture other factors, such as 'the prosecutorial discretion in relation to choice of situations and cases, the scope of defendants' rights and the balance between Judge-led and Prosecution-led inquiry'.[135] In other words, the relevance of commissions' information is more significant during those stages of proceedings where the Prosecutor enjoys more discretion and the Defence does not have the possibility to challenge the evidence submitted by fact-finding commissions. This is true in relation to the phase related to the prosecutorial choice of situations to investigate, when formally a suspect has not yet been identified. By contrast, the use of commissions' investigations starts to appear less significant at the confirmation of charges stage of proceedings, which is deliberately envisaged as an adversarial hearing, whereby the person charged has the right to be present and contest the evidence before a Pre-Trial Chamber composed of three judges.

Therefore, the work of the commissions of inquiry constituted a significant source at the pre-investigative phase, by offering a general overview of the situation, and revealing the (alleged) existence of the contextual elements of international crimes. With a focus on the situations in Sudan, Kenya and Ivory Coast, this study examined how the commissions' sources assumed, even if in different degrees, relevance to paving the way to proceedings before the ICC. In Sudan, the Commission's investigation played a key role within the context of the UN Security Council's decision to refer the situation to the ICC. The examination of the situation in Kenya showed the strict cooperation between the Commission and the Court. The Commission's information had a significant weight on the Prosecutor's decision to open an investigation, by using his *proprio motu* powers under the Article 15 of the Rome Statute. With respect to the Ivory Coast, the relevance of the UN commission of inquiry's information to the ICC's proceedings appeared less evident. Still, the commission of inquiry's information constituted one of the several reports by third parties, which were used by the Pre-Trial Chambers in order to authorise the Prosecution to open the investigation.

In addition, this chapter assessed also the role of commissions' materials during the investigative stage before the ICC. It ascertained that the decision by the Pre-Trial Chamber under Article 58 was strongly influenced by third party sources, as it follows an *ex parte* application conducted with the absence of the Defence, which cannot object to the relevance and admissibility of the evidence. Particularly in the Darfur cases, the commissions' information was used not only to establish that there were reasonable grounds to believe that the crimes had been committed, but also to establish the link between this commission and the alleged perpetrators.

[135] Stahn and Jacobs (n 134) 13.

To conclude, as commissions' sources appeared to assume a central relevance in the issuance of arrest warrants or summons to appear under Article 58, it is important that commissions of inquiry are provided with clear and transparent guidelines and procedures, considering, in most circumstances, the anonymous and unknown nature of the witnesses. However, it is no less certain that commissions of inquiry are not mandated to establish whether individuals are guilty. Thus, in the application for an arrest warrant, it is of the utmost importance that the Prosecutor does not become a mere rubber stamping of commissions' findings or, more generally, that she does not only rely on inferences or types of indirect evidence. She should rather always be able to corroborate with her own evidence the information of the commissions of inquiry.

This is necessary in light of the strong impact that the issuance of the arrest warrant has on the fundamental rights of an individual, by bringing a restriction to his personal liberty. The deprivation of personal liberty could also last for a long time before the Pre-Trial Chamber decides whether or not to confirm the charges. In addition, an arrest warrant or summons issued by international criminal tribunals may also have strong political implications, when the alleged perpetrator is a political leader.[136] Also, with respect to the application under Article 58, the fact-finding sources should always be corroborated by the Prosecutor's own evidence, considering that the commissions' information is confined to the ascertainment of the contextual elements and actus reus of international crimes, whilst it generally puts little emphasis on the attribution of criminal liability.[137] Indeed, in establishing that the investigated facts amount to international crimes, the fulfillment of further elements of international crimes, such as modes of liability and mens rea, receives very poor attention by fact-finding missions.

[136] See M Marsden and C Chung, 'Reasonable Grounds to Believe: An Unreasonably Unclear Evidentiary Threshold in the Rome Statute' (2015) 13 *Journal of International Criminal Justice* 555, 573.

[137] C Harwood, 'Human Rights in Fancy Dress? The Use of International Criminal Law by Human Rights Council Commissions of Inquiry in Pursuit of Accountability' (2015) 58 *Japanese Yearbook of International Law* 71.

Section 3

Issues in the Substantive Engagement of Commissions of Inquiries with International Law

8

The Interplay between International Human Rights Law and International Humanitarian Law in the Practice of Commissions of Inquiry

MARCO ODELLO

8.1. INTRODUCTION

COMMISSIONS OF INQUIRY are bodies created ad hoc, usually by international organisations, often by the United Nations (UN), sometimes by two or more states, or by a single state.[1] They fit, in part, within the traditional international legal mechanisms that deal with the international solution of disputes.[2] Sometimes they have been identified as fact-finding commissions, which are defined as 'any activity designed to obtain detailed knowledge of the relevant facts of any dispute or situation which the competent UN organs needs in order to exercise effectively their functions in relation to the maintenance of international peace and security'.[3] These activities are mainly aimed at reporting back to the body that established them with the purpose of adopting further action. It seems that these forms of inquiry should mainly identify and clarify the facts rather than adopting specific measures or providing an evaluation of the situation.

However, commissions of inquiry have also been used for more comprehensive activities. According to Bassiouni: 'Commissions of Inquiry are fact-finding mechanisms intended to correct violations of human

[1] See Ch 1.

[2] C Hellestveit, 'International Fact-Finding Mechanisms: Lighting Candles or Cursing Darkness?' in CM Baillet and KM Larsen, *Promoting Peace Through International Law* (Oxford, Oxford University Press, 2015).

[3] UN General Assembly Resolution 46/59, *Declaration on Fact-finding by the United Nations in the Field of the Maintenance of International Peace*, UN Doc A/RES/46/59 (9 December 1991).

rights and humanitarian law by investigating and reporting on a particular situation and providing recommendations to the mandating body'.[4]

This definition seems to identify specific aims and tasks for individual commissions of inquiry. They are mainly focused on violations of international humanitarian law and international human rights law, and their function would include the suggestion of recommendations for the body that established them. In this context, they would perform a kind of quasi-judicial function, with the scope of addressing, and correcting, the violations that they are asked to investigate.

It seems therefore that two main purposes may be given to commissions of inquiry: one is the mere impartial collection of information about the facts that are investigated; the other shows a more proactive role, which may include the collection of evidence, the identification of the law applicable to the facts and potential individual responsibilities, and the possible suggestion of outcomes and solutions. This is also reflected in the wording of the mandates that have established different commissions of inquiry, as will be seen later when considering specific activities of commissions of inquiry.

Commissions of inquiry are set up to consider a variety of situations in a variety of contexts. Sometimes they are established to address the situation within a specific country,[5] and in other cases they address more than one state or territories.[6] Usually, those situations may concern violations of international human rights law and international humanitarian law, particularly in cases of international and non-international armed conflict and internal disturbances, riots and generalised armed violence which may be difficult to classify in international law, due to the fluidity of the events, as the recent situations in Libya and in Syria demonstrated. The initial mandate of the Syrian commission of inquiry did not mention international humanitarian law at all.[7] Therefore, because the types of events under investigation can vary, the reference to legal obligations that may apply to those events may change as well including, in particular, international criminal law.

The present chapter looks at the work that commissions of inquiry do, with a particular attention to their use of international human rights law,

[4] M Cherif Bassiouni and C Abraham (eds), *Siracusa Guidelines for International, Regional and National Fact-Finding Bodies* (Cambridge, Intersentia, 2013) 8.

[5] For instance, UN Human Rights Council Resolution S-2/1, Commission of Inquiry of Lebanon (11 August 2006); UN Human Rights Council Resolution S-15/1, Independent Commission of Inquiry on Libya (25 February 2011); UN Security Council Resolution 2127, Commission of Inquiry for the Central African Republic (5 December 2013).

[6] For instance, UN Security Council Resolution 39, Commission for India and Pakistan (20 January 1948); UN Human Rights Council Resolution 19/17, United Nations Fact-finding Mission on West Bank Settlements (10 April 2012).

[7] UN Human Rights Council, *Situation of Human Rights in the Syrian Arab Republic*, UN Doc A/HRC/RES/S-17/1 (23 August 2011).

international humanitarian law and other related rules and principles, in particular international criminal law, due to the possible consequences of individual criminal responsibility linked to the events under consideration. As these sets of rules are defined under international law, the mandates and the reports of the commissions of inquiry are relevant to see how they refer to, interpret and apply those norms in their work. It is also relevant to mention that the two main sets of international rules, despite the fact that they are well defined in international law, are also the object of discussion with regard to their possible relationship.[8] In particular which rules would apply in borderline situations, when the armed conflict is not clearly recognised, and the possible clash of international humanitarian law and international human rights law may occur? This chapter looks at the possible relationship within the context of commissions of inquiry that have dealt with situations that have been, at a certain point, identified as armed conflict.

This chapter looks at a selection of commissions of inquiry which have addressed situations involving both human rights violations and armed conflict: the Commission of Experts Established Pursuant to Security Council Resolution 780;[9] the Independent Inquiry into the actions of the United Nations during the 1994 Genocide in Rwanda;[10] the International Commission of Inquiry to investigate all alleged violations of international human rights law in the Libyan Arab Jamahiriya;[11] the International Commission of Inquiry on Côte d'Ivoire;[12] and the Independent International Commission of Inquiry on the Syrian Arab Republic.[13] Some other relevant examples include the 'Tagliavini Commission',[14] established by

[8] There is a vast literature on this issue: see, among others, R Arnold and N Quénivet (eds), *International Humanitarian Law and Human Rights Law* (Martinus Nijhoff, 2008); R Kolb and G Gaggioli (eds), *Research Handbook on Human Rights and Humanitarian Law* (Edward Elgar, 2013); GIAD Draper, 'The Relationship between the Human Rights Regime and the Laws of Armed Conflict' (1971) 1 *Israel Yearbook on Human Rights* 191; L Doswald-Beck and S Vité, 'International Humanitarian Law and Human Rights Law' (1993) 94 *International Review of the Red Cross* 293; RE Vinuesa, 'Interface, Correspondence and Convergence of Human Rights and International Humanitarian Law' (1998) 1 *Yearbook of International Humanitarian Law* 69; H-J Heintze, 'On the Relationship between Human Rights Law Protection and International Humanitarian Law' (2004) 86 *International Review of the Red Cross* 798.

[9] *Final Report of the Commission of Experts Established Pursuant to Security Council Resolution 780 (1992)*, UN Doc S/1994/674 (27 May 1994) (*Yugoslavia Final Report*).

[10] *Report of the Independent Inquiry into the Actions of the United Nations During the 1994 Genocide in Rwanda*, UN Doc S/1999/1257 (15 December 1999).

[11] UN Human Rights Council, *Report of the International Commission of Inquiry to investigate all Alleged Violations of International human rights law in the Libyan Arab Jamahiriya*, UN Doc A/HRC/17/44 (1 June 2011) 23 (*First Libya Report*); *Report of the International Commission of Inquiry on Libya*, UN Doc A/HRC/19/68 (2 March 2012) (*Final Libya Report*).

[12] *Rapport de la Commission d'enquête Internationale Indépendante sur la Côte d'Ivoire*, UN Doc A/HRC/17/48 (1 July 2011) (*Ivory Coast Report*).

[13] *Report of the Independent International Commission of Inquiry on the Syrian Arab Republic*, UN Doc A/HRC/27/60 (13 August 2014).

[14] EU Council Decision 2008/901/CFSP (2 December 2008).

the Council of the European Union for the first time, to investigate the conflict in Georgia, and including possible violations of both international humanitarian law and international human rights law. They are not the only ones, of course, but they cover different geographical areas and different periods of time. In particular, the Rwanda and Former Yugoslavia Commissions were actively involved in the developments of international criminal law and led to the creation of international criminal tribunals.

The analysis will focus upon the mandates, the use of relevant provisions, their interpretation and application to the facts, and the conclusions in the final reports of commissions of inquiry. This work will also take into consideration the possible evolution over time of mandates and the ways in which commissions of inquiry have made reference to international human rights law, international humanitarian law and international criminal law, which may affect the application and the interplay between international humanitarian law and international human rights law. This is a still unclear relationship as the two sets of rules may be applicable at different times, in situations of armed violence, when often commissions of inquiry are established to address the types of violations and possible responsibilities of individuals involved in the events. The question is whether, and how, several commissions of inquiry refer to or use the rules of international law that may apply to certain situations, which limitations should they have, if any, and the possible justifications that are provided when using different legal provisions in their reports. Also, it may be useful to see if the work of commissions of inquiry gives some indications, raises problems and provides some perspectives on the interaction between international humanitarian law and international human rights law.

8.2. GENERAL CONSIDERATIONS ON THE EVOLUTION AND ROLE IN APPLYING THE RULES OF INTERNATIONAL LAW

The initial examples of commissions of inquiry have dealt mainly with armed conflict situations, when international human rights law was not even foreseen under international law. An earlier example of a commission of inquiry was the commission to investigate violations of international law committed during the Second Balkan War (1913–14) established by the Carnegie Endowment for International Peace (29 June–10 August 1913).[15]

[15] Carnegie Endowment for International Peace, *Report of the International Commission to Inquire into the Causes and Conduct of the Balkan Wars*, Endowment, Washington DC, 1914, available at archive.org/stream/reportofinternat00inteuoft#page/n0/mode/2up, accessed 14 November 2016.

With the codification and development of international humanitarian law, particularly the four 1949 Geneva Conventions[16] and their two 1977 Additional Protocols,[17] and the adoption of international and regional human rights treaties and protection mechanisms, the problems related to the application of the rules to and by states in situations of armed violence have been acknowledged.[18] In particular, since the insertion of the general prohibition of the use of force among states in Article 2(4) of the UN Charter, the questions related to the legality of the use of force by states has been more relevant. In addition, the development of detailed legal obligations in the field of human rights has been accompanied by a wide number of institutions—either in the form of regional courts or international monitoring bodies—which provide more systematic approaches to the interpretation and application of international human rights law. This evolution has not been accompanied by a parallel development in the assessment of the application of international humanitarian law by states. The International Humanitarian Fact Finding Commission,[19] based on Article 90 of Additional Protocol I to the four 1949 Geneva Conventions, is the only permanent institution that could be used by states in relation to the ascertainment of facts related to international armed conflicts. However, it should be stressed that states have never used its services, and it is also unclear whether the International Humanitarian Fact Finding Commission would be able to assert its competence in dealing with non-international armed conflicts, which are the main cases where today's armed violence tends to occur.

Due to the lack of interest by states in using the International Humanitarian Fact Finding Commission, and with the increasing international concern for the protection of human rights in all situations, the UN has

[16] International Committee of the Red Cross (ICRC), Geneva Convention for the Amelioration of the Condition of the Wounded and Sick in Armed Forces in the Field, 75 UNTS 31; Geneva Convention for the Amelioration of the Condition of Wounded, Sick and Shipwrecked Members of Armed Forces at Sea, 75 UNTS 85; Geneva Convention Relative to the Treatment of Prisoners of War, 75 UNTS 135; Geneva Convention Relative to the Protection of Civilian Persons in Time of War (Fourth Geneva Convention), 12 August 1949, 75 UNTS 287,

[17] Protocol Additional to the Geneva Conventions of 12 August 1949, and Relating to the Protection of Victims of International Armed Conflicts (Protocol I) 1125 UNTS 3; Protocol II Additional to the Geneva Conventions of 12 August 1949 and Relating to the Protection of Victims of Non-International Armed Conflicts (Protocol II), 1125 UNTS 609.

[18] See T Meron, *Human Rights and Humanitarian Norms as Customary Law* (Oxford, Clarendon Press, 1989) in particular Ch III; SR Ratner, JS Abrams, JL Bischoff, *Accountability for Human Rights Atrocities in International Law: Beyond the Nuremberg Legacy* (Oxford, Oxford University Press, 2009); W Abresch, 'A Human Rights Law of Internal Armed Conflict: The European Court of Human Rights in Chechnya' (2005) 16(4) *European Journal of International Law* 741.

[19] See C Garraway, 'The International Humanitarian Fact-Finding Commission' (2008) 34(4) *Commonwealth Law Bulletin* 813; E Kussbach, 'The International Humanitarian Fact-Finding Commission' (1994) 43(1) *International and Comparative Law Quarterly* 174.

gradually established its commissions of inquiry, which over time have, on different occasions, referred to international humanitarian law. They are bodies created mainly by the UN Security Council,[20] the UN Human Rights Council[21] and less frequently by the UN Secretary General[22] and the General Assembly.[23] States[24] and regional organisations[25] have also established different types of bodies that may fit in the general category of commission of inquiry. However, it should be noted that UN bodies have competence in relation to the promotion of international human rights law, which derives from the UN Charter.[26] Different main organs, such as the Security Council,[27] the Human Rights Council,[28] the International Court of Justice,[29] and the UN General Assembly[30] have referred to international humanitarian law in situations of armed conflict. However, the majority of institutions and mechanisms established by the UN are essentially human rights bodies, such as the Human Rights Council, and the various human rights monitoring bodies, such as the conventional human rights committees, and the special rapporteurs.

[20] For example, the Commission of Experts on the former Yugoslavia, established by UN Security Council Resolution 780 (6 October 1992), and the International Commission of Inquiry on Darfur, established pursuant to UN Security Council Resolution 1564 (18 September 2004).

[21] For example, the International Commission of Inquiry on the Libyan Arab Jamahiriya, created by UN Human Rights Council Resolution S-15/1, UN Doc A/HRC/S-15/1 (25 February 2011).

[22] For instance, the International Commission of Inquiry for Togo (2000) and the Panel of Inquiry on the 31 May 2010 Flotilla Incident (2010).

[23] UN General Assembly Resolution 52/135, *Situation of Human Rights in Cambodia* (12 December 1997).

[24] An initial example was the famous 'Maine Inquiry' in 1898, which involved Spain and the United States of America, and the recent Chilcot Inquiry (published on 6 July 2016) on the UK role in the 2003 invasion of Iraq.

[25] For instance, the OAS, Permanent Council, *Report of the Commission of Inquiry into the Events of December 17, 2001, in Haiti*, OEA/Ser.G, CP/INF 4702/02 (1 July 2002) and the 2008 European Union's 'Tagliavini Commission' (n 14).

[26] UN Charter, Arts 1(3), 13, 55, 62(2), 68.

[27] See UN Security Council Resolution 764 (13 July 1992) and UN Resolution 2286 (3 May 2016); UN Resolution 1325 (31 October 2000) and UN Resolution 1820 (19 June 2008) on women; UN Resolution 1612 (26 July 2005) on children. See also M Roscini, 'The United Nations Security Council and the Enforcement of International Humanitarian Law' (2010) 43 *Israel Law Review* 330.

[28] UN Human Rights Council, *Protection of the Human Rights of Civilians in Armed Conflict*, UN Doc A/HRC/RES/9/9 (18 September 2008).

[29] See, in particular, *Military and Paramilitary Activities in and against Nicaragua* (Nicaragua v United States of America), Merits [1986] ICJ Rep 14; *Legality of the Threat or Use of Nuclear Weapons* [1996] ICJ Rep 226; *Armed Activities on the Territory of the Congo* (Democratic Republic of the Congo v Uganda), Judgment [2005] ICJ Rep 168; *Legal Consequences of the Construction of a Wall in the Occupied Palestinian Territory*, Advisory Opinion [2004] ICJ Rep 136, paras 24, 25, 47, 50 and 96.

[30] See UN General Assembly Resolution 2675 (9 December 1970); 46/135 (17 December 1991) and 48/152 (20 December 1993).

Before considering specific examples related to the use of different legal rules of international law,[31] in particular international humanitarian law and international human rights law, applied in the context of commissions' work, it may be relevant to briefly refer to the 'legal framework' or 'competence', that in traditional jurisdictional terms is identified as the competence *ratione materiae*, and defines the legal rules and standards that should be used to assess and evaluate the specific situations that are included in the mandate of each commission of inquiry. As commissions of inquiry are more informal mechanisms than judicial bodies, the competence may also be less restrictive and open to changes, according to the fluctuations of the circumstances on the ground. This set of rules, which may include international human rights law, international humanitarian law and other international law obligations, are initially identified by the body or organ that establishes the commission of inquiry, usually in the form of a resolution, when decided by organs of an international organisation.[32] However, sometimes individual commissions of inquiry, as discussed below, have expanded the types of rules that could be applied to the facts. The legal framework is particularly important in determining which type of rules should be taken into consideration by the individual commissions of inquiry, because they would lead the work of the commissioners and their team of practitioners. Furthermore the legal rules 'inform the types of incidents that the mission will examine, the kinds of information that the mission will gather to demonstrate that violations may have occurred, and the process by which the mission evaluates the data'.[33]

It is possible to identify three types of legal frameworks which may affect the work of each commission. The first one is based on the authority of the body establishing the commission of inquiry. Delegation powers derive from the treaty that created a specific organ, which then may establish subsidiary organs, in the form of commissions of inquiry or fact-finding bodies. The second is based on the mandate which is given to individual commissions of inquiry and which defines their scope and areas of competence. Often the mandate provides a certain time framework, which delimits the competence *ratione temporis*, and sometimes a geographical determination where the facts have occurred (competence *ratione loci*), of each commission of inquiry. All these elements may become relevant in the determination of the applicability of rules of international law, as the application of international humanitarian law would depend on the armed

31 See, in particular, the chapters in this section of the book.

32 For instance: UN Security Council Resolution 1564 (2004) on Darfur, Sudan (18 September 2004), S/RES/1564 (2004), para 12; UN Human Rights Council Resolution S-15/1 (n 21) para 11; Human Rights Council Resolution 16/25, *Situation of Human Rights in Côte d'Ivoire*, (13 April 2011) para 10.

33 R Grace, 'The Design and Planning of Monitoring, Reporting, and Fact-Finding Missions' HPCR (Harvard University, December 2013).

activities of states[34] and, in cases of non-international armed conflict, of the 'threshold' defining the level of violence[35] and organisation of armed groups.[36] More relevant, for the application of international humanitarian law and international human rights law, can be the qualification of actions by individuals and groups, which should be assessed by the commission of inquiry. This activity may become problematic because international human rights law rules, particularly in cases of non-international armed conflicts, as discussed below, may not be applicable to non-state actors which are parties to the conflict.[37]

It is also possible to identify a third legal framework that sometimes is defined by the individual commission of inquiry. Some commissions of inquiry define their terms of reference, and in some cases they tend to expand or interpret the original mandate that established them. For instance, the Commission on Libya decided to include international humanitarian law because the level of violence increased after the original mandate was adopted.[38] This could be considered as a form of *ultra vires* violation, as the commission of inquiry receives its mandate from the organ with the authority to establish it, and the mandate is agreed by the members of the organ. In principle, the commission of inquiry itself does not have a specific authority to determine its own mandate, as it is a subsidiary organ, particularly when it is established by an international organisation.[39] For instance Article 29 of the UN Charter does not provide much detail on the powers of subsidiary organs created by the Security Council. The Human Rights Council Advisory Committee, which was established by the Human Rights Council, has a more detailed structure and definition of its mandate as a subsidiary organ.[40] However, in cases where commissions of inquiry have apparently expanded the rules of international law that they have referred to, as discussed later in this chapter, there has not been any strong reaction or censorship of that decision, in particular when international humanitarian law and international criminal law have been used despite the fact that the mandate referred only to international human rights law, as in the previously-mentioned case regarding Libya.[41]

[34] 1949 Geneva Conventions, Common Art 2.

[35] See the ICTY judgment in *Haradinaj* IT-04-08-T, paras 40–49.

[36] 1949 Geneva Conventions, Common Art 3.

[37] On this issue, see A Clapham (ed), *Human Rights and Non-State Actors* (Cheltenham, Edward Elgar, 2013); WA Schabas, 'Punishment of Non-State Actors in Non-International Armed Conflict' (2002) 26(4) *Fordham International Law Journal* 907.

[38] *First Libya Report* (n 11) 2 and 4; para 4.

[39] See D Sarooshi, 'The Delegation of Powers to UN Subsidiary Organs' in D Sarooshi, *The United Nations and the Development of Collective Security* (Oxford, Oxford University Press, 2000).

[40] UN Human Rights Council Resolution 5/1, *Institution-building of the United Nations Human Rights Council* (18 June 2007).

[41] See also AU Commission of Inquiry on South Sudan, *Final Report of the African Union Commission of Inquiry on South Sudan*, Addis Ababa (15 October 2014) para 10.

This may be linked to the fact that the exact classification of the situation under consideration is often not very clear, and a certain amount of flexibility may be needed to address a variety of circumstances in often very volatile and fast-changing contexts. The fact that commissions of inquiry can adapt more easily to the context which they have to assess may be a positive factor. However, it would be advisable that the mandates should be clearer on the rules that should be considered relevant, as most of the mandates refer generally to international law obligations, without providing more detailed guidelines.

Before looking at more specific examples, it is relevant to mention the debate on the application and relationship between international human rights law and international humanitarian law, and possibly other related rules, as this is the main focus of the analysis in the present chapter.

8.3. INTERPLAY OF HUMAN RIGHTS, HUMANITARIAN LAW AND OTHER LEGAL RULES

The traditional approach of international law has been that the law applicable in the context of armed conflicts is different from the law that applies in peace time. Until the adoption of the two 1977 Additional Protocols[42] the influence and relevance of human rights in the context of international humanitarian law has been quite marginal, as this was considered to be the law applicable in peace time. Despite the potential use of the Martens Clause,[43] in relation to the protection of individuals, and the use of common Article 3 to the four 1949 Geneva Conventions, which provides a basic protection to victims of any type of armed conflict, there has traditionally been a sort of partition between human rights lawyers and humanitarian lawyers. For instance, human rights lawyers have often looked at the use of force and the rules of international humanitarian law as incompatible, or at odds, with the protection of fundamental rights, such as life and property, as defined in the international covenants on human rights.

[42] International Committee of the Red Cross (ICRC), Protocol Additional to the Geneva Conventions of 12 August 1949, and relating to the Protection of Victims of International Armed Conflicts (Protocol I), 8 June 1977, 1125 UNTS 3; Protocol Additional to the Geneva Conventions of 12 August 1949, and relating to the Protection of Victims of Non-International Armed Conflicts (Protocol II), 8 June 1977, 1125 UNTS 609.

[43] Convention (II) with Respect to the Laws and Customs of War on Land and its annex: Regulations concerning the Laws and Customs of War on Land. The Hague, 29 July 1899, Preamble; Convention (IV) respecting the Laws and Customs of War on Land and its annex: Regulations concerning the Laws and Customs of War on Land. The Hague, 18 October 1907. See further VV Pustogarov, 'Fyodor Fyodorovich Martens (1845–1909)—a Humanist of Modern Times' (1996) *International Review of the Red Cross* 300; A Cassese, 'The Martens Clause: Half a Loaf or Simply Pie in the Sky?' (2000) 11(1) *European Journal of International Law* 187.

Meanwhile, international humanitarian law lawyers tend to provide a broad interpretation of military activities 'by reference to the law applicable in armed conflict and not deduced from the terms of the Covenant'.[44] New developments in the characteristics of armed conflict and the idea of a 'global battlefield', sometimes justified in the case of anti-terrorist activities by states, have raised the problem of human rights protection in cases of antiterrorist actions by states which resort to military measures.[45] This has certainly affected the way in which international humanitarian law and international human rights law have been applied by different bodies, and their relevance in the context of modern armed conflicts.

The possible relationship between international humanitarian law and international human rights law has been addressed by academics[46] and by judicial bodies in the past decades, particularly since the discussion of minimum humanitarian standards[47] and with the work of international criminal tribunals in the early 1990s. It is not within the scope of this chapter to provide a detailed discussion of the possible solutions and distinctions that have been formulated. However, it is relevant to provide a short account of the legal debate, so that the analysis of the work of commissions of inquiry can be viewed with regard to the problems that emerge in relation to the applicability of international humanitarian law and international human rights law. It may be useful to look at possible solutions and developments that can be identified in clarifying this relationship through the work of commissions of inquiry, because the problems regarding the possible application of international humanitarian law and international human rights law in very specific situations show the need, if possible, for a clearer definition of the rules that should apply in situations of armed violence, which trigger the application of international humanitarian law.

It is also relevant to remember that the discussion on the application of international humanitarian law has been difficult due to the lack of a

[44] See *Legality of the Threat or Use of Nuclear Weapons*, Advisory Opinion [1996] ICJ Rep 226, 240.

[45] See, for instance, the debate on the topic at the 32nd International Conference of the Red Cross and Red Crescent, 'International Humanitarian Law and the Challenges of Contemporary Armed Conflicts', Report Document prepared by the International Committee of the Red Cross (Geneva, 8–10 December 2015) 15–20.

[46] T Meron, 'The Humanisation of Humanitarian Law' (2000) 94 *AJIL* 239; Y Dinstein, 'Human Rights in Armed Conflict: International Humanitarian Law' in T Meron (ed), *Human Rights in International Law*, vol 2 (Oxford, Oxford University Press, 1986) 346; L Doswald-Beck and S Vité, 'International Humanitarian Law and Human Rights Law' (1993) *International Review of the Red Cross* 94; GIAD Draper, 'Humanitarian Law and Human Rights' (1979) *Acta Juridia* 199; R Emilio Vinuesa, 'Interface, Correspondence and Convergence of Human Rights and International Humanitarian Law' (1998) 1 *Yearbook of International Humanitarian Law* 69; R Provost, *International Human Rights and Humanitarian Law* (Cambridge, Cambridge University Press, 2002).

[47] Institute for Human Rights at Åbo Akademy University, *Declaration on Minimum Humanitarian Standards* (1990), submitted to the UN Sub-Commission on Prevention of Discrimination and Protection of Minorities, UN Doc E/CN/Sub.2/1991/55.

specialised adjudicatory body (either court or tribunal) that can specifically deal with international humanitarian law cases. The International Court of Justice, which has a general competence in the application of international law, has also been limited in its jurisdiction by several states in assessing situations of armed conflict.[48] Other courts, which have dealt with the possible link between international humanitarian law and international human rights law, are regional courts, like the European Court of Human Rights[49] and the Inter-American Human Rights system,[50] which are specialised in the application of human rights, international criminal tribunals, and national courts, which have a more general competence, as it is shown by the extensive case law in UK courts based on the 1998 Human Rights Act and the occupation of Iraq.[51] However, the application of international humanitarian law by international courts has not been as extensive as in the case of human rights law, with the exception of the Inter-American Court, which has affirmed its competence to apply international humanitarian law in related cases, showing that the two types of rules are subject to different types of enforcement.

The discussion on the possible relationship between international humanitarian law and international human rights law has assumed three main positions, as also expressed by the International Court of Justice in the *Wall* opinion.[52] At one extreme is the total reciprocal exclusion: law of peace (international human rights law) and law of war (international humanitarian law) without any possible situation in the middle. At the other extreme is the idea that both human rights and humanitarian law would apply at the same time, blurring the two regimes. A third position considers that international humanitarian law and international human rights law may apply in parallel, depending on the specific circumstances of the case.

The first position is considered outdated. However, the US has tried to use that approach in the justification of Guantanamo Bay exclusion of judicial reviews for detainees in the US military base in Cuba.[53] The other

[48] C Tomuschat, 'Specificities of Human Rights Law and International Humanitarian Law regarding State Responsibility' in R Kolb and G Gaggioli (eds), *Research Handbook on Human Rights and Humanitarian Law* (Edward Elgar, 2013) 198, 200.

[49] ECtHR, *Isayeva, Yusupova and Bazayeava v Russia*, Case No 57947/00, 57948/00 and 57949/00 (24 February 2005), para 171; *Bankovic v Belgium* (2001) 11 BHRC 435, (2007) 44 EHRR SE5.

[50] See Inter-Am CHR, *Juan Carlos Abella v Argentina*, Case No 11.137, Report No 55/97 (18 November 1997), para 271; IACHR, *Bamaca Velazquez v Guatemala*, Judgment, Case No 70 (25 November 2000).

[51] *R (Al-Jedda) v Secretary of State for Defence* [2007] UKHL 58, [2008] 1 AC 332; *R (Al-Skeini) v Secretary of State for Defence* [2007] UKHL 26, [2008] 1 AC 153.

[52] *Legal Consequences of the Construction of a Wall in the Occupied Palestinian Territory*, Advisory Opinion, [2004] ICJ Rep 136, para 106.

[53] Response of the United States to Request for Precautionary Measures—Detainees in Guantanamo Bay, Cuba, 15 April 2002 (2002) 41 *International Legal Materials* 1015.

extreme position seems to forget the specific conditions under which the use of force can be exercised. For instance, under international human rights law any killing, even if committed in combat situations, would be a violation of the right to life, therefore it would not be possible to justify most military actions under international human rights law. The third position has been defined by the International Court of Justice and tries to find a way to manage potentially overlapping regimes, particularly in situations of non-international armed conflict and of military occupation. The International Court of Justice referred to the relationship between the two sets of rules as *lex generalis* (international human rights law) and *lex specialis* (international humanitarian law) in the *Wall* advisory opinion.[54] Several subsequent cases[55] and academic commentaries[56] have usually endorsed this position of the International Court of Justice. However, the decision has attracted some criticism based on the difficulty in an operational context of using both branches of law,[57] and the fact that there is 'a fundamental incompatibility in what the two systems set out to achieve [because] [t]here is no over-reaching axiology, no value system that unifies the objectives of these fields of international law'.[58] The debate on the relationship between the two branches of international law is ongoing and not fully settled. However, it is important to remember that human rights law may be still applicable in situations of armed conflict.[59] Apart from the possible derogation clauses in relation to civil and political rights,[60] other human rights, including economic and social rights, and more specific rights, such as refugee law, would still be applicable as these treaties do not foresee exceptions and derogations in case of armed conflict.

[54] *Legal Consequences of the Construction of a Wall in the Occupied Palestinian Territory*, Advisory Opinion [2004] ICJ Rep 136, 178, para 106.

[55] *Legal Consequences of the Construction of a Wall in the Occupied Palestinian Territory*, Advisory Opinion, [2004] ICJ Rep (9 July), at para 106; *Case Concerning Armed Activities on the Territory of the Congo* (DRC v Uganda) [2005] ICJ Rep 116, para 119; *Al-Skeini v Secretary of State for Defence* [2005] EWCA (Civ) 1609, para 48.

[56] F Hampson, 'The Relationship between International Humanitarian Law and Human Rights Law from the Perspective of a Human Rights Treaty Body' (2008) 90 *International Review of the Red Cross* 558.

[57] M Milanović, 'A Norm Conflict Perspective on the Relationship between International Humanitarian Law and Human Rights Law' (2010) 14(3) *International Conflict & Security Law* 459.

[58] I Scobbie, 'Principle or Pragmatics? The Relationship between Human Rights Law and the Law of Armed Conflict' (2010) 14(3) *International Conflict & Security Law* 449, 450.

[59] ICJ, *Legality or Threat of Use of Nuclear Weapons*, Advisory Opinion [1996] ICJ (8 July 1996), para 25; ICJ, *The Legal Consequences of the Construction of a Wall in the Occupied Palestinian Territory*, Advisory Opinion, 9 July 2004, para 106; ICJ, *Case Concerning Armed Activity on the Territory of the Congo* (n 29) paras 216–220; UN Human Rights Committee General Comment No 31, *Nature of the General Legal Obligation on States Parties to the Covenant*, CCPR/C/21/Rev.1/Add.13 (29 March 2004) para 11.

[60] ICCPR, Art 4, and UN Human Rights Committee, General Comment No 29 (2001), *States of Emergency (Article 4)*, UN Doc CCPR/C/21/Rev.1/Addl11 (2001) para 3.

Finally, it could be argued that there is a trend in some recent international treaties to refer both to international humanitarian law and international human rights law to ensure the protection of individuals, as in the cases of the 1989 Convention on the Rights of the Child[61] and its 2000 protocol,[62] and the Convention on the Rights of Persons with Disabilities.[63] This trend is even more evident in the case of certain international criminal law provisions, such as the prohibition of torture, the prohibition of genocide, the prohibition of slavery and deportation to slave labour and rules on individual accountability, which are customary rules included also in the Rome Statute of the ICC[64] that would be applicable either as crimes against humanity or as war crimes. This means that despite the different categorisation of crimes, under international criminal law certain acts deserve punishment regardless of the specific definition of the situation on the ground.

8.4. THE MANDATES

The mandates that establish each commission of inquiry usually include reference to the type of violations and the legal rules that should be taken into consideration to investigate the facts in the specific situation in hand. It can be pointed out that if commissions of inquiry are bodies that only should address and identify a list of facts, without any specific connotation of the legal elements attached to them, the determination of the law should be less relevant than the facts and the circumstances in which those facts occur. However, it has been noted that there is a trend of 'juridification of the mandates'[65] which is justified on the basis of two elements:

(1) commissions' mandates 'refer to legal standards as a yardstick for collection and evaluation of relevant facts';[66]
(2) commissions of inquiry 'are increasingly expressly mandated to make legal findings and determinations'.[67]

This means that the work of commissions of inquiry should be based on the assessment of facts in relation to the applicable law. However, it

61 Convention on the Rights of the Child, 20 November 1989, 1577 UNTS 3, Art 38.

62 UN General Assembly Resolution 54/263, *Optional Protocol to the Convention on the Rights of the Child on the Involvement of Children in Armed Conflict*, UN Doc A/RES/54/263 (25 May 2000).

63 UN General Assembly Resolution 61/106, *Convention on the Rights of Persons with Disabilities*, UN Doc A/RES/61/106 (24 January 2007) Art 11.

64 Rome Statute of the International Criminal Court, 1 July 2002, 2187 UNTS 3.

65 LJ van den Herik, 'An Inquiry into the Role of Commissions of Inquiry in International Law: Navigating the Tensions between Fact-Finding and Application of International Law' (2014) 13 *Chinese Journal of International Law* 507, 531.

66 van den Herik (n 65) 531.

67 van den Herik (n 65) 531

is quite common that the mandates provide very broad reference to the types of violations and the law which should apply. In some cases there is a general reference to violations of international law, as in the case of the Israel commission concerning the naval blockade of Gaza and the flotilla raid, which was asked to provide:

a. An examination of the security circumstances for imposing a naval blockade on the Gaza Strip and whether the naval blockade complies with the rules of international law.
b. Whether the acts carried out by Israel to enforce the naval blockade on May 31, 2010, complied with the rules of international law.[68]

In some cases there is a reference only to human rights violations, as in the case of Libya, where the resolution asks the Commission 'to investigate all alleged violations of international human rights law in the Libyan Arab Jamahiriya … and, where possible, to identify those responsible',[69] and in the case of Syria, where the mandate repeats the wording used in the case of Libya, but also includes a reference to 'crimes against humanity'.[70]

Early examples of the reference to international humanitarian law can be found in the Commissions of Experts for the former Yugoslavia[71] and for Rwanda,[72] which were asked to gather, examine and analyse information in relation to evidence of violation of international humanitarian law and, in the case of Rwanda, also of possible acts of genocide.

More frequently, when the situation on the ground shows levels of protracted violence, which usually involves armed groups, in the case of non-international armed conflicts, mandates refer to violations of international humanitarian law and require the commission of inquiry to take it into consideration. For instance, the Commission of Inquiry for Timor-Leste, established by the Human Rights Commission, was also asked to compile information on possible human rights and international humanitarian law violations.[73] It seems that this trend is becoming more common than in the past, but there may be several reasons for that, which are discussed below.

Sometimes, there are references to the three areas of international law, international human rights law and international humanitarian law, as

[68] Israel, Resolution 1796 of the 32nd Government 'Appointment of an independent public Commission, chaired by the supreme court judge (ret), Jacob Turkel, to examine the maritime incident of May 31, 2010' (14 June 2010) Art 4.

[69] UN Human Rights Council Resolution S-15/1 (n 21) para 11.

[70] UN Human Rights Council Resolution S-17/1 (n 7) para 13.

[71] UN Security Council Resolution 780 (1992) and the *Yugoslavia Final Report* (n 9) Annex, Section II.

[72] UN Security Council Resolution 935 (1 July 1994) and the *Final Report*, UN Doc S/1994/1125 (4 October 1994) Annex, Section IV.

[73] UNCHR Resolution 1999/S-4/1, International Commission of Inquiry on East Timor, UN Commission on Human Rights (27 September 1999) and UN ECOSOC, decision 1999/293 (15 November 1999).

in the case of the Flotilla inquiry established by the UN Human Rights Council[74] that was asked to 'investigate violations of international law, including international humanitarian law and human rights law, resulting from the Israeli attacks on the flotilla of ships carrying humanitarian assistance'.[75]

These various examples show that there may be difficulties in determining the legal framework that should guide the work of the commission of inquiry. This can be due to the initial unclear situation on the ground, and whether, for instance, an armed conflict has actually started, as in the cases of Libya and Syria. The determination of the existence of an armed conflict is sometimes a difficult task, particularly in the case of non-international armed conflicts. However, it is essential for the application of international humanitarian law[76] to the facts that are investigated by individual commissions of inquiry. In these cases, it is possible to argue that it could be useful to refer to human rights and international criminal law obligations of the parties involved in situations of violence, due to the fact that several rules of both branches may have a customary international law status, which therefore may be applicable to them in unclear situations under international law. As the ICTY pointed out, the use of international human rights law 'is generally a welcome and needed assistance to determine the content of customary international law in the field of humanitarian law. With regard to certain of its aspects, international humanitarian law can be said to have fused with human rights law'.[77] For instance, the prohibition of torture,[78] crimes against humanity[79] and genocide[80] are covered by both branches of law. Sometimes the facts evolve quite quickly before the commission of inquiry has started its work, and the commissioners and experts may have to consider the facts in the light of the new situation, as in the cases of Libya and Syria.

In some cases, the mandate refers also to violations of international criminal law, particularly due to the developments in this area of law since the early 1990s and when the commission of inquiry is asked to identify those individuals who may be responsible for internationally defined

[74] UN Doc A/HRC/RES/14/1.

[75] ibid para 8.

[76] According to Art 6, GC IV: '(t)he present Convention shall apply from the outset of any conflict or occupation …'; see also Additional Protocol I, Art 3(a).

[77] *Kunarac*, IT-96-23-T, Judgment of 22 February 2001, para 467.

[78] J-M Henckaerts and L Doswald-Beck, *Customary International Humanitarian Law* ICRC (Cambridge University Press) vol I, r 90: Torture and Cruel, Inhuman or Degrading Treatment.

[79] ICC Statute, Art 7; M Cherif Bassiouni, *Crimes against Humanity: Historical Evolution and Contemporary Application* (Cambridge, Cambridge University Press, 2011) 186.

[80] ICC Statute, Art 6; UN General Assembly, *Convention on the Prevention and Punishment of the Crime of Genocide*, 9 December 1948, United Nations, Treaty Series, vol 78, p 277, Art 2.

crimes.[81] For instance, the Darfur Commission mandate authorised the mission 'to investigate reports of violations of international humanitarian law and human rights law' and 'determine also whether or not acts of genocide have occurred'.[82]

However, there are some problems in relation to the mandates of commissions of inquiry, in particular, the possible pre-determination that violations have occurred, prior to the establishment of the facts and an investigation. As pointed out by the Flotilla inquiry, which was set up by the Human Rights Council 'to investigate *violations* of international law, international humanitarian and human rights law, resulting from the Israeli *attacks* on the flotilla carrying humanitarian assistance' (emphasis added).[83] In this case the Commission re-interpreted its mandate as being to investigate 'the facts and circumstances surrounding the boarding by Israeli military personnel of a flotilla of ships bound for Gaza and to determine whether in the process violations occurred of international law, including international humanitarian law and human rights law'.[84]

In the case of Syria, different subsequent resolutions were adopted in relation to the mandate of the commission of inquiry. The first one decided to

> dispatch urgently a mission to the Syrian Arab Republic to investigate all alleged violations of international human rights law and to establish the facts and circumstances of such violations and of the crimes perpetrated, with a view to avoiding impunity and ensuring full accountability.[85]

A second resolution decided to

> dispatch urgently an independent international commission of inquiry, to be appointed by the President of the Human Rights Council, to investigate all alleged violations of international human rights law since March 2011 in the Syrian Arab Republic, to establish the facts and circumstances that may amount to such violations and of the crimes perpetrated and, where possible, to identify those responsible with a view to ensuring that perpetrators of violations, including those that may constitute crimes against humanity, are held accountable.[86]

In a subsequent resolution of June 2012, the Human Rights Council asked the Syria commission of inquiry to investigate the specific cases

[81] Commission of Inquiry for the Central African Republic, UN Security Council Resolution 2127 (5 December, 2013); Group of Experts for Cambodia, General Assembly Resolution 52/135 (12 December 1997).

[82] UN Security Council Resolution 1564, UN Doc S/RES/1564 (2004) (18 September 2004) para 12.

[83] Report, UN Doc A/HRC/15/21 (27 September 2010) paras 5–6.

[84] ibid paras 4–7.

[85] UN Human Rights Council Resolution S-16/1 (29 April 2011), UN Doc A/HRC/RES/S-16/1 (4 May 2011), para 7.

[86] UN Human Rights Council Resolution S-17/1 (n 7) para 13.

concerning the killings which occurred in El-Houleh, close to the city of Hom. In the same resolution it referred to the 'responsibility to protect' the population by the Syrian government (paragraph 5), and in paragraph 8 asked the commission to

> urgently conduct a comprehensive, independent and unfettered special inquiry, consistent with international standards [...] and, if possible, to publicly identify those who appear responsible for these atrocities, and to preserve the evidence of crimes for possible future criminal prosecutions or a future justice process.

However, not all the mandates are clear in identifying the rules that should be taken into consideration, and the question is whether a commission of inquiry may take into consideration violations of different areas of international law, including international human rights law, international humanitarian law and international criminal law, when this is not explicitly mentioned in the mandate. This is particularly relevant, because many of the situations which include widespread violations of human rights and humanitarian law may trigger the possible application of international criminal law. The mandates very rarely provide specific guidelines, as in the case of North Korea where specific human rights violations were identified,[87] and usually refer broadly to international law, international human rights law, international humanitarian law and international criminal law, without specific clarification on their possible relationships. Such a broad mandate can be justified by the fact that commissions of inquiry may need a certain degree of flexibility[88] in their work, as they have no authority to take further action after the presentation of their reports. Therefore, it is useful, at this stage, to consider the reports of some commissions of inquiry as they may provide some clarification on this relationship, and how the different sets of rules have been identified and used to provide a qualification of the facts under consideration.

8.5. THE REPORTS

Reports by commissions of inquiry are the main outcome of their work and are submitted to the body which established them. There are no standard rules and formats for the reports. Some are quite short and some are very long. Sometimes only one report is provided to the body which established the mandate, sometimes several reports are published, depending on the length of the mandate, or when mandates are extended

[87] UN Human Rights Council Resolution 22/13, *Situation of Human Rights in the Democratic People's Republic of Korea*, UN Doc A/HRC/RES/22/13 (21 March 2013).

[88] OHCHR, *Commissions of Inquiry and Fact-Finding Missions on International Human Rights and Humanitarian Law: Guidance and Practice* (New York, 2015) 9.

or amended. One relevant feature is that they are made publicly available, compared to other types of fact-finding activities that may require confidentiality, as in the case of the International Humanitarian Fact Finding Commission.[89] The main issue to consider here is how reports reflect the mandates and how different applicable rules of international human rights law and international humanitarian law are used to determine and qualify the facts under investigation.

Reports by commissions of inquiry have referred to the legal obligations of states which they were investigating, because certain states are not bound by some treaties, but may be bound by customary rules of international law.[90] They have also made reference to decisions adopted by the International Court of Justice, often in relation to the definition of applicable international customary law. For example, the Commissions on Darfur[91] and on Sri Lanka[92] referred to the *Nicaragua* case to support the customary nature of common Article 3 to the four 1949 Geneva Conventions.[93] In relation to the principle of distinction under international humanitarian law,[94] the Commissions on Darfur,[95] Gaza,[96] and Libya stated that 'the International Court of Justice in its Advisory Opinion … on … Nuclear Weapons, recognised this principle as "intransgressible" in customary international law'.[97] The Commission on Libya made reference to the *Nuclear Weapons* advisory opinion to reaffirm the customary rule on the prohibition of weapons causing superfluous injury,[98] and the Commission on the Georgia-Russia conflict referred to the *Wall* advisory opinion to underline the customary nature of rules expressed in the Hague Regulations.[99] In this way, the commissions of inquiry have restated the use of customary law principles without further exploring the complex relationship between international humanitarian law and international human rights law.

There may be different reasons why international humanitarian law and international criminal law have been incorporated in the reports of several

[89] 1977 Additional Protocol I, Art 90(5)(c).

[90] *Report of the International Commission of Inquiry on Darfur*, (25 January 2005) paras 165–66 (*Darfur Report*).

[91] *Darfur Report* (n 90) para 157.

[92] *Report of the Secretary-General's Panel of Expert on Accountability in Sri Lanka*, (31 March 2011) para 189.

[93] *Case Concerning Military and Paramilitary Activities in and against Nicaragua* (Nicaragua v United States of America) [1986] ICJ Rep 1, para 218.

[94] Additional Protocol I, Arts 48, 51(2) and 52(2) and Additional Protocol II, Art 13(2).

[95] *Darfur Report* (n 90) para 166, note 79.

[96] UN Human Rights Council, *Report of the United Nations Fact-Finding Mission on the Gaza Conflict*, UN Doc A/HRC/12/48 (25 September 2009) para 430.

[97] *Final Libya Report* (n 11) para 539.

[98] *First Libya Report* (n 11) para 182.

[99] Independent International Fact-Finding Mission on the Conflict in Georgia, Report, vol II (September 2009) 299.

commissions of inquiry, despite the fact that, in their mandates, there was only a general reference to investigate violations of human rights. One of the possible reasons is that certain violations of international human rights law, international humanitarian law and international criminal law are much related areas of international law, as mentioned above. Typical examples are violations, such as rape and torture, which may amount to crimes against humanity and war crimes, depending on the context, the victims and the extent (widespread or systematic practice)[100] of the acts. For instance, the Cote d'Ivoire Commission was mandated to investigate 'allegations of serious abuses and violations of human rights'.[101] However, the final report includes a brief examination of violations of both international humanitarian law[102] and international criminal law[103] in addition to human rights violations. This addition was justified at the beginning of the Report, when defining the legal framework of the commission of inquiry, by the fact that Côte d'Ivoire is a party to most international and regional instruments relating to international human rights law and international humanitarian law.[104] It was later supported by the fact that the commissioners perceived the three types of legal rules to be closely linked.[105] The Commission identified the activities of FDS(-CI) Forces de défense et de sécurité (de Côte d'Ivoire) and FAFN (Forces armées des forces nouvelles) as a non-international armed conflict, to which both common Article 3 GCs and Additional Protocol II would be applicable and determined the specific starting date of the armed conflict (23 February 2011).[106] The Commission also mentioned the possible identification of crimes against humanity (para 91) and war crimes (paras 92–93).[107] The Report refers to the fact that:

> The parties to the conflict together with their auxiliary armed forces violated the provisions of statutory and customary international humanitarian law, in particular the right to life and to the physical integrity of protected persons; in some cases, the protected persons were raped and their property plundered,[108]

and that

> acts committed during the fighting in Abidjan and other towns since late March 2011 are attacks on life and corporal integrity, cruel treatment and torture, and

[100] See, eg, *Naletilić and Martinović* (ICTY Trial Chamber), 31 March 2003, para 236; *Akayesu* (ICTR Trial Chamber), 2 September 1998, para 579.
[101] UN Human Rights Council Resolution 16/25 (n 32) para 10.
[102] *Ivory Coast Report* (n 12) paras 88–90.
[103] *Ivory Coast Report* (n 12) paras 91–93.
[104] *Ivory Coast Report* (n 12) para 10.
[105] *Ivory Coast Report* (n 12) paras 88–93.
[106] *Ivory Coast Report* (n 12) para 88.
[107] Identified as 'serious violations of common article 3 of the four Geneva Conventions of 12 August 1949 within the meaning of article 8 of the Rome Statute' (para 92).
[108] *Ivory Coast Report* (n 12) para 90.

> humiliating and degrading treatment violating the dignity of persons who took no direct part in the hostilities.[109]

In the case of the Libya Commission, two mandates were provided by the Human Rights Council[110] and two reports were submitted.[111] The Commission was mandated only

> to investigate all alleged violations of international human rights law in the Libyan Arab Jamahiriya, to establish the facts and circumstances of such violations and of the crimes perpetrated and, where possible, to identify those responsible […].[112]

UN Security Council Resolution 1970, which was adopted on 26 February 2011 (one day after the creation of the Libya Commission), did not mention the existence of an armed conflict, even if it referred extensively to the arms embargo,[113] asked for the respect of international humanitarian law[114] and referred, for the first time, the investigation to the prosecutor of the International Criminal Court.[115] It was only on 17 March 2011 that the Security Council adopted Resolution 1973, which referred to the 'escalation of violence' and the duty of the Libyan authorities 'to comply with their obligations under international humanitarian law'. It mentioned 'crimes against humanity' and authorised the use of force to protect civilians.[116] Clearly, the wording of the resolutions did not help in clarifying the type of situation in Libya. Reference to the obligation to respect international humanitarian law, but not clearly to the existence of an armed conflict, the reference to crimes against humanity, but not to war crimes, shows that the Security Council may be not always the best place to determine the existence of an armed conflict. This fact may limit the work of individual commissions of inquiry in determining the applicable law for the case.

Philip Kirsch, who chaired the Libya Commission, affirmed that

> we did not think it was stepping outside the mandate. We concluded the broad human rights legal framework encompassed human rights and international humanitarian law as *lex specialis* applicable in times of armed conflicts. Also, the resolution that created the commission required us to establish the facts and

[109] *Ivory Coast Report* (n 12) para 92.

[110] UN Human Rights Council Resolution S-15/1 (n 21), extended by A/HRC/RES/17/17, 17 June 2011.

[111] *First Libya Report* (n 11); *Final Libya Report* (n 11).

[112] UN Human Rights Council Resolution S-15/1 (n 21) para 11.

[113] UN Security Council Resolution 1970, UN Doc S/RES/1970 (2011) (26 February 2011) para 9.

[114] UN Security Council Resolution 1970 (n 113) para 2(a).

[115] UN Security Council Resolution 1970 (n 113) para 4.

[116] UN Security Council Resolution 1973, UN Doc S/RES/1973 (2011) (17 March 2011) para 4.

circumstances not only of human rights violations but also "of the crimes perpetrated", regardless of their nature.[117]

This decision was also justified by the fact that the evolution of the situation over time was not necessarily foreseen at the time when the UN Human Rights Council adopted the initial mandate of the commission. Furthermore, because 'The Commission's temporal mandate is not limited and therefore includes violations before, during and after the demonstrations witnessed in a number of cities in Libya in February 2011',[118] the commission's report noted that an armed conflict developed since February 2011. In its First Report of 1 June 2011, the Commission identified three specific scenarios which could define the situation in Libya and to which different legal rules should be applied:

(1) 'The first demonstrations and Government reaction (from 15 February 2011) took place during a time of peace, requiring analysis on the basis of international human rights law.'
(2) Then, 'a non-international armed conflict had commenced by or around 24 February 2011, bringing into play both international humanitarian law alongside international human rights law'.
(3) A separate coexisting international armed conflict commenced with external military action pursuant to Security Council Resolution 1973 (17 March 2011) 'for which the norms of international humanitarian law relating to international armed conflicts are applicable'.[119]

The Commission justified the determination of the applicable law in the following terms:

> With an armed conflict having developed in late February in Libya and continuing during the Commission's operations, the Commission looked into both violations of international human rights law and relevant provisions of international humanitarian law, the *lex specialis* which applies during armed conflict.[120]

The Commission provided a detailed consideration of the international legal framework that would apply to the situation in Libya,[121] on the basis of the three periods that were identified. It stated, accordingly, 'In legal terms, the periods can be demarked as (i) "peacetime," (ii) "non-international armed conflict" and (iii) "co-existing international armed conflict"'.[122] The Commission, in its Second Report, considered that

[117] Harvard Program CR, Interview with Philippe Kirsch, Chair UN Commission of Inquiry on Libya (22 March 2013) cited in Grace (n 33) 14.
[118] *First Libya Report* (n 11) para 4.
[119] *First Libya Report* (n 11) Executive Summary, 4.
[120] *First Libya Report* (n 11) para 4; in this case, the Commission referred to the definition provided in the *Legal Consequences of the Construction of a Wall in the Occupied Palestinian Territory*, Advisory Opinion [2004] ICJ Rep 178, para 106.
[121] *First Libya Report* (n 11) Section D, paras 60–80.
[122] *First Libya Report* (n 11) para 60.

'[w]ith the end of armed conflict (Phase III), international human rights law became predominant'.[123] These clarifications of different stages, degrees and types of violence contribute to the definition of the application of legal rules, and confirm the idea that international humanitarian law is a *lex specialis*, which can be applied only when specific conditions, concerning the level of violence and organisation of the armed groups, which are defined in international humanitarian law, are met. It could be considered that the determination of these elements, which are based on factual evidence, may be one the main functions of each commission of inquiry when exploring the facts, also because it is an essential precondition, as has been mentioned above, when defining the legal regimes applicable to the facts.

The Libya Commission stated that 'International human rights law continued to apply throughout the period being examined by the Commission, albeit with some potential variation during the period of armed conflict'.[124] This was justified by the fact that Libya did not notify the UN Secretary General of any state of emergency and subsequent derogations made to its obligations under Article 4 of the ICCPR. In the first part of the situation in Libya, the Commission considered that 'Government forces engaged in excessive use of force against demonstrators'[125] and found violations of human rights law, in particular arbitrary deprivation of life,[126] failure to guarantee security of persons[127] and violations of the prohibitions on cruel, inhuman or degrading treatment or punishment of persons.[128] It considered that 'excessive use of force by law enforcement officials (whether police or military or other members of State security forces) impinges on these fundamental guarantees'. It also referred to 'specialised soft law standards, in particular the Code of Conduct for Law Enforcement Officials and the Basic Principles on the Use of Force and Firearms by Law Enforcement Officials'.

In relation to the starting date of the armed conflict, the Commission mentioned documents that were published by two main other institutions, the International Criminal Court Prosecutor[129] and the International Commission of the Red Cross (ICRC),[130] which mentioned that an armed

[123] *Final Libya Report* (n 11) para 5.
[124] *First Libya Report* (n 11) para 68.
[125] *First Libya Report* (n 11) para 99.
[126] ICCPR, Art 6.
[127] ICCPR, Art 9.
[128] ICCPR, Art 7.
[129] International Criminal Court, Office of the Prosecutor, *First Report of the Prosecutor of the International Criminal Court to the UN Security Council Pursuant to UNSCR 1970*, (4 May 2011) para 37.
[130] Jakob Kellenberger, President of the ICRC, stated on 10 March 2011 that a non-international armed conflict existed in Libya but without indicating the commencement date, see ICRC, 'Libya: Urgent to Apply the Rules of War', *News Release 11/53*, 10 March 2011.

conflict was taking place in Libya between the end of February and the beginning of March 2011, underlying also the fact that an exact date for the starting of the armed conflict was difficult to assess. The Commission justified its findings on the basis of the escalation of violence, and on the definition of armed conflict provided by international humanitarian law, international criminal law and the *Tadić* case.[131] The main provision of international humanitarian law is Additional Protocol II to the Geneva Conventions Relating to the Protection of Victims in Non-International Armed Conflict (to which Libya is a party). This refers to conflicts

> which take place in the territory of a High Contracting Party between its armed forces and dissident armed forces or other organized armed groups which, under responsible command, exercise such control over a part of its territory as to enable them to carry out sustained and concerted military operations and to implement this Protocol.

The *Tadić* case referred to 'protracted armed violence between governmental authorities and organized armed groups or between such groups within a State'.[132] Further reference was made to Article 8(2)(f) of the ICC Statute.[133]

The Libya Commission also provided a classification of categories of security groups participating in the events, which were in some way related to the official government of Libya,[134] and also considered the level of organisation and structure of opposition armed groups which intervened in the non-international armed conflict,[135] to determine the possible application of international humanitarian law rules. The commission of inquiry affirmed that it 'reached the preliminary view that by or around 24 February, a non-international armed conflict had developed sufficient to trigger the application of Additional Protocol II and Common Article 3 of the Geneva Conventions'.[136] However, this determination is not supported by adequate findings, as also admitted in the same report,[137] regarding the level of organisation of the opposition group.

[131] *Prosecutor v Tadić*, Jurisdiction Decision, ICTY (Appeals Chamber), Decision of 2 October 1995.

[132] *Prosecutor v Tadić* (n 131) para 70.

[133] ICC Statute, Art 8(2)(f): 'Paragraph 2 (e) applies to armed conflicts not of an international character and thus does not apply to situations of internal disturbances and tensions, such as riots, isolated and sporadic acts of violence or other acts of a similar nature. It applies to armed conflicts that take place in the territory of a State when there is protracted armed conflict between governmental authorities and organized armed groups or between such groups'.

[134] *First Libya Report* (n 11) paras 46–55.

[135] *First Libya Report* (n 11) paras 56–58.

[136] *First Libya Report* (n 11) para 65.

[137] *First Libya Report* (n 11) para 65.

The starting date has been debated in legal writings.[138] However, the role of the commission of inquiry should be to ascertain the facts, and under the relevant provisions of international humanitarian law this may become quite an important issue. It would have been useful if the commission of inquiry could have spent more time clarifying this element in its report. It would be useful to define when the armed conflict started, as this is relevant also in relation to the qualification of certain acts committed by the parties involved. The only certain date provided by the Commission was 19 March 2011, when NATO strikes started,[139] to determine the existence of the international armed conflict between the states of the coalition and Libya.

Due to the fact that NATO and other foreign states involved were 'not exercising control over the military actions of either of the parties to the non-international armed conflict' it concluded that 'the international armed conflict is legally separate to the continuing non-international armed conflict, and is thus a "co-existing international armed conflict"'.[140]

It is also worth noting that a second commission of inquiry subsequently addressed the situation in Libya. Established by the Human Rights Council in 2015,[141] this second mission was asked to address human rights violations and abuses after the end of the Ghaddafi regime,

> to investigate violations and abuses of international human rights law committed in Libya since the beginning of 2014, and to establish the facts and circumstances of such abuses and violations with a view to avoiding impunity and ensuring full accountability.[142]

Also in this case, the commission of inquiry did not limit its legal analysis of the facts to violations of international human rights law, but included also international humanitarian law due to the fact that it considered that there was 'a non-international armed conflict occurring in Libya during the mandate period'.[143] Despite the fact that the report confirms that the Libyan official government has not enacted any state of emergency, it considers that the facts on the ground showed the existence of a non-international armed conflict. However, the report does not mention any specific official document that defines the situation in Libya in 2014–15 as

[138] See K Mačák and N Zamir, 'The Applicability of International Humanitarian Law to the Conflict in Libya' (2012) 14(4) *International Community Law Review* 405; KA Johnston, 'Transformation of Conflict Status in Libya' (2012) 17(1) *Journal of Conflict and Security Law* 9.

[139] Establishment of the 'no-fly zone' over Libya, and authorisation to adopt 'all necessary measures' to protect civilians were included in UN Security Council Resolution 1973 (17 March 2011).

[140] *First Libya Report* (n 11) para 66.

[141] UN Human Rights Council Resolution 28/30 (27 March 2015).

[142] UN Human Rights Council Resolution 28/30 (n 141) para 18.

[143] Investigation by the Office of the United Nations High Commissioner for Human Rights on Libya: detailed findings, UN Doc A/HRC/31/CRP.3 (15 February 2016) para 21.

an armed conflict, but it identified actions that are attributable to various armed groups.[144]

However, from a legal point of view it may be difficult to accept these conclusions, for two main reasons. One is that neither the Libyan government nor the Human Rights Council defined the situation in Libya as a non-international armed conflict. In fact, the Human Rights Council mandate refers to violations of international human rights law and not international humanitarian law. Second, and more importantly, the existence of an armed conflict has to be based on the internationally defined criteria given by international humanitarian law, namely Common Article 3 of the Geneva Conventions and the 1977 Additional Protocol II, supported by the interpretation of international courts, such as the famous *Tadić* case.[145] These criteria include the assessment of the level of violence, the control over a portion of territory by armed groups, 'as to enable them to carry out sustained and concerted military operations',[146] and the level of organisation of the groups. This last element, at least in the interpretation of the *Tadić* case, when applying Common Article 3 of the Geneva Conventions, has become less relevant, as the ICTY considered that 'protracted armed violence between governmental authorities and organized armed groups or between such groups within a State' triggers the application of Common Article 3, but not the Additional Protocol II, that would not apply to armed activities between organised armed groups.[147]

The commission of inquiry seemed to assess the level of violence, which was based on the facts that were investigated, and the control over a certain territory, but the structure and organisation of the armed groups were not adequately addressed. This is probably quite different from what a court or tribunal would do in assessing the existence of an armed conflict, as demonstrated by the case law of the international criminal tribunals.[148] It seems that in this case the commission of inquiry assessed and evaluated the situation on the ground. This was not foreseen by the mandates, which asked the commission of inquiry to collect the facts rather than make a legal qualification of those facts. However, it seems also difficult to define which law would apply to a situation if the situation is not assessed in some way.

As mentioned above, some situations of violence change over time and, due to the nature of international humanitarian law that is applicable only

[144] For a description of the groups see ibid Section IV.

[145] See n 131.

[146] Additional Protocol II, Art 1(1).

[147] *Prosecutor v Tadić* (Decision on the Defence Motion for Interlocutory Appeal) (2 October 1995), IT-94-1, para 70.

[148] For an elaboration of the required degree of organisation, see ICTY, *Prosecutor v Boškoski and Tarčulovski*, Case No ICTY-IT–04–82-T, Judgment (Trial Chamber) (10 June 2008) paras 194–205; ICTY, *Prosecutor v Limaj* (IT-03-66-T) (30 November 2005) paras 94–129.

when an armed conflict occurs, it may be difficult to assess whether or not it applies to specific facts. However, it is not clear if a commission of inquiry can, or should, make such an assessment if the mandate is not explicit on that point. It would be advisable that the organ which establishes the commission of inquiry could either pre-determine the existence of the conflict, and ask the commission of inquiry to apply the relevant law to the facts, or ask the commission of inquiry to determine the existence of the conflict, based on the internationally accepted criteria under international humanitarian law, and then assess the application of the relevant law. Leaving the determination of the existence of the armed conflict to the commission may generate some level of inconsistency among different commissions of inquiry, and also it can attract more criticism by the parties involved in the armed conflict. However, it is also difficult, as mentioned above, to determine the existence of an armed conflict, particularly those of a non-international nature, as states are often politically sensitive about their existence[149] and sometimes deny that such a level of violence exists within their territory.[150] This might limit the explicit reference to international humanitarian law (such as the examples of Libya and Syria), when the decisions of international political bodies are taken to establish commissions of inquiry.

Referring to other legal frameworks, which are related to the sometimes imprecise and broad wording of each mandate, may be crucial to provide a more comprehensive analysis of the facts and violations that may have occurred in the specific circumstances. The reference to international criminal law in relation to Libya was justified by the fact that the first HRC mandate asked the Commission 'to make recommendations, in particular, on accountability measures, all with a view to ensuring that those individuals responsible are held accountable'.[151] The risk of not considering international humanitarian law and international criminal law rules, and their alleged violations, might attract criticism based on the fact that certain violations had not been adequately considered by the commission of inquiry. According to Kirsch, this is a major reason for the reference to legal rules that were not included in the original mandate.[152] Therefore, the justification for these extensions of the legal frameworks that are

[149] For a discussion on different types of armed conflicts, see A Paulus and M Vashakmadze, 'Asymmetrical War and the Notion of Armed Conflict—A Tentative Conceptualization' (2009) 91(873) *International Review of the Red Cross* 95.

[150] For instance, in cases related to Turkey, see 'Letter from Ambassador Türkekul Kurttekin Concerning the Activities of PKK', *Landmine Monitor Report* (15 December 2005); and to Russia in Chechnya, see Report of the Secretary General, *Children and Armed Conflict*, UN Doc A/58/546-S/2003/1053 (10 November 2003) para 61.

[151] UN Human Rights Council Resolution S-15/1 (n 21) para 11.

[152] Harvard Program CR, interview with Philippe Kirsch, Chair UN Commission of Inquiry on Libya (22 March 2013), cited in Grace (n 33) 14.

considered by commissions of inquiry could be based on completeness of the final report, to avoid criticism, and therefore to attract more credibility in relation to their work.

Finally, it may be worth looking at the composition of commissions of inquiry to determine the format and content of their reports. Individuals who are appointed as commissioners have different backgrounds and experiences. They include diplomats, politicians, legal experts and academics. Some may be human rights activists and others may have military backgrounds. It may be possible to infer that the knowledge and professional experience of the commissioners could influence the way reports are drafted, and how different branches of international law are taken into consideration. For instance, it is difficult not to link the detailed analysis of legal rules that would apply to the situation in Darfur, with plenty of footnotes referring to international criminal law cases,[153] to the fact that Antonio Cassese, academic and international judge, was chairing the commission of inquiry. Similarly, the definition of the legal framework applicable in Libya and the inclusion of international humanitarian law and international criminal law,[154] the list of violations under specific headings,[155] may have been influenced by the presence of Cherif Bassiouni in the first commission of inquiry on Libya. The report on the Conflict in Georgia shows a much more detailed technical analysis of the facts and legal framework of the events, particularly on the analysis of the rules of international law related to armed conflict,[156] probably due to the fact that the conflict was involving two States and that several legal experts had been involved in the preparation of the report. However, even in this report the relationship between international humanitarian law and international human rights law has not been further explored, apart from the general reference to the *lex specialis* role of international humanitarian law.[157]

8.6. CONCLUSIONS REGARDING THE USE OF INTERNATIONAL HUMAN RIGHTS LAW AND INTERNATIONAL HUMANITARIAN LAW BY COMMISSIONS OF INQUIRY

It seems that there is not a consistent pattern in mandates regarding the legal rules that should be used by commissions of inquiry. Sometimes there is a general reference to violations of international law. Often there is

153 *Darfur Report* (n 90) 40–53.
154 *First Libya Report* (n 11) paras 60–80.
155 *First Libya Report* (n 11) paras 81–235.
156 Independent International Fact-Finding Mission on the Conflict in Georgia, Report, vol II (September 2009) 99–294.
157 ibid 318.

a general reference to violations of international human rights law. Sometimes there is a reference also to international humanitarian law and international criminal law. This variety of options is present in mandates and reports by commissions of inquiry, which usually deal with situations that show widespread violations of human rights. The reference to international humanitarian law is more frequent when an armed-conflict situation is already identified, either by the UN Security Council or by some other international institution, in particular the International Committee of the Red Cross.

Sometimes mandates are subsequently amended or expanded, including reference to international humanitarian law due to the evolution of the situation over time. In other cases, the original mandates are kept as they were originally formulated, but the members of the commission of inquiry re-interpret or somehow expand their original mandate to include also international humanitarian law and/or international criminal law due to the fact that the type of events and violence lead to the escalation of the conflict, which may therefore fit into new legal categorisations.

In some cases, commissions of inquiry have not spent too much time on determining the type of armed conflict which they are supposed to address, and have focused on the types of violations. In other cases, the commission of inquiry has investigated in much more detail the elements of the armed conflict, as in the case of Syria. This raises different issues in relation to the powers of commissions of inquiry, as already mentioned. A first question is whether the commissions of inquiry can, or should, determine the existence of an armed conflict. This may depend on the mandate. However, if the situation in the specific country is changing, should the commission of inquiry wait for a new mandate or, either implicitly or explicitly, interpret its mandate and include in its terms of reference the possible determination of the existence of an armed conflict, based on the facts which are under its consideration? Would this lead to an *ultra vires* situation, as the body acts beyond its mandate? Or to a necessary fine-tuning of the powers that derive from the function of the commission of inquiry?

The conclusion would depend very much on the nature and purpose of the commission of inquiry. If the commission has been established only with the scope of registering and collecting facts, which should be reported back to the body that established it, without any determination of possible responsibilities and accountability for the violations, the determination of the existence of an armed conflict, its classification and the rules applicable to it, would probably exceed its mandate.

However, if the original mandate referred to broader functions, including the determination of violations of international law (which may include international human rights law, international humanitarian law and international criminal law), and the possible identification of individuals

responsible of those violations, then the commissions of inquiry should be allowed to determine the facts and also the legal qualification of the situation on the ground. Depending on the legal rules which are applicable to the case and to the facts, there could be different outcomes and responsibilities, particularly for those individuals allegedly involved in the commission of international crimes. Also, in relation to the type of evidence and witnesses that should be collected, if a criminal prosecution could follow, special attention should be paid to collecting information according to international standards for criminal investigation.[158]

This apparent logical paradigm, however, may face some criticism. If the function of the commission of inquiry is mainly to collect information, including a factual account of events, it might be exceeding its powers when using different sources of international law, as it might become a sort of adjudicatory or quasi-judicial body, as it would apply the law to the facts. If this is the case, or at least the trend in more recent commissions of inquiry, as the examples provided seems to show, it is relevant to determine which legal rules should be applied by the commission of inquiry. This strict approach applies to international judicial bodies to define their jurisdiction *ratione materiae*. Should the commissions of inquiry therefore be regulated and subjected to the same type of legal conditions and limitations? If the mandate refers generally to possible 'violations of international law', should each commission define, at the very outset of its work, the legal rules that it is going to apply, depending on its determination of the facts in the specific context? If commissions of inquiry may expand the rules that are taken into consideration, could they also refer, for instance, to other specific areas of international law, like refugee law or environmental law? But this is not the main area of this chapter and will not be discussed further. However, it is important to notice that this is a possible issue of concern and should be properly addressed when determining the future perspectives, powers, mandates and functions of commissions of inquiry.

As far as international human rights law and international humanitarian law are concerned, the theoretical and practical distinctions in legal regulations may present some problematic issues when used by commissions of inquiry:

- the application of international humanitarian law presupposes the existence of an armed conflict;
- if a state of emergency has not been declared in the territory under consideration, or security operations are conducted using armed force, the full application of international human rights law is, in

[158] See Chs 5–7.

theory, still valid (see the case law of the European Court of Human Rights in the Turkish and Chechen cases);[159]

— the application of international humanitarian law may be limited to some areas of the territory of the state, as it may be applicable only where the actual armed conflict activities are taking place;
— however, could the commission of inquiry determine the existence of an armed conflict, due to the fact that the existence of an armed conflict is not a matter of law (and on the acceptance by the parties to the conflict) but is based on factual elements, based on the GCs and the Additional Protocols?
— in relation to criminal accountability, which is increasingly used in commissions' mandates, including the possible identification of individuals responsible for those crimes, it is true that most international crimes can be committed either in peace or in conflict situations. However, war crimes and grave breaches of international humanitarian law are necessarily based on the existence of an armed conflict, so it may be relevant to determine the existence of the conflict;
— the commissions of inquiry, when justifying the reference and expansion of their legal standards to international humanitarian law, have referred to the *lex specialis* nature of that branch of law, as defined in the International Court of Justice case law (ie *The Wall* advisory opinion). It is often said that international humanitarian law and international human rights law should be used in the same context, on the basis of increasing interplay and, possibly, convergence. Commissions of inquiry have not further elaborated on those concepts. However, some of the reports show that it is difficult to divide the two branches of international law, and they should both be considered in situations of armed conflict;
— finally, it may be relevant to underline the fact that the investigation should be conducted in a fair and, as far as possible, impartial way. It would be particularly important that experts and personnel involved in the investigation were experts in international humanitarian law and not only in international human rights law. Otherwise, this could 'lead to distortion with respect to the evaluation of the lawfulness of the conduct of military operations'.[160]

[159] See, for instance, ECtHR, *Ergi v Turkey*, Application No 23818/94 (Judgment 28 July 1998) para 7; *Varnava v Turkey*, Application Nos 16064/90, 16065/90, 16066/90, 16068/90, 16069/90, 16070/90, 16071/90, 16072/90 and 16073/90 (Judgment 18 September 2009) para 185; *Akhmadov v Russia*, Application No 21586/02 (Judgment 14 November 2008) paras 9–16, 86–88, 91, 97.

[160] M Frulli, 'Fact-Finding or Paving the Road to Criminal Justice?' (2012) 10 *Journal of International Criminal Justice* 1323, 1326; see also T Boutruche, 'Credible Fact-Finding and Allegations of International Humanitarian Law Violations: Challenges in Theory and Practice' (2011) 16(1) *Journal of Conflict and Security Law* 105.

In conclusion, it could be suggested that two types of bodies might be identified, depending on their role. A purely fact-finding body could be defined as a body that exclusively looks at the facts. Those facts should be included in a report, which would then be used by the mandating institution, and which could provide a legal qualification of the facts. A commission of inquiry, or more investigative body, could be established when specific violations are identified, and the assessment of the situation on the ground is more clearly defined, including the existence of an armed conflict, which would involve the application of international humanitarian law.

However, this formal subdivision may be counterproductive, as the monitoring and fact-finding bodies have been conceived as quite informal institutions, when compared to adjudicatory bodies. Therefore, it could be useful to give them a broad mandate, with the idea that the same body, or the mandating organ, can change their competence, depending on the changes of the facts on the ground. It could be left to individual commissions of inquiry to qualify the facts, and to justify their use of different branches of international law. This could be done by defining this power more clearly in the mandate, and by providing the commission of inquiry with the necessary expertise in international humanitarian law and international human rights law, and possibly international criminal law, so that the criteria identified in the reports are properly applied to the facts that are analysed. This would avoid the possible risk of *ultra vires* accusations, as the evolution of the situation should imply a change in the rules that would apply to the facts. Certainly, what can be seen from the practice of commissions of inquiry is that the two branches of international humanitarian law and international human rights law tend to be used in a variety of contexts, particularly when the situation on the ground shows a certain level of violence. It may be difficult to distinguish the applicability of the two branches, in particular when international criminal law should be considered as a possible remedy for the prosecution of individuals involved in the violations. This supports the idea that both branches of international law have been developed to protect the rights of persons affected by a conflict and that international human rights law and international humanitarian law 'are complementary and mutually reinforcing'.[161]

161 UN Human Rights Council, *Outcome of the Expert Consultation on the Issue of Protecting the Human Rights of Civilians in Armed Conflict: Report of the United Nations High Commissioner for Human Rights*, A/HRC/11/31 (4 June 2009) para 5.

9

Laying the Foundations: Commissions of Inquiry and the Development of International Law

SHANE DARCY

9.1. INTRODUCTION

COMMISSIONS OF INQUIRY are a common feature of the present international legal and political system and have frequently been deployed since the emergence of international law as a means for regulating international affairs. Although primarily concerned with the establishment of facts, such entities will often engage with international law, either by choice or design. While commissions of inquiry for the most part have tended to adhere to conventional interpretations and understandings of international law, there may have been times where such bodies can be said to have contributed to the substantive development of international law. In particular, the legal analysis conducted by fact-finding bodies created prior to the establishment of international criminal tribunals in the past century can be said to have had some influence on the drafting of their constitutive instruments and provided a useful resource for the judges sitting in the subsequent trials. Fact-finding by a commission of inquiry, and the attendant application of international law to those facts, has been a precursor to many contemporary international criminal trials. Nonetheless, the value to be ascribed to their factual and legal findings by judicial bodies remains somewhat contested.

This chapter draws on a number of prominent examples of commissions of inquiry to assess whether they can be considered to have made a contribution to the development of international law, specifically international criminal law. It considers illustrative instances of the application of international law by the Commission on the Responsibility of the Authors of the War and on the Enforcement of Penalties (1919), the United Nations War Crimes Commission (1943–48) and the Commission of Experts established by the Security Council to examine alleged

violations of international humanitarian law in the Former Yugoslavia (1992–94). The question of whether commissions of inquiry can be said to have developed, rather than merely applied, international law, is the central concern of this chapter. Consideration will first be given to the legal weight to be ascribed to the findings of commissions of inquiry within the international legal system, before turning to an examination of the three chosen commissions. These examples have been selected primarily because these commissions operated at the beginning of periods that have proven significant for the development of international law, particularly international criminal law. The chapter's analysis will draw upon the jurisprudence of relevant international courts and tribunals, and other sources of international law, in considering the contribution of commissions of inquiry to the development of international law.

9.2. COMMISSIONS OF INQUIRY AND INTERNATIONAL LAW

Commissions of inquiry serve to provide a factual account of disputed events, but are often accompanied by legal analysis which can inform and guide subsequent political, legal and even judicial undertakings. While in theory, 'fact-finding commissions should not engage with law at all', there is an increasing 'juridificiation or even criminalization' of the work of commissions of inquiry.[1] For example, the International Commission of Inquiry on Darfur, established by the United Nations (UN) to examine reports of violations of international human rights and humanitarian law, undertook an analysis of the facts through the lens of international criminal law, which it acknowledged was 'an approach proper to a judicial body', even though the Commission was clearly not such an entity.[2] Given the mandates of contemporary commissions of inquiry, the application and therefore interpretation of international law can hardly be avoided. Legal knowledge and expertise are essential requirements for the fulfillment of the mandates of commissions of inquiry. Théo Boutruche has stated that it is 'virtually impossible to conduct fact-finding without knowledge of the law because it is only through legal expertise that one can select the relevant facts from the huge quantity of information around a given incident'.[3] As the examples below will demonstrate, commissions of inquiry have

[1] LJ van den Herik, 'An Inquiry into the Role of Commissions of Inquiry in International Law: Navigating the Tensions between Fact-Finding and Application of International Law' (2014) 13 *Chinese Journal of International Law* 507, 508.

[2] *Report of the International Commission of Inquiry on Darfur to the United Nations Secretary-General* (Geneva, 25 January 2005) para 14 (*Darfur Report*).

[3] T Boutruche, 'Selecting and Applying Legal Lenses in Monitoring, Reporting and Fact-Finding Missions', *HPCR Working Paper* (October 2013) 1.

not limited their use of international law to a framework for the establishment of relevant facts. They have also engaged in detailed analysis of the law itself, at times offering progressive interpretations of its scope and content, and even suggesting novel legal means of accountability.

The approach of contemporary commissions of inquiry to the application and interpretation of international law is said to be 'generally fairly flexible and progressive'.[4] Aspects of their reports might be seen to progressively develop the law on a range of matters, such as the application of international human rights law to non-state actors, the joint application of international humanitarian and human rights law during armed conflict and the interpretation of international crimes.[5] Such claims are heard frequently, even though practitioners in the field of fact-finding, monitoring and reporting have demonstrated a 'cautious approach' to participating in the development of international law.[6] Research by Boutruche reveals that a significant majority of such individuals felt that

> as a matter of principle, [monitoring, reporting and fact-finding] bodies should not engage in any progressive development of international law, nor would MRF actors decide on a progressive interpretation with regard to an unsettled area of international law. The interviewees stressed the critical need to apply existing law to avoid unnecessary critiques and to ensure the credibility and legitimacy of the mission's findings.[7]

Strict adherence to this principle is challenged by fact-finders being tasked with inquiring into the alleged commission of international crimes, and the attendant range of legal issues with which commissions are confronted. This difficulty was even more pronounced in the past when international law itself was far less developed, with recourse often made to ever-changing customary international law. Contemporary commissions of inquiry have had a tendency 'to shy away from customary law, except when practitioners felt required to rely on this source of law due to a lack of applicable treaty provisions'.[8]

The legal analyses to be found in the reports of commissions of inquiry may prove to be a useful resource, particularly where the subject matter they have engaged with has not been previously addressed by an official body. Amongst the formal sources of international law, reports of commission of inquiry would seem comparable to those set out in Article 38(1)(d) of the Statute of the International Court of Justice, which describes 'judicial

[4] van den Herik (n 1) 533.

[5] Boutruche (n 3) 20–21; van den Herik (n 1) 534–35; T Rodenhäuser, 'Progressive Development of International Human Rights Law: The Reports of the Independent International Commission of Inquiry on the Syrian Arab Republic' (*EJIL: Talk!* 13 April 2013).

[6] Boutruche (n 3) 15.

[7] ibid, 21.

[8] ibid, 15.

decisions and the teachings of the most highly qualified publicists of the various nations, as subsidiary means for the determination of rules of law'. Commissions of inquiry might be considered as a hybrid of these recognised subsidiary sources. Their approach is quasi-judicial, in that they comprise a detached assessment of facts through the lens of applicable international legal standards, and the analysis is often undertaken by leading jurists in the field of international law.[9] The reports produced by commissions of inquiry may 'inadvertently wind up serving jurisprudential purposes' if they have addressed disputed or uncertain international law questions.[10] That being said, while the reports of contemporary commissions are frequently described as authoritative,[11] international courts have been quite conservative when it comes to relying upon their findings. Judge Ušacka of the International Criminal Court commented that the legal conclusions of such commissions 'may be relevant only by analogy', in the same way that the jurisprudence of the ad hoc tribunals 'is not directly applicable before this Court without "detailed analysis"'.[12] van den Herik and Harwood have similarly put it that:

> no immediate precedential value should be attached to detailed legal findings of commissions of inquiry. [...] legal findings and interpretations from commissions of inquiry can only be transposed to the context of a criminal trial with a certain care and diligence.[13]

Although the legal findings of contemporary commissions of inquiry are less commonly relied upon by international courts and tribunals, the historical examples outlined below proved more influential on subsequent legal developments. The explanation may lie in the fact that members of the two earlier commissions comprised representative of states and thus acted on their behalf within the commissions. Accordingly, these bodies might not meet the standards espoused for fact-finding bodies today, in that they were not independent, and neither were they impartial, given that the states they represented were mostly the Allied nations.[14] An

[9] See D Akande and H Tonkin, 'International Commissions of Inquiry: A New Form of Adjudication?' (*EJIL: Talk!* 6 April 2012).

[10] Boutruche (n 3) 21.

[11] M Frulli, 'Fact-Finding or Paving the Road to Criminal Justice? Some Reflections on United Nations Commissions of Inquiry' (2012) 10 *Journal of International Criminal Justice* 1323, 1329.

[12] *Prosecutor v Al Bashir*, Case No ICC-02/05-01/09, Pre-Trial Chamber I, (Decision on the Prosecution's Application for a Warrant of Arrest against Omar Hassan Ahmad Al Bashir, Separate and Partially Dissenting Opinion of Judge Anita Ušacka) (4 March 2009) para 6 (footnotes omitted).

[13] LJ van den Herik and C Harwood, 'Sharing the Law: The Appeal of International Criminal Law for International Commissions of Inquiry', *Grotius Centre Working Paper 2014/016-ICL* (2014), 2–3.

[14] See, for example, UN General Assembly Resolution 46/50, *Declaration on Fact-finding by the United Nations in the Field of the Maintenance of International Peace and Security*, UN Doc A/RES/46/59 (9 December 1991).

analysis of their work is relevant, nevertheless, to understanding how the reception given to the legal findings of commissions of inquiry often depends on the extent to which such holdings align with the views of the states or authorities that have created them.

9.3. COMMISSION ON THE RESPONSIBILITY OF THE AUTHORS OF THE WAR AND THE ENFORCEMENT OF PENALTIES (1919)

Prior to the First World War, official commissions of inquiry, such as those envisaged by the 1899 Hague Convention on the Peaceful Settlement of Disputes, were usually concerned with relatively minor incidents—'differences of an international nature involving neither honor nor vital interests, and arising from a difference of opinion on points of fact', as the 1899 Convention put it.[15] The International Commission to Inquire into the Causes and Conduct of the Balkan Wars, established in 1913, marked a departure from previous approaches, although it was not created by states, but rather by the Carnegie Endowment for International Peace.[16] This Commission drew heavily on international law in its consideration of the lawfulness of the resort to armed force in the Balkans, the treatment of prisoners of war and other practices as occurred during the conflict.[17] The Commission also foresaw and advocated for the deployment of commissions of inquiry during times of war by states:

> Were it possible for there to be a commission of inquiry with the belligerent armies, during war, not in the shape of an enterprise provided by a private initiative, but as an international institution, dependant on the great international organization of governments, which is already in existence, and acts intermittently through Hague Conferences, and permanently through the Hague Tribunal,—the work of such a body would possess an importance and a utility such as cannot attach to a mere private commission.[18]

A standing commission of inquiry along these lines, the report stated, 'could foresee offences, instead of condemning them after they take place'.[19] No such international mechanism was to operate during the First World War.

[15] Convention (I) for the Pacific Settlement of International Disputes (Hague I), 29 July 1899, Art 9.

[16] *Report of the International Commission to Inquire into the Causes and Conduct of the Balkan Wars*, Carnegie Endowment for International Peace (Washington DC, 1914) (*Report of the Commission on the Balkans War*). See further F Trix, 'Peace-mongering in 1913: the Carnegie international commission of inquiry and its report on the Balkan wars' (2014) 5 *First World War Studies* 2, 147.

[17] *Report of the Commission on the Balkans War* (n 16) 208–34 (Chapter 5: 'The War and International Law').

[18] ibid, 234.

[19] ibid.

After the War, and continuing with the retrospective approach of commissions of inquiry of the time, the Commission on the Responsibility of the Authors of the War and the Enforcement of Penalties was created by a decision adopted at the Paris Peace Conference on 25 January 1919. The Commission was comprised of 15 members, two representatives each from the United States, Britain, France, Italy and Japan, and the five remaining members representing Belgium, Greece, Poland, Romania and Serbia.[20] The Commission was tasked with inquiring and reporting on the following:

1. the Responsibility of the authors of war;
2. the facts as to the breaches of the laws and customs of war committed by the forces of the German Empire and their Allies, on land, on sea and in the air during the present war;
3. the degree of responsibility for these offences attaching to particular members of the enemy forces, including members of the General Staffs and other individuals, however highly placed;
4. the Constitution and procedure of a tribunal appropriate to the trial of these offences; and
5. any other matters cognate or ancillary to the above which may arise in the course of the enquiry, and which the Commission finds it useful and relevant to take into consideration.[21]

With such a mandate, the 1919 Commission was required not only to consider existing international law, primarily the laws and customs of war, but also to propose how the law might evolve in the context of a potential judicial mechanism to try offences. Although the proposals put forward by the Commission were partially reflected in the Treaty of Versailles, and other subsequent legal developments, there was considerable divergence amongst the Commission's members on some of the key legal questions with which it was confronted.

The 1919 Commission issued its report on 29 March 1919, a little over two months after it had been brought into existence. The report's annexes included memorandums from both the United States and Japanese representatives, outlining their reservations to the findings of the majority. The legal innovations which the majority put forward were at times a departure from the admittedly rudimentary international law which existed at the time, even though in many respects they have now become part and parcel of the modern international legal landscape, albeit with some refinement. Key contested issues the Commission debated included the

[20] 'Commission on the Responsibility of the Authors of the War and on the Enforcement of Penalties, Report Presented to the Preliminary Peace Conference, March 19, 1919' (1920) 14 *American Journal of International Law* 95–96 (*1919 Commission Report*).

[21] ibid, 95.

proposal that an international tribunal be established, that heads of state should not be immune from prosecution and that high-ranking officials could be criminally responsible for the acts of their subordinates. The Commission included in its list of violations of the laws and customs of war practices which had not previously been explicitly outlawed, and the majority drew criticism, from the United States in particular, for suggesting the laws of humanity as a legal basis for criminal prosecution.

9.3.1. Head of State Immunity

The 1919 Commission's majority report began its discussion on the subject of criminal responsibility by dismissing the idea that 'rank, however exalted, should in any circumstances protect the holder of it from responsibility when that responsibility has been established before a properly constituted tribunal'.[22] This would extend to heads of state, in the Commission's view, as to conclude otherwise would lay down a principle that some of the 'greatest outrages' ever committed could go unpunished.[23] This would 'shock the conscience of civilized mankind'.[24] Removing head of state immunity in this way was certainly an innovation in international law and one with which the United States members disagreed. Doing so would impose 'a degree of responsibility hitherto unknown to municipal or international law, for which no precedents are to be found in the modern practice of nations'.[25] The drafters of the Treaty of Versailles were persuaded by the majority, however, with the former German Emperor arraigned under Article 227 'for a supreme offence against international morality and the sanctity of treaties'.[26] According to the treaty, William II was to be tried by a 'special tribunal' made up of five judges, one from each of the Great Powers. This was a modification of the 1919 Commission's proposal for 'a high tribunal composed of judges drawn from many nations'.[27] The Japanese members had raised questions about this suggestion, while the United States members argued that there was a lack of precedent for creating 'an international criminal court for the trial of individuals'.[28] The Treaty of Versailles entailed a watered-down version of the

22 ibid, 116.
23 ibid.
24 ibid.
25 ibid, 135.
26 Treaty of Versailles, 28 June 1919, Art 227.
27 *1919 Commission Report* (n 20) 122.
28 ibid, 145, 151–52. See further H Rhea, 'The Commission on the Responsibility of the Authors of the War and on Enforcement of Penalties and its Contribution to International Criminal Justice after World War II' (2014) 25 *Criminal Law Forum* 147, 164.

Commission's proposed tribunal, one which never come into existence in any event.[29]

9.3.2. Command Responsibility

The 1919 Commission also addressed the question of the criminal responsibility of superiors for offences committed by subordinates. In doing so, according to a leading text on international criminal law, the majority report of the Commission contains '[t]he foundation of the modern law of command responsibility'.[30] The majority considered that the German Emperor and others 'in high authority' were aware of violations taking place and they could 'at least have mitigated the barbarities committed during the course of the war'.[31] With regard to violations of the laws and customs of war, the majority recommended charges against

> all authorities, civil or military, belonging to enemy countries, however high their position may have been, without distinction of rank, including the heads of states, who ordered, or, with knowledge thereof and with power to intervene, abstained from preventing or taking measures to prevent, putting an end to or repressing, violations of the laws or customs of war.[32]

The United States members refused to agree to this 'doctrine of negative criminality',[33] and stated in their memorandum of reservations that the delegation was 'unalterably opposed' to this form of liability:

> It is one thing to punish a person who committed, or, possessing the authority, ordered others to commit an act constituting a crime; it is quite another thing to punish a person who failed to prevent, to put an end to, or to repress violations of the laws and customs of war. In one case the individual acts or orders others to act, and in doing so commits a positive offence. In the other he is to be punished for the acts of others without proof being given that he knew of the commission of the acts in question or that, knowing them, he could have prevented their commission.[34]

The Japanese members emphasised the importance of strict interpretation in the context of penal law, as they opposed 'abstention' as a basis for criminal liability for war crimes.[35] Although the 1919 Commission's

[29] JN Maogoto, *War Crimes and Realpolitik: International Justice from World War I to the 21st Century* (Boulder, Lynne Rienner, 2004) 56.

[30] R Cryer, H Friman, D Robinson and E Wilmshurst, *An Introduction to International Criminal Law and Procedure* (3rd edn, Cambridge, Cambridge University Press, 2014) 384.

[31] *1919 Commission Report* (n 20) 117.

[32] ibid, 121.

[33] ibid, 129.

[34] ibid, 143.

[35] ibid, 152.

majority report provided an authoritative conceptual basis for superior responsibility, its recommendations on this count were not reproduced in the Treaty of Versailles, nor relied upon in the so-called *Leipzig* trials which followed. Nonetheless, the doctrine of superior responsibility has become well-established in international law.[36]

9.3.3. Substantive Law

In addition to its innovative approach as to who could be prosecuted, and how this might be done, the 1919 Commission also sought to identify, in both factual and legal terms, what might form the substance of such prosecutions. The Commission devised a list of violations of the laws and customs of war and the laws of humanity which illustrated how Germany and its allies had 'piled outrage upon outrage' during the First World War.[37] The list of 32 violations drew on existing treaties, customary law and the 'dictates of the public conscience', a phrase taken from the Martens clause of the Hague Regulations. The Commission's view that these acts were punishable is in itself significant, given that the existing treaties of international humanitarian law had not expressly provided for criminal liability. Moreover, the list included violations that states had not prohibited in the clearest terms when drafting such treaties. The Hague Regulations were deliberately silent on the common wartime practice of hostage-taking for example, yet the 1919 Commission included 'putting hostages to death' as one of the violations of the laws and customs of war committed during the War.[38] The list of violations also addressed sexual violence more forthrightly than the law of war itself had, listing rape and the abduction of women and girls for enforced prostitution as violations.[39] The imposition of collective penalties was also designated as an offence for the first time, despite the ambiguous nature of the rule in Article 50 of the Hague Regulations.[40]

The United States took issue with the majority's invocation of the laws of humanity in compiling the list of violations because this meant the Commission exceeded its given mandate and it also raised concerns regarding

[36] See, for example, G Mettraux, *The Law of Command Responsibility* (Oxford, Oxford University Press, 2009).

[37] *1919 Commission Report* (n 20) 113. Annex I, containing the detailed list of violations was not reprinted in the *American Journal of International Law*, but can be seen in *Violations of the Laws and Customs of War: Reports of the Majority and Dissenting Reports of American and Japanese Members of the Commission of Responsibilities, Conference of Paris, 1919*, Carnegie Endowment for International Peace, Division of Law: Pamphlet No 32 (Oxford, Clarendon Press, 1919).

[38] *1919 Commission Report* (n 20) 114.

[39] ibid.

[40] ibid.

nullum crimen sine lege.[41] The delegation accepted that belligerent parties could prosecute offenders against the laws of war before national courts or military tribunals, but stated that:

> The American representatives know of no international statute or convention making a violation of the laws and customs of war—not to speak of the laws or principles of humanity—an international crime, affixing a punishment to it, and declaring the court which has jurisdiction over the offence.[42]

The Treaty of Versailles reflects the United States view, with Article 227 acknowledging the right of the Allied powers to try persons accused of violating the laws and customs of war before military tribunals. In practice, such trials never occurred and only relatively few individuals were ever tried by the defeated countries for crimes committed during the First World War.[43] Nevertheless, the list of violations devised by the 1919 Commission proved influential in subsequent legal endeavours. This so-called 'Versailles List' was used as a precedent by the United Nations War Crimes Commission established during the Second World War and was said to serve as an 'inspiration for improving international efforts' concerning accountability for war crimes.[44] Relying on the work of the 1919 Commission after the Second World War 'diminished the risk of criticism on the grounds that the UN were inventing new crimes after the acts had been perpetrated'.[45] By providing a 'starting point and practical basis for the immediate commencement of the work of the Commission',[46] the 1919 Commission's list of violations, as well as the various other contributions detailed in this section, provided a valuable foundation for the task of prosecuting the crimes of the Second World War.

9.4. UNITED NATIONS WAR CRIMES COMMISSION (1943–1948)

In line with the stated commitment of Allied governments to try suspected war criminals for the abuses of the Second World War, the United Kingdom and United States committed to the establishment of a 'United Nations

[41] ibid, 133–35, 144–46.
[42] ibid, 146.
[43] See, generally, M Lewis, *The Birth of the New Justice: The Internationalisation of Crime and Punishment, 1919–1950* (Oxford, Oxford University Press, 2014).
[44] See D Plesch and S Sattler, 'A New Paradigm of Customary International Criminal Law: The UN War Crimes Commission of 1943–1948 and its associated Courts and Tribunals' (2014) 25 *Criminal Law Forum* 17, 20.
[45] AJ Kochavi, *Prelude to Nuremberg: Allied War Crimes Policy and the Question of Punishment* (Chapel Hill, University of North Caroline Press, 1998) 96.
[46] ibid, 96.

Commission for the Investigation of War Crimes' in October 1942.[47] The Soviet Union joined with the other two major Allies in issuing the Moscow Declaration on 1 November 1943, which entrenched this commitment to prosecution and identified the need to compile information necessary for that purpose.[48] The United Nations War Crimes Commission (UNWCC) had been established a few days previously at a diplomatic conference of Allied and Dominion countries held at the Foreign Office in London.[49] The Commission had 17 members at the outset, comprising the delegates of the 14 represented states, but excluding the Soviets, who were said to be in general agreement with the Commission's establishment.[50] The narrow mandate given to the Commission belies the extent to which it engaged with international law:

1. it should investigate and record the evidence of war crimes, identifying where possible the individuals responsible;
2. it should report to the Governments concerned cases in which it appeared that adequate evidence might be expected to be forthcoming.[51]

It quickly became apparent that the Commission should also address legal matters concerning war crimes and not merely investigate the facts concerning their commission. The states that created the UNWCC in turn explicitly acknowledged its advisory role on questions of law and policy.[52] Robert Wright, who served as Chair of the Commission, explained that fulfillment of its duty to advise governments on legal questions meant that the Commission 'had to deliberate on fundamental issues of international law, issues which were of practical importance in regard to war crimes'.[53] According to the official *History of the United War Crimes Commission*, this advisory role 'tended, in the course of time, to exceed in importance its original task of investigation'.[54]

[47] The United Nations War Crimes Commission, *History of the United Nations War Crimes Commission and the Development of the Laws of War* (London, HM Stationery Office, 1948) 105–106.

[48] *Statement Signed by President Roosevelt, Prime Minister Churchill and Premier Stalin Regarding Atrocities*, Annex to 'Memorandum to President Roosevelt from the Secretaries of State and War and the Attorney General, January 22, 1945' (Document I), *Report of Robert H Jackson United States Representative to the International Conference on Military Trials* (Washington, US Government Printing Office, 1949) 11–12.

[49] *History of the United Nations War Crimes Commission* (n 47) 112–14.

[50] ibid, 120.

[51] ibid, 113.

[52] ibid, 124–26.

[53] ibid, 3.

[54] ibid, 126.

While the UNWCC could only make recommendations to the Allied powers on matters of international law, Wright considered that its work in this area was of 'prime importance', as it had prepared the groundwork for the prosecution and punishment of war criminals once the war ended.[55] Recent scholarship has analysed the extent of the contribution of the Commission to the development of international law in general and international criminal justice in particular.[56] Without doubt the work of the Commission constitutes a rich source of information and legal analysis of international law as it relates to the prosecution of international crimes. At the 1945 London conference on military trials, which culminated in the adoption of the Nuremberg Charter, the United States representative Robert Jackson, later Chief Prosecutor at Nuremberg, acknowledged the work of the Commission:

> We have felt very keenly that the War Crimes Commission has been doing excellent work and that the War Crimes Commission ought to have some opportunity to present its work if a way could be found.[57]

Jackson and David Maxwell Fyfe, the British representative at the London conference, met with the Commission in July 1945 and discussed 'the problem of utilising the great mass of experience and information accumulated by the Commission'.[58] Despite this praise and engagement, key United States officials had earlier noted the considerable criticism of the Commission for 'the paucity of the results of its work', which had become characterised by disagreement amongst its members.[59] They considered in January 1945 that the Commission had fulfilled its purpose and suggested its dissolution.[60] The Commission did continue to operate until after the end of the war, but once the defeat of Germany was imminent, the four main Allied powers assumed overall control of the task of advancing the law relating to prosecuting international crimes. Nevertheless, the preparatory work of the Commission should not be discounted, for it was not without influence.

As with the 1919 Commission, the UNWCC's legal analysis mainly involved consideration of substantive crimes, potential modes of criminal liability and the constitution of a mechanism for prosecuting alleged war

[55] *History of the United Nations War Crimes Commission* (n 47) 3.

[56] See for example W Schabas et al, 'The United Nations War Commission and the Origins of International Criminal Justice' (2014) 25 *Criminal Law Forum* 1, which provides an overview to a special issue of the journal devoted to the work of the Commission.

[57] 'Minutes of Conference Session of July 13, 1945', *Report of Robert H Jackson* (n 48) 225.

[58] *History of the United Nations War Crimes Commission* (n 47) 456.

[59] 'Memorandum to President Roosevelt from the Secretaries of State and War and the Attorney General, January 22, 1945' *Report of Robert H Jackson* (n 48) 3.

[60] ibid, 8.

crimes. The Commission had conducted its work based on an acceptance of the existence of individual criminal responsibility under international law,[61] even if this somewhat debatable proposition was not confirmed until the Nuremberg Charter and judgment, and their later endorsement by the UN General Assembly.[62] In relation to the Commission's engagement with substantive law, this was primarily through its Legal Committee, which provided advice to member governments on numerous issues arising from German conduct during the war.[63] Considerable attention was focused on the definition of war crimes, the criminal nature of wars of aggression and what subsequently became known as crimes against humanity.[64] For war crimes, the Commission added to the 'Versailles List', by adopting an approach which entailed 'avoiding strict and binding definitions of the concept of war crimes'.[65] The Commission broke new ground in addressing sexual and gender-based war crimes.[66] Its flexible approach, which is not without problems in the context of criminal proceedings,where the principle of legality requires certainty, also allowed the Commission to address the new concept of crimes against humanity:

> … the rule stressed during the first days of the Commission's activities, that narrow legalisms were to be disregarded and the field of the violations of the laws of war extended so as to meet the requirements of justice, was applied in respect of this class of crimes.[67]

While the members of the Commission were initially divided on whether abuses against German nationals were within its jurisdiction, the Legal Committee devised a definition of crimes against humanity, which was 'adopted in substance in Article 6 of the Nuremberg Charter'.[68] Legal advice was offered by the UNWCC to a number of national governments concerning such crimes.[69]

9.4.1. Crimes Against Peace

Crimes against peace proved to be a far more contested subject for the UNWCC. The question of whether criminal liability arose for aggressive

61 *History of the United Nations War Crimes Commission* (n 47) 9.
62 See UN General Assembly Resolution 95(1), 11 December 1946.
63 *History of the United Nations War Crimes Commission* (n 47) 169–70, 485–98.
64 ibid, 170.
65 ibid, 170–74.
66 See D Plesch, S Sàcouto and C Lasco, 'The Relevance of the United Nations War Crimes Commission to the Prosecution of Sexual and Gender-Based Crimes Today' (2014) 25 *Criminal Law Forum* 349.
67 *History of the United Nations War Crimes Commission* (n 47) 174.
68 ibid, 176.
69 ibid, 176–80.

war was '[b]y far the most important issue of substantive law to be studied by the Commission and its Legal Committee', according to the official *History*, and one which generated a clear divergence of opinion amongst the Commission members.[70] A special sub-committee tasked with studying the issue produced majority and minority reports, an approach reminiscent of its 1919 predecessor, whose lack of unanimity the UNWCC had noted.[71] The majority concluded that preparatory acts and the launching of a war of aggression were not 'war crimes' (which formed the basis of the Commission's mandate), and that '[i]t is desirable that for the future penal sanctions should be provided for such grave outrages against the elementary principles of international law'.[72] The minority opinion of the delegate of Czechoslovakia was that international law had developed recently such that individual criminal responsibility arose for aggressive war.[73] His view found favour with other members of the Commission, including Wright, who sought to compare the development of international law to that of the English common law.[74] The Commission, however, remained divided and decided that resolution of this question rested with the governments themselves, and thus the subject was effectively dropped.[75] The absence of agreement does not devalue the work of the Commission on crimes against peace, as it provides a considered appraisal of the state of existing law, and foreshadowed the debates on aggression that were to take place at the London conference in 1945. Wright later wrote of the significance of the Commission's work on crimes against peace, and how he was told that 'these discussions were not without influence in determining the scope of the prosecution and in putting "crimes against peace" in the fore-front of the Charter of the Tribunal'.[76]

9.4.2. Constitutive Law for a Potential International Criminal Court

The UNWCC also considered the constitutive law that might be required for an international criminal court to prosecute war crimes, in addition to national prosecutions by the Commission's member states.[77] Work on this subject included the preparation and detailed consideration of a draft statute for a UN War Crimes Court which might be established

[70] ibid, 180.
[71] ibid, 181–82.
[72] ibid, 182.
[73] ibid.
[74] ibid.
[75] ibid, 184.
[76] ibid, 10.
[77] ibid, 442–54.

by treaty.[78] Despite the effort, this particular proposal received a 'lukewarm' response from the British government, which indicated its desire to work closely with the United States on this matter.[79] Both the Justice and War Departments of the United States had devised proposals regarding prosecutions of Nazi war criminals.[80] William Schabas has noted how the four major Allied powers took a different approach to the format of a tribunal as suggested by the Commission, and how the smaller countries which had contributed to the work of the UNWCC were excluded from the London conference.[81] The four Allies were 'essentially ignoring the proposal of the United Nations War Crimes Commission as they concluded an agreement on the Nuremberg Tribunal behind closed doors'.[82] The *History of the United Nations War Crimes Commission* concedes that the Commission only played only an 'indirect part' in the preparation of the London Agreement on the establishment of the International Military Tribunal.[83]

9.4.3. Superior Orders and Potential Modes of Liability

The legal work undertaken by the UNWCC also included tackling thorny issues such as the doctrine of superior orders and potential modes of criminal liability. The 1919 Commission had left open the question of whether superior orders might be a defence in a criminal trial,[84] but the issue was considered of such importance at the UNWCC, that its Legal Committee appointed a special sub-committee to address it.[85] In the end, differing approaches to superior orders amongst the member states meant that the Commission could not propose a clear principle or rule on the matter. There was unanimity, however, that 'the mere fact of having acted in obedience to the orders of a superior does not of itself relieve a person who has committed a war crime from responsibility'.[86] The Nuremberg Charter reflected this approach and added that superior orders could be considered in mitigation of punishment, while the judges at Nuremberg

[78] For an overview see WA Schabas, 'The United Nations War Crimes Commission's Proposal for an International Criminal Court' (2014) 25 *Criminal Law Forum* 171.

[79] ibid, 186.

[80] See generally BF Smith, *The American Road to Nuremberg; The Documentary Record 1944–1945* (Stanford, Hoover Institution Press, 1982).

[81] Schabas (n 78) 177.

[82] ibid, 188.

[83] *History of the United Nations War Crimes Commission* (n 47) 454.

[84] *1919 Commission Report* (n 20) 117.

[85] *History of the United Nations War Crimes Commission* (n 47) 278.

[86] ibid, 280.

felt that superior orders had to be considered in tandem with the question of duress.[87] Modern international criminal law has modified the approach taken at Nuremberg, and allows the defence in limited circumstances.[88]

9.4.4. Collective Responsibility

The collective nature of the mass commission of crimes during the Second World War had prompted consideration by the Commission of 'the problem of collective responsibility for war crimes', including the idea of criminal organisations.[89] Professor Andre Gros, who later represented France at the London conference, explained that the principle of individual culpability could not be applied to 'the entirely new phenomenon of mass crime':

> One is led to the conception of a collective responsibility corresponding to the collective character of the crimes. The war has furnished plenty of examples of the collective character of the war crimes, of the fact that they have been committed not by isolated individuals but by groups, units or organised formations. Such crimes amount to organised collective violation of international public order.[90]

Gros suggested that membership of criminal associations could be punishable, as provided for under the French Penal Code, although he seemed to favour membership serving to establish a presumption of guilt, in itself a highly controversial proposition, rather than as a stand-alone crime.[91] The Commission debated these proposals and recognised that 'countless crimes have been committed by organised gangs, Gestapo groups, S.S. or military units'.[92] Although it recommended prosecution of both planners of atrocities and members of such entities implicated therein, the Commission stopped short of calling for the trial of organisations themselves, or for declaring membership itself as a crime.[93] The criminal organisations proposal which had emanated from the United States War Department had suggested such an approach.[94] It was taken up at the London conference, eventually appearing in Articles 9 and 10 of the Nuremberg Charter, although the judges at Nuremberg showed notable

[87] See Charter of the International Military Tribunal, Art 8; International Military Tribunal (Nuremberg) *Judgment and Sentences*, 1 October 1946, *reprinted in* (1947) 41(1) *American Journal of International Law* 172, 221.

[88] See Rome Statute of the International Criminal Court, Art 33.

[89] United Nations War Crimes Commission 'Memorandum by Professor Andre Gros on the Problem of Collective Responsibility for War Crimes' (translation), Document C 85 (28 March 1945).

[90] ibid 1–2.

[91] *History of the United Nations War Crimes Commission* (n 47) 294.

[92] ibid, 296.

[93] ibid.

[94] See 'Subject: Trial of European War Criminals (by Colonel Murray C. Bernays, G-1)', 15 September 1944 (Document 16) in Smith (n 80) 33.

caution in their application of this concept.[95] The restraint demonstrated by the Commission on this controversial concept bolsters the argument that when it comes to certain modes of liability, the UNWCC's 'interpretive and precedential value is manifest'.[96]

***

The work of the United Nations War Crimes Commission made an important contribution to the development of international law, albeit one that should not be overstated. It was sidelined by the main Allied powers when it came to the preparation of the Nuremberg Charter, and was not referenced in the Nuremberg judgment.[97] Nonetheless, the Commission's output and engagement with international law remains a valuable source for scholars and practitioners of international criminal law. Given that its members were representative of their states, albeit with a certain degree of distance, their ruminations can be considered as a source for determining customary international law:

> … the Commission was both an international forum for informed diplomatic discussions about what the law is—or should be—on a plethora of issues relevant to war crimes prosecutions and a managing body that evaluated and counseled tens of thousands of war crimes prosecutions occurring around the world. Altogether, the Commission resulted in rich diplomatic debate about international law by a large and diverse group of states, as well as the evaluation of thousands of cases where principles were put into practice. As such, both the *opinio juris* and the state practice required to form customary international laws were contained within a single entity, a truly rare phenomenon, now and then.[98]

The relatively uncertain state of the law concerning international crimes and the context of Nazi criminality loosened the strictures that would have otherwise prevailed on developing legal rules and advancing particular arguments or concepts. As the Commission itself put it, 'international law developed in this field under hard pressure of circumstances. It grew of the necessity to meet a new type of criminality which had never before faced human society or on so vast a scale'.[99] As international law developed rapidly by way of treaties adopted after the Second World War, the scope for pushing the development of the law in such a manner would diminish.

[95] For an overview see S Darcy, *Collective Responsibility and Accountability under International Law*, (Transnational, 2007) 257.
[96] K Hale and D Kline, 'Holding Collectives Accountable' (2014) 25 *Criminal Law Forum* 261, 289.
[97] *cf* Plesch and Sattler (n 44) 40.
[98] K Hale and D Kline, 'Holding Collective Accountable' (2014) 25 *Criminal Law Forum* 261, 264. See also D Plesch and S Sattler, 'Changing the Paradigm of International Criminal Law: Considering the Work of the United Nations War Crimes Commission of 1943–1948' (2013) 15(2) *International Community Law Review* 203.
[99] *History of the United Nations War Crimes Commission* (n 47) 289.

9.5. COMMISSION OF EXPERTS ESTABLISHED PURSUANT TO SECURITY COUNCIL RESOLUTION 780 (1992–1994)

In October 1992, the UN Security Council asked the Secretary General to establish a Commission of Experts to examine the alleged abuses occurring in the conflicts in the Former Yugoslavia.[100] The Council requested that an impartial commission be set up as a matter of urgency to examine the available information, 'with a view to providing the Secretary-General with its conclusions on the evidence of grave breaches of the Geneva Conventions and other violations of international humanitarian law committed in the territory of the former Yugoslavia'.[101] In appointing the Commissioners, the Secretary General paid due regard to their qualifications in 'human rights, humanitarian law as well as criminal law and prosecution'.[102] It has been said that there was an 'unspoken understanding' that the creation of the Commission of Experts was the first step towards the establishment of an international criminal tribunal to prosecute crimes in the Former Yugoslavia.[103] In a resolution from November 1992, the Security Council extended the mandate of the Commission of Experts to include the practice of 'ethnic cleansing', and warned that those ordering or committing such violations would be held individually responsible.[104] Cherif M Bassiouni, who was to replace Frits Kalshoven as the Chair of the Commission in 1993, compared the Commission of Experts to the 1919 Commission and the United Nations War Crimes Commission. He wrote in 1994 that there had only been 'three internationally established commissions to investigate war crimes and prepare for eventual prosecution before international and national judicial bodies'.[105] One key difference from the previous commissions of inquiry was that the members of the Commission of Experts were to serve in their personal capacity, and their appointment was to be based on their 'integrity and absolute impartiality'.[106] That being said, the Commission received its mandate from a political body, in the form of the Security Council, albeit one which failed to ensure that sufficient resources were provided to the Commission for it to complete its task.[107]

100 UN Security Council Resolution 780, UN Doc S/RES/780 (6 October 1992).
101 ibid, para 2.
102 *Report of the Secretary-General on the Establishment of the Commission of Experts pursuant to paragraph 2 of Security Council Resolution 780*, UN Doc S/24657 (14 October 1992) para 8.
103 WA Schabas, *The UN International Criminal Tribunals* (Cambridge University Press, 2006) 17.
104 UN Security Council Resolution 787, UN Doc S/RES/787 (16 November 1992) paras 7–8.
105 MC Bassiouni, 'The United Nations Commission of Experts Established Pursuant to Security Council Resolution 780 (1992)' (1994) 88(4) *American Journal of International Law* 784, 784.
106 *Report of the Secretary-General* (n 102) paras 8–9.
107 Bassiouni (n 105) 795–96, 801–802.

In its first Interim Report, the Commission of Experts addressed a number of legal issues, including the applicable law and 'its interpretation in light of the facts'.[108] It offered its view as to the application of international humanitarian law, which was relevant in both treaty and customary form. The Commission noted the divergence in the law of armed conflict concerning international and non-international armed conflicts, and adopted an approach, which it justified on the basis of the particular context in the Balkans, that applied the law of international armed conflicts 'to the entirety of the armed conflicts in the territory of the former Yugoslavia'.[109] The Commission suggested that '[s]pecial importance also attaches to the conventions and customary law on crimes against humanity', as well as the prohibition of genocide.[110] It discussed briefly war crimes and crimes against humanity, and how 'ethnic cleansing' could fall under these headings, as well as the concepts of command responsibility and superior orders.[111] The Commission stated in its first report that it would examine how rape and other forms of sexual assault might be addressed as war crimes or crimes against humanity.[112] It concluded by turning to universal jurisdiction, which it felt could be applied to war crimes, crimes against humanity and genocide, and how states might combine their jurisdiction so that prosecutions could be undertaken by an international tribunal, along the lines as had been done at Nuremberg.[113] The Commission considered that the creation of an ad hoc international criminal tribunal, as had been suggested elsewhere,[114] would be 'consistent with the direction of its work'.[115]

By the time the Commission of Experts issued its second Interim Report in October 1993, the Security Council had already decided to create an international tribunal to try persons responsible for serious violations of international humanitarian law committed in the Former Yugoslavia since 1991.[116] In Resolution 808, which put the ICTY's establishment in motion, the Council took note of the Commission's suggestion that a tribunal be created. The second Interim Report did not broach questions of international law, perhaps because of the imminent coming into existence of an

[108] *Interim Report of the Commission of Experts Established pursuant to Security Council Resolution 780 (1992)*, transmitted by a Letter from the Secretary-General to the President of the Security Council, UN Doc S/25274 (9 February 1993) para 36.
[109] ibid, para 45.
[110] ibid, paras 40, 46.
[111] ibid, paras 47–57.
[112] ibid, paras 58–60.
[113] ibid, para 72.
[114] Schabas (n 103) 13–16.
[115] *First Interim Report* (n 108) para 74.
[116] See UN Security Council Resolution 808, UN Doc S/RES/808 (22 February 1993); UN Security Council Resolution 827, UN Doc S/RES/827 (23 May 1993).

international criminal tribunal.[117] In its Final Report, the Commission of Experts expressed its deference to the ICTY on relevant legal questions, but explained why it had included some analysis of international law:

> The Commission has chosen to comment on selected legal issues because of their particular significance for understanding the legal context related to violations of international humanitarian law committed in the territory of the former Yugoslavia. The Commission's mandate is to provide the Secretary-General with its conclusions on the evidence of such violations and not to provide an analysis of the legal issues. It will be for the International Tribunal to make legal findings in connection with particular cases.[118]

The Commission's final Report provides a précis of key substantive legal issues concerning international crimes and their prosecution.[119] The legal analysis put forward by the Commission of Experts was considered and applied by the ICTY across a range of issues,[120] and although the ICTY effectively agreed with the Commission on several points, it took a different view at times, departing not just from the Commission's analysis, but from prevailing opinion at the time.

9.5.1. Command Responsibility

The Commission of Experts had elaborated on the concept of command responsibility, as provided for in Article 7 of the ICTY Statute, but only briefly touched upon in the Secretary General's Report on the draft statute.[121] Having noted 'with satisfaction' the similarity between the formulation in the Statute and how the Commission described command responsibility in its first Interim Report, the Commission offered its view as to the mental element required for superior responsibility.[122] On constructive knowledge, or the 'must have known' standard, the Commission put forward a number of indices which could be considered in

[117] *Second Interim Report of the Commission of Experts Established pursuant to Security Council Resolution 780 (1992)*, transmitted by a Letter from the Secretary-General to the President of the Security Council, UN Doc S/26545 (1993) (6 October 1993).

[118] *Final Report of the Commission of Experts Established Pursuant to Security Council Resolution 780 (1992)*, Letter dated 24 May 1994 from the Secretary-General to the President of the Security Council, UN Doc S/1994/674 (24 May 1994) para 41.

[119] ibid, paras 42–109.

[120] See D Re, 'Fact-Finding in the Former Yugoslavia: What the Courts Did' in M Bergsmo (ed), *Quality Control in Fact-Finding* (Florence, Torken Opsahl, 2013) 279, 288–94; M Frulli, (n 11) 1327–28.

[121] *Report of the Secretary-General Pursuant to Paragraph 2 of Security Council Resolution 808 (1993)*, UN Doc S/25704 (3 May 1993) para 56.

[122] *Final Report of the Commission of Experts* (n 118) paras 56, 58.

determining the presence of such knowledge.[123] The ICTY relied on these indicia on more than one occasion[124] and was challenged for doing so in the *Galić* case. The defence considered that the Commission of Experts' report on this matter was based on 'assumptions and superficial information'.[125] The Commission had not cited any evidence to support its interpretation of constructive knowledge, yet the Appeals Chamber upheld the Trial Chamber's use of the indicia and dismissed the appeal:

> The factors mentioned in the Report are not factual findings, they are indicia that can be used along with other factors. These indicia were not considered by the Trial Chamber to be in any way binding upon it because they were contained in the Report.[126]

The Commission's report thus proved to be a persuasive precedent of sorts for the ICTY. It has also been cited approvingly by a Pre-Trial Chamber of the International Criminal Court on this particular issue.[127]

9.5.2. Differences between the Commission and the ICTY

While the ICTY has relied upon the Commission of Experts to buttress its legal arguments on occasion, it has shown little hesitancy in adopting differing interpretations. In one of the first genocide cases, an ICTY Trial Chamber argued that protected groups could be defined negatively, that it 'concurs here with the opinion already expressed by the Commission of Experts'.[128] The Appeals Chamber expressly disagreed with this approach, and found that reliance on the Commission of Experts Report alone was 'not persuasive' here.[129] The Commission's view that targeting the leadership of a group might be sufficient for genocide has gained some traction in the jurisprudence.[130] For crimes against humanity, the Commission of Experts had taken the view that a nexus was required with an

[123] *Final Report of the Commission of Experts* (n 118) para 58.

[124] See for example *Prosecutor v Delalic* et al, Case No IT-96-21-T, Trial Chamber, (Judgment, 18 November 1998) para 386; *Prosecutor v Blaškić*, Case No IT-95-14-T, Trial Chamber, (Judgment, 3 March 2000) para 307.

[125] *Prosecutor v Galic*, Case No IT-98-29-A, Appeals Chamber, (30 November 2006) para 180.

[126] ibid, para 183.

[127] *Prosecutor v Bemba Gombo*, Case No ICC-01/05/-01/08, Decision Pursuant to Art 61(7) (a) and (b) of the Rome Statute on the Charges, Pre-Trial Chamber II, (15 June 2009) para 431.

[128] *Prosecutor v Jelisic*, Trial Chamber, Judgment, Case No IT-95-10-T, (14 December 1999) para 71.

[129] *Prosecutor v Stakic*, Appeals Chamber, Judgment, Case No IT-97-24-A, (22 March 2006) para 27. See, however, Partly Dissenting Opinion of Judge Shahabuddeen, paras 8–18.

[130] See *Final Report of the Commission of Experts* (n 118) para 94; *Jelisic* (n 128) para 82; Schabas (n 103) 170–71.

armed conflict, as specified in the ICTY Statute, although it considered that no link was needed with war crimes or crimes against peace, as had been the case at Nuremberg.[131] The ICTY shunned such conventional legal wisdom regarding the nexus in the ground-breaking *Tadić* case, where the Appeals Chamber held that customary international law no longer required a connection between crimes against humanity and an international armed conflict, or perhaps with any armed conflict.[132] The Commission had also seemingly considered that discrimination was a requirement for crimes against humanity, as had the Report of the Secretary General,[133] although the ICTY Statute had not included such an element. The ICTY Appeals Chamber held that discrimination was only an element of the crime against humanity of persecution.[134] David Re rightly notes that such differences of opinion are 'quite explicable as these issues were judicially undefined when the Commission expressed its opinion'.[135] The energetic judicial creativity demonstrated by the ad hoc international criminal tribunals might also explain such divergence.[136]

The differing views of the Commission and the Tribunal is most apparent in the context of war crimes. In its Final Report, the Commission had reiterated its view that the law applicable to international armed conflicts should be applied to 'the entirety' of the armed conflicts in the Former Yugoslavia.[137] This stance may have been taken because of the accepted opinion at the time, which the Commission gave expression to, that 'there does not appear to be a customary international law applicable to internal armed conflicts which includes the concept of war crimes'.[138] The Commission considered that violations of the laws or customs of war as set out in Article 3 of the ICTY Statute were 'offences when committed in international, but not in internal armed conflicts'.[139] Both the Secretary General and the International Committee of the Red Cross shared this view.[140] The ICTY Appeals Chamber, once again in *Tadić*, argued to the

[131] *Final Report of the Commission of Experts* (n 118) para 75.

[132] *Prosecutor v Tadić*, Case No IT-9-1-AR72, Appeals Chamber, Decision on the Defence Motion for Interlocutory Appeal on Jurisdiction, (2 October 1995) para 141.

[133] *Final Report of the Commission of Experts* (n 118) para 84; *Report of the Secretary-General* (n 121) para 48.

[134] *Prosecutor v Tadić*, Case No IT-94-1-A, Appeals Chamber, (Judgment, 15 July 1999) paras 282–305.

[135] D Re (n 120) 288.

[136] See generally S Darcy and J Powderly (eds), *Judicial Creativity at the International Criminal Tribunals* (Oxford, Oxford University Press, 2010).

[137] *Final Report of the Commission of Experts* (n 118) para 44.

[138] ibid, para 52.

[139] ibid, para 54.

[140] See *Report of the Secretary-General Pursuant to Paragraph 5 of Security Council Resolution 955 (1994)*, UN Doc S/1995/134 (13 February 1994) para 12; 'Some Preliminary Remarks by the International Committee of the Red Cross', DDM/JUR/442 b (25 March 1993) para 4, *reprinted in* V Morris and MP Scharf, *An Insider's Guide to the International Criminal Tribunal for the Former Yugoslavia*, vol 2 (New York, Transnational Publishers, 1995) 391.

contrary and concluded that customary international law had evolved such that 'serious violations of international humanitarian law governing internal armed conflicts entail individual criminal responsibility'.[141] The Commission's Final Report was relied upon by Judge Li in his dissenting opinion on the interpretation of Article 3 of the ICTY Statute.[142] What he saw as an 'unwarranted assumption of legislative power' by the *Tadić* majority,[143] undoubtedly contributed to the extension of war crimes to non-international armed conflict when states exercised their legitimate legislative authority at the Rome Conference in 1998.[144]

***

The Commission of Experts operated as international criminal law was entering a period of rapid growth and, as had happened with the UNWCC, its efforts were overtaken by other legal developments. The establishment of the ICTY during the mandate of the Commission was a milestone in the evolution of international criminal law which overshadowed the Commission's work, even if it offered the Commission a clearer legal framework within which to conduct its analysis of applicable international law. The Commission's reports proved useful as official and authoritative documents which could be referred to by the ICTY where necessary, given the relatively rudimentary state of international criminal law as the trials began. The Tribunal's judges were not tied by the views of the Commission, of course, and they departed from its legal analysis more than once. This is not a negative reflection on the legal activity of the Commission itself, for it arguably provided an interpretation of certain legal issues that was more faithful to the views of states, and in keeping with the principle of legality, than that entailed in the progressive approach of the ICTY. While the Tribunal's jurisprudence prompted certain significant changes in international law, it has not always been successful in this regard and the more conservative view of the Commission of Experts has prevailed on occasion.[145] The legal work of the Commission was not 'overly influential' at the Tribunal, especially when compared with the extensive fact-finding which it had also undertaken.[146] It can also be seen as an example

[141] *Tadić* (n 132) para 135.

[142] ibid, Separate Opinion of Judge Li on the Defence Motion for Interlocutory Appeal on Jurisdiction, para 8.

[143] ibid, para 13.

[144] See Rome Statute of the International Criminal Court, Art 8.

[145] For example, with regard to the concept of belligerent reprisals. See *Final Report of the Commission of Experts* (n 118) paras 63–66; S Darcy, *Judges, Law and War; the Judicial Development of International Humanitarian Law* (Cambridge, Cambridge University Press, 2014) 257–263.

[146] D Re (n 120) 286; R Kerr, *The International Criminal Tribunal for the Former Yugoslavia; An Exercise in Law, Politics and Diplomacy* (Oxford, Oxford University Press, 2004) 56.

of the declining influence of commissions of inquiry on the development of international law, as the law itself has become more well-established, and more emphasis is placed on the fact-finding role of these bodies.

9.6. CONCLUSION

In the international legal system, only states are formally endowed with lawmaking power. Nevertheless, the development of international law is not solely the domain of states in practice, and commissions of inquiry can be counted amongst the various other entities, such as international courts, which have contributed to this multi-faceted process. The historical examples considered in this chapter demonstrate that the legal analysis undertaken by commissions of inquiry can serve to clarify the application, scope and meaning of international law in particular contexts. Their reports comprise official and authoritative sources which can inform, guide and even push states, judges and practitioners in their application of international law. This chapter has sought to consider both the treatment of international law by the chosen commissions, as well as subsequent adherence, or otherwise, to their findings. In each case, the commissions can be said to have made discrete contributions to the development of international law, as evidenced, for example, by the subsequent reliance on those legal analyses by international courts and tribunals. The reports of these commissions of inquiry continue to be cited many years after the fulfillment of their mandates. In a 2011 decision of the International Criminal Court, for example, the Pre-Trial Chamber cited the 1919 Commission's report to bolster its argument that international law does not afford immunity to heads of state before international courts.[147]

The reports of commissions of inquiry can be compared to the recognised subsidiary sources of international law—judicial decisions and scholarly writings—and as such, can carry significant persuasive value and prove influential in the development of international law. States would likely be more receptive to the legal findings of a commission of inquiry if they were to accord with their own understandings of the state of international law. Certain progressive interpretations by commissions of inquiry may be more palatable for states, such as, for example, when they expand the obligations of certain non-state actors under international law.[148]

[147] *Prosecutor v Al Bashir*, Pre-Trial Chamber I, Decision Pursuant to Art 87(7) of the Rome Statute on the Failure by the Republic of Malawi to Comply with the Cooperation Requests Issued by the Court with Respect to the Arrest and Surrender of Omar Hassan Ahmad Al Bashir, ICC-02/05-01/09-139, 12 December 2011, para 23.

[148] Boutruche (n 3) 32.

At the same time, as with the established subsidiary sources, other entities may not be convinced of the interpretations adopted and may choose to depart from them or simply ignore them. This is evident for each of the three commissions examined in this chapter. It is not inconceivable either that commissions of inquiry make erroneous or unfounded statements concerning international law.[149] The concern about the fragmentation of international law because of differing interpretations by international courts could also be applied to commissions of inquiry; the two commissions of inquiry established by the UN to investigate the attack on the Gaza Flotilla came to opposite conclusions regarding the legality of Israel's blockade of the territory.[150] Such divergence of opinion is unfortunate but not surprising. Just as judges are not reticent about lodging separate or dissenting opinions, members of commissions of inquiry have also disagreed on matters of law, including internally, as happened at both the 1919 Commission and the United Nations War Crimes Commission.

The development of international law has become an infrequent by-product of the work of contemporary commissions of inquiry. It is notable that the International Criminal Court makes little use of the legal analyses by commissions of inquiry which have addressed situations over which the Court has jurisdiction.[151] The International Criminal Court did not follow the Darfur Commission's analysis that protected groups in the context of genocide could include any 'stable and permanent groups', as had been mooted by the ICTR in *Akayesu*, or, more broadly, that there was sufficient evidence of a genocidal policy on the part of the Sudanese government.[152] The detailed nature of the legal instruments of the International Criminal Court diminish its need to consult external sources, although this has not prevented extensive reliance by the Court on the jurisprudence of the ad hoc tribunals. The fact-finding efforts of commissions of inquiry remain a valuable reference for the Prosecutor and judges in the preliminary stages of proceedings. Nevertheless, the credibility of their work also depends on

[149] See for example KJ Heller, 'The International Commission of Inquiry on Libya: A Critical Analysis' in J Meierhenrich (ed), *International Commissions: The Role of Commissions of Inquiry in the Investigation of International Crimes* (forthcoming) 30; V Koutrolis, 'The Prohibition of the Use of Force in Arbitrations and Fact-Finding Reports' in M Weller (ed), *The Oxford Handbook of the Use of Force in International Law* (Oxford, Oxford University Press, 2015) 619–20; Boutruche (n 3) 18–21; van den Herik (n 1) 534.

[150] See *Report of the Secretary-General's Panel of Inquiry on the 31 May 2010 Flotilla Incident, September 2011*, paras 69–82; *Report of the international fact-finding mission to investigate violations of international law, including international humanitarian and human rights law, resulting from the Israeli attacks on the flotilla of ships carrying humanitarian assistance*, UN Doc A/HRC/15/21 (27 September 2010) paras 51–54.

[151] For an example, see Office of the Prosecutor, *Situation on Registered Vehicles of Comoros, Greece and Cambodia; Article 53(1)* (6 November 2014) para 27.

[152] *Darfur Report* (n 2) paras 498–501, 513–18.

the quality of the legal analysis, which could be undermined by an overly creative approach which seeks to progress the law's development.[153] As Larissa van den Herik has put it:

> … in the most politically sensitive dossiers, there is a set need to interpret and apply the law quite meticulously and to develop legal reasoning at some length. Such rigor adds to the authority of the report and is also required by the general inclination of the States concerned not to co-operate and subsequently dismiss the report. Rigorous legal reasoning may help to forestall, or at least de-legitimize, unilateral dismissal on legal grounds.[154]

The development of international law is not one of the purposes behind the contemporary establishment of international commissions of inquiry. If a historical view is taken, however, it can be seen that commissions have at times made valuable contributions to the evolution of international law, in particular international criminal law as examined above. While this may have been deliberate and feasible in the earlier stages of the law's development, such an approach is now cautioned against and less likely as the law has advanced. The contribution of commissions of inquiry to the future development of international law is more likely to be inconspicuous and inadvertent.

153 Boutruche (n 3) 1.
154 van den Herik (n 1) 535 (footnotes omitted).

10

Quo Vadis? Commissions of Inquiry and their Implications for the Coherence of International Law

RUSSELL BUCHAN

10.1. INTRODUCTION

STATES ARE RATIONAL actors that formulate international legal rules in order to protect and promote values and interests that they hold in common.[1] At its outset international law was a rudimentary regulatory framework because it was designed principally to safeguard the most fundamental interest that was shared by states, namely the protection of their sovereignty from external intervention, especially violent intervention. International law was therefore originally intended to secure the peaceful co-existence of states in an otherwise anarchic world order that did not possess any overarching central authority capable of guaranteeing the security and safety (that is, the sovereignty) of its member states.[2]

Over time states came to recognise that many of the problems they faced were actually community problems that were common to them all. As a result, international law was expanded and its overriding objective became not just enabling states to co-exist peacefully but, in addition, to achieve effective cooperation over a host of international issues,[3] such as abuses of fundamental human rights, environmental degradation, pandemic health crises, economic insecurity etc. The product was the formation of various international legal regimes dedicated to addressing

1 See the work of the so-called English School theorists, notably H Bull, *The Anarchical Society: A Study of Order in World Politics* (Basingstoke, Palgrave, 2002).

2 This is what Depuy calls the 'law of co-existence': P-M Depuy, 'The Place and Role of Unilateralism in International Law' (2004) 11 *European Journal of International Law* 19, 22.

3 For an excellent discussion of the transition of international law from coexistence to cooperation see W Friedman, *The Changing Structure of International Law* (London, Stevens & Sons, 1964).

key areas of international concern, giving rise to relatively 'self-contained regimes'[4] such as international human rights law, international environmental law, international economic law etc.[5]

As with any system of law, in order to be effective it is imperative that international law is subject to authoritative interpretation and application. The 'principal judicial organ of the United Nations'[6] (UN) is the International Court of Justice, which is generally considered to have emerged as 'the supreme court of international law'.[7] However, in a world order predicated upon the principle of the sovereign equality of states,[8] the jurisdiction of the International Court of Justice is limited to disputes between states; furthermore, its jurisdiction can only be activated where states provide their consent.[9]

The consent-based jurisdiction of the International Court of Justice has seriously impeded its potential to authoritatively interpret and apply international law. In order to circumvent this restriction states have sought alternative ways to ensure that international disputes are subjected to authoritative adjudication, most notably through the creation of treaty tribunals. This is when states conclude an international agreement which establishes a tribunal that is competent to hear disputes arising under that treaty and, in certain circumstances, possesses compulsory jurisdiction in relation to those disputes. Take for example the International Tribunal for the Law of the Sea (ITLOS), which was created by the United Nations Convention on the Law of the Sea (UNCLOS) and which exercises broad jurisdictional competence extending to any dispute concerning the interpretation or application of UNCLOS as well as to disputes concerning any 'international agreement related to the purposes of th[e] Convention' and principles of customary international law.[10] Although the dispute resolution machinery of UNCLOS is complicated, it is important to note that in certain instances, such as those relating to the prompt release of vessels

[4] B Simma, 'Self-Contained Regimes' (1985) 16 *Netherlands Yearbook of International Law* 111.

[5] 'Presently there is no homogenous system of international law. International law consists of erratic blocks and elements; different partial systems; and universal, regional, or even bilateral subsystems and sub-subsystems of different levels of legal integration': G Hafner, 'Pros and Cons Ensuing from Fragmentation of International Law' (2003–2004) 25 *Michigan Journal of International Law* 849, 850.

[6] Statute of the International Court of Justice 1945, Art 1.

[7] J Charney, 'Is International Law Threatened by Multiple International Tribunals?' (1998) *Recueil des Cours* 101, 115.

[8] United Nations Charter 1945, Art 2(1).

[9] As the PCIJ (which was the predecessor to the International Court of Justice) explained in the *East Carelia* case, 'it is well established in international law that no State can, without its consent, be compelled to submit its dispute with other States either to mediation or top arbitration, or to any other kind of pacific settlement': *Status of East Carelia Case* (*Finland v USSSR*) 1923 PCIJ (series B) No 5 at 27 (Advisory Opinion of 23 July).

[10] United Nations Convention on the Law of the Sea 1982, Art 288(2).

and crews[11] and the prescription of provisional orders,[12] ITLOS possesses compulsory jurisdiction.

However, the integration of tribunals within treaty regimes often deters states from becoming parties to that treaty, especially when the treaty touches upon particularly politically sensitive issues. Consider, for example, the refusal of Russia, USA, Israel and China to become parties to the Rome Statute Establishing the International Criminal Court, not because of the substantive definition of the international crimes per se, but instead because these states are concerned that that their nationals (and in particular their military personnel) could potentially face criminal proceedings before an international criminal tribunal sitting in a foreign jurisdiction.[13] Indeed, in highly politicised areas there have been no attempts to create treaty tribunals, a good example being the absence of an international tribunal that is authorised to interpret and apply international humanitarian law.[14]

In order to expose international disputes which implicate regimes of international law to international adjudication there has been a dramatic increase in the use of commissions of inquiry in recent years, especially by organs of the UN, which are mandated to pursue fact-finding in relation to a particular international dispute and, almost always since the end of the Cold War, to interpret and apply relevant principles of international law to the determined facts.[15] Although decisions of commissions of inquiry are not (generally) binding upon the parties to the dispute and are thus not enforceable, the combination of their recent proliferation with the fact that they exercise 'quasi-judicial'[16] powers means that their contribution

[11] United Nations Convention on the Law of the Sea 1982, Art 292.

[12] United Nations Convention on the Law of the Sea 1982, Art 290.

[13] Strictly speaking, the International Criminal Court does not possess compulsory jurisdiction. This is because the International Criminal Court system is based upon the principle of complementarity; the International Criminal Court is only able to engage its jurisdiction where a signatory state is 'unable or unwilling' to investigate or prosecute allegations that international crimes have been committed: Rome Statute Establishing the International Criminal Court 1998, Art 17(1)(a).

[14] Although 1977 Additional Protocol I, Art 70 to the 1949 Geneva Conventions establishes an International Humanitarian Fact Finding Commission (IHFFC), the mandate of this commission is to engage in fact-finding rather than to apply and enforce international humanitarian law. Note that whilst the International Criminal Court, ICTY and ICTR are authorised to interpret and apply international humanitarian law they are not properly categorised as treaty tribunals in the sense that they are tribunals created by international humanitarian law treaties for the purpose of interpreting and applying the provisions of those treaties.

[15] 'In the absence of universal compulsory jurisdiction by international judicial bodies, these commissions of inquiry are a way in which the international community can obtain an authoritative determination of whether these violations have taken place and who is responsible'; D Akande and H Tonkin, 'International Commissions of Inquiry: A New Form of Adjudication?' (*EJIL: Talk!* 6 April 2012), available at www.ejiltalk.org/international-commissions-of-inquiry-a-new-form-of-adjudication/.

[16] J Alvarez, *International Organizations as Law-Makers* (Oxford, Oxford University Press, 2005) 516.

to the interpretation and application of international law is nevertheless 'considerable'.[17]

Evidently, the increased utilisation of commissions of inquiry raises many important international political and legal questions. In the political context, questions arise such as who should be appointed to these commissions and against which criteria should they be selected? Moreover, at what point in time should commissions be deployed, especially given that their deployment may exacerbate tensions already existing within volatile areas? Pertinent international law questions include whether commissions are created by international organisations (or more accurately organs of international organisations) that are imbued with the legal authority to establish them[18] and whether these commissions adhere to internationally acceptable standards of due process when they collect and assess testimonies and evidence.[19]

Due to time and space restrictions this chapter cannot consider all of these issues. Instead, the focus of this chapter is to assess whether interpretations of international law rendered by commissions of inquiry are consistent with interpretations delivered by other organs of the international dispute resolution machinery, and whether commissions of inquiry thereby reaffirm and strengthen existing international law, or whether the commissions demonstrate a tendency to diverge from existing interpretations, thereby posing a threat to the overall coherence of international law. In addressing this issue, this chapter is structured as follows. To set the scene, section 10.2 situates commissions of inquiry within their broader historical and theoretical context. In particular, section 10.2 argues that although commissions of inquiry were originally intended to be purely fact-finding missions that were designed to have a pacifying effect on potentially combustible inter-state disputes, since the end of the Cold War they have increasingly exhibited a human rights focus and have been largely deployed to determine the responsibility of actors for violations of international human rights law, international humanitarian

[17] Alvarez (n 16): 'These contemporary CoIs, while not producing legally binding outcomes, nevertheless carry out various adjudicative functions, from determining applicable legal frameworks and the scope of the legal rules and norms in question to determining whether particular acts amount to violations of these rules and norms'; C Henderson, 'Commissions of Inquiry: Flexible Temporariness or Permanent Predictability?' (2014) 45 *Netherlands Yearbook of International Law* 287, 288.

[18] On this see R Buchan, 'The *Mavi Marmara* Incident and the Application of International Humanitarian Law by Quasi-Judicial Bodies' in D Jinks, JN Maogoto and S Solomon, *Applying International Humanitarian Law in Judicial and Quasi-Judicial Bodies: International and Domestic Aspects* (Asser Press, 2014).

[19] On this see S Wilkinson, 'Standards of Proof in International Humanitarian and Human Rights Fact-Finding and Inquiry Missions' (Geneva Academy of International Law and Human Rights, 2012).

law and international criminal law. Section 10.3 illustrates the potential of commissions of inquiry to engage in diverging interpretations of international law and suggests that this is particularly visible where different commissions are established to assess the same international dispute yet arrive at very different interpretations of international law, a situation which occurred in relation to the four commissions of inquiry that were established to determine the legality of Israel's enforcement of its naval blockade against the *Mavi Marmara* on 31 May 2010. With this in mind, section 10.4 suggests that the work of commissions of inquiry can threaten the integrity and unity of international law which, in turn, can create legal insecurity and foster less accountability. Whilst this chapter concedes in section 10.4 that commissions of inquiry are an indispensable part of the international dispute resolution architecture, I propose that the threat they represent to the coherency of international law can be largely averted if the commissions were to better appreciate the adjudicatory nature of their mandates, and thus their role within international adjudication and international law making more generally. Section 10.5 offers some conclusions.

10.2. THE END OF THE COLD WAR AND THE PROLIFERATION OF COMMISSIONS OF INQUIRY

Commissions of inquiry have long been utilised to address inter-state disputes. Indeed, the use of commissions of inquiry can be traced back to the *Maine* inquiries of 1898, which were inquiries established by the US and Spain in order to determine the cause of an explosion which resulted in the sinking of a US battleship. Recognizing the utility of these types of commissions to clarify the facts surrounding important international incidents, the framers of the 1899 Hague Convention placed commissions of inquiry on a more formal basis.[20] Article 9 of the Hague Convention provides that

> in differences of an international nature involving neither honor nor vital interests, and arising from a difference of opinion on points of fact, the Signatory Powers recommend that the parties, who have not been able to come to an agreement by means of diplomacy, should as far as circumstances allow, institute an International Commission of Inquiry, to facilitate a solution of these differences by elucidating the facts by means of an impartial and conscientious investigation.

[20] As Merrills explains, the impact of the *Maine* inquiries 'sufficient impressed the delegates to the Hague Peace Conference of 1898 for them to give serious attention to the issue of fact-finding in international disputes': J Merrills, *International Dispute Settlement* (Cambridge, Cambridge University Press, 2011) 41–42.

Article 14 further explains that '[t]he report of the International Commission of Inquiry is limited to a statement of facts, and has in no way the character of an Arbitral Award'. Importantly, commissions of inquiry were intended to comprise a body of experts, with each party having a representative and at least one member being independent, to determine the facts of incident. 'The principal idea was to win time, to pre-empt an exacerbation of the conflict and to clarify facts before diverging appreciations and presentations of the situation would lead to complete deadlock.'[21]

This being said, a number of commissions of inquiry established under the Hague Convention found it difficult to pursue an exclusively fact-finding role. The Dogger Bank Inquiry, for example, was created in order to investigate the firing by a Russian warship at a UK fishing fleet which it mistakenly believed to be Japanese torpedo boats. The parties to the dispute created a commission of inquiry pursuant to Article 9 of the Hague Convention, but conferred a mandate that did not just require the commission to identify and clarify the circumstances surrounding the event but, in addition and deviating considerably from the strictures of Article 9, mandated the commission to determine who was responsible for the incident and the extent of their culpability.

Building upon the Hague experience, commissions of inquiry were also embedded within other international treaties. The League of Nations, for example, provided for the use of commissions of inquiry and the Council of the League established commissions on various occasions, including the Aaland Islands dispute between Finland and Sweden in 1921 and the Mosul dispute between Turkey and the UK in 1925. As with the commissions of inquiry established under the Hague Convention, the principal objective of these inquiries was to examine and determine the facts of the incident under consideration. Once the facts were settled, this would provide the necessary foundation for the organs of the League to formally address and attempt to resolve the dispute. However, as with many of the inquiries established under the Hague Convention, more often than not those 'commissions did not limit their exercises to pure fact-finding and often they developed a comprehensive dispute settlement regime'.[22] Instead, these commissions often sought to apply international legal rules to the determined facts and on this basis adjudicate liability.

Notwithstanding that commissions of enquiry often strayed beyond their fact-finding role and into the field of international legal

[21] LJ van den Herik, 'An Inquiry into the Role of Commission of Inquiry in International Law: Navigating the Tensions between Fact-Finding and Application of International Law' (2014) 13 *Chinese Journal of International Law* 507, 511.

[22] van den Herik (n 21) 518.

adjudication,[23] van den Herik is correct when she explains that, between 1899 and the end of the Cold War,

> [e]ven if trends towards the use of legal terms and the inevitable intertwined blurring of the fact/law divide was already visible, overall the inquiries functioned as mechanisms of peace rather than as instruments of law fully embedded in a legal framework and procedure. They were predominantly transactional in nature and facts were established with a view of settling a given dispute or facilitating the settlement thereof. Their primary goal was thus not to condemn and/or impose an objective and formal legal truth, but rather to appease and calm animosities. Even inquiries that did not manage to fully disclose 'the truth' could have a pacifying effect because of the cooling off-period that came along with their operation or because they helped States to accept certain findings in the name of truth.[24]

As we shall see as this chapter progresses, in recent times there has been a 'significant shift'[25] in the *raison d'etre* of commissions of enquiry. Nowadays, almost invariably, commissions are mandated to determine whether violations of international law have been committed. The key date in this transition is the end of the Cold War.

The end of the Cold War is rightly regarded as a seminal moment in the trajectory of international relations and international law. The end of the Cold War is such a significant date because it marked the end of the ideological contestation between East and West and, in particular, signalled the 'triumph' of liberal democracy as the only legitimate form of political governance.[26] In the years following the end of the Cold War we witnessed the formation of an international community of liberal states within the broader, politically pluralist international society of sovereign states, and which has demonstrated a tendency to consider only those states that exhibit respect for the liberal values of democracy, human rights and the rule of law as legitimate. Moreover, this international community has campaigned, often aggressively, for the promotion of liberal values to non-liberal states. Importantly, the international community's campaign for liberal development has been centralised in the United Nations (UN);

[23] By international legal adjudication I mean the interpretation and application of principles of international law by a body that is 'characterized by some serious attempt, primarily through rules for the type of expertise required of the dispute settlers, their method of selection, or their tenure in office (or all three), to recognize [its] "independent" status'; Alvarez (n 16) 459.

[24] van den Herik (n 21) 519.

[25] Henderson (n 17) 292.

[26] C Brown, '"Really Existing Liberalism", Peaceful Democracies and International Order' in R Fawn and J Larkins (eds), *International Society after the Cold War: Anarchy and Order Reconsidered* (Macmillan, 1996) 30.

since the end of the Cold War the UN has emerged as an active promoter of liberal values, in particular respect for fundamental human rights.[27]

Under the influence of the international community the UN has sought to promote respect for liberal values through a number of different mechanisms, such as authorising coalitions of willing states to use military force to intervene in internal conflicts to protect human rights,[28] deploying peacebuilding missions to assist with, and even international administrations that become responsible for, reconstructing war-torn societies upon a liberal basis[29] and creating international criminal tribunals such as the ICTY[30] and ICTR[31] to punish individuals accused of egregious violations of human rights. In a similar vein, we have increasingly witnessed the UN deploy commissions of inquiry, which are bodies that can be

> characterized by some serious attempt, primarily through rules for the type of expertise required of the dispute settlers, their method of selection, or their tenure in office (or all three), to recognize the 'independent' status of the third party decision-maker from the governments involved in their creation.[32]

Overwhelmingly, UN-authorised commissions of inquiry have been deployed in relation to incidents that involve the egregious violation of fundamental human rights. Like their predecessors, a core feature of UN-authorised commissions is to engage in fact-finding. Unlike their predecessors, however, in addition to fact-finding these commissions of inquiry are also *expressly* mandated to determine whether violations of international human rights law and international humanitarian law have been committed and, increasingly, whether these violations are sufficiently serious to amount to violations of international criminal law. In this sense, then, UN-authorised commissions of inquiry can be regarded as another mechanism devised by the UN to help promote respect for human rights, and can be thus seen as a product of the UN's post-Cold War liberal identity.

Commissions of inquiry have been established by various UN organs, including the Security Council, the General Assembly, the Human Rights Council (and its predecessor the Commission on Human Rights), the Secretary General and the High Commissioner for Human Rights. This being said, it is certainly correct that in recent years the

[27] R Buchan, *International Law and the Construction of the Liberal Peace* (Hart Publishing, 2013) Ch 2.

[28] UN Security Council Resolution 1973 (2011).

[29] UN Security Council Resolution 1244 (1999); UN Security Council Resolution 1272 (1999).

[30] UN Security Council Resolution 827 (1993).

[31] UN Security Council Resolution 995 (1994).

[32] Alvarez (n 16) 459.

UN Human Rights Council has 'taken the lead'[33] in deploying commissions of inquiry, which is perhaps unsurprising given that the Human Rights Council possesses an explicit mandate to promote respect for fundamental human rights.

It should be noted that it is not just UN organs that create commissions of inquiry: other international organisations, such as the EU, have utilised commissions of inquiry to address disputes that fall within their competence.[34] As we shall see below, states have also deployed commissions of inquiry to address incidents implicating international law, especially when such incidents involve allegations that fundamental human rights have been egregiously violated.[35]

10.3. ADJUDICATION OF INTERNATIONAL LAW

Given that commissions of inquiry now exercise powers of legal adjudication, combined with the fact that the use of such commissions has dramatically increased in recent years, it is important that we examine the impact that decisions of commissions of inquiry have upon the content and trajectory of international law. In short, the question posed is whether they produce decisions that offer interpretations of international law that differ from established and settled interpretations.

Many commissions of inquiry have been criticised for reaching decisions that deviate from established interpretations of international law.[36] However, the potential for them to produce diverging interpretations of international law is especially apparent where multiple commissions of inquiry are established and mandated to interpret and apply international law in relation to the same factual incident yet reach very different

[33] C Harwood, 'Human Rights in Fancy Dress? The Use of International Criminal Law by Human Rights Council Commissions of Inquiry in Pursuit of Accountability' (2015) *Grotius Working Paper* 2015/043-ICL 1, 2.

[34] See for example European Union (EU), *Independent International Fact-Finding Mission on the Conflict in Georgia* (September 2009) Volumes I, II and III.

[35] Although note that commissions of inquiry established by states to investigate the legality of its conduct are more susceptible to being criticised that the panel leading the commission does not comprise individuals sufficiently independent of the state to be regarded as a *bona fida* commission of inquiry.

[36] Arguably the most controversial has been the Goldstone Commission, which was established by the UN Human Rights Council to determine whether Israel had committed violations of international humanitarian law during its 2008–2009 conflict in Gaza. The commission found that Israel had committed violations of international humanitarian law which, in certain instances, amounted to war crimes. For a critical discussion of how this commission interpreted and applied international humanitarian law see J-P Kot, 'Israeli Civilians versus Palestinian Combatants? Reading the Goldstone Report in light of the Israeli Conception of the Principle of Distinction' (2011) 24 *Leiden Journal of International Law* 961.

conclusions. This occurred in relation to Israel's interception of the *Mavi Marmara*, where four commissions of inquiry were established to examine the compatibility of Israel's conduct with prevailing principles of international law.

After years of in-fighting between Fatah and Hamas, two political parties competing for control over Palestine, in June 2007 Hamas was elected to power in Gaza whilst Fatah retained control over the West Bank. As a result of its belligerent stance towards Israel, Israel declared Hamas a 'terrorist organisation' and determined Gaza 'hostile territory'.[37] Concerned that Hamas was seeking to arm itself in order to commit violence against Israel, Israel imposed a land blockade against Gaza on 14 November 2001.[38] To reinforce this land blockade, Israel imposed a naval blockade against the Gazan coast on 3 January 2009.[39] Concerned that a humanitarian crisis was occurring in Gaza, in May 2010 the Free Gaza Movement dispatched a flotilla of ships with the express intention of violating the naval blockade and delivering humanitarian aid to Gaza. On 31 May 2010 the flotilla approached the naval blockade and was advised by Israeli forces to either turn back or to dock at a nearby Israeli port in order for their cargo to be inspected. With the flotilla rejecting the offer, Israel sought to enforce its naval blockade. In general, this occurred relatively peacefully. However, one boat, the *Mavi Marmara*, resisted the interception and violence erupted between the crew members and Israeli forces. Nine crew members were killed and several Israeli military personnel were injured. Israel eventually assumed control of the situation, confiscated the boat and detained the crew members.[40]

This event raises a number of important international law questions. Was Israel entitled to deploy a naval blockade against Gaza under international humanitarian law and was the degree of force used to enforce the blockade justifiable? Did Israel's treatment of crew members whilst they were detained violate international human rights law? Did the use of violence during the takeover of the *Mavi Marmara* and, subsequently,

[37] *Statement of Israel's Foreign Minister Regarding Israel's Policy towards Hamas and its Terrorism* (1 October 2007), available at www.mfa.gov.il/MFA/About+the+Ministry/Foreign+Minister+Livni/Speeches+interviews/Statements+by+Israeli+FM+Livni+regarding+Israeli+policy+toward+the+Hamas+and+its+terrorism+11-Sep-20.htm.

[38] These land crossings were implemented in response to the Second Intifada, which began in September 2000. See generally J Pressman, 'The Second Intifada: Background and Causes of the Israeli-Palestinian Conflict' (2003) 23(2) *Journal of Conflict Studies* 114.

[39] Number 1/2009 Blockade of the Gaza Strip (3 January 2009), publicised by the Israeli government at en.mot.gov.il/index.php?option=com_content&view=article&id=124:no12009&catid=17:noticetomariners&Itemid=12.

[40] These facts have been determined by a fact-finding mission established by the UN Human Rights Council, *Report of the International Fact-Finding Mission to Investigate Violations of International Law, Including International Humanitarian and Human Rights Law, Resulting from the Israeli Attacks on the Flotilla of Ships Carrying Humanitarian Assistance*, UN Doc A/HRC/15/21 (27 September 2010) (*HRC Report*).

against detained crew members engage the individual criminal responsibility of certain members of the Israeli military?

Without any realistic prospect of an international tribunal being given the opportunity to authoritatively examine the incident and thus pronounce upon the international legality of Israel's conduct, various commissions of inquiry were established to examine whether Israel had committed violations of international law. Two of these reports are domestic and two are international. On the domestic level, both Israel[41] and Turkey[42] established commissions of inquiry which produced reports into the incident. On the international plain, the UN Human Rights Council[43] and the UN Secretary General[44] both established commissions of inquiry to investigate the incident.

Space and time constraints do not afford the opportunity to compare and contrast how these four commissions interpreted and applied the various international legal frameworks implicated by Israel's interception of the *Mavi Marmara*. Instead, this chapter will focus upon how these four commissions interpreted and applied international humanitarian law to the incident, namely the law of naval blockade, an issue that all four reports considered in detail.

10.3.1. The Law of Naval Blockade

A fundamental principle of the law of the high seas is that ships are subject to the exclusive sovereignty of the state of the flag under which the ship sails.[45] This principle is, however, subject to a number of recognised exceptions. A well-recognised exception is that, as a principle of *lex specialis*, during times of armed conflict, international humanitarian law permits states to interdict ships on the high seas where they violate or intend to violate a lawfully established blockade. Indeed, Israel justified its interception of the *Mavi Marmara* on the basis of the law of naval blockade.[46]

41 The Public Commission to Examine the Maritime Incident of 31 May 2010 (23 January 2011), available at www.turkel-committee.gov.il/files/wordocs/8808report-eng.pdf (*Turkel Commission Report*).

42 *Report of Turkish National Commission of Inquiry* (11 February 2011), available at www.mfa.gov.tr/data/Turkish%20Report%20Final%20-%20UN%20Copy.pdf (*Turkish Report*).

43 *HRC Report* (n 40).

44 *Report of the Secretary-General's Panel of Inquiry on the 31 May 2010 Flotilla Incident* (July 2011), available at www.un.org/News/dh/infocus/middle_east/Gaza_Flotilla_Panel_Report.pdf (referred to as the *Palmer Report*, after the Chair of the Panel, Sir Geoffrey Palmer).

45 UNCLOS, Art 92.

46 'We were acting totally within our legal rights. The international law is very clear on this issue … if you have a declared blockade, publicly declared, legally declared, publicised as international law requires, and someone is trying to break that blockade and though you have warned them … you are entitled to intercept even on the high seas' (Mark Regev,

A crucial question, then, is whether Israel's naval blockade was lawfully deployed. The law of naval blockade is located in customary international humanitarian law. However, although not formally a binding document, the *San Remo Manual* is often considered to represent a codification of customary international law that is applicable during times of armed conflict at sea.[47] In this sense, the *Manual* is considered authoritative.[48] The *Manual* explains that in order for a naval blockade to be lawfully deployed it must be publically announced, enforced and effective. It must also apply impartially and cannot be imposed against the ports or coasts of neutral states. Furthermore, the blockade must be in response to an international armed conflict and in all cases must be proportionate.[49]

Again, time and space restrictions preclude an assessment of how the four commissions interpreted and applied these criteria of the law of naval blockade. Instead, my focus will be upon how these commissions of inquiry classified the armed conflict between Israel and Hamas, an issue of immense importance to determining how the Israeli-Hamas conflict is to be regulated and which has been much debated in international legal literature, and in particular to reveal the considerable discrepancies between them.

10.3.2. International Armed Conflict

International humanitarian law is structured according to a bifurcation between international armed conflicts and non-international armed conflicts. International armed conflicts are defined as 'the resort to armed force between states',[50] whereas non-international armed conflicts are defined as 'protracted armed violence between governmental authorities and organized groups or between such groups'.[51] Significantly, different international legal rules govern international and non-international armed conflicts. As has already been noted above, the *San Remo Manual* explains that customary international law only permits naval blockades

Spokesman for Israeli Prime Minister Binyamin Netanyahu, quoted in *The Washington Post*). See C Lynch, 'Israel's Raid Revives Questions of International Law' *The Washington Post* (1 June 2010), available at www.washingtonpost.com/wp-dyn/content/article/2010/06/01/AR2010060102934.html.

[47] See *San Remo Manual on International Law Applicable to Armed Conflicts at Sea*, Introduction (12 June 1994).

[48] L Doswald-Beck, *San Remo Manual on International Law Applicable to Armed Conflicts at Sea* (Cambridge, Cambridge University Press, 1995).

[49] *San Remo Manual on International Law* (n 47) Section II.

[50] *Prosecutor v Tadić*, Case No IT-94-I-I, (Judgment 15 July 1999) para 70.

[51] *Tadić* (n 50).

to be deployed in international armed conflicts,[52] which is a product of international humanitarian law's historical preoccupation with regulating armed conflict between states as opposed to conflict between state and non-state actors.

In relation to the *Mavi Marmara* incident, the pertinent question therefore becomes whether Israel and Hamas were engaged in an international armed conflict on 31 May 2010. As we shall see, the four commissions of inquiry arrived at very different conclusions and it is interesting to compare and contrast their approaches and findings.

Both the Turkish Report and the Human Rights Council Report determined that Israel and Hamas were engaged in an armed conflict on 31 May 2010 in the sense that the violence being perpetrated was of sufficient intensity to engage the application of international humanitarian law. However, neither of these two reports address the issue of whether the armed conflict was of an international character, namely, whether it was an armed conflict between two states. Instead, both reports imply that because an armed conflict was occurring, Israel possessed the right to blockade and that it is unnecessary to classify the legal status of this armed conflict.[53]

This is a strange conclusion. It is well established that international humanitarian law distinguishes between international and non-international armed conflicts, though the maintenance of this distinction has been subject to criticism in recent years. Critics argue that although historically international humanitarian law was concerned with regulating inter-state violence and was thus agonistic to what occurred within states, however violent the situation was, under the pressures of globalisation the international/domestic divide has all but dissolved and that international humanitarian law should apply regardless of which actors are perpetrating the violence and instead on the basis that the violence reaches a certain intensity.[54] Whilst this maybe a normatively attractive position, such an approach is certainly *lex ferenda*. Although certain principles applicable in international armed conflicts are now reflected, either via treaty or custom, in non-international armed conflicts, in terms of

[52] The *Explanation to the San Remo Manual* explains that 'although the provisions of the Manual are primarily meant to apply to international armed conflicts at sea, this has intentionally not been expressly indicated in paragraph 1 in order to dissuade the implementation of these rules in non-international armed conflicts involving naval operations': Doswald-Beck (n 48) 73.

[53] *Turkish Report* (n 42) 33 ff; *HRC Report* (n 40) para 51 ff.

[54] JG Stewart, 'Towards a Single Definition of Armed Conflict in International Humanitarian Law: A Critique of Internationalized Armed Conflict' (2003) 85 *International Review of the Red Cross* 313; E Crawford, *The Treatment of Combatants and Insurgents under the Law of Armed Conflict* (Oxford, Oxford University Press, 2010) Ch 1.

lex lata international humanitarian law incontrovertibly requires that armed conflicts are classified as either international or non-international in character. In light of this, it would seem that the decision of the Turkish and Human Rights Council Reports to dispense with the need to classify the armed conflict as international or non-international in character is legally erroneous and instead represents an attempt to progressively develop international humanitarian law.

The Turkel Report concluded that on 31 May 2010 Israel and Hamas were engaged in an international armed conflict.[55] The armed conflict was classified as international on the basis of the *Targeted Killings* case.[56] In this case, Israel's Supreme Court held that although Hamas is not the governing authority of a state, Israel and Hamas were nevertheless engaged in an international armed conflict because the violence crossed the Israeli border.[57] This decision, however, has been heavily criticised, not least because it is inconsistent with the history of state practice which reveals that 'the single defining feature of international armed conflicts has not been their cross-border, but their interstate, nature'.[58]

The Turkel Report goes on to explain that even if this is not grounds for internationalising the armed conflict, a naval blockade can still be imposed in the realms of a non-international armed conflict,[59] thereby deviating from the requirement of the *San Remo Manual* that naval blockades can only be utilised in international armed conflicts.

This interpretation is justified on the basis that there is sufficient state practice to substantiate the claim that customary international humanitarian law now recognises the right to impose naval blockades in non-international armed conflicts. As the Turkel Report notes

> [n]aval blockades have, nevertheless, been imposed in non-international armed conflict … In certain situations, States have imposed a military or economic blockade against an enemy that is not a *de jure* government.[60]

The Turkel Report provides three examples. The first example refers to the Union's blockade of southern ports controlled by the Confederates during

55 *Turkel Report* (n 41) para 38.

56 HCJ 769/02 *Public Committee Against Torture v Government* [2006] (2) IsrLR 459. In actual fact, the *Turkel Report* identifies two grounds for internationalising an armed conflict between a state and an organised armed group: the *Targeted Killings* scenario and where the state occupies the territory within which the armed group is located. However, the report clearly states that Gaza was not occupied by Israel on 31 May 2010, and therefore the only conclusion is that the *Turkel Report* sought to internationalise the armed conflict on the basis of the *Targeted Killings* judgment.

57 ibid para 18.

58 M Milanovic, 'Lessons for Human Rights and Humanitarian Law in the War on Terror: Comparing Hamdan and the Israeli Targeted Killings Case' (2007) 89 *International Review of the Red Cross* 373, 384.

59 *Turkel Report* (n 41) para 44.

60 *Turkel Report* (n 41) para 39.

the American Civil War.[61] However, to read the American Civil War as a non-international armed conflict is to fundamentally misconceive the nature the hostilities. The Confederates were regarded as a belligerent power by many foreign governments and so the armed conflict between the Union and the Confederates is in fact a well-known example of an *international* armed conflict.[62]

The second example given by the Turkel Report is the Chinese government's blockade of ports under control of the Communist forces in 1949.[63] However, careful inspection of the correspondence between the Chinese government and Communist forces reveals that the government was not imposing a naval blockade of the ports.[64]

The third example offered by the Turkel Report is Israel's blockade of Lebanon in 2006.[65] The Turkel Report suggests that this was a blockade by a state, namely Israel, in the realms of its armed conflict with Hezbollah, a non-state actor. However, before the UN Security Council the Israeli representative unambiguously stated that because of the close relationship between the Lebanese government and Hezbollah, Israel was actually in an armed conflict with Lebanon.[66] In other words, the conflict was between two states and was thus technically an international armed conflict.

In conclusion, then, the Turkel Report identifies little state practice to substantiate the claim that customary international humanitarian law now recognises the right to impose a naval blockade in times of non-international armed conflict. Instead, as the *San Remo Manual* explains, international humanitarian law only permits the use of naval blockades in the context of international armed conflict.

The Palmer Report considers that on 31 May 2010 the conflict between Israel and Hamas had 'all the trappings of an international armed conflict', justifying this determination on the basis that Hamas was in control of territory and possessed state-like features.[67] In essence, the Palmer Report implies that Hamas amounts to a belligerent power under international

[61] *Turkel Report* (n 41) fn 131.

[62] US Department of State: Office of the Historian, *The Blockade of Confederate Ports, 1861–1865*, available at history.state.gov/milestones/1861-1865/Blockade.

[63] *Turkel Report* (n 41) fn 131.

[64] LC Woosley, 'Closure of Ports by the Chinese National Government' (1950) 44 *American Journal of International Law* 350, 350.

[65] *Turkel Report* (n 41) para 43.

[66] 'Responsibility for this belligerent act of war lies with the Government of Lebanon, from whose territory these acts have been launched into Israel'; Permanent Representative of Israel to the United Nations, *Identical Letters Dated July 12 2006 from the Permanent Representative of Israel to the United Nations Addressed to the Secretary-General and the President of the Security Council*, UN Doc A/60/937, S/2006/515, 12 July 2006.

[67] *Palmer Report* (n 44) para 73.

humanitarian law[68] and thus the conflict between Israel and Hamas should be viewed as an international armed conflict.[69]

It is indeed correct that international humanitarian law recognises that where a non-state actor is engaged in an armed conflict with a state but the non-state actor is recognised as a 'belligerent' under international law then this otherwise non-international armed conflict will be transformed into an international armed conflict. The reason for this is because, as Falk explains, '[i]nternational law treats an internal war with the status of belligerency as essentially identical to a war between sovereign states'.[70] This notwithstanding, it is unlikely that Hamas exhibits the necessary features in order to be regarded as a belligerent. Lauterpacht identifies four characteristics that an organised armed group must possess in order to be classified as a belligerent power under international humanitarian law:

> [F]irst, there must exist within the State an armed conflict of a general (as distinguished from purely local) character; secondly, the insurgents must occupy and administer a substantial portion of national territory; thirdly, they must conduct hostilities in accordance with the rules of war and through organized armed forces acting under a reasonable authority; fourthly, there must exist circumstances which make it necessary, for outside states to define their attitude by means of recognition of belligerency.[71]

According to this definition, Hamas cannot be regarded as a belligerent power. First, belligerency status is intended to apply to organised armed groups that are participating in a particularly fierce and entrenched civil war against the government (note the requirement that this 'must exist within a state'). Demonstrably, Hamas is not 'within' Israel. Secondly, Hamas does not comply with the third requirement that it conducts hostilities in accordance with the rules of war. As is well known and documented,[72] Hamas frequently engages in the indiscriminate firing of mortar shells into Israel, with wanton disregard for civilian damage. Such conduct is manifestly inconsistent with the basic tenets of international humanitarian law; in particular, the requirement to distinguish between civilians and combatants and between civilian objects and military

[68] M Milanovic, 'Palmer Committee Report on the Mavi Marmara Incident' (*EJIL: Talk!* 2 September 2011), available at www.ejiltalk.org/palmer-committee-report-on-the-mavi-marmara-incident/.

[69] Interestingly, note that the *Turkel Report* concludes that the doctrine of belligerency is 'almost irrelevant' under contemporary international humanitarian law: *Turkel Report* (n 40) para 39.

[70] R Falk, 'Janus Tormented: The International Law of Internal War' in JN Rosenau (eds) *International Aspects of Civil Strife* (Princeton, Princeton University Press, 1964) 203.

[71] H Lauterpacht, *Recognition in International Law* (Cambridge, Cambridge University Press, 1947) 176.

[72] See, for example, EU Council Commons Position 2001/931/CFDSP, 27 December 2001.

objects.[73] Accordingly, in determining that Hamas is a belligerent power, the Palmer Report engages in an erroneous interpretation of international humanitarian law.

Moreover, like the Turkel Report, the Palmer Report also finds it necessary to consider whether naval blockades can be imposed in the realms of non-international armed conflicts. As such, it concludes that customary international law now recognises such a right.[74] Thus, even if Israel and Hamas were engaged in a non-international armed conflict on 31 May 2010, Israel still possessed the right to impose a naval blockade. The report justifies this approach on the basis that there are 'a few examples'[75] of state practice where naval blockades have been imposed in non-international armed conflicts. As it happens, the report only provides one example: the Union's naval blockade of Southern ports during the American Civil War.[76] As we saw above however in relation to the Turkel Report, this incident cannot be regarded as an example of state practice contributing to the formation of a customary international law that permits the use of naval blockades in a non-international armed conflict.

10.3.3. International Criminal Court

An interesting development occurred on 14 May 2013 when the Comoros referred the incident that occurred on 31 May 2010 to the International Criminal Court, asserting that international crimes were committed and urged the Office of the Prosecutor (OTP) to open a formal investigation into the incident.[77] On 15 May 2013 the OTP announced that it would conduct a preliminary investigation into the situation under Article 53(1) of the Rome Statute with the view to determining whether a formal investigation should be opened.[78] On 6 November 2014 the OTP determined that there was a reasonable basis to believe that Israeli forces had committed war crimes on 31 May 2010 but decided against proceeding with a formal investigation, on the basis that the situation referred to it was of insufficient gravity to warrant engaging the jurisdiction of the

[73] The use of weapons in an indiscriminate manner constitutes a clear violation of international humanitarian law: J-M Henckaerts and L Doswald-Beck, *Customary International Humanitarian Law* (Cambridge, Cambridge University Press, 2005) r 11.

[74] *Palmer Report* (n 44) App I, para 23.

[75] *Palmer Report* (n 44) App I, para 21.

[76] *Palmer Report* (n 44) App I, para 21.

[77] *Letter of Referral of the Situation that occurred on 31 May 2010* (14 May 2013), available at www.icc-cpi.int/iccdocs/otp/Referral-from-Comoros.pdf (*Letter of Referral*).

[78] ICC Press Release, 'ICC Prosecutor Receives Referral by the authorities of the Union of the Comoros in relation to the events of May 2010 on the vessel "Mavi Marmara"' (14 May 2013), available at www.icc-cpi.int/en_menus/icc/press%20and%20media/press%20releases/Pages/otp-statement-14-05-2013.aspx.

International Criminal Court.[79] Importantly, in concluding that there was a reasonable basis to believe that international crimes had been committed (and in particular that war crimes had been committed) the OTP was required to make an important determination in relation to legal character of the armed conflict between Israel and Hamas.

Article 8 of the Rome Statute defines the offence of war crimes and distinguishes between war crimes committed in an international and a non-international armed conflict. In addressing whether there was a reasonable basis to believe that Israeli forces had committed war crimes the OTP was therefore required to classify whether the *Mavi Marmara* interdiction that occurred on 31 May 2010 was committed in the context of an international armed conflict or a non-international armed conflict according to the rules of international humanitarian law. Given the extensive consideration of this issue by the four commissions of inquiry, it is interesting to consider the approach of the OTP.

Importantly, the OTP held that on 31 May 2010 'the situation in Gaza can be considered within the framework of an international armed conflict in view of the continuing military occupation of Israel'.[80] This conclusion is based upon the well-established view that international humanitarian law regards occupied territory as being subject to the rules of international armed conflict.[81] Whether or not territory is occupied depends upon whether the belligerent state exercises effective control over the said territory.[82] Since Israel's unilateral disengagement from Gaza in 2005 Israel has argued that it no longer possesses effective control over Gaza on the basis that it no longer has a physical presence in Gaza.[83] The OTP subscribed to the opposite view and determined that a state can still exercise effective control over a territory even though it is not physically present on the territory in question. Although the OTP did not provide any justification for this approach, instead simply asserting that 'the prevalent view within the international community is that Israel remains an occupying

[79] OTP, *Situation of Registered Vessels of Comoros, Greece and Cambodia: Article 53(1) Report* (6 November 2014), available at www.icc-cpi.int/iccdocs/otp/OTP-COM-Article_53%281%29-Report-06Nov2014Eng.pdf. Note, however, that the Pre-Trial Chamber has since requested that the OTP reconsider its determination that the situation is of insufficient gravity; *Situation on the Registered Vessels of the Union of the Comoros, the Hellenic Republic, and the Kingdom of Cambodia*, Case No ICC-01/13, Decision on the Request of the Union of the Comoros to Review the Prosecutor's Decision not to Initiate an Investigation (16 July 2015), available at www.icc-cpi.int/iccdocs/doc/doc2015869.pdf.

[80] *Situation of Registered Vessels of Comoros* (n 79) para 16.

[81] Hague Regulations Respecting the Laws and Customs of War on Land 1907, Art 42.

[82] *Armed activities on the territory of the Congo* (*Democratic Republic of the Congo v Uganda*) [2005] ICJ Rep, 19 December 2005, paras 172, 175–76.

[83] Israel Military of Foreign Affairs, 'The Disengagement Plan—General Outline' (18 April 2004), available at www.mfa.gov.il/mfa/foreignpolicy/peace/mfadocuments/pages/disengagement%20plan%20-%20general%20outline.aspx.

power in Gaza despite the 2005 disengagement',[84] it would seem that this decision was made on the basis that Israel nevertheless continues to impose considerable control over Gaza because of its stringent land and naval blockade against Gaza and the fact that it reserves the right to make unilateral military incursions into Gaza.

This is not the place to discuss the complicated issue of whether Israel exercises effective control over Gaza and is therefore an occupying power. For the purpose of this chapter, what is interesting is that the OTP arrived at the decision that Israel and Hamas were engaged in an international armed conflict on the basis of the law of occupation, yet this basis for internationalising an otherwise non-international armed conflict was not identified by any of the four reports as being a ground on which the Israeli-Hamas armed conflict could be internationalised.

Both the Turkish and Human Rights Council Reports did determine that Gaza was occupied by Israel but, crucially, only in the context of reaffirming the obligations by Israel to the population of Gaza under the law of occupation, not in terms of internationalising their armed conflict.[85] As I have already noted, both these reports determined that Israel possessed the right to blockade Gaza on the basis that an armed conflict (in and by itself) was occurring. The Palmer Report expressly rejects that Israel is an occupying power on the basis that it is Hamas, an elected authority that is responsible for administering Gaza, which enjoys effective control over the territory.[86] The Turkel Commission gives this issue the most consideration by recognising that the law of occupation internationalises an otherwise non-international armed conflict but swiftly and decisively rejects this argument on the basis that, absent Israeli boots on the ground in Gaza, Israeli does not exercise effective control over Gaza.[87]

10.4. ANALYSIS

In light of the difficulties associated with accessing international tribunals, commissions of inquiry have emerged as a necessary feature of the international dispute architecture, providing a crucial forum within which legal debates can be conducted and thereby ensuring the continued relevance of international law. The contribution of commissions of inquiry to revitalising international human rights law, international humanitarian law and international criminal law has been particularly dramatic given that these are branches of international law that have historically lacked

84 *Situation of Registered Vessels of Comoros* (n 79) para 16.
85 *Turkish Report* (n 42) 81 ff; *HRC Report* (n 40) para 63.
86 *Palmer Report* (n 43) para 73.
87 *Turkel Report* (n 41) 50 ff.

effective enforcement before international tribunals. In the words of the UN:

> The work of commissions/mission is crucial for strengthening human rights protection in multiple ways. The commissions/missions can provide an historical record of serious violations of human rights law and international humanitarian law, and influence changes in law and practice in advance of human rights. Critically, they assist in ensuring accountability for serious violations, which is fundamental in order to deter future violations, promote compliance with the law and provide avenues of justice and redress for victims. They have done so in the inquiries of ad hoc international tribunals and of the International Criminal Court. Many of them have delved into the root causes of the violence and violations, triggering transitional justice mechanisms that address the rights to the truth, justice, remedies and reparations, and guarantees of non-recurrence, and have thus informed more sustainable peacebuilding and reconciliation efforts, and assisted in the political settlement of conflicts.[88]

Notwithstanding the clear benefits associated with the use of commissions of inquiry, this chapter has illustrated that commissions have instigated a 'new form of adjudication'[89] and that there is the potential for commissions of inquiry to reach differing interpretations of international law. An important question that needs to be assessed is what is the impact of these differing interpretations upon the overall coherency and unity of international law.

At the outset it should be noted that any threat that commissions of inquiry may represent to the unity of international law is not alleviated and certainly not avoided simply because the reports produced by the commissions are not binding. As Henderson explains

> CoI do seem to be an additional form of not only resolving contested facts but also obtaining authoritative determinations as to whether violations of international law have taken place and, if so, who is responsible, as well as the making of important pronouncements upon international law. Their interventions may not only embolden one of the parties to the conflict in its particular claims but also influence public perceptions as to the legality of the actions of those involved. Indeed, the reports of commissions and the decisions reached, though not formally binding may end up being just as authoritative, whether in the public, political or legal realm, as more formal permanent judicial processes.[90]

[88] UN Human Rights Office of the High Commissioner, 'Commissions of Inquiry and Fact-Finding Missions on International Human Rights and Humanitarian Law: Guidance and Practice' (2015) 7.

[89] Akande and Tonkin (n 15) ('[t]hese commissions do seem to be an additional form of resolving, and obtaining authoritative pronouncements on, contested facts and issues of international law').

[90] Henderson (n 17) 294. See also Akande and Tonkin (n 15).

It is important to note that the fact that commissions of inquiry arrive at different (and even erroneous) interpretations of international law is not something unique to commissions. International tribunals have also demonstrated a propensity to produce interpretations of international law that deviate from established jurisprudence. An often cited example in this context is the tussle between the International Court of Justice and the ICTY in relation to the rules pertaining to state responsibility and in particular the degree of control a state must exercise over a private actor in order for internationally wrongful acts committed by that private actor to be attributed to the state.

In the *Nicaragua* case in 1986 the International Court of Justice was required to determine whether the human rights abuses committed by the *contra* rebels could be attributed to the US.[91] The International Court of Justice explained that customary international law provides that a state must exercise 'effective control' over an internationally wrongful act in order for that act to be attributed to the state—in this context the International Court of Justice defined the meaning of effective control stringently, requiring that a state 'directed or enforced' the perpetration of the unlawful act.[92]

The question of attribution came before the ICTY in the *Tadić* case in 1999.[93] The ICTY, an international tribunal established by UN Security Council Resolution in order to prosecute international crimes committed in the former Yugoslavia, was required to determine whether the conduct of *Tadić* was attributable to the former Republic of Yugoslavia (FRY), and thus transformed an otherwise non-international armed conflict into an international armed conflict for the purpose of establishing liability under the Fourth Geneva Convention. Looking to the rules on state responsibility under general international law,[94] the ICTY concluded that the conduct of *Tadić* could be attributed to FRY, on the basis that the state exercised 'overall control' over the conduct of the private actor.[95] According to the ICTY, overall control requires that the state: (a) provides financial and military assistance to the private actors, and (b) participates in the planning and supervision of the unlawful acts in question.[96] Clearly, the ICTY deviated from the International Court of Justice's decision that the rules on state responsibility require attribution to be determined on

[91] *Military and Paramilitary Activities in and Against Nicaragua (Nicaragua v USA)* (Merits) [1986] ICJ Rep 14.

[92] *Nicaragua v USA* (n 91) para 115.

[93] *Tadić* (n 50).

[94] The Appeals Chamber explained that it was basing its ruling on 'general international rules on State responsibility which set out the legal criteria for attributing to a State acts performed by individuals not having the formal status of State officials'; *Tadić* (n 50) para 98.

[95] *Tadić* (n 50) para 115.

[96] *Tadić* (n 50) paras 131, 137.

the basis of effective control, instead preferring the 'less strict standard' of overall control.[97] However, the ICTY avoided a head on clash with the International Court of Justice's earlier jurisprudence by factually distinguishing the *Nicaragua* case. The ICTY explained that whilst the *Nicaragua* case was concerned with private actors, in *Tadić* it was an organised armed group that was under consideration, which required a lower standard of overall control.

The question of attribution came before the International Court of Justice again in 2007. In the *Bosnian Genocide* case the Court concluded that a paramilitary group had committed genocidal acts in Srebrenica and then sought to determine whether those genocidal acts could be attributed to FRY in order to establish FRY's responsibility for genocide under the Genocide Convention.[98] The International Court of Justice explained that the overall control test identified by the ICTY in *Tadić* was used to determine whether the armed conflict was of an international character or not under international humanitarian law and its applicability should be strictly limited to this international legal context.[99] By suggesting that the test of overall control extends to legal questions concerning state responsibility the ICTY had 'addressed an issue which was not indispensable for the exercise of its jurisdiction'.[100] To this end, the International Court of Justice was disinclined to follow the ICTY's decision concerning 'issues of general international law [ie the rules relating to state responsibility] which do not lie within the specific purview of its jurisdiction and, moreover, the resolution of which is not always necessary for deciding the criminal case before it'.[101] The International Court of Justice therefore concluded that the question of attribution of unlawful conduct under the rules on state responsibility was to be determined according to the test of effective control outlined in the *Nicaragua* case, regardless of whether the acts were committed by private individuals or an organised group.

97 S Wittich, 'The International Law Commission's Articles on the responsibility of States for Internationally Wrongful Acts Adopted on Second Reading' (2002) 15 *Leiden Journal of International Law* 891, 894.

98 *Application of the Convention on the Protection and Punishment of the Crime of Genocide (Bosnia v Serbia)* [2007] ICJ Rep 1.

99 *Bosnia v Serbia* (n 98) para 403.

100 *Bosnia v Serbia* (n 98) para 403.

101 *Bosnia v Serbia* (n 98) para 403. 'Following the ICJ's judgement in the *Genocide* case, it appears that the application of the 'overall control' test is restricted only to the use which it was originally put in the *Tadić* case, namely that an armed conflict may be qualified as international if a state exercise overall control over a group that is involved in an otherwise non-international armed conflict on another state's territory. The test…cannot be used to establish state responsibility. In the ICJ's view, therefore, the "effective control" test in Nicaragua is the proper test under Article 8 of the Articles on State Responsibility': K Larsen, 'Attribution of Conduct in Peace Operations: The 'Ultimate Authority and Control' Test' (2008) 19 *European Journal of International Law* 509, 515.

The ICTY and the International Court of Justice therefore propounded different articulations of the same legal test. As Talmon has correctly identified, the consequence is that in recent years these decisions have caused 'a lot of confusion'[102] over whether the correct test for determining attribution of internationally wrongful conduct under the rules on state responsibility is effective control or overall control.

The potential for international tribunals to produce conflicting jurisprudence is often regarded as a symptom of the process that has become known as the 'fragmentation of international law'.[103] Broadly speaking, fragmentation describes the diversification of international law into self-contained regimes. As I noted in the introduction to this chapter, such regimes will often establish tribunals that are empowered to arbitrate disputes arising under that treaty. More specifically, then, fragmentation describes the situation where these treaty tribunals provide differing interpretations of principles of international law, especially, although not exclusively in relation to secondary norms of international law.

The potential for treaty tribunals to render conflicting interpretations of the same rules of international law has been subject to sustained criticism, most notably by members of the International Court of Justice. ICJ President Judge Schwebel, for example, has expressed concern that the emergence of new international tribunals 'might produce substantial conflict among them'.[104] Similarly, in 2000 International Court of Justice President Judge Guillaume explained that the proliferation of international tribunals 'exacerbates the risk of conflicting judgments' and 'gives rise to a serious risk of conflicting jurisprudence as the same rule of law might be given different interpretations in different cases'. Such developments, he opined, would 'generate unwanted confusion' and 'distort the operation of justice'.[105] As we have seen above in relation to the rules of attribution, these concerns seem well-founded.[106]

[102] S Talmon, 'The Responsibility of Outside Powers for Acts of Secessionist Entities' (2008) 58 *International and Comparative Law Quarterly* 493, 497.

[103] ILC Report, *Fragmentation of International Law: Difficulties Arising from the Diversification and Expansion of International Law* (13 April 2006) A/CN.4/L.682.

[104] Address to the Plenary Session of the General Assembly of the United Nations by Judge Stephen M Schwebel, President of the International Court of Justice, 26 October 1999.

[105] Address by Judge Gilbert Guillaume, President of the International Court of Justice to the United Nations General Assembly, 26 October 2000.

[106] Charney offers a more positive perspective on the fragmentation of international law. Although he concedes that the proliferation of international tribunals inevitably has an adverse impact upon the coherence of international law, he explains that this is an acceptable cost for a healthy 'level of experimentation in a collective effort to find the best rule to serve the international community as a whole'. For Charney, the multiplication of international tribunals allows for 'a collective consideration of the legal issues, thus leading to an improvement in the quality of law': Charney (n 7) 130. For a similar approach also see M Koskenniemi and P Leino, 'Fragmentation of International Law? Postmodern Anxieties' (2002) 15 *Leiden Journal of International Law* 553.

As my discussion above has revealed, commissions of inquiry are likely to exacerbate and 'magnif[y]'[107] the fragmentation of international law because they create additional forums for adjudicating international legal disputes and can provide differing interpretations of international law.

This leaves us in a difficult conundrum because, on the one hand, we have already conceded that adjudicatory bodies such as commissions of inquiry are indispensable to the effectiveness of international law yet, on the other, we have concluded that commissions of inquiry can produce a conflicting decision which 'jeopardizes the credibility, reliability, and, consequently, the authority of international law'.[108] All in all, the question becomes whether the use of commissions of inquiry should continue unabated or, instead, whether their use should be restricted or even eliminated? As the title of this chapter postulates, *quo vadis*?

In his important contribution to the discussion of the fragmentation of international law, Charney emphasises that whilst international tribunals are a necessary and desirable feature of the international dispute resolution architecture they must remember that when discharging this role 'all participants in the system need to be sensitive to the risks inherent in the decentralized system and be careful to avoid actions that might pull the system apart'.[109] What Charney is saying is that when making decisions international tribunals must do so fully aware of the possible impact of their decisions upon the broader international legal framework and be sensitive to ensure that the coherency of international law is maintained. This chimes with Depuy's approach, when he suggests that it is crucial that international tribunals acknowledge their adjudicatory role and be cognisant of the threat they potentially represent to the unity of international law. In light of this recognition, Depuy implores that a culture of decision making must emerge where international tribunals 'shar[e] a legal philosophy according to which there is some kind of international legal order that should be respected, under any circumstances, by each and every subject of that law'.[110] Similarly Rao, who like Charney does not regard as problematic the possibility of international tribunals arriving at different interpretations of international law but, on the contrary, considers it a 'sign of the

[107] P-M Dupuy, 'The Danger of Fragmentation or Unification of the International Legal System and the International Court of Justice' (1999) 31 *New York University Journal of International Law and Politics* 791, 792.

[108] Hafner (n 5) 856.

[109] J Charney, 'The Impact on the International Legal System of the Growth of International Courts and Tribunals' (1999) 31 *New York University Journal of International Law and Politics* 697, 708.

[110] Dupuy (n 107) 806.

growing maturity of international law',[111] explains that an 'important caveat' is that

> judges of these diverse tribunals, when they interpret and apply, rights and obligations under international law, should be conscious of the overarching international judicial system that is emerging, which they should creatively and energetically promote. Furthermore, judges must show good faith and exhibit respect, not only to their own previous holdings on a subject, but show equal respect to the relevant holdings of other international tribunals in the interest of judicial harmony, certainty, and the predictability of law. In this respect judicial restraint and economy should play just as important role as judicial activism plays to help bridge gaps in law. The ultimate justification for the existence of a diversity of international tribunals is to achieve unity of the international legal system, which is dedicated to justice and equity in international relations.[112]

These arguments, I suggest, apply *mutatis mutandis* to commissions of inquiry. The benefits associated with commissions of inquiry are undeniable and, without some major overhaul in the way in which allegations of violations of international law are adjudicated, their use must continue. But their potential to compromise the integrity of international law can be largely averted providing that they recognise that they exercise (quasi) judicial powers and, when exercising these powers, they do so with an awareness of the broader international legal framework within which they operate and the need to ensure and secure the unity and predictability of international law.

With specific reference to the activities of commissions of inquiry, Boutruche suggests that

> [w]hile it would be problematic to expect such bodies to address all legal issues or provide details for every single rule considered, greater awareness on what those legal issues—and their implications—are, and stronger legal justifications could help strengthen the quality of [monitoring, reporting and fact-finding] reports.[113]

The issue is not that commissions of inquiry should feel precluded from suggesting alternative interpretations of international law, filling gaps in international law or even (exceptionally) attempting to progressively develop international law. Such activism is both necessary and desirable but must be pursued cautiously and where differing interpretations of

[111] PS Rao, 'Multiple International Judicial Forums: A Reflection of the Growing Strengths of International Law or its Fragmentation?' (2004) 25 *Michigan Journal of International Law* 929, 930.

[112] Rao (n 111), 961.

[113] T Boutruche, 'Selecting and Applying Legal Lenses in Monitoring, Reporting and Fact-Finding Missions', *HPCR Working Paper* (October 2013) 35.

international law are offered they must be substantiated by clear legal reasoning and justified in light of previous decisions in alternative adjudicatory forums.

10.5. CONCLUSION

As states sought to increasingly regulate their international relations through international legal rules it became quickly apparent that an independent, authoritative body competent to interpret and apply these rules was essential in order for this international legal system to be effective. The 'first generation' of international adjudication, as Born refers to it, was the Permanent Court of International Justice, which subsequently became the International Court of Justice.[114] As international law fragmented and diversified into self-contained regimes the 'second generation' of international adjudication emerged, these being those specialised international tribunals that were established by specific treaties in order to arbitrate disputes arising under those treaties. I would argue that we have now moved into a third generation of international adjudication, namely the use of commissions of inquiry. Yes, commissions of inquiry have long been used to address international disputes. Originally, however, commissions of inquiry pursued a largely fact-finding role and only occasionally strayed into the field of international legal adjudication. But since the end of the Cold War it has been suggested here that commissions of inquiry have been increasingly deployed (and especially by organs of the UN) in order to not just pursue fact-finding but, in addition, to determine whether violations of international law have been committed, particularly in relation to international human rights law, international humanitarian law and international criminal law. I argue that this dramatic transformation in the role of commissions of inquiry, and thus signalling the dawn of the third generation of international adjudication, can be regarded as an expression of the liberal triumph that occurred at the end of the Cold War, with commissions of inquiry having been reconfigured in order to act as a mechanism via which the international community can promote respect for fundamental human rights.

Whilst undoubtedly commissions of inquiry provide an important contribution to the adjudication of international law, especially given the relative unavailability of the International Court of Justice and even specialised treaty tribunals, this chapter has sought to demonstrate that commissions of inquiry can threaten the unity and coherence of the international

[114] G Born, 'A New Generation of International Adjudication' (2012) 61 *Duke Law Journal* 775, 791 ff.

legal order where they provide differing interpretations of international law. Furthermore, it has been suggested that this threat can be averted providing that commissions of inquiry better appreciate the role they play in the international dispute resolution machinery and that, when making decisions, they take care to ensure that any interpretations of international law they offer are justified by reference to decisions of other adjudicatory bodies and that this is especially the case where they offer interpretations of international law that diverge from existing interpretations.

Section 4

Procedural Questions and Working Methods

11

Selectivity and Choices in Human Rights Fact-finding: Reconciling Subjectivity with Objectivity?

THÉO BOUTRUCHE

11.1. INTRODUCTION

ON 1 SEPTEMBER 2014 the Human Rights Council convened a special session on 'the human rights situation in Iraq in light of abuses committed by the Islamic State in Iraq and the Levant and associated groups'. During this meeting it mandated the High Commissioner for Human Rights (OHCHR) to:

> dispatch a mission to Iraq to investigate alleged violations and abuses of international human rights law committed by the so-called Islamic State in Iraq and the Levant and associated terrorist groups, and to establish the facts and circumstances of such abuses and violations, with a view to avoiding impunity and ensuring full accountability (…).[1]

Such a one-sided mandate may be highly questionable when considering that violations were also carried out by other parties to the conflict, in particular Shia pro-government militias outsourced by the Iraqi authorities to fight the 'Islamic State'.[2] Certainly this results from the growing concern within the international community over the extent and types of abuses committed by this group in Iraq. Interestingly, the final OHCHR investigative report went beyond the mandate limitations, in part due to the general human rights mandate of this agency, and provided information on violations committed by the 'Islamic State' as well as other parties

[1] UN Human Rights Council Resolution 22/1, UN Doc A/HRC/RES/S-22/1 (1 September 2014) para 10.

[2] See, for example, 'Iraq: Militias Escalate Abuses, Possibly War Crimes—Killings, Kidnappings, Forced Evictions', (*Human Rights Watch* 15 February 2015), available at www.hrw.org/news/2015/02/15/iraq-militias-escalate-abuses-possibly-war-crimes.

to the conflict.[3] However, it illustrates the recurring issue of selectivity in human rights fact-finding. While this does impact the scope of commission of inquiry mandates, it also plays a role beforehand in the decision whether to establish a fact-finding body or not. The Human Rights Council's failure to create a commission of inquiry over alleged human rights and international humanitarian law violations committed in Yemen is only the most recent example.

However selectivity is only one issue out of many that may affect the very essence of fact-finding. If human rights fact-finding is about 'methods of ascertaining facts'[4] on alleged human rights violations and abuses, it ought to do so as objectively as possible. However, as a process, fact-finding encompasses a myriad of stages and aspects that require choices to be made, from the decision to create a fact-finding body and the composition of a commission of inquiry to the selection of sources of information, the interpretation of a particular norm and the way the final report is drafted. It therefore comes as no surprise that the findings of a fact-finding mission are met with criticism as being 'biased' or 'lacking in objectivity'. Here lies the constant fundamental tension within human rights fact-finding work, that is, the coexistence of the imperative of objectivity with so many potential risks of appearing subjective.

Instead of focusing on a specific aspect, this Chapter adopts a broad perspective to map and analyse the various points of tension between objectivity and subjectivity in human rights fact-finding. After explaining the terms of the debate and clarifying certain notions such as selectivity and objectivity, this contribution offers an analysis of the most prominent issues that may question the objective character of fact-finding. These include methodological problems such as choosing and selecting sources of information and applying unsettled human rights or international humanitarian law norms to factual conclusions. It finally addresses a few avenues to help reconciling subjectivity and choices that are inherent to fact-finding processes with objectivity imperatives. Central to this is the need for a rigorous, explicitly stated and sound methodology not only to justify certain choices and pre-empt any perceived subjectivity, but to also ensure that those deciding to create a fact-finding body and fact-finders themselves can constantly act as objectively as possible. This is crucial, as subjective considerations are inherent to the fact-finding work.

[3] OHCHR, *Report of the Office of the United Nations High Commissioner for Human Rights on the human rights situation in Iraq in the light of abuses committed by the so-called Islamic State in Iraq and the Levant and associated groups*, UN Doc A/HRC/28/18 (13 March 2015) 11–14.

[4] M Aksenova and M Bergsmo, 'Non-Criminal Justice Fact-Work in the Age of Accountability' in M Bergsmo (ed), *Quality Control in Fact-Finding* (Torkel Opsahl Academic EPublisher, 2013) 1, 2.

11.2. UNDERSTANDING THE TERMS OF THE DEBATE: THE MYTH OF FULL OBJECTIVITY IN FACT-FINDING?

While terms such as 'selectivity', 'objectivity' and 'subjectivity' are common within the human rights fact-finding landscape, it is essential to clarify their status and the way they operate. In that respect, a fundamental distinction arises between on the one hand notions that pertain to principles and requirements guiding the fact-finding work as methodological and professional standards, and on the opposite terms that relate to what can affect the essence of fact-finding work. However, the reality is far more complex, in that subjectivity, for example, is not merely a negative term in human-rights fact-finding. By nature, this work carries a subjective dimension that is somehow intrinsically linked to the human-driven character of this process, which gives way to perceptions and sensitivity, not least because it involves traumatised victims of human rights violations. Ultimately, a fundamental issue pervades the whole process as to the extent to which fact-finding can be a perfectly and purely objective task.

11.2.1. Non-Selectivity, Objectivity, Impartiality and Independence as Principles in Human Rights Fact-Finding

Human rights monitoring and reporting in general and fact-finding in particular are guided by standards of objectiveness and impartiality. These principles are deeply rooted in the essence of human rights, conceived as legal entitlements that pertain to any human being. The very nature of human rights commands considering all situations that raise allegations of violations and abuses irrespective of political, economic or strategic factors. Furthermore, human rights law itself contains fundamental norms on equality and non-discrimination that underpin the notions of objectiveness and impartiality. For example, the International Covenant on Civil and Political Rights and the International Covenant on Economic Social and Cultural Rights both state that those rights are guaranteed 'without distinction of any kind, such as race, colour, sex, language, religion, political or other opinion, national or social origin, property, birth or other status'.[5]

The principles of non-selectivity, objectivity, impartiality and independence reflect those values. Despite being at times seen as overlapping, notably for the standard of objectivity that may encompass the other principles, they all have a specific and distinct meaning that must be considered in the field of fact-finding.

[5] Respectively Arts 2.1 and 2.2.

Non-selectivity is commonly defined as considering all states' human rights records equally without focusing on particular states in this regard. It means 'in consideration of human rights issues that the state/forum will not pick only certain states to criticize'.[6] When creating the Human Rights Council in 2006, the UN General Assembly linked the mandate of this body 'for promoting universal respect for the protection of all human rights and fundamental freedoms for all, without distinction of any kind and in a fair and equal manner' with its work to 'be guided by the principles of universality, impartiality, objectivity and non-selectivity'.[7] This would mean that the Human Rights Council is to treat states equally when reviewing human rights concerns. This includes both the substantive discussions before this organ as well as the way the panoply of measures to be taken would be used. For example, the decision to create a fact-finding mission or a commission of inquiry should not be limited to certain states, nor should their mandate be limited to certain parties allegedly involved in violations.

While the principles of objectivity, independence and impartiality are also relevant for the work of the Human Rights Council or other human rights institutions, they play a crucial role at the stage of the fact-finding work itself. Fact-finders' major concern is to ensure that when they establish facts, it is done in a transparent, independent, objective, and impartial manner to ensure their findings will not be disputed. Those principles are therefore primarily driven by quality control and methodological considerations. They should be understood as core values for a professional and credible work. These concerns are relevant be it for fact-finding work conducted by non-governmental organisations (NGOs) or for ad hoc fact-finding missions and commissions of inquiry. For example the United Nations Fact-Finding Mission on the Gaza Conflict stated that it

> based its work on an independent and impartial analysis of compliance by the parties with their obligations under international human rights and humanitarian law in the context of the recent conflict in Gaza, and on international investigative standards developed by the United Nations.[8]

Similarly, Human Rights Watch, when describing its research methodology considers impartiality as a key guiding principle in the specific context of conducting interviews with victims and witnesses.[9]

[6] HV Condé, 'Nonselectivity (vs. Selectivity)' in *A Handbook of International Human Rights Terminology* (Nebraska University Press, 2004) 178.

[7] Resolution adopted by the General Assembly on 15 March 2006, Un Doc A/RES/60/251, paras 2 and 4.

[8] UN Human Rights Council, *Report of the United Nations Fact-Finding Mission on the Gaza Conflict*, UN Doc A/HRC/12/48 (25 September 2009) para 158 (*Gaza Report*).

[9] Human Rights Watch, 'Our Research Methodology', available at www.hrw.org/node/75141.

The notions of independence, impartiality, and objectivity are identified as 'principles' by the OHCHR Guidance and Practice that UN-mandated commissions and missions should adhere to in their terms of reference, methods of work and rules of procedure.[10] According to this document, under the principle of independence members and staff of the commission or mission shall not be influenced or seek or accept instructions from anyone in carrying out their mandate. Impartiality requires fact-finders to look thoroughly at alleged violations by all parties. Finally, objectivity is to

> collect all relevant facts from all relevant sources, objectively consider all the facts and information gathered and base its conclusions on the facts gathered. It should take into consideration only information that is gathered in an unbiased and impartial manner.[11]

Those principles are therefore closely linked and intertwined. For example the *Siracusa Guidelines for International, Regional and National Fact-Finding Bodies* refer to both independence and impartiality as principles any fact-finding body should maintain at all times. The term independent is defined as being 'free from outside influence', while being 'impartial' means to 'adopt and implement a methodology that allows it to gather facts and draw conclusions in an objective manner'.[12] They are to be applied and guaranteed in various dimensions, including in the way the fact-finders act.[13] The notion of objectivity may also have a restricted understanding as a fact-finding methodological imperative regarding the scope of facts being covered and the sources of information.[14]

11.3. CHOICES AND SUBJECTIVITY: BEYOND MERE CRITICISMS

Criticising a fact-finding report for being subjective and biased, be it from an international NGO or a commission of inquiry, became a common exercise following publication. While some of those criticisms may be well

[10] OHCHR, *Commissions of Inquiry and Fact-Finding Missions on International Human Rights and Humanitarian Law: Guidance and Practice*, 2015, 43, available at www.ohchr.org/Documents/Publications/CoI_Guidance_and_Practice.pdf.

[11] OHCHR, *Guidance and Practice* (n 10) 33–34.

[12] M Cherif Bassiouni and C Abraham (eds) *Siracusa Guidelines for International, Regional and National Fact-Finding Bodies* (Cambridge, Intersentia, 2013) 43.

[13] International Bar Association: Human Rights Institute, *Guidelines on International Human Rights Fact-Finding Visits and Reports* ('Lund-London Guidelines'): 'The NGO should ensure that all members of the delegation are aware that they must, at all times, act in an independent, unbiased, objective, lawful and ethical manner.'

[14] See Lund-London Guidelines on secondary sources: 'Where the delegation relies upon information gathered by a third party, the delegation should take all reasonable measures to verify the objectivity of that information gathering process in order to rely on the evidence collected'.

founded, the ground of subjectivity too often offers an easy way to reject factual or legal findings in whole without having to justify it. Subjectivity would be seen as self-evident without requiring any evidence of how fact-finders failed to be objective. This may be because fact-finding is inherently subjective as a core task. However, this is not so in the negative connotation commonly associated with the term subjectivity. Here lies a critical issue for the topic of this contribution: if fact-finding work contains multiple areas or elements that run the risk of being or being seen as subjective, it is also in nature a task that requires selecting and making choices. There is, therefore, a need to distinguish between those two dimensions in order to avoid the former through a credible methodology and to acknowledge the latter not to render any fact-finding process fundamentally flawed.

By definition choices and selections, if objectively justified, do not amount to being subjective. In that respect it is worth recalling the broader definition of being objective for a person (or a judgment) who is 'not influenced by personal feelings or opinions in considering and representing facts'.[15] However, some form of subjectivity, not negatively connoted, is unavoidable in fact-finding, which despite its professionalisation remains a mental operation conducted by human beings. Fact-finding methodology itself often relies on a common sense approach coupled with fundamental standards, such as the 'do no harm' principle and the need to avoid re-traumatisation of victims and witnesses. In that respect, Simon De Smet highlights that 'most international fact-finders, like their lawyer and journalist counterparts, engage in their fact-finding tasks largely "intuitively"', without being fully conscious of the mental processes that this work involves, while they 'should be more aware of the basic epistemic principles that are at play'.[16] This is particularly relevant in the context of how factual findings are reached on the basis of available evidence and what type of inferences are drawn from it.[17]

This is not to say that any fact-finding work is meant to fail against an unattainable fully objective standard. However, this shows the need to approach issues of subjectivity within this field with much more caution and nuances. One thing is to ensure opinions do not influence factual or legal determination, another is to recognise that selection and choice are part of the fact-finding work, from the selection of facts to be investigated to the selection of witnesses and the decision to adopt a particular interpretation of a controversial norm of international law when applying it to the facts. For example, the Commission of Inquiry on Darfur noted that

[15] Oxford Dictionaries, available at www.oxforddictionaries.com/definition/english/objective.

[16] S De Smet, 'Justified Belief in the Unbelievable' in M Bergsmo (ed), *Quality Control in Fact-Finding* (Torkel Opsahl Academic EPublisher, 2013) 73–74.

[17] De Smet (n 16) 74.

'It was not possible for the Commission to investigate all of the many hundreds of individually documented incidents reported by other sources.'[18]

In many cases, these choices are therefore justified by practical and methodological imperatives. It is nevertheless crucial to be aware of the potential pitfalls that risk affecting the objectivity and credibility of the fact-finding work. The section below provides an overview of selected issues that pertain to both clear-cut cases of subjectivity and questions where a careful methodological approach is required in order to anticipate the risks of losing one's objective sight.

For the purpose of this contribution, the notion of 'subjectivity' will therefore primarily be used in the negative sense of the term—being influenced by opinions and personal feelings—but it would also reflect on a more fluid understanding of this notion when considering that fact-finders have different backgrounds and profiles. 'Objectivity', on the other hand, will be considered in its most general sense, covering also the notions of independence and impartiality.

11.3.1. Navigating the Pitfalls of Selectivity and Choices in Human Rights Fact-Finding

This section aims at focusing on some of the key issues that display or may be perceived as displaying a form of subjectivity throughout the fact-finding process, from the very decision to create a fact-finding mission to the application of the law to the facts.

11.3.1.1. The Original Sin of Subjectivity: The Creation of Commissions of Inquiry

Selectivity in Establishing Commissions of Inquiry

With the very limited use of the 'enquiry procedure' under the four 1949 Geneva Conventions[19] and the absence of any resort to the permanent International Humanitarian Fact-Finding Commission (IHFFC), established under Article 90 of Additional Protocol I of 1977[20], fact-finding

[18] *Report of the International Commission of Inquiry on Darfur to the United Nations Secretary-General* (25 January 2005) para 223 (*Darfur Report*).

[19] T Boutruche, 'Good Offices, Conciliation, and Enquiry' in A Clapham, P Gaeta, and M Sassòli (eds) *The 1949 Geneva Conventions—A Commentary* (Oxford, Oxford University Press, 2015) 561–74.

[20] F Kalshoven, 'The International Humanitarian Fact-Finding Commission: A Sleeping Beauty' (2002) 4 *HV* 215; L Condorelli, 'The International Humanitarian Fact-Finding Commission: An Obsolete Tool or a Useful Measure to Implement International Humanitarian Law?' (2001) 83 *International Review of the Red Cross* 405.

missions and commissions of inquiry were created outside the scope of international humanitarian law treaties to document international humanitarian law violations.

The lack of agreement between parties to a conflict to set up an 'enquiry procedure' has indeed led to states imposing investigative bodies through the UN system. The establishment of an ad hoc fact-finding body constitutes one of the various measures that may be taken to address a human rights situation of concern. Recent years have seen the UN Human Rights Council, and the UN Security Council create fact-finding missions and commissions of inquiry specifically mandated to investigate alleged violations of international human rights and humanitarian law in conflict or post-conflict contexts. For example, the Security Council created the International Commission of Inquiry on Darfur in 2004, and the Human Rights Council established fact-findings missions and commissions of inquiry to address alleged violations committed during the war in Lebanon in 2006, the Gaza conflict in 2009, and the conflicts in Libya and Syria in 2011. Similar missions were also created by the UN Secretary General, such as the Panel of Experts on Accountability in Sri Lanka, and by the European Union with the International Independent Fact-Finding Mission on the Conflict in Georgia, respectively in 2011 and 2008.

As highlighted by an expert, '[s]ince international mechanisms are only intended to address the most serious violations of international law, their application is inherently selective'.[21] However, this criterion cannot account for the selectivity issue regarding commissions of inquiry. While selectivity in creating a fact-finding body within the UN Security Council lies in the political nature of this organ, as explained above, the Human Rights Council was established on the basis of the principle of non-selectivity. However, to date it has been widely criticised for being selective in addressing human rights,[22] including when deciding to set up a commission of inquiry. The Human Rights Council remains a body comprised of states whereby decisions are not merely guided by human rights considerations.

The latest example can be found in some western states dropping an initiative for the establishment of a Human Rights Council commission of inquiry during the Human Rights Council's 30th session in September 2015, to investigate alleged violations of international humanitarian law in Yemen. Following pressure from Saudi Arabia and its coalition partners,

[21] J Brooks, 'Why No International Inquiry in Yemen?' (*ATHA*, 4 November 2015), available at atha.se/blog/why-no-international-inquiry-yemen.

[22] 'Curing the Selectivity Syndrome—The 2011 Review of the Human Rights Council' (*Human Rights Watch* 24 June 2010), available at www.hrw.org/report/2010/06/24/curing-selectivity-syndrome/2011-review-human-rights-council.

who launched a military campaign in March 2015, the Netherlands withdrew a draft resolution on 30 September 2015 to create such a commission. Instead it rallied a consensus resolution supporting the exiled Yemeni government's call for appointing a national commission of inquiry.[23] This alternative does not offer the same guarantees of independence and objectivity and was widely criticised.[24] At the same session, the Human Rights Council adopted a resolution supporting Sri Lanka's accountability initiatives to deal with alleged international humanitarian law and human rights violations committed during the decades-long conflict with the Tamil Tigers. This follows the Report of the OHCHR Investigation on Sri Lanka,[25] submitted to the Human Rights Council during that session, on the basis of a mandate received by Human Rights Council's resolution A/HRC/25/1 in March 2014. The difference of treatment between Yemen and Sri Lanka was rather seen as the result of a combination of factors, notably politics and the ongoing nature of the conflict in the Yemeni case.[26] However, in January 2016, in light of the ever-worsening humanitarian crisis and increasing reports of international humanitarian law and human rights violations, the UN Group of Experts on Yemen monitoring the UN Security Council's sanctions regime recommended the creation of a commission of inquiry by the UN Security Council itself.[27]

Interestingly, it has been argued that the selectivity issue affecting the very creation of a commission of inquiry, and its related politicised nature, tend not to affect the ability of fact-finders to carry out their work objectively and independently once the organ has been set up.[28] This is, however, more challenging when the commission is set up on the basis of a one-sided mandate.

The Issue of One-sided Mandates

While politics may present an obstacle for the creation of a commission of inquiry, it may also account for choosing to design a one-sided mandate,

23 N Cumming-Bruce, 'Saudi Objections Halt U.N. Inquiry of Yemen War', *The New York Times* (30 September 2015), available at mobile.nytimes.com/2015/10/01/world/middleeast/western-nations-drop-push-for-un-inquiry-into-yemen-conflict.html?ref=middleeast&_r=5&referer=.

24 Brooks (n 21).

25 *Report of the OHCHR Investigation on Sri Lanka*, UN Doc A/HRC/30/CRP.2 (16 September 2015).

26 Brooks (n 21).

27 C Anna, 'UN panel on Yemen: Consider creating commission of inquiry' (*Associated Press*, 26 January 2016), available at bigstory.ap.org/article/02871bd8d9b94569a53f4586e364e37e/un-panel-yemen-consider-creating-commission-inquiry.

28 R Grace, 'From Design to Implementation: The Interpretation of Fact-finding Mandates' (2015) 20(1) *Journal of Conflict Security Law* 27.

focusing on only one or certain categories of perpetuators. This impacts significantly upon the objective character of the fact-finding work.

In the case of the Commission of Inquiry on Lebanon (hereafter the Lebanon Commission), the Human Rights Council Resolution defining the mandate specifically focuses on the conduct of Israel, excluding other parties to the conflict, notably Hezbollah, from the scope of the mission's work. The commissioners, mindful of this limitation, specifically addressed this issue in the final report, expressing concerns about the mission's lack of authority to examine the behavior of Hezbollah.[29] Though, as a way to mitigate this shortcoming, the report does make reference to the international humanitarian law and human rights obligations of Hezbollah.

Interestingly, a similar limitation contained in the Human Rights Council resolution creating the Gaza Fact-finding Mission was adjusted in the letter of the Human Rights Council President that slightly redefined the mandate.[30] Based on this letter, which the mission considered to be the operative mandate, the mission, as the final report states,

> determined that it was required to consider any actions by all parties that might have constituted violations of international human rights law or international humanitarian law. The mandate also required it to review related actions in the entire Occupied Palestinian Territory and Israel.[31]

[29] See *Report of the Commission of Inquiry on Lebanon pursuant to Human Rights Council Resolution S-2/1*, UN Doc A/HRC/3/2 (23 November 2006) para 16, which notes: 'A fundamental point in relation to the conflict and the Commission's mandate as defined by the Council is the conduct of Hezbollah. The Commission considers that any independent, impartial and objective investigation into a particular conduct during the course of hostilities must of necessity be with reference to all the belligerents involved. Thus an inquiry into the conformity with international humanitarian law of the specific acts of IDF [Israeli Defense Forces] in Lebanon requires that account also be taken of the conduct of the opponent. That said, taking into consideration the express limitations of its mandate, the Commission is not entitled, even if it had wished, to construe it as equally authorizing the investigation of the actions by Hezbollah in Israel.'

[30] UN Human Rights Council Resolution S-9/1, para 14 states that the mandate is 'to investigate all violations of international human rights law and international humanitarian law by the occupying Power, Israel, against the Palestinian people throughout the Occupied Palestinian Territory, particularly in the occupied Gaza Strip, due to the current aggression.' However, the subsequent letter of the UN Human Rights Council president to the Chair of the Mission offers a broader mandate 'to investigate all violations of international human rights law and international humanitarian law that might have been committed at any time in the context of the military operations that were conducted in Gaza during the period from 27 December 2008 and 18 January 2009'. See *Gaza Report* (n 8) p 13. It is reported that, following Mary Robinson's refusal to head the mission, and after the first objection by Justice Goldstone, both of whom criticized the bias of the mandate, the UN Human Rights Council president widened the mandate's scope to encompass the conduct of Hamas. See 'Goldstone's UN inquiry team arrives in Gaza' (*BBC* 1 June 2009), available at news.bbc.co.uk/1/hi/world/middle_east/8076690.stm.

[31] *Gaza Report* (n 8) para 14.

Beyond the issue of objectivity, one-sided mandates pose a series of additional challenges, including potentially hindering the ability of the commission of inquiry to comprehensively address certain international humanitarian law rules on the conduct of hostilities that, by definition, require consideration of the acts of both the attacker and the party being attacked.

The fact-finding work itself also contains numerous aspects that imply some form of interpretation, selection and choices that may challenge the objectivity of the findings. The following part, while not exhaustive, focuses on the most prominent challenges.

11.3.1.2. The Challenging Task of Objective Fact-Finding

Ironically, any attempt to reconcile subjectivity and objectivity in fact-finding requires looking at this process from an objective point of view to identify the key areas and issues that either properly or potentially impact the objective nature of fact-finding.

Real and Apparent Subjectivity

An analogy with the principles of independence and impartiality as standards of judicial conduct for judges can provide useful lenses through which to understand the challenges at play for fact-finders.

Judges are required to be independent and impartial. The 2002 Bangalore Principles on Judicial Conduct refer to the principle of independence as requiring from a judge to 'uphold and exemplify judicial independence in both *its individual and institutional aspects*' and specify that the principle of impartiality 'applies not only *to the decision itself* but also to *the process by which the decision is made*' (emphasis added).[32] This underlines the need to take into account those two distinctions when considering objectivity within fact-finding work.

Furthermore, and most importantly, in the 2002 Bangalore Principles, for both independence and impartiality, the appearance matters as much as the reality. These qualities must also be perceived to be respected. The standard used is whether judges appear to be independent and impartial 'to a reasonable observer',[33] 'viewing the matter realistically and practically'.[34]

32 *The Bangalore Code of Judicial Conduct*, adopted by the Judicial Group on Strengthening Judicial Integrity, as revised at the Round Table Meeting of Chief Justices held at the Peace Palace, The Hague (25–26 November 2002) 3.

33 Bangalore Code (n 32) 3–4.

34 UNODC, *Commentary* on the *Bangalore Code of Judicial Conduct* (September 2007) para 56. See also Human Rights Committee, *General Comment no 32*, CCPR/C/GC/32 (2007) para 21.

Without putting into question every single aspect of the fact-finding exercise, one must consider some key stages of the process that bear the risk of casting subjectivity over the work of fact-finders. The above distinction between reality and perception could also be applied in the fact-finding context. In that regard, while most of the challenges addressed below pertain to risks of fact-finders being perceived as lacking objectivity, few relate to issues that can affect their real objectivity.

Selection of Facts

Fact-finding, by nature, requires multiple selections of facts, some of which carry a risk of appearing subjective. Certain selections are inherent to the task, in particular for fact-finding about alleged human rights violations for obvious reasons, only the facts related to a potential violation would be considered.

However, beyond that natural selection comes a more challenging exercise. Human rights fact-finding is about investigating individual and specific cases. Finding facts in this context requires the establishment of a number of factual elements related to the individual cases, ranging from information on the victim to the time, location and circumstances of the incident.[35] Consequently, the key question is how to identify the incidents and related facts to be investigated out of a huge quantity of allegations, despite those being all relevant under the mandate of the commission of inquiry.

First, one must acknowledge that a critical aspect of human rights fact-finding is also often to establish patterns of violations.[36] This may be the primary focus of fact-finding bodies. As noted by a UN senior official, UN commissions of inquiry, '[c]ommonly … examine whether there are consistent accounts of recurrent patterns of human rights violations that could be widespread or systematic'.[37]

This being said, the selection also results from a recurring practical and realistic necessity for most of fact-finding bodies as noted above by the Commission of Inquiry on Darfur.[38] The same organ further explained that:

> [It], therefore, selected incidents and areas that were most representative of acts, trends and patterns relevant to the determination of violations of international

[35] For a list of the elements to be established in the case of an alleged murder, see DJ Ravindran et al (eds), *Handbook on Fact-Finding and Documentation of Human Rights Violations* (Bangkok, Asian Forum for Human Rights and Development, 1994) 13.

[36] Amnesty International and CODESRIA, 'UKWELI: Monitoring and Documenting Human Rights Violations in Africa' (2000) 18, available at www.hrea.org/erc/Library/Ukweli/ukweli-en.pdf.

[37] M Rishmawi, 'The role of human rights fact finding in the prevention of genocide' in *International Conference on Prevention of Genocide, Brussels* (31 March–1 April 2014) 3: www.genocideprevention.be/sites/default/files/content/rishmawi_brussels_final.pdf.

[38] *Darfur Report* (n 18) para 223.

> human rights and humanitarian law and with greater possibilities of effective fact-finding. In making this selection, access to the sites of incidents, protection of witnesses and the potential for gathering the necessary evidence were, amongst others, of major consideration'.[39]

Similarly, the UN Fact-Finding Mission on the Gaza Conflict stressed that:

> In view of the time frame within which it had to complete its work, the Mission necessarily had to be selective in the choice of issues and incidents for investigation. The report does not purport to be exhaustive in documenting the very high number of relevant incidents that occurred in the period covered by the Mission's mandate and especially during the military operations in Gaza. Nevertheless, the Mission considers that the report is illustrative of the main patterns of violations.[40]

Establishing patterns may also be required by the norm itself as a condition for its application. For example, for certain acts to constitute a crime against humanity they have to be 'committed as part of a widespread or systematic attack directed against any civilian population'.[41]

Conversely, purposely deciding to ignore certain patterns could also be seen as a form of subjectivity, as such patterns of violations contribute to accurately representing the truth. Certain types of violations are characterised by different patterns of violence that need to be identified to correctly reflect the reality. For instance, the OHCHR fact-finding mission in Kenya identified 'three patterns of violence—spontaneous, organised and retaliatory' following the elections.[42] Similarly, in the context of the violence, which included torching and looting houses, during and after the conflict in Georgia in 2008, the Independent International Fact-Finding Mission on the Conflict in Georgia noted that 'patterns of violence differed depending on the area concerned' and that '[t]he most extensive destruction and brutal violence seem to have taken place in South Ossetia, with certain characteristics that appear to be different from what happened in the buffer zone'.[43] It is therefore essential to consider both the individual case of a violation and the possible pattern to which it may be related. Discussing the work and selection carried out by the UN Truth Commission for El Salvador, Thomas Buergenthal underlined that '[t]he more we learned about El Salvador's civil war (…) the clearer it became that some cases were paradigmatic of a practice of violence that terrorized

[39] *Darfur Report* (n 18) para 223.
[40] *Gaza Report* (n 8) para 157.
[41] Statute of the International Criminal Court, Art 7(1).
[42] OHCHR, *Report from OHCHR Fact-finding Mission to Kenya 6–28 February 2008*, para 8.
[43] Independent International Fact-Finding Mission on the Conflict in Georgia (2009) 353; see also 369.

the country'.[44] Under the mandate of the Truth and Reconciliation Commission of Liberia, this commission had to determine

> whether these were isolated incidents or part of a systematic pattern; establishing the antecedents, circumstances, factors and context of such violations and abuses; and determining those responsible for the commission of the violations and abuses and their motives as well as their impact on victims.[45]

Finally, the applicable relevant norms themselves require the selection and investigation of certain facts from the huge quantity of information around a given incident. The facts covered through the inquiry are framed by the elements of the very rule allegedly violated. Otherwise, a legal conclusion cannot be reached.[46] Investigating facts with an explicit or implicit link with a violation requires, to a certain extent, a minimum amount of legal evaluation for the mere purpose of defining the scope of the facts at stake. For fact-finding bodies mandated to address facts about alleged violations, the question would then rather be to what extent the two operations should be strictly independent of one another. This question touches on the core of the theory of law and legal reasoning. According to one prominent scholar, the expression 'ascertaining' facts is misleading, as this term suggests that the operation is about ascertaining an objective phenomenon that would then be 'confronted' with the legal norm. On the contrary, this author stresses the influence of law on facts in several respects; for example, he suggests that the relevance of a fact is linked to the choice of the applicable law.[47]

Addressing the selection of facts the OHCHR *Guidance and Practice* for Commissions of Inquiry and Fact-Finding Missions on International Human Rights and Humanitarian Law noted that 'commissions/missions are required to prioritize the issues and incidents they will investigate, within the broad terms of their mandate, to ensure that their tasks are completed within the limited resources and time at their disposal'.[48] It further highlights that 'The commission/mission will have to adopt criteria for

[44] T Buergenthal, 'The United Nations Truth Commission for El Salvador' (1994) 27 *Vanderbilt Journal of Transnational Law* 506.

[45] Truth and Reconciliation Commission of Liberia Mandate, enacted on 12 May 2005, by the National Transitional Legislative Assembly, Section 4(a), available at trcofliberia.org/about/trc-mandate.

[46] S Vité, 'L'expertise au service du droit: comment la norme façonne le processus d'enquête dans la mise en œuvre des droits de l'homme et du droit des conflits armés' in D Debons et al (eds) *Katyn et la Suisse: Experts et Expertises Médicales dans les Crises Humanitaires, 1920–2007* (Geneva, Georg, 2009) 251–58.

[47] See JJA Salmon, 'Le fait dans l'application du droit international' in *The Collected Courses of the Hague Academy of International Law*, vol 175 (Boston, Brill Nijhoff, 1982) 261 and 296.

[48] OHCHR, *Guidance and Practice* (n 10) 38.

prioritization'.[49] This latter example illustrates the need to justify any from of selection to avoid being labeled as 'subjective'.

Subjectivity and the Use of Sources of Information

In as much as fact-finding aims at establishing facts about certain incidents, sources of information used in that regard play a central role in the process. Unsurprisingly, most of the criticisms against fact-finding reports revolve around dismissing those sources as biased or unreliable so as to discredit factual conclusions.[50]

Among the various types of sources of information, namely physical, documentary and testimonial evidence, the latter carries the greatest potential for criticisms about the impartiality and objectivity of a commission of inquiry. However, victim and witness' testimonies remain prevalent for human rights fact-finding. It is not surprising in that first-hand accounts by direct eyewitnesses often constitute the easiest or most accessible way to clarify and establish the narrative and circumstances of what happened. The practice of UN monitoring bodies, international commissions of inquiry and NGOs involved in fact-finding, and even international criminal courts and tribunals, consistently relies primarily on witness testimonies. The OHCHR *Guidance and Practice* for Commissions of Inquiry and Fact-Finding Missions on International Human Rights and Humanitarian Law states that 'the testimony of victims and witnesses constitutes the most valuable information available to the investigation'.[51]

A first challenge lies with the selection of witnesses to be interviewed. This in itself could be seen as a subjective process if the witnesses predominantly belong to a particular ethnic group within the context of a conflict which is fought on ethnic lines. Furthermore, certain categories of witnesses may be seen as too subjective due to their status. This is the case of alleged perpetrators or members belonging to the same group or army. Following the mass rape committed in Minova, in the Democratic Republic of Congo, in November 2012, by government soldiers, a debate arose questioning the reliability of accounts given by combatants themselves to establish that orders were given to carry out those acts, arguing that 'testimonies, regardless the story-teller, are also performances informed by

[49] OHCHR, *Guidance and Practice* (n 10) 38.

[50] See, for example, 'Note verbale dated 5 August 2011 from the Permanent Mission of the Syrian Arab Republic addressed to the United Nations High Commissioner for Human Rights', annexed to *Report of the United Nations High Commissioner for Human Rights on the situation of human rights in the Syrian Arab Republic*, UN Doc A/HRC/18/53 (11 September 2011) 90.

[51] OHCHR, *Guidance and Practice* (n 10) 43.

various interests and assumptions'.[52] Furthermore, it is not uncommon for institutions to whom alleged perpetrators belong or for parties to a conflict to provide information to commissions of inquiry. For example, the International Independent Fact-Finding Mission on the Conflict in Georgia received hundreds of documents and pictures from all sides to the conflict. While the source of the information might be seen as unreliable, and must be corroborated by other sources, the information itself might prove useful and it is imperative from a methodological point of view to consider all views of a given allegation, not least to be able to better rebuke the versions given by the parties involved.

This latter example relates to a fundamental distinction between credibility and reliability, referring to the quality of the sources of information fact-finders seek to obtain. However, those two notions do not appear to be distinguished consistently or bear the same meaning from one fact-finding body to another. Nevertheless they appear to be commonly used to describe the assessment of the information collected. For example the International Commission of Inquiry on Libya noted that 'the quality of the evidence and information obtained by the Commission varied in its accuracy and reliability'.[53] However, in the Mapping Exercise Report on the DRC, the OHCHR stressed:

> Assessing the reliability of the information obtained was a two-stage process involving evaluation of the reliability and credibility of the source, and then the pertinence and truth of the information itself. This method is known as the *admiralty scale*.[54]

The information provided by a given source might therefore be relevant and accurate, whereas the source itself could be questionable. As a result, relying solely on this source to make a finding would be seen as a sign of subjectivity.

The Issue of the Standard of Proof: Reaching a Factual Conclusion with a Degree of Certainty

Fact-finding being about establishing facts, the essence of the process revolves around the question related to determining at which point

[52] M Eriksson Baaz, 'Was the Congolese army ordered to rape in Minova?' (*Congo Siasa Blog*, 15 April 2013), available at congosiasa.blogspot.com/2013/04/was-congolese-army-ordered-to-rape-in.html.

[53] UN Human Rights Council, *Report of the International Commission of Inquiry on Libya*, UN Doc A/HRC/19/68 (8 March 2012) para 116.

[54] OHCHR, *Report of the Mapping Exercise documenting the most serious violations of human rights and international humanitarian law committed within the territory of the Democratic Republic of the Congo between March 1993 and June 2003*, (August 2010) para 102.

fact-finders can reach their factual conclusions. This, surely, is an operation where subjective views can play a role as to whether one is convinced or not that a given incident happened?

This is the very purpose of the notion of 'standard of proof' in fact-finding.[55] It is usually defined as the degree of certainty fact-finders set and at which point they can make factual determinations; in other words the type of threshold they use to consider they are convinced an incident happened a certain way. Various standards of proof exist.[56] The least demanding standard of proof commonly used by fact-finders is called the 'balance of probabilities'[57] which consists of comparing information that confirms a fact or violation with information that questions it. If the former is the most convincing, the fact will be considered 'established'. The terms 'reasonable suspicion' or 'reasonable grounds to believe' are also sometimes used and are defined as 'a reliable body of material consistent with other verified circumstances tending to show that an incident or event did happen'.[58]

The standard of proof lies at the heart of the objective nature of any fact-finding conclusion. Adopting a standard of proof is as much a methodological requirement for fact-finders to carry out their mandate pertaining to the establishment of facts as it is a guarantee to ensure their findings are systemically based on the same objective standard to consider the various evidence at hand.

However, one must consider a fundamental underlying dilemma which could be described as follows: Fact-finders are expected to consistently rely on the same standard of proof to make factual determinations, apart from the particular situation where they may decide to apply a higher standard of proof, different from the one used to ascertain facts, to make determinations on identifying alleged perpetrators of international crimes. However, such a standard of proof is spelled out as a general and abstract threshold guiding the fact-finding work. When applying a given standard of proof, numerous elements may influence one's ability to implement it in a consistent manner, such as the difficulty of gathering certain types of evidence, say when the fact-finders cannot access the country or when investigating specific incidents where evidence is scarce.

[55] D Mar, 'The International Court of Justice and Standards of Proof' in K Bannelier et al (eds), *The ICJ and the Development of International Law. The Lasting Impact of the Corfu Channel Case* (Routledge, 2011) 98.

[56] S Wilkinson, 'Finding the Facts' Standards of Proof and Information Handling in Monitoring, Reporting and Fact-Finding Missions' (1 February 2014), available at ssrn.com/abstract=2400927.

[57] B Ramcharan, 'Evidence', in B Ramcharan (ed), *International Law and Fact-Finding in the Field of Human Rights* (1982) 78.

[58] OHCHR, *Report of the Mapping Exercise* (n 54) para 39.

The coherent application of a given standard of proof indeed raises significant challenges. Usually commissions of inquiry and fact-finding missions merely state the standard of proof they use when describing their methodology. However, the International Commission of Inquiry on the Central African Republic recognised this need for flexibility in applying a standard of proof. It noted:

> The standard of proof applied by the Commission in its work is that there are 'reasonable grounds to believe' that a particular incident occurred or that a given pattern of violations prevailed. The Commission has endeavoured to apply this standard with an appropriate degree of rigor, although the feasibility of different techniques of verification, cross-checking, and corroboration inevitably differs according to the context involved. This approach is fully consistent with that commonly used in international fact-finding inquiries of this sort. (…)
>
> The rigorous application of this standard of proof has meant, for example, that the Commission has not been able to make full use of some of the photographic and video materials to which it has been given access, because it has not been able to authenticate or situate the materials in accordance with the required standard.[59]

The standard of proof being closely linked to the sources of information or evidence used to establish facts, this unsurprisingly focuses on the questions of verification and cross-checking of sources. The wording used ('feasibility', 'context') may suggest that all efforts were made to apply this standard with rigour but that it was not always possible to do so. This hints at the fact that despite its purpose to guarantee objectivity in findings, it is necessary to be realistic in that fact-finders may not be able to apply a given standard of proof systematically the same way. By definition the body of information or evidence available and deemed credible and reliable will vary from one incident to another.

Furthermore, when it comes to the legal qualification of facts, fact-finding on alleged violations of some specific international norms may complicate further the ability to apply a standard of proof in a consistent manner. This is particularly the case in the field of international humanitarian law on the conduct of hostilities. Due to the way those norms are drafted, they require taking into account the perspective of the attacker, in order to establish whether a violation occurred. This of course raises difficulties as to the ability of fact-finders to have access to information about this component. In addition, the wording of those norms might also prove to be challenging. For example, regarding the obligations of precaution in attacks, the rules refer to feasible precautions, or what was practically

[59] *The International Commission of Inquiry on the Central African Republic: Final Report*, UN Doc S/2014/928 (22 December 2014) paras 16–17.

possible at the time of the attack, in order to assess whether precautionary measures were taken, making those obligations relative in nature. In that case, even if the same standard of proof is applied throughout the work of a commission of inquiry, it may be difficult to reach a similar degree of certainty when investigating those elements on precaution compared to reaching factual and legal conclusions on incidents where governmental soldiers deliberately killed civilians. This may be a subtle difference, but fact-finders might be satisfied with less evidence although they apply the same standard.

As noted by a scholar, 'having a standard of proof on its own will not provide clarity for all findings, it simply sets out a broad understanding of the threshold required to assess findings of fact and law'.[60] Ultimately a standard of proof only provides a framework to ensure overall consistency.

Applying and Interpreting the Law on the Basis of Facts

Once fact-finders have ascertained facts, they often must classify whether those facts amount to a violation of human rights law or international humanitarian law. While the tension of subjectivity and objectivity in fact-finding is focused on the process of establishing facts, its legal dimension is equally important. This may be at first paradoxical. Findings in law ought to be more straightforward and carry less risk than establishing facts. After all, it would merely be about applying the law to the facts. However this part of fact-finding increasingly becomes a credibility and legitimacy test for commissions of inquiry. This is particular true in areas of legal analysis that are open to various interpretations under existing international law.

The 'lawfare' critique—the use or misuse of the law as a means of achieving a military objective—against the UN Fact-finding Mission on the Gaza Conflict is a salient example of the controversial legal implications of commission of inquiry work.[61] The 2014 Israeli operation 'Protective Edge' against the Gaza Strip gave rise to a further example of diverging interpretations of the same norms, with a specific legal narrative focusing on precautions under international humanitarian law. This is facilitated by the nature of those norms. Unlike most of the norms on the conduct of hostilities that are framed in prohibitive terms and for which allegations must be rebutted by proving that a given prohibition was not breached, precautionary obligations require positive measures to be taken to demonstrate compliance with relevant norms. In that respect, the Israeli authorities

[60] Wilkinson (n 56) 12.

[61] See, generally, LR Blank, 'Finding Facts But Missing the Law: The Goldstone Report, Gaza and Lawfare' (2011) *Case Western Reserve Journal of International Law* 43.

engaged in a discourse which, in addition to accusing Palestinian armed groups of endangering civilians, insisted on how 'the [Israeli Defense Forces] goes to extraordinary lengths to avoid civilian casualties'[62] by taking more precautionary measures than they are required to do under international humanitarian law.

Members of commissions of inquiry, as a matter of principle, tend to avoid engaging in progressive developments of international law, in particular taking a stance with regard to an issue governed by unsettled norms or concepts, which could result in the commission of inquiry adopting a progressive interpretation of international law.[63] Applying only existing law prevents unnecessary critiques and ensures the credibility and legitimacy of the mission's findings. However given the numerous issues addressed by commissions of inquiry, it may actually be unavoidable for such bodies to, at times, adopt a progressive interpretation or to take a stand on a certain unsettled area of international law.

Recent analysis demonstrates that some of the legal findings of the Independent International Commission of Inquiry on Syria constitute a telling example. The manner in which the Commission has addressed questions of the obligations of armed groups under international human rights law and under the Optional Protocol to the Convention on the Rights of the Child, according to one scholar, constitutes a contribution to the progressive development of international human rights law.[64] The most striking example is the final report of the Libya Commission, which stresses: 'international human rights law obligations remain in effect and operate to limit the circumstances when a state actor—even a soldier during internal armed conflict—can employ lethal force'.[65] By employing an approach whereby international human rights law limits the use of force against legitimate lawful targets under international humanitarian law, the Libya Commission adopted a very progressive interpretation of the interplay between international humanitarian law and international human rights law regarding the use of lethal force. Despite a cautious approach adopted by numerous commissions of inquiry when addressing unsettled areas of

[62] 'Exclusive Interview With IAF Pilots: How They Limit Casualties' (*IDF Official Blog* 20 July 2014), available at www.idfblog.com/blog/2014/07/20/exclusive-interview-iaf-pilots-limit-casualties/.

[63] T Boutruche, 'Selecting and Applying Legal Lenses in Monitoring, Reporting, and Fact-Finding Missions' (8 October 2013) 7, available at ssrn.com/abstract=2337437.

[64] See T Rodenhäuser, 'Progressive Development of International Human Rights Law: The Reports of the Independent International Commission of Inquiry on the Syrian Arab Republic' (*EJIL: Talk!* 13 April 2013), available at www.ejiltalk.org/progressive-development-of-international-human-rights-law-the-reports-of-the-independent-international-commission-of-inquiry-on-the-syrian-arab-republic.

[65] *Report of the International Commission of Inquiry on Libya* (n 53) para 60.

international law and efforts to justify certain interpretations under international law[66], those choices may be seen as subjective.

Furthermore, this issue is not limited to unsettled areas of international law and extends to the application by commissions of inquiry of certain norms that are inherently difficult to apply as they require a complex assessment, the result of which could be seen as subjective. In that regard the principle of proportionality under international humanitarian law, in the context of the prohibition of indiscriminate attacks, is particularly relevant. This principle requires an assessment of two elements, both being per se challenging to grasp; on the one hand the expected incidental loss of civilian life, injury to civilians, and damage to civilian objects and, on the other hand, the anticipated concrete and direct military advantage associated with this attack. It is then necessary to compare both elements to undertake a proportionality analysis and decide whether the former is excessive vis-à-vis the latter. It seems that, rather than carrying out a proportionality test in some questionable cases, MRF bodies focused on manifest and clear-cut incidents or patterns of violations of this principle.[67]

11.4. CONCLUDING REMARKS: RECONCILING SUBJECTIVITY WITH OBJECTIVITY IN HUMAN RIGHTS FACT-FINDING

This contribution has shed some light on the tension between subjectivity and objectivity inherent to human rights fact-finding. While this process aims at being as objective as possible, numerous stages or operations within this task risk raising criticisms of 'subjectivity' against the commissions of inquiry. That being said, this chapter also shows that subjectivity carries different meanings and that choices made within the fact-finding work are not all about being influenced by opinions. This leads to somehow downplaying the risks associated with subjectivity. It also argues that objectivity in fact-finding corresponds more to a constant concern and state of mind from fact-finders rather than a theoretical and ideal concept excluding any form of choices and selection.

In particular, the analysis contributes to providing a better understanding of the complex manifestations of subjectivity and choices within fact-finding work. It is argued that being aware of the potential traps of subjectivity is imperative. Most importantly this chapter highlights the

[66] *Report of the international fact-finding mission to investigate violations of international law, including international humanitarian and human rights law, resulting from the Israeli attacks on the flotilla of ships carrying humanitarian assistance*, UN Doc A/HRC/15/21 (27 September 2010) 13–14, and *Independent International Fact-Finding Mission on the Conflict in Georgia Report* vol II (September 2009) 305–306.

[67] *Darfur Report* (n 18) para 73.

need to further consider the key guiding principles of fact-finding as guarantees to limit the risks associated with subjectivity. The overly generic fundamental principles and requirements in fact-finding, such as those of impartiality and of a sound methodology, are to be further operationalised to address the specific issues and find practical solutions to questions arising in the actual work of fact-finding. This is particularly true when it comes to problems identified in this chapter in relation to selectivity and choices. The selection of relevant facts to be investigated, the prevalence of witness testimonies, the intuitive choices made when dealing with certain sources of information, or the interpretation of the relevant norms, are some of the many aspects that need to be carefully considered to ensure strong, convincing and objective findings by commissions of inquiry.

Ultimately this contribution suggests that despite the exponential professionalisation and standardisation of the field of fact-finding, further work is needed to address persistent mistakes and risks associated directly or indirectly with matters of selectivity and subjectivity. The current focus on methodology and consistency of practices in various initiatives and manuals on fact-finding is to be welcomed. In that regard a professional requirement for fact-finders emerges where they are expected to justify choices made in a transparent manner and upon objective criteria, from the selection of facts and the type of evidence used to the interpretation of international norms.

12

Commissions of Inquiry and Procedural Fairness

ALISON BISSET

12.1. INTRODUCTION

THE OPERATION OF commissions of inquiry raises a host of concerns related to procedural fairness. They frequently interview and record the statements of large numbers of victims and witnesses, and sometimes perpetrators, and can publish findings of individual,[1] institutional[2] and state responsibility.[3] Although they are non-judicial bodies, in order to fulfil their fact-finding mandates commissions of inquiry are sometimes created with quasi-judicial powers such as subpoena, search and seizure and abilities to receive information confidentially.[4] Their reports not only have important standing in political and legal bodies and amongst the wider public,[5] they may act as a springboard for a series of other initiatives, notably national or international prosecutions.[6]

[1] *Report of the United Nations Independent Special Commission of Inquiry for Timor-Leste* (Geneva, 2 October 2006) paras 109–34.

[2] UN Human Rights Council, *Report of the international fact-finding mission to investigate violations of international law, including international humanitarian and human rights law, resulting from the Israeli attacks on the flotilla of ships carrying humanitarian assistance*, UN Doc A/HRC/15/21 (27 September 2010) para 262.

[3] UN Security Council, *Report of the International Commission of Inquiry mandated to establish the facts and circumstances of the events of 28 September 2009 in Guinea*, UN Doc S/2009/693 (18 September 2009) paras 201–11.

[4] D Akande and H Tonkin, 'International commissions of inquiry: a new form of adjudication?' (*EJIL Talk!* 6 April 2012), available at www.ejiltalk.org /international-commissions-of-inquiry-a-new-form-ofadjudication/, accessed 12 January 2016.

[5] See Ch 4: J Green and S Samuel, 'Domestic Commissions of Inquiry and International Law: The Importance of Normative Authority'.

[6] For example the commissions of inquiry for the former Yugoslavia and Rwanda led to the creation of ad hoc tribunals for those conflicts. The Porter Commission report was used by the International Court of Justice in *Case Concerning Armed Activities on the Territory of the Congo (Democratic Republic of the Congo v Uganda)* ICJ, (Judgment of 19 December 2005); C Henderson, 'Commissions of Inquiry: Flexible Temporariness or Permanent Predictability?' (2014) 45 *Netherlands Yearbook of International Law* 287, 311.

Despite this, there is no single set of standardised guidelines that apply to commission practice.[7] Commissions of inquiry do not typically operate in accordance with pre-determined standards of procedural fairness and those established to date have adopted different methods and worked to different standards.[8] Yet, as Franck and Fairley note, sound procedures are not merely desirable but a functional prerequisite of effective fact-finding because efficacy rests on credibility and 'credibility emanates primarily from … integrity of process'.[9]

Surprisingly, the procedural aspects of commission of inquiry operation have received limited attention in academic scholarship.[10] In light of their increasingly high profile and the frequency of their establishment as a means of investigating violations of international human rights and humanitarian law, particularly by United Nations (UN) bodies, this chapter revisits this important issue and considers commission of inquiry adherence to standards of procedural fairness. The chapter will begin by considering the importance of procedural fairness and its reflection within commission of inquiry terms of reference. It will then examine international rules and regulations governing fact-finding missions, in order to build a model of procedural fairness for commissions of inquiry. The chapter will demonstrate the problems caused by the absence of overarching guidelines, with a particular focus on: (a) standards of proof and corroboration; (b) guarantees for those implicated; and (c) protections for victims and witnesses. It will argue that in order to enhance their credibility and the reliability of their findings commissions of inquiry ought to operate to a predetermined and robust set of procedural safeguards.

As a result of their efforts to ensure procedural fairness, the chapter will additionally draw on the experience of one particular form of investigative commission, the truth commission,[11] in order to evaluate the possibilities

[7] Even the recently published OHCHR Guidelines, discussed below, do not set out rules of procedural fairness for all commissions of inquiry. See OHCHR, *Commissions of Inquiry and Fact Finding Missions on International Human Rights and Humanitarian Law: Guidance and Practice* (New York, 2015) (*OHCHR Guidance*).

[8] M Cherif Bassiouni, 'Appraising UN Justice-Related Fact-Finding Missions' (2001) 5 *Journal of Law and Policy* 35.

[9] TM Franck and HS Fairley, 'Procedural Due Process in Human Rights Fact-Finding by International Agencies' (1980) 74 *American Journal of International Law* 308, 310.

[10] See M Cherif Bassiouni and C Abraham (eds), *Siracusa Guidelines for International, Regional and National Fact-Finding Bodies* (Cambridge, Intersentia, 2013); M Martin and L Villareal Sosa, *An Empirical Analysis of United Nations Commissions of Inquiry: Towards the Development of a Standardized Methodology* (Dominican University of River Forest Graduate School of Social Work, Working Paper, 2013); S Wilkinson, *Standards of Proof in International Humanitarian and Human Rights Fact-Finding and Inquiry Missions* (Geneva Academy of International Humanitarian and Human Rights Law, 2012).

[11] For definitions of truth commissions see M Freeman, *Truth Commissions and Procedural Fairness* (Cambridge, Cambridge University Press, 2006) 12–18; PB Hayner, *Unspeakable Truths: Transitional Justice and the Challenge of Truth Commissions* (2nd edn, Abingdon, Routledge, 2010) 11.

and identify the difficulties of adhering to standards of fairness in fact-finding proceedings. There are sufficient similarities between truth commissions and commissions of inquiry to make this experience relevant and instructive. Both truth commissions and commissions of inquiry are ad hoc bodies established with context-specific mandates and priorities. Both have to process enormous quantities of data from multiple sources, rely on the testimony of victims and witnesses and publish findings accompanied by recommendations. Both typically suffer from time constraints and under-resourcing and may operate in volatile security settings. However, truth commission proceedings have been subjected to a closer level of study than those of commissions of inquiry,[12] which has required them to develop more robust and transparent processes. Analysis of past truth commission practice demonstrates the complexities of ensuring procedural fairness with limited resources, a demanding mandate and a short life span. Indeed, adherence to standards of procedural fairness has, in the past, created onerous administrative burdens for truth commissions and has resulted in the eventual exclusion of information from the final report where standards have not been met. The chapter will therefore show that while ensuring procedural fairness is desirable, it can be difficult to achieve in practice without compromising other aspects of mandate fulfilment.

12.2. PROCEDURAL FAIRNESS

In any investigation, whether judicial, quasi-judicial or non-judicial, procedures are necessary to channel the issue under consideration to the right conclusion. In some senses procedures can be considered purposive in that they are directed towards ends and goals.[13] They should not, however, be thought of as 'steps leading inexorably to outcomes, but more like signposts indicating the direction to take and the issues to consider'.[14] Procedures are shaped and influenced by the context in which the investigation takes place, meaning that they are informed by context-specific values; values that may be considered to be served by the application of rules and those that determine the manner in which the outcomes are to

[12] See for example, UNHCHR, *Rule of Law Tools for Post-Conflict States: Truth Commissions* (Geneva, United Nations, 2006); E González and H Varney, *Truth Seeking: Elements of Creating an Effective Truth Commission* (Brasilia, Amnesty Commission of the Ministry of Justice of Brazil; New York, International Center for Transitional Justice, 2013).

[13] On this idea see J Bentham and E Dumont, *A Treatise on Judicial Evidence* (London, 1825).

[14] DJ Galligan, *Due Process and Fair Procedures: A Study of Administrative Procedures* (Oxford, Clarendon Press, 1997) 6.

be reached.[15] In legal settings, values are typically understood as authoritative standards. Procedures are also related to issues of fairness, with fairness being achieved when the required outcome is achieved and when values that inform the process are respected.[16] The concept of procedural fairness therefore consists in the relationship between procedures, fair treatment and authoritative standards.[17] Procedures are the means by which standards of fair treatment are applied in legal processes.[18]

The issue is determining the parameters and measures of fairness relevant to a particular procedure or investigation, as procedures are fair or unfair only by reference to standards of fairness and those standards are based on the values that inform the context.[19] In relation to commissions of inquiry, this means that their objectives of information gathering, analysis and formulation of reforms should be carried out properly, with accurate information collected, impartial and objective analysis of that information and proposals made in good faith. There is a common social value in these tasks being executed properly, as the findings or outcomes will then be more robust and any action that flows from the recommendations will be based on solid foundations. This has implications for those involved in the process. Additional values therefore emerge that suggest that those involved should be treated in a way that enhances the accuracy, objectivity and impartiality of the outcome.[20] In essence, they should be afforded procedural rights.

Ensuring fairness in procedures is linked to giving a person what is due to them or treating them in a way to which they have a justifiable claim. The term 'due process' pertains primarily to the rights of the accused at criminal trial within Anglo-American models and endows accused persons with an array of procedural pre-trial, trial and post-trial rights.[21] There has been argument that due process standards should apply in non-criminal proceedings.[22] However, it seems to be generally accepted that, as discussed above, the process 'due' to an individual is dependent on the nature of the proceedings. Non-criminal contexts will attract a less stringent set of standards as the penalties arising are less severe and adherence to full due process standards would impose a disproportionate burden on fact-finding bodies.[23] Nonetheless, convincing argument has been

[15] Galligan (n 14) 6–7.
[16] Galligan (n 14) 8 and 53–65.
[17] Galligan (n 14) 52.
[18] Galligan (n 14) 54.
[19] Galligan (n 14) 55.
[20] Galligan (n 14) 47–48.
[21] J Orth, *Due Process of Law: A Brief History* (Lawrence, Kansas, University Press of Kansas, 2003).
[22] *Hannah* v *Larche* 363 US 240 (1960).
[23] *Hannah* v *Larche* (n 22) 451; *Morrissey v Brewer* 408 US 471 (1972); *Board of Curators University of Missouri* v *Horowitz* 435 US 78 (1978).

advanced that if there is an overlap between a right implicated in a trial and one implicated in non-judicial proceedings, for example where a commission of inquiry might have powers to compel self-incriminating information, 'due process standards provide a useful benchmark of fairness'.[24]

While the full assortment of due process standards may not apply in commission of inquiry proceedings, the requirements of natural justice suggest that adherence to some standards is nevertheless required. Natural justice is most closely associated with administrative proceedings and typically is not applicable where the proceedings are preliminary or advisory in nature and do not lead to a final determination of rights.[25] Yet the case law conveys no real clarity on what amounts to a preliminary proceeding, with some being judged to require adherence to standards of natural justice while others are not.[26] Generally, natural justice applies to any proceeding where rights to liberty,[27] property,[28] employment and livelihood[29] or reputation[30] are implicated or where economic privileges,[31] membership of clubs and associations[32] and legitimate expectations might be affected.[33] Commissions of inquiry, while they do not serve formal adjudicative functions or issue final, binding orders, may well impact upon rights to reputation and their proceedings may have repercussions in the longer term for a range of rights.[34] Thus, natural justice may be relevant as a framework for the operation of commissions of inquiry.

In general terms, natural justice requires an absence of bias, reasonable notice, the right to cross-examination, legal representation, and a duty to give reasons. Absence of bias requires that decision makers do not have a pecuniary or personal interest in the case and must not have prejudged the outcome.[35] Reasonable notice requires that a person is given both notice of proceedings in which they are adversely implicated[36] and an opportunity to present his or her case.[37] What is 'reasonable' in any particular situation will depend on the facts and severity of the consequences that might

[24] Freeman (n 11) 110.
[25] G Flick, *Natural Justice: Principles and Practical Application* (2nd edn, Sydney, Butterworths, 1984) 36.
[26] Freeman (n 11) 120.
[27] Flick (n 25) 27.
[28] Flick (n 25) 28.
[29] Flick (n 25) 29–30.
[30] Flick (n 25) 30–31.
[31] Flick (n 25) 31.
[32] Flick (n 25) 32–33.
[33] Flick (n 25) 33–36. On the meaning of 'legitimate expectation' see Lord Denning MR in *Schmidt* v *Secretary of State for Home Affairs* [1969] 2 Ch 149, 170–71.
[34] This will be discussed further below.
[35] Flick (n 25) 147–70.
[36] Flick (n 25) 51–61.
[37] Flick (n 25) 68–76.

flow from the findings. A written right to reply may be sufficient.[38] Likewise, the rights to cross-examination and legal counsel are restricted and dependent upon the nature of the case. Generally, the efficiency of non-judicial inquiries must be guarded and the introduction of trial-like rights to cross-examination and legal counsel threaten that efficiency.[39] Finally, the extent of the obligation to provide reasons also appears unsettled, but seems most likely to be required where fundamental rights are at issue.[40] In sum, there are no universal rules and the requirements of natural justice will be dependent on, among other factors, the circumstances of the case, the nature of the inquiry and the subject matter.[41]

It is, therefore, clear that procedural fairness is important for the investigation itself and for those involved, but it is difficult to ascertain precisely the standards that commissions of inquiry ought to work to. Indeed, there would seem to be some flexibility determined by the nature of the proceedings and their likely consequences.

12.3. STANDARDS OF PROCEDURAL FAIRNESS IN COMMISSIONS OF INQUIRY

Uncertainty around standards of procedural fairness is demonstrated starkly in commission of inquiry practice. Examination of founding resolutions, terms of reference and even final reports provides little assistance in determining which standards, if any, commissions of inquiry are working to. Founding resolutions, whether of the Security Council,[42] Secretary General[43] or Human Rights Council[44] typically do little more than create the commission of inquiry, endow it with a broad investigatory mandate and set a deadline for the submission of its report. The terms of reference,[45] set for commissions of inquiry by their establishing bodies, tend to be concerned with empowering the commission of inquiry itself. They contain issues such as freedom of movement, the ability to access places, people and information, security for commission of inquiry personnel

[38] Freeman (n 11) 122.
[39] Flick (n 25) 179.
[40] Freeman (n 11) 124.
[41] Flick (n 25) 47.
[42] UN Security Council Resolution 1564, UN Doc S/Res 1564 (18 September 2004) para 12.
[43] *Letter of the Secretary General to the UN Security Council*, UN Doc S/PV.5457 (12 June 2006) 3.
[44] UN Human Rights Council Resolution S-17/1, *Situation of Human Rights in the Syrian Arab Republic* (22 August 2011) paras 13 and 14.
[45] These are also sometimes referred to as standard operating procedures.

and documentation and protection for victims and witnesses.[46] They are, therefore, focused on enhancing fact-finding abilities, rather than ensuring procedural fairness for those who come into contact with commissions of inquiry, or imposing any standards upon commission of inquiry operations.

Commission of inquiry reports are often vague in their efforts to explain their standards of procedure or do so by reference to other sources in which relevant standards are apparently contained. The 2006 Commission of Inquiry for Timor-Leste 'conducted its work in an impartial and independent manner in accordance with international standards'.[47] Yet the report neither explains what those are nor where they might be found. The UN Fact-Finding Mission on the Gaza Conflict in 2009, stated that it had 'for the most part' been 'guided by best practice methodology developed in the context of United Nations Investigations'.[48] The Commission of Inquiry for Libya explained that it had based its work on 'international investigative standards developed by the United Nations'.[49] In the operations of the commission of inquiry for Democratic People's Republic of Korea 'best practices were applied with regard to witness protection, outreach, rules of procedure, report writing, international investigation standards, and archiving.'[50] In a footnote,[51] the commission of inquiry clarified that it followed the best practices outlined in an unpublished OHCHR document.[52]

In short, commissions of inquiry do not appear to be working to an overarching set of UN or international standards that govern their proceedings. Instead, standards and guidelines appear to be spread over a host of instruments.[53] Interestingly, the recently published guidance of the

[46] See eg, *Report of the Commission of Inquiry for Timor-Leste* (n 1) para 5; *Terms of reference for the Commission of Inquiry for Guinea, Annex to the Letter dated 28 October 2009 from the Secretary General addressed to the President of the Security Council*, UN Doc S/2009/556 (28 October 2009); *Report of the Commission of Inquiry on Lebanon pursuant to Human Rights Council Resolution S-2/1*, UN Doc A/HRC/3/2 (23 November 2006) Annex II.

[47] *Report of the Commission of Inquiry for Timor-Leste* (n 1) para 14.

[48] *Report of the United Nations Fact-Finding Mission on the Gaza Conflict*, UN Doc A/HRC/12/48 (25 September 2009) para 161.

[49] *Full Report of the International Commission of Inquiry to investigate all alleged violations of international law in Libya*, annexed to *Report of the International Commission of Inquiry on Libya*, UN Doc A/HRC/19/68 (2 March 2012) Annex I, para 6 (*Final Libya Report*).

[50] *Report of the detailed findings of the commission of inquiry on human rights in the Democratic People's Republic of Korea*, UN Doc A/HRC/25/CRP.1 (7 February 2014) para 29.

[51] *DPRK Report* (n 50) n 11.

[52] Office of the High Commissioner for Human Rights, *International Commissions of Inquiry and Fact-Finding Missions on International Human Rights Law and International Humanitarian Law* (2013).

[53] A full list is available at www.ohchr.org/EN/PublicationsResources/Pages/MethodologicalMaterials.aspx, accessed 7 December 2015.

UN Office of the High Commissioner for Human Rights for Commissions of Inquiry and Fact Finding Missions on International Human Rights and Humanitarian Law[54] purports to provide a broad 'set of principles, policies, practices and methodologies' that guide the work of commissions of inquiry.[55] It aims to assist commissions of inquiry 'in applying a consistent methodology based on best practice and maximizing their potential to successfully fulfill their mandates'.[56] The Guidance calls for commissions of inquiry to establish methodological tools,[57] terms of reference that include standards of proof and the protection of victims and witnesses,[58] and methods of work that determine how it will gather, assess and verify information, ensure confidentiality and ascertain the consent of sources on the various uses to which information may be put.[59]

Yet the Guidance, much like the commission of inquiry reports, suffers from vagueness. It comes with a general disclaimer that the uniqueness of each commission of inquiry requires adaptability and flexibility.[60] Many methodological issues are, apparently, dealt with in more detail within other OHCHR resources,[61] which, while referenced broadly within the text are not always publicly available and therefore somewhat unsatisfactory in the effort to identify the standards of procedural fairness to which commissions of inquiry ought to be operating. The Guidance is generally light on stipulating the standards to which commissions of inquiry should operate, presumably in line with its policy on the need for flexibility in light of variability. Thus, it often gives an overview of the standards adopted by various commissions of inquiry, for example in relation to standards of proof[62] and corroboration,[63] while failing to endorse any in particular.[64] Indeed, the formulation of any specific rules of procedure is left to the particular commission of inquiry, with the suggestion that the 1970 Model Rules, which will be discussed below, be consulted.[65] There is, therefore, a lack of coherence in approach to ensuring procedural fairness in commission of inquiry operations.

54 *OHCHR Guidance* (n 7).
55 *OHCHR Guidance* (n 7) v.
56 *OHCHR Guidance* (n 7) 3.
57 *OHCHR Guidance* (n 7) 65–66.
58 *OHCHR Guidance* (n 7) 67–68.
59 *OHCHR Guidance* (n 7) 69.
60 *OHCHR Guidance* (n 7) 4.
61 *OHCHR Guidance* (n 7) 5.
62 *OHCHR Guidance* (n 7) 62.
63 *OHCHR Guidance* (n 7) 59.
64 *OHCHR Guidance* (n 7) 62.
65 *OHCHR Guidance* (n 7) 69 and Annex II.

12.4. RULES OF PROCEDURE UNDER INTERNATIONAL LAW

12.4.1. International Standards

Matters of procedure are somewhat fragmented in international law generally. A host of international adjudicatory bodies including the International Court of Justice,[66] International Tribunal for the Law of the Sea,[67] the ad hoc international criminal tribunals[68] and the International Criminal Court[69] operate in accordance with their own statutes and rules of procedure and evidence. Specialised organisations, such as the International Labour Organization[70] and World Trade Organization[71] are governed in fact-finding and dispute settlement by unique procedural rules. Within the UN system, treaty monitoring bodies[72] and special rapporteurs[73] work to their own rules of procedure and codes of conduct. It is logical for international institutions with differing mandates, aims and objectives to work to different rules and procedures. Yet even where there may be significant overlap in purpose and function, there is no shared set of processes and protocols guiding investigation at international levels.[74] International human rights law lays down a broad and well-developed set of procedural rights for those accused of criminal offences,[75] some of which

[66] Statute of the International Court of Justice 1945, I UNTS 993, Arts 39–64.

[67] Statute of the International Tribunal for the Law of the Sea, (Annex VI of the United Nations Convention on the Law of the Sea); Rules of the Tribunal (ITLOS/8), as amended 17 March 2009.

[68] Updated Statute of the International Criminal Tribunal for the former Yugoslavia, as last amended by UN Security Council Resolution 1877 (7 July 2009); Updated Rules of Procedure and Evidence, IT/32/Rev.44 (10 December 2009); Statute of the International Criminal Tribunal for Rwanda, UN Security Council Resolution 955 (8 November 1994); Rules of Procedure and Evidence, MICT/1 (8 June 2012).

[69] Rome Statute of the International Criminal Court 1998, 2187 UNTS 90, Arts 53–61; Rules of Procedure and Evidence 2002, ICC-ASP/1/3 ad Corr 1.

[70] Constitution of the International Labour Organisation 1919, as amended, Arts 26–34.

[71] Rules of Conduct for the Understanding on Rules and Procedures Governing the Settlement of Disputes, WT/DSB/RC/1 (96-5267) (11 December 1996).

[72] See for example the Human Rights Committee, *Rules of Procedure of the Human Rights Committee*, CCPR/C/3/Rev.10 (11 January 2012).

[73] UN Human Rights Council, *Code of Conduct for Special Procedures Mandate-Holders of the Human Rights Council*, UN Doc A/HRC/RES/5/2 (18 June 2007); *Manual of Operations of the Special Procedures of the Human Rights Council* (August 2008).

[74] On this in relation to commissions of inquiry see Bassiouni (n 8) 48.

[75] Universal Declaration of Human Rights (adopted 10 December 1948 UN General Assembly Resolution 217 A(III), Arts 10 and 11; International Covenant on Civil and Political Rights, 16 December 1966, 999 UNTS 171, Art 14; United Nations Convention on the Rights of the Child, 20 November 1989, 1577 UNTS 3, Art 40; American Convention on Human Rights, 22 November 1969, 1144 UNTS 123, Art 8; African Charter on Human and Peoples' Rights, 27 June 1981, 1520 UNTS 217; Art 7; European Convention for the Protection of Human Rights and Fundamental Freedoms, 213 UNTS 222, Art 6.

extend to civil proceedings.[76] However, these do not per se deal with commissions of inquiry or the standards that they ought to adhere to in their proceedings.

This is not to say that there are no discernable rules of procedure governing international fact-finding initiatives. Efforts to codify fact-finding procedures can be seen as early as 1899[77] and 1907[78] in the Hague Conventions for the Pacific Settlement of Disputes. These treaties enable states parties to establish an international commission of inquiry to investigate the claims of each side in the event of a dispute.[79] Although concerned with international torts rather than the subject matter now typically considered by commissions of inquiry, the 1907 Convention in particular includes rules of procedure for any established inquiry.[80] It sets out the right to be heard,[81] rules on the role of counsel,[82] a duty to cooperate with the inquiry,[83] rules on the summoning and examination of witnesses[84] and the modalities of testifying[85] and the procedure by which findings are to be rendered.[86]

The procedural rules of the Hague Conventions served as a model for subsequent fact-finding instruments. In 1970, the UN Secretary General issued Draft Model Rules of Procedure for ad hoc bodies of the UN entrusted with studies of particular situations alleged to reveal a consistent pattern of violations of human rights.[87] The debates surrounding their adoption show a division between those who sought the introduction of rules to ensure impartiality and objectivity in the hearing of witnesses and collection of evidence and those who considered that investigating bodies had sufficient guidance in their terms of reference to accomplish their task and should not be subject to rules of procedure of a rigid, juridical

[76] International Covenant on Civil and Political Rights, Art 14(1); United Nations Convention on the Rights of the Child, Art 12(2); American Convention on Human Rights, Art 8(1); European Convention for the Protection of Human Rights and Fundamental Freedoms, Art 6(1).

[77] Hague Convention for the Pacific Settlement of Disputes 1899, 1 Bevans 230.

[78] Hague Convention for the Pacific Settlement of Disputes 1907, 36 Stat 2199, TS no 536.

[79] Art 9 of both Conventions.

[80] SB Kaufmann, 'The Necessity for Rules of Procedure in ad hoc United Nations Investigations' (1969) 18 *The American University Law Review* 740, 741–42.

[81] Hague Convention 1907, Art 19.

[82] Hague Convention 1907, Arts 14, 21, 25 and 26.

[83] Hague Convention 1907, Art 23.

[84] Hague Convention 1907, Arts 25 and 26.

[85] Hague Convention 1907, Arts 27 and 28.

[86] Hague Convention 1907, Arts 33–35.

[87] Draft Model Rules of Procedure for ad hoc bodies of the United Nations entrusted with studies of particular situations alleged to reveal a consistent pattern of violations of human rights, E/CN.4/1021/Rev.1 (30 October 1970).

nature.[88] It was feared that the imposition of such rules on all future bodies might hamper their operation and reduce their efficiency.[89] Ultimately, the latter position prevailed and the rules were adopted in abbreviated form as Model Rules of Procedure for UN Bodies Dealing with Violations of Human Rights in 1974. They are not mandatory and cover constitution, agenda of meetings, officers, secretariat, languages, voting, conduct of business, cooperation with member states, sources of information, records and reports.[90] In addition, the establishing organ or the ad hoc body *may* draw up rules of procedure in relation to sources of information.[91] This is far weaker than the Secretary General's proposal, which sought to draft procedural rules pertaining directly to the sources of information.[92] Yet, the Model Rules, which view rules of procedure as an optional extra in fact-finding, continue to be referenced by OHCHR as a guidance tool for commissions of inquiry in drawing up their rules of procedure and evidence.[93]

Some years later, in 1992, the General Assembly adopted the Declaration on Fact Finding in the Field of Maintenance of International Peace and Security.[94] The Declaration contains useful guidance on the need for impartiality,[95] clear terms of reference,[96] confidentiality,[97] protection for witnesses[98] and the need for cooperation between the commission and states concerned.[99] It states that where 'fact-finding includes hearings, appropriate rules of procedure should ensure their fairness,'[100] although there is no specification on the nature of the envisaged rules.

Thus, these instruments, while they may lay down some guidelines for international fact-finding, do not provide guidance on how commissions

88 Economic and Social Council, Question of the Violation of Human Rights and Fundamental Freedoms Including Policies of Racial Discrimination and Segregation and of Apartheid, in all Countries, with particular reference to Colonial and other Dependent Territories, E/Cn.4/1021/Rev.1 (30 October 1970) 2.

89 ibid.

90 Model Rules of Procedure for United Nations bodies dealing with violations of human rights: prepared by a Working Group of the UN Commission on Human Rights. Contained in the Report of the Working Group established under resolutions 14 (XXVII) and 15 (XXIX) of the Commission on Human Rights, E/CN.4/1134 (1 February 1974).

91 Model Rules (n 90) r 18.

92 H Thoolen and B Verstappen, *Human Rights Missions: A Study of the Fact-Finding Practice of Non-governmental Organisations* (Dordrecht, Martinus Nijhoff Publishers, 1986) 20–21.

93 *OHCHR Guidance* (n 7) 69 and Annex II.

94 UN General Assembly Declaration, *Fact-finding by the United Nations in the Field of the Maintenance of International Peace and Security*, UN Doc A/RES/46/59 (9 December 1991) Annex (*Fact-finding Declaration*).

95 *Fact-finding Declaration* (n 94) 25.

96 *Fact-finding Declaration* (n 94) 25.

97 *Fact-finding Declaration* (n 94) 25.

98 *Fact-finding Declaration* (n 94) 23.

99 *Fact-finding Declaration* (n 94) 22, 24 and 26.

100 *Fact-finding Declaration* (n 94) 27.

might reach findings, the standard of proof to which they should work or how they might afford protections to those who appear before them or are implicated in their reports. They therefore leave many questions unanswered on how commissions of inquiry should ensure procedural fairness.

12.4.2. Subject-specific Standards

In contrast, some of the subject specific international legal principles contain more detailed guidance on standards for non-judicial investigations. The 1989 UN Principles on the Effective Prevention and Investigation of Extra-Legal, Arbitrary and Summary Executions[101] include some aspects of procedural fairness, albeit only in relation to extra-legal, arbitrary and summary executions. The principles stipulate the requirement for impartiality, afford protection rights to complainants and witnesses[102] and participation rights for families of the deceased.[103] A written report is required within a reasonable period of time, detailing the scope of the inquiry, procedures and methods used to evaluate evidence as well as conclusions and recommendations based on findings of fact and on applicable law.[104] From the reporting requirements it can be seen that inquiries should be carried out in accordance with procedures that test the veracity of evidence in order to ensure the accuracy and credibility of findings.

The Principles are supplemented by the UN Manual on the Effective Prevention and Investigation of Extra-Legal, Arbitrary and Summary Executions (1991),[105] which includes a model protocol (the Minnesota Protocol). It too stresses the need for impartiality and independence[106] and the importance of ensuring the safety of victims and witnesses, including through the use of confidentiality guarantees and *in camera* hearings.[107] The Protocol gives all interested parties a right to be heard, with the possibility for compelled witnesses to be represented through legal counsel where there is risk of exposure to criminal or civil liability.[108] It lays down

[101] *Principles on the Effective Prevention and Investigation of Extra-Legal, Arbitrary and Summary Executions*, UN Doc E/1989/65 (25 May 1989) (*UN Principles*). UN General Assembly Resolution 55/89 (2000), *UN Principles on the Effective Investigation and Documentation of Torture and Other Cruel, Inhuman or Degrading Treatment or Punishment* contains very similar guidelines.

[102] *UN Principles* (n 101) Principle 15.

[103] *UN Principles* (n 101) Principle 16.

[104] *UN Principles* (n 101) Principle 17.

[105] *UN Manual on the Effective Prevention and Investigation of Extra-Legal, Arbitrary and Summary Executions*, UN Doc E/ST/CSDHA/.12 (1991) (containing the *Minnesota Protocol*).

[106] *Minnesota Protocol* (n 105) Art 4.

[107] *Minnesota Protocol* (n 105) Art 10.

[108] *Minnesota Protocol* (n 105) Art 13.

detailed guidelines on the evaluation of evidence requiring corroboration and assessment of its 'relevance, veracity, reliability and probity'.[109] It stipulates that hearsay evidence, *in camera* testimony and testimony not subject to cross-examination should be treated with caution and afforded less weight.[110] As under the Principles, the Protocol states that the commission's final report should explain the procedures and methods used in evaluating evidence.[111]

In investigations of serious human rights violations, the Impunity Principles,[112] which include a section dedicated to commission of inquiry operation, are considered to encompass standards of best practice.[113] As above, these also include discussion of the need for impartiality, independence and competence.[114] They include a series of safeguards for those implicated in commissions' findings, requiring the commission to corroborate information before publicly naming individuals and to afford a right to reply to any accusations made.[115] Everyone is provided with a right to know whether his or her name appears in the archives. If it does, the validity of the information may be challenged, following which the alternative version of events is to be attached to the challenged document.[116] The Principles also contain guarantees for victims and witnesses,[117] which require commissions of inquiry to take effective measures to provide physical and psychological protection and support and to ensure that testimony given confidentially is offered pursuant to understanding of the rules that govern disclosure.[118]

12.4.3. International Guidelines

Alongside these international instruments and principles, there are a number of authoritative compilations of guidelines, which, based on analysis

109 *Minnesota Protocol* (n 105) Art 14.
110 *Minnesota Protocol* (n 105) Art 14.
111 *Minnesota Protocol* (n 105) Art (15b).
112 L Joinet, *Set of Principles for the Protection and Promotion of Human Rights Through Action to Combat Impunity*, UN Doc E/CN.4/Sub.2/1997/20/Rev.1 (1997) (*Joinet Principles*). The Principles were updated in 2005: D Orentlicher, *Updated Set of Principles for the Protection and Promotion of Human Rights Through Action to Combat Impunity*, UN Doc E/CN.4/2005/102. Add.1 (2005) (*Updated Principles*).
113 F Haldemann, P Gaeta and T Unger, *Commentary on the UN Principles to Combat Impunity* (Oxford, Oxford University Press, 2017).
114 *Joinet Principles* (n 112) Principle 6; *Updated Principles* (n 112) Principle 7.
115 *Joinet Principles* (n 112) Principle 8; *Updated Principles* (n 112) Principle 9.
116 *Joinet Principles* (n 112) Principle 16; *Updated Principles* (n 112) Principle 17.
117 *Joinet Principles* (n 112) Principle 9; *Updated Principles* (n 112) Principle 10.
118 Note that only the *Updated Principles* contain explicit discussion of the need to inform witnesses of the disclosure rules.

of fact-finding practice and reports, have developed standards to inform inquiry proceedings.[119] The *Lund-London Guidelines*,[120] although primarily aimed at NGO investigations, set out to provide direction for all engaged in human rights fact-finding and aim to enhance accuracy, objectivity, transparency and credibility.[121] The Guidelines suggest that fact-finding missions should be staffed to ensure a lack of bias.[122] Missions should take account of the safety and security of witnesses[123] and ensure that testimony is given in full understanding of the extent of any confidentiality guarantee and the possibilities for disclosure.[124] They should verify the facts upon which findings are based[125] and the final report should detail the standards against which information was weighed.[126]

Similar standards are identified within the 2013 *Siracusa Guidelines*, which seek to promote an effective approach to human rights fact-finding.[127] The *Siracusa Guidelines* provide extensive guidance on the need to establish clear methods of work,[128] including the methods that will be used to collect evidence and information,[129] the standards to which it will be reviewed and evaluated,[130] the standard of proof on which findings will be based[131] and the need to distinguish hearsay from direct evidence.[132] They call for the protection and support of witnesses[133] and for comprehensive reporting that presents the purpose, formation, operations and methods of work,[134] as well as for secure archiving.[135]

[119] 'Belgrade Minimum Rules of Procedure for International Human Rights Fact-Finding Visits' (1981) 75 *American Journal of International Law* 163; Chicago Principles on Post-Conflict Justice 2007, in M Cherif Bassiouni and D Rothenberg, *Facing Atrocity: The Importance of Guiding Principles on Post-Conflict Justice* (The International Human Rights Law Institute, De Paul University, 2007), Part II; Guiding Principles for Human Rights Field Officers Working in Conflict and Post-Conflict Environments (Human Rights Law Centre, University of Nottingham, 2008).

[120] *Guidelines on International Human Rights Fact-Finding Visits and Reports* (the *Lund-London Guidelines*) 2009.

[121] *Lund-London Guidelines* (n 120) Preamble, para 3.

[122] *Lund-London Guidelines* (n 120) Guidelines 8, 10, 15, 23.

[123] *Lund-London Guidelines* (n 120) Guideline 38.

[124] *Lund-London Guidelines* (n 120) Guidelines 42, 45, 52.

[125] *Lund-London Guidelines* (n 120) Guideline 54.

[126] *Lund-London Guidelines* (n 120) Guidelines 59 and 60(vii).

[127] *Siracusa Guidelines for International, Regional and National Fact-Finding Bodies*, in Bassiouni and Abraham (n 10) 37.

[128] Guideline 5.

[129] Guideline 7.3.

[130] Guideline 8.

[131] Guideline 8.3.

[132] Guideline 8.4.

[133] Guideline 10.

[134] Guideline 13.

[135] Guideline 14.

Likewise, the HPCR *Advanced Practitioner's Handbook on Commissions of Inquiry*[136] contains guidance on interpreting mandates to ensure impartiality,[137] the need to adopt a clear methodology to apply legal frameworks[138] and the centrality of standard of proof to systematic analysis of the information obtained.[139] These, and the explanation of them within the report,[140] the HPCR considers, are essential to the credibility of the commission of inquiry's findings, in situations that are likely to be controversial.[141] The *Handbook* provides detailed guidance on how to ensure the protection of the physical security and psychological well-being of victims and witnesses through the training of staff, the use of confidentiality in statement-taking and reporting, and implementing a system of follow-up measures.[142] It also notes the need to respect due process in relation to the naming of individuals suspected of involvement in violations of international law.[143]

Standards of procedural fairness relevant to commissions of inquiry are, therefore, spread disparately, over a wide range of different international legal instruments. Nonetheless, from analysis of the procedural rules contained across international legal instruments and principles, common standards emerge to enable the deduction of a model of procedural fairness for commissions of inquiry. This chapter will consider three key aspects:

(1) in carrying out investigations, commissions of inquiry ought to assess and evaluate evidence in accordance with pre-determined standards that test and ensure the reliability of information and findings. This involves the adoption of a standard of proof and the corroboration of information. Reports should explain the methods and standards worked to and the basis on which findings were reached;
(2) those implicated should be notified and provided with a right to reply before findings are published;
(3) there should be protection and support, both physical and psychological, during and following the dissolution of the commission of inquiry for victims and witnesses who testify. While confidentiality should be available, the commission of inquiry must make clear the extent of that guarantee, obtain consent in relation to any potential uses of the information provided and have in place procedures to ensure its protection.

136 HPCR *Practitioner's Handbook on Commissions of Inquiry, Monitoring, Reporting and Fact-Finding* (PHPCR, Harvard, March 2015).
137 *Practitioner's Handbook* (n 136) 15–17.
138 *Practitioner's Handbook* (n 136) 7–13.
139 *Practitioner's Handbook* (n 136) 27–31.
140 *Practitioner's Handbook* (n 136) 68.
141 *Practitioner's Handbook* (n 136) 20 and 41.
142 *Practitioner's Handbook* (n 136) 45–51.
143 *Practitioner's Handbook* (n 136) 69.

12.5. PROCEDURAL FAIRNESS IN PRACTICE

The remainder of this chapter assesses commission of inquiry practice in relation to the standards identified above. In order to demonstrate the practical dilemmas and difficulties in adhering to procedures while maintaining efficiency, this section additionally draws upon the experience of truth commissions.

12.5.1. Standards of Proof and Corroboration

The need to document methods and procedures is stipulated in many of the instruments surveyed above. The methodology adopted by commissions of inquiry is integral to the reliability and integrity of the fact-finding process and the significance attached to their findings and recommendations. Central to this are the standards of proof by which commissions of inquiry reach their findings and the means by which they test and validate the evidence and information that forms the basis of their conclusions. Although there have been some notable improvements in recent years,[144] many commission of inquiry reports have paid minimal attention to explaining their methodologies, adopted standards or how they have ensured procedural fairness. This particular aspect of the report has typically been discharged in a brief section that will explain what the commission of inquiry has done, often accompanied by a statement that commissions of inquiry are not judicial bodies and do not work to the standards of criminal trials.[145] How information is assessed is seldom explained. For example, the Beit Hanoun Fact Finding Mission report contains four brief paragraphs under the section entitled 'methodology', which outline in the broadest terms how the mission sought to fulfil its mandate. There is no mention of the standard of proof to which it worked.[146] The report of the Libyan Commission of Inquiry, which goes to some lengths to explain how it interpreted its mandate and carried out its work, stresses that its information must be distinguished from evidence capable of use in prosecutions but does not explain the standard against which it assessed its sources to reach its findings.[147]

[144] *DPRK Report* (n 50) 3–23.

[145] See also *OHCHR Guidance* (n 7) 62.

[146] *Report of the high-level fact-finding mission to Beit Hanoun established under Council Resolution S-3/1*, UN Doc A/HRC/9/26 (1 September 2008) paras 6–9.

[147] *Report of the International Commission of Inquiry to investigate all alleged violations of international human rights law in the Libyan Arab Jamahiriya*, UN Doc A/HRC/14/44 (1 June 2011) 2–3.

The OHCHR Guidance states that it 'is important for commissions/missions to clearly indicate in their methods of work the standard of proof they adopt and to include an explicit reference and explanation in their report'.[148] This recommendation follows that of a recent independent study on standards of proof in fact-finding and inquiry missions.[149] In the past, the absence of a single set of procedural guidelines meant that where commissions of inquiry have discussed the standard of proof, they have used a multitude of terminologies in relation to it. These include 'sufficient credible and reliable information',[150] 'overwhelming evidence',[151] 'substantial evidence', 'clear evidence' and 'concrete evidence'.[152] Some commissions have worked to a 'reasonable grounds to believe' standard,[153] some to one of 'reasonable suspicion'[154] and others 'on the balance of probabilities'.[155] Sometimes no overarching standard is laid down and the report is peppered with a variety of terms. For example, the Darfur and Libya inquiries assigned different standards to different tasks, with higher standards adopted in relation to assigning individual responsibility.[156]

Corroboration is also often overlooked. Where it is addressed varying standards have been adopted. The Commission of Inquiry for Guinea required a primary source supported by one other piece of information.[157] The DRC Mapping Exercise required at least two independent sources[158] and, in relation to findings against individuals, the Darfur Commission of Inquiry required a reliable body of information consistent with other verified circumstances.[159] The recent OHCHR Guidance emphasises the desirability of 'corroborating any given piece of information by obtaining concurring information from two other independent and reliable sources', but stresses that this 'may not always be necessary or possible' and that in

148 ibid.

149 Wilkinson (n 10) 47.

150 *Report of the United Nations Fact-Finding Mission on the Gaza Conflict* (n 48) para 24.

151 *From Madness to Hope: The Twelve Year War in El Salvador: Report of the Commission on the Truth for El Salvador*, UN Doc S/25500 (1993) 24.

152 See generally the *Independent International Fact-Finding Mission on the Conflict in Georgia Report 2009*. See also Wilkinson (n 10) 25.

153 *DPRK Report* (n 50) para 22.

154 *Report of the Mapping Exercise documenting the most serious violations of human rights and international humanitarian law committed within the territory of the Democratic Republic of the Congo between March 1993 and June 2003* (August 2010) para 7; *Report of the International Commission of Inquiry in Guinea* (n 3) para 22; *Report of the International Commission of Inquiry on Darfur to the United Nations Secretary-General*, UN Doc S/2005/60 (1 February 2005) para 15 (*Darfur Report*).

155 *Report of the international fact-finding mission to investigate Israeli attacks on the flotilla of ships* (n 2) para 24; *Final Libya Report* (n 49) para 6.

156 UN Human Rights Council, *Situation of Human Rights in the Libyan Arab Jamahiriya*, S/15-1 (25 February 2011).

157 *Report of the International Commission of Inquiry in Guinea* (n 3) para 22.

158 *Report of the Mapping Exercise in DRC* (n 154) para 10.

159 *Darfur Report* (n 154) para 15.

some circumstances 'information from a reliable primary source may need corroboration by only one additional independent and reliable source'.[160]

It might be considered that, as suggested by the OHCHR Guidance, the lack of clarity in relation to standards of proof and corroboration can be explained and justified by the diversity of contexts in which commissions of inquiry operate, their differing mandates and the variety of practical constraints that impact their operation. However, like commissions of inquiry, truth commissions are also endowed with context specific mandates and operate in difficult settings. Yet since the mid-1990s, truth commission reports have, with few exceptions, documented the standards to which they have worked within their final reports.[161] In accordance with their non-judicial status, the majority of truth commissions have stated that their findings do not amount to civil or criminal culpability.[162] Some have explained that they have made factual findings in relation to responsibility and accountability.[163] Others have referred to different categories of responsibility, such as political, historical and moral.[164] Some have created different categories of evidence, such as 'overwhelming', 'substantial' and 'sufficient'.[165] Generally, modern practice reveals a general adherence to a balance of probabilities standard in making findings[166] which seems logical. While truth commission conclusions are not without repercussion, they do not carry the potential consequences of court findings. To impose trial standards would therefore be overly onerous. At the same time, adherence to a balance of probabilities standard means that a relatively robust threshold must be met before truth commissions publish conclusions of individual or institutional culpability, thereby enhancing the credibility of the truth commission findings and providing a solid basis on which to found recommendations.

Corroboration requirements have varied in truth commission practice. Some have worked to high standards, requiring two credible and independent sources on which to base findings.[167] Others have required only one reliable source to corroborate accounts.[168] Both truth commission and

[160] *OHCHR Guidance* (n 7) 59.

[161] For a list of final reports see Hayner (n 11) App 2, Chart 1.

[162] *Witness to Truth: Report of the Sierra Leone Truth and Reconciliation Commission* (Accra, Graphic Packaging Ltd, 2004) vol 2, Ch 2, para 7.

[163] ibid.

[164] *Chega!*, Report of the Commission for Reception, Truth and Reconciliation for East Timor, January 2006, Part 2, para 40.

[165] *From Madness to Hope* (n 151) Annex.

[166] *Truth and Reconciliation Commission of South Africa Report* (Cape Town, Truth and Reconciliation Commission, distributed by Juta and Co, 2002) vol 1, Ch 4, s 155, 91 (*TRC Report*); *Witness to Truth* (n 162) vol 2, Ch 2, para 7.

[167] *From Madness to Hope* (n 151) Annex.

[168] Hayner (n 11) 142. The 2004 version of the Impunity Principles (n 112) (Principle 9) requires only that commissions of inquiry should try to corroborate information. This is weaker than the 1998 version (Principle 8), where two pieces of independent information were suggested.

commission of inquiry reports document a host of practical difficulties associated with investigating in volatile security situations with little time and few resources.[169] Those pressures frequently make it difficult to undertake the verification of information and materials necessary to reach a particular standard of proof. For truth commissions, such difficulties have resulted in the exclusion of information from final reports.[170]

It is clear from a comparison of truth commissions and commission of inquiry practice that while context diversity may explain some variation across adopted methodology, it cannot excuse failure to record and explain operating procedures and standards. Commissions of inquiry working to different mandates, with different objectives and priorities and under a range of operational pressures may adopt slightly different standards. Nevertheless, the standards to which they have worked and the degree of certainty should be explained within the final report. Without such explanation it is impossible to ascertain how much significance should be attached to commission of inquiry findings. Following the truth commission model, it is acceptable, as additionally indicated in the OHCHR Guidance, for commissions of inquiry to adopt different standards of proof. In line with truth commission practice, it has been suggested, and indeed is considered here, that 'balance of probability' is the most appropriate and realistic.[171] Anything higher involves commissions of inquiry in a level of judicial scrutiny that they are not designed to deliver, and lower standards may lead to the reporting of any violation suspected of having occurred.[172] It is also foreseeable that commissions of inquiry may be more certain of some findings than others and that in light of operational challenges or the nature of the violations being investigated they may consider it necessary to work to higher or lower standards in some instances. What is important is that the report makes clear the standards and procedures worked to in order to maintain the credibility and integrity of their findings and to indicate how much weight should be attached to particular findings.

12.5.2. Guarantees for those Implicated

Another key element of procedural fairness is ensuring that those affected by a particular process are afforded the rights and protections due to them. This is particularly important for those who may be adversely implicated in commission of inquiry proceedings. Many, if not most, commissions of inquiry become involved in assigning responsibility either to states,

169 *Final Libya Report* (n 49) para 11.
170 This is discussed further below.
171 Wilkinson (n 10) 50–51.
172 Wilkinson (n 10) 50–51.

institutions or individuals. Some, such as the Commissions for Guinea, Darfur, East Timor, Libya and Syria (2011) have been specifically tasked with identifying those responsible for violations of international law. Where there is a possibility that commissions of inquiry will name specific individuals this raises a host of due process related concerns.

There are some convincing justifications for naming. Exposing those responsible for past violations can be a key element of fulfilling the public's right to know the truth about what has happened.[173] Assigning individual responsibility can act as a measure of accountability and contribute to victims' sense of justice,[174] which is particularly important where there is little chance of trials. The importance of identifying those responsible for past violations has been confirmed by human rights courts and monitoring bodies in their consideration of the rights of victims to an effective remedy[175] and the obligations of states to guarantee human rights,[176] as well as in relation to the wider right to truth.[177] However, the public interest in knowing the truth must be balanced with the rights of those implicated. International human rights law protects rights to privacy, family life and respect for reputation under a host of instruments.[178] Being implicated in the perpetration of violations of human rights or humanitarian law may have far-reaching consequences for an individual's reputation and family life.[179] Naming might also impact on an individual's employment through dismissal from public service or a temporary bar on future reemployment if findings are used to support other initiatives, such as vetting.[180] It can

[173] UN Commission on Human Rights, *Study on the Right to Truth, Report of the Office of the United Nations High Commissioner for Human Rights*, UN Doc E/CN.4/2006/91 (8 February 2006).

[174] On truth commissions and acknowledgement, see JR Quinn, *The Politics of Acknowledgement: Truth Commissions in Uganda and Haiti* (Vancouver, University of British Columbia Press, 2010).

[175] ECtHR, *Aksoy v Turkey*, Application No 21987/93, (Judgment, 18 December 1996) para 98; Human Rights Committee, *Rodríguez v Uruguay*, Communication No 322/1988, UN Doc CCPR/C/51/D/322/1988 (1994) para 14.

[176] IACtHR, *Velasquez Rodriguez Case*, (Judgment, 29 July 1988) (1988) Inter-AmCtHR (Ser C) No 4 (1988) para 174.

[177] Human Rights Committee, *Concluding Comments on Guatemala*, UN Doc CCPR/C/79/Add.63, para 25; IACHR, *Monsenor Oscar Arnulfo Romero and Galdamez v El Salvador*, Case 11.481, Report N° 37/00, OEA/Ser.L/V/II.106 Doc. 3 rev. 671 (1999), para 148. Note the concerns raised by UNHCHR on extending the right to truth to include the identification of individuals. UN Commission on Human Rights, *Study on the Right to Truth* (n 173) para 39.

[178] Universal Declaration of Human Rights, Art 12; International Covenant on Civil and Political Rights, Art 17; United Nations Convention on the Rights of the Child, Art 16; European Convention for the Protection of Human Rights and Fundamental Freedoms, Art 8; American Convention on Human Rights, Arts 11 and 14.

[179] Hayner (n 11) 122.

[180] P de Greiff and A Mayer-Rieckh, *Justice as Prevention: Vetting Public Employees in Transitional Societies* (Chicago, Social Science Research Council, 2007) Chs 12 and 13.

therefore be argued that commissions of inquiry should conduct their proceedings in accordance with standards that ensure fairness.

Commissions of inquiry have taken different approaches to naming individuals. The 2006 Commission of Inquiry for Timor Leste named those considered responsible for inciting violence and widespread human rights violations.[181] The Commission of Inquiry for Guinea named those it deemed as having been involved directly or indirectly.[182] The Commission of Inquiry for Darfur gave names of individuals to the UNSG in a sealed document[183] and the Commission of Inquiry for Syria (2011) noted that it had compiled a list of perpetrators, which could be shared with OHCHR in the event of future investigations and indictments.[184] The OHCHR Guidance states that it is 'usual' for lists of names to be presented in sealed envelopes to the Secretary General or High Commissioner for Human Rights.[185] While this does not amount to public naming, significant ramifications may nevertheless flow from being included on such a list, not least due to the link between commissions of inquiry and prosecuting bodies. It is notable then that commission of inquiry reports contain no information on efforts to notify those implicated or afford them an opportunity to respond before naming them, despite the fact that international guidelines suggest this as best practice. Nor does the OHCHR Guidance contain information on the procedures to be followed prior to naming.

Following the experience of the South African Truth and Reconciliation Commission, truth commissions have taken a prudent approach to affording procedural protections to those implicated. The Truth and Reconciliation Commission's enacting legislation required it to provide those implicated with an opportunity to submit representations within a specified time or to give evidence at a hearing.[186] The requirements of this clause led to legal proceedings[187] and a ruling that those expected to be named during public hearings should be given sufficient notice so as to allow them to be present to hear the evidence, have the opportunity to rebut it, and see the demeanour of the witness. It was also held that alleged perpetrators ought to be afforded a prior view of the findings the

[181] *Report of the Independent Special Commission of Inquiry for Timor-Leste* (n 1) paras 109–34.

[182] *Report of the International Commission of Inquiry for Guinea* (n 3) paras 212–53.

[183] *Darfur Report* (n 154) para 5.

[184] *Report of the United Nations High Commissioner for Human Rights on the situation of human rights in the Syrian Arab Republic,* UN Doc A/HRC/18/53 (15 September 2011) para 13.

[185] *OHCHR Guidance* (n 7) 90.

[186] Promotion of National Unity and Reconciliation Act 1995, s 30(1).

[187] *Nieuwoudt v Chairman, South African Truth and Reconciliation Commission* (1996) 2 All SA 660 (SE); *Du Preez and Van Rensburg v Chairman, South African Truth and Reconciliation Commission,* Case No 4443/96 (unreported decision of Cape of Good Hope Provisional Division, 30 April 1996) and 1996 (3) SA 997 (C).

Commission intended to publish.[188] The Truth and Reconciliation Commission therefore gave 21 days' written notice to those likely to be implicated in hearings. However, many of those implicated could not be traced and the Commission had to delete from its report the names of a large number of alleged perpetrators and descriptions of the incidents in which they were allegedly involved.[189] The Commission was critical of the ruling and its imposition of administrative burdens.[190] Truth commissions established subsequently have also encountered difficulties in providing a right to reply, whether due to practical tracing problems within transitional states[191] or simply due to the large numbers of allegations received.[192] They have not publicly named individuals where the opportunity to reply has not been possible.[193]

The truth commission experience demonstrates the difficulties associated with publishing findings on individual responsibility where there is also adherence to procedural rights of notification and reply for those implicated. To date, commissions of inquiry appear to have avoided these onerous administrative requirements by failing to afford procedural rights to those implicated. This not only falls short of international standards but raises questions as to the credibility of commissions of inquiry and their findings. As with working to standards of proof and corroborating information, there are challenges for resource, time constrained bodies in meeting demanding standards. However, simply ignoring the requirements of procedural fairness is not the solution.

Moving forward, it must be questioned whether it is necessary and, indeed, appropriate, for unaccountable, non-judicial bodies working to relatively low standards of proof to publish, or pass to prosecuting bodies, lists of individuals. Their short life spans make it extremely difficult to fulfil the various aspects of notification and reply necessary to comply with international standards. The contribution that commissions of inquiry might make to accountability through naming is undermined if individual rights have not been respected as part of the fact-finding process and doubt is cast on the integrity of the commission of inquiry and the credibility of its findings. In light of such difficulties, truth commissions have sought alternative means of assigning responsibility. In Argentina,

[188] *Du Preez and Van Rensburg v Chairman, South African Truth and Reconciliation Commission*, 1997 (3) SA 204 (SCA).

[189] *TRC Report* (n 166) vol 5, Ch 6, 260.

[190] *TRC Report* (n 166) vol 1, 185.

[191] *Chega!* (n 164) pt 2, para 34.

[192] *Report of the Truth, Justice and Reconciliation Commission* (Kenya, TJRC, 2013) vol 1, Ch 2 para 61. See also *Witness to Truth* (n 162) vol 1, Ch 5, 154–55; *Final Report of the Truth and Reconciliation Commission for Liberia* (2009) vol II, 190.

[193] *Chega!* (n 164) paras 37–39. The list was also sent to the President with a recommendation that those named be prohibited from holding public office.

the commission assumed a reporting role, summarising information and including names mentioned in testimony where they held credibility.[194] The commissions for Peru and Sierra Leone documented specific crimes and the individuals and units in charge of the areas in which the crimes were committed at the relevant time,[195] leading readers to infer responsibility. While this eases procedural administrative burdens, it is not risk free and individuals may still be tarnished, with implications for their privacy and reputation rights. Whatever solution is reached, commissions of inquiry cannot simply continue to name individuals without affording them procedural rights to rebut the allegations against them. It may be better to omit this aspect of commission of inquiry work than to damage perceptions of the commission of inquiry altogether.

12.5.3. Protections for Victims and Witnesses

Fairness in procedure is important not only for those implicated but also for those who come into contact with commissions of inquiry as victims and witnesses. The need to protect victims and witnesses who testify can be seen in many of the international instruments discussed above.[196] It is also discussed at length in the OHCHR's Guidance.[197] While the Guidance states that the primary responsibility for the protection of those cooperating with commissions of inquiry is that of the government of the state concerned,[198] this will be unrealistic in many situations, particularly where conflict is ongoing, where states are fragile or if the government is opposed to the commission of inquiry.[199] Again, however, practical limitations around time and resources means that commissions of inquiry will not often be in a position to provide the necessary support systems. Truth commissions have experienced similar issues. A small number have been endowed with witness protection powers,[200] but few have had sufficient resources to develop strong programmes.[201]

[194] Hayner (n 11) 143.

[195] Peru, *Informe Final de la Comisión de la Verdad y Reconciliación*, 2003, Annex; *Witness to Truth*, (n 162) vol I, para 34.

[196] See also *Basic Principles and Guidelines on the Right to a Remedy and Reparation for Victims of Violations of International Human Rights and Humanitarian Law* annexed to UN General Assembly Resolution A/C.3/60/L.24, Principle 12(b); General Assembly Resolution 40/34 (1985), *UN Declaration of Basic Principles of Justice for Victims of Crime and Abuse of Power*, Principle 14.

[197] *OHCHR Guidance* (n 7) 74–82.

[198] *OHCHR Guidance* (n 7) 75.

[199] See, for example, *Report of the United Nations High Commissioner for Human Rights on Syria* (n 184) para 9.

[200] Hayner (n 11) 232; Freeman (n 11) 260.

[201] *Final Report of the Truth and Reconciliation Commission for Liberia* (n 192) vol II, 62.

Guarantees of confidentiality can act as an important means of protection and both truth commission[202] and commission of inquiry reports evidence extensive use of the ability to grant confidentiality. The OHCHR Guidance states that interviewees should be informed of the commission of inquiry's confidentiality policy and potential uses of their testimony and that consent should be gained in relation to specific ways in which testimony might be used.[203] It is hoped that this practice is indeed followed in commission of inquiry practice, particularly in light of the links between commissions of inquiry and prosecutorial bodies and the eventuality that those who testify may become of interest to other bodies. Yet, although they very often explain that testimony was taken confidentially, commission of inquiry reports do not document how policies on confidentiality are explained to those who testify, nor how informed consent is obtained. The careful approach of the Timorese truth commission is of note here. It informed every deponent of the possible uses of statements, allowing individuals to decide whether their statement could be included in the final report, whether it would be accessible through the commission's archives and whether to give information confidentially or anonymously.[204] This was done through an information sheet, with a consent form at the bottom, which included tickable boxes. The sheet was then attached to the statement.[205] Such measures also ensure the testimony is being given willingly and freely.

The provision of emotional and psychological support to those testifying is also now considered an important aspect of best practice.[206] The notion that victims of past violations should receive any necessary medical, psychological or social assistance is internationally recognised.[207] The OHCHR Guidance acknowledges the need to ensure psychological support to those testifying,[208] but the focus of discussion within the Guidance is on securing physical, rather than psychological wellbeing. Commission of inquiry reports do not discuss how psychological support has been provided, if at all. Providing emotional and psychological support to those

202 Agreement on the establishment of the Commission to clarify past human rights violations and acts of violence that have caused the Guatemalan Population to suffer, Oslo (17 June 1994), (1997) 36 ILM 283; *Witness to Truth* (n 162) vol 1, Ch 5, paras 22 and 27; *Report of the Truth, Justice and Reconciliation Commission* (n 192) vol IIA, Ch 6, para 19.

203 *OHCHR Guidance* (n 7) 52.

204 *Chega!* (n 164) Part 1, para 150.

205 Freeman (n 11) 174–75.

206 Impunity Principles (n 112), Principle 10.

207 *UN Declaration of Basic Principles of Justice for Victims of Crime* (n 184) Principle 14; *Basic Principles and Guidelines on the Right to a Remedy and Reparation* (n 184) Principles 21 and 24; IACHR, *Annual Report of the Inter-American Court of Human Rights* (San Jose, Costa Rica, OAS, 2010) 11.

208 *OHCHR Guidance* (n 7) 55.

testifying is something that has also challenged truth commissions. While some established specific divisions and units to provide services,[209] others noted a lack of available services at national levels, particularly beyond the life-span of the commission,[210] and called for strengthening of national systems in final reports.[211] Testifying before commissions of inquiry may be traumatic[212] and the commissions must therefore give careful consideration to the psychological support they can provide to those who enable them to fulfill their information-gathering mandates. If commissions of inquiry cannot provide the necessary support, serious questions must be asked as to whether they ought to be interviewing vulnerable victims and witnesses. It has been suggested that longer term monitoring of cases should be referred to a permanent institution such as OHCHR.[213] That may be a solution in some cases, but probably not in all.

12.6. CONCLUSION

In sum, procedural fairness within commission of inquiry practice is disordered, with relevant standards spread over a multitude of international instruments. The absence of a single set of overarching guidelines is problematic and has led to a lack of transparency in practice that casts doubt on the integrity and credibility of commission of inquiry findings. The 2015 OHCHR Guidance has offered some clarity on how commissions of inquiry are working to protect and support victims and witnesses, but it leaves many questions unanswered in relation to standards of proof, corroboration and guarantees for those implicated.

Commissions of inquiry have been subjected to considerable criticism for their lack of consistency and clarity. However, analysis of truth

[209] *TRC Report*(n 166) vol 1, Ch 6, 146 and Ch 10; *Ghana National Reconciliation Commission Final Report* (2004) vol 1, Ch 2, 2.3.3.5.2 and vol 2, Ch 2, 2.5.3.1; Kingdom of Morocco, Justice and Reconciliation Commission, *National Commission for Truth, Justice and Reconciliation, Summary of the Final Report* (2006) 37; *Chega!* (n 164) Part 10; *Final Report of the Truth and Reconciliation Commission for Liberia* (n 192) vol 2, 37.

[210] *TRC Report* (n 166) vol 1, Ch 10, 289; *Final Report of the Truth and Reconciliation Commission for Liberia* (n 192) 84.

[211] Morocco, *National Commission for Truth, Justice and Reconciliation, Summary of the Final Report* (n 209) 45.

[212] The impact of testifying before truth commissions has received more attention than testifying before commissions of inquiry. See AR Chapman, 'Truth Commissions as Instruments of Forgiveness and Reconciliation' in RG Helmick and RL Peterson, (eds) *Forgiveness and Reconciliation: Religion, Public Policy and Conflict Transformation* (Radnor, Pennsylvania Templeton Foundation Press, 2002) 257–79; R Picker, *Victims Perspectives about the Human Rights Violations Hearings* (Johannesburg, Centre for the Study of Violence and Reconciliation, 2005).

[213] T Boutruche, 'Credible Fact-Finding and Allegations of International Humanitarian Law Violations: Challenges in Theory and Practice' (2011) 16 *Journal of Conflict and Security Law* 105, 119.

commission practice shows that some variation in practice, whether in relation to standards of proof adhered to, the adoption of a number of different standards or corroboration requirements, is to be expected in light of mandate and context differentiation and that this may not necessarily be problematic. Thus, criticisms aimed at commissions of inquiry on the basis that they operate to different standards may not be well founded. What is problematic is the failure to explain fully the standards that have been adopted and the methodologies followed to reach findings. In this respect, commission of inquiry reporting practice is wanting both generally and in comparison with that of truth commissions, which have taken a more careful and considered approach to creating categories of responsibility and outlining their procedures. However, presuming that commissions of inquiry do in fact work to predetermined standards, but simply do not always fully explain them in reports, this is something that can easily be remedied by bolstering methodology sections of final reports, rather than treating this section as one that can be dismissed with minimal input.

More troublesome is the failure to ensure the rights of those implicated, which appears to have been overlooked entirely within commission of inquiry practice and is barely mentioned within the OHCHR Guidance. This is a significant problem, with implications for both individuals and the integrity of commissions of inquiry. Where a commission of inquiry is mandated or decides to name, whether publicly or in sealed lists, they must ensure fairness in the form of rights to notification and reply and corroboration of implicating information in order to comply with international standards and best practice. That said, affording procedural rights of this nature brings onerous administrative requirements for commissions of inquiry, which are very often time and resource constrained. Those constraints also impact the abilities of commissions of inquiry to ensure the appropriate protections for those who testify, highlighting the central dilemma for commissions of inquiry in relation to procedural fairness: the tension between fulfilling a fact-finding mandate in a short time with limited funding and resources and adhering to strict standards of procedure.

The truth commission experience echoes the difficulties. Truth commissions have, often because their actions can be subject to national legal challenge, had to confront these dilemmas directly and make difficult decisions as to how to balance individual rights with truth telling. The lack of accountability of commissions of inquiry means that they have, to date, managed to avoid these difficult decisions. In light of the increasingly frequent establishment and high profile of commissions of inquiry and their connection to prosecutorial institutions it seems time for a reevaluation of not only the procedural standards to which commissions of inquiry work but whether, in light of the need to adhere to procedural fairness, commissions of inquiry should be working in the same way.

Some of the procedural problems identified within this chapter might be remedied simply by more thorough reporting on the procedures, standards and methodologies worked to, particularly in relation to standards of proof, corroboration and confidentiality policies. Issues related to the rights of implicated persons, naming individuals and the provision of long-term support for those who testify raise more complex and fundamental questions, which are complicated by the practical limitations around commission of inquiry work. Going forward, a realistic assessment of what commissions of inquiry can and should achieve is needed. Procedural fairness is not an option to be adhered to when there is time and adequate resourcing but a set of requirements that ought to guide operations to ensure robust and credible fact-finding. The procedures required to ensure fairness in any given context are determined by the nature of the process in question and the implications for those affected by and involved within that process. For those creating future commissions of inquiry, the abilities of such commissions to adhere to standards of procedural fairness ought to act as a key factor in determining their mandates, resourcing needs and lifespan and tasks ought to be assigned on the basis that the procedural fairness aspects can and will be fulfilled. Importantly, if this is to include the assignation of individual responsibility, future commissions of inquiry will require not only additional time and resources but enhanced guidance on how to respect and ensure individual rights. There are no easy answers, rather a delicate balancing of what the priorities of commissions of inquiry ought to be and what is desirable, achievable and credible with the time and resources they have available.

13

A Visible College: The Community of Fact-finding Practice

CORINNE HEAVEN

13.1. INTRODUCTION

ON 4 APRIL 2013, Philip Alston, Professor of Law at New York University and United Nations (UN) Special Rapporteur on extreme poverty and human rights, introduced a panel on *The Future of Human Rights Fact-Finding* at the Annual Meeting of the American Society of International Law by outlining a generational shift in human rights fact-finding. Following Alston, the first generation of fact-finding developed when international lawyers and diplomats started to inform different parts of the UN about potential crisis situations during the early beginnings of the organisation.[1] A second generation emerged in the 1970s and 1980s when non-governmental organisations (NGOs) such as Amnesty International and Human Rights Watch began to interview victims of human rights violations and advocate on their behalf. The most recent form of fact-finding, the third generation, somewhat changed again through

> the proliferation of fact-finding bodies whose basic legitimacy is not convincingly contested, radical changes in information and communication technologies (ICTs), the growing range of actors ready to consider and perhaps act upon findings, and the role of the media and popular mobilization [that] are all helping to transform the nature of this enterprise.[2]

[1] This chapter focuses on a practice that is currently known as human rights (and international humanitarian law) fact-finding. This is not to say that fact-finding is a recent development. The Hague Treaties, as well as the Covenant of the League of Nations, included provisions for fact-finding, though limited in scope. For a historical overview see LJ van den Herik, 'An Inquiry into the Role of Commissions of Inquiry in International Law: Navigating the Tensions between Fact-Finding and Application of International Law' (2013) 13 *Chinese Journal of International Law* 507.

[2] P Alston, 'Introduction: Third Generation Human Rights Fact-Finding' (2013) 107(3) *Proceedings of the Annual Meeting (American Society of International Law)* 61.

Alston concluded

> all that is clear is that the field of human rights fact-finding is changing very quickly and that it is assuming an inter-disciplinary dimension that was largely lacking not so long ago. Anthropologists, information scientists, architects, forensic scientists, statisticians, and many other professionals are now increasingly elevating fact-finding to a much more complex and sophisticated art and science.[3]

We might think of the UN Commission of Inquiry on Human Rights in the Democratic People's Republic of North Korea (2013) as a paradigmatic case of third generation fact-finding. Mandated 'to investigate the systematic, widespread and grave violation of human rights, with a view to ensuring full accountability,'[4] the commission made use of satellite imagery provided by Amnesty International, given that it was not granted access to the Democratic People's Republic of North Korea. It also provided the wider public with supporting documentation on its website, ranging from aforementioned satellite imagery, drawings by a former prisoner detailing scenes in a prison, to video excerpts of the public hearings. Michael Kirby, the chair of the commission, gave numerous interviews and press statements, and took part in a live web chat with Reddit users.[5] The commission received considerable media attention, with many expressing support for the commission's key recommendation that the UN Security Council refer the case to the International Criminal Court.[6]

Alston is right to point out that information and communication technologies have changed the field of human rights fact-finding. 'Facts' (or the evidence constituting a 'fact') can now be generated with a variety of information and communication technologies, such as Twitter, Facebook, crowdsourcing and crisis mapping tools as well as geospatial technologies.[7] These technologies also engage individuals in novel ways with fact-finding practice, such as the Reddit users interacting with Michael Kirby. The transformation of fact-finding has certainly been enabled by new technologies, which emerge in a changing international political and social

[3] Alston (n 2) 62.

[4] UN Doc A/HRC/RES/22/13 (9 April 2013).

[5] Available at www.reddit.com/r/IAmA/comments/25nlt5/i_am_michael_kirby_chair_of_the_un_inquiry_on/?limit=500, accessed 4 September 2015. Reddit is a social news site that allows users to post links to stories.

[6] See, for example, www.theguardian.com/world/2014/may/16/reddit-michael-kirby-north-korea-human-rights-abuses, accessed 27 March 2016; www.nytimes.com/2014/03/29/world/asia/un-north-korea.html, accessed 27 March 2016; www.hrw.org/news/2016/02/17/joint-letter-un-human-rights-council-members, accessed 27 March 2016; eeas.europa.eu/delegations/un_geneva/press_corner/all_news/news/2015/20150316_dprk_en.htm, accessed 27 March 2016.

[7] For an overview of the current use of information and communication technologies see P Alston and C Gillespie, 'Global Human Rights Monitoring, New Technologies and the Politics of Information' (2012) 23 *European Journal of International Law* 1089.

order. Broader structural changes, such as complex patterns of conflict and violence, the rise of 'new' security challenges or the mainstreaming of human rights in conflict-affected states have enabled the proliferation of interventions such as fact-finding. But such interventions also shape the social and political context they function in. For example, practitioners regularly make reference to 'successful' inquiries, such as the International Commission of Inquiry on Darfur (2004), which are then constituted as 'best practice'.[8] Thus, fact-finding experts also promote ideas and push for new agendas and open up the possibility of interventions such as fact-finding. Some have even concluded that fact-finding has emerged as one of the core mechanisms to address violations of human rights (and international humanitarian law) in conflict-affected states today.[9] In other words, conflicts are now increasingly viewed through a human rights lens, (re)constituting a reality that fact-finding experts are describing.

Against this background, this chapter suggests that the generational shift Alston identifies has been driven by practitioners and experts who continuously create, learn, develop and transform the complex art and science of fact-finding in a somewhat loose collective. In doing so, these individuals have shaped, diffused and proliferated a practice that is currently known as third generation fact-finding. This chapter invokes the concept of 'communities of practice' to shed light on the collective that has shaped and is shaping the current practice of fact-finding. Communities of practice are 'groups of people informally bound together by shared expertise and passion for a joint enterprise'.[10] They are not formal organisations, but may overlap with them. Individuals do not require official membership to be part of a community of practice. The primary driver of communities of practice is to develop and foster the learning processes of its members as well as to exchange knowledge with the community's environment.

Communities of practice engage with and potentially change the social and political context they function in, but are simultaneously shaped and changed by it. Whilst information and communication technologies, for example, have enabled fact-finders to 'find' facts differently than with interviews alone, it takes certain members of the community, such as the Special Rapporteur on extrajudicial, summary or arbitrary executions, Christof Heyns, to cite Alston and further reinforce the need for those technologies.[11] Whilst communities of practice are made up of individuals

[8] P Alston, 'The Darfur Commission as a Model for Future Responses to Crisis Situations' (2005) 3(3) *Journal of International Criminal Justice* 600.

[9] HPCR, *Advanced Practitioner's Handbook on Commissions of Inquiry: Monitoring, Reporting, Fact-Finding* (Cambridge MA, Harvard TH Chan School of Public Health, 2015).

[10] E Wenger and W Snyder, 'Communities of Practice: The Organizational Frontier', *Harvard Business Review* (2000).

[11] UN Doc A/HRC/29/37 (24 April 2015).

who can affect social and political events, they exist in a social and political context and are shaped by the powers and hierarchies of that context, as well as by the powers and hierarchies within the collective. A Special Rapporteur possesses a certain degree of discursive power to reify the need for information and communication technologies—a power that a different member of the community may not have. Communities of practices are thus jointly shaped by the context they function in as well as by the work of their members.

This chapter outlines the specific practices that undergird the fact-finding community. I identify three key practices: standardisation, professionalisation and transparency, which carry the main weight in explaining this community. Given the limitations of this chapter, the emphasis lies on the community that engages with fact-finding missions and commissions of inquiry that are established ad hoc by a UN organ or agency.[12] However, some of the arguments may also pertain to the regular human rights monitoring regime of the UN, such as the Universal Periodic review, commissions of inquiry by regional organisations such as the African Union or the Organization for Economic Co-operation and Development, or fact-finding missions carried out by states and NGOs.[13] The distinction made is not a conceptual one—especially given that communities of practice do not have formal boundaries—but a pragmatic choice. Against this background, the chapter is organised as follows: First, I will briefly outline the origins of the concept of 'communities of practice' and illustrate its uptake in international relations and international legal scholarship. I then turn to the three core practices that sustain the community of fact-finding practice. I conclude with an outlook on future challenges and prospects for the community.

13.2. COMMUNITIES OF PRACTICE IN INTERNATIONAL RELATIONS AND INTERNATIONAL LAW

The concept of 'communities of practice' was first introduced by Jean Lave and Etienne Wenger who sought to understand how humans learn. As a critique of cognitive learning theories that emphasise the mental processes of individuals, the authors argued that learning is necessarily situated and occurs through the participation in so-called communities of practice.

[12] The terms fact-finding and commission of inquiry are used interchangeably.

[13] For a discussion of the regular human rights monitoring regime see M Scheinin, 'Improving Fact-Finding in Treaty-Based Human Rights Mechanisms and the Special Procedures of the United Nations Human Rights Council' in M Bergsmo (ed) *Quality Control in Fact-Finding* (Florence, Torkel Opsahl Academic EPublisher, 2013) 54. For a discussion of NGO fact-finding see GM Steinberg, A Herzberg and J Berman, *Best Practices for Human Rights and Humanitarian NGO Fact-Finding* (Leiden, Martinus Nijhoff, 2012).

Learning, in this understanding, is first and foremost a social activity between individuals. Through their shared practices and understandings, individuals produce collectives. These collectives have no formal boundaries; and newcomers to the collective become a member by socialisation and learning its respective practices. Members do not require an invitation or a membership card, they do not carry an official title and are not necessarily close to each other (whether socially or geographically). What holds a community of practice together is a shared commitment to particular forms of practice. With new members joining the collective, knowledge and practice is also reconfigured; and new practices emerge.[14] In short, 'any community of practice is produced and re-produced in a collective process of learning'.[15]

Practices, understood as meaningful patterns of action, are both agential and structural.[16] Although the interview of an eye-witness as part of a fact-finding mission is carried out by an individual, it only gains meaning through 'collectively shared understandings of competency, of what is well done or poorly done'.[17] The *practice* of interviewing an eye-witness is only recognised as such when members of the community acknowledge its structural meaning. Thus, '[p]ractices enable agency, namely, they translate structural background intersubjective knowledge into intentional acts end endow them with social meaning. Structure, in turn, shows up in practices in the forms of standards of competence that are socially recognised'.[18] Practitioners sharing a specific understanding of interview techniques form a community of fact-finding practice.

Wenger further developed the concept as a general organisation theory by suggesting that communities of practice constitute a unit (of analysis) that is bound together in three core dimensions. First, a community of practice requires people that 'are engaged in actions whose meanings are negotiated with one another. […] Membership in a community of practice is therefore a matter of mutual engagement'.[19] Hence, a neighbourhood might be a community, but not necessarily a community of practice, if neighbours are not engaged with each other in some practical and meaningful way. Second, communities of practice negotiate a joint enterprise. Following Wenger, practices of the community are always deliberated as

[14] J Lave and E Wenger, *Situated Learning: Legitimate Peripheral Interaction* (Cambridge, Cambridge University Press, 1991). For an overview see also C Bueger and F Gadinger, *International Practice Theory: New Perspectives* (Basingstoke, Palgrave Macmillan, 2014) 29–36.

[15] Bueger and Gadinger (n 14) 30.

[16] E Adler and V Pouliot, 'Introduction and framework' in E Adler and V Pouliot (eds), *International Practices* (Cambridge, Cambridge University Press, 2011) 15.

[17] J Gross Stein, 'Background knowledge in the foreground: conversations about competent practice in "sacred space"' in Adler and Pouliot (eds) (n 16) 89.

[18] Adler and Pouliot, 'Introduction and framework' (n 16) 15.

[19] E Wenger, *Communities of Practice: Learning, Meaning and Identity* (Cambridge, Cambridge University Press, 1998) 73.

a collective, even when the community of practice 'arises in response to some outside mandate'.[20] For example, whilst commissions of inquiry receive their mandate by political bodies such as the UN Security Council or the UN Human Rights Council, the specific working methods are primarily negotiated amongst the members of the fact-finding community. Third, Wenger argues that communities of practice develop a shared repertoire that includes 'routines, words, tools ways of doing things, stories, gestures, symbols, genres, actions or concepts that the community of practice has produced or adopted in the course of its existence and which have become part of its practice'.[21]

Thus, communities of practice have lifecycles:

> They come together, they develop, they evolve, they disperse, according to their timing, the logic, the rhythms, and the social energy of learning. Thus, unlike more formal organisational structures, it is not clear where they begin and end. They do not have launching and dismissal dates.[22]

How then does knowledge and practice change within a community? Janice Gross Stein, for example, shows how within the humanitarian relief community 'change in practices occurs when new problems arise that challenge existing knowledge and/or when some of the influential members of the community want to "do better"'.[23] Antonio Cassese, arguably an influential member of the community of fact-finding practice, for example argued to strengthen UN fact-finding in at least three ways: setting up a roster of experts, a finance system as well as regulations on the structure, powers and functions of fact-finding missions.[24] As will be demonstrated in the remainder of this chapter, two of the three mechanisms are in place today. Communities of practices are therefore social entities that allow for the imagination and creation of new ideas, as members engage with each other.

Members of the community can also push the taken-for-granted knowledge to the foreground, by challenging, analysing and reflecting upon it. This book is, after all, an example of a critical engagement by some members of the collective. Communities of practice know '"the way we do things", but in response to criticism, to failure, or new knowledge, or discovery from doing—are open to new experiences, to new practical knowledge of what works better […]'.[25] What is more, members of a community do not necessarily have to agree with each other when it comes to their joint enterprise. The latter may be continuously negotiated, and the

20 Wenger (n 19) 80.
21 Wenger (n 19) 83. For a critique of the concept see Bueger and Gadinger (n 14) 34–36.
22 Wenger (n 19) 96.
23 Gross Stein (n 17) 89.
24 A Cassese (ed), *Realizing Utopia: The Future of International Law* (Oxford, Oxford University Press, 2012) 303.
25 Gross Stein (n 17) 90.

members may disagree on the substantive content or on desired outcome. All it takes is that they agree on certain rules to negotiate.[26]

Emanuel Adler was the first to introduce the concept to the discipline of international relations. He suggested that communities of practice 'cut across state boundaries and mediate between states, individuals, and human agency, on the one hand, and social structures and systems, on the other.'[27] These transnational communities of practice, then, are not formal international organisations, such as the UN, but coexist or overlap with them: 'If we think about our world as composed of communities of practice we see, for example, transnational communities of diplomats sharing a diplomatic culture, common values, and interests that are intrinsic to their practice.'[28] As an approach to studying international relations, the concept of communities of practices thus invites us to think about the world not as a system of states, but made up of transnational communities of practices, 'based on what people actually *do* rather than on where they happen to live […].'[29]

For Adler, communities of practice are not only engaged in a learning process, but also share a moral commitment to a set of values. In his interpretation of security communities as communities of practice, Adler argues that they 'spread by the co-evolution of background knowledge and subjectivities of self-restraint.'[30] Specifically, he demonstrates how the North Atlantic Treaty Organization's (NATO) expansion from a core of 'western' states to central and eastern European states in the 1990s can be read as a security community whose members learned and diffused cooperative security practices and thereby spread geographically.

International legal scholarship has also begun to engage with the concept of communities of practice. This development is particularly driven by the observation that international lawyers no longer form an 'invisible college', as was envisaged by Oscar Schachter more than 30 years ago.[31] Schachter defined the invisible college of international lawyers as a 'professional community, though dispersed throughout the world and engaged in diverse occupations, constitutes a kind of invisible college dedicated to a common intellectual enterprise.'[32] Whilst at first sight this notion bears

[26] HG Cohen, 'Finding International Law, Part II: Our Fragmenting Legal Community' (2012) 44 *NYU Journal of International Law and Politics* 1066.

[27] E Adler, *Communitarian International Relations: The Epistemic Foundations of International Relations* (Abingdon, Routledge, 2005) 15.

[28] E Adler, 'The Spread of Security Communities: Communities of Practice, Self-Restraint and NATO's Post-Cold War Transformation' (2008) 14(2) *European Journal of International Relations* 200.

[29] Adler and Pouliot, 'Introduction and framework' (n 16) 24.

[30] Adler (n 28) 197.

[31] O Schachter, 'The Invisible College of International Lawyers' (1977) 77:2 *Northwestern University Law Review* 217. See also J D'Aspremont, *Epistemic Forces in International Law: Foundational Doctrines and Techniques of International Legal Argumentation* (Cheltenham, Edward Elgar, 2015) 16–18.

[32] Schachter (n 31) 217.

similarity to Wenger's community of practice, Schachter believed in an objective and unified discipline, where international lawyers stand outside politics (of expertise). However, it is, first, fair to say that international lawyers no longer form an invisible college giving objective advice from the outside, but rather play a key role in international relations, by shaping legal interpretations and definitions or by using international law as a medium for political communication and manoeuvre.[33] International lawyers are, in short, quite visible. After all, the UN Fact-Finding Mission on the Gaza Conflict (2009) is better known as the Goldstone Mission/Report, named after the chair of the commission, Richard J Goldstone. Second, international law has become increasingly fragmented and, as some would argue, no longer represents a unified discipline.[34] Third, whilst Schachter believed that the profession of international law could be strengthened by the engagement with experts, that is, scientific experts, international lawyers are now increasingly seen as (legal) experts themselves that partake in the politics of expertise.[35] Legal experts thus interact with a variety of other experts, such as scientists, journalists, investigators, activists as well as diplomats in the joint endeavour of fact-finding.

Against this background, international legal scholars have begun to make use of Wenger's and Adler's concepts. Harlan Grant Cohen, for example, employs the framework to shed light on the increasing fragmentation of international law. He discusses three international legal communities—human rights law, global administrative law, and the law applied by international tribunals—and argues that in each of these legal communities traditional sources of doctrine have been replaced by alternative legitimate law-making rules.[36] Jutta Brunnée and Stephen J Toope engage the concept to explain that the compliance with legal norms results from the work of legal communities of practice that uphold specific criteria of legality. In addition to research on the formal sources of international law, their account demonstrates how 'legal obligation must be built and continuously reinforced by communities of practice'.[37] Ian Johnstone analyses a specific legal community of practice, the 'interpretive community', arguing that 'the use of international law is part of a broader discursive process

[33] See for example O Kessler and W Werner, 'Expertise, Uncertainty, and International Law: A Study of the Talin Manual on Cyberwarfare' (2013) 26:4 *Leiden Journal of International Law* 793 and A Bianchi, D Peat and M Windsor (eds), *Interpretation in International Law* (Oxford, Oxford University Press, 2015).

[34] Cohen (n 26) 1050.

[35] A Leander and T Aalberts, 'Introduction: The Co-Constitution of Legal Expertise and International Security' (2013) 26(4) *Leiden Journal of International Law* 783.

[36] Cohen (n 26) 1053.

[37] J Brunnée and SJ Toope, 'Interactional international law and the practice of legality' in Adler and Pouliot (eds) (n 16) 110.

in which norms are invoked to explain, defend, justify and persuade'.[38] Focusing on UN Security Council deliberations, he finds that legal arguments play a decisive role in shaping the 'better argument', and often impact, more or less directly, on decision-making within the Council.

In sum, the communities of practice approach offers, as Christian Bueger and Frank Gadinger note, a rich analytical vocabulary. The authors urge researchers to make use of the latter and 'study the multifold socialization processes in international practices, […] the interaction between communities of practice, […] which may also produce policy recommendations on how communities can be facilitated'.[39] Similarly, Adler invites researchers to use the concept to focus on the 'practices that undergird these communities',[40] as this chapter will do in the following sections.

13.3. A COMMUNITY OF FACT-FINDING PRACTICE

A community of practice is not just a concept, but can also be translated into a very practical activity.[41] Having dual character, the concept can be used as analytical framework, but may also be invoked as a practical device by actors aiming to create and shape a collective. With regards to the community of fact-finding practice, this is evident in the call for action by Rob Grace and Claude Bruderlein, Researchers in the Program on Humanitarian and Conflict Research at the Harvard TH Chan School of Public Health. In a working paper on monitoring, reporting and fact-finding (MRF), the authors make the following recommendation:

> Build a Community of Practice: MRF actors lack a forum to share information and learn from one another's experiences. This partly results from the fact that MRF mechanisms originate from a diverse array of intergovernmental, regional, and domestic mandating bodies. While some individual entities have established processes for learning lessons from past practice—for example, the OHCHR's methodology unit—the world of MRF as a whole does not yet possess the capacity for developing an institutional memory. The ability to learn lessons from past practice is particularly important given that the world of MRF is in a perpetual state of change, with each mission teaching MRF actors new lessons.[42]

It is worth pointing out how closely Lave and Wenger's original idea has been translated into a call for action by Grace and Bruderlein. In very

[38] I Johnstone, 'Security Council Deliberations: The Power of the Better Argument' (2003) 14(3) *European Journal of International Law* 439.

[39] Bueger and Gadinger (n 14) 34.

[40] Adler (n 28) 199.

[41] Wenger and Snyder, for example, suggest using it as a tool to enhance performance in business.

[42] R Grace and C Bruderlein, *Building Effective Monitoring, Reporting and Fact-Finding Mechanisms*, HPCR Draft Working Paper (Cambridge, MA, Harvard University) 45.

similar terms, they describe the situated learning process between individuals, how their interaction can improve their joint learning practice and how the MRF community is constantly changing and adapting, thus incorporating new ideas through experience. Improving the work of fact-finding is achieved through situated learning in a community.

But let us take a step back first: for a community of practice to come together, there must be at least some shared understanding of the community's core practice(s). Old and new members need to be able to recognise social practices as legitimate forms of action within a community. How, then, do members of the fact-finding community identify (with) the practice of fact-finding? This section suggests that this occurs through a process of standardisation. This takes place in three main ways: first, the practice of fact-finding is described by general authoritative texts, such as UN declarations and guidelines, which give this practice a particular meaning. Second, policy guidelines and practice manuals develop concrete working methods to further develop a shared understanding of practice. Third, fact-finding practitioners not only negotiate an understanding of fact-finding in general terms (through the generation and publication of documents), but also develop the practice through mandate interpretation on a case-by-case basis.

13.3.1. Standardisation

The 1991 Declaration on Fact-Finding by the United Nations in the Field of the Maintenance of International Peace and Security defines fact-finding as

> any activity designed to obtain detailed knowledge of the relevant facts of any dispute or situation which the competent United Nations organs need in order to exercise effectively their functions in relation to the maintenance of international peace and security.[43]

The recently published document *Commissions of Inquiry and Fact-Finding Missions on International Human Rights and International Humanitarian Law: Guidance and Practice* refers to fact-finding missions and/or commissions of inquiry as

> a variety of temporary bodies of a non-judicial nature, established either by an intergovernmental body or by the Secretary-General or the High Commissioner for Human Rights, and tasked with investigating allegations of violations of international human rights, international humanitarian law or international

[43] UN Doc A/RES/46/59 (9 December 1991).

> criminal law and making recommendations for corrective action based on their factual and legal findings.[44]

The 2013 *Siracusa Guidelines for International, Regional and National Fact-Finding Bodies* describe the practice in the following way: 'Commissions of Inquiry … are fact-finding mechanisms intended to correct violations of human rights and humanitarian law by investigating and reporting on a particular situation and providing recommendations to the mandating body.'[45]

The HPRC *Advanced Practitioner's Handbook on Commissions of Inquiry* views commissions of inquiry as part of a 'broader proliferation of monitoring, reporting and fact-finding mechanisms' established by various parts of the UN.[46] These mechanisms are established 'for the purpose of gathering information on alleged serious violations of IHL or IHRL'.[47] Elsewhere, fact-finding is understood as an 'in-depth examination of specific incidents in order to establish evidence of responsibility'[48] or as 'a method of ascertaining facts, whereby an impartial investigative body elucidates the facts relating to a dispute between states in order to produce a finding of disputed facts for the purpose of a successful peaceful settlement of the dispute'.[49]

As previously stated, fact-finding has also become a key mechanism for NGOs, in particular those working in the human rights field. Against this background, guidelines such as the *Lund-London Guidelines* developed by the International Bar Association and the *Best Practices for Human Rights and Humanitarian NGO Fact-Finding*, published by NGO monitor, also contribute to the standardisation of the practice, thus creating a shared understanding for the collective. Here, fact-finding is understood as 'a mission, visit or activity mandated by an NGO to ascertain the relevant facts relating to and elucidating a situation of human rights concern, whether allegedly committed by State or non-State actors'.[50] The importance of fact-finding, it is argued, lies in the need for 'credible factual claims concerning the behaviour and intentions of states and conflict parties [that] are essential to reduce the adverse humanitarian and human rights impacts of armed conflicts'.[51]

[44] OHCHR, *Commissions of Inquiry and Fact-Finding Missions on International Human Rights and Humanitarian Law* (New York, OHCHR, 2015) 7.

[45] M Cherif Bassiouni and C Abraham, *Siracusa Guidelines for International, Regional and National Fact-Finding Bodies* (Cambridge, Intersentia, 2013) 8.

[46] HPRC *Practitioner Handbook* (n 9) 1.

[47] HPRC *Practitioner Handbook* (n 9) 7.

[48] Grace and Bruderlein (n 42) 13.

[49] BA Boszek, *International Law: A Dictionary* (Lanham, Scarecrow Press, 2005) 365.

[50] *Lund-London Guidelines* (2009), available at www.ibanet.org/Fact_Finding_Guidelines.aspx, accessed 5 April 2016.

[51] GM Steinberg, A Herzberg and J Berman, *Best Practices for Human Rights and Humanitarian NGO Fact-Finding* (Leiden, Martinus Nijhoff Publishers, 2012) 3.

With this in mind, it is clear that commissions of inquiry include more than just the 'finding of' facts, as they also entail corrective and recommendatory functions as well as findings of the law. This is as fact-finding is not just carried out as an end in and of itself, but is seen as a means to achieve a variety of additional goals. The negotiation of these goals forms a crucial part of the community's mutual engagement and commitment. Some observers, for example, argue that fact-finding constitutes a valuable and efficient instrument for promoting peace.[52] In this reading, fact-finding may contribute to successful conflict resolution, since recommendations are made for follow-up mechanisms and root causes of violence are addressed, thus assisting in the political settlement of conflicts.[53] Others argue that fact-finding entails a preventive function, specifically when carried out as an instrument of early warning in order to identify situations that might turn into possible conflicts.[54] This aspect was also envisaged in the UN Report *An Agenda for Peace*, where fact-finding is seen as a substantial part of preventive diplomacy.[55] Advocates of transitional justice hold that fact-finding may also have a therapeutic effect. Truth-telling, it is argued, leads to the recognition of victims and may enhance reconciliation.[56] Richard J Goldstone and M Cherif Bassiouni, for example, point to the link between justice and peace, stating that peace cannot be achieved without an account of what happened in the past, though it is widely recognised that this relationship is less straightforward than the authors hold.[57]

In addition, commissions of inquiry are said to unfold an 'alerting function' as they are aimed at raising awareness for stakeholders to take action in situations of serious violations of international humanitarian law and human rights law.[58] As Larissa van den Herik and Catherine Harwood note: 'Concepts of international criminal law, such as genocide and crimes against humanity, have an acute emotive value. They are thus explicitly suitable to place certain situations on the international agenda, to mobilize

[52] See, for example, WI Shore, *Fact-Finding in the Maintenance for International Peace* (Dobbs Ferry, New York, Oceana Publications, 1970).

[53] A Berg, 'The 1991 Declaration on Fact-Finding by the United Nations' (1993) 4(1) *European Journal of International Law* 107.

[54] WA Dorn, 'Keeping Tabs on a Troubled World: UN Information-Gathering to Preserve Peace' (1996) 27(3) *Security Dialogue* 270.

[55] UN Doc A/47/277—S/24111 (17 June 1992).

[56] PB Hayner, *Unspeakable Truth. Facing the Challenge of Truth Commissions* (New York, Routledge, 2002).

[57] RJ Goldstone, 'Justice as a Tool for Peace-Making: Truth Commissions an International Criminal Tribunals' (1996) 28(3) *New York University Journal of International Law and Politics* 485; M Cherif Bassiouni, 'Appraising UN Justice-Related Fact-Finding Missions' (1997) 5(35) *Journal of Law and Policy* 35.

[58] LJ van den Herik and C Harwood, '"Sharing the Law": The Appeal of International Criminal Law for International Commissions of Inquiry' *Grotius Centre Working Paper 2014/016-ICL* (Leiden, Grotius Centre for International Legal Studies, 2014) 9.

public opinion and to prepare a case for action.'[59] Commissions of inquiry are therefore also understood as a means to implement and ensure compliance with international criminal law, as well as to determine individual responsibility for the commitment of crimes:

> Commissions of inquiry appear to have become a new mechanism for determining the responsibility of both states and individuals for violations of human rights and IHL. In the absence of universal compulsory jurisdiction by international judicial bodies, these commissions of inquiry are a way in which the international community can obtain an authoritative determination of whether these violations have taken place and who is responsible.[60]

However, the authors acknowledge that this has taken place in a selective manner. Whilst those commissions of inquiry that are mandated to ensure accountability for individuals utilise 'the legal categories pertaining to the crime definitions',[61] they more often than not neglect procedural international criminal law. Additionally, most commissions of inquiry do not deploy the same legal analysis as international courts would do, and therefore take on an 'interpretive approach' to international criminal law. This leads van den Herik and Harwood to conclude that whilst commissions of inquiry 'borrow certain terms from international criminal law [it] does not mean they do or must copy-paste the entire system'.[62] Put differently, whilst commissions of inquiry refer to the language of international law to enhance their authority and legitimacy, they should not be understood as legal bodies proper.

Second, in an effort to further standardise current working methods, some of the guidelines have developed recommendations for the working procedures of fact-finding missions and commissions of inquiry, in particular the OHCHR *Guidance on Commissions of Inquiry*. The most current forms of fact-finding may range from interviews with victims, witnesses and alleged perpetrators to field and site visits as well as public hearings. Fact-finding may include the analysis of official documents, video material, photographs, satellite images, social media, reports by the UN and other regional and international organisations.[63] These activities are to be guided by specific principles: independence, impartiality, transparency and do no harm. These principles are shared by all major guidelines and policy reports.

Third, the practice of fact-finding has not only been shaped by authoritative declarations, technical guidelines or academic studies, but also

[59] van den Herik and Harwood (n 58) 9.

[60] D Akande and H Tonkin, 'International Commissions of Inquiry: A New Form of Adjudication?' (*EJIL: Talk!* 6 April 2012), available at www.ejiltalk.org/international-commissions-of-inquiry-a-new-form-of-adjudication/, accessed 13 November 2016.

[61] van den Herik and Harwood (n 58) 15–17.

[62] van den Herik and Harwood (n 58) 18.

[63] OHCHR, *Commissions of Inquiry* (n 44) 36–58.

through the ways in which practitioners have interpreted their mandates. Leading up to the investigation, two aspects in particular are considered: the relevant legal framework that guides the analysis; and the adoption of an adequate standard of proof. With regard to the former, mandate-holders will have to determine the bodies of law that are relevant to their investigation, for example, international humanitarian law, IHRL or ICL. What is more, as there is no universal standard of proof that commissions of inquiry need to adhere to (and none of them employ the threshold of 'beyond reasonable doubt'), it falls to the fact-finding experts to establish a standard they deem as appropriate. After analysing 15 different commissions of inquiry, Steven Wilkinson finds a range of different standards that were employed by the commissions: some identified the standard as 'balance of probalities', 'reasonable grounds to believe', 'reasonable basis to believe', 'reasonable suspicion', whilst some commissions did not identify a standard of proof at all.[64] Against this background, the OHCHR Handbook notes that commissions of inquiry should 'clearly indicate' the standard of proof adopted,[65] whilst the HPCR *Advanced Practitioner's Handbook on Commissions of Inquiry* additionally points out that the public articulation of the level of standard of proof may enhance the (perceived) credibility of the commissions' reports.[66] However, practitioners not only interpret the most appropriate standard of proof, but also the temporal and geographical scope of their mandate and the actors that are considered during the investigation.[67] The interpretation of specific mandates thus also forms part of the community's knowledge and practice, and practitioners jointly developed the tools, skills and resources to achieve the mandate they set out. These tools and skills are constantly negotiated, and have come under increased scrutiny, as the majority of contemporary fact-finding missions now includes a section on their working methods in the final report. In turn, the expertise that is developed in the interpretation of mandates becomes part of the community's repertoire and of the 'way of doing things', and may inform future investigations.

13.3.2. Professionalisation

The second practice that sustains the fact-finding community is a shared commitment to professionalisation. This is one of the ways in which

[64] S Wilkinson, 'Finding the facts: Standards of proof and information handling in monitoring, reporting and fact-finding missions' (HPCR, 2014), available at papers.ssrn.com/sol3/papers.cfm?abstract_id=2400927.

[65] OHCHR (n 44) 62.

[66] HPRC *Practitioner Handbook* (n 9) 27.

[67] R Grace, 'The Design and Planning of Monitoring, Reporting, and Fact-Finding Missions' (HPCR, 2013), available at papers.ssrn.com/sol3/papers.cfm?abstract_id=2365435.

communities of practice learn, invent new practices and potentially also expand, as they incorporate new members. What might this practice look like in concrete terms? The following section illustrates one of the core learning and training processes of the fact-finding community.

Members of the community not only include individuals who are active in the field, but also those who establish various other relations with them. This is especially crucial for those who contribute to the professionalisation of fact-finding experts working in the field. Justice Rapid Response, for example, is an intergovernmental organisation that trains and supplies a roster of experts for investigations. Operational since 2009, Justice Rapid Response was founded in 'an effort to pool the collective strengths of the entire international community in order to ensure that no investigation of a mass atrocity is denied the prompt, trained expertise it needs […]'.[68] The organisation is run by a secretariat based in Geneva and New York and governed by an Executive Board of states that provides strategic guidance and oversight. Justice Rapid Response is funded by voluntary contributions from states and other donors, such as the Greenbaum Foundation, the International Association of Forensic Sciences, the International Criminal Court for the former Yugoslavia (ICTY), the International Organisation of La Francophonie (OIF) and UN Women.[69]

As noted above, the community of fact-finding practice has not only evolved around particular forms of practice and legitimate forms of action, but also a normative commitment to accountability and justice. Justice Rapid Response operates under this paradigm too, thus further promoting the idea of accountability mechanisms as justice and conflict resolution tools:

> Unless we secure evidence to hold perpetrators accountable, we will not be able to bring justice to victims, their families, their communities. Nor can we create credible deterrence against the commission of similar crimes in the future. Bringing justice is essential to breaking the cycle of atrocity-laced violence in countries whose populations have too long suffered under this burden. This, in turn, can be the spark that generates a real chance for lasting peace for these societies.[70]

According to its 2014 Annual Report, Justice Rapid Response has assisted in 47 missions worldwide and has deployed a total of 77 experts since it became operational. In 2014 alone, the organisation sent 37 experts to 21 missions at the request of various entities, such as UN Women, the UN Development Programme, the Office of the High Commissioner of Human Rights (OHCHR) or the International Criminal Court. Justice

68 www.justicerapidresponse.org/who-we-are/about-us/, accessed 8 Septembers 2015.

69 Justice Rapid Response, *Annual Report 2014* (Geneva, Justice Rapid Response, 2014) 15.

70 www.justicerapidresponse.org/what-we-do/making-justice-possible/, accessed 6 September 2015.

Rapid Response currently provides a roster of approximately 500 experts from 95 countries, ranging from military, legal, justice and witness protection experts to forensic scientists, investigators and interpreters.

Before becoming a member of the rooster of experts, individuals are required to complete a training programme. To this end, Justice Rapid Response issues a call for nominations for particular expertise sought. In order to take part in the training programme, potential candidates require the nomination of their employer. Their applications are then selected by Justice Rapid Response. Once candidates have completed their training, they are certified to the roster of experts and can be deployed upon request. In 2014, Justice Rapid Response carried out five training courses, a general investigation course with the US State Department, two courses with ICTR and ICTY staff (plus nine additional experts), a sexual and gender-based violence investigations course in Bogota and a forensics certification workshop in Seoul.[71]

Following Stein, communities of practice change when members of the community 'want to do better' or when crisis situations challenge existing knowledge and practice. Like many other members of the fact-finding community, Justice Rapid Response is also driving for innovation. The organisation is, for example, currently developing ways to incorporate asset recovery into the work of their investigations. As Justice Rapid Response argues, 'in order for survivors of mass atrocities to have the best chance of reparations, the assets of perpetrators must be identified and recovered'.[72] Members of the fact-finding community can push for new practices and new knowledge to become part of the community's common repertoire. The success of such attempts, however, is determined by the extent to which other members engage with the idea. As Wenger reminds us, communities of practice are characterised by mutual engagement, where members of the collective jointly negotiate what constitutes a legitimate form of action.

The training courses offered by Justice Rapid Response are carried out in collaboration with the Institute for International Criminal Investigations. The Institute, founded in 2003, is an international NGO based in Geneva that offers training courses on 'the techniques and knowledge necessary to impartially investigate and adjudicate egregious human rights violations, war crimes, crimes against humanity and genocide, and for the purpose of quickly deploying multi-disciplinary teams to investigate such violations or crimes'.[73] Similarly to Justice Rapid Response, it is funded by donations, primarily from private foundations, government agencies

[71] Justice Rapid Response, *Annual Report 2014* (n 69) 12–13.

[72] www.justicerapidresponse.org/what-we-do/breaking-new-ground/, accessed on 6 September 2015.

[73] www.iici.info/, accessed 8 September 2015.

and individuals.[74] The Institute for International Criminal Investigations is governed by a Board of Directors, consisting of military officers, human rights investigators, academics, criminal investigators and legal experts. Many of these individuals are prominent members of the fact-finding community and have served as fact-finders in the field, such as Hina Jilani, who served on the International Commission of Inquiry on Darfur (2004), and William Schabas, who has served on several fact-finding missions for Amnesty International. In addition to the Board of Directors, the organisation comprises a Council of Advisors which also includes a range of fact-finding experts, such as M Cherif Bassiouni and Richard J Goldstone. The staff of the Institute for International Criminal Investigations is headed by John Ralston, former founding member of the ICTY as well as chief investigator for the International Commission of Inquiry on Darfur (2004). Ralston was also involved in the establishment of Justice Rapid Response and designed the training programmes for the organisation. Currently, the Institute for International Criminal Investigations offers five training courses: an international investigator course; an investigative interview course; a course on analysis skills including sexual and gender-based violence; a course on documenting scenes for war crimes; and a course on the investigation of cases of sexual and gender-based violence.[75]

Both Justice Rapid Response and the Institute for International Criminal Investigations jointly contribute to the community's development by bringing together individuals around shared notions of 'best practice' and a common repertoire of knowledge. These are also ways of enlarging the community and including new members that partake in the joint enterprise. Prominent fact-finding experts teach from their own experience and new members learn from the community's experience. The latter identify with the community through participation in its practices. The training sessions also offer the opportunity to reflect on practices and possibly improve them, and explore new ideas, concepts and actions.

13.3.3. Transparency

The third practice that sustains the fact-finding community is a commitment to transparency. Members of the community increasingly strive for making information public, thus making it easy for others to see what actions have been carried out and that these actions have followed certain rules and regulations. Again, several guidelines include transparency as

[74] www.iici.info/about/financing-and-support, accessed 6 September 2015.
[75] The syllabi of the courses are available at www.iici.info/courses/upcoming-activities, accessed 8 September 2015.

one of the core principles of fact-finding practice. The *OHCHR Handbook* recommends that:

> The commission/mission should, as far as possible without detriment to its work or the security of its staff, information and persons cooperating with it, make information about its mandate, methodology and work publically available. Commissions/missions do not work in secrecy and undertake activities in a country only with the consent of the government.[76]

And the *Siracusa Guidelines* note:

> A fact-finding body should be established in a transparent manner that is appropriate to the context for which is was created. The following should be made publically available for the period the fact-finding body is in operation and should be included in the final report: The organ, body, or agency that established the fact-finding body; official establishing instrument (authorizing resolution(s)/Decree/Law, etc).[77]

The commitment to transparency does not come as a surprise, given that it has become one of the cornerstones of good governance.[78] It is easy to understand why the community of fact-finding practice places an emphasis on transparency: after all, creating transparency and accountability lies at the core of its enterprise. The very logic of fact-finding is that knowing and telling the 'truth' to others constitutes a desirable end in and of itself. In turn, by fostering transparency of their own practices fact-finding experts may enhance their accountability and authority.[79] As Grace suggests, this is also vital given that commissions of inquiry regularly face criticisms of being biased, restrictive, ineffective and lacking objectivity.[80]

However, as Andrew Barry and others have pointed out, transparency is more than a concept.[81] It is also an organising practice of the fact-finding community itself. It is, first and foremost, a crucial way of how the community learns. Given that the fact-finding community is geographically and professionally dispersed, transparency is an important tool to establish

[76] OHCHR (n 44) 34.

[77] Cherif Bassiouni and Abraham, *Siracusa Guidelines* (n 45) 37–38.

[78] See for example OHCHR, *Good Governance Practices for the Protection of Human Rights* (New York, United Nations).

[79] Jennifer Welsh and Dominik Zaum, for example, argue that the UN Security Council dispatches fact-finding missions to improve its epistemic foundations as a source of legitimacy. In this reading, the Council generates specialised knowledge that is viewed as valid and credible by its core audience in order to enhance its perception of legitimacy. See J Welsh and D Zaum, 'Legitimation and the UN Security Council' in J Welsh and D Zaum (eds) *Legitimising International Organizations* (Oxford, Oxford University Press, 2013) 76–77.

[80] R Grace, 'Communication and Report Drafting in Monitoring, Reporting, and Fact-Finding Missions', *HPCR Working Paper* (Cambridge, MA, Harvard School of Public Health, 2013) 7.

[81] See, for example, A Barry, *Transparency as a political device*, available at books.openedition.org/pressesmines/721?lang=en, accessed 8 September 2015 and M Power, *The Audit Society: Rituals of Verification* (Oxford, Oxford University Press, 1997).

relations between the members. They can follow each other's actions and respond to or challenge them. Fact-finding experts can only learn from 'best practice' and 'past experience' when these are documented and made accessible in some form. They can only write manuals and guidelines when they are able to refer to the description of 'past experience' in order to suggest improvements and alterations.

How then is transparency in the fact-finding community employed? First, the fact-finding community uses evermore fora for its members to speak and write about their experience, like Morten Bergsmo's *Quality Control in Fact-Finding* that lets, for example, Richard J Goldstone speak about his personal experience, or *The Transformation of Human Rights Fact-Finding*, edited by Philip Alston and Sarah Knuckey. Research institutions give fact-finding practitioners an opportunity to discuss their knowledge. For example, in 2013, the Center for Human Rights and Global Justice of the NYU School of Law hosted a conference on 'International Human Rights Fact-Finding in the Twenty-First Century', giving more than 20 academics, activists, lawyers and other professionals to speak about and share their expertise.[82] In 2014, the Royal Institute of International Affairs hosted a talk on 'UN Fact-Finding and International Criminal Investigations: Do Either Bring Accountability?', providing Sir Nigel Rodley, Member of the Bahrain International Commission of Inquiry and former UN Special Rapporteur on Torture, and Professor Alex Whiting, former Investigation Coordinator and Prosecution Coordinater at the Office of the Prosecutor of International Criminal Court, with a forum to discuss their views.[83] These events are occasions for the fact-finding community to come together in one place and also engage with a broader audience.

Other members of the community, such as academics and activists, report and comment on development in the community on internet blogs, such as the *Leiden Law Blog*, *EJIL: Talk!* and *Opinio Juris*.[84] Of course, most of the research literature is publically available, and so are the guidelines that have been developed in the past five years. Organisations such as Justice Rapid Response and the Institute for International Criminal Investigations provide information about their work online and conduct outreach activities to engage with the community's environment. In some cases, members of the fact-finding community take on various roles at the same time: Théo Boutrouche, for example, one of the contributors to this book, has published his work in academic journals and spoken at public events

[82] chrgj.org/event/factfindingconference/, accessed 5 September 2015.

[83] www.chathamhouse.org/events/view/195695, accessed 5 September 2015.

[84] See, for example, leidenlawblog.nl/articles/international-commissions-of-inquiry-in-conflict-situations-go-betweens-of, accessed 27 March 2016; www.ejiltalk.org/international-commissions-of-inquiry-a-new-form-of-adjudication/, accessed 27 March 2016; opiniojuris.org/2014/12/23/guest-post-accountability-impact-impasse-curious-case-north-korean-inquiry/, accessed 27 March 2016.

about fact-finding.[85] After taking on various roles in the fact-finding community, he is currently legal advisor to the International Commission of Jurists. He also blogs about fact-finding on *The Art of Facts*.[86] The call for transparency has helped to create and diffuse practices, institutions and persons that are in a position to engage with public information about fact-finding practice.

Second, as noted above, there has been a push towards more transparency for concrete missions. Today, the majority of commissions of inquiry publish a final report. Besides the inclusion of the 'findings' and recommendations of the commission of inquiry, information about the mandate, the working methods, the members of a commission and its field work are made available in the report. Here, transparency unfolds an additional function. The publication of the report directly relates to the normative commitment of the fact-finding community—to impact on the social and political context they function in, by furthering accountability and justice. Without the document of a fact-finding mission, there would be no policy to follow.[87]

Third, the practice of transparency also creates new knowledge and new practical experiences. As lifecycles, communities of practice adapt, change and potentially integrate new 'ways of doing'. By incorporating new ideas, communities of practice also socialise their old and new members. The idea of transparency, of making things known to others, has allowed information and communication technologies to play an increasing role, by enabling not only trained lawyers, investigators and scientists, but other individuals to make possible violations known and transparent. WITNESS, a non-profit organisation that trains and supports citizens to use video footage to expose human rights violations, is a vivid example of this development. The organisation has established a wide set of practices: it responds to crisis situations by training local activists and human rights NGOs in the use of video footage to document human rights violations. WITNESS also undertakes advocacy work to promote the use of information technology and to this end cooperates with private technology companies.[88] Together with the Guardian Project, for example, WITNESS has developed the application InformaCam, an app that records additional data as a form of 'digital fingerprint' when a picture or video is taken in order to verify the authenticity of the media.[89] The WITNESS media lab

[85] See, for example, T Boutruche, 'Credible Fact-Finding and Allegations of International Humanitarian Law Violations: Challenges in Theory and Practice' (2011) 16(1) *Journal of Conflict and Security Law* 105.

[86] www.theartoffacts.org/facts-about-the-author/, accessed 5 September 2015.

[87] For this argument see R Freeman and J Maybin, 'Documents, practices and policy' (2011) 7(2) *Evidence and Policy* 155.

[88] witness.org/, accessed 6 September 2015.

[89] guardianproject.info/apps/informacam/, accessed 6 September 2015.

is dedicated to research on video documentation and aims 'to develop, model and support innovative approaches to sourcing, verifying, and contextualising eyewitness videos'.[90] It is fair to say that WITNESS is pushing the boundaries of human rights fact-finding, and challenges 'the way things are done' and how 'facts are found' in a profound way, as it raises a series of questions of what constitute evidence for 'facts' and how the former is verified. In sum, as Heyns observes, 'there is a much wider community of human rights monitors at work than ever before'.[91] The community of fact-finding practice might undergo yet another generational shift.

13.4. CONCLUDING REMARKS

Fact-finding is one of the central epistemic practices of the UN today, one which has also found a place within regional organisations and states.[92] Epistemic practices are, following Bueger, practices 'that produce and maintain (explicit) knowledge or facts'.[93] They are a crucial means for international organisations such as the UN to organise international political life. Fact-finding provides the vocabulary to speak about a situation and offers common standards to assess a situation. Commissions of inquiry are regularly established in situations of epistemic uncertainty and contestation in an attempt to settle disputed 'facts' by providing, what is seen by some, an authoritative reading of events.

In this chapter it has been argued that the proliferation of fact-finding and commissions of inquiry in the field of international human rights and humanitarian law has been driven by a community of fact-finding practice. The chapter identified three key practices that undergird this community: standardisation, professionalisation and transparency. The three key practices provide a common language for different actors to speak and possibly cooperate with each other. The community has become more pluralist, transparent and creative. In an ongoing effort to learn, develop and diffuse knowledge, the community of fact-finding practice is continuously re-inventing itself.

However, the fact-finding community is also faced with two key challenges: First, the key practices outlined in this chapter run the danger of leading to a technocratisation of fact-finding practice. Standardisation and professionalisation give fact-finding a technical character, when clearly it

90 lab.witness.org, accessed 6 September 2015.

91 UN Doc A/HRC/29/37 (24 April 2015).

92 See, for an overview, C Hellestveit, 'International Fact-Finding Mechanisms: Lighting Candles or Cursing Darkness?' in CM Bailliet and KM Larsen (eds) *Promoting Peace through International Law* (Oxford, Oxford University Press, 2015) 368.

93 C Bueger, 'Making Things Known: Epistemic Practices, the United Nations, and the Translation of Piracy' (2015) 9(1) *International Political Sociology* 6.

is not. The technical character of fact-finding masks the agency that goes into 'finding' and selecting facts, the pragmatic choices that fact-finding experts are required to do every single day when the situation on the ground constrains their work. Often, fact-finding missions are dispatched in ongoing or recent armed conflicts which poses a range of practical challenges to their members. As Philip Alston and Colin Gillespie point out: 'there can be no such thing as neutral, objective "finding" of facts, as though they were items of debris which had been widely scattered by the elements but could be recovered and reconstructed by well-equipped and assiduous sleuths.'[94] For pragmatic (and also epistemological) reasons, facts do not exist independently from our thought and practice.[95] Technocratisation also suggests that there is such a thing as an 'authoritative reading of events': once a fact has been established, an agreement is reached. Yet, it is easy to see that fact-finding does not necessarily lead to agreement or constitute an effective response in situations of epistemic contestation, but may simply stipulate a politics of expertise.

Second, the technocratisation of fact-finding may also lead to a de-politicisation of the practice. The growing repertoire of the community, consisting of manuals, guidelines, 'best practice' cases, training courses and outreach activities as well as the inclusion of method sections in the final reports of commissions of inquiry runs the danger of presenting knowledge as separable from politics (and power). Commissions of inquiry are established by political bodies, for political goals. They are not just technical devices that report about a phenomenon, they are themselves means through with governance is exercised. Given the range of recommendations and follow-up mechanisms current fact-finding missions propose, they are most evidently attempts to change (and govern) the world, especially since human rights violations do not take place in isolation from the political and social context they occur in. Technocratisation and de-politicisation divorce the practical activity of 'finding facts' from the normative commitment to prevention, reconciliation and peace that underwrites much of contemporary fact-finding practice.

The community of fact-finding practice is, however, well-equipped to address these challenges. As pointed out above, the approach to communities of practice not only offers an analytical framework to study how practices such as fact-finding are organised in collectives, but may also be engaged in a very practical way by the members of the community themselves to foster their learning processes and strengthen their mutual engagement. Wenger and Snyder suggest that communities of practice

[94] Alton and Gillespie (n 7) 1093.

[95] For this line of argument, see also F Mégret, 'Do Facts Exist, Can They Be "Found", and Does It Matter?' in P Alston and S Knuckey (eds), *The Transformation of Human Rights Fact-Finding* (Oxford, Oxford University Press, 2016) 27.

can solve problems and drive strategy. In order to achieve these goals in mutual engagement and negotiation, communities of practice can create innovative ways to bring members of the community together. This chapter has outlined some of the infrastructures that the community currently uses to develop fact-finding practice. The task ahead lies precisely in mobilising these infrastructures not only to further develop and negotiate the working methods of commissions of inquiry but, crucially, the various political goals (and the possible tensions between them) they are expected to achieve. This aspect is currently side-lined in both practice and theory, but requires renewed attention to make fact-finding a meaningful and effective practice for international politics.

Index

Printed by Libri Plureos GmbH in Hamburg,
Germany

9 781509 932207